Fourth Edition

ADVANCED ACCOUNTING

COMPREHENSIVE VOLUME

Harry Simons, M.A., C.P.A.
Professor of Accounting
University of California, Los Angeles

Wilbert E. Karrenbrock, Ph.D.

Published By

SOUTH-WESTERN PUBLISHING COMPANY

Cincinnati **Chicago**
Burlingame, Calif. **Dallas** **New Rochelle, N.Y.**

A88

Library of Congress Catalog Card Number 68-14565

678K321

Printed in the United States of America

PREFACE

Advanced Accounting — Comprehensive Volume is a textbook for the student who has completed introductory and intermediate studies and who possesses an understanding of the theoretical framework of accounting. The Fourth Edition of *Advanced Accounting*, like preceding editions, describes special forms of organizations, both profit and nonprofit, and seeks to prepare the student to apply basic accounting principles to the special problems that are found in such organizations. The textbook is designed to serve both the business student who wishes to be able to interpret the full product of accounting and the accounting major who seeks an understanding of theory and practice so that he may qualify for admission to the accounting profession.

Chapter sequence and subject matter in the Third Edition of *Advanced Accounting* have generally been continued in this Fourth Edition. Every part of the book was carefully reviewed and sections were rewritten wherever it was felt that improvement was possible; every illustration was reviewed and modifications were made wherever more effective presentation could be provided. References to the most recent statements and pronouncements by authorities are included throughout the book. Terminology gives expression to current practice. Problems have been revised, and a number of new problems have been added, including problems selected from recent AICPA examinations.

The following may be regarded as the principal changes in the revision. The chapters on governmental accounting have been supplemented by a new chapter on accounting for nonprofit service organizations; the book now provides a broad treatment of the subject of fund accounting. The description of business combinations has been expanded; the pooling-of-interests concept is fully described and illustrated and the differences between purchase and pooling arrangements are presented and evaluated. Accounting for joint ventures has been condensed and now is treated within the chapters on partnership accounting.

Other major changes in the revision are worthy of note. The section on partnership liquidation by installment has been modified to provide for a comparison of alternative methods and procedures. Recommendations by authorities on the recognition of gross profit by the installment method have been included, and the use of the installment method solely for income tax purposes, together with accompanying interperiod tax allocation procedures, is described and illustrated. In the discussion of consolidated statements, certain sections dealing with theoretical considerations underlying financial statement presentations have been expanded. The special difficulties arising in accounting for foreign branches and subsidiaries are explored, and alternative procedures to deal effectively with the translation problem are described and evaluated. A special form of the statement of affairs has been introduced that provides an efficient presentation of the position of the different creditor groups. Terminology in reporting for estates and trusts has been modified to conform with present practice.

Those who have used the companion volume in this series, *Intermediate Accounting — Comprehensive Volume*, will be familiar with the style and the sequence of materials that is found in *Advanced Accounting*. Each chapter discussion is followed by a related set of questions, exercises, and problems. Problems range in difficulty from those reviewing the essential elements in the chapter to those calling for the application of a broad theoretical background. Each set of problems is concluded with selected problems from the Uniform Examination for Certified Public Accountants.

The authors are grateful to the many persons who have contributed to the development of succeeding editions of this textbook. Earlier editions have named those who made particularly important contributions in the past. To this list, the authors wish to name the following for their help in the Fourth Edition. Deep appreciation is expressed to S. Zachary Samuels and to Michael W. Sandberg who assisted throughout the course of the revision and contributed importantly to both the development of the textbook and the preparation of problems. Particular thanks are expressed to the following professors of accounting who made valuable suggestions for the revision: Joe R. Fritzemeyer, Harold Q. Langenderfer, Richard W. Metcalf, and John B. Ross.

The authors express their appreciation to the American Institute of Certified Public Accountants for permission to quote from AICPA Research Bulletins and Opinions and to use problems from the Uniform Certified Public Accountants Examination. Thanks are also extended to the American Accounting Association, the National Association of Accountants, the National Committee on Governmental Accounting, the American Council on Education, and the American Hospital Association for references and quotations from their various publications.

HARRY SIMONS
WILBERT E. KARRENBROCK

CONTENTS

[1]Questions, exercises, and problems are given at the end of each chapter.

Chapter 1

PARTNERSHIPS

FORMATION AND OPERATION

The partnership is defined as "an association of two or more persons to carry on as co-owners a business for profit."[1] "Persons" are considered to include individuals, partnerships, corporations, and other associations. The partnership is a legal relationship originating from a voluntary contract between parties, which may be oral or written or simply implied from the acts of the parties. No formal sanction or recognition by a governmental unit is required in its formation.

NATURE OF THE PARTNERSHIP

The partnership form of organization is widely used. As in the case of the corporate form, the partnership makes possible the pooling of resources for some common business purpose. The partnership has been employed for both small and large-scale operations. Many partnerships represent an association of no more than two persons; some units, however, represent an association of dozens of persons. The partnership may be a small enterprise selling goods or services at a single location, or it may be a large enterprise with branches or offices at many different locations. Within the latter group are accounting, legal, and brokerage firms with offices throughout the nation, as well as sales, construction, and engineering firms of national scope.

Certain important characteristics of the partnership form of organization deserve special note:

Mutual agency. Each partner is an agent of the partnership for the purpose of its business. Acts of a partner bind the partnership, provided these are within his express or implied authority. Acts of a partner that do not fall into the category of carrying on business in the usual manner will not bind the partnership unless there is special authorization from copartners.

Limited life. Since the partnership is a relationship originating from a contract between certain parties, any change in the relationship

[1]This is the definition given in the Uniform Partnership Act, which has been adopted by all of the states except Alabama, Florida, Georgia, Hawaii, Iowa, Kansas, Louisiana, Maine, Mississippi, and New Hampshire. The discussion of partnerships in this and succeeding chapters is based upon the Uniform Partnership Act except where reference is made to other law.

terminates the contract and dissolves the partnership. The withdrawal of a partner or the death of a partner, for example, automatically dissolves the partnership.

Unlimited liability. The liability of a partner is not limited to the amount of his investment. Persons entering into contracts with an "association of individuals" can look to these separate individuals for payment of their claims if partnership property is insufficient to satisfy such claims. Partners, therefore, may be held personally liable and their separate assets may be attached to meet partnership obligations.

Ownership of an interest in a partnership. Properties invested in a partnership are no longer separately owned but now belong to the association of individuals comprising the partnership. The party who invests property in a partnership gives up his right to the separate enjoyment and use of such property. In transferring property, he does acquire an *interest* as a co-owner in properties identified with the partnership. Unless otherwise provided by agreement, this interest gives him an equal voice in the management of the partnership, the right to inspect the books of account of the firm, and the right to obtain an accounting of firm activities. Under certain circumstances, a partner may pledge, transfer, or sell his interest in partnership properties.

Participation in partnership profits. Each partner shares in the profits of the partnership. However, an agreement that calls for a sharing of profits alone does not of itself create a partnership. A party may agree to accept a share of business profits as compensation for services or for the use of certain properties, but a partnership will not be recognized in the absence of definite intent on the part of the parties to enter into this form of relationship.

PARTNERSHIP AS AN ASSOCIATION OF INDIVIDUALS AND AS A SEPARATE ENTITY

The partnership is defined as an association of persons. It involves a pooling of assets and calls for an accounting for each partner's interest in pooled assets. It is founded upon an agreement between persons, and it terminates with the expiration of the agreement or a change in the parties to the agreement. Furthermore, a contractual relationship between a partnership and other parties is actually a contract between partners, jointly and individually, and such other parties, since partners can be held liable in their private capacities for claims that cannot be satisfied by the firm. For certain purposes, however, the partnership takes on the attributes of a separate entity. For example, it acquires, holds, and transfers properties in its own name. It enters into contracts with others and may sue and be sued as a separate entity. Partners act as agents of the firm. The partnership is thus alternately viewed as an association of individuals and as a separate business entity.

CHOOSING BETWEEN PARTNERSHIP AND CORPORATE FORM

When several persons decide to pool their resources in a single business venture, they will have to choose between organizing as a partnership or as a corporation. This decision calls for a careful evaluation of the relative advantages and disadvantages of the two forms of enterprise under the particular circumstances. Among the advantages to be considered in choosing the partnership form are the relative ease both in its formation and dissolution, the personal character of the organization in its relationships with others, and the relative freedom and flexibility that it enjoys in its activities. Such favorable factors will have to be weighed against certain disadvantages, including the personal liability of partners for debts of the organization, the lack of business continuity, and the difficulties that are found in the transfers of ownership interests. When there is a need for a large amount of capital in establishing a business, parties will normally find it necessary to adopt the corporate form of organization.

The relative income tax positions of the two forms of business also require careful consideration. Under present federal income tax laws, the partnership is a tax-reporting entity but not a tax-paying entity. Income tax laws require the partnership to file an informational return that summarizes partnership operations and shows the distribution of income among owners. Partners must report their distributive shares of the partnership income on their individual income tax returns, whether or not such income is distributed and made available to the partners. The partner's share of partnership income thus becomes a part of his total income subject to tax. Corporations, on the other hand, are tax-paying entities. Business income of the corporation is subject to corporate tax rates. Corporate income after income taxes is taxed once again, this time as income of the stockholder, when it is distributed as dividends or when it is distributed in liquidation.

It may be observed that federal income tax legislation provides that under certain circumstances and subject to special limitations, sole proprietorships and partnerships may elect to be taxed as corporations.[1]

[1]One of the important qualifications for such election is the following: the enterprise must be one in which capital is a material income-producing factor, or 50% or more of the gross income of such enterprise consists of profits derived from trading as a principal or from buying or selling real property, stock, securities, or commodities for the account of others. It may be pointed out that where the corporate form offers tax advantages as compared with the partnership form, participants will normally decide to organize as a corporation and thus realize the other advantages that are found in the corporate form.

On the other hand, corporations that can qualify as "tax-option" corporations may elect a special tax status whereby their income or loss is attributed to stockholders and they pay no federal income taxes. When a corporation can qualify as a "tax-option" corporation and elects such special tax status, the corporate tax return becomes no more than an informational return, and each stockholder reports as income subject to individual tax rates his pro-rata share of the taxable income of the corporation, whether distributed by the corporation or retained by it.[1]

Income tax factors, both those that normally apply as well as those that are elective under special conditions, may play important parts in choosing between the partnership and corporate forms of organization. A review of the tax factors relating to the partnership and to the corporation should be made with each change of the tax laws and tax rates to determine whether there would be any advantage in changing the form of an existing business.

KINDS OF PARTNERSHIPS

Partnerships are classified as trading and nontrading partnerships, and distinctions are made among general partnerships, limited partnerships, and joint-stock companies.

Trading and nontrading partnerships. A partnership whose main activity is the manufacture or the purchase and the sale of goods is known as a *trading partnership*. A partnership that is organized for the purpose of rendering services is known as a *nontrading partnership*. A firm of accountants, attorneys, or realtors, then, would be considered a nontrading partnership. The distinction between trading and nontrading partnerships is significant in determining the proper limits of a partner's implied powers to act on behalf of the firm.

General and limited partnerships. A *general partnership* is one in which all partners may publicly act on behalf of the firm and in which each partner can be held individually liable for obligations of the firm. Such partners are known as *general partners*. Statutes of most of the states permit the formation of a *limited partnership*, wherein the activities of certain partners are limited and the personal liability of these parties in turn is limited to a stated amount, which may be the amount actually invested.[2]

---

[1]Several requirements must be met if a corporation is to qualify as a "tax-option" corporation. The corporation may not have more than one class of stock or more than 10 stockholders. It must derive no more than 20% of its gross receipts from royalties, rents, dividends, interest, annuities, and gains from the sales or exchanges of stock or securities during the taxable year. Furthermore, not more than 80% of its gross receipts can originate from sources outside of the United States.

[2]The Uniform Limited Partnership Act has been formulated to bring about uniformity in the formation and operation of the limited partnership. All of the states except Alabama, Delaware, Kansas, Kentucky, Louisiana, Maine, Mississippi, Oregon, and Wyoming have adopted this act.

Such partners are known as *limited* or *special partners*. Laws under which limited partnerships may be organized provide that at least one member of the firm shall be a *general partner* whose liability is unlimited. When a limited partner acts in a manner that would indicate to others that he is a general partner, his liability to outsiders becomes that of a general partner. A limited partnership must hold itself out to the public as such and must comply with the provisions of the limited partnership act under which it is formed.

Joint-stock companies. A partnership may be formed with a capital structure in the form of transferable shares. Such an organization is known as a *joint-stock company*. Ownership of shares is usually evidenced by a stock certificate and gives a party the right to participate in the management of the firm, to share in the profits, and to transfer his holdings. Transfer of shares does not affect the continuity of the organization. The liability of each member of a joint-stock company is unlimited, as in the case of a general partnership. The joint-stock company, then, has features of both the partnership and corporate forms of organization. The joint-stock company has its origin in the common law, although in a number of states it is now regulated by statutory law.

ARTICLES OF COPARTNERSHIP

The partnership is created by an agreement that must possess all of the essential elements required of any enforceable contract. Although a partnership may be formed by an oral agreement, it is always preferable that the agreement be in writing so that misunderstandings and disputes between parties as to the nature and the terms of the contract may be avoided or reduced to a minimum. The agreement in writing is referred to as the *articles of copartnership*.

The articles of copartnership should contain all of the terms relating to the establishment of the partnership. The articles should set forth fully and clearly the agreement that has been reached on important matters, such as:

(1) The partnership name, the parties entering into the agreement, and the location of the business.
(2) The effective date of partnership formation and the duration of the contract.
(3) The character and the scope of the business and its location.
(4) The investments by each partner and the values assigned to such investments.
(5) The rights, powers, and duties of the partners, as well as any limitations upon the authority of partners.
(6) The books and accounts of the partnership and the fiscal year that is adopted.

(7) The profit-and-loss-sharing ratio, including any special provisions for the recognition of differences in investment and service contributions.
(8) Special interest charges and credits relating to investments by partners, and special compensation allowed for services rendered by partners.
(9) Partners' investments and withdrawals subsequent to formation and their treatment in the accounts.
(10) Life insurance on partners and treatment of insurance premiums, recoveries on policies, etc.
(11) Special procedures for settlement of a partner's interest upon his withdrawal or death.
(12) Methods for resolving disputes between partners.

If any change is made in the partnership agreement after formation, such a change requires the approval of all of the parties. When certain matters are not covered by agreement, reference is made to partnership law in resolving any differences between the partners.

INTEREST IN CAPITAL AND SHARE IN PROFITS

The accounting problems peculiar to a partnership relate to the measurement of the individual partners' ownership equities or *interests* in the firm.

A partner's interest in a firm should be distinguished from his share in firm profits. A partner's interest is summarized in his capital account and consists of his original investment, subsequent investments and withdrawals, and his share of firm profits and losses. A partner's profit share determines the extent to which his interest will go up or down as a result of profits and losses. Partners may agree to share profits and losses in any manner, irrespective of capital interests. In the absence of an express agreement, partnership law provides that profits and losses shall be divided equally; when there is an express agreement as to profits but none as to losses, losses are divided in the same ratio as profits.

The significance of the foregoing is indicated in the following illustration. A and B enter into partnership. A and B invest assets and are to receive credit of $30,000 and $10,000 respectively for their contributions. The partners agree to share profits and losses equally. Partnership activities are summarized at this point as follows:

	Net Assets	A, Capital	B, Capital
Investments..................	$40,000	$30,000	$10,000

A has a $30,000 interest in the firm, which has a total capital of $40,000; A's interest may be referred to as a ¾ or 75% interest. B's interest is $10,000, which is a ¼ or 25% interest.

Assume that subsequent partnership activities result in a net income of $25,000. Partnership accounts will report the following:

	Net Assets	A, Capital	B, Capital
Investments	$40,000	$30,000	$10,000
Net income	25,000	12,500	12,500
Total	$65,000	$42,500	$22,500

The agreement between A and B provides that profits are to be divided equally and the interests of both A and B increase by $12,500. Not only have interests changed in amount, but they have also changed relative to each other and are no longer in a 3:1 relationship. The changes in interests, absolute or relative, however, have no effect on the profit-and-loss ratio; the partners will continue to share future profits and losses equally. If liquidation takes place at this point and assets realize book value, A is entitled to $42,500 and B to $22,500, as reported in their capital accounts.

Assume in the example above that instead of net income of $25,000, operations result in a net loss of $25,000. The loss is divided equally, and the accounts will report the following:

	Net Assets	A, Capital	B, Capital
Investments	$40,000	$30,000	$10,000
Net loss	(25,000)	(12,500)	(12,500)
Total	$15,000	$17,500	($ 2,500)

B's capital account now shows a debit balance of $2,500. This balance may be regarded as a receivable because it represents a claim by the partnership against B. If the firm is liquidated at this point and net assets realize book value, B will be required to contribute $2,500 in settlement of his capital deficiency; A will receive $17,500, consisting of the proceeds from asset realization, $15,000, and the amount recoverable from B, $2,500.

The problems arising in the determination of partners' respective ownership interests as a result of investments, withdrawals, and profits and losses are discussed in detail in the remaining pages of this chapter. The significance of the respective ownership interests when a partnership dissolves is considered in the chapters that follow.

RECORDING PARTNERS' INVESTMENTS

Investments by partners may be made in the form of cash or other assets as provided in the partnership contract. When assets other than cash are invested, it is necessary for the partners to agree upon the value of such assets. The assets are recorded in accordance with the agreement, and the partners' capital accounts are credited for the amounts of the respective investments.

The importance of proper valuation of assets invested by partners cannot be overemphasized. The values originally assigned to assets are credited to the partner investing the assets and become a measurement of his interest; subsequent sales of these assets at amounts other than book value result in profit and loss items that are divided in the profit and loss ratio. If equity is to be achieved, then, assets invested by partners should be reported at their fair market values; only increases or decreases in the values of such assets taking place during the term of partnership will be allocated among the partners.

CHANGE FROM SOLE PROPRIETORSHIP TO PARTNERSHIP

Frequently an individual who operates a business joins with others in forming a partnership. Here a transfer may be made to the newly formed partnership of both the assets and the liabilities of the business. When the individual's business books are to be employed for the newly formed partnership, entries are made on these books to give effect to the new organization. When new books are to be opened for the partnership, entries are required on the individual's books to record the transfer of the net assets to the firm, and entries are made on the new books to show the opening asset, liability, and capital balances of the partnership.

To illustrate, assume that E and F form a partnership. E has been operating a business that is to be carried on by the new partnership; F is to invest cash of $25,000. Just before the partnership is formed, a balance sheet is drawn up for E's business as follows:

E
Balance Sheet
June 30, 1967

Assets			Liabilities and Capital	
Cash		$16,200	Liabilities	
Accounts receivable	$20,000		Accounts payable	$24,000
Less allowance for bad debts	1,200	18,800	Capital	
Merchandise inventory		21,400		
Supplies inventory		1,600	E, capital	40,400
Furniture and fixtures	$12,000			
Less allowance for depreciation	5,600	6,400		
Total assets		$64,400	Total liabilities and capital	$64,400

It is agreed that E shall withdraw the cash and that the partnership shall take over the remaining assets and assume the liabilities. However, the following adjustments are to be made in recognizing the asset transfer and in establishing E's interest:

Accounts receivable: Bad accounts of $1,000 are to be written off; a 4% allowance for bad debts is to be recognized on remaining accounts.

Merchandise inventory: Goods previously valued at cost calculated in terms of last-in, first-out are to be recognized at their present market value of $26,600.

Furniture and fixtures: Replacement value is $15,000, but the asset is considered to be 50% depreciated and has a sound value of $7,500.

Goodwill: E is to be allowed credit for goodwill of $10,000 that is considered to be related to his business.

Participant's books are retained for partnership. If E's books are retained for the newly formed partnership, the following entries may be made:

Transaction		Entry		
To record the restatement of E's investment as agreed:		Allowance for Bad Debts. .	440	
Decrease in accounts receivable.	$ 1,000	Merchandise Inventory. . .	5,200	
Decrease in allowance for bad debts (to report allowance at 4% of $19,000, or $760).	440	Allowance for Depreciation	5,600	
Increase in merchandise inventory.	5,200	Goodwill.	10,000	
Increase in furniture and fixtures	1,100	Accounts Receivable. . . .		1,000
Decrease in cost balance $4,500		Furniture and Fixtures. .		4,500
Elim. of allow. for depr. 5,600		E, Capital.		15,740
Establishment of goodwill.	10,000			
To record the withdrawal of cash by E.		E, Capital.	16,200	
		Cash.		16,200
To record the investment of cash by F.		Cash.	25,000	
		F, Capital.		25,000

A balance sheet for the newly organized partnership follows:

E and F
Balance Sheet
June 30, 1967

Assets			Liabilities and Capital		
			Liabilities		
Cash.		$25,000			
Accounts receivable.	$19,000		Accounts payable.		$24,000
Less allowance for bad debts.	760	18,240			
			Capital		
Merchandise inventory. . . .		26,600			
Supplies inventory.		1,600	E, capital.	$39,940	
Furniture and fixtures. . . .		7,500	F, capital.	25,000	64,940
Goodwill.		10,000			
Total assets.		$88,940	Total liabilities and capital.		$88,940

New books are opened for the partnership. If new books are opened for the partnership, entries on the new books are made as follows:

Transaction	Entry		
To record investment by E.	Accounts Receivable	19,000	
	Merchandise Inventory	26,600	
	Supplies Inventory	1,600	
	Furniture and Fixtures	7,500	
	Goodwill	10,000	
	Allowance for Bad Debts		760
	Accounts Payable		24,000
	E, Capital		39,940
To record investment by F.	Cash	25,000	
	F, Capital		25,000

If new books for the partnership are opened, books for the sole proprietorship must be closed. Asset, liability, and capital accounts may be closed by a single compound entry. If desired, it would be possible to record the restatement of assets and the recognition of goodwill on the individual's books. This would be followed by a compound entry to close all of the account balances as adjusted.

CONSOLIDATION OF BUSINESSES

The accounting procedures described in the preceding section are also applied when two or more businesses are consolidated in the formation of a partnership. The articles of copartnership should indicate clearly how the interests of the partners are to be determined. It is also important that the parties agree upon the valuations to be assigned to assets and liabilities. Books of one of the constituent units may be used for the newly formed partnership or a new set of books may be opened.

PARTNERS' ACCOUNTS

Accounts that are maintained with partners consist of (1) capital accounts, (2) drawing or personal accounts, and (3) receivable and payable accounts.

Capital and drawing accounts. Partners' original investments are reported in capital accounts for each partner. Transactions between the partnership and the individual partners resulting in changes in the partners' ownership interests may be summarized in the capital accounts or in separate drawing accounts. Changes in partners' interests arise from transactions such as the following:

Increases

(1) Investments in the partnership of cash, merchandise, or other assets.
(2) Assumption or payment by the individual partners of partnership obligations.

(3) Collection by the partnership of personal claims of partners.
(4) Profits from partnership operations.

Decreases

(1) Withdrawals from the partnership of cash, merchandise, or other assets.
(2) Collection of partnership claims by individual partners.
(3) Assumption or payment by the partnership of personal indebtedness of partners (individual income taxes, life insurance premiums, etc.).
(4) Losses from partnership operations.

The partnership agreement should indicate clearly those special considerations that are to apply as a result of absolute and relative changes in partners' interests. Entries can then be made in the accounts in a manner that will appropriately recognize changes in interests.

Normally, increases or decreases in capital that are interpreted as permanent capital changes are recorded directly in the capital accounts. Drawings by partners in anticipation of profits, and other increases and decreases of relatively minor amounts that are not viewed as of a permanent character, are recorded in the drawing accounts. At the end of the accounting period, profit or loss is summarized in the profit and loss account and the balance in this account is transferred to the drawing accounts. The resulting debit and credit balances in the drawing accounts are transferred to the partners' capital accounts.

In certain instances it may be desirable to maintain a permanent distinction between the original or fixed capitals and subsequent increases or decreases in capitals resulting from partners' investments and withdrawals and from profits and losses. This is the case, for example, when it is agreed that partners are to be credited with interest on capital balances that exceed original or fixed balances and are to be charged with interest on capital deficiencies. When a permanent distinction betweeen original balances and changes in those balances is to be maintained, profits, losses, investments, and withdrawals may be summarized in the drawing accounts and these balances may be left open and carried into succeeding fiscal periods. A credit balance in a drawing account would indicate that the partner had withdrawn less than the increases that took place in his interest; a debit balance would indicate that he had withdrawn more than such increases. When only profits, losses, and withdrawals against profits are summarized in the drawing accounts and these accounts are left open, the distinction between the capital and the drawing accounts of the partnership parallels the distinction between the invested capital and the retained earnings accounts of the corporation. Individual partner's capital and drawing balances would be combined in reporting each partner's total interest on the balance sheet.

Receivable and payable balances. A withdrawal by a partner that is made with the assumption of ultimate repayment to the firm normally calls for the recognition of a special receivable balance. The amount receivable from the partner may be recorded by a charge to the account Advances to Partner or the account Notes Receivable from Partner, whichever is appropriate.

An advance to the firm by a partner that is made with the assumption of ultimate repayment by the firm normally calls for recognition of a special payable balance. The amount owed to the partner may be recorded by a credit to the account Loans Payable to Partner or the account Notes Payable to Partner, whichever is appropriate. In certain instances, partners may agree to invest fixed amounts, any subsequent withdrawals or investments to be recognized as partnership receivables and payables. Receivables from partners may be reported on the balance sheet as assets; payables to partners, as liabilities. When current settlement of these balances is anticipated, they would be recognized as current assets or current liabilities.

The partnership agreement should state clearly any interest provisions with respect to fluctuating capital balances. In the absence of a special agreement, the Uniform Partnership Act provides that a partner is entitled to interest on capital that exceeds the amount he agreed to contribute; however, the Act does not require that a partner be charged for interest on withdrawals that reduce his invested capital. When partner receivable and payable balances are recognized, special agreements should be made concerning the rate of interest that is applicable on these balances.

DISTRIBUTION OF PROFITS AND LOSSES

Partners may agree to the distribution of profits and losses in any manner they wish. The agreement on this matter should be specific and complete so that misunderstandings and disputes may be avoided.

Profits and losses are generally divided in one of the following ways:

(1) Equally.
(2) In an arbitrary ratio.
(3) In the ratio of partners' capitals.
(4) Interest to be allowed on partners' capitals, the balance to be divided on some arbitrary basis as agreed.
(5) Salaries or bonus to be allowed for partners' services, the balance to be divided on some arbitrary basis as agreed.
(6) Interest to be allowed on partners' capitals, salaries to be allowed for partners' services, the balance to be divided on some arbitrary basis as agreed.

The remainder of this chapter illustrates distributions under each of the foregoing bases. Examples are based on the following assumptions:

A profit of $36,000 is determined for the firm of A and B at the end of a fiscal year. Regular withdrawals by partners in anticipation of profits have been summarized in the drawing accounts; permanent capital changes have been summarized in the capital accounts. Drawing and capital accounts at the end of the year appear as follows:

A, Drawing

Jan. 1 to Dec. 31	6,000		

B, Drawing

Jan. 1 to Dec. 31	19,000		

A, Capital

		Jan. 1	50,000
		Apr. 1	10,000

B, Capital

Mar. 1	5,000	Jan. 1	70,000
		Nov. 1	10,000

Profit and loss division equally. Agreements between partners frequently call for the division of profits and losses equally. In the absence of a specific agreement to the contrary, both common and statutory law provide that profits and losses shall be divided equally, regardless of asset and service contributions. The entry for the partnership of A and B to record the division of the profit of $36,000 equally would be as follows:

Profit and Loss	36,000	
A, Drawing		18,000
B, Drawing		18,000

A's share of profits: ½ of $36,000 =	$18,000
B's share of profits: ½ of $36,000 =	18,000
Total	$36,000

The resulting balances in the drawing accounts may now be closed into the capital accounts.

Profit and loss division in arbitrary ratio. In order that differences in partners' capital or service contributions may be recognized, partners may agree to share profits in some arbitrary ratio that expresses such differences. For example, assume that, since the experience, ability, and reputation of A are factors of special significance to the success of the firm, A and B agree to divide profits in the ratio of 3:2. The entry to record the division of the profit of $36,000 is:

Profit and Loss	36,000	
A, Drawing		21,600
B, Drawing		14,400

A's share of profits: ⅗ of $36,000 =	$21,600
B's share of profits: ⅖ of $36,000 =	14,400
Total	$36,000

It should be noted that if operations had resulted in a loss of $36,000, A would have borne 3/5 of the loss and B 2/5 unless the agreement provided that losses were to be distributed in a manner other than the profit ratio. It would be possible, of course, for A and B to agree to share profits 3:2 but to share losses equally or in some other manner.

In certain cases, partners may agree to share part of the earnings in a particular ratio and the balance differently. For example, A and B could agree to divide profits up to $20,000 in the 3:2 ratio and any profits in excess of this amount equally.

Profit and loss division in the ratio of partners' capitals. When properties invested by the partners represent the particularly significant contributions to the success of the firm, partners may agree to divide profits in the ratio of partners' capitals. When profits are to be divided in the capital ratio, the agreement should indicate specifically whether the ratio is to be defined in terms of:

(1) Original capitals.
(2) Capitals at the beginning of each fiscal period.
(3) Capitals at the end of each fiscal period.
(4) Average capitals for each fiscal period.

Original capitals. If the agreement between A and B provides that the periodic division of profits shall be based upon original capitals, reference would be made to the amounts originally invested by the partners.

Capitals at the beginning of each fiscal period. If the periodic division of profits is to be based upon capitals at the beginning of each period, current opening balances as reported by the capital accounts would provide the basis for allocation. Assuming this agreement for A and B, the entry to record the division of the profit of $36,000 for the year is:

Profit and Loss	36,000	
A, Drawing		15,000
B, Drawing		21,000

A, Capital, January 1	$ 50,000
B, Capital, January 1	70,000
Total capitals, January 1	$120,000
A's share of profits: 50,000/120,000 of $36,000 =	$15,000
B's share of profits: 70,000/120,000 of $36,000 =	21,000
Total	$36,000

Capitals at the end of each fiscal period. If the partnership agreement provides for a division of profits based upon partners' capitals at the end of each year, calculations for the division of profits will be made as follows:

A, Capital, December 31	$ 60,000
B, Capital, December 31	75,000
Total capitals, December 31	$135,000

A's share of profits: 60,000/135,000 of $36,000 =	$ 16,000
B's share of profits: 75,000/135,000 of $36,000 =	20,000
Total..............................	$ 36,000

Average capitals for each fiscal period. If the division is to be based upon average capitals for the year, calculations will be made as follows:

	Date	Investment Balance		Number of Months Unchanged	Months × Investment	Total Month-Dollars
A:	Jan. 1	$50,000	×	3	$150,000	
	Apr. 1	60,000	×	9	540,000	$ 690,000
				12		
B:	Jan. 1	$70,000	×	2	$140,000	
	Mar. 1	65,000	×	8	520,000	
	Nov. 1	75,000	×	2	150,000	810,000
		Total		12		$1,500,000

A's share of profits: 690,000/1,500,000* of $36,000 =	$ 16,560
B's share of profits: 810,000/1,500,000 of 36,000 =	19,440
Total....................................	$ 36,000

*It should be observed that it would be possible to determine each partner's average capital for the year by dividing the sum of the month-dollar products for each by 12. (For example: A's average capital = $690,000 ÷ 12, or $57,500; B's average capital, $810,000 ÷ 12, or $67,500.) Or average capitals may be calculated by multiplying the investment balances during the year by the fractions of the year for which such balances are unchanged. (For example, A's average capital = ($50,000 × 3/12) + ($60,000 × 9/12), or $57,500; B's average capital = ($70,000 × 2/12) + ($65,000 × 8/12) + ($75,000 × 2/12), or $67,500.) But the use of balances reduced to year-dollars will not change the ratio between partners and will result in exactly the same profit or loss for each partner.

When partners wish to distribute profits in terms of relative investments, the use of average capitals, which provides for the recognition of capital changes during the period, normally offers the most equitable method. An agreement for the use of average capitals also acts as an incentive for additional investments when these can be profitably employed. When this method is to be used, the agreement should indicate clearly what investments and withdrawals are to be recognized in calculating average capitals. For example, an agreement may provide that all of the changes in partners' interests are to be recognized; here recognition would be given to investments and withdrawals reported in partners' drawing accounts as well as in capital accounts. Or, the agreement may provide that regular drawings are to be permitted in anticipation of accruing profit and that calculations shall be made without regard to drawings. Under the latter agreement, it would be desirable to limit entries in the drawing accounts to regularly allowed drawings, with amounts withdrawn in excess of such allowances, as well as amounts invested, being recorded directly in the capital accounts. The capital accounts will then reflect the data that are to be considered in calculating the average capital ratio.

In the example, partners' investments were expressed in terms of month-dollars. In making month-dollar calculations, partners may agree to consider investments and withdrawals made during the month as having been made as of the beginning of the month, as of the beginning of the following month, or as of one of these dates depending upon whether the change took place before or after the middle of the month. Any unit of time can be used in calculating the ratio of average capitals. Thus, when investments and withdrawals are made during the month, greater accuracy in calculating respective investments can be obtained by using weeks or the actual number of days, thereby determining the ratio of partners' capitals in terms of week-dollars or day-dollars.

Profit and loss division with allowance of interest on partners' capitals. In the preceding section it was suggested that when investments in properties represent the particularly significant contributions to a firm, partners can agree to distribute profits or losses in accordance with relative capital contributions. For example, when individuals pool their cash for investment in the commodities or securities markets, they may feel that an equitable allocation of profit or loss calls for division according to relative investments. However, there are instances when partners may feel that, while respective capitals need to be considered, division of profits in the capital ratio will not be equitable for the following reasons: (1) investments represent only one factor contributing to the success of the joint enterprise and the arrangement for profit distribution should recognize all of these factors; (2) in the event of loss, the partner making the larger investment absorbs the greater part of the loss with no recognition of his special capital contribution.

Interest on capital balances. In providing for the recognition of differences in investments as well as the other factors responsible for successful operations, partners may agree to allow interest on capitals, with any profit or loss after interest divided in some arbitrary ratio. An agreement for interest should indicate the interest rate that is to be applied. It should also indicate whether calculations are to be made in terms of capital balances as of a certain time or on average capitals for the period. The law makes no provision for remuneration to partners for their investments in the absence of an agreement to that effect.

To illustrate the allowance of interest on partners' capitals, assume that A and B agree to allow interest on average investments at 6%; any profit or loss balance is to be divided equally. Assuming no entries for interest during the course of the period, entries to record the allowance of interest and the remaining distribution of profit follow:

Profit and Loss			7,500	
A, Drawing				3,450
B, Drawing				4,050
A: Interest on $50,000 at 6% for 3 months	$ 750			
Interest on $60,000 at 6% for 9 months	2,700	$ 3,450		
B: Interest on $70,000 at 6% for 2 months	$ 700			
Interest on $65,000 at 6% for 8 months	2,600			
Interest on $75,000 at 6% for 2 months	750	4,050		
Total interest allowable		$ 7,500		

Profit and Loss		28,500	
A, Drawing			14,250
B, Drawing			14,250
Original balance in profit and loss account	$36,000		
Less allowance for interest	7,500		
Balance, to be distributed equally	$28,500		

The profit distribution may be summarized in a single entry as follows:

Profit and Loss	36,000	
A, Drawing		17,700
B, Drawing		18,300

It should be observed that the effect of an allowance for interest is to distribute only a limited amount of the profit in the capital ratio. In the case of A and B, 6% of combined average capitals, or $7,500, was distributed in the ratio of average capitals, the balance being distributed equally.

When the partnership agreement provides without qualification that interest is to be allowed on investments, interest must be allowed even though operations have resulted in earnings that are less than the allowable interest or in a loss. After the entry for interest in such a case, the debit balance in the profit and loss account is transferred to the partners' drawing accounts in the profit and loss ratio. For example, assume that operations for A and B prior to the recognition of interest had resulted in a loss of $10,000. Entries to close the profit and loss account would have been as follows:

Profit and Loss			7,500	
A, Drawing				3,450
B, Drawing				4,050
Interest allowable on capitals.				
A, Drawing			8,750	
B, Drawing			8,750	
Profit and Loss				17,500
Original balance in profit and loss account	(Dr.)	$10,000		
Allowance for interest	(Dr.)	7,500		
Balance distributable equally	(Dr.)	$17,500		

The net effect of the foregoing on capitals is:

		A		B		Total
Allowance for interest	(Cr.)	$3,450	(Cr.)	$4,050	(Cr.)	$ 7,500
Less distribution of resulting loss	(Dr.)	8,750	(Dr.)	8,750	(Dr.)	17,500
Net effect	(Dr.)	$5,300	(Dr.)	$4,700	(Dr.)	$10,000

If profit and loss were distributed in the ratio of partners' capitals, B would have been charged with the greater share of the loss. If profit and loss were distributed equally, B would have absorbed a loss of $5,000. The provision for interest, however, secured a $600 advantage for B over A.

Assume that partnership operations had resulted in a loss of only $500. The allowance for interest and the distribution of the total loss would result in an increase in B's capital with a reduction in A's capital equal to the loss plus the increase accruing to B.

The net effect on capitals would be:

		A		B		Total
Allowance for interest	(Cr.)	$3,450	(Cr.)	$4,050	(Cr.)	$7,500
Less distribution of resulting loss	(Dr.)	4,000	(Dr.)	4,000	(Dr.)	8,000
Net effect	(Dr.)	$ 550	(Cr.)	$ 50	(Dr.)	$ 500

Here, too, the agreement for interest resulted in a $600 advantage for B. Partners can provide by agreement, of course, that profit or loss shall be distributed in some arbitrary manner without recognition of interest when the results from operations fail to cover a specified interest allowance.

Interest on excess investments. It may be agreed to allow interest on the excess of the average investment of one partner over that of another. If this were the agreement between A and B, the profit and loss account would be debited for $600 and the drawing account of B would be credited for this amount. Any profit and loss balance would then be transferred to the partners' drawing accounts in the agreed ratio.

Distributions under an agreement to recognize interest on only excess investments will differ from the distributions that would be obtained with a full allowance of interest on capital investments when profit and loss is distributed in a manner other than equally. When interest is allowed only on excess investments, the portion of the profit that would otherwise be distributed equally in recognition of equal amounts of partners' capitals remains to be distributed in the profit and loss ratio.

The agreement for interest may take still other forms. For example, an agreement may provide for fixed capital contributions from individual partners with interest allowed on amounts in excess of such fixed amounts and interest charged on any deficiencies. In other instances, interest may be allowed on capitals in excess of a fixed proportion of total capital, or interest may be charged on capital deficiencies in terms of such a fixed proportion.

Interest on temporary advances or loans. When a partnership makes a temporary advance to a partner or receives an amount as a temporary loan from a partner and these transactions are recognized as creating debtor or creditor relationships between the partner and the firm, interest charges and credits on such transactions are recognized as interest expense and interest income. Interest accruals are recognized periodically on these items just as on other receivable and payable balances. When settlement for interest is made by cash, entries to record the collection of interest or the payment of interest are made in the usual manner. When settlement is not to be made in cash but by adjustments to partners' capitals, interest on an advance to a partner is recorded by a charge to the partner's drawing account and a credit to Interest Income; interest on a loan made by a partner to the firm is recorded by a charge to Interest Expense and a credit to the partner's drawing account.

Recognition of revenue and expense items may be called for in other relationships between a partnership and the individual partners. In certain instances, for example, a partnership and an individual partner may enter into a landlord-tenant relationship. In other instances, the parties may enter into a seller-buyer relationship. Such relationships call for accounting procedures similar to those just described.

Profit and loss division with allowance of salaries or bonuses to partners. Partners may wish to provide for a division of profits that recognizes differences in the ability and the experience of the different members or in the time devoted by them to the business. Partners may agree to an arbitrary ratio for this purpose. However, the use of an arbitrary ratio to recognize personal differences is subject to the same limitations as those found in the use of the capital ratio to recognize capital differences: it may fail to provide satisfactory recognition of the several factors contributing to the success of the enterprise and it may prove inequitable in the event of loss when the partner who has made the greater personal contribution to the firm is charged with the greater part of the loss.

Salaries. In recognizing differences in personal contribution as well as other factors that are responsible for the success of the enterprise, it may be agreed that partners shall be allowed salaries, with any profit or loss balance after salaries divided in some arbitrary ratio. The law makes no provision for remuneration for partners' services in the absence of an agreement thereto; however, the Uniform Partnership Act does provide that, when a partnership must be liquidated as a result of the death of a partner, a surviving partner is entitled to reasonable compensation for his services in winding up the business.

To illustrate the application of a salary arrangement, assume that A and B agree to the allowance of monthly salaries of $1,500 and $1,250 respectively; any profit or loss balance is to be shared equally. Amounts actually withdrawn by partners during the year were recorded in their drawing accounts as summarized on page 13. The profit of $36,000 before recognition of salaries is distributed to the partners by the following entries:

Profit and Loss		33,000	
A, Drawing			18,000
B, Drawing			15,000
A: Salary for 12 months at $1,500	$18,000		
B: Salary for 12 months at $1,250	15,000		
Total salaries allowable	$33,000		

Profit and Loss		3,000	
A, Drawing			1,500
B, Drawing			1,500
Original balance in profit and loss account	$36,000		
Less allowance for salaries	33,000		
Balance distributable equally	$ 3,000		

The foregoing may be summarized in a single entry as follows:

Profit and Loss	36,000	
A, Drawing		19,500
B, Drawing		16,500

When an agreement provides for salaries without qualification, salary distributions must be made even though profit is inadequate to cover salaries or there is a loss. After salaries are recorded in such a case, the profit and loss account shows a debit balance that is transferred to the partners' accounts as agreed.

The allowance of salaries to A and B of $18,000 and $15,000 will provide a $3,000 advantage to A in all distributions. If the partners do not wish such an advantage to remain effective when profit does not cover salaries or when a loss is incurred, their agreement should include provisions for scaling down or suspending salaries under these circumstances.

When fixed salary amounts are paid to partners at regular weekly or monthly intervals, a salary account for each partner may be charged. After nominal accounts are closed into Profit and Loss and the net profit is determined, the salary accounts may be transferred to the profit and loss account in determining the balance of the profit that remains to be distributed. When salaries are allowed but the partners do not necessarily withdraw the allowed amounts at regular intervals, the partners' drawing accounts instead of salary accounts should be debited for all cash withdrawals. Consideration of the amounts allowed as salaries should be deferred until the books are closed. At that time the profit and loss account is debited and each partner's drawing account is credited with the amount allowed as salary for the entire period. The balance in the profit and loss account is then divided as agreed.

It should be pointed out that when an agreement permits partners to make withdrawals, it is important that the nature of such withdrawals be clearly defined. For example, assume that an agreement permits partners to withdraw specified amounts periodically. Is it the intent of the parties simply to permit partners to draw cash out of the business in anticipation of accruing profits? Or is it their intent to consider allowed withdrawals as partial profit distributions? If the first interpretation is applicable, profit or loss distribution will be made without regard to drawing account balances, and withdrawals will be subtracted from distributive profit shares in arriving at each partner's capital change for the period. If the second interpretation is applicable, drawing account balances will be closed into Profit and Loss and the profit or loss balance will be distributed to partners as agreed.

Bonuses. In some instances a managing partner is allowed a bonus that is to be based on the earnings of the business. The bonus is commonly stated as a percentage of profits, but the agreement should indicate whether the percentage is to be applied to the profit determined before deduction of the bonus or after deduction of the bonus. To illustrate, assume that A, the managing partner, is allowed as a bonus 20% of the profit before deducting the bonus. The bonus would be $7,200, determined by applying the 20% rate to the profit from operations, $36,000. But if A is allowed a bonus of 20% of the profit after deduction of the bonus, the bonus would be calculated as follows:

The bonus plus the net profit after deduction of the bonus = $36,000.
Let X = the net profit after deduction of the bonus
And .20X = the bonus allowed to A.
Then: 1.20X = $36,000
X = $30,000
.20X = $6,000, the bonus allowed to A.

To record the bonus allowed to A, the profit and loss account is charged and A's drawing account is credited. The balance in the profit and loss account is then distributed as agreed.

In addition to the statement as to how the bonus calculation is to be made, the bonus agreement should indicate whether the bonus rate is to be applied to the full increase in capital, including all extraordinary and nonrecurring items that receive current recognition, or only to the net income as measured by normally recurring revenue and expense items.

Profit and loss division with allowances for interest and salaries. Partners may agree to allowances of both interest and salaries as a means for dividing profits equitably. When both salaries and interest are allowed, the profit and loss account may be charged and the drawing accounts credited for both classes of allowances at the end of each period. Any balance in the profit and loss account is then divided in the agreed ratio. The entries for salaries, interest, and the transfer of a remaining balance in the profit and loss account are the same as those illustrated in earlier sections.

Profit distribution on the income statement. Partners contribute their capitals, times, and skills in the attempt to realize a profit. Special agreements for interest and salaries make it possible to distribute earnings with appropriate recognition of differences in the partners' contributions. A full analysis of the distribution of earnings may be reported at the bottom of the income statement. Assume that the firm of A and B previously referred to has agreed to the following: monthly salaries of $1,500 and $1,250 respectively; interest at 6% on average capitals; and any profit or loss balance to be divided equally. This can be reported on the income statement as follows:

Net income for year			$36,000
Net income divided as follows:	A	B	Total
Amount allowed as salaries	$18,000	$15,000	$33,000
Amount allowed as interest	3,450	4,050	7,500
	$21,450	$19,050	$40,500
Less reductions made equally for amount by which salaries and interest exceed net income	2,250	2,250	4,500
Net income distribution	$19,200	$16,800	$36,000

Interest for partners' investments and salaries for partners' services treated as expenses. In the foregoing discussions, net income was viewed as the return to the partners for their full contribution to the business as owners — capital as well as personal service. Interest and salary allowances to partners were regarded as means of providing for an equitable distribution of such income. The partnership was viewed as an association of individuals; accounting for the partnership paralleled that for the sole proprietorship where no compensation to an owner for capital or services was recognized in measuring net income.

It is possible to record allowances to partners for interest and salaries as expense items rather than as distributions of net income. If the partnership is viewed as a separate entity, special compensation allowed to partners may be regarded the same as the compensation accruing to the stockholders of a corporation who, at the same time, have entered into relationships with the corporation as creditors and employees. Frequently the partners themselves may prefer to view interest and salary allowances as expenses of operation and may call for statements that summarize net income after such charges. It may be noted that federal income tax laws provide that fixed or guaranteed payments to partners for the use of capital or for services must be reported for tax purposes just as though they were paid to outsiders.

When partners' interest and salaries are treated as expenses, charges for these items are made to expense accounts rather than to the partners' drawing accounts; expense balances are then closed into the profit and loss account in arriving at the earnings distributable in the agreed profit and loss ratio. On the income statement, partners' interest and salaries would be listed with the other expenses in arriving at the net income or loss balance. Whether partners' interest and salaries are treated in the accounts as expense items or as distributions of net income, the ultimate distributions of partnership earnings among the partners are exactly the same.

CORRECTIONS IN PROFITS OF PRIOR PERIODS

When a misstatement of earnings for a prior period is discovered, the profit-and-loss-sharing agreement for the fiscal period in which earnings were misstated must be considered in correcting the capital accounts. The correct earnings for the prior period, as well as the proper share of the profit or loss to which each of the partners was entitled, should be calculated. The share of the profit that each partner actually received is compared with the share that he should have received in arriving at the corrections that are required in the capital accounts.

In certain instances, questions may arise as to whether extraordinary items call for current profit and loss recognition or for the restatement of profit and loss of prior fiscal periods. These questions arise in instances such as the sale of securities at a gain or loss that may be considered to have accrued over a number of years during which the assets were held, or the disposal of a depreciable asset at a gain or loss that may be considered to arise from a failure to measure depreciation satisfactorily in prior periods. The answer to such questions may be anticipated by appropriate provisions in the partnership agreement.

STATEMENT OF CHANGES IN PARTNERS' CAPITAL ACCOUNTS

The balance sheet and the income statement for a partnership are accompanied by a third statement that reports the changes that have taken place in the partners' interests during the period. The statement of changes in partners' capital accounts may be prepared in the following form:

A and B
Statement of Changes in Partners' Capital Accounts
For Year Ended December 31, 1967

	A	B	Total
Capitals, January 1, 1967	$50,000	$70,000	$120,000
Additional capital investments	10,000	10,000	20,000
	$60,000	$80,000	$140,000
Less capital withdrawals		5,000	5,000
Balance	$60,000	$75,000	$135,000
Net income for year	19,200	16,800	36,000
	$79,200	$91,800	$171,000
Less personal drawings	6,000	19,000	25,000
Capitals, December 31, 1967	$73,200	$72,800	$146,000

QUESTIONS

1. What are the essential characteristics of a partnership?

2. In what respects is the partnership form of organization similar to the corporate form? What are the essential differences between the two forms of organization?

3. Under what circumstances is the partnership viewed as a separate entity? Under what circumstances is the partnership viewed as an association of individuals?

4. Distinguish between (a) trading and nontrading partnerships; (b) general and limited partnerships.

5. What is the nature of the joint-stock company?

6. State at least twelve matters in regard to the partnership relationship that should be fully covered in the partnership agreement.

7. What is the significance of a partner's *interest* in a firm? What is the significance of a partner's *share in the profits* of a firm?

8. Give four sources for (a) an increase in a partner's interest in a firm, (b) a decrease in a partner's interest.

9. (a) Indicate the source of partner receivable and payable balances and the treatment of such balances on the statements. (b) How would you record interest charges and credits emerging from such relationships?

10. State the common bases employed in the distribution of partnership profits. Under what circumstances would each of the bases named be the most acceptable?

11. In the absence of an agreement:

(a) Is interest allowed on capital investments?
(b) Is interest charged on partners' drawings?
(c) Is interest allowed on advances to the firm made by partners beyond agreed investments?
(d) Is compensation allowed partners for extra time devoted to the partnership?
(e) Is compensation allowed for special services of a partner relative to firm liquidation?

12. (a) What is the purpose of allowing interest on invested capital? (b) What are the possible treatments for such interest in the accounts? (c) What is the effect of the allowance of interest when operations result in a loss?

13. In forming a partnership with Jackson, Macey suggests that interest of 6% be allowed on average capitals, the balance of any profit to be distributed in the ratio of average capitals. Jackson insists that there is no need for the interest provision if profits are to be distributed in the ratio of average capitals. Is this correct?

14. Martin and McCrea are partners sharing profits 2:1 respectively. Martin borrows cash from the firm and ultimately returns the amount borrowed together with interest. McCrea insists that he should be credited for the full amount of the interest collected. Do you agree?

15. A partnership agreement permits partners A and B to withdraw $100 per week. The profit and loss ratio is 2:1 respectively. What two interpretations may be made of this agreement? Which interpretation will A prefer?

16. (a) What is the purpose of allowing salaries to partners? (b) What is the ultimate effect upon capitals if partners' salaries are treated as an expense as compared with their treatment as distributive shares of profit?

17. The partnership of S and T uses buildings that are owned by T, for which T is to receive rent of $10,000 per year. At the close of the first year of operations, the accountant charges rent and credits T for $10,000. T insists that the full charge for rent is properly made against S; with a charge to an expense account, his advantage will be limited to only $5,000. Comment on T's statement.

18. What are the advantages of reporting partners' salaries and interest on the income statement as expenses as compared with recognition of these items as partial distributions of net income?

19. X and Y divide profits and losses according to capital balances at the beginning of each year. In 1967, securities acquired in 1957 at a cost of $10,000 are sold for $35,000. Partner X insists that the profit should be recognized as having accrued over a 10-year period at the rate of $2,500 per year; the profit and loss ratio for the past 10 years, then, should be applied to the annual increments in arriving at the distribution of the $25,000 gain. (a) Evaluate this proposal. (b) How should a controversy on this point have been avoided?

EXERCISES

1. Peters admits Quarles to a partnership interest in his business. Accounts in the ledger for Peters on November 30, 1967, just before the admission of Quarles show the following balances:

	Debits	Credits
Cash	$ 2,600	
Accounts Receivable	12,000	
Merchandise Inventory	18,000	
Accounts Payable		$ 6,200
Peters, Capital		26,400

It is agreed that for purposes of establishing Peters' interest the following adjustments shall be made:

(1) An allowance for doubtful accounts of 2% of accounts receivable is to be established.
(2) The merchandise inventory is to be valued at $20,200.
(3) Prepaid expenses of $650 and accrued expenses of $400 are to be recognized.

Quarles is to invest sufficient cash to give him a ⅓ interest in the partnership.

(a) Give the entries to adjust the account balances in establishing Peters' interest and to record the investment by Quarles. (b) Prepare a balance sheet for Peters and Quarles.

2. P and R, partners, divide profits and losses on the basis of average capitals. Capital accounts for the year ended December 31, 1967, are shown below. The net profit for 1967 is $13,500. Prepare summaries to show how the profit is divided. (Changes in capitals during the first half of a month are regarded as effective as of the beginning of the month; changes during the second half of a month are regarded as effective as of the beginning of the following month.)

P, Capital

Mar. 9	5,000	Jan. 1	30,000
Oct. 26	7,500	July 1	10,000
		Sept. 22	10,000

R, Capital

Sept. 4	4,000	Jan. 1	33,000
		Apr. 14	15,000

3. Boyle and Clark are partners sharing profits in the ratio of 3:2. The partnership agreement states that each partner is to be allowed drawings of $3,000 annually. Each partner withdrew this amount during 1967, drawing accounts being charged. The net profit for 1967 was $10,000. What entries are necessary to close the accounts at the end of the year if the balances in the drawing accounts are recognized as (a) partners' drawings and (b) partners' salaries?

4. A, B, and C form a partnership and agree to maintain average investments of $100,000, $50,000, and $50,000 respectively. Interest on an excess or on a deficiency in a capital contribution is to be computed at 6%. After the interest allowances, A, B, and C are to share any balance in the ratio of 5:3:2. Average amounts invested during the first six months were as follows: A, $120,000; B, $55,000; C, $40,000. A loss from operations of $2,500 was incurred for the first six months. How is this loss distributed among the partners?

5. Allen and Powers are partners. The partnership agreement provides that Allen "shall receive a bonus of 25% of the profits." What two interpretations of this phrase are possible? Assuming a profit of $20,400, what amount would be allowed as a bonus in each case?

6. R, S, and T, attorneys, decide to form a partnership and agree to distribute profits in the ratio of 5:3:2. It is agreed, however, that R and S shall guarantee fees from their own clients of $60,000 and $50,000 respectively, that any deficiency is to be charged directly against the account of the partner failing to meet his guarantee, and that any excess is to be credited directly to the account of the partner exceeding his guarantee. Fees earned during 1967 are classified as follows:

From clients of R.	$100,000
From clients of S.	40,000
From clients of T.	10,000

Operating expenses for 1967 are $20,000. Give the entries to close the nominal accounts into the profit and loss account and the latter into the capital accounts at the end of 1967.

7. Partners A and B share profits 3:1 after annual salary allowances of $4,000 and $6,000 respectively; however, if profits are not adequate to meet the salary allowances, the entire profit is to be divided in the salary ratio. Profits of $9,000 were reported, for the year 1967. In 1968 it is ascertained that in calculating net income for the year ended December 31, 1967, depreciation was overstated by $3,600 and the ending inventory was understated by $800. Give the correcting entry that is required in 1968.

PROBLEMS

1-1. Allen and Bailey entered into partnership on March 1, 1967, investing $62,500 and $37,500 respectively. It was agreed that Allen, the managing partner, was to receive a salary of $15,000 per year and also 10% of the net profit after adjustment for the salary; the balance of the profit was to be divided in the ratio of original capitals. On December 31, 1967, account balances were as follows:

Cash	$ 35,000	Payables	$ 30,000
Receivables.	33,500	Sales	116,500
Fixtures.	22,500	Allen, Capital.	62,500
Purchases	98,000	Bailey, Capital.	37,500
Returns and Allowances	2,500		
Operating Expenses. . . .	30,000		
Drawings.	25,000		
	$246,500		$246,500

Inventories on December 31, 1967, were: merchandise, $36,500; supplies, $1,250. Prepaid taxes and insurance were $475 and accrued expenses totaled $775. Depreciation on fixtures is to be computed at 20%

per year. Drawings were made as follows: Allen, $1,000 per month; Bailey, $1,500 per month.

Instructions: (1) Give the adjusting and closing entries on December 31, 1967.

(2) Prepare an income statement, a balance sheet, and a statement of changes in partners' capital accounts for the period ended December 31, 1967.

1-2. On July 1, 1967, Baker and Carr decide to pool their assets and form a partnership. The firm is to take over business assets and assume business liabilities, and capitals are to be based on net assets transferred after the following adjustments:

(1) Carr's inventory is to be valued at $14,000.
(2) An allowance for bad debts of 5% is to be established on the customer accounts of each party.
(3) Accrued expenses of $800 are to be recognized on Baker's books.
(4) Carr is to be allowed goodwill of $10,000 and is to invest additional cash so that he will have a 60% interest in the new firm.

Balance sheets for Baker and Carr on July 1 before adjustment are given below:

	Baker	Carr
Cash	$ 7,500	$ 4,500
Customers	18,000	15,000
Inventory	16,000	12,000
Equipment	10,000	12,000
Allowance for depreciation	(4,500)	(1,500)
	$47,000	$42,000
Creditors	$13,800	$10,000
Capital	33,200	32,000
	$47,000	$42,000

Carr's books are to be continued as the partnership books after July 1.

Instructions: (1) Give the entries to adjust and close Baker's books.

(2) Give the required entries on the books of Carr upon the formation of the partnership.

(3) Prepare a balance sheet for the firm of Baker and Carr as of July 1, 1967.

1-3. The capital accounts for Cross and Deming at the end of 1967 are as follows:

Cross

January 1	Balance		35,000
May 1	Investment		15,000
October 1	Withdrawal	10,000	

Deming

January 1	Balance		25,000
April 1	Withdrawal	5,000	

Net income for the year ended December 31, 1967, is $30,000.

Instructions: Give journal entries to record the transfer of net income to the capital accounts under each of the following assumptions. (Show the procedure used in calculating the respective amounts in the explanation after each entry.)

(1) Net income is divided 65% to Cross, 35% to Deming.

(2) Net income is divided in the ratio of investments at the beginning of the period.

(3) Net income is divided in the ratio of average investments.

(4) Interest at 8% is allowed on average investments and the balance of net income is divided equally.

(5) Salaries of $20,000 and $16,000 are allowed to Cross and Deming respectively, and the balance of net income is divided in the ratio of investments at the end of the period.

(6) Cross is allowed a bonus of 33⅓% of net income after bonus, and the balance of the net income is divided in the ratio of investments at the beginning of the period.

1-4. The capital accounts of Clark and Dobson show the following facts for the fiscal year ended December 31, 1967:

Clark

Jan. 1	Balance	$26,000
Mar. 30	Investment	3,000
May 10	Investment	7,000
July 25	Withdrawal	4,000
Dec. 31	Balance	32,000

Dobson

Jan. 1	Balance	$16,500
May 18	Investment	5,000
Aug. 24	Withdrawal	2,000
Dec. 31	Balance	19,500

The profit and loss account shows a credit balance of $23,800 on December 31.

Instructions: Give the journal entries to transfer the balance in the profit and loss account to the capital accounts if the profit is to be distributed on each of the following bases. (Show the procedure used in calculating the respective amounts in the explanation after each entry.)

(1) In the ratio of investments at the beginning of the fiscal period.

(2) In the ratio of average capitals. Investments and withdrawals are to be considered as made at the beginning of the month if made before the middle of the month and are to be considered as made at the beginning of the following month if made after the middle of the month.

(3) Interest of 6% on average capitals, salaries to Clark and Dobson of $15,000 and $10,000 respectively, and any balance equally. (Investments and withdrawals are to be considered as in part [2].)

(4) Allowance to Clark of a bonus of 25% of the net profit after bonus, interest of 6% to be allowed on the excess of the average investment of one partner over that of the other, and any balance in ratio of 3:2 to Clark

and Dobson respectively. (Investments and withdrawals are to be considered as in part [2].)

(5) Salaries of $1,500 and $1,000 a month to Clark and Dobson respectively, provided annual earnings are sufficient to cover the allowance; if earnings are insufficient, the profit shall be distributed in the salary ratio; if operations result in a loss, it shall be distributed equally.

1-5. The following account balances appear in the ledger for the firm of Evans and Gale at the end of 1967 before the profit for the year has been transferred to the partners' accounts:

Evans, Drawing	$ 7,200	
Gale, Drawing	12,500	
Evans, Loan		$17,500
Evans, Capital		50,000
Gale, Capital		50,000
Profit and Loss		30,250

The following information is to be considered in closing the profit and loss account and the drawing accounts:

(1) The cost of installing equipment at the beginning of 1967, $2,700, was charged to expense. The installation relates to equipment with a 10-year life.

(2) The loan to the firm was made by Evans on March 1, 1967. No entry has been made for interest on the loan, which is 6% and is to be paid to Evans at the time the loan is repaid.

(3) The partnership agreement permits Evans and Gale to withdraw weekly sums of $150 and $225 respectively, these amounts to be regarded as salaries. Actual withdrawals by partners differed from allowed amounts and are summarized in the drawing accounts.

(4) Gale, the managing partner, is entitled to a special bonus of 25% of the net profit after deduction of all special allowances to partners (including the bonus), and any remaining profit is to be distributed equally.

Instructions: (1) Give the entries required in closing the accounts.
(2) Prepare a statement of changes in partners' capital accounts for 1967.

1-6. Miller, Nash, and Otis formed a partnership on January 1, 1965, investing $40,000, $24,000, and $20,000 respectively. Partners agreed to the following distribution of profits:

(1) Annual salaries are to be allowed partners as follows:
Miller, $4,800
Nash, $6,000
Otis, $6,000

(2) Interest is to be allowed on partners' capitals as of the beginning of each year at the rate of 6%.

(3) Miller, the managing partner, is to be allowed a bonus of 20% of the net profit after treating as expenses partners' salaries, interest, and bonus.

(4) Profits after partners' salaries, interest, and bonus are to be divided equally.

The partnership fiscal period is to be the calendar year. Activities of the partnership for 1965, 1966, and 1967 are summarized below:

	Profit or Loss Before Interest, Salaries, and Bonus	Cash Withdrawals		
		Miller	Nash	Otis
1965	Loss — $ 2,760	$ 6,000	$ 7,240	$ 8,000
1966	Profit — 12,000	6,980	8,160	8,860
1967	Profit — 29,400	10,200	12,000	10,600

Instructions: Prepare a statement of changes in partners' capital accounts covering the three-year period, 1965–1967.

1-7. Bedford and Brown formed a partnership on January 1, 1965, investing $40,000 and $60,000 respectively. Partners agreed to share profits as follows:

(1) Bedford and Brown are to be allowed salaries of $800 and $1,000 per month respectively, and each salary allowance is to be increased by $100 per month beginning January 1, 1967.

(2) Interest is to be allowed on partners' capital balances as of the beginning of each year at the rate of 5%.

(3) Profits after salaries and interest are to be divided equally.

The partnership fiscal period is the calendar year. Net income for the firm and drawings of the partners for the period January 1, 1965, to September 1, 1967, are summarized below.

	Net Income Before Salaries and Interest	Drawings	
		Bedford	Brown
Jan. 1 — Dec. 31, 1965	$35,000	$8,800	$14,200
Jan. 1 — Dec. 31, 1966	24,000	6,500	8,000
Jan. 1 — Sept. 1, 1967	8,500	4,000	5,500

On September 1, 1967, the partners received a cash offer of $90,000 for total net assets of the firm and accepted the offer. Net assets were turned over to the purchaser, and the cash was distributed to the partners in final settlement.

Instructions: Prepare a statement of the partners' capital accounts that shows all of the changes in capital accounts that took place over the period January 1, 1965, to September 1, 1967, when the firm was dissolved.

1-8. Balance sheet data for the firm of M, N, and O as of January 1, 1967, follow:

Assets	$122,500	Liabilities	$ 62,500
		M, Capital	20,000
		N, Capital	20,000
		O, Capital	20,000
	$122,500		$122,500

Partners share profits equally after the allowance of a salary to O, the managing partner, of $750 monthly.

As a result of operating losses sustained at the beginning of 1967, M advanced $15,000 to the firm on April 1; it was agreed that he would be allowed interest at 6%. With continued losses, the members decided to liquidate. O agreed to take over partnership equipment in part settlement of his interest, the transfer being made at an agreed value of $4,000. On November 1, $20,000 cash was available for distribution to partners after sale of remaining assets and the payment of partnership obligations to outsiders. O had withdrawn his salary for January and February but had not received his salary for the period March 1 to November 1; no other cash payments had been made to partners. Available cash was distributed on November 1 and the firm was declared dissolved.

Instructions: Prepare a statement of partners' capital accounts showing partners' capital and loan balances together with all of the changes in such balances that took place during 1967.

1-9. Marsh, Norton, Olin, and Parks are partners. Their interests in the capital and their profit and loss ratios are as follows:

Marsh	40%
Norton	30%
Olin	20%
Parks	10%

To provide a means by which the remaining partners might purchase a deceased partner's interest from his estate, a life insurance program was inaugurated whereby life insurance proceeds would be paid to the remaining partners in proportion to their percentage ownership in the partnership. Since each partner was in effect insuring the life of each of the other partners, it was agreed that no partner would pay any part of the premiums on policies covering his own life.

In 1967 the premium on all policies amounted to $9,000, which was charged as an expense on the books and thereby deducted from the year's profit. The profit was then credited to each partner in proportion to his ownership percentage. Investigation of the insurance premiums revealed:

Premium on life of Marsh	$3,500
Premium on life of Norton	1,400
Premium on life of Olin	2,300
Premium on life of Parks	1,800

Instructions: Prepare the correcting entry that should be made to the partners' capital accounts in order to reflect properly the agreement as to the insurance. Give your supporting computations in good form.

(AICPA adapted)

1-10. The Trading Company, a partnership, was formed on January 1, 1967, with four partners, D, E, F, and G. Capital contributions were as follows:

D	$100,000
E	50,000
F	50,000
G	40,000

The partnership agreement provides that each partner shall receive 5% interest on the amount of his capital contribution. In addition, D is to receive a salary of $10,000 and E a salary of $6,000, which are to be charged as expenses of the business.

The agreement further provides that F shall receive a minimum of $5,000 per annum from the partnership and G a minimum of $12,000 per annum, both including amounts allowed as interest on capital and their respective shares of profits. The balance of the profit is to be shared in the following proportions:

D	30%
E	30
F	20
G	20

Instructions: Calculate the amount that must be earned by the partnership during 1967, before any charge for interest on capital or partners' salaries, in order that D may receive an aggregate of $25,000, including interest, salary, and share of profits. Show your calculations in statement form.

(AICPA adapted)

1-11. X, Y, and Z have been partners throughout the year 1967. Their average balances for the year and their balances at the end of the year before closing the nominal accounts are as follows:

	Average Balances	Balances Dec. 31, 1967
X	(Cr.) $90,000	(Cr.) $60,000
Y	(Cr.) 3,000	(Dr.) 1,000
Z	(Cr.) 7,000	(Cr.) 10,000

The profit for 1967 is $75,000 before charging partners' drawing allowances and before interest on average balances at the agreed rate of 4% per annum. X is entitled to a drawing account credit of $10,000, Y of $7,000, and Z of $5,000 per annum. The balance of the profit is to be distributed at the rate of 60% to X, 30% to Y, and 10% to Z.

It is intended to distribute amounts of cash to the partners so that, after credits and distributions as indicated in the preceding paragraph, the balances in the partners' accounts will be proportionate to their profit-sharing ratios. None of the partners is to pay in any money, but it is desired to distribute the lowest possible amount of cash.

Instructions: Prepare a statement of the partners' accounts, showing balances at the end of 1967 before closing, the allocations of the net profit for 1967, the cash distributed, and the closing balances.

(AICPA adapted)

1-12. The law firm of B, C, and D has decided to dissolve partnership as of June 30, 1967, and has called you in to render an accounting. The only records maintained are the checkbook and a daily record of cash received. The firm has been in existence for 4 years. Partners have equal capital investments and profits are divided equally. The prior year's tax return indicates that the following expenditures had been capitalized for tax purposes prior to January 1, 1967:

	Asset	Allowance January 1, 1967
Office furniture and fixtures	$1,500	$ 450
Books	900	180
Automobile — B	2,000	600
Automobile — C	1,000	200
Automobile — D	3,000	600
	$8,400	$2,030

Cash receipts to June 30, 1967, amount to $60,000. A summary of cash disbursements follows:

Rent	$ 1,400
Wages and salaries	2,102
Entertainment	4,000
Automobile and miscellaneous	1,000
Withdrawals — B	9,000
Withdrawals — C	10,000
Withdrawals — D	12,000
	$39,502

The capital accounts of the partners as of January 1, 1967, were equal. Depreciation has been charged against partnership profits. Automobiles are depreciated over a 5-year period and office furniture and fixtures and books over a 10-year period. The bank balance at June 30, 1967, is $29,998. The three partners have agreed to distribute the office furniture and fixtures in kind and they feel that the distribution will be equal. The automobiles, which were purchased from partnership funds, will be retained by the partners to whom they have been assigned. The books will be distributed to B.

Instructions: Prepare a statement of changes in partners' capital accounts from January 1, 1967, to June 30, 1967, and the final cash distribution to each partner.

(AICPA adapted)

1-13. The Hope-Ivar-Jones partnership was formed in 1959, with partner Hope contributing the major portion of the capital and partners Ivar and Jones providing the knowledge and experience necessary for the operation of the business. The partnership agreement specifies that the accounting records shall be maintained on the accrual basis and that the net income shall be distributed to the partners as follows:

(1) Each partner shall receive 5% interest on the balance in his capital account at the beginning of the year.

(2) Partners Ivar and Jones shall each receive a commission of 20% of an amount representing net income determined by the cash basis method of accounting after deducting the normal allowance for depreciation and the interest on capital. For this purpose all merchandise purchased is to be treated as an expense.

(3) The net income remaining after deducting the interest on capital and the commissions due to Ivar and Jones, shall be distributed to the three partners equally, except that the total portion of income distributed to partner Hope must not be less than 50% of the net income determined by the accrual basis method of accounting.

During the year, $150 of acccunts receivable were considered uncollectible and were charged off to the allowance for doubtful accounts, and $10 was collected on accounts that had been charged to the allowance for doubtful accounts in prior years.

There were no changes in the partners' capital accounts during the year.

Hope-Ivar-Jones Partnership
Balance Sheets

	December 31, 1966		December 31, 1967	
Assets				
Cash		$ 7,000		$ 11,120
Accounts receivable — customers	$ 5,000		$ 6,000	
Deduct — Allowance for doubtful accounts	100	4,900	120	5,880
Inventory		26,000		24,000
U.S. Government bonds — at cost		—		8,000
Fixed assets — at cost	$120,000		$120,000	
Deduct — Accumulated depreciation	42,500	77,500	46,300	73,700
Prepaid expenses		1,000		800
Total assets		$116,400		$123,500
Liabilities and Capital				
Accounts payable — trade		$ 7,000		$ 4,000
Accrued wages		3,000		5,000
Accrued taxes		500		500
Deferred income		5,900		—
Net income year 1967		—		14,000
Partners' capital:				
Hope	$ 80,000		$ 80,000	
Ivar	12,500		12,500	
Jones	7,500	100,000	7,500	100,000
Total liabilities and capital		$116,400		$123,500

Instructions: (1) Prepare a schedule supported by clearly detailed computations showing the adjustments necessary to convert the net income for the year 1967 from an accrual basis to a cash basis.

(2) Prepare a statement supported by clearly detailed computations showing the distribution to the partners of net income for the year 1967.

(AICPA adapted)

1-14. A, B, and C, attorneys, agreed to consolidate their individual practices as of January 1, 1967. The partnership agreement included the following features:

(1) Each partner's capital contribution was the net amount of the assets and liabilities taken over by the partnership, which were as follows:

	A	B	C
Cash	$ 5,000	$ 5,000	$ 5,000
Accounts receivable	14,000	6,000	16,000
Furniture and library	4,300	2,500	6,200
	$23,300	$13,500	$27,200
Allowance for depreciation	$ 2,400	$ 1,500	$ 4,700
Accounts payable	300	1,400	700
	$ 2,700	$ 2,900	$ 5,400
Capital contributions	$20,600	$10,600	$21,800

Each partner guaranteed the collectibility of his receivables.

(2) C had leased office space and was bound by the lease until June 30, 1967. The monthly rental was $600. The partners agreed to occupy C's office space until the expiration of the lease and to pay the rent. The partners concurred that the rent was too high for the space and that a fair rental value would be $450 per month. The excess rent was to be charged to C at year end. On July 1 the partners moved to new quarters with a monthly rental of $500.

(3) No salaries were to be paid to the partners. The individual partners were to receive 20% of the gross fees billed to their respective clients during the first year of the partnership. After deducting operating expenses, the balance of the fees billed was to be credited to the partners' capital accounts in the following ratios: A, 40%; B, 35%; C, 25%.

On April 1, 1967, D was admitted to the partnership; he was to receive 20% of the fees from new business obtained after April 1 after deducting expenses applicable to that new business. Expenses were to be apportioned to the new business in the same ratio that total expenses, other than bad debt losses, bore to total gross fees.

The following information pertains to the partnership's activities in 1967:

(1) Fees were billed as follows:

A's clients	$22,000
B's clients	12,000
C's clients	11,000
New business:	
Prior to April 1	3,000
After April 1	12,000
Total	$60,000

(2) Total expenses, excluding depreciation and bad debt expenses, were $19,350, including the total amount paid for rent. Depreciation was to be computed at the rate of 10%. Depreciable assets purchased during 1967, on which one-half year's depreciation was to be taken, totaled $5,000.

(3) Cash charges to the partners' accounts during the year were:

A	$ 5,200
B	4,400
C	5,800
D	2,500
	$17,900

(4) Of A's and B's receivables, $1,200 and $450 respectively proved to be uncollectible. A new client billed in March for $1,600 had been adjudged bankrupt and a settlement of 50 cents on the dollar was made.

Instructions: Prepare a statement of changes in partners' capital accounts for the year ended December 31, 1967. Supporting computations should be in good form.

(AICPA adapted)

Chapter 2

PARTNERSHIPS

DISSOLUTION UPON OWNERSHIP CHANGES

A partnership is said to be dissolved when the original association for purposes of carrying on activities has ended. For example, a partnership is automatically dissolved by the death of a partner. When there is dissension among partners, a court may decree the dissolution of a partnership upon the request of one or more of the partners. The withdrawal of a partner through the sale of his interest also dissolves the original association.

With dissolution of a partnership, the authority of the partners to carry on business as a going concern is ended. Although dissolution brings to an end the association of individuals for their original purpose, it does not mean the termination of business or even an interruption in its continuity. Upon the death of a partner, surviving partners still act on behalf of the partnership in completing transactions already begun and in winding up business affairs. Upon the retirement of a partner, the business may be continued without interruption as a new partnership composed of the remaining members.

CONDITIONS RESULTING IN DISSOLUTION

The conditions that result in the dissolution of a partnership are classified and summarized below.

Dissolution by act of the parties. Certain acts by members of a partnership result in dissolution. Under this heading may be included:

(1) Termination of time or accomplishment of purpose. If a definite time for termination is stated in the partnership agreement, or if a particular objective is to be accomplished, termination of the time or accomplishment of the objective fulfills the partnership contract and the firm may dissolve. When a partnership does not have a fixed life or when it continues after stipulated conditions have been fulfilled, it is known as a *partnership at will.*

(2) Mutual agreement. Partners may mutually agree at any time to a change in membership or to termination of their association.

(3) Withdrawal of a partner. A partner has the power to withdraw from a partnership at any time, thus dissolving the firm. If, however, a partner exercises this power in contravention of the partnership agreement, he becomes liable to his copartners for damages that may be sustained through such action. In other words, the partner has the *power* to with-

draw from a partnership at any time, but he must also have the contractual *right* to do so if he is to avoid liability for damages. An exception to this rule is found in the *partnership at will*, from which a partner may withdraw at any time without liability to his copartners. A partner may also withdraw from a partnership without liability upon the unanimous consent of all partners.

Dissolution by operation of the law. A partnership is automatically dissolved upon the occurrence of certain contingencies recognized by law, namely:

(1) Death of any member of the partnership.
(2) Bankruptcy of any partner or of the partnership.
(3) Any event that makes it unlawful for the business to be carried on or for individual members to carry on as a partnership.
(4) War against a country of which a member is a citizen.

Dissolution by judicial decree. A court may decree dissolution on application by or for a partner upon evidence of any of the following circumstances:

(1) Insanity of a partner or the inability of a partner for any cause to fulfill his part of the partnership contract.
(2) Conduct of a partner that affects unfavorably the business being carried on.
(3) Internal dissension among partners.
(4) Impossibility of profitable continuation of the business.
(5) Other reasons that render dissolution equitable, for example, fraud or misrepresentation in the formation of the partnership.

ACCOUNTING FOR DISSOLUTION

The remaining pages of this chapter consider the problems that arise upon dissolution as a result of (1) the admission of a new partner, (2) the withdrawal of a partner, (3) the death of a partner, and (4) the incorporation of a partnership. The special accounting problems incident to the winding up of a business, including those relating to the realization of business assets, liquidation of obligations, and settlement with respective partners, are considered in the two chapters that follow.

ADMISSION OF NEW PARTNERS

Admission of a new partner is possible only with the consent of all of the partners. Such an admission brings about a new association of individuals and hence represents the formation of a new partnership; the original partnership is considered dissolved by common consent. A partnership agreement is binding only while the relationship between the original parties to the agreement remains unchanged. Upon the admission of a new partner, an agreement should be drawn up that states the partners' interests upon formation of the partnership, the distribution of future profits and losses among partners, and all of the other considerations relative to the new association.

The newly formed partnership may continue to use the books and the records of the original firm, but certain account balances will generally require restatement. As long as the original partnership continues in operation, conventional practice does not call for the current recognition of changes in asset values; gains or losses on properties owned by the business emerge only upon ultimate disposition of the properties. But the admission of a new partner involves the formation of a new firm wherein contributions by the participating members must be completely and accurately recognized. Present market values should be determined for the assets that are to be identified with the new organization and account balances should be restated to report such values. Inventories should be restated at present replacement values. Adequate allowances should be established for receivables. Marketable securities should be reported at their current market values. Noncurrent assets should be reported at present appraised values. All liabilities should be determined and reported on the books. The foregoing changes give rise to profit or loss allocable to the original partners in the original profit-and-loss-sharing ratio. If such changes are not reported in the accounts, an incoming partner will participate in gains and losses that took place prior to his admission.

Ordinarily an incoming partner makes some asset contribution for an interest in the newly organized firm. However, a person may be admitted as a partner without an investment and without the recognition of a capital interest. Under such circumstances, a capital interest will emerge only in the future as a result of investments, withdrawals, and profit and loss distributions.

Although a person admitted into a partnership becomes a co-owner in all of the partnership property as of the date of his admission, his liability on existing debt is limited under the provisions of the Uniform Partnership Act. The Act provides, "A person admitted as a partner into an existing partnership is liable for all the obligations of the partnership arising before his admission as though he had been a partner when such obligations were incurred, except that this liability shall be satisfied only out of partnership property." In the event of business insolvency, then, personal assets of a new partner cannot be seized in satisfaction of claims related to the original organization; but his personal assets can be seized in satisfaction of liabilities that arise from activities of the new organization.

A person may acquire an interest in a partnership by (1) the purchase of such an interest from one or more of the original owners, or (2) the investment of assets resulting in an increase in the capital of the partnership.

ACQUISITION OF INTEREST BY PURCHASE

A partner has the power to sell part or all of his interest in a firm. If all the partners agree to the admission of the buyer of the interest as a partner, the admission dissolves the old partnership and brings into existence a new one. If the partners do not agree to the admission of the new party as a partner, the Uniform Partnership Act provides that he simply acquires, in accordance with his contract, the profits, and upon dissolution, the interest, to which the original partner would have been entitled; the transfer of the interest does not, of itself, dissolve the firm, nor does it entitle the buyer to interfere in the management of the business. If, under terms of the partnership agreement, the original partner does not have the right to transfer his interest but nevertheless exercises his power to do so, claims may be raised against him by the remaining partners for any losses that they incur through his action.

When an individual acquires a portion or all of the interest of a partner in a business, the interest acquired is recorded as the capital of the new partner and the capital of the selling partner is correspondingly reduced. The payment for the interest is not recorded on the books of the partnership, for this is simply a transaction between two individuals acting in their private capacities. To illustrate, assume that A and B are partners, each with a capital of $30,000 and sharing profits equally. C purchases ½ of B's interest for $18,000. A approves the admission of C as a partner. The original partnership books are to be retained by the new firm of A, B, and C. The only entry required on the books is:

B, Capital....................................	15,000	
C, Capital..................................		15,000

This entry is made regardless of the amount paid by C to B. The total capital of the partnership remains $60,000. A has a 50% interest in the new firm, B a 25% interest, and C a 25% interest.

The fact that C has acquired a 25% interest in the partnership of A, B, and C does not mean that his participation in profits and losses will be equal to this percentage. Upon C's admittance, the partners should agree upon the future distribution of profits and losses. In the absence of an agreement, A, B, and C will share profits and losses equally.

Parties may feel that accounts fail to report the value of net assets satisfactorily and may decide to adjust valuations prior to the admission of the new partner. Net assets should be restated and the revaluation gain or loss recognized in the capital accounts of the original partners in their profit and loss ratios. When the price paid by an incoming partner is regarded to offer evidence of goodwill identified with the business but not reflected on the books, this intangible may be established on the books before the transfer of the interest is recorded.

ACQUISITION OF INTEREST BY INVESTMENT

When an individual acquires an interest by making an investment, the assets and the capital of the partnership are thereby increased. For example, assume that D and E have capitals of $20,000 and $10,000 respectively and share profits equally. Assets are properly valued. F is admitted as a partner upon investing $12,000. Profits and losses of the new firm are to be divided equally. The original partnership books are to be maintained for the new firm of D, E, and F. The investment is recorded as follows:

Cash....................................	12,000	
F, Capital..................................		12,000

In recording the investment by the new party, the terms of the agreement with respect to his admittance must be observed. In the absence of a specific agreement, the investment by F would be recorded as indicated. F here receives credit for the actual amount invested; the interests of D, E, and F in the newly formed partnership are $20,000, $10,000, and $12,000. F's interest is 12/42, or approximately 29%.

Assume that the agreement between D, E, and F provides that F is to invest a sum sufficient to give him a ¼ or 25% interest in the new firm. In this case, the combined capitals of the original members, $30,000, would represent ¾ of the new capital, and the incoming partner would be required to invest $10,000 for a ¼ interest. Capitals for partners D, E, and F, then, would be $20,000, $10,000, and $10,000 respectively; interests of D, E, and F would be $20,000/$40,000 or 50%, $10,000/$40,000 or 25%, and $10,000/$40,000 or 25% respectively.

Investment with allowance of bonus or goodwill to old partners. When a partnership has operated with considerable success, the partners may admit a new member with the provision that (1) part of the new partner's investment shall be allowed as a bonus to the old partners, or (2) partnership goodwill shall be established and credited to the old partners.

Bonus. In the preceding section, capitals for D and E totaled $30,000 and F was credited for the amount of his investment, $10,000, in acquiring a ¼ interest in the new partnership. Assume, however, that the partnership of D and E has operated with such success that F is willing to invest $12,000 for a ¼ interest. Inasmuch as the net firm assets prior to F's investment are $30,000, an additional investment by F of $12,000 will increase the net assets to $42,000. If a capital account for F is credited with $12,000 and no change is made in the capital accounts of D and E, F's interest in the partnership will be 12/42, which is greater than the ¼ interest to be allowed to him. Since net assets after F's admission total $42,000, a credit of $10,500 to F will give him a ¼ interest. The amount by which the investment exceeds the interest allowed F may be considered a bonus to the old partners. The bonus is divided between the old partners in the original profit and loss ratio. Since D and E shared profits equally, the bonus of $1,500 results in an increase in each partner's capital of $750. Assuming that the original books are to be used for the new partnership, the entry to record the investment by F is as follows:

Cash	12,000	
D, Capital		750
E, Capital		750
F, Capital		10,500

Goodwill. But assume that F insists that his capital account report his actual investment of $12,000 although he is willing to accept a ¼ interest. The valuation by F of a ¼ interest at $12,000 may be used as a basis for recording goodwill identified with the net asset contribution made by D and E to the new organization. If F's capital of $12,000 is to represent ¼ of the total capital, this total will have to be $48,000 and the combined capitals of D and E will have to be $36,000. Since the capitals of D and E now total $30,000, these balances must be increased by $6,000. Goodwill is debited and the original partners' capital accounts are credited for $6,000. The profit and loss ratio is used in distributing the capital increase of $6,000. The entries to record F's investment are as follows:

Goodwill	6,000	
D, Capital		3,000
E, Capital		3,000
Cash	12,000	
F, Capital		12,000

Since nothing is said about the profit-and-loss-sharing ratio in the foregoing, it is assumed that future profits and losses will be divided equally among D, E, and F.

Comparison of bonus and goodwill methods. Partner F obtains a ¼ interest in assets and a ⅓ share of profits upon his admission by the use of either the bonus method or the goodwill method in the previous examples. Although either method can be used in achieving the required interest for the new partner, the two methods offer the same ultimate results only (1) when the incoming partner's percentage share of profit and loss is to be equal to his percentage interest in assets upon admission, and (2) when the former partners continue to share profits and losses between themselves in the original ratio. For example, if in the preceding examples F's share of profits was limited to 25% and D and E were to share remaining profits 37½% and 37½%, both the bonus and the goodwill methods would give the same ultimate results. To illustrate, balances in the examples were found to be as follows:

	Goodwill	Other Assets	D, Capital	E, Capital	F, Capital
When bonus method is used.		$42,000	$20,750	$10,750	$10,500
When goodwill method is used..................	$6,000	$42,000	$23,000	$13,000	$12,000

Assume that assets ultimately realize no more than $42,000, failing to confirm the existence of goodwill. If the goodwill method is used in recording F's investment, the failure to realize goodwill will result in a loss distributable to partners in the profit and loss ratio. Ignoring intervening changes in proprietorship, capital balances for D, E, and F in each case will be:

	Goodwill	Other Assets	D, Capital	E, Capital	F, Capital
When bonus method is used.		$42,000	$20,750	$10,750	$10,500
When goodwill method is used..................	$6,000	$42,000	$23,000	$13,000	$12,000
Deduct write-off of goodwill (loss distributed in profit and loss ratio, 37½%, 37½%, 25%).........	6,000		2,250	2,250	1,500
		$42,000	$20,750	$10,750	$10,500

The goodwill method ultimately gives account balances that are identical with those obtained through use of the bonus method.

On the other hand, assume that assets ultimately realize $48,000, validating the existence of goodwill. If the bonus method is used in recording F's investment, the realization of $6,000 in excess of asset book values will result in a gain distributable to partners in the profit and loss ratio. Ignoring intervening changes in proprietorship, capital balances for D, E, and F in each case will be:

	Goodwill	Other Assets	D, Capital	E, Capital	F, Capital
When goodwill method is used..................	$6,000	$42,000	$23,000	$13,000	$12,000
When bonus method is used.		$42,000	$20,750	$10,750	$10,500
Add recognition of goodwill (gain distributed in profit and loss ratio, 37½%, 37½%, 25%).........	$6,000		2,250	2,250	1,500
	$6,000	$42,000	$23,000	$13,000	$12,000

Whether goodwill proves to be existent or nonexistent, then, the goodwill and the bonus methods give identical results when the incoming partner's share of profits is equal to the original interest acquired and the former partners continue to share profits and losses in their original ratio. If these conditions are not fully met, however, results will be different.

When an incoming partner's percentage share in profits exceeds the percentage interest allowed him in assets upon admission, choice of the bonus method as compared with the goodwill method results in ultimate advantage to the new partner and corresponding disadvantage to the original partners; recognition of goodwill upon admission increases the new partner's capital by his percentage share in assets, while recognition of goodwill later increases his capital by his percentage share in profits, which is larger than his percentage share in assets. When the new member's share in subsequent profits is less than his share in assets upon admission, the goodwill method results in ultimate advantage to the new member and disadvantage to the others; recognition of goodwill upon admission provides the new partner with a greater capital increase than recognition of goodwill later, which would be limited to his profit and loss percentage. Further advantages and disadvantages may accrue to the original partners through a change in the profit and loss ratio between them.

To illustrate, in the original examples previously given, it was stated that, upon admission, F was granted a ¼ interest in assets but a ⅓ share in future profits; D and E were to share remaining profits equally. Under these circumstances, use of the bonus method offers ultimate advantage to F and corresponding disadvantage to D and E. Assume that assets ultimately realize only $42,000 and thus fail to confirm the existence of goodwill. The ultimate write-off of goodwill results in capital balances as follows:

	Goodwill	Other Assets	D, Capital	E, Capital	F, Capital
When bonus method is used.		$42,000	$20,750	$10,750	$10,500
When goodwill method is used.	$6,000	$42,000	$23,000	$13,000	$12,000
Deduct write-off of goodwill (loss distributed equally).	6,000		2,000	2,000	2,000
		$42,000	$21,000	$11,000	$10,000
Gain or (loss) through use of bonus method.			($ 250)	($ 250)	$ 500

The same advantages and disadvantages will emerge assuming that assets ultimately realize $48,000, thus validating the existence of goodwill. Capital balances in each case will be as follows:

	Goodwill	Other Assets	D, Capital	E, Capital	F, Capital
When goodwill method is used..................	$6,000	$42,000	$23,000	$13,000	$12,000
When bonus method is used.		$42,000	$20,750	$10,750	$10,500
Add recognition of goodwill (gain distributed in profit and loss ratio, equally)..	$6,000		2,000	2,000	2,000
	$6,000	$42,000	$22,750	$12,750	$12,500
Gain or (loss) through use of bonus method..........			($ 250)	($ 250)	$ 500

Asset revaluation. It must be observed that the foregoing discussion assumes that values assigned to net assets on the original partnership books are acceptable. If F's investment of $12,000 for a ¼ interest in the firm is based upon a recognition of the fact that net assets on the books at $30,000 are actually worth $36,000, appropriate entries would be required to restate assets at their current values and to raise the capitals of the original owners accordingly. Neither bonus nor goodwill then requires recognition in recording the investment of the new partner.

The importance of a fully detailed agreement between partners has already been emphasized. Complete statements as to the profit-and-loss-sharing agreement as well as partners' interests in firm assets upon partnership formation are particularly important. In the latter case, not only the fractional interest but also the precise dollar interest should be indicated.

Investment with allowance of bonus or goodwill to new partner. A partnership may be in urgent need of additional funds or the partners may desire the services of a certain individual. In such instances a new member may be admitted with the provision that (1) part of the capitals of the old partners shall be allowed as a bonus to the new partner, or (2) goodwill shall be established and credited to the new partner.

Bonus. Assume that the firm of D and E in the previous examples needs additional capital as well as the services of F. D and E agree to allow F a ⅖ interest upon his investment of $12,000. If a capital account for F is credited with $12,000 and no change is made in the capital accounts of D and E, F's interest will be 12/42, which is less than a ⅖ interest. Since the net assets of the partnership after F's admission total $42,000, a credit of $16,800 to F will give him a ⅖ interest. The amount by which the interest allowed F exceeds his investment may be considered a bonus contributed by the old partners. The bonus is subtracted from the capitals of D and E in the original profit and loss ratio. Assuming that the original partnership books are to be used for the new firm, the entry to record the investment by F is as follows:

Cash	12,000	
D, Capital	2,400	
E, Capital	2,400	
F, Capital		16,800

Goodwill. Assume, however, that D and E are unwilling to have their capital accounts reduced, although they are willing to allow F a 2/5 interest in the firm on his investment of \$12,000. The present capital balances of the partners may be used as the basis for determining the interest to be allowed F and the goodwill that he is considered to bring into the firm. If the sum of the capitals of D and E, \$30,000, is to represent 3/5 of the total capital, the total capital will have to be \$50,000 and F's interest will have to be \$20,000. Goodwill is debited for the difference between the amount invested by F and the amount to be credited to his capital account. The entry to record F's admission is:

Cash	12,000	
Goodwill	8,000	
F, Capital		20,000

Comparison of bonus and goodwill methods. Partner F obtains a 2/5 interest in assets and a 1/3 share of profits upon his admission by the use of either the bonus method or the goodwill method in the previous example. Although either method can be used in achieving the required interest for the new partner, the ultimate effects upon the partners' capitals will not be the same. Under the circumstances given, F will prefer to be admitted with an allowance for goodwill because his percentage interest in assets upon admission to the firm is greater than his percentage share in subsequent profits. The nature of the comparisons that might be made in evaluating the two methods from the points of view of the different parties is similar to that described in the previous section.

Asset revaluation. The foregoing discussion assumes that values of net assets on the original partnership books are acceptable. If F's investment of \$12,000 for a 2/5 interest in the firm is based upon a recognition of the fact that net assets reported on the books at \$30,000 are actually worth only \$18,000, appropriate entries would be required to restate these assets and to reduce the capital balances of the original owners accordingly. Neither bonus nor goodwill, then, requires recognition in recording the investment of the new partner.

Bonus and goodwill determinations when not specifically stated. An agreement may indicate that an incoming partner is to receive an interest that is greater or smaller than that which would be recognized if the partner were simply to receive credit for the amount invested. Such an agreement, however, may fail to point out whether the required interest is to be accomplished through recognition of bonus or goodwill. In the absence of an express statement, the conditions for admission must be carefully analyzed in recording the partner's interest in the firm. A series of examples follow.

Assume that X and Y share profits equally. Capital accounts are as follows just before Z's admission:

X, Capital..........	$25,000
Y, Capital..........	$35,000

Example	Analysis	Entry		
(1) Z invests $20,000 for a ¼ interest.	Since recognition of Z's investment at $20,000 will give him a ¼ interest (20,000/80,000), neither bonus nor goodwill is implied by the agreement.	Cash......	20,000	
		Z, Capital		20,000
(2) Z invests $30,000 for a ¼ interest.	Since recognition of Z's investment at $30,000 will give him more than a ¼ interest (30,000/90,000), a ¼ interest is achieved either by (1) crediting him with $22,500 (¼ x $90,000) and recording the excess as a bonus to original partners or (2) crediting him with $30,000 by recording goodwill and raising capitals of the original partners $30,000 (capital of original partners to be ¾ of new capital, or 3 x $30,000, or $90,000; present capital, $60,000).	Cash......	30,000	
		X, Capital		3,750
		Y, Capital		3,750
		Z, Capital		22,500
		or		
		Cash......	30,000	
		Goodwill..	30,000	
		X, Capital		15,000
		Y, Capital		15,000
		Z, Capital		30,000
(3) Z invests $30,000 for a $25,000 interest; total capital $90,000.	Since total capital is limited to $90,000, the sum of the original capital and Z's investment, then an investment of $30,000 by Z for a $25,000 interest implies a $5,000 bonus to original partners.	Cash......	30,000	
		X, Capital		2,500
		Y, Capital		2,500
		Z, Capital		25,000
(4) Z invests $30,000 for a ¼ interest in a total capital of $100,000.	Since Z is to receive an interest of $25,000, which is $5,000 less than the amount invested, and since total capital is to be $10,000 more than total invested capital, the implication is a bonus of $5,000 to original partners together with goodwill of $10,000 to original partners.	Cash......	30,000	
		Goodwill..	10,000	
		X, Capital		7,500
		Y, Capital		7,500
		Z, Capital		25,000
(5) Z invests $30,000 for a ½ interest.	Since recognition of Z's investment of $30,000 gives him less than a ½ interest (30,000/90,000), a ½ interest is achieved either by (1) crediting him with $45,000 (½ x $90,000), representing the sum of his investment, $30,000, together with a bonus of $15,000, or (2) crediting him with $60,000 representing the sum of his investment, $30,000, and goodwill of $30,000 (capital of the new partner to be ½ of the new capital, or $60,000, since present capital is $60,000).	Cash......	30,000	
		X, Capital.	7,500	
		Y, Capital.	7,500	
		Z, Capital		45,000
		or		
		Cash......	30,000	
		Goodwill..	30,000	
		Z, Capital		60,000

Example	Analysis	Entry		
(6) Z invests $30,000 for a $40,000 interest in a total capital of $90,000.	Since the total capital is limited to $90,000, the sum of the original capital and Z's investment, then an investment of $30,000 for a $40,000 interest implies a bonus of $10,000 allowed to the incoming partner.	Cash......	30,000	
		X, Capital.	5,000	
		Y, Capital.	5,000	
		Z, Capital		40,000
(7) Z invests $30,000 for a ½ interest in a total capital of $100,000.	Since Z is to receive a $50,000 interest (½ x $100,000), which is $20,000 more than the amount invested, and since total capital is to be $10,000 more than total invested capital, the conditions for admission imply goodwill of $10,000 and also a bonus of $10,000 to the new partner.	Cash......	30,000	
		Goodwill..	10,000	
		X, Capital.	5,000	
		Y, Capital.	5,000	
		Z, Capital		50,000

SETTLEMENT WITH A WITHDRAWING PARTNER

A partner has the power to withdraw from a firm at any time. If the partner has the right to withdraw under the terms of the contract, he is entitled to claim the full amount of his interest in the firm. If the partner exercises his power to withdraw in violation of the partnership agreement and without the mutual consent of all participants, he becomes liable to his copartners for any damages they sustain through his action. Under the latter circumstances, a withdrawing partner's claim for his interest may suffer impairment in part or in whole by the damages attributable to his withdrawal.

The withdrawal of a partner may bring about the complete termination of the business. On the other hand, the business may be continued without interruption, settlement being made with the withdrawing partner by (1) the purchase of his interest by another member of the firm or (2) transfer to him of partnership cash or other assets in satisfaction of his interest. Under the latter circumstances, withdrawal of the partner would be considered to dissolve the old partnership and bring into existence a new one. The purchase of a withdrawing partner's interest by a remaining partner results in a transfer of the retiring member's capital to the capital account of the partner making the purchase; the actual amount paid to the retiring partner is a transaction outside of the partnership and is not recognized on the partnership books. Settlement by partnership payment to the withdrawing member results in a reduction in firm assets accompanied by cancellation of the withdrawing partner's capital. If settlement is deferred beyond the date of withdrawal, the capital account of the withdrawing partner is closed and a liability account is credited for the amount to be paid in settlement.

The partnership agreement should indicate any special procedures that are to be applied in measuring the interest of a withdrawing partner. The agreement should indicate what recognition is to be made of market values of property items as well as of any partnership goodwill in arriving at a settlement. It should also indicate how payments are to be made in settlement of the interest. Failure to anticipate these problems in the original agreement may give rise to controversy among partners. In the absence of appropriate provisions in the original agreement, parties will have to make special agreements for settlement at the time a withdrawal occurs.

It should be observed that the withdrawal of a member from a partnership and settlement with the firm does not relieve the withdrawing partner of personal liability on existing partnership claims in the absence of an agreement with creditors to that effect.

The withdrawal of a partner ordinarily calls for an appraisal of partnership assets and a restatement of asset and capital balances in terms of the revaluation. Losses and gains from revaluation are carried to the partners' capitals in the profit and loss ratio. The interest of a withdrawing partner, then, will include changes that have taken place in asset values during the time of his participation, changes that in a going concern would normally await the realization of assets.

Revaluation of assets is required, not only in arriving at a fair determination of a retiring partner's interest, but also in stating properly the interests of the continuing partners. With the formation of a new firm and with new arrangements for profit and loss distribution, opening capital balances should report fairly the investments of the partners.

Partners may agree to pay a withdrawing partner an amount equal to his capital balance. On the other hand, partners may agree to pay a withdrawing partner an amount that is greater or smaller than the balance reported in his capital account.

Payment to withdrawing partner of amount that exceeds capital balance. A partner who withdraws from a firm that has been unusually prosperous may demand an amount that exceeds his capital balance. Remaining partners may be willing to settle on this basis instead of terminating the business, a procedure that might otherwise be forced upon them by the retiring partner. Under such circumstances, partners may agree that (1) the excess amount paid shall be treated as a bonus to be absorbed by the continuing partners, or (2) the excess amount paid shall be used as a basis for recording partnership goodwill.

Bonus. Assume that the capital accounts of J, K, and L are \$10,000 each, that assets are properly valued, and that the partners share profits 50%, 25%, and 25% respectively. The partners agree to pay L \$11,500 in settlement of his interest. If the excess of \$1,500 is to be considered a bonus chargeable to J and K, the entry is:

L, Capital	10,000	
J, Capital	1,000	
K, Capital	500	
Payable to L		11,500
To record agreement to pay $11,500 to L in full settlement of his interest, the bonus allowed being charged to J and K in the ratio existing between them, 50:25.		

Goodwill. Assume, however, that J and K are unwilling to have their capital accounts reduced, although they are willing to pay L $11,500 in settlement of his interest. The allowance to L of $1,500 in excess of his interest may be regarded as a payment for goodwill related to the partnership but not recorded on its books. Since L shares in net asset increases to the extent of 25%, $1,500 may be regarded as 25% of the presently existing goodwill; the total goodwill, then, is $6,000. The following entries may be made to recognize the partnership goodwill as thus determined and to report the obligation to the withdrawing partner:

Goodwill	6,000	
J, Capital		3,000
K, Capital		1,500
L, Capital		1,500
To set up partnership goodwill of $6,000 as determined by settlement with L who is allowed $1,500 for his 25% interest in goodwill.		
L, Capital	11,500	
Payable to L		11,500
To record agreement to pay L $11,500.		

The recognition of goodwill of $6,000 and its distribution to all of the partners is consistent with the practice of recognizing the full change in other asset values and of carrying the effects of such changes to all of the capital balances. But there are some who would support the recognition of goodwill only to the extent of the amount allowed to the withdrawing partner; the books, then, will report only the goodwill that is actually "purchased" by the continuing organization. Those who support this approach to goodwill do not suggest that revaluation of other assets be limited to only that portion of the change that is applicable to the equity of the withdrawing partner; however, to counter the charge of inconsistency, this group would raise the argument of conservatism. If, in the previous illustration, goodwill is to be recognized only to the extent of the excess payment to L, the entry would be as follows:

L, Capital	10,000	
Goodwill	1,500	
Payable to L		11,500
To record agreement to pay L $11,500 for his interest in the firm, the excess allowed L being regarded as payment for his share of goodwill.		

Comparison of bonus and goodwill methods. Although either the bonus method or the goodwill method can be used in recording the withdrawal of L, the two methods offer the same results only when the remaining partners continue to share profits between themselves in the original ratio. For example, assume in the preceding examples that J and K agree to share profits of the firm of J and K in the same manner between themselves as in the past, or 2:1 (50:25) respectively. If the bonus method is employed and any goodwill is recognized at a later date, its recognition will have exactly the same effect upon the capitals of J and K as its recognition upon the withdrawal of L. On the other hand, if the goodwill method is employed and goodwill has to be written off as a loss, reductions in the capitals of J and K will be the same as those made in using the bonus method upon L's withdrawal. But assume that J and K decide to divide profits of the new firm equally. With a change in the profit and loss arrangement providing an advantage to K, the bonus method will result in ultimate gain to K: if the bonus method is employed and any goodwill is recognized at a later date, K's share of the increase will be greater than the charge to K's capital upon L's withdrawal. On the other hand, if the goodwill method is employed and goodwill has to be written off as a loss, K's share of the decrease will be greater than the credit to K's capital upon L's withdrawal. In view of the differences that are found in each case, it is important that the parties agree to the exact procedure that is to be followed.

Payment to withdrawing partner of amount that is less than capital balance. A partner who is anxious to withdraw may be willing to accept less than the balance reported in his capital account. His willingness to accept such a reduced amount may arise from his realization that a forced sale of the firm's assets may result in a loss and a decrease in his interest as great as or greater than that which can be effected through agreement. When a withdrawing partner agrees to accept less than the amount reported in his capital account, such a difference may be viewed (1) as a bonus accruing to continuing partners, or (2) where goodwill has been previously recorded, as an offset against the goodwill balance.

Bonus. Assume in the previous example that L agrees to accept $8,500 in full settlement of his $10,000 interest. If the difference of $1,500 is to be regarded as a bonus to the continuing partners, the entry is:

L, Capital....................................	10,000	
Payable to L..............................		8,500
J, Capital..................................		1,000
K, Capital..................................		500
To record agreement to pay L $8,500 in full settlement of his interest, a bonus of $1,500 accruing to J and K in ratio existing between them, 50:25.		

Goodwill. Assume, however, that the partnership books show a goodwill balance. L accepts less than his capital account balance since his capital reflects this intangible in part. Under these circumstances, partners may view the payment to L of an amount that is less than his capital balance as indicating a shrinkage in goodwill rather than an increase in the continuing partners' capitals. Assuming that L is paid $8,500 for an interest reported at $10,000 with the credit excess being treated as an offset to goodwill, the entry would be made as follows:

L, Capital	10,000	
Goodwill		1,500
Payable to L		8,500
To record agreement to pay L $8,500 in full settlement of his interest, the credit of $1,500 arising from settlement being applied against Goodwill.		

It would be possible to recognize the entire shrinkage in partnership goodwill implicit in the settlement with L. Since a reduction of $1,500 applies to a 25% interest, the full goodwill shrinkage may be considered to be $6,000, and the following entry may be made:

J, Capital	3,000	
K, Capital	1,500	
L, Capital	10,000	
Goodwill		6,000
Payable to L		8,500

Comparison of bonus and goodwill methods. Although either the bonus or the goodwill method can be used to record the withdrawal of L, it should be observed that here, as in the case of earlier examples involving problems of bonus and goodwill, the alternative methods offer the same ultimate results only when the remaining partners continue to share profits between themselves in the original ratio.

SETTLEMENT WITH AN ESTATE

The death of a partner dissolves the partnership. In the absence of special provisions to the contrary, profit and loss should be summarized, the partnership assets should be appraised, and the decedent's interest in the firm should be established as of the date of his death. Profit or loss from the date the books were last closed is determined and transferred to the capital accounts in the existing profit and loss ratio. The change in asset values arising from revaluation is likewise carried to the capital accounts in the profit and loss ratio. It is then the obligation of the partners to wind up the business. Assets are sold, liabilities are paid off, and settlement is made with the partner's estate and surviving partners.

Partners may provide by agreement that in the event of the death of a partner the business shall be continued by surviving partners. Partners may agree to settle for the interest of the deceased partner (1) by payment from partnership assets, (2) by payment by individual partners who thus acquire the interest, or (3) by payment from partnership insurance proceeds with surviving partners acquiring the deceased partner's interest. When the business is to be continued by the surviving partners, the death of a partner results in the dissolution of the original partnership and the formation of a new partnership. The interest of the deceased partner as of the date of death should be transferred to a liability account. Payments made to the estate are recorded as reductions in the payable balance.

The partnership agreement sometimes provides that the interest of a deceased partner shall not be calculated until the end of the regular fiscal period when the books are closed. In such instances it may be provided that the interest of a deceased partner shall be determined by allowing a prorata share of the profits of the period up to the date of his death with interest on the capital balance from that date until the date of settlement with the estate. In other cases it may be provided that the usual share of profit shall be allowed even though the decedent's services are lost to the firm for part of the fiscal period. The agreement may also provide for the recognition of goodwill in arriving at the interest of the decedent.

In some instances it may be provided that the estate or some heir shall continue in the place of the deceased partner. An entry to transfer the capital of the deceased partner to an account with the new partner is then necessary.

INCORPORATION OF A PARTNERSHIP

Partners may decide to incorporate in order to secure the advantages found in the corporate form of organization. When a charter is granted recognizing a corporation, the corporation will act to acquire the net assets of the partnership in exchange for its stock. The stock received by the partnership is distributed to the partners in settlement of their equities. The corporation thus takes over the assets and assumes the liabilities of the partnership; the partnership is dissolved and the partners now become stockholders in the newly formed corporation.

The partnership books may be retained, or a new set of books may be opened in recording activities of the new unit.

Partnership books retained. If the partnership books are retained, entries are necessary to report (1) the changes in asset and liability values and in the partners' interests prior to incorporation, and (2) the change in the form of proprietorship. A revaluation account may be charged with losses and credited with gains from revaluation, and the balance in this account may subsequently be closed into the capital accounts in the profit and loss ratio. However, with relatively few adjustments, the capital accounts may be charged or credited directly for losses and gains from revaluation. The issuance of stock in exchange for the partners' interests is recorded by charges to the partners' capitals and credits to the appropriate corporate capital accounts.

New books opened for the corporation. If new books are opened for the corporation, all of the accounts of the partnership are closed. In closing the accounts of the partnership, entries are made to record the transfer of assets and liabilities to the corporation, the receipt of stock in payment of net assets transferred, and the distribution of stock to the partners. If it is desired to provide a full summary of the transactions that terminated the partnership, entries may be made to report the restatement of net assets and partners' interests before recording the transfer of assets and liabilities.

Entries are made on the new books of the corporation to report the assets that were acquired, the liabilities that were assumed, and the stock that was issued in payment for net assets.

QUESTIONS

1. What is meant by dissolution of a partnership?

2. Give three causes for dissolution under each of the conditions listed below:

(a) Dissolution by act of parties.
(b) Dissolution by operation of law.
(c) Dissolution by judicial decree.

3. (a) What is a *partnership at will?* (b) Under what circumstances does this factor assume significance?

4. A partner may acquire an interest *by purchase* or *by investment*. (a) How do these differ? (b) What entries are made on the partnership books in each instance?

5. A and B are partners sharing profits equally. C purchases one half of B's interest and the three parties agree to share future profits equally. At the time of C's admission, certain assets have a fair market value that is materially in excess of their book value. C suggests that there is no need to restate assets in the course of recording his admission. Do you agree?

6. What special accounting problems arise in the calculation of a deceased partner's interest and in settlement with his estate?

7. (a) What special accounting problems arise upon the incorporation of a partnership? (b) What opening entries are required, assuming that partnership books are retained for the corporation?

8. R and S are partners. T is admitted with a ¼ interest and is given a capital credit that exceeds his cash investment. (a) What are two methods of recording the investment? (b) What method will T prefer if his share of partnership profits is to be 33⅓%?

9. X, Y, and Z are attorneys. Partner Z decides to retire on January 1, 1968, but claims that statements as of December 31, 1967, fail to measure his interest adequately. (a) What special problems are faced in settlement with Z? (b) How would you recommend that these problems be met?

10. Meadows and Saliers have been partners for many years when Meadows decides to withdraw. The firm has followed the practice of reporting inventories for statement purposes at cost or market, whichever is lower. Meadows feels that, for purposes of withdrawal, his interest should be measured with regard to the replacement value of the inventory, which is considerably in excess of cost; Saliers is opposed to the recognition of the inventory at its higher replacement value since such a procedure is inconsistent with past practice. What position do you support?

11. Partner Z retires from the firm of X, Y, and Z. What are the possible positions that may be taken in recording the settlement, assuming that (a) Z is paid more than the balance in his capital account and (b) Z is paid less than the balance in his capital account?

EXERCISES

1. Burke, Carter, and Drew are partners sharing profits 40%, 35%, and 25%. Partners' original capitals were in this ratio, but on June 30, 1967, capital balances are as follows: Burke, $60,000; Carter, $50,000; and Drew, $50,000. Partners want to bring capital balances into the profit and loss ratio.

(a) Assuming that the capital balances are to be brought into the profit and loss ratio by payments outside of the firm among partners, the total firm capital to remain the same, what cash transfers are required between partners and what entry would be made on the firm books?

(b) Assuming that the capital balances are to be brought into the profit and loss ratio by the lowest possible cash investments in the firm by partners, what additional investments are required and what entry would be made on the firm books?

2. O, P, and Q are partners sharing profits in the ratio of 3:3:2. R is admitted as a partner and is to be allowed ¼ of the profits, the remaining profits to be divided between O, P, and Q in the original ratio. What is the new profit and loss ratio for the firm of O, P, Q, and R?

3. Bell and Myers are partners who have capitals of $10,000 each and who share profits in the ratio of 60:40. Rand pays Myers $4,000 for ½ of his interest in the firm. (a) What are the capital balances of each partner after Rand's admission? (b) How will profits be shared in the absence of express agreement?

4. The capital balances for Cook and Dempsey are $40,000 each; partners divide profits equally. Evans is admitted to a ⅓ interest in net assets and in net earnings upon investing cash of $25,000. Record Evans' admission employing three alternative procedures and indicate the conditions that would support each alternative.

5. Fears and Harper are partners who have capitals of $30,000 and $20,000 and who share profits 75% and 25% respectively. They agree to admit Landis as a partner upon his payment of $30,000. What entries would be made on the firm books, assuming that:

(a) One third of the capital balances of the old partners are transferred to the new partner, Fears and Harper dividing the cash between themselves.

(b) One third of the capital balances of the old partners are transferred to the new partner, Fears and Harper dividing the cash between themselves. However, before recording the admission of Landis, goodwill is recorded on the firm books so that his capital may be equal to the amount paid for the interest.

(c) The cash is invested in the business and Landis is credited with a ¼ interest in the firm, the bonus method being used in recording his investment.

(d) The cash is invested in the business and Landis is credited with the full amount of his investment, which is to be 25% of the new firm capital.

(e) The cash is invested in the business and Landis is credited for $40,000, which is to be 33⅓% of the new firm capital.

6. Mason and Norris are partners who have capitals of $6,000 and $4,800 and who share profits in the ratio of 3:2. Oster is admitted as a partner upon investing cash of $5,000, profits to be shared equally.

(a) Assume that Oster is allowed a 25% interest in the firm. (1) What entries would be made in recording his investment if the goodwill method is used? (2) What entries would be made if the bonus method is used? (3) Which method will be preferred by Oster? How much will he gain by the use of this method?

(b) Assume that Oster is allowed a 40% interest in the firm. (1) What entries would be made in recording his investment if the goodwill method is used? (2) What entries would be made if the bonus method is used? (3) Which method will be preferred by Oster? How much will he gain by the use of this method?

7. A, B, and C are partners sharing profits in the ratio of 3:3:2. Investments are $60,000, $40,000, and $30,000 respectively. The partners agree to admit D on the following basis: D is to pay A $40,000 for ½ of A's interest; D is also to invest $30,000 in the business. The total capital of the partnership is to be $200,000, of which D's interest is to be $50,000 upon his admission. What are the entries to record D's admission?

8. A, B, and C have capital balances of $11,200, $13,000, and $5,800 respectively and share profits in a ratio of 3:2:1. D invests cash in the partnership for a ¼ interest. Give the entry to record D's admission under each of the following conditions:

(a) D receives a ¼ interest in the assets of the partnership, which includes a credit of $2,000 for goodwill that is recognized upon his admission.

(b) D receives a ¼ interest in the assets of the partnership and B is credited with $2,000 of the bonus to the old partners that is recognized on D's admission.

(c) D receives a ¼ interest in the assets of the partnership and B is credited with $2,000 of the goodwill that is recognized prior to D's admission.

9. Halls, Jones, and Kepple are partners with capital balances on June 30, 1967, of $30,000, $30,000 and $20,000. Profits are shared equally. Kepple wishes to withdraw and it is agreed that he is to take certain furniture and fixtures at their second-hand value of $1,200 and a note for the balance of his interest. The furniture and fixtures are carried on the books as fully depreciated. What entry would be made to record the settlement with the withdrawing partner?

10. Roades, Stone, and Tracy are partners sharing profits in the ratio of 3:2:1 respectively. Capital accounts are $50,000, $30,000, and $20,000 on December 31, 1967, when Tracy decides to withdraw. It is agreed to pay Tracy $30,000 for his interest. Profits after the retirement of Tracy are to be shared equally. (a) Give three possible entries to record Tracy's retirement. (b) Which of these methods will be preferred by Stone? What is the amount of the gain to Stone through use of this method as compared with the other alternatives?

11. Carter, Doyle, and Eton share profits in the ratio of 5:3:2. Eton is permitted to withdraw from the firm on December 31, 1967. The partnership balance sheet on this date is as follows:

Assets		Liabilities and Capital	
Due from Eton	$ 5,000	Liabilities	$ 40,000
Goodwill	40,000	Due to Doyle	15,000
Other assets	95,000	Carter, capital	35,000
		Doyle, capital	30,000
		Eton, capital	20,000
Total assets	$140,000	Total liabilities and capital	$140,000

(a) Give three alternative solutions to record the withdrawal of Eton, assuming that he is paid $22,000 in full settlement of the capital interest and $5,000 claim balance. Which solution do you prefer?

(b) Give three alternative solutions to record the withdrawal of Eton, assuming that he is paid $12,000 in full settlement. Which solution do you prefer?

PROBLEMS

2-1. Collins and Cox are partners sharing profits 60:40. A balance sheet prepared for the partners on April 1, 1967, shows the following:

Cash		$ 24,000	Payables		$ 44,500
Receivables		46,000	Collins:		
Inventories		82,500	Capital account	$75,000	
Equipment	$35,000		Less drawing account balance	8,500	66,500
Less allowance for depreciation	22,500	12,500			
			Cox:		
			Capital account	$50,000	
			Plus drawing account balance	4,000	54,000
Total assets		$165,000	Total liabilities and capital		$165,000

On this date the partners agreed to admit Curry as a partner. Terms of the agreement are summarized below.

Assets and liabilities are to be restated as follows:

(a) An allowance of $2,300 is to be established for possible uncollectibles.

(b) Inventories are to be restated at their present replacement values of $86,250.

(c) Equipment is to be restated at a value of $17,500.

(d) Accrued expenses of $1,950 are to be recognized.

Collins, Cox, and Curry will divide profits in the ratio 5:3:2. Capital balances for the new partners are to be in this ratio, with Collins and Cox making cash settlement outside of the partnership for the required capital adjustment between themselves, and Curry investing cash in the partnership for his interest.

Instructions: (1) Give the entries on the partnership books to give effect to the foregoing.

(2) Prepare a balance sheet for the newly formed partnership.

2-2. Caine, Osman, and Roberts formed a partnership on January 1, 1964, agreeing to distribute profits and losses in the ratio of original capitals. Original investments were $62,500, $25,000, and $12,500 respectively. Earnings of the firm and drawings by each partner for the period 1964–1966 follow:

	Net income (loss)	Drawings: Caine	Drawings: Osman	Drawings: Roberts
1964	$44,000	$15,000	$7,800	$5,200
1965	18,500	15,000	7,800	5,200
1966	(10,500)	10,000	5,200	5,200

At the beginning of 1967, Caine and Osman agreed to permit Roberts to withdraw from the firm. Since the books of the firm had never been audited, the partners agreed to an audit in arriving at the settlement amount. In withdrawing, Roberts was allowed to take certain furniture with a book value of $4,500 for which he was charged $1,500; the balance of his interest was paid in cash.

The following items were revealed in the course of the audit:

	End of 1964	End of 1965	End of 1966
Understatement of accrued expenses.	$ 400	$ 500	$ 650
Understatement of accrued revenue.	250	100	150
Overstatement of inventories.......	1,500	2,000	2,000
Understatement of charge for depreciation on assets still held........	150	350	200

Instructions: (1) Prepare a statement of changes in partners' capital accounts covering the period January 1, 1964, to the time of Roberts' withdrawal, reporting corrected earnings balances for each year and corrected capital balances for each partner.

(2) Give the entries that are required at the beginning of 1967 to correct the books and to record the transfer of assets to Roberts in final settlement.

2-3. The balance sheet for the firm of A, B, and C shows capitals on December 31, 1967, of $22,500, $24,000, and $40,000 respectively. A, B, and C had shared profits equally since the firm was organized in 1960, but beginning January 1, 1967, partners had agreed to share profits in the ratio 1:1:2 respectively. On December 31, 1967, C decided to retire and the partners agreed to make the following corrections in arriving at the amount to be paid to him for his interest:

(1) Accounting for the partnership in past years had not recognized accrued revenue and accrued expense items. It was agreed that capitals should be restated in terms of accrual accounting. Accrued items were:

	December 31, 1966	December 31, 1967
Accrued revenues......	$ 600	$ 800
Accrued expenses.......	2,400	6,000

(2) Certain expenditures had been recognized as expenses, but it was agreed that these are to be capitalized as additions to buildings and depreciated at 5% per year. Such expenditures totaled $6,000 in 1966 and $8,000 in 1967. Depreciation for only one-half year was to be recognized for the year in which the expenditures were made.

(3) The merchandise inventories had been reported annually on a *lifo* basis. It was agreed that these are to be restated on a *fifo* basis. Inventory values at *lifo* and *fifo* were as follows:

December 31, 1966		December 31, 1967	
Lifo	Fifo	Lifo	Fifo
$38,000	$56,000	$39,500	$62,500

Instructions: (1) Prepare a statement of changes in partners' capital accounts reporting corrections in net incomes for prior years in arriving at corrected capital balances as of December 31, 1967.

(2) Give the entry or entries required on the partnership books to give effect to the foregoing corrections.

2-4. Cross and Dodd are partners sharing profits 60% and 40% respectively. On July 1 their interests in the firm are as follows: Cross, $23,000, Dodd, $18,600. Evans is admitted as a partner upon the investment of $16,000.

Instructions: Record the investment by Evans in journal form, assuming:

(1) The new partner is given credit for the actual investment made.

(2) The new partner is given a ⅓ interest, a bonus being contributed by the old partners.

(3) The new partner is given a ⅓ interest, goodwill being recorded upon his admission.

(4) The new partner is given a ¼ interest, a bonus being allowed to the old partners.

(5) The new partner is given a ¼ interest, goodwill being recorded upon his admission.

2-5. J and K are partners with capitals of $10,000 and $40,000 and sharing profits 1:3.

Instructions: Give the journal entries required to record L's admission under each of the following assumptions:

(1) L invests $30,000 for a ¼ interest, the total firm capital after his admission to be $80,000.

(2) L invests $30,000 for a ⅓ interest, the total firm capital after his admission to be $90,000.

(3) L invests $30,000, $10,000 to be considered a bonus to the old partners. Prior to his admission, goodwill of $12,000 is to be recorded on the firm books.

(4) L purchases a ¼ interest in the firm, ¼ of the capital of each old partner being transferred to the account with the new partner. L pays the partners cash of $20,000, which they divide between themselves.

2-6. M and N are partners with capitals of $40,000 and $20,000. They share profits in the ratio of 3:1. The partners agree to admit O as a member of the firm.

Instructions: Give the required entries on the firm books to record the admission of O under each of the following assumptions:

(1) O purchases a ¼ interest in the firm. One fourth of each partner's capital is to be transferred to the new partner. O pays the partners $15,000, which is divided between them in proportion to the equities given up.

(2) O purchases a ⅓ interest in the firm. One third of each partner's capital is to be transferred to the new partner. O pays the partners $16,000, which is divided between them in proportion to the equities given up.

(3) O purchases a ⅓ interest in the firm. One third of each partner's capital is to be transferred to the new partner. O pays the partners $30,000, which is divided between them in proportion to the equities given up. Before O's admission, however, goodwill is recorded on the firm books so that O's ⅓ interest will be equal to the amount of his payment.

(4) O invests $30,000 for a ¼ interest in the firm. Goodwill is recorded on the firm books prior to his admission.

(5) O invests $30,000 for a 50% interest in the firm. M and N transfer part of their capitals to that of O as a bonus.
(6) O invests $40,000 in the firm. $10,000 is to be considered a bonus to Partners M and N.
(7) O invests $40,000 in the firm and is allowed a credit of $12,000 for goodwill upon his admission.
(8) O invests $25,000 for a ¼ interest in the firm. The total firm capital after his admission is to be $85,000.
(9) O invests $27,500 for a ¼ interest in the firm. The total firm capital after his admission is to be $110,000.
(10) O invests $24,000 for a ⅓ interest in the firm. The total firm capital after his admission is to be $84,000.

2-7. Ross and Sears are partners whose capital accounts on December 31, 1966, before closing the firm's books, are $50,000 and $30,000 respectively. The drawing account for Ross shows a debit balance of $8,200; for Sears, a debit balance of $6,800. The partnership agreement with regard to profits provides that (1) each partner is to be allowed an annual salary of $9,000 and (2) Ross is to receive 60% and Sears 40% of the profits after allowance of salaries.

The profit and loss account on December 31 has a credit balance of $14,000 before any entry for the allowance of salaries, and this balance is closed into the partners' capital accounts. The balances of the drawing accounts are also closed into the capital accounts.

On January 2, 1967, Thomas is admitted as a partner upon the investment of $20,000 in the firm. The partners allow him a bonus on the investment so that he may have a ⅓ interest in the firm. The new agreement provides that profits are to be distributed as follows: Ross, 35%; Sears, 25%; and Thomas, 40%. Salaries are not allowed.

On December 31, 1967, the partners' drawing accounts have debit balances as follows: Ross, $7,500; Sears, $5,000; and Thomas, $6,800. The profit and loss account has a $15,000 debit balance. Accounts are closed.

The partners decide to liquidate. All of the assets are sold in January, 1968. After creditors are fully paid, cash of $17,500 remains available for partners. This is distributed to the proper parties.

Instructions: Prepare a statement of changes in partners' capital accounts showing all of the changes that took place since January 1, 1966.

2-8. X and Y are partners whose capitals on December 31, 1966, before the books are closed are $38,500 and $21,500 respectively. The partnership agreement provides for distribution of profits as follows: monthly salaries of $750 to X and $600 to Y are to be allowed; any balance is to be distributed equally. If profits are insufficient to cover the salary allowance, the profit is to be distributed in the salary ratio; in the event of a loss, distribution is to be made equally.

The profit from operations for 1966 was $18,000, and this was transferred to the capital accounts. Equipment, book value $18,900, was destroyed by fire on December 12. Pending settlement with the insurance company, the full amount of the fire loss was reported as a claim against the insurance company.

On March 1, 1967, the firm recovered $13,500 in full settlement of the fire loss (the fire loss determined at this time is regarded as a correction in the profit for 1966). On April 1, Z was admitted as a partner upon the investment of $48,000 in the firm. Profits after Z's admission are to be divided equally. It was agreed that the books should not be closed until the end of the year, but that the profit determined from operations at that time should be considered to have been earned pro rata during the year. The profit from operations for 1967 was $36,000, and this was transferred to the capital accounts.

Instructions: Prepare a statement of changes in partners' capital accounts showing all of the changes that took place in the capital accounts in 1966 and 1967.

2-9. Partners D, E, F, and G share profits 40%, 30%, 15%, and 15% respectively. Their partnership agreement provides that in the event of the death of a partner the firm shall continue until the end of the fiscal period. Profits shall be considered to have been earned proportionately during this period, and the deceased partner's capital shall be adjusted by the proper share of the profit or loss until the date of death. From that date until the date of settlement with the estate there shall be added interest at 6% computed on the adjusted capital. The remaining partners shall continue to share profits in the old ratio. Payment to the estate shall be made within one year from date of the partner's death.

Partner G died on November 16. On December 31, the end of a six-month period, account balances on the partnership books before the profit and loss account is closed are as follows:

Cash	$ 7,500	Notes Payable	$ 15,000
Accounts Receivable	70,000	Accounts Payable	70,500
Inventories	95,000	D, Capital	42,000
Machinery and Equipment	45,000	E, Capital	37,500
Store Furniture and Fixtures	16,500	F, Capital	24,000
		G, Capital	22,500
		Profit and Loss (7/1–12/31)	22,500
	$234,000		$234,000

The profit and loss account is closed on December 31. On this date, F indicates to the remaining partners that he wishes to retire and is willing to accept in settlement of his interest the balance in his capital account after distribution of profits, less 20%. D and E accept his offer and issue a partnership 60-day, 6% note to F in payment of his interest.

Instructions: (1) Prepare all of the necessary journal entries as of December 31.

(2) Prepare a balance sheet for the firm of D and E as of December 31.

2-10. The partnerships of A & B and of C & D started in business on July 1, 1964; each partnership owns one retail appliance store. It was agreed as of June 30, 1967, to combine the partnerships to form a new partnership to be known as Four Partners' Discount Stores.

The June 30, 1967, post-closing trial balances of the partnerships appear below.

	A & B Trial Balance June 30, 1967		C & D Trial Balance June 30, 1967	
Cash	$ 20,000		$ 15,000	
Accounts receivable	100,000		150,000	
Allowance for doubtful accounts.		$ 2,000		$ 6,000
Merchandise inventory	175,000		119,000	
Land	25,000		35,000	
Buildings and equipment	80,000		125,000	
Allowance for depreciation		24,000		61,000
Prepaid expenses	5,000		7,000	
Accounts payable		40,000		60,000
Notes payable		70,000		75,000
Accrued expenses		30,000		45,000
A, capital		95,000		
B, capital		144,000		
C, capital				65,000
D, capital				139,000
	$405,000	$405,000	$451,000	$451,000

The following additional information is available:

(1) The income-sharing ratios for the former partnerships were 40% to A and 60% to B, and 30% to C and 70% to D. The profit-and-loss-sharing ratio for the new partnership will be A, 20%; B, 30%; C, 15%; and D, 35%.

(2) The opening capital ratios for the new partnership are to be the same as the profit-and-loss-sharing ratios for the new partnership. The capital to be assigned to A & B will total $225,000. Any cash settlements among the partners arising from capital account adjustments will be a private matter and will not be recorded on the partnership books.

(3) The partners agreed that the allowance for doubtful accounts for the new partnership is to be 3% of the accounts receivable balances.

(4) The opening inventory of the new partnership is to be valued by the *fifo* method. The inventory of A & B was valued by the *fifo* method, and the inventory of C & D was valued by the *lifo* method. The *lifo* inventory represents 85% of its *fifo* value.

(5) Depreciation is to be computed by the double-declining balance method with a 10-year life for the depreciable assets. Depreciation for 3 years is to be accumulated in the opening balance of the allowance for depreciation account. A & B computed depreciation by the straight-line method, and C & D used the double-declining balance method. All assets were obtained on July 1, 1964.

(6) After the books were closed, an unrecorded merchandise purchase of $4,000 by C & D was discovered. The merchandise had been sold by June 30, 1967.

(7) The accounts of A & B included a vacation pay accrual. It was agreed that C & D should make a similar accrual for their 5 employees who will receive a 2-week vacation at $100 per employee per week.

Instructions: (1) Prepare a work sheet to determine the opening balances of the new partnership after giving effect to the above information. Formal journal entries are not required. Supporting computations, including the computation of goodwill, should be in good form.

(2) Prepare a schedule computing the cash to be exchanged between A and B, and between C and D in settlement of the affairs of each original partnership.

(AICPA adapted)

2-11. Linden and Mills have been operating a business for several years as partners, during which time they have divided profits equally. They need additional capital to expand their business and have agreed to admit Jackson to the partnership as of January 1, 1968, with a ⅓ interest in profits and in the capital when he pays cash into the business as additional capital in an amount equal to ½ of the combined capital of the present two partners, redetermined as follows:

The average partnership profits, after partners' salaries, for the past two years, are to be capitalized at the rate of 10% per annum, which will redetermine the aggregate capital of the two present partners. Before such capitalization of profits, the accounts are to be adjusted for errors and omissions.

The business has not followed a strict accrual basis of accounting. As a result, the following items have been omitted from the books:

Item	Balance 12/31/65	Balance 12/31/66	Balance 12/31/67
Accrued expenses	$3,201	$2,472	$4,360
Prepaid expenses	1,010	1,226	872
Accrued income	—	250	475

In addition, no provision has been made for loss on uncollectible accounts. It is agreed that a provision of $4,500 is needed as of December 31, 1967, of which $600 is for 1966 accounts. Charge-offs have been made to expense in 1965 of 1964 and prior accounts — $1,200; in 1966 of 1965 accounts — $3,100 and of 1966 accounts — $400; in 1967 of 1966 accounts — $2,280, and of 1967 accounts — $525.

The inventory at December 31, 1967, contains some obsolete goods carried at a cost of $4,300. A 20% write-down is to be made to reduce these items to their present value.

In 1966 and 1967, salaries of $3,000 for each partner were taken out of the business and charged to expense before determining profits. It has been agreed that the salaries should have been $4,000 each.

The following financial data are available:

Balance Sheet
December 31, 1967

Cash	$ 7,000	Accounts payable	$ 43,200
Accounts receivable	42,500	Notes payable	25,000
Notes receivable	6,000	Allowance for depreciation of fixtures	5,300
Merchandise	64,000	Linden, capital	22,000
Store fixtures	12,400	Mills, capital	36,400
	$131,900		$131,900

	1965	1966	1967
Profit per books	$ 8,364	$ 8,585	$10,497
Linden, capital	20,000	24,000	22,000
Mills, capital	25,000	33,000	36,400

Instructions: (1) Prepare working papers to summarize the adjustments for errors and omissions and the redetermination of capital accounts as well as the receipt of Jackson's capital contribution as of January 1, 1968. Prepare a schedule showing the computation of the amount Jackson pays into the partnership in support of the entry on the working papers.

(2) Prepare a balance sheet for the new partnership as of January 1, 1968.

(AICPA adapted)

2-12. Alston and Bailey, equal partners in the A and B Stores, sold a ⅓ interest in Store No. 3 to Carter, manager of that store, on January 1, 1967. The new partnership will operate as the A. B. C. Co. Alston and Bailey will continue to operate other stores. The balance sheet of Store No. 3, at January 1, 1967, was as follows:

Assets			Liabilities and Capital		
Merchandise		$63,000	Liabilities		
Fixtures and equipment	$22,000		Accounts payable		$20,000
Allowance for depreciation	10,000	12,000	Capital		
Prepaid expenses		3,900	Alston	$30,000	
Utility deposits		1,100	Bailey	30,000	60,000
Total assets		$80,000	Total liabilities and capital		$80,000

Furniture and fixtures, which have an estimated remaining life of 5 years, were revalued at $18,000 according to the agreement of sale. Each partner contributed $1,000 as working capital, which was credited to his drawing account.

The following transactions for the year 1967 were all in cash:

Sales	$620,000
Merchandise purchases	493,000
Salaries and wages (including salary of $9,000 to Carter, as manager)	77,000
Expenses	25,400
New equipment purchased 7/1/67 (estimated life — 10 years)	3,000

You are also given the following information:

Merchandise inventory, December 31, 1967	$ 60,000
Prepaid expenses, December 31, 1967	3,000

The check record was kept open until all 1967 bills were paid before closing the books as at December 31, 1967.

The partnership agreement provides for a salary of $750 monthly to Carter. All remaining profits are divided equally.

Partners drawing accounts each show a net debit balance of $3,000.

Instructions: (1) Prepare a schedule showing the cash payment that Carter made to Alston and Bailey.

(2) Prepare an income statement of the A.B.C. Co. for the year ended December 31, 1967, including a schedule showing the distribution of profit and loss to the partners.

(AICPA adapted)

2-13. The Western Company is a family partnership engaged in the wholesale trade. It closes its books at December 31. During the year, all transactions are recorded on a cash receipts and disbursements basis. However, at the end of the fiscal year, adjustment is made to what was termed the "inventory account" for all items necessary to reflect operations and financial position on an accrual basis.

Partner E died on October 31, 1967. His will left equal shares in his estate to partners A and C and an outsider, F. All remaining partners, together with F, agreed that the business of The Western Company would continue as a partnership of A, B, C, D, and F, with partners' interests on November 1, 1967, as computed on a proper accrual basis to October 31, and after distribution of E's interest on that date. (Assume no probate period and the distribution of E's estate immediately.)

Depreciation of fixed assets may be ignored.

Balances as shown by the books of the firm were as follows:

	January 1, 1967	October 31, 1967
Cash	$ 42,000	$ 55,000
Inventory account	195,000	195,000
Fixed assets	60,000	59,000
Accruals	29,000	16,000
Notes payable	100,000	60,000
Partners' equity	168,000	168,000
Sales	—	2,000,000
Purchases	—	1,725,000
Operating expenses	—	210,000

In addition to the foregoing, the following information concerning the inventory account was available:

At January 1, 1967: accounts receivable, $80,000; merchandise, $200,000; freight claims (on incoming merchandise), $2,000; prepaid operating expenses, $10,000; accounts payable, $90,000; allowances due customers, $7,000. At October 31, 1967: accounts receivable, $83,300; merchandise, $221,000; freight claims (on incoming merchandise), $1,500; prepaid operating expenses, $6,000; accounts payable, $85,000; allowances due customers, $8,000.

Partners' equities and profit-and-loss-sharing ratio were as follows:	Equities	Profit and Loss Ratio
A	$10,500	6.25%
B	52,500	31.25%
C	77,000	37.50%
D	7,000	12.50%
E	21,000	12.50%

Instructions: (1) Prepare an income statement for the period January 1 to October 31, 1967.

(2) Prepare a statement of financial position at October 31, 1967.

(3) Prepare a statement of partners' equities on November 1, 1967.

(AICPA adapted)

2-14. The East Bay Motel has been owned by Catron and Johnson on a 50% partnership basis. On April 1, 1967, Catron bought Johnson's interest and dissolved the partnership. You have been engaged to act as a consultant to the accountant of the East Bay Motel. The following trial balance was taken from the books of the motel as of March 31, 1967. The books were last closed December 31, 1966.

	Debit	Credit
Cash	$ 630	
Petty Cash	100	
Prepaid Insurance	1,360	
Land	32,500	
Building	75,000	
Allowance for Depreciation — Building		$ 15,000
Furniture and Fixtures	30,000	
Allowance for Depreciation — Furn. and Fix.		10,800
Mortgage Payable — ABC Life Insurance Co.		53,000
Catron, Capital		28,265
Johnson, Capital		28,265
Room Income		17,249
Wages	3,545	
Advertising and Supplies	2,755	
Repairs and Utilities	2,234	
Office Expense	114	
Taxes	166	
Depreciation	3,770	
Interest	405	
	$152,579	$152,579

Upon a careful inspection of details of the settlement between Catron and Johnson, you learned that no adjustment for supplies, taxes, interest, and insurance had been recorded on March 31, 1967.

The following settlement transactions occurred on April 1, 1967:

(1) The partnership bank account was closed by drawing equal checks payable to each partner.

(2) Catron paid Johnson $235 to be applied as follows: one half of petty-cash, $50; one half of supplies inventory, $185.

(3) It was necessary for Catron to borrow additional funds on the motel property. Complete refinancing was worked out with the Second National Bank as set forth in the following disbursement statement prepared by the bank:

Amount of loan from Second National Bank				$84,000
Amount of check from Catron				500
Total				$84,500
Less: Payoff of mortgage due ABC Life Insurance Co.			$56,150	
Amount due Johnson		$28,950		
Plus ½ unexpired fire insurance premium due Johnson, prorated April 1, 1967, to April 1, 1968; original premium was $3,180		500		
Less:		$29,450		
½ penalty due ABC Insurance Co.	$1,325			
½ interest due ABC Insurance Co. from Feb. 6 to Apr. 1, 1967	250			
½ real estate taxes from Jan. 1 to Apr. 1, 1967	150			
Total		1,725		
Amount due Johnson			27,725	83,875
Total				$ 625
Less financing costs				625

(4) In addition, Johnson accepted a $30,000 second mortgage payable in equal monthly installments.

(5) An appraisal of the motel property indicated the following values:

Land	$ 45,500
Building	78,000
Furniture and fixtures	18,200
Total	$141,700

Instructions: Prepare a work sheet that includes columns to show:

(1) Adjustments necessary to bring accounts into agreement with data as presented, showing facts of dissolution agreement.
(2) Income statement for the period January 1, 1967, to March 31, 1967.
(3) Balance sheet as of March 31, 1967.
(4) Adjustments for dissolution.
(5) Opening balances for Catron's books. (AICPA adapted)

Chapter 3

PARTNERSHIPS

LIQUIDATION

It has already been suggested that the dissolution of a partnership does not mean the formal termination of the business. Dissolution of a partnership was recognized in connection with the reorganization of the business as a new unit. In other instances dissolution was recognized as a condition that called for winding up business affairs. Under the latter circumstances, the association of partners was considered ended for purposes of carrying on activities in the usual manner; but partners could still engage in activities leading to final settlement of business affairs, and the partnership agreement continued to govern the association until such time. The term *dissolution,* then, refers to the termination of the partnership as a going concern.

LIQUIDATION DEFINED

The process of winding up a business normally consists of the conversion of a portion or all of the assets into cash, settlement with creditors, and the distribution of remaining assets to the ownership groups. The conversion of assets into cash is referred to as *realization;* the payment of claims is referred to as *liquidation.* The latter term is also used in a broader sense to refer to the complete winding-up process.

Upon liquidation of a partnership, the accountant must be able to advise as to the proper distribution of assets among individual partners. Improper distributions, resulting in overpayment to certain parties with corresponding loss to others, may result in personal liability on the part of the person authorizing such distributions.

PROCEDURE IN LIQUIDATION

When a partnership is to be liquidated, the books should be adjusted and closed and the net income or loss for the period should be carried to the partners' capital accounts. The partnership is then ready to proceed with liquidation.

As assets are converted into cash, any differences between the book values and the amounts realized represent gains or losses to be divided among partners in the profit and loss ratio. Such gains and losses are carried to the capital accounts. The capital balances then become the basis for settlement.

In the course of liquidation, when a partner's capital account reports a debit balance and such partner has a loan balance, the law permits exercise of *the right of offset*, that is, the offset of a part or all of the loan against the capital deficiency. A debit balance in the capital account in the absence of a loan balance or after offset of a loan balance indicates the need for a contribution by the deficient partner. The inability of a partnership to recover a capital deficiency will mean that remaining partners will have to absorb such an amount.

As cash becomes available for distribution, it is first applied to the payment of outside creditors. It may then be applied in settlement of partners' loan and capital balances. It may be observed that the Uniform Partnership Act provides that partners' loans shall rank ahead of partners' capitals in order of payment. Such a rule, however, should be applied subject to one important limitation: when a distribution of cash is made before all of the losses are known, payment should not be made on loan balances or such portions thereof as may be required to offset possible capital deficiencies. In some instances, then, it may be appropriate to apply cash to the payment of capital balances of certain partners even though loan balances of others remain unpaid.

PAYMENTS TO PARTNERS AFTER REALIZATION IS COMPLETED

The accounting procedures that are followed upon partnership liquidation are illustrated in this and the next chapter. Examples in this chapter assume that distributions are made to partners only after realization of assets has been completed and the full loss or gain from realization is known. Examples in the next chapter illustrate the procedures that are followed when distributions are made to partners during the course of liquidation and before the full loss or gain from realization has been determined.

For purposes of the discussions to follow, it is assumed that the firm of A, B, C, and D decides to liquidate. All partnership assets are to be converted into cash. A, B, C, and D share profits and losses 30%, 30%, 20%, and 20% respectively. A balance sheet prepared on May 1, 1967, just before liquidation, reports the following balances:

Assets		Liabilities and Capital	
Cash	$ 10,000	Liabilities	$ 75,000
Other assets	180,000	B, loan	6,000
		D, loan	5,000
		A, capital	42,000
		B, capital	31,500
		C, capital	20,500
		D, capital	10,000
Total assets	$190,000	Total liabilities and capital	$190,000

A number of examples will be offered that assume the realization of varying amounts of cash for partnership assets. The assumptions are listed below.

Example 1. Realization of assets, $140,000, with loss on realization fully absorbed by partners' capital balances.

Example 2. Realization of assets, $120,000, with loss on realization requiring transfer from partner's loan account to capital.

Example 3. Realization of assets, $100,000, with loss on realization resulting in a capital deficiency for one partner.

Example 4. Realization of assets, $80,000, with loss on realization resulting in capital deficiencies for more than one partner.

Example 5. Realization of assets, $60,000, with cash insufficient to pay creditors:

(a) When all of the partners are personally solvent.

(b) When certain partners are personally solvent and others are personally insolvent.

LOSS ON REALIZATION FULLY ABSORBED BY PARTNERS' CAPITAL BALANCES

Example 1. Assume that the noncash assets of the firm of A, B, C, and D, book value $180,000, ultimately realize $140,000. The loss of $40,000 is distributed in the profit and loss ratio. The capital of each partner, in this case, is large enough to absorb his share of the total loss on realization. Under these circumstances the distribution of cash presents no problem. Cash is first applied to the payment of outside creditors, and the balance is applied to the payment of partners' loan and capital balances.

A statement of liquidation to summarize the foregoing follows:

A, B, C, and D
Statement of Liquidation
May 1–31, 1967

	Cash	Other Assets	Liab.	B Loan	D Loan	Capitals and Profit-Sharing Percentage			
						A, Cap. (30%)	B, Cap. (30%)	C, Cap. (20%)	D, Cap. (20%)
Balances before liquidation	10,000	180,000	75,000	6,000	5,000	42,000	31,500	20,500	10,000
(a) Sale of assets and distribution of loss......	140,000	(180,000)				(12,000)	(12,000)	(8,000)	(8,000)
	150,000		75,000	6,000	5,000	30,000	19,500	12,500	2,000
(b) Payment to creditors..	(75,000)		(75,000)						
	75,000			6,000	5,000	30,000	19,500	12,500	2,000
(c) Payment to partners..	(75,000)			(6,000)	(5,000)	(30,000)	(19,500)	(12,500)	(2,000)

The journal entries to record the sale of the assets and the distribution of cash are as follows:

Transaction	Entry		
(a) Sale of assets for $140,000; loss distributed to A, B, C, and D, 30%, 30%, 20%, and 20% respectively.	Cash	140,000	
	A, Capital	12,000	
	B, Capital	12,000	
	C, Capital	8,000	
	D, Capital	8,000	
	Other Assets		180,000
(b) Payment to creditors.	Liabilities	75,000	
	Cash		75,000
(c) Payment to partners.	B, Loan	6,000	
	D, Loan	5,000	
	A, Capital	30,000	
	B, Capital	19,500	
	C, Capital	12,500	
	D, Capital	2,000	
	Cash		75,000

The following points should be noted in the preceding example:

(1) The loss on the realization of assets is divided among the partners in the same way as losses from operation. If there had been a gain on realization, the partners' capital accounts would have been credited. When assets are sold in a number of lots, a separate account to summarize gains and losses may be opened. After the realization of all assets, the debit or credit balance in the account is transferred to the capital accounts in the profit and loss ratio.

(2) Outside creditors are paid in full before payments are made to partners on either loan or capital balances.

(3) Partners' net interests in firm assets are determined before any payment is made to partners. When the books report amounts receivable by the firm from individual partners as a result of advances or as a result of charges for goods or services, such balances would be offset against partners' capitals. Settlement is then made in accordance with amounts reported by partners' loan and capital accounts.

LOSS ON REALIZATION REQUIRING TRANSFER FROM PARTNER'S LOAN ACCOUNT TO CAPITAL

Example 2. Assume that the assets of the firm of A, B, C, and D realize $120,000. Liquidation is summarized in the statement given on the next page. Observe that the sale of the assets for $120,000 results in a loss of $60,000 that is divided among the partners in the profit and loss ratio. Distribution of this loss requires a charge to D of $12,000 and results in a debit balance in D's capital account of $2,000. Instead of requiring D to make an additional investment of $2,000, a transfer of this amount is made from his loan account to his capital account. Partners are then paid amounts equal to their loan and capital account balances.

A, B, C, and D
Statement of Liquidation
May 1–31, 1967

	Cash	Other Assets	Liab.	B Loan	D Loan	Capitals and Profit-Sharing Percentage: A, Cap. (30%)	B, Cap. (30%)	C, Cap. (20%)	D, Cap. (20%)
Balances before liquidation	10,000	180,000	75,000	6,000	5,000	42,000	31,500	20,500	10,000
Sale of assets and distribution of loss	120,000	(180,000)				(18,000)	(18,000)	(12,000)	(12,000)
	130,000		75,000	6,000	5,000	24,000	13,500	8,500	(2,000)
Payment to creditors	(75,000)		(75,000)						
	55,000			6,000	5,000	24,000	13,500	8,500	(2,000)
Offset of D's loan against debit balance in his capital account					(2,000)				2,000
	55,000			6,000	3,000	24,000	13,500	8,500	
Payment to partners	(55,000)			(6,000)	(3,000)	(24,000)	(13,500)	(8,500)	

The entry to record the application of D's loan to his capital deficiency would be as follows:

Transaction	Entry		
Transfer from D's loan account to his capital account of the amount required to absorb his capital deficiency.	D, Loan	2,000	
	D, Capital		2,000

LOSS ON REALIZATION RESULTING IN CAPITAL DEFICIENCY FOR ONE PARTNER

Example 3. Assume that the assets realize $100,000 and that a loss of $80,000 is incurred. Liquidation would be completed in the manner summarized in the statement of liquidation on the next page.

In distributing the loss of $80,000, D is charged for $16,000. This results in a debit balance in D's capital account of $6,000. The offset of the entire amount of D's loan account against his capital still leaves his capital account with a debit balance of $1,000. If D pays the firm $1,000 at this point, his capital deficiency is canceled and the partners can distribute cash to A, B, and C in final liquidation. If, however, recovery from D is not made at this point and the partners decide to distribute the available cash, the distribution should recognize the possibility that D may fail to meet his obligation to the firm. If D is personally insolvent or if for some other reason the firm finds it impossible to collect $1,000 from D, partners A, B, and C will have to absorb the additional loss. The available cash, then, should be distributed in a manner that leaves the

A, B, C, and D
Statement of Liquidation
May 1–31, 1967

	Cash	Other Assets	Liab.	B Loan	D Loan	Capitals and Profit-Sharing Percentage A, Cap. (30%)	B, Cap. (30%)	C, Cap. (20%)	D, Cap. (20%)
Balances before liquidation	10,000	180,000	75,000	6,000	5,000	42,000	31,500	20,500	10,000
Sale of assets and distribution of loss	100,000	(180,000)				(24,000)	(24,000)	(16,000)	(16,000)
	110,000		75,000	6,000	5,000	18,000	7,500	4,500	(6,000)
Payment to creditors	(75,000)		(75,000)						
	35,000			6,000	5,000	18,000	7,500	4,500	(6,000)
Offset of D's loan against debit balance in his capital account					(5,000)				5,000
	35,000			6,000		18,000	7,500	4,500	(1,000)
Payment to partners (see schedule)	(35,000)			(6,000)		(17,625)	(7,125)	(4,250)	
						375	375	250	(1,000)
Additional investment by D	1,000								1,000
	1,000					375	375	250	
Payment to partners	(1,000)					(375)	(375)	(250)	

A, B, C, and D
Schedule to Accompany Statement of Liquidation
Amounts to be Paid to Partners
May 1–31, 1967

	A (30%)	B (30%)	C (20%)	D (20%)
Capital balances before distribution of cash	18,000	7,500	4,500	(1,000)
Add loan balance		6,000		
Partners' total interests	18,000	13,500	4,500	(1,000)
Restricted interests — possible loss of $1,000 to A, B, and C if D fails to contribute amount of his deficiency (ratio: A, B, C—30:30:20)	(375)	(375)	(250)	1,000
Free interests — amounts to be paid to each partner	17,625	13,125	4,250	
Payment to apply on loan		6,000		
Payment to apply on capital	17,625	7,125	4,250	
Total cash distribution	17,625	13,125	4,250	

capitals of A, B, and C with balances that can absorb the possible loss of $1,000 in the profit and loss ratio existing among them.

If D subsequently contributes $1,000, this cash is paid to A, B, and C according to the balances in their accounts. If it is determined that the claim against D is uncollectible, the debit balance in his capital account is charged against the capitals of the other partners in the profit and loss ratio existing among them. It is assumed in the statement of liquidation that D meets his obligation to the firm by contributing $1,000.

It should be observed that cash of $35,000 was available to pay A, B, and C, whose combined loan and capital balances were $36,000. In determining the amount to be paid to these partners, the loss of $1,000 in the event of D's inability to meet his obligation to the firm was considered. Since A, B, and C share profits 30%, 30%, and 20% respectively, this ratio, or its equivalent of $^3/_8$, $^3/_8$, and $^2/_8$, was used in determining the balances to remain in their accounts.

The amount to be paid to a partner may be referred to as his *free interest.* The free interest is calculated by combining each partner's loan and capital balance prior to the distribution of any cash and subtracting from this total any balance that must remain available to absorb possible future losses. When the amount of cash that may be paid to a partner is determined, cash is first applied to any loan that he may have and any balance is applied to his capital.

In determining the distribution of $35,000 to A, B, C, and D, the free interest for each partner was calculated by means of the separate schedule that appears on page 76. The distribution of cash in any manner other than that shown will result in the overpayment of certain partners and the underpayment of others and will require cash transfers among partners later if D fails to meet his obligation to the firm.

The entries to record the additional investment by D and the distribution of this amount to A, B, and C follow:

Transaction	Entry		
Additional investment by D to meet capital deficiency.	Cash	1,000	
	D, Capital		1,000
Payment to partners in final settlement.	A, Capital	375	
	B, Capital	375	
	C, Capital	250	
	Cash		1,000

If D makes settlement directly with his copartners, the following entry is made:

Transaction	Entry		
Payment by D directly to A, B, and C in settlement of indebtedness to copartners.	A, Capital	375	
	B, Capital	375	
	C, Capital	250	
	D, Capital		1,000

If the firm cannot collect its claim against D, the loss must be borne by A, B, and C in their profit and loss ratio. This contingency was considered in distributing the cash, and the capital accounts of A, B, and C were left with balances that can absorb the loss in the ratio of 30:30:20. The entry to record the loss would be:

Transaction	Entry		
Charge-off of D's uncollectible balance against capitals of A, B, and C, in the ratio 30:30:20 respectively.	A, Capital	375	
	B, Capital	375	
	C, Capital	250	
	D, Capital		1,000

LOSS ON REALIZATION RESULTING IN CAPITAL DEFICIENCIES FOR MORE THAN ONE PARTNER

Example 4. Assume that assets realize $80,000 and that a loss of $100,000 is incurred. Under these circumstances, liquidation would be completed as summarized in the statement of liquidation that appears on the following page.

In distributing the loss of $100,000, D's capital account is charged for $20,000. This results in a debit balance of $10,000 in D's capital account. The offset of D's entire loan balance of $5,000 against his capital still leaves a capital deficiency of $5,000. If $5,000 is recovered from D at this point, the capital deficiency is canceled and the partners can wind up activities by distributing the cash to partners A, B, and C. If, however, recovery from D is not made at this point and the partners decide to distribute the available cash, the interests of A, B, and C should be left with balances sufficient to absorb the possible loss from D. The recognition of such a loss will result in a debit balance in C's capital. In anticipating all contingencies, it becomes necessary to consider the possibility of such an additional loss to A and B.

If D subsequently invests $5,000, this cash may be distributed to the partners according to the balances reported in their capital accounts. Under these circumstances C would not be required to make a further contribution. An investment by D was assumed in the statement.

It should be noted that cash of $15,000 was available to pay A, B, and C, whose combined loan and capital balances totaled $20,000. In determining how the cash was to be distributed, the free interest for each partner was calculated by means of a schedule. The possible loss of $5,000 in the event of D's inability to meet his obligation to the partnership was first considered. Since A, B, and C share profits 30%, 30%, and 20%, this ratio was applied in arriving at the partners' restricted interests of $1,875, $1,875, and $1,250 respectively. C's capital, however, was inadequate to absorb his share of the possible additional loss. The loss that C might be unable to absorb, $750, was then considered a fur-

A, B, C, and D
Statement of Liquidation
May 1–31, 1967

	Cash	Other Assets	Liab.	B Loan	D Loan	Capitals and Profit-Sharing Percentage: A, Cap. (30%)	B, Cap. (30%)	C, Cap. (20%)	D, Cap. (20%)
Balances before liquidation	10,000	180,000	75,000	6,000	5,000	42,000	31,500	20,500	10,000
Sale of assets and distribution of loss	80,000	(180,000)				(30,000)	(30,000)	(20,000)	(20,000)
	90,000		75,000	6,000	5,000	12,000	1,500	500	(10,000)
Payment to creditors	(75,000)		(75,000)						
	15,000			6,000	5,000	12,000	1,500	500	(10,000)
Offset of D's loan against debit balance in capital account					(5,000)				5,000
	15,000			6,000		12,000	1,500	500	(5,000)
Payment to partners (see schedule)	(15,000)			(5,250)		(9,750)			
				750		2,250	1,500	500	(5,000)
Additional investment by D	5,000								5,000
	5,000			750		2,250	1,500	500	
Payment to partners	(5,000)			(750)		(2,250)	(1,500)	(500)	

A, B, C, and D
Schedule to Accompany Statement of Liquidation
Amounts to be Paid to Partners
May 1–31, 1967

	A (30%)	B (30%)	C (20%)	D (20%)
Capital balances before distribution of cash	12,000	1,500	500	(5,000)
Add loan balance		6,000		
Partners' total interests	12,000	7,500	500	(5,000)
Restricted interests — possible loss of $5,000 to A, B, and C if D fails to contribute amount of his deficiency (ratio: A, B, C—30:30:20)	(1,875)	(1,875)	(1,250)	5,000
	10,125	5,625	(750)	
Restricted interests — additional possible loss of $750 to A and B if C fails to contribute amount of his possible deficiency (ratio: A, B — 30:30)	(375)	(375)	750	
Free interests — amounts to be paid to each partner	9,750	5,250		
Payment to apply on loan		5,250		
Payment to apply on capital	9,750			
Total cash distribution	9,750	5,250		

ther restricted interest applicable to A and B. Since the profit and loss ratio for A and B is 30% and 30%, or equal, further reductions of $375 were applied to A and B in arriving at their free interests.

It should be observed that the distribution of $15,000 developed in the schedule resulted in payment on A's capital balance before B's loan was fully liquidated. If B insists that full settlement be made on his loan balance before cash is paid on capital balances in view of the priority given partners' loans in the Uniform Partnership Act, the liquidator must consider all of the contingencies that are faced in terminating the partnership. A future loss through failure to recover cash from deficient partners will give rise to a debit balance in B's capital account. Cash paid to B in satisfaction of his loan balance, then, will have to be recovered to absorb such capital deficiency, and failure to effect such recovery could render the liquidator liable to a partner suffering a loss through such premature distribution. Under these circumstances, the liquidator must insist on one of the following procedures:

(1) Recognize the legal priority of partners' loans but make payment to a trustee under the condition that the cash can be recovered to offset a capital deficiency if one should arise; when the possibility of a need for offset is gone, the cash can be released to the partner.

(2) Defer settlement until the full amount of the loss that each partner will be required to absorb in final settlement including charges arising from failures of coparticipants to meet their proper share of firm losses is ascertained; application of loan balances against capital deficiencies can then be effected and appropriate cash distribution made.

(3) Distribute cash in a manner that recognizes the possibility of future losses including charges that may arise from failures of coparticipants to meet their proper share of firm losses; payment on loan balances, as well as capital balances, then, will be withheld when such balances may be required to absorb losses.

If all parties are informed as to the nature and significance of the problem, they should have no objection to the distribution of cash as suggested in (3) above. Distributions of cash when loan and capital balances are involved, then, are the same as the distributions that would be made if total interests were in the form of capital balances.

REALIZATION RESULTING IN CASH INSUFFICIENT TO PAY CREDITORS

Example 5(a). Assume that assets of the firm of A, B, C, and D realize only $60,000. Assume further that all partners are personally solvent and capable of meeting any obligation to the firm that may emerge from liquidation. A loss of $120,000 is distributed to the partners, and available cash of $70,000 is paid to creditors. Appropriate offset of loan balances against capital deficiencies is made. In this case, creditors are left with unpaid balances totaling $5,000; partners A and B have positive equities in the firm of $6,000 and $1,500 respectively, while partners C and D owe the firm $3,500 and $9,000 respectively. If C and D make payment to the firm in settlement of their obligations, the cash of $12,500 may be distributed to creditors and to A and B in full settlement. A statement of liquidation under these conditions follows:

A, B, C, and D
Statement of Liquidation
May 1–31, 1967

						Capitals and Profit-Sharing Percentage			
	Cash	Other Assets	Liab.	B Loan	D Loan	A, Cap. (30%)	B, Cap. (30%)	C, Cap. (20%)	D, Cap. (20%)
Balances before liquidation	10,000	180,000	75,000	6,000	5,000	42,000	31,500	20,500	10,000
Sale of assets and distribution of loss	60,000	(180,000)				(36,000)	(36,000)	(24,000)	(24,000)
	70,000		75,000	6,000	5,000	6,000	(4,500)	(3,500)	(14,000)
Payment to creditors	(70,000)		(70,000)						
			5,000	6,000	5,000	6,000	(4,500)	(3,500)	(14,000)
Offset of loans against debit balances in capital accounts				(4,500)	(5,000)		4,500		5,000
			5,000	1,500		6,000		(3,500)	(9,000)
Additional investment by C and D	12,500							3,500	9,000
	12,500		5,000	1,500		6,000			
Payment to creditors	(5,000)		(5,000)						
	7,500			1,500		6,000			
Payment to partners	(7,500)			(1,500)		(6,000)			

It has already been suggested that, insofar as business-creditor relationships are concerned, the partnership is not viewed as a separate entity but as an association of individuals, all personally responsible for partnership obligations. In the previous example, settlement with creditors was achieved through contributions to the partnership by capital-deficient partners. Assume, however, that creditors, finding that partnership assets are insufficient to meet partnership liabilities in full, proceed against the individual partners. If they are successful in collecting the balance of $5,000 owed to them from A, for example, A's interest in the partnership would go up by $5,000. Upon ultimate collection of capital deficiencies from partners C and D of $3,500 and $9,000 respectively, A would be paid $11,000 and B $1,500. It should be observed that when liquidation is completed by full recovery from deficient partners, the same results are achieved regardless of who makes payment to creditors. Under each of the previous assumptions, A and B recover \$6,000 and \$1,500 respectively, and C and D contribute \$3,500 and \$9,000 respectively.

Example 5(b). In the foregoing example it was assumed that all of the partners were personally solvent and able to meet whatever indebtedness was incurred in arriving at final settlement. Assume, however, that certain partners are personally insolvent. Under these circumstances the law requires a *marshaling of assets* that calls for the following procedure: partnership assets must first be applied to the settlement of the partnerships's own liabilities, and each partner's separate assets must first be applied to the settlement of the partner's own liabilities. Thus, creditors of an insolvent partnership may claim only that portion of a partner's separate property that is not required for the satisfaction of his personal obligations; such separate property in excess of personal obligations may be claimed by firm creditors regardless of the partner's interest in the firm, whether positive or negative. On the other hand, creditors of an insolvent partner may make claim to partnership property only after firm creditors have been satisfied in full; the claim of separate creditors, however, is limited to the remaining positive interest of the particular partner. The Uniform Partnership Act makes the following further provision:

> When a partner has become bankrupt or his estate is insolvent, the claims against his separate property shall rank in the following order:
>
> I. Those owing to separate creditors.
> II. Those owing to partnership creditors.
> III. Those owing to partners by way of contribution.

A deficiency in a partner's capital account is therefore not to be included in the separate creditor total against which personal property is first applied under the Uniform Partnership Act, but is to be met only after other personal and partnership creditors are fully satisfied.

To illustrate application of the foregoing rules, assume again the sale of the assets of the firm of A, B, C, and D at \$60,000, payment to creditors of \$70,000, and offset of loan balances against capitals. Liabilities of \$5,000 are unpaid. The personal status of each of the partners at this point, together with the interest of each in the firm, both positive and negative, are given at the top of the next page.

The personal assets of A and D must be applied in total to payment of personal creditors. However, the personal assets of B and C exceed the respective personal debts, and partnership creditors have recourse against

Partner	Personal Status Exclusive of Firm Interest		Firm Status	
	Assets	Liabilities	Interest in the Firm	Obligation to the Firm
A	10,000	20,000	6,000	
B	20,000	15,000	1,500	
C	25,000	15,000		3,500
D	10,000	10,000		9,000

either partner for the balance of their claims. The fact that B has a positive interest in the partnership is no defense for B if partnership creditors choose to hold him. Furthermore, personal creditors of partner A who cannot be fully satisfied from A's personal assets will look forward to further satisfaction of their claims through final liquidation of the partnership and ultimate settlement of A's positive interest.

Assume that partnership creditors collect from B. Before final settlement is made by the partners, the claim against D, who is personally insolvent, is written off against the capitals of A, B, and C in the ratio 30:30:20. C, who is indebted to the firm and personally solvent, makes appropriate payment to partners A and B, who have positive equities in the firm; the amount recoverable on A's interest is applied to payment of his individual creditors. Assuming settlement in this manner, the statement of liquidation would be completed as shown below.

A, B, C, and D
Statement of Liquidation
May 1–31, 1967

	Cash	Other Assets	Liab.	B Loan	D Loan	Capitals and Profit-Sharing Percentage			
						A, Cap. (30%)	B, Cap. (30%)	C, Cap. (20%)	D, Cap. (20%)
Balances, (see page 81)...			5,000	1,500		6,000		(3,500)	(9,000)
Payment to creditors by B.			(5,000)				5,000		
				1,500		6,000	5,000	(3,500)	(9,000)
Amount due from D and uncollectible, charged to A, B, and C in the ratio 30:30:20 respectively...						(3,375)	(3,375)	(2,250)	9,000
				1,500		2,625	1,625	(5,750)	
Payment by C to A and B.				(1,500)		(2,625)	(1,625)	5,750	

If partnership creditors collect from C instead of B, final settlement will produce the same net results. B will be required to contribute $1,875, the difference between the charge to his capital for D's deficiency, $3,375, and his unpaid loan balance of $1,500; C, after paying his personal creditors, will be required to contribute $750 to cancel his capital deficiency of $5,750, consisting of a debit balance in his capital account of $3,500, increased by the charge for D's deficiency, $2,250. Contributions by B and C totaling $2,625 will be paid to A.

It should be observed that, under common law decisions, the separate property of a partner must be allocated among all of the separate claims of the partner, including any amount owed to a partnership. Under this rule, referring to the tabulation at the top of page 83, partner D's personal assets of $10,000 would be applied to both personal claims of $10,000 and the firm obligation of $9,000; personal creditors would thus receive 10,000/19,000 × $10,000, or $5,263, and the partnership would receive 9,000/19,000 × $10,000, or $4,737. D's unpaid balance would then be distributed to remaining partners, and settlement would be completed in terms of remaining balances in a manner that has already been indicated.

QUESTIONS

1. What is meant by the *right of offset* as applied to the liquidation of a partnership?

2. (a) What priorities are recognized under the Uniform Partnership Act in the distribution of cash upon partnership liquidation? (b) What limitations would you apply in recognizing such priorities?

3. Burke and Collins invest $25,000 and $5,000 respectively in forming a partnership. No agreement is made concerning profit distribution. A loss of $5,000 is incurred at the end of the first six months of operation. Liquidation of the partnership results in an additional loss of $10,000. Collins insists that operating losses may be divided equally but that losses from liquidation should be divided in the ratio of capital investments. (a) Is there any merit to Collins' contention? (b) What is the status of the partners after the foregoing takes place?

4. Mead and Norris, who share profits equally, have loan and capital balances as follows:

	Mead	Norris
Loan balance	$25,000	$10,000
Capital balance	50,000	60,000

All of the assets are sold for $35,000, and Mead suggests that this be applied to the payment of loan balances in final settlement. Do you approve?

5. A, B, and C are partners sharing profits 3:3:2. The partnership is dissolved. Upon distribution of the partnership loss from liquidation, C's capital account shows a debit balance of $10,000. C is personally insolvent. How is this balance canceled?

6. A, B, and C are partners sharing profits equally. The partnership and also certain partners are insolvent and the partnership is liquidated. Upon distribution of the partnership loss from liquidation, a statement is drawn up summarizing the status of each partner as follows:

	Personal Status (Exclusive of Firm Interest)		Firm Status	
Partner	Assets	Liabilities	Interest in Firm	Amount Owed to Firm
A	$30,000	$10,000	$5,000	
B	5,000	10,000		$ 5,000
C	15,000	10,000		15,000

(a) Assume that provisions of the Uniform Partnership Act apply.

(1) Against whom can firm creditors proceed for the recovery of their unpaid claims?

(2) What are the rights of the individual creditors of each partner?

(3) Against whom can A proceed for the recovery of his interest in the firm?

(b) How would your answers differ in each case assuming that settlement is made under common law decisions?

7. Just before partnership liquidation, capital accounts for A, B, and C, who share profits 2:1:1 respectively, are as follows: A, credit balance, $40,000; B, credit balance, $25,000; C, debit balance, $12,500. Under what circumstances, if any, will C share in the distribution of cash after realization of partnership assets?

EXERCISES

1. Knox and Wheeler are partners, and their capital balances are $15,000 and $10,000 respectively. The firm owes Wheeler $4,000 on a note. Profits are shared equally. Upon liquidation, cash of $6,000 becomes available for distribution to the partners. How is this cash to be distributed?

2. A, B, C, and D are partners with capitals of $5,500, $5,150, $6,850, and $4,500 respectively. A has a loan balance of $1,000. Profits are shared in the ratio of 4:3:2:1 by A, B, C, and D respectively. Assets are sold, liabilities are paid, and cash of $6,000 remains. How should this cash be divided?

3. X, Y, and Z form a partnership on January 1, 1967, investing $15,000, $10,000, and $10,000 respectively; profits are to be shared in the ratio of 2:1:1 respectively. It is agreed that 6% (½ of 1% per month) is to be charged on withdrawals that decrease capitals below the original investments. On March 1, X withdraws $5,000. Business is unsatisfactory and it is decided to dissolve the partnership. Partnership assets realize $5,000 and the accountant distributes this cash to the proper parties on November 1, 1967. All parties are solvent, and proper settlement is made among partners the same day. Prepare a statement of partners' capitals that summarizes the activities that took place in 1967.

4. The capitals of Ames, Baker, and Caldwell, who are partners, are $14,000, $10,000, and $14,000, and profits are shared 30%, 20%, and 50% respectively. Upon liquidation, all of the partnership assets are sold and sufficient cash is realized to pay all of the claims except one for $2,000. Caldwell is personally insolvent, but the remaining partners are able to meet any indebtedness to the firm. State how settlement would be made.

5. A, B, and C formed a partnership in 1966, agreeing to divide profits 2:1:1 respectively. In the middle of 1967, with operations going unfavorably, the partners decided to dissolve the relationship. From the following facts, prepare a summary of partners' capital balances that indicates what, if anything, remains to be done in final settlement.

	A	B	C
Value of net assets contributed to firm	$50,000	$22,500	$20,000
Partnership net income, 1966, $30,000, divided 2:1:1	15,000	7,500	7,500
Drawings — 1966	15,000	10,000	10,000
Net assets at time of dissolution valued at $65,000, distributed to partners 2:1:1	32,500	16,250	16,250

6. J and K share profits 40% and 60% respectively. After sale of all firm assets, ledger accounts show the balances reported below. Both partners are personally insolvent and unable to contribute to the partnership. Give all of the entries to summarize partnership activities, including the appropriate distribution of cash on hand.

Cash	$ 2,000	Salary Due to J	$ 500
Due from K	1,500	J, Capital	9,500
Loss from Liquidation	24,500	K, Capital	18,000
	$28,000		$28,000

7. L, M, and N are partners sharing profits 3:3:2 respectively. The partners decide to liquidate. The partnership books report the following balances with respect to land and buildings:

Land		$15,000	Mortgage Payable (secured by land and buildings)	$16,000
Buildings	$25,000			
Less Allowance for Depreciation	7,500	17,500	Accrued Interest on Mortgage	160

The land and buildings are worth $30,000 on the market, and L agrees to take over the property at this value; he also agrees to assume all the indebtedness on the property. Record the transfer on the firm books.

PROBLEMS

3-1. A, B, and C, who share profits and losses in the ratio of 2:2:1 respectively, decide to liquidate on December 31, 1967. Below is a condensed balance sheet prepared just prior to liquidation:

A, B, and C
Balance Sheet
December 31, 1967

Assets		Liabilities and Capital	
Cash	$ 20,000	Trade creditors	$112,000
Other assets	340,000	B, loan	5,000
		C, loan	8,000
		A, capital	95,000
		B, capital	60,000
		C, capital	80,000
Total assets	$360,000	Total liabilities and capital	$360,000

Instructions: For each case below prepare a statement of liquidation, with supporting schedules where necessary, assuming that cash is realized for the other assets as indicated and that all available cash is immediately distributed to the proper parties. Assume that partners who find themselves indebted to the firm invest additional cash and such cash is distributed as a second installment to the proper parties.

(a) $250,000.
(b) $185,000.
(c) $170,000.
(d) $125,000.
(e) $ 90,000.

3-2. Carl, Decker, and Eaton form a partnership on July 1, 1967, each partner investing $25,000. On August 1, 1967, Carl was advanced $10,000 by the firm. On September 1, 1967, Decker made a loan to the firm of $20,000. Interest is to be charged on advances to partners and credited on loans by partners at the rate of 6%. Business is unsatisfactory and the partners decide to dissolve. Eaton is allowed special compensation of $2,500 for managing the sale of assets and settlement with creditors. On December 31, all assets have been sold, outside creditors have been paid, and cash of $35,000 is distributed to partners. All partners are personally solvent and final settlement is made among partners on February 10, 1968.

Instructions: Prepare a statement of changes in partners' capital accounts covering the period July 1, 1967 to February 10, 1968.

3-3. A balance sheet for the partnership of A, B, C, and D just prior to liquidation and dissolution is given at the top of the following page. Profits are shared by A, B, C, and D in the ratio of 4:2:1:1 respectively.

A, B, C, and D
Balance Sheet
April 30, 1967

Assets		Liabilities and Capital	
Cash	$ 20,000	Liabilities	$180,000
Other assets	380,000	D, loan	12,500
Receivable from A	25,000	A, capital	155,000
		B, capital	37,500
		C, capital	20,000
		D, capital	20,000
Total assets	$425,000	Total liabilities and capital	$425,000

"Other assets" are sold for $200,000 and available cash is distributed to the proper parties. It is ascertained that partner B is personally insolvent, but the other partners are able to meet any personal indebtedness to the partnership. The solvent partners make appropriate contributions to the partnership, and this cash is distributed in final settlement.

Instructions: (1) Prepare a statement of liquidation, together with a supporting schedule if necessary.

(2) Give the entries that would be made to record the dissolution of the partnership.

3-4. Gordon and Haller began partnership operations on January 3, 1967, investing cash of $25,000 and $15,000 respectively. Gordon is to be allowed an annual salary of $12,000, and the balance of any profit or loss is to be distributed in the ratio of original capitals. Operations are unsuccessful and a balance sheet prepared on December 31, 1967, shows the following:

Gordon and Haller
Balance Sheet
December 31, 1967

Assets		Liabilities and Capital	
Cash	$ 13,350	Accounts payable	$ 17,500
Accounts receivable (net)	10,000	Gordon, capital	25,000
Merchandise	17,500	Haller, capital	15,000
Equipment (net)	8,500		
Advance to Haller	5,000		$ 57,500
		Less loss for 1967	3,150
Total assets	$ 54,350	Total liabilities and capital	$ 54,350

Interest at 6% is to be charged on the withdrawal of $5,000 made by Haller on July 1. No entries have been made for the interest charge or for the salary allowance to Gordon.

Liquidation takes place at the beginning of 1968. Gordon agrees to take over the merchandise at a value of $14,000 in partial settlement of his interest. Accounts receivable are sold at a 20% discount and equipment is sold for $6,800. Payment is made to creditors and the remaining cash is distributed to the partners.

Instructions: Prepare the entries to close the loss for the year and to record the dissolution of the partnership.

3-5. M, N, O, and P share profits in the ratio of 2:1:1:1 respectively. The partnership cannot meet its obligations to creditors, and dissolution is authorized on November 1, 1967. A balance sheet for the partnership on this date shows balances as follow:

M, N, O, and P
Balance Sheet
November 1, 1967

Assets		Liabilities and Capital	
Cash	$12,500	Liabilities	$30,000
Other assets	40,000	P, Loan	2,500
		M, Capital	5,000
		N, Capital	5,000
		O, Capital	5,000
		P, Capital	5,000
Total assets	$52,500	Total liabilities and capital	$52,500

The personal status of partners on this date is determined to be as follows:

	Cash and Cash Value of Personal Assets	Personal Liabilities
M	$30,000	$20,000
N	5,000	15,000
O	20,000	17,500
P	15,000	20,000

"Other assets" of the partnership are sold and $12,000 is realized.

Instructions: (1) Assuming dissolution under provisions of the Uniform Partnership Act and contributions by appropriate parties in meeting the claims of partnership creditors, give the entries that would appear on the partnership books in winding up the business.

(2) State the amounts that will be paid to the personal creditors of each of the partners.

3-6. The balance sheet for the firm of W, X, Y, and Z on June 15, 1967, just prior to liquidation is as follows:

W, X, Y, and Z
Balance Sheet
June 15, 1967

Assets			Liabilities and Capital	
Cash		$14,000	Accounts payable	$40,000
Merchandise inventory		27,500	W, loan	1,000
Accounts receivable		30,000	Z, loan	2,500
Store fixtures	$15,000		W, capital	13,500
Less allowance for			X, capital	7,500
depreciation	12,500	2,500	Y, capital	5,000
			Z, capital	4,500
Total assets		$74,000	Total liabilities and capital	$74,000

W, X, Y, and Z share profits in the ratio of 5:5:3:2 respectively. Noncash assets realize a total of $24,000. The personal status of partners exclusive of firm equities is determined by firm creditors to be as follows:

	Cash and Cash Value of Personal Assets	Personal Liabilities
W	$30,000	$16,500
X	15,000	18,500
Y	20,000	17,500
Z	5,000	8,500

Instructions: (1) Give the journal entries to record the sale of the assets, the distribution of the loss on the sale of the assets, and the payment of available cash to creditors.

(2) Assuming dissolution under provisions of the Uniform Partnership Act, give the journal entries to complete the liquidation if the creditors collect their unpaid balance from W and the partners then make proper settlement among themselves.

(3) Assuming dissolution under provisions of the Uniform Partnership Act, give the journal entries to complete the liquidation, assuming that the creditors collect their unpaid balance from Y instead of W and the partners then make proper settlement among themselves.

3-7. A and B, a trading partnership, decide to admit C as a partner on January 1, 1967. They agree with C as follows:

> C is not to contribute any tangible assets as his capital investment, but he is to allow his share of the profits to be credited to his capital account until he shall have a 1/5 interest. C is to share profits and losses to the extent of 1/5. C is to receive a salary of $3,000 per year, payable monthly, in addition to his share of the profits. A and B are to receive no salary; they are to share profits and losses equally.

The balance sheet of A and B at December 31, 1966, is as follows:

A and B
Balance Sheet
December 31, 1966

Assets		Liabilities and Capital		
Cash	$ 1,500	Accounts payable		$ 8,000
Accounts receivable	10,000	Capital accounts:		
Merchandise	7,500	A	$10,000	
Furniture and fixtures	1,500	B	5,000	15,000
Goodwill	2,500			
Total assets	$23,000	Total liabilities and capital		$23,000

During the six months ended June 30, 1967, the business has sustained unusual losses and it is decided to dissolve the partnership.

The balance sheet at June 30, 1967, is as follows:

A and B
Balance Sheet
June 30, 1967

Assets		Liabilities and Capital		
Cash	$ 500	Accounts payable		$12,500
Accounts receivable	12,500	Capital accounts:		
Merchandise	5,000	A	$10,000	
Furniture and fixtures	1,500	B	5,000	
Goodwill	2,500			
			$15,000	
		Less deficit (loss on trading for 6 mos.)	5,500	9,500
Total assets	$22,000	Total liabilities and capital		$22,000

Accounts receivable were sold for $9,000, the buyer assuming all responsibility for collection and loss, if any. Merchandise realized $6,500; furniture and fixtures, $500.

Examination of the books discloses that C has not drawn his salary for four months and that B has advanced to the partnership $2,500 by way of a temporary loan. These liabilities are included in the sum of $12,500 shown as accounts payable. C is ascertained to be insolvent.

Instructions: Prepare a statement to summarize the realization of assets, the adjustment of partners' capitals, and the distribution of available funds in termination of the business.

(AICPA adapted)

3-8. You are engaged to assist in terminating the affairs of A and B Discount Sales, a partnership under liquidation. Allen owns Toy Wholesalers and contributed $10,000 in inventory for a 50% interest in A and B Discount Sales on January 3, 1967. Ball owns Appliance Wholesalers and contributed $2,000 cash and $8,000 in inventory for a 50% interest on the same date. All profits and losses are to be shared equally.

A and B Discount Sales was an unsuccessful operation, so it was decided to dissolve the partnership after the Christmas shopping season.

In the course of your examination you determine the following facts:

(1) An incompetent part-time bookkeeper had discarded all cash register tapes and invoices for expenses and purchases. He was also the bookkeeper for Appliance Wholesalers.

(2) The partners state that the only existing payables are to themselves, as follows:

Toy Wholesalers	$ 9,740
Appliance Wholesalers	5,260
	$15,000

(3) You are able to prepare the following summary of cash transactions from bank statements and canceled checks:

Opening cash balance		$ 2,000
Receipts:		
Sales	$70,000	
Inventory liquidation	7,000	77,000
		$79,000
Disbursements:		
Purchases	$36,000	
Operating expenses	26,000	
Leasehold improvements (5-year lease)	6,000	
Liquidating expense	4,000	72,000
Balance, December 31, 1967		$ 7,000

(4) On December 31, 1967, $7,000 was paid to the partners, $3,500 to each, to apply on the $15,000 liability.

(5) The partners state that the dollar amounts of regular sales of toys and appliances were approximately equal and that the dollar amounts of liquidating sales of toys and appliances were also approximately equal. There was a uniform markup of 40% of cost on toys and 25% of cost on appliances. All sales were for cash. The ending inventory of shopworn merchandise was liquidated on December 31, 1967, for 50% of the retail sales price.

(6) The partners believe that some appliances may have been returned to Appliance Wholesalers, but the bookkeeper failed to record the returns on the books of either organization.

Instructions: (1) Compute the unrecorded amount of appliances returned to Appliance Wholesalers, if any.

(2) Prepare an income statement for A and B Discount Sales for the period January 3 to December 31, 1967.

(3) Prepare a statement of partners' capital accounts.

(AICPA adapted)

3-9. M owns a 75% interest in MN partnership and N owns a 25% interest. The partnership is to dissolve and the only assets to be distributed are 145 shares of Arthur Co. with a cost basis to the partnership of $14,500 and a market value of $35,000; 45 shares of Bay Corporation with a cost basis to the partnership of $4,500 and a market value of $15,000; and 210 shares of Cory Stores with a cost basis to the partnership of $21,000 and a market value of $30,000. *Under tax rules, the basis of the distributed assets in the hands of the distributee will be in proportion to the partnership's basis.*

Since M is a director in Arthur Co., M and N agree that M is to receive all 145 of those shares.

Instructions: Prepare a schedule showing the distribution of the stocks so that each partner will receive an equitable share from a market value and from an income tax point of view. Submit your supporting computations in good form.

(AICPA adapted)

3-10. X, Y, and Z are partners sharing profits in the ratio of 4:3:2 respectively. The partnership and two of the partners are currently unable to pay their creditors. The partnership balance sheet and the personal status of the partners are as follows:

X, Y, and Z Partnership
Balance Sheet
November 15, 1967

Cash	$ 500	Accounts and bills payable	$37,000
Other assets	60,500	X, capital	10,000
		Y, capital	6,000
		Z, capital	8,000
Total assets	$61,000	Total liabilities and capital	$61,000

Personal Status of Partners
(Excluding Partnership Interests)

Partner	Cash and Cash Value of Personal Assets	Liabilities
X	$31,000	$20,000
Y	9,450	11,900
Z	4,000	5,000

Instructions: (1) Prepare a work sheet showing distributions to partnership and personal creditors in the event of dissolution under provisions of the Uniform Partnership Act, assuming that "Other assets" are sold for $33,500.

(2) Prepare a computation showing the minimum amount that must be realized from the sale of partnership assets other than cash so that the personal creditors of Y will receive full settlement of their claims.

(AICPA adapted)

3-11. Adams, Bell, Clark, and Dean are partners in a firm that has been engaged in jobbing refrigerators and other household appliances.

The firm started operating on January 1, 1966. At that time Adams and Bell contributed $20,000 and $30,000 respectively as capital for the business. On July 1, 1966, Clark was admitted to the firm, paying in $25,000, and on January 1, 1967, Dean was admitted and paid in $12,000. No interest was to be allowed on the partners' investments. All partners devoted their entire effort to the business during the time they were partners and were to be compensated at the following annual rates: $8,000 each for Adams and Bell, $7,500 for Clark, and $6,000 for Dean. Because of the need for increased working capital, salary withdrawals were limited to $300 per month for each partner. The partnership agreement, as finally drawn up, provided for a split of the net profit and loss after salary allowances among the partners involved for each six months in the following ratios: Adams, 3; Bell, 3; Clark, 2; and Dean, 2.

Formal books of account were not maintained, but a running analysis of cash revealed the following facts:

	Six Months Ended			
	6–30–66	12–31–66	6–30–67	12–31–67
Collections on sales made in the six-month period ended:				
June 30, 1966	$36,600	$ 6,200	$ 4,100	$ 2,500
December 31, 1966	—	124,200	34,500	8,200
June 30, 1967	—	—	192,500	53,900
December 31, 1967	—	—	—	347,300
Payments on purchases	65,871	152,382	185,699	338,546
Rent and other fixed costs	5,698	6,550	10,891	12,141
Other expenses	2,620	14,120	22,620	23,341
Withdrawals	3,600	5,400	7,200	7,200

Unpaid customers' accounts considered collectible at December 31, 1967, by period of origin, were:

Sales Made During Six Months Ended	Amount
6–30–66	$ 1,600
12–31–66	3,100
6–30–67	8,600
12–31–67	26,700

A physical inventory on December 31, 1967, showed that the merchandise inventory on hand at cost, including that covered by unpaid invoices of $14,285, amounted to $83,084.

The partners have agreed:

(a) That "rents and other fixed costs" are to be divided equally over the four six-month periods.
(b) That the cost of merchandise sold during these periods may be assumed to have been 70%, 75%, 80%, and 80% respectively of sales.
(c) That any merchandise "loss" resulting from the application of the above amounts and percentages may be regarded as a proper addition to "other expenses."
(d) That "other expenses" are to be spread over the four periods in proportion to sales.

Instructions: (1) Prepare an operating statement for each six-month period of the firm's existence.

(2) Prepare a statement of changes in partners' capital accounts for each six-month period.

(3) Prepare a balance sheet as of December 31, 1967.

(AICPA adapted)

3-12. Lyle, Mason, and Nolan decided to practice law beginning January 1, 1965. They entered into an agreement under which they share profits and losses in the proportion of 50%, 25%, and 25% respectively and agreed to contribute $50,000 in cash in these same proportions to provide working capital. They decided to keep their books on a cash basis.

On January 1, 1966, Mason died and the remaining partners agreed to admit Smith, giving him a 20% share in the profits with a minimum guarantee of $10,000 per year whether operations are profitable or not. Lyle and Nolan had percentages of 45 and 35 respectively. This partnership was of one year's duration and at the end of this period Nolan decided to retire but permitted the use of his name in future partnerships subject to the payment to him of $5,000 per annum to be treated as an expense of the partnership.

As of January 1, 1967, a partnership was formed in which Nolan's name was utilized in accordance with his proposal and to which Drake was admitted. The partners' interests in this partnership were as follows: Lyle, 55%; Smith, 30%; Drake, 15%.

Receipts of fees were as follows:

	Earned by Partnership		
	No. 1	No. 2	No. 3
1965	$ 80,000		
1966	145,000	$40,000	
1967		50,000	$70,000

Since there were no substantial accruals at the end of the year, disbursements for expenses made during any one period were treated as expenses of the then current partnership. These disbursements were $70,000 in 1965, $80,000 in 1966, and $90,000 in 1967.

Each new partnership agreement provided for the newly created partnership to purchase from the old partnership the $50,000 capital originally paid in by Lyle, Mason, and Nolan. The agreements also provided that the partners should bear the cost of acquisition of this amount in the proportion in which they shared profits and losses. However, it was agreed that an incoming partner, or one acquiring an increased percentage, need not make his contribution in cash immediately but could have the same charged to his drawing account. All such partners availed themselves of this privilege. Partners selling all or a part of their interest in capital were credited through their drawing accounts and immediately withdrew the amount of such credit. In addition to drawings made under this agreement, the partners or their heirs made cash drawings as follows:

	Lyle	Mason	Nolan	Smith	Drake
1965........	$10,500	$27,750	$13,750		
1966........	40,000	4,750	5,000	$7,000	
1967........	10,000	5,000	15,000	2,500	$5,000

Instructions: Prepare statements showing the details of transactions in the partners' drawing accounts and capital accounts for each of the years involved. Prepare these accounts in such a form that the balance at the end of each year which was available for withdrawal by each partner is shown in that partner's drawing account. The capital accounts are to reflect only the $50,000 original investment.

(AICPA adapted)

Chapter 4

PARTNERSHIPS

INSTALLMENT LIQUIDATION; JOINT VENTURES

When partnership liquidation takes place over an extended period of time, it is frequently desirable to make cash distributions to partners as cash becomes available. In adopting an installment payment procedure, particular care must be taken to avoid an overpayment to any partner. This calls for special procedures to determine the partners who may properly participate in successive cash distributions. Just as in earlier examples of liquidation, cash can be made available to partners only after the claims of creditors have been fully satisfied or sufficient cash has been set aside for this purpose.

PROCEDURES FOR DETERMINING INSTALLMENT DISTRIBUTIONS

In the examples of liquidation that were given in the preceding chapter, the total loss or gain on asset realization was known and this balance was divided among the partners in the profit and loss ratio. In making distributions it was necessary to consider only the possibility of losses that might arise upon failure of deficient partners or potentially deficient partners to meet their indebtedness to the firm. Distributions were made to partners in a manner that left their accounts with balances sufficient to absorb these possible losses.

When distributions are made during the course of liquidation, the amount that will be realized on assets that remain to be sold is not known and consequently the amount of the loss that partners will have to absorb is not determinable. Under these circumstances, each distribution to partners should be made as though it were the last. Such an assumption calls for the recognition of: (1) the possibility of a total loss on all remaining assets, and (2) the possibility that deficient partners or potentially deficient partners may be unable to meet their indebtedness to the firm. The practical effect of such a procedure is to provide distributions that bring the partners' interests into the profit and loss ratio as rapidly as possible. Once the profit and loss ratio is achieved, further distributions can be made in the profit and loss ratio. The partners' interests will thus remain in the profit and loss ratio and be able to absorb properly any future loss.

Profit and loss ratio achieved with first installment. Assume that A and B are partners sharing profits 60:40 respectively. The balance sheet as of October 1, 1967, is as follows:

A and B
Balance Sheet
October 1, 1967

Assets		Liabilities and Capital	
Cash	$ 15,000	Liabilities	$ 20,000
Other assets	105,000	A, capital	75,000
		B, capital	25,000
Total assets	$120,000	Total liabilities and capital	$120,000

The partners decide to liquidate. During October, assets with a book value of $70,000 realize $55,000. The liabilities of $20,000 are paid. Account balances on the partnership books at the end of October are as follows:

	Cash	Other Assets	Liabilities	A Capital	B Capital
Balances before liquidation	15,000	105,000	20,000	75,000	25,000
Sale of assets and distribution of loss	55,000	(70,000)		(9,000)	(6,000)
	70,000	35,000	20,000	66,000	19,000
Payment to creditors	(20,000)		(20,000)		
Balances	50,000	35,000		66,000	19,000

At this point $50,000 is available for distribution and owners' interests total $85,000. Since the amount to become available to partners in the future is not known, the present distribution is made as though it were the last. A schedule is prepared in arriving at the distribution, as follows:

A and B
Schedule to Accompany Statement of Liquidation
Amounts to be Paid to Partners
October 31, 1967

	A	B
Capital balances before distribution of cash	66,000	19,000
Restricted interests — possible loss of $35,000 if nothing is realized on remaining assets, chargeable to partners 60:40	(21,000)	(14,000)
Free interests — amount to be paid to each partner	45,000	5,000

The distribution of cash in this way leaves A with a capital of $21,000 and B with a capital of $14,000. Capitals now are in the profit and loss ratio of 60:40. No matter what future losses may be, neither partner will have been overpaid and thus be required to return cash to the firm.

With the capital balances in the profit and loss ratio, future cash distributions may be made in the profit and loss ratio. Assume that in November assets with a book value of $25,000 are sold for $10,000 and in December remaining assets of $10,000 are sold for $12,500. A statement summarizing the complete process of liquidation follows:

A and B
Statement of Liquidation
October 1–December 31, 1967

	Cash	Other Assets	Liabilities	Capitals and Profit-Sharing Ratio: A, Cap. (60)	Capitals and Profit-Sharing Ratio: B, Cap. (40)
Balances before liquidation	15,000	105,000	20,000	75,000	25,000
October — sale of assets and distribution of loss	55,000	(70,000)		(9,000)	(6,000)
	70,000	35,000	20,000	66,000	19,000
Payment to creditors	(20,000)		(20,000)		
	50,000	35,000		66,000	19,000
October — installment to partners (see schedule)	(50,000)			(45,000)	(5,000)
		35,000		21,000	14,000
November — sale of assets and distribution of loss	10,000	(25,000)		(9,000)	(6,000)
	10,000	10,000		12,000	8,000
November — installment to partners in profit and loss ratio	(10,000)			(6,000)	(4,000)
		10,000		6,000	4,000
December — sale of assets and distribution of gain	12,500	(10,000)		1,500	1,000
	12,500			7,500	5,000
December — installment to partners in profit and loss ratio	(12,500)			(7,500)	(5,000)

Entries to record the course of liquidation are as follows:

Transaction	Entry		
October — sale of assets, book value $70,000, for $55,000, loss distributed 60:40.	Cash	55,000	
	A, Capital	9,000	
	B, Capital	6,000	
	Other Assets		70,000
Payment to creditors.	Liabilities	20,000	
	Cash		20,000
October — payment to partners, leaving capitals with balances that can absorb any future loss.	A, Capital	45,000	
	B, Capital	5,000	
	Cash		50,000
November — sale of assets, book value $25,000, for $10,000.	Cash	10,000	
	A, Capital	9,000	
	B, Capital	6,000	
	Other Assets		25,000
November — payment to partners in profit and loss ratio.	A, Capital	6,000	
	B, Capital	4,000	
	Cash		10,000
December — sale of assets, book value $10,000, for $12,500.	Cash	12,500	
	Other Assets		10,000
	A, Capital		1,500
	B, Capital		1,000
December — payment to partners in profit and loss ratio.	A, Capital	7,500	
	B, Capital	5,000	
	Cash		12,500

If, in the above example, settlement with the partners had been deferred until all of the assets were sold, the cash distribution would have been exactly the same as the total cash made available through the installment procedure. Sale of the partnership assets, book value $105,000, for $77,500 resulted in a loss of $27,500; A would be charged with 60% of this amount, or $16,500, and B would be charged with 40%, or $11,000. A and B, then, would be entitled to $58,500 and $14,000 respectively, exactly the same amounts they ultimately received through installment distributions.

It should further be observed that a cash distribution that is viewed as though it were the last should be no different when partners' interests are composed of loan and capital balances than when interests are limited to capital balances alone. If the interests of A and B were composed of loan and capital balances, these would be combined and the amounts to be withheld would be applied to the sum of these balances in arriving at the proper cash distribution. However, loan and capital balances should not be merged in the accounts in view of the distinction that is made between loan and capital balances by law and the fact that interest may accrue on loan balances. When it is determined that cash is to be made available to a certain partner, such cash is first applied to the reduction of the loan balance.

Profit and loss ratio achieved subsequent to first installment. In the example in the preceding section, partners' interests were brought into the profit and loss ratio with the first distribution. Thereafter distributions were made in the profit and loss ratio. In considering the possibility of a loss on all remaining assets, it may be found that the interests of certain partners are inadequate to meet such a contingency. The possibility that deficient partners may not meet their indebtedness to the firm must then be recognized. Under these circumstances, the first distribution will not succeed in bringing the partners' interests into the profit and loss ratio. Furthermore, the determination of subsequent distributions will require a consideration of the possible loss on remaining assets. Each distribution, however, should bring partners' interests closer to the profit and loss ratio; upon achieving the profit and loss ratio, further distributions may be made in that ratio.

The procedure that is employed is illustrated in the example that follows. Assume that X, Y, and Z are partners sharing profits in the ratio of 50:30:20. A balance sheet prepared just prior to liquidation follows:

X, Y, and Z
Balance Sheet
July 1, 1967

Assets		Liabilities and Capital	
Cash	$ 10,000	Liabilities	$ 52,500
Other assets	230,000	X, loan	12,500
		Y, loan	10,000
		X, capital	65,000
		Y, capital	50,000
		Z, capital	50,000
Total assets	$240,000	Total liabilities and capital	$240,000

Assets are sold, and the cash from asset realization is distributed at the end of each month. Asset realization takes place as follows:

July:	Assets, book value $ 70,000, are sold for $50,000.
August:	Assets, book value $ 30,000, are sold for $20,000.
September:	Assets, book value $ 25,000, are sold for $12,500.
October:	Assets, book value $105,000, are sold for $50,000.

The course of liquidation is summarized on the statement of liquidation and supporting schedules that follow.

X, Y, and Z
Statement of Liquidation
July 1–October 31, 1967

	Cash	Other Assets	Liab.	X Loan	Y Loan	Capitals and Profit-Sharing Ratio X, Cap. (50%)	Y, Cap. (30%)	Z, Cap. (20%)
Balances before liquidation	10,000	230,000	52,500	12,500	10,000	65,000	50,000	50,000
July — sale of assets and distribution of loss	50,000	(70,000)				(10,000)	(6,000)	(4,000)
	60,000	160,000	52,500	12,500	10,000	55,000	44,000	46,000
Payment to creditors	(52,500)		(52,500)					
	7,500	160,000		12,500	10,000	55,000	44,000	46,000
July — installment to partners (see Schedule A)	(7,500)							(7,500)
		160,000		12,500	10,000	55,000	44,000	38,500
August — sale of assets and distribution of loss	20,000	(30,000)				(5,000)	(3,000)	(2,000)
	20,000	130,000		12,500	10,000	50,000	41,000	36,500
August — installment to partners (see Schedule B)	(20,000)				(10,000)		(500)	(9,500)
		130,000		12,500		50,000	40,500	27,000
September — sale of assets and distribution of loss	12,500	(25,000)				(6,250)	(3,750)	(2,500)
	12,500	105,000		12,500		43,750	36,750	24,500
September — installment to partners (see Schedule C)	(12,500)			(3,750)			(5,250)	(3,500)
		105,000		8,750		43,750	31,500	21,000
October — sale of assets and distribution of loss	50,000	(105,000)				(27,500)	(16,500)	(11,000)
	50,000			8,750		16,250	15,000	10,000
October — installment to partners in profit and loss ratio	(50,000)			(8,750)		(16,250)	(15,000)	(10,000)

X, Y, and Z
Schedule A — To Accompany Statement of Liquidation
Amounts To Be Paid to Partners
July 31, 1967

	X (50)	Y (30)	Z (20)
Capital balances before distribution of cash	55,000	44,000	46,000
Add loan balances	12,500	10,000	
Partners' total interests	67,500	54,000	46,000
Restricted interests — possible loss of $160,000 if nothing is realized on remaining assets	(80,000)	(48,000)	(32,000)
	(12,500)	6,000	14,000
Restricted interests — additional possible loss of $12,500 to Y and Z if X is unable to meet his possible deficiency (ratio Y and Z — 30:20)	12,500	(7,500)	(5,000)
		(1,500)	9,000
Restricted interests — additional possible loss of $1,500 to Z if Y is unable to meet his possible deficiency		1,500	(1,500)
Free interest — amount to be paid Z on capital			7,500

X, Y, and Z
Schedule B — To Accompany Statement of Liquidation
Amounts To Be Paid to Partners
August 31, 1967

	X (50)	Y (30)	Z (20)
Capital balances before distribution of cash	50,000	41,000	36,500
Add loan balances	12,500	10,000	
Partners' total interests	62,500	51,000	36,500
Restricted interests — possible loss of $130,000 if nothing is realized on remaining assets	(65,000)	(39,000)	(26,000)
	(2,500)	12,000	10,500
Restricted interests — additional possible loss of $2,500 to Y and Z if X is unable to meet his possible deficiency (ratio Y and Z — 30:20)	2,500	(1,500)	(1,000)
Free interests — amount to be paid to each partner		10,500	9,500
Payment to apply on loan		10,000	
Payments to apply on capital		500	9,500
Total cash distribution		10,500	9,500

X, Y, and Z
Schedule C — To Accompany Statement of Liquidation
Amounts To Be Paid to Partners
September 30, 1967

	X (50)	Y (30)	Z (20)
Capital balances before distribution of cash	43,750	36,750	24,500
Add loan balance	12,500		
Partners' total interests	56,250	36,750	24,500
Restricted interests — possible loss of $105,000 if nothing is realized on remaining assets	(52,500)	(31,500)	(21,000)
Free interests — amount to be paid to each partner	3,750	5,250	3,500
Payment to apply on loan	3,750		
Payments to apply on capital		5,250	3,500

In arriving at the amounts to be paid to individual partners, effect was given to the possibilities of (1) a complete loss on remaining unsold assets and (2) failure to recover anything from partners who may become deficient under such circumstances. It should be noted that such losses are considered only for purposes of determining the appropriate distribution of cash; partners' capital accounts in the ledger would be affected only by the profits and losses that emerge on the actual disposal of partnership assets.

PROGRAM FOR DISTRIBUTION OF CASH

The procedure that has been described can be used in all cases involving liquidation by installments. Such a procedure requires calculations and the preparation of a schedule for each proposed distribution until partners' interests are brought into the profit and loss ratio. In some instances it may be considered desirable to prepare in advance a program for the distribution of whatever cash may become available during the course of liquidation. As cash is received from the sale of assets, it can then be distributed to partners in accordance with this program.

To indicate the nature of the alternative approach, assume that capital accounts for F and G just before partnership liquidation are as follows:

F, Capital	G, Capital
$30,000	$25,000

Assume further that F and G share profits and losses equally. Since F will not be required to absorb a greater amount of any losses on liquidation than G, it is obvious that the first cash to be made available to partners should be paid to F. F can be paid a total of $5,000 before his capital is reduced to G's balance. Once the capital accounts are in the profit and loss ratio, further cash distributions can be made in the profit and loss ratio — equally in this case.

Assume, however, that F and G share profits 75% and 25% respectively. In this case, G should receive first cash. Losses chargeable against G are only 25/75 or ⅓ of the amount chargeable against F. Under these circumstances there can be no objection to cash distributions to G that reduce his capital to ⅓ of the balance in F's capital account before F is allowed to share in cash distributions. G, then, should receive the first $15,000 of available cash. With capitals in the profit and loss ratio, further cash distributions are properly made to F and G in the profit and loss ratio, 75:25.

The fact that G's prior claim to cash amounted to $15,000 was readily determined in the preceding example. Frequently, however, capital balances and profit and loss ratios do not lend themselves to such ready analysis, and special calculations are necessary to determine a priority program. These calculations applied to the example just given are shown at the top of the following page.

Procedure	Explanation
Calculate loss-absorption abilities of partners:	Each partner's interest is divided by his profit and loss share to find the maximum loss that he can absorb. This calculation shows that a loss of $40,000 will consume all of F's capital, but it will take a loss of $100,000 to consume G's capital.

	Capital		Profit and Loss Ratio		Loss That Will Absorb Each Partner's Interest
F	$30,000	÷	.75	=	$ 40,000
G	$25,000	÷	.25	=	$100,000

Procedure	Explanation
Calculate priorities in terms of excess loss-absorption capacities:	G's loss-absorbing capacity is greater than that of F by $60,000. Payments may be made to G to the point where his loss-absorbing capacity is no greater than that of F. To find the loss-absorbing capacity of a partner's interest, the interest was divided by the partner's share of profit and loss; to find the amount of capital represented by an excess loss-absorbing capacity, such excess is multiplied by the partner's share of profit and loss. G's excess loss-absorbing capacity, $60,000, multiplied by his profit and loss share, .25, gives the interest represented by this excess.

Excess of G's Loss-Absorbing Capacity		G's Share in Profit and Loss		Prior Claim of G
$60,000	×	.25	=	$15,000

Procedure	Explanation
After priorities have been met, further distributions can be made in the profit and loss ratio.	After $15,000 is paid to G, partners' interests are in the profit and loss ratio. Further distributions can now be made in the profit and loss ratio.

Development of priority payment program illustrated. Development and application of a priority payment program when more than two partners are involved is illustrated in the section that follows. The example is based upon the data that were given for the firm of X, Y, and Z on page 101.

In developing a priority payment program for X, Y, and Z at the start of liquidation, the maximum loss that can be absorbed by each partner's interest is first calculated. Loan balances are combined with capital balances in arriving at partners' interests, and these interests are divided by the partners' respective profit and loss ratio expressed in percentages in developing loss-absorption balances. Cash is then applied in a manner that brings the partners' interests ever closer to the point where they can absorb the same partnership loss.

Dividing interests of $77,500, $60,000, and $50,000 by .50, .30, and .20 gives loss-absorption balances for X, Y, and Z of $155,000, $200,000, and $250,000 respectively. This indicates that Z should receive first cash. Z's interest may be reduced by payments to the point where his loss-absorption capacity is no greater than that for Y. At this point cash should be distributed to both Y and Z. The interests of Y and Z may be reduced by the joint payments to the point where the loss-absorption capacity for Y and for Z is no greater than that for X. At this point, the interests of X, Y, and Z will be brought into the profit and loss ratio, and further cash distributions are properly made in the profit and loss ratio.

Development of the payment program appears below.

X, Y, AND Z
Program of Priorities for Cash Distribution in Partnership Liquidation
July 1, 1967

				Payments		
	X	Y	Z	X	Y	Z
Capital balances	65,000	50,000	50,000			
Loan balances	12,500	10,000				
	77,500	60,000	50,000			
Profit and loss ratio	50%	30%	20%			
Loss-absorption balances (interests divided by partner's profit and loss percentage)	155,000	200,000	250,000			
Allocation I: Cash to Z to reduce his loss-absorption balance to amount reported by Y; reduction of $50,000 requires payment of .20 x $50,000			(50,000)			10,000
	155,000	200,000	200,000			
Allocation II: Cash to Y and Z to reduce their loss-absorption balances to amount reported for X; reductions of $45,000 require payments as follows: To Y, .30 x $45,000 or $13,500 To Z, .20 x $45,000, or $9,000		(45,000)	(45,000)		13,500	9,000
	155,000	155,000	155,000		13,500	19,000
Allocation III: Further cash distributions may be made in the profit and loss ratio.						

The information that is provided in the payment program above may be summarized as follows:

(1) The first $10,000 available to partners should be paid to Z.
(2) The next $22,500 should be paid to Y and Z in the ratio of 30:20.
(3) Amounts that exceed $32,500 should be paid to X, Y, and Z in the profit and loss ratio of 50:30:20.

Installment distributions based on payment program. To show the application of the payment program, it will be assumed that cash is available for distribution to partners X, Y, and Z at monthly intervals as indicated in the earlier example. Cash available for partners, then, is as follows:

July	$ 7,500
August	20,000
September	12,500
October	50,000

Installment distributions are calculated as follows:

July Installment — $7,500

		Payable to		
		X	Y	Z
Allocation I — payable to Z	$10,000			
Amount payable to Z in July	7,500			7,500
Allocation I balance	$ 2,500	—	—	7,500

August Installment — $20,000

		Payable to		
		X	Y	Z
Allocation I — balance payable to Z	$ 2,500			
Amount payable to Z in August	2,500			2,500
Allocation II — payable to Y and Z, 30:20	$22,500			
Amount payable to Y and Z in August	17,500		10,500	7,000
Allocation II — balance	$ 5,000	—	10,500	9,500

September Installment — $12,500

		Payable to		
		X	Y	Z
Allocation II — balance payable to Y and Z, 30:20	$ 5,000			
Amount payable to Y and Z in September	5,000		3,000	2,000
Allocation III — payable to X, Y, and Z, 50:30:20	$ 7,500	3,750	2,250	1,500
		3,750	5,250	3,500

October Installment — $50,000

	Payable to		
	X	Y	Z
Allocation III — payable to X, Y, and Z, 50:30:20	25,000	15,000	10,000

It should be observed that the cash distributions to X, Y, and Z developed from the payment program are exactly the same as the distributions on pages 102–103 that were calculated by considering the possible loss on unsold assets and making distributions in terms of partners' free capitals. Just as in the earlier example, cash that is paid to an individual partner would first be applied against any loan balance that he might have. Entries to record the course of liquidation of the firm of X, Y, and Z and a statement of liquidation summarizing activities for the four-month period, then, would be the same as in the earlier example.

There may be instances when it is difficult or actually impossible to determine the loss or gain related to the sale of individual assets during the course of liquidation. In such instances, the recognition of loss or gain may be postponed until all of the assets are sold; at that time the difference between the book value of assets and the total amount realized from their sale would be recognized as the loss or gain from liquidation and would be reported in the capital accounts. Whether losses or gains are recognized currently or upon termination of liquidation will have no effect upon cash distributions, for losses and gains are transferred to capital accounts in the profit and loss ratio and the objective of the cash distribution procedure is to bring partners' interests into the profit and loss ratio at the earliest possible time.

It may be observed that the preparation of a priority payment program and the determination of cash distributions in accordance with such a program may prove relatively complex when there are a great many partners and profits and losses are not shared in a simple manner. In these circumstances, it may prove more convenient to determine cash distributions by use of the first method, which involves the recognition of the possible loss on remaining assets at the time of each cash distribution.

JOINT VENTURES

A special commercial undertaking by two or more individuals or business units that is terminated upon the fulfillment of the established objective is known as a *joint venture*. Thus the term would be applied to a joint undertaking for a specific purpose such as the development or sale of a tract of land, the construction of a bridge or dam, the purchase and sale of a block of securities, or the exploration and drilling for oil or gas.

The association of parties in a joint venture constitutes a partnership, and partnership law governs throughout the course of the relationship. However, since the joint venture exists only for a specific purpose, the powers and the duties of the members are limited to such purpose. Each partner to the venture may contribute cash, merchandise, or services, and in turn shares in the profit or loss resulting from the undertaking. Since this is a partnership, absence of a specific agreement with respect to the sharing of profit and loss results in equal division. Participants may, by agreement, provide for the allowance of interest on investments, commissions or bonuses on sales, and salaries for services so that differences in contributions to the joint venture in the form of capital, ability, and time may be recognized in distributing profits. Generally, one member of the joint venture is designated as the managing partner and is allowed special compensation for acting in this capacity. As managing participant, he submits statements summarizing venture transactions to his copartners.

There are two methods of accounting for a joint venture: (1) separate books for the joint venture are maintained; (2) separate books are not maintained, accounts for the joint venture transactions simply being carried on the individual books of one or more of the participants. When a joint venture is to be carried on over a relatively long period and a number of involved transactions are anticipated, it is best to open a separate set of books. However, when the joint venture is to be of short duration and of a relatively simple character, there may be no need for separate books.

Accounting for the joint venture — separate books. When separate books for the joint venture are maintained, joint venture transactions are recorded on the separate books in exactly the same manner as for partnership relationships discussed earlier. When a partner maintains individual books summarizing his business as well as personal activities, the interest in a joint venture, just as any interest in a partnership, is recognized and accounted for as an investment: the investment account is charged for the original investment in the undertaking and for subsequent investments and shares of profits that increase his interest; the investment account is credited for withdrawals and shares of losses that decrease his interest. The debit balance in the investment account on the partner's individual books, then, will agree with the credit balance measuring his interest on the joint venture books.

Accounting for the joint venture — no separate books. When separate joint venture books are not kept, activities of the venture will have to be summarized on the partners' individual books. If each partner maintains an individual set of books and each set of books is to be complete, it will be necessary for each partner to notify copartners of all of the transactions that he has entered into on behalf of the joint venture. In reporting joint venture activities on the individual books, a joint venture account is charged for all joint venture costs and is credited for all joint venture revenues. Each partner also maintains accounts with each of his copartners to indicate the ownership interests of these parties in the venture. In following these practices, the balances in the joint venture account and in the accounts with copartners will be the same on the books of each member during the course of the venture.

Separate books:

Transactions	Partnership Books		
(1) A transferred land to the joint venture at agreed current value of \$100,000; the land cost A \$75,000.	Land A, Capital	100,000	 100,000
(2) B made settlement on contracts for grading, landscaping, water and sewer, and other land improvements, \$60,000.	Land B, Capital	60,000	 60,000
(3) C transferred cash to A for joint venture purposes, \$40,000.	Cash C, Capital	40,000	 40,000
(4) A paid advertising, commissions, and other selling expenses, \$37,500.	Selling Expenses Cash	37,500	 37,500
(5) The lots were sold for a total of \$250,000; \$50,000 was received in cash and the balance in installment notes.	Cash Notes Receivable Land Gross Profit on Sale of Land	50,000 200,000	 160,000 90,000
(6) The installment notes were sold without recourse at a 10% discount.	Cash Discount on Sale of Notes Notes Receivable	180,000 20,000	 200,000
(7) Net income of the joint venture was summarized and closed into the partners' accounts: Net income . . . \$32,500 Special compensation to A . . . \$ 5,000 Balance, \$27,500 divided 100:60:40 to A, B, and C: A . . . 13,750 B . . . 8,250 C . . . 5,500 \$32,500	Gross Profit on Sale of Land Selling Expenses Discount on Sale of Notes A, Capital B, Capital C, Capital	90,000	 37,500 20,000 18,750 8,250 5,500
(8) A distributed cash in final settlement of the joint venture.	A, Capital B, Capital C, Capital Cash	118,750 68,250 45,500	 232,500

ACCOUNTING FOR THE JOINT VENTURE ILLUSTRATED

The alternative accounting procedures that may be employed for a joint venture are illustrated in the example that follows. Assume that A, B, and C enter into a joint venture for the purchase, development, and sale of a parcel of land. A is designated the managing partner; upon

Separate Books of A	Separate Books of B	Separate Books of C
vestment in rm of ABC... 100,000 Land....... 75,000 Gain on Transfer of Land to Joint Venture (or Capital)..... 25,000		
	Investment in Firm of ABC.. 60,000 Cash...... 60,000	
		Investment in Firm of ABC... 40,000 Cash....... 40,000
vestment in m of ABC... 18,750 Income from Firm of ABC. 18,750	Investment in Firm of ABC.. 8,250 Income from Firm of ABC 8,250	Investment in Firm of ABC... 5,500 Income from Firm of ABC. 5,500
sh......... 118,750 nvestment in irm of ABC. 118,750	Cash....... 68,250 Investment in Firm of ABC 68,250	Cash......... 45,500 Investment in Firm of ABC. 45,500

termination of the joint venture, special compensation of $5,000 is to be allowed to A and the balance of the profit is to be divided in the ratio of the partners' investments. Transactions and the entries that are required under the alternative procedures are given on pages 110–113.

It should be observed in the example on pages 112–113 that when separate joint venture books are not maintained, a joint venture account on the partner's individual books is charged with all joint venture costs and expenses and is credited with all joint venture revenues. A debit

No separate books:

Transactions	Books of A (Managing Participant)		
(1) A transferred land to the joint venture at agreed current value of $100,000; the land cost A $75,000.	Joint Venture..........	100,000	
	Land...............		75,000
	Gain on Transfer of Land to Joint Venture (or Capital).........		25,000
(2) B made settlement on contracts for grading, landscaping, water and sewer, and other land improvements, $60,000.	Joint Venture..........	60,000	
	B..................		60,000
(3) C transferred cash to A for joint venture purposes, $40,000.	Joint Venture Cash......	40,000	
	C..................		40,000
(4) A paid advertising, commissions, and other selling expenses, $37,500.	Joint Venture..........	37,500	
	Joint Venture Cash....		37,500
(5) The lots were sold for a total of $250,000; $50,000 was received in cash and the balance in installment notes.	Joint Venture Cash......	50,000	
	Joint Venture Notes Receivable...............	200,000	
	Joint Venture........		250,000
(6) The installment notes were sold without recourse at a 10% discount.	Joint Venture Cash......	180,000	
	Joint Venture..........	20,000	
	Joint Venture Notes Receivable.............		200,000
(7) Net income of the joint venture was summarized and closed into the partners' accounts:	Joint Venture..........	32,500	
Net income.................... $32,500	Income from Joint Venture (or Capital)......		18,750
Special compensation to A........ $ 5,000	B..................		8,250
Balance, $27,500 divided 100:60:40 to A, B, and C:	C..................		5,500
A.............. 13,750			
B.............. 8,250			
C.............. 5,500			
$32,500			
(8) A distributed cash in final settlement of the joint venture.	Cash..................	118,750	
	B.....................	68,250	
	C.....................	45,500	
	Joint Venture Cash....		232,500

balance in the joint venture account during the course of the venture would be recognized as the net amount invested in the joint venture. A credit balance in the investment account upon conclusion of the venture indicates that revenues of the venture have exceeded costs and expenses and there has been a profit; the investment account is closed by a debit and the partners' accounts are credited. A debit balance in the investment account upon conclusion of the venture indicates that costs and expenses have exceeded revenues and there has been a loss; the

Books of B			Books of C		
Joint Venture	100,000		Joint Venture	100,000	
A		100,000	A		100,000
Joint Venture	60,000		Joint Venture	60,000	
Cash		60,000	B		60,000
A	40,000		A	40,000	
C		40,000	Cash		40,000
Joint Venture	37,500		Joint Venture	37,500	
A		37,500	A		37,500
A	250,000		A	250,000	
Joint Venture		250,000	Joint Venture		250,000
Joint Venture	20,000		Joint Venture	20,000	
A		20,000	A		20,000
Joint Venture	32,500		Joint Venture	32,500	
Income from Joint Venture		8,250	Income from Joint Venture		5,500
A		18,750	A		18,750
C		5,500	B		8,250
Cash	68,250		Cash	45,500	
C	45,500		B	68,250	
A		113,750	A		113,750

investment account is closed by a credit and the partners' accounts are debited. Accounts with copartners report the interests of these parties in the net assets of the joint venture: a credit balance indicates an accountability by the joint venture to the copartner; a debit balance indicates an accountability by the partner to the joint venture.

In reporting joint venture operations on the individual books of the partners, assets and liabilities other than the joint venture investment balance — for example, joint venture cash, joint venture receivables, and joint venture payables — are generally recognized only on the books of the managing participant; balances on the books of the remaining participants are limited to the investment in the joint venture and balances with coparticipants. It would be possible to report all of the joint venture asset and liability balances on the books of each partner, but this would call for extended bookkeeping by all of the parties during the course of the relationship.

If a joint venture runs beyond the end of the regular fiscal period of the individual members, the question of whether any profit is to be recognized upon the uncompleted venture arises. If the venture is highly speculative and a successful outcome is in any way uncertain, conservatism would suggest that no profit be recognized until its completion. In some instances it may be possible to measure the success of the joint venture at a given stage with the certainty that its completion will not result in an impairment of accumulated profits. When this is the case, recognition of profit before completion of the venture is justified. When joint venture activities are recorded on the individual books of the partners, recognition of profit before completion of a venture is recorded by a debit to the joint venture account for the profit accrual and credits to the partners' accounts. Recognition of loss before completion of a venture would require debits to the partners' accounts and a credit to the joint venture account.

When separate books are not kept, a partner calculates his interest in a joint venture from the account balances related to the venture that appear on his individual books. Accounts with debit balances represent joint venture assets, costs yet to be recovered or realized, or claims of the joint venture against copartners; accounts with credit balances represent outsiders' claims or copartners' interests in venture assets. The difference between the debit and the credit balances on each partner's books measures his own interest in the joint venture. For example, interests of partners A, B, and C in the illustration on pages 112 and 113 are calculated after transaction (3) as follows:

A's Interest		
Joint Venture Cash		$ 40,000
Joint Venture......		160,000
		$200,000
Less Credits:		
B......	$60,000	
C......	40,000	100,000
A's Interest........		$100,000

B's Interest		
Joint Venture......		$160,000
Less Credits:		
A......	$60,000	
C......	40,000	100,000
B's Interest.......		$ 60,000

C's Interest		
Joint Venture......		$160,000
Less Credits:		
A......	$60,000	
B......	60,000	120,000
C's Interest......		$ 40,000

It may be observed that maintenance of records by a managing participant alone is sufficient to account for joint venture activities and to give the required data for settlement at the conclusion of the venture. However, when joint venture accounts are maintained by all of the parties, there is a check upon the accuracy of the records of the managing participant and his settlement with coparticipants upon termination of the venture.

QUESTIONS

1. If cash is to be paid to partners as soon as it is available during the course of liquidation, what rules can be stated for making such distributions?

2. What is meant by a partner's "restricted interest"? How are restricted interests shown in the ledger?

3. A, B, and C decide to liquidate. Partner A, who has a substantial loan balance in the partnership, insists that this loan balance be paid off with the first proceeds from liquidation. (a) Under what circumstances would you agree to such an action? (b) Under what circumstances would you oppose such an action?

4. D and E share profits equally. During the course of liquidation, the liquidator determines that available cash should be paid to Partner D on his capital account since the balance in his capital account exceeds the total of Partner E's loan and capital balances combined. Partner E objects to such a distribution, stating that the Uniform Partnership Act provides that available cash must first be applied to partners' loans and that he will insist on such a procedure. Under these circumstances, what action should the liquidator take?

5. In developing schedules for the distribution of available cash, it is found that certain partners' capital balances are insufficient to meet the possibility of a full loss on all remaining assets. The liquidator suggests that such "deficient" partners make contributions to the partnership so that they will be able to meet any possible future contingency. Do you support such a position?

6. (a) Describe the purpose and the advantages of a priority program for the distribution of available cash during the course of liquidation. (b) Give the steps involved in the preparation of such a program.

7. Accounts for the partnership of A, B, C, and D in dissolution show D with an accrued salary balance of $1,500. D maintains that this is a preferred claim that should be paid off with first available cash. Do you agree?

8. Define a joint venture.

9. Describe two methods of accounting for a joint venture. What factors determine the method to be adopted?

10. Parker and Peters join in a venture. Parker invests $10,000 and Peters $2,000; profits are to be shared equally. The venture is unsuccessful and, upon its conclusion, cash of only $2,500 remains to be distributed to members. State how settlement should be completed.

11. Barker, Conway, and Drake join in a venture consisting of the purchase of merchandise and its shipment to Japan. Drake is to act as manager and is to receive a salary for his services. Interest is to be allowed on partners' investments. Any remaining profit is to be distributed equally. Assuming that a separate set of books is kept for the venture, give the entries to be made on the venture books as well as on the books of each member in recording the transactions listed below:

(a) Barker and Conway invest merchandise in the venture.
(b) Drake invests cash in the venture.
(c) Drake borrows cash on behalf of the venture by having a note discounted.
(d) Drake purchases merchandise for the venture for cash.
(e) Drake purchases merchandise for the venture on account.
(f) Drake withdraws some of the merchandise for his own use.
(g) Drake pays expenses for the shipment of the merchandise.
(h) Drake receives cash proceeds from venture sales.
(i) Drake pays the venture note.
(j) Drake pays the venture accounts payable.
(k) The salary allowance to Drake is recorded.
(l) Interest allowances to Barker, Conway, and Drake are recorded.
(m) The distribution of the net profit from the venture is recorded.
(n) Drake pays Barker and Conway in final settlement.

12. Assuming that a separate set of books is not kept for the joint venture described in Question 11, give the entries to be made on the separate books of Barker, Conway, and Drake to record each of the transactions.

EXERCISES

1. Partners A and B share profits 40% and 60% respectively. The receiver in charge of liquidation of the partnership wishes to distribute available cash to the partners. How should the cash be distributed, assuming the following balances:

Cash	$ 5,000	Salary due to A	$ 500
Other assets	32,500	A, capital	12,800
		Loan due to B	5,000
		B, capital	19,200
Total	$37,500	Total	$37,500

2. Partners A, B, C, and D, who share profits 5:3:1:1 respectively, decide to dissolve. Capital balances at this time are $60,000, $40,000, $30,000, and $10,000, respectively. Before selling the firm's assets, the partners agree to the following:

(1) Partnership furniture and fixtures, with a book value of $12,000, is to be taken over by partner A at a price of $15,000.

(2) Partnership claims of $20,000 are to be paid off and the balance of cash on hand, $30,000, is to be divided in a manner that will avoid the need for any possible recovery of cash from a partner.

What entries would be made to record the foregoing?

3. A balance sheet for the partnership of J, K, and L, who share profits 2:1:1 respectively, shows the following balances just before liquidation:

Cash	Other Assets	Liabilities	J, Cap.	K, Cap.	L, Cap.
$12,000	$59,500	$20,000	$22,000	$15,500	$14,000

In the first month of liquidation, $32,000 was received on the sale of certain assets. Liquidation expenses of $1,000 were paid, and additional liquidation expenses of $800 are anticipated before liquidation is completed. Creditors were paid $5,600. Distribution was made to the partners of such cash as was available for the purpose. Give the entries that are called for as a result of the foregoing.

4. Partners D, E, F, and G share profits 50%, 30%, 10%, and 10% respectively. Accounts maintained with partners just prior to liquidation follow:

	Advances (Dr. Balances)	Loans (Cr. Balances)	Capitals (Cr. Balances)
D		$ 5,000	$40,000
E		10,000	30,000
F	$4,500		15,000
G	2,500		25,000

At this point, cash of $18,000 is available for distribution to the partners. Give the entry to record the distribution of cash, together with calculations in support of the distribution.

5. The balance sheet of the partnership of Q, R, S, and T just prior to liquidation shows:

Assets	Liab.	Q, Loan	Q, Cap.	R, Cap.	S, Cap.	T, Cap.
$90,000	$20,000	$5,000	$20,000	$20,000	$20,000	$5,000

Q, R, S, and T share profits in the ratio of 2:1:1:1 respectively. Certain assets were sold for $45,000. Creditors were paid the full amount owed, partners were paid $20,000, and cash of $5,000 was withheld pending future developments. Give the journal entries to record the foregoing, including the distribution of cash to the partners.

6. Capital and loan balances for partners W, X, Y, and Z, who share profits in the ratio of 4:3:2:1 respectively, are as follows just prior to receivership:

Z, Loan	W, Cap.	X, Cap.	Y, Cap.	Z, Cap.
$5,000	$50,000	$55,000	$20,000	$10,000

Prepare a statement for the receiver showing how available cash would be distributed to the partners during the course of liquidation after the creditors are paid in full. State which partner would receive the first cash available and at what point and to what degree each of the remaining partners would participate in cash distributions.

7. Capital and loan balances for partners J, K, and L, who share profits 40%, 40%, and 20% respectively, are as follows just before receivership:

J, Loan	J, Capital	K, Loan	K, Capital	L, Loan	L, Capital
$10,000	$15,000	$10,000	$35,000	$15,000	$20,000

(a) Prepare a program for the receiver to show how available cash would be distributed to the partners during the course of liquidation after creditors are paid in full. State which partner would receive the first cash available and at what point and to what degree each of the remaining partners would participate in cash distributions.

(b) Assuming that cash of $25,000 is available as a first distribution to partners, what entry would be made to record the distribution?

8. Partners A, B, and C have capital balances of $11,200, $13,000, and $5,800 respectively and share profits in the ratio 4:2:1.

(a) Prepare a schedule showing how available cash will be distributed to partners as it becomes available.

(b) How much must the partnership realize on the sale of its assets if A is to receive $10,000 in final settlement of his interest in the firm?

(c) If A receives a total of $3,200 in cash, how much will C have received at this point?

(d) If A is personally insolvent and B receives a total of $1,800 on his interest in final liquidation of the firm, what was the partnership loss on liquidation?

9. Barnes and Carter join in a venture for the sale of football souvenirs at the Rose Bowl game. Partners agree to the following: (1) Barnes shall be allowed a commission of 10% on net purchases made by him, (2) each member shall be allowed a commission of 25% on his own sales, (3) any remaining profit shall be shared equally. Venture transactions follow:

Dec. 30. Barnes makes cash purchases, $95.
Jan. 1. Carter pays venture expenses, $15.
Jan. 1. Sales are as follows: Barnes, $80; Carter, $60 (each member keeps his own cash receipts).
Jan. 6. Barnes returns unsold merchandise and receives cash of $25 on the return.
Jan. 6. The partners make cash settlement.

Separate books for the venture are not kept. What entries would be made on the books of Barnes and Carter?

10. Joint venture activities for M, N, and O having proved to be unprofitable, the parties agree to dissolve the venture. Accounts with the venture and coparticipants on the books of M, the managing partner, are as follows just before dissolution and liquidation:

	Dr.	Cr.
Joint Venture Cash	$12,000	
Joint Venture	6,500	
N, Capital		$14,500
O, Capital		6,500

The balance of joint venture assets on hand is sold by M for $3,500. M is allowed special compensation of $300 for winding up the venture; remaining profit or loss is distributed equally.

(a) Give the entries that will appear on the books of M when he winds up the venture and makes settlement with coparticipants.

(b) Give the entries that would appear on the separate books of N and O upon venture liquidation and settlement.

PROBLEMS

4-1. The balance sheet for Ross, Scott, and Tucker, partners sharing profits in the ratio of 4:3:3 respectively, shows the following balances on April 30, 1967, just before liquidation:

Assets		Liabilities and Capital	
Cash	$ 31,500	Liabilities	$ 43,500
Other assets	125,000	Tucker, loan	3,000
		Ross, capital	60,000
		Scott, capital	35,000
		Tucker, capital	15,000
Total assets	$156,500	Total liabilities and capital	$156,500

In May, part of the assets are sold for $30,000. In June, the remaining assets are sold for $21,000.

Instructions: Prepare a statement of liquidation with supporting schedules as illustrated on pages 102–103. Assume that available cash is distributed to the proper parties at the end of May and at the end of June. Assume further that partners are solvent and that any partner who is deficient makes appropriate payment to the partnership in July and this is distributed in final settlement.

4-2. Fall, Gibson, and Hoffman are partners sharing profits in the ratio of 3:1:1 respectively. On June 30 their capital accounts show balances of $82,500, $40,000, and $15,000 respectively. The partners sell the firm's assets, pay off creditors, and make cash distributions to partners at the end of each month from asset proceeds as follows:

July, $10,000; August, $16,500; September, $25,000.

Instructions: Prepare a statement of liquidation with supporting schedules as illustrated on pages 102–103. Assume that partners are personally solvent and that any partner who is deficient makes appropriate payment to the partnership in October and this is distributed in final settlement.

4-3. Partners A, B, and C share profits in the ratio of 5:3:2 respectively. On June 30, 1967, just before liquidation, assets, liabilities, and capital balances are as follows:

		Capitals		
Assets	Liabilities	A	B	C
$150,000	$30,000	$52,000	$48,000	$20,000

Cash is realized for assets as shown at the top of the following page, and amounts realized are distributed at the end of each month to the appropriate parties.

	Asset Book Value	Cash Proceeds
July	$30,000	$36,500
August	17,500	11,500
September	22,500	10,000
October	80,000	36,500

Instructions: Prepare a statement of liquidation to summarize the course of liquidation. Provide schedules or calculations in support of monthly distributions.

4-4. The balance sheet of the partnership of D, E, and F on January 1, 1967, just prior to liquidation, shows the following balances:

Assets		Liabilities and Capital	
Cash	$ 15,000	Liabilities	$ 80,000
Other assets	265,000	D, loan	10,000
		F, loan	5,000
		D, capital	75,000
		E, capital	60,000
		F, capital	50,000
Total assets	$280,000	Total liabilities and capital	$280,000

D, E, and F share profits in the ratio of 5:3:2 respectively. Noncash assets are sold and all available cash is distributed to the proper parties at the end of each month. Liquidation takes place as follows:

	Book Value of Assets Sold	Cash Realized on Sale of Assets
January	$ 90,000	$ 55,000
February	60,000	22,500
March	65,000	15,000
April	50,000	20,000
	$265,000	$112,500

Instructions: (1) Prepare a statement of liquidation with supporting schedules as illustrated on pages 102–103.

(2) Prepare the necessary monthly journal entries to record the course of realization and liquidation.

4-5. K, L, M, and N are partners sharing profits 2:1:1:1 respectively. On December 31, 1966, they agree to dissolve. A balance sheet prepared on this date follows:

Assets		Liabilities and Capital	
Assets	$151,500	Liabilities	$ 70,000
		K, loan	5,000
		N, loan	2,500
		K, capital	22,000
		L, capital	21,500
		M, capital	17,000
		N, capital	13,500
Total assets	$151,500	Total liabilities and capital	$151,500

The results of liquidation are summarized below.

1967	Book Value of Assets Sold	Cash Realized on Sale of Assets	Costs of Liquidation Paid	Payments to Creditors	Payments to Partners	Cash Balance Withheld (Undistributed)
Jan.	$75,000	$60,000	$1,000	$55,000		$4,000
Feb.	30,000	18,000	1,100	15,000	$4,400	1,500
Mar.	30,000	10,000	1,200		9,300	1,000
Apr.	16,500	4,000	1,600		3,400	

Instructions: (1) Prepare a statement of liquidation with supporting schedules as illustrated on pages 102–103.

(2) Prepare the necessary monthly journal entries to record the course of realization and liquidation.

4-6. Partners F, G, and H divide profits 60%, 25%, and 15% respectively. A balance sheet on June 30, 1967, just before partnership liquidation, shows the following balances:

Assets		Liabilities and Capital	
Cash	$ 5,000	Liabilities	$35,000
Other assets	92,500	F, capital	45,000
		G, capital	10,000
		H, capital	7,500
Total assets	$97,500	Total liabilities and capital	$97,500

Certain assets are sold in July for $50,000 and available cash is distributed to appropriate parties. Remaining assets are sold in August for $15,000, and cash is distributed in final settlement.

Instructions: (1) Prepare a program showing how cash should be distributed to partners as it becomes available.

(2) Give the entries that are required to record the course of liquidation in July and August.

4-7. R, S, and T share profits in the ratio of 5:3:2 respectively. A balance sheet prepared just prior to partnership liquidation shows:

	R	S	T
Capital balances	$60,000	$45,000	$20,000
Loan balances	22,500	15,000	6,500

Assets are sold and cash is distributed to partners in monthly installments during the course of liquidation as follows:

January	$ 7,500
February	20,000
March	45,000
April (final distribution)	15,000

Instructions: (1) Prepare a program to show how cash should be distributed by the receiver during the entire course of liquidation.

(2) Using the program developed above, prepare schedules summarizing the payments to be made to partners at the end of each month.

(3) Prepare a statement of liquidation to summarize the course of liquidation.

4-8. Partners W, X, Y, and Z share profits in the ratio of 3:3:1:1 respectively. A balance sheet prepared just before partnership liquidation shows:

	W	X	Y	Z
Capital balances	$70,000	$70,000	$30,000	$20,000
Loan balances	20,000	5,000	25,000	15,000

Proceeds from the sale of partnership assets during January and February by the receiver in charge of liquidation and distributions of cash to partners at the end of each month are as follows:

	Cash Proceeds from Sale of Assets	Cash Distributed to Partners	Cash Retained by Receiver (Undistributed)
January	$40,000	$25,000	$15,000
February	35,000	40,000	10,000

Instructions: (1) Prepare a program to show how cash should be distributed by the receiver during the entire course of liquidation.

(2) Using the program above, prepare schedules summarizing the payments to be made to partners at the end of January and February; indicate what part of the payments are to be applied against loan balances and what part against capital balances.

4-9. Carter and Drew join in a venture for the sale of certain novelties during a convention. Carter acts as managing partner. Partners agree to the following: Carter shall be allowed a commission of 5% on gross purchases that he makes; members shall be allowed a commission of 30% on their respective sales; any remaining profit is to be shared equally.

Venture transactions follow:

June 12. Drew gives Carter $350 to be used for venture purposes. Carter purchases merchandise for $1,000, paying $400, the balance payable within 10 days.
14. Carter pays expenses chargeable to the venture, $150.
15-18. Sales by Carter and Drew are as follows (cash proceeds are kept by parties making the sales): Carter, $970; Drew, $790.
18. Carter pays additional venture expenses, $120.
20. Unsold merchandise is returned by Carter, credit of $140 being allowed on the return. The balance owed is paid. Settlement between partners is completed.

Instructions: Separate books for the venture are not kept. Give the journal entries to record the foregoing transactions on the books of each member.

4-10. Lane, Morris, and Newman form a joint venture for the sale of certain merchandise. Lane and Morris are to contribute the merchandise. Newman is to act as the sales agent and is to be allowed 5% of gross sales. Lane and Morris are to be allowed 6% a year on their original investment. The balance of any profit on the venture is to be divided equally among the three parties.

On March 1, Lane and Morris contributed merchandise of $22,000 and $30,000 respectively. Between March 1 and June 1, Newman sold venture merchandise on account for $80,000, of which he collected $76,500, allowed sales discounts of $1,350, and wrote off $2,150 as bad debts. Newman paid joint venture expenses of $19,520 out of joint venture cash. On June 1 the venture was terminated and unsold merchandise on hand was returned to Lane and Morris at the following values: Lane, $5,000; Morris, $3,800. Cash settlement was completed by Newman on this date.

Instructions: (1) Assuming that a set of separate books for the venture is not kept, give the journal entries to record the foregoing on the books of each participant.

(2) Assuming that a separate set of books for the venture is kept, give the journal entries to record the foregoing on (a) the joint venture books and (b) the individual books of each participant.

4-11. Moore, Norris, and Olson own adjoining properties of 15, 10, and 6 acres respectively. It is agreed to pool these properties and to develop, subdivide, and sell the land as a joint venture. It is further agreed that a valuation of $3,500 shall be allowed for each acre contributed to the venture. Profits are to be divided as follows:

(1) A bonus of 10% of selling price is to be allowed to partners making lot sales.

(2) Upon conclusion of the venture, a salary of $6,000 is to be allowed Olson, who is to act as managing partner; Olson is to take care of all of the venture receipts and expenditures.

(3) The net profit after allowance of bonus and salaries is to be divided equally.

Olson pays $50,000 for improvements that are completed in April. The property is subdivided into 155 lots that are offered for sale as follows:

	Number	Sales Price per Lot
Lots, Class I	40	$1,900
Lots, Class II	115	1,500

All of the lots are sold for cash in May and June. Sales by members of the venture are as follows:

	Number of Lots Sold	
	Class I	Class II
Sales by Moore	10	30
Sales by Norris	15	40
Sales by Olson	5	10

Remaining lots are sold by salesmen. Advertising, salesmen's salaries and commissions, and miscellaneous selling expenses paid in June are $34,200. The profit from the venture is calculated and Olson distributes cash to members in final settlement.

Instructions: (1) Assuming that a separate set of books for the venture is not kept, prepare the journal entries to record the foregoing on the books of each partner.

(2) Assuming that a separate set of books for the venture is kept, prepare the journal entries to record the foregoing on (a) the venture books and (b) the books of each member.

4-12. The A B C Partnership is being dissolved. All liabilities have been liquidated. The balance of assets on hand is being realized gradually. The following are details of partners' accounts:

	Capital Account (Original Investment)	Current Account (Undistributed Earnings Net of Drawings)	Loans to Partnership	Profit and Loss Ratio
A	$20,000	$1,500 Cr.	$15,000	4
B	25,000	2,000 Dr.	—	4
C	10,000	1,000 Cr.	5,000	2

Instructions: Prepare a schedule showing how cash payments should be made to the partners as assets are realized.

(AICPA adapted)

4-13. Partners Adams, Burke, Cox, and Drake have decided to dissolve their partnership. They plan to sell the assets gradually in order to minimize losses. They share profits and losses as follows: Adams, 40%; Burke, 35%; Cox, 15%; and Drake, 10%. The partnership's trial balance as of October 1, 1967, the date on which liquidation begins, is as follows:

	Debit	Credit
Cash	$ 200	
Receivables	25,900	
Inventory, October 1, 1967	42,600	
Equipment (net)	19,800	
Accounts payable		$ 3,000
Adams, loan		6,000
Burke, loan		10,000
Adams, capital		20,000
Burke, capital		21,500
Cox, capital		18,000
Drake, capital		10,000
	$88,500	$88,500

Instructions: (1) Prepare a statement as of October 1, 1967, showing how cash will be distributed among partners by installments as it becomes available.

(2) On October 31, 1967, cash of $12,700 became available to creditors and partners. How should it be distributed?

(3) Assume that, instead of being dissolved, the partnership continued operations and earned a profit of $23,625. How should that profit be distributed if, in addition to the aforementioned profit-sharing arrangement, it was provided that Drake receive a bonus of 5% of the net income from operations after treating such bonus as an expense?

(AICPA adapted)

4-14. The partners of Stanford Company agreed to dissolve their partnership and to begin liquidation on February 1, 1967. Rogers was designated as the partner in charge of liquidation. It was agreed that distributions of cash to the partners were to be made on the last day of each month during liquidation, provided sufficient cash was available.

The partnership agreement provided that profits and losses were to be shared on the following basis: Quade, 20%; Rogers, 30%; Stanford, 30%; and True, 20%. The firm's condensed balance sheet as of February 1, 1967, was as follows:

Assets		Liabilities and Capital	
Cash	$33,440	Accounts payable	$ 7,120
Goodwill	20,000	Loan from Quade	5,000
Other assets	44,510	Capital:	
		Quade	8,040
		Rogers	32,160
		Stanford	36,340
		True	9,290
Total assets	$97,950	Total liabilities and capital	$97,950

The liquidating transactions for February and March, other than cash distributions to partners, are summarized by months as follows:

	Cash	
	February	March
Liquidation of assets with a book value of:		
$22,020	$16,440	
$14,950		$16,110
Paid liquidation expenses as incurred	2,740	2,460
Paid to creditors on account	5,910	1,210

Instructions: Prepare a statement showing the total amounts of cash distributed to the partners at the end of February and March and the amounts received by each partner in each distribution. Assume that Rogers made the distributions in such a manner that eventual overpayment to any partner was precluded.
(AICPA adapted)

4-15. (1) The partnership of Arthur, Brown, and Cook has called upon you to assist them in winding up the affairs of their partnership. You are able to gather the following information:

The trial balance of the partnership at June 30, 1967, is as follows:

	Debit	Credit
Cash	$ 6,000	
Accounts Receivable	22,000	
Inventory	14,000	
Plant and Equipment (net)	99,000	
Arthur, Loan	12,000	
Cook, Loan	7,500	
Accounts Payable		$ 17,000
Arthur, Capital		67,000
Brown, Capital		45,000
Cook, Capital		31,500
	$160,500	$160,500

The partners share profits and losses as follows: Arthur, 50%; Brown, 30%; and Cook, 20%.

The partners are considering an offer of $100,000 for the accounts receivable, inventory, and plant and equipment as of June 30. The $100,000 would be paid to the partners in installments, the number and amounts of which are to be negotiated.

Instructions: Prepare a cash distribution schedule as of June 30, 1967, showing how the $100,000 would be distributed as it becomes available.

(2) Assume the same facts as above except that, instead of accepting the offer of $100,000, the partners decide to liquidate their partnership. Cash is distributed to the partners at the end of each month. A summary of the liquidation transactions follows:

July

$16,500 — collected on accounts receivable, balance is uncollectible.
$10,000 — received for the entire inventory.
$ 1,000 — liquidation expenses paid.
$ 8,000 — cash retained in the business at end of the month.

August

$ 1,500 — liquidation expenses paid.
As part payment of his capital, Cook accepted a piece of special equipment that he developed which had a book value of $4,000. The partners agreed that a value of $10,000 should be placed on the machine for liquidation purposes.

$ 2,500 — cash retained in the business at end of the month.

September

$75,000 — received on sale of remaining plant and equipment.

$ 1,000 — liquidation expenses paid.
No cash retained in the business.

Instructions: Prepare a schedule of cash payments as of September 30, 1967, showing how the cash was actually distributed.

(AICPA adapted)

4-16. A, B, and C agree to sell hot dogs on July 3 and 4. A agrees to construct a stand on the front lawn of C and charge the cost to operations. C agrees to the use of his front lawn, but asks $25 for the cost of sod replacement and cleaning up his lawn after July 4. A, B, and C decide that profits, if any, will be distributed first by the $25 payment to C and then by a 40% commission on individual sales. The balance will be distributed 75% to A and 25% to B. They agree that a cash box will only complicate matters and that all purchase and sales transactions will be out of pocket and the responsibility of the individual. Sales to A, B, and C are to be at cost, except that the ending inventory may be purchased at 50% of cost. All other sales are to be made at 100% markup on cost.

The activity of the venture is as follows:

July 2: A constructs the stand on the front lawn of C at a cost of $100.

July 3: A pays $1,000 for supplies. C pays $50 for a permit to operate the concession.

July 4: A purchases additional supplies for $1,500, using $500 given to him by B and $1,000 of his own money.

July 4: Sales for the day were as follows:

A	$1,700
B	2,600
C	600

July 5: C pays $90 for fire extinguishers and these are distributed equally between A, B, and C for their personal use at home.
C agrees to pay $50 for the stand.

July 5: The balance of the inventory was taken by A.

Instructions: Prepare a work sheet analysis of the transactions that will give A, B, and C the following information:

(a) Net profit or loss from the operation.
(b) Distribution of profit or loss to A, B, and C.
(c) The final cash settlement.

(AICPA adapted)

Chapter 5

INSTALLMENT SALES

The sale of real property is often made on a deferred payment plan whereby the seller receives a down payment and the balance in the form of a series of payments made over a number of years. Similar installment payment plans have been widely adopted by dealers in personal property as well as by those selling personal services. The installment payment plan is commonly offered on sales ranging from automobiles to air travel. Consumer installment debt outstanding at the beginning of 1967 exceeded 70 billion dollars and was about four times the size of consumer noninstallment debt.

PROTECTION FOR THE SELLER

With collection periods that may range up to 3 years on the sale of personal property and up to 30 years on the sale of real property, a seller usually seeks to protect himself in the event of a buyer's failure to complete payment on the contract. When real or personal property is sold, the risk of loss from failure to complete the contract can be minimized by the repossession of such property. The sales contract usually includes one of the following arrangements for assuring the repossession of property in the event of default by the buyer:[1]

(1) *Conditional sales contract.* Title to the property may be retained by the seller until the full purchase price has been paid. Such an agreement is known as a *conditional sales contract* but is treated for accounting purposes as a sale and transfer of the property.

(2) *Transfer of title with property subject to lien or mortgage.* Title to the property may be transferred to the buyer with the property subject to a lien or a mortgage for the unpaid portion of the selling price. In the event of failure by the buyer to meet his payments under the contract, the lien or the mortgage provides for the reconveyance of title to the seller.

(3) *Transfer of title to trustee.* Title to the property may be conveyed to a trustee until payments on the contract are completed. When the seller receives the final payment on the contract, title is reconveyed by the trustee to the buyer. The instrument forming the basis for such an agreement is known as a *trust indenture* or *trust deed.*

(4) *Lease-purchase arrangement.* The property may be leased until the full purchase price has been paid. At this time title passes to the buyer. This is known as a *lease-purchase arrangement.*

In spite of the ability of a seller to repossess property in the event of contract default, losses in carrying installment contracts may be heavy.

[1]Under the Uniform Commercial Code, which has been adopted by all the states except Louisiana, these various arrangements are called *secured transactions* and the contracts are called *secured agreements.* Under the Code, special forms are used for the various types of installment sales.

The installment contract, offering liberal credit arrangements, may attract many customers whose credit risk is high. Furthermore, with payments spread over an extended period, there is the possibility of a change in the customer's ability to pay. The depreciation or the obsolescence on goods sold may exceed the payments made, and goods subject to repossession may not be worth as much as the unpaid balance of the contract. Repossession itself may be a costly process. Furthermore, sales on the installment basis mean continuing bookkeeping and collection costs, and in certain instances important servicing and repair costs that must be borne by the seller. These are factors that must be considered by the seller in establishing an installment sales policy.

In attempting to reduce or avoid repossession losses, the seller should consider adopting the following safeguards in installment contracts:

(1) The required down payment should be large enough to cover the decline in the value of an article in its change from "new" to "used."
(2) The period between installment payments should not be too long, preferably not more than one month.
(3) The periodic installment payments should exceed the decline in the value of the article that takes place between payments. When the value of an article exceeds the unpaid balance of the contract, the buyer will not want to default on the contract.

METHODS OF GROSS PROFIT RECOGNITION ON INSTALLMENT SALES

Two general approaches may be taken to the recognition of gross profit on installment sales: (1) the gross profit may be related to the period in which the sale is made, or (2) the gross profit may be related to the periods in which cash is collected on the installment contract.

Gross profit recognized in the period of sale. Installment sales may be regarded as calling for treatment that is no different from that employed for regular sales. Gross profit may be recognized at the time of the sale, the point at which goods are exchanged for legally enforceable claims against customers. Such a procedure will call for recognition in the period of sale of the charges involved in carrying installment sales contracts as well as the charges related to contract defaults and uncollectibles. This is done by debiting appropriate expense accounts and crediting allowances for the charges that can be anticipated. The charges that are anticipated will depend on the individual business unit and its own particular experiences with installment contracts. The recognition of gross profit on installment sales in the period in which the sales are made is relatively simple in application and sound in theory.

Gross profit related to the periods in which cash is collected. Installment sales may be regarded as calling for special treatment whereby gross profit is related to the periods in which the installment receivables are collected rather than to the periods in which the receivables are created. The inflow of cash, then, instead of the time of sale becomes the criterion for revenue recognition. In adopting such an approach, several alternative procedures can be applied. The installment sales plan that is employed must be considered carefully in making a choice as to the procedure that will measure net income most satisfactorily.

Procedures that relate gross profit to collection periods are:

(1) *Collections regarded as first the recovery of cost.* Collections on a contract are regarded as representing first the recovery of product cost. After recovery of cost, all further collections are regarded as profit. This procedure is too conservative under most circumstances; it can be supported only when there is doubt as to any recoverable value associated with either the balance of the installment contract or the goods subject to repossession.

(2) *Collections regarded as first the realization of profit.* Collections are regarded as representing first the realization of the gross profit on the contract. After recognition of the full profit on the transaction, all further collections are regarded as a recovery of cost. This procedure lacks sufficient conservatism under most circumstances in view of the probability that defaults and repossessions over the life of contracts will impair the original profit margin.

(3) *Collections regarded as both return of cost and realization of profit.* Each collection on a contract is regarded as representing both a return of cost and a realization of gross profit in the ratio in which these two factors are found in the original sales price. This method serves to spread the gross profit on an installment sale over the full life of the installment contract. Continuing expenses on an installment contract are matched against the gross profit that is recognized in successive periods; the possible failure to realize the full amount of the gross profit in the event of default by the buyer is anticipated.

Method (3) above, providing for the recognition of gross profit in proportion to collections, is referred to as accounting by the *installment method* or *installment basis.* When gross profit is regarded as contingent upon the collection of cash, there is normally stronger support for its recognition over the entire collection period than for the alternative procedures mentioned.

THE INSTALLMENT METHOD

In applying the installment method in the accounts, the difference between the contract sales price and the cost of that sale is recorded as deferred gross profit. This balance is recognized as revenue periodically in the proportion that the cash collections of the period bear to the sales price. Stated differently, the original gross profit percentage on the sale is applied to periodic collections in arriving at the amounts to be recognized as revenue. At the end of each period a deferred gross profit balance remains on the books that is equal to the gross profit percentage applied to the balance of installment receivables as of this date.

The deferral of gross profit is, in effect, the deferral of sales revenue accompanied by the deferral of cost of goods sold related to such sales revenue. The deferral of gross profit may suggest the deferral of expenses that were incurred in the promotion of installment sales. Ordinarily, however, such a practice may be difficult to defend. Although the gross profit is considered to be contingent upon collections, this cannot be said of the expenses already incurred; the conservatism achieved in recognizing revenue would be impaired or nullified by a nonconservative position with respect to expenses. Furthermore, serious difficulties would be faced in selecting the expenses to be deferred and determining the allocation procedures to be applied in such deferrals. It should be observed that revenue on installment sales recognized in periods subsequent to the period of sale will not be free of charges; certain charges will be continuing — bookkeeping, collection, and product servicing, for example — while other charges will emerge at different intervals — losses related to defaults and repossessions and losses from uncollectible accounts. The installment method of accounting normally implies the deferral of gross profit but the recognition of expenses in the period of their incurrence.

The installment method of reporting gross profit can be used for federal income tax purposes by dealers in personal property regularly selling on the installment plan. The installment method is also permitted at the election of the taxpayer in the following instances: (1) upon the casual sale of personal property other than inventory when the selling price exceeds $1,000 and the initial payments do not exceed 30% of the selling price, and (2) upon any sale or other disposition of real property when initial payments do not exceed 30% of the selling price.[1] Expenses cannot be deferred for tax purposes.

The entries that are required in accounting for installment sales are illustrated in the following pages. The installment method of accounting is first illustrated by means of a simple example involving the sale of real estate. This is followed by illustrations involving the sale of merchandise.

SALE OF REAL ESTATE ON INSTALLMENT BASIS

Assume that on October 1, 1966, the Westwood Realty Co. sells to S. F. West for $50,000 property that it owns and carries on its books at $30,000. The company receives $10,000 on the date of the sale and a mortgage note for $40,000 payable in 20 semiannual installments of $2,000 plus interest on the unpaid principal at 6%. Commissions and other expenses on the sale amounting to $1,500 are paid. Regular install-

[1]By initial payment is meant cash or property other than evidences of indebtedness of the purchaser received during the taxable period in which the sale was made.

ments of principal and interest on the mortgage notes are received by the seller in 1967. The entries that follow are those that would appear on the seller's books if (1) gross profit is recognized in the period of sale, and (2) gross profit is recognized periodically in proportion to collections. It is assumed that the seller's fiscal period is the calendar year.

Transaction	Entry: Recognition of Profit in Period of Sale			Entry: Recognition of Profit Periodically in Proportion to Collections		
October 1, 1966 Sold real property (Parcel A), book value, $30,000, for $50,000.	Receivable from S. F. West....... Real Estate (Parcel A)..... Gain on Sale (Parcel A).....	 50,000 	 30,000 20,000	Receivable from S. F. West........ Real Estate (Parcel A)...... Deferred Gross Profit (Parcel A)	 50,000 	 30,000 20,000
Received down payment, $10,000, and mortgage note for balance, $40,000.	Cash............ Mortgage Note... Receivable from S. F. West.....	10,000 40,000 	 50,000	Cash............. Mortgage Note.... Receivable from S. F. West......	10,000 40,000 	 50,000
Paid expenses on sale, $1,500.	Selling Expenses.. Cash..........	1,500	 1,500	Selling Expenses... Cash...........	1,500	 1,500
December 31, 1966 To adjust accounts for: (1) Accrued interest on mortgage note, $40,000, at 6% for 3 months, $600. (2) (Reporting by installment method) Gross profit realized: gross profit rate, 40% ($20,000, gross profit ÷ $50,000, sales price); cash collected, $10,000; gross profit realized, 40% of $10,000, or $4,000.*	Accrued Interest on Mortgage Note Interest Income.	 600 	 600	Accrued Interest on Mortgage Note.... Interest Income.. Deferred Gross Profit (Parcel A).. Realized Gross Profit (Parcel A)	 600 4,000 	 600 4,000
To close nominal accounts.	Gain on Sale (Parcel A)........... Interest Income.. Selling Expenses Profit and Loss.	20,000 600 	 1,500 19,100	Realized Gross Profit (Parcel A) Interest Income.... Selling Expenses. Profit and Loss..	 4,000 600 	 1,500 3,100
January 1, 1967 To reverse accrued interest established at end of previous period.	Interest Income... Accrued Interest on Mortgage Note	600 	 600	Interest Income.... Accrued Interest on Mortgage Note	600 	 600

*For income tax purposes, a nondealer in real estate cannot recognize expenses of a casual sale of real estate as business expenses but can deduct such expenses in computing the "gross profit" on the sale. Sale of the property by a nondealer, then, would be recognized as giving rise to a gross profit of $18,500, or 37% of the sales price; although expenses of $1,500 on the sale would not be recognized in 1966, total profit recognized over the life of the contract would be limited to $18,500.

Transaction	Entry: Recognition of Profit in Period of Sale			Entry: Recognition of Profit Periodically in Proportion to Collections		
April 1, 1967 Received semiannual installment on mortgage note, $2,000, and interest on $40,000 at 6% for 6 months, $1,200.	Cash............. Mortgage Note. Interest Income	3,200	 2,000 1,200	Cash............. Mortgage Note.. Interest Income.	3,200	 2,000 1,200
October 1, 1967 Received semiannual installment on mortgage note, $2,000, and interest on $38,000 at 6% for 6 months, $1,140.	Cash............. Mortgage Note.. Interest Income..	3,140	 2,000 1,140	Cash............. Mortgage Note.. Interest Income..	3,140	 2,000 1,140
December 31, 1967 To adjust accounts for: (1) Accrued interest on mortgage note, $36,000, at 6% for 3 months, $540. (2) (Reporting by installment method) Gross profit realized: gross profit rate, 40%; cash collected, $4,000; gross profit realized, 40% of $4,000, or $1,600.	Accrued Interest on Mortgage Note.... Interest Income..	540	 540	Accrued Interest on Mortgage Note.... Interest Income.. Deferred Gross Profit (Parcel A) Realized Gross Profit (Parcel A)	540 1,600	 540 1,600
To close nominal accounts.	Interest Income.... Profit and Loss..	2,280	 2,280	Realized Gross Profit (Parcel A).. Interest Income... Profit and Loss...	1,600 2,280	 3,880

If installments are collected regularly until the note is paid off, entries would continue to be made in the manner illustrated. The method of accounting for the installment sale does not affect the entries that are made to record the amounts earned each year as interest. However, the net gain on the sale of property is recognized differently under the two methods: recognition of the profit in the period of sale results in a gain in 1966 of $18,500 ($20,000 – $1,500); recognition of profit periodically in proportion to collections results in a gain in 1966 of $2,500 ($4,000 – $1,500) and a gain in each of the next 10 years of $1,600 (40% of $4,000).

If there should be a default on contract payments, the seller may proceed to repossess the property that was sold. The entry that is made upon repossession depends upon the method originally employed in recording the profit on the sale. If the profit on the sale was recognized at the time of the sale, the entry shows the reacquisition of the property at its present fair market value, the cancellation of the balance of the claim against the buyer, and the gain or the loss on the repossession. If profit was recognized by the installment method, cancellation of the balance of the claim against the buyer is accompanied by cancellation of the deferred gross profit balance related thereto; the property would still be recorded at its fair market value, but the gain or the loss upon repossession would be measured by the difference between the property item that is recognized and the installment contract balances that are canceled.

Assume in the previous example that the buyer fails to meet the installment due on April 1, 1968. The seller surrenders the mortgage note with an unpaid balance of $36,000 and repossesses the property. On this date an appraisal of the property shows it to have a fair market value of $28,500. The entries under each method would be as follows:

Transaction	Entry					
	Recognition of Profit in Period of Sale			Recognition of Profit Periodically in Proportion to Collections		
Reacquired real property (Parcel A) valued at $28,500; surrendered mortgage note with unpaid balance of $36,000.	Real Estate (Parcel A)...............	28,500		Real Estate (Parcel A)...............	28,500	
	Loss on Repossession (Parcel A)........	7,500		Deferred Gross Profit (Parcel A)	14,400	
	Mortgage Note. .		36,000	Mortgage Note.		36,000
				Gain on Repossession (Parcel A)		6,900

In each case above, a second entry would also be necessary to write off as a loss the accrued interest of $540 on the mortgage note that was recognized at the end of 1967 but that was found to be uncollectible in 1968.

The loss and gain figures in each case above can be proved by the following calculations:

		Recognition of Profit in Period of Sale	Recognition of Profit Periodically in Proportion to Collections
Total amount collected..........................		$14,000	$14,000
Loss in value of repossessed property:			
Original basis.....................	$30,000		
Fair market value upon recovery.....	28,500	1,500	1,500
Net gain..................................		$12,500	$12,500
Gain recognized prior to repossession..........		20,000	5,600
Gain (loss) on repossession....................		($ 7,500)	$ 6,900

When the installment method is used in reporting profits and a number of properties are sold at different gross profit rates during the year, separate accounts may be maintained to show the deferred gross profit on each sale. Summaries at the end of the year of the amounts collected on individual contracts provide the basis for calculating the gross profits that have been realized.

SALE OF MERCHANDISE ON INSTALLMENT BASIS

The procedures that are employed in accounting for sales of merchandise on an installment basis are similar to those just illustrated. In recording transactions it is necessary to distinguish between regular sales and installment sales and to provide the other data for arriving at the gross profit that is to be recognized as a result of collections on installment accounts.

To illustrate accounting for the sale of merchandise on an installment basis, assume that a balance sheet for the Kelton Sales Co. on January 1, 1967, reports the following balances:

Cash	$ 25,000	Accounts payable	$ 40,000
Merchandise inventory	100,000	Deferred gross profit on installment sales, 1966	22,800
Accounts receivable (regular)	15,000	Deferred gross profit on installment sales, 1965	7,000
Installment contracts receivable, 1966	60,000	Capital stock	100,000
Installment contracts receivable, 1965	20,000	Retained earnings	50,200
Total assets	$220,000	Total liabilities and stockholders' equity	$220,000

Installment sales in 1966 and 1965 were made at gross profit rates of 38% and 35% respectively. On January 1, 1967, with installment contracts receivable of 1966 totaling $60,000 still on hand, the balance sheet reports deferred gross profit of 38% of this amount, or $22,800; with installment contracts receivable of 1965 totaling $20,000, the balance sheet reports deferred gross profit of 35% of this amount, or $7,000.

Transactions and entries for the Kelton Sales Co. relating to regular and installment sales for 1967 follow:

Transaction		Entry		
January 1–December 31 (1) Regular sales consisted of cash sales, $250,000, and sales on account, $200,000; installment sales were $150,000.		Cash	250,000	
		Accounts Receivable (Regular)	200,000	
		Sales (Regular)		450,000
		Installment Contracts Receivable, 1967	150,000	
		Installment Sales		150,000
(2) Purchases of merchandise on account were $425,000.		Purchases	425,000	
		Accounts Payable		425,000
(3) Receipts in addition to those from cash sales were from the following sources:		Cash	325,000	
Accounts receivable (regular)	$190,000	Accounts Receivable (Regular)		190,000
Installment contracts receivable, 1967	80,000	Installment Contracts Receivable, 1967		80,000
Installment contracts receivable, 1966	40,000	Installment Contracts Receivable, 1966		40,000
Installment contracts receivable, 1965	15,000	Installment Contracts Receivable, 1965		15,000

Transaction	Entry		
(4) Payments were applied to the following: Accounts payable .... $435,000 Less discounts taken ... 5,000 $430,000 Operating expenses 120,000	Accounts Payable Operating Expenses Purchases Discounts Cash	435,000 120,000 	 5,000 550,000
Adjusting and closing, December 31 (5) To record cost of goods relating to installment sales, $90,000.	Cost of Installment Sales Shipments on Installment Sales	90,000 	 90,000
(6) To close installment sales and cost of installment sales accounts and to record gross profit on installment sales for year, $60,000 (40% of installment sales).	Installment Sales Cost of Installment Sales Deferred Gross Profit on Installment Sales, 1967	150,000 	 90,000 60,000
(7) To record the gross profit realized as a result of collections on installment contracts of 1967, 1966, and 1965, as follows: 1967 accounts, 40% of $80,000 ..... $32,000 1966 accounts, 38% of $40,000 ..... 15,200 1965 accounts, 35% of $15,000 5,250	Deferred Gross Profit on Installment Sales, 1967 Deferred Gross Profit on Installment Sales, 1966 Deferred Gross Profit on Installment Sales, 1965 Realized Gross Profit on Installment Sales, 1965–1967	32,000 15,200 5,250 	 52,450
(8) To close beginning inventory, purchases, purchases discounts, and shipments on installment sales accounts into Profit and Loss, thus summarizing the goods available for regular sales ($430,000).	Profit and Loss Shipments on Installment Sales Purchases Discounts Merchandise Inventory, January 1, 1967 Purchases	430,000 90,000 5,000 	 100,000 425,000
(9) To record ending inventory, thus summarizing cost of goods relating to regular sales ($310,000).	Merchandise Inventory, December 31, 1967 Profit and Loss	120,000 	 120,000
(10) To close regular sales into Profit and Loss, thus summarizing gross profit on regular sales ($140,000).	Sales (Regular) Profit and Loss	450,000 	 450,000
(11) To close realized gross profits on installment sales of current and prior years into Profit and Loss, thus summarizing total gross profit ($192,450).	Realized Gross Profit on Installment Sales, 1965–1967 Profit and Loss	52,450 	 52,450
(12) To close operating expenses into Profit and Loss, thus summarizing the net income before income taxes ($72,450).	Profit and Loss Operating Expenses	120,000 	 120,000
(13) To record estimated income taxes payable at 40% of net income before taxes of $72,450, or $28,980.	Income Taxes Income Taxes Payable	28,980 	 28,980
(14) To close income taxes into Profit and Loss, thus summarizing net income ($43,470).	Profit and Loss Income Taxes	28,980 	 28,980
(15) To transfer net income to Retained Earnings ($43,470).	Profit and Loss Retained Earnings	43,470 	 43,470

It should be observed that, unless the gross profit on both regular and installment sales is the same, it will be necessary to maintain a record of the cost of merchandise shipped on installment sales. This cost is recorded by a debit to Cost of Installment Sales and a credit to Shipments on Installment Sales. The latter balance will be recognized as a subtraction item from the sum of the beginning inventory and purchases in determining the goods available for regular sales.[1] The ending inventory subtracted from goods available for regular sales gives the cost of regular sales.

In the illustration, the cost of installment sales is determined to be $90,000; the gross profit on such sales is then $60,000, or 40% of installment sales of $150,000. In calculating the cost of goods relating to regular sales, the amount of goods available for such sales is first determined. This is found to be $430,000 — the sum of the beginning inventory, $100,000, and purchases, $425,000, less purchases discounts, $5,000, and shipments on installment sales, $90,000. Cost of goods relating to regular sales is $310,000 — goods available for sale as above, $430,000, less the ending inventory, $120,000.

When a perpetual inventory system is maintained, purchases are recorded directly in the inventory account. Entries for the costs of installment sales and regular sales are made currently, the accounts Cost of Installment Sales and Cost of Regular Sales being charged and the inventory account credited.

There are frequently instances when the gross profit rates vary significantly within the different departments of a particular business. When the gross profit rates are different but the ratio of collections to sales for each department is approximately the same each period, an average gross profit rate can be applied to total collections for each period in arriving at the realized gross profit; however, when the collection ratios are not the same, satisfactory measurement of realized gross profit requires that sales, costs, and collections be summarized separately for each department. Sales and cost figures by departments will supply departmental gross profit rates, and these rates can be applied to collections identified with the respective departments in arriving at realized gross profit.

Alternative procedure for calculating realized gross profit. In the illustration on pages 136 and 137, the realized gross profit was calculated by applying the gross profit percentage for the year in which the con-

[1]It would be possible to credit the purchases account instead of Shipments on Installment Sales. The use of a separate shipments account that is recognized as an offset against the sum of the beginning inventory and purchases, however, preserves the information concerning total purchases for the period.

tracts originated to the amounts collected on such contracts. The realized gross profit can also be determined by calculating the amount of deferred gross profit as of the end of the period and reducing the deferred gross profit account to this balance. This procedure applied to the facts for the Kelton Sales Co. is as follows:

	1967	1966	1965
Balance of deferred gross profit before adjustment	$60,000	$22,800	$ 7,000
Deferred gross profit at the end of 1967:			
On installment contracts receivable of 1967, 40% of uncollected balance of $70,000.....	28,000		
On installment contracts receivable of 1966, 38% of uncollected balance of $20,000.....		7,600	
On installment contracts receivable of 1965, 35% of uncollected balance of $5,000......			1,750
Reduction in deferred gross profit balances at the end of 1967 — gross profit realized as a result of collections during 1967..................	$32,000	$15,200	$ 5,250

Use of special journals in recording installment sales. Sales and cash transactions are normally recorded in special sales and cash journals designed to classify and summarize separately regular and installment sales and collections from each of these sources. The sales journal normally provides special columns for cash sales, regular sales on account, and installment sales. The cash receipts journal provides a column for collections of regular accounts receivable as well as special columns for collections of installment contracts receivable of the current and prior periods. When gross profits are to be determined on a departmental basis, special journals may be designed to offer further classification of sales, costs, and installment contract receivables and collections by departments.

Aging accounts in installment method accounting. In the illustration, accounts were set up for both installment contracts receivable and deferred gross profit by years; collections were related to receivables classified as to date of origin. It is possible to employ a single controlling account and subsidiary ledger for all of the installment accounts and to summarize the entire deferred gross profit in a single account. When such an arrangement is followed, however, it will be necessary at the end of each period to analyze and classify installment receivables according to the year of their origin. The appropriate gross profit percentages can then be applied to the receivable totals by years in arriving at the deferred gross profit balance.

The foregoing procedure may be followed in order to avoid the additional work that is involved in carrying a number of controlling accounts and related subsidiary ledgers for installment receivables as well as the special efforts that are required in analyzing collections and relating them to receivables that are classified according to the period of their origin.

PREPARATION OF FINANCIAL STATEMENTS WHEN THE INSTALLMENT METHOD IS USED

A business with installment sales prepares its balance sheet in the usual manner; however, the balance sheet will include the contracts receivable and the deferred gross profit balances related to sales on the installment plan.

When current assets are held to include those resources "reasonably expected to be realized in cash or sold or consumed during the normal operating cycle of the business," installment contracts receivable qualify for inclusion under the current heading regardless of the length of time required for their collection.[1] In reporting installment contracts receivable under the current heading, disclosure of the maturity dates of such contracts will provide readers of the balance sheet with a better appreciation of the company's financial position; accordingly, annual maturities of receivables should be indicated either by parenthetical or footnote disclosure or by listing receivables according to their annual maturities.

Conflicting positions have been taken with respect to the appropriate classification on the balance sheet of the deferred gross profit balance. It has been suggested that this balance be reported as:

(1) A liability item to be included under the deferred revenues heading.
(2) An asset valuation account to be subtracted from installment contracts receivable.
(3) A capital item to be included as a part of retained earnings.

Deferred gross profit on installment sales is generally reported in the liability section of the balance sheet as deferred revenue. Accountants following this practice take the position that the installment sale has actually increased the working capital position of the company but that the recognition of an increase in capital must await the conversion of the installment receivable into cash.

---

[1]See *Accounting Research Bulletin No. 43*, "Restatement and Revision of Accounting Research Bulletins," 1953 (New York: American Institute of Certified Public Accountants), p. 20. Installment or deferred accounts and notes are specifically mentioned as properly includible in the current asset category when they "conform generally to normal trade practices and terms within the business."

This position, however, is subject to serious challenge. If it is maintained that the installment sales procedure is followed because there is no assurance of the realization of revenue beyond the amount currently recognized, then the deferred gross profit balance is more properly viewed as an asset valuation account. The recovery of cash on installment contracts shrinks the valuation account requirements and thus makes possible the recognition of revenue in periods subsequent to the sale.

On the other hand, when the collection of installment contracts is reasonably assured, it can be maintained that the installment sale has given rise to gross profit as in the case of a regular sale, except that the profit should not be recognized as fully subject to income taxes or available for dividends until collections are made. Such an approach suggests the reclassification of the deferred gross profit into three elements:

(1) An allowance for the continuing expenses that are still anticipated in the collection of installment contracts receivable, including charges arising from defaults and repossessions. Such an allowance would be subtracted from the installment receivable balance.

(2) An obligation for the income taxes on the portion of the gross profit that has not yet been recognized on the tax return. Such income tax liability would not be combined with balances reporting income taxes that have already accrued since this amount will become payable only as installment contract receivables are realized in cash in subsequent periods.

(3) The balance representing net earnings identified with installment contracts. This amount can be reported as a special retained earnings balance that is not to be used as a basis for dividends until installment receivables are collected.

With such a reclassification of the deferred gross profit balance, profits on installment sales would be recognized as having accrued for financial statement purposes although maintaining a deferred status for tax purposes. In the illustrations in this chapter, deferred gross profit is reported as deferred revenue in accordance with generally prevailing practice.

In preparing an income statement for a business with both regular and installment sales, detail summarizing gross profit for each class of sales may be provided separately and such detail summarized in a total column. Data concerning collections on installment contracts, the gross profit rates applying to such collections, and calculations of realized gross profit are reported by means of a supporting schedule.

A balance sheet, an income statement, and a schedule providing an analysis of the gross profit on installment sales for the Kelton Sales Co. prepared at the end of 1967 are given on pages 142 and 143.

Kelton Sales Co.
Balance Sheet
December 31, 1967

Assets		
Current assets:		
Cash		$ 50,000
Accounts receivable (regular)		25,000
Installment contracts receivable:		
1967	$ 70,000	
1966	20,000	
1965	5,000	95,000
Merchandise inventory		120,000
Total assets		$290,000

Liabilities and Stockholders' Equity			
Liabilities			
Current liabilities:			
Accounts payable		$ 30,000	
Income taxes payable		28,980	$ 58,980
Deferred revenues:			
Deferred gross profit on installment sales:			
1967		$ 28,000	
1966		7,600	
1965		1,750	37,350
Total liabilities			$ 96,330
Stockholders' Equity			
Capital stock		$100,000	
Retained earnings:			
Balance, January 1	$ 50,200		
Add net income for 1967	43,470	93,670	
Total stockholders' equity			193,670
Total liabilities and stockholders' equity			$290,000

Kelton Sales Co.
Income Statement
For Year Ended December 31, 1967

			Installment Sales	Regular Sales	Total
Sales			$150,000	$450,000	$600,000
Cost of goods sold:					
Merchandise inventory, Jan, 1, 1967		$100,000			
Purchases	$425,000				
Less purchases discounts	5,000	420,000			
Merchandise available for sale		$520,000			
Less merchandise inventory, Dec. 31, 1967		120,000	90,000	310,000	400,000
Gross profit			$ 60,000	$140,000	$200,000
Less deferred gross profit on 1967 installment sales (see gross profit schedule)			28,000		28,000
Realized gross profit on current year's sales			$ 32,000	$140,000	$172,000
Add realized gross profit on prior years' sales on installment basis (see gross profit schedule)					20,450
Total realized gross profit					$192,450
Operating expenses					120,000
Net income before income taxes					$ 72,450
Income taxes					28,980
Net income					$ 43,470

Kelton Sales Co.
Analysis of Gross Profit on Installment Sales
Schedule to Accompany Income Statement
For Year Ended December 31, 1967

Gross profit rate on installments sales, 1967:			
Gross profit, \$60,000 ÷ installment sales, \$150,000			40%
Deferred gross profit on installment sales, 1967:			
Installment contract receivables, \$150,000, less collections, \$80,000, or \$70,000 × 40%			\$28,000
Realized gross profit:			
	1967	1966	1965
Collections on installment contracts receivable	\$80,000	\$40,000	\$15,000
Installment sales gross profit percentage	40%	38%	35%
Realized gross profit	\$32,000	\$15,200	\$ 5,250

TRADE-INS

In certain sales on the installment plan, companies will accept a trade-in as part payment on a new contract. When the amount allowed on the goods traded in is a value that will permit the company to realize a normal gross profit on its resale, no special problem is involved; the trade-in is recorded at the value allowed, Cash is charged for any payment accompanying the trade-in, Installment Contracts Receivable is charged for the balance of the sales price, and Installment Sales is credited for the amount of the sale. Frequently, as a special sales inducement, an overallowance is given on the trade-in. Such an overallowance is, in effect, a reduction in the sales price, and the accounts should properly report this fact. Under such circumstances, the trade-in should be recorded at no more than the company would pay on its purchase; the difference between the amount allowed and the value of the article to the company should be reported either as a charge to an overallowance account or as a reduction in Installment Sales. In either case, the gross profit on installment sales should be regarded as the difference between the cost of the goods sold and net sales — the installment sales total less any trade-in overallowances.

To illustrate application of the foregoing, assume that a certain article that cost \$675 is sold for \$1,000. A used article is accepted as down payment, \$300 being allowed on the trade-in. The company estimates reconditioning costs on this article of \$20 and a sales price after such reconditioning of \$275. The company normally expects a 20% gross profit on sales of used goods.

The value of the trade-in and the amount of the overallowance are calculated as follows:

Amount allowed on trade-in			$300
Value of article traded-in:			
Sales value of article		$275	
Less: Reconditioning costs	$20		
Gross profit to be realized on resale, 20% of $275	55	75	200
Overallowance			$100

The sale can now be recorded as follows:

Merchandise — Trade-Ins	200	
Overallowances on Installment Sales Trade-Ins	100	
Installment Contracts Receivable, 1967	700	
Installment Sales		1,000
Cost of Installment Sales	675	
Merchandise — New		675

The cost percentage on the installment sale is calculated as follows: cost, $675; net sales, $1,000, less overallowance, $100, or $900; cost percentage, 675/900, or 75%. The gross profit on installment sales, then, is 25%, and 25% of $200, the down payment on the sale, may be considered realized to date. The article traded in is recorded at $200. This cost when increased by reconditioning costs measures the utility of the article to the business and permits a normal gross profit on its resale.

It was assumed in the example just given that the company employs a perpetual inventory system for merchandise. When a periodic inventory system is employed, trade-ins are recorded in a separate nominal account and this balance is added to purchases in summarizing cost of goods sold at the end of the period.

DEFAULTS AND REPOSSESSIONS

Default on an installment contract and repossession of the article sold calls for an entry on the books of the seller that reports the merchandise reacquired, cancels the installment receivable together with the deferred gross profit balance related thereto, and records the gain or the loss on the repossession. As in the case of goods acquired by trade-in, a repossessed article should be recorded at an amount that will permit a normal gross profit on its resale.

To illustrate the procedure for defaults and repossessions, assume the following data:

Total installment sales in 1967	$100,000
Gross profit rate on installment sales in 1967	36%

In 1968 a customer defaults on a contract for $600 that had originated in 1967. A total of $250 had been collected on the contract in 1967 prior to the default. The article sold is repossessed; its value to the company is $180, allowing for reconditioning costs and a normal gross profit on resale. The entry to record the default and the repossession follows:

Merchandise — Repossessions	180	
Deferred Gross Profit, 1967	126	
Loss on Repossessions	44	
Installment Contracts Receivable, 1967		350

It should be observed that cancellation of the installment contracts receivable balance of $350 is accompanied by cancellation of deferred gross profit of $126 (36% of $350). The repossessed merchandise is reported at a value of $180. A loss of $44 is recognized on the repossession representing the difference between the installment contract balances canceled, $224 ($350 – $126), and the value assigned to repossessed goods, $180.

When perpetual inventories are maintained, repossessed goods are charged to the inventory balance; when periodic inventories are employed, repossessions are recorded in a separate nominal account and this balance is added to purchases in calculating cost of goods sold. When goods are repossessed in the year in which the sale is made and before the gross profit percentage has been calculated, it may be necessary to assume a gross profit percentage in recording the gain or the loss from the repossession. A correcting entry is made at the end of the period when the actual gross profit percentage is determined.

If the repossessed merchandise in the preceding example is recorded at a value in excess of $224, the difference between the balance in the installment contracts receivable account and the deferred gross profit account, a gain will be reported on the repossession. Ordinarily, however, conservatism would suggest that no more than the unrecovered cost, the difference between the receivable balance and the deferred gross profit balance, be assigned to the repossessed goods. No gain, then, would be reported at the time of the repossession; recognition of any gain would await the sale of the repossessed goods.

Any gain or loss on defaults and repossessions is normally recognized on the income statement as an addition to or a subtraction from the realized gross profit on installment sales.

USE OF THE INSTALLMENT METHOD

In accounting for installment sales, the accountant is faced with the question: Should gross profit be related to the period in which the sale is made or should it be related to the periods in which the sales price is realized in cash? In answering this question the accountant must consider all of the circumstances that are encountered in the particular situation. He must then select the alternative that in his judgment leads to the fairest expression of financial operations and position.

The following statement relative to the recognition of profit was made by the American Institute of Certified Public Accountants in its original set of rules that was subsequently adopted by the membership:

> . . . Profit is deemed to be realized when a sale in the ordinary course of business is effected, unless the circumstances are such that the collection of the sales price is not reasonably assured.[1]

No direct reference to the installment sales method was made by AICPA committees until 1967 when the Accounting Principles Board in *Opinion No. 10* repeated the above statement and continued:

> The Board reaffirms this statement; it believes that revenues should ordinarily be accounted for at the time a transaction is completed, with appropriate provision for uncollectible accounts. Accordingly, it concludes that, in the absence of the circumstances referred to above, the installment method of recognizing revenue is not acceptable.

In clarification of the circumstances where the installment method could be supported, the following observation was made:

> The Board recognizes that there are exceptional cases where receivables are collectible over an extended period of time and because of the terms of the transactions or other conditions, there is no reasonable basis for estimating the degree of collectibility. When such circumstances exist, and as long as they exist, either the installment method or the cost recovery method of accounting may be used. (Under the cost recovery method, equal amounts of revenue and expense are recognized as collections are made until all costs have been recovered, postponing any recognition of profit until that time.)[2]

The American Accounting Association Committee on Concepts and Standards Underlying Corporate Reports has cautioned against adoption of the installment method unless such a practice can be fully justified. The Committee has commented:

> The tax laws have unduly and unintentionally tended to influence the development of corporate accounting in that to some extent legislative concessions in measuring taxable income have been adopted into accounting practice without justification in principle. An illustration of this is the instalment basis of reporting income, when the consideration is received over a period of time. There is no sound accounting reason for the use of the instalment method for financial statement purposes in the case of closed transactions in which collection is dependent upon lapse of time and the probabilities of realization are properly evaluated. In the opinion of the

---

[1]*Accounting Research and Terminology Bulletins,* 1961 (New York: American Institute of Certified Public Accountants), *Accounting Bulletin No. 43,* p. 11.

[2]*Opinion of the Accounting Principles Board No. 10,* "Omnibus Opinion — 1966," 1967 (New York: American Institute of Certified Public Accountants), p. 149.

Committee, such income has accrued and should be recognized in financial statements, even though deferred for tax purposes.[1]

The authors are in agreement with the positions expressed above. There may be adequate support for the use of the installment method when real estate is sold with a small down payment and installments covering a number of years and there is serious possibility of default through a change in market conditions or the inability or unwillingness of the buyer to complete the contract. However, it would appear that in conventional sales of personal property on the installment plan, the instances where use of the installment method can be justified are rare.

A dealer who sells personal property on the installment plan and recognizes the entire gross profit in the period of sale on his financial statements can still choose to employ the installment method for income tax purposes. The installment method is normally chosen for tax purposes as a means of postponing the recognition of income until installment collections are made and cash is actually available to meet the tax liability.

In using the installment method only for income tax purposes, there may be significant differences between net incomes reported on the successive tax returns and net incomes as stated on the books. Periodic tax payments, then, may be significantly different from the amounts that would be applicable to the net incomes reported on the books. For example, in the year in which the installment method is used for the first time, the income tax that is paid will be less than the amount applicable to book income in view of the income on current sales that is deferred for tax purposes. In subsequent periods, taxes paid may be greater or smaller than amounts applicable to book income depending upon the differences between the amount of income on prior-period sales that is recognized and the amount of income on current sales that is deferred for income tax purposes. Differences between financial and tax reporting for installment sales suggest the application of inter-period income tax allocation procedures whereby periodic adjustments are made to bring the charge for income taxes to the balance that is applicable to net income as reported on the books.[2]

To illustrate application of the foregoing, assume that the Kelton Sales Co. in the illustration on pages 136–138 reports gross profit on installment sales in the period of the sales for financial statement purposes but reports gross profit by the installment method for income tax pur-

---

[1]*Accounting and Reporting Standards for Corporate Financial Statements and Preceding Statements and Supplements, Supplementary Statement No. 4*, "Accounting Principles and Taxable Income," 1952 (Iowa City: American Accounting Association), p. 33.

[2]For a full discussion of inter-period tax allocation, refer to Simons and Karrenbrock, *Intermediate Accounting — Comprehensive Volume*, Fourth Edition, 1964, pages 307–312.

poses. Net income for 1967 before taxes would be reported on the income statement as $80,000 — regular and installment sales, $600,000, less cost of goods sold, $400,000, and operating expenses, $120,000. Receivable balances would require analysis in arriving at deferred gross profit balances requiring recognition for tax purposes. Net income per books would be restated to net income for income tax purposes by the following adjustments:

Net income before income taxes, per books	$ 80,000
Add deferred gross profit at end of 1966	29,800
	$109,800
Deduct deferred gross profit at end of 1967	37,350
Net income by installment method	$ 72,450

Assuming income taxes at 40%, the Kelton Sales Co. in assigning an income tax charge to net income for 1966 would recognize a deferred tax liability of 40% of $29,800, or $11,920. In adjusting the accounts at the end of 1967, an entry to recognize income taxes would be made on the books as follows:

Income Taxes (40% of $80,000, net income per books)	32,000	
Income Taxes Payable (40% of $72,450, net income per tax return)		28,980
Deferred Income Tax Liability (40% of $7,550, increase in deferred gross income balance)		3,020

In employing the installment basis for income tax purposes while recognizing the entire gross profit on installment sales as well as the tax charges assignable to such profit on the books, the Kelton Sales Co. will report operations for 1967 as follows:

Sales	$600,000
Cost of goods sold	400,000
Gross profit	$200,000
Operating expenses	120,000
Net income before income taxes	$ 80,000
Income taxes	32,000
Net income	$ 48,000

INTEREST ON INSTALLMENT CONTRACTS

Installment contracts frequently provide for a charge for interest on the principal amount owed. The interest charge is ordinarily payable together with the installment payment that reduces the principal amount.

The arrangement for the periodic payment of interest generally takes one of the following forms:

(1) Interest is computed on the balance of the principal owed between installment periods. This is sometimes referred to as *long-end* interest.

(2) Interest is computed on the individual installment due, from the date the contract was entered into until the date of the installment payment. This is sometimes referred to as *short-end* interest.

(3) Periodic payments are equal in amount and represent interest on the balance of the principal owed between installment periods, the remainder a reduction in the principal balance.

(4) Interest throughout the payment period is computed on the original principal.

To illustrate the foregoing payment plans, assume that on June 30 equipment is sold for $400 on an installment basis. Terms of the sale call for a down payment of $100, the balance to be paid in 6 monthly installments with interest at 6%. The payments that would be made according to each of the plans listed are described in the following paragraphs.

(1) Periodic interest on balance of principal owed between installments. If 6 principal payments of $50 are to be made together with the interest that is due on the balance of the principal owed between installment dates, payments will be made as shown in the table below.

Date	Interest on Balance Owed (½ of 1% per Month)	Contract Payment Due	Total Payment	Balance of Principal
June 30				$400.00
June 30		$100.00	$100.00	300.00
July 31	$1.50	50.00	51.50	250.00
Aug. 31	1.25	50.00	51.25	200.00
Sept. 30	1.00	50.00	51.00	150.00
Oct. 31	.75	50.00	50.75	100.00
Nov. 30	.50	50.00	50.50	50.00
Dec. 31	.25	50.00	50.25	None
	$5.25	$400.00	$405.25	

Entries to record the foregoing will be made as follows:

Transaction	On the Books of the Buyer			On the Books of the Seller		
June 30 To record the installment sale, $400, and the down payment, $100.	Equipment	400.00		Installment Contracts Receivable	400.00	
	Installment Contracts Payable		400.00	Installment Sales		400.00
	Installment Contracts Payable	100.00		Cash	100.00	
	Cash		100.00	Installment Contracts Receivable		100.00
July 31 To record the first payment of $50 and interest at 6% for 1 month on the balance owed of $300.	Installment Contracts Payable	50.00		Cash	51.50	
	Interest Expense	1.50		Installment Contracts Receivable		50.00
	Cash		51.50	Interest Income		1.50
August 31 To record the second payment of $50 and interest at 6% for 1 month on the balance owed of $250.	Installment Contracts Payable	50.00		Cash	51.25	
	Interest Expense	1.25		Installment Contracts Receivable		50.00
	Cash		51.25	Interest Income		1.25

Similar entries will be made for subsequent installments.

(2) Periodic interest on individual installment due. Assume the same facts except that interest is to be paid periodically upon the installment that is due from contract date to the date of the installment payment. Payments will be made as shown in the table that follows:

Date	Interest from Date of Sale to Date of Payment (½ of 1% per Month)	Contract Payment Due	Total Payment	Balance of Principal
June 30				$400.00
June 30		$100.00	$100.00	300.00
July 31	$ .25	50.00	50.25	250.00
Aug. 31	.50	50.00	50.50	200.00
Sept. 30	.75	50.00	50.75	150.00
Oct. 31	1.00	50.00	51.00	100.00
Nov. 30	1.25	50.00	51.25	50.00
Dec. 31	1.50	50.00	51.50	None
	$5.25	$400.00	$405.25	

It should be noted that interest payments do not agree with the interest actually accruing on the unpaid principal. Assuming the preparation of monthly financial statements, accrued interest based on the principal balance would have to be recognized at the end of each month. The amount of interest paid may then be offset against this balance.

Entries to record the interest accrual as well as the installment payments at the end of July and August will be made as follows:

Transaction	On the Books of the Buyer			On the Books of the Seller		
July 31 To record accrued interest at 6% for 1 month on balance owed of $300.	Interest Expense... Accrued Interest on Contracts Payable..........	1.50	 1.50	Accrued Interest on Contracts Receivable............. Interest Income..	1.50	 1.50
To record the first payment of $50 and interest at 6% for 1 month on payment of $50.	Installment Contracts Payable..... Accrued Interest on Contracts Payable. Cash..........	50.00 .25	 50.25	Cash............. Installment Contracts Receivable. Accrued Interest on Contracts Receivable........	50.25	 50.00 .25
August 31 To record accrued interest at 6% for 1 month on balance owed of $250.	Interest Expense... Accrued Interest on Contracts Payable..........	1.25	 1.25	Accrued Interest on Contracts Receivable............. Interest Income..	1.25	 1.25
To record the second payment of $50 and interest at 6% for 2 months on payment of $50.	Installment Contracts Payable..... Accrued Interest on Contracts Payable. Cash..........	50.00 .50	 50.50	Cash............. Installment Contracts Receivable. Accrued Interest on Contracts Receivable........	50.50	 50.00 .50

Although the charges for interest are greater than the payments for interest in the entries above, the charges go down periodically while the payments go up. After the final payment, total payments for interest will be equal to the sum of the charges that were recognized. Changes in the accrued interest balance are summarized below.

Date	Increase for Accrual (Cr.)	Decrease for Payment (Dr.)	Balance of Accrued Interest on Contracts Payable (Cr.)
July 31..........	$1.50	$ .25	$1.25
Aug. 31.........	1.25	.50	2.00
Sept. 30.........	1.00	.75	2.25
Oct. 31..........	.75	1.00	2.00
Nov. 30.........	.50	1.25	1.25
Dec. 31.........	.25	1.50	None

(3) Equal periodic payments that represent (a) interest on the balance of the principal between interest dates and (b) principal. When periodic payments are to be equal in amount and are to represent interest on the unpaid principal and an amount to be applied against principal, the equal payments are found by actuarial calculations. By the use of actuarial tables it can be determined that an obligation of $300 accruing interest at 6% is discharged by 6 equal monthly payments of $50.88.[1] A table to show payments and the allocation of such payments between interest and principal appears below.

Date	Contract Payment Due	Portion of Payment Applying to Interest Accruing on Principal (½ of 1% per Month)	Balance of Payment Representing Reduction in Principal	Balance of Principal
June 30				$400.00
June 30	$100.00		$100.00	300.00
July 31	50.88	$1.50	49.38	250.62
Aug. 31	50.88	1.25	49.63	200.99
Sept. 30	50.88	1.00	49.88	151.11
Oct. 31	50.88	.76	50.12	100.99
Nov. 30	50.88	.50	50.38	50.61
Dec. 31	50.86*	.25	50.61	None
	$405.26	$5.26	$400.00	

*A final payment of only $50.86 is required to cancel the interest for the last month together with the unpaid principal on this date.

It should be observed that payments apply first to the accrued interest on the principal to the date of payment and then to a reduction in the principal amount owed. Entries to record the equal periodic payments at the end of July and August are shown on the following page.

[1] $300 is the present value of an ordinary annuity of 6 rents at interest of ½ of 1%. The calculation of the equal periodic rents that will cancel the principal indebtedness and pay the interest accruals is described in Chapter 27.

Transaction	On the Books of the Buyer			On the Books of the Seller		
July 31 To record the first regular payment of $50.88, representing payment of accrued interest to date, $1.50 (½ of 1% of $300), and principal, $49.38.	Interest Expense... Installment Contracts Payable..... Cash..........	1.50 49.38	 50.88	Cash.............. Interest Income.. Installment Contracts Receivable.	50.88	 1.50 49.38
August 31 To record the second regular payment of $50.88, representing payment of accrued interest to date, $1.25 (½ of 1% of $250.62), and principal, $49.63.	Interest Expense... Installment Contracts Payable..... Cash..........	1.25 49.63	 50.88	Cash.............. Interest Income.. Installment Contracts Receivable.	50.88	 1.25 49.63

(4) Periodic interest computed on original principal. Assume the same facts except that periodic interest payments are to continue at 6% of the original principal for the duration of the contract. Payments are made as shown in the following table:

Date	Interest Based on Original Principal (½ of 1% per Month)	Contract Payment Due	Total Payment	Balance of Principal
June 30..........				$400.00
June 30..........		$100.00	$100.00	300.00
July 31..........	$ 2.00	50.00	52.00	250.00
Aug. 31..........	2.00	50.00	52.00	200.00
Sept. 30..........	2.00	50.00	52.00	150.00
Oct. 31..........	2.00	50.00	52.00	100.00
Nov. 30..........	2.00	50.00	52.00	50.00
Dec. 31..........	2.00	50.00	52.00	None
	$12.00	$400.00	$412.00	

Although each of the first three methods resulted in interest at 6% per year, the method just illustrated results in an effective interest charge that is actually more than double the 6% rate. While the average amount owed during the course of the contract was $175 [($300 plus $50) ÷ 2], the interest charge for the 6-month period totaled $12, resulting in an interest rate of nearly 14% ($24, interest per year ÷ $175, the average amount owed).

Whatever method is employed in charging interest, use of the installment method requires that only that portion of a payment which reduces the principal balance of the installment contract receivable be considered in computing the gross profit realized.

QUESTIONS

1. What two basic approaches may be taken to the recognition of gross profit on sales made on the installment plan? Give the theory underlying each approach.

2. What three procedures may be followed when the recognition of gross profit is to be related to the cash that is realized on installment contracts? Evaluate each procedure and indicate the circumstances under which each procedure may be considered particularly suitable.

3. What methods may be adopted by the seller to assure himself of the recovery of goods that were sold in the event of default on the part of the buyer?

4. What practices should be followed if losses on the repossessions of merchandise are to be minimized?

5. Would you recommend that expenses related to installment sales be deferred when gross profit on such sales is deferred? Give reasons.

6. (a) Describe the *installment method* of accounting. (b) Give two methods for the periodic calculation of realized gross profit.

7. Describe the form for a cash receipts journal that might be used to record collections on both regular accounts receivable and installment contracts originating over a three-year period.

8. Compare the financial statements for a business that does not sell on the installment basis with those for a business that does sell on the installment basis.

9. State how each of the following balances would be classified on the financial statements: (a) installment contracts receivable, (b) repossessed merchandise, (c) overallowances on trade-ins, (d) loss on repossessions.

10. Describe the positions that may be taken in reporting deferred gross profit on installment sales on the balance sheet. Which position do you favor? Why?

11. Burke and Baggett use the installment method in the accounts and report the entire deferred gross profit balance as a part of the company's capital. Would you have any objections to such a procedure?

12. L. P. Monarch wishes to adopt the installment method for profit recognition on installment sales but wishes to keep bookkeeping detail at a minimum by maintaining a single customer's ledger. What special procedures are required in following such an arrangement?

13. (a) At what value would you recommend that articles traded in be entered on the books? (b) How would you treat trade-in overallowances in the accounts? (c) How should such overallowances be recognized in arriving at the gross profit on installment sales?

14. The Markham Company reports the difference between the installment contract receivable balances and the deferred gross profit balance that is canceled upon a repossession as the cost of the repossessed goods. Under what circumstances, if any, would you object to such a procedure?

15. Describe four different interest plans that may be found in an installment sales contract.

EXERCISES

1. At the end of 1967, R. A. Brady sells for $10,000 property that he acquired in 1960 at a cost of $4,250. Terms of the sale are $4,000 down with the balance to be paid in annual installments of $1,000. Indicate the profit to be recognized by Brady in 1967 and in each of the 6 years that follow, assuming that:

(a) Collections on the contract are first considered a return of the property cost; after recovery of the cost, collections are regarded as profit.
(b) Collections are first considered realization of the profit on the contract; after recovery of the profit, collections are regarded as a return of cost.
(c) Each collection is considered both a return of cost and of profit in the ratio in which these are found in the sales price.

2. In July, 1967, C. P. Walters sold real estate that had cost him $9,000 for $24,000, receiving cash of $3,500 and a mortgage note for the balance payable in monthly installments. Installments received in 1967 reduced the principal of the note to a balance of $20,000. The buyer defaulted on the note at the beginning of 1968, and the property was repossessed. The property had an appraised value of $16,500 at the time of repossession. Give the entries that would be made on the books of the seller in 1967 and 1968, assuming (a) that the full profit is recognized when the sale is made and (b) that the gross profit on the sale is recognized in proportion to the periodic collections.

3. The Fuller Sales Company reports profits on the installment basis. Perpetual inventory records are kept for stock on hand. Sales during 1967 are summarized below. Give the entries that would be made to record the transactions and to close the accounts for 1967.

(a) Sales on installment basis, $250,000.
(b) Collections on installment accounts, $120,000.
(c) Shipments of goods on installment sales; cost $200,000.
(d) Repossessions of goods sold on installment basis; installment accounts canceled, $20,000; repossessed goods valued at $14,500.
(e) Expenses paid, $16,000.

4. J. C. Clendenin accounts for installment sales by reporting income in the proportion of the collections to the selling price. On December 31, 1967, his books show account balances as follows:

Installment Contracts Receivable		Deferred Gross Profit	
1965	$ 10,000	1965	$ 8,000
1966	40,000	1966	26,000
1967	90,000	1967	105,000

The gross profit rates were: 1965, 35%; 1966, 30%; 1967, 40%.

(a) What adjusting entries are required on December 31, 1967?

(b) How much was collected in 1967 on accounts receivable of each year?

5. The Charles B. Croft Store accounts for installment sales on the installment basis. At the beginning of 1967, ledger accounts include the following balances:

Installment Accounts Receivable, 1965	$15,000
Installment Accounts Receivable, 1966	48,000
Deferred Gross Profit, 1965	6,300
Deferred Gross Profit, 1966	18,000

At the end of 1967, account balances before adjustment for realized gross profit on installment sales are:

Installment Accounts Receivable, 1965	None
Installment Accounts Receivable, 1966	$12,000
Installment Accounts Receivable, 1967	65,000
Deferred Gross Profit, 1965	6,300
Deferred Gross Profit, 1966	18,000
Deferred Gross Profit, 1967	30,000

Installment sales in 1967 were made at 66⅔% above cost of merchandise sold. What are the entries to record the gross profit realized in 1967?

6. The books of Donald Murphy show the following balances on December 31, 1967:

Accounts Receivable	$627,500
Deferred Gross Profit (before adjustment)	76,000

Analysis and aging of the accounts receivable reveal the following:

Regular accounts	$415,000
1966 installment accounts	32,500
1967 installments accounts	180,000

Sales on an installment basis in 1966 were made at 30% above cost; in 1967, at 33⅓% above cost. Give the entry to adjust the deferred gross profit account at the end of 1967.

7. The Cook Trading Company recognizes profits on installment sales on its books at the time of sale just as it recognizes profits on regular sales. For income tax purposes the company reports profits on the installment basis. The income statement for 1967 prepared by the company from its accounts showed a net income of $112,000. The following data were recognized at the end of 1966 in preparing the tax return:

Accounts receivable on December 31, 1966, included:

1965 installment accounts of $40,000; deferred gross profit of $12,000 was considered related to this balance.

1966 installment accounts of $80,000; deferred gross profit of $26,000 was considered related to this balance.

The following data are available at the end of 1967:

Accounts receivable on December 31, 1967, includes:

- 1965 installment accounts of \$12,500.
- 1966 installment accounts of \$25,000.
- 1967 installment accounts of \$60,000; installment sales in 1967 were made at approximately 66⅔% above cost.

From the foregoing data calculate the net income to be reported on the income tax return, showing how this amount is developed.

8. The Walsh Co. sells new automobiles. A sale of a new automobile costing \$2,500 was made at the end of 1967. The new car was sold at a price of \$3,600; an old automobile was accepted as down payment and an allowance of \$1,500 was allowed on the trade-in. The company anticipates reconditioning costs on this automobile of \$150 and a resale price of \$1,400. Its used car sales are expected to produce a 25% gross profit. Give entries to record the sale of the automobile, to adjust and close the accounts, and to recognize the gross profit on the sale by the installment method.

9. Weiss and Company sells refrigerators at 20% above cost and accounts for sales by the installment method. In 1967 repossessions were made on unpaid installment contract balances of \$15,000. Repossessed units had a total resale value of \$13,500. The company records such repossessions at a value that will permit the normal margin on sales. Give the entry to summarize the repossessions for 1967.

10. In October, 1967, the Phillips Co. repossessed a piano that had been sold in 1966 at a gross profit of 45%. The uncollected installment contract balance on the date of the repossession was \$800. In 1967, \$300 had been collected, which included interest of \$40; collections had been properly recorded. The repossession was recorded by a charge to Sales Returns and a credit to Installment Contracts Receivable for \$800, closing the latter account. The value of the piano on the date of repossession was \$380. The company recognizes income by the installment method. What entry or entries are required on December 31, 1967, to correct and bring the accounts up to date?

11. On October 31, 1967, Paul A. Barnes sold property that had cost him \$60,000 for \$75,000. He received \$20,000 down; the balance is payable in monthly installments, with the first payment due at the end of November. Barnes decides to report the profit on the sale on the installment basis. What entries would be made for the sale, for the receipt of installments at the end of November and December, and for the recognition of profit for 1967, assuming that:

(a) Monthly payments are sums consisting of \$400 to apply against the principal plus interest on the unpaid balance at 6%.

(b) Monthly payments are equal amounts of \$400 that include interest at 6% on the unpaid amount of the obligation, any excess reducing the principal amount owed.

PROBLEMS

5-1. The Warren Furniture Company reports income on the installment basis and uses perpetual inventory accounts. The following data are available:

Sales Made During	Percent of Gross Profit	Installment Receivables on January 1, 1967	Collected During 1967	Installment Receivables on December 31, 1967
1965	46%	$30,000	$30,000	——
1966	42%	50,000	34,000	$ 16,000
1967	40%	——	60,000	140,000

Instructions: Prepare all the journal entries for 1967 required for the data above, including those required for the recognition of gross profit at the end of the year.

5-2. The Lawrence Appliance Co. recorded installment sales of $600,000 in 1967. A record was kept of the different articles sold on the installment basis. At the end of the year the total cost of goods sold on the installment basis was calculated at $405,000. The total collections on installment sales for the year were $360,000. The estimated value of the merchandise repossessed was $24,000, and balances owed on the repossessions were $40,000. Perpetual inventory accounts were not maintained.

Instructions: Prepare the journal entries required for the data above, including the entries to set up the total realizable gross profit at the end of the year, to record the repossessions, and to record the realized gross profit.

5-3. The Wabash Appliance Co. reports gross profit on the installment basis. The following data are available:

	1965	1966	1967
Installment sales	$240,000	$250,000	$300,000
Cost of goods — installment sales	180,000	181,250	216,000
Gross profit	$ 60,000	$ 68,750	$ 84,000
Collections:			
1965 installment contracts	$ 45,000	$ 75,000	$ 72,500
1966 installment contracts		47,500	80,000
1967 installment contracts			62,500
Defaults:			
Unpaid balance of 1965 installment contracts		$ 12,500	$ 15,000
Value assigned to repossessed goods		6,500	6,000
Unpaid balance of 1966 installment contracts			16,000
Value assigned to repossessed goods			9,000

Instructions: Give all of the entries for 1967 that are required in recording installment sales, collections, defaults and repossessions, and the recognition of gross profit. Assume the use of perpetual inventory accounts.

5-4. On September 30, 1967, A. C. Barr bought an automobile for $3,600. He made a down payment of $1,600, with the balance due in 10 monthly installments, the first to be made at the end of October.

Instructions: (1) Assume that Barr is to make monthly payments of $200 plus interest on the unpaid balance at 6%. Set up a table showing the principal and interest payments and the principal amount owed after each payment.

(2) Assume that Barr is to make monthly payments of $200 plus interest on each installment for the full time the payment was owed. Complete a table with columns showing (a) the interest paid, (b) the principal paid, (c) the total payment, (d) the interest accruing on the balance of the principal between interest dates, (e) the principal balance, and (f) the accrued interest balance.

(3) Assume that Barr is to make equal monthly payments, each payment to apply first as interest on the unpaid principal at 6% and the balance as a reduction in principal. Such equal payments are calculated to be $205.54. Complete a table showing the payments, the interest and principal portions of each payment, and the principal amount owed after each payment.

(4) What is the approximate effective annual interest rate if monthly payments are $200 plus interest at 6% charged on the original principal amount of $3,600?

5-5. The Weber Sales Corporation purchased a machine for $60,000 on July 31, 1967. The company paid $12,000 down and gave a note for the balance payable in 48 monthly installments, the first one due on August 31.

Instructions: (1) Assuming that interest at 6% on the balance of the principal is added to regular monthly payments of $1,000, give the journal entries for the acquisition of the machine and for the payments at the end of August, September, and October, 1967.

(2) Assuming that interest at 6% on the individual payments only from the date of purchase to the date of payment is added to regular monthly payments of $1,000, give the journal entries for the interest adjustments and for the monthly payments at the end of August, September and October, 1967.

(3) Assuming that monthly payments are to be equal amounts of $1,127.28 as calculated actuarially, representing interest at 6% on the unpaid principal and the balance a reduction of principal, give the journal entries for the monthly payments at the end of August, September, and October, 1967.

5-6. Harmony Instruments, Inc. sold a piano, cost $1,000, for $1,600 on September 30, 1967. The down payment was $160, and the same amount was to be paid at the end of each succeeding month. Interest was charged on the unpaid balance of the contract at ½ of 1% a month, payments being considered as applying first to accrued interest and the balance to principal.

After paying a total of $640, the customer defaulted. The piano was repossessed in February 1968. It was estimated that the piano had a value of $560 on a depreciated cost basis. The company uses perpetual inventory accounts and enters the total deferred gross profit at the time of sale.

Instructions: Give the journal entries to record:
(1) The installment sale.
(2) The monthly collections.
(3) The recognition of realized gross profit at the end of 1967.
(4) The repossession in 1968.

5-7. F. A. Sloan purchased two adjoining 75-foot business lots in 1962. Lot No. 1 was purchased early in that year for $36,000 and Lot No. 2 was purchased later in the year for $24,000. Sloan made three 50-foot lots out of the original two by taking 25 feet from each to make Lot No. 3. The cost of this third lot was determined by allocating a portion of the cost of the original two lots to it. Sloan then built a store on Lot No. 3 at a cost of $36,000. It was completed on June 30, 1967, and had an estimated life of 20 years.

The three pieces of property were sold during 1967 on the following terms:

Lot No.	Sales Price	Date of Sale	Down Payment	Equal Installment Payments
1	$36,000	Oct. 31	$ 7,200	$1,200 every 2 months
2	40,000	Mar. 31	3,600	$1,600 every 3 months
3	84,000	June 30	12,000	$4,000 every 6 months

Each installment payment is to be applied first to accrued interest on the principal amount owed at the rate of 6%, the balance to a reduction of principal.

The purchaser of Lot No. 3 did not complete his contract, failing to meet the installment due on June 30, 1968, and the property was repossessed.

Instructions: (1) Prepare journal entries to record the transactions for 1967 on Sloan's books.

(2) Prepare the entry to record the realized gross profit when the books are closed on December 31, 1967.

(3) Record the repossession of Lot No. 3 in 1968. (Assume that upon repossession the lot is recorded at original cost; the building, at original cost less depreciation to date based upon original estimates.)

5-8. A trial balance prepared for Western Equipment, Inc. on December 31, 1967, appears at the top of the following page.

The inventory of merchandise on December 31, 1967, was $60,000.

The following account balances were reported in the post-closing trial balance prepared on January 1, 1967:

Installment Accounts Receivable, 1966	$150,000
Installment Accounts Receivable, 1965	30,000
Deferred Gross Profit, 1966	45,000
Deferred Gross Profit, 1965	9,600

Instructions: (1) Calculate the gross profit percentages on installment sales for 1965, 1966, and 1967.

(2) Prepare a balance sheet and an income statement with a supporting schedule providing an analysis of gross profit on installment sales.

(3) Prepare the adjusting and closing entries.

Cash	27,500	
Installment Accounts Receivable, 1967	55,000	
Installment Accounts Receivable, 1966	12,000	
Installment Accounts Receivable, 1965	3,000	
Accounts Receivable	17,000	
Inventory, December 31, 1966	52,000	
Other Assets	40,000	
Accounts Payable		40,000
Deferred Gross Profit, 1966		45,000
Deferred Gross Profit, 1965		9,600
Capital Stock		100,000
Retained Earnings		68,400
Sales		125,000
Installment Sales		320,000
Purchases	350,000	
Cost of Installment Sales	232,000	
Shipments on Installment Sales		232,000
Operating Expenses	151,500	
	940,000	940,000

5-9. A trial balance prepared for the Grossett Sales Corporation on December 31, 1967, is given below.

Cash	25,000	
Installment Accounts Receivable, 1967	80,000	
Installment Accounts Receivable, 1966	20,000	
Installment Accounts Receivable, 1965	5,000	
Accounts Receivable	40,000	
Inventory, December 31, 1966	30,000	
Other Assets	52,000	
Accounts Payable		75,000
Deferred Gross Profit, 1966		96,000
Deferred Gross Profit, 1965		22,500
Capital Stock		100,000
Retained Earnings		44,500
Sales		192,000
Installment Sales		500,000
Purchases	455,000	
Repossessed Merchandise	10,000	
Cost of Installment Sales	310,000	
Shipments on Installment Sales		310,000
Loss on Repossessions	13,000	
Operating Expenses	300,000	
	1,340,000	1,340,000

The following account balances were found in the post-closing trial balance prepared at the beginning of 1967:

Installment Accounts Receivable, 1966	$240,000
Installment Accounts Receivable, 1965	50,000
Deferred Gross Profit, 1966	96,000
Deferred Gross Profit, 1965	22,500

The inventory of new and repossessed merchandise on December 31, 1967, was $35,000.

At the end of December, before preparing the trial balance, the bookkeeper made the following incomplete entry:

Repossessed Merchandise	10,000	
Loss on Repossessions	13,000	
Installment Accounts Receivable, 1967		5,000
Installment Accounts Receivable, 1966		10,000
Installment Accounts Receivable, 1965		8,000

Instructions: (1) Calculate the gross profit percentages on installment sales for 1965, 1966, and 1967.

(2) Prepare the required correcting entry for the repossessions.

(3) Prepare a balance sheet and an income statement with a supporting schedule providing an analysis of gross profit on installment sales.

(4) Prepare the adjusting and closing entries.

5-10. Wilson Corporation, which operates on the calendar-year basis, purchased business property on June 30, 1962, for $100,000 cash. The appraised value of the land was $10,000 and the remaining life of the building was estimated to be 50 years. Depreciation has been accumulated by use of the straight-line method.

On June 30, 1966, the property was sold for $150,000, for which payment was received as follows:

(1) $25,000 cash on date of sale.
(2) Four non-interest-bearing notes due as follows:

$30,000 — 6/30/67
$30,000 — 6/30/68
$50,000 — 6/30/69
$15,000 — 6/30/70

Wilson Corporation elected to record the gain on the sale of the property by the installment method, inasmuch as the collection of the receivable is not reasonably assured.

Instructions: (1) Prepare the necessary journal entries and computations to record the sale on June 30, 1966.

(2) Furnish the necessary journal entries and computations to record the collection of the notes at their maturities.

(3) State the sections of the balance sheet in which the account balances at December 31, 1966, should be shown. (AICPA adapted)

5-11. The Four Star Investment Company was organized and started operations in January, 1967. It is engaged in acquiring unimproved land and dividing it into lots for sale as home sites. Realizing that the project is speculative, the company decided to take up gross profits on sale of lots (after deducting any commissions payable to salesmen) in the proportion that cash collected each year bears to the sales price. The transactions for 1967 were as follows:

(a) Purchased 120 acres of land for subdivision at a cost of $48,000, payable in cash, and divided the land into lots of 100 ft. width and 120 ft. depth, obtaining a total of 310 lots. The remaining area was devoted to streets and other general purposes. The lots were priced according to location as follows: The A lots were listed to sell for $1,500 each, B lots for $1,000 each and C lots for $800 each. There were 80 A lots, 100 B lots, and the remainder were C lots.

(b) Costs and expenses incurred in 1967 were as follows:

Legal fees for purchasing land, surveying fees, etc.....	$ 6,000
Grading contract......	22,500
Water and sewerage system contract......	18,490
Paving contract......	26,630
Building model home, which is to be offered for sale and is expected to yield a profit......	13,500
Advertising and publicity......	7,300
General office expense of which one fourth is considered applicable to the period after development of the lots has been completed......	23,600
Sales manager's salary......	9,000
Sales commissions......	2,210

(c) Sales during 1967 were as follows, all at the prices listed above:
A lots — 26; B lots — 32; C lots — 12

All lots were sold with a ¼ down payment, except 6 of the A lots that were collected for in full. The notes taken were payable in 3 installments starting 1 year from date of sale. Ignore interest on the notes.

Instructions: Prepare a statement, supported by all necessary computations presented in good form, showing the net profit of the company for the year 1967.

(AICPA adapted)

5-12. The Bledsoe Sales Co. sells goods and accounts for such sales on the installment basis. At the end of each year it takes up gross profit on these sales in the year(s) of collection rather than in the year of sale and considers each collection to be composed of cost and gross profit elements.

The balances of the controlling accounts for installment contracts receivable at the beginning and the end of 1967 were:

	January 1, 1967	December 31, 1967
Installment contracts receivable:		
1965......	$ 24,020	—
1966......	344,460	$ 67,440
1967......	—	410,090

As collections are made, the company debits Cash and credits Installment Contracts Receivable. During 1967, upon default in payment by customers, the company repossessed merchandise having an estimated resale value of $1,700. The sales had been made in 1966 for $5,400, and $3,200 had been collected prior to default. The company recorded the default and repossession by a debit to Inventory of Repossessed Merchandise and a credit to Installment Contracts Receivable — 1966 for the uncollected balance.

The company's sales and cost of sales for the 3 years involved are summarized below:

	1965	1966	1967
Net sales	$380,000	$432,000	$602,000
Cost of sales	247,000	285,120	379,260

Instructions: (1) Prepare journal entries to record at December 31, 1967, the recognition of profits and any other adjustments arising from the above data. Give complete explanations in support of your entries.

(2) Give one acceptable alternative method of handling the repossession and discuss the relative merits of the method used in (1) above and the alternative method suggested here.

(AICPA adapted)

5-13. The Wallace Sales Co. started business on January 1, 1966. Separate accounts were set up for installment and cash sales, but no perpetual inventory record was maintained. On the installment sales, a ⅓ down payment was required, with the balance payable in 18 equal monthly installments. At the end of each year the company adjusted its books to the "installment basis" by use of a deferred gross profit account. When contracts were defaulted, the unpaid balances were charged to a bad debts expense account, and sales of repossessed merchandise were credited to this account. The expense account was adjusted at the year end to reflect the actual loss.

Information about the transactions of the Wallace Sales Co. follows:

	1966	1967
Sales:		
New merchandise for cash	$ 21,348	$ 29,180
New merchandise on installment (including the one-third cash down payment)	188,652	265,320
Repossessed merchandise	600	700
Purchases	154,000	173,585
Physical inventories at December 31:		
New merchandise at cost	36,400	48,010
Repossessions at realizable value	150	160
Unpaid balances of installment contracts defaulted:		
1966 sales	2,865	3,725
1967 sales		3,010
Cash collections on installment contracts, exclusive of down payments:		
1966 sales	42,943	61,385
1967 sales		55,960

Instructions: (1) Compute the gross profit percentages for the years 1966 and 1967.

(2) In T-account form, reproduce the ledger accounts for installment contracts receivable.

(3) Calculate the net loss on defaulted accounts for the year 1966.

(4) Prepare a schedule showing the realized gross profit for the year 1967 that would be reported on the income statement.

(AICPA adapted)

5-14. The Parker Furniture Company commenced business operations on January 1, 1966. All sales are made on installment contracts, and inventory records are on a periodic basis. Contract receivables are kept separate by years. At the end of each year, adjustments for unrealized and realized gross profits are made through a deferred gross profit on installment sales account. Defaulted contracts were recorded by debiting the loss on defaults account and crediting the appropriate contracts receivable account for the amount unpaid at the time of default. All repossessed merchandise and trade-ins should be recorded at realizable values. Presented below is information taken from the accounts of the Parker Furniture Company.

	1966	1967
Contracts receivable (unpaid balances):		
1966 accounts	$ 62,425	$ 3,175
1967 accounts		101,375
Installment sales	138,675	220,925
Purchases	160,000	154,600
New merchandise inventory, December 31, at cost	60,154	73,042
Loss on defaults		5,000

Additional information:

In the process of your audit you find that the following items were not included in the inventory taken on December 31, 1967:

(1) Merchandise received as a trade-in on December 15, 1967, for which an allowance was given. The realizable value of the merchandise is $500, which was the allowance for the trade-in. No entry was made to record this merchandise on the books at the time it was received.

(2) Repossessed merchandise, originally sold in 1966, representing the only default and repossession by the company to date, had a realizable value of $2,000 at the time of repossession and at December 31, 1967. No entry has been made to record this repossessed merchandise.

Instructions: (1) Prepare the adjusting entry to record the trade-in merchandise.

(2) Compute the gross profit percentages for 1966 and 1967.

(3) Reconstruct the deferred gross profit on installment sales account by years through December 31, 1967, showing, in good form, all computations for the amounts included in the account.

(4) Prepare the entry necessary to adjust the loss on defaults account.

(AICPA adapted)

5-15. The Ladero Sales Company was formed on July 31, 1965, and sells household appliances at retail on installment payment contracts.

The following information was taken from the accounts of the Ladero Sales Company at year ends:

	July 31 1967	July 31 1966
Installment contracts receivable:		
1966 contracts	$ 4,000	$ 63,000
1967 contracts	80,000	
Sales	250,000	150,000
Merchandise inventory, new, at cost	42,250	32,250
Purchases	155,000	
Selling and administrative expenses	70,000	
Loss on defaulted contracts	8,550	500
Allowance for defaulted contracts	4,500	4,500

The CPA's audit at July 31, 1967, disclosed the following:

(1) When a contract is in default, the merchandise is repossessed and the contract is written off to Loss on Defaulted Contracts. Information regarding repossessed merchandise is kept on a memo basis and is not recorded on the books. Any income derived from the sale of this merchandise is credited to Loss on Defaulted Contracts. No repossessed merchandise was sold in 1966 or 1967 for more than the unpaid balance of the original contract. An analysis of the loss on defaulted contracts account follows:

Contracts written off:		
1966 contracts		$ 7,500
1967 contracts		3,000
		10,500
Less sale of repossessed merchandise:		
1966 contracts	$1,600	
1967 contracts	350	1,950
Balance		$ 8,550

The market value of the repossessed merchandise inventory on hand at July 31, 1967, was $400, all of which was repossessed from 1966 contracts. There was no merchandise repossessed during the year ended July 31, 1966.

The $4,000 balance of 1966 installment contracts receivable is considered collectible.

(2) The gross profit ratio for 1966 was 40%.

(3) The company's financial statements are prepared on the accrual basis, and the installment method of reporting income is used for income tax purposes. The company is on the charge-off method for losses on defaulted contracts for income tax purposes.

Instructions: (1) Prepare a schedule to compute the adjustment to the balance of the account Allowance for Defaulted Contracts that the CPA would suggest at July 31, 1967. The rate of bad debt losses for 1967 is expected to be the same as the experience rate for 1966 based on sales.

(2) Prepare a schedule computing taxable income on the installment sales method for the year ended July 31, 1967. The following supporting schedules should be in good form:

Computation of realized gross margin on 1966 sales.
Computation of losses on defaults on 1966 contracts and 1967 contracts.

(AICPA adapted)

5-16. The Jackson Appliance Company started business on January 1, 1967. Separate accounts were established for installment and cash sales, but no perpetual inventory record was maintained.

On installment sales, the price was 106% of the cash sale price. A standard installment contract was used whereby a down-payment of ¼ of the installment price was required, with the balance payable in 15 equal monthly installments. (The interest charge per month is 1% of the unpaid cash sale price equivalent at each installment.)

Installments receivable and installment sales were recorded at the contract price. When contracts were defaulted, the unpaid balances were charged to Bad Debt Expense. Sales of defaulted merchandise were credited to Bad Debt Expense.

Sales:	
Cash sales	$126,000
Installment sales	265,000
Repossessed sales	230
Inventory, January 1, 1967:	
Merchandise inventory	58,060
Purchases, 1967:	
New merchandise	209,300
Inventories, physical, December 31, 1967:	
New merchandise	33,300
Repossessed inventory	180
Cash collections on installment contracts, 1967:	
Down payments	66,250
Subsequent installments	79,341
(Average 6 monthly installments on all contracts except on defaulted contracts)	

Five contracts totaling $1,060 were defaulted, in each case after 3 monthly installments were paid.

Interest should be recognized in the period earned.

Instructions: (1) Calculate the gross profit percentage for 1967.

(2) Prepare a schedule showing, by payment for the first 7 months: the cash sale price equivalent, the contract balance, the amount of interest earned, and the cash collected on a $1,060 installment sale contract.

(3) Calculate the net gain or loss on defaulted contracts during 1967.

(4) Calculate the realized gross profit for 1967.

(AICPA adapted)

Chapter 6

CONSIGNMENTS

Arrangements are frequently made for the physical transfer of goods by their owner to another party who is to act as sales agent, legal title to the goods being retained by the owner until their sale. Such a transfer is known as a *consignment.* The party who owns the goods in such a relationship is known as the *consignor;* the party who undertakes to sell the goods is known as the *consignee, factor,* or *commission merchant.*

NATURE OF THE CONSIGNMENT

From a legal point of view the transfer of goods represents a bailment, the consignee having possession of the goods for the purpose of sale as specified in the agreement between the consignor and the consignee. The consignor holds the consignee accountable for goods transferred to the latter's care until the goods are sold to a third party. Upon such sale, the consignor recognizes a transfer of title to the goods and also revenue from the sale. The consignee, on the other hand, cannot regard consigned goods as his own property; nor is there any liability to the consignor other than an accountability for consigned goods. The relationship between the consignor and the consignee is one of principal and agent, and the law of agency governs the determination of the rights and the obligations of the two parties.

The consignment has certain advantages over the direct sale of goods to retailers or merchants that have contributed to its widespread adoption. The consignor may prefer the consignment of goods to dealers over sale for the following reasons:

(1) The consignment may be the only way in which a wider marketing area can be secured by a producer, manufacturer, or distributor, particularly when (a) the goods are just being introduced and the demand for the product is unknown or uncertain; (b) sales in the past have proven unprofitable to the dealer; (c) the goods are costly, requiring a large investment on the part of the dealer if purchased; and (d) price fluctuation or product perishability is such that the dealer will agree to sell goods only if the risk of loss is borne by another. The dealer, incurring neither liability nor risk, is generally willing to accept goods on a consignment basis although he might be unwilling to purchase the goods. Consignments to achieve a wider marketing area are employed for many products including a wide variety of household appliances, books, magazines, newspapers, and novelty items.

(2) Certain risks are avoided by the consignor. Since the consignor has transferred goods to a party who is no more than a sales agent, he can recover unsold goods or the proceeds from sales from the consignee even though the latter becomes insolvent or bankrupt; general creditors of the consignee cannot claim any part of the consigned goods or their proceeds, which are regarded as a fund held in trust for the consignor.

(3) Selling specialists may be obtained by the consignor, particularly for the sale of grain, livestock, and produce. The compensation for such services is frequently a commission, which may be a percentage of sales price or a fixed amount for each unit of goods sold.

(4) The retail selling price of consigned goods can be controlled by the consignor who still owns the goods. This may be difficult or impossible when goods are actually sold to the dealer.

The consignee may favor the acquisition of goods by consignment instead of by purchase for the following reasons:

(1) The consignee is protected from the risk of failure to move the product or its sale at a loss. This factor may be particularly important in the case of new products or products that are being sold in a certain area for the first time.

(2) The risks of physical deterioration as well as of price fluctuation are avoided. These are important considerations where risks are particularly prevalent, as in the trade of livestock, fresh produce, and other perishable products.

(3) Working capital requirements are reduced, the cost of the consignment inventory being carried by the consignor.

OPERATION OF THE CONSIGNMENT

In the transfer of goods on consignment, a written contract should be prepared expressing the nature of the relationship and covering such matters as: credit terms to be granted by the consignee to customers; expenses of the consignee to be reimbursed by the consignor; commissions or profits to be allowed the consignee; care and handling of consignment inventories and proceeds from consignment sales; remittances and settlements by the consignee; and reports to be submitted by the consignee.

The rights and the duties of the consignee are established and defined by the laws of bailments and of agency. Most important among these are the following:

Consignee's rights:

(1) The consignee is entitled to reimbursement for necessary expenditures on consigned goods and also to compensation for sales. Necessary expenditures depend upon the nature of the goods consigned and ordinarily include cartage, freight, insurance, taxes, storage, handling charges, repairs under warranties, and such other charges as are by custom borne by the consignor. Expenditures that are authorized by special agreement or that are chargeable by law to the account of the

consignor, as well as amounts allowed as compensation on sales, represent liens by the consignee on consigned goods or on the sales proceeds. If the proceeds from consignment sales are insufficient to cover such charges, the consignee may claim such deficiency from the consignor.

(2) The consignee has the right to offer the customary warranties on goods that are sold, the consignor being bound by the terms of such warranties.

Consignee's duties:

(1) The consignee must protect the goods of his principal in a reasonable and prudent manner consistent with the nature of the goods and the circumstances of the consignment. If the consignee has been given special instructions, he must carry these out diligently to avoid liability.

(2) The consignee must sell the consigned goods at the price that is authorized or, in the absence of a set price, at a price that will best satisfy the interests of his principal. Ordinarily, as a result of trade custom or contract, the consignee is accountable to the consignor for consignment sales in full, regardless of whether sales are made for cash or on account. On the other hand, there are instances when the consignee may be authorized by agreement or permitted by the custom of the trade to sell goods on account, losses to be borne by the consignor and remittances to be made only after collections on account have been made. But the right of the consignee to sell goods on such a basis does not relieve him of the responsibility of exercising reasonable care in the sale of goods and in the collection of accounts. If these principles are observed, the consignee cannot be held liable for losses on collections. A consignee may agree to guarantee the accounts resulting from consignment sales. If the consignee agrees to absorb such losses when they would otherwise be charged against his principal, he is known as a *del credere agent*. He is normally allowed extra compensation for assuming the additional risk.

(3) The consignee must keep goods of the consignor apart from other merchandise. If physical separation is not practicable, the goods should be marked or records maintained that will make it possible to identify consigned goods. Consignment accounts receivable should not be combined with the consignee's own receivables. From a legal standpoint, cash proceeds from consignment sales should be kept separately until remittance is made. In practice, however, cash from consignment sales is frequently combined with the consignee's own cash in the absence of an agreement specifically calling for separation.

(4) The consignee must report regularly on the progress of consignment sales. The report that is rendered by the consignee is known as an *account sales*. This report lists the goods received on consignment, the goods sold, sales prices, expenses, the amount owed, and the amount remitted. Records must be kept by the consignee to support the information reported on the account sales.

ACCOUNTING FOR THE CONSIGNMENT

The factors that distinguish the consignment from a sale must be recognized in recording the transfer of goods and subsequent transactions. The accounting procedures generally followed by the consignee and the consignor are explained in the following pages.

Books of the consignee. The accounting procedures to be followed by the consignee depend upon whether (1) consignment transactions are to be summarized separately and profits on individual consignments are to be calculated separately from profits on regular sales, or (2) consignment transactions are to be merged with other transactions of the consignee, no attempt being made to distinguish between profits on consignment sales and profits on regular sales.

When profits on consignment sales are to be separately determined, the consignee maintains a consignment-in account for each consignment. This account is charged for all expenses that are to be absorbed by the consignor; it is credited for the full proceeds from consignment sales. The commission or profit on consignment sales is ultimately transferred from the consignment-in account to a separate revenue account, and the resulting balance in the consignment-in account reports the amount that is owed to the consignor in settlement.

When consignment transactions are to be combined with regular transactions, consignment sales are recorded with regular sales. The entries for consignment sales are accompanied by entries charging Purchases or Cost of Goods Sold and crediting the consignor for the amount to be paid for the goods sold. Expenses that are to be absorbed by the consignor are charged to the consignor's account. The resulting balance in the account with the consignor reports the amount owed in final settlement.

Books of the consignor. The accounting procedures to be followed by the consignor depend upon whether (1) consignment transactions are to be summarized separately and profits on individual consignments are to be calculated separately from profits on regular sales, or (2) consignment transactions are to be merged with other transactions of the consignor, no attempt being made to distinguish between profits on consignment sales and profits on regular sales.

If profits on consignment sales are to be separately determined, the consignor maintains a consignment-out account for each consignment. This account is charged for the cost of merchandise shipped to the consignee and for all other expenses related to the consignment; it is credited for sales made by the consignee. Profit or loss from consignment sales is ultimately transferred from the consignment-out account to the profit and loss account in which the net result from all activities is summarized.

If consignment transactions are to be combined with other transactions and a single operating profit or loss is to be calculated, revenues and expenses related to consignment sales are recorded in the accounts that summarize regular operations.

ACCOUNTING FOR THE COMPLETED CONSIGNMENT ILLUSTRATED

The entries that are required on the books of both consignee and consignor upon the transfer of goods, sale of goods, payment of expenses, and final settlement are illustrated in the example that follows.

On June 6, the Western Sales Co. ships 10 radio sets to R. Green, the sets to be sold at an advertised price of $85. The consignee is to be allowed a commission of 20% and is to be reimbursed for any cartage costs. On July 24, Green sends cash to the consignor in settlement of the account together with the following account sales:

ACCOUNT SALES No. 2843

July 24, 19 67

Sales for the account of Western Sales Co.

Address Riverside, California

Below please find account sales of 10 Radio Sets, Model AX 154

Sold By
R. GREEN
Seattle, Washington

Date	Explanation	Amount	
June 6-July 20	Sales:		
	10 Radio Sets @ $85		$850
	Charges:		
	Cartage-in	$ 25	
	Commission (20% of Sales)	170	195
	Balance		$655
	Remittance enclosed		655
	Balance due		—

The transactions and the entries to record the transactions on the books of the consignee and of the consignor are listed on pages 172 and 173. It is assumed that the consignee and the consignor do not maintain perpetual inventory records but use the periodic inventory system in arriving at cost of goods sold.

The entries to be made for a completed consignment on the books of the consignee and the consignor are explained in the following paragraphs. Explanations are identified with transactions in the example by number.

Transactions	Consignee's Books: If consignment profits are separately determined	Consignee's Books: If consignment profits are not separately determined
June 6 (1) Shipment of 10 radio sets on consignment, cost to consignor, $50 each.	(Memorandum) Received 10 radio sets from Western Sales Co. on consignment, to be sold at $85 each. Commission allowed is 20%. Reimbursement to be allowed for costs of cartage.	(Memorandum)
June 6 (2) Expenses of consignor identified with consignment. Freight to consignee...... $60		
June 6–July 20 (3) Expenses of consignee chargeable to account of consignor: Cartage-in.............. $25	Consignment In — Western Sales Co........... 25 Cash................ 25	Western Sales Co....... 25 Cash................ 2
June 6–July 20 (4) Sales of sets for cash, 10 at $85, or $850. (Charge by consignor is sales price, $850, less 20% commission, $170, or $680.)	Cash.................. 850 Consignment In — Western Sales Co..... 850	Cash.................. 850 Sales................ 85 Purchases.............. 680 Western Sales Co..... 68
July 20 (5) Charge by consignee for commissions on sales, 20% of $850, or $170.	Consignment In — Western Sales Co........... 170 Commissions on Consignment Sales....... 170	
July 20 (6) Remittance in settlement of account together with account sales rendered by consignee.	Consignment In — Western Sales Co........... 655 Cash................ 655	Western Sales Co....... 655 Cash................ 65

Consignee's records — if consignment profits are separately determined. ***(1) Transfer of goods to the consignee.*** The consignee records the receipt of goods on consignment by a memorandum in the journal or in a separate book maintained for such purposes. A supplementary record should be kept to show all of the detail with respect to goods received on consignment. Sometimes a memorandum entry is made in recording the receipt of goods. If the goods are billed at cost, at sales price, or at some arbitrary figure, such billed price may be used in making the entry. A memorandum entry in the example, using the sales price, would be:

Merchandise on Consignment........................	850	
Consignments Received — Western Sales Co...........		850

A subsidiary ledger may be maintained offering the detail to support the balance in the consignments received account. When the goods are sold and an account sales is rendered, the memorandum entry is reversed.

Consignor's Books

If consignment profits are separately determined			If consignment profits are not separately determined		
			(Memorandum)		
Consignment Out — R. Green	500		Shipped 10 radio sets to R. Green on consignment, sets to be sold at $85 each. Consignee is to be allowed commission of 20% and is to be reimbursed for costs of cartage.		
Merchandise Shipments on Consignment		500			
Consignment Out — R. Green	60				
Freight-Out *		60			
Cash	655		Cash	655	
Consignment Out — R. Green	195		Cartage	25	
Consignment Out — R. Green		850	Commissions	170	
			Sales		850
Consignment Out — R. Green	95				
Consignment Profit and Loss		95			

*It is assumed that the freight-out account was originally charged for freight on consignment sales as well as on other sales.

(2) Expenses of the consignor identified with the consignment. The consignee is not affected by transactions of the consignor.

(3) Expenses of the consignee identified with the consignment. The consignee records expenses that are to be absorbed by the consignor by charges to Consignment In and credits to appropriate asset or liability accounts. When an expense account on the consignee's books was originally charged with an expense that is to be absorbed entirely or in part by the consignor, Consignment In is charged and the expense account is credited for the amount chargeable to the consignor.

(4) Sales by the consignee. The consignee records consignment sales by charges to the appropriate asset account and credits to Consignment In.

(5) Commission or profit accruing to the consignee. The consignee records the commission or profit on consignment sales by a debit to

Consignment In and a credit to an appropriate revenue account. After recording the commission or profit, the credit balance in Consignment In shows the amount that is owed to the consignor in final settlement.

It should be observed that since no part of the consignee's expenses has been assigned to consignment commissions or profits, the consignment revenue account must be regarded as a gross profit balance. Such revenue, then, should be added to the gross profit from the consignee's own sales in preparing an income statement. In certain instances, the consignee may wish to develop net earnings balances for consignment operations and for regular operations. Such an income statement presentation will call for an allocation of operating expenses between the two classes of operations.

(6) Remittance and account sales rendered by the consignee. The consignee records remittances of cash to the consignor by debits to Consignment In and credits to Cash. If payment is made for the full amount owed, the entry to record the payment closes the consignment-in account.

In some instances a consignee is required to advance cash to the consignor upon receiving goods on consignment. Such advances are recognized as reductions in the amount owed to the consignor when settlement is made. Advances may be recorded by a debit to an asset account, Advances to Consignor, and a credit to Cash. When remittance is made by the consignee for the difference between the amount owed on consignment sales and the amount originally advanced, the account reporting the liability to the consignor is debited, the advances account is credited, and Cash is credited.

If goods are received on a consignment basis from a number of different parties, Consignments In may be set up as a controlling account, charges and credits being recorded in individual consignment accounts in a subsidiary ledger. When there are relatively few consignments, a separate account for each one may be carried in the general ledger.

Consignee's records — if consignment profits are not separately determined. ***(1) Transfer of goods to the consignee.*** The consignee records the receipt of goods on consignment by a memorandum entry.

(2) Expenses of the consignor identified with the consignment. The consignee is not affected by the transactions of the consignor.

(3) Expenses of the consignee identified with the consignment. The consignee debits the consignor's account for expenses chargeable to the consignor and credits appropriate asset or liability accounts or expense accounts if expenses were originally recorded in expense accounts.

(4) Sales by the consignee. The consignee records consignment sales like regular sales. Each sales entry is accompanied by an entry to record the charge made by the consignor for goods sold: Purchases or Cost of Goods Sold is debited and the consignor's account is credited.

(5) Commission or profit accruing to the consignee. The consignee makes no entry for commission or profit on consignment sales. The earnings on consignment sales will be reflected in the consignee's gross profit as a result of the entries made above.

(6) Remittance and account sales rendered by the consignee. The consignee records payments to the consignor by charges to the consignor's account and credits to Cash.

Consignor's records — if consignment profits are separately determined. ***(1) Transfer of goods to the consignee.*** The consignor records the transfer of goods to the consignee by a debit to Consignment Out and a credit to Merchandise Shipments on Consignment or to an inventory account when perpetual inventory balances are maintained. Merchandise Shipments on Consignment would be treated as a subtraction item from the sum of the beginning inventory and purchases in determining the cost of goods available for regular sales. Transfers are recorded at cost even though selling or other arbitrary prices are assigned to the goods in statements sent to the consignee.

(2) Expenses of the consignor identified with the consignment. The consignor records expenses that are related to the consignment by debits to Consignment Out and credits to Cash or to liability accounts. When an expense account was originally charged for an expense that is related to the consignment, Consignment Out is charged and the expense account is credited for the amount identified with the consignment.

(3), (4), (5) Expenses of the consignee identified with the consignment— sales by the consignee — commission charge by the consignee. The consignor makes no entries for transactions of the consignee until he receives a statement from the consignee.

(6) Remittance and account sales rendered by the consignee. When the consignor receives an account sales, Cash is debited for the cash remittance, Consignment Out is debited for the total expenses charged to the consignor's account by the consignee, and Consignment Out is credited for the gross sales reported by the consignee. It would be possible to debit Cash and credit Consignment Out for the net proceeds from consignment sales. If this procedure were followed, the entry for transaction (6) in the example would be:

Cash..	655	
Consignment Out — R. Green.....................		655

The balance in the consignment-out account would be the same in either case.

When the consignor requires cash advances on consignment shipments, the receipt of cash representing an advance may be recorded by a debit to Cash and a credit to a liability account, Advances from Consignee. The receipt of cash in settlement of the consignment, then, will call for debits to Cash and to the advances account accompanied by entries to the consignment-out account recognizing revenues and expenses reported by the consignee.

When all of the consigned goods have been sold, the consignment account shows the net result from consignment transactions: a credit balance indicates that consignment revenue has exceeded consignment expenses, resulting in a profit; a debit balance indicates that expenses have exceeded revenue, resulting in a loss. The balance in the consignment account may now be transferred to a consignment profit and loss account. The balance of the latter account is subsequently closed into the general profit and loss account in which other operations of the business are summarized. The balance in the profit and loss account reporting the profit or loss from regular as well as consignment operations is ultimately transferred to capital.

If consignments are numerous, Consignments Out may be set up as a controlling account and data relating to each consignment may be recorded in an individual account in a subsidiary ledger. If consignments are relatively few, a separate account for each consignment may be carried in the general ledger.

Consignor's records — if consignment profits are not separately determined. ***(1) Transfer of goods to the consignee.*** When the consignor does not maintain perpetual inventory records, the transfer of goods to the consignee is recorded by a memorandum entry in the journal or in a separate book maintained for this purpose. A supplementary record should be kept that shows all of the detail with respect to goods on consignment. Sometimes a memorandum entry is made in recording shipments. Such an entry for transaction (1) in the example would be:

Merchandise on Consignment — R. Green	500	
Consignment Transfers		500

A subsidiary record would provide the detail to support the balance in the account Merchandise on Consignment. When the consigned goods are sold, the memorandum entry is reversed.

If perpetual inventory records are maintained, transfer of goods would require an entry as follows:

Merchandise on Consignment — R. Green	500	
Merchandise Inventory (or Finished Goods)..........		500

(2) Expenses of the consignor identified with the consignment. The usual accounts are charged for consignment expenses, no attempt being made to distinguish between consignment expenses and expenses related to regular sales.

(3),(4),(5) Expenses of the consignee identified with the consignment — sales by the consignee — commission charge by the consignee. The consignor makes no entries for transactions completed by the consignee until he receives a statement from the consignee.

(6) Remittance and account sales rendered by the consignee. When the consignor receives an account sales, Cash is debited for the cash accompanying the statement, expense accounts are debited for expenses charged to the consignor's account by the consignee, and Sales is credited for the gross sales reported by the consignee. In the absence of perpetual inventories, an entry is made for the ending inventories and this establishes cost of goods sold for the period. If perpetual inventories are employed, the cost of goods sold balance on the books relating to regular sales must be increased by the cost of goods sold relating to consignment sales by the following entry:

Cost of Goods Sold	500	
Merchandise on Consignment — R. Green		500

With sales, cost of goods sold, and expenses reflecting combined consignment and regular operations, further adjustments are made in the usual manner. Nominal accounts may then be closed into the profit and loss account, and the profit or loss from combined operations is ultimately transferred to capital.

ACCOUNTING FOR AN UNCOMPLETED CONSIGNMENT

In the illustration on pages 172 and 173, the profit from consignment sales was not recognized by consignee or consignor until all the consigned goods were sold and full remittance was made. If all the consigned goods are not sold at the time the parties to a consignment prepare financial statements, it becomes necessary to compute the profit realized on the part that was sold. The nature of the problems that arise and the entries that are made on the books of the consignee and the consignor for an uncompleted consignment are illustrated in the following example. Assume the consignment of goods as in the previous example but assume that both consignee and consignor prepare financial statements on June 30. On this date 6 sets have been sold, the consignee submitting the following account sales:

ACCOUNT SALES No. 2671

June 30, 19 67

Sales for the account of Western Sales Co.

Address Riverside, California

Below please find account sales of 6 Radio Sets, Model AX 154

Sold By

R. GREEN

Seattle, Washington

Date	Explanation	Amount	
June 6-June 30	Sales:		
	6 Sets @ $85		$510
	On Hand:		
	4 Sets		
	Charges:		
	Cartage-in	$ 25	
	Commission (20% of Sales)	102	127
	Balance		$383
	Remittance enclosed		383
	Balance due		—

The entries to record the transactions on the books of the consignee and the consignor are given on pages 180 and 181. The entries to be made for an uncompleted consignment on the books of the consignee and the consignor are explained in the following paragraphs.

Consignee's records — if consignment profits are separately determined. The consignee should recognize the earnings on consignment sales before preparing financial statements at the end of each period by charging Consignment In and crediting revenue for the commissions or profit on consignment sales to date. A credit balance in the consignment-in account after this entry indicates that proceeds from consignment sales exceeded the charges to the consignor, resulting in an obligation to the consignor; a credit balance is reported on the balance sheet as a current payable. A debit balance in the consignment-in account would indicate that proceeds from consignment sales were less than the charges to the consignor. The consignee may hold the consignor for reimbursement of this amount if it is not covered by subsequent sales. A debit balance in the consignment-in account would be reported on the balance sheet as a current receivable.

Consignee's records — if consignment profits are not separately determined. No entry is necessary at the end of the period if entries are made at the time consigned goods are sold recognizing purchases or cost of goods sold and the obligation to the consignor. A credit balance in the consignor's account at the end of the period is reported on the balance sheet as a current payable; a debit balance would be reported as a current receivable.

Consignor's records — if consignment profits are separately determined. An account sales is required by the consignor as of the close of his own fiscal period so that he may record the profit or loss on sales of consigned goods to date. The data disclosed by the account sales are recorded in the usual manner. The consignment-out account then shows expenses identified with the consignment and revenue from consignment sales. The profit on consignment sales to date must now be removed from the consignment-out account; this will leave the account with a debit balance representing the charges identified with the goods not yet sold. The balance in the consignment-out account is reported on the balance sheet as a part of the company's inventories.

In the example, the consignment-out account shows charges of $687 consisting of the cost of the consigned goods, $500, freight to the consignee, $60, cartage-in, $25, and commissions, $102. Those charges relating to consigned goods sold should be applied against current revenue; those charges relating to consigned goods still on hand are properly deferred so that they can be assigned to revenue of subsequent periods. Freight and cartage are applicable to all of the goods shipped and hence are assigned to current and future revenues in the same manner as the original cost of consigned goods; the commission charge is limited to consignment sales of the current period and hence is assigned in total to current revenues. The charges to current revenue and to revenue of subsequent periods are summarized below.

	Total Charges	Charges Identified With Consignment Sales (6 sets)	Charges Identified With Consignment Inventory (4 sets)
Charges by consignor:			
Cost of consigned merchandise	$500	$300	$200
Freight to consignee	60	36	24
Charges by consignee:			
Cartage-in	25	15	10
Commissions	102	102	
Totals	$687	$453	$234

Transactions	Consignee's Books: If consignment profits are separately determined			Consignee's Books: If consignment profits are not separately determined		
June 6 Shipment of 10 radio sets on consignment, cost to consignor, $50 each.	(Memorandum)			(Memorandum)		
June 6 Expenses of consignor identified with consignment: Freight to consignee...... $60						
June 6–June 30 Expenses of consignee chargeable to account of consignor: Cartage-in.............. $25	Consignment In — Western Sales Co........... Cash................	25	 25	Western Sales Co....... Cash................	25	 25
June 6–30 Sales of sets for cash, 6 at $85, or $510. (Charge by consignor is sales price, $510, less 20% commission, $102, or $408.)	Cash.................. Consignment In — Western Sales Co.....	510	 510	Cash.................. Sales............... Purchases............. Western Sales Co.....	510 408	 510 408
June 30 Charge by consignee for commissions on sales, 20% of $510, or $102.	Consignment In — Western Sales Co........... Commissions on Consignment Sales.......	102	 102			
June 30 Remittance for balance owed together with account sales rendered by consignee.	Consignment In — Western Sales Co........... Cash................	383	 383	Western Sales Co....... Cash................	383	 383

The tabulation at the bottom of page 179 shows charges of $453 relating to consignment sales. The sales figure of $510 recorded by the consignor as a credit to Consignment Out then represents a recovery of consignment costs of $453 and a profit of $57. The entry to transfer the profit of $57 from the consignment-out account to a consignment profit and loss account increases the debit balance in Consignment Out from $177 to $234. Consignment Out then reports the charges relating to unsold goods on consignment, and this balance is carried into the next period.

The consignment-out account with R. Green after adjustment at the end of the fiscal period appears as shown at the bottom of the opposite page.

Consignor's Books

If consignment profits are separately determined			If consignment profits are not separately determined		
Consignment Out — R. Green	500		(Memorandum)		
Merchandise Shipments on Consignment		500			
Consignment Out — R. Green	60				
Freight-Out		60			
Cash	383		Cash	383	
Consignment Out — R. Green	127		Cartage	15	
Consignment Out — R. Green		510	Commissions	102	
			Merchandise on Consignment	10	
Consignment Out — R. Green	57		Sales		510
Consignment Profit and Loss		57			
			Merchandise on Consignment	224	
			Profit and Loss		200
			Freight-Out		24

Consignment Out — R. Green

Date				Date			
June 6	Shipped 10 radio sets, cost $50 each		500	June 30	Sales, 6 sets		510
6	Freight		60	30	Balance — cost assigned to inventory of 4 sets:		
June 30	Charges by consignee:				Cost, 4 sets at $50	200	
	Cartage-in	25			Additional charges:		
	Commissions	102	127		Incurred by consignor: freight (4/10 of $60)	24	
30	Profit on sale of 6 sets to Consignment Profit and Loss		57		Incurred by consignee: cartage-in (4/10 of $25)	10	234
			744				744
July 1	Balance — cost assigned to 4 sets		234				

If the consignor does not record the charges to his account by the consignee, simply crediting the consignment account for the net proceeds from consignment sales, the entry on June 30 would be:

Cash	383	
Consignment Out — R. Green		383

The balance in the consignment-out account would be the same as when charges by the consignee and gross sales are reported in the account. The adjustment for profit of $57, then, would be the same as in the previous instances.

The balance in the consignment-out account is reported on the balance sheet as a separate inventory item that is added to the merchandise on hand, as follows:

Inventories:		
Merchandise on hand	$10,000	
Merchandise on consignment	234	$10,234

If preferred, the original cost of the consigned goods, $200, and the additional consignment charges that are deferred, $34, could be reported separately.

During the next period, consignment shipments, expenses, and sales are recorded in the consignment-out account in the usual manner. At the end of the period this account is adjusted once more in recognizing the profit on consignment sales of the period and the charges that are to be related to the goods still on consignment.

There may be instances in which the consignee, in rendering a statement to the consignor, fails to remit the full amount owed. When this is the case, the consignor debits Accounts Receivable instead of Cash. For example, if Green, in the example on page 181, reports the sale of 6 sets but remits only $150, an entry would be made as follows:

Cash	150	
Accounts Receivable — R. Green	233	
Consignment Out — R. Green	127	
Consignment Out — R. Green		510

The receipt of cash at a later date would be recorded by a charge to Cash and a credit to Accounts Receivable — R. Green.

Consignor's records — if consignment profits are not separately determined. When consignment profits are not separately determined by the consignor, the charges made by the consignee against the proceeds from consignment sales are recognized on the books of the consignor by debits to appropriate expense accounts. When the consigned goods have not all been sold at the end of a fiscal period, however, those expenses that are identified with the unsold goods on consignment should be deferred. Data on the account sales are analyzed and a compound entry is made as follows: Cash is debited for the cash remitted by the consignee or Accounts Receivable is debited for the amount due from the consignee; expense accounts are debited for charges made by the consignee on goods that have been sold; Merchandise on Consignment is debited for the consignee's charges on goods not yet sold; and Sales is credited for the total consignment sales.

Those charges incurred by the consignor that relate to unsold goods on consignment must also be set up as consignment inventory at the end of the period. In the absence of perpetual inventories, Merchandise on Consignment is charged for the sum of the original cost of merchandise and the other charges relating to the unsold goods; the profit and loss account is credited for the original cost of these goods, and the consignor's expense accounts are credited for the portion of the expenses relating to this inventory. If perpetual inventory records are maintained, the transfer of goods to the consignee would have been recorded originally by a debit to Merchandise on Consignment and a credit to the inventory account. Instead of recording the amount of the goods in the hands of the consignee at the end of the period, then, it would be necessary to reduce the consignment inventory balance and charge Cost of Goods Sold for the goods sold by the consignee. This entry would be accompanied by an entry to defer expenses reported on the consignor's books relating to the portion of goods still unsold.

Merchandise on Consignment, after adjustments on the books of the consignor, includes the original cost of the goods increased by the deferred expenses of both consignee and consignor relating to the unsold goods. In the example, the $234 balance for merchandise on consignment consists of: original cost of goods, $200; deferred expenses of the consignee, $10; and deferred expenses of the consignor, $24.

CONSIGNMENT RESHIPMENTS

It should be observed in the previous examples that freight and cartage charges, whether incurred by consignor or consignee, were costs of bringing goods to the point of the sale and hence were properly viewed as acquisition costs and assignable to the inventory. When consigned goods are returned to a consignor, expenditures identified with the original shipment of goods as well as with their return should be recognized as charges to current revenue; the reshipment of goods to a consignee, then, calls for charges that are no more than those which would normally apply to such transfer. Expenditures for the repair of defective units returned should likewise be regarded as charges to current revenue, with subsequent transfer of such units to a consignee calling for charges that are no more than normal costs. Shipping charges to customers that are necessary in completing sales, when paid by the consignor or when chargeable to his account by a consignee, require recognition as expenses of the period.

ALTERNATIVE ACCOUNTING PROCEDURES

While this chapter has dealt with the standard procedures that are employed in the consignment relationship, other methods of accounting may be employed as long as the accounts properly report the personal and legal relationships of the parties. Variations from standard procedures are often introduced to meet special requirements or to provide particular information concerning consignment activities for reporting purposes.

Alternative procedures — consignee's records. For example, assume that the consignee desires to maintain consignment profit and loss detail but does not want to combine this information with data summarizing regular profit and loss activities for reporting purposes. The procedure for the consignee outlined at the extreme right of pages 172 and 180 can be followed, but consignment sales, consignment purchases, and consignment expenses would be summarized in separate accounts. This detail can then be reported in a separate section of the income statement or it can be summarized in a supporting schedule with only the net income from consignment sales reported on the income statement.

Alternative procedures — consignor's records. Similarly, the consignor, while wishing to maintain consignment profit and loss detail, may wish to distinguish between these data and other profit and loss data on the income statement. When this is the case, the procedure for the consignor illustrated at the extreme right of pages 173 and 181 can be followed, but separate accounts would be maintained for consignment sales, consignment cost of sales, and consignment expenses. Such procedure permits full information concerning both consignment and regular operations. Consignment profit and loss data may be reported separately on the income statement, or these data may be summarized on a supporting schedule with only the net results from consignment operations reported on the income statement.

QUESTIONS

1. Distinguish between a sale and a consignment.

2. "A consignment is regarded as a bailment." "The relationship of consignor and consignee is one of principal and agent." Explain.

3. What are the duties of the consignee?

4. What are the advantages of a consignment over a sale from the point of view of (a) the consignor and (b) the consignee?

5. Explain two methods for recording consignment activities on the books of the consignee. What will determine the procedure that is to be used?

6. Explain two methods for recording consignment activities on the books of the consignor. What will determine the procedure to be used?

7. What entries are made on the books of the consignee and the consignor for each transaction listed below, assuming that each party summarizes consignment transactions separately and calculates consignment profit apart from profit on other sales?

(a) Goods are transferred by the consignor to the consignee.
(b) The consignor pays expenses relating to the consignment.
(c) The consignee pays expenses relating to the consignment, but he is to be reimbursed for such disbursements by the consignor.
(d) The consignee pays expenses relating to the consignment that are not reimbursable.
(e) The consignee sells consigned merchandise on account.
(f) The consignee collects consignment accounts receivable.
(g) The consignee makes settlement with the consignor.

8. What entry would be made on the books of the consignee and the consignor for each transaction listed in Question 7, assuming that each party combines consignment transactions with other transactions and calculates a single profit for both consignment and regular sales?

9. State for each account below: (a) whether it would appear on the books of the consignee or the books of the consignor, and (b) how it would be reported on the financial statements that are prepared at the end of the fiscal period.

(1) Consignment In (credit balance).
(2) Consignment In (debit balance).
(3) Consignment Out (debit balance).
(4) Commissions on Consignments (credit balance).
(5) Profit on Consignment Sales.
(6) Merchandise on Consignment.
(7) Consignment Expenses Deferred.
(8) Merchandise Shipments to Consignees.

10. The Burkhart Co. is advised by a consignee that sales of consigned merchandise have been made on account and that reimbursement will follow in a later period. What treatment will this require on the books of the consignor?

11. Justify the practice of showing merchandise on consignment on the consignor's balance sheet at a figure above the original invoice cost of such goods.

12. The Burnside Co. transfers merchandise to a number of dealers on a consignment basis. At the end of each period, goods on consignment are reported on the balance sheet at cost, all consignment expenses of the period being regarded as chargeable to current revenue. Would you approve such statements?

13. A consignee returns a shipment of goods that he is unable to sell. How would you recommend that the consignor treat the original charges in transferring goods to the consignee and the subsequent charges when goods are returned?

14. The Paulson Co. transfers merchandise on a consignment basis and records such transfers in the same manner as sales on account. (a) Do you object to this procedure? (b) What adjustments are required at the end of the period for consigned goods still in the hands of the consignee under these circumstances?

15. The Garrett Company makes the following entry upon shipping merchandise on a consignment basis:

Accounts Receivable — Consignees....................	xxx	
Merchandise..................................		xxx
Deferred Gross Profit on Consignment Sales...........		xxx

Do you object to this procedure? What entries would you assume are made during the period and at the end of the period?

EXERCISES

1. In December, the Whitworth Publishing Company ships 20 sets of books to a book dealer on consignment. The consignor maintains a cost accounting system and perpetual inventories; the cost of manufacturing each set is $30. At the end of December the dealer reports the sale of 6 sets at $49.75 each and remits sales proceeds less 20% representing commissions and $15 for freight paid by the consignee on the receipt of the sets. What are the entries on the books of the consignor, assuming that profits from consignments are not recorded separately on the consignor's books?

2. A. M. Anderson submits the following information on an account sales. The cost of each unit to the consignor is $60. Consignee and consignor take physical inventories at year-end in calculating cost of goods sold. (a) Give the entries that will appear on the books of the consignee and the consignor, assuming that each party calculates consignment profits separately. (b) Give the entries on each party's books, assuming that consignment profits are not calculated separately.

Account Sales, Dec. 31, 1967 — Sales by A. M. Anderson for the account of Warner and Sloan

Date	Explanation	Amount	
Dec. 5-31	Sales: 4 Electric Stoves @ $110		$440
	On hand: 6 Electric Stoves		
	Freight in	$ 61	
	Commission (25% of Sales)	110	171
	Remittance enclosed		$269

3. A consignment-out account on the books of Parks, Inc., appears below. What entry would be made on November 30 to adjust the account?

Consignment Out — T. A. Fuller

Nov. 15	10 radio sets		400	Nov. 30	Sales, 4 sets	340
15	Cartage out		20		(Remittance by consignee, $340, less charges, $123)	
30	Charges by consignee:					
	Freight in	40				
	Cartage in	15				
	Commissions	68	123			

4. Assume that Parks, Inc., in Exercise 3 does not maintain consignment-out accounts but merges consignment transactions with other transactions on its books. Assume, further, that the consignor maintains perpetual inventory records. What entries would be made on the consignor's books to record the consignment transactions?

5. On May 1 the Select Sales Products Co. ships 5 appliances to the Jones Hardware Co. on consignment. Each unit is to be sold at $250, payable $50 in the month of purchase and $10 per month thereafter. The consignee is to be entitled to 20% of all amounts collected on consignment sales. Jones Hardware sells 3 appliances in May and 1 in June. Regular monthly collections are made by the consignee, and appropriate cash remittances are made to the consignor at the end of each month. The cost of the appliances shipped by the consignor was $155 per unit. The consignor paid shipping costs to the consignee totaling $50. The consignor recognizes profits in the period in which the consignment sales are made. Assuming that both consignee and consignor report consignment profits separately, give the entries that would be made on each party's books to record the above transactions for the months of May and June, including any adjustments that would be made at the end of June in preparing semiannual financial statements.

PROBLEMS

6-1. The Wilson Publishing Company ships 4-volume sets of *Management Encyclopaedia* to book dealers on consignment. The sets are to be sold at an advertised price of $49.50. The estimated cost per set is $25. Consignees are allowed a commission of 30% of the sales price and are to be reimbursed for cartage relating to consigned goods.

On December 8, 100 sets were sent to the Culver Book Store on consignment. The consignor estimated that packing charges of $85 were related to the books shipped. The shipment cost paid by the consignor was $200. The consignee paid $30 for cartage on sets received. Sixty sets were sold in December for cash. Remittance of the amount owed to the consignor was made on December 31. Both consignee and consignor take physical inventories and adjust and close their books at year-end.

Instructions: (1) Prepare an account sales to be submitted by the consignee at the end of December.

(2) Give the journal entries for December on the books of the consignee, assuming that (a) consignment profits are calculated separately and (b) consignment profits are not calculated separately.

(3) Give the journal entries for December on the books of the consignor, assuming that (a) profits from consignments are calculated separately, and (b) profits are not calculated separately.

6-2. Television, Inc., agrees to transfer television sets to Brooks Bros. on a consignment basis. The consignee is to sell sets at $398 and is to receive a 25% commission on sales price. The consignor agrees to reimburse the consignee for all expenses related to the consignment. The agreement also calls for an advance payment of $100 per set by the consignee; the $100 advance is to be deducted as settlement is made for each set sold. The consignee is to provide an account sales quarterly and is to make cash remittance for the amount owed at that time.

Transactions for the period October 1–December 31, 1967, are listed below.

(a) The consignor shipped 10 sets to the consignee. The consignor maintains a cost accounting system and perpetual inventories; records show a cost for each set of $210.

(b) The consignor paid freight charges on the shipment, $165.

(c) The consignee made advance payments on the sets received.

(d) The consignee sold 6 sets for cash; expenses of delivery and installation chargeable to the consignor were $75.

(e) The consignee returned 2 sets representing a model that could not be sold and paid freight charges of $40 on the return.

(f) The consignee prepared an account sales and made cash settlement on December 31.

Instructions: (1) Prepare the account sales to be submitted by the consignee.

(2) Give the entries that would be made by the consignee assuming (a) con-

signment profits are calculated separately and (b) consignment profits are not calculated separately.

(3) Give the entries that would be made by the consignor assuming (a) consignment profits are calculated separately and (b) consignment profits are not calculated separately.

6-3. The Duncan Corporation manufactures refrigerators and maintains a cost accounting system and perpetual inventory records. On July 3, 1967, 10 refrigerators were sent to the Victory Electric Store on consignment. Account sales, together with remittances, at the end of July and August were as follows:

Account Sales, July 31, 1967 — Sales by Victory Electric Store for the account of Duncan Corporation

Date	Explanation	Amount	
July 7-31	Sold: 4 Refrigerators @ $280		$1,120
	On hand: 6 Refrigerators		
	Freight	$150	
	Cartage in	60	210
	Balance		$ 910
	Remittance enclosed		60
	Balance due		$ 850

Account Sales, August 31, 1967 — Sales by Victory Electric Store for the account of Duncan Corporation

Date	Explanation	Amount
July 31	Balance Due	$ 850
Aug. 1-31	Sold: 3 Refrigerators @ $280	840
	On hand: 3 Refrigerators	
	Freight	
	Cartage in	
	Balance	$1,690
	Remittance enclosed	330
	Balance due	$1,360

The consignee was allowed to set the sales price but was charged $280 for each refrigerator sold. The consignee was to be reimbursed for freight and transportation charges. The consignor's cost to manufacture each unit was $196.

Sales on account by the Victory Electric Store were as follows:

July 7–July 31	4 refrigerators at $400	$1,600
Aug. 1–Aug. 31	3 refrigerators at $370	1,110

Collections on account were as follows:

July	$750
August	600

Both consignor and consignee prepare financial statements at the end of each month.

Instructions: (1) Give the journal entries required on the books of the consignee for July and August, assuming that consignment sales are merged with regular sales.

(2) Give the journal entries required on the books of the consignor for July and August assuming that records show separately the profit on consignments.

6-4. The Aristocrat Sales Co. ships electric shavers to Ray E. Jensen on consignment. The cost of shavers to the consignor is $10.80. Sales are to be made at an advertised price of $24. The consignee is allowed a commission of 25% of sales plus an allowance for advertising not to exceed $100. The following transactions take place in December:

100 shavers were shipped to Jensen.
The Aristocrat Sales Co. paid shipment charges on goods sent to consignee, $50.
Jensen paid for advertising consigned goods, $150.
Jensen accepted a sight draft drawn by Aristocrat Sales Co., $400.
Jensen sold 80 shavers during the month at the advertised price.
Jensen made remittance at the end of the month for the balance owed to date.

Both consignor and consignee prepare financial statements at the end of December.

Instructions: (1) Prepare an account sales to be submitted by the consignee at the end of December.

(2) Give the journal entries on the books of the consignee, assuming that (a) consignment profits are calculated separately and (b) consignment profits are not calculated separately.

(3) Give the journal entries on the books of the consignor, assuming that (a) consignment profits are calculated separately and (b) consignment profits are not calculated separately. Assume that the consignor does not maintain perpetual inventory records but takes year-end physical inventories.

6-5. On June 1, Lee Sales Co. shipped 25 radio sets to A. M. Fields on consignment, sets to be sold at an advertised price of $200. The cost of each set to the consignor was $100. The cost of shipment paid by the consignor was $75. The consignor agreed to absorb consignee's expenditures for cartage and also to allow the consignee $10 for delivery and installation of each set. Commission is to be 25% of sales price. On

June 30, Fields submitted a summary of consignment sales showing the following:

Sets received			25
Sets sold		8	
Sets returned to consignor (defective)		2	10
Sets on hand			15
June 3–30	Sales, 8 sets at $200		$1,600
	Charges:		
	Cartage in	$ 50	
	Deliveries and installation expense	80	
	Commissions, 25% of sales	400	530
			$1,070
	Remittance enclosed		250
	Balance owed (collections from customers not yet made)		$ 820

Instructions: Give all of the entries to record the foregoing, as well as any adjustments that are required at the end of the period, on (1) the consignee's books and (2) the consignor's books. Assume that consignment profits are separately determined by both parties; neither party maintains perpetual inventories.

6-6. In examining the accounts of the Mack Sales Co., the auditor determined that consignments of Product A had been recorded as sales during the fiscal period. As consignment shipments were made, receivable accounts with consignees were charged and Sales was credited. At that time, Cost of Goods Sold was charged and Inventories was credited for the cost of the merchandise shipped. Receivable accounts were credited when cash was received from consignees; costs incurred by the consignees but chargeable to the consignor were recognized when remittances were recorded. The trial balance of the Mack Sales Co. on December 31, 1967, follows:

Cash	18,000	
Receivables — Customers	24,000	
Receivables — Consignees	18,200	
Inventories	46,500	
Plant and Equipment (net)	50,000	
Accounts Payable		25,000
Capital Stock, $1 par		50,000
Retained Earnings, January 1, 1967		47,500
Sales		236,000
Cost of Goods Sold	165,000	
Operating Expenses	36,800	
	358,500	358,500

An analysis of account sales as of this date revealed that 2,000 units of Product A were still unsold and in the hands of consignees. This product was charged to consignees at $5 per unit but had a cost of $3.25. Consignees had incurred expenses of $400 chargeable to the consignor that had not been recognized; of this total $125 represents expenses on consigned goods not yet sold. In addition, expenses of $260 on the consignor's books were related to consignment inventories. Because of a loss carryover from 1966, the company will not pay any income taxes for 1967.

Instructions: (1) Give the journal entries that are required on the books of the Mack Sales Co. to bring the accounts up to date and to close the accounts on December 31.

(2) Prepare a balance sheet and an income statement for the year ended December 31, 1967.

6-7. The Morrison Co. records shipments to consignees A, B, and C as sales on account. When the sale is recorded, Cost of Goods Sold is charged and Inventories is credited for the cost of goods shipped to consignees. Expenses incurred by consignees and to be absorbed by the consignor are recognized when remittances are made by the consignees. The trial balance of the Morrison Co. on December 31, 1967, follows:

Cash	$ 57,750	
Accounts Receivable	50,000	
Inventories	56,000	
Plant and Equipment	85,000	
Accounts Payable		$ 12,500
Capital Stock, $100 par		100,000
Retained Earnings, January 1, 1967		28,500
Sales		365,000
Cost of Goods Sold	213,250	
Operating Expenses	44,000	
	$506,000	$506,000

The product sold by the corporation is charged to consignees at $30 but costs only $16 per unit. The consignee sets the retail price. Account sales and accompanying remittances from A, B, and C on December 31 are reported below. Remittances and supplementary data have not yet been recorded.

	A	B	C
Units received	15	40	5
Units sold	10	25	1
Units returned (now in transit)	5	0	4
Units on hand	0	15	0
Sales	$300	$750	$ 30
Cartage in	20	80	18
Cost of returning sets to consignor	25		30
Remittance enclosed	$255	$670	
Balance due from consignor			$ 18

Expenses of $85 on the consignor's books are estimated to be related to the 15 units in the hands of B. Income taxes are estimated at $45,000.

Instructions: (1) Give the journal entries that are required on the books of the Morrison Co. to bring the accounts up to date and to close the accounts on December 31.

(2) Prepare a balance sheet and an income statement for the year ended December 31, 1967.

6-8. You are examining the December 31, 1967, financial statements of the Kelly Sales Company, a new client. The company was established on January 1, 1966, and is a distributor of air conditioning units. The company's income statements for 1966 and 1967 were presented to you as follows:

Kelly Sales Company

Statements of Income and Expense

For the Years Ended December 31, 1967 and 1966

	1967	1966
Sales	$1,287,500	$1,075,000
Cost of sales	669,500	559,000
Gross profit	$ 618,000	$ 516,000
Selling and administrative expense	403,500	330,000
Net income before income taxes	$ 214,500	$ 186,000
Provision for income taxes @ 50%	107,250	93,000
Net income	$ 107,250	$ 93,000

Your examination disclosed the following:

(1) Some sales were made on open account; other sales were made through dealers to whom units were shipped on a consignment basis. Both sales methods were in effect in 1966 and 1967. In both years, however, the company treated all shipments as outright sales.

(2) The sales price and cost of the units were the same in 1966 and 1967. Each unit had a cost of $130 and was uniformly invoiced at $250 to open account customers and to consignees.

(3) During 1967 the amount of cash received from consignees in payment for units sold by them was $706,500. Consignees remit for the units as soon as they are sold. Confirmations received from consignees showed that they had a total of 23 unsold units on hand at December 31, 1967. Consignees were unable to confirm the unsold units on hand at December 31, 1966.

(4) The cost of sales for 1967 was determined by the client as follows:

		Units	
Inventory on hand in warehouse, December 31, 1966		1,510	
Purchases		4,454	
Available for sale		5,964	
Inventory on hand in warehouse, December 31, 1967		814	
Shipments to: open account customers	3,008		
consignee customers	2,142	5,150 @ $130 =	$669,500

Instructions: (1) Compute the total amount of the Kelly Sales Company's inventory at:

(a) December 31, 1967.
(b) December 31, 1966.

(2) Prepare the auditor's work sheet journal entries to correct the financial statements for the year ended December 31, 1966.

(3) Prepare the formal adjusting journal entries to correct the accounts at December 31, 1967. (The books have not been closed. Do not prepare the closing journal entries.)

(AICPA adapted)

6-9. The Stacy Company is closing its books as of December 31, 1967. In making an investigation of the accounts of the company, you discover the following facts:

(1) During November and December, the company shipped out stoves to two dealers, A and B, on a consignment basis. The consignment agreements provided that the stoves were to be sold by the consignee at a list price of $180 each. The consignee was to be allowed a 25% commission on each sale and was to be reimbursed for all expenses paid in connection with the shipment of the stoves to him. Sales on account are at the risk of the consignee.

(2) At the time of each shipment, the company debited a trade account receivable and credited Sales $120 for each stove, this being the usual sale price received by the company, on the basis of which a gross profit of 20% on cost is realized.

(3) All cash received from these two consignees was credited to the trade accounts receivable accounts. No other entries have been made in these accounts receivable.

(4) Information as to all of the transactions with the consignees is as follows:
- (a) Stoves shipped out: to A — 100, to B — 40.
- (b) Stoves unsold by consignees as of 12/31/67: A — 35, B — 25.
- (c) Crating and shipping cost to company — $84.
- (d) Freight paid by consignees: A — $130, B — $100.
- (e) Cash advanced by A at date of receipt of the first 80 stoves — $4,000. Cash subsequently remitted by A — $5,395.
- (f) Cash remitted by B — $575.

Instructions: Prepare any adjusting entries that should be made by the Stacy Company and list each account affected by these transactions and adjustments, showing the corrected balances after adjustment. (Assume that (1) inventories are maintained on a perpetual basis, and (2) consignment profits are not separately determined.)

(AICPA adapted)

6-10. On June 1, 1967, the Adams Corporation consigned 100 refrigerators to the Burke Company, to be sold as follows:

Cash price: $180 less 5% discount.

Time-payment plan: $180 net, ⅓ in cash on delivery, the balance in 24 monthly payments of $5. All credit sales are subject to the approval of the Adams Corporation as to credit risk. Refrigerators will be repossessed when time-payment contracts are 2 months in default and will be returned to the manufacturer for reconditioning.

The manufacturing cost of each refrigerator was $60, and $400 freight was prepaid on the shipment.

The Burke Company paid $200 truckage and deposited with the consignor $7,500 cash, thus advancing in all $7,700 to secure the consignment. This sum is to remain credited to the Burke Company until all refrigerators are sold and fully paid or repossessed. However, on December 31 of the current year, and thereafter on the last day of each month, the consignor must refund to the Burke Company the amount, if any, by which the original deposit exceeds the aggregate of (1) the full sales price of the unsold refrigerators and (2) the uncollected installments on time-payment contracts.

The Burke Company will receive a commission of $30 on each refrigerator sold for cash or on approved time-payment contract. The Burke Company will promptly remit all collections, less commissions in full, on all such sales. Commissions on defaulted contracts that had been approved by the Adams Corporation will not be recoverable from the Burke Company.

On June 30 the Burke Company reported that it had sold 60 refrigerators, 20 for cash and 40 on the time-payment plan. The latter sales had been duly approved by the Adams Corporation. The amounts collected had been remitted according to agreement.

Installments on the 40 time-payment contracts were collected for July, August, and September and were remitted.

In October and November, collections were made and remitted on only 30 of these contracts, and the refrigerators sold on the 10 defaulting contracts were repossessed and returned to the Adams Corporation on November 30. The latter expects to sell these refrigerators at $100 each after spending $10 each for inward freight and cost of reconditioning.

December collections on time-payment contracts were made in full, and the Burke Company reported cash sales of 20 refrigerators, with 20 remaining in stock. The Adams Corporation received these collections and the net proceeds from the cash sales on December 31.

In accounting for installment sales, the Adams Corporation follows the plan of recognizing income only in terms of amounts collected.

Instructions: (1) Give the entries that will record the transactions on the books of the Adams Corporation.

(2) Prepare comprehensive summaries of these entries showing and explaining the following resulting balances at December 31, 1967:

(a) Consignments out.
(b) Repossessed refrigerators.
(c) Cash.
(d) Accounts receivable — Burke Co.
(e) Profit realized.
(f) Profit not realized.
(g) Gain on defaults.

(AICPA adapted)

6-11. The West Company, which manufactures and sells gas burners to be installed in coal-burning furnaces, arranged in September, 1967, to sell some of its product through three dealers to whom it consigned burners packed with their related parts and fixtures, each such package being identified as a burner. The contract with the consignee provides that:

(a) He shall fix the sales price for all burners to be sold in his territory, such price to be approved by the West Company.

(b) He shall pay all expenses incident to handling, selling, and collecting for the burners after delivery to him, except for repairs and expenses pertinent thereto required because of defective production.

(c) He shall retain as commission 25% of the amount for which he sells the burners, exclusive of installation charges.

(d) He shall be responsible for the proper installation of burners sold and may make therefor suitable charges in which the West Company shall not participate.

(e) He shall render, within 10 days after the end of each month, an account sales, accompanied by a check for the amount due the West Company as the result of transactions during the month to which the report relates.

A condensed trial balance of the West Company's accounts at September 30, 1967, follows:

	Dr.	Cr.
Cash	$ 58,910	
Accounts receivable	241,964	
Inventories:		
Finished burners and related parts and fixtures	21,200	
Work in process, materials and supplies	42,271	
Prepaid expenses	3,007	
Plant	128,762	
Accounts payable		$ 31,742
Accrued liabilities		138,798
Capital stock		100,000
Retained earnings		18,978
Sales		643,947
Sales returns and allowances	2,648	
Manufacturing	129,384	
Selling expense	139,637	
Administrative expense	89,423	

	Dr.	Cr.
Allowance for bad debts		$ 9,398
Allowance for depreciation		27,632
Nonoperating income		318
Nonoperating expense	$ 3,607	
Provision for income taxes	110,000	
	$970,813	$970,813

All shipments charged to Accounts Receivable were credited to Sales.

Accounts Receivable included accounts with the three consignees, which, upon examination, revealed the following:

Hale Plumbing Co.

Debits:			
9/ 4/67	18 burners shipped on consignment		$3,600.00
9/20/67	Transportation charges paid on two burners returned as defective		22.00
9/27/67	Cost of repairing two burners returned as defective		18.00
			$3,640.00
Credits:			
9/30/67	Cash received for 13 burners		1,767.75
Balance, 9/30/67			$1,872.25

Lord Heating Equipment Co.

Debits:			
9/ 6/67	6 burners shipped on consignment		$1,200.00
9/15/67	Transportation charges on one burner returned as defective		28.00
			$1,228.00
Credits:			
9/15/67	1 burner returned as defective	$200.00	
9/30/67	Cash received for 3 burners	544.50	744.50
Balance, 9/30/67			$ 483.50

Quade Furnace Company

Debits:			
9/ 5/67	12 burners shipped on consignment		$2,400.00
9/ 5/67	Freight prepaid on consigned burners		36.00
9/30/67	Commission on 9 burners		450.00
			$2,886.00
Credits:			
9/30/67	Cash received for 9 burners		1,344.00
Balance, 9/30/67			$1,542.00

Consignees reported burners on hand at 9/30/67 as follows:

Hale Plumbing Co.	3
Lord Heating Equipment Co.	2
Quade Furnace Co.	3

Shipping records show that on September 27, 1967, the West Company shipped burners, freight prepaid, to replace those returned by consignees, as follows:

To:	Hale Plumbing Co.	2
	Lord Heating Equipment Co.	1

Burners on hand at the West Company's plant at September 30, 1967, numbered 212 and were inventoried at manufacturing cost. Inventories at the beginning of the period have been closed into Manufacturing, while those at the end of the period have been closed out of Manufacturing. All normal adjusting entries have been made for the fiscal year ended September 30, 1967. Unpaid commissions on sales were credited to Accrued Liabilities.

Account sales for September, 1967, with related checks, were received by the West Company as follows:

From:	Hale Plumbing Co.	October 7, 1967
	Lord Heating Equipment Co.	October 12, 1967
	Quade Furnace Co.	October 9, 1967

Those from Hale Plumbing Co. and Lord Heating Equipment Co. reflect payments of $36 and $18, respectively, for transportation charges that they paid upon receiving their consignments; that from Quade Furnace Company includes a charge for the cost of repairs to a defective burner in the amount of $6.

All entries in the West Company's accounts with the consignees, which are dated September 30, 1967, were based on checks received and data recorded in their account sales received on the dates stated above.

Instructions: (1) Prepare an account sales for September, 1967, as rendered by each of the three consignees.

(2) Prepare a columnar work sheet showing corrections to the accounts of the West Company, as of September 30, 1967; no adjustment of the provision for income taxes is required.

(3) Prepare a balance sheet for the West Company as of September 30, 1967.

(4) Prepare a condensed income statement for the West Company for the year ended September 30, 1967.

(AICPA adapted)

Chapter 7

HOME OFFICE AND BRANCH RELATIONSHIPS

GENERAL PROCEDURES

In their search for increased sales, business organizations are constantly reaching out into more distant areas. Frequently the development of these areas cannot be adequately accomplished by salesmen traveling from a central office. The use of catalogs with mail orders or shipments on consignment may further sales but may still fail to accomplish the desired results. The establishment of sales headquarters in these districts may be the means of achieving marketing objectives.

Selling activities are conducted from sales offices at different locations under the direction of the home office. Customers deal, not with the headquarters of the business, but with an outlying sales unit. Contact with the organization is more easily and quickly made. The desired goods or services are more readily available.

AGENCY AND BRANCH DISTINGUISHED

The establishment of an outlying selling unit may take the form of an *agency* or a *branch*. The distinction between an agency and a branch is based upon the functions assigned to the organization as well as the degree of independence that it assumes in the exercise of such functions. An organization that merely takes orders for goods and that operates under the direct supervision of officers of the home office is called an agency. An organization that sells goods out of a stock that it maintains and that possesses the authority to engage in transactions as an independent business unit is known as a branch.

OPERATIONS OF AN AGENCY

An agency that operates solely as a local sales organization under the direction of a home office generally carries no stock other than samples of the lines that are offered for sale. Samples of the merchandise offerings as well as advertising materials are provided by the home office. The agency is normally provided with a working fund that is to be used for the payment of expenses that can be more conveniently settled through the agency. The imprest system is often adopted for the control of agency cash.

Orders for merchandise obtained by the agency are sent to the home office for approval. If the sales price and credit terms are acceptable, the home office fills the orders and ships the goods to customers. The home office may bear the responsibility for maintaining the accounts that arise out of sales, billing the customers, and making collections. Expenses of operating the agency other than those paid by the agency from its working fund are met by the home office.

ACCOUNTING FOR AN AGENCY

The typical agency does not require a complete set of books. Ordinarily, summaries of working fund receipts and disbursements and records of sales to customers are sufficient. Summaries of working fund disbursements accompanied by supporting evidence in the form of paid vouchers are sent to the home office. When the local manager or salesmen are to be paid according to the volume of sales completed, sales records supply this information.

In adopting the imprest system for the agency working fund, the home office writes a check to the agency for the amount of the fund. Establishment of the fund is recorded on the home office books by a charge to the agency working fund account and a credit to Cash. The agency will request fund replenishment whenever the fund runs low and at the end of each fiscal period. Such a request is normally accompanied by an itemized and authenticated statement of disbursements and the paid vouchers. Upon sending the agency a check in replenishment of the fund, the home office charges expense or other accounts for which disbursements from the fund were reported and credits Cash.

When the home office transfers assets other than cash to the agency, it charges asset accounts identified with the agency, such as "Agency Furniture," "Agency Samples," and "Agency Supplies," and credits the appropriate asset accounts for the cost of the items transferred.

The home office may record transactions of the agency in the revenue and expense accounts used for its own transactions if there is no desire to summarize agency operations separately. In closing the books, the profit or loss balance reports the result of combined operations.

If the home office wishes to determine the net earnings of each of its agencies as well as of the home office, it will maintain separate revenue and expense accounts for the individual sales units. A supplementary record of the cost of goods sold by each sales unit must also be kept. This record provides the data for the entries charging individual agencies and the home office with the cost of goods identified with the respective sales.

The entries required as a result of the establishment of an agency and the entries to record subsequent activities of such a unit are illustrated in the example that follows.

Assume that on March 1 General Traders, Inc., established a sales agency in Toledo. Agency revenues and expenses are recorded in separate agency accounts, and the operating results for each agency as well as for the home office are determined at the end of each month. Agency transactions for March and the entries to record the transactions on the books of the home office are listed below:

Agency Transaction	Home Office Books		
March 1 Receipt of working fund from home office.	Working Fund — Toledo Agency	1,000	
	Cash		1,000
March 1–31 Orders submitted by agency, approved and filled by home office.	Accounts Receivable	5,000	
	Sales — Toledo Agency		5,000
Collections by home office on agency sales.	Cash	3,000	
	Accounts Receivable		3,000
Disbursements by home office on behalf of agency.	Salaries and Commissions — Toledo Agency	250	
	Rent — Toledo Agency	200	
	Advertising Supplies — Toledo Agency	450	
	Cash		900
March 31 Replenishment of working fund by home office, paid expense vouchers being submitted by the agency.	Salaries and Commissions — Toledo Agency	350	
	Misc. Expense — Toledo Agency	200	
	Cash		550
Entries summarizing agency transactions — Data for agency adjustments: Cost of goods identified with agency sales, $3,500. Advertising supplies on hand, approximately ⅔ of amount received.	Cost of Goods Sold — Toledo Agency	3,500	
	Merchandise Shipments — Toledo Agency		3,500
	Advertising Supplies Used — Toledo Agency	150	
	Advertising Supplies — Toledo Agency		150
	Sales — Toledo Agency	5,000	
	Profit and Loss — Toledo Agency		5,000
	Profit and Loss — Toledo Agency	4,650	
	Cost of Goods Sold — Toledo Agency		3,500
	Salaries and Commissions — Toledo Agency		600
	Rent — Toledo Agency		200
	Advertising Supplies Used — Toledo Agency		150
	Misc. Expense — Toledo Agency		200
	Profit and Loss — Toledo Agency	350	
	Profit and Loss		350

It will be noted in the example that the cost of the goods sold by the agency is recorded by a debit to Cost of Goods Sold — Agency and a credit to Merchandise Shipments — Agency. The merchandise shipments account balance is subtracted from the sum of the home office beginning inventory and purchases in determining the merchandise available for home office sales. The ending inventory, when subtracted from merchandise available for home office sales, gives the cost of goods identified with home office sales.

Following the adjusting entries, agency revenue and expense balances are closed into a profit and loss account for each agency. Agency profit and loss accounts are subsequently transferred to the general profit and loss account in which the profit or loss from home office activities will also be summarized.

OPERATIONS OF A BRANCH

Although a branch operates as a separate business unit, it is subject to control by the home office. The degree of self-management to be exercised by a branch is determined by the home office. General policies and standards adopted by the business are usually applied to all of the branches. Outside of this realm, however, the branch manager may be given complete authority, the effectiveness of his management and control being judged on the basis of the branch financial reports.

A branch is supplied by the home office with cash and merchandise and such other assets as may be needed. The branch may purchase merchandise from outsiders to satisfy certain local needs for goods not available from the affiliated unit. The branch ships merchandise, bills its customers, and makes collections on account, such sums being deposited in its own bank account. The bank balance is drawn upon in making payment for purchases of goods and services.

Although the foregoing are typical branch functions, there are instances where certain limitations are imposed upon such activities. For example, in some cases the home office may assume the responsibility of collecting branch receivables, or a branch may be required to deposit branch receipts to the credit of the home office and to make branch disbursements from a working fund operated on the imprest system. Such restrictions upon the authority of a branch serve to give it some of the characteristics of an agency. On the other hand, some agencies are assigned special functions that extend beyond the scope of the typical agency, such as maintaining accounts with customers and making collections on accounts. The accounting procedures that are illustrated in this chapter are those that would be employed for a typical agency or branch. These procedures may be modified to meet special conditions.

ACCOUNTING SYSTEMS FOR BRANCHES

Branch accounting systems may provide for (1) maintenance of branch records at the home office, (2) maintenance of branch records at both branch and home office, and (3) maintenance of branch records at the branch.

Records maintained at the home office. The home office sometimes keeps the complete records summarizing branch activities. Branch transactions may be recorded in the home office journals and ledgers or in a separate set of records. Data to be recorded are supplied by the branch in the form of either original documents evidencing branch transactions or memorandum records summarizing branch transactions supported by the original vouchers. Duplicate copies of vouchers and summaries sent to the home office are usually retained by the branch. Accounting centralization at the home office is particularly appropriate when the branch bears some resemblance to the agency form of organization.

Records maintained at both branch and home office. A system whereby both the branch and the home office maintain detailed records of branch transactions is sometimes adopted. The branch may maintain the books of original entry for all transactions in duplicate. Copies of the books of original entry are sent to the home office where data are posted to branch accounts maintained separately or included in the home office general ledger. At the end of the period the home office adjusts and closes the branch accounts and determines the branch earnings.

Records maintained at the branch. Generally, the branch accounting system is maintained at the branch. The branch keeps the books of original entry and posts to ledger records. Financial statements are prepared by the branch periodically and are submitted to the home office. Statements that are submitted by the branch are usually verified by the company's internal auditors.

When complete self-balancing books are kept by the branch, an account called Home Office or Home Office Current takes the place of the customary capital accounts. This account is credited for cash, goods, or services received from the home office and for profits resulting from branch operations. The account is charged for remittances made by the branch to the home office and for losses from operations. The home office account, then, indicates the extent of the accountability of the branch to the home office.

The home office, in turn, keeps a reciprocal account, called Branch, Investment in Branch, or Branch Current. This account is charged for cash, goods, or services transferred to the branch and for branch profits;

it is credited for remittances from the branch and for branch losses. The branch account, then, indicates the amount invested in the branch. When a number of branches are maintained, a separate account is established for each branch.

Depreciable branch assets are sometimes carried on the home office books. This procedure may be followed when depreciation rates are to be uniformly applied to certain groups of assets, whether used by the branch or the home office, and when insurance policies are to be acquired by the home office for all assets.

Certain expenses relating to branch operations are sometimes paid by the home office. Branches are notified by the home office of expenses incurred in their behalf, and such charges are recorded on the branch books so that branch income statements may provide complete summaries of the operations of the separate sales organizations. Certain items can be directly identified with individual branches and are immediately charged to the branches. Such items include taxes and insurance paid by the home office on branch assets. Other charges resulting in benefits that are not directly identified with certain branches, such as advertising for the different lines being sold, may be summarized on the home office books and be charged periodically to the branches according to the volume of branch sales, the volume of shipments of merchandise by the home office to branches, or on some other equitable basis. When a home office does not sell to customers itself but acts solely in a supervisory capacity, it may be desirable to charge all of its expenses to the branches. Expenses that are not directly identified with branches may be combined and distributed in total as an indirect charge. When charges reported on home office books are taken up on the branch books, home office accounts should be relieved of the amounts transferred.

The home office may charge the individual branches for interest and rent on the working capital and the properties and equipment transferred to the branches. Such charges are made so that earnings of the different sales units may be reported on a comparable basis in view of the differences that are found in the investments by the home office in these units. When such charges are made, the branch recognizes these charges as expense items, while the home office reports corresponding revenue.

Accounting for a branch illustrated. The entries that are required on the books of a branch and a home office in accounting for the operations of the branch are illustrated in the example that follows. Assume that on October 1 the Southern Supply Company of Los Angeles establishes its first branch in San Diego. Additional branches are planned for the future. Separate books are to be kept by the branch, and financial statements are to be submitted to the home office at the end of each month. Merchandise is to be billed at cost. Branch furniture and fixtures are to be carried on the books of the home office. The branch is to be charged interest at the rate of 6% on the home office investment in the branch as of the beginning of each month. Transactions of Branch #1 and the entries to record the transactions on the books of the branch and the home office are listed below and on the following page. Explanations for the transactions are given beginning on page 206.

Branch Transactions		Home Office Books			Branch Books		
October 1							
(1) Receipt of cash from home office.		Branch #1	6,000		Cash	6,000	
		Cash		6,000	Home Office		6,000
(2) Receipt of merchandise from home office, billing at cost.		Branch #1	12,000		Mdse. Shipments from Home Office	12,000	
		Mdse. Shipments to Branch #1		12,000	Home Office		12,000
(3) Purchase of furniture and fixtures by branch for cash, the asset to be carried on the home office books.		Furniture and Fixtures, Branch #1	3,000		Home Office	3,000	
		Branch #1		3,000	Cash		3,000
October 2–31							
(4) (a) Sales on account.					Accounts Receivable	6,500	
					Sales		6,500
(b) Collections on account.					Cash	3,500	
					Accounts Receivable		3,500
(5) Payment of expenses.					Sales Salaries and Commissions	400	
					Rent	200	
					Miscellaneous Expense	150	
					Cash		750
(6) Remittance to home office.		Cash	2,000		Home Office	2,000	
		Branch #1		2,000	Cash		2,000
(7) Branch charges submitted by home office:		Branch #1	500		Insurance	35	
(a) Insurance on branch assets	$ 35	Unexpired Insurance		35	Depreciation of Furniture and Fixtures	50	
(b) Depreciation of furniture and fixtures	50	Allowance for Depreciation of Furniture and Fixtures, Branch #1		50	Taxes	25	
(c) Taxes on branch assets	25	Accrued Taxes		25	Advertising	300	
(d) Advertising	300	Advertising		300	Interest Expense, Home Office	90	
(e) Interest at 6% for one month on investment in branch on Oct. 1, $18,000.	90	Interest Income, Branch #1		90	Home Office		500

Branch Transactions	Home Office Books	Branch Books
(8) Adjusting and closing entries — data for branch adjustments: Merchandise inventory, Oct. 31.............. $8,400		Merchandise Inventory.............. 8,400 Profit and Loss... 8,400
		Sales.............. 6,500 Profit and Loss... 6,500
		Profit and Loss..... 13,250 Mdse. Shipments from Home Office 12,000 Sales Salaries and Commissions..... 400 Rent........... 200 Misc. Expense... 150 Insurance....... 35 Depr. of Furniture and Fixtures. 50 Taxes.......... 25 Advertising...... 300 Interest Expense, Home Office..... 90
	Branch #1......... 1,650 Profit and Loss, Branch #1....... 1,650	Profit and Loss..... 1,650 Home Office..... 1,650
	Profit and Loss, Branch #1......... 1,650 Profit and Loss... 1,650	

Reference to the example illustrates the following procedures (explanations are identified with transactions by number):

(1) Transfer of assets other than merchandise by home office to branch.

Home office books. When an asset other than merchandise is transferred and the asset is to be carried on the branch books, the home office charges the branch account and credits the appropriate asset account. When the asset transferred is to be carried on the home office books, an asset account identified with the branch, such as Furniture and Fixtures — Branch, is charged and the original asset account is credited.

Branch books. Upon receiving an asset other than merchandise that is to be carried on the branch books, the branch charges the asset account and credits the home office account. No entry is required when the asset transferred is to be carried on the home office books. However, the branch would maintain a memorandum record for assets of this class.

(2) Transfer of merchandise by home office to branch.

Home office books. When merchandise is transferred to the branch, the home office charges the branch account and credits Merchandise Shipments to Branch. At the end of the period, the balance of the account

Merchandise Shipments to Branch will be subtracted from the sum of the beginning inventory, purchases, and freight-in in calculating the merchandise available for home office sales. When the home office maintains a perpetual inventory system, appropriate inventory accounts are credited for the goods transferred to the branch. Illustrations in this chapter assume that a branch is charged for no more than merchandise cost on interoffice transfers. Such cost should include any freight and transportation charges paid by the home office in acquiring the goods as well as in transferring the goods to the branch. There are instances when the home office follows the practice of billing a branch for an amount that exceeds cost. Such a practice calls for special accounting procedures that are described in the next chapter.

Branch books. Upon receiving merchandise from the home office, the branch charges Merchandise Shipments from Home Office at billed price and credits the home office account. At the end of the period, merchandise received from the home office together with merchandise purchases from outsiders is added to the beginning inventory in determining the goods available for branch sale. If the branch maintains a perpetual inventory system, inventory accounts are charged for the goods acquired from the home office.

(3) Purchase of assets by branch to be carried on home office books.

Home office books. When the home office is notified by the branch of a purchase of an asset that is to be used by the branch but that is to be carried on the books of the home office, the home office charges an appropriate asset account identified with the branch and credits the branch account.

Branch books. Upon purchase of an asset that is to be carried on the home office books, the branch charges the home office account and credits Cash or an appropriate liability account.

(4), (5) Current transactions involving only branch and outsiders.

Home office books. Transactions that involve only the branch and outsiders during the period require no entries on the books of the home office.

Branch books. Transactions of the branch and outsiders during the period are recorded on the branch books in the usual manner.

(6) Remittances by branch to home office.

Home office books. Upon receiving cash from the branch, the home office charges Cash and credits the branch account. Receipt of an asset other than cash is recorded by a charge to an appropriate asset account and a credit to the branch account.

Branch books. Upon remitting cash to the home office, the branch charges the home office account and credits Cash. Transfer of some other branch asset to the home office is recorded by a charge to Home Office and a credit to the appropriate asset account.

(7) Branch charges submitted by home office.

Home office books. When the home office charges the branch for items that are to be recognized by the branch as expenses, the home office charges the branch account and credits appropriate asset, asset valuation, liability, expense, or revenue accounts, whichever may be appropriate; thus (a) a charge to the branch for insurance that has been paid in advance by the home office is accompanied by a credit to Unexpired Insurance; (b) a charge for depreciation on branch furniture and fixtures carried on the home office books is accompanied by a credit to Allowance for Depreciation of Furniture and Fixtures, Branch; (c) a charge for taxes on branch assets that are to be paid by the home office at some future date is accompanied by a credit to Accrued Taxes; (d) a charge for branch advertising that has been paid for by the home office and is included in the advertising expense account is accompanied by a credit to Advertising; (e) a charge to the branch for interest on the amount invested in the branch is accompanied by a credit to Interest Income, Branch.

Branch books. Upon notification of expenses that are to be recognized on the branch books, the branch debits the appropriate expense accounts and credits the home office account.

(8) Determination of branch net income or loss.

Home office books. When the branch reports net income for the period, the home office debits the branch account and credits Profit and Loss, Branch. A net loss is recorded by a debit to Profit and Loss, Branch and a credit to the branch account. The profit and loss account for each branch is subsequently closed into the general profit and loss account in which operations of the home office are also summarized.

Branch books. At the end of the period the necessary adjustments are made, and the revenue and expense accounts are closed into the profit and loss account in the usual manner. The balance in the profit and loss account is then transferred to the home office account.

PREPARATION OF BRANCH AND HOME OFFICE STATEMENTS

The branch normally prepares a balance sheet and an income statement at the end of the fiscal period. The home office also prepares statements to show its financial condition and operating results. The branch investment accounts appear as assets on the home office balance sheet. Branch balance sheets may be attached as schedules in support of the branch balances. The individual branch earnings may be shown on the home office income statement immediately after operating results of the home office, as follows:

Net income from own operations	$6,140
Add: Income of branches:	
Net income — Branch #1	1,650
Total income	$7,790

The branch income statements may be attached to the home office income statement as schedules offering the detail to support the net amounts reported on the statement.

PREPARATION OF COMBINED STATEMENTS FOR HOME OFFICE AND BRANCHES

Although separate statements offer significant information to both home office and branch officials, such statements must be combined in fully stating a company's financial position and the results of its operations. The financial position of the business unit as a whole is fully presented only when the individual asset and liability items of the various branches are substituted for the branch investment balances and combined with the home office items; operating results for the business as a whole are fully presented only when the individual revenue and expense items of the various branches are substituted for the branch net income or loss and combined with the home office data. Stockholders, creditors, and taxing authorities require combined statements; these parties normally have little or no interest in the separate status and operating results of individual departments or branches of a business.

In combining branch data with home office data, the elimination of certain reciprocal interoffice items is necessary. In preparing a combined balance sheet, the home office account and the branch account are eliminated since these are without significance when the related units are recognized as a single entity. Any other interbranch receivable and payable balances that may have been established are also irrelevant and without significance in stating the financial position of the business and are eliminated.

In preparing a combined income statement, the accounts Merchandise Shipments from Home Office and Merchandise Shipments to Branch are eliminated, since these balances summarize interoffice transfers that are of no significance when the related units are reported as a single entity. Other interoffice revenue and expense items are also eliminated so that the combined statement may report only the results of transactions of the organization with outsiders.

Working papers facilitate the elimination of interoffice items and the combining of like items. Working papers for the Southern Supply Company and its branch are illustrated below and on page 211. The combined statements prepared from the working papers are given on pages 211 and 212. Branch data are obtained from the information on pages 205 and 206. It will be noted on the working papers that an item with a debit balance is canceled or eliminated by a credit; an item with a credit balance is canceled by a debit.

Southern Supply Company
Working Papers for Combined Balance Sheet
October 31, 1967

	Home Office	Branch #1	Eliminations Dr.	Eliminations Cr.	Combined Balance Sheet
Debits					
Cash	6,250	3,750			10,000
Accounts Receivable	18,000	3,000			21,000
Merchandise Inventory	30,000	8,400			38,400
Unexpired Insurance	150				150
Branch #1	15,150			15,150	
Furniture and Fixtures, Home Office	14,000				14,000
Furniture and Fixtures, Branch #1	3,000				3,000
	86,550	15,150			86,550
Credits					
Allowance for Depr. of Furniture and Fixtures, Home Office	9,100				9,100
Allowance for Depr. of Furniture and Fixtures, Branch #1	50				50
Accounts Payable	23,300				23,300
Accrued Taxes	200				200
Home Office		15,150	15,150		
Capital Stock	25,000				25,000
Retained Earnings	28,900				28,900
	86,550	15,150	15,150	15,150	86,550

Southern Supply Compay
Working Papers for Combined Income Statement
For Month Ended October 31, 1967

	Home Office	Branch #1	Eliminations Dr.	Eliminations Cr.	Combined Income Statement
Sales	24,000	6,500			30,500
Cost of Goods Sold:					
Merchandise Inventory, October 1	38,000				38,000
Purchases	16,000				16,000
Merchandise Shipments from Home Office		12,000		12,000	
	54,000				54,000
Less Merchandise Shipments to Branch #1	12,000		12,000		
Merchandise Available for Sale	42,000	12,000			54,000
Less Mdse. Inventory, October 31	30,000	8,400			38,400
Cost of Goods Sold	12,000	3,600			15,600
Gross Profit on Sales	12,000	2,900			14,900
Expenses:					
Sales Salaries and Commission	1,900	400			2,300
Rent	1,000	200			1,200
Advertising	800	300			1,100
Depreciation of Furniture and Fixtures	400	50			450
Insurance	250	35			285
Taxes	150	25			175
Miscellaneous Expense	1,450	150			1,600
Total Expenses	5,950	1,160			7,110
Net Operating Income	6,050	1,740			7,790
Add Interest Income, Branch #1	90		90		
Deduct Interest Expense, Home Office		90		90	
Net Income	6,140	1,650	12,090	12,090	7,790

Southern Supply Company
Combined Balance Sheet for Home Office and Branch
October 31 ,1967

Assets			Liabilities and Stockholders' Equity		
			Liabilities		
Cash		$10,000			
Accounts receivable		21,000	Accounts payable		$23,300
Merchandise inventory		38,400	Accrued taxes		200
Unexpired insurance		150			
Furniture and fixtures	$17,000				$23,500
Less allowance for depreciation	9,150	7,850	Stockholders' equity		
			Capital stock	$25,000	
			Retained earnings	28,900	53,900
Total assets		$77,400	Total liab. and stockholders' equity		$77,400

Southern Supply Company
Combined Income Statement for Home Office and Branch
For Month Ended October 31, 1967

Sales		$30,500
Cost of goods sold:		
Merchandise inventory, October 1	$38,000	
Purchases	16,000	
Merchandise available for sale	$54,000	
Less merchandise inventory, October 31	38,400	15,600
Gross profit on sales		$14,900
Expenses:		
Sales salaries and commissions	$ 2,300	
Rent	1,200	
Advertising	1,100	
Depreciation of furniture and fixtures	450	
Insurance	285	
Taxes	175	
Miscellaneous expense	1,600	7,110
Net income		$ 7,790

ADJUSTMENT OF RECIPROCAL ACCOUNTS

The balances in the branch account on the home office books and in the home office account on the branch books may not show reciprocal balances at any one time because of certain interoffice data that have been recorded by one office but not by the other. The home office, for example, debits the branch immediately upon the shipment of merchandise to the branch. The branch, however, does not credit the home office account until it receives the merchandise, which may be several days after shipment by the home office. The fact that the account balances are not reciprocal is of no concern during the fiscal period. At the end of the fiscal period, however, the causes for any differences in the balances must be investigated and appropriate entries made to bring interoffice accounts into agreement before accounts for each office can be closed and individual and combined statements prepared.

The data to be considered in reconciling the two accounts may be classified as follows:

(1) Debits in the branch account without corresponding credits in the home office account.
(2) Credits in the branch account without corresponding debits in the home office account.
(3) Debits in the home office account without corresponding credits in the branch account.
(4) Credits in the home office account without corresponding debits in the branch account.

To illustrate the procedure to be followed in reconciling the branch and the home office accounts, assume that on December 31, the end of a fiscal year, but before accounts are closed, branch and home office accounts are as follows:

On Home Office Books

Branch

	Nov. 30	Balance..............	10,500		Dec. 17	Cash received from branch...............	1,500
(1)	Dec. 28	Merchandise shipped to branch..............	3,000	(2)	Dec. 22	Collection of branch receivables...........	750

On Branch Books

Home Office

	Dec. 15	Cash sent to home office.	1,500		Nov. 30	Balance..............	10,500
(3)	Dec. 30	Cash sent to home office.	500	(4)	Dec. 26	Correction — Understatement of net income for prior year.........	200

Analysis of the accounts discloses the following:

(*1*) *Debit in the branch account without corresponding credit in the home office account.* The home office has charged Branch and credited Merchandise Shipments to Branch with $3,000 for merchandise shipped to the branch at the end of the year. The shipment has not reached the branch by December 31 and consequently no entry for the shipment appears on its books. The following entry is required on the branch books on December 31:

Merchandise Shipments from Home Office — In Transit	3,000	
Home Office..................................		3,000

The account Merchandise Shipments from Home Office — In Transit is closed into the profit and loss account. When the income statement for the branch is prepared, the balance of the account Merchandise Shipments from Home Office — In Transit is added to the balance of the account Merchandise Shipments from Home Office. The total of the two accounts is then equal to the balance of the account Merchandise Shipments to Branch shown on the books of the home office, and these reciprocal balances can be eliminated in preparing a combined income statement.

In addition to the entry above, the branch in recording its ending inventory must increase its merchandise on hand by the amount of goods in transit. The merchandise in transit thus appears on the branch balance sheet and will be included as a part of the total inventory in the preparation of combined statements. If the branch maintains a perpetual inventory system, instead of the above procedure, a special inventory in transit account would be charged and the home office account credited. Upon receipt of the goods, the inventory account would be charged and the inventory in transit balance closed.

(2) *Credit in the branch account without corresponding debit in the home office account.* The home office has charged Cash and credited Branch for $750 upon collecting an account that is carried on the branch books. This transaction has not been entered on the books of the branch. The following entry is required on the branch books on December 31:

Home Office	750	
Accounts Receivable		750

(3) *Debit in the home office account without corresponding credit in the branch account.* The branch has charged Home Office and credited Cash for $500 upon remitting cash to the home office. This cash has not reached the home office by December 31. The following entry is required on the home office books on December 31:

Cash in Transit	500	
Branch		500

(4) *Credit in the home office account without corresponding debit in the branch account.* The branch has credited Home Office upon correcting the accounts for an understatement of net income for the preceding period. This information has not been reported on the books of the home office. The following entry is required on the home office books on December 31:

Branch	200	
Corrections in Profits of Prior Periods (or Retained Earnings)		200

After the foregoing entries have been made, the reciprocal accounts are in agreement as indicated below:

	Home Office Books	Branch Books
	Branch account	Home office account
Balances before adjustments	$11,250	$ 8,700
Adjustments:		
Additions:		
Merchandise shipped to branch		3,000
Understatement of branch net income — prior period	200	
	$11,450	$11,700
Deductions:		
Transfer of cash to home office	500	
Collection of branch receivable by home office		750
Corrected balances	$10,950	$10,950

It should be observed that, in addition to data relative to differences, there may be other data that require recognition on both home office and branch ledgers in bringing the interoffice accounts up to date. After entries have been made to bring the accounts up to date, individual and combined statements may be prepared and the revenue and expense accounts for each office closed.

QUESTIONS

1. What are the factors that would be considered by a company in deciding whether it should adopt a policy of sales by consignment, the establishment of an agency, or the establishment of a branch form of organization?

2. Distinguish between typical agency and typical branch operations.

3. Indicate the kind of an accounting system that might reasonably be adopted by a home office and its sales office, assuming that:

(a) An agency is organized, the home office to take care of merchandise shipments, billing of customers, and collections on account.
(b) An agency is organized, the home office to take care of merchandise shipments but the agency to bill customers and make collections.
(c) A branch is established, the branch to maintain a stock of merchandise, to make collection on accounts, and to make payments for expenses from its own cash.
(d) A branch is established, the branch to maintain a stock of merchandise, to make collections that are deposited to the credit of the home office, and to make payments from an imprest working fund.

4. The Baker Sales Co. adopts the imprest system for cash that is sent to its newly organized sales agencies. Describe the operation of such a system.

5. What special problems result when a home office wishes to determine the degree of success of operations for each of its agencies?

6. (a) Describe the nature of the branch and the home office accounts. (b) How are these balances reported on the separate statements of the home office and the branch? (c) How are these balances reported on the combined statements?

7. (a) Describe the nature of the accounts Shipments to Branch on the home office books and Shipments from Home Office on the branch books. (b) How are these balances reported on the separate statements of the home office and the branch? (c) How are these balances reported on the combined statements?

8. Give the entries that will appear on the books of the home office and the branch for each of the following transactions:

(a) The home office sends cash and merchandise to a newly organized branch.
(b) The branch purchases merchandise from outsiders.
(c) The branch pays expenses.
(d) The branch sells merchandise on account.
(e) The branch makes remittance to the home office.
(f) The home office charges the branch with certain expenses previously paid by the home office.
(g) The branch reports a loss from operations.

9. (a) Give four different transactions originating with the home office that affect the branch-home office reciprocal accounts. (b) Give four different transactions originating with the branch that affect the reciprocal accounts.

10. The Webster Co. carries all of the furniture and fixtures that are in use by its branches on the home office books. What are the entries required by both the home office and a branch when:

(a) The home office purchases branch fixtures for cash.
(b) The branch pays for the installation of the fixtures.
(c) The branch pays for insurance on the fixtures.
(d) The home office pays personal property taxes on the fixtures.
(e) The home office records depreciation on the fixtures.

11. The Walters home office charges its individual branches for interest on the net amount invested. (a) What is the purpose of such a charge? (b) What entries are made by the home office and the respective branch in recognizing such a charge? (c) How is the transaction reported on the separate statements of the home office and the branch? (d) How is the transaction reported on the combined statements?

12. What are the relative merits of separate statements for the home office and for the related branches as compared with combined statements for the home office and the branches?

13. (a) What eliminations are required in the development of working papers for the preparation of combined statements for a home office and its related branches? (b) Why are such eliminations necessary?

14. The home office and the branch reciprocal accounts for the Peters Sales Corporation are not in agreement at the end of the fiscal period. Give four possible categories within which the reason for any differences might be found. Give an example of a situation under each that might arise in reconciling the accounts.

EXERCISES

1. Give the entries that are required on the home office books of the Millings Sales Company to record:

(a) The transfer of $500 to an agency to establish a working fund.
(b) Receipt of sales orders from the agency, $5,000.
(c) Collections by the home office of agency accounts, $3,500.
(d) Disbursements by the home office representing agency expenses, $450.
(e) Replenishment of the agency working fund upon receipt of expense vouchers for $225.
(f) Cost of goods identified with agency sales, $3,600.

2. Give the entries that are required on the books of the Parker Company and the separate books of its branch to record:

(a) Transfer by home office to the branch of cash, $1,500, and merchandise, $6,000.
(b) Purchases of merchandise on account by branch, $1,500.
(c) Payments on account by branch, $750.
(d) Sales for cash by branch, $6,500.
(e) Payment of expenses by branch, $2,200.
(f) Disbursements by home office representing branch expenses, $350.
(g) Determination of a loss from branch operations, $225.

3. The home office of the Meadows Company carries all branch equipment items in its own ledger. Give the entries that would appear on the books of the home office and the branch as a result of the following transactions:

(a) At the beginning of 1966 the branch office acquires branch furniture on account, $2,500, terms 2/10, n/30.
(b) The home office makes payment on the invoice within the discount period.
(c) Depreciation on the equipment is recorded at the end of the year at 10%.
(d) At the beginning of 1967 the branch furniture is traded in for new branch furniture costing $4,000; an allowance of $1,500 is received on the old furniture and the home office pays the balance.

4. The following account is found on the home office books of the Ford Corporation at the end of January. Give the entries affecting the home office account that will appear on the branch books for the month of January.

Alexandria Branch

1967			1967		
1/1	Balance	67,500	1/16	Remittance from branch	2,000
1/10	Payment of branch note	2,500	1/20	Return of goods by branch	1,200
1/10	Payment for branch furniture and fixtures	10,000	1/25	Collection of branch account	150
1/16	Shipments of goods to branch	6,500	1/31	Branch loss for month	750
1/30	Expenses charged to branch	800			

5. Give the entries that are required on the books of the Price Co. home office and Westwood branch as a result of the following transactions:

(a) The branch writes off bad accounts of $600. The allowance for bad debts account is maintained on the books of the home office.

(b) The home office analyzes the balance of its general and administrative expenses account and finds that $1,250 of this balance is chargeable to the Westwood branch.

(c) The shipments from home office account on the branch books is found to include a charge of $1,200 for merchandise intended for shipment by the home office to the Westwood branch but shipped to the Beverly Hills branch by mistake and retained by the latter branch.

(d) The branch authorizes the home office to increase the allowance for bad accounts of the branch by $850 as a result of sales for the month.

6. On December 31 the branch account on the home office books of the Ward Co. shows a balance of $8,400 and the home office account on the branch books shows a balance of $9,735. The following data are determined in accounting for the difference:

(1) Merchandise billed at $615 was shipped by the home office to the branch on December 28. The merchandise is in transit and has not been recognized on the books of the branch.

(2) The branch collected a home office account receivable of $2,500, but failed to notify the home office of this collection.

(3) The home office recorded the branch net income for November at $1,125. This was in error, as the branch reported net income of $1,215.

(4) The home office was charged $640 when the branch returned merchandise to the home office on December 31. The merchandise is in transit.

(a) Prepare a statement reconciling the branch and the home office accounts. (b) What entries would be made on the branch and the home office books before financial statements are prepared?

PROBLEMS

7-1. On July 1, 1967, the Crawford Company of New York, establishes an organization in Boston to act as a sales agency. The following assets are sent to the agency on July 1:

A working fund to be operated under the imprest system....	$1,000
Samples from the merchandise stock..........................	5,000
Advertising materials and literature..........................	1,250
	$7,250

During July the agency submits sales on account of $17,600 that are approved by the home office; cost of merchandise shipped in filling orders is $10,500. Home office disbursements chargeable to the agency are as follows:

Furniture and fixtures for agency	$2,400
Manager's and salesmen's salaries and commissions	1,750
Rent	800
	$4,950

On July 31 the agency working fund is replenished, paid expense vouchers being submitted by the agency as follows:

Advertising expense	$ 325
Miscellaneous expense	600
	$ 925

The following information is used in adjusting the agency accounts on July 31:

Agency samples will be useful until December 31; at that time it is believed they will have a salvage value of 40% of cost.

Approximately ⅖ of the advertising materials and literature remain on hand.

Furniture and fixtures are to be depreciated on a 5-year basis.

The agency manager is to receive a bonus of 5% of all sales above $10,000 a month, the bonus to be paid by the home office at quarterly intervals.

Instructions: (1) Give the journal entries on the home office books to record the transactions and to adjust and close the accounts kept with the agency.

(2) Prepare a statement summarizing agency activities for the month of July, 1967.

7-2. The branch account on the home office books of the Sunset Sales Co. and the home office account on the branch books on January 31, 1967, are shown below.

Wilshire Branch

1967				1967		
Jan. 1	Balance	62,815		Jan. 15	Remittance	10,600
5	Merchandise shipments: 100 units of Product A @ $37.85	3,785		22	Merchandise returns	410
12	Merchandise shipments: 200 units of Product A @ $37.85 200 units of Product B @ $44.95	16,560				
15	Advertising chargeable to branch	600				
29	Merchandise shipments	4,400				

Home Office

1967				1967		
Jan. 13	Remittance	10,600		Jan. 1	Balance	62,815
18	Merchandise returns	410		8	Merchandise shipments	3,785
22	Understatement of depreciation in 1966	540		16	Merchandise shipments	16,650
31	Remittance	16,000		20	Collection of home office account	750

Instructions: (1) Prepare a statement reconciling the reciprocal accounts as of January 31, 1967.

(2) Give whatever entries may be necessary for the books of the home office as well as for the branch before combined statements can be prepared.

7-3. The branch account on the home office books of Block and Decker, Inc., and the home office accounts on the branch books on January 31, 1967, are shown below.

Beverly Hills Branch

1967			1967			
Jan. 1	Balance	50,615	Jan. 20	Cash received from branch	14,000	
16	Merchandise shipments	22,600		Remittance received from branch customer in settlement of branch account	65	
31	Expenses chargeable to branch	215				

Home Office — Current

1967			1967		
Jan. 10	Bad accounts written off	1,200	Jan. 1	Balance	28,415
20	Cash remittance to home office	14,000	21	Correction for profit understatement for December	310
			31	Cost of merchandise sold	21,400
			31	Profit for January	1,440

Home Office — Merchandise

1967			1967		
Jan. 31	Cost of merchandise sold	21,400	Jan. 1	Balance	22,200
31	Shipment returns to home office	840	16	Shipments from home office	21,200

The following additional data are available in reconciling the accounts:

(a) A shipment of goods of $1,400 charged by the home office to the Beverly Hills branch was actually sent to the Brentwood branch.

(b) The goods returned by the branch are in transit and hence do not appear on the home office records.

(c) The branch failed to recognize expenses incurred by the home office and chargeable against profits, $215, in calculating its profit for January.

(d) The allowance for doubtful accounts on branch receivables is maintained by the home office.

Instructions: (1) Prepare a statement reconciling the reciprocal accounts as of January 31, 1967.

(2) Give whatever entries may be necessary to correct and bring the accounts up to date on (a) the books of the branch and (b) the books of the home office.

7-4. The Wesley Co. of San Francisco operates a branch in Sacramento. A branch balance sheet on December 31, 1966, showed the following balances:

Cash		$ 3,500	Accounts payable	$ 2,000
Accounts receivable	$12,200		Accrued expenses	600
Less allow. for bad debts	850	11,350	Home office	30,250
Merchandise inventory		16,500		
Prepaid expenses		350		
Furniture and fixtures	$ 3,850			
Less allow. for depr.	2,700	1,150		
Total assets		$32,850	Total liabilities	$32,850

Branch transactions during 1967 are summarized below:

(a) Sales on account, $40,000.
(b) Purchases on account, $10,500.
(c) Goods received from home office, billing at cost, $20,000.
(d) Collections on account, $38,000.
(e) Payments on account, $10,100.
(f) Bad accounts written off, $600.
(g) Cash remittances to home office, $15,000.
(h) Expenses paid, $12,400.
(i) Expenses paid by home office and charged to branch, $800.
(j) Year-end adjusting data:
Merchandise on hand, $19,400.
Prepaid expenses, December 31, $450.
Accrued expenses, December 31, $400.
Receivables estimated to be uncollectible, December 31, $800.
Depreciation for 1967, $600.

Instructions: (1) Give the entries to be made by the branch for the year to record the transactions and to adjust and close the accounts at the end of the year.

(2) Prepare a balance sheet, an income statement, and a statement of changes in the home office account for the branch for the year ended December 31, 1967.

(3) Give all of the entries that would be made by the home office in 1967 affecting the branch account.

7-5. A balance sheet for the Eagle Sales Co. as of January 1, 1967, is given below.

Balance Sheet

Assets			Liabilities and Stockholders' Equity	
Cash		$ 15,000	Accrued expenses	$ 250
Accounts receivable	$42,000		Accounts payable	33,750
Less allow. for bad debts	1,200	40,800	Capital stock	50,000
			Retained earnings	28,200
Merchandise inventory		46,000		
Store furn. and fixtures	$15,000			
Less allow. for depr.	4,600	10,400		
Total assets		$112,200	Total liab. and stockholders' equity	$112,200

On this date a branch sales office is established in Miami. The branch is sent the following assets by the home office upon its organization:

(a) Cash, \$1,500.
(b) Merchandise, cost, \$10,200.
(c) Store furniture and fixtures previously used by the home office — cost, \$3,000; age, 2½ years; depreciation rate used in the past, 10% a year. The cost of shipment and installation, \$900, is paid by the branch. This cost is to be written off over the remaining life of the asset. The equipment accounts are to be carried on the books of the home office.
(d) Accounts receivable, \$2,600. Accounts arose from sales by the home office to customers in Miami. The branch is authorized to take over the accounts and make collections.

Home office and branch transactions with outsiders during January were:

	Home Office	Branch
Sales on account	\$34,600	\$6,200
Collections on own accounts	40,000	2,600
Purchases on account	31,600	3,000
Payments on account	36,200	1,450
Payments of expenses (including accruals as of January 1)	9,200	1,250

The following took place with respect to accounts received by the branch from the home office: collections of \$1,600 were made; accounts of \$150 were uncollectible and were written off; it is believed that remaining accounts of \$850 are collectible.

Interoffice transactions during January were:

Merchandise shipments to branch, cost	\$1,250
Cash remittance to home office	1,000

The following information is to be recorded on January 31:

(a) Merchandise costing \$600 was shipped by the home office to the branch on January 31; this merchandise is in transit and will not reach the branch until February 2. (This shipment is not included in transfers previously mentioned.)
(b) Expenses paid by the home office during the month that are chargeable to the branch total \$475. (These are included in the \$9,200 amount.)
(c) Depreciation on furniture and fixtures is recorded at the rate of 10% a year.
(d) Merchandise inventories, excluding merchandise in transit, are: home office, \$44,500; branch, \$9,800.
(e) Accrued expenses are: home office, \$750; branch, \$350.

Instructions: (1) Prepare journal entries to record the foregoing transactions for (a) the branch and (b) the home office.

(2) Prepare individual statements for the branch and for the home office.

(3) Prepare combined statements for the branch and the home office.

(4) Prepare the journal entries to adjust and close the books at the end of the month for (a) the branch and (b) the home office.

7-6. On January 1, 1967, the Barton Sales Co. opened a new branch in a neighboring city. The balance sheet for the home office on January 1 and a summary of transactions for the home office and the branch for 1967 are given below.

Balance Sheet

Assets			Liabilities and Stockholders' Equity	
Cash		$ 59,300	Accrued expenses	$ 1,250
Accounts receivable		27,650	Accounts payable	22,800
Merchandise inventory		40,120	Capital stock, $20 par	50,000
Prepaid expenses		1,800	Retained earnings	70,420
Furniture and fixtures	$20,000			
Less allowance for depr.	4,400	15,600		
Total assets		$144,470	Total liab. and stockholders' equity	$144,470

Home Office Transactions

(a) Transfers of cash to branch, $42,500.
(b) Transfers of merchandise to branch (billing at cost), $50,200.
(c) Sales on account, $105,000.
(d) Purchases on account, $122,500.
(e) Collections on account, $113,600.
(f) Payments on account, $124,000.
(g) Expenses paid, $26,600.
(h) Cash received from branch, $53,400.
(i) Dividends paid, $10,000.

Adjusting data on December 31:
Depreciation for year, $1,180.
Merchandise inventory, $48,500.
Prepaid expenses, $2,050.
Accrued expenses, $1,350.

Branch Transactions

(a) Cash received from home office, $42,500.
(b) Merchandise received from home office, $50,200.
(c) Sales on account, $66,000.
(d) Purchases on account, $22,500.
(e) Collections on account deposited to the credit of the home office, $53,400.
(f) Payments on account, $12,250.
(g) Purchase of furniture and fixtures for cash, $8,000.
(h) Expenses paid, $18,000.

Adjusting data on December 31:
Depreciation, $650.
Merchandise inventory, $23,500.
Prepaid expenses, $750.
Accrued expenses, $300.

Instructions: (1) Prepare journal entries to record the foregoing transactions for (a) the branch and (b) the home office.

(2) Prepare individual statements for the branch and for the home office.

(3) Prepare combined statements for the branch and the home office.

(4) Give the journal entries to adjust and close the books for (a) the branch and (b) the home office.

7-7. Comparison between the interoffice account of the Walsh Wholesale Company with its suburban branch and the corresponding account carried on the latter's books shows the following discrepancies at the close of business on September 30, 1967:

(a) A charge of $870 (Office Furniture) on the home office books is taken up by the branch as $780.

(b) A credit by the home office for $300 (Merchandise Allowances) is taken up by the branch as $350.

(c) The home office charges the branch $325 for interest on open account, which the branch fails to take up in full; instead, the branch sends to the home office an incorrect adjusting memo, reducing the charge by $75, and sets up a liability for the net amount.

(d) A charge for labor by the home office, $433, is taken up twice by the branch.

(e) A charge of $785 is made by the home office for freight on merchandise, but the amount is entered by the branch as $78.50.

(f) The branch incorrectly sends the home office a debit note for $293, representing its proportion of a bill for truck repairs; the home office does not record it.

(g) The home office receives $475 from the sale of a truck, which it erroneously credits to the branch; the branch does not charge the home office therewith.

(h) The branch accidentally receives a copy of the home office entry dated October 10, 1967, correcting item (g), and enters a credit in favor of the home office as of September 30, 1967.

The balance of the account with the branch on the home office books shows $131,690 receivable from the branch at September 30, 1967. The interoffice accounts were in balance at the beginning of the year.

Instructions: (1) Give the balance on the branch books before adjustment.

(2) Give the correct amount of the interoffice balance.

(3) Prepare working papers reconciling the amount of $131,690 on the home office books with the adjusted balance.

(4) Prepare the journal entry or entries necessary to adjust the branch office books.

(AICPA adapted)

7-8. The Signal Telephone Company operated two departments — Communications and Manufacturing. The Manufacturing division kept a complete set of accounts, which were controlled by the general ledger of the Communications division.

As of November 30, 1967, the Signal Telephone Company sold to the Peet Manufacturing Company the current and plant assets, except cash, of the Manufacturing division, the purchaser assuming all of the department's liabilities to outsiders. On the date of sale the Peet Manufacturing Company issued to the Signal Telephone Company, in full payment of the purchase price, 5,000 shares of no-par common stock.

The Peet Manufacturing Company was organized on November 30, 1967, with a capital of 6,000 shares of no-par common stock and 1,000 shares of 4% cumulative preferred stock, $100 par, having a liquidating and call value of $110 a share. On that date it received cash for the remaining 1,000 shares of common and the 1,000 shares of preferred in the amounts of $60,000 and $100,000 respectively.

The physical transfer of the assets was not made until a month later (December 31, 1967), and the Signal Telephone Company operated the Manufacturing division during December for the account of the Peet Manufacturing Company.

The books of both the Signal Telephone Company and the Peet Manufacturing Company are to be kept on a calendar year basis.

Condensed divisional balance sheets of the Signal Telephone Company at November 30, 1967, and December 31, 1967, before recording the transfer, were as follows:

	November 30, 1967		December 31, 1967	
Assets	Communications	Manufacturing	Communications	Manufacturing
Cash	$ 50,000	$ 10,000	$ 60,000	$ 20,000
Accounts receivable	100,000	50,000	110,000	40,000
Inventories	50,000	100,000	50,000	80,000
Investments in subsidiary companies	20,000	—	20,000	—
Plant and property	500,000	350,000	500,000	350,000
Allowances for depreciation	(250,000)	(150,000)	(252,000)	(152,000)
Total	$470,000	$360,000	$488,000	$338,000

	November 30, 1967		December 31, 1967	
Liabilities and Stockholders' Equity	Communications	Manufacturing	Communications	Manufacturing
Accounts payable	$ 60,000	$ 40,000	$ 78,000	$ 22,000
Sundry accruals	120,000	10,000	110,000	10,000
Reserves for federal income taxes	40,000	—	40,000	—
Interdepartmental control	(300,000)	300,000	(308,000)	308,000
Capital stock	300,000	—	300,000	—
Retained earnings:				
Balance 12/31/66	200,000	—	200,000	—
Profit or (loss)	50,000	10,000	68,000	(2,000)
Total	$470,000	$360,000	$488,000	$338,000

Instructions: (1) Give the journal entries:

(a) To open the books of the Peet Manufacturing Company.
(b) To effect the transfer of the assets acquired and the liabilities assumed by the Peet Manufacturing Company from the Signal Telephone Company for the books of each company.
(c) To effect the elimination of the Manufacturing division of the Signal Telephone Company.
(d) To close the books of each company at December 31, 1967.

(2) Prepare a balance sheet at December 31, 1967, for each company, including any pertinent explanatory notes.

(AICPA adapted)

7-9. Boyle is a processor of steel parts for machines, trading as the Boyle Company, and Kamp is an assembler of machine parts, trading as the Kamp Company.

On January 1, 1966, Boyle and Kamp decided to form a partnership, to be known as the Master Manufacturing Company. It was contemplated that each partner would continue his own business, dealing both with the partnership and with outsiders. The profit and loss ratio was Boyle, 40%, and Kamp, 60%.

No audit was made of the accounts before the following income statements for the year 1966 were prepared:

	Boyle Company	Kamp Company	Master Mfg. Company
Sales	$265,000	$540,000	$870,000
Cost of sales	154,000	372,000	525,000
Gross profit	$111,000	$168,000	$345,000
Expenses	78,000	93,000	210,000
Net profit from operations	$ 33,000	$ 75,000	$135,000
Gain on sale of business property	3,500		3,000
Loan by Kamp Company deemed worthless on account of adjudication in bankruptcy		2,000	
	$ 36,500	$ 73,000	$138,000

An audit of the accounts and the records of the three companies at December 31, 1966, disclosed the following:

(1) Included in cost of sales of Master Manufacturing Company were purchases from Boyle Company of $135,000. Sales to Master Manufacturing Company on the books of Boyle Company were $145,000. Analysis of the discrepancy discloses that Boyle Company had billed Master Manufacturing Company for $8,000, which Master Manufacturing Company claimed was fictitious. In addition, Master Manufacturing Company took a credit of $2,000 for defective merchandise, not recorded by Boyle Company.

(2) Kamp Company also purchased parts from Boyle Company and sold them to Master Manufacturing Company. The books of the three companies involved showed the following entries in connection with these transactions:

On the books of Boyle Company:

Kamp Company	55,000	
Sales		55,000

On the books of Kamp Company:

Purchases	40,000	
Boyle Company		40,000
Master Manufacturing Company	85,000	
Sales		85,000

On the books of Master Manufacturing Company:

Purchases	65,000	
Kamp Company		65,000

(3) Kamp Company disbursed substantial sums on behalf of Master Manufacturing Company during the first 3 months of the latter's existence. An "Advances" account was used by both companies. An analysis of the "Advances" accounts follows:

	Charges to Master Mfg. Co. on books of Kamp Company	Credits to Kamp Company on books of Master Mfg. Co.
Sale of machine for Kamp Co. by Master Manufacturing Co.	$ 3,000	
Insurance	2,000	$ 2,000
Legal expenses	200	
Freight	430	
Advertising	125	
Machinery		25,000
Supplies	10,050	
Payroll	11,190	
	$26,995	$27,000

Boyle and Kamp were unable to reconcile their differences and a Special Master in Chancery was appointed in January, 1967, to find an equitable reconciliation. His findings were as follows:

(a) Boyle Company's bill to Master Manufacturing Company of $8,000 was entirely unsupported and therefore disallowed.

(b) Master Manufacturing Company was entitled to $1,000 credit for defective merchandise.

(c) As to sales by Boyle Company to Kamp Company and by Kamp Company to Master Manufacturing Company, Boyle Company should have charged

Kamp Company $50,000 and Kamp Company should have charged Master Manufacturing Company $70,000.

(d) Expenses disbursed by Kamp Company on behalf of Master Manufacturing Company were allowed, except for the following:

(1) Legal expense to be borne equally.
(2) Advertising allowed in amount of $25 only.
(3) Payroll overstated on Kamp Company's books by $325.

(e) The machine recorded on the books of Master Manufacturing Company actually was owned by Kamp Company. Master Manufacturing Company had deducted $625 depreciation for the 3-month period. Kamp Company had also deducted $625 depreciation. This machine was used by Master Manufacturing Company from date of acquisition on July 1, 1966, to October 1, 1966, when it was sold by Master Manufacturing Company for $27,375, or $3,000 in excess of adjusted book value. Kamp Company charged Master Manufacturing Company with $3,000, representing actual profit of $2,375 plus rental charges of $625. This was allowed. The $3,000 was credited to Cost of Sales on Kamp Company's books.

Instructions: Submit pertinent working papers, a reconciliation of all reciprocal accounts of the three companies, and an accounting of the differences between original and corrected net income figures in summary form for use in preparing the income tax returns of Boyle and Kamp.

(AICPA adapted)

Chapter 8

HOME OFFICE AND BRANCH RELATIONSHIPS

SPECIAL PROBLEMS

In addition to the general branch-home office relationships described in the preceding chapter, there are other relationships that create special accounting problems. These relationships are: (1) interbranch transfers of cash, (2) interbranch transfers of merchandise, and (3) merchandise shipments to branches involving billings at arbitrary rates above cost or at retail sales price.

INTERBRANCH TRANSFERS OF CASH

Ordinarily, branch activities are limited to transactions with the home office and with outsiders. On certain occasions, however, the home office may authorize the transfer of certain assets from one branch to another. Instead of opening special accounts with member branches, branches will normally clear such transfers through the home office account. To illustrate, assume that upon authorization by the home office Branch #1 sends cash of $1,000 to Branch #2. The entries to record this transfer on the home office and branch books are:

Home Office			Branch #1			Branch #2		
Branch #2..........	1,000		Home Office........	1,000		Cash..............	1,000	
Branch #1........		1,000	Cash............		1,000	Home Office......		1,000

When this procedure is followed, settlement between individual branches is not required; the net extent of branch accountability so far as affiliated units are concerned is summarized in a single account, the home office account.

INTERBRANCH TRANSFERS OF MERCHANDISE

When merchandise is supplied by the home office to its branches, it may become necessary in certain instances for the home office to authorize the transfer of goods from one branch to another. Interbranch transfers of merchandise, the same as interbranch transfers of cash, are normally cleared through the home office account rather than through special accounts with member branches.

In the case of interbranch merchandise transfers, a special problem arises with respect to the handling of freight charges. A branch is properly charged with the cost of freight on goods it receives. In arriving at the cost of the merchandise inventory at the end of the period, freight charges are properly recognized as a part of such cost. But a branch should not be charged with excessive freight when, because of indirect routing, excessive costs are incurred. Under such circumstances, the branch acquiring the goods should be charged for no more than the normal freight from the usual shipping point; the office directing the interbranch transfer and responsible for the excessive cost should absorb the excess as a charge to profit and loss. The procedure to be followed is illustrated below.

The Superior Manufacturing Co. ships goods to Branch #5, billing the branch for the goods at $4,500 plus freight charges incurred, $600. At a subsequent date, the home office authorizes the transfer of these goods to Branch #8. Branch #5 pays the freight charge on the transfer, $450. If the shipment had been made by the home office directly to Branch #8, the freight charge would have been $650. Entries on the books of the home office, Branch #5, and Branch #8 to record this interbranch transfer of merchandise would be as follows:

Books of Home Office

Transactions	Entry		
Original shipment of goods and charge to Branch #5 for cost of goods and freight.	Branch #5	5,100	
	Merchandise Shipments to Branch #5		4,500
	Cash		600
Authorization by home office of transfer of goods from Branch #5 to Branch #8: Branch #8 charged for cost of goods and normal freight; Branch #5 credited for original charges plus freight paid on transfer to Branch #8.	Merchandise Shipments to Branch #5	4,500	
	Merchandise Shipments to Branch #8		4,500
	Branch #8	5,150	
	Excess Freight on Interbranch Transfers of Merchandise	400	
	Branch #5		5,550

Books of Branch #5

Transactions	Entry		
Original receipt of goods and charges for cost of goods and freight.	Merchandise Shipments from Home Office	4,500	
	Freight-In	600	
	Home Office		5,100
Transfer of goods at order of home office; charge to home office for original charges plus freight paid on reshipment to Branch #8.	Home Office	5,550	
	Merchandise Shipments from Home Office		4,500
	Freight-In		600
	Cash		450

Books of Branch #8

Transactions	Entry		
Receipt of goods from Branch #5; charges recognized for cost of goods and normal freight.	Merchandise Shipments from Home Office	4,500	
	Freight-In	650	
	Home Office		5,150

In preparing the income statement for the home office, the excess freight charge may be reported as a subtraction from the summary of branch earnings in the lower section of the statement; on the combined income statement, the charge may be reported in the cost of goods sold, selling expense, or general and administrative expense section, depending on the division of the company that is responsible for such transfers.

In the example, it was assumed that neither branch was responsible for the excess freight and the charge was therefore reported on the home office books. If excess freight results from a mistake in an order for goods by a branch or from some other branch failure, the charge should be borne by the branch and be reported on its books.

BRANCH BILLING AT AMOUNTS OTHER THAN COST

When a home office bills the branch for merchandise at a figure other than cost, billing is usually made at an arbitrary rate above cost or at the retail sales figure.

Billing at an arbitrary rate above cost. Billing by the home office may be made at some arbitrary rate above cost in order to withhold from branch officials complete information concerning the actual earnings from branch operations. In other instances, this policy is followed as a means of assigning a charge for goods procurement and handling as well as for the special costs that are related to the home office-branch relationship.

Upon acquiring merchandise from the home office, the branch records the charges that are listed on the invoices accompanying the goods. When billings to the branch exceed cost, the earnings determined by the branch will be less than actual earnings; the inventories reported by the branch at the billed figures will exceed cost. These factors must be recognized by the home office and given effect upon its accounting records in summarizing branch operations.

Assume that goods, cost $10,000, are shipped by a home office to a branch, and the branch is billed for the goods at 20% above cost, or $12,000. The shipment may be recorded as shown at the top of the following page.

Transaction	Home Office Books			Branch Books		
Transfer of merchandise to branch: Home office cost, $10,000. Billing to branch, $12,000.	Branch #1.........	12,000		Mdse. Shipments from Home Office..	12,000	
	Mdse. Shipments to Branch #1.....		10,000	Home Office.....		12,000
	Allowance for Overvaluation of Branch Mdse.....		2,000			

The branch records the goods at their billed price. The home office makes the following entry: Branch #1 is debited for the billed amount; Merchandise Shipments to Branch #1 is credited for the actual cost of the merchandise; an Allowance for Overvaluation of Branch Merchandise is credited for the difference between the billed price and the cost of the goods shipped. Branch and home office accounts, then, are reciprocal. Merchandise shipments reported at cost can be subtracted from the sum of the beginning inventory and the purchases in arriving at the cost of merchandise available for home office sales. The balance in the allowance for overvaluation of branch merchandise account is properly recognized as an offset against the branch account in arriving at the actual investment in the branch.

As the branch sells the goods acquired from the home office and recognizes profit for the difference between the fictitious billed price and the sales price, the difference between the cost and the billed price reported by the home office in the allowance account is properly recognized as earned. Ordinarily, the home office defers recognition of such earnings until the end of the fiscal period. At that time the allowance for overvaluation of branch merchandise account is reduced to a balance equal to the overvaluation actually present in the branch inventory, and the amount of the reduction is added to the net income reported by the branch.

To illustrate, referring again to the example, an allowance of $2,000 is recorded on the books of the home office upon the shipment of merchandise, cost $10,000, at a billed price of $12,000. At the end of the period the branch reports an inventory of $8,400. The actual cost of the branch inventory is $7,000 ($8,400 ÷ 1.20): the allowance for overvaluation of branch merchandise of $2,000 is excessive and should be reduced to a balance of $1,400. In arriving at net income, the branch recognizes cost of goods sold at $3,600 ($12,000 − $8,400). The actual cost of goods sold by the branch is $3,000 ($3,600 ÷ 1.20); the earnings reported by the branch are understated and should be increased by $600. Assuming that the branch books report net income of $5,000, entries to summarize branch activities are made on the branch and home office books as follows:

Transaction	Home Office Books			Branch Books		
(a) To close branch earnings to home office account on branch books. (b) To recognize branch earnings on home office books.	(b) Branch #1 . . . . . . Profit and Loss, Branch #1	5,000	5,000	(a) Profit and Loss . . Home Office . .	5,000	5,000
To bring allowance for overvaluation of branch inventory to required balance and to correct branch earnings.	Allowance for Overvaluation of Branch Mdse. . . . . Profit and Loss, Branch #1	600	600			
To close branch earnings into general profit and loss account.	Profit and Loss, Branch #1 . . . . Profit and Loss. . . .	5,600	5,600			

The balance of Allowance for Overvaluation of Branch Merchandise is now $1,400 and reports the overstatement in the branch investment balance at the end of the period. The credit of $600 to the branch profit and loss account on the home office books corrects the branch earnings for the overstatement of the branch cost of goods sold.

When the branch inventory consists of goods acquired from the home office at a fictitious price and also goods purchased from outsiders at cost, it is necessary to distinguish between the two classes of goods in order that the home office may be able to determine the overvaluation in that portion of the branch inventory acquired from the home office.

Billing at retail sales price. The home office may bill a branch for merchandise at its retail sales price not only to conceal information concerning branch earnings from branch officials, but also to provide a more effective control over merchandise handled by the branch. The home office, when informed of branch sales currently, is provided with a continuous record of the goods in the hands of the branch; the inventory position is calculated by subtracting sales to date from the retail sales price of goods made available to the branch. At the end of the period, a physical inventory for the branch at retail sales price should be equal to the difference between the billed price of goods available for sale and net sales for the period. If the inventory reported by the branch is not equal to this difference, the discrepancy must be investigated and explained to the satisfaction of the home office.

Obviously, if the branch is billed for goods at the sales price, the branch cost of goods sold will be equal to sales and branch activities will show a loss from operations equal to the expenses of operation. Branch accounts may be adjusted and closed in the usual manner at the end of the fiscal period, the home office account being debited for the reported loss. Branch statements may be prepared and submitted to the home office. Since the branch income statement gives no indication of the actual profitability of branch activities, its value to the branch is limited to its use for statistical and comparative purposes.

In accounting for shipments that are billed at sales price, the home office may follow a procedure that is similar to that employed for shipments at an arbitrary rate above cost. A memorandum record is maintained by the home office showing both the cost and the billed prices for all goods sent to the branch. Upon shipping goods to a branch, the allowance for overvaluation of branch merchandise account is credited for the difference between the cost and the billed price. The home office will require the branch to submit a detailed summary of the goods on hand at the end of each period. By reference to the memorandum record of shipments, merchandise items comprising the inventory may be converted from sales prices to costs and the balance that should remain in the allowance account determined. The laborious process of converting sales price to cost for each item or class of merchandise may be avoided if the selling price of all merchandise is fixed by applying a uniform percentage markup on cost. The cost of the inventory may then be calculated as illustrated in the previous section.

The amount transferred from the allowance account to the branch profit and loss account reports the gross profit that has been realized as a result of branch sales. This transfer converts the loss taken up as a result of the branch report into a net income if branch operations have actually proved profitable. The balance remaining in the overvaluation account reports the overstatement in the branch investment balance.

COMBINED STATEMENTS WHEN GOODS ARE BILLED AT AMOUNTS OTHER THAN COST

When affiliated units record interoffice transfers of goods at cost, the preparation of combined financial statements is a relatively simple matter. Reciprocal home office and branch account balances are eliminated and balance sheet data are then combined; reciprocal interoffice revenue and expense balances are eliminated and income statement data are combined. When goods are billed to a branch at amounts other than cost, special problems are encountered in the preparation of combined statements. The ending inventory on the branch balance sheet reported at an amount other than cost must be restated in terms of cost in preparing the combined balance sheet; the beginning and the ending inventory balances on the branch income statement reported at amounts other than cost must be restated in terms of cost in preparing the combined income statement.

When the preparation of combined statements calls for the restatement of real and nominal accounts as well as the elimination of reciprocal accounts, it is generally desirable to develop such summaries through the preparation of working papers that include both balance sheet and income statement data. Such working papers are illustrated in the remaining pages of this chapter.

WORKING PAPERS FOR COMBINED STATEMENTS ILLUSTRATED

Separate balance sheets prepared from the ledgers of the Rodger Sales Corporation and its branch on December 31, 1966, are given below. A combined balance sheet prepared from the separate balance sheets is given at the top of page 236. The branch inventory on December 31 was composed of goods acquired from both the home office and outsiders: goods, cost $20,000, were acquired from outsiders; the balance, $25,000, was acquired from the home office and is stated at billed price, which is 25% above cost.

Rodger Sales Corporation
Balance Sheet — Home Office
December 31, 1966

Assets			Liabilities and Stockholders' Equity		
Cash		$ 25,000	Liabilities		
Accounts receivable		60,000	Accounts payable		$ 40,000
Merchandise inventory		100,000			
Furniture and fixtures	$30,000		Stockholders' equity		
Less allowance for depreciation	12,000	18,000	Capital stock	$200,000	
			Retained earnings	36,500	236,500
Branch	$78,500				
Less allowance for overvaluation of branch merchandise	5,000	73,500			
Total assets		$276,500	Total liab. and stockholders' equity		$276,500

Rodger Sales Corporation
Balance Sheet — Branch
December 31, 1966

Assets			Liabilities	
Cash		$ 10,000	Accounts payable	$ 10,000
Accounts receivable		20,000	Home office	78,500
Merchandise inventory		45,000		
Furniture and fixtures	$22,500			
Less allowance for depreciation	9,000	13,500		
Total assets		$ 88,500	Total liabilities	$ 88,500

Rodger Sales Corporation

Combined Balance Sheet for Home Office and Branch

December 31, 1966

Assets			Liabilities and Stockholders' Equity		
Cash		$ 35,000	Liabilities		
Accounts receivable		80,000	Accounts payable		$ 50,000
Merchandise inventory		140,000	Stockholders' equity		
Furniture and fixtures	$52,500		Capital stock	$200,000	
Less allowance for depreciation	21,000	31,500	Retained earnings	36,500	236,500
Total assets		$286,500	Total liab. and stockholders' equity		$286,500

Transactions of the home office and the branch during 1967 are listed and recorded below.

Transactions	Home Office Books			Branch Books		
Purchases on account.	Purchases	220,000		Purchases	25,000	
	Accounts Payable		220,000	Accounts Payable		25,000
Goods shipped to branch by home office: cost, $48,000; billed price, 25% above cost, or $60,000.	Branch	60,000		Merchandise Shipments from Home Office	60,000	
	Merchandise Shipments to Branch		48,000	Home Office		60,000
	Allowance for Overvaluation of Branch Merchandise		12,000			
Sales on account.	Accounts Receivable	300,000		Accounts Receivable	125,000	
	Sales		300,000	Sales		125,000
Collections on account.	Cash	305,000		Cash	115,000	
	Accounts Receivable		305,000	Accounts Receivable		115,000
Payments on account.	Accounts Payable	200,000		Accounts Payable	30,000	
	Cash		200,000	Cash		30,000
Payment of expenses.	Expenses	47,000		Expenses	17,750	
	Cash		47,000	Cash		17,750

Transaction	Home Office Books	Branch Books
Declaration and payment of dividends by home office.	Dividends Declared........ 25,000 Cash......... 25,000	
Remittances by branch to home office.	Cash........... 30,000 Branch........ 30,000	Home Office..... 30,000 Cash......... 30,000
Adjusting data: Depreciation for year.	Expenses........ 3,000 Allowance for Depreciation... 3,000	Expenses........ 2,250 Allowance for Depreciation... 2,250
To close beginning merchandise inventories.	Profit and Loss... 100,000 Merchandise Inventory, Jan. 1........ 100,000	Profit and Loss... 45,000 Merchandise Inventory, Jan. 1........ 45,000
To record ending merchandise inventories: Home office.......... $80,000 Branch: Acquired from outsiders.............. $10,000 Acquired from home office at billed price. 20,000 Total.............. $30,000	Merchandise Inventory, Dec. 31......... 80,000 Profit and Loss. 80,000	Merchandise Inventory Dec. 31......... 30,000 Profit and Loss. 30,000

Working papers for the preparation of combined statements are illustrated on page 238.

The balances listed in the first two columns of the working papers report the account balances of the home office and the branch as of December 31, 1967. It will be noted that the trial balances are adjusted and brought up to date except for the ending merchandise inventories. Beginning inventories are reported in the adjusted trial balances as debits; these are to be recognized in arriving at cost of goods sold. Ending inventories are listed following both trial balance debit and credit sections: ending inventories are reported as debits so that they may be recognized as assets in the development of the balance sheet; ending inventories are also reported as credits so that they may be recognized as subtractions from the cost of goods available for sale (beginning inventories and purchases) in arriving at cost of goods sold.

Rodger Sales Corporation

Working Papers for Combined Statements for Home Office and Branch

December 31, 1967

	Home Office	Branch	Adjustments and Eliminations Dr.	Adjustments and Eliminations Cr.	Income Statement Dr.	Income Statement Cr.	Retained Earnings Dr.	Retained Earnings Cr.	Balance Sheet Dr.	Balance Sheet Cr.
Debits										
Cash	88,000	47,250							135,250	
Accounts Receivable	55,000	30,000							85,000	
Mdse. Inventory, Jan. 1, 1967	100,000	45,000		(c) 5,000	140,000					
Furniture and Fixtures	30,000	22,500							52,500	
Branch	108,500			(a) 108,500						
Purchases	220,000	25,000			245,000					
Mdse. Shipments from Home Office		60,000		(b) 60,000						
Expenses	50,000	20,000			70,000					
Dividends Declared	25,000						25,000			
	676,500	249,750								
Mdse. Inventory, December 31, 1967 (Balance Sheet)	80,000	30,000		(d) 4,000					106,000	
Credits										
Allowance for Overvaluation of Branch Merchandise	17,000		(b) 12,000 (c) 5,000							
Allowance for Depr. of Furniture and Fixtures	15,000	11,250								26,250
Accounts Payable	60,000	5,000								65,000
Home Office		108,500	(a) 108,500							
Capital Stock	200,000									200,000
Retained Earnings, January 1, 1967	36,500							36,500		
Sales	300,000	125,000				425,000				
Mdse. Shipments to Branch	48,000		(b) 48,000							
	676,500	249,750								
Mdse. Inventory, December 31, 1967 (Income Statement)	80,000	30,000	(d) 4,000			106,000				
			177,500	177,500	455,000	531,000	25,000	36,500	378,750	291,250
Net Income to Retained Earnings					76,000			76,000		
					531,000	531,000				
Balance of Retained Earnings to Balance Sheet							87,500			87,500
							112,500	112,500	378,750	378,750

The transactions that were given on pages 236 and 237 resulted in an allowance for overvaluation of branch merchandise on the home office books as follows:

Allowance for Overvaluation of Branch Merchandise

	1967 Jan. 1 Balance relating to goods acquired from home office at 25% above cost; billed price \$25,000, cost \$20,000 (\$25,000 – [\$25,000 ÷ 1.25]). 5,000 Jan. 1– Dec. 31 Merchandise, cost \$48,000, billed at 25% above cost... 12,000 *(Balance in account, \$17,000)*

The branch account on the home office books appeared as follows:

Branch

1967 Jan. 1 Balance.................. 78,500 Jan. 1– Dec. 31 Merchandise shipments to branch.................. 60,000 *(Balance in account, \$108,500)*	1967 Jan. 1– Dec. 31 Remittances from branch.. 30,000

The home office account on the branch books appeared as follows:

Home Office

1967 Jan. 1– Dec. 31 Remittances to home office. 30,000	1967 Jan. 1 Balance.................. 78,500 Jan. 1– Dec. 31 Mdse. shipments from home office.................... 60,000 *(Balance in account, \$108,500)*

In developing combined statements, the affiliated units are recognized as a single unit. Accounts for the home office and the branch must be restated so that, when combined, they will offer those balances that would have resulted if the transactions of the related units had been recorded in a single set of books. In this process any balance sheet accounts that report interoffice charges and credits and that have no meaning when the related units are recognized as one unit are eliminated. Any income statement accounts that report transfers of merchandise or charges for services between affiliated units similarly require elimination. Furthermore, when merchandise accounts report values other than cost and an allowance for overvaluation of branch merchandise has been established, merchandise accounts will require restatement to cost and the allowance account will require cancellation.

The adjustments and the eliminations that were made on the working papers for the Rodger Sales Corporation and its branch in arriving at a summary of the activities of the related units are described below.

(a) The reciprocal accounts Home Office and Branch are canceled by the following elimination:

Home Office	108,500	
Branch		108,500

(b) Account balances resulting from the transfer of merchandise between offices are canceled by the following elimination:

Merchandise Shipments to Branch	48,000	
Allowance for Overvaluation of Branch Merchandise	12,000	
Merchandise Shipments from Home Office		60,000

(c) The original balance of $5,000 in the allowance for overvaluation of branch merchandise account is applied to the beginning inventory balance to reduce it to cost as follows:

Allowance for Overvaluation of Branch Merchandise	5,000	
Merchandise Inventory, Jan. 1, 1967		5,000

(d) The ending inventory, both as a balance sheet value and an income statement value, is reduced by $4,000 to its actual cost as follows:

Merchandise Inventory, Dec. 31, 1967 (Income Statement)	4,000	
Merchandise Inventory, Dec. 31, 1967 (Balance Sheet)		4,000

Combining branch and home office accounts now gives those balances that would have been obtained if a single set of accounts had been maintained in recording activities of both the branch and the home office. Combined account balances are carried to appropriate Income Statement, Retained Earnings, and Balance Sheet columns on the working papers. Following such transfers, the Income Statement columns are summarized and the net income is carried to the Retained Earnings columns. The retained earnings balance may now be determined and carried to the Balance Sheet columns. The statement columns are used in preparing the combined statements illustrated on page 241.

It should be noted that the adjustments and the eliminations just described are made only on the working papers. The accounts and the ledgers of the home office and the branch are not affected. Home office and branch accounts are closed in the usual manner. Transactions of subsequent periods will continue to be recorded on the books of the home

Rodger Sales Corporation
Combined Balance Sheet for Home Office and Branch
December 31, 1967

Assets			Liabilities and Stockholders' Equity		
Cash		$135,250	**Liabilities**		
Accounts receivable		85,000	Accounts payable		$ 65,000
Merchandise inventory		106,000			
Furniture and fixtures	$52,500		**Stockholders' equity**		
Less allowance for depreciation	26,250	26,250	Capital stock	$200,000	
			Retained earnings	87,500	287,500
Total assets		$352,500	Total liabilities and stockholders' equity		$352,500

Rodger Sales Corporation
Combined Income Statement for Home Office and Branch
For Year Ended December 31, 1967

Sales		$425,000
Cost of goods sold:		
Merchandise inventory, Jan. 1, 1967	$140,000	
Purchases	245,000	
Merchandise available for sale	$385,000	
Less merchandise inventory, Dec. 31, 1967	106,000	279,000
Gross profit on sales		$146,000
Expenses		70,000
Net income		$ 76,000

Rodger Sales Corporation
Combined Retained Earnings Statement for Home Office and Branch
For Year Ended December 31, 1967

Retained earnings balance, January 1, 1967	$ 36,500
Add net income for year	76,000
	$112,500
Deduct dividends declared	25,000
Retained earnings balance, December 31, 1967	$ 87,500

office and the branch with appropriate recognition of the special requirements that are found in employing separate self-balancing records for each of the related units.

Continuing the previous example, the accounts for the home office and the branch are closed by the following entries:

Transaction	Home Office Books			Branch Books		
Closing entries: To close nominal accounts.	Sales . . . . Merchandise Shipments to Branch . . . . Purchases . . . . . Expenses . . . . . . Profit and Loss.	300,000 48,000	 220,000 50,000 78,000	Sales . . . . Purchases . . . . . Merchandise Shipments from Home Office . . . Expenses . . . . . . Profit and Loss.	125,000	 25,000 60,000 20,000 20,000
To close branch earnings to home office account.				Profit and Loss . . . Home Office . . .	5,000	 5,000
To recognize branch earnings on home office books: (a) Branch net income per branch books, $5,000.	(a) Branch . . . . Branch Profit and Loss	5,000	 5,000			
(b) To bring allowance for overvaluation of branch inventory to required balance and to correct branch earnings: Balance in allowance before adjustment, 12/31/67 $17,000 Required balance, 12/31/67 (billed price $20,000 – cost [$20,000 ÷ 1.25]) 4,000 Transfer to branch profit and loss $13,000	(b) Allowance for Overvaluation of Branch Merchandise . . . . . Branch Profit and Loss	13,000	 13,000			
To close branch earnings into general profit and loss account.	Branch Profit and Loss . . . . Profit and Loss.	18,000	 18,000			
To close combined earnings for the period to Retained Earnings.	Profit and Loss . . . Retained Earnings	76,000	 76,000			
To close dividends declared balance.	Retained Earnings Dividends Declared	25,000	 25,000			

QUESTIONS

1. A home office frequently authorizes the transfer of cash from one branch to another. How should such transfers be reported on the books of the home office and the respective branches?

2. Describe the nature of the special problem that arises when a home office authorizes interbranch transfers of merchandise.

3. How would you recommend that the balance of the account Excess Freight on Interbranch Transfers of Merchandise be reported on (a) the income statement for the home office and (b) the combined income statement?

4. The branches of the Bolton Co. find it necessary to borrow from banks in their respective cities at frequent intervals. The home office, however, wishes to maintain a complete record of all bank obligations on its own books. What accounting procedure would you recommend on the books of the branches and the home office when (a) an amount is borrowed by a branch from a bank and (b) the branch repays the loan together with interest?

5. The Martin Department Store maintains three branch stores in outlying suburban districts. While merchandise is sold at an average markup on cost of 25%, certain classes of merchandise are sold at some special sales at a smaller margin, at cost, or in some instances below cost. Retail prices are also changed as a result of wholesale price fluctuations. What are the advantages and the disadvantages to be found in billing the branches for merchandise (a) at cost, (b) at a uniform percentage above cost, and (c) at selling price?

6. The home office ships merchandise to its branch, billing the branch for such goods at a standard percentage above cost. (a) What entries are made on the books of the home office and the branch in recording the transfer? (b) What entries will be required by the home office in recognizing the sale to outsiders of a portion of such a shipment?

7. A branch acquires goods for sale from both its home office and outside suppliers. The home office bills the branch for merchandise at sales price, which involves varying markups on the different classes of goods shipped. How can the home office arrive at branch inventory cost at the end of the period?

8. Welson, Inc., bills its branch for merchandise at an amount in excess of cost and establishes an allowance for overvaluation of branch merchandise on its books. The branch subsequently finds that it does not require all of the goods and returns part of the shipment. (a) What entries would be required for such a return on both the branch and the home office books? (b) How would you recognize freight charges incurred by the home office and subsequently by the branch on the transfer and the return of the goods?

9. The home office of Frank Co. bills branches for merchandise at amounts in excess of cost and establishes an allowance for overvaluation of branch merchandise on such transfers. At the end of each period, the balance of this account is reduced to the excess still reported in the branch inventory. (a) How would you treat this balance in preparing a balance sheet for the home office? (b) How would you treat this balance in preparing a combined balance sheet for home office and branch?

10. The New York branch of the Suprex Products Co. receives remittances from customers whose accounts originated in sales made by other branches. This branch keeps the cash from such collections, simply notifying the home office and the other branches of such collections. What entries would you recommend be made by the home office and the related branches in accounting for the collections?

11. What point of view is taken in the restatement of branch and home office activities for purposes of combined statement presentation?

12. In listing adjusted trial balance data for home office and branch in the development of working papers for combined statements, home office and branch balances are not reciprocal if the home office has recognized branch earnings but the branch has not yet closed its nominal accounts. What effect does this have on the elimination of the reciprocal accounts?

13. What special adjustments are required in the preparation of working papers for combined statements when an allowance for overvaluation of branch merchandise is found on the home office trial balance?

14. What is the effect of the preparation of combined statements on the closing entries for home and branch office books?

EXERCISES

1. Branch A is authorized by its home office to send cash of $1,500 that it can spare to Branch B. How is this transfer best recorded on the books of (a) Branch A, (b) Branch B, and (c) the home office?

2. The McCall Manufacturing Company maintains branches that market the products that it produces. Merchandise is billed to the branches at manufacturing cost, the branches paying freight charges from the home office to the branch. On November 15, Branch No. 1 ships part of its stock to Branch No. 5 upon authorization by the home office. Originally Branch No. 1 had been billed for this merchandise at $1,600 and had paid freight charges on the shipment from the home office of $350. Branch No. 5, upon receiving the merchandise, pays freight charges on the shipment from Branch No. 1 of $250. If the shipment had been made from the home office directly to Branch No. 5, the freight cost to Branch No. 5 would have been $400. How should the merchandise transfers be recorded on the books of (a) Branch No. 1, (b) Branch No. 5, and (c) the home office?

3. The ledger of the Phillips Branch Store #5 shows the following balances on December 31:

Merchandise inventory, January 1 (cost)	$40,000
Shipments from home office (at cost)	30,000
Freight in	5,000
Sales	50,000
Sales returns	2,000

A closing inventory is taken on December 31, and the merchandise at sales price is determined to be $52,000. At what cost should the ending merchandise inventory be recorded?

4. Trial balances before adjustment for the home office and the branch of the Ace Company show the following items on December 31. Differences in the shipments account balances result from the home office policy of billing the branch for merchandise at 20% above cost.

	Home Office Books	Branch Books
Allowance for overvaluation of branch merchandise.	$3,600	
Shipments to branch.	8,000	
Purchases (outsiders).		$ 2,500
Shipments from home office.		9,600
Merchandise inventory, December 1		15,000

(a) What part of the branch inventory as of December 1 represented purchases from outsiders and what part represented goods acquired from the home office?

(b) Assuming that the branch ending inventory is $10,000, composed of merchandise from home office at billed price, $8,400, and merchandise from outsiders at cost, $1,600, what entry is necessary on the home office books to adjust the allowance account at the end of the fiscal period?

5. The Marsh Co. bills its branch for merchandise at 135% of cost. On December 31 the balance in the inventory allowance account is to be calculated from the following information reported by the branch:

	Merchandise from Home Office (at billed price)	Merchandise Purchased from Outsiders (at cost)	Merchandise Total
Mdse. inventory, Dec. 1.	$16,200	$ 4,000	$20,200
Mdse. into stock, Dec. 1–31.	20,250	12,000	32,250
Mdse. inventory, Dec. 31.	18,900	5,000	23,900

(a) What is the balance of the allowance account on the home office books before any adjustment is made for branch sales for December?

(b) What entry is required on the home office books to adjust the allowance account at the end of December?

(c) Assuming that the branch had returned to the home office merchandise originally acquired at a billed price of $540, what entries would be made on the branch and home office books to record this return?

6. The Berkeley branch of the Bruin Co. is billed for merchandise by the home office at 20% above cost. The branch in turn prices merchandise for sales purposes at 25% above billed price. On January 17 all of the branch merchandise is destroyed by fire. No insurance was maintained. Branch accounts show the following information:

Merchandise inventory, Jan. 1, (at billed price)	$26,400
Shipments from home office (Jan. 1–17)	20,000
Sales	15,000
Sales returns	2,000
Sales allowances	1,000

(a) What was the cost of the merchandise destroyed?

(b) Give the entries on both the branch books and the home office books to record the loss. (Assume perpetual inventory records.)

7. On December 1, Walsh Co. opened a branch in Newark, shipping to the branch merchandise billed at $30,000. During the month additional shipments were made at billed prices of $12,000. During December the branch returned merchandise that was defective and received credits of $750 on the returns. At the end of the month the branch records its inventory at $18,500, as follows:

Merchandise acquired from home office at billed price	$16,500
Merchandise acquired from outsiders	2,000
Total inventory	$18,500

A branch loss for December is calculated at $2,600.

The home office has followed the practice of billing the branch at 20% above merchandise cost. Further, the home office has recorded branch merchandise shipments and returns in its regular sales and sales returns accounts at this billed price.

Give the journal entries that are necessary on the books of the home office at the end of December to recognize the results of branch operations and to correct and bring its books up to date.

PROBLEMS

8-1. On December 31, the end of a monthly period, the trial balance for the Burnside Sales Co. Branch No. 1 reported balances as listed below. The home office bills the branch for merchandise at 33⅓% above cost.

Cash	$ 2,510	Notes Payable	$ 1,000
Merchandise Inventory	16,000	Home Office	23,180
Store Supplies	400	Sales	20,500
Store Furniture	8,000	Purchases	5,000
Allowance for Depreciation of Store Furniture	320	Shipments from Home Office	10,500
		Selling Expenses	4,250
Accounts Payable	3,500	General Expenses	1,840

The following data were available on December 31:

Store supplies inventory, $140.
Depreciation of furniture, 1% a month.
Accrued selling expenses, $120.
Prepaid selling expenses, $150.

Merchandise inventories:	On Dec. 1	On Dec. 31
Amount received from home office (at billed price)	$12,500	$14,200
Amount purchased from outsiders (at cost)	3,500	2,750
Total on hand	$16,000	$16,950

The home office notified the branch on December 31 that it had paid off the branch note for $1,000.

Instructions: (1) Prepare the adjusting and closing entries for the branch. (2) Give the journal entries on the home office books summarizing branch operations for the month.

8-2. Branch No. 12 was established by Royal Sales, Inc., on March 1. Merchandise was billed to the branches by the home office at 30% above cost. Branch transactions during March were as follows:

Mar. 1. Received from home office $8,500 cash and merchandise billed at $28,600.

1. Paid $800 representing first and last months' rent on lease.

1. Purchased furniture and fixtures for $6,500, paying $2,000 cash, the balance to be paid in 90 days. The home office is informed of this purchase, all branch fixed assets being carried on the home office books.

Mar. 1–31. Purchased merchandise from outsiders on account, $9,500.
Paid on account, $3,500.
Sold merchandise on account, $16,025.
Received in payment of accounts: cash, $8,000; notes, $1,500.
Paid expenses:

Advertising	$ 320
Sales salaries and commissions	750
Miscellaneous selling expenses	350
Miscellaneous general expenses	300
Total	$ 1,720

Remitted to home office cash of $2,500 and returned merchandise billed at $1,040 that was unsuited for branch.
Received summary of charges to branch made by home office for March:

Depreciation of furniture and fixtures	$ 65
Insurance on branch assets (the home office originally debited Prepaid Insurance for payment of insurance premiums)	50
Taxes on branch assets (accrued by home office)	40
Advertising	450
Total	$ 605

On March 31 the branch had stock on hand as follows:

Merchandise received from home office (at billed amounts).....	$18,850
Merchandise purchased from outsiders (at cost)...............	4,800
Total inventory..................................	$23,650

Sales salaries of $40 had accrued on this date.

Instructions: (1) Give the journal entries for the branch to record the transactions listed and to adjust and close the books at the end of the month.

(2) Give the journal entries that are required on the books of the home office as a result of the foregoing.

8-3. Profit and loss data for Paxton Sales Co. of Cincinnati and its Dayton branch for 1967 follow:

	Cincinnati Office	Dayton Office
Sales...	$1,060,000	$315,000
Inventory, January 1 (at cost).....................	115,000	
(at billed price)..............		44,500
Purchases....................................	820,000	
Shipments to Dayton Office (at cost)..............	210,000	
Shipments from Cincinnati Office (at billed price)....		252,000
Inventory, December 31 (at cost)..................	142,500	
(at billed price)............		58,500
Operating expenses..............................	382,000	101,500

Records show that the Dayton Branch was billed for merchandise shipments as follows:

In 1966, cost + 25%
In 1967, cost + 20%

Instructions: (1) Prepare income statements for the branch and for the home office for the year ended December 31, 1967.

(2) Prepare a combined income statement.

(3) Give the closing entries for the branch.

(4) Give the entries that are required on the home office books to summarize branch and home office operations and to close the books.

8-4. The Ruggles Co. operates a branch in Cleveland. Profit and loss data for the home office and the branch for 1967 follow:

	Home Office	Branch
Sales.................................	$256,000	$78,500
Purchases from outsiders....................	210,000	20,000
Shipments to branch:		
Cost to home office......................	30,000	
Billing price to branch....................		40,000
Expenses................................	60,000	12,500

Inventories, January 1, 1967:		
Home office, acquired from outsiders, at cost..	80,000	
Branch:		
Acquired from outsiders, at cost...........		7,500
Acquired from home office, at billed price, which averaged 22½% above cost.......		24,500
Inventories, December 31, 1967:		
Home office, acquired from outsiders, at cost..	55,000	
Branch:		
Acquired from outsiders, at cost...........		5,500
Acquired from home office, at 1967 billed price.............................		26,000

Instructions: (1) Prepare an income statement for the branch and an income statement for the home office for the year ended December 31, 1967.

(2) Prepare a combined income statement for branch and home office.

(3) Give the closing entries on the books of the branch.

(4) Give the entries recognizing the branch net income followed by the closing entries on the books of the home office.

8-5. On December 31, 1967, the end of a monthly period, trial balances were prepared for the Spencer Sales Co. and its branch as shown below. Merchandise was billed to the branch by the home office at 120% of cost.

	Home Office		Branch	
	Dr.	Cr.	Dr.	Cr.
Cash	10,350		2,650	
Accounts Receivable	26,200		12,850	
Merchandise Inventory (December 1)	31,500		14,400	
Home Office Furniture and Fixtures	8,500			
Allowance for Depreciation of Home Office Furniture and Fixtures		2,500		
Branch Furniture and Fixtures			3,600	
Allowance for Depreciation of Branch Furniture and Fixtures				540
Allowance for Overvaluation of Branch Merchandise		3,700		
Store Supplies	940		580	
Branch	33,760			
Accounts Payable		35,400		4,200
Home Office				32,040
Capital Stock		65,000		
Retained Earnings	6,850			
Sales		44,850		20,000
Shipments to Branch		8,500		
Purchases	27,600		4,100	
Shipments from Home Office			10,200	
Advertising	2,850		2,800	
Sales Salaries and Commissions	4,250		2,350	
Miscellaneous Selling Expense	1,850		1,050	
Rent	2,700		1,500	
Miscellaneous General Expense (includes taxes and insurance)	2,600		700	
	159,950	159,950	56,780	56,780

The following data were available on December 31:

Merchandise inventories: home office, cost $24,200; branch, $14,600, composed of merchandise received from the home office (at billed price), $11,700, and merchandise purchased from outsiders (at cost), $2,900.

Store supplies on hand: home office, $380; branch, $300.

Prepaid expenses (credit Miscellaneous General Expense): home office, $350; branch, $120.

Accrued expenses (charge Miscellaneous General Expense): home office, $260; branch, $105.

Depreciation of furniture and fixtures is recorded at 1% a month.

A cash remittance of $1,500 had been recorded on the branch books; this cash has not yet been received by the home office and no entry has been made.

The home office had charged the branch with the following expenses that have not yet been recorded by the branch: taxes and insurance, $220.

Instructions: (1) Prepare individual statements for the branch and the home office for the month of December, 1967.

(2) Prepare working papers for combined statements.

(3) Prepare combined statements for the branch and the home office.

(4) Give the entries to adjust and close the books of (a) the branch and (b) the home office.

8-6. The Joy Music Company, a Washington corporation, operates two retail music stores, one located in Seattle, Washington, and the other in Tacoma, Washington. Each store maintains a separate set of accounting records; intercompany transfers or transactions are recorded in an intercompany account carried on each set of records.

Purchases of major items of inventory, such as organs and pianos, are made under a financial arrangement with a local bank advancing 90% of the invoice price and the company paying 10%. If the bank note remains unpaid at the end of 90 days, the company is required to pay an additional 10% of the invoice price as a payment on the note.

In August, 1967, the Seattle store purchased an organ for which the seller's draft in the amount of $6,300 was sent to The First National Bank of Seattle, which refused to finance the purchase of the instrument. Arrangements were made through the Tacoma store with The Citizens Bank of Tacoma to provide the financing. The bank lent the Tacoma store 90% of the invoice price, or $5,670, which the Tacoma store deposited and credited to Notes Payable. The Seattle store drew a check payable to the Tacoma store for $630, or 10% of the invoice price, charging the Tacoma intercompany account on its books. The Tacoma store took up the deposit, crediting the intercompany account with the Seattle store.

The Tacoma store, using the 10% received from the Seattle store and the 90% advanced by the bank, drew a check payable to The First National Bank of Seattle in full payment of the draft, charging Notes Payable.

In November, the Seattle store made the second payment of $630 directly to the Tacoma bank, charging the Tacoma intercompany account, and also notified the Tacoma bookkeeper that the payment had been made. The Tacoma store took up the transaction, charging Organ Purchases and crediting the Seattle intercompany account. In December, the Seattle store paid off the balance on the note, charging Organ Purchases.

Instructions: Give the entries that are required on each set of books to correct the account balances.

(AICPA adapted)

8-7. The trial balances of the home office and the branch office of The Allen Company appear below.

The Allen Company
Trial Balance
For the Year Ended December 31, 1967

Debits	Home	Branch
Cash	$ 17,000	$ 200
Inventory — Home	23,000	
Inventory — Branch		11,550
Sundry Assets	200,000	48,450
Branch Current Account	60,000	
Purchases	190,000	
Purchases from Home		105,000
Freight-in from Home		5,500
Sundry Expenses	42,000	24,300
	$532,000	$195,000

Credits	Home	Branch
Sundry Liabilities	$ 35,000	$ 3,500
Home Current Account		51,500
Sales	155,000	140,000
Sales to Branch	110,000	
Allowance for Markup in Branch Inventory	1,000	
Capital Stock	200,000	
Retained Earnings	31,000	
	$532,000	$195,000

The audit at December 31, 1967, disclosed the following:

(1) The branch office deposits all cash receipts in a local bank for the account of the home office. The audit work sheet for the cash cut-off revealed:

Amount	Deposited by Branch	Recorded by Home Office
$1,050	December 27, 1967	December 30, 1967
$1,100	December 29, 1967	January 2, 1968
$ 600	December 30, 1967	January 3, 1968
$ 300	January 2, 1968	January 6, 1968

(2) The branch office pays expenses incurred locally from an imprest bank account that is maintained with a balance of $2,000. Checks are drawn once a week on this imprest account and the home office is notified of the amount needed to replenish the account. At December 30 an $1,800 reimbursement check was mailed to the branch office.

(3) The branch office receives all of its goods from the home office. The home office bills the goods at cost plus a markup of 10% of cost. At December 31 a shipment with a billing value of $5,000 was in transit to the branch. Freight costs are typically 5% of billed values. Freight costs are considered to be inventoriable costs.

(4) The trial balance opening inventories are shown at their respective costs to the home office and to the branch office. The inventories at December 31, excluding the shipment in transit, are

Home office, at cost	$30,000
Branch office, at billing value	$10,400

Instructions: Prepare a work sheet for The Allen Company and its branch office with columns for "Trial Balance," "Adjustments and Eliminations," "Home Income Statement," "Branch Income Statement," and "Combined Balance Sheet." The branch income statement should be prepared on the basis of home cost. (Formal journal entries are not required. Supporting computations must be in good form.) Number your work sheet adjusting and eliminating entries. Disregard income taxes.

(AICPA adapted)

8-8. You are engaged to audit the records of the Western Import Company, which has not previously been audited. The trial balance at December 31, 1967, follows:

Debits	Home Office	Branch
Cash	$ 15,000	$ 2,000
Accounts receivable	20,000	17,000
Inventory — December 31, 1967	30,000	8,000
Fixed assets — net	150,000	
Branch office current account	44,000	
Cost of sales	220,000	93,000
Expenses	70,000	41,000
Total	$549,000	$161,000
Credits		
Accounts payable	$ 23,000	
Mortgage payable	50,000	
Capital stock	100,000	
Retained earnings — January 1, 1967	26,000	
Sales	350,000	$150,000
Accrued expenses		2,000
Home office current account		9,000
Total	$549,000	$161,000

The following additional information is to be considered:

(1) The branch receives all of its merchandise from the home office. The home office bills goods to the branch at 125% of cost. During 1967 the branch was billed for $105,000 on shipments from the home office.

(2) The home office credits sales for the invoice price of goods shipped to the branch.

(3) On January 1, 1967, the inventory of the home office was $25,000. The branch books showed a $6,000 inventory.

(4) The home office billed the branch for $12,000 on December 30, 1967, representing the branch's share of expenses paid at the home office. The branch has not recorded this billing.

(5) All cash collections made by the branch are deposited in a local bank to the account of the home office. Deposits of this nature included the following:

Amount	Date Deposited by Branch	Date Recorded by Home Office
$5,000	December 28, 1967	December 30, 1967
3,000	December 29, 1967	January 2, 1968
7,000	December 30, 1967	January 3, 1968
2,000	January 2, 1968	January 5, 1968

(6) Expenses incurred locally by the branch are paid from an imprest bank account that is reimbursed periodically by the home office. Just prior to the end of the year, the home office forwarded a reimbursement check in the amount of $3,000, which was not received by the branch office until January, 1968.

(7) It is not necessary to make provisions for federal income tax.

Instructions: (1) Prepare a columnar work sheet for the company and its branch with columns for "Trial Balance," "Adjustments and Eliminations," "Branch Income Statement," "Home Office Income Statement," and "Balance Sheet," Complete the work sheet, keying and explaining all adjustments and eliminations. (The income statement should be on a *cost* basis.)

(2) Prepare a reconciliation of branch office and home office current accounts showing the *corrected* book balances.

(AICPA adapted)

8-9. The Boston Branch, an outlet of Jones Sales Co., receives its merchandise from its out-of-state home office at an interoffice billing price determined at 133⅓% of cost at home office shipping point. Branch inventories are carried on the branch books at the interoffice billing price.

The Boston Branch is required to file a separate state franchise report, and for this purpose inventories are to be based on cost at home office shipping point without regard to transportation costs.

The trial balance before closing for the Boston Branch of Jones Sales Co. at August 31, 1967, appears at the top of the following page.

	Dr.	Cr.
Cash	$ 13,930	
Imprest Cash Fund	200	
Notes Receivable	8,000	
Accrued Interest Income (October 1, 1966)	190	
Accounts Receivable	18,000	
Inventory (October 1, 1966, at interoffice billing price)	12,000	
Sales		$ 56,200
Sales Returns	2,500	
Sales Allowances	3,815	
Shipments from Home Office and Other Branch (at interoffice billing price)	61,840	
Freight-In	3,064	
Home Office Merchandise Account		61,840
Home Office Current Account		11,309
Selling Expenses	2,910	
Administrative and General Expenses	4,150	
Interest Income		1,250
	$130,599	$130,599

Related accounts in the books of the home office of Jones Sales Co. show balances at September 30, 1967, before year-end closing, as follows:

	Dr.	Cr.
Allowance for Bad Debts — Boston Branch Accounts Receivable (to be adjusted at year-end closing to 2% of accounts receivable)		$ 850
Allowance for Interoffice Profit on Inventories — Boston Branch 10/1/66		3,000
Branch Furniture and Fixtures (at cost, acquired 10/1/62)	$ 4,500	
Allowance for Depreciation — Boston Branch Furniture and Fixtures (depreciation accumulated through 9/30/66)		1,800
Boston Branch Current Account	11,423	
Boston Branch Merchandise Account	64,800	
Shipments to Branch (at billing price)		64,800

Transactions of the branch for September, 1967, as yet unrecorded because of illness of the branch bookkeeper, are summarized as follows:

(1) Gross sales on credit, $12,000.

(2) Sales returns, $600; sales allowances, $885.

(3) Shipments from home office at billing price, $2,960; freight paid by branch, $195.

(4) Selling expenses, $390, and administrative and general expenses, $750, paid in cash.

(5) Cash collected from customers, $6,570; notes received on account, $2,100.

(6) Cash remitted to home office on September 30, 1967, $2,500.

Other Branch Data at September 30, 1967

(7) Interest accrued on notes receivable, $204.

(8) Accounts determined to be worthless and to be charged off, $595.

(9) Actual petty cash on hand, $86. The petty cash paid out was for miscellaneous administrative expenses. A check to replenish the imprest cash fund was in transit from the home office at September 30, 1967.

(10) Inventory of Boston Branch, September 30, 1967, at interoffice billing price, $16,000.

Additional Facts

(11) During the year, the home office incurred clerical and other expenses of $1,270 applicable to the Boston Branch, also insurance on direct shipments to the branch of $185. These items, recorded in the home office account Administrative and General Expenses Control, are charged currently to branch operations subsidiary accounts on the books of the home office.

(12) The freight-in account on the branch books is found to include $300 of freight on merchandise intended for shipment to Boston Branch but erroneously shipped to Wilmington Branch and retained by the latter.

Instructions: (1) Prepare columnar working papers for both branch and home office, reflecting thereon the account balances, transactions, and adjustments as these would be recorded on the books of the separate offices.

(2) Prepare a balance sheet and an income statement for the branch for the year ended September 30, 1967, that will be required for the state franchise report.

(AICPA adapted)

8-10. The preclosing general ledger trial balances at December 31, 1967, for the Gorman Wholesale Company and its Atlanta Branch Office are shown at the top of the following page. Your audit disclosed the following data:

(1) On December 23 the branch office manager purchased $4,000 of furniture and fixtures but failed to notify the home office. The bookkeeper, knowing that all fixed assets are carried on the home office books, recorded the proper entry on the branch office records. It is the company's policy not to take any depreciation on assets acquired in the last half of a year.

(2) On December 27 a branch office customer erroneously paid his account of $2,000 to the home office. The bookkeeper made the correct entry on the home office books but did not notify the branch office.

(3) On December 30 the branch office remitted cash of $5,000, which was received by the home office in January, 1968.

(4) On December 31 the branch office erroneously recorded the December allocated expenses from the home office as $500 instead of $1,500.

(5) On December 31 the home office shipped merchandise billed at $3,000 to the branch office, which was received in January, 1968.

(6) The entire opening inventory of the branch office had been purchased from the home office. Home office 1967 shipments to the branch office were pur-

Accounts	Trial Balance Home Office Dr. (Cr.)	Trial Balance Branch Office Dr. (Cr.)
Cash	36,000	8,000
Accounts Receivable	35,000	12,000
Inventory — Home Office	70,000	
Inventory — Branch Office		15,000
Fixed Assets, net	90,000	
Branch Office	20,000	
Accounts Payable	(36,000)	(13,500)
Accrued Expenses	(14,000)	(2,500)
Home Office		(9,000)
Capital Stock	(50,000)	
Retained Earnings	(45,000)	
Home Office:		
Sales	(440,000)	
Purchases	290,000	
Expenses	44,000	
Branch Office:		
Sales		(95,000)
Purchases		24,000
Purchases from Home Office		45,000
Expenses		16,000
	—0—	—0—

chased by the home office in 1967. The physical inventories at December 31, 1967, excluding the shipment in transit, are:
Home office — $55,000 (at cost)
Branch office — $20,000 (comprised of $18,000 from home office and $2,000 from outside vendors.)

(7) The home office consistently bills shipments to the branch office at 20% above cost. The sales account is credited for the invoice price.

Instructions: Prepare a work sheet with a pair of columns for each of the following: (1) Trial Balance (as listed above), (2) Adjustments and Eliminations, (3) Home Office Income Statement, (4) Branch Office Income Statement, (5) Combined Balance Sheet. The work sheet should show branch office income data on the basis of home office cost. Disregard income taxes. Number your work sheet adjusting and eliminating entries. (Formal journal entries are not required. Supporting computations, including the computation of ending inventories, must be in good form.)

(AICPA adapted)

Chapter 9

BUSINESS COMBINATIONS

There has been a steady trend in the United States for many decades toward business combination. However, since the end of World War II there has been a wave of business combination without parallel in history, and this movement promises to continue unabated. Business combination takes many different forms. The combination of business units is often achieved through fusion of different companies into a larger single unit. Such fusion is accomplished through mergers or consolidations. Business combination is also achieved by the acquisition of control by one company over the operations of another. Control of corporate units is achieved through stock ownership or through interlocking directorates. Such control results in unified and integrated operation of business enterprises while permitting component units to retain their separate corporate identities.

The trend towards business combination has been stimulated by a variety of objectives. These include: acquisition of a wider marketing area and higher sales volume; acquisition or development of a stronger organization and better production and management talent; reduction of costs through economies and efficiencies in operating on a larger scale; increased control over the market and improved competitive position; diversification of product lines; improved position with respect to sources of raw materials supply; better access to capital for growth as well as lower costs on borrowings. In recent years many business units have combined in order to obtain certain income tax advantages.

Business combination through merger or consolidation is described in this chapter; business combination through control over other units by stock ownership is described in the chapters that follow.

MERGERS

A *merger* is effected upon the direct acquisition of the properties of one or more companies by another. The company taking over the properties of others retains its identity and continues operations as a larger unit; the other companies are dissolved and lose their separate identities.

Ordinarily, the acquiring unit takes over all assets and assumes all liabilities of the companies to be absorbed. Upon transfer of assets and liabilities, the acquiring company makes payment for the acquisition with cash, securities of the acquiring company, or both. Such payments are distributed to the stockholders of the companies that are to be dissolved.

Before there can be a merger, the terms of the proposed arrangement must be approved by the board of directors of each company that is a party to the action. Normally, the merger agreement will have to be ratified by the stockholders of the company to be dissolved, and under certain circumstances by the stockholders of the company making the acquisition. Merger agreements must also meet state statutory provisions, and in certain instances will require approval by the Securities and Exchange Commission and perhaps by other regulatory agencies.

In recording the merger on the books of a company being absorbed, nominal accounts are adjusted and closed so that the earnings to the date of the merger may be determined and transferred to retained earnings; property accounts may be revised to conform to appraised values according to the merger agreement. Asset and liability accounts are closed, and an account with the transferee is debited for the claim resulting from the transfer of net assets. Entries follow to record the receipt of cash or securities in payment of the claim and to record the distribution of such assets to stockholders in final settlement. On the books of the company making the acquisition, asset accounts are debited for the values of assets taken over, liability accounts are credited for the liabilities assumed, and an account with the transferor is credited for the net amount owed. Payment for the net assets acquired may then be recorded and the account with the transferor closed.

When payment exceeds the appraised value of assets acquired, the excess is regarded by the acquiring company as payment for goodwill. Presumably, the reason for paying an amount in excess of the net asset values that have been identified rests in the superior earnings ability of the business to be absorbed.

CONSOLIDATIONS

A *consolidation* is effected when a corporation is specifically organized to acquire the assets and to assume the liabilities of two or more previously existing companies. A new corporation is formed; the original companies are dissolved.

Ordinarily, the newly formed company issues securities that are given in exchange for properties acquired. Stockholders of the original companies thereby become stockholders of the new unit. In some cases the new corporation may sell its stock and with such proceeds acquire the net assets of the companies to be combined.

As in the case of a merger, terms of a proposed consolidation will have to be approved by the board of directors of each company that is a party to the action. The proposal will also require approval by stockholders in accordance with legal provisions. Before an agreement for consolidation is completed, investigations, audits, and appraisals may be called for by the negotiating parties. Information from these sources may provide bases for determination of the relative contributions that are made by each of the companies joining in the consolidation.

A set of books is established for the new enterprise. With the transfer of assets and liabilities to the new unit, entries are made on the books of the constituent companies just as for absorbed companies that are parties to a merger. The new company debits asset accounts for the value of the assets that it takes over, credits liability accounts for the liabilities that it assumes, and credits appropriate capital accounts for the capital identified with the new enterprise.

Results of the merger and the consolidation are similar, one unit emerging from a fusion of two or more previously existing units. Frequently, a distinction between the two forms of combination is not made in practice, a combination of either form being referred to as a merger.

PROBLEMS ARISING IN COMBINATION OF BUSINESS UNITS

Problems that arise in the course of business combination may be simple or complex. For example, a proposal for the outright purchase of one company by another may involve little more than an agreement as to the price to be paid for the company and the terms for such payment. On the other hand, a proposal for a consolidation that involves a number of companies and payment to dissolving units in the form of different securities may raise complex problems as to the relative contributions of the constituent units and the means for recognizing such contributions. The assistance of company managements, lawyers, accountants, appraisers, and financial analysts may be required in the course of reaching an agreement. The problems that arise in the course of a combination of several companies and the approaches that may be adopted in resolving such problems are described in the following section. Although the discussion is related to a consolidation, it is equally applicable to a merger in which similar problems may be encountered.

CONTRIBUTIONS BY CONSTITUENT MEMBERS TO A COMBINATION

When equities in an enlarged unit are to be allowed to former ownership groups, a basis for the equitable assignment of such equities will normally be sought in (1) relative net asset contributions and (2) relative earnings contributions. Although both of these factors may receive close consideration in the course of negotiations, final settlement may be influenced in no small part by the relative bargaining strength of the different parties.

The determination of relative net asset contributions frequently calls for special assistance by accountants and by appraisers. Statements of financial position prepared by the constituent companies offer a starting point in arriving at relative contributions. Individual items on these statements require special analysis and investigation by independent accountants so that they may be restated, when necessary, in a manner that will make them both complete and comparable. The discovery of clerical errors or omissions as well as errors in the application of accounting principles calls for corrections to achieve a full and satisfactory accounting. When differences in practices and procedures are encountered, items will have to be restated to offer a comparable accounting. The following matters, in particular, warrant attention and modification when necessary in achieving statement comparability: valuation methods for investments; allowances for receivables; cost determination and valuation procedures for inventories; capitalization policies for plant and equipment charges; depreciation methods for plant and equipment items; amortization policies for intangibles; provisions for contingencies; and policies for recognizing deferrals and accruals. Although alternative procedures in each of the foregoing areas may be acceptable for general accounting purposes, the special purpose for which the statements are to be employed calls for the selection of particular procedures that will provide a comparable accounting.

Having obtained accounting comparability, further inquiry into the adequacy of these data as a basis for measuring relative net asset contributions may be in order. Asset book values summarize past costs; however, assets must be recognized not in terms of their past costs but in terms of current fair values. A new accounting entity is to be created and net asset contributions to the new unit in terms of current values are to be determined. With unrecorded changes in plant and equipment values, such as those emerging from changes in monetary values and technological advances, and with different uses to be made of such property items, special assistance by independent appraisers will be required in arriving at fair valuations for respective contributions. Inventories reported at lifo or fifo will require restatement at a fair market value. Investments reported at the lower of cost or market will require recognition at current market value. Intangibles at amortized cost balances will require recognition at their value to the new unit.

The determination of relative earnings contributions to the new organization calls for special analyses by the accountant. Income statements for the constituent units must be recast as were the balance sheets to achieve a complete and comparable accounting. The discovery of past errors and omissions calls for appropriate corrections. When differences in income measurement procedures are found, restatement of revenues and expenses in terms of comparable procedures may be required. The following matters, in particular, warrant attention and modification when necessary in achieving a comparable accounting: measurements of cost of goods manufactured and sold, including inventory pricing and valuation methods; charges for depreciation on plant and equipment items; amortization of intangibles; recognition of bad debts; charges for management salaries; and charges relating to retirement plans.

With earnings reported on a comparable basis, further analyses are necessary in projecting past earnings of individual companies forward. Earnings of the past are significant only insofar as they can be employed in evaluating the relative earnings contributions that will be made by the individual units to the new organization. In arriving at the relative earnings contributions to the new organization, modification of past earnings, then, may be in order. Items deemed extraordinary and non-recurring may require adjustment or elimination. If depreciable assets have been restated in arriving at the individual net asset contributions, appropriate restatement of depreciation charges relating to such assets is required for purposes of income measurement. Management salaries and also interest charges arising from financing activities must be reviewed in terms of the new organization. Fixed and variable costs must be analyzed in terms of the new organization. With comparable earnings available for a number of years, the earnings trend for each unit can be determined and applied to earnings data in projecting these forward.

With statements that provide financial data on a comparative basis, parties must now determine how the new company shall recognize the contributions by the individual participants. In certain instances, parties may decide that asset and earnings contributions can be satisfactorily recognized by issuing a single class of stock. In other instances, parties may decide that a satisfactory recognition of individual contributions is possible only through the issue of two or more classes of securities. The problems that arise in an equitable distribution of securities under each of these arrangements are discussed in the sections that follow.

ISSUANCE OF A SINGLE CLASS OF STOCK IN BUSINESS COMBINATION

When the earnings rates on assets of the constituent parties are approximately the same and a single class of stock is to be issued, parties may agree that such shares shall be issued in relation to the net asset contributions. However, when earnings rates vary and a single class of stock is to be issued, parties may provide that earnings regarded as above normal shall be used as a basis for calculating goodwill and that such goodwill shall be added to the other net assets in measuring a company's full contribution.

To illustrate the foregoing, assume that stockholders of Companies A, B, and C agree to consolidate and form Company D. Net assets at appraised values and average adjusted earnings of the past five years, which the parties believe offer the most reliable estimate of future earnings, follow:

	Co. A	Co. B	Co. C	Total
Net asset contribution	$200,000	$300,000	$500,000	$1,000,000
Percentage of asset contribution to total assets	20%	30%	50%	
Earnings contribution	$ 30,000	$ 30,000	$ 40,000	$ 100,000
Percentage of earnings contribution to total earnings	30%	30%	40%	

If Company D issues a single class of stock in the net asset ratio, stockholders of Companies A, B, and C will receive stock in the ratio of 20:30:50 respectively. Although an equitable division of the interest in the assets of $1,000,000 is achieved, earnings of $100,000 in the future will accrue to stockholders in the asset ratio, resulting in a loss to original stockholders of Company A and a gain to original stockholders of Company C.

On the other hand, if a single class of stock is issued in the earnings ratio, stockholders of Companies A, B, and C will receive stock in the ratio of 30:30:40 respectively. Although an equitable division of future earnings is achieved, stockholders will fail to maintain their original interests in assets: stockholders of Company A will acquire an interest that exceeds their investment, while stockholders of Company C will acquire an interest that is less than their investment.

To avoid the inequities resulting from the distribution of a single class of stock either in the net asset ratio or in the earnings ratio, the parties decide that respective contributions shall be measured by the values assigned to net assets as increased by goodwill. It is agreed that contributions are to be determined as follows: (1) a 6% return is to be regarded as a fair return on identifiable net assets; (2) excess earnings are to be capitalized at 20% in arriving at a value for goodwill. Contributions considering net asset and earnings factors are then calculated as follows:

	Co. A		Co. B		Co. C		Total
Net assets other than goodwill		$200,000		$300,000		$500,000	$1,000,000
Goodwill:							
Average annual earnings..	$30,000		$30,000		$40,000		
Normal annual return on assets, 6%............	12,000		18,000		30,000		
Excess annual earnings...	$18,000		$12,000		$10,000		
Excess annual earnings capitalized at 20%.......		90,000		60,000		50,000	200,000
Total contributions........		$290,000		$360,000		$550,000	$1,200,000

In recording the issuance of stock by Company D, it will have to be determined whether goodwill is actually to be recognized in the accounts of the new company or whether goodwill is not to be recognized, goodwill calculations simply being made to assure an equitable allotment of shares to the various units in view of their varying earnings records. Regardless of how the investments are recorded, stock is issued in the ratio of total contributions as calculated. The first entry that is given below records the issuance of stock by Company D and the allotment of shares assuming that goodwill is recognized in the accounts at the amount of capitalized excess earnings; entries (2) and (3) record the issuance of stock on alternative assumptions involving the nonrecognition of goodwill in the accounts.

(1) Goodwill is recognized — 12,000 shares, $100 par, are issued:

Goodwill....................................		200,000	
Other Assets..................................		1,000,000	
Capital Stock, $100 par.........................			1,200,000
Distribution of shares to:			
Co. A: $290,000 ÷ $100.........	2,900 shares		
Co. B: $360,000 ÷ $100.........	3,600 shares		
Co. C: $550,000 ÷ $100.........	5,500 shares		
Total.........................	12,000 shares		

(2) Goodwill is not recognized — 10,000 shares, $100 par, are issued:

Assets.......................................		1,000,000	
Capital Stock, $100 par.......................			1,000,000
Distribution of shares to:			
Co. A: 290,000/1,200,000 × 10,000.........	2,417 shares		
Co. B: 360,000/1,200,000 × 10,000.........	3,000 shares		
Co. C: 550,000/1,200,000 × 10,000.........	4,583 shares		
Total...................................	10,000 shares		

(3) Goodwill is not recognized — 25,000 shares, $30 stated value, are issued:

Assets	1,000,000	
Capital Stock, $30 stated value		750,000
Paid-In Capital from Issuance of Stock in Excess of Stated Value		250,000

Distribution of shares to:

Co. A: 290,000/1,200,000 × 25,000	6,042 shares
Co. B: 360,000/1,200,000 × 25,000	7,500 shares
Co. C: 550,000/1,200,000 × 25,000	11,458 shares
Total	25,000 shares

Although the number of shares in each case above varies, each company's share in the total remains the same. A comparison of the relative net asset and earnings contributions by Companies A, B, and C and the relative claims upon net assets and earnings of the new company in each case is as follows:

	Co. A	Co. B	Co. C
Net asset contribution	20%	30%	50%
Earnings contribution	30%	30%	40%
Claim upon net assets and earnings of new company	24%	30%	46%

When relative earnings contributions differ from relative net asset contributions, original relationships in both earnings and net asset contributions of the individual companies cannot be preserved by the issuance of a single class of stock. It may be observed in the preceding example that Company A with above-normal earnings gains an increased share in net assets; however, it fails to retain its original share in earnings. Company C fails to maintain its interest in net assets but gains an increased share in earnings. Company B, whose asset and earnings shares were the same, retains its original relative status in both assets and earnings.

ISSUANCE OF SEVERAL CLASSES OF STOCK IN BUSINESS COMBINATION

If original relationships in both net assets and earnings are to be preserved, it will be necessary to issue more than a single class of stock. The following procedures must be applied in the allocation of several classes of stock of the new company to the constituent groups:

(1) Earnings contributions of the constituent companies should be capitalized at a certain rate, but this rate must not exceed the earnings rate

of any of the constituent companies. This procedure determines the total stock to be issued to each company.[1]

(2) Preferred stock should be distributed to constituent companies in proportion to the net assets that they contribute. Such stock should be preferred as to assets upon dissolution, the preferences being equal to the values of properties contributed. The dividend rate should not exceed the rate used in capitalizing profits. Shares should be fully participating with common.

(3) Common stock should be issued to each company for the difference between the company's total stock as calculated in (1) above, and the amount it receives in preferred stock as calculated in (2) above.

The issuance of stock that is preferred as to assets results in the preservation of claims in the new organization that are equal to the net asset contributions. Participating preferred stock supplemented by common stock so that the total stock issued is in the earnings ratio makes possible a distribution of earnings in the earnings ratio.

To illustrate the above procedure, assume contributions to Company D by Companies A, B, and C as previously indicated:

	Co. A	Co. B	Co. C	Total
Net asset contribution.........	$200,000	$300,000	$500,000	$1,000,000
Earnings contribution.........	$ 30,000	$ 30,000	$ 40,000	$ 100,000
Earnings rate on net assets.....	15%	10%	8%	10%

It is agreed that earnings are to be capitalized at 8% in determining the total stock to be issued. Fully participating 6% preferred stock, $100 par, and preferred as to assets of this par value, is to be issued in exchange for net assets transferred; common stock, $100 par, is to be issued to each company for the difference between the total stock to which it is entitled and the preferred stock that it is to receive. The common stock is regarded as payment for goodwill. The stock allotment is made as follows:

	Co. A	Co. B	Co. C	Total
Total stock to be issued (earnings ÷ .08)................	$375,000	$375,000	$500,000	$1,250,000
Amount of preferred stock to be issued (equal to asset contribution)..................	200,000	300,000	500,000	1,000,000
Amount of common stock to be issued (balance, representing payment for goodwill).......	$175,000	$ 75,000	——	$ 250,000

[1]It should be observed again that "earnings" as used in the discussions represent the estimated earnings contribution to the new unit. A company may have experienced losses in the past. However, for purposes of the business combination, it is attractive only if its properties will make some contribution to earnings of the combined unit.

Company D makes the following entry:

Goodwill	250,000	
Other Assets	1,000,000	
Preferred Stock, $100 par		1,000,000
Common Stock, $100 par		250,000

The preferred stock issued to stockholders of Companies A, B, and C preserves their claims to assets in the new organization in amounts equal to assets contributed. The preferred and common issues provide for a distribution of earnings in the earnings contribution ratio. Annual earnings of $100,000 by the new organization will permit an 8% dividend on both participating preferred stock and common stock. Such earnings would be distributed as follows:

	Co. A	Co. B	Co. C	Total
On 6% preferred participating stock (8%)	$16,000	$24,000	$40,000	$ 80,000
On common stock (8%)	14,000	6,000	—	20,000
Total distribution	$30,000	$30,000	$40,000	$100,000
Original earnings contribution	30%	30%	40%	100%

Several observations need to be made:

(1) Earnings distributions must not be less than the preferred rate on the *total* capital stock if distributions are to be made in the original earnings ratio. For example, if only $60,000 were earned and distributed, the distribution would be limited to preferred stock, earnings accruing in the ratio of preferred holdings, or 20%, 30%, and 50%. A distribution of $70,000 comes closer to the original earnings ratio, but still fails to meet it:

	Co. A	Co. B	Co. C	Total
On 6% preferred participating stock (6%)	$12,000	$18,000	$30,000	$ 60,000
On common stock (4%)	7,000	3,000		10,000
Total distribution	$19,000	$21,000	$30,000	$ 70,000
Percentage earnings distribution	27%	30%	43%	100%

A distribution of $75,000 would permit the payment to common stockholders of $15,000, or 6%, the earnings distribution then being made in the original ratio.

If the original earnings ratio is to be maintained at any earnings distribution level, two classes of stock would have to be issued, each class offering the same dividend rights but only one class offering a prior claim on assets upon liquidation. Such issues can be designated Class A shares and Class B shares.

(2) Preferred stock must be participating if distributions that exceed the preferred rate on total capital stock are to be made in the original earnings ratio. If, in the example, the 6% preferred stock was non-participating and earnings of $100,000 were to be distributed, the distribution would fail to meet the earnings contribution rate of 30%, 30%, and 40%. Under these circumstances the distribution would be made as follows:

	Co. A	Co. B	Co. C	Total
On preferred stock (6%)	$12,000	$18,000	$30,000	$ 60,000
On common stock (16%)	28,000	12,000		40,000
Total distribution	$40,000	$30,000	$30,000	$100,000
Percentage earnings distribution	40%	30%	30%	100%

(3) It would be possible to enable Company C stockholders to participate in the common stock distribution by capitalizing earnings at a rate that is less than 8%. For example, assume that earnings are capitalized at 5%: 5% fully participating preferred stock is issued in exchange for net assets transferred, and common stock is issued for the balance of the total stock to be issued. Both classes of stock are $100 par. The stock allotment is made as follows:

	Co. A	Co. B	Co. C	Total
Total stock to be issued (average earnings ÷ .05)	$600,000	$600,000	$800,000	$2,000,000
Amount of preferred stock	200,000	300,000	500,000	1,000,000
Amount of common stock	$400,000	$300,000	$300,000	$1,000,000

Earnings of $100,000 would satisfy preferred stock requirements and would make possible a 5% distribution on common stock, earnings being distributed in the original ratio as follows:

	Co. A	Co. B	Co. C	Total
On preferred stock (5%)	$10,000	$15,000	$25,000	$ 50,000
On common stock (5%)	20,000	15,000	15,000	50,000
	$30,000	$30,000	$40,000	$100,000

Capitalization of earnings at 5% in arriving at the total par value of the stock to be issued above requires the recognition of goodwill of $1,000,000. Assume, however, that such a valuation for the intangible is unwarranted. Instead of issuing a certain number of common shares with a "$100 par" designation, an equal number of shares can be issued but designated "no-par." The stated value assigned to the no-par common stock would be determined by the valuation placed upon goodwill. Dividend rights of the common stock would remain the same as when a par value is assigned. If no goodwill is to be recognized, both no-par preferred stock and no-par common stock could be issued. The asset preference rights and the dividend rights of each class should be the same as in the previous cases where par values were assigned and the stock should be issued in the same ratio as in the previous cases. The asset contribution could then be recorded at $1,000,000, and this value could be assigned in some reasonable manner to the preferred and common stock.

No attempt has been made in the foregoing paragraphs to cover all of the problems arising in the allotment of securities to the parties to a business combination. However, some of the major considerations have been mentioned. The individual problems in each case will have to be studied carefully in ascertaining bases for security allotment. In arriving at a satisfactory allotment, there will be concern not only with achieving an equitable arrangement with the individual parties but also with establishing a sound financial structure for the new organization. The latter objective must be fulfilled if the company is to prosper and stock issues are to be received favorably on the securities market. The agreement that is finally reached will be a product of theoretical considerations, practical considerations, and then compromises by the parties to the negotiation.

BUSINESS COMBINATIONS REGARDED AS "POOLING OF INTERESTS"

A combination brings the assets of two or more companies under single ownership and control. In certain instances the combination involves a change in original ownership, as, for example, when assets of one company are sold for cash to another. However, in other instances, the combination provides for a continuation of the original ownership; this would be the case, for example, when assets of a company are transferred to another company in exchange for stock that offers the original ownership a continued interest in and control of assets. A combination that involves the elimination of an important part of the original ownership is designated as a combination by *purchase*. A combination that involves a continuation of substantially all of the original ownership is designated as a combination by *pooling of interests*. In modern practice, the accounting for a combination may vary depending upon the determination as to whether the combination represents a substantive change in ownership continuity or no more than a change in the form of ownership continuity.

The Committee on Accounting Procedure of the American Institute of Certified Public Accountants in *Accounting Research Bulletin No. 48*, dealing with business combinations, observes:

> For accounting purposes, the distinction between a *purchase* and a *pooling of interests* is to be found in the attendant circumstances rather than in the designation of the transaction according to its legal form (such as a merger, an exchange of shares, a consolidation, or an issuance of stock for assets and businesses), or in the number of corporations which survive or emerge, or in other legal or tax considerations (such as the availability of surplus for dividends).[1]

Among the attendant circumstances to be considered in determining the extent to which a new ownership or a continuity of old ownership exists in a particular case, the Committee would consider the following matters in particular:

Stock issued in exchange for properties in consolidation. When the shares issued are not substantially in proportion to respective interests in predecessor companies, a purchase (new ownership) rather than a pooling of interests is presumed to result; when relative voting rights as between constituents are materially altered, a purchase may be indicated; likewise, a plan to retire a substantial part of the stock issued to owners of the predecessor companies, or substantial changes in ownership occurring shortly before the combination or planned to occur shortly after the combination, would indicate a purchase.

Management. When management of one of the constituents is eliminated or its influence upon overall management is to be very small, a purchase is indicated.

Properties contributed. The abandonment or the sale of a large part of the business of one or more of the constituent companies and the failure thus to achieve a continuity of all of the constituents in one enterprise would lend support to recognition of the consolidation as a purchase.

Size of constituents. Although relative size may not necessarily be determinative, especially where smaller units contribute desired management personnel, the clear domination by one of the constituents (say 90%, 95%, or more of the voting interest in the combined enterprise by stockholders of one of the constituent companies) would offer the presumption of a purchase.

---

[1]*Accounting Research Bulletin No. 48*, "Business Combinations," 1957 (New York: American Institute of Certified Public Accountants), p. 21.

The Committee concludes:

> No one of the factors discussed . . . would necessarily be determinative and any one factor might have varying degrees of significance in different cases. However, their presence or absence would be cumulative in effect. Since the conclusions to be drawn from consideration of these different relevant circumstances may be in conflict or partially so, determination as to whether a particular combination is a purchase or a pooling of interests should be made in the light of all such attendant circumstances.[1]

ACCOUNTING FOR POOLING OF INTERESTS

When a combination is considered to represent a purchase, there is full agreement that a new accountability is in order for those assets acquired; with a transfer of assets through purchase, assets should be recorded at their cost to the buyer, a cost that need not coincide with the values reported on the books of the seller. On the other hand, when a combination is considered to represent a pooling of interests, there is wide agreement that assets may be carried forward at the values at which they are carried on the books of the constituent units. Many authorities have gone beyond this point to support the theory that since the combination is characterized by a continuity of the original ownerships, it is appropriate to carry forward the capital balances of predecessor units. The Committee on Accounting Procedure takes this position. The Committee defines the accounting under conditions of purchase and pooling of interests as follows:

> When a combination is deemed to be a purchase, the assets acquired should be recorded on the books of the acquiring corporation at cost, measured in money, or, in the event other consideration is given, at the fair value of such other consideration, or at the fair value of the property acquired, whichever is more clearly evident. This is in accordance with the procedure applicable to accounting for purchases of assets.
>
> When a combination is deemed to be a pooling of interests, a new basis of accountability does not arise. The carrying amounts of the assets of the constituent corporations, if stated in conformity with generally accepted accounting principles and appropriately adjusted when deemed necessary to place them on a uniform accounting basis, should be carried forward; and the combined earned surpluses and deficits, if any, of the constituent corporations should be carried forward, except to the extent otherwise required by law or appropriate corporate action. Adjustments of assets or of surplus which would be in conformity with generally accepted accounting principles in the absence of a combination are ordinarily equally appropriate if effected in connection with a pooling of interests; however, the pooling-of-interests concept implies a combining of surpluses and deficits of the constituent corporations, and it would be inappropriate and misleading in connection with a pooling of interests to eliminate the deficit of one constituent against its capital surplus and to carry forward the earned surplus of another constituent.[2]

---

[1] *Ibid.*, p. 24.
[2] *Ibid.*, pp. 24–25.

It should be observed that the Committee indicates that retained earnings may be carried forward in a pooling of interests but it does not require that such a practice be followed. The new enterprise may recognize retained earnings of the constituent companies as stated capital or as additional paid-in capital, which is consistent with the action that can be taken by a corporation to transfer retained earnings to paid-in capital balances.

When a combination is recognized as a pooling of interests, the income statement of the continuing business for the period in which the combination occurs should report the combined results of operations of the constituent units for the entire period in which the combination was effected. When comparative financial statements are presented for periods prior to that in which the combination was effected, they should be restated on a combined basis. Financial statements should clearly disclose the fact that a business combination has been treated as a pooling of interests.[1]

ACCOUNTING FOR POOLING OF INTERESTS ILLUSTRATED

The examples that were given earlier in this chapter assumed that combinations were deemed to be purchases. The examples that follow will provide a comparison of the accounting for combinations under conditions of purchase and pooling of interests.

Assume that a combination of Companies D, E, and F is contemplated. Assets, liabilities, and capitals of the companies are reported in conformity with generally accepted accounting principles and are stated on a uniform basis. On July 1, 1967, balance sheets for the three companies are as follows:

		Co. D		Co. E		Co. F
Assets		$2,000,000		$1,250,000		$1,000,000
Liabilities		$ 750,000		$ 400,000		$ 350,000
Capital stock	(no-par)	1,000,000	($100 par)	500,000	($50 par)	500,000
Additional paid-in capital		350,000		150,000		100,000
Retained earnings (deficit)		(100,000)		200,000		50,000
Total liabilities and stockholders' equity		$2,000,000		$1,250,000		$1,000,000

On this date Company D agrees to acquire all of the assets and to assume all of the liabilities of Companies E and F in exchange for shares of stock that it will issue. Stock of Company D is currently selling on the market at $50 per share. Assets of Companies E and F are to be ap-

[1]For specific recommendations on these matters by the Accounting Principles Board, see *Opinion of the Accounting Principles Board No. 10*, "Omnibus Opinion — 1966," 1967 (New York: American Institute of Certified Public Accountants), p. 144.

praised and the companies are to receive Company D shares with a market value equal to that of the net assets transferred. The exchange of shares for net assets is calculated as follows:

	Co. E	Co. F	Total
Assets per books	$1,250,000	$1,000,000	$2,250,000
Asset increase per appraisal	150,000	100,000	250,000
	$1,400,000	$1,100,000	$2,500,000
Liabilities per books	400,000	350,000	750,000
Net assets for purposes of exchange	$1,000,000	$ 750,000	$1,750,000
Number of shares to be issued (net assets ÷ $50)	20,000	15,000	35,000

Entries that would be made on the books of Company D on alternative purchase and pooling assumptions and a balance sheet for Company D reflecting the combination under each assumption follow:

Entries on Company D Books

If combination is deemed a purchase

Assets (at appraised values)	2,500,000	
Liabilities		750,000
Capital Stock, no-par (35,000 shares)		1,750,000

Company D Balance Sheet, July 1, 1967

Assets	$4,500,000
Liabilities	$1,500,000
Capital stock	2,750,000
Additional paid-in capital	350,000
Deficit	(100,000)
Total liabilities and stockholders' equity	$4,500,000

If combination is deemed a pooling of interests

Assets (at original book values)	2,250,000	
Liabilities		750,000
Capital Stock, no-par (35,000 shares)		1,000,000
Additional Paid-In Capital		250,000
Retained Earnings		250,000

Company D Balance Sheet, July 1, 1967

Assets	$4,250,000
Liabilities	$1,500,000
Capital stock	2,000,000
Additional paid-in capital	600,000
Retained earnings	150,000
Total liabilities and stockholders' equity	$4,250,000

In recognizing the merger as a purchase, no special problem is encountered by Company D. As in the case of any other exchange of stock for assets, the assets are recorded at their fair values and invested capital accounts are credited. In recognizing the merger as a pooling of interests, asset, liability, and capital balances reported by Companies E and F are carried without change to the books of Company D.

Upon completion of the merger, entries need to be made on the books of Companies E and F to report the receipt of Company D shares in exchange for net assets and the distribution of such shares to stockholders. When the consideration for net assets is recognized as an amount other than their book value, a gain or a loss is reported on the transfer. Payment by Company D in the transaction that was designated as a purchase, for example, would call for entries on the books of Companies E and F as follows:

Company E Books			Company F Books		
Stock of Co. D.	1,000,000		Stock of Co. D.	750,000	
Liabilities.	400,000		Liabilities.	350,000	
Assets.		1,250,000	Assets.		1,000,000
Retained Earnings. .		150,000	Retained Earnings. .		100,000
Received 20,000 shares of Co. D stock valued at $50 per share in exchange for net assets.			Received 15,000 shares of Co. D stock valued at $50 per share in exchange for net assets.		
Capital Stock.	500,000		Capital Stock.	500,000	
Additional Paid-In Capital.	150,000		Additional Paid-In Capital.	100,000	
Retained Earnings. . . .	350,000		Retained Earnings. . . .	150,000	
Stock of Co. D.		1,000,000	Stock of Co. D.		750,000
Distributed 20,000 shares of Co. D stock in exchange for 5,000 shares of Co. E stock outstanding (4 shares for 1).			Distributed 15,000 shares of Co. D stock in exchange for 10,000 shares of Co. F stock outstanding (1.5 shares for 1).		

In the example that was given for a pooling of interests, capital stock of the acquiring company was no-par and the stated capital for the combination was recognized at an amount equal to the sum of the capital stock balances of the constituent units. This permitted the full recognition of additional paid-in capital and retained earnings balances of the constituent units. When the stated capital of a combination is to be greater or less than the stated capital of the constituent units, adjustments to additional paid-in capital and retained earnings balances are the same that would apply to an increase or a decrease in stated capital where no business combination is involved. Hence, when the stated capital of a combination is to be greater than the total of the stated capitals of the constituent units, the excess should be deducted from the total additional paid-in capital, and when this balance is exhausted, from the total retained earnings; when the stated capital is to be less than the total of the stated capitals of the constituent units, the difference should be recognized as an increase in total additional paid-in capital. In a combination that is deemed to be a pooling of interests, then, establishing a stated capital for the combination may involve a decrease in the retained earnings total but never an increase in this total.

To illustrate the foregoing as well as to provide a comparison of purchase and pooling accounting for a consolidation, assume that Companies D, E, and F referred to on page 271 agree to form Company G and that they transfer their assets and liabilities to this company. Assets of Company D are considered to be fairly valued for purposes of the consolidation; assets of Companies E and F, however, are to be revalued as stated earlier. Shares of Company G are to be issued on the basis of 1 share for every $50 of net assets transferred. Shares, then, are issued as follows:

To Company D, 25,000 shares ($1,250,000 ÷ $50).
To Company E, 20,000 shares ($1,000,000 ÷ $50).
To Company F, 15,000 shares ($ 750,000 ÷ $50).

Purchase and pooling entries below are given on three different assumptions of Company G stock par value: in case (1) par value is $45; in case (2) par value is $35; in case (3) par value is $25.

Entries on Company G Books

If combination is deemed a purchase			If combination is deemed a pooling of interests		
(1) Assets (at appraised values)	4,500,000		Assets (at original book values)	4,250,000	
Liabilities		1,500,000	Liabilities		1,500,000
Capital Stock, $45 par (60,000 shares)		2,700,000	Capital Stock, $45 par (60,000 shares)		2,700,000
Additional Paid-In Capital		300,000	Retained Earnings		50,000
(2) Assets (at appraised values)	4,500,000		Assets (at original book values)	4,250,000	
Liabilities		1,500,000	Liabilities		1,500,000
Capital Stock, $35 par (60,000 shares)		2,100,000	Capital Stock, $35 par (60,000 shares)		2,100,000
Additional Paid-In Capital		900,000	Additional Paid-In Capital		500,000
			Retained Earnings		150,000
(3) Assets (at appraised values)	4,500,000		Assets (at original book values)	4,250,000	
Liabilities		1,500,000	Liabilities		1,500,000
Capital Stock, $25 par (60,000 shares)		1,500,000	Capital Stock, $25 par (60,000 shares)		1,500,000
Additional Paid-In Capital		1,500,000	Additional Paid-In Capital		1,100,000
			Retained Earnings		150,000

When the combination is deemed to be a purchase, capitals are limited to invested capital balances regardless of the par value assigned to the capital stock.

When the combination is deemed to be a pooling of interests, capitals of the constituent units are continued but with the following modifications:

In case (1), the increase in the value assigned to capital stock from the $2,000,000 total reported by the constituent companies to the $2,700,000 balance required elimination of the full amount of additional paid-in capital of $600,000 and a further reduction in total retained earnings of $100,000.

In case (2), the increase in the value assigned to capital stock from \$2,000,000 to \$2,100,000 required a reduction of \$100,000 in total additional paid-in capital; the full amount of retained earnings was carried forward.

In case (3), a reduction in the value assigned to capital stock from \$2,000,000 to \$1,500,000 was accompanied by an increase of \$500,000 in total additional paid-in capital; the full amount of retained earnings was carried forward.

EFFECTS OF ALTERNATIVE COMBINATION PROCEDURES

It is important that the effects of the alternative consolidation procedures be carefully observed. Differences initially appear on the balance sheets. However, differences in balance sheet items are subsequently reflected in revenue and expense accounts and in net income determinations.

With purchase accounting, an exchange of stock for the assets of a going concern in a period of rising prices frequently results in the recognition of assets at amounts significantly above the values reported on the books of the transferor. Furthermore, when shares are selling at high net earnings multiples, the value of the shares may exceed the appraised values of tangible assets, thus calling for the recognition of a variety of intangible assets including goodwill. The recognition of assets at their values at the date of the transfer is accompanied by an increase of the same amount in invested capital balances. On the other hand, pooling accounting results in the recognition of assets at their original book values. Replacement values or current market values are ignored. No recognition is made of intangibles that are not already reflected in the accounts. Transfer of the assets at their original book values is accompanied by transfer of the capital balances relating to such assets. Frequently, then, retained earnings are carried forward. In a merger, this may mean the elimination of a previously existing deficit and the recognition instead of a retained earnings balance; in a consolidation, this may mean the recognition of a retained earnings balance from the very beginning of the new organization.

With purchase accounting, asset balances as restated form the basis for charges to revenue. When intangibles are recognized on the acquisition, they require assignment against revenue and thus affect periodic earnings. With pooling accounting, charges to revenue arising from the use of acquired assets remain unchanged. In failing to recognize any intangibles related to the acquisition, revenue is freed from charges for amortization that would otherwise apply.

The effects of the alternative treatments on the income statement may be regarded as of even greater significance than those on the balance sheet. Final net income determinations are extremely important to management, employees, stockholders, and creditors. Net earnings determine security prices on the stock market. Net earnings also affect management bonuses, employee profit-sharing arrangements, and declarations of dividends to stockholders.

CURRENT POOLING-OF-INTERESTS PRACTICE

With alternative approaches that provide significantly different results in stating a company's financial position and reporting its earnings, it would be expected that the criteria for distinguishing between purchase and pooling forms be clear and unequivocal. Unfortunately, this has not been the case and charges have been made in recent years that the choice between the purchase and the pooling approaches is frequently determined by the accounting consequences relating to each approach.

A distinction between purchase and pooling of interests for reporting purposes was made in accounting literature as early as the 1920's. The earliest reference by the American Institute of Certified Public Accountants to the pooling of interests concept was in 1945. In 1950, the Committee on Accounting Procedure issued its first official pronouncement dealing with this matter. In 1957, the Committee in attempting to clarify both the conditions to be considered in distinguishing between a purchase and a pooling of interests and the accounting procedures that were appropriate for combinations of either class issued *Bulletin No. 48.* Guideposts for distinguishing between purchase and pooling expressed earlier in this chapter are those that were given in this bulletin.

Questions have continued to be raised concerning the factors to be considered in making the distinction between a purchase and a pooling of interests. Certain positions that have been taken by the Committee on Accounting Procedure have been seriously challenged. Among these are the positions it has taken on continuity of management, continuity of properties, and the relative sizes of constituent companies. In view of the Committee's observation that ". . . no one of the factors discussed . . . would necessarily be determinative and any one factor might have varying degrees of significance in different cases," many accounting firms have chosen to ignore certain factors that the Committee would consider in adopting the pooling approach.

Arthur D. Wyatt in his *Accounting Research Study No. 5*, "A Critical Study of Accounting for Business Combinations," describes the accounting practices that he encountered in a study of more than 350 combinations that took place in the United States within the period 1949–1960 and he observes:

> By 1960 most business combinations apparently could be accounted for under either the purchase concept or under the pooling concept, and either treatment would be held to be in accordance with generally accepted accounting principles. This situation is one in which confusion is bound to flourish.[1]

In the acquisition of assets by exchange, generally accepted accounting principles call for reporting assets at the value of the consideration given in exchange or the value of the assets acquired, whichever is more clearly determinable. Pooling provides an exception to this principle, and hence it is important that the criteria for recognizing a pooling be carefully defined. One can hope that the Accounting Principles Board will take a clear and definitive position on this important matter in the near future.

DIVISIVE REORGANIZATIONS

The preceding sections considered the combination of business units with the ownerships in the original units being continued in the combined unit. It was pointed out that such a combination suggested an accounting that would reflect the change as no more than one of form; asset values as well as ownership interests of the original units were identified with the larger unit. Frequently one encounters a reverse situation — one in which an existing corporation is divided, with the ownership of the original unit being continued in the divisive units. Under these circumstances, too, it might well be maintained that asset values together with ownership interests of the original unit should be carried into the smaller units.

Divisive reorganizations are commonly classified as *split-ups*, *split-offs*, and *spin-offs*.

Split-up. A split-up is the transfer by a corporation of all of its assets to two or more new companies in exchange for all of the stock of the new companies. The original unit then distributes the stock to its stockholders as a liquidating settlement and dissolves. Owners of the original company are now owners of the separate units into which it has been divided.[2]

---

[1]*Accounting Research Study No. 5*, "A Critical Study of Accounting for Business Combinations," 1963 (New York: American Institute of Certified Public Accountants), p. 15. Professor Maurice Moonitz, Director of Accounting Research for the American Institute of Certified Public Accountants in 1963, comments in the preface of the study (page xi): "The general conclusion is unavoidable that accounting for business combinations has deteriorated in recent years so that a variety of practices can be described as accepted." The reader should consult *Accounting Research Study No. 5* for a comprehensive review and analysis of business combinations and recommendations for applying the alternative accounting concepts.

[2]The use of the term "split-up" in this sense is to be distinguished from the use of this term to indicate the issuance of an additional number of shares by a corporation without a change in the amount of paid-in capital identified with outstanding shares.

Split-off. A split-off is the transfer by a corporation of a part of its assets to a new company in exchange for the stock of the new company. The original unit subsequently distributes the stock in the new company to its stockholders in exchange for a proportionate part of the stockholdings of each. The latter shares are canceled and the amount of its stock outstanding is thus reduced.

Spin-off. A spin-off is the same as a split-off except that the distribution of stock is made by the original unit to its stockholders without any surrender of stock by them.

Corporate subdivision suggests accounting problems that are similar to those encountered in corporate combination. Under what circumstances should a fresh-start approach be adopted for the new unit in stating assets, liabilities, and capital balances? Under what circumstances should a reverse-pooling approach be employed and original book values be recognized on the records of the new unit for net asset transfers? In employing the latter approach, many problems will arise in allocating the capital balances between the divisive units. Few criteria for such allocation have been suggested, and the accountant will have to consider all of the circumstances of the divisive reorganization in arriving at an approach that can find theoretical as well as practical support.

BUSINESS REORGANIZATION AND TAXES

Proposals for business combination or division cannot be considered without reference to the tax factors that will accompany such action. A choice between several possible courses of action may be influenced in no small part by the tax implications related to the different alternatives. In some instances, tax considerations may actually be the motivating factors in considering a certain course of action. For example, stockholders of a corporation may decide upon a merger or consolidation to lessen the burden of death taxes, to provide a means of converting business profits that would otherwise be taxable as dividends into capital gains, or to utilize operating loss carryovers that might otherwise be lost. Once a course of action providing the desired tax advantages is chosen, the transaction must be carefully planned so that it fully conforms to the particular tax requirements.

In planning either a corporate combination or a division, special attention must be focused on whether such a corporate change will be accompanied by an income tax liability. Certain reorganizations qualify as "tax-free" while others are "taxable." In a tax-free transaction, the transferor recognizes neither gain nor loss on the transfer of assets; assets are reported on the books of the transferee just as they were carried on the books of the original owner. In a taxable transaction, the transferor recognizes a gain or a loss on the transfer of assets; assets are reported on the books of the transferee at the purchase price identified with the transfer.

The Internal Revenue Code provides that a tax-free status for all of the parties to a corporate combination or division is available only under the following circumstances:

(1) A statutory merger or consolidation — an arrangement effected in accordance with the laws of the various states.

(2) An acquisition by one corporation of the stock of another, provided that *voting stock* is exchanged for a controlling interest composed of at least 80% of the stock and the voting power of the acquired company.

(3) An acquisition by one corporation of the properties of another, provided that *voting stock* is exchanged for *substantially all* of the properties of the acquired company.

(4) A transfer of assets to another corporation in exchange for a controlling interest of at least 80% of the stock and the voting power of the acquired company. (This section applies to corporate distributions whether defined as spin-offs, split-offs, or split-ups.)

When there is a tax-free combination or division, pooling or reverse-pooling treatment in the accounts will provide a consistency between book and tax bases for property items and also between book and tax charges representing the amortization of such balances. This argument is frequently advanced as a reason for the application of the pooling approach in the accounts. In choosing between alternative methods, however, the primary question is not whether a method conforms to income tax practices, but whether it leads to the fairest expression of a business unit's financial position and operating results.

STATEMENTS GIVING EFFECT TO TRANSACTIONS NOT CONSUMMATED

The accountant may be called upon to prepare statements to give effect to transactions that are proposed or are projected. Such hypothetical statements are frequently referred to as *pro forma statements* or *"giving effect to" statements.*

A proposal for a combination will normally call for the preparation of a hypothetical balance sheet indicating the financial position that will emerge under the conditions contemplated for the combination. With such a hypothetical statement, the parties to the combination can evaluate their prospective positions in the new unit. When additional financing is required in a merger or a consolidation, a hypothetical balance sheet may be used to inform prospective investors concerning the enterprise. For example, a company acquiring another business for cash may have to raise funds through the sale of additional shares of stock; or a company to be organized for the acquisition of properties of other units may find it necessary to finance such acquisitions through borrowing and through the issue of shares of stock. Under each of these conditions, prospective investors will want information with respect to the financial status to be achieved upon the realization of financial objectives.

The hypothetical statement is frequently employed in the consideration of financial changes other than a combination. For example, a company planning to retire bonded indebtedness through funds from the sale of additional stock may prepare statements to reflect such changed financing: a hypothetical balance sheet may be prepared to report the financial position as modified by such an action; the income statement for the past period may be recast to show the amount of earnings and the earnings per share assuming conditions of an increased stock equity and the elimination of bonded indebtedness. With data available in this form, stockholders are able to evaluate the changes that are contemplated. A hypothetical statement would also be employed to indicate to stockholders the financial status to be achieved under alternative proposals for corporate recapitalization or reorganization.

Pro forma statements may include proposed transactions that may or may not ultimately occur, or they may be prepared to show the effects of transactions actually consummated subsequent to the dates of the reports. A company seeking to sell additional stock in March, 1967, for example, may submit pro forma statements for 1966 representing financial data for 1966 modified by the effects of a significant change in bonded indebtedness that took place in January, 1967.

In drawing up a pro forma statement it is important that the special conditions that are assumed in its preparation be fully and prominently disclosed. The heading of the statement should indicate that it gives effect to certain projected data. The character of the transactions to which effect is given should be clearly disclosed either in the heading or elsewhere in the statement. The hypothetical statement is generally prepared by means of working papers on which account balances for the company as of a certain date are listed, transactions to which effect is to be given are posted, and resulting account balances are determined. Frequently, the pro forma statement is prepared in a form that shows the individual adjustments. A pro forma balance sheet prepared in this form is illustrated on the opposite page.

Company Y
Pro Forma Balance Sheet
To Give Effect to Proposed Issue of Additional Common Stock
and Application of Proceeds Thereof
December 31, 1966

	Balance Sheet (Audited)	Adjustments	Pro Forma Balance Sheet
Assets			
Cash	$ 150,000	(A) $2,812,500 (B) (1,020,000) (C) (1,200,000)	$ 742,500
Receivables	850,000		850,000
Inventories	1,380,000		1,380,000
Total current assets	$2,380,000		$2,972,500
Property, plant, and equipment, less depreciation	1,400,000	(C) 1,200,000	2,600,000
Other assets	100,000		100,000
Total assets	$3,880,000		$5,672,500
Liabilities and Stockholders' Equity			
Accounts payable	$ 500,000		$ 500,000
Estimated federal income tax payable	120,000		120,000
Total current liabilities	$ 620,000		$ 620,000
Long-term debt	1,000,000	(B) (1,000,000)	
Total liabilities	$1,620,000		$ 620,000
Capital stock, $1 par	$ 400,000	(A) 250,000	$ 650,000
Additional paid-in capital	650,000	(A) 2,562,500	3,212,500
Retained earnings	1,210,000	(B) (20,000)	1,190,000
Total stockholders' equity	$2,260,000		$5,052,500
Total liabilities and stockholders' equity	$3,880,000		$5,672,500

Note: The pro forma adjustments give effect to the following proposed transactions:

(A) The sale of 250,000 shares of common stock of Company Y at $12.50 per share less underwriting discounts and commissions of $1.25 per share.
(B) The retirement of long-term indebtedness of $1,000,000 at a call price of 102.
(C) The acquisition of land, buildings, and machinery from Company Z at a cost of $1,200,000.

QUESTIONS

1. (a) Distinguish between combination by company fusion and combination by company control. (b) Distinguish between a combination achieved through merger and a combination achieved through consolidation.

2. Assuming a merger whereby Company A exchanges shares of its stock for the net assets of Company B, describe the entries to be made on the books of Companies A and B.

3. Assuming a consolidation whereby Company C is organized and exchanges shares of its stock for the net assets of Companies D and E, describe the entries to be made on the books of Companies C, D, and E.

4. (a) Describe the nature of the contributions that are made by the parties to a consolidation. (b) What procedures are normally employed in arriving at a satisfactory measurement of relative contributions?

5. (a) What are the limitations in the issue of a single class of stock to constituent parties to a consolidation? (b) Describe the procedure that must be followed in the allotment of securities among parties to a consolidation if both the relative net asset and the relative earnings contributions are to be preserved through such allotment.

6. Stockholders of Companies A, B, and C decide to consolidate. Asset and estimated annual earnings contributions are as follows:

	Co. A	Co. B	Co. C	Total
Asset contribution...........	$300,000	$700,000	$1,000,000	$2,000,000
Estimated annual earnings contribution..............	50,000	100,000	100,000	250,000

Representatives of Companies A and B propose that a single class of stock of the new company should be distributed in the estimated earnings ratio. Representatives of Company C propose that such stock should be distributed in the asset ratio. Criticize these proposals and suggest a more satisfactory plan for consolidation, assuming that (a) a single class of stock is to be issued and (b) two classes of stock are to be issued.

7. (a) Distinguish between a combination achieved through *purchase* and a combination achieved through *pooling of interests*. (b) What factors should be considered in making the distinction? (c) What accounting significance is attached to the distinction?

8. (a) What arguments are made in support of the recognition of original asset values on the books of a new organization viewed as having emerged from a pooling of interests? (b) Give arguments, pro and con, for the recognition of the retained earnings of constituent companies on the books of the new organization.

9. State what treatment would be applied to paid-in capital and retained earnings balances of constituent companies in a consolidation viewed as a pooling of interests (a) when the stated capital for the new unit is to be more than the total of the stated capitals of the constituent companies, and (b) when the stated capital is to be less than the total of the stated capitals of the constituent companies.

10. Describe each of the following: (a) split-up, (b) split-off, and (c) spin-off.

11. What special accounting problems arise in a divisive reorganization?

12. (a) Describe the nature of the pro forma statement. (b) Describe certain conditions under which the preparation of such a statement would be appropriate. (c) What particular precautions must be observed in the preparation of such statements?

EXERCISES

1. The Brooks Corporation acquires net assets of the Wharton Corporation for $360,000, paying cash of $160,000 and issuing 4,000 shares of its stock that have a market value of $50 per share on the date of acquisition. The Wharton Corporation balance sheet on the date of the merger is as follows:

Current assets	$100,000	Current liabilities	$ 20,000
Plant and equipment	125,000	Long-term debt	30,000
		Capital stock, par $10	50,000
		Additional paid-in capital	35,000
		Retained earnings	90,000
Total assets	$225,000	Total liabilities and stockholders' equity	$225,000

The Brooks Corporation common stock has a par value of $20. (a) Give the entries that should be made on the books of the Wharton Corporation and on the books of the Brooks Corporation in recording the merger. (b) How should the cash and the shares of the Brooks Corporation be distributed among the Wharton Corporation stockholders?

2. Asset and estimated annual earnings contributions of Companies M, N, and O, parties to a consolidation, are as follows:

	Co. M	Co. N	Co. O	Total
Asset contribution	$1,000,000	$2,000,000	$2,000,000	$5,000,000
Estimated annual earnings contribution	90,000	200,000	240,000	530,000

Parties agree to the following: a single class of stock, \$10 par, is to be issued by the new corporation; stock is to be exchanged for net assets as indicated plus allowances for goodwill represented by annual earnings in excess of 8% on asset contributions as above, capitalized at 20%. (a) What entry is made by the new corporation assuming that stock is issued equal in amount to the sum of assets and goodwill? How is the stock distributed among constituent companies? (b) What entry is made assuming that stock of \$5,000,000 is issued, goodwill calculations being made simply to assure the equitable allotment of this stock? How is the stock distributed among constituent companies?

3. Assume in Exercise 2 that two classes of stock are to be issued by the new corporation, 5% fully participating preferred stock and common stock, both issues with a par value of \$10. Preferred stock is to be issued to each company in an amount equal to the asset contributions as shown. Earnings are to be capitalized at 8% in determining the total of preferred stock and common stock to be issued to each company. Common stock is to be issued for the difference between totals so determined and the preferred stock to which each company is entitled. State the number of shares of preferred stock and common stock of the new corporation to be issued to stockholders of Companies M, N, and O.

4. Balance sheet data for Companies R and S, prior to their consolidation, follow:

	Co. R	Co. S
Assets	\$850,000	\$600,000
Liabilities	\$250,000	\$200,000
Capital stock, \$100 par	400,000	250,000
Additional paid-in capital	50,000	100,000
Retained earnings	150,000	50,000
Total liabilities and stockholders' equity	\$850,000	\$600,000

Stockholders of the two companies agree to a consolidation whereby Company T is to be organized to acquire the net assets of Companies R and S. Company T stock is to be no-par with a stated value, and shares are to be issued in exchange for the stock of Companies R and S on a 5 for 1 basis. The consolidation is deemed a pooling of interests, and asset, liability, and stockholders' equity balances of the predecessor companies are to be continued on the new company books.

(a) Give the entries that are made on the books of Company T under each of the following assumptions:

(1) The no-par shares are given a stated value of \$20 per share.
(2) The no-par shares are given a stated value of \$15 per share.
(3) The no-par shares are given a stated value of \$25 per share.

(b) Give the entries that are made on the books of Companies R and S in recording the transfers of net assets and the distribution of Company T stock in final liquidation.

5. Stockholders of Allen Company, Bay Company, and Cook Company agree to a merger. Bay Company and Cook Company are to accept shares of Allen Company in exchange for all of their assets and liabilities on the basis of 1 share for every $125 of net assets transferred. On December 31, 1967, the date of the transfer, balances on the books of the separate companies are as follows:

	Allen Co.	Bay Co.	Cook Co.
Assets			
Current assets	$230,000	$200,000	$230,000
Plant and equipment (net)	450,000	250,000	370,000
Goodwill	20,000		50,000
Total assets	$700,000	$450,000	$650,000
Liabilities and Stockholders' Equity			
Current liabilities	$175,000	$120,000	$190,000
Bonds payable		100,000	200,000
Common stock, $100 par	500,000	150,000	200,000
Additional paid-in capital	45,000	90,000	
Retained earnings (deficit)	(20,000)	(10,000)	60,000
Total liabilities and stockholders' equity	$700,000	$450,000	$650,000

The following adjustments are to be made in arriving at the net asset contributions of Bay Company and Cook Company for purposes of the merger:

(1) The inventory of the Bay Company is presently stated on a lifo basis at $100,000; the inventory is to be recognized at $160,000, representing cost calculated on a fifo basis consistent with the costing procedures of the other companies.

(2) No value is to be assigned to goodwill reported on the books of the Cook Company.

Assuming that the merger is construed as a pooling of interests and that predecessor companies' asset, liability, and stockholders' equity items are to be continued, give the entries that are required on the books of the Allen Company and prepare a balance sheet upon consummation of the merger.

6. Balance sheets for Companies G and H on June 30, 1967 appear at the top of the following page.

Assets	Co. G	Co. H
Cash	$ 150,000	$ 300,000
Other current assets	1,050,000	2,200,000
Property, plant, and equipment (net)	900,000	1,000,000
Other assets	250,000	
Total assets	$2,350,000	$3,500,000
Liabilities and Stockholders' Equity		
Current liabilities	$ 650,000	$ 700,000
Long-term debt	500,000	300,000
Capital stock, $1 par	600,000	
Capital stock, no par		50,000
Additional paid-in capital	450,000	
Retained earnings	150,000	2,450,000
Total liabilities and stockholders' equity	$2,350,000	$3,500,000

Company G proposes to issue 250,000 shares, which can be sold at $12.50 per share less underwriting discounts and commissions of $1.25 per share. It then proposes to acquire all of the assets of Company H with the exception of its cash balance and to assume all of the obligations of the latter for an aggregate consideration of $3,000,000, payable $2,250,000 in cash and the balance in long-term notes.

Prepare a pro forma balance sheet that gives effect to the proposed transactions.

7. Company Y offers to sell to Company X its assets at their book value plus $150,000, the latter amount representing payment for goodwill. Operating data for the past year for the two companies are as follows:

		Co. X		Co. Y
Sales		$960,000		$800,000
Cost of goods sold		672,000		600,000
Gross profit on sales		$288,000		$200,000
Selling expense	$168,000		$117,600	
General and administrative expenses	72,000	240,000	50,400	168,000
Net income		$ 48,000		$ 32,000

Company X estimates the following operating changes if Company Y is merged through purchase:

(1) After the merger, the sales volume of Company X will be 20% in excess of the present combined sales volume, and the sales price per unit will be decreased by 10%.

(2) Fixed manufacturing cost has been 30% of cost of goods sold for each company. After the merger, the fixed manufacturing costs of Company X will be increased by 90% of the current fixed manufacturing cost of Company Y. The current variable manufacturing cost of Company X, which is 70% of cost of goods sold, is expected to increase in proportion to the increased sales volume.
(3) Selling expenses of Company X are expected to be 90% of the present combined selling expenses.
(4) General and administrative expenses of Company X will increase by 80% as a result of the merger.

Excess of the estimated net income over the combined present net income of the two companies is to be capitalized at 20%. If this amount exceeds the price set by Company Y for goodwill, Company X will accept the offer. Prepare a projected income statement for Company X assuming a condition of merger and state whether Company X should accept the offer.

PROBLEMS

9-1. A merger was effected on June 1 whereby the Columbia Corporation took over the assets and assumed the liabilities of the Decker Company in exchange for 8,000 shares of its own stock. A balance sheet for the Columbia Corporation just prior to the merger shows the following:

Cash, receivables, inventories	$365,000	Current liabilities	$105,000
Investments	120,000	Long-term debt	180,000
Plant and equipment (net)	400,000	Preferred stock, $100 par	100,000
Goodwill and other intangibles	100,000	Common stock, $5 stated value	250,000
		Additional paid-in capital	90,000
		Retained earnings	260,000
Total assets	$985,000	Total liabilities and stockholders' equity	$985,000

The Decker Company balance sheet consists of the following:

Cash, receivables, inventories	$ 80,800	Current liabilities	$ 40,000
Plant and equipment (net)	140,000	Long-term debt	60,000
Goodwill	40,000	Common stock, $10 par	100,000
		Additional paid-in capital	30,000
		Appraisal capital	50,000
		Deficit	(19,200)
Total assets	$260,800	Total liabilities and stockholders' equity	$260,800

The Columbia Corporation records the assets of the Decker Company at appraised values as follows: cash, receivables, inventories, $56,000; plant and equipment, $120,000. Liabilities are understated by certain accrued items totaling $1,200. The stock of the Columbia Corporation is selling at $12 per share, and this figure is used in recording the purchase of the Decker Company net assets.

Instructions: (1) Give the entries that would appear on the books of the Columbia Corporation as a result of the merger.

(2) Prepare a balance sheet for the Columbia Corporation after the merger.

(3) Give the entries to close the books of the Decker Company.

(4) State how stock of the Columbia Corporation should be distributed to owners of Decker Company stock upon the dissolution of the latter company.

9-2. Stockholders for Companies D, E, and F agree to the following plan in effecting a consolidation:

The new company, DEF, Inc., shall acquire all of the assets of Companies D, E, and F and shall assume all of the liabilities, issuing 6% preferred stock, $100 par value, in an amount equal to the net assets transferred excluding intangible assets. Assets are to be valued at current market or reproduction costs. Average profits for 1964, 1965, and 1966 in excess of 6% of net tangible assets after revaluation are to be capitalized at 25% in determining the valuation to be placed on goodwill; 150,000 shares of no-par common are to be issued in payment of goodwill.

Balance sheets on March 31, 1967, when the consolidation is to be made effective, follow:

	Co. D	Co. E	Co. F
Cash	$ 120,000	$ 100,000	$ 30,000
Receivables	280,000	160,000	220,000
Inventories	700,000	400,000	650,000
Plant and equipment (net)	2,200,000	1,000,000	1,500,000
Goodwill	200,000	100,000	
Total assets	$3,500,000	$1,760,000	$2,400,000
Accounts payable	$ 350,000	$ 310,000	$ 300,000
Bonds payable	1,500,000		500,000
Common stock, $100 par	1,000,000	500,000	2,000,000
Retained earnings (deficit)	650,000	950,000	(400,000)
Total liabilities and stockholders' equity	$3,500,000	$1,760,000	$2,400,000

Assets are revalued as follows for purposes of the consolidation:

	Co. D	Co. E	Co. F
Inventories	$ 950,000	$ 500,000	$ 800,000
Plant and equipment	3,000,000	1,300,000	1,750,000

Average earnings for the three-year period ended December 31, 1966, were as follows: Company D, $160,000; Company E, $120,000; Company F, $125,000.

Instructions: (1) Give the journal entries for Companies D, E, and F to record the revaluation of assets and the adjustments for goodwill. (Give calculations to show how respective goodwill balances are determined.)

(2) Give the journal entries for each company to record the receipt of new stock from DEF, Inc. and its distribution to stockholders in exchange for their stock. Calculate the number of shares of preferred and common stock of DEF, Inc. to be distributed to stockholders in exchange for each share of common stock in Companies D, E, and F.

(3) Give the journal entries for DEF, Inc. to record the net assets acquired and the distribution of stock for assets acquired.

(4) Prepare a balance sheet for DEF, Inc.

9-3. Asset and estimated earnings contributions by Companies A, B, and C, parties to a consolidation in 1967, are as follows:

	Co. A	Co. B	Co. C
Assets as appraised (before goodwill)......	$3,000,000	$1,500,000	$1,500,000
Estimated annual earnings contribution...	300,000	165,000	135,000

The new corporation is to be known as the ABC Corporation. Two plans are suggested for the distribution of stock in the new company to stockholders of Companies A, B, and C.

Plan A: The ABC Corporation shall issue a single class of stock in exchange for assets. Earnings of each company in excess of 6% of assets as appraised are to be capitalized at 20% in calculating the goodwill contribution by constituent parties. Stock is to have a par value of $10 and is to be issued in an amount equal to total assets transferred including goodwill.

Plan B: Two classes of stock, 6% fully participating preferred and common, are to be issued. Earnings are to be capitalized at 7½% in determining the total stock to be issued in exchange for the assets of each company. Preferred stock, par $10, is to be issued in an amount equal to assets at their appraised values. Common stock, par $10, is to be issued for the difference between the total stock to be issued to each company and the amount it is to receive in preferred. The issue of common stock is to be regarded as payment of goodwill.

Instructions: (1) Give the required entries on the books of the ABC Corporation and state how the stock should be distributed among Companies A, B, and C under each of the plans considered.

(2) If earnings and dividends of the new corporation are estimated for 1967 at $750,000, state how this total would be distributed among former stockholders of Companies A, B, and C under each of the plans considered.

9-4. Stockholders of Company R and Company S agree to consolidate. Under the agreement, a new company, Company T, is to be formed with a single class of $100 par stock. Shares of Company T will be issued to Company R and Company S in par value amounts equal to the net asset contributions made by these companies. In order to secure additional capital for expansion, it is planned to place 20,000 additional shares on sale to the public at par.

Balance sheets of Companies R and S as of December 31, 1967, are given below.

	Co. R	Co. S
Assets		
Cash	$ 28,500	$ 22,500
Notes receivable	52,500	30,500
Notes receivable discounted	(50,000)	
Accounts receivable	158,000	90,000
Inventories	50,500	77,500
Plant expansion fund	50,000	
Land	15,000	20,000
Buildings (net)	124,000	140,000
Machinery (net)	205,000	119,000
Other assets		7,500
Total assets	$633,500	$507,000
Liabilities and Stockholders' Equity		
Notes payable	$ 42,500	$ 22,000
Accounts payable	155,500	72,000
Bonds payable		100,000
Capital stock, $10 par	300,000	
Capital stock, $20 par		300,000
Treasury stock, Co. S, 1,000 shares at cost		(20,000)
Premium on capital stock	75,000	
Retained earnings	60,500	33,000
Total liabilities and stockholders' equity	$633,500	$507,000

It is agreed that the following adjustments are to be made in arriving at the net asset contributions by the two companies:

(a) Company R employs the lifo method of inventory valuation. The inventory of December 31, 1967, is to be increased to $65,000 to be uniform with the fifo valuation method used by Company S.

(b) The buildings of Company S were acquired in January, 1964, and have been depreciated at the rate of $10,000 per year. Depreciation is to be recognized on the buildings on the basis of an estimated life of 20 years, the same as that recognized for buildings by Company R.

(c) Company S has been depreciating its machinery on a decreasing-charge basis. The machinery cost $200,000 when purchased 4 years ago and was estimated to have a scrap value of $20,000 at the end of 15 years. Depreciation is to be recognized by the straight-line method consistent with the depreciation method used by Company R.

Shares are sold to the public as planned and the consolidation is consummated on December 31, 1967.

Instructions: (1) Give all of the entries required on the books of Company R and Company S, including those to record the distribution of Company T shares to stockholders. (State the number of Company T shares that are issued to Company R and to Company S, and the basis of exchange with each stockholder.)

(2) Give all of the entries necessary on the books of Company T.

(3) Prepare a balance sheet for Company T as of December 31, 1967.

9-5. Stockholders of Companies L, M, and N are considering alternative arrangements for a combination. Balance sheets reflecting uniform accounting procedures that are to be used as a basis for the combination are prepared on September 1, 1967, as follows:

	Co. L	Co. M	Co. N
Assets	$4,000,000	$5,500,000	$500,000
Liabilities	$2,850,000	$1,500,000	$175,000
Capital stock (all $10 par)	1,500,000	1,000,000	250,000
Additional paid-in capital		400,000	125,000
Retained earnings (deficit)	(350,000)	2,600,000	(50,000)
Total liabilities and stockholders' equity	$4,000,000	$5,500,000	$500,000

Company L shares have a market price of $15. A market price is not available for shares of Company M and Company N since stock of these companies is closely held.

Instructions: Prepare a balance sheet for the combination giving effect to each of the assumptions that follow:

(1) Company L acquires all of the assets and assumes all of the liabilities of Company M and Company N by issuing in exchange for the acquisitions 300,000 shares of its stock to Company M and 25,000 shares of its stock to Company N. The transaction is treated in the accounts as a purchase.

(2) Company L shares are issued as in (1) above, but the transaction is treated in the accounts as a pooling of interests.

(3) A new corporation, L and M Company, is formed to take over the assets and to assume the liabilities of Companies L, M, and N. The new company issues no-par stock with a stated value of $5 in payment of acquisitions, as follows: to Company L, 150,000 shares; to Company M, 300,000 shares; to Company N, 25,000 shares. The transaction is treated as a pooling of interests.

9-6. The stockholders of Companies X, Y, and Z are considering a combination of their companies. Accordingly, they authorize the preparation of financial statements giving effect to uniform procedures. Balance sheets on November 1, 1967, that are to be used in arriving at terms for a combination follow:

	Co. X	Co. Y	Co. Z
Assets	$10,000,000	$2,000,000	$1,500,000
Liabilities	$ 3,500,000	$1,250,000	$ 500,000
Capital stock	1,000,000	1,000,000	500,000
Additional paid-in capital	500,000	250,000	150,000
Retained earnings (deficit)	5,000,000	(500,000)	350,000
Total liabilities and stockholders' equity	$10,000,000	$2,000,000	$1,500,000

Stock of each company is no-par. Shares issued and outstanding are as follows: Company X, 1,000,000; Company Y, 20,000; Company Z, 50,000. Company X shares are quoted on the market at $10; Company Y and Company Z shares are closely held and there are no quotations for them.

Instructions: Prepare a balance sheet giving effect to the combination under each of the following assumptions:

(1) Company X acquires all of the assets and assumes all of the obligations of Company Y and Company Z, and in payment issues 100,000 shares of its stock to Company Y and 150,000 shares to Company Z. The transaction is treated as a purchase.

(2) Company AAA is formed to acquire all of the assets and to assume all of the liabilities of the three companies. Payment is made by Company AAA by the issue of shares with a par value of $2.50 as follows: to Company X, 1,000,000 shares; to Company Y, 100,000 shares; to Company Z, 150,000 shares. The transaction is treated as a pooling of interests.

9-7. Balance sheets for Richards, Inc. and the Scott Corporation on June 30, 1967, appear at the top of the following page.

On this date the Scott Corporation is offered 400,000 shares of Richards, Inc. in exchange for its net assets. Richards, Inc. stock has a market value of $10.50 per share. The offer is accepted and the shares transferred to the Scott Corporation are distributed to its stockholders in final liquidation.

Instructions: (1) (a) Give entries on the books of Richards, Inc. to record the acquisition of the Scott Corporation, assuming that the merger is recognized as a purchase and the stock issued in exchange for net assets is recorded at its market value. Net assets of the Scott Corporation are recorded at their book values; the difference between the market value of the stock and the net assets acquired for such stock is to be recognized as goodwill. (b) Prepare a balance sheet for Richards, Inc. after the purchase.

(2) (a) Give the entries on the books of Richards, Inc. to record the acquisition of the Scott Corporation, assuming that the merger is recognized as a pooling of interests. (b) Prepare a balance sheet for Richards, Inc. after the pooling of interests.

	Richards, Inc.	Scott Corporation
Assets		
Cash	$ 140,000	$ 950,000
Receivables	450,000	730,000
Inventories	580,000	980,000
Prepaid expenses	25,000	66,500
Total current assets	$1,195,000	$2,726,500
Property, plant, and equipment, less depreciation	900,000	720,000
Other assets	100,000	20,000
Total assets	$2,195,000	$3,466,500
Liabilities and Stockholders' Equity		
Current portion of long-term debt	$ 25,000	$ 40,000
Accounts payable	500,000	146,500
Estimated federal income taxes payable	50,000	400,000
Total current liabilities	$ 575,000	$ 586,500
Long-term debt	50,000	180,000
Total liabilities	$ 625,000	$ 766,500
Capital stock, $1 par, 1,600,000 shares issued and outstanding	$1,600,000	
Capital stock, no par, 5,000 shares issued and outstanding		$ 50,000
Retained earnings (deficit)	(30,000)	2,650,000
Total stockholders' equity	$1,570,000	$2,700,000
Total liabilities and stockholders' equity	$2,195,000	$3,466,500

9-8. Balance sheets for Company Y and Company Z on June 30, 1967, are shown at the top of the following page.

The companies are contemplating a merger in which the net assets of Company Z are to be acquired by Company Y in exchange for 120,000 shares of stock of the latter company; stock of Company Y is subsequently to be distributed to stockholders of Company Z in liquidation of Company Z.

Instructions: Prepare a pro forma balance sheet to give effect to the merger, assuming that it is to be regarded as a pooling of interests. (Prepare the statement in a form that shows the adjustments that are made in reflecting the merger.)

	Co. Y	Co. Z
Assets		
Cash	$ 100,000	$ 50,000
Receivables	350,000	250,000
Inventories	940,000	560,000
Property, plant, and equipment, less depreciation	1,100,000	650,000
Total assets	$2,490,000	$1,510,000
Liabilities and Stockholders' Equity		
Accounts payable	$ 750,000	$ 160,000
Taxes and accruals	100,000	40,000
Long-term debt	600,000	200,000
Total liabilities	$1,450,000	$ 400,000
Capital stock, $5 stated value	$1,000,000	
Capital stock, $1 par		$ 100,000
Additional paid-in capital		250,000
Retained earnings	40,000	760,000
Total stockholders' equity	$1,040,000	$1,110,000
Total liabilities and stockholders' equity	$2,490,000	$1,510,000

9-9. Effective December 31, 1967, X Corporation proposes to acquire, in exchange for common stock, all of the assets and liabilities of Y Corporation and Z Corporation, after which the latter two corporations will distribute the X Corporation stock to their shareholders in complete liquidation and dissolution. X Corporation proposes to increase its outstanding stock for purposes of these acquisitions. Balance sheets of each corporation immediately prior to merger on December 31, 1967, are given below. The assets of each corporation are deemed to be worth their book values.

	X Corporation	Y Corporation	Z Corporation
Current assets	$ 2,000,000	$ 500,000	$ 25,000
Fixed assets (net)	10,000,000	4,000,000	200,000
Total assets	$12,000,000	$4,500,000	$225,000
Current liabilities	$ 1,000,000	$ 300,000	$ 20,000
Long-term debt	3,000,000	1,000,000	105,000
Capital stock ($10 par)	3,000,000	1,000,000	50,000
Retained earnings	5,000,000	2,200,000	50,000
Total liab. and stockholders' equity	$12,000,000	$4,500,000	$225,000

	X Corporation	Y Corporation	Z Corporation
Other data relative to acquisition:			
Shares outstanding	300,000	100,000	5,000
Fair market value per share	$40	$40	$30
Number of shares of X Corporation to be exchanged —			
for Y Corporation assets		100,000	
for Z Corporation assets			5,000
Old management to continue		Yes	No
Old shareholders to elect director on X Corporation Board		Yes	No

Instructions: Prepare journal entries for the X Corporation to record the combination of the X Corporation, the Y Corporation, and the Z Corporation.

(AICPA adapted)

9-10. Financial statements of G Corporation and D Corporation appear below.

Balance Sheets
June 30, 1967

	G Corporation	D Corporation
Assets		
Cash	$ 25,500	$ 1,500
Receivables, net	24,500	7,500
Inventories	42,000	8,800
Due from D Corporation	7,600	—
Fixed assets, less depreciation	59,500	35,800
Other assets	4,500	200
Total assets	$163,600	$53,800
Liabilities and Stockholders' Equity		
Accounts and notes payable	$ 22,600	$35,400
Due to G Corporation	—	7,600
Accrued expenses	1,500	2,200
Federal income tax payable	9,500	—
Total liabilities	$ 33,600	$45,200
Capital stock, $10 par value	$ 50,000	—
Capital stock, $100 par value	—	$25,000
Capital contributed in excess of par value	30,000	32,000
Retained earnings, December 31, 1966	43,000	(42,300)
Net income (loss) from January 1, 1967	9,500	(6,100)
Dividends paid	(2,500)	—
Total stockholders' equity	$130,000	$ 8,600
Total liabilities and stockholders' equity	$163,600	$53,800

Statements of Income and Expense
For the Six Months Ended June 30, 1967

	G Corporation	D Corporation
Sales	$150,000	$60,000
Cost of sales	105,000	54,000
Gross profit	$ 45,000	$ 6,000
Operating expenses	31,000	8,200
Operating profit (loss)	$ 14,000	($ 2,200)
Other income (deductions)	5,000	(3,900)
Net income (loss) before taxes	$ 19,000	($ 6,100)
Provision for income taxes	9,500	—
Net income after taxes (loss)	$ 9,500	($ 6,100)

The net incomes (losses) before income taxes for the two corporations for the last 6 years are as follows (net income per books and net taxable income are the same):

	G Corporation	D Corporation
1961	$18,000	($10,000)
1962	(7,500)	4,000
1963	12,600	(15,000)
1964	14,900	(6,000)
1965	31,200	(7,000)
1966	28,900	(11,100)

On July 1, 1967, D Corporation transferred to G Corporation all of its assets, subject to all liabilities, in exchange for unissued G Corporation capital stock. Both corporations have been owned since their inception in 1961 by the same group of stockholders, although in different proportions as to individuals. The terms of the merger provided that the fair value of the stock in each case is to be its book value, except that an allowance is to be made for the value of any net operating carry-forward losses. Obtaining the benefit of the loss carryover deduction was not the principal purpose for the merger. (Assume a 50% income tax rate and a 5-year loss carry-forward period.)

Instructions: (1) Compute (a) the number of shares of G Corporation to be distributed to shareholders of D Corporation, and (b) the number of shares of G Corporation stock to be exchanged for each share of D Corporation stock.

(2) Prepare the journal entry for the books of G Corporation, recording the merger with D Corporation as a pooling of interests.

(3) Prepare the journal entries for the books of D Corporation, recording the merger with G Corporation and the distribution of G Corporation stock to the stockholders of D Corporation.

(AICPA adapted)

9-11. Y Corporation acquired all of the outstanding stock of Z Corporation as of June 30, 1967. As consideration for the acquisition, Y Corporation gave the stockholders of Z Corporation $550,000 and 500,000 shares of previously unissued common stock in exchange for all the outstanding stock of the Z Corporation. The Y Corporation stock had a par value of $1 and a quoted market value of $2.50 both before and after this transaction.

The balance sheet of Z Corporation as of June 30, 1967, was as follows:

Assets

Current assets:				
Cash			$120,000	
Accounts receivable			240,000	
Inventories			210,000	$ 570,000
Fixed assets:				
	Cost	Allowance for Depreciation	Net	
Property A	$ 310,000	$160,000	$150,000	
Property B	370,000	170,000	200,000	
Property C	480,000	180,000	300,000	
Property D	250,000	150,000	100,000	
	$1,410,000	$660,000	$750,000	750,000
Total assets				$1,320,000

Liabilities and Stockholders' Equity

Accounts payable		$ 470,000
Stockholders' equity:		
Common stock — authorized and outstanding, 500,000 shares of $1 par value	$500,000	
Paid-in capital in excess of par value	100,000	
Retained earnings	250,000	850,000
Total liabilities and stockholders' equity		$1,320,000

All receivables are considered collectible. Inventories are stated at cost, which is also equivalent to replacement cost and is not in excess of market. Properties B, C and D have been appraised at $600,000, $800,000 and $200,000 respectively. Goodwill is not considered to be a significant factor in this business.

An engineer of the Y Corporation estimates that the properties of the Z Corporation will have a 10-year useful life from July 1, 1967, with no salvage value at the end of that period. Y Corporation uses the straight-line method of depreciating its assets.

On July 1, 1967, Z Corporation sold property A for $500,000 and for the 6 months ended December 31, 1967, reported a net income of $450,000, which included the gain from the sale of property A and depreciation of $55,000.

The balance sheet of Z Corporation at December 31, 1967, was as follows:

Assets

Current assets:		
Cash	$390,000	
Accounts receivable	355,000	
Inventories	260,000	$1,005,000

Fixed assets:

	Cost	Allowance for Depreciation	Net	
Property B	$ 370,000	$188,500	$181,500	
Property C	480,000	204,000	276,000	
Property D	250,000	162,500	87,500	
	$1,100,000	$555,000	$545,000	545,000
Total assets				$1,550,000

Liabilities and Stockholders' Equity

Accounts payable		$ 250,000
Stockholders' equity:		
Common stock	$500,000	
Paid-in capital in excess of par value	100,000	
Retained earnings	700,000	1,300,000
Total liabilities and stockholders' equity		$1,550,000

On January 1, 1968, Z Corporation was dissolved and all of its assets were transferred to and its liabilities assumed by Y Corporation. The transaction is to be accounted for as a purchase and not as a pooling of interests.

Instructions: (1) Prepare the journal entry of Y Corporation to record its investment in Z Corporation as of June 30, 1967, and explain the basis for the value assigned to the investment.

(2) Prepare the journal entries to record the accounts of Z Corporation on the books of Y Corporation upon dissolution of Z Corporation and explain how the amounts were determined. (Disregard income tax implications.)

(AICPA adapted)

9-12. Presented below are balance sheets for the Ace Company at December 31, 1966, and May 31, 1967:

Ace Company
Balance Sheets

	December 31, 1966	May 31, 1967
Assets		
Cash	$ 1,038,000	$ 472,000
Receivables	2,550,000	3,105,000
Inventories	5,592,000	6,028,000
Prepaid expenses	308,000	297,000
Total current assets	$ 9,488,000	$ 9,902,000
Property (net)	6,927,000	6,804,000
Other assets	635,000	604,000
Total assets	$17,050,000	$17,310,000
Liabilities and Stockholders' Equity		
Accounts payable	$ 2,427,000	$ 3,052,500
Current maturities — long-term debt	600,000	600,000
Accrued liabilities	1,096,000	922,000
Dividends payable — preferred stock	63,000	0
Estimated federal income taxes	417,000	333,500
Total current liabilities	$ 4,603,000	$ 4,908,000
Long-term debt	4,200,000	4,050,000
Stockholders' equity:		
Preferred cumulative stock — 21,000 shares of $100 par, 3%, outstanding; redeemable at $102	2,100,000	2,100,000
Common stock — 100,000 shares of $10 par outstanding	1,000,000	1,000,000
Capital contributed in excess of par value of common stock	587,000	587,000
Retained earnings	4,560,000	4,665,000
Total liabilities and stockholders' equity	$17,050,000	$17,310,000

Note: The increase in Retained Earnings is net of a dividend of $.20 per share paid March 15, 1967, on common stock.

The Ace Company proposes to sell all of its assets except cash and receivables to the Jones Company on July 31, 1967. The sales price shall be $10,000,000 adjusted by the change in book value for inventories and property from December 31, 1966, to May 31, 1967. The May 31 book values of prepaid expenses and other assets are to be added to the sales price.

The settlement shall be:

(1) Jones Company 4% note for $3,000,000 payable in semiannual installments of $150,000 commencing January 31, 1968.
(2) Assumption of all liabilities except the estimated federal income taxes payable and long-term debt.
(3) Balance payable in cash immediately.

The company intends to retire the preferred stock and to establish a $300,000 reserve for contingencies. The net profit for June and July is estimated at $150,000 before income taxes (assume that a 50% tax rate has been in effect since 1962).

The last preferred stock dividend was declared on December 31, 1966. The regular common stock dividend was paid on June 15, 1967.

Taxable income for the past 4 years follows:

1963	$1,481,000
1964	412,400
1965	639,600
1966	842,500

Instructions: (1) Compute the total sales price and settlement to be made.

(2) Compute Ace Company's gain or loss on the sale giving effect to income taxes. (Assume that a loss can be carried back three years prior to the loss year; the taxpayer may claim a refund for taxes paid in the years in which the carry-back may be applied.)

(3) Prepare a work sheet with columnar headings "Per Books," "Adjustments," and "Estimated Balance Sheet, July 31, 1967", giving effect to the proposed sale and other information given. Support your adjustments with schedules or computations you deem necessary. Formal journal entries are not required.

(AICPA adapted)

Chapter 10

CONSOLIDATED STATEMENTS

ACQUISITION OF SUBSIDIARY COMPANY

In the previous chapter, discussion was limited to the joint control and operation of corporate units through merger or consolidation. The practical effects of a merger or a consolidation are frequently achieved through the ownership by one company of a majority or all of the voting stock of other corporate units. A company owning more than 50% of the voting stock of another is in a position to elect the board of directors of the latter unit and thus to control the resources and the operations of the company. While the fusion of separate companies frequently offers serious practical difficulties, acquisition of control by means of stock ownership may be relatively simple to arrange and may require a smaller investment. Furthermore, control through stock ownership may be preferred over the other possibilities because of certain financial, administrative, tax, or legal advantages found in this relationship.

CORPORATE CONTROL THROUGH STOCK OWNERSHIP

The power of a corporation to acquire stock of other corporations is generally granted by the laws of the state.[1] State law may specifically permit the organization of companies that are formed for the sole purpose of acquiring and holding stock of other corporations.

Even though a corporation may acquire a majority or all of the stock issued by other corporations, the latter units continue to retain their separate identities. From a practical point of view, the acquisition by one company of a controlling interest in the stock of another company may be equivalent to a merger or a consolidation since properties are now under unified management and control. From a legal point of view, however, regardless of the degree of corporate control that may be exercised, each company continues to be regarded as a separate entity.[2]

---

[1]Section 802 (d) of the California Corporations Code (as amended through 1965), for example, provides that the general business corporation can "acquire, subscribe for, hold, own, pledge, and otherwise dispose of and represent shares of stock, bonds, and securities of any other corporation, domestic or foreign."

[2]The legal conception of the separateness of the corporation and its stockholders and those circumstances that may call for a denial of such separateness was stated in the case of *Majestic Co. vs. Orpheum Circuit, Inc.* (21 F.2d 720). Quoting from this case, " . . . a corporation has an entity separate and distinct from its stockholders; and the act of the corporation is not that of the stockholders. . . . A corporation is not liable for the acts or the obligations of another cor-

Parent and holding company. A corporation that holds the stock of others and controls their activities is called a *parent company*. When a corporation is organized for the sole purpose of holding the stock of others and supervising their activities, it is known as a *holding company*. The chief source of revenue of the holding company is the dividends on the securities it holds; expenses are entirely of an administrative nature. A company that exercises control over others while engaged in its own trading or manufacturing activities is sometimes called an *operating holding company* to distinguish it from a pure holding company. The companies that are controlled by a parent or holding company are known as *subsidiaries*. Parent and subsidiary companies are referred to as *affiliated companies*. A company that holds a major part or all of the voting stock of another is referred to as the *controlling interest*. Those holding any remaining interest in the controlled company are referred to as the *minority interest*. A controlled company whose stock is wholly owned by affiliated units is called a *wholly owned subsidiary*.

Ownership of a majority of the voting stock of a company assures control over that unit. In practice, however, ownership of a lesser amount generally offers control for all practical purposes, particularly when remaining stockholders are widely scattered, unorganized, and willing to delegate their voting power to the dominant group. When ownership is not complete, control must be exercised in a manner that is not prejudicial to the minority interest.

Recording an investment in a subsidiary company. A corporation acquires the stock of other companies by purchase for cash, by exchange for other assets, or by exchange for its own securities. An investment account is charged for the cost of the stock acquired. When cash is paid, the investment account is charged for the amount paid. When other assets are given in exchange, the investment should be recorded at the fair value of the assets given up. When a company's own securities are issued in exchange for stock acquired, the investment should be recorded at the fair value of the securities given in exchange or at the fair value of the stock acquired, whichever is more clearly evident; any difference between the value assigned to the investment and the par or stated value of the securities should be recognized as a premium or a discount on the

---

poration, merely because it controls such other by reason of ownership of its stock. . . . The corporate entity will not be ignored at law nor in equity, whether the control is in the hands of one or many stockholders. . . . The corporation will be regarded as a legal entity as a general rule, and the courts acting cautiously and only when the circumstances justify it, will ignore the fiction of corporate entity, where it is used as a blind or instrumentality to defeat public convenience, justify wrong, or perpetrate a fraud, and will regard the corporation as an association of persons. . . ."

securities issued. Investments in the stock of subsidiary companies are reported under the "Investments" heading on the parent company balance sheet.

NATURE OF CONSOLIDATED STATEMENTS

A parent company balance sheet that reports subsidiary holdings as investments and subsidiary company balance sheets that report interests held by a parent as capital stock are complete statements of the related units as separate legal entities. However, such statements fail to afford a view of the related units as a single business or a single economic entity. If a comprehensive view of the affiliated companies in relation to the outside world is to be provided, the legal view of separateness of the different units must be cast aside and the practical implications of the ownership of a controlling interest must be incorporated in the presentation. The statement that erases the legal boundaries between a parent and its subsidiaries and presents the financial position of the affiliates as a single unit is known as the *consolidated balance sheet.*

In preparing a combined balance sheet for a home office and its branches, individual asset and liability balances of the branch were combined with similar home office balances; reciprocal balances arising from interoffice transactions and having no asset, liability, or proprietorship significance in viewing the related units as a single entity were eliminated. The effect of such a procedure was to substitute for the branch investment balance on the home office books those assets and liabilities represented by this balance. In developing a consolidated balance sheet for a parent and its subsidiary companies, the subsidiary units are viewed just as though they were branches: individual assets and liabilities of the subsidiary units are combined with similar items of the parent; reciprocal items that have no significance when the related units are viewed as a single entity are eliminated. The parallel approach to consolidation for home office-branch and parent-subsidiary relationships is illustrated in the example that follows.

Assume that the Ward Appliance Company of New York wishes to establish a sales outlet in Boston, and on January 2, 1967, establishes an unincorporated branch in that city. In establishing the branch, the home office transfers to it cash of $125,000 and merchandise of $100,000. Working papers for a combined balance sheet for the home office and the branch are shown at the top of the following page. A combined balance sheet follows the working papers.

Assume that the Ward Appliance Company establishes the Boston office as a separately incorporated unit. The new company is to be known as the Boston Sales Company. The Ward Appliance Company acquires

Ward Appliance Company
Working Papers for Combined Balance Sheet for Home Office and Branch
January 2, 1967

	Home Office	Boston Branch	Eliminations		Combined Balacne Sheet	
			Dr.	Cr.	Dr.	Cr.
Debits						
Cash	75,000	125,000			200,000	
Receivables	150,000				150,000	
Merchandise	200,000	100,000			300,000	
Boston Branch	225,000			225,000		
Plant and Equipment	350,000				350,000	
	1,000,000	225,000				
Credits						
Payables	250,000					250,000
Home Office		225,000	225,000			
Capital Stock	500,000					500,000
Additional Paid-in Capital	100,000					100,000
Retained Earnings	150,000					150,000
	1,000,000	225,000	225,000	225,000	1,000,000	1,000,000

Ward Appliance Company
Combined Balance Sheet for Home Office and Branch
January 2, 1967

Assets		
Cash		$ 200,000
Receivables		150,000
Merchandise		300,000
Plant and equipment		350,000
Total assets		$1,000,000
Liabilities and Stockholders' Equity		
Payables		$ 250,000
Capital stock	$500,000	
Additional paid-in capital	100,000	
Retained earnings	150,000	750,000
Total liabilities and stockholders' equity		$1,000,000

all the capital stock of the Boston Sales Company for cash of $125,000; the stock is recorded on the Boston Sales Company books at a stated value of $100,000, the excess being reported as additional paid-in capital. Merchandise of $100,000 is transferred to the Boston Sales Company, open accounts for this balance being established on the books of the two companies. Statements expressing the financial position of the parent and the subsidiary as one unit are just as necessary here as when the related unit is a branch. Working papers for a consolidated balance sheet for the parent company and its wholly owned subsidiary may be prepared as shown below.

Ward Appliance Company and Subsidiary Boston Sales Company
Working Papers for Consolidated Balance Sheet
January 2, 1967

	Ward Appliance Co.	Boston Sales Co.	Eliminations Dr.	Eliminations Cr.	Consolidated Balance Sheet Dr.	Consolidated Balance Sheet Cr.
Debits						
Cash	75,000	125,000			200,000	
Receivables	150,000				150,000	
Receivable from Boston Sales Co.	100,000			(b) 100,000		
Merchandise	200,000	100,000			300,000	
Investment in Stock of Boston Sales Co.	125,000			(a) 125,000		
Plant and Equipment	350,000				350,000	
	1,000,000	225,000				
Credits						
Payables	250,000					250,000
Payable to Ward Appliance Co.		100,000	(b) 100,000			
Capital Stock, Ward Appliance Co.	500,000					500,000
Additional Paid-in Capital, Ward Appliance Co.	100,000					100,000
Retained Earnings, Ward Appliance Co.	150,000					150,000
Capital Stock, Boston Sales Co.		100,000	(a) 100,000			
Additional Paid-in Capital, Boston Sales Co.		25,000	(a) 25,000			
	1,000,000	225,000	225,000	225,000	1,000,000	1,000,000

In viewing the parent and the subsidiary as a single entity, reciprocal intercompany balances must be eliminated to avoid a duplication of assets, liabilities, and ownership equities. The investment balance and the subsidiary capital accounts are without significance when the related units are viewed as one and are eliminated. The intercompany receivable and payable balances are also without significance when the related units are viewed as one; ultimate settlement of these balances will simply result in the transfer of cash from one company to another without any effect upon total net resources or stockholders' equities. Remaining account balances are combined. A consolidated balance sheet for the Ward Appliance Company and its wholly owned subsidiary will show exactly the same balances as those in the example on page 304 where the Boston office was organized as a branch.

It was suggested in an earlier chapter that separate balance sheets for home office and branch units were incomplete as expressions of financial position in view of the fact that these units represent a single legal entity; such legal identity is reflected only through the combination of data as illustrated. In the case of parent and subsidiary companies, however, the consolidation of financial data must be viewed as presenting no more than the economic unity of the related companies. This summary of economic resources subject to central direction and control is of vital significance to both management and stockholders; nevertheless, it must be considered as complementing the separate statements of the related units, not as substituting therefor. The separate balance sheets retain their validities as presentations of the assets, liabilities, and stockholders' equities of the different legal entities. A creditor must make reference to the separate balance sheet of the particular debtor in determining the degree of protection related to his claim. A stockholder must make reference to the separate balance sheet of his particular company in determining the amount that may be available for dividends. Taxing and regulatory authorities must make reference to the separate statements of the particular companies in applying specific regulations. Only when the consolidated balance sheet is accompanied by separate statements of each of the affiliated companies is full information made available concerning the legal positions of the individual units as well as the composite economic position of such units.

It may be observed that although a consolidated balance sheet for the parent-subsidiary relationship cannot be offered as a statement of legal position, such a legal position can frequently be attained if this should prove desirable. For example, in the previous illustration the Boston Sales Company will continue to operate as a separate legal entity only as long as this is the desire of the parent company; should advantages emerge for a home office-branch relationship, the parent through exercise of its voting power can authorize the dissolution of the subsidiary and the distribution of assets in kind to its stockholder. The subsidiary company is thus converted into a branch; the balance sheet that was previously limited to an expression of economic position is now valid as an expression of both legal and economic position.

Preceding paragraphs have referred to the need for expressing the financial position of a parent and its subsidiaries as a single unit by means of a consolidated balance sheet. There is also a need for expressing the operations of the related units as one. This is done by the preparation of a consolidated income statement. In preparing a consolidated income statement, revenue and expense balances reporting transactions between affiliated units are eliminated and remaining balances summarizing operations with outsiders are combined. The consolidated income statement may be supplemented by a consolidated statement of retained earnings to explain the change in retained earnings that is found on consolidated balance sheets prepared at the end of successive periods.

Although a complete reporting would call for consolidated financial statements accompanied by separate statements for a parent and its subsidiaries, statements to stockholders in recent years have normally been limited to consolidated statements. The New York Stock Exchange rules require that no more than consolidated statements be made available to stockholders of listed companies with majority-owned subsidiaries; separate statements may be provided in lieu of consolidated statements only under unusual conditions making consolidated statements inappropriate. The Committee on Accounting Procedure of the American Institute of Certified Public Accountants in commenting on the purpose of consolidated statements observes, "There is a presumption that consolidated statements are more meaningful than separate statements and that they are usually necessary for a fair presentation when one of the companies in the group directly or indirectly has a controlling financial interest in the other companies."[1] The American Accounting Association Committee on Concepts and Standards in viewing the growing tendency to present consolidated statements unaccompanied by separate statements of constituent units points out, "These trends strongly imply that the consolidated statements are more useful than the separate statements, and may now be primary rather than secondary or supplemental."[2]

Conditions for preparation of consolidated statements. Consolidated financial statements can normally be justified only when (1) a controlling financial interest is present, continuing, and assured, (2) the operations of the related companies are those of an integrated unit, and (3) consolidation offers a valid reflection of the financial status of the related companies.

(1) *A controlling financial interest must be present, continuing, and assured.* It is the ownership of voting stock that affords control. This factor alone, however, does not afford an index of the control that is actually exercised. A company may have a majority ownership of the voting stock of another company and yet fail to exert a dominant role in electing the board of directors, in developing policy, or in directing operations of the latter

---

[1]*Accounting Research Bulletin No. 51*, "Consolidated Financial Statements," 1959 (New York: American Institute of Certified Public Accountants), p. 41.

[2]*Accounting and Reporting Standards for Corporate Financial Statements and Preceding Statements and Supplements*, "Consolidated Financial Statements," 1954 (Columbus: American Accounting Association), p. 42.

company. For example, a company may obtain a majority interest in an established and well-managed company and may permit this company to continue its activities as an independent unit completely free from influence or control by the parent under present favorable circumstances. Or a company may have dominant interests in foreign companies, but the foreign government may place various restrictions upon the operations of such units, including restrictions upon the transfer of properties outside of such countries. In other instances, control may be temporary in view of an impending sale of shares by the parent, issue of additional shares by a subsidiary, or legal reorganization faced by a subsidiary. In each of the foregoing circumstances, consolidated statements indicating an economic unity with full and centralized control may not be appropriate. On the other hand, a company may have less than a majority ownership in the stock of another, yet be in a position to exert effective domination over the latter. Remaining majority stockholders may be completely satisfied with the policies set by the controlling company; patent rights and leasehold arrangements may afford special influence to the controlling company; conditions of interlocking directorates may contribute to unified direction. In spite of the absence of a controlling interest in the voting stock of the related company, unity under effective control is present and the preparation of consolidated statements may be appropriate.

In general, as the degree of ownership of stock in a subsidiary rises, the arguments supporting the preparation of consolidated statements become more persuasive. A number of companies exercising control authorize consolidated statements only when stock in a subsidiary is wholly owned; when ownership is less than 100%, holdings in the subsidiary are recognized as no more than an investment. Many other companies feel that consolidation requires ownership of a substantial majority interest, such as holdings of 75%, 80%, 85%, or more of the stock of a subsidiary. In practice one rarely encounters consolidated statements for related companies when majority stock ownership by a parent is not present even though there may be unified control. Some authorities maintain that majority stock ownership is a prerequisite for consolidation; control must be legally assured if the assumption of a single economic entity is to be valid.[1]

---

[1]The American Institute Committee on Accounting Procedure in discussing consolidation policy states, "The usual condition for a controlling financial interest is ownership of a majority voting interest, and, therefore, as a general rule ownership by one company, directly or indirectly, of over fifty per cent of the outstanding voting shares of another company is a condition pointing toward consolidation." (*Accounting Research Bulletin No. 51*, "Consolidated Financial Statements," 1959, New York: American Institute of Certified Public Accountants, p. 41). The Securities and Exchange Commission in Regulation S-X has adopted the rule that registrants may consolidate only *majority-owned* subsidiaries. A majority-owned subsidiary is defined as "a subsidiary more than fifty per cent of whose outstanding securities representing

(2) *Operations of the related companies must be those of an integrated unit.* When a parent holds a controlling interest in the stock of another company but the operations of the companies are not related or complementary and the organizations do not make up a homogeneous unit, a single combined presentation of financial data might be unrealistic and without value. For example, assume that a manufacturing company owns all the stock of an insurance company, a savings and loan company, or a bank. To combine the balance sheets and the income statements of a financial institution with those of a manufacturing organization would hardly provide meaningful financial data. Although each organization has profitable operations as its objective, the means and the operations for attaining this objective are not related.[1]

(3) *Consolidation must afford a valid reflection of the financial status of the related units.* Legal lines can be erased only so long as these lines are not relevant in an economic overall view; when these lines have certain implications that affect the overall view, the implications must be recognized either by foregoing the consolidation procedure or by their disclosure on the consolidated statements. For example, assume that a parent controls a subsidiary that is insolvent and on the verge of bankruptcy. The unsatisfactory financial position of the subsidiary may be obliterated in the process of consolidation; the consolidated statement may thus suggest a financial position for the related organizations that is not supported by the separate legal parts. Although it may be possible for healthy associates to restore solvency to an insolvent member, there

---

the right, other than as affected by events of default, to vote for the election of directors, is owned by the subsidiary's parent and/or one or more of the parent's other majority-owned subsidiaries." It may be noted that the Internal Revenue Code recognizes consolidated statements as a means for expressing the financial position and operations for "an affiliated group," and permits the filing by a parent and its subsidiaries of a consolidated income tax return reporting the combined taxable income. For tax purposes "an affiliated group" that is granted permission to file a consolidated return is defined as one or more chains of "includible corporations" having a common parent company which is an "includible corporation" and which owns at least 80% of the voting power and at least 80% of each class of nonvoting stock (except nonvoting stock which is limited and preferred as to dividends) of at least one of the other "includible corporations," provided at least 80% of the voting power and 80% of each class of nonvoting stock of any other "includible corporation" is owned by the parent corporation and/or other "includible corporation."

[1]The American Institute Committee on Accounting Procedure comments, "In deciding upon consolidation policy, the aim should be to make the financial presentation which is most meaningful in the circumstances. The reader should be given information which is suitable to his needs, but he should not be burdened with unnecessary detail. Thus, even though a group of companies is heterogeneous in character, it may be better to make a full consolidation than to present a large number of separate statements. On the other hand, separate statements or combined statements would be preferable for a subsidiary or group of subsidiaries if the presentation of financial information would be more informative to shareholders and creditors of the parent company than would be the inclusion of such subsidiaries in the consolidation. For example, separate statements may be required for a subsidiary which is a bank or insurance company and may be preferable for a finance company where the parent and other subsidiaries are engaged in manfacturing operations." (*Accounting Research Bulletin No. 51*, "Consolidated Financial Statements," 1959, New York: American Institute of Certified Public Accountants, p. 42).

is no assurance that such a course will prove to be in the best interests of the individual units and that it will be followed. Consolidation under these conditions would not provide a full appreciation of the status of the parent and its related subsidiaries as a unit but would actually serve to obscure certain facts and to misrepresent financial position.

Judgment will have to be exercised in the determination of when the preparation of consolidated statements is appropriate. Consolidated statements can be justified only when they afford a view of the related companies as a single enterprise that is both valid and informative. In preparing consolidated statements, the consolidation policies that are applied should be disclosed in some satisfactory manner. Consolidation limited to wholly owned subsidiaries, for example, may be disclosed in the heading of the statement; the exclusion of an important unit in view of its heterogeneous character may be disclosed by special note.

Problems in preparation of consolidated statements. There are many problems that arise in the preparation of consolidated statements. These problems vary with the time at which the statements are prepared, the ownership interests in affiliated units and the direct or indirect controls that are afforded through such ownership interests, and the nature of intercompany transactions. The discussion in the remaining pages of this chapter is limited to the problems that arise in the preparation of a consolidated balance sheet at the date that control of a subsidiary is acquired. The problems that arise in the preparation of the consolidated balance sheet at dates subsequent to the acquisition of control and the special problems that are encountered in the preparation of consolidated income and retained earnings statements are considered in the chapters that follow.

ACQUISITION OF THE STOCK OF A GOING CONCERN

In the example for the preparation of a consolidated balance sheet on page 303, a parent-subsidiary relationship arose as a result of the acquisition by the parent of subsidiary company stock at the time the subsidiary was formed. The interest acquired was complete or 100%. The amount paid by the parent was equal to the book value of the subsidiary interest. A parent-subsidiary relationship often arises through the purchase of stock from stockholders of a going concern. In the latter instance, the interest acquired by the parent may be 100% or it may be a lesser percentage. With less than 100% ownership, eliminations against subsidiary capital balances will be less than 100% and the portion of subsidiary capital that is not eliminated will be recognized on the consolidated balance sheet as *minority interest* — the equity in consolidated assets related to stockholders who have retained their shares in the subsidiary. Furthermore, in a purchase of stock from a previous ownership group, the amount paid for the stock may be equal to the book value of the interest acquired, it may be more than the book value of the interest, or it may be less than the book value of the interest. When there is a difference between investment cost and the book value of the net assets that are to replace such cost, the reasons for this must be carefully analyzed so that the difference may be properly expressed on the consolidated balance sheet.

Before proceeding with the preparation of a consolidated balance sheet, a careful examination should be made to determine whether investment cost on the parent's books and assets, liabilities, and stockholders' equity on the subsidiary's books are satisfactorily stated. When errors or accounting failures are discovered, they should be corrected. This is necessary if assets and liabilities as well as the equities of both the controlling interest and the minority interest are to be accurately reported on the consolidated balance sheet.

Corrections on parent company's books. Assume that a parent exchanges marketable securities that it owns for all the stock of another company. The marketable securities have a fair current value of \$400,000, and the book value of the subsidiary stock is also \$400,000. However, the securities are carried by the parent at a cost of \$500,000, and this balance is carried to the investment account when the exchange is made. A determination of these facts calls for a correcting entry on the parent company's books reducing the investment balance and recognizing a loss on the securities of \$100,000; the apparent excess of investment cost over the book value of the subsidiary interest has thus been resolved as a reduction in parent company retained earnings.

Or, assume that a company issues its own stock, par \$1,000,000, in exchange for all the stock of another company with a book value of \$1,200,000. The investment in the subsidiary company stock is recorded by the parent at \$1,000,000 and the capital stock account is credited for this amount. Examination reveals, however, that the parent company's shares have a current fair value of \$1,500,000. Under these circumstances, a correcting entry is required on the parent's books raising the investment account by \$500,000 and recognizing additional paid-in capital of this amount. The apparent excess of book value of the subsidiary interest over investment cost has been converted into an excess of investment cost over book value of the subsidiary interest, and appropriate recognition of the latter balance will be required in preparing a consolidated balance sheet.

Corrections on subsidiary company's books. Assume that a parent acquires all the stock of a subsidiary for $1,000,000. Subsidiary company capital accounts report a total of $800,000. A careful review of subsidiary records shows that excessive depreciation has been recognized on plant and equipment, intangibles with a continuing value have been written off, certain estimated liabilities are overstated, and contingency reserves properly recognized as appropriations of retained earnings are reported as liabilities. Accounts should be restated to reflect acceptable accounting practices. With such restatement, the parent's equity in the subsidiary is raised; in preparing the consolidated balance sheet, the excess of investment cost over book value of the subsidiary interest is reduced or is actually converted into an excess of book value over cost; minority interest is stated in terms of the corrected balances for subsidiary company capital.

Or, assume that a parent acquires 80% of the stock of a subsidiary for $1,000,000; subsidiary company capital balances related to this interest total $1,200,000. Examination of subsidiary records shows that certain costs have been improperly capitalized, depreciation charges on plant and equipment have been inadequate, intangible assets without continuing value are reported at original cost, and certain liabilities are understated. Subsidiary company records require restatement to reflect acceptable accounting practices. In developing a consolidated balance sheet, the excess of book value of the subsidiary interest over investment cost is reduced or is actually converted into an excess of cost over book value; minority interest is stated in terms of the corrected balances.

The preparation of the consolidated balance sheet when stock is acquired in a going concern is illustrated in a series of examples in the section that follows. It will be assumed in the examples that investment costs are accurately stated and that balance sheets of the subsidiary companies reflect acceptable accounting practices.

ACQUISITION OF 100% OF SUBSIDIARY STOCK AT BOOK VALUE

To illustrate the procedure that is followed when all the stock of a company is acquired at book value, assume that the capital of Company S consists of 1,000 shares of capital stock, $100 par, or capital stock of $100,000, and retained earnings of $50,000. On December 1, 1967, Company P acquires all the stock of Company S at a cost of $150,000. Working papers for a consolidated balance sheet are shown at the top of the following page. A consolidated balance sheet prepared from the working papers follows.

It should be noted on the working papers that the investment account and the subsidiary capital stock and retained earnings balances are can-

Company P and Subsidiary Company S
Working Papers for Consolidated Balance Sheet
December 1, 1967

	Co. P	Co. S	Eliminations		Consolidated Balance Sheet	
			Dr.	Cr.	Dr.	Cr.
Debits						
Investment in Co. S Stock	150,000					
Eliminate 100% of Capital Stock				100,000		
Eliminate 100% of Retained Earnings				50,000		
Other Assets	300,000	250,000			550,000	
	450,000	250,000				
Credits						
Liabilities	150,000	100,000				250,000
Capital Stock, Co. P	200,000					200,000
Retained Earnings, Co. P	100,000					100,000
Capital Stock, Co. S		100,000				
Eliminate 100%			100,000			
Retained Earnings, Co. S		50,000				
Eliminate 100%			50,000			
	450,000	250,000	150,000	150,000	550,000	550,000

Company P and Subsidiary Company S
Consolidated Balance Sheet
December 1, 1967

Assets		$550,000
Liabilities		$250,000
Stockholders' equity:		
Capital stock	$200,000	
Retained earnings	100,000	300,000
Total liabilities and stockholders' equity		$550,000

celed. Remaining balances for the two companies are then combined. The assets and the liabilities of the subsidiary are thus substituted for the investment account.

Assume that the capital of Company S consists of capital stock of $200,000 and a deficit of $50,000 and that Company P acquires all the stock at book value of $150,000. The consolidated balance sheet would be exactly the same as in the preceding example, but eliminations on the working papers would be made as shown on the working papers on the following page.

Company P and Subsidiary Company S
Working Papers for Consolidated Balance Sheet
December 1, 1967

	Co. P	Co. S	Eliminations		Consolidated Balance Sheet	
			Dr.	Cr.	Dr.	Cr.
Debits						
Investment in Co. S Stock	150,000					
Eliminate 100% of Capital Stock				200,000		
Eliminate 100% of Deficit			50,000			
Other Assets	300,000	250,000			550,000	
	450,000	250,000				
Credits						
Liabilities	150,000	100,000				250,000
Capital Stock, Co. P	200,000					200,000
Retained Earnings, Co. P	100,000					100,000
Capital Stock, Co. S		200,000				
Eliminate 100%			200,000			
Deficit, Co. S		(50,000)				
Eliminate 100%				50,000		
	450,000	250,000	250,000	250,000	550,000	550,000

ACQUISITION OF LESS THAN 100% OF STOCK AT BOOK VALUE

When the stock of a subsidiary is only partly owned and a consolidated balance sheet is to be prepared, the assumption of a single entity would still require that all assets and liabilities of the related companies be combined. However, if all assets and liabilities of the subsidiary company are to be reflected on the consolidated statement, a minority interest in the net assets so combined must be recognized.

To illustrate the procedure that is followed, assume in the previous example that Company P had acquired only 90% of the stock of Company S, paying an amount equal to the book value of the interest, or $135,000. In recognizing subsidiary net assets of $150,000 on the consolidated balance sheet, it is also necessary to recognize an accompanying minority interest of $15,000 in such assets. Working papers for a consolidated balance sheet would be prepared as shown at the top of the next page. A consolidated balance sheet follows the working papers.

In combining home office and branch accounts, balances in the home office and branch accounts were always equal in amount and thus were fully eliminated. In the consolidation of a parent and its related subsidiary, eliminations applied to the parent investment account and to the subsidiary company capital accounts must be limited to the interest acquired by the parent in the subsidiary. Thus, in the example, eliminations are made against subsidiary capital balances of $135,000. This

Company P and Subsidiary Company S
Working Papers for Consolidated Balance Sheet
December 1, 1967

	Co. P	Co. S	Eliminations Dr.	Eliminations Cr.	Consolidated Balance Sheet Dr.	Consolidated Balance Sheet Cr.
Debits						
Investment in Co. S.	135,000					
Eliminate 90% of Capital Stock				90,000		
Eliminate 90% of Retained Earnings				45,000		
Other Assets	315,000	250,000			565,000	
	450,000	250,000				
Credits						
Liabilities	150,000	100,000				250,000
Capital Stock, Co. P	200,000					200,000
Retained Earnings, Co. P	100,000					100,000
Capital Stock, Co. S		100,000				
Eliminate 90%			90,000			
Minority Interest, 10%						10,000
Retained Earnings, Co. S		50,000				
Eliminate 90%			45,000			
Minority Interest, 10%						5,000
	450,000	250,000	135,000	135,000	565,000	565,000

Company P and Subsidiary Company S
Consolidated Balance Sheet
December 1, 1967

Assets			$565,000
Liabilities			$250,000
Stockholders' equity:			
Minority interest:			
Capital stock	$ 10,000		
Retained earnings	5,000	$ 15,000	
Controlling interest:			
Capital stock	$200,000		
Retained earnings	100,000	300,000	315,000
Total liabilities and stockholders' equity			$565,000

leaves $15,000 that is recognized as minority interest. The minority interest does not appear on the books or on the separate financial statements of any of the affiliated companies; it is recognized only on the consolidated working papers and on the consolidated balance sheet prepared from the working papers.

Minority interest is reported on the consolidated balance sheet in practice in a number of different ways. This balance is sometimes reported as a liability. Occasionally it is included as a part of the stockholders' equity. However, in most instances minority interest is reported under a separate heading between liabilities and the parent company stockholders' equity. The authors are of the opinion that there is no theoretical support for viewing the interest of minority stockholders as a liability. Minority interest is not a claim to be liquidated. Quite the contrary, it points to an interest by a special group of stockholders in the assets reported on the consolidated balance sheet. In presenting the combined resources for a number of related companies, it would appear that minority interest is best regarded as a part of the total stockholders' equity. The stockholders' equity should be reported in two parts — one part summarizing the interest of the minority group and a second part summarizing the interest of the controlling group.[1]

Minority balances in invested capital and in retained earnings may be combined for reporting purposes, or these balances may be separately listed paralleling the presentation of the interest of the controlling group. The latter presentation indicates whether operations of the affiliates have given rise to undistributed earnings or have resulted in an impairment of invested capital. It may be noted that the Securities and Exchange Commission rules require such separation. When a consolidated balance sheet includes minority interests in a number of subsidiaries, such interests are normally reported in total and the detail is provided on a supporting schedule.

The minority interest on the consolidated balance sheet on page 315 is reported as a part of the stockholders' equity.

---

[1]The view that the minority interest expresses a part of an enlarged stockholders' equity rather than an accountability to an outside group is frequently associated with the "entity theory of consolidations." For a full statement of the entity theory of consolidations and the support advanced for this approach, see *The Entity Theory of Consolidated Statements* by Maurice Moonitz (Foundation Press, 1951).

In a survey of consolidated financial statement practices of a group of American industrial corporations conducted by the Research Department of the American Institute of Certified Public Accountants, the position of minority interest on the balance sheet was tabulated as follows:

	No. of Cases
As a liability	23
Below "Total Liabilities" and just above parent company stockholders' equity	3
Classified as part of stockholders equity	3
Unclassified — just above capital stock of parent:	
Total parent company stockholders' equity shown	48
Total parent company stockholders' equity not shown	8
	85

("Survey of Consolidated Financial Statement Practices," 1956, New York: American Institute of Certified Public Accountants, p. 18.)

Assume that the capital of Company S is $150,000, composed of capital stock of $200,000 and a deficit of $50,000, and that Company P acquires a 90% interest for $135,000. Working papers for a consolidated balance sheet would be prepared as follows:

Company P and Subsidiary Company S
Working Papers for Consolidated Balance Sheet
December 1, 1967

	Co. P	Co. S	Eliminations		Consolidated Balance Sheet	
			Dr.	Cr.	Dr.	Cr.
Debits						
Investment in Co. S Stock	135,000					
Eliminate 90% of Capital Stock				180,000		
Eliminate 90% of Deficit			45,000			
Other Assets	315,000	250,000			565,000	
	450,000	250,000				
Credits						
Liabilities	150,000	100,000				250,000
Capital Stock, Co. P	200,000					200,000
Retained Earnings, Co. P	100,000					100,000
Capital Stock, Co. S		200,000				
Eliminate 90%			180,000			
Minority Interest, 10%						20,000
Deficit, Co. S		(50,000)				
Eliminate 90%				45,000		
Minority Interest, 10%					5,000	
	450,000	250,000	225,000	225,000	570,000	570,000

A prorata share of each of the capital balances is recognized in stating the minority interest. When a subsidiary has a deficit, a prorata share of such deficit, then, is recognized as a subtraction item in arriving at the minority interest. The consolidated balance sheet for Company P and Company S above would be the same as that appearing on page 315 except for the detail composing minority interest: minority interest would consist of a capital stock interest of $20,000 less a share in the deficit of $5,000.

ACQUISITION OF SUBSIDIARY INTEREST AT MORE THAN BOOK VALUE

The cost of a parent's interest in a subsidiary may exceed the book value of such an interest. The reason for the difference between the amount paid and the book value of the interest acquired should be determined before the consolidated balance sheet is prepared. This explanation will determine how the excess is to be reported. The explanation may be any of the following:

(1) *Failure of subsidiary accounts to report asset value increases at time of stock acquisition.* Subsidiary company asset balances may properly report past costs and satisfactory depreciation and amortization practices, but such balances may fail to reflect advances that have taken place in the values of the individual assets. If a company's assets were acquired through merger, asset balances would be restated in terms of the price that was paid for the assets. With a purchase price for stock of the subsidiary company that recognizes added values identified with subsidiary assets, a formal appraisal of subsidiary assets and a recognition of the increases would be in order. Entries on the books of the subsidiary to report appraisal values may be authorized by the parent upon assuming control. Asset and capital balances of the subsidiary could thus be raised and the parent's interest brought into agreement with the investment account balance. It should be noted that, unlike the condition of merger, the subsidiary company books continue to report the account balances of a separate legal entity; an appraisal involving an increase in net assets must be accompanied by a credit to an appraisal capital balance. Subsequent to such action, procedures appropriate to appraisal accounting will be required. When practical difficulties in the restatement of subsidiary account balances are found, the parent may prefer to recognize appraisal values only on the working papers for consolidation. Adjustments that provide a projection of appraisal accounting to the date of the consolidation will be required on consolidated working papers prepared in subsequent periods.

(2) *Failure of subsidiary accounts to reflect certain intangible assets.* Subsidiary net assets may report tangible assets satisfactorily, but they may fail to reflect the existence of goodwill or other intangible assets that were recognized by the parent in its acquisition of subsidiary holdings. Again, if the company's assets were to be acquired through merger, goodwill and other intangibles recognized in the purchase price would be given accounting recognition. With the acquisition of stock of a subsidiary at a price that recognizes unrecorded goodwill and other intangibles, such intangibles may be established on the books of the subsidiary and appraisal capital may be credited. If such a practice is considered objectionable, the intangibles may be recognized by means of adjustments on the consolidated working papers. When intangible assets are subject to amortization, adjustments to reflect such amortization will be required on consolidated working papers prepared in subsequent periods.

It should be observed that, in each of the categories listed above, a full restatement of subsidiary net assets is required regardless of the degree of parent ownership in the subsidiary. When assets are undervalued, they should be brought up to their full fair values. When certain intangibles are not reported, they should be established at their full amounts. Assume in the last instance, for example, that a company acquires 80% of the stock of a subsidiary at a price that is $100,000 in excess of the book value of this interest; such excess payment, it is assumed, fairly recognizes the high earnings of the subsidiary and the goodwill that attaches to the interest acquired. Under these circumstances, the subsidiary goodwill should be recognized at $125,000 ($100,000 ÷ .80). With such recognition, the full amount of the intangible as indicated by the price paid for the subsidiary interest will be reported on the consolidated balance sheet, together with a minority interest calculated in terms of subsidiary assets as restated.

(3) *Payment for achieving centralized control.* Subsidiary net assets, tangible and intangible, may be satisfactorily reported and payment by the parent of an amount that exceeds the book value of the interest acquired may be viewed as the price paid to achieve the desired centralized control and the economic advantages accompanying integrated operations. Accordingly, the amount by which the investment cost exceeds the book value of the subsidiary interest may be regarded as the amount paid by the parent for goodwill. The goodwill is recognized on the consolidated working papers in eliminating reciprocal balances: offsetting the book value of the interest acquired in the subsidiary against the investment account balance leaves a debit excess that is extended to the consolidated balance sheet columns as goodwill.

The price that is paid by the parent to achieve the advantages of affiliation is frequently referred to or designated as "goodwill from consolidation" to distinguish this from the goodwill identified with specific companies. The balance for goodwill from consolidation regarded as the cost to the parent of acquiring this intangible would be limited to the amount reflected in the investment balance. Both consolidated goodwill and goodwill reported by the separate companies are generally combined for statement purposes.

(4) *Excess representing a combination of factors.* In certain instances an investment excess over subsidiary book value may represent a combination of factors and it may not be possible to arrive at a satisfactory basis for assigning the excess to such factors. For example, an excess may represent a price paid to secure control, but it may also include in part a recognition of subsidiary assets that are undervalued. Under these conditions, a designation of the difference between cost and book value as "Excess of Cost over Book Value of Subsidiary Interest" may be more appropriate than the alternative reporting procedures that have been described. This balance is properly reported as an asset on the consolidated balance sheet, for it must be assumed that the payment for the

interest in the subsidiary did not exceed values received; the balance would be listed under the "Intangibles" or "Other Assets" heading.

Whether the difference between cost and book value is expressed as goodwill or as an excess of cost over book value of the subsidiary interest, the difference if regarded as representing the cost of benefits of limited duration should be amortized over such benefit period. Amortization to reduce the investment account and retained earnings may be accomplished by periodic entries on the books of the parent company or by adjustments limited to the successive consolidated working papers. When amortization is indicated, periodic adjustments on the working papers that leave the investment account unchanged on the books of the parent are normally preferred.

The Committee on Accounting Procedure of the American Institute of Certified Public Accountants in considering the treatment of investment cost that exceeds the book value of a subsidiary interest in *Accounting Research Bulletin No. 51* has made the following recommendations:

> Where the cost to the parent of the investment in a purchased subsidiary exceeds the parent's equity in the subsidiary's net assets at the date of acquisition, as shown by the books of the subsidiary, the excess should be dealt with in the consolidated balance sheet according to its nature. In determining the difference, provision should be made for specific costs or losses which are expected to be incurred in the integration of the operations of the subsidiary with those of the parent, or otherwise as a result of the acquisition, if the amount thereof can be reasonably determined. To the extent that the difference is considered to be attributable to tangible assets and specific intangible assets, such as patents, it should be allocated to them. Any difference which cannot be so applied should be shown among the assets in the consolidated balance sheet under one or more appropriately descriptive captions. When the difference is allocated to depreciable or amortizable assets, depreciation and amortization policies should be such as to absorb the excess over the remaining life of related assets.[1]

When investment cost is more than the book value of the interest that is acquired, the difference is frequently regarded in practice as payment for goodwill. This approach may be followed in the interests of expediency rather than from an identification of the specific factors that explain the purchase of stock at a price above book value. Some companies apply an excess of cost over book value against retained earnings. This is done either by reducing the investment account on the parent company books by a charge against Retained Earnings at the time of stock acquisition or by reducing the investment account on the consolidated working papers by a similar charge whenever a consolidated balance

---

[1]*Accounting Research Bulletin No. 51*, "Consolidated Financial Statements," 1959 (New York: American Institute of Certified Public Accountants), p. 43.

sheet is to be prepared. Although conservatism is offered as support for the immediate disposition of the investment excess, the practice cannot be justified on theoretical grounds.[1]

It will be assumed in each of the illustrations and problems to follow that, in the absence of qualifications to the contrary, a cost that exceeds the book value of a subsidiary interest may be designated on the consolidated balance sheet as "Excess of Cost over Book Value of Subsidiary Interest." It will further be assumed that amortization of this balance is not required on successive statements.

WORKING PAPERS WHEN SUBSIDIARY INTEREST IS ACQUIRED AT MORE THAN BOOK VALUE

To illustrate the eliminations that are required when stock is acquired at more than its book value, assume that Company S has 1,000 shares of capital stock, $100 par, or capital stock of $100,000, outstanding, and retained earnings of $50,000. Company P acquires 90% of the stock for $175,000. Working papers for a consolidated balance sheet are shown at the top of the following page. A consolidated balance sheet follows the working papers.

Elimination of reciprocal elements on the working papers leaves an investment balance of $40,000 that is carried to the consolidated balance sheet columns as the excess of cost over the book value of the subsidiary interest acquired. This balance does not appear on the books or on the separate financial statements of any of the affiliated companies but only on the consolidated working papers and the consolidated balance sheet. The investment account with a balance of $175,000 has been replaced for purposes of the consolidated balance sheet by the following items:

Debits		Credits		Net Debit Excess
Assets	$250,000	Liabilities	$100,000	
Excess of Cost over Book Value	40,000	Minority Interest	15,000	
	$290,000		$115,000	$175,000

[1]The American Institute of Certified Public Accountants in *Accounting Research Bulletin No. 43,* "Restatement and Revision of Accounting Research Bulletins," page 40, in considering intangibles, whether emerging from separate purchase or from an investment in excess of an equity acquired in a subsidiary as shown by the latter's books, states: "Lump-sum write-offs of intangibles should not be made to earned surplus immediately after acquisition, nor should intangibles be charged against capital surplus. If not amortized systematically, intangibles should be carried at cost until an event has taken place which indicates a loss or a limitation on the useful life of the intangibles."

Company P and Subsidiary Company S
Working Papers for Consolidated Balance Sheet
December 1, 1967

	Co. P	Co. S	Eliminations Dr.	Eliminations Cr.	Consolidated Balance Sheet Dr.	Consolidated Balance Sheet Cr.
Debits						
Investment in Co. S Stock	175,000					
Eliminate 90% of Capital Stock				90,000		
Eliminate 90% of Retained Earnings				45,000		
Excess of Cost over Book Value					40,000	
Other Assets	275,000	250,000			525,000	
	450,000	250,000				
Credits						
Liabilities	150,000	100,000				250,000
Capital Stock, Co. P	200,000					200,000
Retained Earnings, Co. P	100,000					100,000
Capital Stock, Co. S		100,000				
Eliminate 90%			90,000			
Minority Interest, 10%						10,000
Retained Earnings, Co. S		50,000				
Eliminate 90%			45,000			
Minority Interest, 10%						5,000
	450,000	250,000	135,000	135,000	565,000	565,000

Company P and Subsidiary Company S
Consolidated Balance Sheet
December 1, 1967

Assets			$525,000
Excess of cost over book value of subsidiary interest			40,000
Total assets			$565,000
Liabilities			$250,000
Stockholders' equity:			
Minority interest:			
Capital stock	$ 10,000		
Retained earnings	5,000	$ 15,000	
Controlling interest:			
Capital stock	$200,000		
Retained earnings	100,000	300,000	315,000
Total liabilities and stockholders' equity			$565,000

If the subsidiary capital of $150,000 had consisted of capital stock of $200,000 and a deficit of $50,000 and the parent had acquired 90% of the stock for $175,000, the consolidated balance sheet would be exactly the same except for the detail composing minority interest.

ACQUISITION OF SUBSIDIARY INTEREST AT LESS THAN BOOK VALUE

When stock of a subsidiary is acquired at less than its book value, the treatment of the difference on the consolidated balance sheet will be determined by the reasons that can be assigned for the difference between cost and book value.

(1) *Failure of subsidiary accounts to reflect asset value declines at time of stock acquisition.* Subsidiary asset balances may properly report past costs and satisfactory depreciation and amortization practices, but such balances may fail to reflect declines that have taken place in the values of individual assets. If a merger of the two companies had been effected, asset balances would have been restated in terms of costs as established by the purchase price. With a purchase price for stock of the subsidiary that recognizes declines in asset values, a formal appraisal of subsidiary assets and a recognition on the subsidiary company's books of the declines would be in order. Asset and capital balances of the subsidiary would thus be reduced and the parent's interest brought into agreement with the investment account balance. When practical difficulties are found in restating account balances on the books of the subsidiary, the parent may prefer to recognize such adjustments only on the consolidated working papers. Adjustments that provide a projection of the write-downs to the date of the consolidation will be required on consolidated working papers prepared in subsequent periods.

In certain instances assets as reported on the subsidiary books may be regarded as generally overvalued but the restatement of the individual asset items may be both difficult and impractical. In such circumstances, the parent may choose to report the assets at book value but recognize a valuation account related to assets as a whole designated "Allowance for Overvaluation of Assets." The allowance for overvaluation is recognized on the consolidated working papers in the course of eliminating reciprocal accounts: offsetting the interest acquired in the subsidiary company against the investment account balance gives rise to a credit excess that is extended to the consolidated balance sheet as an overvaluation allowance. The allowance would be reported as a subtraction item from total assets in preparing the consolidated balance sheet. When the interest acquired by a parent is less than 100%, the difference between the investment cost and the related subsidiary book value will measure only the asset overstatement related to the parent's interest; here it would be appropriate to reduce the minority interest and raise the allowance for the overvaluation that may be related to the minority group. When the allowance is related to assets that are to be consumed or sold or to assets subject to depreciation or amortization, it should be adjusted on successive working papers consistent with the reductions that are applied to such assets.

(2) *Negative goodwill.* When the stock of a subsidiary is acquired at less than its book value and the subsidiary shows goodwill on its books, it is normally fair to assume that such goodwill is overvalued. Under these circumstances, the difference between cost and the book value of the parent company's interest would be recognized as *negative goodwill* and applied as an offset to the goodwill balance reported by the subsidiary. When the interest acquired by the parent is less than 100%, a difference between cost and the book value of the parent's interest recognized as negative goodwill will show only the shrinkage applicable to the parent's interest, and further reduction should be made for the goodwill related to the minority interest. To illustrate, assume purchase of 75% of the stock of a subsidiary at a cost that is $120,000 less than the book value of the interest acquired; the subsidiary company reports goodwill of $200,000. Under these circumstances a shrinkage of goodwill by $160,000 ($120,000 ÷ .75) is indicated. Goodwill may be written down on the books of the subsidiary company by a charge to Retained Earnings. If this practice is objectionable, Goodwill may be reduced by a similar charge on the working papers for a consolidated balance sheet whenever these are prepared.

(3) *Capital from consolidation.* Assume the purchase of stock at less than book value where subsidiary assets are satisfactorily valued and earnings are considered satisfactory; assume, further, that there is evidence to support the fact that a "bargain purchase" was made. Under these circumstances, a difference between the book value and cost of subsidiary holdings may be regarded as Capital from Consolidation. Again the answer to the disposition of the difference between the book value of the interest acquired and the cost of the investment is found in an analogous situation involving a merger of two companies. Assume that a company purchases assets for $75,000 but reports them at $100,000, the value at which they had been carried by their former owner and a value that is considered to involve no overstatement. The acquisition of the assets, then, would be recorded by a charge to the asset balances of $100,000, a credit to cash of $75,000, and a credit to appraisal capital of $25,000. Capital from Consolidation emerging from a substitution of subsidiary net assets for a smaller investment account balance should likewise be regarded as appraisal capital. The investment in the subsidiary will be carried in the accounts without change and the original difference between book value and cost will continue to be recognized as Capital from Consolidation on successive working papers for a consolidated balance sheet.

(4) *Difference representing a combination of factors.* In certain instances, a difference between the amount paid for stock and its book value is explained by a combination of factors and it may not be possible to reach a satisfactory basis for assigning the difference to such factors. For example, a purchase price may be viewed as involving a recognition of assets that are overvalued counterbalanced in part by the cost of securing control of such properties. Under such circumstances, designation of the difference between book value and cost as "Excess of Book Value of Subsidiary Interest over Cost" may be more appropriate than the alternative reporting procedures that have been considered. This balance, recognized as a valuation account applicable to net assets as a whole, should be reported separately following the listing of liabilities on the consolidated balance sheet. When the balance is considered related in part to depreciable or amortizable assets or to liabilities, adjustments to the balance in successive consolidated working papers would be appropriate.

The American Institute Committee on Accounting Procedure in considering investments in subsidiaries at costs that are less than their book values has commented as follows:

> In general, parallel procedures should be followed in the reverse type of case [investments in purchased subsidiaries at less than book value as compared with investments at more than book value]. Where the cost to the parent is less than its equity in the net assets of the purchased subsidiary, as shown by the books of the subsidiary at the date of acquisition, the amount at which such net assets are carried in the consolidated statements should not exceed the parent's cost. Accordingly, to the extent that the difference . . . is considered to be attributable to specific assets, it should be allocated to them, with corresponding adjustments of the depreciation or amortization. In unusual circumstances there may be a remaining difference which it would be acceptable to show in a credit account, which ordinarily would be taken into income in future periods on a reasonable and systematic basis. A procedure sometimes followed in the past was to credit capital surplus with the amount of the excess; such a procedure is not now considered acceptable.[1]

When investment cost is less than the book value of a subsidiary interest, the difference is frequently regarded in practice as negative goodwill to be subtracted from any goodwill of the parent or of the affiliated companies. Although this practice is defended as conservative it is not theoretically sound since the so-called negative goodwill is in no way related to goodwill arising from other independent transactions. In the absence of any goodwill against which it can be offset, a credit excess has frequently been recognized as a special capital item arising from the consolidation. It should be observed that the latter treatment

---

[1]*Accounting Research Bulletin No. 51*, "Consolidated Financial Statements," 1959 (New York: American Institute of Certified Public Accountants), p. 43–44.

is now considered objectionable by the Committee on Accounting Procedure of the American Institute of Certified Public Accountants; in the Committee's view, net assets of the subsidiary that are reported on the consolidated balance sheet should not exceed the parent's cost.[1]

It will be assumed in each of the illustrations and problems to follow that, in the absence of qualifications to the contrary, a book value of a parent's interest that exceeds investment cost may be designated on the consolidated balance sheet as "Excess of Book Value of Subsidiary Interest over Cost." It will further be assumed that amortization of this balance is not required on successive statements.

WORKING PAPERS WHEN SUBSIDIARY INTEREST IS ACQUIRED AT LESS THAN BOOK VALUE

To illustrate the eliminations that are required when stock is acquired at an amount that is less than book value, assume that Company S has 1,000 shares of stock, $100 par, or capital stock of $100,000, outstanding, and retained earnings of $50,000. Company P acquires 90% of the stock for $125,000. Working papers are prepared as shown on the top of the next page.

---

[1]The survey of consolidated financial statement practices conducted by the Research Department of the American Institute of Certified Public Accountants disclosed a variety of different practices that were employed by a group of American industrial corporations in treating the difference between the costs to the parent for shares of a subsidiary and the amounts shown on the books of the subsidiary for the underlying assets. The different practices were tabulated as follows:

Cost of Investment in Excess of Underlying Assets	No. of Cases
Charged to earned surplus (parent or consolidated)	31*
Charged to capital surplus	20*
Assigned to assets of subsidiary (usually fixed assets), with corresponding adjustment of depreciation	32†
Described as goodwill or similar intangible	16
Charged against income of parent company in year of consolidation	4
Charged against negative goodwill	3
Set up as a deferred charge and amortized	3
Described as excess of cost of investment over underlying assets	11

*Since the publication of *Accounting Research Bulletin No. 43*, such procedures are considered improper.

†In seven of these cases, the amounts of the assets were adjusted on the books of the subsidiary. In the others, adjustments were made only for consolidated statement purposes.

Cost of Investment Less than Underlying Assets	No. of Cases
Described as capital surplus	46
Deducted from assets (usually fixed assets) of subsidiary, with corresponding adjustment of depreciation	23
Offset against excesses in the opposite direction in connection with other subsidiaries	34
Added to appreciation surplus	1
Added to reserve for anticipated loss on liquidation of certain assets	1
Described as excess of underlying assets over the cost of the investment	5

("Survey of Consolidated Financial Statement Practices," 1956, New York: American Institute of Certified Public Accountants, p. 20.)

Company P and Subsidiary Company S
Working Papers for Consolidated Balance Sheet
December 1, 1967

	Co. P	Co. S	Eliminations Dr.	Eliminations Cr.	Consolidated Balance Sheet Dr.	Consolidated Balance Sheet Cr.
Debits						
Investment in Co. S Stock......	125,000					
Eliminate 90% of Capital Stock				90,000		
Eliminate 90% of Retained Earnings................				45,000		
Excess of Book Value over Cost						10,000
Other Assets.................	325,000	250,000			575,000	
	450,000	250,000				
Credits						
Liabilities....................	150,000	100,000				250,000
Capital Stock, Co. P............	200,000					200,000
Retained Earnings, Co. P........	100,000					100,000
Capital Stock, Co. S............		100,000				
Eliminate 90%..............			90,000			
Minority Interest, 10%.......						10,000
Retained Earnings, Co. S........		50,000				
Eliminate 90%..............			45,000			
Minority Interest, 10%.......						5,000
	450,000	250,000	135,000	135,000	575,000	575,000

A consolidated balance sheet prepared from the working papers follows:

Company P and Subsidiary Company S
Consolidated Balance Sheet
December 1, 1967

Assets.......................................			$575,000
Liabilities..................................			$250,000
Excess of book value of subsidiary interest over cost.......			10,000
Total liabilities............................			$260,000
Stockholders' equity:			
Minority interest:			
Capital stock.................	$ 10,000		
Retained earnings............	5,000	$ 15,000	
Controlling interest:			
Capital stock.................	$200,000		
Retained earnings............	100,000	300,000	315,000
Total liabilities and stockholders' equity................			$575,000

Crediting the investment account for $135,000 results in a credit excess of $10,000 that is carried to the consolidated balance sheet columns as "Excess of Book Value over Cost." This balance does not appear on the books or on the separate financial statements of any of the affiliated companies but only on the consolidated working papers and on the consolidated balance sheet. The investment account with a balance of $125,000 has been replaced for purposes of the consolidated balance sheet by the following items:

Debits		Credits		Net Debit Excess
Assets	$250,000	Liabilities	$100,000	
		Excess of Book Value over Cost	10,000	
		Minority Interest	15,000	
	$250,000		$125,000	$125,000

If capital of the subsidiary had consisted of capital stock of $200,000 and a deficit of $50,000 and the parent had acquired this stock for $125,000, the consolidated balance sheet would be exactly the same except for the detail composing minority interest.

ALTERNATIVE WORKING PAPER AND ELIMINATION PROCEDURES

The working papers that have been illustrated have provided a pair of columns for consolidated balance sheet data. Working papers may be constructed with a single column for consolidated balance sheet data. Credit balances that result from eliminations applied against accounts with debit balances would be extended to the consolidated balance sheet column as contra or negative balances within a debit section; debit balances resulting from eliminations applied against accounts with credit balances would be extended to the consolidated balance sheet column as contra or negative balances within a credit section. In indicating a contra balance, a value is recorded in red, or it is encircled, bracketed, or asterisked. Both debit sections and credit sections would be totaled.

As an alternative procedure to the elimination on the working papers of the interest acquired in the subsidiary, it would be possible (1) to cancel the entire subsidiary company investment balance and list separately a cost or book value excess requiring recognition on the consolidated balance sheet in the debits or credits section of the working papers, and (2) to cancel the entire subsidiary company capital balances and list separately the minority interest in the credits section of the working papers. Referring to the illustration on page 327, for example, a single elimination can be applied on the working papers as follows:

Capital Stock, Co. S	100,000	
Retained Earnings, Co. S	50,000	
Investment in Co. S Stock		125,000
Excess of Book Value over Cost		10,000
Minority Interest		15,000

SUBSIDIARY ACQUISITION VIEWED AS POOLING OF INTERESTS

It was assumed in the previous pages that the acquisition of stock in a subsidiary involved the elimination of an important part of the original ownership. Under these circumstances, the "purchase" concept as previously described in Chapter 9 on business combinations was applied in the development of consolidated balance sheets: modification of subsidiary company book values in terms of the parent company acquisition costs was considered appropriate; no recognition was made of past accumulated earnings of the company acquired. In certain instances a parent-subsidiary relationship may be effected with no substantial change in the original ownership, and attendant circumstances may point to such an arrangement as no more than a "pooling of interests." Under the latter conditions, it has been held that, as in the case of a merger or consolidation deemed a pooling of interests, the need for a new accountability does not arise: assets and liabilities of the constituent units when stated in conformity with generally accepted accounting principles and properly adjusted so that they are on a uniform basis may be combined without adjustment for purposes of the consolidated statement; retained earnings and deficit balances may be similarly combined for consolidated reporting.

The Committee on Accounting Procedure of the American Institute of Certified Public Accounts in *Accounting Research Bulletin No. 48* on "Business Combinations" comments on the application of the pooling-of-interests concept to the parent-subsidiary relationship as follows:

> Where one or more of the constituent corporations continues in existence in a subsidiary relationship, and the requirements of a pooling of interests have been met, the combination of earned surpluses in the consolidated balance sheet is proper since a pooling of interests is not an acquisition as that term is used in paragraph 3 of Chapter 1 (a) of Accounting Research Bulletin No. 43 which states that earned surplus of a subsidiary corporation created prior to acquisition does not form a part of the consolidated earned surplus. Under the pooling-of-interests concept, the new enterprise is regarded as a continuation of all of the constituent corporations and this holds true whether it is represented by a single corporation or by a parent corporation and one or more subsidiaries. If, however, prior to the origin of a plan of combination one party to the combination had been acquired by another such party as a subsidiary in circumstances which precluded the transactions from being considered a pooling of interests, the parent's share of the earned surplus of the subsidiary prior to such acquisition should not be included in the earned surplus of the pooled corporations.[1]

To illustrate the application of the pooling-of-interests concept in the preparation of consolidated statements, assume balance sheet data for

[1]*Accounting Research Bulletin No. 48*, "Business Combinations," 1957 (New York: American Institute of Certified Public Accountants), p. 25.

Company A and Company B on June 30, 1967, as given in the following tabulation:

	Co. A	Co. B
Assets	$1,000,000	$ 400,000
Liabilities	$ 300,000	$ 100,000
Capital stock	500,000	250,000
Retained earnings	200,000	50,000
Total liabilities and stockholders' equity	$1,000,000	$ 400,000

On this date Company A acquires 90% of the stock of Company B, issuing to stockholders of Company B in exchange for such interest its own capital stock with a par value of $240,000. The investment is recorded at the par value of the stock issued. Working papers for a consolidated balance sheet may be prepared as shown below.

Company A and Subsidiary Company B
Working Papers for Consolidated Balance Sheet
June 30, 1967

	Co. A	Co. B	Eliminations		Consolidated Balance Sheet	
			Dr.	Cr.	Dr.	Cr.
Debits						
Investment in Co. B Stock	240,000					
To cancel investment balance				240,000		
Other Assets	1,000,000	400,000			1,400,000	
	1,240,000	400,000				
Credits						
Liabilities	300,000	100,000				400,000
Capital Stock, Co. A	740,000					740,000
Retained Earnings, Co. A	200,000			30,000		230,000
Capital Stock, Co. B		250,000				
Eliminate 90%			225,000			
Minority Interest, 10%						25,000
Retained Earnings, Co. B		50,000				
Eliminate 90%			45,000			
Minority Interest, 10%						5,000
	1,240,000	400,000	270,000	270,000	1,400,000	1,400,000

Assets, liabilities, and capitals are combined on the working papers. The combining of capitals calls for special analysis. Subsidiary capital to be carried into the consolidated balance sheet in the example consists of 90% of subsidiary capital balances, or capital stock, $225,000, and retained earnings, $45,000. With an increase in capital stock of $240,000 already reflected in the capital stock account of the parent company, the increase in retained earnings is limited to $30,000. An elimination is made on the working papers to cancel the investment balance, to cancel the interest of the parent in subsidiary capital balances, and to restate remaining capital balances in accordance with the foregoing analysis.

Assume credits to invested capital balances on the books of the parent upon acquisition of the 90% interest of less than $225,000. Under these circumstances, invested capital balances would be raised to $225,000 and the full amount of subsidiary retained earnings identified with the controlling interest would be recognized on the consolidated balance sheet. The issue of parent company stock of $100,000 in exchange for the subsidiary interest, for example, would call for the following adjustment on the consolidated working papers:

Capital Stock, Co. B.	225,000	
Retained Earnings, Co. B.	45,000	
Investment in Co. B Stock.		100,000
Additional Paid-in Capital.		125,000
Retained Earnings, Co. A.		45,000

On the other hand, assume credits to the invested capital accounts of the parent of more than $270,000. In maintaining subsidiary asset values for consolidated statement purposes, an increase in capital stock that exceeds the net assets recognized would have to be accompanied by a shrinkage in parent company retained earnings. The issue of parent company stock of $300,000 in exchange for the 90% subsidiary interest, for example, would call for the following adjustment on the working papers:

Capital Stock, Co. B	225,000	
Retained Earnings, Co. B	45,000	
Retained Earnings, Co. A.	30,000	
Investment in Co. B Stock		300,000

It will be assumed in the discussions as well as in exercises and problems to follow that a consolidation is to be regarded as arising from a purchase unless it is specifically designated as a "pooling of interests."

QUESTIONS

1. What advantages are found in the unified operation of related units through stock control instead of through merger?

2. (a) What is the nature and the purpose of the consolidated balance sheet? (b) What part of the stock of a corporation should be held to justify the preparation of such a statement?

3. What factors must be present to justify the preparation of a consolidated balance sheet?

4. State whether a consolidated balance sheet should be prepared under each of the following circumstances:

(a) Company A, operating a chain of retail stores, owns 100% of the stock of a subsidiary that has been established to assist stores in financing sales to customers.
(b) Company B, operating a chain of theaters, owns 100% of the stock of a savings and loan association.
(c) Company C owns 90% of the stock of a subsidiary company that owns 90% of the stock of a third company; all companies are engaged in the manufacture and sale of electronic components.
(d) Company D, a manufacturing company, owns 90% of the stock of a subsidiary that engages in research and development related to operations of its parent; the subsidiary has reported losses ever since its organization.
(e) Company E, a construction company, owns 50% of the stock of a company that engages in exploration of oil and gas; operations of the latter company have been profitable ever since its organization.

5. The Carlson Co., a company with a controlling interest in a number of subsidiaries, makes available to its stockholders only consolidated statements, since it feels that these are superior to its own separate statements. Do you have any criticism of this policy?

6. The Morton Co. recognizes minority interest on the consolidated balance sheet as a liability. Would you consider this practice acceptable? Give reasons.

7. (a) In preparing a consolidated balance sheet, what possibilities can you suggest for reporting the portion of the cost of an investment that exceeds the book value acquired? Indicate the circumstances under which each of the methods suggested would be appropriate.

(b) What possibilities can you suggest for reporting an excess of book value over cost of an investment? Indicate the circumstances under which each of the methods suggested would be appropriate.

8. Under what circumstances would you suggest the amortization of an "excess of cost over book value of subsidiary interest"? What procedure would you follow in amortizing such a balance?

9. Would capital from consolidation be regarded as paid-in capital, retained earnings, or appraisal capital? Explain.

10. What objection can be raised to the recognition of an excess of book value over investment cost as "capital from consolidation"?

11. What is meant by "negative goodwill"? Would you limit the recognition of negative goodwill to the difference between the investment cost and the subsidiary interest acquired? Explain.

12. In preparing working papers for a consolidated balance sheet for Company P, what eliminations are made and what balances are extended to the consolidated balance sheet column under each of the following assumptions:

(a) Company P acquires all of the stock of Company S, paying more than book value; Company S has a deficit.
(b) Company P acquires all of the stock of Company S, paying less than book value; Company S books report additional paid-in capital and retained earnings balances.
(c) Company P acquires 80% of the stock of Company S, paying book value; Company S has a retained earnings balance.
(d) Company P acquires 80% of the stock of Company S, paying less than book value; Company S books report additional paid-in capital and deficit balances.

13. Give two alternative procedures that may be followed in recording eliminations on consolidated working papers.

14. (a) What circumstances would suggest that consolidation be viewed as a pooling of interests? (b) What differences are found in the preparation of a consolidated balance sheet under circumstances indicating a pooling of interests as compared with a purchase?

15. On November 15 the Murdock Company acquired 8,000 shares of the stock of the Norris Corporation at a price of $20 per share. On November 1, the Norris Corporation had declared a dividend of 50 cents per share payable on December 1 to stockholders of record November 20. How should the Murdock Company record the investment and the subsequent receipt of the dividend? Give reasons for your answer.

EXERCISES

1. On June 15, Norton, Inc. purchases 8,000 shares of Burke Company common stock at 12½.

(a) Assuming that the outstanding stock of Burke Company consists of 10,000 shares, $10 par, and its books show a retained earnings balance of $45,000, (1) what eliminations would be made and (2) what balances will appear on the consolidated balance sheet?

(b) Assuming that the books of the Burke Company show a deficit of $45,000, (1) what elimination would be made and (2) what balances will appear on the consolidated balance sheet?

2. The Wexler Company seeks a sales outlet in Cincinnati. Articles of incorporation are obtained in Ohio for a company to be known as the Major Sales Company; authorization is received for the issuance of 10,000 shares of no-par stock. On April 1, 1967, the Wexler Company acquires all the stock of the Major Sales Company at a price of $250,000; a stated value of $10 per share is assigned to the issue. A balance sheet for the Wexler Company just prior to the formation of the separately incorporated sales office follows:

Cash	$ 420,000	Liabilities		$ 250,000
Other assets	780,000	Stockholders' equity:		
		Capital stock	$500,000	
		Additional paid-in capital	150,000	
		Retained earnings	300,000	950,000
Total assets	$1,200,000	Total liabilities and stockholders' equity		$1,200,000

(a) Give the entries that will appear on the books of the two companies as a result of the formation of the Major Sales Company.

(b) Prepare a separate balance sheet for the parent company and for its subsidiary.

(c) Prepare a consolidated balance sheet.

3. Give the elimination that would be made on the working papers for a consolidated balance sheet for the Marsh Company and its subsidiary, the Nater Company, for each set of conditions listed below (give the elimination in a form that cancels fully the investment and the subsidiary company capital balances):

Investment by Parent		Subsidiary Capital Balances		
Amount Paid	Interest Acquired	Capital Stock	Additional Paid-in Capital	Retained Earnings (Deficit)
(a) $160,000	100%	$100,000	$20,000	$25,000
(b) 140,000	100%	100,000	80,000	(30,000)
(c) 120,000	75%	100,000	40,000	(5,000)
(d) 100,000	75%	100,000	25,000	15,000

4. Balance sheet items of The Palmer Corporation and the Quinn Company are summarized below:

The Palmer Corporation

Assets	$ 1,000,000	Liabilities		$ 300,000
		Stockholders' equity:		
		Capital stock	$400,000	
		Retained earnings	300,000	700,000
Total assets	$1,000,000	Total liabilities and stockholders' equity		$1,000,000

Quinn Company

Assets	$380,000	Liabilities		$ 60,000
		Stockholders' equity:		
		Capital stock (12,000 shares no par)	$100,000	
		Retained earnings	220,000	320,000
Total assets	$380,000	Total liabilities and stockholders' equity		$380,000

Prepare a consolidated balance sheet for The Palmer Corporation and its subsidiary assuming that:

(a) All the stock of the Quinn Company is purchased for $360,000.
(b) All the stock of the Quinn Company is purchased for $310,000.
(c) 9,000 shares of Quinn Company stock are purchased at 30.
(d) 9,000 shares of Quinn Company stock are purchased at 35.

5. The Culligan Company acquires 80% of the stock of Demby, Inc. The investment in the subsidiary is recorded at a cost of $1,000,000. A balance sheet for the subsidiary on the date of acquisition shows the following:

Goodwill	$ 150,000	Liabilities	$ 350,000
Other assets	850,000	Capital stock	500,000
		Additional paid-in capital	50,000
		Retained earnings	100,000
Total assets	$1,000,000	Total liabilities and stockholders' equity	$1,000,000

Give any entries that would be made on the books of the parent and the subsidiary prior to the preparation of a consolidated balance sheet under each of the conditions stated below:

(a) Culligan Company issues 100,000 shares of its own stock, par $10, for its interest; Culligan Company shares are selling on the market at 8½ on the date of acquisition. Any difference between investment cost and the book value of the subsidiary interest acquired is to be considered as the cost of the special advantages to emerge from integrated operations of the two companies.
(b) Culligan Company pays cash for its interest. Any difference between the investment cost and the book value of the subsidiary interest acquired is to be considered as evidence of the understatement of subsidiary company tangible assets.
(c) Culligan Company pays cash for its interest. Any difference between the investment cost and the book value of the subsidiary interest acquired is to be considered as evidence of the understatement of subsidiary company goodwill.

6. The Barnett Company on March 1 acquires 8,000 shares of the Clair Company for $165,000 cash. Each company has 10,000 shares outstanding. Account balances of the two companies on this date are as follows:

	Barnett Co.	Clair Co.
Assets	$820,000	$210,000
Liabilities	$200,000	$ 60,000
Capital stock	400,000	100,000
Additional paid-in capital	100,000	20,000
Retained earnings	120,000	30,000
Total liabilities and stockholders' equity	$820,000	$210,000

Prior to the preparation of a consolidated balance sheet, it is authorized that appraisal values for plant and equipment items are to be entered in the accounts. Accordingly, asset appraisal increases are recorded in the accounts of the two companies as follows:

Barnett Company	$60,000
Clair Company	45,000

Prepare a consolidated balance sheet.

7. Balance sheets for the Porter Company and the Ross Company on July 1, 1967, are as follows:

	Porter Co.	Ross Co.
Cash	$100,000	$ 50,000
Goodwill	50,000	40,000
Other assets	350,000	60,000
Total assets	$500,000	$150,000
Liabilities	$150,000	$ 35,000
Capital stock, $10 par	300,000	50,000
Retained earnings	50,000	65,000
Total liabilities and stockholders' equity	$500,000	$150,000

On this date Porter Company acquires 80% of the stock of Ross Company for $70,000. Prepare a consolidated balance sheet on the assumption that the purchase of Ross Company stock at less than book value is considered evidence of the overstatement of goodwill on Ross Company books.

8. The Carter Company on July 1 acquires 90% of the stock of Dome, Inc., issuing its own stock in exchange for such interest. Balance sheets for the two companies just before the acquisition are as shown at the top of the following page.

	Carter Co.	Dome, Inc.
Assets	$1,200,000	$750,000
Liabilities	$ 500,000	$300,000
Capital stock	450,000	100,000
Additional paid-in capital	100,000	250,000
Retained earnings	150,000	100,000
Total liabilities and stockholders' equity	$1,200,000	$750,000

Assuming that the combination is viewed as a pooling of interests, prepare a consolidated balance sheet under each of the following assumptions:

(a) Carter Company stock with a par value of $300,000 is issued in exchange for Dome, Inc. shares and the investment is recorded at this amount.
(b) Carter Company stock with a par value of $400,000 is issued in exchange for Dome, Inc. shares and the investment is recorded at this amount.
(c) Carter Company stock with a par value of $500,000 is issued in exchange for Dome, Inc. shares and the investment is recorded at this amount.

PROBLEMS

10-1. Balance sheets for Companies A, B, and C on December 31, 1967, are as follows:

	Co. A	Co. B	Co. C
Cash	$300,000	$ 50,000	$ 25,000
Goodwill	100,000	25,000	25,000
Other assets	350,000	275,000	250,000
Total assets	$750,000	$350,000	$300,000
Liabilities	$150,000	$100,000	$125,000
Capital stock, par $10	300,000	150,000	200,000
Additional paid-in capital	100,000	50,000	25,000
Retained earnings (deficit)	200,000	50,000	(50,000)
Total liabilities and stockholders' equity	$750,000	$350,000	$300,000

On this date, Company A acquired all of the stock of Company B for cash of $275,000 and acquired 80% of the stock of Company C in exchange for 6% notes of $125,000 that are payable by Company A in 5 years.

Instructions: Prepare a consolidated balance sheet as of December 31, 1967, under each of the assumptions listed below:

(1) Differences between investment balances and the book values of subsidiary holdings are attributed to the undervaluation or the overvaluation of subsidiary company "other assets," and subsidiary accounts are restated.

(2) Differences between investment balances and the book values of subsidiary holdings are regarded as evidence of "goodwill" or "negative goodwill" identified with subsidiary companies.

(3) Subsidiary company net assets are regarded as fairly valued; accordingly, an amount paid for shares in excess of book value is recognized as the cost of achieving integrated operations; the purchase of shares at less than book value is recognized as a "bargain purchase."

(4) Differences between investment balances and book values of subsidiary holdings cannot be applied to specific balance sheet items and hence are reported as separate items appropriately designated.

10-2. Balance sheets for Companies D and E on December 31, 1967, are as follows:

	Co. D	Co. E
Cash	$ 850,000	$ 75,000
Other assets	2,200,000	425,000
Total assets	$3,050,000	$500,000
Liabilities	$1,200,000	$100,000
Capital stock	(par $50) 2,000,000	(par $10) 250,000
Additional paid-in capital	500,000	
Retained earnings (deficit)	(650,000)	150,000
Total liabilities and stockholders' equity	$3,050,000	$500,000

On this date, Company D acquired 80% of the stock of Company E.

Instructions: Prepare a consolidated balance sheet as of December 31, 1967, under each set of conditions listed below.

(1) Subsidiary stock is acquired for cash of $350,000. The difference between the investment balance and the book value of the interest acquired is regarded as evidence of the goodwill identified with the subsidiary company.

(2) Subsidiary stock is acquired in exchange for 5,000 shares of the parent company stock, and the investment account is recorded at $300,000, the current market value of the shares that are issued. The difference between the investment balance and the book value of the interest acquired is regarded as evidence of the overstatement of certain assets of Company E, and asset accounts are adjusted to bring the book value of subsidiary shares into agreement with the amount paid for them by the parent.

(3) Subsidiary stock is acquired in exchange for cash of $200,000 and 6% notes of $250,000 payable by Company D in 10 years. Inventories of Company E, reported at lifo, are restated at fifo and increased by $75,000. The difference between the investment balance and the book value of the interest acquired is regarded as the cost of achieving integrated operations.

(4) Subsidiary stock is acquired by exchanging 5,000 shares of Company D stock for 20,000 shares of Company E stock; the investment is recorded at the par value of the stock issued. The difference between the investment balance and the book value of the interest acquired is regarded as arising from a "bargain purchase" of Company E.

10-3. The balance sheet data for Companies P and S as of June 1, 1967, are summarized below.

Company P

Assets	$1,250,000
Liabilities	$ 650,000
Capital stock	500,000
Retained earnings	100,000
Total liabilities and stockholders' equity	$1,250,000

Company S

Assets	$350,000
Liabilities	$100,000
Capital stock (20,000 shares, no par)	200,000
Retained earnings	50,000
Total liabilities and stockholders' equity	$350,000

Instructions: Prepare a consolidated balance sheet for Company P and Company S for each case below. (Assume that Company P has sufficient cash to make the purchase indicated.)

(1) Company P purchases all of the stock of Company S at $14 a share.
(2) Company P purchases all of the stock of Company S at $11 a share.
(3) Company P purchases 19,000 shares of Company S stock at $14 a share.
(4) Company P purchases 19,000 shares of Company S stock at $11 a share.

10-4. The balance sheets of Companies A and B on March 1, 1967, follow:

	Co. A	Co. B
Cash	$200,000	$ 20,000
Other assets	450,000	80,000
Total assets	$650,000	$100,000
Liabilities	$150,000	$ 20,000
Capital stock ($10 par)	200,000	50,000
Additional paid-in capital	40,000	10,000
Retained earnings	260,000	20,000
Total liabilities and stockholders' equity	$650,000	$100,000

Instructions: Prepare a consolidated balance sheet based on each of the assumptions below.

(1) Company A purchases all of the stock of Company B for cash, $95,000.
(2) Company A purchases 80% of the stock of Company B for cash, $60,000.
(3) Company A acquires all of the stock of Company B by issuing additional shares of its own stock and exchanging these for the outstanding stock of Company B, share for share. The market value of Company A stock at this time is $18.50 per share and this value is used in recording the investment.

10-5. The balance sheets for Rush Company and Sloan, Inc. on December 1, 1967, the date that the former acquired stock in Sloan, Inc. from the stockholders of the latter company, are as follows:

	Rush Co.	Sloan, Inc.
Cash	$ 105,000	$ 50,000
Accounts receivable	180,000	110,000
Inventories	250,000	225,000
Land, machinery, and equipment	600,000	260,000
Investment in Sloan, Inc. stock	320,000	
Total assets	$1,455,000	$645,000
Accounts payable	$ 155,000	$ 65,000
Bonds payable		200,000
Capital stock	1,000,000	480,000
Additional paid-in capital	200,000	80,000
Retained earnings (deficit)	100,000	(180,000)
Total liabilities and stockholders' equity	$1,455,000	$645,000

The stock of Sloan, Inc. has a stated value of $30 per share. The Rush Company acquired 12,800 shares at 25.

Instructions: Prepare consolidated working papers and a consolidated balance sheet.

10-6. Balance sheets on September 30, 1967, immediately after Company P acquires stock in Companies X, Y, and Z, follow:

	Co. P	Co. X	Co. Y	Co. Z
Investment in Co. X stock	$ 315,000			
Investment in Co. Y stock	177,500			
Investment in Co. Z stock	66,000			
Other assets	1,000,000	$500,000	$260,000	$200,000
Total assets	$1,558,500	$500,000	$260,000	$200,000
Liabilities	$ 233,500	$180,000	$ 50,000	$ 75,000
Preferred stock ($100 par)			50,000	
Common stock ($10 par)	1,000,000	250,000	100,000	150,000
Retained earnings (deficit)	325,000	70,000	60,000	(25,000)
Total liabilities and stockholders' equity	$1,558,500	$500,000	$260,000	$200,000

Stock was acquired by Company P as follows:

22,500 shares of Company X stock at 14.
10,000 shares of Company Y common stock at 12.50.
500 shares of Company Y preferred stock at 105.
12,000 shares of Company Z stock at 5.50.

Instructions: Prepare consolidated working papers and a consolidated balance sheet.

10-7. The balance sheets for Companies R, S, and T on November 1, 1967, immediately after Company R acquired control of Companies S and T, appear below.

	Co. R	Co. S	Co. T
Cash	$ 90,000	$ 35,000	$ 20,000
Accounts receivable	167,500	45,000	50,000
Inventories	350,000	100,000	85,000
Plant and equipment	400,000	160,000	135,000
Investment in Co. S stock	192,000		
Investment in Co. T stock	165,000		
Total assets	$1,364,500	$340,000	$290,000
Accounts payable	$ 160,000	$ 30,000	$ 40,000
Bonds payable	150,000	100,000	60,000
Capital stock	600,000	100,000	200,000
Additional paid-in capital	200,000	30,000	20,000
Retained earnings (deficit)	254,500	80,000	(30,000)
Total liabilities and stockholders' equity	$1,364,500	$340,000	$290,000

Stock of each of the companies is no-par, total shares having been issued as follows: by Company R, 60,000; by Company S, 8,000; by Company T, 12,500. Company R acquired Company S stock at $30 per share and Company T stock at $15 per share on the open market.

Instructions: Prepare consolidated working papers and a consolidated balance sheet.

10-8. The balance sheets for Companies L and M on November 15, 1967, immediately after Company L acquired control of Company M, are shown below. Upon securing control, Company L authorized that Company M's books be audited and its plant and equipment appraised. The audit disclosed that a general contingency reserve for $25,000 was carried on the books as a payable. Appraisers reported a sound value for plant and equipment of $350,000.

Company L

Cash	$ 120,000	Payables		$ 410,000
Receivables	340,000	Capital stock		1,000,000
Inventories	550,000	Additional paid-in capital		250,000
Plant and equipment	600,000	Retained earnings:		
Investment in Company M stock, 7,500 shares	390,000	Appropriated	$200,000	
		Unappropriated	140,000	340,000
Total assets	$2,000,000	Total liabilities and stockholders' equity		$2,000,000

Company M

Cash	$ 40,000	Payables		$145,000
Receivables	105,000	Capital stock, 10,000 shares		200,000
Inventories	115,000	Additional paid-in capital		100,000
Plant and equipment	225,000	Retained earnings:		
		Appropriated	$30,000	
		Unappropriated	10,000	40,000
Total assets	$485,000	Total liabilities and stockholders' equity		$485,000

Instructions: (1) Give the entries that would be made on the books of Company M to correct its books and to show plant and equipment on the appraised basis.

(2) Prepare consolidated working papers and a consolidated balance sheet for parent and subsidiary after the books of the subsidiary are adjusted.

10-9. The balance sheets for Companies P and Q on November 30, 1967, immediately after the acquisition by Company P of its holdings in Company Q, follow:

Company P

Current assets	$1,160,000	Current liabilities	$ 350,000
Plant and equipment	1,800,000	Long-term debt	500,000
Investment in Company Q stock (90,000 shares)	540,000	Capital stock, 68,000 shares, $20 par	1,360,000
		Additional paid-in capital	2,040,000
		Deficit	(750,000)
Total assets	$3,500,000	Total liabilities and stockholders' equity	$3,500,000

Company Q

Current assets	$ 750,000	Current liabilities	$ 300,000
Plant and equipment	1,750,000	Long-term debt	350,000
		Capital stock, 100,000 shares, $2.50 stated value	250,000
		Additional paid-in capital	400,000
		Retained earnings	1,200,000
Total assets	$2,500,000	Total liabilities and stockholders' equity	$2,500,000

Company Q shares were acquired by exchanging Company P shares for Company Q shares on a 1-for-5 basis. Company P shares were selling on the market at $30 and the investment in stock of Company Q was recorded on this basis.

Instructions: (1) Prepare consolidated working papers and a consolidated balance sheet assuming that the combination is recognized as a pooling of interests.

(2) Prepare consolidated working papers and a consolidated balance sheet assuming that the combination is recognized as a purchase.

10-10. The balance sheets for Company R and Company S as of December 31, 1967, are as follows:

Company R

Cash	$ 50,000	Payables	$1,750,000
Receivables, less reserves	300,000	Accruals	450,000
Inventories	1,600,000	Common stock, 10,000 shares	1,000,000
Prepayments	47,000	Retained earnings	800,000
Fixed assets, less reserves	2,003,000		
Total assets	$4,000,000	Total liabilities and stockholders' equity	$4,000,000

Company S

Cash and investments (including stock of R)	$ 7,000,000	Payables	$ 7,872,000
Receivables, less reserves	2,400,000	Accruals	1,615,000
Inventories	11,200,000	Common stock, 100,000 shares	10,000,000
Prepayments	422,000	Retained earnings	20,513,000
Fixed assets, less reserves	18,978,000		
Total assets	$40,000,000	Total liabilities and stockholders' equity	$40,000,000

An appraisal on December 31, 1967, which was carefully considered and approved by the boards of directors of Company R and Company S, placed a total replacement value, less sustained depreciation, of $3,203,000 on the fixed assets of Company R.

Company S offered to purchase all the assets of Company R, subject to its liabilities, as at December 31, 1967, for $3,000,000. However, 40% of the stockholders of Company R objected to the price on the ground that it did not include any consideration for goodwill, which they believe to be worth at least $500,000. A counter-proposal was made and final agreement was reached on the basis that Company S acquired 60% of the common stock of Company R at a price of $300 a share.

Instructions: Prepare a consolidated balance sheet for the two companies as at December 31, 1967.

(AICPA adapted)

10-11. Companies D and E are engaged in the exploitation, development, and production of minerals. They decide to consolidate and form Company Z with a capital stock of 100,000 shares of no-par value.

Under certain rights, acquired for nominal considerations, the holdings of Companies D and E have proved to be very valuable, principally because of discoveries of extensive underground deposits, the cost of which was considerably less than the present intrinsic values.

A disinterested appraisal has been made, and, based upon this appraisal and other assets apart from those appraised, the capital stock of Z is to be issued to the stockholders of the subsidiary companies in the following proportions: for each share of D, 2 shares of Z; and for each share of E, 4 shares of Z.

The appraisal shows the value of the properties of D to be $2,600,000 and those of E, $4,400,000.

All the stock is exchanged, with the exception of 100 shares of D. Later, 20,000 shares of Z stock are sold for cash at $100 a share.

The accounts of D and E, as at the date of consolidation, were:

	D	E
Cash	$ 200,000	$ 100,000
Property	1,600,000	1,800,000
Sundry other assets	500,000	100,000
Total	$2,300,000	$2,000,000
Reserves for depletion and depreciation	$ 800,000	$ 600,000
Sundry liabilities	300,000	600,000
Capital stock ($100 par)	1,500,000	1,000,000
Retained earnings (deficit)	(300,000)	(200,000)
Total	$2,300,000	$2,000,000

Instructions: (1) Prepare journal entries to record transactions on books of Z.

(2) Prepare a consolidated balance sheet with explanations for eliminations and adjustments.

(AICPA adapted)

10-12. On April 30, 1967, Securities Company agrees to purchase the common stock of Consolidated Company for a tentative price of $180,000. The purchase price is to be reduced by the amount, if any, by which the total book value of the shares of Consolidated Company as of January 31, 1967, exceeded the total book value as of April 30, 1967.

The balance sheets of Consolidated Company were as follows:

Assets	April 30, 1967	Jan. 31, 1967
Current assets	$ 55,000	$ 56,000
Fixed assets, less accumulated depreciation	76,000	78,000
Investment in and advances to Industries, Inc.	20,200	14,100
	$151,200	$148,100
Liabilities and Owners' Equity		
Current liabilities	$ 27,000	$ 30,000
Capital stock	17,000	17,000
Retained earnings	107,200	101,100
	$151,200	$148,100

The balance sheets of Industries, Inc., a subsidiary of Consolidated Company, were as follows:

Assets	April 30, 1967	Jan. 31, 1967
Current assets	$ 10,000	$ 18,100
Other assets	1,200	1,200
Fixed assets. less accumulated depreciation	4,300	18,600
	$15,500	$ 37,900
Liabilities and Owners' Equity		
Notes payable	$ 5,000	$ 14,300
Accounts payable — trade	5,800	8,600
Accrued liabilities	2,000	2,200
	$ 12,800	$ 25,100
Long-term debt:		
Notes payable	$ 18,500	$ 19,400
Advance from Consolidated Co.	250	6,400
	$ 18,750	$ 25,800
Capital stock	$ 700	$ 1,000
Paid-in capital	$ 19,250	$ 10,000
Deficit	($ 36,000)	($ 24,000)
	$ 15,500	$ 37,900

The agreement provided that the book value of Consolidated Company should be determined in accordance with generally accepted accounting principles except that the shares of Industries, Inc., should be included at their book value, if any. In the absence of a book value, the liabilities of Consolidated Company are to be increased by a proportionate amount of the excess of the liabilities of Industries, Inc., over its assets; the proportion shall be the percentage of outstanding stock owned. The excess of liabilities over assets shall be reduced by any loss sustained by Industries, Inc., in the transfer of certain assets to its sole minority stockholder in cancellation of its promissory note.

During the period from January 31, 1967, to April 30, 1967, accumulated advances made by Consolidated Company in the amount of $12,250 were transferred to Paid-in Capital by Industries, Inc.

On March 31, 1967, Industries, Inc. sold certain assets to its minority stockholder in consideration of the cancellation of a note payable to him. The transaction resulted in a book loss of $6,100. As part of this transaction, the minority stockholder surrendered all his stock, 30% of the outstanding stock, to Industries, Inc., for cancellation.

Instructions: (1) Prepare schedules showing the net book value of Consolidated Company at January 31, 1967, and April 30, 1967, computed in accordance with the terms of the sales agreement.

(2) Compute the adjustment, if any, to the tentative purchase price.

(AICPA adapted)

Chapter 11

CONSOLIDATED STATEMENTS

INVESTMENTS CARRIED BY EQUITY METHOD

When stock of a subsidiary company is acquired, the cost of the stock acquisition is recorded in an investment account. Thereafter the parent company may choose to recognize the changes that take place in its ownership equity in the subsidiary by periodic adjustments to the investment account, or it may choose to carry the investment account at its original cost. The term *equity method* is used to indicate that the parent follows the practice of adjusting the investment account for changes in its equity; the term *cost method* is used to indicate that the investment account is carried without adjustment.

In developing working papers for a consolidated balance sheet, the method that is employed in carrying the investment must be known, for this determines the nature of the eliminations to be made. Regardless of the method employed in carrying the investment, development of the consolidated balance sheet is based on the assumption that parent and subsidiary constitute a single economic entity. Whether the investment is carried by the equity method or the cost method, then, the consolidated balance sheet must be the same.

The equity method and the development of the consolidated balance sheet when this method is used are described in this chapter. The cost method and the development of the consolidated statement when the cost method is used are described in the next chapter.

EQUITY METHOD

The equity method is based on the theory that the accounting for an investment in a subsidiary company should parallel the accounting for an investment in a branch. In support of the equity approach, it is maintained that parent and controlled subsidiaries are parts of an integrated whole just as are home office and branch units: changes in the stockholders' equity of a subsidiary company, then, need to be recognized on the parent's books if the position and the progress of the parent company are to be fully reported. Although there is a legal distinction between parent and subsidiary, the accounting is based upon the economic and practical applications of the relationship.

Adoption of the equity method calls for the following accounting procedures:

Subsidiary net income or net loss. Net income increases a subsidiary's net assets and increases its retained earnings; a net loss decreases net assets and decreases retained earnings. The parent recognizes its share of the net income of a subsidiary by a debit to the investment account and a credit to a nominal account, Income — Company X; it recognizes its share of the net loss of a subsidiary by a debit to a nominal account, Loss — Company X, and a credit to the investment account. Subsidiary net incomes and net losses are thus accrued periodically on the books of the parent. Income or loss from subsidiary operations is ultimately transferred to Retained Earnings.

Subsidiary dividends. The declaration of dividends by a subsidiary decreases its retained earnings and increases its liabilities; payment of dividends reduces cash and cancels the dividend liability. The parent company recognizes its share of the dividends declared by a subsidiary by a debit to Dividends Receivable and a credit to the investment account; the receipt of cash is recorded by a debit to Cash and a credit to Dividends Receivable. A dividend is recognized by a parent, then, as a recovery of a portion of its investment in the subsidiary.

The equity method of accounting for a subsidiary relationship parallels the accounting that is employed for a branch relationship. The similarity of accounting for investments, income, losses, and remittances (or dividends) is shown below.

Home Office Books		*Parent Company Books*	
Branch X		Investment in Stock of Co. X	
Investment in branch Branch net income	Branch net loss Branch remittances	Investment in subsidiary stock Share of subsidiary net income	Share of subsidiary net loss Share of subsidiary dividends
Retained Earnings		Retained Earnings	
Branch net loss	Own net income Branch net income	Share of subsidiary net loss	Own net income Share of subsidiary net income

EQUITY METHOD ILLUSTRATED

The use of the equity method in carrying investments in subsidiaries and the preparation of a consolidated balance sheet subsequent to the acquisition of control are illustrated in the example that follows.

Assume that on January 1, 1967, Company P acquires 80% of the stock of Company S for $100,000. On this date Company S has capital stock outstanding of $100,000 and a retained earnings balance of

$20,000. Company S reports net income for the 6-month period ended June 30, 1967, of $20,000. A dividend of $10,000 is declared by Company S on December 5 and is paid on December 20. Company S reports a net loss for the 6-month period ended December 31, 1967, of $5,000.

The net income of Company P for 1967, excluding subsidiary income, is $25,000. Company P declares no dividends during the year.

Working papers for a consolidated balance sheet are prepared by Company P on the date of acquisition of stock of Company S as follows:

Company P and Subsidiary Company S
Working Papers for Consolidated Balance Sheet
January 1, 1967

	Co. P	Co. S	Eliminations		Consolidated Balance Sheet	
			Dr.	Cr.	Dr.	Cr.
Debits						
Investment in Co. S Stock	100,000					
Eliminate 80% of Capital Stock				80,000		
Eliminate 80% of Retained Earnings				16,000		
Excess of Cost over Book Value					4,000	
Other Assets	250,000	200,000			450,000	
	350,000	200,000				
Credits						
Liabilities	200,000	80,000				280,000
Capital Stock, Co. P	100,000					100,000
Retained Earnings, Co. P	50,000					50,000
Capital Stock, Co. S		100,000				
Eliminate 80%			80,000			
Minority Interest, 20%						20,000
Retained Earnings, Co. S		20,000				
Eliminate 80%			16,000			
Minority Interest, 20%						4,000
	350,000	200,000	96,000	96,000	454,000	454,000

Entries that are required on the books of the parent in 1967 as a result of its 80% interest in Company S are shown at the top of the following page.

When working papers for a consolidated balance sheet are prepared at the time of acquisition of holdings in the subsidiary, elimination is made for the equity originally acquired in the subsidiary: subsidiary company capital balances are charged and the investment account is credited. When the parent employs the equity method for an investment

Transaction	Equity Method in Carrying Investment Account		
June 30 Announcement of net income of $20,000 for 6-month period by Co. S.	Investment in Co. S Stock.	16,000	
	Income—Subsidiary Co. S		16,000
December 5 Declaration of dividend of $10,000 by Co. S.	Dividends Receivable from Co. S.	8,000	
	Investment in Co. S Stock.		8,000
December 20 Payment of dividend by Co. S.	Cash	8,000	
	Dividends Receivable from Co. S. . . .		8,000
December 31 Announcement of net loss of $5,000 for 6-month period by Co. S.	Loss — Subsidiary Co. S	4,000	
	Investment in Co. S Stock.		4,000

in a subsidiary, the investment account balance reflects the original equity in the subsidiary adjusted for changes that have taken place in this equity. In preparing working papers for a consolidated balance sheet subsequent to stock acquisition, eliminations must be made in terms of the equity as of the date of the consolidated balance sheet: charges are made to each of the subsidiary company capital balances for the percentage ownership identified with the parent, the remaining capital balances being extended to the consolidated balance sheet columns as minority interest; credits for corresponding amounts are made to the investment account, any difference between the investment account balance and the eliminations against it being extended to the consolidated balance sheet columns as the cost or book value excess. On December 31, 1967, working papers for a consolidated balance sheet for Company P and Company S would be prepared as shown at the top of the following page.[1]

It should be noted that Company P took up 80% of Company S's net income of $15,000, or $12,000. Company P's retained earnings at the end of the year, then, were composed of its balance as of January 1, $50,000, subsidiary income, $12,000, and its own net income for the year,

[1]Balance sheet figures are based on the assumption that liabilities of each company remain unchanged for the year.

Company P and Subsidiary Company S
Working Papers for Consolidated Balance Sheet
December 31, 1967

	Co. P	Co. S	Eliminations Dr.	Eliminations Cr.	Consolidated Balance Sheet Dr.	Consolidated Balance Sheet Cr.
Debits						
Investment in Co. S Stock	104,000					
Eliminate 80% of Capital Stock				80,000		
Eliminate 80% of Retained Earnings				20,000		
Excess of Cost over Book Value					4,000	
Other Assets	283,000	205,000			488,000	
	387,000	205,000				
Credits						
Liabilities	200,000	80,000				280,000
Capital Stock, Co. P	100,000					100,000
Retained Earnings, Co. P	87,000					87,000
Capital Stock, Co. S		100,000				
Eliminate 80%			80,000			
Minority Interest, 20%						20,000
Retained Earnings, Co. S		25,000				
Eliminate 80%			20,000			
Minority Interest, 20%						5,000
	387,000	205,000	100,000	100,000	492,000	492,000

$25,000, a total of $87,000. The investment account was increased by the parent's share of the subsidiary net income, $12,000, and decreased by the parent's share of dividends declared by the subsidiary, $8,000. Offset of 80% of the subsidiary capital account balances as of the end of the year against the investment account balance left a debit excess of $4,000 to be carried to the consolidated balance sheet columns as Excess of Cost over Book Value of Subsidiary Interest. Cancellation of 80% of the subsidiary capital account balances left credit excesses totaling $25,000 to be carried to the consolidated balance sheet columns as Minority Interest.

A consolidated balance sheet prepared from the working papers is shown at the top of the following page.

A cost or book value excess on an investment in a subsidiary is determined at the time the controlling interest is acquired. If there is no amortization of this balance, it will remain unchanged on the consolidated balance sheet prepared in subsequent periods.

Company P and Subsidiary Company S
Consolidated Balance Sheet
December 31, 1967

Assets			$488,000
Excess of cost over book value of subsidiary interest			4,000
Total assets			$492,000
Liabilities			$280,000
Stockholders' equity:			
Minority interest:			
Capital stock	$ 20,000		
Retained earnings	5,000	$ 25,000	
Controlling interest:			
Capital stock	$100,000		
Retained earnings	87,000	187,000	212,000
Total liabilities and stockholders' equity			$492,000

MODIFICATIONS IN THE EQUITY METHOD

The equity method in its conventional application as illustrated provides for accruing subsidiary profit and loss in the investment account and recognizing subsidiary capital distributions as investment realization. The investment balance, then, reflects the original cost of the investment adjusted for the parent's share of the change in subsidiary net assets since the date the interest was acquired.

Justification for the equity method is made in terms of the economic unity that is represented by the two units as well as the full control that the parent exercises over subsidiary company activities. Subsidiary net income improves the position of the parent and can actually be made available to the parent in view of its control over the financial activities of the subsidiary; losses of a subsidiary affect the parent adversely. With recognition of subsidiary earnings in the parent company accounts, it follows that the receipt of dividends from a subsidiary must be regarded as the recovery of accrued earnings or the partial realization of the investment balance.

However, the fact still remains that, from a legal point of view, periodic net incomes and losses of a subsidiary have no effect upon a parent's capital or upon its ability to declare dividends; furthermore, all dividends received by the parent from a subsidiary, whether distributions of earnings accumulated prior to affiliation or after affiliation, represent income to the parent. The same positions are taken by federal income tax laws: a parent cannot recognize subsidiary profits and losses in calculating its taxable income, and a parent must include in its taxable income any dividends representing a distribution of the subsidiary's earnings.[1]

The equity method can be modified to offer a more satisfactory accounting for parent company capital by providing a distinction between capital that is related to changes in interests in the subsidiaries and capital that is legally realized and available for dividends. Such modification calls for the use of appraisal accounting procedures. In the example that follows, the conventional procedure is compared with an alternative procedure that can be applied.

Assume that on January 1, 1967, Company H acquires 90% of the stock of Company S. Company S's net income for 1967 is $50,000, but dividends to stockholders for the year are only $10,000. Company H may regard itself as better off by 90% of the net income of the subsidiary, or $45,000; however, from a legal point of view its earnings and its ability to declare dividends to its own stockholders at this time is limited to $9,000.

Appraisal accounting procedures call for the following:

(1) Net income of a subsidiary is regarded as support for the recognition of an appraisal increment in the subsidiary investment; a parent, then, debits the investment account and credits appraisal capital for its share of subsidiary net income.

(2) The subsequent distribution of earnings as dividends by a subsidiary is regarded as realization of the appraisal increment: the parent, then, debits Dividends Receivable or Cash and credits the investment account for its share of subsidiary dividends; this is accompanied by a second entry debiting the appraisal capital balance and crediting income.

The alternative procedure is compared with the conventional procedure in the entries for Company H at the top of the following page.

Use of the alternative procedure results in summarizing subsidiary operations in appraisal capital and in retained earnings accounts: earnings of the subsidiary that are not distributed in the form of dividends are recognized as appraisal capital; earnings that are distributed and made available to the parent are recognized as retained earnings. Although the total assets and the total capital of the parent company are the same in each case, the alternative method affords a clarification of the parent company's capital.

[1]It should be observed, however, that a corporation is entitled to a specific deduction from gross income for dividends received from other domestic corporations subject to income taxes. This deduction is 85% of dividends received but 100% of "qualifying dividends" received from corporations of an "affiliated group" that do not file consolidated tax returns.

Transaction	Equity Method in Carrying Investment Account: Conventional Procedure — Subsidiary Profit and Loss Recognized as Retained Earnings			Equity Method in Carrying Investment Account: Alternative Procedure — Subsidiary Profit and Loss Recognized as Appraisal Capital		
Announcement of net income of $50,000 by Co. S.	Investment in Co. S Stock.....	45,000		Investment in Co. S Stock.....	45,000	
	Income — Co. S...........		45,000	Appraisal Capital Increase—Undistributed Earnings of Company S...		45,000
Payment of dividends of $10,000 by Co. S.	Cash...........	9,000		Cash...........	9,000	
	Investment in Co. S Stock...		9,000	Investment in Co. S Stock...		9,000
				Appraisal Capital Increase — Undistributed Earnings of Co. S	9,000	
				Dividend Income........		9,000

The preceding description was limited to a consideration of subsidiary net incomes and their recognition by a parent. But assume that subsidiary net losses exceed net incomes. In applying the equity method in its conventional manner, such losses are recognized as decreases in retained earnings even though the legal ability of the parent to declare dividends remains unimpaired. In fact, the amount available to the parent company for payment of dividends may exceed the balance of retained earnings even before its reduction for subsidiary losses. This is the case if the subsidiary has declared dividends out of retained earnings accumulated prior to date of control, for the receipt of dividends legally enables the parent to redistribute such amounts to its own stockholders. Here, too, appraisal accounting procedures can provide for a presentation of capital in terms of amounts that are unrealized and amounts that are realized and legally available for dividends.

To illustrate, assume that on January 1, 1967, Company H acquires 80% of the stock of Company T. Company T reports a net loss for 1967 of $30,000 but pays dividends during the year of $10,000. Company H may regard itself as worse off by 80% of the loss, or $24,000; however, the dividend distribution by the subsidiary has made $8,000 available to the parent for distribution to its own stockholders. Appraisal accounting procedures would call for (1) a negative appraisal capital balance to show the excess of subsidiary losses and dividends over income accruing to the parent since acquisition, and (2) a retained earnings balance that reflects the income that may be used as a basis for dividends. The alternative procedure for recognizing the loss and the dividend is compared with the conventional procedure below.

Transaction	Equity Method in Carrying Investment Account					
	Conventional Procedure — Subsidiary Profit and Loss Recognized as Retained Earnings			Alternative Procedure — Subsidiary Profit and Loss Recognized as Appraisal Capital		
Announcement of net loss of $30,000 by Co. T.	Loss — Co. T. . .	24,000		Appraisal Capital Decrease — Losses and Dividends of Co. T in Excess of Earnings	24,000	
	Investment in Co. T Stock . .		24,000	Investment in Co. T Stock . . .		24,000
Payment of dividends of $10,000 by Co. T.	Cash	8,000		Cash	8,000	
	Investment in Co. T Stock . .		8,000	Investment in Co. T Stock . . .		8,000
				Appraisal Capital Decrease — Losses and Dividends of Co. T in Excess of Earnings	8,000	
				Dividend Income		8,000

Although net assets and total capital for the parent company are the same in each case above, again a clarification of capital is achieved through use of the alternative method. Use of the conventional method results in a reduction in retained earnings of $24,000. Use of the alternative method results in an $8,000 increase in parent retained earnings as a result of the receipt of a dividend from the subsidiary; a negative appraisal capital balance reports a $32,000 impairment in the parent company's capital as a result of the $40,000 decrease in the subsidiary capital for the year. The negative capital balance reflecting the net write-down in the subsidiary investment would be subtracted from the sum of invested capital and retained earnings in reporting total capital on the parent company's balance sheet.

Subsidiary earnings of $40,000 will serve to restore the investment balance to its original amount and to cancel the negative appraisal capital balance; subsidiary earnings in excess of this amount will result in an increase in the investment balance above its original amount and an accompanying recognition of a positive appraisal capital balance. When impairment in the investment in the subsidiary is material and appears to be permanent, it would be appropriate to apply the negative capital balance against parent company retained earnings.

When the conventional equity procedures are followed and both parent and subsidiary earnings are summarized in the retained earnings account, changes in the investment accounts will have to be analyzed in determining the portion of parent company retained earnings that can be used as a basis for dividends. When the alternative procedures are used, income that is not available for dividends is reported as an appraisal capital balance. However, for purposes of the consolidated balance sheet, this balance is properly regarded as earned, since here the legal distinction between the parent and the subsidiary disappears. When the alternative procedure is used, then, appraisal capital balances arising from the restatement of investments in subsidiaries should be combined with retained earnings of the parent company in preparing the consolidated balance sheet.

Application of the conventional equity procedures are assumed in the discussions and in the examples in the text.

ELIMINATIONS FOR INTERCOMPANY INDEBTEDNESS

The preparation of the consolidated balance sheet generally requires the elimination of items other than investment and reciprocal capital balances. Transactions among affiliated companies frequently give rise to receivables on the statements of certain members of the group and corresponding payables on the statements of others. Reciprocal asset and liability balances arise from such transactions as sales, advances, and loans among affiliated companies and the declaration of dividends by subsidiaries. Such reciprocal balances simply call for the transfer of cash from one party to another; transfers will have no effect upon net assets or the capital balances of the respective units. When the legal positions are disregarded and the parent company and its subsidiaries are viewed as a single unit, the intercompany balances lose their significance and require elimination in the same manner as interbranch items.

The eliminations for intercompany items are made only on the consolidated working papers. In making the eliminations, liability accounts are debited and the reciprocal asset balances are credited. This procedure is illustrated for advances between affiliated companies on the working papers below.

	Co. P	Co. S	Eliminations		Consolidated Balance Sheet	
			Dr.	Cr.	Dr.	Cr.
Debits						
Advances to Co. S	15,000			15,000		
Credits						
Advances from Co. P.		15,000	15,000			

When only a portion of an asset or a liability balance is identified with an affiliate, the elimination is limited to such a portion, leaving the balance related to outsiders to be shown on the consolidated balance sheet. For example, a subsidiary that is 80% owned has declared dividends of $5,000. An elimination is made as follows:

	Co. P	Co. S	Eliminations		Consolidated Balance Sheet	
			Dr.	Cr.	Dr.	Cr.
Debits						
Dividends Receivable	4,000			4,000		
Credits						
Dividends Payable		5,000	4,000			1,000

ELIMINATIONS FOR DISCOUNTED NOTES

A note issued by one affiliate and held by another would be eliminated. However, a special problem is encountered when a note transferred to an affiliate is subsequently acquired by an outsider. Here it is necessary to recognize a liability to the outsider on the consolidated balance sheet. The elimination may be made as follows:

	Co. P	Co. S	Eliminations		Consolidated Balance Sheet	
			Dr.	Cr.	Dr.	Cr.
Debits						
Notes Receivable (acquired from Co. S)	5,000			(a)5,000		
Credits						
Notes Payable (issued to Co. P)		5,000	(a)5,000			
Notes Receivable Discounted (Co. S note)	5,000		(b)5,000			
Notes Payable				(b)5,000		5,000

The intercompany notes receivable and notes payable balances are canceled. Notes Receivable Discounted is shown on the consolidated balance sheet as Notes Payable, since discounting the note results in an obligation to an outsider. An alternative procedure on the working papers would be simply to offset the balance of Notes Receivable Discounted against Notes Receivable, leaving the notes payable balance to be carried to the consolidated balance sheet columns.

Assume that a customer's note held by one company is discounted by an affiliated company. Notes Receivable Discounted on the original company's books and Notes Receivable on the books of the company discounting the note are offset against each other. If the note is subsequently taken to a bank or to some other party outside the affiliated group and discounted, no further eliminations are required. Notes Receivable Discounted is carried to the consolidated balance sheet columns. To illustrate, assume that Company P discounts customers' notes of $10,000 held by Company S. Company P, in turn, has $5,000 of these notes discounted by a bank. Eliminations would be made as follows:

	Co. P	Co. S	Eliminations		Consolidated Balance Sheet	
			Dr.	Cr.	Dr.	Cr.
Debits						
Notes Receivable	10,000	10,000		10,000	10,000	
Credits						
Notes Receivable Discounted	5,000	10,000	10,000			5,000

CORRECTIONS AND ADJUSTMENTS PRIOR TO ELIMINATIONS

Before eliminations can be made, it is necessary that balances resulting from transactions between affiliated companies be reciprocal as of the date chosen for reporting the consolidated position. It may be determined upon an examination of the books of the parent and the subsidiary that certain balances are not reciprocal because (1) one of the companies has failed to record certain information or (2) items are in transit, only one of the companies having recognized and recorded the transfer.

Failure to record information. When a company has failed to record certain information, it is necessary that this information be recorded in its accounts and reported on its statements. For example, assume that a subsidiary has declared a dividend at the end of the year and shows Dividends Payable on its balance sheet. The balance sheet for the parent is incomplete if it fails to show the dividends receivable from the subsidiary. Before any attempt is made to consolidate the statements, this information should be recorded and the parent's statements brought up to date.

Items in transit. When items such as cash or merchandise are in transit, the company initiating the transfer may have recorded the transaction but the other company may have no information concerning the transfer until receipt of the item, at which time the proper entry will be made. Failure by one company to recognize such a transfer at the end of a period will result in intercompany balances that are not reciprocal; examination and analysis of the related balances will disclose the failure and the need for adjustment.

Items in transit may be recognized only on the consolidated working papers, since they will be recorded in due course by the transferee. A pair of adjustment columns may be provided on the working papers for this purpose. To illustrate, assume that on December 31 a parent advances $10,000 to a subsidiary. The parent records the transfer on December 31. The subsidiary company makes no entry until the cash is received in January. The adjustment and the elimination may be shown on the working papers as of December 31 as follows:

	Co. P	Co. S	Adjustments		Eliminations		Consolidated Balance Sheet	
			Dr.	Cr.	Dr.	Cr.	Dr.	Cr.
Debits								
Advances to Co. S.	10,000					10,000		
Cash.			10,000				10,000	
Credits								
Advances from Co. P				10,000	10,000			

PREPARATION OF CONSOLIDATED BALANCE SHEET ILLUSTRATED — EQUITY METHOD

The concepts that have been developed in this chapter are reviewed in the illustration that follows. Assume that Company P acquires a controlling interest in the stock of two companies as listed below.

April 1, 1966, purchased 900 shares of Company S1 at $130	$117,000
July 1, 1966, purchased 800 shares of Company S2 at $90. . .	$ 72,000

Capital stock, retained earnings, or deficit balances on December 31, 1965, and earnings and dividends for 1966 and 1967 are as follows:

	Co. P	Co. S1	Co. S2
Capital stock (all $100 par)	$300,000	$100,000	$100,000
Retained earnings (deficit) balances, December 31, 1965	60,000	25,000	(10,000)
Dividends declared December 30, 1966, payable January 15, 1967.	10,000		5,000
Net income (loss) from own operations, 1966.	(30,000)	(20,000)	15,000
Dividends declared December 30, 1967, payable January 15, 1968.	10,000		5,000
Net income (loss) from own operations, 1967.	15,000	(10,000)	20,000

As a result of the foregoing, the investment and the retained earnings accounts of the parent company are affected in the manner shown in the table below.

	Equity Method in Carrying Investment Accounts		
	Investment in Co. S1 (90% Owned)	Investment in Co. S2 (80% Owned)	Retained Earnings Co. P
December 31, 1965:			
Balance of retained earnings			60,000
April 1, 1966:			
Purchase of 900 shares of Co. S1 stock at $130	117,000		
July 1, 1966:			
Purchase of 800 shares of Co. S2 stock at $90		72,000	
December 30, 1966:			
Dividend declared:			
Co. S2, $5,000		(4,000)	
Co. P, $10,000			(10,000)
December 31, 1966:	117,000	68,000	50,000
Net income (loss), 1966:			
Co. S1, ($20,000)	(13,500)		(13,500)
Co. S2, $15,000		6,000	6,000
Co. P, ($30,000)			(30,000)
December 30, 1967:	103,500	74,000	12,500
Dividends declared:			
Co. S2, $5,000		(4,000)	
Co. P, $10,000			(10,000)
December 31, 1967:	103,500	70,000	2,500
Net income (loss), 1967:			
Co. S1, ($10,000)	(9,000)		(9,000)
Co. S2, $20,000		16,000	16,000
Co. P, $15,000			15,000
Balances, December 31, 1967	94,500	86,000	24,500

It should be observed that when a parent acquires a controlling interest in a subsidiary during a year, the parent recognizes profit or loss only for the period from the date of purchase of stock to the date of the balance sheet. When the subsidiary company prepares interim statements, specific data with respect to the accrual of earnings during the year are available. In the absence of such statements and in the absence of any other specific information to the contrary, it would be assumed that profit or loss accrues evenly throughout the year. A prorata share of the profit or loss for the period is considered to have accrued prior to date of purchase, the balance subsequent to purchase. In the example, subsidiary profit and loss balances and retained earnings balances for 1966 are calculated as follows:

Company S1

Retained earnings, December 31, 1965	$25,000
Net loss for 1966, $20,000.	
Prorata share of net loss to April 1, 1966, date of acquisition of interest by Co. P, 3/12 × $20,000	(5,000)
Retained earnings, April 1, 1966 (date of acquisition)	$20,000
Prorata share of net loss, April 1 to December 31, 1966, 9/12 × $20,000	(15,000)
Retained earnings, December 31, 1966	$ 5,000
Loss to be taken up by parent company: 90% of net loss of $15,000, April 1–December 31, 1966	($13,500)

Company S2

Deficit, December 31, 1965	($10,000)
Net income for 1966, $15,000.	
Prorata share of net income to July 1, 1966, date of acquisition of interest by Co. P, 6/12 × $15,000	7,500
Deficit, July 1, 1966 (date of acquisition)	($ 2,500)
Prorata share of net income, July 1 to December 31, 1966, 6/12 × $15,000	7,500
	$ 5,000
Dividends declared December 30, 1966	(5,000)
Retained earnings, December 31, 1966	None
Income to be taken up by parent company: 80% of net income of $7,500, July 1 to December 31, 1966	$ 6,000

Although, in the absence of data to the contrary, profit or loss may be considered to accrue evenly over the year, this is not the case for dividends; dividends reduce retained earnings as of the date of their declaration.

Assuming that the equity method is used in carrying subsidiary investments, working papers for the consolidated balance sheet of Company P on December 31, 1967, are prepared as shown on pages 362 and 363. A consolidated balance sheet prepared from the working papers is shown on page 364.

EQUITY METHOD — PROVING COST OR BOOK VALUE EXCESS ON SUBSIDIARY INVESTMENT

When the equity method is used, the cost or book value excess after investment account elimination should be compared with the balance that was determined on the date of the stock acquisition. If entries to

Equity Method:

Company P and Subsidiary Companies S1 and S2
Working Papers for Consolidated Balance Sheet
December 31, 1967

	Co. P	Co. S1	Co. S2	Eliminations		Consolidated Balance Sheet	
				Dr.	Cr.	Dr.	Cr.
Debits							
Cash	10,000	3,000	12,000			25,000	
Notes Receivable	20,000	5,000	15,000			40,000	
Accrued Interest on Notes Receivable	300	150	350			800	
Notes Receivable from Co. S1			10,000		(a) 10,000		
Accrued Interest on Notes Receivable — Co. S1			200		(b) 200		
Accounts Receivable	45,000	30,000	47,000			122,000	
Allowance for Bad Debts	(900)	(600)	(1,000)				2,500
Advances to Co. S1	5,000				(c) 5,000		
Dividends Receivable from Co. S2	4,000				(d) 4,000		
Merchandise Inventory	44,000	35,000	56,000			135,000	
Machinery and Equipment	90,000	60,000	40,000			190,000	
Allowance for Depreciation of Mach. and Equip.	(24,000)	(20,000)	(6,000)				50,000
Land	24,500	20,000	16,500			61,000	
Investment in Co. S1 Stock	94,500						
Eliminate 90% of Capital Stock					(e) 90,000		
Eliminate 90% of Deficit				(f) 4,500			
Excess of Cost over Book Value						9,000	
Investment in Co. S2 Stock	86,000						
Eliminate 80% of Capital Stock					(g) 80,000		
Eliminate 80% of Retained Earnings					(h) 12,000		
Excess of Book Value over Cost							6,000
	398,400	132,550	190,050				

Credits							
Notes Payable	25,000	5,000					30,000
Accrued Interest on Notes Payable	600	150					750
Notes Payable to Co. S2		10,000		(a) 10,000			
Accrued Interest on Notes Payable to Co. S2		200		(b) 200			
Accounts Payable	38,300	17,200	21,550				77,050
Advances from Co. P		5,000		(c) 5,000			
Dividends Payable	10,000		5,000	(d) 4,000			11,000
Bonds Payable			50,000				50,000
Discount on Bonds Payable			(1,500)			1,500	
Capital Stock, Co. P	300,000						300,000
Retained Earnings, Co. P	24,500						24,500
Capital Stock, Co. S1		100,000					
Eliminate 90%				(e) 90,000			
Minority Interest, 10%							10,000
Deficit, Co. S1		(5,000)					
Eliminate 90%					(f) 4,500		
Minority Interest, 10%						500	
Capital Stock, Co. S2			100,000				
Eliminate 80%				(g) 80,000			
Minority Interest, 20%							20,000
Retained Earnings, Co. S2			15,000				
Eliminate 80%				(h) 12,000			
Minority Interest, 20%							3,000
	398,400	132,550	190,050	205,700	205,700	584,800	584,800

Company P and Subsidiary Companies S1 and S2
Consolidated Balance Sheet
December 31, 1967

Assets			
Current assets:			
Cash		$ 25,000	
Notes receivable		40,000	
Accrued interest on notes receivable		800	
Accounts receivable	$122,000		
Less allowance for bad debts	2,500	119,500	
Merchandise inventory		135,000	$320,300
Plant and equipment:			
Machinery and equipment	$190,000		
Less allowance for depreciation	50,000	$140,000	
Land		61,000	201,000
Excess of cost over book value of subsidiary interest			9,000
Total assets			$530,300
Liabilities and Stockholders' Equity			
Liabilities			
Current liabilities:			
Notes payable		$ 30,000	
Accrued interest on notes payable		750	
Accounts payable		77,050	
Dividends payable		11,000	$118,800
Long-term debt:			
Bonds payable		$ 50,000	
Less discount on bonds payable		1,500	48,500
Excess of book value of subsidiary interest over cost			6,000
Total liabilities			$173,300
Stockholders' Equity			
Minority interest:			
Capital stock	$ 30,000		
Retained earnings	2,500	$ 32,500	
Controlling interest:			
Capital stock	$300,000		
Retained earnings	24,500	324,500	
Total stockholders' equity			357,000
Total liabilities and stockholders' equity			$530,300

the investment account have been properly made in the past and if eliminations are properly recorded on the working papers, the cost or book value excess should be equal to the balance originally determined, adjusted for any amortization of such balance since the date of stock acquisition. In the example for Company P and its subsidiaries where no amortization was recognized, cost and book value excesses are proved as shown below.

Proof of Cost and Book Value Excesses — Equity Method

	Co. S1		Co. S2	
Amount paid for interest		$117,000		$72,000
Subsidiary capital on date of acquisition:				
Capital stock	$100,000		$100,000	
Retained earnings (deficit)	20,000		(2,500)	
Total	$120,000		$ 97,500	
Ownership interest	90%		80%	
Book value of stock acquired		108,000		78,000
Excess of cost over book value (book value over cost) on date of subsidiary acquisition		$ 9,000		($ 6,000)

QUESTIONS

1. Explain how the parent company accounts for subsidiary profits, losses, and dividends when investments are carried by the equity method. What theoretical support can you offer for such procedures?

2. (a) How are eliminations to be made on the working papers for a consolidated balance sheet when investments in subsidiaries are carried by the equity method? (b) What check is available on the accuracy of the eliminations against the investment account?

3. (a) What objections can be raised to the equity method in its conventional application? (b) What modifications can be made in this method to overcome these objections?

4. Give four different transactions that result in reciprocal intercompany balances that require elimination in preparing a consolidated balance sheet.

5. State for each of the following items whether, in the preparation of a consolidated balance sheet, it will be reflected as minority interest, retained earnings, additional paid-in capital, or appraisal capital:

(a) Retained earnings (on parent's books).
(b) Retained earnings (on subsidiary's books).

(c) Additional paid-in capital (on parent's books).
(d) Additional paid-in capital (on subsidiary's books).
(e) Appraisal capital — plant and equipment (on parent's books).
(f) Appraisal capital — undistributed earnings of subsidiary (on parent's books).
(g) Appraisal capital — plant and equipment (on subsidiary's books).
(h) Capital from consolidation.

6. A minority stockholder of the Phillips Co., a subsidiary of Tevis, Inc., believes that the elimination of subsidiary company receivables in the preparation of a consolidated balance sheet affects adversely the measurement of the minority interest. Evaluate this opinion.

7. Customer notes acquired by subsidiary companies of the Landsdale Corporation are discounted by the parent company as a regular practice. The parent collects the notes at their maturity. (a) What entries are made on the books of a subsidiary company and the parent upon discounting a note? (b) How are the notes receivable and the notes receivable discounted balances reported on each company's separate balance sheet and on the consolidated balance sheet?

8. Company M, a wholly owned subsidiary of Company L, is unable to borrow cash from the bank. Accordingly, it requests an accommodation note from the parent. The parent complies with the request and the subsidiary then discounts the note at the bank. (a) What entries will appear on the books of Company L and Company M as a result of the foregoing? (b) How will these transactions be reported (1) on Company L's separate balance sheet, (2) on Company M's separate balance sheet, and (3) on the consolidated balance sheet?

9. Give the entries that would be made on the books of Company A and Company B, parent and subsidiary respectively, for each of the transactions that are listed below, and indicate in each case the eliminations that would be required in the preparation of consolidated working papers, assuming that settlement of open balances is not completed currently.

(a) Company B sells merchandise on account to Company A.
(b) Company B borrows cash from Company A, issuing a note for the amount borrowed.
(c) Company B declares a cash dividend.
(d) Company B issues first-mortgage bonds, Company A acquiring a block of the bonds directly from Company B at face value.
(e) Company A discounts notes that had been acquired by Company B, and in turn has these rediscounted at the bank.

10. The Morrison Company shipped merchandise of $5,000 to its parent, the Doheny Company, on December 29. The Doheny Company did not receive the shipment until January 6. How would you suggest this transfer be reported on the balance sheets of the two companies before balance sheet data are consolidated?

EXERCISES

1. The Brown Corporation and the Curtis Corporation each have 1,000 shares of stock outstanding, $100 par. Changes in capital from January 1, 1966, to December 31, 1967, were as follows:

	Brown Corp.	Curtis Corp.
Retained earnings (deficit), January 1, 1966....	$50,000	($15,000)
Dividends declared and paid in December, 1966	(10,000)	
	$40,000	($15,000)
Net income (loss) for 1966..................	30,000	(5,000)
Retained earnings (deficit), Dec. 31, 1966......	$70,000	($20,000)
Dividends declared and paid in June, 1967.....	(10,000)	
	$60,000	($20,000)
Net income (loss) for 1967..................	(5,000)	15,000
Retained earnings (deficit), Dec. 31, 1967......	$55,000	($ 5,000)

The Lucas Corporation acquired 800 shares of the Brown Corporation stock at $200 and 900 shares of the Curtis Corporation stock at $100 on July 1, 1966. What is the cost or book value excess on each investment for purposes of the consolidated balance sheet?

2. Assuming that investments in Exercise 1 are carried by the equity method, what entries are required on the books of the parent company for earnings, losses, and dividends of each of the subsidiaries?

3. Company A acquired 80% of the stock of Companies B and C on July 1, 1966, for $75,000 and $120,000 respectively. Capital stock outstanding of each subsidiary is $100,000. Retained earnings changes for the companies were as follows:

	Company B	Company C
Retained earnings (deficit), January 1, 1966.....	($20,000)	$30,000
Dividends paid April 1, 1966..................		(5,000)
	($20,000)	$25,000
Net income (loss), 1966......................	(10,000)	30,000
	($30,000)	$55,000
Dividends paid April 1, 1967..................		(5,000)
	($30,000)	$50,000
Net income (loss), 1967......................	15,000	(10,000)
Retained earnings (deficit), January 1, 1968.....	($15,000)	$40,000

The parent company carries investment accounts on the equity basis.

(a) What eliminations would be made in preparing consolidated working papers on July 1, 1966?

(b) What entries would be made on the books of the parent for 1966 and 1967?

(c) What eliminations would be made in preparing consolidated working papers on December 31, 1967?
(d) What is the cost or book value excess on each investment that will appear on the consolidated balance sheet?

4. (a) Explain the meaning and the use of the appraisal capital accounts (1) Undistributed Earnings of Subsidiary Company and (2) Subsidiary Company Losses and Dividends in Excess of Earnings. (b) If these accounts are used in adopting the equity method, what entries would be made on the books of Company P in recording the following:

(1) Company P purchased 80% of the stock of Company S for $220,000 on January 2, 1965. Company S reported capital stock of $150,000 and retained earnings of $100,000 on this date.
(2) Company S announced a net loss from operations of $15,000 for 1965.
(3) Company S declared and paid a dividend of $10,000 in 1965.
(4) Company S announced net income from operations of $20,000 for 1966.
(5) Company S declared and paid a dividend of $10,000 in 1966.
(6) Company S announced net income from operations of $30,000 for 1967.
(7) Company S declared and paid a dividend of $10,000 in 1967.

5. Give the elimination that is required in each case below. Company P owns 80% of the stock of Company S.

(a) Company P's books: Advances to Company S, $15,000.
Company S's books: Advances from Company P, $15,000.
(b) Company P's books: Notes Receivable Discounted (discounted by Company S), $10,000.
Notes Receivable, $20,000.
Company S's books: Notes Receivable (received from Company P), $10,000.
Notes Receivable Discounted (discounted by bank), $8,000.
(c) Company P's books: Notes Payable (issued to Company S), $5,000.
Company S's books: Notes Receivable (received from Company P), $5,000.
Notes Receivable Discounted (Company P's note discounted by bank), $5,000.
(d) Company P's books: Dividends Receivable from Company S, $1,600.
Company S's books: Dividends Payable, $2,000.

PROBLEMS

11-1. Stockholders' equities on January 1, 1965, on the books of Companies A, B, and C were as follows:

	Company A		Company B		Company C	
Capital stock	($100 par)	$800,000	($10 par)	$100,000	($20 par)	$50,000
Retained earnings (deficit)		350,000		110,000		(10,000)
Stockholders' equity		$1,150,000		$210,000		$40,000

On April 1, 1965, Company A purchased for cash 7,500 shares of Company B stock at 16½, and on May 1, 1965, it purchased 2,000 shares of Company C stock at 22.

Earnings announced at the end of each year and dividends declared at the end of each year, payable in January of the following year, were:

	Company A		Company B		Company C	
	Net income (loss) from own operations	Dividends per share	Net income (loss)	Dividends per share	Net income	Dividends per share
1965...	($50,000)	$6	($10,000)	Passed	$ 6,000	Passed
1966...	10,000	6	12,000	15¢	14,000	$1.00
1967...	32,000	6	20,000	50¢	20,000	2.50

Instructions: (1) Assuming that investment accounts are carried by the equity method, give all the entries that would be made on the books of Company A at the end of 1965, 1966, and 1967.

(2) Calculate: (a) the cost or book value excess on each investment; (b) the minority interest of each company at the end of 1965, 1966, and 1967; and (c) the balance of retained earnings for the controlling interest that will appear on the consolidated balance sheet at the end of 1965, 1966, and 1967.

11-2. Company W accounts for investments in its subsidiaries by the equity method. On December 31, 1967, balance sheet data for the parent and its subsidiaries were as follows:

	Co. W	Co. X	Co. Y	Co. Z
Investment in subsidiaries..................	$ 905,000			
Other assets..............................	875,000	$285,000	$525,000	$635,000
Total assets..............................	$1,780,000	$285,000	$525,000	$635,000
Liabilities...............................	$ 895,000	$110,000	$160,000	$185,000
Capital stock.............................	1,000,000	250,000	300,000	300,000
Retained earnings (deficit)................	(115,000)	(75,000)	65,000	150,000
Total liabilities and stockholders' equity.....	$1,780,000	$285,000	$525,000	$635,000

Data relative to subsidiary investments follow:

	Co. X	Co. Y	Co. Z
Investment balance, December 31, 1967...............	$160,000	$305,000	$440,000
Interest of parent represented by investment............	100%	90%	85%
Total net income (net loss) of subsidiary since date of investment by parent..............................	($225,000)	$140,000	$100,000
Total dividends paid by subsidiary since date of investment by parent..............................	—	60,000	120,000

Instructions: (1) Prepare a consolidated balance sheet. (Working papers are not required.)

(2) Calculate the amount that was paid by the parent for the investment in each of the three subsidiaries.

11-3. Comparative balance sheets for Company H and its 90% owned subsidiary Company A appear below.

	Company H		Company A	
	Dec. 31 1966	Dec. 31 1967	Dec. 31 1966	Dec. 31 1967
Investment in Company A	$ 950,000	$1,062,500		
Other assets	3,650,000	3,850,000	$1,655,000	$1,880,000
Total assets	$4,600,000	$4,912,500	$1,655,000	$1,880,000
Liabilities	$1,200,000	$1,475,000	$ 650,000	$ 750,000
Capital stock	3,000,000	3,000,000	1,000,000	1,000,000
Additional paid-in capital	250,000	250,000	50,000	50,000
Retained earnings — free (deficit)	120,000	137,500	(45,000)	60,000
Retained earnings — appropriated	30,000	50,000		20,000
Total liabilities and stockholders' equity	$4,600,000	$4,912,500	$1,655,000	$1,880,000

The controlling interest in Company A was acquired by Company H at the end of 1966. Company A paid dividends of $25,000 during 1967. Company H has employed the equity method in carrying the investment in the subsidiary.

Instructions: (1) Give the entries that were made by Company H to recognize dividends and earnings of subsidiary Company A in 1967.

(2) Prepare a balance sheet in comparative form reporting the consolidated financial position of Company H and Company A at the end of 1966 and 1967. (Working papers are not required.)

11-4. Balance sheet data on December 31, 1967, for Companies A and B appear below.

		Company A		Company B
Investment in Company B (32,000 shares)		$ 416,000		
Other assets		1,350,000		$685,000
Total assets		$1,766,000		$685,000
Liabilities		$ 480,000		$235,000
Capital stock	(no par)	1,000,000	($2.50 par)	100,000
Additional paid-in capital		500,000		160,000
Retained earnings (deficit)		(214,000)		190,000
Total liabilities and stockholders' equity		$1,766,000		$685,000

The investment by Company A in Company B was made on January 2, 1967. Company B's retained earnings on this date were $145,000. Company A received dividends of $30,000 from Company B during the year and recorded these by crediting the investment account. No other entries were made in the investment account in 1967.

Instructions: (1) Using balance sheet data that are brought up to date, prepare working papers for a consolidated balance sheet as of December 31, 1967.

(2) Prepare a consolidated balance sheet as of December 31, 1967.

(3) Prove the investment cost or book value excess on the consolidated balance sheet by calculating this balance as of the date of purchase.

11-5. Balance sheet data for Abbott Corporation and its subsidiaries, the Burr Co. and Carl, Inc., as of December 31, 1967, appear below.

Abbott Corporation

Current assets	$1,250,000	Current liabilities	$ 233,500
Investments:		Bonds payable	600,000
In Burr Co. (4,500 shares)	75,000	Capital stock (no par)	1,000,000
In Carl, Inc. (7,000 shares)	175,000	Additional paid-in capital	200,000
Plant and machinery	1,000,000	Retained earnings	500,000
Other assets	33,500		
Total assets	$2,533,500	Total liabilities and stockholders' equity	$2,533,500

Burr Co.

Current assets	$ 85,000	Current liabilities	$ 70,000
Plant and machinery	105,000	Bonds payable	50,000
Other assets	15,000	Capital stock (no par, 5,000 shares)	100,000
		Deficit	(15,000)
Total assets	$205,000	Total liabilities and stockholders' equity	$205,000

Carl, Inc.

Current assets	$190,000	Current liabilities	$ 84,000
Plant and machinery	85,000	Capital stock (no par, 10,000 shares)	100,000
Other assets	10,000	Additional paid-in capital	65,000
		Retained earnings	36,000
Total assets	$285,000	Total liabilities and stockholders' equity	$285,000

Stock of the Burr Co. was acquired at the end of 1963 for $115,500; at this time the Burr Co. showed a retained earnings balance of $40,000. The Burr Co. reported a loss of $10,000 for 1967, but this has not yet been recognized on the books of the parent.

Stock of Carl, Inc. was acquired at the end of 1965 for $161,000; at this time Carl, Inc. showed a retained earnings balance of $5,000. Carl, Inc. reported net income of $15,000 for 1967 and declared a dividend of $4,000, which is included in the current liability total. The parent has made no entries for the subsidiary net income or for the dividend.

The Abbott Corporation current receivables include $6,000 from the Burr Co. and $500 from Carl, Inc.; the subsidiaries show corresponding payable balances.

Instructions: (1) Prepare working papers for a consolidated balance sheet.
(2) Prepare a consolidated balance sheet.
(3) Prove any cost or book value excess on subsidiary investments.

11-6. Balance sheets for the Ellis Co. and its subsidiary, the Fair Co., as of December 31, 1967, are given below.

	Ellis Co.	Fair Co.
Current assets	$1,800,000	$1,150,000
Investment in Fair Co. stock	1,220,000	
Investment in Fair Co. bonds	200,000	
Plant and equipment (net)	1,000,000	850,000
Other assets	105,000	50,000
Total assets	$4,325,000	$2,050,000
Current liabilities	$1,285,000	$ 450,000
Mortgage bonds payable	500,000	250,000
Capital stock:		
100,000 shares, $10 par	1,000,000	
100,000 shares, no par		650,000
Additional paid-in capital	1,800,000	
Retained earnings (deficit)	(260,000)	700,000
Total liabilities and stockholders' equity	$4,325,000	$2,050,000

The Ellis Co. has owned 90% of the stock of the Fair Co. since 1948. The parent company follows changes in its equity in the subsidiary by adjustments to its investment account.

Analysis of the Ellis Co. data discloses that this company has not recognized the net income of the Fair Co. for 1967 and the dividend declared in December. Net income for the Fair Co. for 1967 was $65,000. A dividend of 40¢ a share was announced by the Fair Co. on December 30, payable February 1, 1968; dividends declared are included in the current liabilities total.

The parent company acquired Fair Co. bonds of $200,000 at face value upon their issuance by the subsidiary.

There are intercompany trade balances totaling $65,000 at the end of the year.

Instructions: (1) Give the journal entries to bring the books of the parent company up to date.
(2) Prepare working papers for a consolidated balance sheet.
(3) Prepare a consolidated balance sheet.

11-7. Balance sheet data for the Gale Corporation and its subsidiaries, Harris, Inc. and the Ingram Corporation, as of December 31, 1967, are given below.

Gale Corporation

Cash	$ 65,000	Accrued interest on notes payable	$ 800
Accounts receivable	50,000	Notes payable	50,000
Advances to Ingram Corporation	5,000	Accounts payable	45,000
Merchandise inventory	65,000	Capital stock ($10 par)	300,000
Plant and equipment	120,000	Additional paid-in capital	60,000
Investment in Harris, Inc. (35,000 shares)	105,000	Retained earnings	136,200
Investment in Ingram Corporation (14,400 shares)	172,000		
Investment in Ingram Corporation bonds (face value, $10,000)	10,000		
Total assets	$592,000	Total liabilities and stockholders' equity	$592,000

Harris, Inc.

Cash	$ 30,000	Accounts payable	$ 76,000
Notes receivable	15,000	Capital stock (no par, 40,000 shares)	100,000
Accounts receivable	41,000	Additional paid-in capital	35,000
Merchandise inventory	50,000	Retained earnings	15,000
Plant and equipment	90,000		
Total assets	$226,000	Total liabilities and stockholders' equity	$226,000

Ingram Corporation

Cash	$ 9,800	Dividends payable	$ 1,500
Accounts receivable	60,200	Accrued interest on notes payable	600
Merchandise inventory	85,000	Notes payable	25,300
Plant and equipment	120,000	Accounts payable	37,600
		Bonds payable	50,000
		Capital stock (no-par, 18,000 shares)	100,000
		Retained earnings	60,000
Total assets	$275,000	Total liabilities and stockholders' equity	$275,000

The Ingram Corporation has just remitted payment in full of the advance by the Gale Corporation. The latter company has not yet received the check.

The Ingram Corporation owes Harris, Inc., $10,000 on a note. This amount is included in the balances on the statements of the respective companies. Interest of $120 has accrued on this note and is included as accrued interest on the Ingram Corporation books, but the accrued interest has not been recognized by Harris, Inc.

The investment accounts are carried by the Gale Corporation on the equity basis. However, neither the net incomes of the subsidiaries for the year nor the dividend declared by the Ingram Corporation have been recorded. Additional paid-in capital and retained earnings accounts at the beginning of the year were as follows:

	Gale Corp.	Harris, Inc.	Ingram Corp.
Additional paid-in capital	$ 60,000	$35,000	
Retained earnings (deficit)	112,000	(5,000)	$50,000

Instructions: (1) Prepare consolidated working papers from corrected balance sheets.

(2) Prepare a consolidated balance sheet.

11-8. The balance sheets on December 31, 1967, for Company P and its subsidiaries, Company X and Company Y, are given at the top of the following page.

Company P acquired its controlling interest in subsidiary Companies X and Y in 1964 and has maintained the investment accounts on the equity basis. However, Company P has not recognized on its books the net income of its subsidiaries for 1967. Dividends of $30,000 paid by Company X during the year were properly recorded by the subsidiary and the parent; but a year-end dividend of $15,000 declared by Company X has not been recorded on the books of either the subsidiary or the parent.

The charge to the account, Advance to Co. Y, on Company P's books arose as the result of an accommodation note for $50,000 issued to Company Y so that Company Y might obtain working capital by discounting this paper.

Company X owes Company P $15,500. This balance is included in the other asset and other liability totals for Company P and Company X.

Instructions: (1) Prepare consolidated working papers from corrected balance sheets.

(2) Prepare a consolidated balance sheet.

(3) Prove the cost or book value excess on each investment as of December 31, 1967, by calculating the balances for these items that were determined in the preparation of the consolidated balance sheet at the end of 1966.

	Co. P	Co. X	Co. Y
Assets			
Investment in Co. X, 80% interest	$ 225,000		
Investment in Co. Y, 95% interest	142,500		
Advance to Co. Y	50,000		
Notes receivable (acquired from Co. P)			$ 50,000
Notes receivable discounted (notes originally acquired from Co. P)			(50,000)
Other assets	1,230,000	$375,000	330,000
Total assets	$1,647,500	$375,000	$330,000
Liabilities			
Notes payable (issued to Co. Y)	$ 50,000		
Advance from Co. P			$ 50,000
Other liabilities	277,500	$100,000	75,000
Total liabilities	$ 327,500	$100,000	$125,000
Stockholders' Equity			
Capital stock	$1,000,000	$250,000	$200,000
Retained earnings (deficit), January 1, 1967	300,000	30,000	(10,000)
Net income for 1967	60,000	25,000	15,000
	$1,360,000	$305,000	$205,000
Dividends, 1967	40,000	30,000	
Stockholders' equity, December 31, 1967	$1,320,000	$275,000	$205,000
Total liabilities and stockholders' equity	$1,647,500	$375,000	$330,000

11-9. Syndicate X controls Company B through the ownership of 75,600 shares of the latter's capital stock, out of a total of 96,000 shares outstanding at June 30, 1967. The authorized capital stock of Company B is 150,000 shares, all of one class.

Company B controls Company C through the ownership of 6,250 shares of the latter's capital stock out of a total of 10,000 shares outstanding at June 30, 1967.

The sum of the capital stock and surplus of Company B at June 30, 1967, is $5,894,706, and of Company C, $2,132,470.

Company B wishes to acquire the minority interest in Company C through the issuance of shares of its capital stock at a value equal to its book value at June 30, 1967, taking into account the book value of capital stock of Company C, Company B's investment in which is carried on Company B's books at a total cost of $687,500.

Instructions: (1) Determine the number of shares to be issued by Company B, ignoring fractional shares.

(2) Compute the percentage of control held by Syndicate X after such shares have been issued.

(AICPA adapted)

11-10. Company Q has four subsidiaries, Companies A, B, C, and D. For a special purpose a consolidated balance sheet is required at a date interim to the close of the fiscal periods. The balance sheets and the income statements of the subsidiary companies as of the interim date are available, and it is found that the intercompany debtor-creditor account balances do not agree. All differences are traced and are satisfactorily explained as follows:

On the books of Company Q:

Company A was charged with $516.79 for furniture.
Company C was charged with $1,828 for machinery.

On the books of Company A:

Company B was charged with $2,083.16 for furniture.

On the books of Company B:

Company Q was charged with $10,021.02 for cash remitted.
Company C was charged with $1,858.78 for merchandise.

On the books of Company C:

Company Q was charged with $2,020 for commission, but this was not allowed by Company Q.

Company A was credited with $520.50 for a cash sale from Company A's merchandise held on consignment by Company C. Of this amount, 20% was profit.

On the books of Company D:

Company Q was credited with $600 for cash remitted to Company D by a Company Q customer.

Company A was credited with $380 for a sale from Company A's merchandise held on consignment by Company D. Of this amount 25% was profit.

Instructions: Give the entries for each company that would be required in bringing balance sheets up to date prior to the preparation of a consolidated balance sheet.

(AICPA adapted)

Chapter 12

CONSOLIDATED STATEMENTS

INVESTMENTS CARRIED BY COST METHOD

The consolidated balance sheet has already been described as a statement that shows the financial position of two or more affiliated companies as a single unit. This concept for consolidation is the same regardless of how subsidiary company investments are carried on the books of the parent. Whether the parent adopts the equity method or the cost method for carrying investments in subsidiaries, the final product of the consolidation process must be the same. Adoption of the cost method for investment accounting will give account balances that differ from those which result from use of the equity method; eliminations appropriate to cost method accounting will then have to be applied in the development of a consolidated balance sheet.

COST METHOD

The cost method is based on the theory that the accounting for an investment in a subsidiary should be the same as the accounting for any other long-term investment in securities. In support of the cost method, it is maintained that parent and subsidiary are two different companies: dividends received on stock equities require recognition as revenue; gain or loss on the investment should await the sale of the securities owned. Although there may be economic unity between parent and subsidiary, the accounting is an expression of the legal factors that are found in the relationship.

When the cost method is adopted, the parent company accounts for an investment in a subsidiary just as it would for any other long-term investment in securities. Only the original cost of the stock of a subsidiary is reported in the investment account. Changes in the parent company's equity in a subsidiary as a result of subsidiary profits and losses are disregarded. The declaration of a dividend by a subsidiary is recorded on the books of the parent by a debit to Dividends Receivable and a credit to Dividend Income. The subsequent receipt of the dividend is recorded by a debit to Cash and a credit to Dividends Receivable.

COST METHOD ILLUSTRATED

The use of the cost method in carrying investments in subsidiaries and the preparation of the consolidated balance sheet subsequent to the acquisition of control are illustrated in the example that follows.

Assume the same facts as those previously given on page 348 in illustrating the equity method: on January 1, 1967, Company P acquires 80% of the stock of Company S for $100,000; on this date, capital stock of Company S is $100,000 and retained earnings are $20,000. The preparation of consolidated working papers for Companies P and S on the date of acquisition was previously illustrated on page 349.

In employing the cost method for carrying the investment, entries are required on the books of the parent during 1967 as follows:

Transaction	Cost Method in Carrying Investment Account		
June 30: Announcement of net income of $20,000 for 6-month period by Co. S.	No entry		
December 5: Declaration of dividend of $10,000 by Co. S.	Dividends Receivable... Dividend Income....	8,000	 8,000
December 20: Payment of dividend by Co. S.	Cash................ Dividends Receivable.	8,000	 8,000
December 31: Announcement of net loss of $5,000 for 6-month period by Co. S.	No entry		

With the investment carried at cost, working papers for a consolidated balance sheet may be prepared as shown at the top of the following page.

It should be noted that when the cost method is used, the parent company does not recognize the net change that has taken place in its equity in the subsidiary until a consolidated balance sheet is prepared. Subsidiary earnings are recognized only to the extent that these have been made available to the parent as dividends. When the consolidated balance sheet is prepared, the change in the capital of the subsidiary since the date of acquisition still remains to be recognized.

In the development of consolidated working papers, the investment account reports the investment at its cost and thus reflects only the original equity acquired by the parent. In canceling reciprocal balances, then, eliminations are made just as they were made on the date of stock acquisition. Elimination of the original equity acquired against the investment account leaves a balance that reflects the original cost or

Company P and Subsidiary Company S
Working Papers for Consolidated Balance Sheet
December 31, 1967

	Co. P	Co. S	Eliminations		Consolidated Balance Sheet	
			Dr.	Cr.	Dr.	Cr.
Debits						
Investment in Co. S Stock	100,000					
Eliminate 80% of Capital Stock				80,000		
Eliminate 80% of $20,000, Retained Earnings at Acquisition				16,000		
Excess of Cost over Book Value					4,000	
Other Assets	283,000	205,000			488,000	
	383,000	205,000				
Credits						
Liabilities	200,000	80,000				280,000
Capital Stock, Co. P	100,000					100,000
Retained Earnings, Co. P	83,000					83,000
Capital Stock, Co. S		100,000				
Eliminate 80%			80,000			
Minority Interest, 20%						20,000
Retained Earnings, Co. S		25,000				
Eliminate 80% as above			16,000			
Minority Interest, 20% of $25,000						5,000
Retained Earnings to Parent						4,000
	383,000	205,000	96,000	96,000	492,000	492,000

book value excess on the investment, and this is carried to the consolidated balance sheet columns. Elimination of the percentage of stock acquired against the subsidiary capital stock account leaves a credit excess representing the equity of the minority interest in this balance. However, elimination of the share of subsidiary retained earnings originally acquired by the parent against the present retained earnings account leaves a balance that reflects two elements: (1) the minority's equity in retained earnings and (2) a residual amount representing the change in the parent company's equity in the retained earnings since the date of stock acquisition.

In the example, the retained earnings of Company S on December 31, 1967, are $25,000. Elimination of the parent's share of subsidiary retained earnings accumulated prior to date of purchase, $16,000, leaves a balance of $9,000 to be carried to the consolidated balance sheet columns. The minority's interest in retained earnings is 20% of $25,000, or $5,000, and this amount is extended to the consolidated balance sheet columns as a part of the minority interest. The remainder, or $4,000, is the retained earnings increase identified with the parent company holdings; this amount is 80% of the increase in the subsidiary's retained earnings since the date the stock was acquired.

The parent increased its retained earnings by $8,000 upon the receipt of dividends from the subsidiary. In preparing the consolidated balance sheet, the parent now recognizes a further $4,000 retained earnings increase. Retained earnings of the parent company on the consolidated balance sheet, then, reflect a total increase of $12,000, which is 80% of the subsidiary earnings of $15,000 since the stock was acquired.

A consolidated balance sheet prepared from the working papers on page 379 follows:

Company P and Subsidiary Company S
Consolidated Balance Sheet
December 31, 1967

Assets			$488,000
Excess of cost over book value of subsidiary interest			4,000
Total assets			$492,000
Liabilities			$280,000
Stockholders' equity:			
Minority interest:			
Capital stock	$ 20,000		
Retained earnings	5,000	$ 25,000	
Controlling interest:			
Capital stock	$100,000		
Retained earnings	87,000	187,000	212,000
Total liabilities and stockholders' equity			$492,000

The consolidated balance sheet above is identical with that shown on page 352 of the preceding chapter.

ALTERNATIVE CONSOLIDATION TECHNIQUE FOR COST METHOD

Instead of eliminations as shown in the preceding example, it is possible to adjust the investment account on the working papers for the change in the parent's equity in the subsidiary since the date of stock acquisition. With the investment account reporting a balance that would have been obtained if the equity method were used, eliminations are made for the parent's equity as of the date of the balance sheet. To illustrate, in the preceding example the increase in the subsidiary company's retained earnings balance during the period of the parent company's ownership and the portion of this increase accruing to the parent are computed as follows:

Company S retained earnings balance:	December 31, 1967	$25,000
	January 1, 1967	20,000
Retained earnings increase during period of ownership by Company P		$ 5,000
Ownership interest		80%
Retained earnings increase accruing to Company P		$ 4,000

The investment account and the parent company retained earnings are raised by $4,000 on the working papers. The investment account is now on an equity basis: equity method accounting would have resulted in a debit to the investment account for subsidiary earnings of 80% of $15,000, or $12,000, and in a credit for subsidiary dividends of 80% of $10,000, or $8,000, a net debit increase of $4,000. The parent company retained earnings are now on an equity basis: equity method accounting would have resulted in a credit to the parent company's retained earnings of 80% of $15,000, or $12,000, instead of an increase limited to that portion of the subsidiary earnings received as a dividend, $8,000.

Working papers prepared by this alternative procedure follow:

Company P and Subsidiary Company S
Working Papers for Consolidated Balance Sheet
December 31, 1967

	Co. P	Co. S	Adjustments		Eliminations		Consolidated Balance Sheet	
			Dr.	Cr.	Dr.	Cr.	Dr.	Cr.
Debits								
Investment in Co. S Stock	100,000		4,000					
Eliminate 80% of Capital Stock						80,000		
Eliminate 80% of Retained Earnings						20,000		
Excess of Cost over Book Value							4,000	
Other Assets	283,000	205,000					488,000	
	383,000	205,000						
Credits								
Liabilities	200,000	80,000						280,000
Capital Stock, Co. P	100,000							100,000
Retained Earnings, Co. P	83,000			4,000				87,000
Capital Stock, Co. S		100,000						
Eliminate 80%					80,000			
Minority Interest, 20%								20,000
Retained Earnings, Co. S		25,000						
Eliminate 80%					20,000			
Minority Interest, 20%								5,000
	383,000	205,000	4,000	4,000	100,000	100,000	492,000	492,000

DIVIDENDS FROM PRE-ACQUISTION RETAINED EARNINGS

The procedure that has been described for the cost method is normally subject to one departure from an accounting that considers only the legal factors. Authorities are agreed that a subsidiary dividend that represents a distribution of earnings accumulated prior to the date of the subsidiary stock acquisition should be recorded by the parent not as dividend income but as a reduction in the investment balance. Such a dividend is recognized as representing, in effect, a partial return of investment or the equivalent of a liquidating dividend, since the asset transfer is accompanied by a shrinkage of subsidiary company asset and capital balances below the acquired amounts. The source of dividends, whether out of earnings accumulated prior to stock acquisition or after stock acquisition, might be ignored and dividends treated as revenue when stock holdings are relatively small and no control is exercised over dividend declarations; but with significant stock holdings and a parent-subsidiary relationship, dividends that represent no more than a transfer of assets from an affiliate to a controlling company must be recognized as such. The American Institute of Certified Public Accountants has taken this position in adopting the following rule:

> Earned surplus of a subsidiary company created prior to acquisition does not form a part of the consolidated earned surplus of the parent company and subsidiaries; nor can any dividend declared out of such surplus properly be credited to the income account of the parent company.[1]

Earnings of a subsidiary accumulated prior to the date of parent control, whether retained or distributed, then, should not receive recognition as retained earnings either on the separate balance sheet of the parent or on the consolidated balance sheet; only amounts that are earned after the date of company affiliation can be viewed as giving rise to retained earnings.

To illustrate the special procedures that are used when dividends received by a parent require recognition as a return of investment, assume the following: Company P purchases 80% of the stock of Company S for $200,000. Company S has stock of $100,000 outstanding and retained earnings of $100,000. Company P acquires an equity in the subsidiary of 80% of $200,000, or $160,000, thus paying $40,000 in excess of book value of the subsidiary interest acquired. Company S subsequently reports net income of $10,000 and distributes dividends of $30,000.

---

[1] *Accounting Research Bulletin No. 43, Restatement and Revision of Accounting Research Bulletins,* 1953 (New York: American Institute of Certified Public Accountants), p. 11.

Income is recognized by the parent only to the extent that dividends represent earnings of the subsidiary since the date the parent acquired the stock. The receipt of the dividend is recorded as follows:

Cash	24,000	
Dividend Income		8,000
Investment in Company S Stock		16,000

Inasmuch as dividends that reduce the amount of the acquired retained earnings are considered to be a recovery of the investment, the original equity acquired by the parent and reflected in the investment account has now been reduced. Subsequent eliminations on the consolidated working papers must recognize this shrinkage. Although the original investment balance of $200,000 reflected an 80% interest in capital stock of $100,000 and retained earnings of $100,000, the present balance of $184,000 reflects an 80% interest in capital stock of $100,000 and retained earnings of $80,000.

Working papers for a consolidated balance sheet just before the dividend and just after the dividend would be as follows:

Working papers prepared prior to dividend distribution:

Company P and Subsidiary Company S
Working Papers for Consolidated Balance Sheet

	Co. P	Co. S	Eliminations		Consolidated Balance Sheet	
			Dr.	Cr.	Dr.	Cr.
Debits						
Investment in Co. S Stock	200,000					
Eliminate 80% of Capital Stock				80,000		
Eliminate 80% of $100,000, Retained Earnings at Acquisition				80,000		
Excess of Cost over Book Value					40,000	
Other Assets	600,000	310,000			910,000	
	800,000	310,000				
Credits						
Liabilities	250,000	100,000				350,000
Capital Stock, Co. P	500,000					500,000
Retained Earnings, Co. P	50,000					50,000
Capital Stock, Co. S		100,000				
Eliminate 80%			80,000			
Minority Interest, 20%						20,000
Retained Earnings, Co. S		110,000				
Eliminate 80% as above			80,000			
Minority Interest, 20% of $110,000						22,000
Retained Earnings to Parent						8,000
	800,000	310,000	160,000	160,000	950,000	950,000

Working papers prepared after dividend distribution:

Company P and Subsidiary Company S
Working Papers for Consolidated Balance Sheet

	Co. P	Co. S	Eliminations		Consolidated Balance Sheet	
			Dr.	Cr.	Dr.	Cr.
Debits						
Investment in Co. S Stock	184,000					
Eliminate 80% of Capital Stock				80,000		
Eliminate 80% of $80,000, Retained Earnings at Acquisition as adjusted($100,000 less $20,000 recognized as return of investment)				64,000		
Excess of Cost over Book Value					40,000	
Other Assets	624,000	280,000			904,000	
	808,000	280,000				
Credits						
Liabilities	250,000	100,000				350,000
Capital Stock, Co. P	500,000					500,000
Retained Earnings, Co. P	58,000					58,000
Capital Stock, Co. S		100,000				
Eliminate 80%			80,000			
Minority Interest, 20%						20,000
Retained Earnings, Co. S		80,000				
Eliminate 80% as above			64,000			
Minority Interest, 20% of $80,000						16,000
Retained Earnings to Parent						—
	808,000	280,000	144,000	144,000	944,000	944,000

The consolidated balance sheet that is prepared after the dividend distribution continues to show an excess of cost over book value of the subsidiary interest of $40,000 and parent company retained earnings of $58,000. The dividend of $30,000 resulted in a distribution to the minority interest of $6,000 (20%) and to the parent of $24,000 (80%); the consolidated balance sheet reflects a shrinkage in total assets of $6,000 accompanied by a reduction in the minority interest of $6,000.

As long as the investment account continues to reflect the dividend distribution of $20,000 as a return of the investment, eliminations on working papers will continue to be made in terms of a subsidiary retained earnings balance of $80,000.

ARBITRARY ADJUSTMENTS IN INVESTMENT ACCOUNTS

Arbitrary changes in an investment account may sometimes be authorized by management in order to bring the balance in this account closer to the current underlying values that it represents. When it is found that arbitrary changes have been made, the investment account will require adjustment to bring it either to a cost basis or to an equity basis. To illustrate, assume that Company P acquires 80% of Company S for $250,000 at the beginning of 1958. Company S capital stock is $200,000 and retained earnings are $40,000. Cost of the investment exceeds the parent equity in the subsidiary on date of purchase, then, by $58,000 ($250,000 — [80% of $240,000]). The investment is carried at cost. At the end of 1967, in view of profitable activities of the subsidiary that have increased its retained earnings over the 10-year period from $40,000 to $200,000, the parent makes an entry on its books increasing the investment balance and the retained earnings by $100,000. In preparing the consolidated working papers, either of the following procedures may be followed:

(1) The change in the investment balance may be canceled by the following adjustment:

Retained Earnings, Company P	100,000	
Investment in Stock of Company S		100,000

The usual eliminations for an investment that is carried by the cost method can now be made.

(2) The investment account may be adjusted so it shows the investment on an equity basis. In the example, 80% of the $160,000 increase in the subsidiary retained earnings is $128,000. The investment account and the retained earnings are adjusted to the equity basis by the following entry:

Investment in Stock of Company S	28,000	
Retained Earnings, Company P		28,000

The usual eliminations for an investment that is carried by the equity method can now be made.

The foregoing adjustments are made only on the consolidated working papers. When investment balances continue to reflect arbitrary changes, similar analyses and adjustments are required whenever consolidated working papers are prepared.

PREPARATION OF CONSOLIDATED BALANCE SHEET ILLUSTRATED — COST METHOD

In the example to follow, a comparison is offered of the cost method and the equity method, using the same facts given in the extended illustration on pages 359 to 365 in the preceding chapter. It was assumed that shares of subsidiary companies S1 and S2 were purchased by Company P as follows:

April 1, 1966, 900 shares of Company S1 at 130	$117,000
July 1, 1966, 800 shares of Company S2 at 90	$ 72,000

Cost Method:

Company P and Subsidiary Companies S1 and S2
Working Papers for Consolidated Balance Sheet
December 31, 1967

	Co. P	Co. S1	Co. S2	Eliminations		Consolidated Balance Sheet	
				Dr.	Cr.	Dr.	Cr.
Debits							
Cash	10,000	3,000	12,000			25,000	
Notes Receivable	20,000	5,000	15,000			40,000	
Accrued Interest on Notes Receivable	300	150	350			800	
Notes Receivable from Co. S1			10,000		(a) 10,000		
Accrued Interest on Notes Receivable — Co. S1			200		(b) 200		
Accounts Receivable	45,000	30,000	47,000			122,000	
Allowance for Bad Debts	(900)	(600)	(1,000)				2,500
Advances to Co. S1	5,000				(c) 5,000		
Dividends Receivable from Co. S2	4,000				(d) 4,000		
Merchandise Inventory	44,000	35,000	56,000			135,000	
Machinery and Equipment	90,000	60,000	40,000			190,000	
Allowance for Depreciation of Mach. and Equip.	(24,000)	(20,000)	(6,000)				50,000
Land	24,500	20,000	16,500			61,000	
Investment in Co. S1 Stock	117,000						
Eliminate 90% of Capital Stock					(e) 90,000		
Eliminate 90% of $20,000, Retained Earnings on April 1, 1966					(f) 18,000		
Excess of Cost over Book Value						9,000	
Investment in Co. S2 Stock	72,000						
Eliminate 80% of Capital Stock					(g) 80,000		
Eliminate 80% of $2,500 Deficit on July 1, 1966				(h) 2,000			
Excess of Book Value over Cost							6,000
	406,900	132,550	190,050				

Credits							
Notes Payable	25,000	5,000					30,000
Accrued Interest on Notes Payable	600	150					750
Notes Payable to Co. S2		10,000		(a) 10,000			
Accrued Interest on Notes Payable to Co. S2		200		(b) 200			
Accounts Payable	38,300	17,200	21,550				77,050
Advances from Co. P		5,000		(c) 5,000			
Dividends Payable	10,000		5,000	(d) 4,000			11,000
Bonds Payable			50,000				50,000
Discount on Bonds Payable			(1,500)			1,500	
Capital Stock, Co. P	300,000						300,000
Retained Earnings, Co. P	33,000						33,000
Capital Stock, Co. S1		100,000					
Eliminate 90%				(e) 90,000			
Minority Interest, 10%							10,000
Deficit, Co. S1		(5,000)					
Eliminate 90% as above				(f) 18,000			
Minority Interest, 10% of $5,000 deficit						500	
Retained Earnings to Parent						22,500	
Capital Stock, Co. S2			100,000				
Eliminate 80%				(g) 80,000			
Minority Interest, 20%							20,000
Retained Earnings, Co. S2			15,000				
Eliminate 80% as above					(h) 2,000		
Minority Interest, 20% of $15,000							3,000
Retained Earnings to Parent							14,000
	406,900	132,550	190,050	209,200	209,200	607,300	607,300

The effects of earnings and dividends upon the investment and the retained earnings accounts of the parent, assuming use of the cost method, are shown in the tabulation below. The account changes when the equity method was used are repeated so that the effects of the two methods may be compared.

	Equity Method in Carrying Investment Account			Cost Method in Carrying Investment Account		
	Investment in Co. S1	Investment in Co. S2	Retained Earnings Co. P	Investment in Co. S1	Investment in Co. S2	Retained Earnings Co. P
December 31, 1965:						
Retained earnings balances.			60,000			60,000
April 1, 1966:						
Purchase of 900 shares of Co. S1 stock at $130.	117,000			117,000		
July 1, 1966:						
Purchase of 800 shares of Co. S2 stock at $90		72,000			72,000	
December 30, 1966:						
Dividends declared:						
Co. S2, $ 5,000. . . .		(4,000)				4,000
Co. P, $10,000. . . .			(10,000)			(10,000)
	117,000	68,000	50,000	117,000	72,000	54,000
December 31, 1966:						
Net income(loss), 1966:						
Co. S1, ($20,000). . .	(13,500)		(13,500)			
Co. S2, $15,000 . . .		6,000	6,000			
Co. P, ($30,000). . .			(30,000)			(30,000)
	103,500	74,000	12,500	117,000	72,000	24,000
December 30, 1967:						
Dividends declared:						
Co. S2, $ 5,000. . . .		(4,000)				4,000
Co. P, $10,000. . . .			(10,000)			(10,000)
	103,500	70,000	2,500	117,000	72,000	18,000
December 31, 1967:						
Net income(loss), 1967:						
Co. S1, ($10,000). . .	(9,000)		(9,000)			
Co. S2, $20,000 . . .		16,000	16,000			
Co. P, $15,000 . . .			15,000			15,000
Balances, Dec. 31, 1967	94,500	86,000	24,500	117,000	72,000	33,000

Assuming that the cost method is used in carrying subsidiary investments, working papers for a consolidated balance sheet on December 31, 1967, would be prepared as shown on pages 386 and 387. A consolidated balance sheet prepared from these working papers would be the same as the balance sheet prepared from account balances maintained on the equity basis that was given on page 364.

COST METHOD — PROVING SUBSIDIARY EARNINGS ACCRUING TO PARENT

When the cost method is used, the cost or book value excess on a subsidiary investment will be the same as that found at acquisition if there is no amortization of this balance, since the investment balance has remained unchanged and the eliminations are the same as those originally made. When this method is used, the portion of subsidiary retained earnings accruing to the parent may be proved. The retained earnings accruing to the parent reported on the consolidated working papers on pages 386 and 387 are proved as follows:

Proof of Subsidiary Retained Earnings Accruing to Parent

	Co. S1	Co. S2
Retained earnings (deficit) balances, December 31, 1967	($ 5,000)	$15,000
Retained earnings (deficit) balances on date of acquisition.*		
Co. S1, April 1, 1966	20,000	
Co. S2, July 1, 1966		(2,500)
Retained earnings increase (decrease) from date of parent company acquisition to December 31, 1967.	($25,000)	$17,500
Ownership interest	90%	80%
Retained earnings increase (decrease) accruing to parent since date of acquisition	($22,500)	$14,000

*See tabulations on page 361.

REPORTING INVESTMENTS ON PARENT COMPANY STATEMENTS

Both the equity and the cost methods of carrying investment balances in subsidiary companies have been illustrated. It has been demonstrated that the consolidated balance sheet will be the same regardless of the method employed. However, the two methods provide different investment and retained earnings balances on the parent's separate balance sheet and different earnings on the parent's separate income statement. Since this is the case, the parent company's separate financial statements should offer specific information concerning the method employed in carrying investments. Data with respect to financial position and the results of operation can then be interpreted in terms of the effects of the method employed.

When the cost method of accounting for subsidiary investments is used, the financial statements should provide data in parenthetical or note form offering the economic implications of subsidiary stock ownership. The net change in the parent's equity arising from subsidiary earnings since control was achieved should be indicated on the balance sheet, while the portion of such change identified with the current period should be reported on the income statement.

When the equity method of accounting for subsidiary investments is employed, the financial statements should provide data in parenthetical or note form with respect to investment cost and dividend income so that the limitations set by law as relating to the parent-subsidiary relationship may be fully understood. On the balance sheet, data should be presented relative to the cost of the subsidiary investment and to the portion of retained earnings that may be regarded as realized in view of the governing legal factors; on the income statement, further data are required with respect to that portion of current income that can be regarded as realized from a legal point of view.

EVALUATION OF EQUITY AND COST METHODS

Cost is the method that is generally chosen in accounting for investments in subsidiaries and in presenting such investments on the separate statements of the parent company. Objections are raised to the equity method on several grounds. First, the equity method involves basic departures from generally accepted practice in the recognition of revenue. Earnings of the subsidiary are viewed as earnings of the parent, an economic view which, it can be maintained, finds proper expression on the consolidated statement and not on the statement representing the separate legal entity. Second, investment balances fail to offer either costs or current values of subsidiary holdings, since they are composed of a mixture of different elements — costs (or investment values) as of stock acquisition dates, modified by adjustments based upon the changes in capital reported on the books of the subsidiaries following acquisitions. Finally, the equity method calls for analysis of the accounts and special adjustments in arriving at the amount of retained earnings legally available for dividends and the amount of income that is subject to income taxes. The choice of cost is supported as a method consistent with that applied to other investments and one that offers investment and revenue balances that conform with legal and income tax criteria.

UNCONSOLIDATED SUBSIDIARIES ON THE CONSOLIDATED BALANCE SHEET

The previous section dealt with the choice of equity or cost methods in accounting for investments on the books of the parent company. However, a special problem is faced when certain subsidiaries are not consolidated in the preparation of consolidated statements. When the cost method is used by the parent, should investments in unconsolidated subsidiaries continue to be reported at such cost or should they be restated to reflect changes in subsidiary equities?

The consolidated statements purport to show position and operations of a number of related companies from an economic point of view. Ideally, this calls for recognizing subsidiary earnings from the time the relationship was entered into as well as combining account balances of the affiliated units. However, when combining account balances of subsidiaries with those of the parent is considered inappropriate, use of the equity method still affords the parent a means of reflecting the favorable or unfavorable implications of subsidiary ownership on the consolidated statements. The objection to the use of the equity method for separate financial statements because it reflects the economic view becomes invalid when applied to the use of this method for consolidated statements.

The Committee on Accounting Procedure in *Accounting Research Bulletin No. 51* issued in 1959, in considering the problem of reporting unconsolidated subsidiaries in consolidated statements, indicated a preference for use of the equity method but stated that either the cost method or the equity method could be used provided the same method was applied to all of the unconsolidated units.[1] However, the Accounting Principles Board in an omnibus opinion issued in 1967 amended *Accounting Research Bulletin No. 51* and called for the use of the equity method in the following:

> If, in consolidated financial statements, a domestic subsidiary is not consolidated, the Board's opinion is that . . . the investment in the subsidiary should be adjusted for the consolidated group's share of accumulated undistributed earnings and losses since acquisition. This practice is sometimes referred to as the "equity method." In reporting periodic consolidated net income, the earnings or losses of the unconsolidated subsidiary (or group of subsidiaries) should generally be presented as a separate item. The amount of such earnings or losses should give effect to amortization, if appropriate, of any difference between the cost of the investment and the equity in net assets at date of acquisition and to any elimination of intercompany gains or losses that would have been made had the subsidiary been consolidated. If desired, dividends received by members of the consolidated group from the unconsolidated subsidiary may be shown parenthetically or by footnote.[2]

[1] *Accounting Research Bulletin No. 51*, "Consolidated Financial Statements," 1959 (New York: American Institute of Certified Public Accountants), pp. 46–47.

[2] *Opinion of the Accounting Principles Board No. 10*, "Omnibus Opinion — 1966," 1967 (New York: American Institute of Certified Public Accountants), pp. 142–143. It should be observed that the amendment is designed to modify *Accounting Research Bulletin No. 51* insofar as it relates to domestic subsidiaries. The Board has deferred recommendations on the treatment of foreign subsidiaries on consolidated financial statements until a research study on foreign investments is completed and can be considered. The Board has also deferred recommendations on the treatment of jointly owned (50% or less) companies until a research study on accounting for intercorporate investments is completed.

The Accounting Principles Board suggested no change in the following statement in *Accounting Research Bulletin No. 51* relating to the disclosure of assets and liabilities of unconsolidated subsidiaries:

> Where the unconsolidated subsidiaries are, in the aggregate, material in relation to the consolidated financial position or operating results, summarized information as to their assets, liabilities and operating results should be given in the footnotes or separate statements should be presented for such subsidiaries, either individually or in groups, as appropriate.[1]

QUESTIONS

1. Compare the entries for subsidiary profits, losses, and dividends when an investment is carried by the equity method and when it is carried by the cost method.

2. (a) What eliminations are made against the investment account on the consolidated working papers when an investment in a subsidiary is carried at cost? (b) What alternative method for eliminations on the working papers may be employed when the cost method is used?

3. Which method in your opinion provides a more satisfactory portrayal of an ownership interest in a subsidiary — the cost method or the equity method?

4. The chief accountant for the Wharton Co. recommends use of the cost method in accounting for investments in subsidiaries. He suggests that the equity method brings appraisal values into the books and this is contrary to company policy. (a) Evaluate this position. (b) Give other considerations that would suggest use of the cost method.

5. The Wilson Co. reports a retained earnings balance of $100,000 on the date that Dewey, Inc. acquires a controlling interest. This retained earnings balance is subsequently used as a basis for cash dividends. (a) How would you recommend that the parent record such dividends? Give reasons for your answer. (b) What eliminations are made on the working papers subsequent to the receipt of such dividends?

6. When the cost method for a subsidiary investment is used and eliminations are made in terms of original equity acquired, a retained earnings balance accruing to the parent company is recognized on the working papers. How can this balance be proved?

7. What special procedures are required on the working papers when investment balances have been adjusted by arbitrary amounts during the course of subsidiary stock ownership?

---

[1]*Accounting Research Bulletin No. 51*, "Consolidated Financial Statements," 1959 (New York: American Institute of Certified Public Accountants), p. 48.

8. The Webster Co., which is 100% owned by Mason, Inc., has suffered heavy losses since the date control was acquired by Mason, Inc. 10 years ago. (a) How are those losses recognized by the parent if the investment is carried by the equity method? (b) How can such losses be recognized by the parent if the investment is carried by the cost method?

9. What special disclosures are recommended for subsidiary investment balances and subsidiary earnings on the separate financial statements of the parent company when (a) investments in subsidiary companies are carried by the cost method, and (b) investments in subsidiary companies are carried by the equity method?

10. The Walsh Corporation reports investments in majority owned and wholly owned subsidiaries at cost on its separate balance sheet. Only wholly owned subsidiaries are consolidated for purposes of the consolidated balance sheet; but whenever the latter statement is prepared, investment balances for those subsidiaries not consolidated are restated by applying the equity method. Would you support such restatements? Give your reasons.

EXERCISES

1. The Harper Co. and the Jerome Co. each have 1,000 shares of stock outstanding, $100 par. Changes in capital, January 1, 1966, to December 31, 1967, were as follows:

	Harper Co.	Jerome Co.
Retained earnings (deficit) balances, January 1, 1966	$50,000	($20,000)
Dividends paid in December, 1966	(15,000)	
	$35,000	($20,000)
Net income, 1966	40,000	15,000
	$75,000	($ 5,000)
Dividends paid in December, 1967	(10,000)	
	$65,000	($ 5,000)
Net income (loss), 1967	(10,000)	20,000
Retained earnings balances, December 31, 1967	$55,000	$15,000

The King Corporation acquired 800 shares of Harper Co. stock at 100 and 900 shares of Jerome Co. stock at 90 on July 1, 1966.

(a) What is the cost or book value excess on each investment?

(b) What entries would be made by the parent for profits, losses, and dividends of each of the subsidiaries if investments are carried at cost?

(c) What entries would be made if investments are carried by the equity method?

2. The McFarland Corporation, a holding company, carries investments at cost. On July 3, 1967, it acquired 32,000 shares of Jessup Co. stock at 15. Comparative balance sheet data for the Jessup Co. revealed that retained earnings had gone up from $50,000 on January 1, 1967, to $75,000 on December 31, 1967, as a result of profits of $40,000 less two dividends of $7,500 each paid on June 1 and December 1. Capital stock and additional paid-in capital balances remained unchanged at $420,000 and $100,000 respectively; 40,000 shares of stock were outstanding. (a) What entries are required during the year on the books of the holding company? (b) What eliminations are required at the end of the year in preparing a consolidated balance sheet? (c) What is the cost or book value excess on the investment and the retained earnings accruing to the holding company as a result of subsidiary operations?

3. Company P paid $85,000 for a 90% interest in the stock of Company A on January 1, 1967. The investment is carried at cost. During 1967 Company A reported a net income of $30,000 and paid dividends of $10,000. At the end of the year Company A reported a retained earnings balance of $5,000. The capital stock balance remained unchanged at $80,000. (a) What is the elimination on the consolidated working papers? (b) What is the cost or book value excess on the investment and the retained earnings accruing to the parent as a result of subsidiary operations?

4. The Stockton Manufacturing Co. owns an 80% interest in the stock of the Turner Co., acquired on January 1, 1959, at a cost of $400,000. Capital stock of the Turner Co. is $500,000. The subsidiary showed a deficit of $50,000 when the Stockton Manufacturing Co. acquired control, but profitable operations converted the deficit to a retained earnings balance of $350,000 as of December 31, 1967. At the end of 1967, the board of directors of the Stockton Manufacturing Co. authorized that the investment account be written up by $250,000 and that Appraisal Capital be credited for this amount in recognition of past earnings of the subsidiary.

(a) Give two sets of adjustments and eliminations, either of which could be used in developing consolidated working papers.

(b) What is the cost or book value excess that will appear on the consolidated balance sheet on December 31, 1967?

5. Merrihew, Inc. paid $175,000 for a 90% interest in the Doerr Company on January 1, 1967. The capital of the Doerr Company was composed of capital stock, $100,000, and retained earnings, $60,000. Investments are carried by Merrihew, Inc. at cost. The Doerr Company announced a net loss of $20,000 for 1967 and paid a dividend of $10,000. (a) How would you advise that the foregoing be recorded on the books of Merrihew, Inc.? (b) What is the cost or book value excess on January 1 and on December 31?

PROBLEMS

12-1. The Miller Company and the North Company each have 10,000 shares of no-par stock outstanding. Capital stock balances are $80,000 and $100,000 respectively. Changes in capital, January 1, 1966, to December 31, 1967, were as follows:

	Miller Co.	North Co.
Retained earnings (deficit) balances, January 1, 1966	$50,000	($25,000)
Dividends declared and paid in December, 1966	(15,000)	
	$35,000	($25,000)
Net income (net loss), 1966	40,000	(5,000)
Retained earnings (deficit) balances, December 31, 1966	$75,000	($30,000)
Dividends declared and paid in December, 1967	(15,000)	
	$60,000	($30,000)
Net income (net loss), 1967	(10,000)	24,000
Retained earnings (deficit) balances, December 31, 1967	$50,000	($ 6,000)

The Lawrence Corporation acquired 9,000 shares of Miller Co. stock at 14 and 8,000 shares of North Co. stock at 8½.

Instructions: (1) Calculate the cost or book value excess on each purchase, assuming that the investments were made on (a) July 1, 1966; (b) October 1, 1967.

(2) Assume that the investments are carried by the equity method. What entries would be made on the books of the parent to record profits, losses, and dividends of each subsidiary, assuming that the investments were made on (a) July 1, 1966; (b) October 1, 1967?

(3) Assume that the investments are carried by the cost method. What entries would be made on the books of the parent to record profits, losses, and dividends of each subsidiary, assuming that the investments were made on (a) July 1, 1966; (b) October 1, 1967?

12-2. Balance sheets for a parent and its subsidiaries on December 31, 1967, are as follows:

	Co. Z	Co. A	Co. B	Co. C
Investments in subsidiaries	$1,575,000			
Other assets	1,725,000	$715,000	$755,000	825,000
Total assets	$3,300,000	$715,000	$755,000	$825,000
Liabilities	$ 742,500	$150,000	$220,000	$250,000
Capital stock	2,500,000	500,000	500,000	600,000
Retained earnings	57,500	65,000	35,000	(25,000)
Total liabilities and stockholders' equity	$3,300,000	$715,000	$755,000	$825,000

Data relative to subsidiary investment balances are as follows:

	Amount Paid for Stock	Interest Acquired	Subsidiary Capital on Date Parent Acquired Control: Capital Stock	Retained Earnings (Deficit)
Investment in Co. A......	$500,000	100%	$500,000	($ 20,000)
Investment in Co. B......	550,000	95%	500,000	75,000
Investment in Co. C......	525,000	80%	600,000	125,000

Instructions: Prepare a consolidated balance sheet as of December 31, 1967. (Working papers are not required.)

12-3. Balance sheets for parent Company P and its 85%-owned subsidiary Company Q are given below:

	Company P		Company Q	
	Dec. 31 1966	Dec. 31 1967	Dec. 31 1966	Dec. 31 1967
Investment in Company Q.....	$250,000	$250,000		
Other assets..................	735,000	700,000	$475,000	$460,000
Total assets..................	$985,000	$950,000	$475,000	$460,000
Liabilities....................	$265,000	$305,000	$115,000	$175,000
Capital stock..................	500,000	500,000	200,000	200,000
Additional paid-in capital......	100,000	100,000	100,000	100,000
Retained earnings (deficit)......	120,000	45,000	60,000	(15,000)
Total liabilities and stockholders' equity....................	$985,000	$950,000	$475,000	$460,000

Company P acquired its controlling interest in Company Q at the end of 1966. The interest in Company Q was carried at cost despite the unfavorable operations of the subsidiary in 1967.

Instructions: Prepare a balance sheet in comparative form reporting the consolidated financial position of parent and subsidiary at the end of 1966 and at the end of 1967. (Working papers are not required.)

12-4. The Allen Co. acquired 12,500 shares of stock of the Burton Co., $10 par, at 14, and 8,500 shares of stock of the Crow Co., $10 par, at 7½. Purchases were made on January 2, 1966. Retained earnings changes for the three companies for 1966 and 1967 are shown at the top of the following page.

	Allen Co.	Burton Co.	Crow Co.
Retained earnings (deficit) balances, January 2, 1966	$130,000	$ 37,500	($20,000)
Net income (net loss) from own operations, 1966	47,500	15,000	(5,000)
Dividend income from Burton Co.	5,000		
	$182,500	$ 52,500	($25,000)
Dividends declared and paid, 1966	(15,000)	(6,000)	
Retained earnings (deficit) balances, December 31, 1966	$167,500	$ 46,500	($25,000)
Net income from own operations, 1967	57,500	15,000	10,000
Dividend income from Burton Co.	7,500		
	$232,500	$ 61,500	($15,000)
Dividends declared and paid, 1967	(20,000)	(9,000)	
Retained earnings (deficit) balances, December 31, 1967	$212,500	$ 52,500	($15,000)

Condensed balance sheets as of December 31, 1967, were as follows:

	Allen Co.	Burton Co.	Crow Co.
Investment in Burton Co.	$175,000		
Investment in Crow Co.	63,750		
Other assets	361,250	$282,500	$160,000
Total assets	$600,000	$282,500	$160,000
Liabilities	$187,500	$ 80,000	$ 75,000
Capital stock	200,000	150,000	100,000
Retained earnings (deficit)	212,500	52,500	(15,000)
Total liabilities and stockholders' equity	$600,000	$282,500	$160,000

Instructions: (1) Prepare working papers for a consolidated balance sheet.

(2) Revise the investment account balances on the assumption that the equity method is used, and prepare working papers for a consolidated balance sheet.

(3) Prepare a consolidated balance sheet.

(4) Prove (a) retained earnings balances accruing to the parent under the cost method and (b) cost or book value excesses on investments under the equity method.

12-5. The Penn Construction Co. owns controlling interests in the stock of the Roper Co. and the Scott Co. The interests were acquired on May 1, 1967. Balance sheets for the three companies on December 31, 1967, are given at the top of the following page.

The parent company has made no entries to record the profits, losses, or dividend declarations of its subsidiaries.

	Penn Const. Co.		Roper Co.		Scott Co.	
Investment in Roper Co. (3,600 shares)........		$270,000				
Investment in Scott Co. (820 shares).........		125,000				
Other assets...........		570,000		$600,000		$350,000
Total assets............		$965,000		$600,000		$350,000
Liabilities.............		$339,000		$284,000		$220,000[1]
Capital stock...........	(5,000 sh.)	500,000	(4,000 sh.)	380,600	(1,000 sh.)	100,000
Retained earnings (deficit):						
Balance, January 1, 1967.	$116,000		($ 40,000)		$ 20,000	
Net income (loss), 1967...	30,000		(24,600)		15,000	
	$146,000				$ 35,000	
Dividends paid in November, 1967............	(20,000)					
Dividends declared in December, 1967, payable in January, 1968......					(5,000)	
Balance, December 31, 1967		126,000		(64,600)		30,000
Total liabilities and stockholders' equity.......		$965,000		$600,000		$350,000

[1]Includes dividends declared of $5,000.

Instructions: (1) Give the necessary journal entries to adjust the parent company accounts, assuming that the investments are carried by the cost method, and prepare working papers for a consolidated balance sheet.

(2) Give the necessary journal entries to adjust the parent company accounts, assuming that the investments are carried by the equity method, and prepare working papers for a consolidated balance sheet.

(3) Prepare a consolidated balance sheet as of December 31, 1967.

12-6. The Burns Co. owns 25,000 shares of stock of Coogan Co. and 8,000 shares of stock of Dailey, Inc., both acquired on March 1, 1967. Investments are carried at cost. Balance sheets for the three companies on December 31, 1967, are as follows:

	Burns Co.		Coogan Co.		Dailey, Inc.
Investment in Coogan, Co..........	$ 40,000				
Investment in Dailey, Inc..........	82,500				
Goodwill.........................	60,000		$ 25,000		
Other assets.....................	612,500		100,000		$130,000
Total assets.....................	$795,000		$125,000		$130,000
Liabilities......................	$212,500		$ 39,500		$ 60,000
Capital stock..........(15,000 sh.)	450,000	(30,000 sh.)	60,000	(10,000 sh.)	50,000
Retained earnings................	132,500		25,500		20,000
Total liabilities and stockholders' equity......................	$795,000		$125,000		$130,000

Earnings and dividends for the companies for 1967 are listed below.

	Burns Co.	Coogan Co.	Dailey, Inc.
Net income (net loss)	$47,500	$36,000	($15,000)
Dividends paid	50 cents per share on March 15 and the same amount at quarterly intervals thereafter.	7½ cents per share on February 5 and at quarterly intervals thereafter.	None

The foregoing information was properly recorded during the year.

Instructions: Prepare working papers and a consolidated balance sheet Assume that any excess of investment book value over cost is regarded as negative goodwill; however, no reduction in minority interest for negative goodwill is to be made.

12-7. Balance sheet data as of December 31, 1967, for the Fuller Co. and its affiliates, Gulf Co. and Horn Co., are shown below.

Fuller Co.

Cash, receivables, and inventories	$2,050,000	Trade creditors	$ 640,000
Investments:		Long-term debt	1,000,000
Gulf Co. (200,000 shares at cost)	500,000	Preferred stock, $100 par	350,000
Horn Co. (22,000 shares at cost)	150,000	Common stock, $10 par	1,500,000
Plant and equipment	1,480,000	Additional paid-in capital	750,000
Other assets	15,000	Deficit	(45,000)
Total assets	$4,195,000	Total liabilities and stockholders' equity	$4,195,000

Gulf Co.

Cash, receivables, and inventories	$ 680,000	Dividends payable	$ 37,500
Plant and equipment	350,000	Trade creditors	192,500
Other assets	20,000	Long-term debt	150,000
		Capital stock (no par, 250,000 shares)	250,000
		Additional paid-in capital	100,000
		Retained earnings	320,000
Total assets	$1,050,000	Total liabilities and stockholders' equity	$1,050,000

Horn Co.

Cash, receivables, and inventories	$ 120,000	Trade creditors	$ 70,000
Plant and equipment	80,000	Capital stock (no par, 25,000 shares)	120,000
		Retained earnings	10,000
Total assets	$ 200,000	Total liabilities and stockholders' equity	$ 200,000

Stock of Gulf Co. was acquired at the end of 1960 when the retained earnings balance of this company was $65,000. Stock of Horn Company was acquired on June 1, 1967. Horn Co. had reported a deficit on January 1, 1967, of $17,000. The dividend declared by Gulf Co. has not yet been taken up on the books of the parent. Fuller Co. receivables include $15,000 from Gulf Co. and $450 from Horn Co. Corresponding payables are included by subsidiaries in the trade creditor totals.

Instructions: (1) Prepare consolidated working papers.

(2) Prepare a consolidated balance sheet.

(3) Prove the subsidiary retained earnings balances accruing to the parent company.

12-8. On September 30, 1966, the Valley Company acquired a controlling interest in Clark Company at a purchase price of $1,550,000. Balance sheets of the two companies on December 31, 1967, follow:

		Valley Company		Clark Company
Cash, receivables, and inventories		$2,850,000		$1,420,000
Plant and equipment		2,650,000		1,500,000
Investment in Clark Company (165,000 shares)		1,418,000		
Other assets		297,000		145,000
Total assets		$7,215,000		$3,065,000
Accounts payable and accrued items		$1,365,000		$ 450,000
Bonds payable		1,000,000		500,000
Capital stock	($20 par)	2,500,000	($5 par)	1,000,000
Additional paid-in capital		1,500,000		200,000
Retained earnings		850,000		465,000
Appraisal capital				450,000
Total liabilities and stockholders' equity		$7,215,000		$3,065,000

A consolidated balance sheet is to be prepared for the first time on December 31, 1967, and for this purpose the following data are developed by analysis of the accounts of the two companies:

It is determined that Clark Company had retained earnings of $175,000 on the date when Valley Company acquired control. Plant and equipment of the subsidiary was appraised on this date and was written up by $485,000 in accordance with such appraisal; since the date of appraisal, appraisal capital of $35,000 has been transferred to retained earnings.

Since date of control by the Valley Company, Clark Company has paid dividends of $160,000; dividends received from the subsidiary have been recorded by the parent by credits to the investment account.

A remittance of $15,000 in payment of accounts payable to the Valley Company was made by Clark Company on December 31, 1967, and is recorded on the latter company's books; the remittance was in transit on December 31 and hence is not included on the balance sheet of the Valley Company as of this date.

Instructions: (1) Prepare consolidated working papers.

(2) Prepare a consolidated balance sheet.

(3) Prove the subsidiary retained earnings balance accruing to the parent.

12-9. The following are the balance sheets of P, Inc. and S, Inc. as of December 31, 1965:

	P, Inc.	S, Inc.
Cash	$ 432,576	$ 32,569
Accounts receivable	825,620	225,627
Inventories	1,628,429	625,375
Prepaid expenses	36,475	5,648
Total assets	$2,923,100	$889,219
Accounts payable	$ 325,647	$437,989
Federal income tax payable	250,000	15,000
Capital stock	300,000	50,000
Retained earnings	2,047,453	386,230
Total liabilities and stockholders' equity	$2,923,100	$889,219

As of December 31, 1965, P, Inc. acquired from the stockholders all of the shares of stock of S, Inc. in exchange for $550,000 of P's 4%, 10-year debentures. The excess cost of acquisition (excess of the purchase price over the net assets of S) is to be amortized on P's books by charges to income over a ten-year period.

For the years 1966 and 1967, operations of S, Inc. resulted in *losses* of $52,376 and $15,226, respectively, and operations of P, Inc. resulted in *profits* of $387,465 and $420,009, respectively. P provided a reserve on its books by charges to income for the losses of its subsidiary. The profits shown above for P are *before* provision for amortization of the excess cost of acquisition and for the losses of its subsidiary, S. Dividends of $150,000 were paid by P in each of the years 1966 and 1967.

The remaining assets and liabilities of P and S at December 31, 1966 and 1967, were as follows:

	P, Inc.		S, Inc.	
	1966	1967	1966	1967
Assets				
Cash	$ 426,879	$ 490,327	$ 30,194	$ 31,187
Accounts receivable	897,426	940,227	200,525	203,287
Inventories	1,826,162	1,952,173	600,476	535,711
Advances to S, Inc.	165,000	180,000		
Prepaid expenses	32,879	34,327	5,347	4,621
Liabilities				
Accounts payable	$ 357,428	$ 298,627	$287,688	$226,178
Federal income taxes payable	406,000	443,500		
Advances from P, Inc.			165,000	180,000

Instructions: From the information shown above prepare a work sheet for use in preparing a consolidated balance sheet as of December 31, 1967. Key and explain all entries made as adjustments or eliminations and prepare supporting schedules for major computations. (*Disregard any income tax effects of your entries.*)

(AICPA adapted)

12-10. The combined assets and liabilities of Peet, Inc., a parent company, and its subsidiaries were as shown below.

Assets	
Current assets	$ 636,000
Intercompany accounts receivable	258,000
Investment of parent in subsidiaries	1,268,000
Properties, less allowances for depreciation	1,093,000
Deferred charges	13,000
Goodwill	306,000
Total assets	$3,574,000

Liabilities and Stockholders' Equity	
Current liabilities	$ 174,000
Intercompany accounts payable	295,000
Funded debt — subsidiaries	130,000
Funded debt — parent company	696,000
Subsidiaries' capital and surplus at acquisition	1,298,000
Capital stock — parent company	460,000
Capital surplus — parent company	154,000
Earned surplus	367,000
Total liabilities and stockholders' equity	$3,574,000

The balance sheets of 38 "nominal" companies, each showing $1,000 capital stock and $1,000 receivable on intercompany account and nothing else, are not included in this combined balance sheet. However, the parent company carries the investment in these companies among the assets at par and includes the offsetting amount in the intercompany accounts payable.

Among the investments of the parent company is an amount of $6,000 representing bonds of a like principal amount of a subsidiary.

Preferred stocks of three subsidiaries are held by the public in the amounts of $10,000, $5,000, and $5,000, respectively. They are nonparticipating and all dividends had been paid.

The common stocks of all subsidiaries are 100% owned except the stock of one company, of which 10% is held by the public. On the date of the balance sheet, the capital and the earned surplus at acquisition of this company amounted to $40,000 and surplus earned since acquisition amounted to $30,000. No common dividends had ever been paid.

Instructions: Complete the consolidation on a columnar work sheet.

(AICPA adapted)

12-11. Marsh Sales, Inc. and Kelly Realty Corp. are wholly owned subsidiaries of Dodge Manufacturing Co., Inc. The parent corporation manufactures electric refrigerators, electric ranges, and various other electric appliances. Refrigerators and ranges are sold only to Marsh

Sales, Inc., which acts as a distributor. Other appliances are sold directly to outside distributors.

The parent and the subsidiary sales corporation are tenants of property owned by Kelly Realty Corp.

The intercompany accounts on the books of each company as at December 31, 1967, are as follows:

Dodge Manufacturing Co., Inc.	Debit	Credit
Investment in Marsh Sales, Inc. (at cost)	$100,000.00	
Investment in Kelly Realty Corp. (at cost)	175,000.00	
Due from Marsh Sales, Inc.	86,175.97	
Due to Kelly Realty Corp.		$ 1,475.00
Capital stock issued and outstanding, 100,000 shares, no par value		1,000,000.00
Retained earnings		410,169.50
Marsh Sales, Inc.		
Due to Kelly Realty Corp.		$ 800.00
Due to Dodge Manufacturing Co., Inc.		33,910.00
Capital stock issued and outstanding, 1,000 shares, $100 par value		100,000.00
Retained earnings		62,501.10
Kelly Realty Corp.		
Due from Dodge Manufacturing Co., Inc.	$ 6,575.00	
Due to Marsh Sales, Inc.		$ 2,800.00
Capital stock issued and outstanding, 1,000 shares, no par value		175,000.00
Retained earnings		34,109.50

An audit of the books of the three companies for the year ended December 31, 1967, revealed the following:

(1) The minute books of the three companies indicate the following with respect to dividends:

(a) The board of directors of Dodge Manufacturing Co., Inc. at a meeting on January 4, 1968, declared a regular quarterly dividend of 50 cents per share, payable January 31, 1968, to stockholders of record on January 23, 1968.

(b) The board of directors of Marsh Sales, Inc. at a meeting on December 28, 1967, declared a 1% dividend, payable in cash on January 15, 1968, to stockholders of record on December 31, 1967.

(c) The board of directors of Kelly Realty Corp. at a meeting on December 1, 1967, declared a dividend of $1.00 per share, payable January 2, 1968, to stockholders of record on December 15, 1967.

No effect has been given to these dividend declarations on the books of the parent company as at December 31, 1967. The subsidiary companies recorded the dividend declarations pertaining to their respective companies at date of declaration.

(2) Marsh Sales, Inc., received from one of its customers a check for $4,200 covering its own invoices aggregating $2,400 and invoices of Dodge Manufacturing Co., Inc. aggregating $1,800. The sales corporation recorded this transaction as follows:

Cash	4,200	
Accounts Receivable		4,200

(3) Marsh Sales, Inc. advanced $5,000 in cash to Kelly Realty Corp. and made the following entry:

Dodge Manufacturing Co., Inc.	5,000	
Cash		5,000

(4) On September 15, 1967, Dodge Manufacturing Co., Inc. shipped 100 appliances of a new design on consignment at $20 each to Marsh Sales, Inc. Marsh Sales, Inc. made no entry upon receipt of the goods. During October, 1967, Marsh Sales, Inc. sold all of the appliances at $25 each, crediting sales for the total thereof. Dodge Manufacturing Co., Inc. made no entries on its books, but included the 100 appliances in its inventory at December 31, 1967, at its cost of $14 each.

(5) The parent corporation filed a consolidated federal income tax return for the year ended December 31, 1966. The results of operations for the respective companies that year, before consolidation, were as follows:

Dodge Manufacturing Co., Inc., net loss	$13,280
Marsh Sales, Inc., net profit	42,260
Kelly Realty Corp., net profit	21,130

The federal income tax, amounting to $21,000, was paid by the parent corporation, which recorded the transaction as follows:

Federal Income Taxes Payable	21,000	
Cash		21,000

An agreement in the files indicates that federal income taxes should be apportioned among the companies based upon unconsolidated net profit. A company having a loss year is to pay no tax nor charge the other companies for the benefit derived from the use of its loss in the return. The proper liability of each company was recorded as at December 31, 1966.

(6) Kelly Realty Corp. sold certain of its furniture to Marsh Sales, Inc. at current market value, which was 75% of net book value. The realty corporation had purchased the furniture for $3,500 exactly 2 years prior to the date of sale and had taken depreciation at the rate of 10% per annum. It billed Marsh Sales, Inc. for $2,800 and recorded the transaction as follows:

Marsh Sales, Inc.	2,800	
Furniture and Fixtures		2,800

Marsh Sales, Inc. recorded the purchase as follows:

Furniture and Fixtures	2,800	
Kelly Realty Corp.		2,800

(7) As at December 31, 1967, the books of the parent corporation and the sales subsidiary do not reflect rent for the month of December, 1967, in the amounts of $6,100 and $1,400, respectively, due to Kelly Realty Corp.

(8) Marsh Sales, Inc. had not recorded December, 1967, purchase invoices submitted by the parent corporation in the amount of $48,265.97.

Instructions: (1) Prepare an itemized reconciliation of the intercompany accounts.

(2) Prepare the adjusting journal entries necessary to correct each set of books at the end of 1967.

(AICPA adapted)

Chapter 13

CONSOLIDATED STATEMENTS

SPECIAL PROBLEMS IN CONSOLIDATION

Special problems arise in the preparation of consolidated statements when (1) stock is acquired directly from a subsidiary, (2) stock is acquired in a company that has two or more classes of stock outstanding, and (3) stock of a subsidiary is received in the form of a stock dividend. The acquisition of merchandise and other assets from affiliated companies and the acquisition of bonds of affiliated units also give rise to special problems. The factors that must be considered in each of these instances are explained and illustrated in this chapter.

PURCHASE OF STOCK DIRECTLY FROM SUBSIDIARY

Instead of acquiring stock by purchase on the open market, a parent may acquire part or all of its holdings directly from the company to be controlled. The interest that is acquired may consist of treasury stock or newly issued stock. In either case, the capital of the subsidiary is increased by the amount paid for the stock, and subsequent eliminations in the preparation of the consolidated balance sheet are based on the capital of the subsidiary after the sale of the stock.

To illustrate, assume that the capital of Company S is as follows:

Capital stock (10,000 shares, no par)...................	$150,000
Retained earnings....................................	40,000
	$190,000
Less treasury stock, 2,500 shares at cost.................	30,000
Total...	$160,000

Company P acquires the 2,500 shares of treasury stock from Company S at $20 per share and also 5,000 shares on the open market at the same price. The entries on the books of Companies P and S are:

On Company P's books:

Investment in Co. S Stock..................	150,000	
Cash..................................		150,000

On Company S's books:

Cash.....................................	50,000	
Treasury Stock..........................		30,000
Paid-In Capital from Sale of Treasury Stock in Excess of Cost.........................		20,000

Eliminations on working papers for a consolidated balance sheet on the date of the stock acquisition will be made as follows:

	Co. P	Co. S	Eliminations		Consolidated Balance Sheet	
			Dr.	Cr.	Dr.	Cr.
Debits						
Investment in Co. S Stock	150,000					
Eliminate 75% of Capital Stock				112,500		
Eliminate 75% of Additional Paid-in Capital				15,000		
Eliminate 75% of Retained Earnings				30,000		
Excess of Book Value over Cost						7,500
Credits						
Capital Stock, Co. S		150,000				
Eliminate 75%			112,500			
Minority Interest, 25%						37,500
Additional Paid-In Capital, Co. S		20,000				
Eliminate 75%			15,000			
Minority Interest, 25%						5,000
Retained Earnings, Co. S		40,000				
Eliminate 75%			30,000			
Minority Interest, 25%						10,000

SUBSIDIARIES WITH PREFERRED AND COMMON STOCK

When control is acquired in a subsidiary that has issued both preferred and common stock, it is necessary to apportion the capital of the subsidiary between the two classes of stock. The apportionment is required on the date control is acquired and regularly thereafter when consolidated statements are prepared. Changes in the equities identified with the particular holdings of the parent can then be recognized in the development of the consolidated statements.

The procedures that are followed in assigning capital to preferred and common stock are the same as those followed in calculating book values for preferred and common stock. The rights and the priorities of each issue must be carefully analyzed. The portion of the capital that is related to the preferred stock is first calculated. This amount is subtracted from the total capital in arriving at the capital related to the common stock.

Preferred stock usually has a liquidating value equal to par, par plus a premium, or a stated dollar amount. Capital equal to this value is identified with the preferred equity. When the preferred shareholders have additional priorities upon the distribution of corporate capital, such additional amounts should be recognized as a part of the preferred stockholders' equity. Remaining capital is regarded as the common stockholders' equity. Capital apportionment procedures are described in a series of cases that follow. It is assumed that, upon liquidation, preferred stock has a value equal to its par value and, when cumulative, is entitled to the payment of dividends in arrears.

(1) *Noncumulative, nonparticipating preferred stock.* When preferred stock is noncumulative and nonparticipating, the preferred equity is limited to the preferred stock balance; remaining capital balances are identified with the common stock. A deficit would be entirely identified with the common stock.

(2) *Cumulative, nonparticipating preferred stock.* When preferred stock is cumulative and nonparticipating and when dividends on the preferred have been paid to date, the preferred equity is limited to the preferred stock balance. When there are dividends in arrears on preferred stock, the preferred stock balance and an amount equal to the dividends in arrears is assigned to the preferred; the balance of capital is assigned to common. In the event of a deficit and dividends in arrears, the amount of dividends in arrears would still be included in the preferred equity; the residual common equity would thus be impaired by the deficit as well as the dividends in arrears.

(3) *Noncumulative, participating preferred stock.* When preferred stock is noncumulative but participates with common stock in dividends in excess of a stipulated rate, a retained earnings balance should be assigned to the preferred and common stocks in accordance with the specific participation features of the preferred. A deficit would be identified with the common stock.

(4) *Cumulative, participating preferred stock.* When preferred stock is both cumulative and participating, a retained earnings balance is again assigned to the preferred stock and the common stock in accordance with the participation features of the preferred. If there are dividends in arrears on preferred stock, however, an amount equal to the dividends in arrears is first assigned to the preferred stock. In the event of a deficit and dividends in arrears on preferred stock, the amount of dividends in arrears would still be included in the preferred equity; the common equity would thus be reduced by both the deficit and the dividends in arrears.

The capital apportionments are illustrated in the examples that follow. Assume that on December 31, 1967, the capital of a subsidiary company is as follows:

6% preferred stock, 2,000 shares, $50 par	$100,000
Common stock, 20,000 shares, $10 par	200,000
Retained earnings	30,000

Capital of the subsidiary would be apportioned as follows:

	Total Capital	Preferred Stock Equity	Common Stock Equity
(1) Preferred — noncumulative, nonparticipating	$330,000	$100,000	$230,000
(2) Preferred — cumulative, nonparticipating, dividends in arrears $12,000 (including 1967)	330,000	112,000	218,000
(3) Preferred — noncumulative, fully participating	330,000	110,000	220,000
(4) Preferred — cumulative, fully participating, dividends in arrears $12,000 (including 1967)	330,000	114,000	216,000

In example (4) above, the retained earnings balance was allocated to preferred and common equities as though it were to be distributed currently, as follows:

	To Preferred	To Common
Prior year's dividend requirements, 6%	$ 6,000	
Current year's dividend requirement, 6%	6,000	
Preferred rate to common for current year, 6%		$12,000
Balance ratably to preferred and common	2,000	4,000
	$14,000	$16,000

Assume that the capital of the subsidiary referred to above is composed of preferred and common stock as indicated and a deficit of $30,000 instead of retained earnings of this amount. The capital would be apportioned as follows:

	Total Capital	Preferred Stock Equity	Common Stock Equity
(1) Preferred — noncumulative, nonparticipating	$270,000	$100,000	$170,000
(2) Preferred — cumulative, nonparticipating, dividends in arrears $12,000 (including 1967)	270,000	112,000	158,000
(3) Preferred — noncumulative, fully participating	270,000	100,000	170,000
(4) Preferred — cumulative, fully participating, dividends in arrears $12,000 (including 1967)	270,000	112,000	158,000

The example that follows illustrates the procedure that may be employed in the preparation of working papers for a consolidated balance sheet when a subsidiary company has two or more classes of stock. Assume that on January 1, 1967, the capital of Company S consists of the following:

6% preferred stock, cumulative and nonparticipating, $100 par (dividends in arrears for 1965 and 1966)	$100,000
Common stock, $100 par	200,000
Retained earnings	30,000

Company S was legally able to pay dividends on preferred stock in 1965 and 1966; however, in view of the working capital requirements of the company, dividends on preferred stock were passed.

On January 1, 1967, Company P acquires 400 shares of preferred stock at 115 and 1,800 shares of common stock at 125. Preferred and common equities are calculated on the date of acquisition in preparing a consolidated balance sheet. The retained earnings balance is apportioned as follows:

Retained earnings, January 1, 1967	$30,000
Retained earnings identified with preferred — amount required to meet dividends in arrears for 1965 and 1966	12,000
Retained earnings identified with common — balance	$18,000

Working papers for a consolidated balance sheet on January 1, 1967, are prepared as follows:

	Co. P	Co. S	Eliminations		Consolidated Balance Sheet	
			Dr.	Cr.	Dr.	Cr.
Debits						
vestment in Co. S Preferred Stock	46,000					
Eliminate 40% of Preferred Stock				40,000		
Eliminate 40% of Retained Earnings Identified with Preferred Stock, $12,000				4,800		
Excess of Cost over Book Value					1,200	
vestment in Co. S Common Stock	225,000					
Eliminate 90% of Common Stock				180,000		
Eliminate 90% of Retained Earnings Identified with Common Stock, $18,000				16,200		
Excess of Cost over Book Value					28,800	
Credits						
referred Stock, Co. S		100,000				
Eliminate 40%			40,000			
Minority Interest, 60%						60,000
ommon Stock, Co. S		200,000				
Eliminate 90%			180,000			
Minority Interest, 10%						20,000
etained Earnings Identified with Co. S Preferred		12,000				
Eliminate 40%			4,800			
Minority Interest, 60%						7,200
etained Earnings Identified with Co. S Common		18,000				
Eliminate 90%			16,200			
Minority Interest, 10%						1,800

Assume that the subsidiary company reports a loss of $20,000 for 1967 and once more passes the dividends on preferred stock. The change in the common and preferred stockholders' equities for 1967 must be calculated before a consolidated balance sheet can be prepared at the end of the year. The retained earnings allocation to preferred and common stock on December 31, 1967, is made as follows:

Retained earnings, December 31, 1967	$10,000
Retained earnings identified with preferred — amount required to meet dividends in arrears, 1965–1967 inclusive	18,000
Deficit identified with common — balance	($ 8,000)

It should be observed that the preferred stockholders' equity in the subsidiary capital is considered to have increased by $6,000 in view of the increase in dividends in arrears on preferred stock from $12,000 to $18,000; the common stockholders' equity has decreased by the loss, $20,000, and also by the amount of the dividend requirement on preferred stock for the current year, $6,000, a total of $26,000. The view adopted here is one of continued operations within the original capital framework. A corporate reorganization at some future date might conceivably result in a settlement with preferred stockholders whereby this group agrees to accept less than its full equity as calculated here. However, assuming profitable operations in the future and the ability of the company to pay off preferred dividend arrearages, earnings of $26,000 will be required to restore the common stockholder group to the status that it occupied at the beginning of the year.

Equity method. Since Company P controls Company S through ownership of the latter company's common stock, it may carry the investment in preferred in the same manner that it carries the investment in common. If the equity method is used in carrying investments in subsidiaries, entries are made by the parent as follows:

Investment in Co. S Preferred Stock	2,400	
Income — Co. S		2,400
To record increase in preferred stock equity in subsidiary, 40% of $6,000, additional dividend arrearage on preferred stock.		
Loss — Co. S	23,400	
Investment in Co. S Common Stock		23,400
To record decrease in common stock equity in subsidiary, 90% of $26,000, consisting of loss for year, $20,000, and dividend requirements on preferred stock for year, $6,000.		

Consolidated working papers at the end of the year may be prepared as shown at the top of the following page.

Cost method. If the cost method were used in the previous example, no entries would appear on the books of the parent during the year since

Assuming investments are carried by the equity method:

	Co. P	Co. S	Eliminations Dr.	Eliminations Cr.	Consolidated Balance Sheet Dr.	Consolidated Balance Sheet Cr.
Debits						
Investment in Co. S Preferred Stock	48,400					
Eliminate 40% of Preferred Stock				40,000		
Eliminate 40% of Retained Earnings Identified with Preferred Stock, $18,000				7,200		
Excess of Cost over Book Value					1,200	
Investment in Co. S Common Stock	201,600					
Eliminate 90% of Common Stock				180,000		
Eliminate 90% of Deficit Identified with Common Stock, $8,000			7,200			
Excess of Cost over Book Value					28,800	
Credits						
Preferred Stock, Co. S		100,000				
Eliminate 40%			40,000			
Minority Interest, 60%						60,000
Common Stock, Co. S		200,000				
Eliminate 90%			180,000			
Minority Interest, 10%						20,000
Retained Earnings Identified with Co. S Preferred		18,000				
Eliminate 40%			7,200			
Minority Interest, 60%						10,800
Deficit Identified with Co. S Common		(8,000)				
Eliminate 90%				7,200		
Minority Interest, 10%					800	

no dividends were declared by the subsidiary. However, in preparing consolidated working papers, retained earnings would be allocated between preferred and common stock issues just as was done on page 410. Eliminations are made for preferred and common equities originally acquired, minority interests in the two classes of equities are calculated and extended to the consolidated balance sheet columns, and the earnings accruing to the parent on each class of stock are then calculated and listed.

Consolidated working papers would be prepared as shown at the top of the following page.

It should be noted that preferred and common stock issues may provide for rights and privileges that vary with certain conditions and with specified dates. Under such circumstances an apportionment of capital between preferred and common equities may be possible only if certain assumptions are made with respect to such special factors. When it is necessary to make certain assumptions in arriving at the preferred and common equities, such assumptions should be disclosed by special note on the consolidated balance sheet.

Assuming investments are carried by the cost method:

	Co. P	Co. S	Eliminations		Consolidated Balance Sheet	
			Dr.	Cr.	Dr.	Cr.
Debits						
Investment in Co. S Preferred Stock	46,000					
Eliminate 40% of Preferred Stock				40,000		
Eliminate 40% of Retained Earnings Identified with Preferred Stock on Jan. 1, 1967, $12,000				4,800		
Excess of Cost over Book Value					1,200	
Investment in Co. S Common Stock	225,000					
Eliminate 90% of Common Stock				180,000		
Eliminate 90% of Retained Earnings Identified with Common Stock on Jan. 1, 1967, $18,000				16,200		
Excess of Cost over Book Value					28,800	
Credits						
Preferred Stock, Co. S		100,000				
Eliminate 40%			40,000			
Minority Interest, 60%						60,000
Common Stock, Co. S		200,000				
Eliminate 90%			180,000			
Minority Interest, 10%						20,000
Retained Earnings Identified with Co. S Preferred		18,000				
Eliminate 40% as above			4,800			
Minority Interest, 60% of $18,000						10,800
Retained Earnings to Parent						2,400
Deficit Identified with Co. S Common		(8,000)				
Eliminate 90% as above			16,200			
Minority Interest, 10% of $8,000 Deficit					800	
Retained Earnings to Parent					23,400	

STOCK DIVIDENDS BY SUBSIDIARY

A dividend in the form of like stock has no effect upon the total capital of a corporation. Such a stock dividend likewise does not change the respective equities of the individual stockholders. The parent company, then, should recognize no change in the investment account balance or revenue upon receipt of such a dividend. However, a memorandum entry is made to record the additional shares received in the form of a dividend. The special problems that arise in preparing a consolidated balance sheet after distribution of a subsidiary stock dividend are illustrated in the examples that follow.

Assume that on January 1, 1967, Company P purchased 800 shares of Company S stock at 180. On this date, the capital of Company S is:

Capital stock (1,000 shares)	$100,000
Retained earnings	60,000

Working papers for a consolidated balance sheet on the date of stock acquisition are prepared as follows:

	Co. P	Co. S	Eliminations Dr.	Eliminations Cr.	Consolidated Balance Sheet Dr.	Consolidated Balance Sheet Cr.
Debits						
Investment in Co. S Stock	144,000					
Eliminate 80% of Capital Stock				80,000		
Eliminate 80% of Retained Earnings				48,000		
Excess of Cost over Book Value					16,000	
Credits						
Capital Stock, Co. S		100,000				
Eliminate 80%			80,000			
Minority Interest, 20%						20,000
Retained Earnings, Co. S		60,000				
Eliminate 80%			48,000			
Minority Interest, 20%						12,000

Assume that the subsidiary reports net income for 1967 of $30,000 and distributes a 50% stock dividend.

Equity method. If the investment account is carried by the equity method, the parent recognizes the subsidiary earnings by raising the investment account and also its retained earnings by 80% of $30,000, or $24,000. The receipt of the stock dividend of 400 shares is recorded by a memorandum entry. Subsequent eliminations on the working papers for a consolidated balance sheet are made in the usual manner, for the total capital of the subsidiary did not change with the transfer from Retained Earnings to Capital Stock. Eliminations at the end of 1967 are made as follows:

Assuming investments are carried by the equity method:

	Co. P	Co. S	Eliminations Dr.	Eliminations Cr.	Consolidated Balance Sheet Dr.	Consolidated Balance Sheet Cr.
Debits						
Investment in Co. S Stock	168,000					
Eliminate 80% of Capital Stock				120,000		
Eliminate 80% of Retained Earnings				32,000		
Excess of Cost over Book Value					16,000	
Credits						
Capital Stock, Co. S		150,000				
Eliminate 80%			120,000			
Minority Interest, 20%						30,000
Retained Earnings, Co. S		40,000				
Eliminate 80%			32,000			
Minority Interest, 20%						8,000

Cost method. If the investment is carried at cost, the parent makes no entry for the subsidiary earnings for the year. The receipt of the stock dividend is recorded by a memorandum entry. Subsequent eliminations on the working papers must continue to be made in terms of the total subsidiary capital of $160,000 as of the date of the stock acquisition. Elimination of the parent's ownership in a capital stock balance of $150,000, then, must be accompanied by an elimination against retained earnings of only $10,000, the retained earnings balance as of date of acquisition reduced by the amount transferred to the capital stock account. Eliminations at the end of 1967 are made as follows:

Assuming investments are carried by the cost method:

	Co. P	Co. S	Eliminations		Consolidated Balance Sheet	
			Dr.	Cr.	Dr.	Cr.
Debits						
Investment in Co. S Stock	144,000					
Eliminate 80% of Capital Stock, $150,000 (Capital Stock, date of acquisition, $100,000, plus stock dividend, $50,000)				120,000		
Eliminate 80% of Retained Earnings, $10,000 (Retained Earnings, date of acquisition, $60,000, less stock dividend, $50,000)				8,000		
Excess of Cost over Book Value					16,000	
Credits						
Capital Stock, Co. S		150,000				
Eliminate 80%			120,000			
Minority Interest, 20%						30,000
Retained Earnings, Co. S		40,000				
Eliminate 80% as above			8,000			
Minority Interest, 20% of $40,000						8,000
Retained Earnings to Parent						24,000

When a subsidiary transfers to the capital stock account earnings that have accumulated after the date the parent acquired control, it would be appropriate to disclose on the consolidated balance sheet that retained earnings of the controlling interest represent in part earnings that have been formally capitalized by the subsidiary. Such disclosure can be made by parenthetical remark or special note, or by reporting retained earnings in two parts. However, a transfer of retained earnings to paid-in capital of the controlling interest would not be appropriate. The Committee on Accounting Procedure of the American Institute of Certified Public Accountants comments on this matter as follows:

> Occasionally, subsidiary companies capitalize earned surplus arising since acquisition, by means of a stock dividend or otherwise. This does

not require a transfer to capital surplus on consolidation, inasmuch as the retained earnings in the consolidated financial statements should reflect the accumulated earnings of the consolidated group not distributed to the shareholders of, or capitalized by, the parent company.[1]

INTERCOMPANY PROFITS

The sale of merchandise as well as of other properties often takes place between affiliated companies. An intercompany sale normally involves a profit to the company making the sale. This profit is properly recognized on the separate financial statements of the selling company. However, such a profit can be recognized for consolidated statement purposes only if the goods or other properties have been resold outside of the affiliated group. If the asset is still held by an affiliate, the sale must be viewed as no more than a transfer between affiliates; any intercompany profit, together with the related increase in asset cost emerging from such a transfer, must be canceled.

Intercompany profits on inventories. When merchandise is acquired from a related company and such goods are sold to outsiders, profit is fully realized by the company originally selling the goods as well as by the company making the sale to outsiders. These transactions need not be considered in preparing consolidated statements. For example, assume that Company P sells goods costing $6,000 to Company S, an 80% owned subsidiary, for $7,500; Company P recognizes a profit on its books of $1,500. Company S, in turn, sells the goods to outsiders for $10,000; Company S recognizes a profit on its books of $2,500. In preparing a consolidated balance sheet, assets have increased by $4,000 and this asset increase is balanced by the assignment of retained earnings of $4,000 between the minority interest and the controlling interest: 20% of the retained earnings of $2,500 shown by Company S, or $500, is reported as retained earnings of the minority interest; 80% of the retained earnings of $2,500 of Company S, or $2,000, together with the retained earnings of $1,500 shown by Company P, or a total of $3,500, is reported as retained earnings of the controlling interest. The income of $4,000 is fully realized and its ultimate distribution in the form of dividends to stockholders representing the minority interest and the controlling interest will be made as reported on the consolidated balance sheet.

However, assume that goods that were sold to an affiliated company have not been resold and are included in the inventory of the affiliate on the date that the consolidated balance sheet is being prepared. When

[1] *Accounting Research Bulletin No. 51*, "Consolidated Financial Statements," 1959 (New York: American Institute of Certified Public Accountants), p. 46.

a subsidiary is wholly owned and when the sale is made by a parent to a subsidiary or by a subsidiary to a parent, the need for the elimination of the full amount of the profit that was recognized on the sale is obvious. Such a transaction must be regarded for consolidated statement purposes as no different from a transfer of goods between a home office and a branch with neither profit nor an increase in the original cost of the goods arising from the transfer.

What portion of the profit should be eliminated, however, when a subsidiary is not wholly owned? When the sale is made by a parent to a subsidiary, elimination of the full amount of the profit would still be in order; even though the affiliate is not wholly owned, the controlling interest can hardly maintain that it has realized a profit on a transaction that constitutes no more than an intercompany transfer of goods. However, conflicting views are held with respect to the amount of the profit that is to be eliminated when the sale is made by a subsidiary to a parent. Some authorities maintain that since a minority interest is entitled to a portion of the profit reported by the subsidiary regardless of whether the buyer is an affiliated company or an outsider, recognition on the consolidated balance sheet of the minority interest's share in such profit and a corresponding increase in the original cost of goods is warranted; eliminations, then, should be limited to that portion of the profit that accrues to the parent. Others insist that no profit should be assigned either to a minority interest or to a controlling interest as long as goods are held by companies within the affiliated group. It should be observed that if a minority interest is recognized on the consolidated balance sheet as an outside or quasi-liability group, this would offer support for eliminating no more than the profit identified with the parent. On the other hand, when a minority interest is viewed as a part of the ownership group, it would follow that intercompany profit accruing to the minority interest as well as the intercompany profit accruing to the controlling interest should be eliminated.

Committees of both the American Institute of Certified Public Accountants and the American Accounting Association have taken the position that the full amount of intercompany profit should be eliminated regardless of the degree of ownership in affiliated units. The Committee on Accounting Procedure of the American Institute of Certified Public Accountants in *Accounting Research Bulletin No. 51* makes the following observations:

> . . . As consolidated statements are based on the assumption that they represent the financial position and operating results of a single business enterprise, such statements should not include gain or loss on transactions among the companies in the group. Accordingly, any

intercompany profit or loss on assets remaining within the group should be eliminated; the concept usually applied for this purpose is gross profit or loss.[1]

The amount of intercompany profit or loss to be eliminated . . . is not affected by the existence of a minority interest. The complete elimination of the intercompany profit or loss is consistent with the underlying assumption that consolidated statements represent the financial position and operating results of a single business enterprise. The elimination of the intercompany profit or loss may be allocated proportionately between the majority and minority interests.[2]

The Committee on Accounting Concepts and Standards of the American Accounting Association in *Supplementary Statement No. 7* on "Consolidated Financial Statements" expresses a similar view:

In the consolidated financial statements, no gain or loss should be recognized as the result of transactions among affiliates. From a combined point of view, these transactions result merely in a shift of assets from one department or branch to another department or branch of the same entity. Therefore:

(1) The elimination of intercompany markups in assets should be complete, irrespective of the presence or absence of an outside (minority) interest. This procedure is necessary to insure a cost basis which, properly, should not be affected by the pattern of share ownership.

(2) The amount of intercompany markup to be eliminated is the intercompany gross margin, reduced by any inventoriable costs incurred in the movement of the goods from one affiliate to another.

(3) The intercompany gain to be eliminated from assets logically is applied in consolidation as a reduction of the income or retained earnings of the affiliates that have recorded the gain. If any such affiliate is a subsidiary with a minority interest, the per share equity of that interest is thus reduced, in the consolidated statements, in the same manner and in the same proportionate amount as the controlling interest. The practice of reflecting a minority interest's share of unrealized intercompany profit as if realized, while widely accepted, conflicts with the underlying purpose of consolidated financial statements as herein contemplated, namely, to reflect the activities of a group of companies as though they constituted a single unit.[3]

The elimination of intercompany profit on inventories is illustrated in the examples that follow.

Sale by parent to wholly owned subsidiary. Assume that Company P sells merchandise to its 100% owned subsidiary, Company S. At the

[1] *Accounting Research Bulletin No. 51*, "Consolidated Financial Statements," 1959 (New York: American Institute of Certified Public Accountants), p. 43.

[2] *Ibid.*, p. 45.

[3] *Accounting and Reporting Standards for Corporate Financial Statements and Preceding Statements and Supplements*, "Consolidated Financial Statements," 1957 (Columbus: American Accounting Association), pp. 44–45.

date of the consolidated balance sheet, the subsidiary has merchandise that it acquired from the parent at a price of $10,000; the cost of the goods to the parent was $6,000.

In the preparation of separate financial statements, the parent company properly recognizes a profit of $4,000 on the merchandise transfer, and the subsidiary company properly shows the goods as part of its inventory at a cost of $10,000. In preparing a consolidated balance sheet, the intercompany profit is canceled and the merchandise inventory of the subsidiary is reduced to its original cost. The following elimination is made on the working papers:

	Co. P	Co. S	Eliminations		Consolidated Balance Sheet	
			Dr.	Cr.	Dr.	Cr.
Debits						
Merchandise Inventory		10,000		4,000	6,000	
Credits						
Retained Earnings, Co. P			4,000			

It would be possible to reduce the inventory balance by means of a valuation account. Instead of crediting Merchandise Inventory on the working papers, a credit would be made to an allowance for intercompany profits on inventories account. Reporting the inventory balance less the valuation account on the consolidated balance sheet offers disclosure of the reduction for intercompany profits that has been applied to the inventory.

The elimination for intercompany profit does not appear on the books of any company but is shown only on the consolidated working papers. Sale of the merchandise by the subsidiary to outsiders in the following period results in the full realization of the intercompany profit. At the end of the next fiscal period, inventories are analyzed once more and eliminations are made on the working papers for any intercompany profits included in the inventories at that time.

Sale by parent to partially owned subsidiary. Assume the facts in the preceding example but ownership by Company P of only 80% of Company S stock. Here, too, the parent company reports a profit on the merchandise transfer of $4,000, and the goods are shown on the subsidiary's books at $10,000. However, with neither a profit nor an increase in the original cost of the inventory to be recognized on the consolidated balance sheet, the intercompany profit is canceled as in the preceding example. Sale of the goods by the subsidiary to outsiders in the next period will result in full realization by the parent of the profit on the original transfer as well as a participation with the minority interest in any profit or loss on the ultimate sale.

Sale by wholly owned subsidiary to parent. Assume that Company S, a wholly owned subsidiary, sells merchandise to its parent, Company P. At the date of the consolidated balance sheet, the parent has merchandise of $10,000 that it acquired from the subsidiary; the cost of the goods to the subsidiary was $6,000. Inasmuch as the parent owns 100% of the subsidiary, the entire profit of $4,000 reported on the books of the subsidiary accrues to the parent. In preparing the consolidated balance sheet, the full amount of the profit must be canceled and the inventory

Assuming investments are carried by the equity method:

	Co. P	Co. S	Eliminations		Consolidated Balance Sheet	
			Dr.	Cr.	Dr.	Cr.
Debits						
Merchandise Inventory	10,000			4,000	6,000	
Investment in Co. S	140,000					
Eliminate 100% of Capital Stock				100,000		
Eliminate 100% of Retained Earnings				25,000		
Excess of Cost over Book Value					15,000	
Credits						
Capital Stock, Co. P	200,000					200,000
Retained Earnings, Co. P	15,000		4,000			11,000
Capital Stock, Co. S		100,000				
Eliminate 100%			100,000			
Retained Earnings, Co. S		25,000				
Eliminate 100%			25,000			

Assuming investments are carried by the cost method:

	Co. P	Co. S	Eliminations		Consolidated Balance Sheet	
			Dr.	Cr.	Dr.	Cr.
Debits						
Merchandise Inventory	10,000			4,000	6,000	
Investment in Co. S	125,000					
Eliminate 100% of Capital Stock				100,000		
Eliminate 100% of $10,000, Retained Earnings at Acquisition				10,000		
Excess of Cost over Book Value					15,000	
Credits						
Capital Stock, Co. P	200,000					200,000
Retained Earnings, Co. P						
Capital Stock, Co. S		100,000				
Eliminate 100%			100,000			
Retained Earnings, Co. S		25,000	4,000			
Eliminate 100% as above			10,000			
Retained Earnings to Parent						11,000

reduced to its original cost. If the equity method is employed in carrying the subsidiary investment, subsidiary earnings have been recognized by the parent and summarized in its retained earnings account and the charge to cancel the profit on the intercompany sale is made to parent company retained earnings. If the cost method is employed, the subsidiary earnings have not yet been recognized by the parent and the charge may be made to subsidiary company retained earnings. Working papers may be developed as shown on the preceding page.

Retained earnings of the parent for consolidation in each case reflect $15,000, the earnings accruing from profitable activities of the wholly owned subsidiary, less $4,000, the adjustment for intercompany profits included in this balance.

Sale by partially owned subsidiary to parent. Assume that Company S is only 80% owned and that, on the date of the consolidated balance sheet, Company P has merchandise of $10,000 that it acquired from the subsidiary company; cost of the goods to the subsidiary was $6,000. If the full amount of the intercompany profit is to be canceled and the inventory reported at its original cost, the charge cannot be applied in total to retained earnings of the parent. With ownership by the parent of 80% of the subsidiary stock, only 80% of the earnings will be reported as retained earnings of the parent while 20% will be reported as retained earnings of the minority interest. In canceling the intercompany profit, then, retained earnings of the parent should be reduced by $3,200 and retained earnings of the minority interest should be reduced by $800.

If the equity method is employed, charges are made to retained earnings of both the parent and the minority interest. The charge to the minority interest can be made by a charge directly to the retained earnings of the subsidiary company that will reduce the balance to be extended to the consolidated balance sheet columns as minority interest. The charge can also be reported on a separate line on the working papers; such a charge would be carried to the consolidated balance sheet columns and ultimately subtracted from the unadjusted retained earnings of the minority interest that is extended to the consolidated balance sheet columns. If the cost method is employed, subsidiary earnings accruing to the parent are still to be recognized and the full charge for intercompany profits is made to the subsidiary retained earnings account; amounts that are extended to the consolidated balance sheet columns as retained earnings of the minority interest and retained earnings of the parent will then be based upon the subsidiary retained earnings balance after adjustment for intercompany profits. Working papers in each case may be developed as follows:

Assuming investments are carried by the equity method:

	Co. P	Co. S	Eliminations Dr.	Eliminations Cr.	Consolidated Balance Sheet Dr.	Consolidated Balance Sheet Cr.
Debits						
Merchandise Inventory	10,000			4,000	6,000	
Investment in Co. S.	112,000					
Eliminate 80% of Capital Stock				80,000		
Eliminate 80% of Retained Earnings				20,000		
Excess of Cost over Book Value					12,000	
Credits						
Capital Stock, Co. P	200,000					200,000
Retained Earnings, Co. P	12,000		3,200			8,800
Capital Stock, Co. S		100,000				
Eliminate 80%			80,000			
Minority Interest, 20%						20,000
Retained Earnings, Co. S		25,000	800			
Eliminate 80%			20,000			
Minority Interest, 20% of $25,000, less $800						4,200

Assuming investments are carried by the cost method:

	Co. P	Co. S	Eliminations Dr.	Eliminations Cr.	Consolidated Balance Sheet Dr.	Consolidated Balance Sheet Cr.
Debits						
Merchandise Inventory	10,000			4,000	6,000	
Investment in Co. S.	100,000					
Eliminate 80% of Capital Stock				80,000		
Eliminate 80% of $10,000, Retained Earnings at Acquisition				8,000		
Excess of Cost over Book Value					12,000	
Credits						
Capital Stock, Co. P	200,000					200,000
Retained Earnings, Co. P						
Capital Stock, Co. S		100,000				
Eliminate 80% of Capital Stock			80,000			
Minority Interest, 20%						20,000
Retained Earnings, Co. S		25,000	4,000			
Eliminate 80% as above			8,000			
Minority Interest, 20% of $21,000						4,200
Retained Earnings to Parent						8,800

Net earnings of the subsidiary company for the year for consolidation purposes are $11,000, consisting of $15,000, the change in subsidiary retained earnings, less $4,000, the adjustment for intercompany profits. Parent company retained earnings in each case reflect 80% of the subsidiary company net earnings of $11,000, or $8,800.

Sale by one subsidiary to another subsidiary. Assume that Company S2, 80% owned by Company P, holds merchandise acquired for $10,000 from Company S1, 90% owned by Company P; the cost of the goods to Company S1 was $6,000. Inasmuch as Company P owns 90% of the stock of Company S1, 90% of the profit of $4,000, or $3,600, would be identified with the parent; 10% of the profit, or $400, would be identified with the minority interest of Company S1. In the preparation of the consolidated balance sheet, the intercompany profit of $4,000 is eliminated.

If the equity method is used for the subsidiary investment, the elimination on the working papers is as follows:

Retained Earnings, Company P	3,600	
Retained Earnings, Company S1 (Reducing Minority Interest)	400	
Merchandise Inventory		4,000

If the cost method is used for the subsidiary investment, the elimination would be:

Retained Earnings, Company S1 (Reducing Controlling and Minority Interests)	4,000	
Merchandise Inventory		4,000

More than one transfer within affiliated group. Calculation of the amount to be eliminated is somewhat more complicated when there has been more than one transfer within the affiliated group. For example, assume that Company P holds merchandise that was acquired at a price of $10,000 from subsidiary Company S1, 90% owned by Company P. Company S1 acquired the goods at a price of $8,000 from subsidiary Company S2, 80% owned by Company P. The cost of the goods to Company S2 was $6,000. In this case, the profit recognized by the parent on intercompany transfers is calculated as follows:

Profit recognized by parent on transfer of goods by Company S1 to Company P, 90% of $2,000	$1,800
Profit recognized by parent on transfer of goods by Company S2 to Company S1, 80% of $2,000	1,600
Total profit recognized by Company P	$3,400

If investments are carried by the equity method, the elimination on consolidated working papers for Company P and subsidiary Companies S1 and S2 would be as follows:

Retained Earnings, Company P	3,400	
Retained Earnings, Company S1 (Reducing Minority Interest)	200	
Retained Earnings, Company S2 (Reducing Minority Interest)	400	
Merchandise Inventory		4,000

If investments are carried by the cost method, the elimination would be as follows:

Retained Earnings, Company S1 (Reducing Controlling and Minority Interests)	2,000	
Retained Earnings, Company S2 (Reducing Controlling and Minority Interests)	2,000	
Merchandise Inventory		4,000

The merchandise is reported on the consolidated balance sheet at its original cost, $6,000.

Alternative procedure for sales by partially owned subsidiaries. In the previous examples, the position was taken that inventories acquired from related companies should be decreased by the full amount of the intercompany profit; eliminations were made for any profit identified with a minority interest as well as for any profit identified with a controlling interest.

It was suggested earlier that there are some who would view the minority interest as an outside interest and would regard profits that accrue to the minority as realized for consolidated statement purposes. Such a position would call for the elimination of no more than the portion of the intercompany profit that accrues to the parent company. For example, assume an inventory in the hands of the parent that includes merchandise of $10,000 on which an 80%-owned subsidiary made a profit of $4,000. If only the parent company share of the profit is to be eliminated, a reduction of $3,200 would be applied to the merchandise inventory and to retained earnings of the parent. The resulting inventory value of $6,800 would be regarded as composed of $6,000, original cost, increased by $800, the profit accruing to the minority interest on the transfer; stated differently, the inventory value would be $10,000, the purchase price of the goods, less $3,200 (80% of $4,000), the amount recoverable from the subsidiary when the latter distributes dividends whose source is the profit made on the transfer. Although the minority interest suffers no reduction for intercompany profits if the latter procedure is followed, the method that is chosen is of no importance to this group; the minority interest is concerned, not with the financial position and minority interest measurements reported on the consolidated statement, but with the financial data reported on the separate statements of the company in which they have an ownership interest.

For purposes of illustrations and problems in this and in succeeding chapters, it will be assumed that eliminations for intercompany profits are to be complete and are to be assigned to both the minority interest and the controlling interest.

Intercompany profits on depreciable assets. The practices that are followed in eliminating intercompany profits on inventories are also applicable in eliminating intercompany profits on other assets. When a profit is recognized by an affiliated company on the sale of an asset that remains within the affiliated group, it is necessary in reporting the consolidated position to reduce the asset to cost and to reduce retained earnings by the amount of the intercompany profit. The elimination of intercompany profits when depreciable assets are involved presents special problems. These are illustrated in the examples that follow.

Depreciable asset constructed by parent for wholly owned subsidiary. Assume that Company P constructs certain equipment for subsidiary Company S, 100% owned. Company S is charged $10,000; the cost to Company P is $6,000. If a consolidated balance sheet is prepared at the date of the asset acquisition, it is necessary to reduce the equipment to the actual cost of construction and to eliminate the intercompany profit on the transfer. The elimination on the working papers follows:

	Co. P	Co. S	Eliminations		Consolidated Balance Sheet	
			Dr.	Cr.	Dr.	Cr.
Debits						
Equipment		10,000		4,000*	6,000	
Credits						
Retained Earnings, Co. P			4,000			

*If it is considered desirable to report the reduction for intercompany profits on property items on the consolidated balance sheet, the credit would be made to a separate allowance for intercompany profits account as in the case of intercompany profits on inventories.

The elimination appears only on the working papers; the books of Company P properly show the profit of $4,000, and the books of Company S properly show the equipment at a cost of $10,000.

On consolidated working papers prepared in subsequent periods, the intercompany profit identified with the asset decreases in proportion to the decrease taking place in the asset as a result of the recorded depreciation. For example, if the equipment has a 5-year life, the asset would be reported at only 4/5 of its original cost at the end of the first year, and the intercompany profit included in such cost is correspondingly only 4/5 of the profit originally recognized. Instead of applying the reduction to the equipment account at this point, the reduction must be applied both to the asset balance and to the allowance for depreciation balance, each of these accounts now being overstated. The elimination would be made as follows:

	Co. P	Co. S	Eliminations Dr.	Eliminations Cr.	Consolidated Balance Sheet Dr.	Consolidated Balance Sheet Cr.
Debits						
Equipment		10,000		4,000	6,000	
Allowance for Depreciation of Equipment		(2,000)	800			1,200
Credits						
Retained Earnings, Co. P			3,200			

The asset is reduced by the intercompany profit, $4,000; the allowance is reduced by the depreciation on such intercompany profit, 20% of $4,000, or $800. Asset and allowance balances are now reduced to a cost basis and equipment is reported on the consolidated balance sheet as follows:

Equipment	$6,000	
Less allowance for depreciation of equipment	1,200	
Book value		$4,800

The annual depreciation recognized by the subsidiary is 20% of $10,000, or $2,000; depreciation in terms of actual cost, however, is 20% of $6,000, or $1,200. Inasmuch as the parent company recognizes 100% of the subsidiary earnings, the parent company's retained earnings are adversely affected each year by the excessive charge of $800. Although the intercompany profit at the time of the asset sale was $4,000, the intercompany profit at the end of the first year has been reduced to $3,200. Reduction of the asset book value to cost cancels this balance. All reference to intercompany profit is thus canceled.

The eliminations for intercompany profit that are required on the working papers over the life of the asset are listed below.

	Retained Earnings, Company P Dr.	Allowance for Depreciation of Equipment Dr.	Equipment Cr.
Date of transfer	$4,000	$ —	$4,000
End of first year	3,200	800	4,000
End of second year	2,400	1,600	4,000
End of third year	1,600	2,400	4,000
End of fourth year	800	3,200	4,000
End of fifth year	—	4,000	4,000

At the end of the fifth year, the cost of the equipment is completely written off. The profit of $4,000 recognized by the parent at the time of construction has been canceled entirely by excessive depreciation of $4,000 recorded by the subsidiary and recognized by the parent. No further eliminations are required.

Depreciable asset constructed by parent for partially owned subsidiary. If, in the previous example, the parent had owned only 80% of the stock of the subsidiary, eliminations each year would be the same as those given. For consolidated statement purposes, then, the asset is reported at its actual cost and the allowance for depreciation reflects amortization of such cost. Here, too, the subsidiary records annual depreciation that is excessive in terms of cost by $800; however, since the parent recognizes only 80% of the earnings of the subsidiary, the parent company's retained earnings are adversely affected by only $640 each year. Since the elimination for intercompany profit decreases annually by $800, the parent company's retained earnings are left each year with a $160 credit excess. This is the periodic profit that accrues to the parent through charging the minority interest with depreciation on the asset at its sales price. At the end of 5 years, the cost of the asset will have been written off entirely; the parent company retained earnings will reflect an $800 net increase resulting from the original profit of $4,000 on the sale less the charges on this addition to cost carried back to the parent, 80% of $4,000, or $3,200. The increase in the parent interest was accompanied by a shrinkage in the minority interest as a result of the charges that were absorbed by the latter on the amount added to the asset cost, 20% of $4,000.

Depreciable asset constructed by wholly owned subsidiary for parent. Assume that Company P acquires certain equipment from its subsidiary Company S, 100% owned. Company P is charged $10,000; the cost to Company S is $6,000. Equipment has a 5-year life. Here, the subsidiary recognizes a profit of $4,000 on the transfer. Since the parent owns all of the stock of the subsidiary, the entire profit accrues to the parent and subsequent eliminations of intercompany profit must be assigned in full to the parent. In preparing a consolidated balance sheet at the date of asset acquisition, intercompany profit of $4,000 is eliminated. In subsequent periods, the amounts to be eliminated will be the same as those in the first example. The intercompany profit of $4,000 recognized by the parent on the original transfer is canceled annually, then, through (1) the excess depreciation recorded by the subsidiary and subsequently recognized by the parent and (2) the charge that is made to the parent in reducing the asset to cost.

Depreciable asset constructed by partially owned subsidiary for parent. Assume the same facts as in the preceding example except that the subsidiary is only 80% owned. In this case, 80% of the profit of $4,000 will be recognized as retained earnings of the parent and 20% as retained earnings of the minority interest. In preparing working papers for a consolidated balance sheet on the date of asset acquisition, the equipment is reduced to cost and the intercompany profit is canceled by reductions in the retained earnings of the parent of $3,200 and in the retained earnings of the minority interest of $800.

Eliminations on working papers in subsequent periods will also be applied against the asset balance and the related parent and minority interests. However, as the asset balance goes down, the intercompany profit in the asset and in the parent and minority interests goes down correspondingly. Eliminations that are required on the working papers over the life of the asset are listed below.

	Retained Earnings, Company P Dr.	Retained Earnings, Company S Minority Interest Dr.	Allowance for Depreciation of Equipment Dr.	Equipment Cr.
Date of transfer..	$3,200	$800	$ —	$4,000
End of first year.	2,560	640	800	4,000
End of second year	1,920	480	1,600	4,000
End of third year	1,280	320	2,400	4,000
End of fourth year	640	160	3,200	4,000
End of fifth year.	—	—	4,000	4,000

It may be noted that although a charge of $800 is applied against the minority interest at the time of the asset transfer for consolidated statement purposes, subsequent charges are reduced by $160 each year (1/5 of $800) and the minority interest shows a corresponding increase of $160. This is the periodic profit that accrues to the minority interest through charging the parent with depreciation on the asset at its sales price. At the end of 5 years the full cost of the asset will be written off; the minority interest will reflect an $800 net increase representing the original profit on the sale of $4,000 less the portion of the profit that was carried back to the parent, 80% of $4,000, or $3,200. On the other hand, a charge of $3,200 is applied to the parent company retained earnings at the time of the asset transfer, but subsequent charges are reduced by $640 per year (1/5 of $3,200) and retained earnings of the parent are thus increased by $640 annually. At the same time the parent recognizes annual depreciation on the asset at 20% of $10,000, or $2,000; depreciation in terms of actual asset cost, however, is 20% of $6,000, or $1,200. A charge for depreciation of $800 counterbalanced only in part by an increase in retained earnings of $640 results in an annual shrinkage in parent company retained earnings of $160. This is the periodic cost to the controlling interest resulting from a purchase made from a subsidiary on which a profit is shared with a minority interest.

As in the case of eliminations for intercompany profits on inventories, if the parent employs the equity method in carrying subsidiary investments, eliminations for intercompany profits are applied to retained earnings of the parent and of the subsidiary companies; if the parent employs the cost method, the full charge for intercompany profits may be made to the subsidiary retained earnings and retained earnings identified with the minority and with the parent calculated in terms of such adjusted balance.

Other transfers. When a depreciable asset is acquired by a subsidiary company from another subsidiary or when such an asset is acquired after a series of transfers within the affiliated group, careful analysis is required in arriving at the intercompany profit to be eliminated. The analyses involved are similar to those described in the earlier section on inventory eliminations.

Income taxes on intercompany profits. Federal income tax regulations provide that under certain conditions "affiliated corporations" may elect to file a consolidated income tax return. The Internal Revenue Code defines "affiliated corporations" and prescribes the special conditions under which such a group can file a consolidated return. In filing a consolidated income tax return, intercompany profits arising from the sale of merchandise, plant and equipment items, or other assets are eliminated. When affiliated companies do not choose to file a consolidated return or when they are not eligible for such filing, each company is required to file a separate return. In such separate filings, individual companies are required to include profits arising from sales to affiliated units.

When income taxes are paid on profits on intercompany sales of assets, and assets are still in the hands of an affiliate at the time of consolidation, the taxes should be deferred or they should be recognized as increasing the costs of the assets for consolidated purposes. Eliminations against parent and minority interests, then, should be limited to the intercompany profits after income taxes.[1] For purposes of illustrations and problems, eliminations are made without regard to the income tax adjustments that would be appropriate under the circumstances mentioned.

Acquisition of property prior to date of effective control. When inventories or other properties are acquired from an affiliated company

[1]The Committee on Accounting Procedure comments: "If income taxes have been paid on intercompany profits on assets remaining within the group, such taxes should be deferred or the intercompany profits to be eliminated in consolidation should be appropriately reduced." (*Accounting Research Bulletin No. 51*, "Consolidated Financial Statements," 1959, New York: American Institute of Certified Public Accountants, p. 46.)

prior to the date of affiliation, such assets are properly shown on the consolidated balance sheet at the prices at which they were transferred. No eliminations for intercompany profits are required in such instances inasmuch as the companies were not affiliated at the time the sales were completed.

INTERCOMPANY BOND HOLDINGS

The acquisition by one company of bonds of an affiliated unit gives rise to an intercompany debtor-creditor relationship similar to those already described. However, certain features of this relationship and the problems that result from such features require consideration.

When bonds of one company are acquired by an affiliated company, intercompany holdings should be eliminated and only the bonds held by outsiders should be shown on the consolidated balance sheet. The investment in bonds may be offset against bonds payable, only the bonds held by outsiders being reported on the statement. However, in view of the fact that bonds held within the affiliated group can be pledged or issued to outsiders and thus represent a ready source of cash, it may be preferable to report holdings separately as a deduction from the full amount of bonds issued in the same manner as treasury bonds. When the latter procedure is to be followed, both bond investment and liability balances are extended to the consolidated balance sheet columns of the working papers. Bonds held can then be reported on the consolidated balance sheet as follows:

Bonds payable	$200,000	
Less bonds held by affiliated company	50,000	
Bonds outstanding		$150,000

Bonds may be issued at a premium or a discount. Bonds of an affiliated company may be acquired on the market at a price that differs from the amount at which they are carried by the issuing company. Such conditions serve to complicate matters. In viewing parent and subsidiary as one company, both the intercompany bonds and any premium or discount balance related to such holdings lose their significance and must be eliminated. The amount paid for bonds is viewed as the cost of bond retirement; a difference between investment cost and the carrying value of the obligation is recognized as a loss or a gain from bond retirement. Furthermore, such a loss or a gain must be identified as a parent company item or as a subsidiary company item so that it may be properly assigned to controlling and minority interests.

The examples that follow illustrate the nature of the analysis that is required.

Subsidiary acquisition of parent company bonds. Assume that Company P issued 10-year bonds of $100,000 at 90. Two years after the issue, bonds of $10,000 are acquired on the market by subsidiary Company S for $9,400. In preparing working papers for a consolidated balance sheet, the elimination for intercompany bonds can be made as follows:

	Co. P	Co. S	Eliminations		Consolidated Balance Sheet	
			Dr.	Cr.	Dr.	Cr.
Debits						
Investment in Co. P Bonds (face value, $10,000)		9,400		9,400		
Credits						
Bonds Payable	100,000		10,000			90,000
Discount on Bonds Payable	(8,000)			800	7,200	
Retained Earnings, Co. P			200		200	

The liability balance appears on the books of Company P; regardless of who acquires the bonds, then, the reacquisition must be viewed as the retirement of Company P bonds, with any gain or loss accruing to the latter company. The elimination on the working papers gives effect to such an analysis. The entire loss is identified with the parent company; no gain or loss can be related to the subsidiary company that has simply made an investment. If the parent company were to authorize the acquisition of the bonds from the subsidiary at $9,400 and their retirement, the $200 loss would actually be recorded on the books of the parent company and no further reference to such intercompany holdings would be required.

If it is desired to report intercompany bond holdings as treasury bonds, only reciprocal discount balances are eliminated. The entire discount is canceled in the bond investment balance by a charge to the bond account that raises the investment to par; 1/10 of the discount on bonds payable is canceled since 1/10 of the issue is held within the affiliated group. The bond investment balance at par can then be subtracted from bonds payable at par in drawing up the consolidated balance sheet. The balance of the discount on bonds payable represents the discount on bonds held by outsiders. Working papers will appear as shown at the top of the following page.

Assume that a consolidated balance sheet is prepared one year after the acquisition of the bonds by the subsidiary. Amortization of the discount on the books of Company P has reduced the discount balance by $1,000 (the original discount of $10,000 is amortized over a 10-year bond

	Co. P	Co. S	Eliminations Dr.	Eliminations Cr.	Consolidated Balance Sheet Dr.	Consolidated Balance Sheet Cr.
Debits						
Investment in Co. P Bonds (face value, $10,000)		9,400	600		10,000	
Credits						
Bonds Payable	100,000					100,000
Discount on Bonds Payable	(8,000)			800	7,200	
Retained Earnings, Co. P			200		200	

period); accumulation of the discount on the books of Company S has raised the investment balance by $75 (the discount on the acquisition of $600 is accumulated over an 8-year holding period). Assuming that intercompany bond holdings are to be recognized as treasury bonds, working papers for a consolidated balance sheet would be prepared as follows:

	Co. P	Co. S	Eliminations Dr.	Eliminations Cr.	Consolidated Balance Sheet Dr.	Consolidated Balance Sheet Cr.
Debits						
Investment in Co. P Bonds (face value, $10,000)		9,475	525		10,000	
Credits						
Bonds Payable	100,000					100,000
Discount on Bonds Payable	(7,000)			700	6,300	
Retained Earnings, Co. P			175		175	

Interest transactions were recorded on the books of the two companies during the year in terms of a debtor-creditor relationship; in developing the consolidated statements, however, amounts applying to intercompany bond holdings are canceled to give effect to the single company view.

Parent acquisition of subsidiary company bonds. Assume that it is subsidiary Company S that issues 10-year bonds of $100,000 at 90. Two years after the issue, the parent acquires bonds of $10,000 at $9,400. Again, for consolidation purposes the acquisition of the bonds is considered analagous to a company's retirement of its own bonds. Here, too, the price of such a retirement differs from the carrying value of the bonds and a loss must be recognized. In this case, however, it is bonds of the subsidiary that are retired at a loss; the loss, then, is related to the subsidiary company and not to the parent. If the subsidiary is wholly owned, the full amount of the loss must be assigned to the parent company. If the subsidiary is only partly owned, the loss must be assigned in part to the minority interest and in part to the parent. Assuming that the parent owns 80% of the stock of the subsidiary and that intercompany bond holdings are to be recognized as treasury bonds, working papers for a consolidated balance sheet may be prepared as follows:

Assuming investments are carried by the equity method:

	Co. P	Co. S	Eliminations		Consolidated Balance Sheet	
			Dr.	Cr.	Dr.	Cr.
Debits						
Investment in Co. S Bonds (face value, $10,000)	9,400		600		10,000	
Credits						
Bonds Payable		100,000				100,000
Discount on Bonds Payable		(8,000)		800	7,200	
Retained Earnings, Co. P	50,000		160			49,840
Retained Earnings, Co. S		10,000	40			
Eliminate 80%			8,000			
Minority Interest, 20% of $10,000, less $40						1,960

Assuming investments are carried by the cost method:

	Co. P	Co. S	Eliminations		Consolidated Balance Sheet	
			Dr.	Cr.	Dr.	Cr.
Debits						
Investment in Co. S Bonds (face value, $10,000)	9,400		600		10,000	
Credits						
Bonds Payable		100,000				100,000
Discount on Bonds Payable		(8,000)		800	7,200	
Retained Earnings, Co. P	46,000					46,000
Retained Earnings, Co. S		10,000	200			
Eliminate 80% as above			4,000			
Minority Interest, 20% of $9,800						1,960
Retained Earnings to Parent						3,840

The loss of $200 by Company S is identified with the equities that must absorb this loss: 80% of $200, or $160, is assigned to the parent company, and 20% of $200, or $40, is assigned to the minority interest. If the parent were to authorize the transfer of the bonds to the subsidiary for $9,400 and their retirement, the $200 loss would actually be recorded in the subsidiary's books and no further reference to such intercompany holdings would be required.

When bonds of a related company are acquired at a price that is less than that at which they are carried on the books of the debtor, instead of treating the credit that emerges from the elimination of reciprocal items as an increase in the parent and minority equities, conservatism might suggest that such an excess be recognized as a deferred revenue balance under a heading such as "Unrealized Gain on Intercompany Bond Holdings." If the affiliate holding the bonds were to sell these to the issuing company at cost, a gain would emerge on the books of the latter company; however, if the sale were to be made to outsiders at cost, the gain would not be realized. Treatment of a credit excess as deferred revenue recognizes the latter possibility.

QUESTIONS

1. (a) A company establishes a subsidiary and acquires all of the stock of the latter company at a price in excess of the par value of the stock. How will the premium on the subsidiary's books be reported on the consolidated balance sheet? (b) Assume that a company acquires an 80% interest in a subsidiary by the purchase of two blocks of stock at amounts in excess of par value, one block of 60% from original stockholders of the company and one block of 20% directly from the corporation. How will the premium on the subsidiary's books be reported on the consolidated balance sheet?

2. Describe the special problem that arises in the preparation of a consolidated balance sheet when a parent's holdings in a subsidiary company consist of both preferred and common shares.

3. In the preparation of a consolidated balance sheet, explain how the retained earnings balance of a subsidiary company would be apportioned between preferred stock and common stock, assuming that:

(a) Preferred is noncumulative and nonparticipating.
(b) Preferred is cumulative and nonparticipating; dividends are 3 years in arrears.
(c) Preferred is noncumulative and participates ratably with common.
(d) Preferred is cumulative and participates ratably with common; only dividends for the current year are unpaid.

4. Assume a deficit instead of a retained earnings balance in Question 3. How would such a deficit be apportioned between preferred and common shares under each of the assumptions listed?

5. (a) How does a parent recognize the receipt from a subsidiary company of a stock dividend of common shares on common held? (b) In preparing working papers for a consolidated balance sheet subsequent to the stock dividend, how are eliminations made assuming that investments are carried by (1) the equity method and (2) the cost method?

6. What special problem arises in the preparation of a consolidated balance sheet when inventories include goods acquired from affiliated units?

7. What eliminations for intercompany profit are required in the preparation of a consolidated balance sheet assuming each of the conditions listed below? Where alternative procedures are possible, describe these.

(a) A parent's inventory includes goods acquired from a wholly owned subsidiary.
(b) A parent's inventory includes goods acquired from a partly owned subsidiary.
(c) The inventory of a wholly owned subsidiary includes goods acquired from a parent.
(d) The inventory of a partly owned subsidiary includes goods acquired from a parent.
(e) The inventory of a partly owned subsidiary includes goods acquired from a wholly owned subsidiary.
(f) The inventory of a wholly owned subsidiary includes goods acquired from a partly owned subsidiary.

8. What special problems are found in the elimination of intercompany profits on depreciable assets?

9. Company P controls Company S through ownership of the stock of the latter company. The parent has acquired certain depreciable assets from the subsidiary and these are 25% depreciated on the date a consolidated balance sheet for the affiliated companies is prepared. Describe the eliminations that are required in canceling the intercompany profit on the depreciable assets, indicating alternative procedures where possible, assuming that (a) the subsidiary company is wholly owned and (b) the subsidiary is partly owned.

10. The London Company acquires 90% of the outstanding common stock of the James Company on April 10, 1967. The James Company had completed a building for the London Company at the end of 1966 at a cost of $60,000, receiving $85,000 on the contract. Would you recommend any elimination for intercompany profits in preparing a consolidated balance sheet at the date of stock acquisition? Explain.

11. What elimination is made on the consolidated working papers when bonds of an 80%-owned subsidiary are acquired by a parent at an amount that exceeds that at which they are carried on the books of the subsidiary?

12. Give two alternative procedures that may be employed for reporting a credit excess that emerges from the elimination of bonds of an affiliate acquired at an amount that is less than that at which they are carried on the books of the issuing company. Evaluate the alternatives and indicate your preference.

EXERCISES

1. Fields, Inc. acquired control of the Goodyear Manufacturing Company through purchases of stock of the latter company as follows:

5,000 shares on the market, cost	$635,000
2,500 shares directly from the corporation at 130	325,000
Total investment	$960,000

Just before purchase of the stock by Fields, Inc. the capital of the Goodyear Manufacturing Company was:

Capital stock, $100 par (10,000 shares authorized, 6,500 shares issued)	$650,000	
Additional paid-in capital	300,000	$950,000
Less deficit		45,000
Total capital		$905,000

Determine as of the date of purchase (a) the cost or book value excess on the investment, and (b) the minority interest.

2. The Ardmore Company has stock outstanding as follows:

Common, 5,000 shares, $100 par	$500,000
6% Preferred, 1,000 shares, $100 par (liquidating value of shares is equal to par value)	100,000

Assuming a retained earnings balance at the end of 1967 of $60,000, state what part of such retained earnings should be recognized as preferred stockholders' equity and what part as common stockholders' equity if the preferred stock is:

(a) Noncumulative and nonparticipating.
(b) Cumulative, dividends paid to date, and nonparticipating.
(c) Cumulative, dividends two years in arrears (1966 and 1967), and nonparticipating.
(d) Noncumulative and fully participating.
(e) Noncumulative, dividends not paid for two years (1966 and 1967), and fully participating.
(f) Cumulative, dividends paid to date, and fully participating.
(g) Cumulative, dividends two years in arrears (1966 and 1967), and fully participating.

3. Assume in Exercise 2 that there is a deficit of $60,000 at the end of 1967 instead of the retained earnings balance. How should the deficit be apportioned between preferred and common equities in each instance listed?

4. On January 1, 1967, the Webley Corporation purchased 500 shares of Vinson Corporation preferred stock at 90 and 1,600 shares of Vinson Corporation common stock at 50. Investments are carried by the equity method. The capital of the Vinson Corporation on December 31, 1967, was as follows:

6% Preferred stock, 1,000 shares, $100 par............... (Dividends of $12,000 are in arrears on December 31, 1967; liquidating value of shares is equal to par)	$100,000
Common stock, 2,000 shares, $100 par.................	200,000
Additional paid-in capital...........................	30,000
Retained earnings....................................	15,000

Retained earnings of the Vinson Corporation on January 1, 1967, were $40,000. At the beginning of 1967 there were dividends in arrears on the preferred stock of $36,000. Dividend distributions to preferred stockholders in 1967 totaled $30,000.

From the foregoing information, give:

(a) The eliminations that would be made on consolidated working papers (1) on the date of acquisition of the stock and (2) on December 31, 1967.
(b) The cost or book value excess on the investment to be reported on the consolidated balance sheet as a result of the purchases.
(c) The change in the parent company retained earnings as a result of subsidiary operations during 1967.

5. The R. E. Whitaker Corporation, a holding company, carries investments at cost. On June 30, 1966, it purchased 16,000 shares of Lowell Company stock at 12. Capital changes of the Lowell Company were:

	Capital Stock ($5 par)	Retained Earnings
Balances, January 1, 1966...............	$100,000	$120,000
Profit for 1966..........................		30,000
	$100,000	$150,000
Cash dividends, December 1966..........		(10,000)
Balances, December 31, 1966.............	$100,000	$140,000
Profit for 1967..........................		20,000
	$100,000	$160,000
Stock dividend issued in June, 1967.......	50,000	(50,000)
	$150,000	$110,000
Cash dividends, December, 1967..........		(10,000)
Balances, December 31, 1967.............	$150,000	$100,000

(a) What elimination is required on the working papers for a consolidated balance sheet on December 31, 1967?
(b) In preparing the consolidated balance sheet on December 31, 1967, what is (1) the cost or book value excess on the investment, (2) the minority interest, and (3) the retained earnings accruing to the parent since date of acquisition?

6. The Thurston Corporation issued 10-year 5% bonds of $500,000 at 90 on April 1, 1965. Interest is payable semiannually on April 1 and October 1. L. D. Scott Corporation owns 80% of the stock of the Thurston Corporation. The parent company acquired Thurston Corporation bonds, face value $100,000, at 94 on April 1, 1967. (a) What adjusting entries are required to record the accrued interest on bonds on the books of the two companies on December 31, 1967? (b) What eliminations will be made on the working papers for a consolidated balance sheet on this date if the investment in the subsidiary is carried by the equity method?

7. Company P owns 90% of the stock of Company S1 and 80% of the stock of Company S2. Investments are carried by the equity method. Intercompany sales of merchandise are made at a gross profit of 20% of sales. (a) Give the elimination in each case below to cancel the intercompany profit. (b) Give the elimination in each case if only the profit recognized by the parent is to be canceled.

(1) Merchandise held by Company P, acquired from Company S1 for $10,000.
(2) Merchandise held by Company S1, acquired from Company P for $10,000.
(3) Merchandise held by Company S2, acquired from Company S1 for $10,000.
(4) Merchandise held by Company S2, acquired from Company S1 for $10,000; merchandise was originally purchased by Company S1 from Company P for $8,000.
(5) Merchandise held by Company P, acquired from Company S1 for $10,000; merchandise was originally purchased by Company S1 from Company S2 for $8,000.

8. On December 31, 1966, the Anderson Corporation completed the construction of a building for the Jenkins Company. The charge made for construction was $100,000. The cost of construction was $80,000. The life of the building is estimated at 20 years.

What elimination will be made on the working papers for a consolidated balance sheet on December 31, 1966, on December 31, 1967, and on December 31, 1968, assuming that:

(a) Anderson Corporation is the parent company and owns 100% of the stock of the Jenkins Company.
(b) Anderson Corporation is the parent company and owns 80% of the stock of the Jenkins Company.
(c) Jenkins Company is the parent company and owns 100% of the stock of the Anderson Corporation. (Assume that the investment is carried at equity.)
(d) Jenkins Company is the parent company and owns 80% of the stock of the Anderson Corporation. (Assume that the investment is carried at equity.)

9. Company P owns 80% of the stock of Company Y and 90% of the stock of Company Z. Both holdings were acquired prior to 1956 and are carried at cost. Give any adjustments and eliminations that are required on the consolidated working papers on December 31, 1967, as a result of the following information available on this date:

(a) Company P has in its inventory goods of $48,300 acquired from Company Z. Merchandise is sold by Company Z at 15% above cost.
(b) Company Y has in its inventory goods of $6,000 acquired from Company P. The cost of the goods was $5,000.

(c) Company P owns Company Y bonds. The investment is shown at $9,700; the face value of the bonds owned is $10,000. On this date the books of Company Y show bonds payable of $100,000 and an unamortized premium on bonds payable of $2,500.
(d) Company P shows equipment of $40,000 acquired from Company Y at the end of March, 1958. The equipment was constructed by Company Y and was sold at a gross profit of 25% of sales price. The equipment is being depreciated on a 20-year basis.
(e) Company Z announced a dividend of $5,000 but Company P has not yet recognized the dividend.
(f) Company Z remitted $6,000 to Company Y in payment of an advance. Company Y has not yet received the remittance.
(g) Company P as an accommodation to Company Z gave the latter company a note for $50,000. Company Z then discounted the note at the bank to obtain cash. As a result of the two transactions, Company Z shows on its books Notes Receivable, $50,000, Notes Receivable Discounted, $50,000, and Advances from Company P, $50,000.

PROBLEMS

13-1. At the beginning of 1967, the Johnson Company acquired all of the treasury stock of the Sperry Company at a purchase price of $195,000 and also 70,000 shares on the open market at a price of 12½. A balance sheet for the Sperry Company on December 31, 1966, showed the following:

Assets			$1,650,000
Liabilities			$ 375,000
Stockholders' equity:			
Capital stock, $5 par, 100,000 shares issued	$500,000		
Less treasury stock, 15,000 shares at par	75,000		
Outstanding, 85,000 shares		$425,000	
Additional paid-in capital		250,000	
Retained earnings		600,000	1,275,000
Total liabilities and stockholders' equity			$1,650,000

At the end of 1967, balance sheets for the Johnson Company and the Sperry Company were as follows:

		Johnson Co.		Sperry Co.
Investment in Sperry Co. stock		$1,070,000		
Other assets		5,000,000		$1,940,000
Total assets		$6,070,000		$1,940,000
Liabilities		$1,200,000		$ 385,000
Capital stock	($10 par)	2,500,000	($5 par)	750,000
Additional paid-in capital		720,000		370,000
Retained earnings		1,650,000		435,000
Total liabilities and stockholders' equity		$6,070,000		$1,940,000

An analysis of changes in retained earnings in 1967 for each company follows:

	Johnson Co.	Sperry Co.
Balances, January 1, 1967	$1,590,000	$ 600,000
Stock dividend declared June 1, payable June 15, 1967		(250,000)
Cash dividends declared December 1, payable December 15, 1967	(375,000)	(150,000)
Net income for year (including dividends received from affiliates)	435,000	235,000
Balances, December 31, 1967	$1,650,000	$ 435,000

Instructions: Prepare working papers and a consolidated balance sheet as of December 31, 1967.

13-2. The Patterson Company owns controlling interests in the Carey Company, the Drake Company, and Eaton, Inc. These interests were acquired in 1958. Balance sheets prepared for these companies on December 31, 1967, were as follows:

	Patterson Co.	Carey Co.	Drake Co.	Eaton, Inc.
Investment in Carey Co. (18,000 shares)	$ 295,000			
Investment in Drake Co. (20,500 shares)	240,000			
Investment in Eaton, Inc. (17,500 shares)	140,000			
Other assets	1,265,000	$475,000	$410,000	$285,000
Total assets	$1,940,000	$475,000	$410,000	$285,000
Payables	$ 750,000	$180,000	$125,000	$100,000
Capital stock	1,280,000	200,000	250,000	200,000
Additional paid-in capital	75,000	50,000	15,000	25,000
Retained earnings (deficit)	(165,000)	45,000	20,000	(40,000)
Total liabilities and stockholders' equity	$1,940,000	$475,000	$410,000	$285,000

Stock of the Patterson Company is no par, 50,000 shares being outstanding. Capital stock of each of the subsidiaries has a stated value of $10 per share.

The parent company recognizes profits and losses of subsidiary companies in its investment accounts and treats dividends as a reduction in investment balances. No entries had been made, however, to record changes in subsidiary equities that took place in 1967, including the dividends declared by the Carey Company in December, 1967. Changes in capital in 1967 were as follows:

	Patterson Co.	Carey Co.	Drake Co.	Eaton, Inc.
Retained earnings (deficit), January 1, 1967	($245,000)	$ 50,000	$ 35,000	($50,000)
Net income (loss), 1967	80,000	25,000	(15,000)	10,000
	($165,000)	$ 75,000	$ 20,000	($40,000)
Dividends declared in December, 1967, payable in January, 1968		(30,000)		
Retained earnings (deficit), Dec. 31, 1967	($165,000)	$ 45,000	$ 20,000	($40,000)

The parent company's inventories on December 31, 1967, included merchandise of \$75,000 acquired from the Carey Company and merchandise of \$30,000 acquired from the Drake Company. Merchandise was sold to the parent by subsidiaries at a 20% gross profit on sales price. Intercompany advances and current trade balances on December 31, 1967, totaled \$100,000.

Instructions: (1) Give the entries to bring the parent company's books up to date on December 31, 1967.

(2) Prepare working papers and a consolidated balance sheet as of December 31, 1967.

13-3. Account balances as of December 31, 1967, for Reagon Company and Sears Company appear below:

	Reagon Co.	Sears Co.
Current assets	\$ 652,500	\$ 560,000
Investment in Sears Co. common stock	200,000	
Investment in Sears Co. bonds	87,500	
Plant and equipment	1,400,000	685,000
Allowance for depreciation	(260,000)	(420,000)
Total assets	\$2,080,000	\$ 825,000
Current liabilities	\$ 310,000	\$ 125,000
6% bonds payable	500,000	250,000
Discount on bonds payable	(20,000)	(15,000)
6% cumulative nonparticipating preferred stock, \$50 par		100,000
Common stock, \$10 par	650,000	300,000
Additional paid-in capital	200,000	
Retained earnings	440,000	65,000
Total liabilities and stockholders' equity	\$2,080,000	\$ 825,000

Reagon Company acquired 90% of the common stock of Sears Company at the end of 1960 for \$200,000. At that time Sears Company reported a deficit of \$35,000 and dividends on preferred stock were \$21,000 in arrears. However, dividends in arrears were cleared up at the end of 1965 and the company has paid dividends on common as well as on preferred in 1966 and 1967.

At the beginning of 1967, Reagon Company acquired land and buildings from Sears Company at a price of \$100,000; land was recorded at \$60,000 and buildings were recorded at \$40,000. The buildings were expected to have a remaining life of 8 years and Reagon Company recorded depreciation for 1967 at the rate of 12½%. Sears Company had carried the land at a cost of \$50,000 and the buildings at a cost of \$200,000 less accumulated depreciation of \$180,000, and it reported a gain on the sale of \$30,000.

At the end of 1967, Reagon Company purchased $100,000 of Sears Company bonds on the market, paying $90,000, which included $2,500 representing accrued interest for 5 months. The accrued interest on the investment is included in Reagon Company current assets; current liabilities of Sears Company include accrued interest on bonded debt of $6,250.

During 1967, sales of merchandise by Sears Company to Reagon Company totaled $75,000; cost of the goods to Sears Company was $60,000. On December 31, 1967, Reagon Company inventory included goods of $12,500 acquired from Sears Company. However, the accounts for Reagon Company do not show goods of $2,500 that are in transit; these goods had been recorded as a sale by Sears Company and had been shipped on December 30. On December 31, Sears Company showed a total of $8,500 due from Reagon Company on open account.

Current liabilities of Sears Company include a payable for dividends of $1.25 per share on common stock declared on December 20, 1967, and payable on February 5, 1968; no entry for the dividends has been made by Reagon Company.

Instructions: Prepare working papers and a consolidated balance sheet as of December 31, 1967.

13-4. Balance sheet data for the Madison Company and the Norwalk Company on December 31, 1967, follow:

	Madison Co.	Norwalk Co.
Current assets	$1,175,000	$500,000
Investment in Norwalk Co. stock	215,000	
Plant and equipment	525,000	200,000
Allowance for depreciation of plant and equipment	(335,000)	(50,000)
Goodwill	100,000	
Total assets	$1,680,000	$650,000
Current liabilities	$ 550,000	$260,000
6% preferred stock, cumulative and nonparticipating	250,000	100,000
Common stock:		
500,000 shares, no par	500,000	
50,000 shares, no par		250,000
Additional paid-in capital	120,000	
Retained earnings	180,000	40,000
Appraisal capital	80,000	
Total liabilities and stockholders' equity	$1,680,000	$650,000

The Madison Company acquired 80% of the common stock and 40% of the preferred stock of the Norwalk Company at the end of 1963 for a total of $215,000. At the date of acquisition the Norwalk Company showed retained earnings of $15,000. At this time there were dividends in arrears on preferred for the years 1961, 1962, and 1963. Since the date of acquisition of its stock by the Madison Company, the Norwalk Company has paid dividends on preferred totaling $30,000.

On December 31, 1967, Madison Company held merchandise of $80,000 acquired from the Norwalk Company. There was also merchandise in transit of $14,000 that the Madison Company had not recognized on its books. In its accounts receivable the Norwalk Company showed claims of $35,000 against the Madison Company, which included the charge for merchandise in transit. The gross profit on sales for 1967 reported by the Norwalk Company was 32%.

Instructions: Prepare working papers and a consolidated balance sheet on December 31, 1967.

13-5. On January 1, 1967, the Ryan Corporation acquired stock of Shell, Inc. as follows:

7,000 shares of common, $50 par, at 60
200 shares of 6% noncumulative and nonparticipating preferred, $100 par, at 150

On this date the Ryan Corporation also acquired 4,000 shares of Todd, Inc. no-par stock at 75. This represented an 80% interest.

Balance sheets of the three companies on December 31, 1967, were as follows:

	Ryan Corporation		Shell, Inc.		Todd, Inc.	
Cash		$ 178,000		$ 20,000		$ 25,000
Accounts receivable		520,000		115,000		90,000
Merchandise inventory		1,150,000		280,000		185,000
Machinery and equipment	$1,350,000		$400,000		$350,000	
Less allowance for depreciation	400,000	950,000	180,000	220,000	180,000	170,000
Buildings	$ 600,000		$260,000		$245,000	
Less allowance for depreciation	150,000	450,000	135,000	125,000	145,000	100,000
Land		60,000		40,000		35,000
Investment in Shell, Inc. stock		450,000				
Investment in Todd, Inc. stock		300,000				
Investment in Todd, Inc. bonds (face value, $20,000)		22,000				
Total assets		$4,080,000		$800,000		$605,000
Accounts payable		$1,000,000		$150,000		$ 79,800
Bonds payable		300,000				100,000
Premium on bonds payable						5,200
Preferred stock		500,000		100,000		
Common stock		1,500,000		400,000		220,000
Retained earnings		780,000		150,000		200,000
Total liabilities and stockholders' equity		$4,080,000		$800,000		$605,000

Changes in retained earnings for 1967 were as follows:

	Ryan Corporation	Shell, Inc.	Todd, Inc.
Balances, Jan. 1, 1967	$645,000	$116,000	$195,000
Dividends, 1967	(80,000)	(16,000)	(20,000)
	$565,000	$100,000	$175,000
Profits, 1967	215,000[1]	50,000	25,000
Balances, Dec. 31, 1967	$780,000	$150,000	$200,000

[1]Includes dividends received from subsidiaries.

On February 1, 1967, the Ryan Corporation began the construction of machinery for Todd, Inc. Construction and installation of the machinery was completed on June 1 at a cost to the Ryan Corporation of $75,000; the subsidiary was charged $90,000. The subsidiary recorded depreciation from June 1 at the rate of 10% a year.

Instructions: Prepare working papers and a consolidated balance sheet as of December 31, 1967.

13-6. Company P owns 85% of the stock of Company A and 90% of the stock of Company B. Account balances on December 31, 1967, were as follows:

	Co. P	Co. A	Co. B
Cash	$ 195,000	$ 40,000	$ 20,000
Accounts receivable	115,000	150,000	160,000
Inventories	310,000	207,500	270,000
Buildings, machinery and equipment (net)	500,000	415,000	300,000
Land	40,000	40,000	30,000
Investment in Co. A stock	425,000		
Investment in Co. B stock	460,000		
Investment in Co. A bonds	105,000		
Total assets	$2,150,000	$852,500	$780,000
Notes payable	$ 100,000	$ 45,000	$ 20,000
Accounts payable	150,000	90,000	170,000
Bonds payable	250,000	250,000	
Discount on bonds payable		(12,500)	
Capital stock	1,000,000	500,000	250,000
Retained earnings (deficit)	650,000	(20,000)	340,000
Total liabilities and stockholders' equity	$2,150,000	$852,500	$780,000

Stock in Companies A and B was acquired at the end of June, 1966. Changes in retained earnings have been as follows:

	Co. P	Co. A	Co. B
Retained earnings (deficit) balances, June 30, 1966	$564,000	($30,000)	$290,000
Profit (loss) from own operations, June 30–December 31, 1966	30,000	(15,000)	40,000
	$594,000	($45,000)	$330,000
Dividends paid by Co. P, December, 1966	(30,000)		
	$564,000	($45,000)	$330,000
Dividends paid by Co. B, December, 1966	13,500		(15,000)
Retained earnings (deficit) balances, December 31, 1966	$577,500	($45,000)	$315,000
Profit (loss) from own operations, 1967	90,000	25,000	50,000
	$667,500	($20,000)	$365,000
Dividends paid by Co. P, 1967	(40,000)		
	$627,500	($20,000)	$365,000
Dividends paid by Co. B, 1967	22,500		(25,000)
Retained earnings (deficit) balances, December 31, 1967	$650,000	($20,000)	$340,000

Intercompany sales of merchandise were made at 25% above cost. On December 31, 1967, the following information was available:

Co. B inventory includes:	merchandise acquired from Co. A for	$30,000
	merchandise acquired from Co. P for	25,000
Co. A inventory includes:	merchandise acquired from Co. P for	10,000
Co. P inventory includes:	merchandise acquired from Co. A for	35,000

Accounts receivable and accounts payable balances included $12,500 owed by Company B to Company A, $20,000 owed by Company B to Company P, and $5,000 owed by Company P to Company A.

The parent company acquired Company A bonds of $100,000 in July, 1966, at a premium and has been amortizing the premium properly. Company A originally issued the bonds at the beginning of 1958 at 90; the discount is being amortized over 20 years.

Instructions: Prepare working papers and a consolidated balance sheet as of December 31, 1967.

13-7. Prior to January 1, 1967, the stockholders of Large Company and Small Company approved the merger of the two companies. On January 1, 1967, 5,000 shares of Large Company common stock were issued to the Small Company stockholders in exchange for the 3,000 shares of Small Company common stock outstanding.

Balance sheets of the two companies on December 31, 1967, were as follows:

	Large Company	Small Company
Cash	$ 36,400	$ 28,200
Notes receivable	22,000	9,000
Accounts receivable	20,900	21,700
Accruals receivable	13,000	3,300
Inventories	81,200	49,600
Plant and equipment	83,200	43,500
Accumulated depreciation	(12,800)	(9,300)
Investment in Small Company	50,000	
Total assets	$293,900	$146,000
Notes payable	$ 4,000	$ 12,000
Accounts payable	42,000	19,600
Dividends payable		4,500
Accruals payable	2,600	2,100
Notes receivable discounted	8,100	
Capital stock, $10 par value	120,000	
Capital stock, $20 par value		60,000
Capital in excess of par	28,500	20,000
Retained earnings	88,700	27,800
Total liabilities and stockholders' equity	$293,900	$146,000

The following additional information is available:

(1) Net income for 1967 (disregard income taxes):

Large Company	$21,700
Small Company	10,200

(2) On December 31, 1967, Small Company owed Large Company $16,000 on open account and $8,000 in interest-bearing notes. Large Company discounted $3,000 of the notes received from Small Company with the First State Bank.

(3) On December 31, 1967, Small Company accrued interest payable of $120 on the notes payable to Large Company: $40 on the notes of $3,000 discounted with the bank and $80 on the remaining notes of $5,000. Large Company did not accrue interest receivable from Small Company.

(4) During 1967, Large Company sold merchandise that cost $30,000 to Small Company for $40,000. Small Company's December 31 inventory included $10,000 of this merchandise priced at Small Company's cost.

(5) On July 1, Small Company sold equipment that had a book value of $15,000 to Large Company for $17,000. Large Company recorded depreciation on it in the amount of $850 for 1967. The remaining life of the equipment at the date of sale was 10 years.

(6) Small Company shipped merchandise to Large Company on December 31, 1967, and recorded an account receivable of $6,000 for the sale. Small Company's cost for the merchandise was $4,800. Because the merchandise was in transit, Large Company did not record the transaction. The terms of the sale were f.o.b. shipping point.

(7) Small Company declared a dividend of $1.50 per share on December 30, 1967, payable on January 10, 1968. Large Company made no entry for the declaration.

Instructions: Prepare working papers for a consolidated balance sheet, assuming that the consolidation is to be accounted for as a pooling of interests. Formal journal entries are not required.

(AICPA adapted)

13-8. Four years ago The Astor Company acquired 50% of the preferred stock of the Barnes Corporation for $55,000 and 90% of that corporation's common stock for $195,000. At acquisition date the Barnes Corporation had retained earnings of $60,000, and dividends on the 5% cumulative preferred stock were not in arrears. The investments were recorded by The Astor Company at the book value shown by the Barnes Corporation at date of acquisition.

Consolidated statements are now being prepared as of December 31, 1967, for The Astor Company and its subsidiary. The financial position of the individual companies was as follows on that date:

The Astor Company

Miscellaneous assets	$116,000	Liabilities	$ 50,000
Investments:		Preferred stock (4%)	100,000
Barnes preferred	50,000	Common stock	100 000
Barnes common	234,000	Retained earnings	150,000
		Total liabilities and stock-	
Total assets	$400,000	holders' equity	$400,000

Barnes Corporation

Miscellaneous assets	$400,000	Liabilities	$ 60,000
		Preferred stock (5%)*	100,000
		Common stock	200 000
		Retained earnings	40,000
		Total liabilities and stock-	
Total assets	$400,000	holders' equity	$400,000

*Preferred stock dividends are 3 years in arrears. No dividends have been paid on common since acquisition by The Astor Company. Profit in 1964 was $8,000, but losses during the past 3 years have totaled $23,000.

Instructions: Prepare a consolidated balance sheet of the above companies as of December 31, 1967, in which all significant details given in the above information are fully disclosed. Present in good form schedules showing all computations needed. Comment on any items that require explanation.

(AICPA adapted)

13-9. The balance sheets of Company A and its subsidiaries, Companies B and C, as of December 31, 1967, are given at the top of the next page.

The dividends on the preferred stocks of the respective companies have all been paid during the year 1967.

	Companies		
	A	B	C
Assets			
Investments:			
Preferred capital stock of Co. B — 60%	$ 300,000		
Common capital stock of Co. B — 90%	800,000		
Common capital stock of Co. C — 90%	1,300,000		
Bonds of Co. B at cost	270,000		
Notes receivable — Co. B	20,000		
Other assets	2,000,000	$2,180,000	$2,000,000
Total assets	$4,690,000	$2,180,000	$2,000,000
Liabilities and Stockholders' Equity			
Capital stock:			
Preferred — 6%	$ 500,000	$ 500,000	$ 500,000
Common	1,100,000	150,000	500,000
Total capital stock	$1,600,000	$ 650,000	$1,000,000
Retained earnings:			
Balance — January 1, 1967	$1,100,000	$ 150,000	$ 300,000
Net profits for the year 1967	400,000	200,000	300,000
	$1,500,000	$ 350,000	$ 600 000
Dividends deducted	12,000	30,000	30,000
Retained earnings, December 31, 1967	$1,488,000	$ 320,000	$ 570,000
First mortgage 6% bonds outstanding	$1,000,000	$ 600,000	
Notes receivable discounted — Co. B	10,000		
Notes payable — Co. A		20,000	
Other liabilities	592,000	590,000	$ 430,000
Total liabilities	$1,602,000	$1,210,000	$ 430,000
Total liabilities and stockholders' equity	$4,690,000	$2,180,000	$2,000,000

The bonds of Company B, which mature December 31, 1974, were acquired by Company A on July 1, 1967, at 90.

Company A acquired its holding of the stock in Companies B and C in 1964 and has taken up its share of the earnings of these companies.

Instructions: Prepare a consolidated balance sheet as of December 31, 1967.

(AICPA adapted)

13-10. The following information pertains to Company A and its subsidiaries, Companies S-1 and S-2:

(1) Post-closing trial balances for Company A and its subsidiaries as of December 31, 1967, are given at the top of page 448.
(2) The investment accounts are carried at cost.
(3) At acquisition, dividends on preferred stock for 1964 and 1965 were in arrears. Preferred stock has a liquidation value of par plus all dividends in arrears and is nonvoting.

	Co. A	Co. S-1	Co. S-2
Investment in Co. S-1 (acquired January 1, 1966)			
Common Stock (90%)	$200,000		
Preferred Stock (40%)	40,000		
Investment in Co. S-2 (70%, acquired January 1, 1967)	59,300		
Current Assets	50,000	$ 50,000	$ 40,000
Machinery and Equipment	40,000	20,000	30,000
Allowance for Depreciation — Machinery and Equipment	(20,000)	(15,000)	(10,000)
Bonds of Co. S-2 (par $10,000)	10,100		
All Other Assets	600	313,000	70,180
Current Liabilities	(20,000)	(20,000)	(20,000)
Bonds Payable — 10 yrs., 4%, due December 31, 1972			(30,000)
Premium on Bonds Payable			(180)
Capital stock — Common, $100 par	(300,000)	(250,000)	(60,000)
Capital Stock — Preferred, 5%, $100 par, cumulative and nonparticipating		(100,000)	
Premium on Preferred Stock		(10,000)	
Retained Earnings	(60,000)	12,000	(20,000)

(4) On January 1, 1967, Company S-1 declared a common stock dividend of $50,000 from Premium on Preferred Stock.

(5) The retained earnings accounts showed the following:

	Co. S-1	Co. S-2
Balance, January 1, 1966	($10,000)	$ 14,000
Profit, 1966	7,000	7,000
Cash dividends, 1967 — on January 1, 1967	(5,000)	
Cash dividends, 1967 — on December 31, 1967		(6,000)
Profit and Loss, 1967	(4,000)	5,000
Balance, December 31, 1967	($12,000)	$20,000

(6) The inventory of Company A includes $5,000 of merchandise purchased from Company S-2; cost to Company S-2 is marked up 25%.

(7) The inventory of Company S-2 includes $2,000 of merchandise purchased from Company S-1; markup by Company S-1 is 10% in selling price.

(8) Current liabilities include the following: Company S-1 owes Company A $1,000; Company S-2 owes Company A $2,000; Company S-1 owes Company S-2 $3,000; and Company A owes Company S-1 $2,000.

(9) Machinery having a life of 10 years was purchased by Company A from Company S-1 on January 1, 1966, for $10,000. Cost to Company S-1 was $7,000.

(10) Company S-2 neglected to amortize Premium on Bonds Payable for 1967.

Instructions: (1) Prepare working papers for a consolidated balance sheet as of December 31, 1967.

(2) Prepare a consolidated balance sheet as of December 31, 1967.

(AICPA adapted)

Chapter 14

CONSOLIDATED STATEMENTS

CHANGES IN INTEREST IN SUBSIDIARY

Illustrations in previous chapters have assumed that control of a subsidiary is achieved through a single purchase of stock and that the parent's interest remains unchanged throughout the period of control. A parent may acquire control of a subsidiary through several purchases of stock at different times and at varying prices. A parent may sell part of its holdings in the subsidiary, thus reducing its interest. A parent's interest may change as a result of the issuance of additional shares or the retirement of outstanding shares by the subsidiary company. The problems that arise in the preparation of the consolidated balance sheet when changes have taken place in the interests held in subsidiary companies are considered in this chapter.

SEVERAL PURCHASES: CONTROL ACHIEVED UPON FIRST PURCHASE

In some instances a parent may have a controlling interest in a subsidiary company and may subsequently increase this interest by the purchase of additional stock. Assume that Company P acquires stock of Company S as follows:

January 1, 1966, 800 shares at 120	\$ 96,000
July 1, 1967, 100 shares at 130	13,000
Total investment	\$109,000

The capital stock of each company is \$100,000, the shares having a par value of \$100. Retained earnings balances on December 31, 1965, and earnings and dividends for 1966 and 1967 are as follows:

	Co. P	Co. S
Retained earnings, December 31, 1965	\$60,000	\$15,000
Net income from own operations, 1966	15,000	20,000
Dividends declared, December, 1967	10,000	5,000
Net income from own operations, 1967	25,000	20,000

The investment account and the retained earnings of the parent company are affected by the foregoing information as follows:

	If Equity Method is Used		If Cost Method is Used	
	Investment in Co. S	Retained Earnings, Co. P	Investment in Co. S	Retained Earnings, Co. P
December 31, 1965:				
Balances		60,000		60,000
January 1, 1966:				
Purchase of 800 shares of Co. S stock at 120	96,000		96,000	
	96,000	60,000	96,000	60,000
December 31, 1966:				
Net income, 1966:				
Co. S, $20,000	16,000	16,000		
Co. P, $15,000		15,000		15,000
	112,000	91,000	96,000	75,000
July 1, 1967:				
Purchase of 100 shares of Co. S stock at 130	13,000		13,000	
	125,000	91,000	109,000	75,000
December, 1967:				
Dividends declared:				
Co. S, $5,000	(4,500)			4,500
Co. P, $10,000		(10,000)		(10,000)
	120,500	81,000	109,000	69,500
December 31, 1967:				
Net income, 1967:				
Co. S, $20,000	17,000	17,000		
Co. P, $25,000		25,000		25,000
December 31, 1967, Balances	137,500	123,000	109,000	94,500

Equity method. When the equity method is used in carrying the investment, special care is necessary in taking up earnings of the subsidiary. Earnings are taken up to the extent of the percentage of stock owned. When holdings of the parent are increased, the percentage of earnings to be taken up is increased as of the date of the additional purchase. In the example, Company P held 80% of Company S stock during all of 1966 and took up 80% of earnings of Company S for 1966. However, Company P increased its holdings to 90% on July 1, 1967. After July 1, then, the parent recognizes 90% of the earnings of the subsidiary. The net income taken up by Company P for 1967 is calculated as follows:

January 1–June 30, 1967: 80% × ($\frac{6}{12}$ × $20,000)	$ 8,000
July 1–December 31, 1967: 90% × ($\frac{6}{12}$ × $20,000)	9,000
Net income identified with parent's interest, January 1–December 31, 1967	$17,000

Working papers for a consolidated balance sheet on December 31, 1967, would be prepared as follows:

Equity method:

Company P and Subsidiary Company S
Working Papers for Consolidated Balance Sheet
December 31, 1967

	Co. P	Co. S	Eliminations		Consolidated Balance Sheet	
			Dr.	Cr.	Dr.	Cr.
Debits						
Investment in Co. S Stock	137,500					
Eliminate 90% of Capital Stock				90,000		
Eliminate 90% of Retained Earnings				45,000		
Excess of Cost over Book Value					2,500*	
Other Assets	205,500	220,000			425,500	
	343,000	220,000				
Credits						
Liabilities	120,000	70,000				190,000
Capital Stock, Co. P	100,000					100,000
Retained Earnings, Co. P	123,000					123,000
Capital Stock, Co. S		100,000				
Eliminate 90%			90,000			
Minority Interest, 10%						10,000
Retained Earnings, Co. S		50,000				
Eliminate 90%			45,000			
Minority Interest, 10%						5,000
	343,000	220,000	135,000	135,000	428,000	428,000

*An investment cost or book value excess in the illustrations in this and in the following chapter should be proved as already explained. In this case the excess of cost over the book value of the subsidiary interest is proved as follows:

Amount paid for 800 shares on January 1, 1966	$96,000	
Less book value of stock acquired, 80% of $115,000 ($100,000 + $15,000)	92,000	
Excess of cost over book value of subsidiary interest		$4,000
Amount paid for 100 shares on July 1, 1967	$13,000	
Less book value of stock acquired, 10% of $145,000 ($100,000 + $35,000 + [$\frac{6}{12}$ × $20,000])	14,500	
Excess of book value of subsidiary interest over cost		(1,500)
Net excess of cost over book value of subsidiary interest		$2,500

Cost method. If Company P uses the cost method in carrying the investment in Company S, working papers for a consolidated balance sheet would be prepared as shown on the next page.[1]

[1]The consolidated balance sheet obtained when the cost method is used should be compared with the consolidated balance sheet when the equity method is used for each of the cases in this and in the following chapter. Consolidated statements will be found to be the same.

Cost method:

Company P and Subsidiary Company S
Working Papers for Consolidated Balance Sheet
December 31, 1967

	Co. P	Co. S	Eliminations Dr.	Eliminations Cr.	Consolidated Balance Sheet Dr.	Consolidated Balance Sheet Cr.
Debits						
Investment in Co. S Stock	109,000					
Eliminate 90% of Capital Stock				90,000		
Eliminate 80% of $15,000, Retained Earnings Jan. 1, 1966				12,000		
Eliminate 10% of $45,000, Retained Earnings July 1, 1967				4,500		
Excess of Cost over Book Value					2,500	
Other Assets	205,500	220,000			425,500	
	314,500	220,000				
Credits						
Liabilities	120,000	70,000				190,000
Capital Stock, Co. P	100,000					100,000
Retained Earnings, Co. P	94,500					94,500
Capital Stock, Co. S		100,000				
Eliminate 90%			90,000			
Minority Interest, 10%						10,000
Retained Earnings, Co. S		50,000				
Eliminate as above			16,500			
Minority Interest, 10% of $50,000						5,000
Retained Earnings to Parent						28,500*
	314,500	220,000	106,500	106,500	428,000	428,000

*The retained earnings accruing to the parent in the illustrations in this and in the following chapter should be proved as already explained. In this case retained earnings accruing to Company P are proved as follows:

Retained earnings, July 1, 1967, date of change in percentage owned, $35,000 + ($\frac{6}{12}$ × $20,000)	$45,000	
Retained earnings, January 1, 1966, date stock was originally acquired	15,000	
Net increase in retained earnings, January 1, 1966, to July 1, 1967	$30,000	
Ownership interest during this period	80%	
Retained earnings accruing to parent, January 1, 1966, to July 1, 1967		$24,000
Retained earnings, December 31, 1967	$50,000	
Retained earnings, July 1, 1967, date when the additional 10% lot was acquired	45,000	
Net increase in retained earnings, July 1, 1967, to December 31, 1967	$ 5,000	
Ownership interest during this period	90%	
Retained earnings increase accruing to parent, July 1, 1967, to December 31, 1967		4,500
Total retained earnings accruing to parent, January 1, 1966, to December 31, 1967		$28,500

Eliminations on the working papers are based upon the retained earnings balances at the time each purchase of stock was made. The retained earnings balance on July 1, 1967, when the second purchase was made, is calculated as follows:

Retained earnings, January 1, 1967	$35,000
Add estimated earnings, January 1–July 1, 1967 ($\frac{6}{12}$ × $20,000, net income for year)	10,000
Retained earnings, July 1, 1967	$45,000

SEVERAL PURCHASES: CONTROL NOT ACHIEVED UPON FIRST PURCHASE

A company may obtain control of a subsidiary only after a second or subsequent purchase of the stock of that company. If the first purchase fails to give control, the preparation of a consolidated balance sheet and the recognition of the earnings on the investment equity are not warranted. Upon a subsequent purchase that makes control effective, however, consolidation is proper.

Upon the acquisition of control, the parent company properly recognizes the earnings that have accrued on the interests previously held from the dates of such acquisitions. In the absence of control in the past, equity changes relating to a noncontrolling interest in the subsidiary could be viewed as only of a contingent nature and could not be given accounting recognition; when control is achieved, recognition of past changes in the parent's equity is justified. For purposes of the consolidated balance sheet, then, the parent company recognizes the earnings of the subsidiary relating to each lot of stock from the date it was acquired to the balance sheet date just as when control is acquired on the first of several purchases.[1]

To illustrate, assume that Company P acquires stock of Company S as follows:

January 1, 1966, 250 shares at 130	$ 32,500
July 1, 1967, 600 shares at 140	84,000
Total	$116,500

The capital stock of each company is $100,000, each share with a par value of $100. Retained earnings balances on December 31, 1965, and earnings and dividends for 1966 and 1967 are:

[1]The Committee on Accounting Procedure of the American Institute of Certified Public Accountants in *Accounting Research Bulletin No. 51* observes that there may be circumstances calling for exceptional treatment. The Committee states, "If two or more purchases are made over a period of time, the earned surplus of the subsidiary at acquisition should generally be determined on a step-by-step basis; however, if small purchases are made over a period of time and then a purchase is made which results in control, the date of the latest purchase, as a matter of convenience, may be considered as the date of acquisition." (*Accounting Research Bulletin No. 51*, "Consolidated Financial Statements," 1959, New York: American Institute of Certified Public Accountants, p. 44.)

	Co. P	Co. S
Retained earnings, December 31, 1965	$65,000	$25,000
Dividends declared, December, 1966	10,000	5,000
Net income from own operations, 1966	20,000	10,000
Dividends declared, December, 1967	10,000	5,000
Net income from own operations, 1967	25,000	15,000

The investment account and retained earnings of the parent are affected by the foregoing as follows:

	If Equity Method is Used		If Cost Method is Used	
	Investment in Co. S	Retained Earnings, Co. P	Investment in Co. S	Retained Earnings, Co. P
December 31, 1965:				
Balances		65,000		65,000
January 1, 1966:				
Purchase of 250 shares of Co. S stock at 130	32,500		32,500	
	32,500	65,000	32,500	65,000
December, 1966:				
Dividends declared:				
Co. S, $5,000		1,250		1,250
Co. P, $10,000		(10,000)		(10,000)
	32,500	56,250	32,500	56,250
December 31, 1966:				
Net income, 1966:				
Co. S, $10,000				
Co. P, $20,000		20,000		20,000
	32,500	76,250	32,500	76,250
July 1, 1967:				
Purchase of 600 shares of Co. S stock at 140	84,000		84,000	
	116,500	76,250	116,500	76,250
December, 1967:				
Dividends declared:				
Co. S, $5,000	(4,250)			4,250
Co. P, $10,000		(10,000)		(10,000)
	112,250	66,250	116,500	70,500
December 31, 1967:				
Adjustment for earnings on 25% interest in Co. S held during 1966	1,250	1,250		
Net income, 1967:				
Co. S, $15,000	8,250	8,250		
Co. P, $25,000		25,000		25,000
December 31, 1967, Balances	121,750	100,750	116,500	95,500

Equity method. Earnings of the subsidiary company are disregarded and dividends are recognized as revenue until the parent acquires sufficient stock to give it a controlling interest. Upon obtaining a controlling interest, earnings accruing on the interest previously held are taken up in the investment account and thereafter the equity method is employed in the usual manner. In the example, the parent recognized earnings of the subsidiary at the end of 1967 as follows:

Earnings, 1966 (recognized by adjustment to investment account and to retained earnings): 25% of $5,000, this balance being determined as follows: Co. S net income, 1966, $10,000, less dividends paid in this period, $5,000 (parent recognized its share of dividends as revenue in 1966)		$1,250
Earnings, 1967: 25% of $7,500, Co. S net income January 1 — June 30 ($\frac{6}{12}$ × $15,000)	$1,875	
85% of $7,500, Co. S net income July 1 — December 31 ($\frac{6}{12}$ × $15,000)	6,375	$8,250

Working papers for a consolidated balance sheet on December 31, 1967, would be prepared as follows:

Equity method:

Company P and Subsidiary Company S
Working Papers for Consolidated Balance Sheet
December 31, 1967

	Co. P	Co. S	Eliminations Dr.	Eliminations Cr.	Consolidated Balance Sheet Dr.	Consolidated Balance Sheet Cr.
Debits						
Investment in Co. S Stock	121,750					
Eliminate 85% of Capital Stock				85,000		
Eliminate 85% of Retained Earnings				34,000		
Excess of Cost over Book Value					2,750	
Other Assets	159,000	200,000			359,000	
	280,750	200,000				
Credits						
Liabilities	80,000	60,000				140,000
Capital Stock, Co. P	100,000					100,000
Retained Earnings, Co. P	100,750					100,750
Capital Stock, Co. S		100,000				
Eliminate 85%			85,000			
Minority Interest, 15%						15,000
Retained Earnings, Co. S		40,000				
Eliminate 85%			34,000			
Minority Interest, 15%						6,000
	280,750	200,000	119,000	119,000	361,750	361,750

Cost method. When investments in subsidiaries are carried by the cost method, accounting for an investment in the stock of a company after control is achieved is the same as that employed before such control: earnings of the subsidiary are disregarded and dividends are recognized as revenue. The investment balance, then, reports only the costs of the different lots purchased. In preparing working papers for a consolidated balance sheet, the equities related to each lot in the investment account are eliminated. Working papers for a consolidated balance sheet would be prepared as follows:

Cost method:

Company P and Subsidiary Company S
Working Papers for Consolidated Balance Sheet
December 31, 1967

	Co. P	Co. S	Eliminations		Consolidated Balance Sheet	
			Dr.	Cr.	Dr.	Cr.
Debits						
Investment in Co. S Stock	116,500					
Eliminate 85% of Capital Stock				85,000		
Eliminate 25% of $25,000, Retained Earnings on January 1, 1966				6,250		
Eliminate 60% of $37,500, Retained Earnings on July 1, 1967				22,500		
Excess of Cost over Book Value					2,750	
Other Assets	159,000	200,000			359,000	
	275,500	200,000				
Credits						
Liabilities	80,000	60,000				140,000
Capital Stock, Co. P	100,000					100,000
Retained Earnings, Co. P	95,500					95,500
Capital Stock, Co. S		100,000				
Eliminate 85%			85,000			
Minority Interest, 15%						15,000
Retained Earnings, Co. S		40,000				
Eliminate as above			28,750			
Minority Interest, 15% of $40,000						6,000
Retained Earnings to Parent						5,250
	275,500	200,000	113,750	113,750	361,750	361,750

PURCHASE AND SALE OF HOLDINGS IN SUBSIDIARY

A parent may acquire stock in a subsidiary and subsequently sell a part or all of its holdings. For example, assume that Company P completed the following transactions in stock of Company S:

	Total
January 1, 1966, purchased 900 shares at 140	$126,000
July 1, 1967, sold 100 shares at 160	$ 16,000

Each company has capital stock of $100,000 and the shares of each company have a par value of $100. Retained earnings balances on December 31, 1965, and earnings and dividends for 1966 and 1967 are as follows:

	Co. P	Co. S
Retained earnings, December 31, 1965	$145,000	$50,000
Dividends declared in December, 1966		10,000
Net income from own operations, 1966	30,000	20,000
Dividends declared in December, 1967		10,000
Net income from own operations, 1967	35,000*	20,000

*Before gain on sale of Company S stock.

The investment and retained earnings accounts of the parent company are affected by the foregoing as follows:

	If Equity Method is Used		If Cost Method is Used	
	Investment in Co. S	Retained Earnings, Co. P	Investment in Co. S	Retained Earnings, Co. P
December 31, 1965:				
Balances		145,000		145,000
January 1, 1966:				
Purchase of 900 shares of Co. S stock at 140	126,000		126,000	
December, 1966:				
Dividends declared:				
Co. S, $10,000	(9,000)			9,000
	117,000	145,000	126,000	154,000
December 31, 1966:				
Net income, 1966:				
Co. S, $20,000	18,000	18,000		
Co. P, $30,000		30,000		30,000
	135,000	193,000	126,000	184,000
July 1, 1967:				
Sale of 100 shares at 160. Equity Method: carrying value (Jan. 1, 1967), $15,000; gain $1,000	(15,000)	1,000		
Cost Method: carrying value, $14,000; gain, $2,000			(14,000)	2,000
	120,000	194,000	112,000	186,000
December, 1967:				
Dividends declared:				
Co. S, $10,000	(8,000)			8,000
	112,000	194,000	112,000	194,000
December 31, 1967:				
Net income, 1967:				
Co. S, $20,000	16,000	16,000		
Co. P, $35,000		35,000		35,000
December 31, 1967, Balances	128,000	245,000	112,000	229,000

Equity method. When a sale is made, the investment account is reduced by the carrying value of the stock that is sold. When the equity method is employed, the carrying value consists of the original cost adjusted by earnings and dividends that have been recorded in the investment account. If there have been several purchases of stock and a part of the investment is sold, the carrying value of the specific lot sold is found or the carrying value is determined by the first-in, first-out method or by some other method. It is assumed in the illustrations in this chapter that the carrying value of stock sold is determined by the first-in, first-out method.

The sale of stock for cash is recorded by a debit to Cash for the cash proceeds, a credit to the investment account for the carrying value of the stock sold as calculated, and a debit or a credit to a loss or a gain account for the difference. Thereafter the parent takes up earnings and dividends upon the percentage of stock retained. In the example, the carrying value of the stock of Company S is $150 a share; this value was established at the close of 1966, after recording the subsidiary earnings for 1966. The sale of 100 shares is recorded as follows:

Cash	16,000	
Investment in Co. S Stock		15,000
Gain on Sale of Co. S Stock		1,000

When a sale is made during a fiscal period, it would be possible to take up the estimated subsidiary earnings to the date of sale before recording the sale. Assuming that the earnings to July 1, 1967, are estimated at $11,000, the tabulation would appear:

	If Equity Method is Used	
	Investment in Co. S	Retained Earnings, Co. P
December 31, 1966:		
Balances	135,000	193,000
July 1, 1967:		
Estimated net income, Co. S, Jan. 1, 1967–July 1, 1967, $11,000	9,900	9,900
	144,900	202,900
July 1, 1967:		
Sale of 100 shares at 160 — carrying value of stock, $161 ($144,900 ÷ 900); loss, $100	(16,100)	(100)
	128,800	202,800
December, 1967:		
Dividends paid by Co. S	(8,000)	
	120,800	202,800
December 31, 1967:		
Net income, Co. S, July 1–December 31, $9,000 (Net income for year, $20,000, less income already recognized, January 1–June 30, $11,000)	7,200	7,200
Net income, Co. P, for 1967, $35,000		35,000
December 31, 1967, Balances	128,000	245,000

Here the parent takes up 90% of the estimated earnings to July 1, 1967. The investment account is then reduced by the carrying value of the lot sold as of that date. Thereafter 80% of earnings and dividends are recorded. Although this procedure would seem more logical, the procedure illustrated in the tabulation on page 457 may be preferred since it does not require an estimate of the earnings to date of sale and results in the same balances at the end of the year.

Working papers for Company P and Company S are shown below.

Equity method:

Company P and Subsidiary Company S
Working Papers for Consolidated Balance Sheet
December 31, 1967

	Co. P	Co. S	Eliminations Dr.	Eliminations Cr.	Consolidated Balance Sheet Dr.	Consolidated Balance Sheet Cr.
Debits						
Investment in Co. S Stock	128,000					
Eliminate 80% of Capital Stock				80,000		
Eliminate 80% of Retained Earnings				56,000		
Excess of Book Value over Cost						8,000
Other Assets	467,000	270,000			737,000	
	595,000	270,000				
Credits						
Liabilities	250,000	100,000				350,000
Capital Stock, Co. P	100,000					100,000
Retained Earnings, Co. P	245,000					245,000
Capital Stock, Co. S		100,000				
Eliminate 80%			80,000			
Minority Interest, 20%						20,000
Retained Earnings, Co. S		70,000				
Eliminate 80%			56,000			
Minority Interest, 20%						14,000
	595,000	270,000	136,000	136,000	737,000	737,000

Cost method. When the cost method is used, the investment account is reduced by the cost of the shares sold. When there have been several purchases, the cost identified with the lot that is sold is found or cost is calculated by the first-in, first-out method or by some other method. In the example, the investment account is credited for $14,000, the cost of 100 shares, and a gain is recognized for $2,000, the amount by which the sales price exceeds the cost. Working papers are prepared as shown at the top of the following page.

It will be noted that when the cost method is used, eliminations are made for only the percentage of stock owned on the date of consolidation. The retained earnings that accrued to the parent company on the 10% lot held from January 1, 1966, to June 30, 1967, have now by virtue of the sale become a part of the minority interest. The gain of $2,000 recog-

Cost method:

Company P and Subsidiary Company S
Working Papers for Consolidated Balance Sheet
December 31, 1967

	Co. P	Co. S	Eliminations Dr.	Eliminations Cr.	Consolidated Balance Sheet Dr.	Consolidated Balance Sheet Cr.
Debits						
Investment in Co. S Stock	112,000					
Eliminate 80% of Capital Stock				80,000		
Eliminate 80% of $50,000, Retained Earnings on January 1, 1966				40,000		
Excess of Book Value over Cost						8,000
Other Assets	467,000	270,000			737,000	
	579,000	270,000				
Credits						
Liabilities	250,000	100,000				350,000
Capital Stock, Co. P	100,000					100,000
Retained Earnings, Co. P	229,000					229,000
Capital Stock, Co. S		100,000				
Eliminate 80%			80,000			
Minority Interest, 20%						20,000
Retained Earnings, Co. S		70,000				
Eliminate 80% as above			40,000			
Minority Interest, 20% of $70,000						14,000
Retained Earnings to Parent						16,000
	579,000	270,000	120,000	120,000	737,000	737,000

nized by the parent on the sale may be considered to represent (1) the earnings during the period of stock ownership, plus or minus (2) the gain or the loss attributable to the change in market price since the holdings were acquired.

SUBSIDIARY ISSUE OR REACQUISITION OF STOCK AFFECTING PARENT'S INTEREST

A parent's interest in a subsidiary may change as a result of the issuance of additional stock or the reacquisition of stock outstanding by the subsidiary company. For example, a parent may own 15,000 shares in a subsidiary company whose shares outstanding total 18,000. The sale by the subsidiary of 2,000 additional shares to outsiders changes the interest of the parent from 15,000/18,000 or 83⅓%, to 15,000/20,000 or 75%; on the other hand, the reacquisition by the subsidiary of 2,000 shares from outsiders, whether such shares are held as treasury stock or whether they are formally retired, changes the interest of the parent from 15,000/18,000 or 83⅓%, to 15,000/16,000 or 93¾%. Changes in the interest of a parent arising from changes in the capital structure of the subsidiary require special analysis in the preparation of the consolidated balance sheet. The nature of the problems that arise under the foregoing circumstances are illustrated in the example that follows.

Assume that Company P acquires stock of Company S as follows:

January 1, 1966, 900 shares at 120 .... $108,000

Capital balances for Company P and Company S on December 31, 1965, and changes in these balances for 1966 and 1967 follow. Capital stock of each company is $100 par.

	Co. P		Co. S		
	Capital Stock	Retained Earnings	Capital Stock	Additional Paid-in Capital	Retained Earnings
Balances, December 31, 1965	$100,000	$150,000	$100,000		$10,000
Net income from own operations, 1966		40,000			15,000
Sale of additional stock, 200 shares at 150 on January 1, 1967			20,000	$10,000	
Dividends declared, December, 1967		(20,000)			(15,000)
Net income from own operations, 1967		45,000			20,000

The effect of the foregoing on the investment and retained earnings accounts of the parent are shown in the tabulation below.

	If Equity Method is Used		If Cost Method is Used	
	Investment in Co. S	Retained Earnings, Co. P	Investment in Co. S	Retained Earnings, Co. P
December 31, 1965:				
Balances		150,000		150,000
January 1, 1966:				
Purchase of 900 shares of Co. S stock at 120	108,000		108,000	
	108,000	150,000	108,000	150,000
December, 1966:				
Net income, 1966:				
Co. S, $15,000	13,500	13,500		
Co. P, $40,000		40,000		40,000
	121,500	203,500	108,000	190,000
January 1, 1967:				
Adjustment resulting from change in parent company's interest upon sale of additional stock by subsidiary	3,750	3,750		
	125,250	207,250	108,000	190,000
December, 1967:				
Dividends declared:				
Co. S, $15,000	(11,250)			11,250
Co. P, $20,000		(20,000)		(20,000)
	114,000	187,250	108,000	181,250
December 31, 1967:				
Net income, 1967:				
Co. S, $20,000	15,000	15,000		
Co. P, $45,000		45,000		45,000
December 31, 1967, Balances	129,000	247,250	108,000	226,250

Equity method. When the equity method is employed, it is necessary to determine the change in the parent company's equity resulting from the change in its ownership interest in the subsidiary. The increase or the decrease in the parent's equity is taken up in the investment account in the same manner as regular earnings reported by the subsidiary. In the example, just before the issue of additional stock by the subsidiary company, the parent had a 90% interest in subsidiary company capital of $125,000; after the issue, the parent had a 75% interest in capital of $155,000. The parent company recognizes an increase in its equity as follows:

Equity in subsidiary capital after sale of stock, 75% of $155,000 . . .	$116,250
Equity in subsidiary capital just prior to sale of stock, 90% of $125,000	112,500
Increase in parent's equity as a result of change in interest.	$ 3,750

Working papers for a consolidated balance sheet at the end of 1967 will be prepared as follows:

Equity method:

Company P and Subsidiary Company S
Working Papers for Consolidated Balance Sheet
December 31, 1967

	Co. P	Co. S	Eliminations		Consolidated Balance Sheet	
			Dr.	Cr.	Dr.	Cr.
Debits						
Investment in Co. S Stock	129,000					
Eliminate 75% of Capital Stock				90,000		
Eliminate 75% of Additional Paid-in Capital.				7,500		
Eliminate 75% of Retained Earnings				22,500		
Excess of Cost over Book Value.					9,000	
Other Assets	338,250	260,000			598,250	
	467,250	260,000				
Credits						
Liabilities.	120,000	100,000				220,000
Capital Stock, Co. P.	100,000					100,000
Retained Earnings, Co. P.	247,250					247,250
Capital Stock, Co. S		120,000				
Eliminate 75%.			90,000			
Minority Interest, 25%.						30,000
Additional Paid-in Capital, Co. S.		10,000				
Eliminate 75%.			7,500			
Minority Interest, 25%.						2,500
Retained Earnings, Co. S.		30,000				
Eliminate 75%.			22,500			
Minority Interest, 25%.						7,500
	467,250	260,000	120,000	120,000	607,250	607,250

Cost method. When the cost method is used, eliminations are made in the usual manner for the equity originally acquired. The minority interest is calculated in terms of the current minority percentage. Subsidiary capital balances after deductions for eliminations and for the minority interest as thus determined indicate the change in the parent's interest from the date control was acquired.

Working papers for a consolidated balance sheet at the end of 1967 will be prepared as follows:

Cost method:

Company P and Subsidiary Company S
Working Papers for Consolidated Balance Sheet
December 31, 1967

	Co. P	Co. S	Eliminations Dr.	Eliminations Cr.	Consolidated Balance Sheet Dr.	Consolidated Balance Sheet Cr.
Debits						
Investment in Co. S Stock	108,000					
Eliminate 90% of $100,000, Capital Stock on date of acquisition, Jan. 1, 1966				90,000		
Eliminate 90% of $10,000, Retained Earnings on date of acquisition, Jan. 1, 1966				9,000		
Excess of Cost over Book Value					9,000	
Other Assets	338,250	260,000			598,250	
	446,250	260,000				
Credits						
Liabilities	120,000	100,000				220,000
Capital Stock, Co. P	100,000					100,000
Retained Earnings, Co. P	226,250					226,250
Capital Stock, Co. S		120,000				
Eliminate as above			90,000			
Minority Interest, 25%						30,000
Additional Paid-in Capital, Co. S		10,000				
Minority Interest, 25% of $10,000						2,500
Retained Earnings to Parent						7,500*
Retained Earnings, Co. S		30,000				
Eliminate as above			9,000			
Minority Interest, 25% of $30,000						7,500
Retained Earnings to Parent						13,500
	446,250	260,000	99,000	99,000	607,250	607,250

*The subsidiary's increase in paid-in capital is recognized by the controlling interest as an increase in retained earnings. It would be possible to recognize this increase separately in reporting the controlling interest on the consolidated balance sheet, but such an increase should not be regarded as a part of the paid-in capital of the controlling interest. It was observed on page 414 that an increase in a parent company's equity in a subsidiary, even when reflected as a part of the subsidiary company's capital stock, is properly reported as retained earnings on the consolidated balance sheet.

SUBSIDIARY COMPANY TREASURY STOCK TRANSACTIONS

When a parent acquires stock in a subsidiary company that holds treasury stock, the parent's interest in the subsidiary is calculated in terms of the subsidiary company shares outstanding. In developing a consolidated balance sheet, the cost of the treasury stock must be assigned to subsidiary capital stock, additional paid-in capital, and retained earnings balances as though the stock were actually retired, and eliminations must be developed in terms of resulting balances. Upon the subsequent sale of treasury stock, there is a change in the parent company's equity in the subsidiary, and special analysis of the effects of such a change on the parent's equity is required in developing the consolidated statement. The nature of the problems that arise under the foregoing circumstances are illustrated in the example that follows.

Assume that Company P acquires stock of Company S as follows:

January 1, 1966, 750 shares at 140 .... $105,000

The capital stock of each company is $100 par. Capital stock, treasury stock, additional paid-in capital, and retained earnings balances for each company on December 31, 1965, and changes in these balances during 1966 and 1967 follow:

	Co. P		Co. S			
	Capital Stock	Retained Earnings	Capital Stock Issued	Treasury Stock	Additional Paid-in Capital	Retained Earnings
Balances, December 31, 1965......	$100,000	$80,000	$100,000	$15,000	$10,000*	$25,000
Dividends declared, December, 1966		(20,000)				(9,000)
Net income from own operations, 1966........................		25,000				15,000
Sale of all treasury stock, 100 shares, at 165 on January 1, 1967......				(15,000)	1,500	
Dividends declared, December, 1967		(20,000)				(10,000)
Net income from own operations, 1967........................		30,000				25,000

*Capital stock was originally issued at 110, resulting in a $10,000 premium on the sale of the stock.

The purchase on January 1, 1966, of 750 shares of Company S stock when 900 shares were outstanding gave the parent a $\frac{750}{900}$ or $83\frac{1}{3}\%$ interest. In preparing a consolidated balance sheet on the date of stock acquisition, subsidiary capital balances are restated in terms of capital stock outstanding and the additional paid-in capital and retained earnings balances relating to such outstanding stock. Treasury stock, then, is viewed as retired stock; the payment of $15,000 for reacquired stock is viewed as a contraction of capital stock and additional paid-in capital balances recognized on the original sale of stock of $10,000 and $1,000 respectively and a reduction of retained earnings for the balance. Subsidiary capital balances are restated as follows:

	Capital Stock Issued	Treasury Stock	Additional Paid-in Capital	Retained Earnings
Balances per subsidiary books	$100,000	$15,000	$10,000	$25,000
Cancellation of treasury stock balance	(10,000)	(15,000)	(1,000)	(4,000)
Balances for consolidation purposes	$ 90,000	——	$ 9,000	$21,000

Working papers for a consolidated balance sheet on the date of acquisition of control would be prepared as follows:

Company P and Subsidiary Company S
Working Papers for Consolidated Balance Sheet
January 1, 1966

	Co. P	Co. S	Eliminations Dr.	Eliminations Cr.	Consolidated Balance Sheet Dr.	Consolidated Balance Sheet Cr.
Debits						
Investment in Co. S Stock	105,000					
Eliminate $83\frac{1}{3}\%$ of Capital Stock				75,000		
Eliminate $83\frac{1}{3}\%$ of Additional Paid-in Capital				7,500		
Eliminate $83\frac{1}{3}\%$ of Retained Earnings				17,500		
Excess of Cost over Book Value					5,000	
Other Assets	140,000	160,000			300,000	
	245,000	160,000				
Credits						
Liabilities	65,000	40,000				105,000
Capital Stock, Co. P	100,000					100,000
Retained Earnings, Co. P	80,000					80,000
Capital Stock, Co. S		90,000				
Eliminate $83\frac{1}{3}\%$			75,000			
Minority Interest, $16\frac{2}{3}\%$						15,000
Additional Paid-in Capital, Co. S		9,000				
Eliminate $83\frac{1}{3}\%$			7,500			
Minority Interest, $16\frac{2}{3}\%$						1,500
Retained Earnings, Co. S		21,000				
Eliminate $83\frac{1}{3}\%$			17,500			
Minority Interest, $16\frac{2}{3}\%$						3,500
	245,000	160,000	100,000	100,000	305,000	305,000

The investment and retained earnings accounts of the parent company are affected by transactions in 1966 and 1967 as follows:

	If Equity Method is Used		If Cost Method is Used	
	Investment in Co. S	Retained Earnings, Co. P	Investment in Co. S	Retained Earnings, Co. P
December 31, 1965:				
Balances		80,000		80,000
January 1, 1966:				
Purchase of 750 shares of Co. S stock at 140	105,000		105,000	
	105,000	80,000	105,000	80,000
December, 1966:				
Dividends declared:				
Co. S, $9,000	(7,500)			7,500
Co. P, $20,000		(20,000)		(20,000)
	97,500	60,000	105,000	67,500
December 31, 1966:				
Net income, 1966:				
Co. S, $15,000	12,500	12,500		
Co. P, $25,000		25,000		25,000
	110,000	97,500	105,000	92,500
January 1, 1967:				
Adjustment arising from change in parent company's interest upon sale of treasury stock by subsidiary company	1,875	1,875		
	111,875	99,375	105,000	92,500
December, 1967:				
Dividends declared:				
Co. S, $10,000	(7,500)			7,500
Co. P, $20,000		(20,000)		(20,000)
	104,375	79,375	105,000	80,000
December 31, 1967:				
Net income, 1967:				
Co. S, $25,000	18,750	18,750		
Co. P, $30,000		30,000		30,000
December 31, 1967, Balances	123,125	128,125	105,000	110,000

Equity method. When the equity method is employed, it is necessary to determine the change in the parent's equity resulting from the sale of treasury stock. The increase or the decrease in the parent company's equity is calculated in a manner similar to that illustrated upon the sale of unissued shares in a previous example. The parent company, in this case, recognizes an increase in its equity as follows:

Equity in subsidiary capital after resale of treasury stock, 75% of $142,500	$106,875
Equity in subsidiary capital just prior to resale of treasury stock, 83⅓% of $126,000	105,000
Increase in parent's equity as a result of change in interest	$ 1,875

Working papers for a consolidated balance sheet at the end of 1967 would be prepared as follows:

Equity method:

Company P and Subsidiary Company S
Working Papers for Consolidated Balance Sheet
December 31, 1967

	Co. P	Co. S	Eliminations		Consolidated Balance Sheet	
			Dr.	Cr.	Dr.	Cr.
Debits						
Investment in Co. S Stock	123,125					
Eliminate 75% of Capital Stock				75,000		
Eliminate 75% of Additional Paid-in Capital				8,625		
Eliminate 75% of Retained Earnings				34,500		
Excess of Cost over Book Value					5,000	
Other Assets	185,000	207,500			392,500	
	308,125	207,500				
Credits						
Liabilities	80,000	50,000				130,000
Capital Stock, Co. P	100,000					100,000
Retained Earnings, Co. P	128,125					128,125
Capital Stock, Co. S		100,000				
Eliminate 75%			75,000			
Minority Interest, 25%						25,000
Additional Paid-in Capital, Co. S		11,500				
Eliminate 75%			8,625			
Minority Interest, 25%						2,875
Retained Earnings, Co. S		46,000				
Eliminate 75%			34,500			
Minority Interest, 25%						11,500
	308,125	207,500	118,125	118,125	397,500	397,500

Cost method. When the cost method is used, eliminations for the equity originally acquired are made in the usual manner. The minority interest is calculated in terms of the current minority percentage. Subsidiary capital balances after deductions for eliminations and for the minority interest as thus determined indicate the change in the parent's present interest.

Working papers for a consolidated balance sheet would be prepared as shown at the top of the following page.

Cost method:

Company P and Subsidiary Company S
Working Papers for Consolidated Balance Sheet
December 31, 1967

	Co. P	Co. S	Eliminations Dr.	Eliminations Cr.	Consolidated Balance Sheet Dr.	Consolidated Balance Sheet Cr.
Debits						
Investment in Co. S Stock	105,000					
Eliminate 83⅓% of $90,000, Capital Stock on date of acquisition, Jan. 1, 1966				75,000		
Eliminate 83⅓% of $9,000, Additional Paid-in Capital on date of acquisition, Jan. 1, 1966				7,500		
Eliminate 83⅓% of $21,000, Retained Earnings on date of acquisition, Jan. 1, 1966				17,500		
Excess of Cost over Book Value					5,000	
Other Assets	185,000	207,500			392,500	
	290,000	207,500				
Credits						
Liabilities	80,000	50,000				130,000
Capital Stock, Co. P	100,000					100,000
Retained Earnings, Co. P	110,000					110,000
Capital Stock, Co. S		100,000				
Eliminate as above			75,000			
Minority Interest, 25%						25,000
Additional Paid-in Capital, Co. S		11,500				
Eliminate as above			7,500			
Minority Interest, 25%						2,875
Retained Earnings to Parent						1,125
Retained Earnings, Co. S		46,000				
Eliminate as above			17,500			
Minority Interest, 25% of $46,000						11,500
Retained Earnings to Parent						17,000
	290,000	207,500	100,000	100,000	397,500	397,500

QUESTIONS

1. (a) What eliminations are made on working papers for a consolidated balance sheet when an investment account shows the acquisition of an 80% interest in a subsidiary followed by the acquisition at a later date of a 10% interest, assuming that the investment is carried by the equity method? (b) What eliminations would be made under the foregoing circumstances assuming that the investment is carried by the cost method?

2. Some accountants maintain that when control of a subsidiary is not achieved until a second or later purchase of stock, earnings should be recognized for consolidation purposes only from the date control is acquired; some others maintain that, with acquisition of control, it is proper to recognize earnings that have accrued on noncontrolling interests from the date of the original acquisitions. Which position do you support? Give reasons.

3. (a) What entry is made when a parent sells a portion of an investment in a subsidiary and the investment is carried by the equity method? (b) What entry is made assuming that the investment is carried by the cost method?

4. An investment account reports the purchase of two lots of subsidiary stock, 8,000 shares or an 80% lot, followed by 1,500 shares or a 15% lot. The parent subsequently sells 1,000 shares of the second lot purchased. Describe the eliminations that are to be made on working papers for a consolidated balance sheet assuming (a) investments are carried by the cost method and (b) investments are carried by the equity method.

5. The Westwood Corporation acquires 80,000 shares of stock of the Bel Air Company; the latter company's books show 100,000 shares to be outstanding. At a later date the Bel Air Company sells 20,000 additional shares on the market. (a) What entry is made on the parent company books upon the additional stock issue assuming (1) the investment account is carried by the equity method and (2) the investment is carried by the cost method? (b) What eliminations are required on the working papers for consolidated statements assuming (1) the investment is carried by the equity method and (2) the investment is carried by the cost method?

6. The Palmer Company has owned 400,000 shares or an 80% interest in the stock of Travel, Inc., for a number of years. Travel, Inc. acquires 50,000 shares of its stock on the market and formally cancels and retires these shares. How is this recognized on the books of the parent and in the preparation of consolidated statements?

7. The Mason Company, with 10,000 shares outstanding, reacquires 1,000 shares of its own stock on the market at a price below its book value. The Burton Corporation subsequently acquires 7,500 shares of Mason Company stock. In preparing a consolidated balance sheet for the Burton Corporation, what disposition will be made of the treasury stock balance?

8. In Question 7, assuming that the treasury stock is resold by the Mason Company at a price in excess of its cost, (a) what entry will be made on the subsidiary company's books and (b) what entry will be made on the parent's books assuming that the investment account is carried by the equity method?

EXERCISES

1. The Parker Company made purchases of the stock of the Marlow Corporation as follows:

January 1, 1966, 3,000 shares at 12	$36,000
January 1, 1967, 6,000 shares at 15	90,000

The Marlow Corporation has 10,000 shares of stock outstanding. Its net earnings for 1966 and 1967 were $15,000 and $20,000 respectively, and dividends of $10,000 were paid in 1966 and also in 1967. (a) Assuming that the Parker Company carries investments by the equity method, what entries relating to the investments would be made in 1966 and 1967? (b) Assuming that investments are carried by the cost method, what entries would be made in 1966 and 1967?

2. An investment account on the books of Paul and Pearson, Inc. on December 1, 1967, appeared as follows:

Investment in Ronald Company Stock

1/1/67	9,500 shares (95% interest) at 16	152,000	7/15/67	Cash dividend	1,900

On this date the company sold 2,000 shares of its Ronald Company stock at 18. (a) What entry would be made to record the sale? (b) Assuming that the subsidiary announces net income of $30,000 for 1967, what entry would be made to record the earnings accruing to the parent?

3. Company H carries its investment accounts at cost. On December 31, 1966, it purchased 800 shares of the stock of Company R at 220. On this date it also purchased 600 shares of the stock of Company S at 70, and on July 1, 1967, it purchased an additional 200 shares at 90. Par values of stock of Companies H, R, and S are $100 each. Below is an analysis of the retained earnings accounts of Companies R and S.

	Co. R	Co. S
Retained earnings (deficit), December 31, 1966	$100,000	($25,000)
50% stock dividend declared June 15, distributable June 30, 1967	(50,000)	
	$ 50,000	($25,000)
Net income (loss), year ended December 31, 1967 (earned proportionately during the year)	(20,000)	12,000
Retained earnings (deficit), December 31, 1967	$ 30,000	($13,000)

Company H recorded the receipt of the stock dividend by a charge to the investment account and a credit to Retained Earnings. Account balances on the books of Companies H, R, and S as of December 31, 1967, are given at the top of the following page. Give the eliminations that would appear on the working papers and give the balances that would appear on the consolidated balance sheet after eliminations.

December 31, 1967

	Co. H	Co. R	Co. S
Investment in Co. R Stock	216,000		
Investment in Co. S Stock	60,000		
Capital Stock, Co. H	250,000		
Retained Earnings, Co. H	200,000		
Capital Stock, Co. R		150,000	
Retained Earnings, Co. R		30,000	
Capital Stock, Co. S			100,000
Deficit, Co. S			(13,000)

4. The Star Company purchased stock of Waldon, Inc. as follows:

Mar. 1, 1966, 700 shares at 60
Sept. 1, 1966, 150 shares at 70
July 1, 1967, 50 shares at 90

Waldon, Inc. has 1,000 shares outstanding. The company reported a net loss from operations for 1966 of $15,000 and net income from operations for 1967 of $40,000. The Star Company carries the investment account by the equity method. What entries would be made by the Star Company at the end of each year?

5. In Exercise 4, assume the first two purchases as indicated but a sale of 50 shares at 90 on July 1, 1967. (a) How would the sale be recorded? (b) What entries would be made at the end of each year to record the earnings for the year?

6. On March 1, 1967, the Sears Corporation purchased 9,000 shares of Thurston Company stock at 12. Thurston Company capital on January 1, 1967, and changes in capital were as follows:

Capital stock (no par), 10,000 shares		$ 80,000
Retained earnings, January 1, 1967	$ 20,000	
Net income, 1967	15,000	
	$ 35,000	
Dividends, October, 1967	7,500	27,500
Capital, December 31, 1967		$107,500

The investment account was carried on the Sears Corporation's books at cost. Give as of December 31, 1967: (a) the eliminations required on the working papers, (b) the cost or book value excess on the investment, (c) the minority interest, and (d) the subsidiary earnings accruing to the parent.

7. Assume in Exercise 6 that 500 shares of Thurston Company stock were sold on November 1, 1967, at 15. (a) What entry would be made to record the sale? (b) Give as of December 31, 1967: (1) the eliminations required on the working papers, (2) the cost or book value excess on the investment, (3) the minority interest, and (4) the subsidiary earnings accruing to the parent.

8. The Glenn Development Company acquired 7,500 shares of the Ever Ready Company on the market for $160,000 at the beginning of 1967. At this time the books of the Ever Ready Company showed the following: 10,000 shares of stock outstanding, $10 par; additional paid-in capital, $30,000; and retained earnings, $10,000. In December, 1967, the subsidiary issued 2,500 additional shares, which were sold to outsiders at 20. Net income for 1967 was $20,000. (a) What entries should be made on the books of the parent for 1967 assuming that the investment is carried by the equity method? (b) What entries should be made for 1967 assuming use of the cost method?

9. Assume in Exercise 8 that the additional issue of 2,500 shares was sold to the parent instead of to outsiders. (a) What entries should be made for 1967 if the equity method is used for the investment? (b) What entries should be made for 1967 assuming use of the cost method?

10. The Holmes Company owns 9,000 shares of Pacific Wholesalers acquired at a cost of $150,000 in 1960. At the time of purchase, Pacific Wholesalers had stock outstanding of $100,000, $10 par, and retained earnings of $60,000. On January 1, 1967, Pacific Wholesalers issued 2,000 additional shares at par to raise funds. At this time the company's retained earnings were $20,000. During 1967 the subsidiary paid dividends of $12,000 and reported a net income of $15,000. (a) What entries should be made on the books of the Holmes Company in 1967 assuming that the investment is carried on the equity basis? (b) What entries should be made in 1967 assuming use of the cost method? (c) What is the cost or book value excess on the investment? (d) What were the retained earnings of the parent company after consolidation on December 31, 1967, assuming that the cost basis was used and that its own retained earnings before considering subsidiary activities were $100,000?

11. The Berry Company purchased 9,000 shares of Stern, Inc. at 15 on July 1, 1967. On this date the capital of Stern, Inc. was as follows:

Capital stock issued, 12,000 shares, $10 par.....		$120,000
Premium on stock..........................		24,000
Retained earnings — Appropriated...........	$ 60,000	
Free...................	15,000	75,000
		$219,000
Less treasury stock, 2,000 shares at cost........		18,000
Capital, July 1, 1967......................		$201,000

(a) Assuming that a consolidated balance sheet is prepared on the date of stock acquisition, (1) give the elimination that is required on the working papers, and (2) calculate the cost or book value excess on the investment and the minority interest that will be reported on the consolidated balance sheet. (b) Assuming that the investment is carried by the equity method and that the subsidiary sells its treasury stock on the market at 14, how will the sale be recognized by the parent company?

PROBLEMS

14-1. On January 2, 1967, the Kirby Company purchased 15,000 shares of Kroger Company stock at 16 and on July 1, 1967, purchased an additional 1,500 shares at 17. The following information is available on December 31, 1967:

		Kirby Co.		Kroger Co.
Investment in Kroger Co.		$265,500		
Other assets		645,000		$475,000
Total assets		$910,500		$475,000
Liabilities		$230,500		$160,000
Capital stock (50,000 shares)		500,000	(20,000 shares)	300,000
Retained earnings (deficit):				
Balance, January 1, 1967	$135,000		($ 7,500)	
Net income for 1967	65,000		35,000	
	$200,000		$27,500	
Dividends declared and paid in November, 1967	(20,000)		(12,500)	
Balance, December 31, 1967		180,000		15,000
Total liabilities and stockholders' equity		$910,500		$475,000

Instructions: Prepare working papers and a consolidated balance sheet as of December 31, 1967.

14-2. On December 31, 1966, Company A purchased 1,200 shares of the stock of Company B at $120 a share. On April 1, 1967, Company A purchased 600 shares of the stock of Company B at $80 a share and 1,500 shares of the stock of Company C at $70 a share. Balance sheets of the three companies on December 31, 1967, are as follows:

	Co. A	Co. B	Co. C
Cash	$ 64,000	$ 40,000	$ 15,000
Notes receivable	30,000	30,000	20,000
Accounts receivable	60,000	50,000	40,000
Inventories	110,000	91,000	65,000
Investment in Co. B stock	192,000		
Investment in Co. C stock	105,000		
Bonds of Co. B (face value $20,000)	19,000		
Plant and equipment	200,000	150,000	100,000
Total assets	$780,000	$361,000	$240,000

	Co. A	Co. B	Co. C
Notes payable	$ 74,000	$ 35,000	$ 20,000
Dividends payable	28,000	9,000	
Accounts payable	60,000	55,000	70,000
Bonds payable		50,000	
Discount on bonds payable		(4,000)	
Preferred stock, Co. A ($100 par)	100,000		
Common stock, Co. A ($100 par)	300,000		
Retained earnings, Co. A	218,000		
Capital stock, Co. B ($50 par)		150,000	
Retained earnings, Co. B		66,000	
Capital stock, Co. C (2,000 shares, no par)			180,000
Deficit, Co. C			(30,000)
Total liabilities and stockholders' equity	$780,000	$361,000	$240,000

Company A has not recognized the dividend declared by Company B on December 31, 1967. The notes payable by Company C represent loans from Companies A and B.

An analysis of the retained earnings accounts reveals the following:

	Co. A	Co. B	Co. C
Retained earnings (deficit) December 31, 1966	$210,000	$95,000	($40,000)
Stock dividend declared June 15, 1967, distributable June 30		(50,000)	
	$210,000	$45,000	($40,000)
Net income, year ended December 31, 1967	36,000	30,000	10,000
	$246,000	$75,000	($30,000)
Cash dividends declared December 31, payable January 15, 1968	(28,000)	(9,000)	
Retained earnings (deficit), December 31, 1967	$218,000	$66,000	($30,000)

Instructions: Prepare working papers and a consolidated balance sheet as of December 31, 1967.

14-3. The following information is available for Companies P, A, and B on December 31, 1967:

	Co. P	Co. A	Co. B
Investment in Co. A	$105,000		
Investment in Co. B	135,000		
Other assets	698,500	$150,000	$265,000
Total assets	$938,500	$150,000	$265,000

	Co. P	Co. A	Co. B
Liabilities	$120,000	$ 52,500	$ 95,000
Capital stock (all $10 par)	500,000	100,000	100,000
Additional paid-in capital	150,000		20,000
Retained earnings (deficit)	168,500	(2,500)	50,000
Total liabilities and stockholders' equity	$938,500	$150,000	$265,000

Investment accounts are carried at cost.

Stock of Co. A was purchased as follows:

September 1, 1966, 7,000 shares at 10.
January 1, 1967, 2,500 shares at 14.

Stock of Co. B was purchased as follows:

January 1, 1966, 4,000 shares at 15.
April 1, 1967, 5,000 shares at 18.

One thousand shares of Company B stock were sold on July 1, 1967, at 12.

Changes in retained earnings for the three companies were as follows:

	Co. P	Co. A	Co. B
Balance of retained earnings (deficit), January 1, 1966	$222,500	($20,000)	$35,000
Dividends, November, 1966	(20,000)		(10,000)
	$202,500	($20,000)	$25,000
Increase (decrease) from operations, for 1966	(45,000)	7,500	15,000
	$157,500	($12,500)	$40,000
Dividends, November, 1967	(14,000)		(10,000)
	$143,500	($12,500)	$30,000
Increase from operations, 1967	25,000	10,000	20,000
Balance of retained earnings (deficit), December 31, 1967	$168,500	($ 2,500)	$50,000

Instructions: Prepare working papers and a consolidated balance sheet as of December 31, 1967.

14-4. Accounts of the Dodge, Elgin, and Fuller companies show the following balances on December 31, 1967:

	Dodge Co.	Elgin Co.	Fuller Co.
Investment in Elgin Co.	$172,000		
Investment in Fuller Co.	98,500		
Other assets	389,000	$275,000	$145,000
Liabilities	164,000	80,000	50,000
Capital stock (all $100 par)	400,000	150,000	100,000
Retained earnings (deficit)	95,500	45,000	(5,000)

Changes in retained earnings for the three companies follow:

	Dodge Co.	Elgin Co.	Fuller Co.
Retained earnings, December 31, 1965	$ 82,500	$ 10,000	$ 5,000
Dividends, 1966	(16,000)		
	$ 66,500	$ 10,000	$ 5,000
Increase (decrease) from operations, 1966	25,000	10,000	(15,000)
Retained earnings (deficit), December 31, 1966	$ 91,500	$ 20,000	($ 10,000)
Dividends paid in December, 1967	(16,000)	(5,000)	
	$ 75,500	$ 15,000	($ 10,000)
Increase from operations, 1967	20,000	30,000	5,000
Retained earnings (deficit), December 31, 1967	$ 95,500	$ 45,000	($ 5,000)

The investment accounts appear as follows:

Investment in Elgin Co.

April 1, 1966	1,200 shares at 125	150,000			
July 1, 1966	50 shares at 130	6,500			
Nov. 1, 1967	100 shares at 155	15,500			

Investment in Fuller Co.

Jan. 2, 1966	900 shares at 110	99,000	Oct. 1, 1966	150 shares at 110	16,500[1]
July 1, 1967	100 shares at 160	16,000			

[1]The sale was made at $150 a share; the investment account was credited at cost, and profit and loss for 1966 was credited for the gain on the sale.

Instructions: Prepare working papers and a consolidated balance sheet as of December 31, 1967.

14-5. Balance sheets for Companies W, X, Y, and Z on December 31, 1967, are given below. Investments in subsidiaries were carried at cost.

	Co. W	Co. X	Co. Y	Co. Z
Investment in Co. X (800 shares)	$ 71,600			
Investment in Co. Y (950 shares)	68,000			
Investment in Co. Z (900 shares)	143,500			
Inventories	120,000	$ 55,000	$ 50,000	$ 75,000
Plant and equipment (net)	100,000	80,000		100,000
Co. X bonds (face value, $20,000)	20,400			
Other assets	200,000	115,000	105,000	130,000
Total assets	$723,500	$250,000	$155,000	$305,000
Bonds payable		$100,000		
Discount on bonds payable		(4,000)		
Other liabilities	$238,500	34,000	$100,000	$150,000
Capital stock (all $100 par)	250,000	100,000	100,000	100,000
Additional paid-in capital		10,000		
Retained earnings (deficit)	235,000	10,000	(45,000)	55,000
Total liabilities and stockholders' equity	$723,500	$250,000	$155,000	$305,000

Retained earnings changes have been as follows:

	Co. W	Co. X	Co. Y	Co. Z
Retained earnings (deficit), December 31, 1965	$185,000	($30,000)	($35,000)	$ 60,000
Net income (loss), 1966	40,000	20,000	(25,000)	60,000
	$225,000	($10,000)	($60,000)	$120,000
Dividends paid in December, 1966	(20,000)			(20,000)
Retained earnings (deficit), December 31, 1966	$205,000	($10,000)	($60,000)	$100,000
Net income (loss), 1967	50,000	30,000	15,000	(45,000)
	$255,000	$ 20,000	($45,000)	$ 55,000
Dividends paid in December, 1967	(20,000)	(10,000)		
Retained earnings (deficit), December 31, 1967	$235,000	$ 10,000	($45,000)	$ 55,000

Company X stock was purchased on January 2, 1966.

Company Y stock was purchased as follows:

Jan. 2, 1966, 850 shares at 70	$ 59,500
May 1, 1967, 100 shares at 85	8,500
Balance in account	$ 68,000

The Company Z investment account shows:

April 1, 1966, purchased 850 shares at 160	$136,000
July 1, 1967, sold 100 shares at 210	(21,000)
	$115,000
Sept. 1, 1967, purchased 150 shares at 190	28,500
Balance in account	$143,500

An analysis of inventories on hand on December 31, 1967, disclosed the following:

	Inventory Total	Acquired from				
		Outsiders	Co. W	Co. X	Co. Y	Co. Z
Co. W	$120,000	$ 90,000		$20,000	$10,000	
X	55,000	40,000	$15,000			
Y	50,000	35,000	10,000	5,000		
Z	75,000	50,000	15,000	10,000		
	$300,000	$215,000	$40,000	$35,000	$10,000	

All intercompany sales were made at a 20% gross profit on sales price.

Intercompany receivables on December 31 totaled $65,000.

Plant and equipment of Company W included assets of $30,000 constructed by Company X in 1966. The cost of construction to Company X was $24,000. These assets had been depreciated by Company W since July 1, 1966, at 10% per year.

Instructions: From the foregoing balance sheets and supplementary information, construct working papers and a consolidated balance sheet at December 31, 1967.

14-6. Balance sheets for Companies P, R, and S on December 31, 1967, were as follows:

	Co. P	Co. R	Co. S
Investment in Co. R (1,600 shares)	$ 205,000		
Investment in Co. S (1,250 shares)	140,000		
Other assets	1,250,000	$565,000	$425,000
Total assets	$1,595,000	$565,000	$425,000
Liabilities	$ 645,000	$175,000	$204,000
Capital stock (all $100 par)	600,000	250,000	200,000
Additional paid-in capital	50,000	10,000	
Retained earnings	300,000	130,000	21,000
Total liabilities and stockholders' equity	$1,595,000	$565,000	$425,000

Company P acquired 1,600 shares of Company R stock in 1963 and has carried the investment account on the equity basis. At the beginning of 1967, Company R sold to outsiders 500 shares of its stock at 120. In 1964, Company P acquired 1,250 shares of stock of Company S; this investment was also carried on the equity basis. On July 1, 1967, Company S sold to outsiders 500 shares of its stock at par. On December 31, 1967, Company P owes Company R $100,000.

No entries had been made in the investment accounts for 1967. Changes in retained earnings for the three companies for 1967 were as follows:

	Co. P	Co. R	Co. S
Retained earnings (deficit), January 1	$265,000	$100,000	($ 9,000)
Net income for 1967	65,000	30,000	30,000
	$330,000	$130,000	$ 21,000
Dividends paid in 1967	(30,000)		
Retained earnings, December 31	$300,000	$130,000	$ 21,000

Instructions: (1) Give the entries on December 31, 1967, to bring the investment accounts on the books of Company P up to date.

(2) Prepare working papers and a consolidated balance sheet as of December 31, 1967.

14-7. In April, 1960, Craig, Inc. organized two subsidiaries, South Company and West Company. Each subsidiary issued 30,000 shares of stock, $10 par, and all of the shares were acquired by the parent company. At the beginning of 1967, South Company acquired properties that were recorded at a value of $150,000 in exchange for 6,000 shares of its stock, and West Company sold 7,500 shares of its stock at 12½; parties to the exchange and to the sale were outsiders.

Balance sheet data for the parent and its subsidiaries on December 31, 1967, were as follows:

	Craig, Inc.	South Co.	West Co.
Investment in South Co.	$ 300,000		
Investment in West Co.	300,000		
Other assets	5,575,000	$2,650,000	$993,750
Total assets	$6,175,000	$2,650,000	$993,750
Liabilities	$1,825,000	$ 850,000	$650,000
Capital stock (all $10 par)	2,500,000	360,000	375,000
Additional paid-in capital	1,000,000	90,000	18,750
Retained earnings (deficit)	850,000	1,350,000	(50,000)
Total liabilities and stockholders' equity	$6,175,000	$2,650,000	$993,750

Instructions: Prepare working papers and a consolidated balance sheet as of December 31, 1967.

14-8. Balance sheets on December 31, 1967, for the Wells Company and its subsidiary, the Wiley Company appear below.

	Wells Co.	Wiley Co.
Investment in Wiley Co. (4,500 shares)	$ 230,000	
Other assets	2,235,000	$360,000
Total assets	$2,465,000	$360,000
Liabilities	$ 600,000	$115,000
Capital stock (all $20 par)	1,000,000	120,000
Additional paid-in capital	350,000	42,000
Accumulated earnings	515,000	83,000
Total liabilities and stockholders' equity	$2,465,000	$360,000

The Wells Company carries its investment in the Wiley Company at cost. Its interest in the subsidiary was acquired on July 1, 1962, when the stockholders' equity of the latter company was as follows:

Capital stock issued, 6,000 shares	$120,000
Additional paid-in capital (premium on stock issued)	30,000
Accumulated earnings	75,000
	$225,000
Less treasury stock, 1,000 shares at cost	16,500
Stockholders' equity, July 1, 1962	$208,500

The treasury stock was sold to outsiders by the Wiley Company in 1966 at $12,000 in excess of its cost.

Instructions: Prepare working papers and a consolidated balance sheet as of December 31, 1967.

14-9. Company A, the parent company, has a substantial interest in Company B. The earnings of Company A have been declining in recent years and the prospects for growth are poor. Conversely, Company B has been prospering and the prospects for growth are excellent.

For management purposes, the two companies are to be merged as of July 1, 1967. The following facts are available as of June 30, 1967:

(1) Both companies have only one class of capital stock outstanding. Company A owns 72% of Company B's capital stock.
(2) Net book value of capital stock:

Company A (consolidated)	$1,415,000
Company B	$1,230,000

(3) Shares of capital stock outstanding:

Company A	80,000 shares
Company B	100,000 shares

(4) Each company has agreed to purchase the stock of dissenting stockholders at current market value. The following stock will be purchased on July 1, 1967, prior to the merger and treated as treasury stock:
Company A — 400 shares @ $20 per share.
Company B — 10,000 shares @ $24 per share.
(5) The owners of Company A wish to exchange on an equitable basis Company A capital stock for the Company B capital stock held by the surviving minority interest.

Instructions: Taking into consideration the percentage change in ownership caused by the purchase of the treasury stock, prepare schedules to compute the total number of shares of Company A capital stock that would be exchanged for the Company B capital stock held by minority interests on each of the following bases:

(1) Current market value of stock. (Assume that the market price of the stock will not be affected by the treasury stock purchases.)
(2) Net book value of stock.

(AICPA adapted)

14-10. The following balances appear on the books of the Bishop Company and its subsidiary, the Carey Company, on the dates stated:

	Jan. 1 1965	Dec. 31 1965	Dec. 31 1966	Dec. 31 1967
Bishop Company:				
Investment in Carey Co.	$128,000	$128,000	$119,000	$140,000
Retained earnings	135,000	160,000	148,000	155,000
Carey Company:				
Capital stock	100,000	100,000	100,000	100,000
Retained earnings	50,000	62,000	70,000	80,000

The Carey Company's capital stock consists of 1,000 shares of $100 par each. The Bishop Company purchased 800 shares on January 1, 1965, sold 50 shares on January 1, 1966, and purchased 100 shares on January 1, 1967.

The investment account was charged with the cost of stock purchased and was credited with the proceeds from the stock sold. The Bishop Company has made no other entries in the investment account and has credited income for all dividends received from the Carey Company. The difference between investment cost and the subsidiary equity acquired is recognized on the consolidated balance sheet as goodwill.

Instructions: Prepare statements showing the composition of the amounts of goodwill, retained earnings, and minority interest appearing on the consolidated balance sheets prepared on: (1) December 31, 1965; (2) December 31, 1966; (3) December 31, 1967.

(AICPA adapted)

14-11. Company L acquired 90% of the outstanding stock of Company N on March 31, 1967, for $162,000. Previously Company L acquired 30% of the outstanding stock of Company M on January 1, 1966, for $25,000. On July 1, 1967, Company L purchased an additional 40% of the outstanding stock of Company M for $42,000, thereby gaining effective control of Company M as of that date. In order further to increase its stockholdings in Company M without impairing working capital, Company L sold 100 shares of Company N stock on October 1, 1967, for $20,500 and immediately used $13,800 of the proceeds to secure an additional 15% of Company M outstanding stock.

The balance sheets of the respective companies as at December 31, 1967, are as follows:

	Co. L	Co. M	Co. N
Cash in banks	$ 86,000	$ 12,500	$ 35,000
Notes receivable	18,000	6,000	8,000
Accounts receivable (less allowance)	52,000	13,000	34,000
Inventories	89,500	16,000	51,000
Investment in Co. M (at cost)	80,800		
Investment in Co. N (at book value)	149,320		
Plant and equipment (less allowances)	225,000	56,500	101,000
Total assets	$700,620	$104,000	$229,000
Notes payable	$ 9,000	$ 8,000	$ 12,000
Accounts payable	73,600	22,400	46,200
Accrued liabilities	5,320	2,600	4,800
Capital stock — common, $100 par	400,000	60,000	100,000
Retained earnings	212,700	11,000	66,000
Total liabilities and stockholders' equity	$700,620	$104,000	$229,000

A summary of retained earnings (deficit) from January 1, 1966, to December 31, 1967, follows:

	Co. L	Co. M	Co. N
Balance, January 1, 1966	$150,000	($ 10,000)	$ 40,000
Net profit (loss) — 1966:			
1st quarter	7,000	(2,000)	3,000
2nd quarter	9,000	1,000	4,000
3rd quarter	15,000	3,000	6,000
4th quarter	12,000	6,000	5,000
Total	$193,000	($ 2,000)	$ 58,000
Dividends declared and paid on July 1, 1966	(12,000)		(3,000)
Balance, January 1, 1967	$181,000	($ 2,000)	$ 55,000
Net profit (loss) — 1967:			
1st quarter	6,000	2,500	4,500
2nd quarter	11,500	3,000	7,000
3rd quarter	13,000	3,600	6,200
4th quarter	16,200	5,900	5,300
Total	$227,700	$ 13,000	$ 78,000
Dividends declared June 1, 1967, and paid on June 15, 1967	(15,000)		(12,000)
Dividends declared December 1, 1967 and paid on December 15, 1967		(2,000)	
Balance, December 31, 1967	$212,700	$ 11,000	$ 66,000

Net profit of Company L for the fourth quarter of 1967 includes $2,500 representing the gain on the sale of 100 shares of Company N stock. (Proceeds $20,500, less March 31, 1967, cost, $18,000.)

Inventories at December 31, 1967, include intercompany items as follows, all goods having been acquired from affiliated companies in the last quarter of 1967:

Company		Amount	
Purchaser	Seller	Inventory	Seller's Cost
L	M	$13,600	$12,000
L	N	5,000	4,500*
M	N	13,000	11,000
N	M	16,000	14,000

*Acquired by Company N from Company M, Company M's cost then being $4,200.

Instructions: Prepare working papers and a consolidated balance sheet for Companies L, M, and N, as of December 31, 1967.

(AICPA adapted)

14-12. On January 1, 1967, the Riggs Company purchased 90% of the stock of the Scott Company and 80% of the stock of the Tolle Company. Wishing to acquire the remaining stock of the more profitable Tolle Company, the Riggs Company on June 30, 1967, disposed of 200 shares of its holdings in the Scott Company at a price of $160 per share, and on that date was successful in acquiring an additional 10% of the stock of the Tolle Company in exchange for the entire proceeds of the sale of the Scott Company stock.

The investment accounts on the books of the Riggs Company are carried at cost except the account representing the investment in capital stock of the Scott Company; this account has been credited with the proceeds of the 200 shares sold.

Balance sheets of the three companies at December 31, 1967, are as follows:

	Riggs Co.	Scott Co.	Tolle Co.
Assets			
Current assets	$152,500	$150,000	$105,000
Investment in subsidiary companies —			
Scott Co.			
Capital stock	220,000		
Advances	25,000		
Tolle Co.			
Capital stock	214,000		
Advances	40,000		
Buildings and equipment		170,000	235,000
Total	$651,500	$320,000	$340,000
Liabilities and Stockholders' Equity			
Capital stock:			
Riggs Co. — 3,000 shares	$300,000		
Scott Co. — 2,000 shares		$200,000	
Tolle Co. — 1,000 shares			$100,000
Due to parent company		25,000	40,000
Accounts payable	235,000	40,000	25,000
Retained earnings at beginning of year	166,500	60,000	145,000
Profit for the year	*20,000	15,000	40,000
Dividends (paid Dec. 31, 1967)	(70,000)	(20,000)	(10,000)
Total	$651,500	$320,000	$340,000

*Dividends received from subsidiary companies, less expenses of parent company.

It is assumed that the profits of the companies for the year 1967 were divided equally between the two 6-month periods.

Instructions: (1) Prepare a consolidated balance sheet.
(2) Prepare a statement of consolidated retained earnings.

(AICPA adapted)

Chapter 15

CONSOLIDATED STATEMENTS

INDIRECT AND MUTUAL HOLDINGS

A parent company may control another company that itself is a parent company. Such a condition is described as one of *indirect ownership*. Sometimes a company's holdings are supplemented by those of an affiliated company. Control that is achieved through a connecting affiliate may also be regarded as a condition of indirect ownership. Occasionally one may find that a subsidiary holds a block of the stock of the parent company. Such a situation is described as one of *mutual* or *reciprocal ownership*. This chapter considers the special problems that arise in the preparation of consolidated statements when indirect and mutual holdings are encountered.

INDIRECT HOLDINGS — SUBHOLDINGS ACQUIRED AFTER PARENT COMPANY CONTROL

When a parent company owns controlling interests in companies that themselves are parents, the preparation of consolidated statements for the parent at the apex of the system requires careful analysis of capitals, earnings, and dividends beginning with the companies on the lowest tier. Illustrations here will be limited to the accounting for relationships involving a parent company, a subparent company, and a subsidiary company. In the first set of examples it is assumed that a controlling interest is acquired in a company that subsequently acquires control over another unit. In the second set of examples it is assumed that a controlling interest is acquired in a company that already exercises control over an affiliate.

Assume the data that follow. On January 1, 1966, Company P purchases 800 shares of Company SP stock at 150, paying $120,000. On January 1, 1967, Company SP purchases 900 shares of Company S stock at 140, paying $126,000. The capital stock of each company is $100,000, consisting of 1,000 shares with a par value of $100. Retained earnings balances on December 31, 1965, and earnings and dividends for 1966 and 1967 are as follows:

	Co. P	Co. SP	Co. S
Retained earnings, December 31, 1965........	$240,000	$60,000	$10,000
Net income (loss) from own operations, 1966...	30,000	(15,000)	10,000
Dividends declared in December, 1967........	10,000	10,000	5,000
Net income (loss) from own operations, 1967...	(20,000)	30,000	15,000

Changes in the investment accounts and the retained earnings accounts of the parent and the subparent companies as a result of the foregoing are given in the tabulation below.

	If Equity Method Is Used				If Cost Method Is Used			
	Co. P Books		Co. SP Books		Co. P Books		Co. SP Books	
	Inv. in Co. SP	Retained Earnings Co. P	Inv. in Co. S	Retained Earnings Co. SP	Inv. in Co. SP	Retained Earnings Co. P	Inv. in Co. S	Retained Earnings Co. SP
cember 31, 1965, balances.......		240,000		60,000		240,000		60,000
uary 1, 1966: Purchase by Co. P of 800 shares of Co. SP stock at 150..........	120,000				120,000			
	120,000	240,000		60,000	120,000	240,000		60,000
cember 31, 1966: Net income (loss), 1966: Co. SP, ($15,000)............	(12,000)	(12,000)		(15,000)				(15,000)
Co. P, $30,000..............		30,000				30,000		
	108,000	258,000		45,000	120,000	270,000		45,000
uary 1, 1967: Purchase by Co. SP of 900 shares of Co. S stock at 140.........			126,000				126,000	
	108,000	258,000	126,000	45,000	120,000	270,000	126,000	45,000
cember, 1967: Dividends paid: Co. S, $5,000..............			(4,500)					4,500
Co. SP, $10,000..............	(8,000)			(10,000)		8,000		(10,000)
Co. P, $10,000..............		(10,000)				(10,000)		
	100,000	248,000	121,500	35,000	120,000	268,000	126,000	39,500
cember 31, 1967: Net income (loss), 1967: Co. S, $15,000..............			13,500	13,500				
Co. SP: Own operations...... $30,000				30,000				30,000
Through ownership of Co. S............ 13,500								
To Co. P, 80% of.... $43,500	34,800	34,800						
Co. P, ($20,000)............		(20,000)				(20,000)		
cember 31, 1967, balances......	134,800	262,800	135,000	78,500	120,000	248,000	126,000	69,500

Equity method. When the equity method of carrying investments is used, no special problem arises until a subsidiary company acquires control over another company and thus becomes a subparent. Upon assuming control, the subparent now recognizes the changes in the capital of the company it controls. The parent, in turn, recognizes changes in the capital of the subparent; such changes arise from (1) the subparent's own operations and (2) the subparent's recognition of the earnings of the company it controls.

In the example, beginning in 1967 Company P records its share of the earnings of Company SP only after the latter has recognized the earnings accruing from operations of Company S. Earnings of Company S for 1967 are $15,000. Company SP takes up in its investment and retained earnings accounts 90% of this amount, or $13,500. Company P may now take up 80% of the retained earnings increase of Company SP of $43,500, consisting of earnings from the latter's own operations,

$30,000, and earnings that are recognized as a result of operations of subsidiary Company S, $13,500.

The parent company is affected by the earnings of the subsidiaries of the subparent company. It is not affected by the dividends of such subsidiaries, however, since dividends have no effect upon the capital of the recipient when the equity method is employed. Declaration of a dividend by Company S, then, simply results in an entry on the books of Company SP to take up such a dividend. Declaration of a dividend by Company SP results in an entry on the books of Company P.

Working papers for a consolidated balance sheet at the end of 1967 for Company P, Company SP, and Company S are prepared as follows:

Equity method:

Company P and Subsidiary Companies
Working Papers for Consolidated Balance Sheet
December 31, 1967

	Co. P	Co. SP	Co. S	Eliminations		Consolidated Balance Sheet	
				Dr.	Cr.	Dr.	Cr.
Debits							
Investment in Co. SP Stock	134,800						
Eliminate 80% of Capital Stock					80,000		
Eliminate 80% of Retained Earnings					62,800		
Excess of Book Value over Cost							8,000
Investment in Co. S Stock		135,000					
Eliminate 90% of Capital Stock					90,000		
Eliminate 90% of Retained Earnings					27,000		
Excess of Cost over Book Value						18,000	
Other Assets	428,000	143,500	190,000			761,500	
	562,800	278,500	190,000				
Credits							
Liabilities	200,000	100,000	60,000				360,000
Capital Stock, Co. P	100,000						100,000
Retained Earnings, Co. P	262,800						262,800
Capital Stock, Co. SP		100,000					
Eliminate 80%				80,000			
Minority Interest, 20%							20,000
Retained Earnings, Co. SP		78,500					
Eliminate 80%				62,800			
Minority Interest, 20%							15,700
Capital Stock, Co. S			100,000				
Eliminate 90%				90,000			
Minority Interest, 10%							10,000
Retained Earnings, Co. S			30,000				
Eliminate 90%				27,000			
Minority Interest, 10%							3,000
	562,800	278,500	190,000	259,800	259,800	779,500	779,500

The working papers above are employed in the preparation of a consolidated balance sheet for parent Company P and its affiliates. If a consolidated balance sheet for Company SP and its subsidiary Company S were desired, balance sheets for the two companies could be consolidated. The consolidated balance sheet for the subparent could then be consolidated with the balance sheet for the parent in obtaining a statement for the three companies. This statement would be the same as that which was developed by means of the single set of working papers.

Cost method. If the cost method is used, working papers for a consolidated balance sheet would be prepared as follows:

Cost method:

Company P and Subsidiary Companies
Working Papers for Consolidated Balance Sheet
December 31, 1967

	Co. P	Co. SP	Co. S	Eliminations		Consolidated Balance Sheet	
				Dr.	Cr.	Dr.	Cr.
Debits							
Investment in Co. SP Stock	120,000						
Eliminate 80% of Capital Stock					80,000		
Eliminate 80% of $60,000, Retained Earnings on 1/1/66					48,000		
Excess of Book Value over Cost							8,000
Investment in Co. S Stock		126,000					
Eliminate 90% of Capital Stock					90,000		
Eliminate 90% of $20,000, Retained Earnings on 1/1/67					18,000		
Excess of Cost over Book Value						18,000	
Other Assets	428,000	143,500	190,000			761,500	
	548,000	269,500	190,000				
Credits							
Liabilities	200,000	100,000	60,000				360,000
Capital Stock, Co. P	100,000						100,000
Retained Earnings, Co. P	248,000						248,000
Capital Stock, Co. SP		100,000					
Eliminate 80%				80,000			
Minority Interest, 20%							20,000
Retained Earnings, Co. SP		69,500			(x)9,000		
Eliminate 80% as above				48,000			
Minority Interest, 20% of $78,500							15,700
Retained Earnings to Co. P							14,800
Capital Stock, Co. S			100,000				
Eliminate 90%				90,000			
Minority Interest, 10%							10,000
Retained Earnings, Co. S			30,000				
Eliminate 90% as above				18,000			
Minority Interest, 10% of $30,000							3,000
Retained Earnings to Co. SP				(x)9,000			
	548,000	269,500	190,000	245,000	245,000	779,500	779,500

The investment account eliminations are based, as usual, upon capital balances as of the date of acquisition of a controlling interest.

Beginning with the most remote subsidiary, however, the retained earnings accruing to its respective parent, instead of being extended to the consolidated balance sheet columns, are carried to the retained earnings account of such subparent. This amount, then, is included in the determination of the subparent's retained earnings. The calculation of the subparent minority interest is based upon the subparent's retained earnings as so adjusted, and the balance of retained earnings, if accruing to a top parent, may be extended to the consolidated balance sheet columns. If the balance accrues to a company that is in turn controlled by another, it is carried to the retained earnings of such subparent as was done in the first instance.

In the example, after elimination of $18,000, the share of the retained earnings originally acquired, and after extension of the minority interest in the retained earnings, 10% of $30,000, or $3,000, the balance of earnings accruing to the subparent, $9,000, is carried to Company SP retained earnings (entry [x]). The minority interest in Company SP is calculated on the retained earnings balance of Company SP as adjusted by the increase accruing from its subsidiary.

Of the retained earnings of Company SP, $14,800 represents the increase accruing to Company P since the date of acquisition. This figure is obtained by adding to Company SP retained earnings, $69,500, the $9,000 accruing to it by virtue of its ownership of 90% of Company S. The total retained earnings of Company SP, thus, is $78,500. This total is reduced by the retained earnings acquired by Company P at the time of acquisition, $48,000, and a minority interest of 20% of $78,500, or $15,700. The balance, $14,800, is the retained earnings increase that accrues to Company P as a result of the change in the capital of Company SP, which includes the earnings accruing to the latter company from the operations of Company S.

As in the preceding case, it would be possible first to construct a consolidated balance sheet for Company SP and its subsidiary, Company S. This balance sheet, when consolidated with that of Company P, would be the same as the consolidated balance sheet developed from the working papers on page 487.

INDIRECT HOLDINGS — SUBHOLDINGS ACQUIRED PRIOR TO PARENT COMPANY CONTROL

To illustrate the problems that arise when control is achieved over a company that already exercises control over an affiliate, assume the data that follow. On January 1, 1966, Company SP purchases 800 shares of Company S stock at 120, paying $96,000. On January 1, 1967, Company P purchases 850 shares of Company SP stock at 160, paying

$136,000. The capital stock of each company is $100,000, consisting of 1,000 shares with a par value of $100. Retained earnings balances on December 31, 1965, and earnings and dividends for 1966 and 1967 are as follows:

	Co. P	Co. SP	Co. S
Retained earnings (deficit), December 31, 1965	$250,000	$20,000	($15,000)
Net income (loss) from own operations, 1966 . .	20,000	10,000	(5,000)
Dividends declared in December, 1967.	10,000	5,000	
Net income from own operations, 1967.	15,000	10,000	10,000

Changes in the investment accounts and the retained earnings accounts of the parent and the subparent companies as a result of the foregoing follow.

	If Equity Method Is Used				If Cost Method Is Used			
	Co. P Books		Co. SP Books		Co. P Books		Co. SP Books	
	Inv. in Co. SP	Retained Earnings Co. P	Inv. in Co. S	Retained Earnings Co. SP	Inv. in Co. SP	Retained Earnings Co. P	Inv. in Co. S	Retained Earnings Co. SP
December 31, 1965, balances.		250,000		20,000		250,000		20,000
January 1, 1966:								
Purchase by Co. SP of 800 shares of Co. S stock at 120.			96,000				96,000	
		250,000	96,000	20,000		250,000	96,000	20,000
December 31, 1966:								
Net income (loss), 1966:								
Co. S, ($5,000).			(4,000)	(4,000)				
Co. SP, $10,000.				10,000				10,000
Co. P, $20,000.		20,000				20,000		
		270,000	92,000	26,000		270,000	96,000	30,000
January 1, 1967:								
Purchase by Co. P of 850 shares of Co. SP stock at 160.	136,000				136,000			
	136,000	270,000	92,000	26,000	136,000	270,000	96,000	30,000
December, 1967:								
Dividends paid:								
Co. SP, $5,000.	(4,250)			(5,000)		4,250		(5,000)
Co. P, $10,000.		(10,000)				(10,000)		
	131,750	260,000	92,000	21,000	136,000	264,250	96,000	25,000
December 31, 1967:								
Net income, 1967:								
Co. S, $10,000.			8,000	8,000				
Co. SP:								
Own operations. $10,000				10,000				10,000
Through ownership of Co. S. 8,000								
To Co. P, 85% of. . . . $18,000	15,300	15,300						
Co. P, $15,000.		15,000				15,000		
December 31, 1967, balances.	147,050	290,300	100,000	39,000	136,000	279,250	96,000	35,000

Equity method. Company SP recognizes earnings of the subsidiary from the date stock in Company S is acquired. Company P became a parent at the beginning of 1967, and at the end of 1967 it recognizes Company SP's earnings for the year as increased by the latter company's share in the earnings of Company S. Company P is thus affected by changes in the capital of Company S only from the date it acquires control of Company SP. Working papers for a consolidated balance sheet for Company P, Company SP, and Company S are illustrated below.

Equity method:

Company P and Subsidiary Companies
Working Papers for Consolidated Balance Sheet
December 31, 1967

	Co. P	Co. SP	Co. S	Eliminations		Consolidated Balance Sheet	
				Dr.	Cr.	Dr.	Cr.
Debits							
Investment in Co. SP Stock	147,050						
Eliminate 85% of Capital Stock					85,000		
Eliminate 85% of Retained Earnings					33,150		
Excess of Cost over Book Value.						28,900	
Investment in Co. S Stock		100,000					
Eliminate 80% of Capital Stock					80,000		
Eliminate 80% of Deficit				8,000			
Excess of Cost over Book Value.						28,000	
Other Assets	423,250	139,000	90,000			652,250	
	570,300	239,000	90,000				
Credits							
Liabilities	180,000	100,000					280,000
Capital Stock, Co. P	100,000						100,000
Retained Earnings, Co. P.	290,300						290,300
Capital Stock, Co. SP		100,000					
Eliminate 85%				85,000			
Minority Interest, 15%							15,000
Retained Earnings, Co. SP.		39,000					
Eliminate 85%				33,150			
Minority Interest, 15%							5,850
Capital Stock, Co. S			100,000				
Eliminate 80%				80,000			
Minority Interest, 20%							20,000
Deficit, Co. S			(10,000)				
Eliminate 80%					8,000		
Minority Interest, 20%						2,000	
	570,300	239,000	90,000	206,150	206,150	711,150	711,150

Cost method. If the cost method is employed, working papers will appear as illustrated at the top of the following page.

Eliminations for the investment of the subparent in the subsidiary are made in terms of the capital of the subsidiary at the date the subparent acquired control. Reference is made to the account balances reported by the subsidiary for this purpose. The earnings accruing from the subsidiary since the date of acquisition of control are transferred directly to the subparent retained earnings. Eliminations for the investment of the parent in the subparent are made in terms of the capital of the subparent at the date the parent acquired control. For this purpose, retained earnings of the subparent include the change in the capital of *ost method:*

Company P and Subsidiary Companies
Working Papers for Consolidated Balance Sheet
December 31, 1967

	Co. P	Co. SP	Co. S	Eliminations		Consolidated Balance Sheet	
				Dr.	Cr.	Dr.	Cr.
Debits							
vestment in Co. SP Stock	136,000						
Eliminate 85% of Capital Stock					85,000		
Eliminate 85% of $26,000, Retained Earnings on 1/1/67 ($30,000 − $4,000)					22,100		
Excess of Cost over Book Value						28,900	
vestment in Co. S Stock		96,000					
Eliminate 80% of Capital Stock					80,000		
Eliminate 80% of $15,000, Deficit on 1/1/66				12,000			
Excess of Cost over Book Value						28,000	
ther Assets	423,250	139,000	90,000			652,250	
	559,250	235,000	90,000				
Credits							
abilities	180,000	100,000					280,000
apital Stock, Co. P	100,000						100,000
etained Earnings, Co. P	279,250						279,250
apital Stock, Co. SP		100,000					
Eliminate 85%				85,000			
Minority Interest, 15%							15,000
etained Earnings, Co. SP		35,000			(x)4,000		
Eliminate 85% as above				22,100			
Minority Interest, 15% of $39,000							5,850
Retained Earnings to Co. P							11,050
apital Stock, Co. S			100,000				
Eliminate 80%				80,000			
Minority Interest, 20%							20,000
eficit, Co. S			(10,000)				
Eliminate 80% as above					12,000		
Minority Interest, 20% of $10,000 Deficit						2,000	
Retained Earnings to Co. SP				(x)4,000			
	559,250	235,000	90,000	203,100	203,100	711,150	711,150

the subsidiary accruing to the subparent up to the date the parent acquired control.

In the example, after the elimination of the subparent's share of the deficit on acquisition, $12,000, and after extension of the deficit relating to the minority interest, $2,000, the balance, or a $4,000 retained earnings increase, is carried to Company SP retained earnings (see entry [x]). The elimination of Company SP retained earnings is based on a balance of $26,000, or Company SP's balance of $30,000 as shown by the books, less $4,000, which is 80% of the $5,000 decrease in Company S retained earnings from the date the subparent's holdings were acquired to the date the parent acquired control of the subparent. The elimination, then, is 85% of $26,000, or $22,100. The minority interest in Company SP is stated at $5,850, which is 15% of $39,000, Company SP retained earnings of $35,000 as increased by subsidiary earnings of $4,000. The earnings accruing to Company P may now be extended to the consolidated balance sheet columns. This balance is $11,050, or the subparent retained earnings as adjusted, $39,000, less the elimination, $22,100, and less the subparent minority interest in retained earnings, $5,850.

CONTROL ACHIEVED BY MEANS OF CONNECTING AFFILIATES

Previous illustrations in this chapter provided for three-tier arrangements, sometimes referred to as father-son-grandson relationships, where direct control was exercised by the parent over the subparent and direct control was exercised in turn by the subparent over the subsidiary. There are instances when control is not achieved through direct ownership of the stock of another company as illustrated, but through the holdings of a connecting affiliate. When structures are complicated, they should be analyzed diagrammatically before the process of consolidation is begun. The previous example is diagramed at the left below; the example to follow is diagramed at the right.

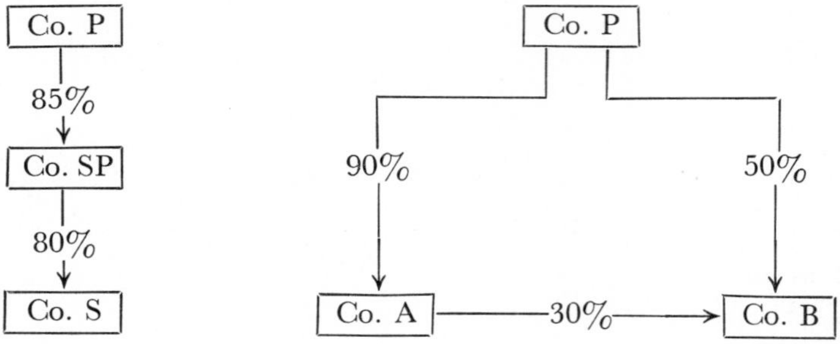

Assume the data that follow. On January 1, 1966, Company A purchases 300 shares of Company B stock at 125, paying $37,500. On January 1, 1967, Company P purchases 900 shares of Company A stock at 150, paying $135,000, and also 500 shares of Company B stock at 160, paying $80,000. The capital stock of each company is $100,000, consisting of 1,000 shares with a par value of $100. Retained earnings balances on December 31, 1965, and earnings and dividends for 1966 and 1967 follow:

	Co. P	Co. A	Co. B
Retained earnings, December 31, 1965	$180,000	$10,000	$20,000
Net income from own operations, 1966	40,000	30,000	20,000
Dividends declared in December, 1967	20,000	10,000	10,000
Net income from own operations, 1967	35,000	25,000	15,000

Company P exercises direct control over Company A beginning in 1967. In spite of the absence of a majority interest by Company P in Company B, Company P is assured of control over Company B through its ownership of a controlling interest in the connecting affiliate, Company A. Investment and retained earnings accounts of the parent and subsidiary companies are affected by earnings and dividends in 1966 and 1967 as shown on pages 494 and 495.

Equity method. No problem arises until 1967 when Company P acquires 90% of the stock of Company A and 50% of the stock of Company B. Company P now exercises direct control over Company A. It is also assured of control over Company B as a result of its control of Company A. If investments are to be carried by the equity method, investment balances should be adjusted to an equity basis as soon as control is achieved, and the subsequent accounting should follow normal equity procedures. As of January 1, 1967, Company A, viewing its investment in Company B as now converted into an interest expressing an affiliation with Company B, may take up its share of the capital change in Company B from the date it acquired its holdings in Company B: Company B's retained earnings have increased by $20,000 since the date the stock was acquired and Company A recognizes an increase in its investment account of 30% of $20,000, or $6,000. Henceforth Companies P and A continue to recognize earnings and dividends of affiliated units, and eliminations on the consolidated working papers are made in terms of capital balances as of the date of the consolidation.

Working papers for a consolidated balance sheet on December 31, 1967, are illustrated on page 496.

Cost method. If the cost method is employed, working papers will appear as illustrated on page 497.

The elimination of the investment of Company A in Company B is made in terms of the capital balances reported by the latter at the date Company A acquired control. For purposes of the elimination of the investment of Company P in Company A, however, the retained earnings balance of Company A must include its share of the increase in the capital of Company B up to the date of Company P control.

In the example on page 497, eliminations for the capital stock of Company B held by Companies P and A are followed by eliminations for retained earnings of Company B as of the dates of the respective stock acquisitions. After the extension of Company B retained earnings of $9,000 as minority interest, the balance, $10,000, represents the retained earnings increase accruing to Companies P and A. The retained earnings increase accruing to Company A is 30% of $25,000, the difference be-

	If Equity Method Is Used				
	Co. P Books			Co. A Books	
	Inv. in Co. A	Inv. in Co. B	Retained Earnings Co. P	Inv. in Co. B	Retained Earnings Co. A
December 31, 1965, balances			180,000		10,000
January 1, 1966:					
Purchase by Co. A of 300 shares of Co. B Stock at 125				37,500	
			180,000	37,500	10,000
December 31, 1966:					
Net income, 1966:					
Co. B, $20,000					
Co. A, $30,000					30,000
Co. P, $40,000			40,000		
			220,000	37,500	40,000
January 1, 1967:					
Purchase by Co. P of 900 shares of Co. A stock at 150	135,000				
Purchase by Co. P of 500 shares of Co. B stock at 160		80,000			
Recognition by Co. A of 30% of Co. B retained earnings increase for 1966 upon achieving control of Co. B through holdings of Companies P and A				6,000	6,000
	135,000	80,000	220,000	43,500	46,000
December, 1967:					
Dividends paid:					
Co. B, $10,000		(5,000)		(3,000)	
Co. A, $10,000	(9,000)				(10,000)
Co. P, $20,000			(20,000)		
	126,000	75,000	200,000	40,500	36,000
December 31, 1967:					
Net income, 1967:					
Co. B, $15,000		7,500	7,500	4,500	4,500
Co. A:					
Own operations $25,000					25,000
Through ownership of Co. B 4,500					
To Co. P, 90% of $29,500	26,550		26,550		
Co. P, $35,000			35,000		
December 31, 1967, balances	152,550	82,500	269,050	45,000	65,500

tween the present balance of retained earnings of $45,000 and the balance on the date of the original stock acquisition by Company A of $20,000, and this increase, $7,500, is carried to Company A retained earnings (entry [x]); the retained earnings increase accruing to Company P is 50% of $5,000, the difference between the present balance of retained earnings of $45,000 and the balance on the date of the original stock acquisition by Company P of $40,000, and this increase, $2,500, is

If Cost Method Is Used				
Co. P Books			Co. A Books	
Inv. in Co. A	Inv. in Co. B	Retained Earnings Co. P	Inv. in Co. B	Retained Earnings Co. A
		180,000		10,000
			37,500	
		180,000	37,500	10,000
				30,000
		40,000		
		220,000	37,500	40,000
135,000				
	80,000			
135,000	80,000	220,000	37,500	40,000
		5,000 9,000 (20,000)		3,000 (10,000)
135,000	80,000	214,000	37,500	33,000
				25,000
		35,000		
135,000	80,000	249,000	37,500	58,000

carried to the consolidated balance sheet columns. In eliminating the investment in Company A, retained earnings of the subsidiary are recognized as $46,000, or Company A's balance of $40,000 as reported on its books increased by $6,000, which is 30% of the increase in Company B's retained earnings from the date Company A acquired stock in Company B until the date Company P acquired control of Company A. The working papers are completed as in earlier examples.

Equity method:

Company P and Subsidiary Companies
Working Papers for Consolidated Balance Sheet
December 31, 1967

	Co. P	Co. A	Co. B	Eliminations		Consolidated Balance Sheet	
				Dr.	Cr.	Dr.	Cr.
Debits							
Investment in Co. A Stock......	152,550						
Eliminate 90% of Capital Stock					90,000		
Eliminate 90% of Retained Earnings................					58,950		
Excess of Cost over Book Value.						3,600	
Investment in Co. B Stock......	82,500						
Eliminate 50% of Capital Stock					50,000		
Eliminate 50% of Retained Earnings................					22,500		
Excess of Cost over Book Value.						10,000	
Investment in Co. B Stock......		45,000					
Eliminate 30% of Capital Stock					30,000		
Eliminate 30% of Retained Earnings................					13,500		
Excess of Cost over Book Value.						1,500	
Other Assets.................	284,000	220,500	225,000			729,500	
	519,050	265,500	225,000				
Credits							
Liabilities.....................	150,000	100,000	80,000				330,000
Capital Stock, Co. P...........	100,000						100,000
Retained Earnings, Co. P.......	269,050						269,050
Capital Stock, Co. A...........		100,000					
Eliminate 90%.............				90,000			
Minority Interest, 10%.......							10,000
Retained Earnings, Co. A.......		65,500					
Eliminate 90%.............				58,950			
Minority Interest, 10%.......							6,550
Capital Stock, Co. B...........			100,000				
Eliminate 50%.............				50,000			
Eliminate 30%.............				30,000			
Minority Interest, 20%.......							20,000
Retained Earnings, Co. B.......			45,000				
Eliminate 50%.............				22,500			
Eliminate 30%.............				13,500			
Minority Interest, 20%.......							9,000
	519,050	265,500	225,000	264,950	264,950	744,600	744,600

MUTUAL HOLDINGS

Occasionally it may be found that a company holds a controlling interest in a subsidiary, and the latter, in turn, holds a part of the stock of the parent company. When there are mutual holdings, the retained earnings change of the parent for any period depends upon the retained earnings change of the subsidiary, while the retained earnings change of the subsidiary may be viewed as similarly affected by the retained earnings change of the parent. With each change dependent upon the other,

Cost method:

Company P and Subsidiary Companies
Working Papers for Consolidated Balance Sheet
December 31, 1967

	Co. P	Co. A	Co. B	Eliminations Dr.	Eliminations Cr.	Consolidated Balance Sheet Dr.	Consolidated Balance Sheet Cr.
Debits							
Investment in Co. A Stock	135,000						
Eliminate 90% of Capital Stock					90,000		
Eliminate 90% of $46,000, Retained Earnings on 1/1/67 ($40,000 + $6,000)					41,400		
Excess of Cost over Book Value						3,600	
Investment in Co. B Stock	80,000						
Eliminate 50% of Capital Stock					50,000		
Eliminate 50% of $40,000, Retained Earnings on 1/1/67					20,000		
Excess of Cost over Book Value						10,000	
Investment in Co. B Stock		37,500					
Eliminate 30% of Capital Stock					30,000		
Eliminate 30% of $20,000, Retained Earnings on 1/1/66					6,000		
Excess of Cost over Book Value						1,500	
Other Assets	284,000	220,500	225,000			729,500	
	499,000	258,000	225,000				
Credits							
Liabilities	150,000	100,000	80,000				330,000
Capital Stock, Co. P	100,000						100,000
Retained Earnings, Co. P	249,000						249,000
Capital Stock, Co. A		100,000					
Eliminate 90%				90,000			
Minority Interest, 10%							10,000
Retained Earnings, Co. A		58,000					
Add Retained Earnings from Co. B					(x)7,500		
Eliminate 90% as above				41,400			
Minority Interest, 10% of $65,500							6,550
Retained Earnings to Co. P							17,550
Capital Stock, Co. B			100,000				
Eliminate 50% owned by Co. P				50,000			
Eliminate 30% owned by Co. A				30,000			
Minority Interest, 20%							20,000
Retained Earnings, Co. B			45,000				
Eliminate 50% as above				20,000			
Eliminate 30% as above				6,000			
Minority Interest, 20% of $45,000							9,000
Retained Earnings to Co. A, 30% of $25,000 ($45,000 Retained Earnings, 12/31/67 — $20,000, Retained Earnings 1/1/66)				(x)7,500			
Retained Earnings to Co. P, 50% of $5,000 ($45,000, Retained Earnings 12/31/67 — $40,000, Retained Earnings 1/1/67							2,500
	499,000	258,000	225,000	244,900	244,900	744,600	744,600

algebraic calculations are required in determining the respective changes. To illustrate, assume the following facts:

On January 1, 1966, date of organization of Co. S, Co. P acquired 800 shares of Co. S stock at par	$80,000
On January 1, 1967, Co. S purchased 100 shares of Co. P stock at 200	$20,000

The capital stock of each company is $100,000, consisting of 1,000 shares with a par value of $100. Retained earnings balances on December 31, 1965, and earnings and dividends for 1966 and 1967 are:

	Co. P	Co. S
Retained earnings, December 31, 1965	$40,000	—
Net income from own operations, 1966	15,000	$10,000
Dividends declared in December, 1967	5,000	5,000
Net income from own operations, 1967	20,000	10,000

Changes in the investment and retained earnings accounts of the parent and the subsidiary company are shown on this and the following page.

	If Equity Method Is Used			
	Co. P Books		Co. S Books	
	Inv. in Co. S	Retained Earnings Co. P	Inv. in Co. P	Retained Earnings Co. S
December 31, 1965, balances		40,000.00		
January 1, 1966:				
Purchase by Co. P of 800 shares of Co. S stock at 100	80,000.00			
	80,000.00	40,000.00		
December 31, 1966:				
Net income for 1966:				
Co. S, $10,000	8,000.00	8,000.00		10,000.00
Co. P, $15,000		15,000.00		
	88,000.00	63,000.00		10,000.00
January 1, 1967:				
Purchase by Co. S of 100 shares of Co. P stock at 200			20,000.00	
	88,000.00	63,000.00	20,000.00	10,000.00
December, 1967:				
Dividends paid:				
Co. S, $5,000	(4,000.00)			(5,000.00)
Co. P, $5,000		(5,000.00)	(500.00)	
	84,000.00	58,000.00	19,500.00	5,000.00
December 31, 1967:				
Net income for 1967:				
Co. S, $10,000	10,434.78	10,434.78		10,000.00
Co. P, $20,000		20,000.00	3,043.48	3,043.48
December 31, 1967, balances	94,434.78	88,434.78	22,543.48	18,043.48

Equity method. No special problem arises until 1967 when Companies P and S record the earnings accruing to each as a result of the transactions of the other. The earnings to be recorded by each company may be computed algebraically in the following manner:

Let P = P's *increase in retained earnings*, consisting of P's net income plus the share of S's earnings accruing to P.

Let S = S's *increase in retained earnings*, consisting of S's net income plus the share of P's earnings accruing to S.

$$\text{Then: } P = \$20{,}000 + .8S$$
$$S = \$10{,}000 + .1P$$

To solve for P:

$$P = \$20{,}000 + .8\,(\$10{,}000 + .1P)$$
$$P = \$20{,}000 + \$8{,}000 + .08P$$
$$P - .08P = \$28{,}000$$
$$.92P = \$28{,}000$$
$$P = \$30{,}434.78$$

To solve for S:

$$S = \$10{,}000 + .1P$$
$$S = \$10{,}000 + .1\,(\$30{,}434.78)$$
$$S = \$10{,}000 + \$3{,}043.48$$
$$S = \$13{,}043.48$$

S takes up 10% of this increase in P's retained earnings:
10% of $30,434.78, or $3,043.48

P takes up 80% of this increase in S's retained earnings:
80% of $13,043.48, or $10,434.78

If Cost Method Is Used

Co. P Books		Co. S Books	
Inv. in Co. S	Retained Earnings Co. P	Inv. in Co. P	Retained Earnings Co. S
	40,000.00		
80,000.00			
80,000.00	40,000.00		
			10,000.00
	15,000.00		
80,000.00	55,000.00		10,000.00
		20,000.00	
80,000.00	55,000.00	20,000.00	10,000.00
	4,000.00		(5,000.00)
	(5,000.00)		500.00
80,000.00	54,000.00	20,000.00	5,500.00
			10,000.00
	20,000.00		
80,000.00	74,000.00	20,000.00	15,500.00

It would be possible to solve for P in an alternative manner as follows:

$$P = \$20{,}000 + .8S$$
$$S = \$10{,}000 + .1P$$

Multiplying the first equation by 5 and the second equation by 4:

$$5P - 4S = \$100{,}000$$
$$-.4P + 4S = \$\ 40{,}000$$

Adding the two equations:

$$4.6P = \$140{,}000.00$$
$$P = \$\ 30{,}434.78$$

Since Company P's retained earnings increase is \$30,434.78, Company S will take up 10% of this amount, or \$3,043.48. Company S's retained earnings increase is now \$10,000.00 + \$3,043.48, or \$13,043.48, and Company P takes up 80% of this amount, or \$10,434.78. These entries result in total retained earnings increases on the books of Com-

Equity method:

Company P and Subsidiary Company S
Working Papers for Consolidated Balance Sheet
December 31, 1967

	Co. P	Co. S	Eliminations		Consolidated Balance Sheet	
			Dr.	Cr.	Dr.	Cr.
Debits						
Investment in Co. S Stock	94,434.78					
Eliminate 80% of Capital Stock				80,000.00		
Eliminate 80% of Retained Earnings				14,434.78		
Investment in Co. P Stock		22,543.48				
Eliminate 10% of Capital Stock				10,000.00		
Eliminate 10% of Retained Earnings				8,843.48		
Excess of Cost over Book Value					3,700.00	
Other Assets	244,000.00	195,500.00			439,500.00	
	338,434.78	218,043.48				
Credits						
Liabilities	150,000.00	100,000.00				250,000.00
Capital Stock, Co. P	100,000.00					
Eliminate 10%			10,000.00			90,000.00
Retained Earnings, Co. P	88,434.78					
Eliminate 10%			8,843.48			79,591.30
Capital Stock, Co. S		100,000.00				
Eliminate 80%			80,000.00			
Minority Interest, 20%						20,000.00
Retained Earnings, Co. S		18,043.48				
Eliminate 80%			14,434.78			
Minority Interest, 20%						3,608.70
	338,434.78	218,043.48	113,278.26	113,278.26	443,200.00	443,200.00

pany P and Company S of \$30,434.78 and \$13,043.48 respectively, the amounts that were calculated algebraically.

Working papers for a consolidated balance sheet are illustrated at the bottom of page 500. The combined earnings for the year for Company P and Company S were \$30,000 (\$20,000 + \$10,000). After eliminations on the working papers, the earnings related to the controlling and minority interests are equal to this sum: earnings reflected in an increase in retained earnings for the controlling interest are \$27,391.30 (90% of \$30,434.78); earnings reflected in an increase in retained earnings for the minority interest are \$2,608.70 (20% of \$13,043.48).

Cost method. When the cost method is adopted, there is no need to calculate the earnings to be recorded as a result of the operations of the affiliate. However, after eliminations have been made for the parent's equity in the subsidiary at date of acquisition, it is necessary to calculate the minority interest in the subsidiary. This figure will not be the minority percentage of the subsidiary retained earnings balance as shown, since this balance does not include the earnings accruing to the subsidiary as a result of its interest in the parent.

To calculate the minority interest, the subsidiary retained earnings balance may first be computed as follows:

Let P = P's *total retained earnings* balance on December 31, 1967.
Let S = S's *total retained earnings* balance on December 31, 1967.

Company P's total retained earnings consist of its present retained earnings balance, \$74,000, plus 80% of Company S's total retained earnings, since it has owned the subsidiary since its formation. Company S's total retained earnings consist of its present balance, \$15,500, plus 10% of Company P's retained earnings increase for the current year. Company P's retained earnings increase for the current year is represented by its present balance as adjusted by its share of the change in subsidiary company capital, less its balance at the end of the preceding year as adjusted by its share of the change in the subsidiary company capital at that time. Company P's retained earnings balance at the end of the preceding year was \$63,000: the reported balance, \$55,000, plus its share of the increase in the retained earnings of Company S since date of stock acquisition, 80% of \$10,000, or \$8,000.

Total retained earnings balances of the two companies on December 31, 1967, may be stated as follows:

$$P = \$74{,}000 + .8S$$
$$S = \$15{,}500 + .1\ (P - \$63{,}000)$$

The retained earnings of Company S can now be calculated as follows:

$$
\begin{aligned}
S &= \$15{,}500 + .1\ (P - \$63{,}000)\\
S &= \$15{,}500 + .1\ (\$74{,}000 + .8S - \$63{,}000)\\
S &= \$15{,}500 + \$7{,}400 + .08S - \$6{,}300\\
S - .08S &= \$16{,}600\\
.92S &= \$16{,}600\\
S &= \underline{\underline{\$18{,}043.48}}
\end{aligned}
$$

The retained earnings of Company P are computed as follows:

$$
\begin{aligned}
P &= \$74{,}000 + .8\ (\$18{,}043.48)\\
P &= \$74{,}000 + \$14{,}434.78\\
P &= \underline{\underline{\$88{,}434.78.}}
\end{aligned}
$$

The subsidiary retained earnings balance has been calculated at $18,043.48. The minority interest of 20% of this balance, or $3,608.70, is now extended to the consolidated balance sheet columns. The difference between $15,500.00, the retained earnings for Company S, and $3,608.70, the minority interest, or $11,891.30, represents the increase in retained earnings of the subsidiary accruing to the parent company since acquisition. The working papers are illustrated below.

Cost method:

Company P and Subsidiary Company S
Working Papers for Consolidated Balance Sheet
December 31, 1967

	Co. P	Co. S	Eliminations Dr.	Eliminations Cr.	Consolidated Balance Sheet Dr.	Consolidated Balance Sheet Cr.
Debits						
Investment in Co. S Stock	80,000.00					
Eliminate 80% of Capital Stock				80,000.00		
Investment in Co. P Stock		20,000.00				
Eliminate 10% of Capital Stock				10,000.00		
Eliminate 10% of $63,000, Retained Earnings on 1/1/67				6,300.00		
Excess of Cost over Book Value					3,700.00	
Other Assets	244,000.00	195,500.00			439,500.00	
	324,000.00	215,500.00				
Credits						
Liabilities	150,000.00	100,000.00				250,000.00
Capital Stock, Co. P	100,000.00					
Eliminate 10%			10,000.00			90,000.00
Retained Earnings, Co. P	74,000.00					
Eliminate 10% as above			6,300.00			67,700.00
Capital Stock, Co. S		100,000.00				
Eliminate 80%			80,000.00			
Minority Interest, 20%						20,000.00
Retained Earnings, Co. S		15,500.00				
Minority Interest, 20% of $18,043.48, Retained Earnings as computed						3,608.70
Retained Earnings to Co. P						11,891.30
	324,000.00	215,500.00	96,300.00	96,300.00	443,200.00	443,200.00

MUTUAL HOLDINGS ARISING WITHIN FISCAL PERIOD

Purchase of stock resulting in mutual holdings may take place within the fiscal period. When this is the case, the increases in retained earnings are computed on a mutual basis for only the portion of the period during which the reciprocal ownership existed.

Assume the following data. On January 1, 1966, Company P acquired 900 shares (90%) of Company S stock for $150,000. On April 1, 1967, Company S acquired 100 shares (10%) of Company P stock for $25,000. Capital stock of each company is $100,000, consisting of 1,000 shares with a par value of $100. Retained earnings balances on December 31, 1965, and earnings for 1966 and 1967 follow:

	Co. P	Co. S
Retained earnings, December 31, 1965	$ 50,000	$20,000
Net income from own operations, 1966	30,000	10,000
Retained earnings, December 31, 1966	$ 80,000	$30,000
Net income from own operations, 1967	40,000	20,000
Retained earnings, December 31, 1967	$120,000	$50,000

Equity method. Assuming use of the equity method, changes in the investment accounts and retained earnings accounts are as follows:

	If Equity Method Is Used			
	Co. P Books		Co. S Books	
	Inv. in Co. S	Retained Earnings Co. P	Inv. in Co. P	Retained Earnings Co. S
December 31, 1965, balances		50,000.00		20,000.00
January 1, 1966:				
Purchase by Co. P of 900 shares of Co. S stock	150,000.00			
	150,000.00	50,000.00		20,000.00
December 31, 1966:				
Net income for 1966:				
Co. S, $10,000	9,000.00	9,000.00		10,000.00
Co. P, $30,000		30,000.00		
	159,000.00	89,000.00		30,000.00
April 1, 1967:				
Purchase by Co. S of 100 shares of Co. P stock			25,000.00	
	159,000.00	89,000.00	25,000.00	30,000.00
December 31, 1967:				
Net income, January 1–April 1:				
Co. S, ¼ of $20,000	4,500.00	4,500.00		5,000.00
Co. P, ¼ of $40,000		10,000.00		
Net income, April 1–December 31:				
Co. S, ¾ of $20,000				15,000.00
10% of Co. P earnings			4,780.22	4,780.22
Co. P, ¾ of $40,000		30,000.00		
90% of Co. S earnings	17,802.20	17,802.20		
December 31, 1967, balances	181,302.20	151,302.20	29,780.22	54,780.22

It will be observed that Company P took up 90% of Company S earnings for the first three months of 1967. Since there were mutual holdings of stock thereafter, company earnings are determined algebraically for the balance of the year as shown below.

Let P and S represent earnings of respective companies for the nine-month period, April 1–December 31:

$$P = \$30,000 + .9S$$
$$S = \$15,000 + .1P$$

To solve for P:

$$P = \$30,000 + .9\ (\$15,000 + .1P)$$
$$P = \$30,000 + \$13,500 + .09P$$
$$P - .09P = \$43,500$$
$$.91P = \$43,500$$
$$P = \$47,802.20$$

To solve for S:

$$S = \$15,000 + .1\ (\$47,802.20)$$
$$S = \$15,000 + \$4,780.22$$
$$S = \$19,780.22$$

S takes up 10% of these earnings:
10% of \$47,802.20 = \$4,780.22

P takes up 90% of these earnings:
90% of \$19,780.22 = \$17,802.20

Working papers for a consolidated balance sheet would be prepared as follows:

Equity method:

Company P and Subsidiary Company S
Working Papers for Consolidated Balance Sheet
December 31, 1967

	Co. P	Co. S	Eliminations Dr.	Eliminations Cr.	Consolidated Balance Sheet Dr.	Consolidated Balance Sheet Cr.
Debits						
Investment in Co. S Stock	181,302.20					
Eliminate 90% of Capital Stock				90,000.00		
Eliminate 90% of Retained Earnings				49,302.20		
Excess of Cost over Book Value					42,000.00	
Investment in Co. P Stock		29,780.22				
Eliminate 10% of Capital Stock				10,000.00		
Eliminate 10% of Retained Earnings				15,130.22		
Excess of Cost over Book Value					4,650.00	
Other Assets	200,000.00	150,000.00			350,000.00	
	381,302.20	179,780.22				
Credits						
Liabilities	130,000.00	25,000.00				155,000.00
Capital Stock, Co. P	100,000.00					
Eliminate 10%			10,000.00			90,000.00
Retained Earnings, Co. P	151,302.20					
Eliminate 10%			15,130.22			136,171.98
Capital Stock, Co. S		100,000.00				
Eliminate 90%			90,000.00			
Minority Interest, 10%						10,000.00
Retained Earnings, Co. S		54,780.22				
Eliminate 90%			49,302.20			
Minority Interest, 10%						5,478.02
	381,302.20	179,780.22	164,432.42	164,432.42	396,650.00	396,650.00

Cost method. Assuming use of the cost method, changes in the investment and retained earnings accounts would be as follows:

	If Cost Method Is Followed			
	Co. P Books		Co. S Books	
	Inv. in Co. S	Retained Earnings Co. P	Inv. in Co. P	Retained Earnings Co. S
December 31, 1965, balances		50,000.00		20,000.00
January 1, 1966: Purchase by Co. P of 900 shares of Co. S stock	150,000.00			
	150,000.00	50,000.00		20,000.00
December 31, 1966: Net income for 1966: Co. S, $10,000				10,000.00
Co. P, $30,000		30,000.00		
	150,000.00	80,000.00		30,000.00
April 1, 1967: Purchase by Co. S of 100 shares of Co. P stock			25,000.00	
	150,000.00	80,000.00	25,000.00	30,000.00
December 31, 1967: Net income for 1967: Co. S, $20,000				20,000.00
Co. P, $40,000		40,000.00		
December 31, 1967, balances	150,000.00	120,000.00	25,000.00	50,000.00

The Company S retained earnings balance for the purpose of computing the minority interest in this company is calculated at the end of 1967 as follows:

Let P and S represent total retained earnings balances of Companies P and S respectively. Company P acquired Company S stock when the Company S retained earnings balance was $20,000. Company P's retained earnings total consists of its balance on the books plus 90% of the increase in Company S's retained earnings since January 1, 1966. P, then, may be stated:

$$P = \$120,000 + .9\,(S - \$20,000)$$

Company S acquired Company P stock on April 1, 1967, when Company P's retained earnings were $90,000: $80,000 as of December 31, 1966, plus ¼ of $40,000, the net income for 1967. However, the earnings of Company S from January 1, 1966, to April 1, 1967, although not appearing on Company P's books when the cost method is used in carrying investments, nevertheless require recognition in stating Company P's retained earnings on the date Company S acquired an interest in Company P. Company P's retained earnings on April 1, then, are $103,500, or $90,000 plus 90% of $15,000 ($10,000 + $5,000, subsidiary earnings for 1966 and for January 1–April 1, 1967). Company S's retained earnings consist of its balance on the books plus 10% of the increase in Company P's retained earnings since April 1, 1967. S, then, may be stated:

$$S = \$50{,}000 + .1\ (P - \$103{,}500)$$

To solve for S:

$$\begin{aligned} S &= \$50{,}000 + .1\ (\$120{,}000 + .9S - \$18{,}000 - \$103{,}500) \\ S &= \$50{,}000 + \$12{,}000 + .09S - \$1{,}800 - \$10{,}350 \\ S - .09S &= \$50{,}000 + \$12{,}000 - \$1{,}800 - \$10{,}350 \\ .91S &= \$49{,}850 \\ S &= \underline{\underline{\$54{,}780.22}} \end{aligned}$$

Working papers would be prepared as follows:

Cost method:

Company P and Subsidiary Company S
Working Papers for Consolidated Balance Sheet
December 31, 1967

	Co. P	Co. S	Eliminations		Consolidated Balance Sheet	
			Dr.	Cr.	Dr.	Cr.
Debits						
Investment in Co. S Stock	150,000.00					
Eliminate 90% of Capital Stock				90,000.00		
Eliminate 90% of $20,000, Retained Earnings on Jan. 1, 1966				18,000.00		
Excess of Cost over Book Value					42,000.00	
Investment in Co. P Stock		25,000.00				
Eliminate 10% of Capital Stock				10,000.00		
Eliminate 10% of $103,500, Retained Earnings on April 1, 1967				10,350.00		
Excess of Cost over Book Value					4,650.00	
Other Assets	200,000.00	150,000.00			350,000.00	
	350,000.00	175,000.00				
Credits						
Liabilities	130,000.00	25,000.00				155,000.00
Capital Stock, Co. P	100,000.00					
Eliminate 10%			10,000.00			90,000.00
Retained Earnings, Co. P	120,000.00					
Eliminate 10% as above			10,350.00			109,650.00
Capital Stock, Co. S		100,000.00				
Eliminate 90%			90,000.00			
Minority Interest, 10%						10,000.00
Retained Earnings, Co. S		50,000.00				
Eliminate 90% as above			18,000.00			
Minority Interest, 10% of $54,780.22, Retained Earnings as computed						5,478.02
Retained Earnings to Co. P						26,521.98
	350,000.00	175,000.00	128,350.00	128,350.00	396,650.00	396,650.00

MUTUAL HOLDINGS — SHARES OF PARENT HELD BY AFFILIATE REGARDED AS TREASURY STOCK

The preceding pages have described the approach that has generally been taken when there are mutual holdings within an affiliated group of companies. Equities of the parent company stockholders and the minority interests in consolidated assets are developed as of the date of the consolidated statements; equities are determined on the assumption that net earnings are fully distributed on the date of the consolidated balance sheet, successive distributions by the companies to their stockholders ultimately resulting in participation in earnings by the controlling interest and by the minority interest as indicated by the application of the simultaneous equations.

It is possible, however, to take a quite different approach in preparing the consolidated statement. The statement can be developed on the assumption that the shares of a parent held by a subsidiary will ultimately be resold by the subsidiary either to outsiders or directly to the parent. Such an assumption calls for the recognition of parent company shares held by an affiliate as treasury stock. There is no participation by the minority interest in parent company earnings; instead, the minority interest remains unchanged until the subsidiary sells its interest in the parent at an amount other than its cost.

In adopting the treasury stock approach, the parent company carries the investment in the subsidiary on its books just like any other controlling interest; the subsidiary company carries the investment in stock of the parent company as a long-term investment. In preparing a consolidated balance sheet, the investment in subsidiary company stock is eliminated. The investment in parent company stock is reported as treasury stock.

To illustrate the application of the treasury stock approach, assume the same facts as in the preceding example. Changes in the investment accounts and the retained earnings accounts of the parent and the subsidiary company would be as shown at the top of the following page.

If Company P carried the investment in Company S at equity, working papers for a consolidated balance sheet would be prepared as shown at the top of page 509; if the investment is carried at cost, working papers would be prepared as shown at the bottom of page 509.

In preparing the working papers, investments in parent company stock are carried to the consolidated balance sheet columns at their cost. In preparing the consolidated balance sheet, the cost of such investments may be recognized as reductions in parent company paid-in capital and retained earnings balances. Capital balances of the controlling interest are thus reported in terms of the shares that are actually outstanding.

	If Equity Method Is Used				If Cost Method Is Used			
	Co. P Books		Co. S Books		Co. P Books		Co. S Books	
	Inv. in Co. S	Retained Earnings Co. P	Inv. in Co. P	Retained Earnings Co. S	Inv. in Co. S	Retained Earnings Co. P	Inv. in Co. P	Retained Earnings Co. S
December 31, 1965, balances		50,000		20,000		50,000		20,000
January 1, 1966: Purchase by Co. P of 900 shares of Co. S stock	150,000				150,000			
	150,000	50,000		20,000	150,000	50,000		20,000
December 31, 1966: Net income for 1966:								
Co. S, $10,000	9,000	9,000		10,000				10,000
Co. P, $30,000		30,000				30,000		
	159,000	89,000		30,000	150,000	80,000		30,000
April 1, 1967: Purchase by Co. S of 100 shares of Co. P stock			25,000				25,000	
December 31, 1967: Net income for 1967:								
Co. S, $20,000	18,000	18,000		20,000				20,000
Co. P, $40,000		40,000				40,000		
December 31, 1967, balances	177,000	147,000	25,000	50,000	150,000	120,000	25,000	50,000

In the example, ownership of 10% of the outstanding stock of Company P at a cost of $25,000 calls for reductions in capital stock of $10,000 and retained earnings of $15,000. The controlling interest will appear on the consolidated balance sheet as follows:

Controlling interest:		
Capital stock, 900 shares	$ 90,000	
Retained earnings	132,000	$222,000

It would be possible to report the cost of the holdings in Company P as a subtraction from the sum of the capital balances of the parent company in stating the controlling interest on the consolidated balance sheet. If holdings in Company P are to be reported in this manner, the controlling interest would be presented as follows:

Controlling interest:		
Capital stock, 1,000 shares	$100,000	
Retained earnings	147,000	
	$247,000	
Less capital stock held by affiliated unit, 100 shares, at cost	25,000	$222,000

The American Institute Committee on Accounting Procedure in referring to mutual holdings merely observes, "Shares of the parent held by a subsidiary should not be treated as outstanding stock in the consolidated balance sheet."[1] The American Accounting Association

[1]*Accounting Research Bulletin No. 51*, "Consolidated Financial Statements," 1959 (New York: American Institute of Certified Public Accountants), p. 45.

Equity method:

Company P and Subsidiary Company S
Working Papers for Consolidated Balance Sheet
December 31, 1967

	Co. P	Co. S	Eliminations Dr.	Eliminations Cr.	Consolidated Balance Sheet Dr.	Consolidated Balance Sheet Cr.
Debits						
Investment in Co. S Stock	177,000					
Eliminate 90% of Capital Stock				90,000		
Eliminate 90% of Retained Earnings				45,000		
Excess of Cost over Book Value					42,000	
Investment in Co. P Stock		25,000			25,000	
Other Assets	200,000	150,000			350,000	
	377,000	175,000				
Credits						
Liabilities	130,000	25,000				155,000
Capital Stock, Co. P	100,000					100,000
Retained Earnings, Co. P	147,000					147,000
Capital Stock, Co. S		100,000				
Eliminate 90%			90,000			
Minority Interest, 10%						10,000
Retained Earnings, Co. S		50,000				
Eliminate 90%			45,000			
Minority Interest, 10%						5,000
	377,000	175,000	135,000	135,000	417,000	417,000

Cost method:

Company P and Subsidiary Company S
Working Papers for Consolidated Balance Sheet
December 31, 1967

	Co. P	Co. S	Eliminations Dr.	Eliminations Cr.	Consolidated Balance Sheet Dr.	Consolidated Balance Sheet Cr.
Debits						
Investment in Co. S Stock	150,000					
Eliminate 90% of Capital Stock				90,000		
Eliminate 90% of $20,000, Retained Earnings on Jan. 1, 1966				18,000		
Excess of Cost over Book Value					42,000	
Investment in Co. P Stock		25,000			25,000	
Other Assets	200,000	150,000			350,000	
	350,000	175,000				
Credits						
Liabilities	130,000	25,000				155,000
Capital Stock, Co. P	100,000					100,000
Retained Earnings, Co. P	120,000					120,000
Capital Stock, Co. S		100,000				
Eliminate 90%			90,000			
Minority Interest, 10%						10,000
Retained Earnings, Co. S		50,000				
Eliminate 90% as Above			18,000			
Minority nterest, 10% of $50,000						5,000
Retained Earnings to Parent						27,000
	350,000	175,000	108,000	108,000	417,000	417,000

Committee on Concepts and Standards has gone further and recommends that holdings of parent company shares be treated as treasury stock. The Committee comments:

> Shares of the controlling company's capital stock owned by a subsidiary before the date of acquisition of control should be treated in consolidation as treasury stock. Any subsequent acquisition or sale by a subsidiary should likewise be treated in the consolidated statements as though it had been the act of the controlling company.[1]

The recognition of investments in parent company shares as treasury stock on the consolidated balance sheet is both sound in theory and simple in application. There is strong theoretical support for viewing parent company holdings by a subsidiary company as, in effect, reacquired shares. The need for assigning earnings to controlling and minority interests on the assumption of a simultaneous distribution of earnings is avoided. There is some evidence that the treasury stock approach is finding preference in contemporary practice.

COMPLEX RELATIONSHIPS

More complex indirect and mutual relationships than those illustrated in this chapter are sometimes encountered. When more involved ownership problems are encountered, the accounting and the preparation of consolidated statements are possible by careful analysis of the relationships involved and application of the rules developed in this chapter.

QUESTIONS

1. Distinguish between a condition of direct ownership and one of indirect ownership.

2. The Farris Company acquired control of the Gross Company in 1962. The Gross Company is a parent company, controlling activities of the Hardin Company and the Irwin Company. Investments in subsidiary companies are carried at cost. (a) What eliminations are made for the investment in the Gross Company in preparing working papers for a consolidated balance sheet for the Farris Company on December 31, 1967, assuming that subsidiary company investments were made by the Gross Company after the Farris Company acquired control? (b) How would your answer differ if subsidiary company investments were made by the Gross Company prior to the date the Farris Company acquired control?

---

[1]Accounting and Reporting Standards for Corporate Financial Statements and Preceding Statements and Supplements, "Consolidated Financial Statements, 1954" (Columbus: American Accounting Association), p. 44.

3. Company A has owned 90% of the stock of Company B since 1962. Company B acquired 80% of the stock of Company C upon its formation on January 1, 1964. (a) What percentage of Company C's retained earnings will be reported as retained earnings of the controlling interest on a consolidated balance sheet for Companies A, B, and C prepared on January 1, 1968? (b) Assuming control by Company B over Company C as indicated but acquisition of Company A's interest in Company B on January 1, 1968, what percentage of Company C's retained earnings will be reflected as retained earnings of the controlling interest on the consolidated balance sheet prepared on this date?

4. Company Q owns 90% of the stock of Company R and 80% of the stock of Company S. Each of the latter companies owns 40% of the stock of Company T. Can the net assets of Company T be properly included in a consolidated balance sheet prepared for Company Q? Give reasons for your answer.

5. What is meant by a condition of "mutual holdings"?

6. (a) What two views may be adopted in developing a consolidated balance sheet for two affiliates with mutual holdings? (b) Give the arguments that may be raised in support of each. (c) Which view do you support? Why?

7. Assuming that two affiliated companies have mutual holdings and recognize the earnings of each other in consolidation, what special calculations are required in the preparation of a consolidated balance sheet when (a) investments are carried by the equity method and (b) investments are carried by the cost method?

8. The Price Company, a subsidiary of Phillips, Inc., holds 500 shares representing a 2½% interest in the stock of the latter company. The shares were acquired at a price in excess of their book value and are carried at cost. Assuming that holdings of the subsidiary are not eliminated in the preparation of a consolidated balance sheet, explain two methods for reporting such acquisition on the consolidated balance sheet.

EXERCISES

1. On January 2, 1966, the Cokely Corporation acquired 900 shares of the Gable Corporation stock at 140. On January 2, 1967, the Gable Corporation acquired 800 shares of Hall Company stock at 90. The capital stock of each company is $100,000 and shares have a par value of $100. Retained earnings balances on December 31, 1965, and earnings and dividends for 1966 and 1967 were as shown at the top of the following page.

	Cokely	Gable	Hall
Retained earnings (deficit), December 31, 1965	$140,000	$50,000	($10,000)
Dividends declared in November, 1966	20,000	10,000	
Net income from own operations, 1966	30,000	20,000	15,000
Dividends declared in November, 1967	20,000	10,000	10,000
Net income from own operations, 1967	40,000	25,000	20,000

Give the entries affecting the investment accounts and retained earnings accounts on the books of the Hall Company, the Gable Corporation, and the Cokely Corporation if investments are carried by (a) the equity method and (b) the cost method.

2. Retained earnings changes for Companies A, B, and C are summarized below:

	Co. A	Co. B	Co. C
Retained earnings, January 1, 1967	$85,000	$60,000	$10,000
Net income, 1967	14,500	25,000	15,000
	$99,500	$85,000	$25,000
Dividends declared and paid in December, 1967	(20,000)	(15,000)	(10,000)
Retained earnings, December 31, 1967	$79,500	$70,000	$15,000

Give the entries that would be made on the books of the parent company and the subparent company during 1967, assuming use of the equity method and facts as indicated in each case below.

(a) Company A acquired 90% of the stock of Company B on January 2, 1966; Company B acquired 80% of the stock of Company C on July 1, 1967.

(b) Company A acquired 90% of the stock of Company B on July 1, 1967; Company B had acquired 80% of the stock of Company C on January 2, 1966.

3. Give the entries that would appear in each case in Exercise 2, assuming that investments are carried by the cost method.

4. Company F owns 90% of the stock of Company G, the stock having been acquired on January 2, 1960, when Company G showed on its books a deficit of $200,000. Company P acquired 90% of the stock of Company F on January 2, 1965, when Company F showed on its books retained earnings of $300,000. Company G's deficit had been reduced to $60,000 on this date. Investment accounts are carried at cost. On December 31, 1967, retained earnings balances for Companies P, F, and G are as follows: Company P, $3,000,000; Company F, $280,000; Company G, $40,000. (a) What is the amount of retained earnings of the controlling interest to be reported on the consolidated balance sheet prepared for Company P and its affiliates on December 31, 1967? (b) What is the amount of retained earnings of the minority interest on this date?

5. Company A owns 90% of the stock of Company B, and Company B owns 80% of the stock of Company C. What elimination for intercompany profits is required on the working papers for a consolidated balance sheet for each case below, assuming that merchandise is sold at a gross profit on sales of 15%? (Assume that investment accounts are carried by the equity method.)

(a) Merchandise held by Co. C, acquired from Co. A, $25,000.
(b) Merchandise held by Co. B, acquired from Co. A, $25,000.
(c) Merchandise held by Co. C, acquired from Co. B, $25,000.
(d) Merchandise held by Co. A, acquired from Co. C, $25,000.

6. On January 2, 1967, the Marsh Manufacturing Company acquired 800 shares of stock in Lowell, Inc. at 80. On the same date the latter corporation acquired 100 shares of parent company stock at 90. Capital stock and retained earnings accounts on December 31, 1967, are:

	Marsh Mfg. Co.		Lowell, Inc.	
Capital stock (1,000 shares)		$100,000		$100,000
Retained earnings, January 2, 1967	$40,000		$10,000	
Net income for 1967	20,000	60,000	5,000	15,000
Total capital, December 31, 1967		$160,000		$115,000

Each company recognizes the earnings of the other on consolidated statements.

(a) Assuming that investments are carried by the equity method, give the entry for each company to recognize the earnings of the affiliate for the year. (b) Assuming that the investment in the subsidiary is carried at cost, calculate the total minority interest that will be reported on the consolidated balance sheet at the end of 1967.

7. Company Y owns 800,000 shares of the stock of Company Z. Company Z in turn owns 250,000 shares of the stock of Company Y. Each company has 1,000,000 shares of stock outstanding. Earnings for Companies Y and Z for 1967 were $100,000 and $40,000 respectively before considering the earnings in each other. (a) What are the earnings of Company Y and of Company Z for the year after recognition by each company of earnings of the other? (b) Assuming that the earnings of $140,000 are ultimately distributed as dividends, how much will be received by the outside stockholders owning Company Y shares and by the outside stockholders owning Company Z shares?

8. Capital stock and retained earnings balances of Companies A and B on December 31, 1967, follow:

	Co. A	Co. B
Capital stock, $100 par	$200,000	$100,000
Retained earnings (deficit)	50,000	(10,000)
	$250,000	$ 90,000

Company A acquired a 90% interest in Company B on June 1, 1963, when Company B's retained earnings were $15,000. Company B acquired a 5% interest in Company A on January 2, 1965; on this date Company B showed retained earnings of $5,000 and Company A showed retained earnings of $30,000. Investments are carried at cost. In preparing consolidated statements each company recognizes its share of the earnings of the other.

(a) What is the total to be reported for the controlling interest on a consolidated balance sheet prepared on December 31, 1967? (b) What is the total to be reported for the minority interest on December 31, 1967?

PROBLEMS

15-1. Company X acquired 80% of the capital stock of Company Y on January 2, 1966, at a cost of $600,000. On this date Company Y held 75% of the stock of Company Z. This interest had been acquired for $187,500 on January 2, 1960, the date Company Z had been organized. On January 2, 1967, Company X purchased 15% of Company Z stock from a stockholder for $85,000. Balance sheet data for the three companies and a summary of changes in retained earnings for the period 1965–1967 follow.

	Co. X	Co. Y	Co. Z
Investment in stock of Co. Y	$ 600,000		
Investment in stock of Co. Z	85,000	$187,500	
Other assets	640,000	637,500	$560,000
Total assets	$1,325,000	$825,000	$560,000
Liabilities	$ 350,000	$265,000	$160,000
Capital stock	1,000,000	500,000	200,000
Premium on issue of stock			50,000
Retained earnings (deficit)	(25,000)	60,000	150,000
Total liabilities and stockholders' equity	$1,325,000	$825,000	$560,000
Retained earnings (deficit), Jan. 1, 1966	($ 115,000)	($ 20,000)	$140,000
Net income (loss), 1966	40,000	60,000	60,000
Dividends, 1966		(15,000)	(20,000)
Retained earnings (deficit), Jan. 1, 1967	($ 75,000)	$ 25,000	$180,000
Net income (loss), 1967	50,000	65,000	(30,000)
Dividends, 1967		(30,000)	
Retained earnings (deficit), Dec. 31, 1967	($ 25,000)	$ 60,000	$150,000

Instructions: Prepare working papers and a consolidated balance sheet as of December 31, 1967.

15-2. Balance sheets for Companies P, A, and B on December 31, 1967, are given below. Investments in subsidiaries are carried at cost.

	Co. P	Co. A	Co. B
Investment in Co. A stock (90%)	$125,000		
Investment in Co. B stock (15%)	7,500		
Investment in Co. B stock (80%)		$ 40,000	
Other assets	367,500	210,000	$ 75,000
Total assets	$500,000	$250,000	$ 75,000
Liabilities	$145,000	$ 95,000	$ 45,000
Capital stock (all $100 par)	300,000	100,000	50,000
Premium on capital stock	60,000	25,000	
Retained earnings (deficit)	(5,000)	30,000	(20,000)
Total liabilities and stockholders' equity	$500,000	$250,000	$ 75,000

Company A's stock was purchased by Company P as follows:
March 1, 1959, 60%, when Company A had a deficit of $15,000.
January 1, 1963, 30%, when Company A had retained earnings of $10,000.

Company B's stock was purchased by Companies P and A on the date of Company B's organization, September 1, 1965.

Instructions: Prepare working papers and a consolidated balance sheet as of December 31, 1967.

15-3. Information for the Lane, Meyer, and Norton companies follows:

Balance Sheets — December 31, 1967

	Lane Co.	Meyer Co.	Norton Co.
Investment in Meyer Co. (42,000 shares)	$ 315,000		
Investment in Norton Co. (16,000 shares)		$160,000	
Other assets	1,400,000	400,000	$320,000
Total assets	$1,715,000	$560,000	$320,000
Liabilities	$ 480,000	$214,500	$140,000
Capital stock	1,000,000	250,000	120,000
Additional paid-in capital			35,000
Retained earnings	235,000	95,500	25,000
Total liabilities and stockholders' equity	$1,715,000	$560,000	$320,000

Capital stock outstanding of the three companies is as follows: Lane Company, 50,000 shares; Meyer Company, 50,000 shares; and Norton Company, 20,000 shares.

Holdings of the Lane Company in stock of the Meyer Company were obtained on January 2, 1966. The Norton Company stock had been acquired by the Meyer Company on July 1, 1965. Investments are carried at cost.

Analysis of Changes in Retained Earnings and Additional Paid-in Capital Balances

	Lane Co.	Meyer Co.	Norton Co.	
	Retained Earnings	Retained Earnings	Additional Paid-in Capital	Retained Earnings
Balances, Dec. 31, 1964	$215,000	$ 60,000		($30,000)
Net income (loss), 1965	40,000	18,000		(15,000)
Capital from reduction in stated value of capital stock, Dec. 31, $80,000:				
Recognized as additional paid-in capital . . . $35,000			$35,000	
Applied to cancellation of deficit 45,000				45,000
	$255,000	$ 78,000	$35,000	
Cash dividends paid in December	(30,000)	(5,000)		
Balances, Dec. 31, 1965	$225,000	$ 73,000	$35,000	
Net income, 1966	35,000	15,000		$10,000
	$260,000	$ 88,000	$35,000	$10,000
Cash dividends paid in December	(30,000)	(7,500)		
Balances, Dec. 31, 1966	$230,000	$ 80,500	$35,000	$10,000
Net income, 1967	35,000	25,000		15,000
	$265,000	$105,500	$35,000	$25,000
Cash dividends paid in December	(30,000)	(10,000)		
Balances, Dec. 31, 1967	$235,000	$ 95,500	$35,000	$25,000

Instructions: Prepare working papers and a consolidated balance sheet for the Lane Company and its affiliates on December 31, 1967.

15-4. Companies A, B, C, and D show account balances at the end of 1967 as listed below. Company A owns an 80% interest in Company B

	Co. A	Co. B	Co. C	Co. D
Cash	$ 65,000	$ 50,000	$ 45,000	$ 40,000
Notes Receivable	45,000	25,000	5,000	10,000
Accounts Receivable	78,000	72,000	40,000	35,000
Merchandise Inventory, January 1	85,000	70,000	35,000	30,000
Furniture and Fixtures	30,000	20,000	15,000	15,000
Allowance for Depreciation of Furniture and Fixtures	15,000	12,000	5,000	4,000
Land	20,000	15,000	10,000	
Buildings	110,000	80,000	40,000	
Allowance for Depreciation of Buildings	12,000	22,000	15,000	
Investment in Stock of Co. B	200,000			
Investment in Stock of Co. C	80,000			
Investment in Stock of Co. D			30,000	
Goodwill	15,000	10,000		
Notes Payable	20,000	15,000	25,000	10,000
Accounts Payable	65,000	79,000	55,000	60,000
Bonds Payable	60,000		40,000	
Capital Stock	300,000	100,000	100,000	50,000
Retained Earnings (Deficit)	235,000	105,000	(10,000)	(5,000)
Sales	540,000	360,000	230,000	145,000
Purchases	290,000	180,000	140,000	80,000
Operating Expenses	220,000	165,000	95,000	50,000
Other Revenues	15,000	15,000	10,000	6,000
Other Expenses	24,000	21,000	15,000	10,000

and an 80% interest in Company C. Company C owns a 90% interest in Company D. All stock is $100 par. Investments are carried by the equity method, but no entries were made in the investment accounts during 1967.

The following information is to be recorded before the books are closed:

(a) Depreciation (same rates are used by each company):

Furniture and fixtures	20%
Buildings	2½%

(b) Merchandise inventories, December 31:

Company A	$100,000
Company B	85,000
Company C	35,000
Company D	30,000

(c) Dividends were declared payable January 15, 1968, to stockholders of record December 28, 1967, as follows:

	Per Share
Company A	$1.50
Company B	2.00
Company D	1.00

Instructions: Prepare working papers and a consolidated balance sheet as of December 31, 1967.

15-5. Balance sheets on December 31, 1967, for Star Properties, Inc. and Turf Corporation are as follows:

	Star Properties Inc.		Turf Corp.
Investment in stock of Turf Corp., 15,000 shares at cost	$ 225,000		
Investment in stock of Star Properties, Inc. 10,000 shares at cost			$115,000
Other assets	1,250,000		405,000
Total assets	$1,475,000		$520,000
Liabilities	$ 425,000		$180,000
Capital stock (100,000 sh.)	1,000,000	(20,000 sh.)	300,000
Retained earnings	50,000		40,000
Total liabilities and stockholders' equity	$1,475,000		$520,000

Star Properties, Inc. acquired Turf Corporation stock when the latter company was formed in May, 1961. Turf Corporation purchased its shares in Star Properties, Inc. on July 1, 1964. The Star Properties, Inc. showed a deficit of $10,000 on this date, while Turf Corporation retained earnings were $15,000.

Instructions: (1) Prepare working papers and a consolidated balance sheet as of December 31, 1967, assuming that each company recognizes its share of earnings on investments.

(2) Prepare working papers and a consolidated balance sheet as of December 31, 1967, assuming that the subsidiary company's investment in parent company stock is treated as treasury stock.

15-6. Balance sheets on December 31, 1967, for Companies E and F are as follows:

	Co. E		Co. F
Investment in Co. F stock (18,000 shares at cost)	$ 270,000		
Investment in Co. E stock (2,500 shares at cost)			$ 72,500
Other assets	1,480,000		227,500
Total assets	$1,750,000		$300,000
Liabilities	$ 450,000		$100,000
Capital stock, no par . . . . (50,000 shares)	1,000,000	(20,000 sh.)	200,000
Additional paid-in capital	100,000		50,000
Retained earnings (deficit)	200,000		(50,000)
Total liabilities and stockholders' equity	$1,750,000		$300,000

Company F stock was acquired by Company E on January 2, 1962, when Company F showed retained earnings of $30,000. Company E stock was acquired by Company F on January 2, 1965. On this date Company E and Company F retained earnings balances were $140,000 and $10,000 respectively.

Instructions: Prepare working papers and a consolidated balance sheet as of December 31, 1967, assuming that each company recognizes earnings on its investment in the affiliate.

15-7. Company X and Company Y prepare balance sheets on December 31, 1967, as follows:

	Co. X	Co. Y
Investment in Co. Y stock (900 shares)	$120,000	
Investment in Co. X stock (200 shares)		$ 30,000
Other assets	385,000	220,000
Total assets	$505,000	$250,000
Liabilities	$240,000	$115,000
Capital stock (all $100 par)	200,000	100,000
Retained earnings	65,000	35,000
Total liabilities and stockholders' equity	$505,000	$250,000

Investments in subsidiaries are carried at cost. Company X acquired Company Y stock on January 2, 1967, when Company Y's retained earnings showed a balance of $20,000. Company Y acquired Company X stock on July 1, 1967. Company X's retained earnings on January 1, 1967, were $45,000. (It may be assumed that earnings accrue proportionately throughout the year and that each company recognizes earnings on its investment in the affiliate.)

Instructions: (1) Prepare working papers for a consolidated balance sheet as of December 31, 1967.

(2) Revise the above balances on the assumption that the equity method is used and prepare working papers for a consolidated balance sheet.

(3) Prepare a consolidated balance sheet.

15-8. Parent and subparent companies take up earnings and dividends of subsidiaries through the investment accounts. Give any journal entries affecting the investment accounts in 1967 as a result of the following:

(1) Company P owns 4,500 shares of Company A stock, $100 par, purchased at 125. Company A has 5,000 shares outstanding. On December 31, Company A announces a net loss from operations for 1967 of $30,000, declares a cash dividend of $1.25 per share, and declares a stock dividend of one share for every five held by stockholders.

(2) Company P owns 17,000 shares of Company B no-par common stock, purchased at 11, and 500 shares of Company B 6% cumulative and nonparticipating preferred, $100 par, purchased at 110. Company B has outstanding 20,000 shares of common and 1,000 shares of preferred. On December 31, Company B announces a net income from operations for 1967 of $24,000.

(3) Company P owns 9,000 shares of Company C stock acquired as follows: July 1, 1963, 8,000 shares; March 1, 1967, 1,000 shares. Company C has 10,000 shares outstanding. On December 31, Company C announces a net loss from operations for 1967 of $30,000.

(4) Company P owns 1,600 shares of Company D stock. Company D has 2,000 shares of stock outstanding. Company D owns 8,000 shares of Company E common. Company E has 10,000 shares of common outstanding. Company E announces a net income from operations of $20,000 for 1967 and on December 31, 1967, declares a cash dividend of 50 cents per share. Company D's net income for the year, before considering its earnings as a result of its ownership of Company E stock, is $30,000. (Give entries for Company P and Company D.)

(5) Company P owns 9,000 shares of Company F stock acquired as follows: January 1, 1966, 8,000 shares; July 1, 1967, 1,000 shares. Company F owns 1,000 shares of Company P stock acquired on October 1, 1967. Company P and Company F each have 10,000 shares outstanding. Company P's net income for 1967, before considering its earnings as a result of ownership of Company F stock, is $30,000; Company F's net income for 1967 is $18,000. (Assume net incomes are earned proportionately throughout the year and that both parent and subsidiary companies recognize earnings of each other. Give entries for Company P and Company F.)

15-9. Balance sheets and summaries of retained earnings for Company P and its affiliates appear below. All stock is $100 par. Investments in subsidiaries are carried at cost.

Balance Sheets — December 31, 1967

	Co. P	Co. A	Co. B	Co. C	Co. D	Co. E
Investment in Co. A	$120,000					
Investment in Co. B	42,000					
Investment in Co. C	99,500					
Investment in Co. D	270,000					
Investment in Co. E					$100,000	
Other assets	188,500	$285,000	$215,000	$320,000	395,000	$205,000
	$720,000	$285,000	$215,000	$320,000	$495,000	$205,000
Liabilities	$310,000	$145,000	$120,000	$155,000	$210,000	$100,000
Capital stock, Co. P	250,000					
Retained earnings, Co. P	160,000					
Capital stock, Co. A		150,000				
Deficit, Co. A		(10,000)				
Capital stock, Co. B			100,000			
Deficit, Co. B			(5,000)			
Capital stock, Co. C				100,000		
Retained earnings, Co. C				65,000		
Capital stock, Co. D					200,000	
Retained earnings, Co. D					85,000	
Capital stock, Co. E						100,000
Retained earnings, Co. E						5,000
	$720,000	$285,000	$215,000	$320,000	$495,000	$205,000

Analysis of Retained Earnings Balances

	Co. P	Co. A	Co. B	Co. C	Co. D	Co. E
Retained earnings (deficit), Dec. 31, 1965	$145,000	$20,000	($60,000)	$15,000	$ 60,000	$15,000
Net income (loss), 1966	25,000	60,000	25,000	30,000	20,000	(30,000)
	$170,000	$80,000	($35,000)	$45,000	$ 80,000	($15,000)
50% stock dividend distributed in Dec. 1966		(50,000)				
Cash dividend paid in Dec., 1966	(20,000)			(10,000)	(20,000)	
Retained earnings (deficit), Dec. 31, 1966	$150,000	$30,000	($35,000)	$35,000	$ 60,000	($15,000)
Net income (loss), 1967	35,000	(40,000)	30,000	40,000	40,000	20,000
	$185,000	($10,000)	($ 5,000)	$75,000	$100,000	$ 5,000
Cash dividend paid in Dec., 1967	(25,000)			(10,000)	(15,000)	
Retained earnings (deficit), Dec. 31, 1967	$160,000	($10,000)	($ 5,000)	$65,000	$ 85,000	$ 5,000

Company P acquired 400 shares of Company A stock on July 1, 1966, at 100, and an additional 400 shares on November 1, 1966, at 105. A stock dividend received by Company P on this stock was recorded by a debit to the investment account and a credit to a revenue account for $38,000, the market value of the 400 shares received.

Company P acquired Company B's stock as follows: on January 2, 1966, 800 shares at 45; March 1, 1967, 100 shares at 60.

The investment in Company C on Company P's books shows: (debit) January 2, 1966, 900 shares at 120; (debit) October 1, 1967, 50 shares at 130; (credit) July 1, 1967, 100 shares at 150.

Company P acquired 1,800 shares of Company D stock on January 2, 1966, at 150. Company D had acquired 800 shares of Company E stock on April 1, 1966, at 125.

Company P and Company A inventories (included under the heading "Other Assets") include merchandise of $22,000 and $38,500 respectively acquired from Company D during 1967. Company D sells merchandise at 25% above cost.

Company P owns equipment (included at its depreciated value under the heading "Other Assets") acquired from Company A on January 2, 1967. Company P was charged $30,000 for the equipment and is depreciating the asset on a 10-year basis. Company A reported a gross profit of $6,000 on the sale.

Instructions: Prepare working papers and a consolidated balance sheet as of December 31, 1967.

15-10. Information about the Dodge Company, the Ely Company, and the Fields Company follows:

Balance Sheets
December 31, 1967

	Dodge Co.	Ely Co.	Fields Co.
Cash in banks and on hand	$ 30,000	$ 10,000	$ 15,000
Customers' notes and accounts receivable	90,000	50,000	60,000
Inventories	70,000	60,000	50,000
Investments at cost			
Stock of Ely Co. — 75%	100,000		
Stock of Fields Co. — 80%	200,000		
Stock of Ely Co. — 15%			30,000
Property, plant and equipment, less allowance for depreciation	500,000	200,000	120,000
Deferred charges	10,000	5,000	5,000
Total assets	$1,000,000	$325,000	$280,000
Notes payable	$ 60,000	$ 50,000	$ 30,000
Accounts payable	40,000	45,000	20,000
Mortgage on plant			90,000
Capital stock — par value $100 a share	500,000	200,000	100,000
Retained earnings	300,000	30,000	40,000
Appraisal capital	100,000		
Total liabilities and stockholders' equity	$1,000,000	$325,000	$280,000

The Dodge Company acquired its holdings in Ely Company and Fields Company on December 31, 1966.

The Fields Company's holdings of Ely Company stock were purchased at an earlier date at par, which was also the book value.

Analysis of Retained Earnings Balances
Year Ended December 31, 1967

	Dodge Co.	Ely Co.	Fields Co.
Retained earnings at December 31, 1966	$ 280,000	$ 10,000	$ 50,000
Income for year 1967	70,000	20,000	30,000
	$ 350,000	$ 30,000	$ 80,000
Dividends paid	(50,000)		(40,000)
Retained earnings at December 31, 1967	$ 300,000	$ 30,000	$ 40,000

Instructions: From the foregoing data prepare a consolidated balance sheet of the Dodge Company and its subsidiaries as of December 31, 1967.

(AICPA adapted)

15-11. The following condensed balance sheets of Company A, Company B, and Company C were prepared as of December 31, 1967:

	Co. A	Co. B	Co. C
Current assets	$1,234,567	$ 731,282	$340,274
Investments:			
80% of Co. B stock, at cost	1,400,000	—	—
75% of Co. C stock, at cost	—	540,200	—
Fixed assets — net	3,030,933	1,322,607	514,987
Total assets	$5,665,500	$2,594,089	$855,261
Current liabilities	$ 400,500	$ 275,389	$ 93,261
Bonds payable	—	750,000	—
Retained earnings appropriation for redemption of bonds	—	250,000	—
Capital stock, $100 par value	3,000,000	1,000,000	600,000
Additional paid-in capital	710,300	—	45,600
Retained earnings	1,554,700	318,700	116,400
Total liabilities and stockholders' equity	$5,665,500	$2,594,089	$855,261

The stock of Company C was acquired by Company B on January 31, 1966. Since that date Company C had total earnings of $28,400 and paid cash dividends of $40,000. Company B credited all dividends received to its income account.

Company A acquired the stock of Company B on December 31, 1967.

Instructions: Prepare the journal entries necessary for the preparation of a consolidated balance sheet for Company A and subsidiairies as of the close of business December 31, 1967. Show all supporting computations in good form.

(AICPA adapted)

15-12. On December 31, 1966, the Lance Paper Company bought 90% of the $500,000 capital stock of the Miller Supply Company for $370,080 and 80% of the $200,000, 7% preferred stock of the North Printing Company for $176,000.

The Miller Supply Company had acquired on December 31, 1965, 90% of the $200,000 common stock of the North Printing Company for $126,000.

Balance sheets and other data are given below:

Lance Paper Company
Balance Sheet
December 31, 1967

Investments:		Accounts payable:	
Miller Supply Co.	$ 397,080	North Printing Co.	$ 10,000
North Printing Co.	187,200	Capital stock:	
Notes receivable:		Preferred	400,000
North Printing Co.	20,000	Common	800,000
Other assets (net)	708,520	Retained earnings	102,800
		Total liabilities and	
Total assets	$1,312,800	stockholders' equity	$1,312,800

Miller Supply Company
Balance Sheet
December 31, 1967

Investments:		Notes receivable dis-	
North Printing Co.	$ 126,000	counted	$ 10,000
Notes receivable:		Capital stock	500,000
North Printing Co.	10,000	Retained earnings	26,000
Other assets (net)	400,000		
		Total liabilities and	
Total assets	$ 536,000	stockholders' equity	$ 536,000

North Printing Company
Balance Sheet
December 31, 1967

Goodwill	$ 20,000	Notes payable:	
Accounts receivable:		Lance Paper Co.	$ 20,000
Lance Paper Co.	15,000	Miller Supply Co.	10,000
Other assets (net)	425,000	Dividends payable:	
		Preferred	14,000
		Common	16,000
		Capital stock:	
		7% Preferred	200,000
		Common	200,000
		Total liabilities and	
Total assets	$ 460,000	stockholders' equity	$ 460,000

Lance consistently takes on its books its share of Miller's profits.

The difference of $5,000 between the current accounts of Lance and North represents North merchandise in transit to Lance.

Miller does not take upon its books its share of the North profits but credits to income the North dividends when received.

Miller made a profit of $50,000 in 1967, before considering income from its investment in North, and on December 20, 1967, paid a dividend of 4% ($20,000) on its $500,000 capital stock.

North made a profit of $20,000 in 1966, which was paid out in dividends that were duly received by the shareholders before December 31, 1966.

North made a profit of $30,000 in 1967 and on December 20, 1967, declared dividends of 7% on the preferred stock and 8% on the common stock, both payable January 10, 1968.

Provision had been made by the three companies for all known liabilities and accruals, including 1967 federal income taxes.

Instructions: (1) Prepare working papers for a consolidated balance sheet.
(2) Prepare a consolidated balance sheet as of December 31, 1967.
(3) Prepare a statement of minority interest.
(4) Prepare a statement of the book value or cost excess on each investment.

(AICPA adapted)

15-13. The following financial facts pertain to Corporations R and S, which had mutual holdings during and at the end of the fiscal year 1967:

	Corporation	
	R	S
Of the issued capital stock,		
R owns	10%	50%
S owns	20%	10%
Net assets (exclusive of investment accounts) — December 31, 1967	$540,000	$590,000
Dividends declared during 1967	?	18,000
1967 net income (after taxes), exclusive of dividends	53,000	60,000

There has been no change in the mutual holdings during the year. Each corporation carries its investment account at cost.

Instructions: (1) Compute the dollar equity of outside shareholders in the total net assets of R and S respectively.

(2) Compute the dollar amount of dividends declared in 1967 to which the outside shareholders of R are entitled, assuming that R declared as dividends its *total* 1967 net income after taxes.

(AICPA adapted)

15-14, Company P has 500,000 shares of capital stock issued and outstanding, owns 350,000 shares of capital stock of Company Q, and has retained earnings of $1,050.

Company Q has 400,000 shares of capital stock issued and outstanding, owns 45,000 shares of capital stock of Company P, and has a deficit of $2,100.

Instructions: A consolidated balance sheet is being prepared. Determine the amount of the deficit of Company Q applicable to the minority stockholders' interest in that company.

(AICPA adapted)

15-15. Company H has agreed to purchase the minority interest in Company S. Their balance sheets show:

	Co. H		Co. S
Tangible assets.	$3,764,513		$2,264,718
Goodwill.	500,000		
91,000 shares of Co. S.	1,270,000	(5,373 shares Co. H)	622,443
Total assets.	$5,534,513		$2,887,161
Creditors.	$ 367,423		$ 133,675
Capital stock . . . . . (40,000 sh.)	4,000,000	(100,000 shares)	2,500,000
Retained earnings	1,167,090		253,486
Total liabilities and stockholders' equity	$5,534,513		$2,887,161

The stock is to be acquired at asset value, but in the computation the goodwill of either company is not to be considered.

Instructions: Compute the amount that should be paid to the minority stockholders per share of Company S. Do not carry your computation further than whole cents per share.

(AICPA adapted)

15-16. The following is a summary of the balance sheets of three corporations at a given date:

	R	S	T
Total assets.	$1,500,000	$2,000,000	$3,500,000
Total liabilities.	$ 250,000	$ 750,000	$1,100,000
Capital stock, $100 par.	1,000,000	750,000	2,000,000
Retained earnings	250,000	500,000	400,000
Total liabilities and stockholders' equity.	$1,500,000	$2,000,000	$3,500,000

Each corporation owned a part of the capital stock of the others, carried on their respective books as follows:

	Capital Stock In		
	R	S	T
R owned		15%	15%
Carried at		$100,000	$300,000
S owned	15%		10%
Carried at	$150,000		$175,000
T owned	5%	5%	
Carried at	$ 50,000	$ 60,000	

The three companies agreed to consolidate and each to accept its pro-rata share in the capital stock of a new corporation (P) having 1,000,000 shares of no-par value.

Instructions: Compute the percentage of the shares of Corporation P that the stockholders of R, S, and T, respectively, will receive, and the total equity or paid-in value of the consolidated capital.

(AICPA adapted)

Chapter 16

CONSOLIDATED STATEMENTS

INCOME AND RETAINED EARNINGS STATEMENTS

The consolidated balance sheet is prepared to offer a composite summary of the financial position of a parent company and its affiliates as of a given date. The considerations that lead to the preparation of the consolidated balance sheet also suggest the need for consolidated income and retained earnings statements that offer a summary of the financial progress of the affiliated units.

The concepts underlying the preparation of consolidated income and retained earnings statements are the same as those already discussed in the previous chapters. In preparing the consolidated income statement, intercompany revenue and expense items are eliminated. Remaining balances are then combined. As in the case of the consolidated balance sheet, the consolidated income and retained earnings statements are based on the premise that the parent company and its subsidiaries represent a single operating unit. A complete and integrated set of statements is prepared for the parent and its subsidiaries viewed as one entity.

CONTINUITY IN CONSOLIDATED STATEMENTS

It should be recognized throughout the process of consolidation that there is a need for continuity in consolidated statements for successive periods that parallels the continuity that is found in the separate company statements for successive periods. Consolidated statements for any one period are the product of the consolidated balance sheet prepared at the end of the preceding period and all of the transactions of the current period. The consolidated balance sheet prepared at the end of the current period is the starting point for the financial statements to be developed for the succeeding period. In such a continuity, the retained earnings balance of the minority interest reported on the consolidated balance sheet must be the retained earnings balance of the minority interest reported on the consolidated balance sheet prepared at the end of the preceding period increased by that portion of the consolidated income accruing to the minority interest and reduced by dividends to the minority interest for the current period; in turn, the retained earnings balance for the controlling interest must be the retained earnings balance of the controlling interest as of the end of the preceding period increased by that portion of the consolidated income accruing to the controlling interest and reduced by dividends to the controlling interest for the current period.

Consolidated statements may be prepared by combining balance sheet, income statement, and retained earnings statement data on separate sets of working papers. Ordinarily, however, it is more convenient to prepare these statements by means of a single set of working papers. Eliminations for purposes of consolidation are applied to adjusted trial balances for the affiliated companies in a manner similar to that employed previously in the preparation of combined statements for a home office and its branches.

PREPARATION OF CONSOLIDATED STATEMENTS

The preparation of consolidated statements will be illustrated by means of two sets of examples. A relatively simple set of facts for a trading company and its subsidiary covering a two-year period is presented in the first set of examples, and working papers are illustrated for investments carried by the equity method and for investments carried by the cost method. A more complex set of facts for a manufacturing company and its subsidiary for a two-year period is given in the second set of examples; here, too, working papers are illustrated for investments carried by the equity method and by the cost method.

For purposes of the first set of examples, assume the facts listed below. The letter designation that precedes each item is used later in describing the elimination required for that item and also in identifying the elimination on the working papers.

(a) Company A acquired 80% of the stock of Company B on January 1, 1966, at a cost of $125,000. Capital stock of Company B on this date was $100,000; retained earnings were $25,000.

(b) Company A purchased merchandise from Company B as follows: during 1966, $15,000; during 1967, $25,000.

(c) Amounts owed by Company A to Company B on open account were as follows: December 31, 1966, $3,500; December 31, 1967, $6,500.

(d) Intercompany profits in inventories related to goods acquired by Company A from Company B were as follows: December 31, 1966, $1,000; December 31, 1967, $2,500.

(e) Company B paid dividends of $25,000 in 1967, Company A receiving 80% of this amount.

Working papers for a consolidated balance sheet for Companies A and B on the date of acquisition of control are shown at the top of the following page.

Company A and Subsidiary Company B
Working Papers for Consolidated Balance Sheet
January 1, 1966

	Co. A	Co. B	Eliminations Dr.	Eliminations Cr.	Consolidated Balance Sheet Dr.	Consolidated Balance Sheet Cr.
Debits						
Cash	25,000	15,000			40,000	
Accounts Receivable (net)	60,000	40,000			100,000	
Merchandise Inventory	85,000	40,000			125,000	
Plant and Equipment (net)	200,000	85,000			285,000	
Investment in Co. B Stock	125,000					
Eliminate 80% of Capital Stock				80,000		
Eliminate 80% of Retained Earnings				20,000		
Excess of Cost over Book Value					25,000	
	495,000	180,000				
Credits						
Accounts Payable	75,000	55,000				130,000
Bonds Payable	100,000					100,000
Capital Stock, Co. A	250,000					250,000
Retained Earnings, Co. A	70,000					70,000
Capital Stock, Co. B		100,000				
Eliminate 80%			80,000			
Minority Interest, 20%						20,000
Retained Earnings, Co. B		25,000				
Eliminate 80%			20,000			
Minority Interest, 20%						5,000
	495,000	180,000	100,000	100,000	575,000	575,000

Working papers for consolidated statements illustrated — equity method. Assume that the parent has carried its investment in the subsidiary by the equity method. Financial statements for Companies A and B for the years ended December 31, 1966 and 1967, are shown on pages 530 and 531.

Working papers for consolidated statements for 1966 and 1967 appear on pages 532 and 533. It should be observed that the accounts taken from the financial statements are restated in pre-closing form; furthermore, any items that may have been recorded directly in the retained earnings account are listed separately. Thus: retained earnings balances are shown as of the beginning of the period; nominal accounts are listed in the appropriate debit and credit sections; when dividends declared have been recorded by charges to retained earnings, such dividends would be listed as a separate debit item.

After listing the pre-closing trial balance figures, the ending inventory is recorded both as a balance sheet value and as an income statement value. The ending inventory is recorded as a debit immediately below the total of other debit items and in this position represents the asset to

Income Statements
For Year Ended December 31, 1966

	Co. A		Co. B	
Sales		$600,000		$210,000
Cost of goods sold:				
Merchandise inventory, January 1	$ 85,000		$ 40,000	
Purchases	380,000		160,000	
Merchandise available for sale	$465,000		$200,000	
Deduct merchandise inventory, December 31	90,000	375,000	75,000	125,000
Gross profit on sales		$225,000		$ 85,000
Expenses		145,000		40,000
Net income before income taxes		$ 80,000		$ 45,000
Income taxes		30,000		15,000
Net income		$ 50,000		$ 30,000
Add income — Subsidiary Co. B, 80% of $30,000		24,000		
Net income, including parent company's share of Co. B earnings		$ 74,000		

Retained Earnings Statements
For Year Ended December 31, 1966

	Co. A	Co. B
Balance, January 1	$ 70,000	$ 25,000
Add net income for year	74,000	30,000
Balance, December 31	$144,000	$ 55,000

Balance Sheets
December 31, 1966

	Co. A		Co. B	
Assets				
Cash		$ 35,000		$ 25,000
Accounts receivable (net)		65,000		35,000
Merchandise inventory		90,000		75,000
Plant and equipment (net)		215,000		100,000
Investment in stock of Co. B (carried on equity basis)		149,000		
Total assets		$554,000		$235,000
Liabilities				
Accounts payable		$ 60,000		$ 80,000
Bonds payable		100,000		
Total liabilities		$160,000		$ 80,000
Stockholders' Equity				
Capital stock	$250,000		$100,000	
Retained earnings	144,000		55,000	
Total stockholders' equity		394,000		155,000
Total liabilities and stockholders' equity		$554,000		$235,000

Income Statements
For Year Ended December 31, 1967

	Co. A		Co. B	
Sales		$625,000		$220,000
Cost of goods sold:				
Merchandise inventory, January 1	$ 90,000		$ 75,000	
Purchases	380,000		125,000	
Merchandise available for sale	$470,000		$200,000	
Deduct merchandise inventory, December 31	80,000	390,000	70,000	130,000
Gross profit on sales		$235,000		$ 90,000
Expenses		135,000		35,000
Net income before income taxes		$100,000		$ 55,000
Income taxes		40,000		20,000
Net income		$ 60,000		$ 35,000
Add income — Subsidiary Co. B, 80% of $35,000		28,000		
Net income, including parent company's share of Co. B earnings		$ 88,000		

Retained Earnings Statements
For Year Ended December 31, 1967

	Co. A	Co. B
Balance, January 1	$144,000	$ 55,000
Add net income for year	88,000	35,000
	$232,000	$ 90,000
Deduct dividends declared during year	40,000	25,000
Balance, December 31	$192,000	$ 65,000

Balance Sheets
December 31, 1967

	Co. A		Co. B	
Assets				
Cash		$ 55,000		$ 30,000
Accounts receivable (net)		60,000		35,000
Merchandise inventory		80,000		70,000
Plant and equipment (net)		240,000		90,000
Investment in stock of Co. B (carried on equity basis)		157,000		
Total assets		$592,000		$225,000
Liabilities				
Accounts payable		$ 50,000		$ 60,000
Bonds payable		100,000		
Total liabilities		$150,000		$ 60,000
Stockholders' Equity				
Capital stock	$250,000		$100,000	
Retained earnings	192,000		65,000	
Total stockholders' equity		442,000		165,000
Total liabilities and stockholders' equity		$592,000		$225,000

Equity method:

Company A and Subsidiary Company B
Working Papers for Consolidated Statements
December 31, 1966

	Co. A	Co. B	Eliminations Dr.	Eliminations Cr.	Consolidated Income Statement Dr.	Consolidated Income Statement Cr.	Retained Earnings — Minority Interest Dr.	Retained Earnings — Minority Interest Cr.	Retained Earnings — Controlling Interest Dr.	Retained Earnings — Controlling Interest Cr.	Consolidated Balance Sheet Dr.	Consolidated Balance Sheet Cr.
Debits												
Cash	35,000	25,000									60,000	
Accounts Receivable (net)	65,000	35,000		(c) 3,500							96,500	
Merchandise Inventory, 1/1/66	85,000	40,000			125,000							
Plant and Equipment (net)	215,000	100,000									315,000	
Investment in Stock of Co. B	149,000											
Eliminate 80% of Capital Stock				(a1) 80,000								
Eliminate 80% of Retained Earnings, 1/1/66				(a2) 20,000								
Eliminate 80% of Earnings for 1966				(a3) 24,000							25,000	
Excess of Cost over Book Value												
Purchases	380,000	160,000		(b) 15,000	525,000							
Expenses	145,000	40,000			185,000							
Income Taxes	30,000	15,000			45,000							
	1,104,000	415,000										
Merchandise Inventory, 12/31/66	90,000	75,000		(d) 1,000							164,000	
Credits												
Accounts Payable	60,000	80,000	(c) 3,500									136,500
Bonds Payable	100,000											100,000
Capital Stock, Co. A	250,000											250,000
Retained Earnings, Co. A, 1/1/66	70,000									70,000		
Capital Stock, Co. B		100,000										
Eliminate 80%			(a1) 80,000									
Minority Interest, 20%												20,000
Retained Earnings, Co. B, 1/1/66		25,000										
Eliminate 80%			(a2) 20,000									
Minority Interest, 20%								5,000				
Sales	600,000	210,000	(b) 15,000			795,000						
Income — Subsidiary Co. B	24,000		(a3) 24,000									
	1,104,000	415,000										
Merchandise Inventory, 12/31/66	90,000	75,000	(d) 1,000			164,000						
			143,500	143,500	880,000	959,000						
Consolidated Income					79,000							
Income to Minority Interest, 20% of $29,000, Co. B Net Income after Adjustment (see below)								5,800				
Balance to Controlling Interest										73,200		
					959,000	959,000		10,800		143,200	660,500	506,500
Retained Earnings — Minority Interest to Balance Sheet							10,800					10,800
Retained Earnings — Controlling Interest to Balance Sheet									143,200			143,200
							10,800	10,800	143,200	143,200	660,500	660,500

Calculation of Co. B net income:	
Net income per books	$30,000
Deduct intercompany profit on merchandise transferred to Co. A	1,000
Net income for consolidation purposes	$29,000

Working Papers for Consolidated Statements
December 31, 1967

	Co. A	Co. B	Eliminations Dr.	Eliminations Cr.	Consolidated Income Statement Dr.	Consolidated Income Statement Cr.	Retained Earnings — Minority Interest Dr.	Retained Earnings — Minority Interest Cr.	Retained Earnings — Controlling Interest Dr.	Retained Earnings — Controlling Interest Cr.	Consolidated Balance Sheet Dr.	Consolidated Balance Sheet Cr.
Debits												
Cash	55,000	30,000									85,000	
Accounts Receivable (net)	60,000	35,000		(c) 6,500							88,500	
Merchandise Inventory, 1/1/67	90,000	75,000		(d1) 1,000	164,000							
Plant and Equipment (net)	240,000	90,000									330,000	
Investment in Stock of Co. B	157,000											
Eliminate 80% of Capital Stock				(a1) 80,000								
Eliminate 80% of Retained Earnings, 1/1/67, less dividends				(a2) 24,000								
Eliminate 80% of Earnings for 1967				(a3) 28,000								
Excess of Cost over Book Value											25,000	
Purchases	380,000	125,000		(b) 25,000	480,000							
Expenses	135,000	35,000			170,000							
Income Taxes	40,000	20,000			60,000							
Dividends Declared — Co. A	40,000								40,000			
Dividends Declared — Co. B		25,000		(a2) 20,000			5,000					
	1,197,000	435,000										
Merchandise Inventory, 12/31/67	80,000	70,000		(d2) 2,500							147,500	
Credits												
Accounts Payable	50,000	60,000	(c) 6,500									103,500
Bonds Payable	100,000											100,000
Capital Stock, Co. A	250,000											250,000
Retained Earnings, Co. A, 1/1/67	144,000		(d1) 800							143,200		
Capital Stock, Co. B		100,000										
Eliminate 80%			(a1) 80,000									
Minority Interest, 20%												20,000
Retained Earnings, Co. B, 1/1/67		55,000	(d1) 200									
Eliminate 80%			(a2) 44,000									
Minority Interest, 20% of $55,000, less $200								10,800				
Sales	625,000	220,000	(b) 25,000			820,000						
Income — Subsidiary Co. B	28,000		(a3) 28,000									
	1,197,000	435,000										
Merchandise Inventory, 12/31/67	80,000	70,000	(d2) 2,500			147,500						
			187,000	187,000	874,000	967,500						
Consolidated Income					93,500							
Income to Minority Interest, 20% of $33,500, Co. B Net Income after Adjustment (see below)								6,700				
Balance to Controlling Interest										86,800		
					967,500	967,500	5,000	17,500	40,000	230,000	676,000	473,500
Retained Earnings — Minority Interest to Balance Sheet							12,500					12,500
Retained Earnings — Controlling Interest to Balance Sheet									190,000			190,000
							17,500	17,500	230,000	230,000	676,000	676,000

Calculation of Co. B net income:

Net income per books	$35,000
Deduct adjustment for intercompany profits on merchandise: 12/31/67, $2,500, less 1/1/67, $1,000	1,500
Net income for consolidation purposes	$33,500

Company A and Subsidiary Company B
Consolidated Income Statement
For Year Ended December 31, 1966

Sales		$795,000
Cost of goods sold:		
Merchandise inventory, January 1	$125,000	
Purchases	525,000	
Merchandise available for sale	$650,000	
Deduct merchandise inventory, December 31	164,000	486,000
Gross profit on sales		$309,000
Expenses		185,000
Net income before income taxes		$124,000
Income taxes		45,000
Net income		$ 79,000
Distribution of net income:		
To minority interest		$ 5,800
To controlling interest		73,200
Total net income		$ 79,000

Company A and Subsidiary Company B
Consolidated Retained Earnings Statement
For Year Ended December 31, 1966

	Retained Earnings — Minority Interest	Retained Earnings — Controlling Interest
Balance, January 1, 1966	$ 5,000	$ 70,000
Add net income for year	5,800	73,200
Balance, December 31, 1966	$10,800	$143,200

Company A and Subsidiary Company B
Consolidated Balance Sheet
December 31, 1966

Assets			
Cash			$ 60,000
Accounts receivable (net)			96,500
Merchandise inventory			164,000
Plant and equipment (net)			315,000
Excess of cost over book value of subsidiary interest			25,000
Total assets			$660,500
Liabilities			
Accounts payable			$136,500
Bonds payable			100,000
Total liabilities			$236,500
Stockholders' Equity			
Minority interest:			
Capital stock	$ 20,000		
Retained earnings	10,800	$ 30,800	
Controlling interest:			
Capital stock	$250,000		
Retained earnings	143,200	393,200	
Total stockholders' equity			424,000
Total liabilities and stockholders' equity			$660,500

Company A and Subsidiary Company B
Consolidated Income Statement
For Year Ended December 31, 1967

Sales		$820,000
Cost of goods sold:		
Merchandise inventory, January 1	$164,000	
Purchases	480,000	
Merchandise available for sale	$644,000	
Deduct merchandise inventory, December 31	147,500	496,500
Gross profit on sales		$323,500
Expenses		170,000
Net income before income taxes		$153,500
Income taxes		60,000
Net income		$ 93,500
Distribution of net income:		
To minority interest		$ 6,700
To controlling interest		86,800
Total net income		$ 93,500

Company A and Subsidiary Company B
Consolidated Retained Earnings Statement
For Year Ended December 31, 1967

	Retained Earnings — Minority Interest	Retained Earnings — Controlling Interest
Balance, January 1	$10,800	$143,200
Add net income for year	6,700	86,800
	$17,500	$230,000
Deduct dividends declared during year	5,000	40,000
Balance, December 31	$12,500	$190,000

Company A and Subsidiary Company B
Consolidated Balance Sheet
December 31, 1967

Assets			
Cash			$ 85,000
Accounts receivable (net)			88,500
Merchandise inventory			147,500
Plant and equipment (net)			330,000
Excess of cost over book value of subsidiary interest			25,000
Total assets			$676,000
Liabilities			
Accounts payable			$103,500
Bonds payable			100,000
Total liabilities			$203,500
Stockholders' Equity			
Minority interest:			
Capital Stock	$ 20,000		
Retained earnings	12,500	$ 32,500	
Controlling interest:			
Capital stock	$250,000		
Retained earnings	190,000	440,000	
Total stockholders' equity			472,500
Total liabilities andstockholders' equity			$676,000

be reported on the balance sheet; the ending inventory is also recorded immediately below the other credit items and in this position represents the subtraction item from the beginning inventory and purchases in reporting cost of goods sold on the income statement.

After listing pre-closing balances and ending inventory values, eliminations for intercompany balance sheet and income statement items are recorded in the eliminations columns. When adjustments or corrections of account balances are required, a pair of columns for such purpose may be included to the left of the eliminations columns.

Explanations of the eliminations on the working papers for Companies A and B follow. The letter preceding each explanation corresponds with that used in reporting the elimination on the working papers.

Working papers for consolidated statements — 1966. (a) The investment in subsidiary stock when carried by the equity method reflects full recognition of subsidiary earnings and dividends for the period, but these are not yet reported in the subsidiary retained earnings account. Investment account eliminations, then, must be applied against reciprocal elements that are found in both real and nominal account balances. The eliminations that are required for the investment in stock of Company A follow:

(a1) Eighty percent of the capital stock of Company B is offset against the investment account. The elimination on the working papers is made as follows:

Capital Stock, Co. B (80% of $100,000)	80,000	
Investment in Stock of Co. B................		80,000

(a2) Eighty percent of the retained earnings of Company B as of January 1, 1966, as reported on the working papers, is offset against the investment account. The elimination is made as follows:

Retained Earnings, Co. B, 1/1/66 (80% of $25,000)	20,000	
Investment in Stock of Co. B...............		20,000

(a3) With the detailed profit and loss items for the subsidiary reported on the working papers and ultimately to be combined with like profit and loss items of the parent, the entry that was made by the parent company to recognize the subsidiary profit or loss for the current period may be canceled. The entry made by Company A to recognize its share of Company B earnings for the year is canceled as follows:

Income — Subsidiary Co. B..................	24,000	
Investment in Stock of Co. B................		24,000

(b) Intercompany sales are canceled by an elimination as follows:

Sales (Co. B)	15,000	
Purchases (Co. A)		15,000

(c) Intercompany trade accounts are canceled by an elimination as follows:

Accounts Payable (Co. A)	3,500	
Accounts Receivable (Co. B)................		3,500

(d) The ending inventory is reduced to cost both as a balance sheet value and as an income statement value by the following entry:

Merchandise Inventory, 12/31/66 (income statement value)	1,000	
Merchandise Inventory, 12/31/66 (balance sheet value)		1,000

Account balances on the working papers may now be combined and extended to the income statement, retained earnings, and balance sheet columns. Revenue and expense balances are carried to the income statement columns. The portion of the retained earnings of the subsidiary company identified with the minority interest as of the beginning of the period and any dividends of the subsidiary company identified with the minority interest for the current period are carried to the retained earnings — minority interest columns; the retained earnings of the controlling interest as of the beginning of the period and any dividends identified with the controlling interest for the current period are carried to the retained earnings — controlling interest columns. Remaining balances are carried to the balance sheet columns.

Income statement columns may now be summarized: a debit excess in the income statement columns indicates a net loss from combined activities; a credit excess indicates a net income from combined activities. The portion of the combined earnings accruing to the minority interest is calculated and carried to the retained earnings — minority interest columns; the combined earnings less the portion assigned to the minority interest are carried to the retained earnings — controlling interest columns.

The retained earnings of the minority interest may now be determined and transferred to the balance sheet columns; the retained earnings of the controlling interest are similarly determined and transferred to the balance sheet columns. These transfers bring ending assets and ending liabilities and capital in the balance sheet columns into agreement.

In the example, the amount of the subsidiary earnings that were recognized for consolidation purposes had to be calculated before arriving at the portion of the consolidated earnings to be assigned to the minority interest. Subsidiary earnings that were included in the consolidated earnings total were calculated in a lower section of the working papers. Subsidiary earnings included a profit of $1,000 on goods still in the hands of the parent. Consolidated earnings reflect a reduction of this amount as a result of reductions applied to the ending inventory values. Subsidiary company earnings as originally reported are reduced by the intercompany profit and the adjusted earnings balance is then used in calculating the portion of the consolidated income that is identified with the minority interest.

Working papers for consolidated statements — 1967. (a) Investment account eliminations are made in terms of reciprocal balances that are found in the real and the nominal accounts as of December 31, 1967, as follows:

(a1) Eighty percent of the capital stock of Company B is offset against the investment account. The elimination on the working papers is made as follows:

Capital Stock, Co. B (80% of $100,000)	80,000	
Investment in Stock of Co. B.		80,000

(a2) Subsidiary accounts at the end of 1967 reflect two retained earnings elements that must be applied against the investment account: (1) retained earnings as of January 1, 1967, and (2) the dividends declared balance, in effect, a negative retained earnings balance. Eighty percent of the beginning retained earnings balance is applied against the investment account, 20% of the retained earnings balance being recognized as retained earnings related to the minority interest; 80% of the dividends declared balance is applied against the investment account, 20% of the dividends declared balance being recognized as a decrease in the retained earnings related to the minority interest. An elimination may be made in compound form applying positive and negative retained earnings balances against the investment account as follows:

Retained Earnings, Co. B, 1/1/67 (80% of $55,000)	44,000	
Dividends Declared (Co. B).		20,000
Investment in Stock of Co. B.		24,000

(a3) The entry made by Company A to recognize its share of subsidiary earnings for 1967 is canceled by the following entry:

Income — Subsidiary Co. B.	28,000	
Investment in Stock of Co. B.		28,000

(b) Sales made by Company B to Company A during 1967 are eliminated as follows:

Sales (Co. B)	25,000	
Purchases (Co. A)		25,000

(c) Intercompany trade accounts are canceled by the following elimination:

Accounts Payable (Co. A)	6,500	
Accounts Receivable (Co. B)		6,500

(d) Intercompany profits in both beginning and ending inventories are canceled.

(d1) The inventory at the end of 1966 was reduced by intercompany profits of $1,000; the asset reduction was accompanied by a reduction in earnings of the subsidiary that was assigned 20% to the minority interest and 80% to the controlling interest. Balances on the consolidated statements for inventories and for retained earnings of both minority and controlling interests as of the beginning of 1967 must be the same as those reported at the end of 1966. The following elimination brings beginning balances into agreement with those reported at the end of the previous period:

Retained Earnings, Co. A, 1/1/67 (80% of $1,000)	800	
Retained Earnings, Co. B, 1/1/67 (reducing minority interest — 20% of $1,000)	200	
Merchandise Inventory, 1/1/67		1,000

The beginning inventory is now reduced to $164,000, the balance that was recognized on the consolidated statements at the end of 1966. The beginning retained earnings of the controlling interest is reduced to $143,200, the balance that was reported at the end of 1966. The beginning retained earnings of the minority interest is reduced to $10,800 (20% of $55,000, less $200), the balance that was reported at the end of 1966.

(d2) The restatement of the beginning inventory is accompanied by a restatement of the ending inventory that cancels the intercompany profit in the asset and reduces combined earnings by the intercompany profit. Intercompany profit in the ending inventory is canceled as follows:

Merchandise Inventory, 12/31/67 (income statement value)	2,500	
Merchandise Inventory, 12/31/67 (balance sheet value)		2,500

Account balances are extended to the profit and loss, retained earnings, and balance sheet columns as was done on the working papers for

1966. Consolidated income is calculated and identified with minority and controlling interests. The amount of subsidiary earnings that is included in the consolidated total must be calculated in arriving at the portion that is to be identified with the minority interest. The reduction in inventories at the end of 1966 reduced consolidated earnings for 1966 but will raise consolidated earnings for 1967, the year in which such goods are sold to outsiders. Consolidated earnings for 1967 were raised by $1,000, the intercompany profit related to 1966 inventories, and reduced by $2,500, the intercompany profit related to 1967 inventories. Both of these adjustments arose from intercompany profits that were included in subsidiary earnings, hence these are applied to the net income balance reported by the subsidiary in arriving at the earnings of the minority interest for the year. Working papers can now be completed.

Consolidated statements prepared from the working papers at the end of 1966 and 1967 are given on pages 534 and 535.

Working papers for consolidated statements illustrated — cost method. Assume that Company A has maintained its investment account in Company B at cost. The individual statements for Company A that were given on pages 530 and 531 would be modified as follows: For the year ended December 31, 1966, the income statement would report net income of only $50,000 — earnings limited to its own activities; the balance sheet would show the investment in Company B at cost, $125,000, and retained earnings would be reported at $120,000 — the retained earnings balance, January 1, 1966, $70,000, increased by earnings for 1966, $50,000. For the year ended December 31, 1967, the income statement would report net income of only $80,000 — earnings from its own activities, $60,000, increased by dividends received from Company B, $20,000; the balance sheet would continue to report the investment in Company B at cost of $125,000, and retained earnings would be reported at $160,000 — the retained earnings balance as of January 1, 1967, $120,000, increased by earnings for 1967, $80,000, and reduced by dividends paid in 1967, $40,000.

Working papers for consolidated statements for 1966 and 1967 are shown on pages 542 and 543.

In view of the different recognition that is made of subsidiary activities, certain eliminations differ from those that are required when the equity method is used. Eliminations that differ follow:

(a) The balance of the investment account reports the payment for the subsidiary equity originally acquired, and the parent company's percentage of capital stock and retained earnings as of the date of original acquisition of subsidiary holdings is applied against this balance just as when working papers were limited to the development of the consolidated balance sheet. Eliminations are made as follows:

(a1) Capital Stock, Co. B (80% of $100,000).......	80,000	
Investment in Stock of Co. B..............		80,000
(a2) Retained Earnings, Co. B (80% of $25,000)...	20,000	
Investment in Stock of Co. B..............		20,000

The amount of the minority interest in the subsidiary retained earnings at the beginning of the current period is carried to the retained earnings — minority interest columns. After the first year, a difference between the retained earnings at the beginning of the period and the sum of the elimination against retained earnings and the interest of the minority in retained earnings represents the subsidiary net earnings accruing to the parent from the date of acquisition of holdings to the beginning of the current period. This difference is extended to the retained earnings columns of the controlling interest.

(d) In preparing working papers for 1967, the inventory at the beginning of the period is reduced by intercompany profits of $1,000; the asset reduction is accompanied by a reduction in retained earnings of Company B. The latter charge is recognized in calculating the retained earnings of the minority interest at the beginning of the period and the retained earnings of the subsidiary accruing to the parent as of the beginning of the period. The elimination is made as follows:

(d1) Retained Earnings, Co. B, 1/1/67 (reducing controlling and minority interests)...........	1,000	
Merchandise Inventory, 1/1/67...........		1,000

(e) Dividend income as reported by the parent is offset against dividends declared as reported by the subsidiary. The dividends declared balance on the books of the subsidiary is canceled to the extent of the reciprocal element included therein; the balance left in the account reflects the decrease for current dividends identified with the minority interest, and this balance is carried to the retained earnings — minority interest columns to be recognized as such. The dividend income balance is canceled, this balance losing its significance when parent and subsidiary revenue and expense balances are combined to arrive at the parent's share of earnings for the period. The elimination is made as follows:

(e) Dividend Income — Co. B..................	20,000	
Dividends Declared — Co. B...............		20,000

Remaining eliminations on the working papers are the same as those that were required when the equity method was employed. Working papers are summarized and are then used in preparing the consolidated

Cost method:

Company A and Subsidiary Company B
Working Papers for Consolidated Statements
December 31, 1966

	Co. A	Co. B	Eliminations Dr.	Eliminations Cr.	Consolidated Income Statement Dr.	Consolidated Income Statement Cr.	Retained Earnings — Minority Interest Dr.	Retained Earnings — Minority Interest Cr.	Retained Earnings — Controlling Interest Dr.	Retained Earnings — Controlling Interest Cr.	Consolidated Balance Sheet Dr.	Consolidated Balance Sheet Cr.
Debits												
Cash	35,000	25,000									60,000	
Accounts Receivable (net)	65,000	35,000		(c) 3,500							96,500	
Merchandise Inventory, 1/1/66	85,000	40,000			125,000							
Plant and Equipment (net)	215,000	100,000									315,000	
Investment in Stock of Co. B	125,000											
Eliminate 80% of Capital Stock				(a1) 80,000								
Eliminate 80% of Retained Earnings of $25,000 on 1/1/66				(a2) 20,000								
Excess of Cost over Book Value											25,000	
Purchases	380,000	160,000		(b) 15,000	525,000							
Expenses	145,000	40,000			185,000							
Income Taxes	30,000	15,000			45,000							
	1,080,000	415,000										
Merchandise Inventory, 12/31/66	90,000	75,000		(d) 1,000							164,000	
Credits												
Accounts Payable	60,000	80,000	(c) 3,500									136,500
Bonds Payable	100,000											100,000
Capital Stock, Co. A	250,000											250,000
Retained Earnings, Co. A, 1/1/66	70,000									70,000		
Capital Stock, Co. B		100,000										
Eliminate 80%			(a1) 80,000									
Minority Interest, 20%												20,000
Retained Earnings, Co. B, 1/1/66		25,000										
Eliminate 80% as above			(a2) 20,000									
Minority Interest, 20% of $25,000								5,000				
Sales	600,000	210,000	(b) 15,000			795,000						
	1,080,000	415,000										
Merchandise Inventory, 12/31/66	90,000	75,000	(d) 1,000			164,000						
			119,500	119,500	880,000	959,000						
Consolidated Income					79,000							
Income to Minority Interest, 20% of $29,000, Co. B Net Income after Adjustment (see below)								5,800				
Balance to Controlling Interest										73,200		
					959,000	959,000		10,800		143,200	660,500	506,500
Retained Earnings — Minority Interest to Balance Sheet							10,800					10,800
Retained Earnings — Controlling Interest to Balance Sheet									143,200			143,200
							10,800	10,800	143,200	143,200	660,500	660,500

Calculation of Co. B net income:	
Net income per books	$30,000
Deduct intercompany profit on merchandise transferred to Co. A	1,000
Net income for consolidation purposes	$29,000

December 31, 1967

	Co. A	Co. B	Eliminations Dr.	Eliminations Cr.	Consolidated Income Statement Dr.	Consolidated Income Statement Cr.	Retained Earnings — Minority Interest Dr.	Retained Earnings — Minority Interest Cr.	Retained Earnings — Controlling Interest Dr.	Retained Earnings — Controlling Interest Cr.	Consolidated Balance Sheet Dr.	Consolidated Balance Sheet Cr.
Debits												
Cash	55,000	30,000									85,000	
Accounts Receivable (net)	60,000	35,000		(c) 6,500							88,500	
Merchandise Inventory, 1/1/67	90,000	75,000		(d1) 1,000	164,000							
Plant and Equipment (net)	240,000	90,000									330,000	
Investment in Stock of Co. B	125,000											
Eliminate 80% of Capital Stock				(a1) 80,000								
Eliminate 80% of Retained Earnings of $25,000 on 1/1/66				(a2) 20,000								
Excess of Cost over Book Value											25,000	
Purchases	380,000	125,000		(b) 25,000	480,000							
Expenses	135,000	35,000			170,000							
Income Taxes	40,000	20,000			60,000							
Dividends Declared — Co. A	40,000								40,000			
Dividends Declared — Co. B		25,000		(e) 20,000			5,000					
	1,165,000	435,000										
Merchandise Inventory, 12/31/67	80,000	70,000		(d2) 2,500							147,500	
Credits												
Accounts Payable	50,000	60,000	(c) 6,500									103,500
Bonds Payable	100,000											100,000
Capital Stock, Co. A	250,000											250,000
Retained Earnings, Co. A, 1/1/67	120,000									120,000		
Capital Stock, Co. B		100,000										
Eliminate 80%			(a1) 80,000									
Minority Interest, 20%												20,000
Retained Earnings, Co. B, 1/1/67		55,000	(d1) 1,000									
Eliminate 80% as above			(a2) 20,000									
Min. Int., 20% of $54,000 ($55,000 – $1,000)								10,800				
Retained Earnings to Parent										23,200		
Sales	625,000	220,000	(b) 25,000			820,000						
Dividend Income — Co. B	20,000		(e) 20,000									
	1,165,000	435,000										
Merchandise Inventory, 12/31/67	80,000	70,000	(d2) 2,500			147,500						
			155,000	155,000	874,000	967,500						
Consolidated Income					93,500							
Income to Minority Interest, 20% of $33,500, Co. B Net Income after Adjustment (see below)								6,700				
Balance to Controlling Interest										86,800		
					967,500	967,500	5,000	17,500	40,000	230,000	676,000	473,500
Retained Earnings — Minority Interest to Balance Sheet							12,500					12,500
Retained Earnings — Controlling Interest to Balance Sheet									190,000			190,000
							17,500	17,500	230,000	230,000	676,000	676,000

Calculation of Co. B net income:

Net income per books	$35,000
Deduct adjustment for intercompany profits on merchandise: 12/31/67, $2,500, less 1/1/67, $1,000	1,500
Net income for consolidation purposes	$33,500

statements. The consolidated statements will be the same regardless of whether the investment account is carried at equity or at cost. Consolidated statements for Companies A and B that were given on pages 534 and 535 may be constructed either from the working papers on pages 532–533 or from the working papers on pages 542–543.

PREPARATION OF CONSOLIDATED STATEMENTS — SPECIAL PROBLEMS

In the first set of examples, relatively simple conditions were assumed. In the examples to follow, more complex conditions are given and the special procedures under such conditions are illustrated: consolidated statements are required for manufacturing companies at the end of the first year of a parent-subsidiary relationship and at the end of the second year of such a relationship; eliminations are required for investment and related subsidiary capital balances, for intercompany profits on inventories and plant items, for intercompany indebtedness in the form of bonds, and for other reciprocal asset-liability and revenue-expense balances. The data that follow are to be considered in preparing consolidated statements for Company P and Company S at the end of 1966 and at the end of 1967. Letter designations given below are used on subsequent pages in describing eliminations and in identifying eliminations on the working papers.

(a) Company P acquired 80% of the stock of Company S on January 1, 1966, at a cost of $200,000. Capital stock of Company S on that date was $200,000; retained earnings were $10,000.

(b) Company P acquires part of its raw materials from Company S. Intercompany sales were as follows: 1966, $25,000; 1967, $35,000.

(c) Company S sells raw materials to the parent at a gross profit of 20% of sales prices. It is estimated that Company P inventories included raw materials acquired from Company S as follows:

	December 31, 1966	December 31, 1967
Finished goods	$2,000	$3,000
Goods in process	3,000	5,000
Raw materials	5,000	7,000

(d) Amounts are owed Company S by Company P on open account as follows: 1966, $10,000; 1967, $15,000.

(e) Dividends were declared by Company S as follows: In December of 1966, a dividend of $5,000 was declared, the dividend being paid in January, 1967. In 1967, two dividends of $5,000 each were declared, the first dividend being paid in July and the second to be paid in January, 1968.

(f) Company S issued bonds of $100,000 at 95 at the end of 1966. Company P purchased one fifth of the issue from the subsidiary at this price.

(g) At the end of 1966 Company S sold equipment to Company P for $20,000 and recognized a gain on the sale of $5,000. The parent recognizes depreciation on the asset at the rate of 10% per year.

Working papers for a consolidated balance sheet prepared on the date of stock acquisition follow:

Company P and Subsidiary Company S
Working Papers for Consolidated Balance Sheet
January 1, 1966

	Co. P	Co. S	Eliminations		Consolidated Balance Sheet	
			Dr.	Cr.	Dr.	Cr.
Debits						
Cash	20,000	10,000			30,000	
Accounts Receivable (net)	45,000	40,000			85,000	
Finished Goods Inventory	50,000	30,000			80,000	
Goods in Process Inventory	40,000	20,000			60,000	
Raw Materials Inventory	35,000	15,000			50,000	
Machinery and Equipment	400,000	120,000			520,000	
Buildings	160,000	100,000			260,000	
Land	75,000	40,000			115,000	
Investment in Stock of Co. S	200,000					
Eliminate 80% of Capital Stock				160,000		
Eliminate 80% of Retained Earnings				8,000		
Excess of Cost over Book Value					32,000	
	1,025,000	375,000				
Credits						
Allowance for Depreciation — Machinery and Equipment	120,000	60,000				180,000
Allowance for Depreciation — Buildings	60,000	35,000				95,000
Accounts Payable	75,000	65,000				140,000
Dividends Payable	20,000	5,000				25,000
Capital Stock, Co. P	500,000					500,000
Retained Earnings, Co. P	250,000					250,000
Capital Stock, Co. S		200,000				
Eliminate 80%			160,000			
Minority Interest, 20%						40,000
Retained Earnings, Co. S		10,000				
Eliminate 80%			8,000			
Minority Interest, 20%						2,000
	1,025,000	375,000	168,000	168,000	1,232,000	1,232,000

Working papers for consolidated statements illustrated — equity method. Assume that the parent maintains its investment in the subsidiary by the equity method. Financial data for Companies P and S for the years ended December 31, 1966 and 1967, are shown on pages 546–

549. Working papers for consolidated statements for Companies P and S for 1966 and for 1967 may be developed as illustrated on pages 550–551 and 552–553.

Trial balances that are adjusted for all items with the exception of ending inventories are first listed on the working papers. The ending inventories are then listed in both the debit and credit sections following adjusted trial balance data. The eliminations for intercompany real and nominal account balances may then be recorded.

Explanations of the eliminations that are required on the working papers for Companies P and S follow. The letter preceding each explanation corresponds with that used in reporting the elimination on the working papers.

Working papers for consolidated statements — 1966. (a) Investment account eliminations are made in terms of reciprocal balances that are found in both real and nominal accounts as shown below.

(a1) Eighty percent of the capital stock of Company S is offset against the investment account by the following elimination:

Capital Stock, Co. S (80% of $200,000)......	160,000	
Investment in Stock of Co. S..............		160,000

Income Statements
For Year Ended December 31, 1966

	Co. P		Co. S	
Sales....................................		$575,000		$270,000
Less sales returns and allowances............		10,000		5,000
Net sales..................................		$565,000		$265,000
Cost of goods sold:				
Finished goods inventory, January 1........	$ 50,000		$ 30,000	
Cost of goods manufactured (see schedule)...	385,000		180,000	
Merchandise available for sale..............	$435,000		$210,000	
Deduct finished goods inventory, December 31................................	60,000	375,000	45,000	165,000
Gross profit on sales........................		$190,000		$100,000
Selling and general expenses.................		80,000		65,000
Net income before income taxes..............		$110,000		$ 35,000
Add gain on sale of equipment...............				5,000
Net income and special gain before income taxes.				$ 40,000
Income taxes...............................		45,000		15,000
Net income and special gain.................		$ 65,000		$ 25,000
Add income — Subsidiary Co. S, 80% of $25,000		20,000		
Net income and special gain, including parent company's share of Co. S earnings..........		$ 85,000		

(a2) Eighty percent of Company S beginning retained earnings and dividends declared balances are offset against the investment account as follows:

Retained Earnings, Co. S, January 1, 1966 (80% of $10,000)	8,000	
Dividends Declared — Co. S (80% of $5,000)		4,000
Investment in Stock of Co. S ($8,000 — $4,000)		4,000

(a3) The entry made by Company P to recognize its share of subsidiary earnings for the year is canceled as follows:

Income — Subsidiary Co. S	20,000	
Investment in Stock of Co. S		20,000

(b) Sales that were made by Company S to Company P are eliminated as follows:

Sales (Co. S)	25,000	
Raw Material Purchases (Co. P)		25,000

(c) The profit recognized by Company S on transfers of raw materials to Company P was 20% of the sales price. Intercompany profits in Company P ending inventories are as follows: finished goods, 20% of $2,000, or $400; goods in process, 20% of $3,000, or $600; finished goods,

Income Statements
For Year Ended December 31, 1967

	Co. P		Co. S	
Sales		$620,000		$365,000
Less sales returns and allowances		11,100		9,500
Net sales		$608,900		$355,500
Cost of goods sold:				
Finished goods inventory, January 1	$ 60,000		$ 45,000	
Cost of goods manufactured (see schedule)	415,000		245,000	
Merchandise available for sale	$475,000		$290,000	
Deduct finished goods inventory, December 31	75,000	400,000	65,000	225,000
Gross profit on sales		$208,900		$130,500
Selling and general expenses		90,000		70,000
Net operating profit		$118,900		$ 60,500
Interest income		1,100		
Interest expense				5,500
Net income before income taxes		$120,000		$ 55,000
Income taxes		50,000		20,000
Net income		$ 70,000		$ 35,000
Add income — Subsidiary Co. S, 80% of $35,000		28,000		
Net income, including parent company's share of Co. S earnings		$ 98,000		

Cost of Goods Manufactured Schedules
To Accompany Income Statements
For Year Ended December 31, 1966

	Co. P		Co. S	
Goods in process inventory, January 1		$ 40,000		$ 20,000
Raw materials:				
Raw materials inventory, January 1	$ 35,000		$ 15,000	
Purchases	130,000		55,000	
Total cost of raw materials available for use	$165,000		$ 70,000	
Deduct raw materials inventory, December 31	45,000	120,000	20,000	50,000
Direct labor		135,000		60,000
Manufacturing overhead		145,000		75,000
Total goods in process during year		$440,000		$205,000
Deduct goods in process inventory, December 31		55,000		25,000
Cost of goods manufactured		$385,000		$180,000

Retained Earnings Statements
For Year Ended December 31, 1966

	Co. P	Co. S
Balance, January 1	$250,000	$ 10,000
Add net income for year	85,000	25,000
	$335,000	$ 35,000
Deduct dividends declared during year	40,000	5,000
Balance, December 31	$295,000	$ 30,000

Balance Sheets
December 31, 1966

Assets	Co. P		Co. S	
Cash		$ 10,000		$ 20,000
Accounts receivable (net)		30,000		40,000
Dividends receivable		4,000		
Finished goods inventory		60,000		45,000
Goods in process inventory		55,000		25,000
Raw materials inventory		45,000		20,000
Machinery and equipment	$435,000		$180,000	
Less allowance for depreciation	180,000	255,000	75,000	105,000
Buildings	$180,000		$140,000	
Less allowance for depreciation	65,000	115,000	45,000	95,000
Land		75,000		40,000
Investment in bonds of Co. S		19,000		
Investment in stock of Co. S		216,000		
Total assets		$884,000		$390,000
Liabilities				
Accounts payable		$ 69,000		$ 60,000
Dividends payable		20,000		5,000
5% bonds payable			$100,000	
Less discount on bonds payable			5,000	95,000
Total liabilities		$ 89,000		$160,000
Stockholders' Equity				
Capital stock	$500,000		$200,000	
Retained earnings	295,000		30,000	
Total stockholders' equity		795,000		230,000
Total liabilities and stockholders' equity		$884,000		$390,000

Cost of Goods Manufactured Schedules
To Accompany Income Statements
For Year Ended December 31, 1967

	Co. P		Co. S	
Goods in process inventory, January 1		$ 55,000		$ 25,000
Raw materials:				
Raw materials inventory, January 1	$ 45,000		$ 20,000	
Add purchases	140,000		80,000	
Total cost of raw materials available for use	$185,000		$100,000	
Deduct raw materials inventory, December 31	50,000	135,000	30,000	70,000
Direct labor		145,000		85,000
Manufacturing overhead		150,000		105,000
Total goods in process during year		$485,000		$285,000
Deduct goods in process inventory, December 31		70,000		40,000
Cost of goods manufactured		$415,000		$245,000

Retained Earnings Statements
For Year Ended December 31, 1967

	Co. P	Co. S
Balance, January 1	$295,000	$ 30,000
Add net income for year	98,000	35,000
	$393,000	$ 65,000
Deduct dividends declared during year	40,000	10,000
Balance, December 31	$353,000	$ 55,000

Balance Sheets
December 31, 1967

	Co. P		Co. S	
Assets				
Cash		$ 20,000		$ 25,000
Accounts receivable (net)		45,000		50,000
Dividends receivable		4,000		
Finished goods inventory		75,000		65,000
Goods in process inventory		70,000		40,000
Raw materials inventory		50,000		30,000
Machinery and equipment	$450,000		$190,000	
Less allowance for depreciation	205,000	245,000	90,000	100,000
Buildings	$185,000		$140,000	
Less allowance for depreciation	75,000	110,000	50,000	90,000
Land		75,000		40,000
Investment in bonds of Co. S		19,100		
Investment in stock of Co. S		236,000		
Total assets		$949,100		$440,000
Liabilities				
Accounts payable		$ 76,100		$ 84,500
Dividends payable		20,000		5,000
5% bonds payable			$100,000	
Less discount on bonds payable			4,500	95,500
Total liabilities		$ 96,100		
Stockholders' Equity				
Capital stock	$500,000		$200,000	
Retained earnings	353,000		55,000	
Total stockholders' equity		853,000		255,000
Total liabilities and stockholders' equity		$949,100		$440,000

Equity method:

Company P and
Working Papers for
December

	Co. P	Co. S	Eliminations Dr.	Eliminations Cr.	
Debits					
Cash	10,000	20,000			(1)
Accounts Receivable (net)	30,000	40,000		(d) 10,000	(2)
Dividends Receivable	4,000			(e) 4,000	(3)
Finished Goods Inventory, 1/1/66	50,000	30,000			(4)
Goods in Process Inventory, 1/1/66	40,000	20,000			(5)
Raw Materials Inventory, 1/1/66	35,000	15,000			(6)
Machinery and Equipment	435,000	180,000		(g) 5,000	(7)
Buildings	180,000	140,000			(8)
Land	75,000	40,000			(9)
Investment in Bonds of Co. S	19,000		(f) 1,000		(10)
Investment in Stock of Co. S	216,000				(11)
Eliminate 80% of Capital Stock				(a1) 160,000	(12)
Eliminate 80% of Retained Earnings, 1/1/66, less dividends				(a2) 4,000	(13)
Eliminate 80% of Earnings for 1966				(a3) 20,000	(14)
Excess of Cost over Book Value					(15)
Discount on Bonds Payable		5,000		(f) 1,000	(16)
Sales Returns and Allowances	10,000	5,000			(17)
Raw Material Purchases	130,000	55,000		(b) 25,000	(18)
Direct Labor	135,000	60,000			(19)
Manufacturing Overhead	145,000	75,000			(20)
Selling and General Expenses	80,000	65,000			(21)
Income Taxes	45,000	15,000			(22)
Dividends Declared — Co. P	40,000				(23)
Dividends Declared — Co. S		5,000		(a2) 4,000	(24)
	1,679,000	770,000			(25)
Finished Goods Inventory, 12/31/66	60,000	45,000		(c) 400	(26)
Goods in Process Inventory, 12/31/66	55,000	25,000		(c) 600	(27)
Raw Materials Inventory, 12/31/66	45,000	20,000		(c) 1,000	(28)
Credits					
Allowance for Depreciation of Machinery and Equipment	180,000	75,000			(29)
Allowance for Depreciation of Buildings	65,000	45,000			(30)
Accounts Payable	69,000	60,000	(d) 10,000		(31)
Dividends Payable	20,000	5,000	(e) 4,000		(32)
5% Bonds Payable		100,000			(33)
Capital Stock, Co. P	500,000				(34)
Retained Earnings, Co. P, 1/1/66	250,000				(35)
Capital Stock, Co. S		200,000			(36)
Eliminate 80%			(a1) 160,000		(37)
Minority Interest, 20%					(38)
Retained Earnings, Co. S, 1/1/66		10,000			(39)
Eliminate 80%			(2a) 8,000		(40)
Minority Interest, 20%					(41)
Sales	575,000	270,000	(b) 25,000		(42)
Gain on Sale of Equipment		5,000	(g) 5,000		(43)
Income — Subsidiary Co. S	20,000		(a3) 20,000		(44)
	1,679,000	770,000			(45)
Finished Goods Inventory, 12/31/66	60,000	45,000	(c) 400		(46)
Goods in Process Inventory, 12/31/66	55,000	25,000	(c) 600		(47)
Raw Materials Inventory, 12/31/66	45,000	20,000	(c) 1,000		(48)
			235,000	235,000	(49)
Cost of Goods Manufactured					(50)
					(51)
Consolidated Income					(52)
Income to Minority Interest, 20% of $18,000, Co. S Net Income after Adjustment (see below)					(53)
Balance to Controlling Interest					(54)
					(55)
Retained Earnings — Minority Interest to Balance Sheet					(56)
Retained Earnings — Controlling Interest to Balance Sheet					(57)
					(58)

Calculation of Co. S Net Income:

Net income per books		$25,000
Deduct: Intercompany profit on sale of equipment to Co. P	$5,000	
Intercompany profit on merchandise transferred to Co. P	2,000	7,000
Net income for consolidation purposes		$18,000

Subsidiary Company S
Consolidated Statements
31, 1966

	Consolidated Manufacturing		Consolidated Income Statement		Retained Earnings — Minority Interest		Retained Earnings — Controlling Interest		Consolidated Balance Sheet	
	Dr.	Cr.	Dr.	Cr.	Dr.	Cr.	Dr.	Cr.	Dr.	Cr.
(1)									30,000	
(2)									60,000	
(3)										
(4)			80,000							
(5)	60,000									
(6)	50,000									
(7)										
(8)									610,000	
(9)									320,000	
(10)									115,000	
(11)									20,000	
(12)										
(13)										
(14)										
(15)										
(16)									32,000	
(17)			15,000						4,000	
(18)	160,000									
(19)	195,000									
(20)	220,000									
(21)			145,000							
(22)			60,000							
(23)										
(24)										
(25)					1,000		40,000			
(26)										
(27)									104,600	
(28)									79,400	
									64,000	
(29)										
(30)										255,000
(31)										110,000
(32)										119,000
(33)										21,000
(34)										100,000
(35)										500,000
(36)								250,000		
(37)										
(38)										40,000
(39)										
(40)										
(41)						2,000				
(42)				820,000						
(43)										
(44)										
(45)										
(46)				104,600						
(47)		79,400								
(48)		64,000								
(49)	685,000	143,400								
(50)		541,600	541,600							
(51)	685,000	685,000	841,600	924,600						
(52)	....		83,000							
(53)	....					3,600				
(54)	....							79,400		
(55)			924,600	924,600	1,000	5,600	40,000	329,400	1,439,000	1,145,000
(56)	....				4,600					4,600
(57)	....						289,400			289,400
(58)					5,600	5,600	329,400	329,400	1,439,000	1,439,000

Equity method

Company P and
Working Papers for
December

	Co. P	Co. S	Eliminations Dr.	Eliminations Cr.	
Debits					
Cash	20,000	25,000			(1)
Accounts Receivable (net)	45,000	50,000		(d) 15,000	(2)
Dividends Receivable	4,000			(e) 4,000	(3)
Finished Goods Inventory, 1/1/67	60,000	45,000		(c1) 400	(4)
Goods in Process Inventory, 1/1/67	55,000	25,000		(c1) 600	(5)
Raw Materials Inventory, 1/1/67	45,000	20,000		(c1) 1,000	(6)
Machinery and Equipment	450,000	190,000		(g) 5,000	(7)
Buildings	185,000	140,000			(8)
Land	75,000	40,000			(9)
Investment in Bonds of Co. S	19,100		(f1) 900		(10)
Investment in Stock of Co. S	236,000				(11)
Eliminate 80% of Capital Stock				(a1) 160,000	(12)
Eliminate 80% of Retained Earnings, 1/1/67, less dividends				(a2) 16,000	(13)
Eliminate 80% of Earnings for 1967				(a3) 28,000	(14)
Excess of Cost over Book Value					(15)
Discount on Bonds Payable		4,500		(f1) 900	(16)
Sales Returns and Allowances	11,100	9,500			(17)
Raw Material Purchases	140,000	80,000		(b) 35,000	(18)
Direct Labor	145,000	85,000			(19)
Manufacturing Overhead	150,000	105,000		(g) 500	(20)
Selling and General Expenses	90,000	70,000			(21)
Interest Expense		5,500		(f1) 100	(22)
				(f2) 1,000	(23)
Income Taxes	50,000	20,000			(24)
Dividends Declared — Co. P	40,000				(25)
Dividends Declared — Co. S		10,000		(a2) 8,000	(26)
	1,820,200	924,500			(27)
Finished Goods Inventory, 12/31/67	75,000	65,000		(c2) 600	(28)
Goods in Process Inventory, 12/31/67	70,000	40,000		(c2) 1,000	(29)
Raw Materials Inventory, 12/31/67	50,000	30,000		(c2) 1,400	(30)
Credits					
Allowance for Depreciation of Machinery and Equipment	205,000	90,000	(g) 500		(31)
Allowance for Depreciation of Buildings	75,000	50,000			(32)
Accounts Payable	76,100	84,500	(d) 15,000		(33)
Dividends Payable	20,000	5,000	(e) 4,000		(34)
5% Bonds Payable		100,000			(35)
Capital Stock, Co. P	500,000				(36)
Retained Earnings, Co. P, 1/1/67	295,000		(c1) 1,600		(37)
			(g) 4,000		(38)
Capital Stock, Co. S		200,000			(39)
Eliminate 80%			(a1) 160,000		(40)
Minority Interest, 20%					(41)
Retained Earnings, Co. S, 1/1/67		30,000	(c1) 400		(42)
			(g) 1,000		(43)
Eliminate 80%			(a2) 24,000		(44)
Minority Interest, 20% of $30,000, less $1,400					(45)
Sales	620,000	365,000	(b) 35,000		(46)
Interest Income	1,100		(f1) 100		(47)
			(f2) 1,000		(48)
Income — Subsidiary Co. S	28,000		(a3) 28,000		(49)
	1,820,200	924,500			(50)
Finished Goods Inventory, 12/31/67	75,000	65,000	(c2) 600		(51)
Goods in Process Inventory, 12/31/67	70 000	40 000	(c2) 1,000		(52)
Raw Materials Inventory, 12/31/67	50,000	30,000	(c2) 1,400		(53)
			278,500	278,500	(54)
Cost of Goods Manufactured					(55)
					(56)
Consolidated Income					(57)
Income to Minority Int., 20% of $34,000, Co. S Net Income after Adj., plus $100, Recognized Gain on Sale of Eqpt. to Parent (see below)					(58)
Balance to Controlling Interest					(59)
					(60)
Retained Earnings — Minority Interest to Balance Sheet					(61)
Retained Earnings — Controlling Interest to Balance Sheet					(62)
					(63)

Calculation of Co. S Net Income:

Net income per books	$35,000
Deduct adjustment for intercompany profits on merchandise 12/31/67, $3,000, less 1/1/67, $2,000	1,000
Net income for consolidation purposes	$34,000

Calculation of Recognized Gain on Equipment by Minority Interest:

Gain on sale of equipment to Co. P recognized by Co. S, 12/31/66, $5,000.

Gain identified with minority interest and to be recognized over life of equipment (10 years), 20% of $5,000, or $1,000.

Gain to be recognized in 1967, 1/10 x $1,000, or $100.

Subsidiary Company S
Consolidated Statements
31, 1967

	Consolidated Manufacturing		Consolidated Income Statement		Retained Earnings — Minority Interest		Retained Earnings — Controlling Interest		Consolidated Balance Sheet	
	Dr.	Cr.	Dr.	Cr.	Dr.	Cr.	Dr.	Cr.	Dr.	Cr.
(1)									45,000	
(2)									80,000	
(3)										
(4)			104,600							
(5)	79,400									
(6)	64,000									
(7)									635,000	
(8)									325,000	
(9)									115,000	
(10)									20,000	
(11)										
(12)										
(13)										
(14)										
(15)									32,000	
(16)									3,600	
(17)			20,600							
(18)	185,000									
(19)	230,000									
(20)	254,500									
(21)			160,000							
(22)			4,400							
(23)										
(24)			70,000							
(25)							40,000			
(26)										
(27)					2,000					
(28)									139,400	
(29)									109,000	
(30)									78,600	
(31)										294,500
(32)										125,000
(33)										145,600
(34)										21,000
(35)										100,000
(36)										500,000
(37)								289,400		
(38)										
(39)										
(40)										
(41)										40,000
(42)										
(43)										
(44)										
(45)						4,600				
(46)				950,000						
(47)										
(48)										
(49)										
(50)										
(51)				139,400						
(52)		109,000								
(53)		78,600								
(54)	812,900	187,600								
(55)		625,300	625,300							
(56)	812,900	812,900	984,900	1,089,400						
(57)	....		104,500							
(58)	....					6,900				
(59)	....							97,600		
(60)			1,089,400	1,089,400	2,000	11,500	40,000	387,000	1,582,600	1,226,100
(61)	....				9,500					9,500
(62)	....						347,000			347,000
(63)					11,500	11,500	387,000	387,000	1,582,600	1,582,600

Company P and Subsidiary Company S
Consolidated Income Statement
For Year Ended December 31, 1966

Sales		$820,000
Less sales returns and allowances		15,000
Net sales		$805,000
Cost of goods sold:		
Finished goods inventory, January 1	$ 80,000	
Cost of goods manufactured (see schedule)	541,600	
Merchandise available for sale	$621,600	
Deduct finished goods inventory, December 31	104,600	517,000
Gross profit on sales		$288,000
Selling and general expenses		145,000
Net income before income taxes		$143,000
Income taxes		60,000
Net income		$ 83,000
Distribution of net income:		
To minority interest		$ 3,600
To controlling interest		79,400
Total net income		$ 83,000

Company P and Subsidiary Company S
Cost of Goods Manufactured Schedule
To Accompany Consolidated Income Statement
For Year Ended December 31, 1966

Goods in process inventory, January 1		$ 60,000
Raw materials:		
Raw materials inventory, January 1	$ 50,000	
Purchases	160,000	
Total cost of raw materials available for use	$210,000	
Deduct raw materials inventory, December 31	64,000	146,000
Direct labor		195,000
Manufacturing overhead		220,000
Total goods in process during year		$621,000
Deduct goods in process inventory, December 31		79,400
Cost of goods manufactured		$541,600

Company P and Subsidiary Company S
Consolidated Retained Earnings Statement
For Year Ended December 31, 1966

	Retained Earnings — Minority Interest	Retained Earnings — Controlling Interest
Balance, January 1	$2,000	$250,000
Add net income for year	3,600	79,400
	$5,600	$329,400
Deduct dividends declared during year	1,000	40,000
Balance, December 31	$4,600	$289,400

Company P and Subsidiary Company S
Consolidated Income Statement
For Year Ended December 31, 1967

Sales		$950,000
Less sales returns and allowances		20,600
Net sales		$929,400
Cost of goods sold:		
Finished goods inventory, January 1	$104,600	
Cost of goods manufactured (see schedule)	625,300	
Merchandise available for sale	$729,900	
Deduct finished goods inventory, December 31	139,400	590,500
Gross profit on sales		$338,900
Selling and general expenses		160,000
Net operating profit		$178,900
Interest expense		4,400
Net income before income taxes		$174,500
Income taxes		70,000
Net income		$104,500
Distribution of net income:		
To minority interest		$ 6,900
To controlling interest		97,600
Total net income		$104,500

Company P and Subsidiary Company S
Cost of Goods Manufactured Schedule
To Accompany Consolidated Income Statement
For Year Ended December 31, 1967

Goods in process inventory, January 1		$ 79,400
Raw materials:		
Raw materials inventory, January 1	$ 64,000	
Purchases	185,000	
Total cost of raw materials available for use	$249,000	
Deduct raw materials inventory, December 31	78,600	170,400
Direct labor		230,000
Manufacturing overhead		254,500
Total goods in process during year		$734,300
Deduct goods in process inventory, December 31		109,000
Cost of goods manufactured		$625,300

Company P and Subsidiary Company S
Consolidated Retained Earnings Statement
For Year Ended December 31, 1967

	Retained Earnings — Minority Interest	Retained Earnings — Controlling Interest
Balance, January 1	$ 4,600	$289,400
Add net income for year	6,900	97,600
	$11,500	$387,000
Deduct dividends declared during year	2,000	40,000
Balance, December 31	$ 9,500	$347,000

Company P and Subsidiary Company S
Consolidated Balance Sheet
December 31, 1966

Assets			
Cash			$ 30,000
Accounts receivable (net)			60,000
Finished goods inventory			104,600
Goods in process inventory			79,400
Raw materials inventory			64,000
Machinery and equipment		$610,000	
Less allowance for depreciation		255,000	355,000
Buildings		$320,000	
Less allowance for depreciation		110,000	210,000
Land			115,000
Excess of cost over book value of subsidiary interest			32,000
Total assets			$1,050,000
Liabilities			
Accounts payable			$ 119,000
Dividends payable			21,000
5% bonds payable		$100,000	
Less bonds held by affiliated company		20,000	
		$ 80,000	
Less discount on bonds payable		4,000	76,000
Total liabilities			$ 216,000
Stockholders' Equity			
Minority interest:			
Capital stock	$ 40,000		
Retained earnings	4,600	$ 44,600	
Controlling interest:			
Capital stock	$500,000		
Retained earnings	289,400	789,400	
Total stockholders' equity			834,000
Total liabilities and stockholders' equity			$1,050,000

20% of \$5,000, or \$1,000. The intercompany profits on inventories as of December 31, 1966, are canceled as follows:

Finished Goods Inventory, 12/31/66 (income statement value)	400	
Goods in Process Inventory, 12/31/66 (manufacturing schedule value)	600	
Raw Materials Inventory, 12/31/66 (manufacturing schedule value)	1,000	
Finished Goods Inventory, 12/31/66 (balance sheet value)		400
Goods in Process Inventory, 12/31/66 (balance sheet value)		600
Raw Materials Inventory, 12/31/66 (balance sheet value)		1,000

(d) Accounts receivable from Company P reported by Company S are offset against accounts payable reported by Company P by the following elimination:

Accounts Payable (Co. P)	10,000	
Accounts Receivable (Co. S)		10,000

Company P and Subsidiary Company S
Consolidated Balance Sheet
December 31, 1967

Assets			
Cash			$ 45,000
Accounts receivable (net)			80,000
Finished goods inventory			139,400
Goods in process inventory			109,000
Raw materials inventory			78,600
Machinery and equipment		$635,000	
Less allowance for depreciation		294,500	340,500
Buildings		$325,000	
Less allowance for depreciation		125,000	200,000
Land			115,000
Excess of cost over book value of subsidiary interest			32,000
Total assets			$1,139,500
Liabilities			
Accounts payable			$ 145,600
Dividends payable			21,000
5% bonds payable		$100,000	
Less bonds held by affiliated company		20,000	
		$ 80,000	
Less discount on bonds payable		3,600	76,400
Total liabilities			$ 243,000
Stockholders' Equity			
Minority interest:			
Capital stock	$ 40,000		
Retained earnings	9,500	$ 49,500	
Controlling interest:			
Capital stock	$500,000		
Retained earnings	347,000	847,000	
Total stockholders' equity			896,500
Total liabilities and stockholders' equity			$1,139,500

(e) Dividends receivable of Company S reported by Company P are offset against dividends payable reported by Company S as follows:

Dividends Payable (Co. S)	4,000	
Dividends Receivable (Co. P)		4,000

(f) The investment in bonds of Company S reported by Company P must be raised to par so that it may be offset against the bonds payable account reported at par; one fifth of the discount on bonds payable must be canceled so that the discount reports only the amount related to bonds held by outsiders. The following entry is made on the working papers:

Investment in Bonds of Co. S ($20,000 – $19,000)	1,000	
Discount on Bonds Payable (20,000/100,000 × $5,000)		1,000

(g) Equipment acquired by Company P from Company S at the end of 1966 must be reduced to cost and the profit on the transfer reported by Company S canceled. The following elimination is made:

Gain on Sale of Equipment (Co. S)	5,000	
Machinery and Equipment (Co. P)		5,000

Account balances on the working papers may now be combined and extended to the statement columns. Manufacturing and income statement columns are summarized and the consolidated income determined. Net income is then assigned to minority and controlling interests, and the working papers are completed as in the earlier examples.

Working papers for consolidated statements — 1967. (a) Investment account eliminations are made in terms of the reciprocal balances found in real and nominal accounts as of December 31, 1967, as follows:

(a1) Eighty percent of the capital stock of Company S is offset against the investment account by the following elimination:

Capital Stock (80% of $200,000)	160,000	
Investment in Stock of Co. S		160,000

(a2) Eighty percent of Company S retained earnings as of January 1, 1967, and 80% of the dividend declared balances are offset against the investment account as follows:

Retained Earnings, Co. S, 1/1/67 (80% of $30,000)	24,000	
Dividends Declared — Co. S (80% of $10,000)		8,000
Investment in Stock of Co. S................		16,000

(a3) The entry made by Company P to recognize its share of subsidiary earnings for 1967 is canceled by the following elimination:

Income — Subsidiary Co. S...................	28,000	
Investment in Stock of Co. S................		28,000

(b) Sales that were made by Company S to Company P during 1967 are canceled as follows:

Sales (Co. S)................................	35,000	
Raw Material Purchases (Co. P).............		35,000

(c) The profit recognized by Company S on transfers of raw materials to Company P was 20% of the sales price. Intercompany profits on beginning and ending inventories are calculated as follows:

	January 1, 1967		December 31, 1967	
	Sales Price of Raw Materials	Intercompany Profit 20%	Sales Price of Raw Materials	Intercompany Profit 20%
Finished goods.....	$2,000	$ 400	$3,000	$ 600
Goods in process...	3,000	600	5,000	1,000
Raw materials.....	5,000	1,000	7,000	1,400

(c1) Intercompany profits in the beginning inventories are canceled by the following elimination:

Retained Earnings, Co. P, 1/1/67 (80% of $2,000)	1,600	
Retained Earnings, Co. S, 1/1/67 (reducing minority interest, 20% of $2,000)	400	
Finished Goods Inventory, 1/1/67		400
Goods in Process Inventory, 1/1/67..........		600
Raw Materials Inventory, 1/1/67............		1,000

(c2) Intercompany profits on the ending inventories are canceled as follows:

Finished Goods Inventory, 12/31/67 (income statement value)	600	
Goods in Process Inventory, 12/31/67 (manufacturing schedule value)	1,000	
Raw Materials Inventory, 12/31/67 (manufacturing schedule value)	1,400	
Finished Goods Inventory, 12/31/67 (balance sheet value)		600
Goods in Process Inventory, 12/31/67 (balance sheet value)		1,000
Raw Materials Inventory, 12/31/67 (balance sheet value)		1,400

(d) Intercompany trade balances are canceled by the following elimination:

Accounts Payable (Co. P)	15,000	
Accounts Receivable (Co. S)		15,000

(e) Dividends receivable on the stock of Company S reported by Company P is offset against dividends payable reported by Company S as follows:

Dividends Payable (Co. S)	4,000	
Dividends Receivable (Co. P)		4,000

(f) Intercompany bonded debt must be eliminated; in addition, interest income and interest expense balances relating to the intercompany debt item must be canceled.

(f1) At the end of 1966, intercompany bond holdings were eliminated by canceling reciprocal bond discount balances and applying bonds held by Company P against bonds payable of Company S in preparing the consolidated balance sheet. At the end of 1967, discounts are reflected in both real and nominal balances, since discount balances have been reduced for current amortization. At the end of 1967, then, elimination will involve reciprocal discount balances reflected in the discount account on the books of Company S and the investment account of Company P and also reciprocal interest charges and credits resulting from discount amortization and accumulation on the books of Companies S and P. An elimination is made as follows:

Investment in Bonds of Co. S (Co. P)	900	
Interest Income (Co. P)	100	
Discount on Bonds Payable (Co. S)		900
Interest Expense (Co. S)		100

(f2) Company S paid Company P interest of $1,000 in 1967 on Company S bonds of $20,000 held by Company P. The intercompany interest is canceled as follows:

Interest Income (Co. P)	1,000	
Interest Expense (Co. S)		1,000

(g) Asset values as well as depreciation charges relating to equipment items acquired by Company P from its subsidiary must be restated in terms of cost. In considering eliminations relating to the asset and to the charges to operations arising therefrom, analysis of the asset as of the beginning and end of the period is required as follows:

	At Sales Price to Co. P	At Cost to Co. S	Intercompany Profit
December 31, 1966:			
Equipment	$20,000	$15,000	$5,000
December 31, 1967:			
Equipment	$20,000	$15,000	$5,000
Allowance for depreciation (10%)	(2,000)	(1,500)	(500)
	$18,000	$13,500	$4,500

Assuming the equity method and assuming the preparation of only a consolidated balance sheet at the end of 1966 and 1967, eliminations for intercompany profit on the equipment would be made as follows:

December 31, 1966			December 31, 1967		
Retained Earnings, Co. P	4,000		Retained Earnings, Co. P	3,600	
Retained Earnings, Co. S (reducing minority interest)	1,000		Retained Earnings, Co. S (reducing minority interest)	900	
Machinery and Equipment		5,000	Allowance for Depreciation	500	
			Machinery and Equipment		5,000

This analysis suggests the following elimination in developing consolidated statements at the end of 1967:

(1) Retained earnings of the controlling interest as of January 1, 1967, must be reduced by $4,000, and retained earnings of the minority interest as of January 1, 1967, must be reduced by $1,000, consistent with the reductions that were applied to these balances in stating the asset at cost at the end of 1966.

(2) The asset must be reduced by $5,000 and the allowance for depreciation must be reduced by $500 so that the asset may be reported at its cost, $15,000, less an allowance for depreciation based upon such cost, $1,500.

(3) Depreciation on equipment for the year, recognized at 10% of $20,000, or $2,000, must be reduced by $500 so that the expense may be reflected in terms of asset cost, 10% of $15,000, or $1,500.

The following elimination is made on the working papers:

Retained Earnings, Co. P, 1/1/67	4,000	
Retained Earnings, Co. S, 1/1/67 (reducing minority interest)	1,000	
Allowance for Depreciation of Machinery and Equipment	500	
Machinery and Equipment		5,000
Manufacturing Expenses (Depreciation of Equipment)		500

As indicated in Chapter 13, when a partly owned subsidiary sells a property item to a parent, a profit accrues to the minority interest as depreciation is recognized on asset sales price by the parent. In the example above, although a reduction in the asset value at the date of purchase of $5,000 calls for a charge to the minority interest of $1,000, reductions in the asset value in subsequent periods of smaller amounts call for correspondingly smaller charges to the minority interest; when the asset is fully depreciated, no further charge to the minority interest will be required and this group's interest will have increased by $1,000. In assigning consolidated earnings to minority and controlling interests in the period of asset sale, it is necessary to cancel all reference to any profit on the asset sale and hence to an increase in the minority interest arising from the sale; however, subsequent to the time of sale, as the controlling interest absorbs depreciation in terms of the asset sales price, the earnings related to the minority interest should be increased for the portion of the profit on the sale that will not be carried back to the parent. In the example, the minority interest ultimately gains $1,000; this gain is recognized at the rate of $100 per year. In calculating the portion of consolidated earnings relating to the minority interest for 1967, then, the earnings of the minority interest are increased by $100.

Consolidated statements for 1966 and 1967 prepared from the working papers are illustrated on pages 554–557.

Working papers for consolidated statements illustrated — cost method. Assuming that Company P carries its investment in Company S at cost, working papers for consolidated statements for 1966 and for 1967 may be developed as illustrated on pages 562–563 and 564–565.

In view of the different recognition that is made of subsidiary operations, certain eliminations differ from those that are required when the equity method is used. The eliminations that are made differently are

Cost method:

Company P and
Working Papers for
December

	Co. P	Co. S	Eliminations Dr.	Eliminations Cr.	
Debits					
Cash	10,000	20,000			(1)
Accounts Receivable (net)	30,000	40,000		(d) 10,000	(2)
Dividends Receivable	4,000			(e1) 4,000	(3)
Finished Goods Inventory, 1/1/66	50,000	30,000			(4)
Goods in Process Inventory, 1/1/66	40,000	20,000			(5)
Raw Materials Inventory, 1/1/66	35,000	15,000			(6)
Machinery and Equipment	435,000	180,000		(g) 5,000	(7)
Buildings	180,000	140,000			(8)
Land	75,000	40,000			(9)
Investment in Bonds of Co. S	19,000		(f) 1,000		(10)
Investment in Stock of Co. S	200,000				(11)
Eliminate 80% of Capital Stock				(a1) 160,000	(12)
Eliminate 80% of Retained Earnings of $10,000 on 1/1/66				(a2) 8,000	(13)
Excess of Cost over Book Value					(14)
Discount on Bonds Payable		5,000		(f) 1,000	(15)
Sales Returns and Allowances	10,000	5,000			(16)
Raw Material Purchases	130,000	55,000		(b) 25,000	(17)
Direct Labor	135,000	60,000			(18)
Manufacturing Overhead	145,000	75,000			(19)
Selling and General Expenses	80,000	65,000			(20)
Income Taxes	45,000	15,000			(21)
Dividends Declared — Co. P	40,000				(22)
Dividends Declared — Co. S		5,000		(e2) 4,000	(23)
	1,663,000	770,000			(24)
Finished Goods Inventory, 12/31/66	60,000	45,000		(c) 400	(25)
Goods in Process Inventory, 12/31/66	55,000	25,000		(c) 600	(26)
Raw Materials Inventory, 12/31/66	45,000	20,000		(c) 1,000	(27)
Credits					
Allowance for Depreciation of Machinery and Equipment	180,000	75,000			(28)
Allowance for Depreciation of Buildings	65,000	45,000			(29)
Accounts Payable	69,000	60,000	(d) 10,000		(30)
Dividends Payable	20,000	5,000	(e1) 4,000		(31)
5% Bonds Payable		100,000			(32)
Capital Stock, Co. P	500,000				(33)
Retained Earnings, Co. P, 1/1/66	250,000				(34)
Capital Stock, Co. S		200,000			(35)
Eliminate 80%			(a1) 160,000		(36)
Minority Interest, 20%					(37)
Retained Earnings, Co. S, 1/1/66		10,000			(38)
Eliminate 80% as above			(a2) 8,000		(39)
Minority Interest, 20% of $10,000					(40)
Sales	575,000	270,000	(b) 25,000		(41)
Dividend Income — Co. S	4,000		(e2) 4,000		(42)
Gain on Sale of Equipment		5,000	(g) 5,000		(43)
	1,663,000	770,000			(44)
Finished Goods Inventory, 12/31/66	60,000	45,000	(c) 400		(45)
Goods in Process Inventory, 12/31/66	55,000	25,000	(c) 600		(46)
Raw Materials Inventory, 12/31/66	45,000	20,000	(c) 1,000		(47)
			219,000	219,000	(48)
Cost of Goods Manufactured					(49)
					(50)
Consolidated Income					(51)
Income to Minority Interest, 20% of $18,000, Co. S Net Income after Adjustment (see below)					(52)
Balance to Controlling Interest					(53)
					(54)
Retained Earnings — Minority Interest to Balance Sheet					(55)
Retained Earnings — Controlling Interest to Balance Sheet					(56)
					(57)

Calculation of Co. S Net Income:

Net income per books		$25,000
Deduct: Intercompany profit on sale of equipment to Co. P	$ 5,000	
Intercompany profits on merchandise transferred to Co. P	2,000	7,000
Net income for consolidation purposes		$18,000

Subsidiary Company S
Consolidated Statements
31, 1966

	Consolidated Manufacturing		Consolidated Income Statement		Retained Earnings — Minority Interest		Retained Earnings — Controlling Interest		Consolidated Balance Sheet	
	Dr.	Cr.	Dr.	Cr.	Dr.	Cr.	Dr.	Cr.	Dr.	Cr.
(1)									30,000	
(2)									60,000	
(3)										
(4)			80,000							
(5)	60,000									
(6)	50,000									
(7)									610,000	
(8)									320,000	
(9)									115,000	
(10)									20,000	
(11)										
(12)										
(13)										
(14)									32,000	
(15)									4,000	
(16)			15,000							
(17)	160,000									
(18)	195,000									
(19)	220,000									
(20)			145,000							
(21)			60,000							
(22)							40,000			
(23)					1,000					
(24)										
(25)									104,600	
(26)									79,400	
(27)									64,000	
(28)										255,000
(29)										110,000
(30)										119,000
(31)										21,000
(32)										100,000
(33)										500,000
(34)								250,000		
(35)										
(36)										
(37)										40,000
(38)										
(39)										
(40)						2,000				
(41)				820,000						
(42)										
(43)										
(44)										
(45)				104,600						
(46)		79,400								
(47)		64,000								
(48)	685,000	143,400								
(49)		541,600	541,600							
(50)	685,000	685,000	841,600	924,600						
(51)			83,000							
(52)						3,600				
(53)								79,400		
(54)			924,600	924,600	1,000	5,600	40,000	329,400	1,439,000	1,145,000
(55)					4,600					4,600
(56)							289,400			289,400
(57)					5,600	5,600	329,400	329,400	1,439,000	1,439,000

Cost method:

Company P and
Working Papers for
December

	Co. P	Co. S	Eliminations Dr.	Eliminations Cr.	
Debits					
Cash	20,000	25,000			(1)
Accounts Receivable (net)	45,000	50,000		(d) 15,000	(2)
Dividends Receivable	4,000			(e1) 4,000	(3)
Finished Goods Inventory, 1/1/67	60,000	45,000		(c1) 400	(4)
Goods in Process Inventory, 1/1/67	55,000	25,000		(c1) 600	(5)
Raw Materials Inventory, 1/1/67	45,000	20,000		(c1) 1,000	(6)
Machinery and Equipment	450,000	190,000		(g) 5,000	(7)
Buildings	185,000	140,000			(8)
Land	75,000	40,000			(9)
Investment in Bonds of Co. S	19,100		(f1) 900		(10)
Investment in Stock of Co. S	200,000				(11)
Eliminate 80% of Capital Stock				(a1) 160,000	(12)
Eliminate 80% of Retained Earnings of $10,000 on 1/1/66				(a2) 8,000	(13)
Excess of Cost over Book Value					(14)
Discount on Bonds Payable		4,500		(f1) 900	(15)
Sales and Returns and Allowances	11,100	9,500			(16)
Raw Material Purchases	140,000	80,000		(b) 35,000	(17)
Direct Labor	145,000	85,000			(18)
Manufacturing Overhead	150,000	105,000		(g) 500	(19)
Selling and General Expenses	90,000	70,000			(20)
Interest Expense		5,500		(f1) 100	(21)
				(f2) 1,000	(22)
Income Taxes	50,000	20,000			(23)
Dividends Declared — Co. P	40,000				(24)
Dividends Declared — Co. S		10,000		(e2) 8,000	(25)
	1,784,200	924,500			(26)
Finished Goods Inventory, 12/31/67	75,000	65,000		(c2) 600	(27)
Goods in Process Inventory, 12/31/67	70,000	40,000		(c2) 1,000	(28)
Raw Materials Inventory, 12/31/67	50,000	30,000		(c2) 1,400	(29)
Credits					
Allowance for Depreciation of Machinery and Equipment	205,000	90,000	(g) 500		(30)
Allowance for Depreciation of Buildings	75,000	50,000			(31)
Accounts Payable	76,100	84,500	(d) 15,000		(32)
Dividends Payable	20,000	5,000	(e1) 4,000		(33)
5% Bonds Payable		100,000			(34)
Capital Stock, Co. P	500,000				(35)
Retained Earnings, Co. P, 1/1/67	279,000				(36)
					(37)
Capital Stock, Co. S		200,000			(38)
Eliminate 80%			(a1) 160,000		(39)
Minority Interest, 20%					(40)
Retained Earnings, Co. S, 1/1/67		30,000	(c1) 2,000		(41)
			(g) 5,000		(42)
Eliminate 80% as above			(a2) 8,000		(43)
Minority Interest, 20% of $23,000 ($30,000–$7,000)					(44)
Retained Earnings to Parent					(45)
Sales	620,000	365,000	(b) 35,000		(46)
Interest Income	1,100		(f1) 100		(47)
			(f2) 1,000		(48)
Dividend Income — Co. S	8,000		(e2) 8,000		(49)
	1,784,200	924,500			(50)
Finished Goods Inventory, 12/31/67	75,000	65,000	(c2) 600		(51)
Goods in Process Inventory, 12/31/67	70,000	40,000	(c2) 1,000		(52)
Raw Materials Inventory, 12/31/67	50,000	30,000	(e2) 1,400		(53)
			242,500	242,500	(54)
Cost of Goods Manufactured					(55)
					(56)
Consolidated Income					(57)
Income to Minority Int., 20% of $34,000, Co. S Net Income after Adj., plus $100, Recognized Gain on Sale of Eqpt. to Parent (see below)					(58)
Balance to Controlling Interest					(59)
					(60)
Retained Earnings — Minority Interest to Balance Sheet					(61)
Retained Earnings — Controlling Interest to Balance Sheet					(62)
					(63)

Calculation of Co. S Net Income:

Net income per books	$35,000
Deduct adjustment for intercompany profits on merchandise: 12/31/67, $3,000, less 1/1/67, $2,000	1,000
Net income for consolidation purposes	$34,000

Calculation of Recognized Gain on Equipment by Minority Interest:
Gain on sale of equipment to Co. P recognized by Co. S, 12/31/66, $5,000.
Gain identified with minority interest and to be recognized over life of equipment (10 years), 20% of $5,000, or $1,000.
Gain to be recognized in 1967, 1/10 x $1,000, or $100.

Subsidiary Company S
Consolidated Statements
31, 1967

	Consolidated Manufacturing		Consolidated Income Statement		Retained Earnings — Minority Interest		Retained Earnings — Controlling Interest		Consolidated Balance Sheet	
	Dr.	Cr.	Dr.	Cr.	Dr.	Cr.	Dr.	Cr.	Dr.	Cr.
(1)									45,000	
(2)									80,000	
(3)										
(4)			104,600							
(5)	79,400									
(6)	64,000									
(7)									635,000	
(8)									325,000	
(9)									115,000	
(10)									20,000	
(11)										
(12)										
(13)										
(14)									32,000	
(15)									3,600	
(16)			20,600							
(17)	185,000									
(18)	230,000									
(19)	254,500									
(20)			160,000							
(21)			4,400							
(22)										
(23)			70,000							
(24)							40,000			
(25)					2,000					
(26)										
(27)									139,400	
(28)									109,000	
(29)									78,600	
(30)										294,500
(31)										125,000
(32)										145,600
(33)										21,000
(34)										100,000
(35)										500,000
(36)								279,000		
(37)										
(38)										
(39)										
(40)										40,000
(41)										
(42)										
(43)										
(44)						4,600				
(45)								10,400		
(46)				950,000						
(47)										
(48)										
(49)										
(50)										
(51)				139,400						
(52)		109,000								
(53)		78,600								
(54)	812,900	187,600								
(55)		625,300	625,300							
(56)	812,900	812,900	984,900	1,089,400						
(57)			104,500							
(58)						6,900				
(59)								97,600		
(60)			1,089,400	1,089,400	2,000	11,500	40,000	387,000	1,582,600	1,226,100
(61)					9,500					9,500
(62)							347,000			347,000
(63)					11,500	11,500	387,000	387,000	1,582,600	1,582,600

given below and are designated by the same letter used for the corresponding elimination in the illustration of the equity method.

(a) The parent company's percentage of the capital stock and retained earnings of Company S as of the date of acquisition of subsidiary holdings are eliminated against the investment balance. Eliminations are made on the working papers for 1966 and also on the working papers for 1967 as follows:

(a1) Capital Stock, Co. S (80% of $200,000)	160,000	
Investment in Stock of Co. S		160,000
(a2) Retained Earnings, Co. S (80% of $10,000)	8,000	
Investment in Stock of Co. S		8,000

(c) In preparing working papers for 1967, the intercompany profits in the beginning inventories are canceled by the following elimination:

(c1) Retained Earnings, Co. S 1/1/67 (reducing controlling and minority interests)	2,000	
Finished Goods Inventory, 1/1/67		400
Goods in Process Inventory, 1/1/67		600
Raw Materials Inventory, 1/1/67		1,000

(e) Dividends receivable on stock of Company S reported by Company P is offset against dividends payable reported by Company S just as when the equity method is used. However, an entry is required to offset dividend income reported by the parent against dividends declared reported by the subsidiary. The latter elimination is made on the working papers for 1966 as follows:

(e2) Dividend Income — Co. S	4,000	
Dividend Declared — Co. S		4,000

On the working papers for 1967 the amount that is eliminated is $8,000.

(g) In preparing working papers for 1967, the intercompany profit on the equipment is canceled by the following elimination:

Retained Earnings, Co. S, 1/1/67 (reducing controlling and minority interests)	5,000	
Allowance for Depreciation of Machinery and Equipment	500	
Machinery and Equipment		5,000
Manufacturing Expenses (Depreciation of Equipment)		500

Statements prepared from either the equity or the cost set of working papers are shown on pages 554–557.

SPECIAL PROBLEMS

Special conditions frequently create certain problems in arriving at consolidated income. The problems must be carefully analyzed and solutions developed within the framework defined in the previous pages. The American Institute Committee on Accounting Procedure in *Accounting Research Bulletin No. 51* comments on those problems that arise when a subsidiary is purchased during the year and when a subsidiary is disposed of during the year. In referring to the purchase of a subsidiary, the Committee states:

> When a subsidiary is purchased during the year, there are alternative ways of dealing with the results of its operations in the consolidated income statement. One method, which usually is preferable, especially where there are several dates of acquisition of blocks of shares, is to include the subsidiary in the consolidation as though it had been acquired at the beginning of the year, and to deduct at the bottom of the consolidated income statement the preacquisition earnings applicable to each block of stock. This method presents results which are more indicative of the current status of the group, and facilitates future comparison with subsequent years. Another method of prorating income is to include in the consolidated statement only the subsidiary's revenue and expenses subsequent to the date of acquisition.

In reference to the disposal of a subsidiary interest, the committee makes the following observation:

> Where the investment in a subsidiary is disposed of during the year, it may be preferable to omit the details of operations of the subsidiary from the consolidated income statement, and to show the equity of the parent in the earnings of the subsidiary prior to disposal as a separate item in the statement.[1]

QUESTIONS

1. What reconciliations should be made in the preparation of consolidated statements in assuring that there is a continuity in statements prepared at the end of successive years?

2. Individual statements are available for parent Company X and subsidiary Company Y. What changes will be made in account balances in transferring statement data to working papers for the preparation of consolidated statements?

---

[1]*Accounting Research Bulletin No. 51*, "Consolidated Financial Statements," 1959 (New York: American Institute of Certified Public Accountants), p. 45.

3. Parent Company A maintains its investments in subsidiary companies by the equity method. Working papers for consolidated statements are prepared at the end of 1967. Give the eliminations that would be required under each of the following sets of circumstances:

(a) Company B was organized by Company A at the beginning of 1962, Company A acquiring all of the stock of Company B at par. Company B retained earnings increased during the period 1962–1966; Company B reported a profit for 1967 and paid dividends in 1967.

(b) 80% of the stock of Company C was acquired by Company A at the beginning of 1964 at a price that exceeded its book value. Company C capital balances consisted of capital stock, additional paid-in capital, and retained earnings. Company C retained earnings increased during the period 1964–1966; Company C reported a loss for 1967, but paid dividends from past earnings.

(c) 90% of the stock of Company D was acquired by Company A at the beginning of 1967 at a price that was less than its book value. Company D capital balances consisted of capital stock and a deficit. Company D operated at a loss and paid no dividends in 1967.

4. Assuming in Question 3 that investment accounts are maintained by the parent at cost, what eliminations would be required for each of the circumstances listed?

5. Beginning and ending inventories of the Meadows Co. include goods acquired from an 80%-owned subsidiary on which the latter company made a profit. What procedures would be followed in preparing working papers for consolidated statements if the goods acquired from the affiliate are to be reduced to their original cost to the affiliate?

6. At the end of 1967 a parent company constructed buildings for a partly owned subsidiary at a profit. (a) What elimination for intercompany profit is required in preparing working papers for consolidated statements for 1967? (b) Assuming that it was the partly owned subsidiary that constructed buildings for the parent at a profit, what elimination would be required?

7. In 1962 a parent company sold equipment to a partly owned subsidiary at a profit. The asset has a 10-year life. (a) What elimination for the intercompany profit is required in preparing working papers for consolidated statements for 1967? (b) Assuming that the foregoing facts relate to the sale of equipment by the partly owned subsidiary to the parent, what elimination would be required?

8. Company P owns all of the stock of Company S. At the beginning of 1967 Company S issued 10-year bonds at a discount. Company P acquired half of the bond issue directly from the subsidiary. What eliminations are required on the working papers for consolidated statements prepared at the end of 1967?

EXERCISES

1. Company P owns 80% of the stock of Company S. The information below appears on the working papers for consolidated statements on December 31, 1967. What eliminations are required?

(a) The investment account balance is $240,000. Earnings and dividends have been recorded in the investment account since acquisition, June 30, 1963, and including 1967. Company S capital stock outstanding is $250,000; retained earnings on June 30, 1963, were $20,000; retained earnings on January 1, 1967, were $50,000; net income for the year is $15,000; dividends declared by Company S during the year were $10,000, $2,500 of this amount being payable on January 20, 1968.

(b) Sales made by Company S to Company P totaled $80,000 for 1967. Sales made by Company P to Company S were $16,000. Sales are made at 25% above cost. Inventories on January 1 and December 31 included:

	Jan. 1	Dec. 31
Co. P, merchandise acquired from Co. S	$15,000	$18,000
Co. S, merchandise acquired from Co. P	1,500	4,500

(c) 5% bonds of $20,000 were acquired by Company P from Company S at par on July 1, 1967. Interest is payable semiannually on March 1 and September 1.

(d) Company P owes Company S $30,000 on open account.

2. Assume in Exercise 1 above that the investment balance is carried at cost. Give the eliminations that are required on the working papers for consolidated statements where these would differ from the eliminations that are required under the equity method.

3. Company Y owns 90% of the stock of Company Z. The investment account is carried at cost and shows a balance of $300,000 on December 31, 1967. Company Z capital stock is $300,000; retained earnings on January 1, 1967, were $100,000; the net income for 1967 is $30,000; dividends declared during the year totaled $16,000, including a dividend in the fourth quarter of $4,000 that is payable on January 10, 1968. The stock was acquired on June 30, 1958, when Company Z showed a deficit of $10,000. What eliminations are required on the working papers for consolidated statements prepared on December 31, 1967?

4. Company P owns 80% of the stock of Company A and Company A owns 90% of the stock of Company B, both holdings acquired prior to 1958 and carried at cost. Give any adjustments and eliminations that are required in preparing the working papers for consolidated statements for the year ended December 31, 1967, as a result of the following information available at this time:

(a) Company P has in its inventory merchandise of $48,300 acquired from Company B. Merchandise is sold by Company B at 15% above cost.

(b) Company B has in its inventory merchandise of $8,000 acquired from Company P. The merchandise was sold at a 25% gross profit on sales price.

(c) Company A shows equipment of $20,000 acquired from Company P at the end of October, 1960. The equipment was constructed by Company P and was sold at a gross profit of $5,000. The equipment is being depreciated on a 10-year basis.
(d) Company B has announced a dividend of $5,000, which has not been recognized by affiliates.
(e) Company B has remitted $10,000 to Company A in payment of an advance. Company A has not yet received the remittance.
(f) During the year, sales of merchandise by Company B to Company P totaled $250,000; sales by Company P to Company B were $42,500.

5. The Werner Corporation owns 80% of the stock of the Western Company. The Western Company owns 90% of the stock of the Wilson Company. Investments are carried at equity. An analysis of the inventories of the three companies on December 31, 1966, shows the following:

		Merchandise Acquired from			
	Total	Werner Corp.	Western Co.	Wilson Co.	Non-Affiliated Companies
Werner Corp. inventory......	$100,000		$10,500	$1,500	$88,000
Western Company inventory..	80,000	$ 9,000		3,000	68,000
Wilson Company inventory...	75,000	12,000	15,000		48,000

Merchandise is sold to affiliated units at 20% above cost.

(a) What eliminations would be made on the consolidated working papers for consolidated statements prepared at the end of 1966 to give effect to the foregoing information? (b) What eliminations would be made on the consolidated working papers for consolidated statements prepared at the end of 1967 in recognition of the foregoing?

6. What entries are required on the books of Company P to record the following information? Company P takes up earnings of the subsidiary in its investment account.

Sept. 1, 1966. Company P purchased 1,500 shares of Company S stock, $50 par, at 60. (Company S has 2,000 shares outstanding and retained earnings of $80,000.)
Dec. 15, 1966. Company S paid a cash dividend of $1 and a stock dividend of 1 share for every 5 held.
Dec. 31, 1966. Company S announced net income of $24,000 for 1966.
Mar. 1, 1967. Company P purchased 300 shares of Company S stock at 40.
Sept. 1, 1967. Company P sold 150 shares of Company S stock at 60.
Dec. 31, 1967. Company S announced a net loss for 1967 of $12,000.

7. Company Y has been a subsidiary of Company X since January 1, 1957. On January 1, 1963, Company X completed the construction of buildings for Company Y. The contract price of the buildings was $500,000; the cost of construction was $400,000. Company Y records depreciation on the buildings at 2½% annually. (a) What elimination would appear on the working papers for consolidated statements for the year ended December 31, 1967, assuming that the parent owns 100% of the stock of Company Y? (b) What elimination would be made assuming that the parent owns only 80% of the stock of Company Y?

8. (a) Assuming the same facts as in Exercise 7 but that the construction was completed by Company Y for the parent, Company X, what elimination would be required on December 31, 1967, if the parent owns 100% of the stock of the subsidiary? (b) What elimination would be made if the parent owns only 80% of the stock of the subsidiary?

9. Company L has owned 100% of the stock of Company M for many years. On January 1, 1967, Company M buys on the market $200,000 of Company L's 6% First Mortgage Bonds at 105. Bonds were originally issued by Company L at par on January 1, 1964, and are payable at the end of 10 years. (a) What eliminations would be made on the working papers for consolidated statements prepared for the year ended December 31, 1967? (b) Would the eliminations be any different assuming that the parent company owns only 80% of the stock of the subsidiary? If so, give the eliminations.

PROBLEMS

16-1. Financial statements for Company P and its 80%-owned subsidiary Company S for the year ended December 31, 1967, are summarized below.

	Co. P	Co. S
Balance Sheets		
Investment in Co. S	$ 400,000	
Other assets	2,150,000	$ 550,000
Total assets	$2,550,000	$ 550,000
Liabilities	$ 600,000	$ 130,000
Capital stock	1,500,000	400,000
Retained earnings	450,000	20,000
Total liabilities and stockholders' equity	$2,550,000	$ 550,000
Income Statements		
Sales	$2,000,000	$ 650,000
Cost of goods sold	1,350,000	400,000
Gross profit	$ 650,000	$ 250,000
Operating expenses	500,000	185,000
Net income before income taxes	$ 150,000	$ 65,000
Income taxes	60,000	15,000
Net income	$ 90,000	$ 50,000
Add income — Subsidiary Co. S	40,000	
Net income, including parent company's share of subsidiary earnings	$ 130,000	$ 50,000
Dividends declared	75,000	20,000
Increase in retained earnings	$ 55,000	$ 30,000

The parent has carried the investment in Company S by the equity method since acquisition of the subsidiary in 1960. The inventory of the parent on January 1, 1967, included goods of $40,000 that cost the subsidiary $27,500; the inventory of the parent on December 31, 1967, included goods of $50,000 that cost the subsidiary $31,250. During 1967 purchases by the parent from the subsidiary totaled $135,000. Amounts owed by the parent to the subsidiary at the end of 1967 totaled $22,500.

Instructions: Prepare working papers for consolidated statements for the year ended December 31, 1967.

16-2. Adjusted trial balances for Companies A and B on December 31, 1967, are given below.

	Co. A	Co. B
Debits		
Merchandise Inventory, January 1	$ 15,000	$ 20,000
Investment in Co. B (80% interest)	120,000	
Other Assets	225,000	155,000
Purchases	105,000	60,000
Expenses	60,000	35,000
Dividends Paid	10,000	15,000
	$535,000	$285,000
Merchandise Inventory, December 31	$ 25,000	$ 15,000
Credits		
Liabilities	$ 85,000	$ 40,000
Capital Stock	200,000	100,000
Retained Earnings, January 1	62,000	35,000
Sales	180,000	110,000
Income from Co. B	8,000	
	$535,000	$285,000
Merchandise Inventory, December 31	$ 25,000	$ 15,000

The investment account is carried by the equity method. The January 1 inventory of Company A included merchandise of $5,000 that cost Company B $4,000. During the year Company A made purchases from its subsidiary of $20,000. The ending inventory of Company A includes merchandise of $6,000 that cost Company B $4,500.

Instructions: (1) Prepare working papers for consolidated statements for the year ended December 31, 1967.

(2) Prepare a consolidated balance sheet, income statement, and retained earnings statement.

16-3. Adjusted trial balances for Companies C and D on December 31, 1967, are given below.

	Co. C	Co. D
Debits		
Merchandise Inventory, December 31	$ 15,000	$ 20,000
Investment in Co. D (80% Interest)	100,000	
Other Assets	355,000	240,000
Cost of Goods Sold	210,000	125,000
Expenses	160,000	100,000
Dividends	10,000	
Total	$850,000	$485,000
Credits		
Liabilities	$165,000	$125,000
Capital Stock	300,000	100,000
Retained Earnings (Deficit), January 1	20,000	(15,000)
Sales	325,000	275,000
Income from Co. D	40,000	
Total	$850,000	$485,000

The investment account is carried by the equity method. The January 1 inventory of Company C included merchandise of $5,000 that cost Company D $4,200. During the year Company C made purchases from its subsidiary of $35,000. Its ending inventory includes merchandise of $3,200 that cost Company D $2,500.

Instructions: (1) Prepare working papers for consolidated statements for the year ended December 31, 1967.

(2) Prepare a consolidated balance sheet, income statement, and retained earnings statement.

16-4. Condensed financial statements for the Alpha Corporation and the Beta Corporation for the year ended December 31, 1967, are as follows:

	Alpha Corp.	Beta Corp.
Balance Sheets		
Investment in Beta Corp. (90% interest)	$ 385,000	
Other assets	1,465,000	$ 800,000
Total assets	$1,850,000	$ 800,000
Liabilities	$ 650,000	$ 260,000
Capital stock	1,000,000	500,000
Retained earnings	200,000	40,000
Total liabilities and stockholders' equity	$1,850,000	$ 800,000

	Alpha Corp.	Beta Corp.
Income Statements		
Sales	$1,000,000	$ 600,000
Cost of goods sold	520,000	330,000
Gross profit	$ 480,000	$ 270,000
Operating expenses	250,000	140,000
Net income before income taxes	$ 230,000	$ 130,000
Income taxes	110,000	50,000
Net income	$ 120,000	$ 80,000
Dividends declared	40,000	25,000
Increase in retained earnings	$ 80,000	$ 55,000

The investment in Beta Corporation is carried at cost; Alpha Corporation acquired its holdings in 1962 when the Beta Corporation showed a deficit of $100,000. The January 1 inventory of Alpha Corporation included goods of $12,500 that cost Beta Corporation $10,000. During the year, sales by the subsidiary to the parent totaled $60,000. The December 31 inventory of Alpha Corporation included goods of $27,500 that cost Beta Corporation $20,000. Alpha Corporation owed Beta Corporation $12,500 at the end of 1967. Dividends of $22,500 received by the Alpha Corporation in 1967 were reported directly in retained earnings.

Instructions: Prepare working papers for consolidated financial statements for the year ended December 31, 1967.

16-5. Adjusted trial balances for Companies G and H as of December 31, 1967, are given below.

	Co. G	Co. H
Debits		
Merchandise Inventory, January 1	$ 30,000	$ 15,000
Investment in Co. H (90% Interest)	100,000	
Other Assets	300,000	160,000
Purchases	90,000	60,000
Expenses	60,000	30,000
Dividends Declared	20,000	10,000
Total	$600,000	$275,000
Credits		
Liabilities	$115,000	$ 55,000
Capital Stock	200,000	100,000
Additional Paid-in Capital	60,000	10,000
Retained Earnings, January 1	76,000	5,000
Sales	140,000	105,000
Dividend Income, Co. H Stock	9,000	
Total	$600,000	$275,000

The investment in Company H is carried at cost. Stock of Company H was acquired in 1964 when Company H showed a deficit of $15,000. The January 1 inventory of Company G included merchandise of $6,000 that cost Company H $5,000. During the year Company G made purchases from its subsidiary of $30,000. Its ending inventory includes merchandise of $8,000 that cost Company H $6,500. Inventories on December 31, are: Company G, $35,000; Company H, $25,000.

Instructions: (1) Prepare working papers for consolidated statements for the year ended December 31, 1967.

(2) Prepare a consolidated balance sheet, income statement, and retained earnings statement.

16-6. Adjusted trial balances for Companies L and M on December 31, 1967, appear below.

	Co. L	Co. M
Debits		
Merchandise Inventory, December 31	$ 80,000	$ 60,000
Investments in Co. M (85% Interest)	135,000	—
Other Assets	640,000	335,000
Cost of Goods Sold	420,000	180,000
Expenses	125,000	75,000
Dividends Paid	25,000	10,000
Total	$1,425,000	$ 660,000
Credits		
Liabilities	$ 315,000	$ 185,000
Capital Stock	250,000	200,000
Retained Earnings (Deficit), January 1	251,500	(15,000)
Sales	600,000	290,000
Dividend Income, Co. M Stock	8,500	—
Total	$1,425,000	$ 660,000

Stock of Company M is carried at cost and was acquired in 1960 when Company M showed retained earnings of $30,000. During the year Company L made purchases from Company M totaling $22,500. The January 1 inventory of Company L included merchandise acquired from Company M at $6,000; the December 31 inventory includes merchandise acquired from Company M at $4,800. Company M sells merchandise to Company L at 33⅓% above cost.

Instructions: (1) Prepare working papers for consolidated statements for the year ended December 31, 1967.

(2) Prepare a consolidated balance sheet, income statement, and retained earnings statement.

16-7. Adjusted trial balances for Reed, Inc., and its subsidiaries, the Sterling Corporation and the Taylor Corporation, on December 31, 1967, the end of a fiscal year, appear below.

	Reed, Inc.		Sterling Corporation		Taylor Corporation	
	Dr.	Cr.	Dr.	Cr.	Dr.	Cr.
Cash	63,875		34,500		20,000	
Dividends Receivable	2,125					
Accounts Receivable	117,000		82,500		94,500	
Merchandise Inventory, Jan. 1	140,000		80,000		105,000	
Furniture and Equipment (net)	50,000		40,000		28,000	
Land and Buildings (net)	100,000		85,000			
Investment in Stock of Sterling Corporation (850 shares)	245,000					
Investment in Stock of Taylor Corporation (1,600 shares)	185,000					
Dividends Payable		6,250		2,500		
Accounts Payable		70,250		54,500		37,500
Capital Stock ($100 par)		500,000		100,000		200,000
Retained Earnings (Deficit)		324,000		150,000		(20,000)
Sales		730,000		470,000		420,000
Sales Returns and Allowances	20,000		10,000		10,000	
Sales Discounts	12,000		5,000		4,000	
Purchases	540,000		340,000		300,000	
Purchases Returns and Allowances		15,000		4,000		5,000
Purchases Discounts		8,000		2,000		2,500
Selling Expenses	80,000		50,000		45,000	
General and Administrative Expenses	55,000		25,000		30,000	
Interest Expense	10,000		3,000		5,000	
Interest Income		3,000		2,000		1,500
Dividend Income, Sterling Corporation Stock		8,500				
Income Taxes	20,000		20,000		5,000	
Dividends Declared	25,000		10,000			
	1,665,000	1,665,000	785,000	785,000	646,500	646,500
Merchandise Inventory, Dec. 31	150,000	150,000	90,000	90,000	87,500	87,500

Reed, Inc., carries investment balances at cost. The Sterling Corporation stock was acquired in 1965 when the retained earnings of this company were $140,000 and the Taylor Corporation stock was acquired in 1966 when this company had a deficit of $15,000.

The Taylor Corporation sells merchandise to the parent at approximately 10% above cost. Intercompany sales during 1967 totaled $40,000. Inventories of the parent included merchandise from the Taylor Corporation at billed price as follows:

On January 1 . . . .$6,600 On December 31. . . . .$8,250

Reed, Inc., owes the Taylor Corporation $5,000 on account.

Instructions; (1) Prepare working papers for consolidated statements for the year ended December 31, 1967.

(2) Prepare a consolidated balance sheet, income statement, and retained earnings statement.

16-8. Adjusted trial balances for Company P and its subsidiaries Company Y and Company Z on December 31, 1967, the end of a fiscal year, appear below.

	Co. P		Co. Y		Co. Z	
	Dr.	Cr.	Dr.	Cr.	Dr.	Cr.
Cash	94,500		52,500		25,000	
Dividends Receivable	2,250					
Accounts Receivable (net)	70,000		25,000		15,000	
Finished Goods, Jan. 1	60,000		30,000		22,500	
Goods in Process, Jan. 1	25,000		15,000		10,000	
Raw Materials, Jan. 1	40,000		25,000		12,500	
Land and Buildings (net)	250,000		65,000		30,000	
Machinery and Equipment (net)	300,000		105,000		45,000	
Investment in Stock of Co. Y	164,250					
Investment in Stock of Co. Z	56,000					
Dividends Payable		4,000		2,500		
Accounts Payable		136,000		60,000		70,500
Bonds Payable				100,000		
Capital Stock ($100 par)		450,000		100,000		100,000
Retained Earnings (Deficit)		381,250		30,000		(5,000)
Sales		892,500		245,750		105,000
Sales Returns and Allowances	15,000		5,000		3,000	
Sales Discounts	8,000		3,500		1,500	
Raw Material Purchased	260,000		61,000		30,600	
Purchases Returns and Allowances		10,000		500		1,500
Purchases Discounts		2,500		500		400
Direct Labor	150,000		30,000		15,000	
Manufacturing Overhead	230,000		45,000		25,000	
Selling Expenses	60,000		20,500		15,000	
General Expenses	85,000		25,000		17,500	
Interest Expense	2,000		7,000		5,000	
Interest Income		500		250		200
Gain on Sale of Equipment		10,000				
Income from Co. Y		38,250				
Loss from Co. Z	8,000					
Income Taxes	22,500		15,000			
Dividends Declared	22,500		10,000			
	1,925,000	1,925,000	539,500	539,500	272,600	272,600
Finished Goods, Dec. 31	35,000	35,000	30,000	30,000	20,000	20,000
Goods in Process, Dec. 31	25,000	25,000	20,000	20,000	10,000	10,000
Raw Material, Dec. 31	44,500	44,500	27,500	27,500	10,500	10,500

Company P carries investment balances by the equity method. Stock was acquired as follows:

900 shares of Company Y stock at 145 when Company Y's capital was $125,000.

800 shares of Company Z stock at 90 when Company Z's capital was $105,000.

Companies P and Z acquired part of their raw materials from Company Y. During the year sales were made by Company Y as follows (sales are made at a gross profit of 25% of sales):

Sales to Company P	$45,000
Sales to Company Z	15,000

It is estimated that materials acquired from Company Y are included in Company P and Company Z inventories at costs to these companies as follows:

	Co. P		Co. Z	
	Jan. 1, 1967	Dec. 31, 1967	Jan. 1, 1967	Dec. 31, 1967
Finished goods.......	$3,000	$4,000	$1,000	$1,500
Goods in process.....	2,000	2,000	1,000	1,000
Raw materials.......	5,000	6,000	1,000	3,500

On January 2, 1967, Company Y acquired machinery from Company P for which a charge of $50,000 was made. The cost of the machinery to Company P was $40,000. Company Y is depreciating the machinery on a 10-year life.

On December 31 Company P owed Company Y $12,500 on account, and Company Z owed Company Y $5,000.

Instructions: (1) Prepare working papers for consolidated statements for the year ended December 31, 1967.

(2) Prepare a consolidated balance sheet, a consolidated income statement supported by a manufacturing schedule, and a consolidated retained earnings statement.

16-9. The individual and consolidated statements of Companies A and B for the year ended December 31, 1967, are given on the next page.

Company A purchased its 70% interest in Company B several years ago. Company A sells its product in part to Company B for further processing, and in part to other firms. The inventories of Company B included an intercompany markup at both the beginning and the end of the year. Cash transfers are made between the companies according to working capital needs.

Early in 1967, Company B purchased $100,000 face value of the bonds of Company A as a temporary investment. These are carried on Company B's books at cost.

Instructions: On the basis of the information you can develop from an analysis of the individual and consolidated statements, answer the six questions below. Show clearly *all* computations necessary to support your answers.

(1) Does Company A carry its investment in Company B on the cost basis or the equity (accrual) basis? State the reason for your conclusion.

(2) The appraisal increase represents a revaluation of the total of Company B's assets on the basis of the price paid by Company A for its interest in Company B. What was the balance of Company B's retained earnings at date of acquisition?

(3) Prepare a reconciliation schedule which will explain clearly the difference between Company A's retained earnings at December 31, 1967, $200,000, and the consolidated retained earnings at December 31, 1967, $231,000.

(4) What is the nature of the nonrecurring loss on the consolidated income statement? Show the consolidating elimination entry from which it originated.

	Co. A	Co. B	Consolidated
Cash and receivables	$ 35,000	$108,000	$ 97,400
Inventories	40,000	90,000	122,000
Plant (net)	460,000	140,000	600,000
Appraisal increase in plant (net)			50,000
Investment in Company B	245,000		
Company A bonds owned		103,000	
	$780,000	$441,000	$869,400
Current payables	$ 70,000	$ 23,000	$ 53,000
Dividends payable	10,000	8,000	12,400
Mortgage bonds	200,000	50,000	150,000
Capital stock	300,000	200,000	300,000
Retained earnings	200,000	160,000	231,000
Minority interest			123,000
	$780,000	$441,000	$869,400
Sales	$600,000	$400,000	$760,000
Cost of sales	360,000	280,000	403,000
Gross profit	$240,000	$120,000	$357,000
Operating expense	130,000	54,000	184,000
Operating profit	$110,000	$ 66,000	$173,000
Interest income	1,800	5,000	1,800
Dividend income	11,200		
Total	$123,000	$ 71,000	$174,800
Interest expense	10,000	3,000	8,000
Provision for income taxes	56,000	34,000	90,000
Nonrecurring loss			3,000
Minority share			5,400
Net income	$ 57,000	$ 34,000	$ 68,400
Dividends	20,000	16,000	24,800
Transfer to retained earnings	$ 37,000	$ 18,000	$ 43,600

(5) Show the amounts of intercompany debts, excluding the bonds, and show which company is the debtor and which is the creditor in each instance.

(6) Prepare a schedule reconciling the sum of the cost of sales of Companies A and B individually with the consolidated cost of sales. Show clearly the intercompany markup in the beginning and ending inventories of Company B and how you determined the amounts.

(AICPA adapted)

16-10. Balance sheets and income statements for the year ended December 31, 1967, of Company R and its wholly owned subsidiary Company S are given on the work sheet form on the following page.

	Co. R	Co. S	Eliminations and Adjustments Dr.	Eliminations and Adjustments Cr.	Consolidated
Cash	250,000	130,000			
Marketable Securities	400,000	150,000			
Accounts Receivable — Customers	1,250,000	540,000			
Allowance for Doubtful Accounts	(25,000)	(10,000)			
Subsidiary Current Account	100,000				
Inventories	1,100,000	600,000			
Treasury Stock	50,000				
Stock of Co. S (at cost)	150,000				
Advances to Subsidiary	420,000				
Plant, Property and Equip. (net)	1,525,000	710,000			
	5,220,000	2,120,000			
Accounts Payable	575,000	185,000			
Accrued Expenses	350,000	100,000			
Due to Company R		90,000			
Estimated Federal Income Taxes	525,000	275,000			
Advances from Parent		420,000			
Capital Stock	1,000,000	150,000			
Retained Earnings, 1/1/67	2,420,000	825,000			
Net Income	650,000	250,000			
Dividends Paid	(300,000)	(175,000			
	5,220,000	2,120,000			
Net Sales	10,000,000	4,600,000			
Cost of Goods Sold	(6,700,000)	(3,210,000)			
Selling, General, and Adm. Expenses	(2,400,000)	(900,000)			
Other Income (net)	250,000	20,000			
Estimated Federal Income Taxes	(500,000)	(260,000)			
Net Income	650,000	250,000			

The following additional information is available:

(1) Marketable securities of the subsidiary includes $20,000 cost of shares of the parent company's stock acquired for payment of bonuses.

(2) There is merchandise billed at $10,000 in transit from the parent to the subsidiary which has not been recorded by the subsidiary.

(3) It has been determined that there is intercompany profit of $20,000 in the portion of the subsidiary's inventory purchased from the parent. The equivalent figure at December 31, 1966, was $10,000.

(4) The parent's equity in the subsidiary was $200,000 at the date of acquisition.

(5) Sales by the parent to the subsidiary in 1967 totaled $1,700,000.

(6) The parent has made a service charge of $50,000 to the subsidiary which is included in Other Income of the parent and in Administrative Expenses of the subsidiary.

Instructions: (1) Complete a work sheet in the form given above, making the necessary eliminating and adjusting entries and extending the consolidated figures for statement purposes. *Key the debit and credit side of each entry.*

(2) Prepare a schedule showing the changes for 1967 in retained earnings of the companies and the entries necessary for consolidation.

(AICPA adapted)

16-11. Following are the trial balances of Company A and its subsidiaries Company B and Company C on December 31, 1967:

Debits	Co. A	Co. B	Co. C
Cash	$ 75,000	$ 50,000	$ 60,000
Accounts receivable	350,000	190,000	420,000
Notes receivable	200,000	60,000	40,000
Inventory, raw materials, Jan. 1, 1967	150,000	105,000	160,000
Purchases, raw materials	650,000	400,000	510,000
Labor	450,000	320,000	370,000
Manufacturing expenses	190,000	190,000	205,000
Selling expenses	85,000	40,000	75,000
Administrative expenses	45,000	25,000	35,000
Inventory, goods in process, Jan. 1, 1967	80,000	70,000	75,000
Inventory, finished goods, Jan. 1, 1967	90,000	65,000	80,000
Plant and equipment	900,000	400,000	750,000
Investment in stock of Co. B	875,000		
Investment in stock of Co. C	1,200,000		
	$5,340,000	$1,915,000	$2,780,000
Credits			
Capital stock	$3,000,000	$ 500,000	$ 800,000
Notes payable	110,000	80,000	60,000
Accounts payable	100,000	65,000	250,000
Bonds payable	500,000		
Premium on bonds	5,000		
Allowance for depreciation	100,000	60,000	112,500
Sales	1,400,000	1,050,000	1,250,000
Retained earnings	125,000	160,000	307,500
	$5,340,000	$1,915,000	$2,780,000

The inventories at December 31, 1967, were:

	Co. A	Co. B	Co. C
Raw materials	$ 230,000	$ 175,000	$ 210,000
Goods in process	95,000	80,000	85,000
Finished goods	135,000	145,000	105,000

Company A purchased the entire stock issue of Companies B and C on January 1, 1967, at the prices shown in the trial balance. During the year each of the three companies declared and paid a 5% dividend. Company A took up its dividends from Companies B and C by credits to

Retained Earnings. The various entries for the dividends were the only entries affecting the retained earnings accounts during the year.

On December 31, 1966, Company A's inventory of raw materials included goods from Company B at a price of $60,000, the cost thereof to Company B being $40,000. On the same date Company B's inventory of raw material included goods purchased from Company C for $75,000 on which Company C made a profit of $25,000.

During 1967, Company C sold goods to Company B at a price of $200,000. These goods cost Company C $160,000. Company B still owes $30,000 on these purchases, the indebtedness being included in the accounts payable.

During 1967, Company B sold goods, cost $300,000, to Company A at a sales price of $375,000. Company A made cash advances totaling $400,000 to Company B during the year. The sales just mentioned were charged against the advances account, the $25,000 balance of which is included in Company B's accounts payable.

The inventories on December 31, 1967, include intercompany profits as follows:

	Raw Materials	Goods in Process	Finished Goods
Company A	$20,000	$5,000	$4,000
Company B	30,000	6,000	5,000

Company A's bonds were issued July 1, 1967. They bear 5% interest, payable semiannually, and mature in five years. No interest has been paid.

Allow depreciation at 5% per annum on the cost of the fixed assets.

Instructions: Prepare the following consolidated statements: (1) cost of goods manufactured and sold; (2) income statement; (3) retained earnings statement (showing as the final balance therein the retained earnings balance appearing in the consolidated balance sheet); (4) balance sheet.

(AICPA adapted)

16-12. The trial balances of Company P and its subsidiary Company S as of December 31, 1967, are given at the top of the following page.

The investment in stock of Company S represents a 90% interest that was acquired January 1, 1967, for $175,000. At the same time, $50,000 face amount of bonds of Company S was acquired for $52,000. These bonds had been issued in 1957 at 106 and are due January 1, 1977. Company S has recorded the amortization of the bond premium applicable to 1967 as an adjustment of interest expense. The stock and the bonds were not purchased from Company S but from the public.

Included in the purchases account of Company S is a total of $180,000 of goods bought from Company P, at 120% of cost to Company P. The

	Balances December 31, 1967			
	Co. P		Co. S	
	Debit	Credit	Debit	Credit
Cash	$ 23,000		$ 30,000	
Accounts receivable	94,000		60,000	
Inventory 1/1/67 — cost	105,000		51,000	
Investment in stock of Co. S	175,000			
Investment in bonds of Co. S	51,800			
Other assets	445,000		210,000	
Current liabilities		$ 163,000		$ 17,100
Bonds payable — 5%				200,000
Deferred bond premium				5,400
Sales		630,000		340,000
Purchases	485,000		300,000	
Operating expenses	92,000		70,000	
Other expenses	22,000		15,500	
Interest and dividends		12,800		
Dividends paid	20,000		10,000	
Surplus, 1/1/67		107,000		84,000
Common stock		600,000		100,000
	$1,512,800	$1,512,800	$746,500	$746,500

closing inventory of Company S is estimated to include the same proportion of these purchases as of other purchases.

Inventories at December 31, 1967, at cost to each company, were:

Company P — $80,000.
Company S — $45,000.

Instructions: Prepare working papers showing the income and the expense of each company for the year 1967 and the consolidated income of Company P and its subsidiary.

(AICPA adapted)

16-13. The trial balances at the top of the following page were prepared after completion of the examination of the December 31, 1967, financial statements of Allen Corporation and its subsidiaries, Barth Corporation and Cole Corporation. The subsidiary investments are accounted for by the cost method.

The audit working papers provide the following additional information:

(1) The Barth Corporation was formed by the Allen Corporation on January 1, 1967. To secure additional capital, 25% of the capital stock was sold at par value in the securities market. Allen Corporation purchased the remaining capital stock at par value for cash.

Debits	Trial Balances, December 31, 1967 — Allen Corporation	Barth Corporation	Cole Corporation
Cash	$ 82,000	$ 11,000	$ 27,000
Accounts receivable	104,000	41,000	143,000
Inventories	241,000	70,000	78,000
Investment in Barth Corporation	150,000		
Investment in Cole Corporation	175,000		
Investments — other	185,000		
Fixed assets	375,000	58,000	99,000
Accumulated depreciation	(96,000)	(7,000)	(21,000)
Cost of sales	820,000	300,000	350,000
Operating expenses	60,000	35,000	40,000
Total	$2,096,000	$508,000	$716,000
Credits			
Accounts payable	$ 46,000	$ 33,000	$ 24,000
Sales	960,000	275,000	570,000
Gain on sales of assets	9,000		
Dividend income	18,000		
Capital stock, $20 par value	500,000	200,000	100,000
Retained earnings	563,000		12,000
Appropriation for contingency			10,000
Total	$2,096,000	$508,000	$716,000

(2) On July 1, 1967, Allen Corporation acquired from stockholders 4,000 shares of Cole Corporation capital stock for $175,000. A condensed trial balance for Cole Corporation at July 1, 1967, follows:

	Debit	Credit
Current assets	$165,000	
Fixed assets (net)	60,000	
Current liabilities		$ 45,000
Capital stock, par value $20		100,000
Retained earnings		36,000
Sales		200,000
Cost of sales	140,000	
Operating expenses	16,000	
Total	$381,000	$381,000

(3) The following intercompany sales of certain products were made in 1967:

	Sales	Gross Profit on Sales	Included in Purchaser's Inventory at December 31, 1967 at Lower of Cost or Market
Allen Corp. to Cole Corp.	$ 40,000	20%	$15,000
Barth Corp. to Cole Corp.	30,000	10%	10,000
Cole Corp. to Allen Corp.	60,000	30%	20,000
Total	$130,000		$45,000

In valuing the Allen Corporation inventory at the lower of cost or market, the portion of the inventory purchased from the Cole Corporation was written down by $1,900.

(4) On January 2, 1967, Allen Corporation sold a punch press to Barth Corporation. The machine was purchased on January 1, 1965, and was being depreciated by the straight-line method over a 10-year life. Barth Corporation computed depreciation by the same method based on the remaining useful life. Details of the sale are as follows:

Cost of punch press	$25,000
Accumulated depreciation	5,000
Net book value	$20,000
Sales price	24,000
Gain on sale	$ 4,000

(5) Cash dividends were paid on the following dates in 1967:

	Allen	Cole
June 30	$22,000	$ 6,000
December 31	26,000	14,000
Total	$48,000	$20,000

(6) Allen Corporation billed $6,000 to each subsidiary at year end for executive services in 1967. The billing was treated as an operating expense and reduction of operating expenses. The invoices were paid in January, 1968.

(7) At year end Cole Corporation appropriated $10,000 for a contingent loss in connection with a law suit that had been pending since 1965.

Instructions: Prepare working papers for consolidated statements for Allen Corporation and its subsidiaries for the year ended December 31, 1967. The sales, costs, and expenses of the subsidiaries are to be included in the consolidation as though the subsidiaries had been acquired at the beginning of the year. You plan to deduct the current year's preacquisition earnings of Cole Corporation at the bottom of the consolidated income statement. (Formal journal entries and statements are not required. Supporting computations should be in good form.)

(AICPA adapted)

16-14. During 1967 the Packard Company acquired a controlling interest in Designers, Inc. Trial balances of the companies at December 31, 1967, are as follows:

Debits	Packard Company	Designers, Inc.
Cash	$ 100,000	$ 80,000
Notes receivable	100,000	
Accounts receivable	200,000	100,000
Accrued interest receivable	1,000	
Inventories	924,000	125,000
Investment in Designers, Inc.	475,000	
Plant, property and equipment	1,250,000	500,000
Deferred charges	25,000	
Patents and licenses		50,000
Cost of sales	1,350,000	525,000
Administrative and selling expenses	251,000	174,000
Interest expense		1,000
Total debits	$4,676,000	$1,555,000
Credits		
Accounts payable	$ 425,000	$ 80,000
Notes payable		75,000
Dividend payable		5,000
Allowance for depreciation	500,000	150,000
Capital stock	300,000	100,000
Retained earnings	1,650,000	395,000
Sales and services	1,800,000	750,000
Interest income	1,000	
Total credits	$4,676,000	$1,555,000

The following information is available regarding the transactions and accounts of the companies:

(1) An analysis of the investment in Designers, Inc.:

Date	Description	Amount	Interest Acquired
January 1, 1967	Investment	$325,000	70%
September 30, 1967	Investment	105,000	20%
Total		$430,000	90%
December 31, 1967	90% of Designers, Inc. income for 1967	45,000	
		$475,000	

The net income of Designers, Inc. for the 9 months ended September 30, 1967, was $25,000.

(2) An analysis of the companies' retained earnings accounts:

	Packard Company	Designers, Inc.
Balance, January 1, 1967	$1,605,000	$ 400,000
December 31, 1967:		
Cash dividend declared (payable January 15, 1968)		(5,000)
90% of Designers, Inc. income for 1967	45,000	
Balance, December 31, 1967	$1,650,000	$ 395,000

(3) The patents and licenses of Designers, Inc. have a fair market value of $25,000.

(4) On September 30, 1967, Packard Company loaned its subsidiary $100,000 on a 4% note. Interest and principal are payable in quarterly installments beginning December 31, 1967.

(5) Designers, Inc. sales are principally engineering services billed at cost plus 50%. During 1967, $40,000 was billed to Packard Company, of which $16,500 was treated as a deferred charge at December 31, 1967.

(6) During the year, parent company sales to the subsidiary aggregated $60,000, of which $16,000 remained in the inventory of Designers, Inc. at December 31, 1967.

(7) In 1967 the parent company constructed certain tools at a cost of $15,000 that were sold to Designers, Inc. for $25,000. Designers, Inc. depreciates such tools using the straight-line method over a 5-year life. One-half year's depreciation is provided in the year of acquisition.

Instructions: Prepare working papers for consolidated statements for the year ended December 31, 1967. Construct working papers with the following columns: name of account, 3 columns; Packard Company, 1 column; Designers, Inc., 1 column; adjustments and eliminations, 2 columns; consolidated income statement, 1 column; retained earnings, 1 column; consolidated balance sheet, 1 column. Working papers should be accompanied by explanations and computations in support of each adjustment or elimination given on the working papers. The consolidation is not to be regarded as a pooling of interests. Income tax implications are to be disregarded. (AICPA adapted)

16-15. Following are trial balances of Company A and its subsidiary Company B at December 31, 1967:

Debits	Co. A	Co. B
Cash	$ 545,200	$ 267,300
Receivables, customers	187,000	375,400
War bonds	1,575,300	556,000
Inventories	398,200	146,800
Investment, Co. B —		
Bonds	198,000	
Capital stock	300,000	
Advances	226,600	
Investment, Co. A bonds (at par)		30,000
Fixed assets	2,311,000	714,700
Unamortized bond discount		2,700
Goodwill		90,000
Cost of sales	3,280,500	1,676,100
Selling and administrative expense	333,000	261,000
Depreciation expense	184,000	42,600
Interest expense	24,000	19,700
Bond discount amortized		300
Amortization of premium on Co. B bonds owned	2,000	
Provision for income taxes	600,000	420,000
Dividends paid	100,000	20,000
Total debits	$10,264,800	$4,622,600

Credits	Co. A	Co. B
Accounts payable	$ 79,200	$ 69,500
Accrued income taxes	624,800	431,400
Other accrued expense	10,000	4,000
Advances from Co. A		226,600
Reserve for bad debts	2,500	3,200
Reserve for depreciation	1,420,600	302,300
Reserve for postwar adjustments	1,000,000	445,000
First-mortgage 3% bonds	800,000	
First-mortgage 4% bonds		200,000
Capital stock	1,000,000	200,000
Paid-in surplus	50,200	
Earned surplus, 12/31/66	424,700	90,200
Sales	4,797,300	2,644,500
Interest — war bonds	20,400	5,000
— intercompany bonds	7,200	900
— advances to Co. B	11,700	
Dividend received	16,200	
Net profit		
Total credits	$10,264,800	$4,622,600

Company A on January 1, 1959, purchased from security holders its 81% interest in the capital stock of Company B and its 90% interest in Company B bonds, the total consideration being $516,000 of which $216,000 was allocated to the bonds. The purpose of the purchase was to obtain additional manufacturing facilities and Company B's established markets for products similar to Company A's regular line. The earned surplus of Company B as shown by its books on December 31, 1958, was $150,000. The 25-year first-mortgage 4% bonds had been originally marketed on December 31, 1951, to net 96¼.

For several years a part of the output of Company B has been an intermediate product sold to Company A at a uniform markup of 20% (on sales). Sales of this character recorded on Company B's books were $258,000 for 1967, of which $64,500 remained in Company A's inventory at the end of the year; the corresponding amount in Company A's inventory at the beginning of the year was $82,000.

Company A has made advances to Company B on which the latter pays interest semiannually at the rate of 6% per annum. During 1967 (on July 1) an additional $50,000 was advanced.

Company A constructed a building, at a cost of $100,000, which, on January 1, 1962, was turned over to Company B for its use at a price of $120,000. Annual depreciation of 3% has been accrued thereon since that date.

Instructions: Prepare a columnar consolidating work sheet showing in separate columns a consolidated balance sheet and a consolidated income statement as of December 31, 1967.

(AICPA adapted)

Chapter 17

FOREIGN BRANCHES AND SUBSIDIARIES

Problems of foreign exchange accounting are encountered when a business engages in operations outside the territorial limits of its country. With American government and business extending their activities to every part of the world, problems of foreign exchange assume greater importance to the accountant in the United States today than ever before.

The accountant becomes concerned with problems of foreign exchange when he must express foreign transactions in terms that are meaningful to his domestic client. This involves the translation of transactions that were originally expressed in foreign currencies. Goods may be sold and exported to buyers in foreign lands. Goods may be purchased and imported from abroad. Investments may be made in stocks or bonds issued by corporations in foreign lands or in bonds issued by foreign governments. Domestic enterprises may expand through the establishment of foreign branches and subsidiaries. In each of these relationships, the accountant is faced with the problem of restating transactions that are recorded in a foreign currency in terms of domestic currency equivalents.

RATES OF EXCHANGE

The translation of transactions in terms of domestic currency calls for the use of *rates of exchange* that express the value relationships between a foreign country's basic monetary unit and the domestic unit. At one time, rates of exchange were based directly upon the relative pure gold content of the respective monetary units; these were referred to as the *mint par rates of exchange.* With the abandonment of the gold standard, however, rates of exchange have become the products of various economic factors. *Free market rates of exchange* arise from supply and demand factors. In many countries, the government defines an *official rate of exchange.* An official rate may differ from the rate on the local market where free market conditions determine the exchange of currencies. In some cases, different rates are quoted depending upon the purpose for which the currency exchange is made. Even with government-defined rates of exchange, nations may limit or block the exchange of money or its transfer.

Exchange rates are subject to change. A government may act to change the official rate of exchange from time to time in response to changes that have taken place in economic or political conditions. Free market rates fluctuate daily as changes take place in supply and demand factors.

Different exchange rates, changes in these rates, and the various restrictions that may be imposed by governments upon the exchange of currencies complicate the ordinary conduct of trade between businesses or individuals in different countries. These factors also complicate the problem of restating foreign transactions in meaningful fashion. Special care is necessary in interpreting transactions stated in foreign currency. When more than one exchange rate is encountered, a choice between these rates will have to be made in translating foreign accounts. Here, particular care must be exercised to choose the exchange rate that best expresses the relationship between the two currencies and that provides for the most realistic translation under prevailing circumstances. The free market rate of exchange is frequently found to be the most suitable exchange rate in meeting this objective.

The pages that follow describe the conventional procedures that are employed in the translation of financial data reported in terms of foreign currencies. When special conditions are encountered, modification of conventional procedures to meet such special conditions may be required.

QUOTATIONS OF RATES OF EXCHANGE

Foreign rates of exchange may be quoted *directly* or *indirectly*. A direct quotation states the value of a single unit of foreign currency in terms of equivalent domestic currency. The British pound is stated at an equivalent United States dollar value of $2.7842; the Danish krone is stated at $.14435. These quotations are direct. An indirect quotation, on the other hand, states the domestic currency unit in terms of the equivalent foreign currency. Thus the United States dollar would be quoted as equivalent to .359170 of a pound; the dollar would also be equivalent to 6.927607 kroner.

Rates of exchange may be relatively stable over long periods of time; on the other hand, they may fluctuate widely even over relatively short periods.

The table at the top of the following page lists the monetary units for various foreign countries and the quoted rates of exchange that may be found in the financial pages of our daily newspapers. These are direct quotations expressed in United States dollars.

Foreign Exchange Rates

(Selling prices in dollars for bank transfers in the United States for payment abroad, as quoted at 4 p.m.)

Country	Monetary Unit	Oct. 3, 1967
Canada	Dollar	.930400
Europe		
Great Britain	Pound	2.784200
Austria	Schilling	.038800
Belgium	Franc	.020155
Denmark	Krone	.144350
France	Franc	.203925
Holland	Guilder	.278125
Italy	Lira	.001606
Portugal	Escudo	.034800
Sweden	Krona	.193700
Switzerland	Franc	.230225
West Germany	Deutschemark	.249800
Latin America		
Argentina	"Free" Peso	.002880
Brazil	"Novo" Cruzeiro	.372000
Ecuador	Sucre	.051000
Mexico	Peso	.080100
Peru	Sol	.026500
Venezuela	"Free" Bolivar	.223000
Near East		
Iraq	Dinar	2.791000
Lebanon	Pound	.310500
Far East		
Australia	Dollar	1.113700
Hong Kong	Hong Kong Dollar	.174000
Japan	Yen	.002764
Pakistan	Rupee	.204100
Philippines	Peso	.255700

FOREIGN SALES AND PURCHASES

In selling or buying goods abroad, a sale price or a purchase price is stated in terms of either the domestic currency or the foreign currency. With fluctuation in the exchange rate, one of the parties to the transaction will realize a gain or a loss resulting from the change in the exchange rate between the date the transaction is entered into and the date the account is paid. For example, an American exporter in selling merchandise abroad may bill the buyer in either United States dollars or the foreign currency. If he bills the buyer in United States dollars, there can be no gain or loss accruing to him from exchange rate fluctuations; remittance of the billed dollar amount will be required of the buyer, no matter what change takes place in the exchange rate between the date of sale and the date of payment. If the buyer is billed in foreign currency, however, the American exporter will be subject to a gain or a loss arising from a change in the rate of exchange.

To illustrate, assume that an American exporter sells goods to a merchant in Holland, billing the buyer for $2,750. Assuming a rate of exchange for the guilder at the date of the sale of $.275, the foreign buyer will treat this transaction as a purchase for 10,000 guilders. Assume that on the date of settlement the rate of exchange has changed to $.272. Under these circumstances, it will cost the buyer more than 10,000 guilders to purchase a draft for $2,750 in payment of the invoice. The buyer thus incurs a loss as a result of the fluctuation in the rate of exchange.

But assume in the foregoing example that the buyer was billed at 10,000 guilders instead of $2,750. The seller, although setting a price in foreign currency, must still record the transaction on his books in terms of dollars. Assuming a guilder rate at the time of sale of $.275, the seller will treat the transaction as a sale for $2,750. However, a notation is made in the customer's account stating the number of guilders required in settlement. The seller, then, makes the following entry:

Accounts Receivable — Holland Customer (10,000 guilders)	2,750	
Sales		2,750

Assume now that a draft for 10,000 guilders is received from the buyer at a time when the rate of exchange for the guilder has declined to $.272. Conversion of the draft into dollars results in recovery of $2,720. The seller here must recognize a loss of $30 as a result of the change in the exchange rate. The seller makes the following entry:

Cash	2,720	
Loss on Currency Exchange	30	
Accounts Receivable — Holland Customer (10,000 guilders)		2,750

The foreign buyer in the previous examples has his counterpart in the American importer. An American who imports goods from abroad may be billed in either domestic or foreign currency. If he is billed in domestic currency, he makes settlement in United States dollars in accordance with the sum recognized on the date of purchase; he is not affected by exchange fluctuations. However, if he is billed in foreign currency, he is subject to a gain or a loss from a change in the rate of exchange.

To illustrate, assume that an American importer acquires goods from an Italian manufacturer at a billed price of 1,000,000 lire. The entry on the books of the buyer upon receipt of the goods and the invoice, assuming a rate of exchange for the lira on the date of the receipt of the invoice of $.001610, is:

Purchases	1,610	
Accounts Payable — Italian Creditor (1,000,000 lire)		1,610

Assume that on the date of settlement the rate of exchange for the lira has declined to \$.001595. The buyer pays only \$1,595 for the required lire and makes the following entry:

Accounts Payable — Italian Creditor (1,000,000 lire)......	1,610	
Cash..		1,595
Gain on Currency Exchange........................		15

If the exporter or the importer is faced with the possibility of exchange fluctuations and wishes to protect himself against substantial losses from this source, he may engage in hedging operations involving futures transactions. For example, the exporter in the first example who bills the buyer in guilders may, at the time of the sale of the goods, sell 10,000 guilders for future delivery by him on the date that he expects to receive the remittance from his Dutch customer. The importer in the second example who is billed in lire may, at the time of the purchase of the goods, buy 1,000,000 lire for future delivery to him on the date that he expects to make payment to his Italian creditor.

When gains and losses from exchange transactions are considered to arise from financial management's election to assume the risks of exchange fluctuation, a net gain or loss from these transactions should be recognized on the income statement as Other Revenue or Other Expense. On the other hand, when it is reasonable to regard gains and losses as price adjustments, they may be combined with related purchases and sales balances.

CALCULATIONS FOR MONETARY TRANSLATIONS

When rates involve a foreign currency on a decimal basis, monetary translation is simple. For example, assume 5,150.25 Mexican pesos (5,150 pesos and 25 centavos) and a direct exchange rate for the dollar of \$.0802 pesos. The pesos total is expressed in dollars by the following calculation:

$$5{,}150.25 \times \$.0802 = \$413.05.$$

On the other hand, \$5,000 may be expressed in Mexican pesos by a calculation as follows:

$$\$5{,}000 \div \$.0802 = 62{,}344.14 \text{ pesos.}$$

However, when nondecimal currencies are involved, the translating process is more difficult. For example, the British monetary system is not a decimal currency. One pound (£) equals 20 shillings (s); 1 shilling equals 12 pence (d). For all arithmetic functions, these relationships must be observed. Pounds, shillings, and pence would be added as follows:

£40	– 10s	– 6d
14	– 15	– 8
£55	– 6s	– 2d

The sum of 14 pence in the pence column is recognized as 1 shilling and 2 pence.
The sum of 25 shillings in the shillings column is increased by 1 shilling from the pence column and is recognized as 1 pound and 6 shillings.
The sum of 54 pounds in the pounds column is increased by 1 pound from the shillings column and is recorded as 55 pounds.

Pounds, shillings, and pence are subtracted as follows:

£40	– 10s	– 6d
14	– 15	– 8
£25	– 14s	– 10d

8 pence cannot be subtracted from 6 pence; therefore 10 shillings and 6 pence is regarded as the equivalent of 9 shillings (10 – 1) and 18 pence (12 + 6); 8 pence subtracted from 18 pence leaves 10 pence.
15 shillings cannot be subtracted from 9 shillings (10 – 1); hence 40 pounds and 9 shillings is regarded as 39 pounds (40 – 1) and 29 shillings; 15 shillings subtracted from 29 shillings leaves 14 shillings.
14 pounds subtracted from 39 pounds (40 – 1) leaves 25 pounds.

In translating pounds, shillings, and pence into dollars, shillings and pence will first have to be restated as decimal parts of a pound. A shilling is $\frac{1}{20}$ or .05 of a pound; a pence is $\frac{1}{12}$ of a shilling, or in terms of a pound, $\frac{1}{12} \times \frac{1}{20}$ or $\frac{1}{240}$ of a pound, or as a decimal part, .0041667 of a pound. A sum such as £230 – 14s – 9d would then be expressed as follows:

£230			....	£230.0000
	14s		(14 × .05)..............................	.7000
		9d	(9 × .0041667).........................	.0375
£230 – 14s – 9d				£230.7375

Assuming that the direct rate of exchange for the pound is \$2.815, the dollar equivalent of £230 – 14s – 9d would be:

230.7375 × \$2.815 = \$649.53

On the other hand, the translation of dollars into pounds, shillings, and pence requires that the dollar figure first be divided by the direct rate of exchange for the pound. The decimal part of a pound is then restated in terms of shillings and pence. To illustrate, \$6,000 is expressed in terms of pounds, shillings, and pence as follows:

\$6,000 ÷ \$2.815 = £2,131.4387.
.4387 pounds, expressed as shillings, is .4387 × 20 or 8.774 shillings.
.774 shillings, expressed as pence, is .774 × 12 or 9.288 pence.
\$6,000 translated at the rate of \$2.815 thus gives a value of £2,131 – 8s – 9d.

TRANSLATION OF THE ACCOUNTS OF A FOREIGN AFFILIATE

When a domestic company maintains a branch or a subsidiary company abroad, combined or consolidated financial statements for the related units require a full translation of the accounts on the statements of the foreign unit in terms of the domestic currency.

The general rules for the translation of foreign accounts that have been recommended by the American Institute of Certified Public Accountants in *Accounting Research Bulletin No. 43* are summarized below.[1]

Balance sheet items

Current assets. Cash, accounts receivable, and other current assets should be translated at the rate of exchange prevailing on the date of the balance sheet. Inventory should follow the standard rule of cost or market, whichever is lower. When an inventory is not translated at the rate of exchange prevailing on the date of the balance sheet, the burden of proof is on those following some other procedure.

Noncurrent assets. Fixed assets, permanent investments, and long-term receivables should be translated at the rates prevailing when such assets were acquired or constructed.

Current liabilities. Current liabilities payable in foreign currency should be translated at the rate of exchange prevailing on the date of the balance sheet.

Noncurrent liabilities. Long-term liabilities payable in foreign currency should be translated at the rates prevailing when they were originally incurred.

Capital stock. Capital stock stated in foreign currency should be translated at the rates prevailing when it was originally issued.

Income statement items

Revenues and expenses. Operations stated in foreign currency should be translated at the average rate of exchange. With wide fluctuations in exchange, the transaction should be made at average rates of exchange applicable to each month, or if this is impractical, on the basis of a carefully weighted average.

Depreciation. Depreciation should be computed at the rates of exchange prevailing when the related assets were acquired or constructed.

The application of these rules to the translation of branch accounts is described and illustrated in the following section. The application of these rules to the translation of the accounts of a subsidiary company is described and illustrated in a later section.

ACCOUNTING FOR THE FOREIGN BRANCH

When a domestic business establishes a branch unit in a foreign country, it encounters problems similar to those already described and illustrated in the chapters dealing with branch accounting. It is also

[1]*Accounting Research and Terminology Bulletins*, 1961 (New York: American Institute of Certified Public Accountants), *Accounting Research Bulletin No. 43*, Chapter 12, "Foreign Operations and Foreign Exchange," p. 111–116.

faced with special problems created by branch activities that are expressed in terms of a foreign currency. These special problems arise whenever reports of the combined activities of the home office and the branch are to be prepared. Home office operations and home office relationships with the branch are summarized in terms of the domestic currency; branch operations and branch relationships with the home office are summarized in terms of the foreign currency. Before the home office can take up the earnings of the branch and prepare combined reports, account balances of the branch must be translated into a currency common with that of the home office.

In the example that follows, the procedures that are generally employed in accounting for a foreign branch will be illustrated. Assume that the ABC Company, of New York, establishes a London branch to sell the regular lines of the home office as well as goods acquired from English suppliers. A balance sheet prepared for the home office on December 31, 1966, just before the establishment of the branch, follows:

ABC Company
Balance Sheet
December 31, 1966

Assets			Liabilities and Stockholders' Equity		
Cash		$ 65,000	Accounts payable		$160,000
Accounts receivable		160,000	Capital stock	$200,000	
Merchandise inventory		185,000	Retained earnings	105,000	305,000
Furniture and fixtures	$85,000				
Less allowance for depreciation	30,000	55,000			
Total assets		$465,000	Total liabilities and stockholders' equity		$465,000

Transactions and entries for the home office and the branch for the year 1967 are listed below and on the next page:

Transaction	Home Office Books (Amounts in dollars)			Branch Books (Amounts in pounds)		
(1) Transfer by the home office to the newly organized London branch of a draft for £10,000. The exchange rate on the date of the purchase of the draft was 2.81, the home office paying $28,100.	Remittances to Branch	28,100		Cash	10,000	
	Cash		28,100	Remittances from Home Office		10,000
(2) Transfer by the home office to the branch of a draft for $14,000. The exchange rate upon receipt by the branch was 2.80, the branch deposit in the bank being £5,000.	Remittances to Branch	14,000		Cash	5,000	
	Cash		14,000	Remittances from Home Office		5,000

Transaction	Home Office Books (Amounts in dollars)			Branch Books (Amounts in pounds)		
(3) Shipment by the home office to the branch of merchandise, cost $70,000. The exchange rate when the merchandise was received by the branch was 2.80, the branch recording the shipment at £25,000.	Branch....... Merchandise Shipments to Branch.....	70,000	 70,000	Merchandise Shipments from Home Office... Home Office.	25,000	 25,000
(4) Purchase by the branch of furniture and fixtures for cash, £3,500. (The exchange rate on the date of purchase was 2.80.)				Furniture and Fixtures....... Cash........	3,500	 3,500
(5) Purchases of merchandise on account: Home office.... $200,000 Branch.......... £ 12,000	Purchases..... Accounts Payable....	200,000	 200,000	Purchases...... Accounts Payable.....	12,000	 12,000
(6) Sales on account: Home office..... $360,000 Branch.......... £ 30,000	Accounts Receivable...... Sales.......	360,000	 360,000	Accounts Receivable..... Sales........	30,000	 30,000
(7) Collections on account: Home office..... $345,000 Branch.......... £ 25,000	Cash......... Accounts Receivable....	345,000	 345,000	Cash.......... Accounts Receivable.....	25,000	 25,000
(8) Payments on account: Home office..... $245,000 Branch.......... £ 9,500	Accounts Payable.......... Cash.......	245,000	 245,000	Accounts Payable........... Cash........	9,500	 9,500
(9) Expenses paid in cash: Home office..... $ 75,000 Branch.......... £ 9,000	Expenses...... Cash.......	75,000	 75,000	Expenses....... Cash........	9,000	 9,000
(10) Transfer by the branch to the home office of draft for $28,000. The exchange rate on the date of purchase of the draft was 2.80, the branch paying £10,000.	Cash......... Remittances from Branch.	28,000	 28,000	Remittances to Home Office... Cash........	10,000	 10,000
(11) Transfer by the branch to the home office of draft for £1,000. The exchange rate on the date of receipt of the draft was 2.78, the home office deposit in the bank being $2,780.	Cash......... Remittances from Branch.	2,780	 2,780	Remittances to Home Office... Cash........	1,000	 1,000
(12) Depreciation for year on furniture and fixtures: Home office..... $ 8,500 Branch.......... £ 350	Expenses...... Allowance for Depreciation.	8,500	 8,500	Expenses....... Allowance for Depreciation.	350	 350
(13) To close beginning merchandise inventory.	Profit and Loss. Merchandise Inventory, Jan. 1......	185,000	 185,000			
(14) To record ending merchandise inventories: Home office..... $100,000 Branch.......... £ 18,500	Merchandise Inventory, Dec. 31....... Profit and Loss........	100,000	 100,000	Merchandise Inventory, Dec. 31........ Profit and Loss.........	18,500	 18,500

In accounting for domestic branches, the net investment in a branch was reflected on the home office books in a single branch account and the net accountability of the branch to the home office was reflected on the branch books in a single home office account. In accounting for a foreign branch, however, additional accounts may be introduced to facilitate the subsequent translation of branch account balances into domestic monetary amounts. Remittances by a home office to a branch may be summarized in separate reciprocal accounts on both home office and branch books so that the dollar amount represented by the remittance-from-home-office balance on the branch books may be readily determined; remittances to a home office by a branch may be summarized in separate reciprocal accounts on both home office and branch books so that the dollar amount represented by the remittance-to-home-office balance on the branch books may be readily determined. Remittance account balances are ultimately closed into the related home office and branch accounts.

After the transactions for the ABC Company and its London branch are posted, trial balances for the two offices will appear as shown below.

ABC Company and London Branch
Preclosing Trial Balances
December 31, 1967

	Home Office		Branch	
	Dr.	Cr.	Dr.	Cr.
Cash	$ 78,680		£ 7,000	
Accounts Receivable	175,000		5,000	
Merchandise Inventory, January 1	185,000			
Furniture and Fixtures	85,000		3,500	
Allowance for Depreciation		$ 38,500		£ 350
Accounts Payable		115,000		2,500
Branch	70,000			
Remittances to Branch	42,100			
Remittances from Branch		30,780		
Home Office				25,000
Remittances from Home Office				15,000
Remittances to Home Office			11,000	
Capital Stock		200,000		
Retained Earnings		105,000		
Sales		360,000		30,000
Purchases	200,000		12,000	
Merchandise Shipments to Branch		70,000		
Mdse. Shipments from Home Office			25,000	
Expenses	83,500		9,350	
	$919,280	$919,280	£72,850	£72,850
Merchandise Inventory, December 31[1]				
Acquired from Suppliers	$100,000	$100,000	£ 6,500	£ 6,500
Acquired from Home Office			12,000	12,000
	$100,000	$100,000	£18,500	£18,500

[1]The ending inventory is listed as both a debit and a credit in view of the need for recognizing this balance both as an asset item on the balance sheet and as a subtraction item from the sum of beginning inventory and purchases on the income statement.

TRANSLATION OF BRANCH ACCOUNT BALANCES

At the end of each fiscal period, the home office will require the foreign branch to submit financial statements in terms of the foreign currency. At the same time the home office will require the branch to submit the trial balance and the adjusting data in support of the branch statements. These data will be used by the home office in translating branch operations in terms of the domestic monetary unit.

Financial statements for the London branch of the ABC Company are given below. Preclosing account balances and ending inventory data as originally submitted by the branch in terms of pounds and as restated by the home office in terms of United States dollars are listed at the top of the next page.

ABC Company
Balance Sheet — London Branch
December 31, 1967

Assets			Liabilities	
Cash		£ 7,000	Accounts payable	£ 2,500
Accounts receivable		5,000	Home office	31,150
Merchandise inventory		18,500		
Furniture and fixtures	£3,500			
Less allowance for depreciation	350	3,150		
Total assets		£33,650	Total liabilities	£33,650

ABC Company
Income Statement — London Branch
For Year Ended December 31, 1967

Sales		£30,000
Cost of goods sold:		
Purchases	£12,000	
Merchandise shipments from home office	25,000	
Goods available for sale	£37,000	
Less merchandise inventory, December 31	18,500	18,500
Gross profit on sales		£11,500
Expenses		9,350
Net income		£ 2,150

ABC Company — London Branch
Trial Balance Translated into U.S. Dollars
December 31, 1967

	Adjusted Trial Balance (Pounds)		Translation Rate*	Adjusted Trial Balance (U.S. Dollars)	
	Dr.	Cr.		Dr.	Cr.
Cash	£ 7,000		(C) 2.77	$ 19,390	
Accounts Receivable	5,000		(C) 2.77	13,850	
Furniture and Fixtures	3,500		(H) 2.80	9,800	
Allowance for Depreciation		£ 350	(H) 2.80		$ 980
Accounts Payable		2,500	(C) 2.77		6,925
Home Office		25,000	(R) $70,000		70,000
Remittances from Home Office		15,000	(R) $42,100		42,100
Remittances to Home Office	11,000		(R) $30,780	30,780	
Sales		30,000	(A) 2.78		83,400
Purchases	12,000		(A) 2.78	33,360	
Merchandise Shipments from Home Office	25,000		(R) $70,000	70,000	
Expenses	9,000		(A) 2.78	25,020	
Depreciation[1]	350		(H) 2.80	980	
	£72,850	£72,850		$203,180	$203,405
Exchange Adjustment (to balance)				225	
				$203,405	$203,405
Merchandise Inventory, Dec. 31					
Acquired from Suppliers	£ 6,500	£ 6,500	(C) 2.77	$ 18,005	$ 18,005
Acquired from Home Office	12,000	12,000	(H) 2.80	33,600	33,600
	£18,500	£18,500		$ 51,605	$ 51,605

*Translation rate:

(C) = Current rate — exchange rate at end of period (2.77).

(H) = Historical rate — exchange rate on date transaction was completed (rate on date of purchase of asset, 2.80; rate on date of acquisition of goods from home office, 2.80).

(R) = Reciprocal amount — dollar value on home office books for corresponding transaction.

(A) = Average rate (2.78).

[1]Depreciation is reported as a separate expense item to facilitate conversion of this item in terms of asset cost.

The practices described in the following paragraphs are generally applied in the translation of the foreign branch balances and have been applied in the example.

Current items. Current assets and current liabilities are restated at the rate of exchange that is effective at the end of the accounting period. This is the rate that is expected to prevail as noncash current assets are converted into cash and as cash is applied to the payment of current obligations. The application of the current rate to current assets and to current liabilities affords the closest approximation to the balance that will become available for remittance to the home office.

One exception to restatement at the current rate may be suggested: when a significant part of an inventory consists of goods acquired from a home office, the original dollar cost may be assigned to that part of the inventory and the current rate may be applied to the balance of the inventory. This practice is followed in the example. The rate that is applied to the current assets is also applied to current asset valuation accounts.

Noncurrent items. Noncurrent assets as well as noncurrent liabilities are converted at the rate of exchange prevailing on the dates of the transactions that originated the asset and liability balances. Noncurrent items are thus carried on successive statements at original dollar values without response to fluctuations in the rate of exchange; original balances are expressed regardless of the change in the value of the monetary unit in accordance with generally accepted accounting principles.

Ordinarily the number of long-term debt items is relatively small and the exchange rate that was in effect on the date of the incurrence of each such debt item can be readily determined. However, a special problem is encountered for plant and equipment items. With many different acquisitions at different dates, special procedures must be applied in the accounts to facilitate the restatement of this class of assets. Such procedures normally involve the maintenance of two sets of values for plant and equipment accounts. Accounts may be established with two pairs of money columns, one pair of columns reporting the asset balances in terms of the monetary unit actually employed and the second pair of columns of a memorandum nature reporting the asset balances in terms of equivalent dollar amounts. Accounts will then provide balances that show costs for assets in the foreign currency and costs in equivalent dollar amounts. The dollar amounts are substituted for the foreign currency values when branch accounts are converted.

The allowance for depreciation reported by the branch in terms of the foreign currency represents the application of various depreciation rates to the different asset costs; when assets are restated, an allowance must be provided that will offer an application of the depreciation rates to the equivalent dollar acquisition costs. An allowance balance may be established at the same percentage of dollar cost that the allowance in the foreign currency bears to the asset cost in the foreign currency; restatement of the allowance is thus accomplished without the need for detailed analyses and calculations. For example, an allowance in foreign currency applicable to a number of asset items and constituting 38½% of such total asset cost is restated by simply applying this percentage to the total dollar cost assigned to the assets.

To simplify the process of periodic account balance restatements, branch plant and equipment accounts and related allowance accounts may be carried on the books of the home office. In following this policy, the branch records the purchase of a plant and equipment item by a debit to the home office account and a credit to cash in the foreign currency; the home office is notified and it debits a branch plant and equipment account and credits the branch for the purchase at the exchange rate prevailing at the date of purchase. Periodically, the home office charges the branch for depreciation on the property item by debiting the branch account and crediting an asset allowance account based on the original dollar cost identified with the asset; the branch recognizes the expense by debiting depreciation and crediting the home office, the charge being calculated in terms of the foreign currency cost of the asset.

Reciprocal accounts. Reciprocal branch-home office accounts reporting investments and cash transfers will ultimately be set off against each other and hence must be stated at the same dollar amounts. The values in foreign currency in the accounts of the branch, then, are restated at the dollar balances reported on the home office books. Thus: (1) the home office balance is restated at the dollar balance reported in the reciprocal branch account on the home office books; (2) the remittances-from-home-office balance is restated at the dollar balance reported in the reciprocal remittances-to-branch balance on the home office books; (3) the remittances-to-home-office balance is restated at the dollar balance reported in the reciprocal remittances-from-branch balance on the home office books.

Revenue and expense accounts. Revenue and expense accounts, with certain exceptions that are mentioned later, are restated at average rates. Average rates normally provide the best approximation to the dollar equivalents represented by the nominal account balances. The restatement of revenues and expenses in terms of the original dollar values represented therein would be a formidable task and the results would normally differ little from those obtained when averaging procedures are used.

In the translation of an adjusted trial balance, prepaid and accrued items reported in real accounts are restated at current rates and their nominal counterparts are restated at average rates. Although such a procedure may appear to be inconsistent, analysis of the debits and the credits in the revenue and expense accounts and restatement at both average and current rates would normally be unwarranted in view of the minor differences that would be formed in such a procedure as compared with application of average rates.

An average rate is not applicable to the beginning and the ending inventories that enter into the profit and loss computation. The beginning inventory is restated at the same dollar value that was used for the closing inventory at the end of the previous period. The ending inventory is stated at the value that was used in its recognition as an asset item; the ending inventory, then, is stated at the same dollar value on the balance sheet and on the income statement.

An average rate is not applied to nominal account balances that report transactions between the branch and the home office. Merchandise Shipments from Home Office, for example, is restated at the dollar value that is reported for Merchandise Shipments to Branch on the home office books.

Further exception from the averaging procedure is made in the case of amortization and depreciation of asset values. The debit to the expense account should be the same in dollars as the credit made to the asset account or to the allowance account; the credit to the asset or to the allowance is made in terms of an asset dollar value as of the date of the asset acquisition as described earlier.

The average rate used in restating revenue and expense balances may be an average daily rate, an average weekly rate, or an average monthly rate for the year. In some cases the averaging procedure may be modified by weights to offer adequate recognition of those rates effective during the busy seasons. An average rate is sometimes computed to reflect the rates that are applied to the transfer of earnings to the home office; the dollar balance in the remittances-from-branch account on the home office books divided by the foreign currency balance in the remittances-to-home-office account on the branch books offers such an average.

The exchange adjustment. If all of the accounts of the branch were restated at a single exchange rate, accounts after translation into dollars would be in balance; however, restatement of items at different rates leaves the accounts out of balance. When rates of exchange have fluctuated narrowly during the period, the difference between debits and credits will be small; when rates have fluctuated widely, the difference may be large. In either case, the accounts are brought into balance by recognizing a debit or a credit to an exchange adjustment balance. A required debit to the exchange adjustment balance may be viewed as an expense item, and a credit to this balance may be viewed as a revenue item. Under this procedure, asset and liability balances as translated are accepted as complete and accurate; any trial balance difference calls for adjustment in the nominal account section. The gain or the loss is reported on the income statement as other revenue or other expense.

Some accountants take a different view of the significance of the exchange adjustment. These persons maintain that the exchange rate may change in the new period, thus serving to invalidate the exchange adjustment. Since the gain or the loss from exchange has not yet been realized, a required exchange adjustment debit should be reported as a deferred cost and an exchange adjustment credit as a deferred revenue. With fluctuations in the exchange rate from period to period and a counter-balancing of "expense" and "revenue" in successive periods, exchange adjustments are removed from periodic profit and loss measurements. Still other accountants, placing chief emphasis on accounting conservatism, would recognize a required debit to an exchange adjustment balance as an expense item and a required credit as a deferred revenue balance to be listed on the balance sheet under a heading such as "Reserve for Exchange."[1] In the examples in this chapter, the exchange adjustment balance, whether a debit or a credit, is recognized as a profit and loss item.

It should be recognized that the exchange adjustment, no matter what interpretation is placed upon it, is a balance that emerges only in the translation of branch account balances and receives no recognition on the books of either the home office or the branch. The preparation of combined statements for a home office and its foreign branch in terms

---

[1]The Committee on Accounting Procedure of the American Institute of Certified Public Accountants distinguishes between realized and unrealized exchange losses and gains and makes the following recommendations:

"Realized losses and gains on foreign exchange should be charged or credited to operations.

"Provision should be made, ordinarily by a charge against operations, for declines in translation value of foreign net current and working assets (unrealized losses). Unrealized gains should preferably be carried to a suspense account, except to the extent that they offset prior provisions for unrealized losses, in which case they may be credited to the account previously charged." See *Accounting Research and Terminology Bulletins*, 1961 (New York: American Institute of Certified Public Accountants), *Accounting Research Bulletin No. 43*, p. 113.

There has been no dispute on the position set forth by the Committee for the treatment of realized gains and losses — those arising from the actual exchange of currencies. But its position on the treatment of unrealized gains and losses is challenged. It should be observed that the view of the Committee with respect to the latter is consistent with its general approach to problems of valuation: losses are anticipated; gains must await realization. In its recommendations for the valuation of marketable securities, for example, a decline in the market value of the asset below cost was to be recognized in the accounts as a loss but an advance in the market value of the asset above cost was not to be recognized until asset realization confirmed a gain.

of domestic currency involves a fiction even as did the development of consolidated statements for a parent company and its subsidiaries. In preparing consolidated statements for a parent and its subsidiaries, the accountant adopted the fiction of a single company; in this view, minority interests and differences between investment costs and equities acquired in subsidiary companies required recognition. When combined statements for a parent and its foreign branches are to be prepared, the accountant adopts the fiction of a uniform monetary unit; in this view, an exchange adjustment requires recognition.

Conversion of the account balances for the London branch of the ABC Company in accordance with the foregoing rules resulted in a trial balance in dollars with a credit excess of $225 and hence the recognition of an exchange adjustment debit of this amount.

COMBINED STATEMENTS FOR HOME OFFICE AND FOREIGN BRANCH

With branch trial balance and ending inventory balances translated into dollars, financial statements for the branch in terms of the domestic currency may now be prepared. With branch earnings expressed in terms of dollars, the home office may recognize branch earnings on its books and summarize operations for the period. Branch and home office statements as prepared by the ABC Company home office are given on pages 606 and 607. The closing entries for the home office and the branch units are as follows:

Transactions	Home Office Books (Amounts in dollars)			Branch Books (Amounts in pounds)		
(15) To close nominal accounts summarizing profit and loss activities.	Sales	360,000		Profit and Loss	16,350	
	Merchandise Shipments to Branch	70,000		Sales	30,000	
	Purchases		200,000	Purchases		12,000
	Expenses		83,500	Merchandise Shipments from Home Office		25,000
	Profit and Loss		146,500	Expenses		9,350
(16) To close balance in profit and loss account on branch books into home office account.				Profit and Loss	2,150	
				Home Office		2,150
(17) To recognize branch net income on home office books: Net income per branch books, £2,150; in domestic currency, $5,420.	Branch	5,420				
	Profit and Loss (Branch Profit)		5,420			
(18) To close combined profit and loss on home office books.	Profit and Loss	66,920				
	Retained Earnings		66,920			
(19) To close remittances balances into respective branch and home office accounts.	Branch	11,320		Remittances from Home Office	15,000	
	Remittances from Branch	30,780		Remittances to Home Office		11,000
	Remittances to Branch		42,100	Home Office		4,000

ABC Company
Balance Sheet — London Branch
December 31, 1967

Assets			Liabilities	
Cash		$19,390	Accounts payable	$ 6,925
Accounts receivable		13,850	Home office	86,740
Merchandise inventory		51,605		
Furniture and fixtures	$9,800			
Less allowance for depreciation	980	8,820		
Total assets		$93,665	Total liabilities	$93,665

ABC Company
Income Statement — London Branch
For Year Ended December 31, 1967

Sales		$83,400
Cost of goods sold:		
Purchases	$ 33,360	
Merchandise shipments from home office	70,000	
Merchandise available for sale	$103,360	
Less merchandise inventory, December 31	51,605	51,755
Gross profit on sales		$31,645
Expenses (including exchange adjustment, $225)		26,225
Net income		$ 5,420

ABC Company
Balance Sheet — Home Office
December 31, 1967

Assets			Liabilities and Stockholders' Equity		
Cash		$ 78,680	Accounts payable		$115,000
Accounts receivable		175,000	Capital stock	$200,000	
Merchandise inventory		100,000	Retained earnings	171,920	371,920
Furniture and fixtures	$85,000				
Less allowance for depreciation	38,500	46,500			
Branch		86,740			
Total assets		$486,920	Total liabilities and stockholders' equity		$486,920

ABC Company
Income Statement — Home Office
For Year Ended December 31, 1967

Sales		$360,000
Cost of goods sold:		
Merchandise inventory, January 1	$185,000	
Purchases	200,000	
	$385,000	
Less merchandise shipments to branch	70,000	
Merchandise available for sale	$315,000	
Less merchandise inventory, December 31	100,000	215,000
Gross profit on sales		$145,000
Expenses		83,500
Net income from own operations		$ 61,500
Add net income — London Branch		5,420
Total income		$ 66,920

With branch data translated into dollars, combined financial statements for home office and branch may be prepared. Working papers for the preparation of combined statements for the ABC Company are illustrated on page 608.

ACCOUNTING FOR THE FOREIGN SUBSIDIARY

Domestic companies may establish subsidiary companies in foreign lands under the incorporation laws of such countries or they may acquire controlling interests in foreign companies already organized. The accounting for the foreign subsidiary is similar to that which has already been described for the foreign branch. However, there are certain reciprocal balances that will be found in the parent-subsidiary relationship that were not found in the home office-branch relationship. These special reciprocal balances are illustrated in the example that follows, together with the procedures that are followed in the translation of these special reciprocal balances and the subsequent preparation of consolidated statements for the parent and the foreign subsidiary.

For purposes of illustration assume that the ABC Company in the previous example, instead of establishing an affiliated unit in London in the form of a branch, establishes the unit in the form of a wholly owned subsidiary company known as the ABC Company of London. All of the facts given in the previous example are the same with the exception of the form that the transactions between the affiliates take in view of the different relationship that exists.

ABC Company
Working Papers for Combined Statements for Home Office and Branch
December 31, 1967

	Home Office	Branch	Eliminations		Income Statement		Retained Earnings		Balance Sheet	
			Dr.	Cr.	Dr.	Cr.	Dr.	Cr.	Dr.	Cr.
Debits										
Cash	78,680	19,390							98,070	
Accounts Receivable	175,000	13,850							188,850	
Merchandise Inventory, January 1	185,000				185,000					
Furniture and Fixtures	85,000	9,800							94,800	
Branch	70,000			(a) 70,000						
Remittances to Branch	42,100			(b) 42,100						
Remittances to Home Office		30,780		(c) 30,780						
Purchases	200,000	33,360			233,360					
Merchandise Shipments from Home Office		70,000		(d) 70,000						
Expenses	83,500	26,000			109,500					
Exchange Adjustment		225			225					
	919,280	203,405								
Merchandise Inventory, December 31 (Balance Sheet)	100,000	51,605							151,605	
Credits										
Allowance for Depreciation	38,500	980								39,480
Accounts Payable	115,000	6,925								121,925
Home Office		70,000	(a) 70,000							
Remittances from Home Office		42,100	(b) 42,100							
Remittances from Branch	30,780		(c) 30,780							
Capital Stock	200,000									200,000
Retained Earnings	105,000							105,000		
Sales	360,000	83,400				443,400				
Merchandise Shipments to Branch	70,000		(d) 70,000							
	919,280	203,405								
Merchandise Inventory, December 31 (Income Statement)	100,000	51,605				151,605				
			212,880	212,880	528,085	595,005		105,000	533,325	361,405
Net Income to Retained Earnings					66,920			66,920		
Retained Earnings to Balance Sheet							171,920			171,920
					595,005	595,005	171,920	171,920	533,325	533,325

Assume that the transactions between the home office and the branch are defined for the parent-subsidiary relationship as follows:

(1) Acquisition by the parent of all of the stock of the subsidiary company for £10,000.
(2) Long-term advance by parent to subsidiary company of $14,000.
(3) Sale of merchandise on account by parent to subsidiary for $70,000.
(10) Remittance by subsidiary company to parent on account, $28,000.
(11) Declaration and payment of dividend by subsidiary company to parent, £1,000.

The foregoing transactions would be recorded on the books of the parent and its London subsidiary as shown below. It is assumed that the parent maintains its investment balance at cost. All of the other transactions of the parent and the subsidiary would be recorded as previously illustrated on pages 596 and 597.

Transaction	Parent Company Books (Amounts in dollars)	Subsidiary Company Books (Amounts in pounds)
(1) Acquisition by the ABC Co. of 100% of the stock of a newly organized subsidiary ABC Co. of London, with payment made by a draft for £10,000. The exchange rate on the date of the purchase of the draft was 2.81, the parent paying $28,100.	Investment in Stock of ABC Co. of London...... 28,100 Cash......... 28,100	Cash........... 10,000 Capital Stock.. 10,000
(2) Advance by the parent to the subsidiary, with transfer of draft for $14,000. The exchange rate upon receipt of the advance by the subsidiary was 2.80, the subsidiary deposit in the bank being £5,000.	Advances to ABC Co. of London... 14,000 Cash......... 14,000	Cash........... 5,000 Advances from ABC Co. (New York) ($14,000)..... 5,000
(3) Sale by the parent to the subsidiary of merchandise for $70,000. The exchange rate when the merchandise was received by the subsidiary was 2.80, the subsidiary taking up the shipment at £25,000. (It is assumed that merchandise was sold by the parent at its original cost.)	Accounts Receivable from ABC Co. of London... 70,000 Sales......... 70,000	Purchases....... 25,000 Accounts Payable to ABC Co. (New York) ($70,000)..... 25,000
(10) Payment by the subsidiary to the parent on account, with transfer of draft for $28,000. The exchange rate on the date of the purchase of the draft was 2.80, the subsidiary paying £10,000.	Cash........... 28,000 Accounts Receivable from ABC Co. of London....... 28,000	Accounts Payable to ABC Co. (New York) ($28,000).. 10,000 Cash......... 10,000
(11) Declaration and payment by the subsidiary of a dividend of £1,000. Transfer of a draft for this amount was made by the subsidiary. The exchange rate on the date of receipt of the dividend was 2.78, the parent deposit in the bank being $2,780.	Cash........... 2,780 Dividend Income......... 2,780	Dividends Paid.. 1,000 Cash......... 1,000

After the transactions for the ABC Company and its subsidiary are posted, trial balances for the two companies will appear as follows:

ABC Company (New York) and London Subsidiary
Preclosing Trial Balances
December 31, 1967

	Parent Dr.	Parent Cr.	Subsidiary Dr.	Subsidiary Cr.
Cash	$ 78,680		£ 7,000	
Accounts Receivable	175,000		5,000	
Accounts Receivable from ABC Co. of London	42,000			
Merchandise Inventory, January 1	185,000			
Furniture and Fixtures	85,000		3,500	
Allowance for Depreciation		$ 38,500		£ 350
Advances to ABC Co. of London	14,000			
Investment in Stock of ABC Co. of London	28,100			
Accounts Payable		115,000		2,500
Accounts Payable to ABC Co. (New York)				15,000
Advances from ABC Co. (New York)				5,000
Capital Stock		200,000		10,000
Retained Earnings		105,000		
Dividends Paid			1,000	
Sales		430,000		30,000
Purchases	200,000		37,000	
Expenses	83,500		9,350	
Dividend Income		2,780		
	$891,280	$891,280	£62,850	£62,850
Merchandise Inventory, December 31				
Acquired from Suppliers	$100,000	$100,000	£ 6,500	£ 6,500
Acquired from Parent			12,000	12,000
	$100,000	$100,000	£18,500	£18,500

TRANSLATION OF SUBSIDIARY COMPANY ACCOUNT BALANCES

At the end of the fiscal period, the subsidiary company prepares financial statements in terms of its own currency. At the same time it will submit to the parent company the trial balance and the adjusting data in support of the subsidiary statements so that the parent may be able to translate the data in preparing consolidated statements. Preclosing account balances and ending inventory data as originally submitted by the subsidiary in terms of pounds and restated by the parent company in terms of U.S. dollars are listed at the top of the next page.

ABC Company — London Subsidiary
Trial Balance Translated into U.S. Dollars
December 31, 1967

	Adjusted Trial Balance (Pounds)		Translation Rate*		Adjusted Trial Balance (U.S. Dollars)	
	Dr.	Cr.			Dr.	Cr.
Cash	£ 7,000		(C)	2.77	$ 19,390	
Accounts Receivable	5,000		(C)	2.77	13,850	
Furniture and Fixtures	3,500		(H)	2.80	9,800	
Allowance for Depreciation		£ 350	(H)	2.80		$ 980
Accounts Payable		2,500	(C)	2.77		6,925
Accounts Payable to ABC Co. (New York		15,000	(R)	$42,000		42,000
Advances from ABC Co. (New York)		5,000	(R)	$14,000		14,000
Capital Stock		10,000	(R)	$28,100		28,100
Dividends Paid	1,000		(R)	$ 2,780	2,780	
Sales		30,000	(A)	2.78		83,400
Purchases	37,000		(A) (R)	£12,000 at 2.78 $70,000	103,360	
Expenses	9,000		(A)	2.78	25,020	
Depreciation	350		(H)	2.80	980	
	£62,850	£62,850			$175,180	$175,405
Exchange Adjustment (to balance)					225	
					$175,405	$175,405
Merchandise Inventory, Dec. 31						
Acquired from Suppliers	£ 6,500	£ 6,500	(C)	2.77	$ 18,005	$ 18,005
Acquired from Parent	12,000	12,000	(H)	2.80	33,600	33,600
	£18,500	£18,500			$ 51,605	$ 51,605

*Translation rate:
(C) = Current rate — exchange rate at end of period (2.77).
(H) = Historical rate — exchange rate on date transaction was completed (rate on date of purchase of asset, 2.80; rate on date of acquisition of goods from parent, 2.80).
(R) = Reciprocal amount — dollar value on parent company books for corresponding transaction.
(A) = Average rate (2.78).

The following practices are generally applied in the restatement of subsidiary-parent company reciprocal accounts and have been applied in the example:

Paid-in capital and retained earnings. If the subsidiary company is formed by the parent, the paid-in capital accounts are restated at the exchange rate effective as of the date of organization. At dates subsequent to formation, paid-in capital balances will continue to be converted at original rates; retained earnings as of the beginning of the period will be reported at the amount that was recognized at the end of the preceding period — a dollar balance that brought the balance sheet of the preceding period into balance. If the subsidiary was organized prior to the date control was achieved by the parent, all balance sheet items, including paid-in capital and retained earnings balances, would be translated at the rate prevailing at the time control is achieved in preparing a consolidated balance sheet on this date. At dates subsequent to the acquisition of control, paid-in capital balances would continue to be converted at the rate originally applied; retained earnings as of the beginning of the period would be the amount reported as retained earnings on the balance sheet prepared at the end of the preceding period.

Intercompany trade account balances. Entries on the books of the parent and the subsidiary for intercompany purchases and sales are made just as though the units were not affiliated. Similar practices are followed for settlements between companies. Billing by a parent to a subsidiary in dollars, then, is recognized by an entry on the books of the subsidiary in the equivalent foreign currency at the time the goods are received with a memorandum notation of the dollar settlement required; subsequent payment in dollars when the foreign cost of dollar exchange is more or less than the amount originally recorded results in the recognition of a loss or a gain on exchange on the books of the subsidiary. Billing by a parent to a subsidiary in the foreign currency results in a dollar entry on the parent books at the rate of exchange on the date of the transfer with a memorandum notation of the foreign currency settlement amount; subsequent payment in the foreign currency that provides a greater or a lesser number of dollars than the amount originally recognized results in a gain or a loss on exchange on the books of the parent. When the sale is made by the subsidiary to the parent, similar considerations will apply. When there are open trade account balances between the companies at the end of the period, subsidiary company balances in foreign currency are restated at the dollar balances reported on the books of the parent. Reciprocal dollar balances are then eliminated in the preparation of consolidated statements.

Intercompany advances. Advances between related companies result in intercompany debtor and creditor balances on the books of the parent and the subsidiary. As in the case of trade account balances, when settlement is to be made in currency that is foreign to the particular company, memorandum accounts are maintained to report the foreign monetary settlement requirements; with fluctuations in the exchange rate, a gain or a loss on exchange is recognized upon settlement. At the end of the period, as in the case of trade accounts, advances shown in the foreign currency are restated at the dollar balances reported on the parent's books. Reciprocal dollar balances are then eliminated in the preparation of consolidated statements.

CONSOLIDATED STATEMENTS FOR PARENT AND SUBSIDIARY COMPANY

The parent company investment in the subsidiary may be carried by the cost method or by the equity method. When the cost method is employed, the parent recognizes dividends received from the subsidiary as revenue. The dollars reported as dividend income on the parent company's books provide the basis for restating the dividend paid balance on the subsidiary books. In developing working papers for consolidated statements, eliminations for an investment account maintained at cost are made in the usual manner; dividends received reported by the parent are applied against dividends paid reported by the subsidiary. Working papers and consolidated statements are completed in the usual manner.

When the investment is carried by the equity method, subsidiary earnings need to be restated in terms of the domestic currency and the parent then recognizes its share of such earnings; the investment account is charged and a revenue account is credited. Thereafter, in preparing working papers for consolidated statements, eliminations for an investment account maintained by the equity method are made in the usual manner.

Working papers for the preparation of consolidated statements for the ABC Company and its London subsidiary may be prepared in a form as illustrated on the following page. The closing entries for the parent and subsidiary company follow:

Transactions	Parent Company Books (Amounts in dollars)			Subsidiary Company Books (Amounts in pounds)		
15) To close nominal accounts ummarizing profit and loss activities.	Sales Dividend Income Purchases Expenses Profit and Loss	430,000 2,780	 200,000 83,500 149,280	Profit and Loss Sales Purchases Expenses	16,350 30,000	 37,000 9,350
6) To close balance in profit and ss account on subsidiary company's books to retained earnings, nd to close dividends paid balnce into retained earnings.				Profit and Loss Retained Earnings Retained Earnings Dividends Paid	2,150 1,000	 2,150 1,000
7) To close profit and loss account on parent's books.	Profit and Loss Retained Earnings	64,280	 64,280			

ABC Company (New York) and London Subsidiary
Working Papers for Consolidated Statements
December 31, 1967

	Parent Company	Subsidiary Company	Eliminations Dr.	Eliminations Cr.	Income Statement Dr.	Income Statement Cr.	Retained Earnings Dr.	Retained Earnings Cr.	Balance Sheet Dr.	Balance Sheet Cr.
Debits										
Cash	78,680	19,390							98,070	
Accounts Receivable	175,000	13,850							188,850	
Accounts Receivable from ABC Co. of London	42,000			(c) 42,000						
Merchandise Inventory, January 1	185,000				185,000					
Furniture and Fixtures	85,000	9,800							94,800	
Advances to ABC Co. of London	14,000			(d) 14,000						
Investment in Stock of ABC Co. of London	28,100									
Eliminate 100% of Capital Stock				(a) 28,100						
Dividends Paid		2,780		(b) 2,780						
Purchases	200,000	103,360		(e) 70,000	233,360					
Expenses	83,500	26,000			109,500					
Exchange Adjustment		225			225					
	891,280	175,405								
Merchandise Inventory, December 31 (Balance Sheet)	100,000	51,605							151,605	
Credits										
Allowance for Depreciation	38,500	980								39,480
Accounts Payable	115,000	6,925								121,925
Accounts Payable to ABC Co. (New York)		42,000	(c) 42,000							
Advances from ABC Co. (New York)		14,000	(d) 14,000							
Capital Stock, ABC Co.	200,000									200,000
Retained Earnings, ABC Co.	105,000							105,000		
Capital Stock, ABC Co. of London		28,100								
Eliminate 100%			(a) 28,100							
Sales	430,000	83,400	(e) 70,000			443,400				
Dividend Income	2,780		(b) 2,780							
	891,280	175,405								
Merchandise Inventory, December 31 (Income Statement)	100,000	51,605				151,605				
			156,880	156,880	528,085	595,005		105,000	533,325	361,405
Net Income to Retained Earnings					66,920			66,920		
Retained Earnings to Balance Sheet							171,920			171,920
					595,005	595,005	171,920	171,920	533,325	533,325

RECOMMENDATIONS FOR MODIFYING TRANSLATION PROCEDURES

The principles and the procedures that have been described and illustrated were developed many decades ago when the gold standard prevailed, and they provided a satisfactory approach to accounting for foreign and domestic units when currencies were freely exchangeable and rates of exchange maintained relative stability. However, for some time now, serious questions have been raised as to the adequacy of these rules under conditions that are vastly different from the conditions that prevailed when the rules were formulated.

The distinction that is made between current and noncurrent items for purposes of translation has been the subject of special attention and criticism. Conventional practice calls for the translation of current assets and current liabilities at the current rate of exchange — the rate prevailing at the time the statements are prepared — and for the translation of noncurrent assets and noncurrent liabilities at historical rates — the rates prevailing at the time the asset was acquired or the liability was assumed. A number of authorities have maintained that, for purposes of translation, a distinction should be made, not between current and noncurrent items, but between monetary items and nonmonetary items. It has been argued that, to arrive at meaningful statements, the monetary items — cash and any claims to cash, together with all obligations requiring settlement in cash — should be translated at the rate prevailing on the date of the balance sheet; nonmonetary items should be translated at the rates prevailing at the time the items were recorded. Cash, trade notes and accounts receivable, long-term receivables including investments in bonds, and all of the liabilities, current as well as fixed, would then be reported at the current rate; merchandise inventory, supplies, and plant and equipment would be reported at historical rates.[1]

The conventional procedures, these authorities maintain, fail to deal realistically with the translation problem. Long-term liabilities no less than short-term liabilities need to be reported at the dollar amounts that are anticipated in their settlement. On the other hand, inventories and supplies, like plant and equipment items, should be reported at the dollar amounts involved in their acquisition without reference to changes that have taken place in the exchange rate.

The alternative approach to the translation of foreign accounts may be regarded as essentially a refinement of conventional procedures.

---

[1]It will be recalled that a distinction between monetary items and nonmonetary items was required in the preparation of financial statements adjusted for price-level changes. For further discussion of the monetary-nonmonetary item distinction, refer to the authors' *Intermediate Accounting, Comprehensive Volume*, Fourth Edition, pp. 886–888.

Under conventional procedures, no attempt is made to establish historical dollar costs for working capital items, even when these can be determined; it is felt that a valid statement of working capital calls for applying the current rate to current assets and to current liabilities. The application of the current rate rather than historical rates to working capital items provides, in effect, a revaluation of these items; the exchange gain or loss that emerges in the process of translation, then, is the product of the changes in rates associated with the current assets and the current liabilities. In applying the alternative approach, the net monetary pool is substituted for the working capital pool. An exchange gain or loss is measured by the changes in rates associated with the monetary assets and the monetary liabilities.

The Accounting Principles Board of the American Institute of Certified Public Accountants has recognized that the fair presentation of foreign investments and operations under present conditions may call for some departure from conventional translating procedures and has authorized the preparation of an Accounting Research Study dealing with this matter. Pending completion of this study and the preparation of recommendations that may be deemed desirable on the basis of such a study, the Board, in its *Opinion No. 6* issued in 1965, made the following statement modifying the provisions on foreign operations and foreign exchange as stated in *Accounting Research Bulletin No. 43:*

> The Board is of the opinion that translation of long-term receivables and long-term liabilities at current exchange rates is appropriate in many circumstances.[1]

The authors are in full agreement with those favoring the alternative approach to the translation of foreign accounts and are of the opinion that this may very well be the direction that practice will take in the future.[2] Illustrations in this chapter, however, are developed within the framework of conventional practice, and the problems at the end of the chapter assume application of the procedures that have been illustrated.

---

[1]*Opinion of the Accounting Principles Board No. 6*, "Status of Accounting Research Bulletins," 1965 (New York: American Institute of Certified Public Accountants), p. 42.

[2]Paul Grady in *Accounting Research Study No. 7*, "Inventory of Generally Accepted Accounting Principles for Business Enterprises," 1965 (New York: American Institute of Certified Public Accountants), page 332, comments on the AICPA recommendations on foreign operations and foreign exchange as stated in Chapter 12 of *Accounting Research Bulletin No. 43* as follows: "The foregoing chapter of ARB No. 43 has become outmoded in relation to present practice, particularly in the translation of long-term assets and liabilities, due to the prevalence of major currency revaluations and continued substantial inflation in many countries."

The reader may wish to consult two highly regarded research studies that include important suggestions for improving foreign translation practices: *Research Report No. 36*, "Management Association Problems in Foreign Operations," 1960 (New York: National Association of Accountants), and Samuel R. Hepworth, *Reporting Foreign Operations*, 1956 (Ann Arbor, Michigan: Bureau of Business Research, University of Michigan). The National Associa-

SPECIAL PROBLEMS

In war and postwar years, many serious problems have arisen to complicate foreign exchange accounting. Departures from the gold standard, currency devaluations, inflation, a variety of exchange rates under different conditions and for different purposes, and blocked currencies have created special difficulties. With these conditions, it is important that particular care be taken by the accountant in interpreting statements that summarize foreign activities.

Examples in this chapter have assumed that consolidation provided a valid reflection of the activities and the status of the affiliated units. Frequently, special factors may suggest that foreign affiliates be excluded from consolidation. Investments in the foreign units, then, would be reported on the separate statements of the domestic unit with special presentations, notations, or footnotes offering pertinent data relative to such investments. Consolidation may be given up in favor of some alternative investment presentation as a result of such factors as restrictions on the movement of foreign exchange, restrictions on the transfer of properties, special legislation regulating activities between affiliates, unfavorable legislation affecting foreign units, widely fluctuating rates of exchange, changing governments, or significant time periods between fiscal year closing dates for affiliated companies.[1]

---

tion of Accountants in the March, 1960, issue of the *N.A.A. Bulletin* summarizes its research study conclusions for translation of asset and liability balances as follows:

> From the standpoint of the U.S. shareholder, two classes of items may be distinguished in the balance sheet of a foreign subsidiary. First, there are *financial items* consisting of local currency and claims to receive or to pay a fixed number of local currency units. The dollar equivalent of local currency financial assets and liabilities is immediately affected by a change in the rate of exchange. The reason is that if the local currency declines relative to the U.S. dollar, financial assets in local currency will yield fewer dollars on conversion and debts payable in local currency can be satisfied with fewer dollars. Local currency financial assets are always at risk from unfavorable movements in the exchange rate. This risk can be minimized by keeping net financial assets of the foreign subsidiary as low as possible. Because financial items are immediately and directly affected by fluctuations in the exchange rates, the exchange rate prevailing on the date of the balance sheet yields the best translation for financial items expressed in a foreign currency.
>
> The *physical assets* constitute the second class of items in the balance sheet of a foreign subsidiary. Physical items such as inventories and fixed assets tend to be unaffected by exchange rate fluctuations. Since a substantial decline in value of a foreign currency unit relative to the dollar is usually a consequence of inflation in the foreign country, prices in that country may be expected to rise and physical assets will command increased selling prices in the devalued currency. Such assets are logically translated at the rate of exchange current on the date the foreign subsidiary acquired the assets.

Professor Hepworth maintains that translation procedures should be adopted which "restrict the exchange adjustment to what it should logically represent, namely gains or losses caused by changing dollar value of foreign assets and liabilities which represent contractual rights to cash, or to the receipt of cash, or contractual obligations for the disbursement of cash. Only if this is the case does the exchange adjustment have real significance in terms of managerial action and responsibility assignment."

[1]The Research Department of the American Institute of Certified Public Accountants found U.S. companies employing a variety of forms of disclosure with respect to foreign investments. For a summary of findings, see *Survey of Consolidated Financial Statement Practices*, 1956 (New York: American Institute of Certified Public Accountants), pp. 8, 26–31.

The Committee on Accounting Procedure of the American Institute of Certified Public Accountants has made the following general recommendations relative to accounting for foreign operations:

> A sound procedure for United States companies to follow is to show earnings from foreign operations in their own accounts only to the extent that funds have been received in the United States or unrestricted funds are available for transmission thereto. Appropriate provision should be made also for known losses.
>
> Any foreign earnings reported beyond the amounts received in the United States should be carefully considered in the light of all the facts. The amounts should be disclosed if they are significant, and they should be reserved against to the extent that their realization in dollars appears to be doubtful.
>
> As to assets held abroad, the accounting should take into consideration the fact that most foreign assets stand in some degree of jeopardy, so far as ultimate realization by United States owners is concerned. Under these conditions it is important that special care be taken in each case to make full disclosure in the financial statements of United States companies of the extent to which they include significant foreign items.
>
> Where more than one foreign exchange rate is in effect, care should be exercised to select the one most clearly realistic and appropriate in the circumstances.[1]

The Committee observes that a major change in the exchange rate may call for certain translation procedures other than those that are normally applied. The effects of such a change are stated as follows:

> Long-term liabilities and capital stock stated in foreign currency should not be translated at the closing rate, but at the rates of exchange prevailing when they were originally incurred or issued. This is a general rule, but an exception may exist in respect to long-term debt incurred or capital stock issued in connection with the acquisition of fixed assets, permanent investments, or long-term receivables a short time before a substantial and presumably permanent change in the exchange rate. In such instances it may be appropriate to state the long-term debt or the capital stock at the new rate and proper to deal with the exchange differences as an adjustment of the cost of the assets acquired.[2]

The Committee makes the following observation on the translation of income statement data after a major change in the exchange rate:

> Where a major change in an exchange rate takes place during a fiscal year, there may be situations in which more realistic results will be obtained if income computed in foreign currencies is translated for the entire fiscal year at the new rates in effect after such major fluctuation. . . .[3]

---

[1]*Accounting Research Bulletin No. 43, Restatement and Revision of Accounting Research Bulletins*, 1953 (New York: American Institute of Certified Public Accountants), Chapter 12, "Foreign Operations and Foreign Exchange," pp. 111 and 112.

[2]*Ibid.*, p. 114.

[3]*Ibid.*, p. 115.

QUESTIONS

1. (a) What is meant by the rate of exchange? (b) Distinguish between a market rate of exchange and an official rate of exchange. (c) When more than one rate is in effect, what rate should be employed in translating foreign accounts into dollars?

2. Distinguish between a direct exchange quotation and an indirect quotation.

3. Describe the conversion of a foreign decimal currency into United States dollars and compare this with the conversion of a nondecimal currency.

4. The Boston Company sells goods abroad and bills its customers in terms of their own currencies. (a) How should the company record such sales? (b) How will the company record remittances from such foreign accounts? (c) Would your answers be any different if the customers abroad are subsidiary companies?

5. The Ward House, an importing concern, purchases goods from Italy and is billed for 1,000,000 lire. At the date of purchase the exchange rate for the foreign currency is $.001625. However, at the time of settlement of the account the lira is quoted at $.0016. (a) Does the Ward House gain or lose by the exchange fluctuation? Explain. (b) Would your answer be different if the purchase price had been billed at $1,625?

6. Weedon, Inc. purchases goods regularly from a French supplier. Settlement is made in francs and credit terms are 60 days. On December 31, the end of the fiscal period, Weedon, Inc. books show a liability to the French supplier of $202,000 representing a purchase for 1,000,000 francs that was made when the franc was quoted at $.2020. (a) What adjustment, if any, would you make on December 31 if the franc is quoted on this date at $.2030? (b) What adjustment would you make on this date if the franc is quoted at $.2010? Give reasons.

7. Describe several methods for arriving at an average rate of exchange.

8. Give the practices that are generally followed in translating the following classes of accounts stated in foreign currencies:

(a) Current assets.
(b) Current liabilities.
(c) Allowances applying to current assets.
(d) Noncurrent assets.
(e) Allowances applying to noncurrent assets.
(f) Noncurrent liabilities.

9. (a) Distinguish between realized and unrealized exchange gains and losses. (b) What treatment would you recommend for gains and losses of each category?

10. (a) How do you explain the emergence of an "exchange adjustment" balance in converting a trial balance from a foreign currency standard to the domestic standard? (b) Describe the alternative ways in which this balance may be reported on the combined or consolidated financial statements. Indicate your preference and give reasons for such preference. (c) What disposition is made of the exchange adjustment in the succeeding period?

11. The following balances are found on the books of a foreign branch. Assuming the use of conventional procedures, state how each balance would be translated into domestic currency for purposes of home office and branch combined statements.

(a) Cash
(b) Beginning Merchandise Inventory
(c) Ending Merchandise Inventory
(d) Equipment
(e) Allowance for Depreciation
(f) Accounts Receivable
(g) Allowance for Bad Debts
(h) Prepaid Insurance
(i) Accrued Expenses
(j) Home Office — Current
(k) Remittances to Home Office
(l) Remittances from Home Office
(m) Merchandise Shipments from Home Office
(n) Sales
(o) Expenses
(p) Depreciation

12. The following balances appear on the books of a foreign subsidiary company. The subsidiary was organized by the parent and is wholly owned. Assuming the use of conventional procedures, state how each balance would be translated in preparing consolidated statements for parent and subsidiary.

(a) Capital Stock
(b) Additional Paid-in Capital
(c) Retained Earnings (balance at the beginning of the period)
(d) Advances from Parent
(e) Accounts Payable to Parent
(f) Plant and Equipment
(g) Allowance for Depreciation
(h) Bonds Payable
(i) Dividends Payable

13. Assume in Question 12 that only 80% of the stock of the subsidiary had been acquired several years after its formation. How would each item listed be converted?

14. There is some controversy on the rates to be used in translating balance sheet items. (a) Describe the alternative positions that are taken on this matter. (b) What position would you take? Give reasons.

15. Some have insisted that the translation of long-term debt should be made at the current exchange rate in view of the fact that the liabilities will be paid off in terms of the rate of exchange prevailing at the date of payment and the current rate is the best approximation of such rate. Evaluate this position.

16. The Beals Co. has a foreign branch in a country that is at war. Transfer of the foreign currency is blocked and the branch investment is considered to be in serious jeopardy. How would you recommend that this situation be recognized on the statements of the home office?

EXERCISES

1. Simpson Company, of Detroit, sells merchandise to Burdick Company, of Windsor, Canada, on November 4. The sales price is $26,000; the exchange rate of the Canadian dollar on this date is $.9225. Settlement of the invoice is made by Burdick Company on December 20; the exchange rate for the Canadian dollar on this date is $.93. Give the entries that would be made on the books of the two companies for the transfer of goods and the settlement, assuming that (1) $26,000 represents the sales price in American dollars; (2) $26,000 represents the sales price in Canadian dollars.

2. The following transactions took place between the home office of the Sawyer Company, of Cincinnati, and a branch located in Paris, France. Give the entries required on the books of the home office and on the books of the branch for each of the following transactions:

(a) A draft for 300,000 francs was sent to the branch. The exchange rate for the franc expressed in terms of dollars on the date of the purchase of the draft was $.2041.
(b) Merchandise costing $81,800 was sent to the branch. The exchange rate on the date of shipment was $.2045.
(c) The branch purchased furniture and fixtures for 50,000 francs. This property item is to be carried on the books of the home office, and the home office is informed of the purchase. The exchange rate on the date of the purchase was $.205.
(d) The branch sent a draft for $16,400 to the home office. The exchange rate on the date of purchase of the draft was $.205.
(e) The branch sent a draft for 60,000 francs to the home office. The exchange rate on the date of deposit of the draft in the bank was $.204.
(f) The branch returned merchandise that was unsuited for its use on which the original billing was $4,090.
(g) The home office informed the branch of a charge for depreciation at 10% of the cost of furniture and fixtures (see acquisition in [c]).

3. In January, 1967, the Chang Company, of San Francisco, established a wholly owned subsidiary in Hong Kong. Give the entries that would be required on the books of the two companies for each of the transactions listed below. The Chang Company maintains its investment account in the subsidiary company by the equity method.

(a) In establishing the subsidiary company, the parent sends a draft for 1,000,000 Hong Kong dollars in payment for 10,000 shares. The rate for the Hong Kong dollar in terms of the American dollar is $.176 when the parent purchases the draft.
(b) In February the parent transfers to the subsidiary company merchandise billed at a price of $77,000 in American dollars. The rate of exchange at the time is $.175.
(c) In May the subsidiary sends to the parent a draft for $35,000 in American dollars in partial settlement of the amount owed. The draft is acquired by the subsidiary when the rate of exchange is $.175.
(d) In June the subsidiary company ships to the parent company merchandise billed at 175,000 Hong Kong dollars. The parent company

credits the receivable account that it has with the subsidiary, using an exchange rate of $.175.

(e) In December the subsidiary company sends the parent a draft for 50,000 Hong Kong dollars representing a dividend on the shares held by the parent. The draft is converted into cash by the parent at an exchange rate of $.174.

4. On December 31, the Pakistan Branch of the James Company of Los Angeles reported the trial balance in rupees shown below.

Cash	3,500	
Accounts Receivable	24,000	
Remittances to Home Office	35,000	
Merchandise Inventory, January 1	28,500	
Merchandise Shipments from Home Office	74,000	
Accounts Payable		7,500
Remittances from Home Office		21,500
Home Office — Current		54,000
Sales		102,000
Operating Expenses	20,000	
	185,000	185,000

Exchange rates for the rupee at the beginning of the year and at the end of the year were $.21 and $.20 respectively. The average rate for the year was $.208.

On the home office books, Merchandise Shipments to Branch is shown at $15,530, Remittances to Branch is shown at $4,500, Remittances from Branch is shown at $7,680, and Branch — Current is shown at $12,000.

Prepare a trial balance in United States dollars for the Pakistan branch as of December 31.

5. Transactions of the First State Bank of Wilmington, California, with a foreign correspondent for one month were as follows:

Debits

July 2. Remittance, demand draft, lire 3,500 (lira rate: $.3505).
8. Remittance, sight draft, lire 2,700 (lira rate: $.3525).
20. Remittance, cable, lire 4,260 (lira rate: $.3558).

Credits

July 5. Sight draft, lire 1,900 (lira rate: $.3512).
15. Cable, lire 4,000 (lira rate: $.3547).
26. Demand draft, lire 3,820 (lira rate: $.3572).

Assuming an exchange rate for the lira at the end of July of $.3575, determine the exchange profit or loss for July and give the balances in the account at the end of July in both foreign and domestic currency.

PROBLEMS

17-1. Adjusted trial balances for the Spencer Company and its Canadian branch office on December 31, 1967, follow:

Spencer Company and Canadian Branch
Adjusted Trial Balances
December 31, 1967

	U.S. Dollars		Canadian Dollars	
	Dr.	Cr.	Dr.	Cr.
Cash	55,200		22,000	
Accounts Receivable	61,600		32,500	
Allowance for Bad Debts		1,600		1,000
Merchandise Inventory, Jan. 1	85,000		36,000	
Furniture and Equipment	125,000		60,000	
Allowance for Depreciation		40,000		42,000
Accounts Payable		36,600		20,500
Branch	78,800			
Remittances from Branch		9,350		
Remittances to Home Office			10,000	
Capital Stock		200,000		
Retained Earnings		108,050		
Home Office				80,000
Sales		300,000		172,000
Merchandise Shipments to Branch		30,000		
Purchases	215,000		95,000	
Merchandise Shipments from Home Office			32,000	
Expenses	105,000		28,000	
	725,600	725,600	315,500	315,500
Merchandise Inventory, Dec. 31:				
Acquired from Suppliers	120,000	120,000	22,000	22,000
Acquired from Home Office			10,500	10,500
Total	120,000	120,000	32,500	32,500

The exchange rates for the Canadian dollar were as follows:

Beginning of year	.96
Average for year	.94
End of year	.92
On date of acquisition of furniture and equipment	1.04

All of the branch merchandise on January 1 had been acquired from Canadian suppliers. Branch merchandise from the home office on December 31 had an original cost to the home office of $9,800.

Instructions: (1) Prepare a statement showing the translation of the branch balances into United States dollars.

(2) Give the entries on the home office books to recognize the branch earnings for the year and to close the home office accounts at the end of the year.

17-2. Carr and Hobbs, Inc. opened a branch in Holland at the beginning of 1967. Transactions of the branch in 1967 are summarized below.

(a) Cash received from home office, January 1	$ 27,050
(b) Merchandise received from home office: January 1	$135,250
June 30	$218,400
(c) Cash remitted to home office, June 30	800,000 guilders
(d) Purchase of furniture and fixtures for cash at the beginning of the year	150,000 guilders
(e) Sales on account	2,000,000 guilders
(f) Collections on accounts receivable	1,650,000 guilders
(g) Purchases on account	100,000 guilders
(h) Payments on accounts payable	80,000 guilders
(i) Expenses paid	400,000 guilders

Adjusting data at the end of 1967 were as follows:

Merchandise inventory: acquired in Holland	20,000 guilders
acquired from home office	205,000 guilders
Accrued expenses	10,000 guilders

Furniture and fixtures are depreciated at the rate of 20% per year.

Exchange rates for the guilder in 1967 were:

January 1	.2705
June 30	.2730
December 31	.2765
Average rate	.2735

Instructions: (1) Give the entries for the branch to record transactions for 1967 and to adjust and close the books.

(2) Prepare a statement showing the translation of the branch balances into United States dollars.

(3) Give all of the entries that would be made by the home office, including the entry to recognize branch earnings for 1967.

17-3. The trial balances on December 31, 19––, of South Bay Importers, Inc. and its Philippines branch are shown at the top of the following page.

The branch purchased its building and its furniture and fixtures at the middle of the year, the exchange rate for pesos being $.30 at the time. Both home office and branch recognize depreciation on buildings at the rate of 10% per year and depreciation on furniture and fixtures at the rate of 20% per year. Depreciation charges are divided equally between selling expenses and general and administrative expenses.

South Bay Importers, Inc. and Philippines Branch
Trial Balances
December 31, 19--

	South Bay Importers, Inc.		Philippines Branch (In pesos)	
	Dr.	Cr.	Dr.	Cr.
Cash	$ 62,500		25,000	
Accounts Receivable	85,000		145,000	
Remittances to Philippines Branch	30,000			
Philippines Branch	83,000			
Inventories, January 1	48,000			
Prepaid Expenses	23,500		6,000	
Furniture and Fixtures	14,500		10,000	
Allowance for Depreciation of Furniture and Fixtures		$ 7,000		
Building	150,000		200,000	
Allowance for Depreciation of Building		30,000		
Land	24,000			
Accrued Expenses		2,500		1,500
Accounts Payable		46,000		86,000
Capital Stock, $100 par		300,000		
Retained Earnings		97,000		
Remittances from Home Office				98,500
Home Office				285,500
Sales		209,500		238,500
Merchandise Shipments to Branch (at cost)		83,500		
Purchases	225,000			
Merchandise Shipments from Home Office			278,300	
Selling Expenses	18,000		28,000	
General and Administrative Expenses	12,000		17,700	
	$775,500	$775,500	710,000	710,000

Inventories on December 31 are as follows: home office, $58,400; branch, 133,000 pesos (cost to home office, $43,900).

Exchange rates for pesos during the year were:

January 1	$.32
December 31	.30
Average rate for the year	.31

Instructions: (1) Prepare working papers for combined statements for the home office and the branch.

(2) Prepare a combined income statement and a combined balance sheet.

17-4. At the beginning of 1967 the George Wilson Company establishes a wholly owned subsidiary in West Germany under the name of the Rhine Corporation with a capital of 1,000,000 deutschemarks. During 1967, the following transactions take place:

(a) The parent sells merchandise to the subsidiary at cost, $150,000, billing the subsidiary in deutschemarks. The exchange rate for the deutschemark on the date of sale is $.240.
(b) The subsidary purchases furniture and fixtures at the beginning of 1967 for 20,000 deutschemarks. The rate of exchange on the date of the purchase is $.2375.
(c) The subsidiary sells merchandise on account for 690,000 deutschemarks.
(d) Subsidiary collections on account total 600,000 deutschemarks.
(e) The subsidiary sends drafts to the parent in partial settlement of account as follows:

200,000 deutschemarks ...... exchange rate, $.237
150,000 deutschemarks ...... exchange rate, $.235
100,000 deutschemarks ...... exchange rate, $.233

(f) In December, 1967, the subsidiary acquires buildings for 400,000 deutschemarks and machinery for 450,000 deutschemarks. The rate of exchange on the date of the purchases is $.232.
(g) Operating expenses paid by the subsidiary total 46,000 deutschemarks.

On December 31, 1967, the parent company prepares a trial balance of its accounts after adjustment except for the ending inventory as follows:

Cash	$ 137,500	
Notes Receivable	105,000	
Accounts Receivable	242,500	
Inventories, January 1, 1967	250,000	
Prepaid Expenses	18,000	
Investment in Stock of Rhine Corp., 100% ownership (10,000 shares of 100 deutschemarks par) cost	232,000	
Furniture and Fixtures	58,000	
Allowance for Depreciation of Furniture and Fixtures		$ 17,500
Buildings	400,000	
Allowance for Depreciation of Buildings		205,000
Land	50,000	
Accounts Payable		149,500
Accrued Expenses		5,500
Deposits Received on Machines Leased		86,000
Deferred Income on Leasing		39,500
Capital Stock		500,000
Additional Paid-In Capital		100,000
Retained Earnings		132,500
Sales		1,489,500
Purchases	1,038,000	
Operating Expenses	194,000	
	$2,725,000	$2,725,000

The subsidiary recognizes no depreciation on buildings and machinery for 1967; depreciation on subsidiary furniture and fixtures is to be recognized at 20% per year. Inventories on hand on December 31, 1967, are as follows: parent, $150,000; subsidiary, 165,000 deutschemarks. The average rate of exchange for the deutschemark for 1967 is $.234, and the rate of exchange on December 31, 1967, is $.230.

Instructions: (1) Give the entries that are required on the books of the subsidiary to record the transactions for 1967 and to adjust and close the accounts at the end of 1967.

(2) Prepare trial balances for the subsidiary in deutschemarks and in United States dollars. (Indicate rates used in conversions.)

(3) Prepare working papers for consolidated statements.

(4) Prepare a consolidated income statement and a consolidated balance sheet.

17-5. Following are the balance sheets for The Frost Corporation, of Santa Monica, California, and its Swedish subsidiary, the Belt Company, on December 31, 1967:

The Frost Corporation and Swedish Subsidiary
Balance Sheets
December 31, 1967

	The Frost Corporation	Belt Co. (In kronor)
Assets		
Cash	$ 47,500	125,000
Notes receivable	25,000	80,000
Accounts receivable	69,500	225,000
Inventories	174,000	525,000
Prepaid expenses	3,500	15,000
Investment in Belt Company — 80% of shares outstanding (at cost)	90,000	
Furniture and fixtures (net)	6,000	30,000
Buildings (net)	88,000	
Land	96,500	
Total assets	$600,000	1,000,000
Liabilities and Stockholders' Equity		
Accounts payable	$ 89,600	275,000
Accrued expenses	5,400	25,000
Bonds payable	100,000	
Capital stock	250,000	500,000
Additional paid-in capital	60,000	
Retained earnings	95,000	200,000
Total liabilities and stockholders' equity	$600,000	1,000,000

The Frost Corporation acquired its holdings in the Belt Company on January 2, 1967. The latter company had a capital of 550,000 kronor, including a retained earnings balance of 50,000 kronor, on this date. The exchange rate on January 2, 1967, was $.200.

The Belt Company acquired the furniture and fixtures in May, 1966. The Belt Company owes the parent $25,000 on account as of December 31, 1967. This amount is included in its accounts payable as 125,000 kronor.

The December 31, 1967, inventory of The Frost Corporation includes merchandise of $36,500 acquired from its subsidiary when the exchange rate was $.192. The merchandise cost the Belt Company 155,000 kronor.

The exchange rate on December 31, 1967, was $.194.

Instructions: (1) Prepare working papers for a consolidated balance sheet for the parent and its subsidiary.

(2) Prepare a consolidated balance sheet as of December 31, 1967.

17-6. Trial balances prepared for the Southern Supply Company and its Canadian branch store on December 31, 19--, are listed below.

Southern Supply Company and Canadian Branch
Trial Balances
December 31, 19--

	Home Office (U.S. dollars)		Canadian Branch (Canadian dollars)	
	Dr.	Cr.	Dr.	Cr.
Cash	$ 76,000		$ 10,000	
Accounts Receivable	66,000		20,000	
Merchandise Inventory, January 1	37,200		14,800	
Furniture and Fixtures (net)	14,400		5,000	
Remittances to Branch	24,000			
Branch — Current	23,600			
Accounts Payable		$ 18,800		$ 2,400
Remittances from Home Office				23,850
Home Office — Current				23,550
Allowance for Overvaluation of Branch Merchandise		12,560		
Capital Stock		100,000		
Retained Earnings, January 1		77,440		
Sales		249,600		84,000
Shipments to Branch		41,600		
Purchases	224,000		12,000	
Shipments from Home Office			52,000	
Selling Expenses	22,800		12,000	
General and Administrative Expenses	12,000		8,000	
	$500,000	$500,000	$133,800	$133,800

Merchandise sent by the home office to the branch was billed at 25% above cost. Additional merchandise required by the branch was acquired from United States sources and has been recorded on the books of the branch in terms of American dollars.

The merchandise inventory of the branch at the beginning and the end of the year is composed of the following:

	Jan. 1	Dec. 31
Goods acquired from outsiders, at cost	$ 4,000	$ 3,600
Goods acquired from home office, at billed price	10,800	19,400
Total	$14,800	$23,000

The merchandise inventory of the home office at the end of the year cost $27,000.

The branch acquired its furniture and fixtures when the exchange rate for the Canadian dollar was $1.02.

Exchange rates for the Canadian dollar were as follows:

January 1	$1.02
December 31	1.03
Average during year	1.024

Instructions: (1) Prepare working papers for combined statements for the home office and the branch.

(2) Prepare a combined income statement and a combined balance sheet.

17-7. A branch office was established in Liverpool on January 1, 19--, by the Atlantic Sales Company of Boston. The transactions of the branch for the year are summarized as follows:

Cash received from home office	$10,000 (rate: 2.80) $ 5,000 (rate: 2.78)
Merchandise received from home office	$26,000 (rate: 2.80) $20,000 (rate: 2.76)
Cash remitted to home office	£ 4,000 (rate: 2.78) £ 4,000 (rate: 2.77)
Purchase of furniture and fixtures for cash	£ 500 (rate: 2.80)
Sales on account	£35,000
Accounts receivable collected	£27,000
Purchases on account	£10,000
Accounts payable paid	£ 8,500
Operating expenses paid	£ 6,000

The following adjustments are required at the end of the year:

(a) Merchandise inventory . . . £ 8,450

(b) Accrued operating expenses . . . £ 150

(c) Depreciation on furniture and fixtures, 10%.

(d) The branch manager in addition to his salary is to be allowed a bonus of 10% of the net income accruing to the home office (this amount is to be set up as a liability on the books of the branch).

The average rate of exchange is $2.78. The exchange rate on December 31, is $2.81.

Instructions: (1) Prepare the entries for the branch to record its activities for the year.

(2) Prepare working papers for the branch in both currencies.

(3) Prepare statements for the branch in both currencies.

(4) Prepare the entries to adjust and close the books of the branch.

(5) Prepare all of the entries for the home office resulting from the above information.

17-8. The Pelham Company, Ltd., of Canada, keeps its records in Canadian dollars and presents the following balance sheet as of December 31, 19--:

Assets		
Cash		$ 10,000
Accounts receivable		300,000
Inventories		250,000
Fixed assets (U.S. dollar cost at date of acquisition)		100,000
Total assets		$660,000
Liabilities and Stockholders' Equity		
Notes payable		$ 15,000
Accounts payable		150,000
Due to Parent Company (U.S. dollars)		200,000
Capital stock, $100 par		150,000
Retained earnings:		
Beginning of year	$ 25,000	
Profit for year	120,000	145,000
Total liabilities and stockholders' equity		$660,000

The following further information is available:

Accounts receivable: all Canadian funds.
Notes payable: all Canadian funds.
Accounts payable: $30,000 payable in Canadian funds and $120,000 in United States funds.

Inventories:

Raw material purchased in Canadian funds	$ 20,000
Raw material purchased in United States funds	100,000
Goods in process	130,000

This last item includes material purchased both in the United States and in Canada, with labor all performed in Canada. The total purchases for the year average approximately 85% from the United States and 15% from Canada. The labor cost approximates 13% of the cost of materials.

Assume no intercompany profit on materials purchased from the parent company.

Instructions: Convert this statement to a United States currency basis for consolidation with the balance sheet of the parent company. Assume that the Canadian dollar is worth $1.05 in United States funds.

(AICPA adapted)

17-9. Trial balances as of December 31, 1957, of the Parker Company and its two subsidiaries were as shown below.

Parker Company and Subsidiary Companies
Trial Balances
December 31, 1957

	Parker Company		Domestic Subsidiary		Mexican Subsidiary (Pesos)	
	Dr.	Cr.	Dr.	Cr.	Dr.	Cr.
Cash	$ 10,000		$ 1,500		10,000	
Accounts Receivable — Trade	30,000		8,000		35,000	
Accounts Receivable — Merchandise in Transit to Domestic Subsidiary	4,000					
Inventories	20,000				83,000	
Investments (at cost):						
Domestic subsidiary, 900 shares acquired 12/31/56	9,000					
Foreign subsidiary, 1,000 shares acquired 12/31/56	12,000					
Fixed Assets	45,000		3,500		175,000	
Goodwill			2,000			
Cost of Sales	300,000		15,000		300,000	
Depreciation	3,000		200		7,000	
Taxes	15,000		400		15,000	
Selling Expenses	42,000		2,400		27,000	
Administrative and General Expenses	35,000		2,000		18,000	
Dividends Declared			1,000			
Sales — Trade		$400,000		$21,000		381,000
Sales — Domestic Subsidiary		10,000				
Accounts Payable — Trade		25,000				7,000
Dividend Payable				1,000		
Long-Term Debt (due 1/1/60)						100,000
Reserve for Depreciation		15,000		2,000		75,000
Capital Stock		50,000		*10,000		*100,000
Retained Earnings, 1/1/57		25,000		2,000		7,000
	$525,000	$525,000	$36,000	$36,000	670,000	670,000

*1,000 shares issued and outstanding.

Data:

In April, 1957, the Mexican peso was devalued from United States $.12, the prevailing rate of exchange on December 31, 1956, to $.08, which was also the prevailing rate of exchange on December 31, 1957.

Instructions: (1) Prepare a working trial balance in United States dollars for the Mexican subsidiary.

(2) Prepare working papers for consolidated statements.

(AICPA adapted)

17-10. The Ward Corporation acquired The Pierce Corporation on January 1, 1966, by the purchase at book value of all outstanding capital stock. The Pierce Corporation is located in a Central American country whose monetary unit is the peso. The Pierce Corporation's accounting records were continued without change; a trial balance, in pesos, of the balance sheet accounts at the purchase date follows:

The Pierce Corporation
Trial Balance (in pesos)
January 1, 1966

	Debit	Credit
Cash	P 3,000	
Accounts Receivable	5,000	
Inventories	32,000	
Machinery and Equipment	204,000	
Allowance for Depreciation		P 42,000
Accounts Payable		81,400
Capital Stock		50,000
Retained Earnings		70,600
	P244,000	P244,000

The Pierce Corporation's trial balance, in pesos, at December 31, 1967, is shown at the top of the following page.

The following additional information is available:

(1) All of The Pierce Corporation's export sales are made to its parent company and are accumulated in the account Sales — Foreign. The balance in the account Due from The Ward Corporation is the total of unpaid invoices. All foreign sales are billed in United States dollars. The reciprocal accounts on the parent company's books show total 1967 purchases as $471,000 and the total of unpaid invoices as $70,500.

(2) Depreciation is computed by the straight-line method over a 10-year life for all depreciable assets. Machinery costing P20,000 was purchased on December 31, 1966, and no depreciation was recorded for

The Pierce Corporation
Trial Balance (in pesos)
December 31, 1967

	Debit	Credit
Cash	P 25,000	
Accounts Receivable	20,000	
Allowance for Bad Debts		P 500
Due from The Ward Corporation	30,000	
Inventories, December 31, 1967	110,000	
Prepaid Expenses	3,000	
Machinery and Equipment	210,000	
Allowance for Depreciation		79,900
Accounts Payable		22,000
Income Taxes Payable		40,000
Notes Payable		60,000
Capital Stock		50,000
Retained Earnings		100,600
Sales — Domestic		170,000
Sales — Foreign		200,000
Cost of Sales	207,600	
Depreciation	22,400	
Selling and Administration Expenses	60,000	
Gain on Sale of Assets		5,000
Provision for Income Taxes	40,000	
	P728,000	P728,000

this machinery in 1966. There have been no other depreciable assets acquired since January 1, 1966, and no assets are fully depreciated.

(3) Certain assets that were in the inventory of fixed assets at January 1, 1966, were sold on December 31, 1967. For 1967, a full year's depreciation was recorded before the assets were removed from the books. Information regarding the sale follows:

Cost of assets	P14,000
Accumulated depreciation	4,900
Net book value	P 9,100
Proceeds of sale	14,100
Gain on sale	P 5,000

(4) Notes payable are long-term obligations that were incurred on December 31, 1966.

(5) No entries have been made in the retained earnings account of the subsidiary since its acquisition other than the net income for 1966. The retained earnings account at December 31, 1966, was converted to $212,000.

(6) The prevailing rates of exchange follow:

	Dollars per Peso
January 1, 1966	2.00
1966 average	2.10
December 31, 1966	2.20
1967 average	2.30
December 31, 1967	2.40

Instructions: Prepare a work sheet to convert the December 31, 1967, trial balance of The Pierce Corporation from pesos to dollars. The work sheet should show the unconverted trial balance, the conversion rates, and the converted trial balance.

(AICPA adapted)

Chapter 18

STATEMENT OF AFFAIRS

The inability of an individual or a business to meet maturing obligations frequently results in creditor control and creditor management of all of the debtor's assets. So long as the debtor remains solvent, creditors are unorganized. With insolvency and the possibility of loss to creditors, this group may organize and assume control of the insolvent's assets in an attempt to protect its interests. In such cases the insolvent's financial position and the status of his creditors is shown and analyzed on a statement of affairs.

INSOLVENCY DEFINED

The term *insolvency* as popularly employed and as normally defined by state statute expresses the inability of an individual or a business to meet outstanding debts as they mature. The assets of the business may exceed its liabilities, but if its liquid assets are insufficient to meet maturing obligations, the business is considered insolvent. Insolvency commonly arises because of losses from operations, the overextension of credit to customers, or excessive investments in inventories or in plant and equipment.

The concept of insolvency, as described above, differs from insolvency as defined by federal bankruptcy legislation. For purposes of the National Bankruptcy Act, a person is deemed to be insolvent only when the aggregate of his property at a fair valuation is less in amount than his total liabilities. A business may be temporarily unable to meet maturing obligations, but if its assets at a fair valuation exceed its liabilities, it is not considered insolvent within the provisions of the Bankruptcy Act. On the other hand, a business whose liabilities exceed the fair value of its assets would be insolvent even though for the time being it might be able to meet maturing obligations.

AVAILABLE PROCEDURES IN INSOLVENCY

Creditors and the insolvent may seek to settle difficulties without recourse to the courts. They may agree to the extension of time for payment of debt, a composition of creditors, control of the debtor's assets by a creditors' committee, or other forms of "friendly adjustment." If a settlement without resorting to the courts is not mutually satisfactory, however, the creditors or the insolvent may apply to state or federal courts for legal remedies.

Extensions. If a person cannot meet his obligations as they mature, creditors may agree to allow the insolvent an extension of time in which to pay his debts. Creditors generally favor the allowance of an extension of time when it is probable that, by doing so, the debtor will be enabled to pay his debts and continue in business. The extension, then, may mean for creditors the full recovery of their claims as well as a continuing demand by this sales outlet for their product. When it appears that an extension of time for payment will not succeed in solving the financial difficulties that have arisen, either the creditors or the insolvent will resort to other forms of action.

Composition of creditors. Creditors may agree to accept a certain percentage of their respective claims in full settlement of amounts owed. Settlement may consist of cash payment of the agreed amount or part payment in cash and the balance in the form of notes. An agreement of this kind is known as a *composition of creditors*. Such a composition settlement may be favored by creditors in an effort to avoid the costs and delays that are involved in alternative actions. Further, such a settlement may permit the debtor to continue in business.

Control by creditors' committee. Debtor and creditors may agree to the formation of a creditors' committee for the control of the debtor's business. The committee generally appoints a representative who, under its direction, conducts, reorganizes, or liquidates the business. The agreement may provide for the return of properties to the debtor when claims have been met or when creditors are satisfied with the financial improvement that has been achieved. Trade associations, local credit bureaus, and adjustment bureaus frequently offer specialized services in controlling and operating a debtor's properties or in arranging settlements between the debtor and his creditors without recourse to courts.

Voluntary assignment for benefit of creditors. State insolvency laws provide that an insolvent may execute a voluntary assignment of all of his property in trust for the benefit of his creditors. An *assignee* or *trustee* is named or appointed to take over the debtor's properties on behalf of the creditor group. The assignee converts the properties into cash and makes appropriate distribution of such cash among creditors. If any assets remain after claims have been fully satisfied, such assets are returned to the assignor.

Receivership in equity. An insolvent debtor or his creditors may apply to a court of equity for the appointment of a receiver to take charge of the debtor's business. The receiver, operating as an officer of the court and under its supervision, pays off maturing obligations according to their legal priorities and attempts to restore solvency. If solvency is restored, the receiver can return the business to its owners. If the receiver finds that the business cannot be rehabilitated and solvency restored, the court may permit him to (1) reorganize the business by reducing or eliminating the equity of the debtor, or (2) wind up the business, paying creditors as much as possible from the proceeds of liquidation.

Bankruptcy. Bankruptcy legislation makes it possible for either a debtor or his creditors to file a petition with the court asking that the debtor be declared a bankrupt and that his assets, with the exception of those that are exempt under the law, be sold and the proceeds distributed to the creditors. Action in bankruptcy, rather than other means of settlement, may be preferred by debtors as well as creditors. A debtor who complies with the bankruptcy provisions is legally freed from the payment of past debts even though the assets that he surrenders are not sufficient to cover these. The debtor is thus given a fresh start. Creditors who are parties to bankruptcy proceedings are assured of an orderly and equitable distribution of the debtor's assets.

NATIONAL BANKRUPTCY ACT

The Constitution gives Congress the power to establish uniform laws on the subject of bankruptcies. Prior to the enactment of laws on this subject by Congress, the states had power to enact legislation. The adoption of a bankruptcy law by Congress in 1898, however, supplanted state acts. The law in effect at present is the National Bankruptcy Act of 1898 as amended. Conditions, procedures, and relief under bankruptcy laws, then, are the same throughout the United States. With bankruptcy action, affairs of the insolvent come under the jurisdiction of a federal district court.

Widespread financial difficulties in the 1930's resulted in significant amendments to the National Bankruptcy Act, as well as the incorporation in the Act of certain sections providing special relief for debtors. Among these sections, mention should be made of Chapters X and XI on "Corporate Reorganizations" and "Arrangements" that were added to the Act in 1938.

Corporate reorganization provisions under Bankruptcy Act. A corporation seeking a change in its corporate capital structure with or without a change in its debt structure may apply to a federal court for such reorganization under Chapter X of the Bankruptcy Act. If relief is sought simply with respect to debt, such relief must be applied for under the "Arrangements" section of the Act. A petition for reorganization may be submitted by either stockholders or creditors. The petition may be filed during the course of bankruptcy proceedings or in the absence of such proceedings.

The plan for reorganization must be approved by two thirds of the creditors and a majority of the stockholders affected. After such approval, the court will confirm the plan if it is satisfied that the plan is feasible and is in the best interests of the creditors. The reorganization is then binding upon the corporation, its stockholders, and its creditors. In the event of failure to effect a corporate reorganization, any bankruptcy proceedings that may have been suspended by the petition for reorganization are reopened.

Arrangement provisions under Bankruptcy Act. An *arrangement* is defined by Chapter XI of the Bankruptcy Act as "any plan of a debtor for the settlement, satisfaction, or extension of the time of payment of his unsecured debts, upon any terms." A person who cannot meet his obligations is permitted to file a petition with a federal court proposing an extension, composition of creditors, or other settlement of his financial obligations. As in the case of corporate reorganizations, such a petition may be filed during the course of bankruptcy or in the absence of such proceedings.

The proposed arrangement is submitted to the creditors and must be accepted by a majority of the creditors who also represent a majority in amount of the claims against the debtor. Upon such acceptance, the arrangement will be confirmed by the court if it is satisfied that the plan is feasible and is in the best interests of the creditors. The terms of the arrangement are then binding upon the debtor and all of his creditors. If an arrangement is not effected, bankruptcy proceedings where previously operative are reinstated.

An arrangement permits the settlement of an insolvent's affairs under the jurisdiction of a federal court and the legal provisions of the Bankruptcy Act. Creditors are afforded the protection that they would receive under bankruptcy proceedings without the delays and the costs of such an action. The debtor is freed from his obligations without the stigma that attaches to being named a "bankrupt."

Bankruptcy provisions under Bankruptcy Act. Bankruptcy proceedings begin with the filing of a petition with a federal court asking that some person be adjudged a bankrupt. The Bankruptcy Act provides for voluntary and involuntary actions in instituting bankruptcy proceedings.

The law allows any person except a municipal, railroad, insurance, or banking corporation or a building and loan association to file a petition asking to be adjudged a *voluntary bankrupt* and to be allowed the benefits of the Act. The amount owed by the debtor is immaterial.

Creditors may file a petition asking that a debtor be adjudicated an *involuntary bankrupt*. Such a debtor may be any natural person except a wage earner who works for compensation not exceeding $1,500 a year or a farmer, and any moneyed, business, or commercial corporation except a municipal, railroad, insurance, or banking corporation or a building and loan association. The debtor must have obligations of $1,000 or more.

A partnership may be declared bankrupt without reference to its individual partners, or it may be declared bankrupt together with one or more or all of its partners. When all of a firm's general partners are declared bankrupt, the partnership is likewise adjudged bankrupt.

Insolvency alone is not sufficient grounds in filing a petition asking to have a debtor adjudged an involuntary bankrupt. The petition must set forth the fact that an *act of bankruptcy* was committed by the debtor within four months prior to filing the petition. An act of bankruptcy is considered to have been committed if the debtor has:

(1) Concealed, removed, or permitted to be concealed or removed any part of his property, with intent to hinder, delay, or defraud any of his creditors, or made or suffered a transfer of any of his property that would be considered fraudulent under the Act.
(2) Made or suffered while insolvent and within four months before the initiation of bankruptcy proceedings, a transfer of any property to or for the benefit of a creditor on an antecedent debt, which enables such creditor to obtain a greater percentage of his debt than some other creditor of the same class.
(3) Suffered or permitted, while insolvent, any creditor to obtain a lien upon any of his property through legal proceedings or distraint and not having vacated or discharged such lien within thirty days from the date thereof or at least five days before the date set for any sale or other disposition of such property.
(4) Made a general assignment for the benefit of his creditors.
(5) While insolvent or unable to pay his debts as they mature, procured, permitted, or suffered voluntarily or involuntarily the appointment of a receiver or trustee to take charge of his property.
(6) Admitted in writing his inability to pay his debts and his willingness to be adjudged a bankrupt.

Insolvency within the meaning of the Bankruptcy Act was defined earlier in this chapter. It should be observed that the attempt to effect a settlement without recourse to courts, or, under state laws, by such actions as the general assignment of assets for the benefit of creditors or the transfer of a debtor's assets to a receiver or a trustee, may be offered by a creditor as an act of bankruptcy. Such actions, then, may be made the basis for the commencement of involuntary proceedings in bankruptcy. This means that there must be complete agreement among all of the creditors concerned to settle without resorting to bankruptcy action if the possibility of federal jurisdiction is to be avoided.

BANKRUPTCY PROCEEDINGS

The voluntary or involuntary petition filed with the bankruptcy court indicates the grounds upon which bankruptcy proceedings are sought. In certain cases the court will appoint a *receiver in bankruptcy* or *marshal* to take charge of the debtor's assets. The receiver or marshal preserves the property and safeguards it against loss until the court determines whether the debtor is to be adjudged a bankrupt. When the debtor is adjudged a bankrupt, the creditors appoint a trustee who acquires all of the bankrupt's rights, titles, and interests in his property, real or personal, tangible or intangible. The trustee then disposes of the property and uses the proceeds for the satisfaction of the bankruptcy creditors. A *creditors' committee* may be appointed by the creditors to make recommendations to the trustee and to the court relative to administration of the bankruptcy action. An officer of the court known as a *referee* supervises and reviews the activities of the trustee and authorizes the distribution of the proceeds from the sale of the debtor's property.

Creditors of the bankrupt must prepare statements setting forth their claims and supplying information about the consideration related to such claims, property pledged on the claims, and any other pertinent matters. Such claims and proofs must normally be filed with the court or with the referee within six months from the date of the first meeting of creditors. When there are mutual debts between a bankrupt and a creditor, one balance is set off against the other and only the difference is recognized.

Creditors to whom certain assets have been pledged as security are known as *secured creditors*. Creditors who have no security but who are entitled under the law to priority in payment over general creditors are known as *creditors with priority*.[1] Creditors without security or priority are known as *unsecured* or *general creditors*.

[1]Creditors with priority are sometimes referred to as *preferred creditors*. However, use of the term *preferred creditors* is not desirable because in law a preferred creditor is a transferee who acquired property from the debtor while the debtor was insolvent and within four months of the filing of a petition in bankruptcy and thus was provided with a preference as compared with other creditors in the same group. Such a preference may be voided by the trustee in bankruptcy and the property may be recovered when it can be determined that the creditor had knowledge of the insolvency of the debtor at the time of the transfer.

Unpledged properties are sold by the trustee, and the cash is accumulated for ultimate distribution to creditors with priority and then to unsecured creditors. Properties that have been pledged to creditors as security are converted into cash, and the proceeds are applied first to the respective secured claims. If certain pledged property fails to realize an amount equal to the claim against it, the unpaid balance of the claim becomes an unsecured or general claim against the debtor. If the pledged property realizes more than the amount of the claim, the excess becomes available to the trustee for distribution to creditors with priority and to unsecured creditors.

The claims that are given priority in bankruptcy proceedings and the order of their payment follow:

(1) The costs and expenses of administration, including the actual and necessary costs and expenses of preserving the debtor's estate after filing the petition. Among these costs and expenses would be referee's salary and expenses, filing fees, attorney's and trustee's fees, expenses of recovering concealed or fraudulently transferred assets, etc.
(2) Wages and commissions, not to exceed $600 to each claimant, that have been earned within three months before the date of commencement of proceedings, due to workmen, servants, clerks, or traveling or city salesmen.
(3) Costs and expenses of creditors successful in having the confirmation of an arrangement or wage-earner plan or bankrupt's discharge refused, revoked, or set aside; or in securing the conviction of any person for a bankruptcy offense.
(4) Taxes legally due and owing by the bankrupt to the United States or any state or any subdivision thereof.
(5) Debts owing to any person entitled to priority by laws of the United States; and also rent for actual use and occupancy, accrued within three months before the date of bankruptcy, owing to a landlord who is entitled to priority under applicable state law.

When claims with priority have been provided for in full, the referee will authorize the distribution of such funds as may become available to remaining general creditors. Distributions involve the declaration and the payment of a *dividend* to creditors, such a dividend being a stated percentage payment on all allowed claims with the exception of claims with priority or balances that are secured. Upon receipt of the final dividend, unsecured creditors must regard unpaid balances as losses.

Although bankruptcy is a means of securing release from past obligations, such a release is not applied to all forms of debt. Certain obligations continue in effect and must still be paid after formal discharge of the debtor. The bankrupt is not released from the following:

(1) Taxes due to the United States or any state, county, district, or municipality.
(2) Liabilities for obtaining money or property by false pretenses or false representations, for willful and malicious injuries to the person or the

property of another, for alimony or for maintenance or support of a wife or child, that is due or to become due, etc.

(3) Debts not duly scheduled in time for proof and allowance when a creditor had no notice or actual knowledge of bankruptcy proceedings.

(4) Debts created by fraud, embezzlement, misappropriation, or defalcation while the debtor was acting as an officer or in any fiduciary capacity.

(5) Wages, salaries, or commissions earned within three months before the date of commencement of proceedings due to workmen, servants, clerks, or traveling or city salesmen.

(6) Moneys of an employee received or retained by an employer to secure the faithful performance of the terms of a contract of employment.

The adjudication of a person as a bankrupt operates as an application for his discharge in bankruptcy. The court, after examining the bankrupt, will fix a time for filing objections to a discharge in bankruptcy. In the absence of any valid objections, the court will grant a discharge that releases the bankrupt from all of his obligations with the exception of those classes previously mentioned.

A bankrupt will be denied a discharge if he has been guilty of certain actions. For example, a discharge will be denied if it is proved that the bankrupt:

(1) Destroyed, mutiliated, falsified, concealed, or in certain cases failed to keep or preserve books of accounts or records.

(2) Obtained money or property on credit, or obtained an extension or renewal of credit, by a materially false statement in writing as to his financial condition.

(3) Transferred, removed, destroyed, or concealed any of his property with intent to hinder, delay, or defraud creditors within twelve months prior to the filing of the bankruptcy petition.

(4) Refused to obey any lawful order of, or answer any material question approved by, the court.

(5) Failed to explain satisfactorily any losses of assets or deficiencies of assets to meet his liabilities.

(6) Was granted a discharge or had a composition confirmed under the Act in a bankruptcy proceeding commenced within six years prior to the date of the filing of the bankruptcy petition.

A discharge in bankruptcy will also be denied if the bankrupt during the course of proceedings has committed certain *offenses* as defined by the law. Offenses named include such acts as: knowingly and fraudulently making false oaths in relation to any bankruptcy proceeding; knowingly and fraudulently concealing property belonging to the bankrupt's estate; knowingly and fraudulently concealing, destroying, mutilating, falsifying, or withholding any document affecting the properties or affairs of the bankrupt; and knowingly and fraudulently giving or offering any money, property, remuneration, reward, advantage, or promise thereof, for acting or forbearing to act in a bankruptcy proceeding. In addition to a denial of discharge, offenses are punishable by fines and imprisonment. Fines and imprisonment may be applied not only to the bankrupt but also to any other party committing, advising, or otherwise assisting in such offenses.

STATEMENT OF AFFAIRS

The accountant is frequently asked to prepare a statement providing an analysis of the insolvent's financial position and the status of the creditors with respect to the insolvent's assets. The *statement of affairs* is designed to serve this purpose.

The statement of affairs is, in effect, a statement of position from a "quitting concern" point of view. Assets on the statement of affairs, instead of being reported at their book values, are reported at their estimated realizable values; furthermore, instead of being classified as current and noncurrent, assets are reported as *pledged* with certain creditor groups or *free* and thus available to general creditors. Liabilities are reported at their balance sheet amounts. The liabilities, however, are not classified as current and noncurrent, but are listed in terms of their legal status or rank, being reported as obligations *with priority*, *secured* obligations, and *unsecured* or *general* obligations.

The statement of affairs may be required by creditors as a means of determining what action to take with respect to an insolvent. The statement may also be requested by an assignee, a receiver, or a trustee as a means of informing creditors concerning the possible outcome of a particular course of action.

Before the statement of affairs can be constructed, a balance sheet is prepared and certain supplementary information is assembled. Such supplementary data consist of the following:

(1) Estimates and appraisals from reliable sources of the amounts that will be realized upon each asset.
(2) Pledges of assets that have been made on specific obligations.
(3) Obligations that are expected to emerge in the course of liquidation but that are not reflected on the balance sheet.

Assets on the statement of affairs. The classification of assets and their presentation on the statement of affairs differ from the classification and the presentation of assets on the balance sheet. The availability of assets to unsecured creditors generally forms the basis for classification on the statement of affairs. Asset classifications are related to the liability classifications on the opposite side of the statement. Assets are ordinarily classified in groups and in the following order:

(1) Assets pledged with fully secured creditors. Assets that have been pledged and that are expected to realize an amount equal to or in excess of the claims on which they have been pledged are reported under the heading "Assets pledged with fully secured creditors."

(2) Assets pledged with partly secured creditors. Assets that have been pledged but that are expected to realize less than the amounts of the claims on which they have been pledged are reported under the heading "Assets pledged with partly secured creditors."

(3) Free assets. Assets that have not been pledged and hence are not related to individual liability items are reported under the heading "Free assets."

The asset side of the statement of affairs usually has columns to show (1) the book value of the asset, (2) the name of the asset, (3) the appraised value of the asset, (4) the estimated amount that will become available for unsecured creditors as a result of the realization of the asset, and (5) the estimated loss or gain on the realization of the asset.

Liabilities and capital on the statement of affairs. The classification of liabilities and their presentation on the statement of affairs differ from the classification and the presentation of liabilities on the balance sheet. On the statement of affairs, liabilities are classified according to their legal priority and secured status. Liabilities are followed by capital items. Liability and capital items are normally classified in groups and in the order indicated below.

(1) Creditors with priority. Creditors who must, by law, be provided for in full before anything may be paid to remaining unsecured creditors are reported under the heading "Creditors with priority." Federal and state statutes must be consulted in determining what debts are given priority in settlement with creditors. Creditors who have priority under the Bankruptcy Act were indicated on page 641.

(2) Fully secured creditors. Creditors who have been pledged certain assets that are expected to realize as much as or more than their respective claims are reported under the heading "Fully secured creditors."

(3) Partly secured creditors. Creditors who have been pledged certain assets that are expected to realize less than their respective claims are reported under the heading "Partly secured creditors."

(4) Unsecured creditors. Creditors who are without legal priority and who have been pledged no assets are reported under the heading "Unsecured creditors."

(5) Capital. Balances summarizing the interests of the owners in the business are reported under the heading "Capital" or "Stockholders' equity."

The liabilities and capital side of the statement of affairs has columns to show (1) the book value of the liability or capital item, (2) the name of the liability or capital item, and (3) the amount of the liability that is unsecured.

PREPARATION OF STATEMENT OF AFFAIRS ILLUSTRATED

The preparation of a statement of affairs is illustrated in the example that follows. A balance sheet prepared for Superior Products, Inc., on May 15, 1967, appears on the following page.

Appraisals of the company's assets indicate that forced realization of assets will result in recovery of the amounts set forth below.

Cash	$ 1,750
Notes receivable, $14,000, and accrued interest, $300	14,300
Accounts receivable	19,500
Finished goods	14,000
Goods in process after completion (estimated costs to complete: materials, $2,000; additional labor, etc., $2,500)	25,000
Raw materials remaining after completion of goods in process	8,500
Miscellaneous supplies	500
Prepaid insurance	Nothing
Stock of Hanson Co. ($60 per share)	30,000
Machinery and equipment	18,000
Buildings } Land }	55,000
Goodwill	Nothing
Patents completely written off the books in past years but that have a realizable value	10,000

It is estimated that, in addition to the liabilities shown on the balance sheet, the following amounts will have to be paid:

Liquidation expenses	$12,500
Notes receivable discounted that will probably be dishonored without possibility of recovery by the company	5,000
Probable judgments on damage suits pending	20,000

Obligations of the company are secured as follows:

Obligation	Security
Notes payable of $20,000 on which interest of $400 is accrued	300 shares of Hanson Co. stock
Accounts payable of $30,000	Notes receivable
First mortgage bonds	Land and buildings

Points to be observed in statement of affairs. The statement of affairs for Superior Products, Inc., prepared from the balance sheet and the supplementary data, appears on pages 648 and 649. Special attention should be given to the following matters.

Superior Products, Inc.
Balance Sheet
May 15, 1967

Assets

Current assets:			
Cash		$ 1,750	
Notes receivable		15,000	
Accounts receivable	$35,000		
Less allowance for bad debts	3,500	31,500	
Accrued interest on notes receivable		300	
Inventories:			
Finished goods	$15,000		
Goods in process	22,000		
Raw materials	10,000		
Miscellaneous supplies	1,500	48,500	
Prepaid insurance		1,200	$ 98,250
Investments:			
Stock of Hanson Co. (500 shares)			40,000
Plant and equipment:			
Machinery and equipment	$55,000		
Less allowance for depr. on mach. and equip.	15,000	$ 40,000	
Buildings	$50,000		
Less allowance for depreciation on buildings	5,000	45,000	
Land		35,000	120,000
Intangibles:			
Goodwill			20,000
Total assets			$278,250

Liabilities and Stockholders' Equity

Liabilities

Current liabilities:		
Taxes payable	$ 600	
Wages payable	1,200	
Notes payable	55,000	
Accounts payable	102,000	
Accrued interest on notes payable	1,200	
Accrued interest on bonds	750	$160,750
Long-term debt:		
First mortgage bonds		50,000
Total liabilities		$210,750

Stockholders' Equity

Capital stock	$100,000	
Additional paid-in capital	12,000	
	$112,000	
Less deficit	44,500	
Total stockholders' equity		67,500
Total liabilities and stockholders' equity		$278,250

Presentation of assets and liabilities. It will be observed that the net book value of each asset, liability, or capital item is indicated in the Book Value column. Valuation allowances are deducted from the accounts to which they apply and only the net values are indicated. The gross amount of each item as well as the allowances could be shown if desired. If this were done, the allowances would be shown immediately beneath the items to which they apply, the allowances being recorded in the Book Value column in red to indicate that they represent subtraction items.

Certain items that are not listed on the balance sheet may require recognition on the statement of affairs. Such items would include assets that have been written off but that do have some realizable value upon liquidation, claims for expenses that are expected to emerge as a result of liquidation activities, and claims that have been regarded in the past as contingent but that are expected to make an ultimate claim upon assets in liquidation. When an item that does not appear on the balance sheet is presented on the statement of affairs, the Book Value column is left blank. In the illustration the free asset Patents, the liability with priority Estimated Liquidation Expenses, and the unsecured liabilities Estimated Liability on Notes Receivable Discounted and Estimated Liability on Damage Suits Pending are examples of the foregoing.

Creditors with priority. Balances of creditors who have legal priority are listed and summarized, but balances are not extended to the Amount Unsecured column; this column is used for claims that are both unsecured and without priority. Provision is made for claims with priority by subtracting this total from the total estimated amount to become available to unsecured creditors.

Fully secured creditors. A creditor who is secured by property estimated to realize as much as or more than the amount of the claim is assured of full payment from the proceeds of such property; consequently nothing is reported in the Amount Unsecured column. The property that is pledged as security on such a claim is shown on the asset side of the statement as an asset pledged with a fully secured creditor. If the property is expected to realize more than the claim that will be made against it, such excess is extended to the Estimated Amount Available column; this is a part of the total to become available for payment to unsecured creditors. In the statement of affairs for Superior Products, Inc., the mortgage bonds are reported as fully secured. Land and buildings pledged on the bonds are reported as assets pledged with fully secured creditors.

Partly secured creditors. A creditor who is secured by property estimated to realize less than the amount of the claim is only partly secured.

Superior
Statement
May 15,

Book Value	Assets	Appraised Value	Estimated Amount Available	Loss or (Gain) on Realization
	Assets pledged with fully secured creditors:			
$ 45,000	Buildings	$ 55,000		$ 25,000
35,000	Land			
	Less claim, first mortgage bonds, and accrued interest (see contra)	50,750	$ 4,250	
	Assets pledged with partly secured creditors:			
24,000	Hanson Co. stock, 300 shares (deducted contra)	$ 18,000		6,000
15,000	Notes receivable	$ 14,000		1,000
300	Add accrued interest	300		
	Total (deducted contra)	$ 14,300		
	Free assets:			
1,750	Cash	$ 1,750	1,750	
31,500	Accounts receivable	19,500	19,500	12,000
15,000	Finished goods	14,000	14,000	1,000
22,000	Goods in process			
	Estimated value after completion... $25,000			
	Less costs to complete:			
	Raw materials $2,000			
	Labor, etc. 2,500 4,500	20,500	20,500	1,500
10,000	Raw materials			
	Required to complete goods in process... $ 2,000			
	Balance, estimated to realize 8,500	10,500	10,500	(500)
1,500	Miscellaneous supplies	500	500	1,000
1,200	Prepaid insurance	0		1,200
16,000	Hanson Co. stock (200 shares)	12,000	12,000	4,000
40,000	Machinery and equipment	18,000	18,000	22,000
20,000	Goodwill	0		20,000
	Patents	10,000	10,000	(10,000)
				$ 84,200
	Estimated amount available		$111,000	
	Creditors with priority (see contra)		14,300	
	Estimated amount available to unsecured creditors (approximately 64¢ on the dollar)[1]		$ 96,700	
	Estimated deficiency to unsecured creditors		54,200	
$278,250			$150,900	

[1]Estimated amount available, $96,700, divided by total unsecured liabilities, $150,900, equals estimated amount payable on claims, 64%, or 64 cents on the dollar.

Products, Inc.
of Affairs
967

Book Value	Liabilities and Stockholders' Equity		Amount Unsecured
	Creditors with priority:		
	Estimated liquidation expenses	$12,500	
$ 600	Taxes payable	600	
1,200	Wages payable	1,200	
	Total (deducted contra)	$14,300	
	Fully secured creditors:		
50,000	First mortgage bonds	$50,000	
750	Add accrued interest	750	
	Total (deducted contra)	$50,750	
	Partly secured creditors:		
20,000	Notes payable	$20,000	
400	Add accrued interest	400	
	Total	$20,400	
	Less security: Hanson Co. stock (see contra)	18,000	$ 2,400
30,000	Accounts payable	$30,000	
	Less security: notes receivable and accrued interest (see contra)	14,300	15,700
	Unsecured creditors:		
35,000	Notes payable	$35,000	
800	Add accrued interest	800	35,800
72,000	Accounts payable		72,000
	Estimated liability on notes receivable discounted		5,000
	Estimated liability on damage suits pending		20,000
	Stockholders' equity:		
100,000	Capital stock		
12,000	Additional paid-in capital		
(44,500)	Deficit		
$278,250	Total unsecured liabilities		$150,900

The amount of the claim in excess of the estimated value of the pledged property is extended to the Amount Unsecured column; this is a part of the total of the unsecured or general claims against the debtor. The property that is pledged as security for such a claim is shown on the asset side of the statement as an asset pledged with a partly secured creditor. Inasmuch as total asset proceeds will be required to meet the claim on which the asset has been pledged, none of the asset value is reported as available to unsecured creditors. In the statement of affairs for Superior Products, Inc., certain notes payable and certain accounts payable are reported as partly secured. The notes receivable and the pledged portion of the Hanson Company's stock are reported as assets pledged with partly secured creditors.

Unsecured creditors. Balances for creditors who are unsecured and without priority are extended to the Amount Unsecured column. Items shown under the heading "Unsecured creditors" on the statement of affairs for Superior Products, Inc., are examples of the foregoing. The amounts that are expected to be realized on all assets that are not pledged are extended to the Estimated Amount Available column. Items shown under the heading "Free assets" are examples of the foregoing.

Capital. The capital balances for the enterprise are reported under the heading "Capital" or "Stockholders' Equity," but balances are not extended to the Amount Unsecured column. This column is used for amounts due to creditors. A deficit is reported in the Book Value column in red to indicate that it is a subtraction item.

Calculation of deficiency to unsecured creditors. The amount that is estimated to become available for unsecured creditors is calculated on the asset side of the statement and the total for creditors with priority is subtracted from this amount. The remainder is the estimated amount available for unsecured creditors without priorities. The difference between the total unsecured liabilities and the amount that is available to meet such claims represents the estimated deficiency to be absorbed by the general creditors. The asset and the liability sides of the statement of affairs are brought into balance by adding the deficiency to the amount available to unsecured creditors.

Special column for loss or gain on realization of assets. A column headed "Loss or Gain on Realization of Assets" may be shown on the asset side of the statement as illustrated on page 648. The differences between the book values of assets and the amounts estimated to be realized on their sales are reported in this column. Estimated gains on realization are shown in red so that these may be subtracted from estimated losses in computing the estimated net loss on realization.

Accrued interest on assets and liabilities. Accrued interest items should be added to the principal to which they relate. When an asset has been pledged, both the asset and any interest accumulations thereon are considered as security on the debt. For example, in the illustration both notes receivable of $14,000 and accrued interest on these notes of $300 are shown as pledged on accounts payable of $30,000.

A pledged asset is security for both the principal of the debt and any interest accruals on this principal. For example, bonds payable of $50,000 and accrued interest on the bonds of $750 are shown as fully secured, and the sum of the principal and interest is subtracted from the pledged properties consisting of land and buildings.

Single balance sheet item shown in several places on the statement of affairs. In certain instances an asset or a liability that appears as a single item on the balance sheet appears in several places on the statement of affairs. For example, Superior Products, Inc., owns 500 shares of Hanson Co. stock. Three hundred shares are pledged; the remaining shares are unpledged. The Hanson Co. stock is therefore shown in two sections on the asset side of the statement of affairs: $\frac{3}{5}$ of the value of the asset is shown as pledged; $\frac{2}{5}$ of the value of the asset is shown as free. The balance sheet of Superior Products, Inc., also shows notes payable of $55,000. Notes of $20,000 are secured by assets that are estimated to realize less than the amount of the obligation; remaining notes are unsecured. These facts are indicated by presenting notes of $20,000 as partly secured and notes of $35,000 as unsecured.

Assets requiring additional expenditures before realization. In some instances it may be advisable or necessary to complete the work begun on certain assets before they are offered for sale. When this is the case, the costs to be incurred in completing the assets and the values of the assets upon completion must be estimated. The net amount recoverable can then be estimated. For example, in the illustration it is estimated that the goods in process can be sold for $25,000 after completion costs estimated at $4,500. The goods in process are reported at $20,500, the estimated net recoverable amount.

Preparing estimates of amounts that may be paid to unsecured creditors. An estimate of the amount that may ultimately be paid to unsecured creditors is obtained by dividing the estimated amount available for unsecured creditors by the total unsecured liabilities. In the illustration it is estimated that $96,700 will become available to meet unsecured liabilities of $150,900. Consequently it is estimated that the unsecured creditors will receive 64% of their respective claims, or, stated differently, 64 cents on the dollar. This information may be indicated in the lower section of the statement as illustrated.

Special problems. Mention should be made of several special matters that may arise but that were not illustrated.

Amounts recoverable from partners. In preparing a statement of affairs for a partnership, when individual partners are personally solvent and will be required to make contributions to the partnership towards payment of firm obligations, the amounts estimated to be recoverable from such partners should be reported as free assets.

Amounts recoverable from stockholders. When corporate assets include subscriptions on capital stock, contracts with subscribers will be enforced and amounts estimated to be recoverable should be reported as free assets. When a discount on capital stock is reported in the capital section of the balance sheet and the amount of such a discount is recoverable from stockholders by creditors in the event of insolvency, the recoverable discount should be included as a free asset on the statement of affairs.

Balance sheet reserves. Balance sheet reserves should be carefully identified as asset valuation accounts, estimated liabilities, or appropriations of retained earnings, and their position on the statement of affairs should be determined accordingly.

Interests in affiliated units. When a company has affiliated branch units, assets and liabilities of the branches should be combined with those of the home office for purposes of the statement of affairs in view of the single legal identity represented by such units. When a company has controlling interests in stock of subsidiary companies, consolidation is not appropriate in view of the separate legal entities involved. Investments in stock of subsidiary companies, receivables from subsidiaries, and payables to subsidiaries are reported on the statement of affairs under appropriate asset and liability headings. When a subsidiary is insolvent, the statement of affairs for an insolvent parent would show an ownership interest in such a subsidiary with no value; receivables from the subsidiary would be reported at the amounts recoverable as indicated by the statement of affairs prepared for the subsidiary.

Prepaid expenses. Although prepaid expenses may be included in the asset section at amounts estimated to be recoverable, exceptions are made when it is possible that certain prepaid expenses will expire or be consumed before liquidation is completed. For example, when the length of time required for liquidation is unknown, conservatism would suggest that no realizable value be reported for prepaid insurance items even though refunds on a short-rate basis could possibly result.

Procedure in constructing the statement of affairs. In constructing the statement of affairs, it will prove most convenient to proceed in the following manner:

(1) The section headings for the statement should first be set up, adequate space being left between these for the data to be shown.
(2) Each liability should be considered and reported in the appropriate liability section. If a liability is secured, the related asset should be considered at this time and reported in the appropriate asset section.
(3) After all liabilities have been considered together with assets pledged on such claims, all remaining assets represent unpledged items and may be listed as such.
(4) Asset and liability data are then summarized and the statement is completed.

DEFICIENCY STATEMENT

A *deficiency statement* to indicate the source of the deficiency to unsecured creditors is usually prepared to accompany the statement of affairs. A deficiency statement for Superior Products, Inc., is illustrated below.

Superior Products, Inc.
Deficiency Statement
May 15, 1967

Estimated losses on realization of assets:		
Buildings and land	$ 25,000	
Hanson Co. stock	10,000	
Notes receivable	1,000	
Accounts receivable	12,000	
Finished goods	1,000	
Goods in process	1,500	
Miscellaneous supplies	1,000	
Prepaid insurance	1,200	
Machinery and equipment	22,000	
Goodwill	20,000	$ 94,700
Additional liabilities:		
Estimated liquidation expenses	$ 12,500	
Estimated liability on notes receivable discounted	5,000	
Estimated liability on damage suits pending	20,000	37,500
Estimated gross loss		$132,200
Deduct:		
Estimated gains on realization of assets:		
Raw materials	$ 500	
Additional assets:		
Patents	10,000	10,500
Estimated net loss		$121,700
Loss to be borne by owners:		
Capital stock	$100,000	
Additional paid-in capital	12,000	
	$112,000	
Less deficit	44,500	67,500
Estimated deficiency to unsecured creditors		$ 54,200

STATEMENT OF AFFAIRS — ALTERNATIVE FORM

The statement of affairs has been described and illustrated in its conventional form. Alternative forms for this statement have been suggested; one such form is illustrated on page 655. The statement is prepared from the same data as used in the previous example. Preparation of the statement in the alternative form calls for the following steps:

(1) Account balances are listed at their book values as reported on the balance sheet.
(2) These balances are then restated, assets being listed at their estimated realization values, liabilities at the amounts payable upon liquidation, and the stockholders' equity at the difference between assets and liabilities as restated.
(3) Liabilities as restated are extended to columns headed "Creditors" — (1) "With Priority," (2) "Fully Secured," (3) "Partly Secured," and (4) "Unsecured." When a liability is only partly secured, the portion of the liability that will be satisfied by the pledge is reported in the Partly Secured column and the balance of the liability is reported in the Unsecured column.
(4) Assets as restated are extended to columns headed "Assets Available to Creditors" — (1) "With Priority," (2) "Fully Secured," (3) "Partly Secured," and (4) "Unsecured." When an asset is pledged with a fully secured creditor, the portion of the asset required to satisfy the claim is reported as available to the fully secured creditor and the balance of the asset is reported as available to unsecured creditors.
(5) The amount required to satisfy creditors with priority is transferred from the column "Assets Available to Creditors — Unsecured" to the column "Assets Available to Creditors — With Priority."

The statement of affairs in the alternative form can be prepared in little time and provides a satisfactory presentation of the status of the different creditor groups. However, this form has not yet won wide acceptance, and it should be assumed in questions, exercises, and problems that, in the absence of any specific designation, reference is made to the statement of affairs in its conventional form.

FUNCTIONS SERVED BY THE STATEMENT OF AFFAIRS

The advantages of the statement of affairs over the balance sheet to creditors of an insolvent concern are readily apparent. The statement of affairs will assist creditors in determining just what policy shall be adopted or what action shall be taken with respect to the insolvent. Analysis of this statement will help them to decide whether an extension of time, a composition agreement, or some other form of action is in their best interests.

A solvent enterprise may prepare a statement of affairs to accompany an application for a loan or a credit line. In such instances the statement is utilized to impress prospective creditors with the satisfactory condition of the enterprise and the absence of risk if additional credit is granted.

(ALTERNATIVE FORM)
Superior Products, Inc.
Statement of Affairs
May 15, 1967

Liabilities and Stockholders' Equity	Book Value	Adjusted	Creditors			
			With Priority	Fully Secured	Partly Secured	Un-secured
axes payable	$ 600	$ 600	$ 600			
Vages payable	1,200	1,200	1,200			
Iotes payable	55,000	55,000			$ 18,000	$ 37,000
ccounts payable	102,000	102,000			14,300	87,700
ccrued interest on notes payable	1,200	1,200				1,200
ccrued interest on bonds	750	750		$ 750		
irst mortgage bonds	50,000	50,000		50,000		
stimated liquidation expenses		12,500	12,500			
stimated liability on notes receivable discounted		5,000				5,000
stimated liability on damage suits pending		20,000				20,000
apital stock	100,000	100,000				
dditional paid-in capital	12,000	12,000				
eficit	(44,500)	(166,200)				
Totals	$278,250	$194,050	$ 14,300	$ 50,750	$ 32,300	$150,900

Assets	Book Value	Adjusted	Assets Available to Creditors			
			With Priority	Fully Secured	Partly Secured	Un-secured
ash	$ 1,750	$ 1,750				$ 1,750
Iotes receivable	15,000	14,000			$ 14,000	
ccounts receivable (net)	31,500	19,500				19,500
ccrued interest on notes receivable	300	300			300	
inished goods	15,000	14,000				14,000
oods in process	22,000	20,500				20,500
aw materials	10,000	10,500				10,500
Iiscellaneous supplies	1,500	500				500
repaid insurance	1,200					
tock of Hanson Co. (500 shares)	40,000	30,000			18,000	12,000
Iachinery and equipment (net)	40,000	18,000				18,000
uildings (net) and	45,000 35,000	55,000		$50,750		4,250
oodwill	20,000					
atents		10,000				10,000
	$278,250	$194,050				
reditors with priority			$ 14,300			(14,300)
Totals			$ 14,300	$ 50,750	$ 32,300	$ 96,700

otal unsecured creditors	$150,900
stimated amount available to unsecured creditors	96,700
stimated deficiency to unsecured creditors	$ 54,200
stimated amount payable per dollar of unsecured liability: $96,700 ÷ $150,900	64¢

When the statement of affairs is presented as an exhibit for credit purposes, the usual balance sheet classifications can be used. Assets may be reported at "going concern" values rather than at amounts that would be recovered upon forced liquidation. Obviously, a statement of affairs prepared by a solvent concern will show an amount available to unsecured creditors exceeding the total of unsecured claims. Such excess is reported on the liabilities and capital side of the statement in bringing the statement into balance.

QUESTIONS

1. What is meant by insolvency? How does the definition of insolvency for purposes of the Bankruptcy Act differ from the popular definition?

2. (a) What remedies are available to creditors without resort to the courts when claims are not paid when due? (b) What remedies are available under statutes or court jurisdiction?

3. (a) What is an "arrangement" under the Bankruptcy Act? (b) What are the advantages of arrangement proceedings as compared with bankruptcy proceedings? (c) Distinguish between arrangement and corporate reorganization plans under the Bankruptcy Act.

4. Distinguish between voluntary and involuntary bankruptcy.

5. (a) What are the conditions that must be claimed in petitioning that a debtor be adjudged a bankrupt? (b) Name the "acts of bankruptcy."

6. Explain the order of payment of debts in bankruptcy proceedings.

7. Describe the nature of a dividend authorized by a referee in bankruptcy.

8. Name those classes of obligations that are not released when a debtor is granted a discharge in bankruptcy.

9. (a) What is meant by bankruptcy "offenses"? (b) What is the effect of such offenses upon the bankruptcy action?

10. How does classification and presentation of assets and liabilities on the statement of affairs differ from classification and presentation of these items on the balance sheet?

11. Distinguish between the valuation procedures that are employed on the statement of affairs and those employed on the balance sheet.

12. In preparing a statement of affairs, indicate the sources from which a receiver may obtain reliable estimates or information concerning the probable realization of the following assets:

(a) Merchandise inventory.
(b) Land and buildings.
(c) Securities.
(d) Goodwill.
(e) Unexpired insurance.
(f) Notes receivable.
(g) Patents.
(h) Accounts receivable.

13. (a) Distinguish between secured creditors and creditors with priority. (b) What claims have priority under the Bankruptcy Act?

14. Explain how each item below will appear on a statement of affairs:

(a) *Estimated liquidation costs*, $2,500.
(b) *First mortgage bonds*, $25,000, upon which interest of $300 is accrued, secured by land and buildings, book value $40,000, estimated to realize $30,000.
(c) *Land and buildings* pledged to holders of bonds (see [b]).
(d) *Deficit*, $5,000.
(e) *Cash overdraft*, $1,500.
(f) *Probable judgments on damage suits pending*, $5,000.
(g) *Taxes payable*, $350.
(h) *Goodwill*, $20,000, upon which it is believed nothing will be realized.
(i) *Goods in process*, book value $15,000, estimated to realize $16,000 after additional costs of completion estimated at $1,500.
(j) *Notes receivable*, $15,000.
(k) *Notes receivable*, $20,000, upon which interest of $600 is accrued; notes are estimated to be 80% collectible; one half of the notes are pledged on notes payable of $10,000 on which interest of $400 is accrued.
(l) *Notes payable* secured by notes receivable (see [k]).
(m) *Patents*, previously written off against retained earnings but estimated to realize $5,000.
(n) *Wages payable*, $800.

15. How would each of the following account balances be reported on the statement of affairs?

(a) Reserve for depreciation.
(b) Reserve for income taxes.
(c) Reserve for contingencies.
(d) Reserve for bad debts.
(e) Reserve for container deposits made by customers.
(f) Reserve for self-insurance.
(g) Reserve for bond redemption fund.
(h) Reserve for unclaimed bond principal and interest payments.

16. How would you report the following balances on the statement of affairs for the Burtchett Co.?

(a) Subscriptions receivable — preferred stock.
(b) Discount on common stock.
(c) Deficit.
(d) Paid-in capital from sale of treasury stock.
(e) Appraisal capital — buildings.
(f) Dividends payable on preferred stock.

17. (a) State how the estimated amount payable on unsecured claims is calculated. (b) In developing a statement of affairs for the Coburn Co., accountants summarize their conclusions with the following statement, "It appears that 68.31 cents on the dollar will become available to unsecured creditors if forced liquidation takes place." Do you have any criticism of the foregoing statement?

18. You are asked to prepare a statement of affairs for the Walsh Co. You find the following items under the investments heading on the balance sheet for the Walsh Co.:

(1) A balance with a domestic branch carried at a value of $120,000.
(2) Stock of a 100% owned subsidiary carried at a cost of $300,000.
(3) Advances to the 100% owned subsidiary of $60,000.

State how each balance will be reported on a statement of affairs.

19. You are preparing a statement of affairs for the partnership of X, Y, and Z. In the course of your analysis of financial position, you determine that X and Y are personally solvent and will be able to meet the deficiency of the partnership to its creditors. How will you show this on the statement?

20. What is the nature and the purpose of the deficiency statement?

21. Describe the statement of affairs when it is prepared in its alternative form as illustrated in the chapter. Do you believe that this form has advantages over the conventional form?

22. What use may be made of the statement of affairs by a solvent enterprise?

EXERCISES

1. The Wallace Metals Company is bankrupt. The data listed below are developed in the course of preparation of a statement of affairs. Indicate how these data should be reported on the statement.

(a) Notes payable, $60,000, on which interest of $1,400 is accrued; included in the foregoing are notes of $15,000 on which interest of $300 is accrued and which are secured by U.S. bonds of $10,000 (see [b]).

(b) U. S. bonds, $50,000 par and market value, on which there is accrued interest at 3% for three months.

2. Melody, Inc. has goods in process on hand costing $16,500. Completion of such goods is expected to require materials costing $5,000 and labor and other costs of $8,500. When completed, it is estimated that the goods can be sold for $35,000. Raw materials on hand have a cost of $20,000; materials other than those required for the completion of goods in process are estimated to bring $13,500. Finished goods have a cost of $22,000 and are estimated to have a sales value of $24,500. How would these facts be reported on the statement of affairs?

3. The balances reported below are found on the books of the Mason Company. State how each balance would appear on a statement of affairs prepared for this company.

Cash balance in savings account with Y bank	$ 3,500
Cash overdraft in checking account with Y bank	(4,500)
Cash balance representing sinking fund accumulation with Z bank	16,500
Cash overdraft in checking account with Z bank	(1,500)
Total cash per books	$14,000

4. P. M. Lee, receiver for Craig, Inc., prepares a statement of affairs for this company on January 31. Indicate how the following data would be reported on the statement of affairs prepared on this date:

(a) 200 shares of Griffin stock, cost $20,000, par $100, market value per share, $110; 100 shares are pledged to creditors whose claims total $10,500; remaining shares are unpledged.

(b) Goods in process, cost $20,000, estimated to realize $18,000 after completion, which requires materials of $500 and additional labor of $2,000.
(c) Raw materials, cost $12,000, estimated to realize $12,500 after the withdrawal of materials required to complete goods in process in (b).
(d) Accounts receivable, book value $25,000, estimated to realize $20,000, pledged to holders of notes of $22,500.

5. The receiver for Harrison Mills, Inc. prepares a statement of affairs which shows that unsecured creditors whose claims total $60,000 may expect to receive approximately $36,000 if assets are sold for the benefit of creditors. How much may each of the following creditors hope to receive?

(a) A. G. Payne who is an employee and is owed $150.
(b) C. A. Kambel who holds a note for $1,000 on which interest of $50 is accrued; nothing has been pledged on the note.
(c) F. R. Steel who holds a note of $6,000 on which interest of $300 is accrued; securities, book value, $6,500, present market value, $5,000, are pledged on the note.
(d) R. T. Taylor who holds a note for $2,500 on which interest of $150 is accrued; property, book value, $2,000, present market value, $3,000, is pledged on the note.

6. The land and buildings owned by the Winn Corporation are sold to satisfy creditors and realize $40,000. Liabilities of the Winn Corporation are as follows:

Wages Payable	$ 350
Taxes Payable	150
Accrued Interest on Notes Payable	400
Accrued Interest on Mortgage Payable	500
Notes Payable	22,000
Accounts Payable	53,000
Mortgage Payable (secured by land and buildings)	20,000

State the amount to be paid to each of the creditor groups upon distribution of the proceeds of $40,000 by the trustee in bankruptcy.

7. A statement of affairs for the Fox Company shows an estimated amount available for unsecured creditors of $60,000 and a deficiency to this group of $15,000. What is the estimated amount to become available on each dollar of unsecured claims?

8. Prepare a deficiency statement for the Belflour Company from the data that follow:

Stockholders' equity, per books:	
Capital stock	$100,000
Deficit	15,500
Balance	$ 84,500
Estimated gains on realization of assets:	
Land and buildings	$ 22,500

Estimated losses on realization of assets:

Accounts receivable	$ 6,600
Inventories	24,000
Prepaid insurance and other prepaid expenses	600
Machinery and equipment	20,000
Goodwill and patents	45,000
	$ 96,200

Estimated claims requiring settlement, not recorded on books:

Liquidation costs	$ 5,000
Contingent liabilities	7,500
	$ 12,500

9. A review of the assets and the liabilities of the Chambers Company in receivership on November 30, 1967, discloses the following:

A mortgage payable of $100,000 is secured by land and buildings valued at $160,000.
Notes payable of $50,000 are secured by furniture and equipment valued at $40,000.
Liabilities other than those referred to above total $120,000, which includes claims with priority of $15,000.
Assets other than those referred to above have an estimated value of $45,000.

Prepare a statement of affairs in the alternative form illustrated on page 655.

PROBLEMS

18-1. The following balances are found in the general ledger for the McKinney Company on November 1, 1967:

Accounts Payable	$167,500
Accounts Receivable	62,500
Additional Paid-In Capital — Premium on Sale of Stock	20,000
Allowance for Bad Debts	5,000
Allowance for Depreciation — Buildings	40,000
Allowance for Depreciation — Machinery and Equipment	70,000
Buildings	105,000
Capital Stock	200,000
Cash	15,750
Deficit	71,750
Goodwill	50,000
Inventories	115,000
Investments	45,000
Land	52,500
Machinery and Equipment	125,000
Mortgage Payable, secured by land and buildings	100,000
Notes Payable	40,000

The books do not show the following accruals: wages, $850; taxes, $2,000; interest on notes, $1,250; interest on mortgage, $2,500. The investments have a market value of $27,500 and have been pledged as security to holders of the notes. An offer has been received for land and buildings of $125,000 and for machinery and equipment of $15,000. It is estimated that inventories will realize $85,000 after their completion, which will require additional costs of $12,500. It is estimated that 15% of the accounts receivable will prove uncollectible. Expenses of liquidation are estimated at $15,000.

Instructions: (1) Prepare a statement of affairs.
(2) Prepare a deficiency statement.

18-2. The balance sheet for Barker Supply Company shows the following items on January 31, 1967:

Assets			Liabilities and Stockholders' Equity	
Cash		$ 4,850	Accrued salaries and wages	$ 400
Accrued int. on notes rec.		500	Accrued int. on notes payable	800
Notes receivable		20,000	Notes payable	50,000
Accounts receivable	$45,000		Accounts payable	68,000
Less allow. for bad debts	1,500	43,500	Capital stock	50,000
Merchandise inventory		40,000	Premium on stock	5,000
Prepaid insurance		500	Deficit	(17,850)
Furniture and fixtures	$12,000			
Less allow. for depreciation	8,000	4,000		
Delivery equip.	$20,000			
Less allow. for depreciation	2,000	18,000		
Goodwill		25,000		
Total		$156,350	Total	$156,350

A receiver appointed on January 31 obtains the following data:

It is estimated that assets will realize the following amounts:

Notes receivable and the accrued interest thereon	$13,400
Accounts receivable	37,500
Merchandise inventory	70% of book value
Prepaid insurance	Nothing
Furniture and fixtures	4,500
Delivery equipment	14,000
Goodwill	Nothing

Notes payable of $20,000 on which interest of $200 is accrued are secured by merchandise inventory with a book value of $30,000.

Notes payable of $15,000 on which interest of $450 is accrued are secured by the delivery equipment.

The company is contingently liable on notes receivable discounted of $15,000; however, it is believed that notes of only $2,000 may have to be paid without recovery.

Liquidation expenses are estimated at $6,000.

Instructions: (1) Prepare a statement of affairs.
(2) Prepare a deficiency statement.

18-3. A receiver was appointed on July 1, 1967, to take charge of the Crocker Manufacturing Company. At that time the following balance sheet and supplementary data were available.

Assets			Liabilities and Stockholders' Equity	
Cash		$ 4,050	Accrued wages	$ 3,850
Accounts receivable	$40,000		Accrued interest on notes	2,400
Less allow. for bad debts	500	39,500	Accrued interest on bonds	1,500
			Notes payable	63,500
			Accounts payable	90,000
Raw materials		20,000	First mortgage bonds	60,000
Goods in process		35,000	Common stock	100,000
Finished goods		42,000	Additional paid-in capital	15,500
Prepaid insurance		1,000	Deficit	(60,199)
Patterns, jigs, and tools		20,000		
Machinery and equipment	$75,000			
Less allow. for depreciation	40,000	35,000		
Buildings	$80,000			
Less allow. for depreciation	30,000	50,000		
Land		30,000		
Intangibles		1		
Total		$276,551	Total	$276,551

It is estimated that assets will realize the following amounts: accounts receivable, $36,500; raw materials, $14,000; goods in process after costs of $15,000 required for their completion, $40,000; finished goods, $36,000; prepaid insurance, no value; patterns, jigs, and tools, $4,000; machinery and equipment, $8,000; land and buildings, $70,000; intangibles, $2,500.

One half of the finished goods on hand is pledged to holders of notes of $25,000; interest of $600 is applicable to these notes.

Additional accrued wages of $400 are not shown on the balance sheet. Liquidation expenses are estimated at $12,500.

Instructions: (1) Prepare a statement of affairs.

(2) Prepare a deficiency statement.

(3) Prepare a statement to show how much each creditor may expect to receive upon liquidation.

18-4. A receiver is appointed on March 30, 1967, to take charge of Wentworth Manufacturing Company. The balance sheet on that date is shown at the top of the following page.

Accounts receivable are classified as follows: good, $20,000; doubtful, $18,000 with an estimated value of $4,250; bad, $12,000. Good accounts

Assets			Liabilities and Stockholders' Equity	
		$ 15,400	Accrued int. on mortgage	$ 1,400
ts rec.	$ 50,000		Accrued int. on notes pay.	2,500
allow. for			Accrued wages and salaries	4,500
d debts	7,000	43,000	Mortgage note payable	50,000
			Notes payable	91,500
on stock subscriptions			Accounts payable	95,000
vable		10,000	Preferred stock	50,000
aterials		20,000	Common stock	125,000
n process		24,000	Common stock subscribed	25,000
d goods		40,000	Deficit	(43,500)
insurance		1,000		
		20,000		
ery	$ 70,000			
allow. for				
pr.	12,000	58,000		
gs.	$105,000			
allow. for				
	20,000	85,000		
		20,000		
ill		35,000		
		30,000		
		$401,400	Total	$401,400

000 are pledged to one of the trade creditors who is owed $8,000.
elieved that all common stock subscriptions will be collected.
e Weber Construction Company has offered to purchase certain
or amounts as follows: all of the finished goods, $20,000; goods in
s upon their completion, $26,500; and patents, $5,000. It is esti-
that completion of the goods in process will require materials,
, and wages and other expenditures, $10,000. Finished goods with
value of $18,000 are pledged to holders of notes of $15,000.
st of $300 applies on these notes.
terials that will remain after completion of goods in process are
ted to have a value of $15,000. Tools are estimated to have a value
,000. Machinery is estimated to have a value of $27,500 and the
ged land and buildings a value of $55,000. Nothing will be real-
n goodwill and prepaid insurance. The company is contingently
on notes receivable discounted amounting to $10,000; however, it
nated that notes discounted of only $3,000 will have to be paid
t recovery. The estimated expenses of liquidation are $12,000.

ructions: (1) Prepare a statement of affairs.
Prepare a deficiency statement.
Prepare a statement to show how much each creditor may expect to
upon liquidation.

18-5. The Cummings Company of San Diego has a branch in Santa Ana and a wholly owned subsidiary in Riverside, the Sun Company. The Sun Company was forced into bankruptcy on June 30, 1967. A balance sheet for the Sun Company prepared on this date follows:

Assets		Liabilities and Stockholders' Equity		
Accounts receivable	$ 60,000	Cash overdraft — National Bank		$ 10,000
Merchandise inventory	90,000	Accounts payable		90,000
Plant and equipment	105,000	Due to Cummings Co.		80,000
		Mortgage secured by plant and equipment		30,000
		Capital stock	$75,000	
		Less deficit	30,000	45,000
Total	$255,000	Total		$255,000

The Santa Ana branch balance sheet on this date shows:

Assets		Liabilities	
Cash	$ 10,000	Accounts payable	$ 40,000
Accounts receivable	40,000	Home office	60,000
Merchandise inventory	50,000		
Total	$100,000	Total	$100,000

The balance sheet for the Cummings Company on June 30, 1967, follows:

Assets		Liabilities and Stockholders' Equity	
Cash	$ 20,000	Accounts payable	$140,000
Accounts receivable	80,000	Notes payable — State Bank	60,000
Advances to Sun Co.	80,000	Wages payable	2,500
Branch office current	60,000	Taxes payable	4,500
Investment in stock of Sun Co.	75,000	Mortgage secured by plant and equipment	60,000
Plant and equipment	100,000	Capital stock	100,000
		Retained earnings	48,000
Total	$415,000	Total	$415,000

It is assumed in the case of each business that accounts receivable and inventories will realize 60% of book value; plant and equipment items, 50% of book value.

Instructions: Prepare a statement of affairs for the Cummings Company showing the probable amount available to creditors of this company upon liquidation. (Show all calculations that are required in support of your conclusions.)

18-6. Using the data in Problem 18-1 for the McKinney Company, prepare a statement of affairs in the alternative form illustrated on page 655.

18-7. Using the data in Problem 18-2 for Barker Supply Company, prepare a statement of affairs in the alternative form illustrated on page 655.

18-8. The Peerless Corporation advises you that it is facing bankruptcy proceedings. As the company's CPA you are aware of its condition.

The balance sheet of the Peerless Corporation at June 30, 1967, and supplementary data are presented below.

Assets	
Cash	$ 2,000
Accounts receivable, less allowance for bad debts	70,000
Inventory, raw materials	40,000
Inventory, finished goods	60,000
Marketable securities	20,000
Land	13,000
Buildings, less allowance for depreciation	90,000
Machinery, less allowance for depreciation	120,000
Goodwill	20,000
Prepaid expenses	5,000
Total assets	$440,000

Liabilities and Stockholders' Equity	
Accounts payable	$ 80,000
Notes payable	135,000
Accrued wages	15,000
Mortgages payable	130,000
Common stock	100,000
Retained earnings (deficit)	(20,000)
Total liabilities and stockholders' equity	$440,000

Supplementary data:

(1) Cash includes a $500 travel advance that has been expended.

(2) Accounts receivable of $40,000 have been pledged in support of bank loans of $30,000. Credit balances of $5,000 are netted in the accounts receivable total.

(3) Marketable securities consisted of government bonds costing $10,000 and 500 shares of Bartlett Company stock. The market value of the bonds is $10,000 and of the stock is $18 per share. The bonds have accrued interest due of $200. The securities are collateral for a $20,000 bank loan.

(4) Appraised value of raw materials is $30,000 and of finished goods is $50,000. For an additional cost of $10,000, the raw materials would realize $70,000 as finished goods.

(5) The appraised value of fixed assets is: land, $25,000; buildings, $110,000; machinery, $75,000.

(6) Prepaid expenses will be exhausted during the liquidation period.

(7) Accounts payable include $15,000 of withheld payroll taxes and $6,000 owed to creditors who had been reassured by the president that they

would be paid. There are unrecorded employer's payroll taxes in amount of $500.

(8) Wages payable are not subject to any limitations under bankru laws.

(9) Mortgages payable consist of $100,000 on land and buildings a $30,000 chattel mortgage on machinery. Total unrecorded acc interest for these mortgages amounted to $2,400.

(10) Estimated legal fees and expenses in connection with the liquidatio $10,000.

(11) Probable liability on judgment in a pending damage suit is $50,0C

(12) You have not rendered an invoice for $5,000 for last year's audit you estimate a $1,000 fee for liquidation work.

Instructions: (1) Prepare a statement of affairs.

(2) Compute the estimated settlement per dollar of unsecured liabi

(AICPA ada

18-9. The Hardy Corporation is in financial difficulty because of sales. Its stockholders and principal creditors want an estimate o financial results of the liquidation of assets and liabilities and the dis tion of the corporation.

The corporation's post-closing trial balance on December 31, is as follows:

	Debit	Credi
Cash	$ 1,000	
Accounts Receivable	20,500	
Allowance for Bad Debts		$ 3:
Inventories	40,000	
Supplies Inventory	3,000	
Downhill Railroad 5% Bonds	5,000	
Accrued Bond Interest Rceeivable	750	
Advertising	6,000	
Land	4,000	
Building	30,000	
Accumulated Depreciation — Building		5,0
Machinery and Equipment	46,000	
Accumulated Depreciation — Machinery and Equipment		8,0
Accounts Payable		26,0
Notes Payable — Bank		25,0
Notes Payable — Officers		20,0
Payroll Taxes Payable		8
Wages Payable		1,5
Mortgage Payable		42,0
Mortgage Interest Payable		5
Capital Stock		50,0
Retained Earnings	29,100	
Reserve for Product Guarantees		6,2
	$185,350	$185,3

The following information has been collected in anticipation of a meeting of the stockholders and the principal creditors to be held on January 2, 1968:

(1) Cash includes a $300 protested check from a customer. The customer stated that he would have funds to honor the check in about two weeks.

(2) Accounts receivable include accounts totaling $10,000 that are fully collectible and that have been assigned to the bank in connection with the notes payable. Included in the unassigned receivables is an uncollectible account of $150. The allowance for bad debts account of $350 now on the books will adequately provide for other doubtful accounts.

(3) Purchase orders totaling $9,000 are on hand for the corporation's products. Inventory with a book value of $6,000 can be processed at an additional cost of $400 to fill these orders. The balance of the inventory, which includes obsolete materials with a book value of $1,200, can be sold for $10,500.

(4) In transit at December 31 but not recorded on the books was a shipment of defective merchandise being returned by a customer. Mr. Hardy, president of the corporation, had authorized the return and the refund of the purchase price of $250 after the merchandise had been inspected. Other than this return, Mr. Hardy knows of no other defective merchandise that would bear upon the appropriated reserve for product guarantees account. The merchandise being returned has no salvage value.

(5) The supplies inventory is comprised of advertising literature, brochures, and other sales aids. These could not be replaced for less than $3,700.

(6) The Downhill Railroad bonds are recorded at face value. They were purchased in 1964 for $600, and the adjustment to face value was credited to Retained Earnings. At December 31, 1967, the bonds were quoted at 18 dealt in flat. (Accrued interest, if any, is included in quoted price.)

(7) The advertising account represents the future benefits of a 1967 advertising campaign. Ten percent of certain advertising expenditures were placed in the account. Mr. Hardy stated that this was too conservative and that 20% would result in a more realistic measure of the market that was created.

(8) The land and the building are in a downtown area. A firm offer of $50,000 has been received for the land, which would be used as a parking lot; the building would be razed at a cost of $12,000 to the buyer. Another offer of $40,000 was received for the real estate, which the bidder stated would be used for manufacturing that would probably employ some Hardy employees.

(9) The highest of the offers received from used machinery dealers was $18,000 for all of the machinery and equipment.

(10) One creditor, whose account for $1,000 is included in the accounts payable, confirmed in writing that he would accept 90¢ on the dollar if the corporation paid him by January 10.

(11) Wages payable include year-end adjustments of $325 payable to certain factory employees for their overtime during the busy season.

(12) The mortgage payable is secured by the land and the building. The last two monthly principal payments of $200 each were not made.

(13) Estimated liquidation expenses amount to $3,200.

(14) For income tax purposes the corporation has the following net operating loss carry-overs (tax rate, 50%):

1965	$10,000
1966	$12,000
1967	$ 8,000

Instructions: (1) Prepare a statement of affairs.

(2) Prepare a schedule that computes the estimated settlement per dollar of unsecured liabilities.

(AICPA adapted)

18-10. The Malone Manufacturing Company has been forced into bankruptcy as of April 30, 1967. The following balance sheet was prepared by the company bookkeeper as of April 30, 1967:

Assets	
Cash	$ 2,700
Accounts receivable	39,350
Notes receivable	18,500
Inventories:	
Raw materials	19,600
Work in process	35,100
Finished machines	12,000
Supplies	6,450
Tools	14,700
Prepaid expenses	950
Plant and property:	
Land	20,000
Buildings	75,000
Machinery	80,900
Total	$325,250

Liabilities and Stockholders' Equity	
Note payable to the First National Bank	$ 15,000
Notes payable to suppliers	51,250
Accounts payable	52,000
Accrued salaries and wages	8,850
Accrued property taxes	2,900
Employees' taxes withheld	1,150
Accrued wage taxes	600
Accrued interest on bonds	1,800
First mortgage bonds payable	90,000
Allowance for depreciation — buildings	33,750
Allowance for depreciation — machinery	32,100
Common stock ($100 par value)	75,000
Deficit	(39,150)
Total	$325,250

Additional information:

(1) Of the total accounts receivable, $10,300 are believed to be good. The other accounts are doubtful, but it seems probable that 20% finally can be collected.

(2) A total of $15,000 of the notes receivable has been pledged to secure the note payable to the First National Bank. All except $2,500 of these appear to be good. Interest of $800 is accrued on the $12,500 of good notes pledged and $300 is accrued on the $15,000 payable to the bank. The remaining notes are not considered collectible.

(3) The finished machines are expected to be sold for one third above their cost, but expenses in disposing of them will equal 20% of their sales price. Work in process can be completed at an additional cost of $15,400, of which $3,700 would be material used from the raw materials inventory. The work in process, when completed, will probably sell for $40,000 and selling expenses will be 20% of sales price. The raw materials not used will realize $8,000. Most of the value of tools consists of special items. After completion of work in process, the tools should sell for $3,000. The supply inventory, which will not be needed to complete work, should sell for $1,000.

(4) Land and buildings are mortgaged as security for bonds. They have an appraised value of $95,000. The company recently purchased $20,000 of machinery on a conditional sales contract. They still owe $12,000 principal on this contract, which is included in the notes payable. These machines have a current used value of $10,000. Depreciation taken on these machines amounts to $1,800. The remaining machinery is believed to be salable at $10,000, but the cost of selling it may be $1,000.

Instructions: (1) Prepare a statement of affairs showing the estimated deficiency to unsecured creditors.

(2) Compute the percentage of probable payments to the $52,000 accounts payable.

(AICPA adapted)

18-11. The Circle Furniture Co., Inc., has been finding it more and more difficult to meet its obligations. Although its sales volume appeared to be satisfactory and it was showing a profit, the requirements for capital for inventory and time contracts were greater than the company could provide. Finally, after pledging all of its installment accounts, it found itself unable to meet the bills falling due on October 10, 1967. It is the opinion of the management that if it could obtain an extension of time in which to pay its obligations it could meet its liabilities in full. The corporation has arranged for a meeting of creditors to determine if the company should be granted an extension or be forced into bankruptcy.

The trial balance for the current calendar year of the company on September 30, 1967, is given at the top of the following page.

The following additional data are available:

(1) Depreciation, bad debts, prepaid and accrued items had all been adjusted as of September 30, 1967.

(2) All installment contracts had been pledged with the bank on September 30, 1967; the bank had deducted its interest to date and had in-

Circle Furniture Co., Inc.
Trial Balance
September 30, 1967

	Debit	Credit
Cash on hand	$ 500	
Cash in bank	1,620	
Installment contracts — pledged	215,000	
Allowance for bad contracts		$ 13,440
Accounts receivable — 30 day	20,830	
Allowance for bad debts		1,050
Inventories — January 1, 1967	151,150	
Unexpired insurance	1,490	
Autos and trucks	22,380	
Allow. for depreciation — autos and trucks		14,960
Furniture and equipment	12,500	
Allow. for depreciation — furn. and equip.		2,140
Buildings	89,760	
Allowance for depreciation — building		7,530
Land	10,240	
Organization expense	880	
Trade accounts payable		132,100
Contract payable — furniture and equipment		5,800
Chattel mortgage on auto and trucks		10,000
Bank loan — secured by installment contracts		161,250
Taxes payable		14,220
Accrued salaries and wages		4,680
Accrued interest		10,990
Notes payable — stockholder		100,000
First mortgage		49,000
Capital stock		100,000
Retained earnings	65,290	
Sales		708,900
Purchases	527,630	
Expenses and miscellaneous income (net)	216,790	
	$1,336,060	$1,336,060

creased the company loan to equal 75% of the face amount of the contracts in accordance with a loan agreement. It was estimated that a forced liquidation would result in a loss of $40,000 from the face amount of the contracts.

(3) Thirty-day accounts receivable were not pledged and it was estimated that they would provide $16,500 on a liquidation basis.

(4) It was estimated that since January 1, 1967, the company had made a gross profit of 33⅓%, but that the inventory on hand would provide only $100,000 on a forced liquidation.

(5) Cancellation of the insurance would provide $990.

(6) All the autos and trucks were covered by a chattel mortgage, and their total market value was $8,000.

(7) The store had been remodeled in 1966 and the furniture and equipment had been acquired on contract. Because of its special utility it was estimated that on a forced sale no more than $5,000 could be expected.

(8) The land and the buildings were subject to a 6% first mortgage on which interest had been paid to July 30, 1967. It was estimated the property could be sold for $75,000.

(9) The notes payable to stockholders had not been subordinated to general creditors. The notes carried a 6% rate of interest, but no interest had been paid since December 31, 1965.

(10) Since prior income tax returns disclosed a large available net operating loss carry-over, no current income tax need be considered.

(11) The cost of liquidation proceedings was estimated to be $5,000.

(12) There appeared to be no other values on liquidation and no unrecorded liabilities.

Instructions: (1) Prepare a statement of affairs.

(2) Prepare a statement of estimated deficiency to unsecured creditors.

(3) Compute the percentage of recovery by the unsecured creditors if the company were to be forced into bankruptcy.

(AICPA adapted)

18-12. The Allen-Barnes Partnership, of which Allen is manager, has had difficulty in meeting its obligations as the debts matured. If the business is dissolved, it will require six months. The bookkeeper prepared the following trial balance on April 15, 1967:

	Debit	Credit
Cash in Banks	$ 20,000	
Accounts Receivable	100,000	
Allowance for Bad Debts		$ 4,000
Notes Receivable	58,000	
Notes Receivable Discounted		12,000
Raw Materials	9,000	
Work in Process	20,000	
Finished Goods	15,000	
Prepaid Insurance	1,200	
Property Held in Trust	18,000	
Machinery and Equipment, cost	9,000	
Building	33,000	
Land	12,000	
Accumulated Depreciation		6,000
Interest Receivable	700	
Payroll Taxes Payable		200
Real Estate Taxes		1,200
Wages Payable		3,450
Notes Payable		60,000
Accounts Payable		125,700
Mortgage Payable — 4%		40,000
Equipment Contract Payable (purchased on a conditional sale contract)		6,400
Interest Payable		1,000
Allen, Capital		15,975
Barnes, Capital		1,975
Trust Principal		18,000
	$295,900	$295,900

An analysis of the accounts revealed the following:

(1) Cash in First Bank, \$8,000; in Second Bank, \$12,000.

(2) Of the accounts receivable, 60% are good and fully collectible, 30% are doubtful and considered to be only 80% collectible, and the remaining 10% are worthless.

(3) All notes are good and are pledged as security on notes payable to the Factor House of \$50,000 with accrued interest of \$500.

(4) Of the notes that were discounted at the Manning Bank, it is estimated that one amounting to \$2,000 will not be paid at maturity or thereafter.

(5) All finished goods will be sold for 20% less than their cost. Work in process cannot be sold until finished and can be completed by incurring labor and material costs of \$9,000, of which \$3,000 will be from the raw materials inventory. The balance of the raw materials inventory will realize \$5,000.

(6) The prepaid insurance, which expires October 15, has a short-term cancellation value on April 15 of \$900.

(7) Property held in trust is in the form of stocks and bonds with realizable value of \$24,000. The partnership is entitled to a fee of \$600 per year, payable April 15, for their services. Cash was not available in the trust for the payment; therefore the fee was not recorded.

(8) The machinery and equipment with a book value of \$8,000 will realize \$5,000.

(9) The land and the building may be sold for \$38,000; however the mortgage holder has indicated a willingness to cancel the debt and to assume all encumbrances for the surrender of title to the real estate. Interest on the mortgage was paid on January 15.

(10) Wages and commissions were last paid in full on December 31. Commission salesmen were dismissed on February 15. Accrued wages in the trial balance are:

Carl, bookkeeper (to April 15)	\$1,400
Commission salesmen (to February 15)	300
Allen, managing partner (to April 15)	1,750
	\$3,450

(11) The partnership owes the Second Bank a note of \$10,000.

(12) The estimated administrative expenses are \$3,000.

(13) Although Allen has personal liabilities that are approximately equal to his personal assets, Barnes's personal assets exceed his personal liabilities by \$2,800.

Instructions: (1) Prepare a statement in good form showing the estimated deficiency, if any, to unsecured creditors.

(2) Prepare a statement showing the estimated amounts available for each class of creditors.

(AICPA adapted)

Chapter 19

RECEIVERSHIPS

When an insolvent and his creditors cannot effect a mutually satisfactory settlement without recourse to the courts, legal remedies may be sought through the courts. Either the insolvent or his creditors may apply to a court of equity for the appointment of an assignee, a trustee, or a receiver to take charge of the insolvent's business.

RECEIVER IN EQUITY

Upon recognizing the need for protection to creditors, to owners, or to others having an interest in the business and after application by such parties, the courts will appoint a receiver to assume control of the assets of a person or a company. Such authority is assumed by state and federal courts under powers granted by statute or under the common law. During the period of receivership the debtor is removed from control, while the usual rights of creditors to legal action are suspended. The appointee of the court, operating under the laws relating to receivership and under instructions of the court, acts in a fiduciary capacity to protect the equities and the rights of the different parties.

Although an assignee or a trustee is ordinarily appointed to direct liquidation and settlement with creditors, a receiver is frequently appointed with the expectation that he may be able to restore financial solvency and subsequently return properties to the control of former owners. The receiver assumes control of the assets, converts some or all of these into cash, and compromises and pays off claims. Significant decisions are made only with the advice and the approval of the court having jurisdiction. When rehabilitation of the business is effected, the receiver returns the property to its original management.

If solvency cannot be restored by continued operations of the properties, the receiver may attempt a reorganization of the business, reducing in part or in whole the debtor's equity. If this appears inexpedient or proves unsuccessful, assets are sold and creditors are paid off in accordance with their legal rights.

RECEIVER'S REPORTS

During the receiver's administration, reports of receivership operations are required at regular intervals by the court, creditors, owners, and perhaps governmental agencies and other interested groups. Ordinarily a specific system of accounting is not prescribed by law or by the courts. However, a system should be designed that will provide all of the data that are required in reporting to the different parties. The receiver must be able to offer a full account of his activities if he is to prove that he has properly and faithfully fulfilled his responsibilities.

Upon assuming control, the receiver submits to the court a list of the assets taken over as authorized by court order. Creditors may request a statement of affairs at this time. Thereafter interim statements of position and operations, supported by schedules summarizing receipts, disbursements, and other significant data, are required. Reports that cover the entire period of stewardship are required upon termination of control.

Receivership activities normally call for the adoption of a double-entry system of bookkeeping. Ordinarily, separate books are maintained by the receiver unless liquidation is to take place immediately, in which case the old books may be used to record the winding up process.

When separate books are maintained by the receiver, these ordinarily report the transactions to which he is a party. Eventually, receivership transactions are summarized and entered on the debtor's books. The receivership records are used in preparing periodic summaries of receivership operations. However, in the preparation of financial statements for the business unit as a whole, it will be necessary to combine the account balances on the receiver's books and on the debtor's books.

Whether the company books are continued or a new set of books is opened by the receiver, a careful distinction should be maintained in the records between original assets and liabilities and those emerging in the course of receivership. A distinction should be maintained between original assets taken over by the receiver and new assets acquired by him in view of the difference in the receiver's responsibility with respect to the two classes of assets. In the case of new assets, the receiver's responsibility embraces both their acquisition and their realization; in the case of original assets, the receiver's responsibility is limited only to their realization. In the case of new receivables, for example, the receiver must exercise satisfactory diligence both in granting credit and in realizing such claims; in the case of old receivables, however, losses arising from an unsound credit policy of the past cannot be attributed to the receiver. The responsibilities of the receiver with respect to old and new debt are also different. In the case of new debt, the receiver is responsible both for its incurrence and for its appropriate liquidation; in the case of original debt, the receiver is responsible only for its settlement in accordance with the instructions by appropriate authority. New debt may also have certain legal preferences over old debt, calling for a clear distinction between the two classes of debt in the accounts.

EIVERSHIP ACCOUNTS

Vhen the receiver maintains a set of books summarizing receivership vities, transactions are recorded on the separate receiver's books and he books of the debtor in the following manner.

Assumption of control by receiver. ***Receiver's books:*** When a receiver pointed by a court, he is granted title as a receiver to part or all of assets of the debtor. The receiver debits the appropriate asset acts for those assets transferred to him by the court action; he credits lebtor company. The account with the company summarizes the nt of accountability of the receiver to the debtor. Ordinarily the es of the assets on the company books are retained for purposes of the ver's books. When both an asset account and a valuation account hown for a property item, both asset and valuation account balances established on the receiver's books. Assets taken over and to be zed may be designated "Old" to distinguish them from assets that ubsequently acquired by the receiver. Ordinarily, existing obliga- of the debtor are not transferred but are left on the debtor's books; ver, any liabilities emerging from the receiver's activities are re- d on the receiver's books. A distinction is thus maintained between nal obligations and those incurred by the receiver.

ebtor's books: The debtor credits asset accounts and debits related tion accounts for assets taken over by the receiver; he debits an nt with the receiver. The account with the receiver is a reciprocal nt summarizing the net assets of the debtor that are reported on the ver's books.

perations by the receiver. ***Receiver's books:*** The receiver records actions in the usual manner, with the following exceptions:

Vhen liabilities existing prior to the receivership appear on the riginal books, payment of such liabilities by the receiver should be eported by a debit to the debtor account balance and a credit to Cash. However, instead of reducing the debtor balance directly, the harge is normally made to a temporary account with the debtor, s for example, "Debtor's Liability Paid — Accounts Payable, Old." The receiver's books then offer full data relating to the settlement of he debtor's obligations. Account balances reporting the payment of ebts are closed into the debtor's account at the end of the period.

osses and gains that have accrued prior to the date of receivership ut that are recognized during receivership should be identified with he debtor. Such losses and gains can be recorded directly in the ebtor's account with the losses and gains recognized in nominal accounts on the debtor's books. However, instead of transferring such items to the debtor's books, the losses or gains are normally recorded on the receiver's books in nominal accounts identified with the debtor, as, for example, "Debtor — Loss from Bad Accounts, Old," and "Debtor — Gain on Sale of Securities." These balances are closed into the receiver's profit and loss account at the end of the period.

(3) When the receiver is appointed, he is charged with the administration and the realization of the assets of the debtor; he thus takes credit for the proceeds from asset realization as well as any revenue emerging during the course of administration, including rental income, interest income, dividend income, etc. The receiver, however, is not charged with responsibility for the obligations that were assumed by the debtor; payment of original indebtedness, as well as interest expense, penalties, and debt call premiums, are made by the receiver only upon orders by appropriate authority. Under the circumstances, any charges relating to the old indebtedness are identified with the debtor and are not recognized in the evaluation of the receiver's activities. As in the case of losses in (2), charges arising from an old debt can be transferred to the debtor's books. Ordinarily, however, such charges are recorded on the receiver's books in nominal accounts identified with the debtor, as, for example, "Debtor — Interest Expense on Mortgage." These balances, too, are closed into the receiver's profit and loss account at the end of the period.

Debtor's books: The books of the debtor are not affected by transactions of the receiver that are reported in the usual manner in the receiver's books. For transactions in the three special classes mentioned, the procedures followed on the debtor's books are:

(1) The discharge of obligations reflected on the debtor's books is normally recorded as soon as payment is made by the receiver. Data concerning the unpaid balances of original obligations are thus available at any time. Payment of an obligation by the receiver is recorded by a debit to the liability account and a credit to the receiver's account. When this practice is followed, the balance of the debtor's account on the receiver's books will not be the same as the balance of the receiver's account on the debtor's books until the receiver closes the balances in the debtor's liability paid accounts into the debtor's account at the end of the period.

(2) When losses and gains are considered to be identified with the debtor rather than with receivership activities and are recorded directly in the debtor's account by the receiver, such items are recorded on the

debtor's books by entries to appropriate loss or gain accounts with an offsetting entry to the receiver's account. The debtor's account on the receiver's books and the receiver's account on the debtor's books will be reciprocal, then, insofar as such items are concerned. However, when the receiver maintains a special class of nominal accounts for such special losses and gains, their recognition on the debtor's books is deferred until all activities are summarized at the end of the period.

(3) When charges are incurred by the receiver on old obligations and these are recorded directly in the debtor's account by the receiver, such items would be recorded on the debtor's books in a manner similar to that explained in (2) above. When such expenses are reported in special nominal accounts on the receiver's books, their recognition on the debtor's books is deferred until all activities are summarized at the end of the period.

Adjusting and closing the books. ***Receiver's books:*** The receiver's accounts are adjusted and closed at periodic intervals and also just before control is returned to the original owners. Adjustments are made in the usual manner. Revenue and expense accounts relating to receivership operations are closed into a profit and loss account in ascertaining the net income or loss identified with the receiver's administration. When special debtor loss, gain, and expense balances are reported on the receiver's books, these are closed into the profit and loss account, the balance in the latter account then reflecting the net change in capital for the period. The balance in the profit and loss account is transferred to the debtor's account. Balances in debtor's liability paid accounts are also closed into the debtor's account at this time.

Debtor's books: An increase in capital as summarized on the receiver's books is recognized by a debit to the receiver's account and a credit to the appropriate capital account; a decrease would be recorded by a debit to the capital balance and a credit to the receiver's account. The debtor's account on the receiver's books and the receiver's account on the debtor's books are now reciprocal. When nominal accounts summarizing special profit and loss items are reported on the debtor's books, these too are transferred to capital.

Return of control to debtor. ***Receiver's books:*** Upon return of control to the debtor, the debtor's account, the asset valuation accounts, and the liability accounts are debited and the asset accounts are credited. The books of the receiver are then closed.

Debtor's books: When assets are returned to the debtor and liabil incurred by the receiver are assumed by the debtor, the asset account debited and the asset valuation accounts, the liability accounts, and receiver's account are credited.

STATEMENTS PREPARED BY THE RECEIVER

A balance sheet and an income statement for a business in rece ship are required periodically by the various interested parties. S statements can be prepared only by combining account balance ported on the books of the receiver and on the books of the debtor. balances for the receiver's books and the debtor's books before adju and closing are first drawn up. Balances of the accounts in both s books are then combined by means of working papers.

Working papers may include columns for adjustments and for e nations. Accounts are brought up to date in the adjustment colu The elimination columns are used in eliminating the reciprocal acco In eliminating the reciprocal accounts, the balance of the rece account on the books of the debtor is offset against the account wit debtor on the books of the receiver. If the balances of the debtor' bility paid accounts in the receiver's books have not been closed int account with the debtor, the balance of the receiver's account o debtor's books must be offset against the combined balances of the d account and the debtor's liability paid accounts on the receiver's b Account balances are now extended to the statement columns: rev gain, expense, and loss balances are carried to the profit and los umns; asset, liability, and capital balances are carried to the ba sheet columns. The net increase in capital as a result of receiv operations is calculated and the profit and loss and balance sheet col on the work sheet are brought into balance. The work sheet is then for the preparation of financial statements.

The balance sheet is prepared in its usual form. In preparin income statement, a distinction is normally made between profi loss items identified with the receiver and similar items identified the debtor. Presentation of the net income or loss from receiv operations may be followed by a summary of debtor profit and loss

ACCOUNTING FOR RECEIVER ILLUSTRATED

The entries on the books of the receiver and the debtor ar preparation of financial statements to summarize receivership oper are illustrated in the example that follows.

The Miles Corporation finds itself unable to meet current oblig as they mature, and I. B. Owens is appointed as receiver on Mar

Miles Corporation
Balance Sheet
March 31, 1967

Assets

Current assets:			
Cash			$ 1,000
Notes receivable			15,000
Accounts receivable		$ 25,000	
Less allowance for bad debts		1,000	24,000
Accrued interest on notes receivable			150
Merchandise inventory			50,000
Total current assets			$ 90,150
Investments:			
Common stock of X Co.		$ 16,000	
Preferred stock of Y Co.		4,000	
Total investments			20,000
Plant and equipment:			
Furniture and fixtures	$ 6,000		
Less allowance for depreciation	1,950	$ 4,050	
Buildings	$60,000		
Less allowance for depreciation	7,800	52,200	
Land		15,000	
Total plant and equipment			71,250
Total assets			$181,400

Liabilities and Stockholders' Equity

Liabilities

Current liabilities:		
Notes payable		$ 35,000
Accounts payable		30,000
Accrued interest on notes payable		250
Accrued interest on mortgage		400
Total current liabilities		$ 65,650
Long-term debt:		
6% First mortgage payable		40,000
Total liabilities		$105,650

Stockholders' Equity

Capital stock	$100,000	
Less deficit	24,250	
Total stockholders' equity		75,750
Total liabilities and stockholders' equity		$181,400

Transaction			Receiver's Books			Corporation's Books		
Assumption of Control by the Receiver, March 31, 1967								
(1) Assets taken over by receiver:								
Cash		$ 1,000	Cash	1,000		I. B. Owens, Receiver	181,400	
Notes Receivable		15,000	Notes Receivable, Old	15,000		Allow. for Bad Debts	1,000	
Accounts Receivable	$25,000		Accounts Receiv., Old	25,000		Allow. for Depr. of Furniture and Fixtures	1,950	
Less All. for Bad Debts	1,000	24,000	Accrued Interest on Notes Rec., Old	150		Allow. for Depr. of Bldgs.	7,800	
Accrued Interest on Notes Receiv.		150	Mdse. Inventory	50,000		Cash		1,000
Merchandise Inventory		50,000	Common Stock of X Co.	16,000		Notes Receivable		15,000
Common Stock of X Co.		16,000	Preferred Stock of Y Co.	4,000		Accounts Receivable		25,000
Preferred Stock of Y Co.		4,000	Furniture and Fixtures	6,000		Accrued Interest on Notes Rec.		150
Furniture and Fixtures	$ 6,000		Buildings	60,000		Mdse. Inventory		50,000
Less Allow. for Depr.	1,950	4,050	Land	15,000		Common Stock of X Co.		16,000
Buildings	$60,000		Allow. for Bad Debts, Old		1,000	Preferred Stock of Y Co.		4,000
Less Allow. for Depr.	7,800	52,200	Allow. for Depr. of Furniture and Fixtures		1,950	Furniture and Fixtures		6,000
Land		15,000	Allow. for Depr. of Bldgs.		7,800	Buildings		60,000
		$181,400	Miles Corp. in Receivership		181,400	Land		15,000
Operations of the Receiver, March 31–December 31								
(2) Sales on account		$210,000	Accounts Receivable	210,000				
			Sales		210,000			
(3) Purchases on account		$112,000	Purchases	112,000				
			Accounts Payable		112,000			
(4) Accounts Receivable (new) were reduced by the following:								
Cash collections		$158,500	Cash	158,500				
Notes received in payment		30,000	Notes Receivable	30,000				
Sales returns and allowances		1,500	Sales Returns and Allow.	1,500				
Sales discounts allowed		2,000	Sales Discounts	2,000				
		$192,000	Accounts Receivable		192,000			

Transaction	Receiver's Books			Corporation's Books		
(5) Collection on Accounts Receivable, Old, $22,000; remaining accounts were written off as bad.	Cash Allow. for Bad Debts, Old Corporation — Loss from Bad Debts, Old Accounts Rec., Old	22,000 1,000 2,000	 25,000			
(6) Collection on Notes Receivable, Old, $15,000, and Interest, $450.	Cash Notes Receivable, Old Accrued Interest on Notes Rec., Old Interest Income	15,450	 15,000 150 300			
(7) Collection on Notes Receivable (new), $18,000 and Interest, $200.	Cash Notes Receivable Interest Income	18,200	 18,000 200			
(8) Accounts Payable (new) were reduced by the following: Cash payments ... $46,000 Notes issued in payment ... 40,000 Purchases returns and allowances ... 1,500 Purchases discounts received ... 2,500	Accounts Payable Cash Notes Payable Purchases Returns and Allowances Purchases Discounts	90,000	 46,000 40,000 1,500 2,500			
(9) Payment of Accounts Payable, Old ... $30,000	Corporation Liability Paid — Accts. Pay., Old Cash	30,000	 30,000	Accounts Payable I. B. Owens, Receiver	30,000	 30,000
(10) Payment of Notes Payable, Old, $35,000, and Interest, $950.	Corporation Liability Paid — Notes Payable, Old Corporation Liability Paid — Accrued Interest on Notes Payable, Old Corporation — Interest Expense on Notes Payable, Old Cash	35,000 250 700	 35,950	Notes Payable Accrued Interest on Notes Payable I. B. Owens, Receiver	35,000 250	 35,250
(11) Payment of Notes Payable (new), $15,000, and Interest, $300.	Notes Payable Interest Expense Cash	15,000 300	 15,300			

Transaction	Entry	Debit	Credit	
(12) Sale of securities: Book Value / Amount Realized Common Stock of X Co. . . . . $16,000 / $ 8,500 Preferred Stock of Y Co. . . . . 4,000 / 4,500 $20,000 / $13,000	Cash . . . . Corporation — Loss on Sale of X Co. Stock . . . . Common Stock, X Co. . . . . Preferred Stock, Y Co. . . . . Corporation — Gain on Sale of Y Co. Stock	13,000 7,500	16,000 4,000 500	
(13) Payment of operating expenses: Sales salaries . . . . $22,000 Other selling expense . . . . 18,600 Office expense . . . . 8,000 Other general expense . . . . 12,000 Receivership fees 6,500 $67,100	Sales Salaries . . . . Other Selling Expense . . . . Office Expense . . . . Other General Expense . . . . . . Receivership Fees . . . . Cash	22,000 18,600 8,000 12,000 6,500	67,100	
Adjusting Entries, December 31 (14) To transfer beginning merchandise inventory to Profit and Loss, $50,000.	Profit and Loss . . . . Merchandise Inventory	50,000	50,000	
(15) To record ending inventory, $36,000.	Merchandise Inventory . . . . . . Profit and Loss	36,000	36,000	
(16) To provide for bad debts (new accounts), $450.	Loss from Bad Debts . . . . Allow. for Bad Debts	450	450	
To record depreciation: (17) Furniture and Fixtures . . . . $ 450	Depr. of Furn. and Fixtures . . Allow. for Depr. of Furniture and Fixtures	450	450	
To record depreciation: (18) Buildings . . . . $ 1,800	Depreciation of Buildings . . . . Allow. for Depr. of Bldgs. . .	1,800	1,800	
(19) To record accrued interest on notes receivable . . . . $ 200	Accrued Interest on Notes Receivable . . . . Interest Income	200	200	
(20) To record accrued interest on notes payable (new) . . . . $ 300	Interest Expense . . . . Accrued Interest on Notes Payable	300	300	

Closing Entries, December 31						
(22) To close receiver's revenue and expense accounts into the profit and loss account.	Sales	210,000				
	Pur. Returns and Allow.	1,500				
	Purchases Discounts	2,500				
	Interest Income	700				
	Sales Returns and Allow.		1,500			
	Purchases		112,000			
	Sales Salaries		22,000			
	Other Selling Expense		18,600			
	Office Expense		8,000			
	Depr. of Furn. and Fix.		450			
	Depr. of Building		1,800			
	Loss from Bad Debts		450			
	Other General Expense		12,000			
	Receivership Fees		6,500			
	Sales Discounts		2,000			
	Interest Expense		600			
	Profit and Loss		28,800			
(23) To close corporation expense, loss, and gain accounts into the profit and loss account.	Profit and Loss	11,500				
	Corporation — Gain on Sale of Y Co. Stock	500				
	Corporation — Int. Expense on Notes, Old		700			
	Corporation — Int. Expense on Mortgage, Old		1,800			
	Corporation — Loss from Bad Debts, Old		2,000			
	Corporation — Loss on Sale of X Co. Stock		7,500			
(24) To record increase in retained earnings for the nine-month period.	Profit and Loss	3,300		I. B. Owens, Receiver	3,300	
	Miles Corp. in Receivership		3,300	Retained Earnings		3,300

Transaction			Receiver's Books			Corporation's Books		
(25) To close corporation liabilities paid accounts.			Miles Corp. in Receivership	65,250				
			Corporation Liability Paid — Accounts Payable, Old		30,000			
			Corporation Liability Paid — Notes Payable, Old		35,000			
			Corporation Liability Paid — Accrued Interest on Notes Payable, Old		250			
Return of Control to Debtor, January 2, 1968								
(26) Assets and liabilities returned to corporation:			Miles Corp. in Receivership	119,450		Cash	33,800	
Cash		$ 33,800	Notes Payable	25,000		Notes Receivable	12,000	
Notes Receivable		12,000	Accounts Payable	22,000		Accounts Receivable	18,000	
Accounts Receivable	$18,000		Accrued Interest on Notes Payable	300		Accrued Interest on Notes Receivable	200	
Less Allow. for Bad Debts	450	17,550	Accrued Interest on Mortgage	1,800		Merchandise Inventory	36,000	
Accrued Interest on Notes Receivable		200	Allow. for Bad Debts	450		Furniture and Fixtures	6,000	
Merchandise Inventory		36,000	Allow. for Depr. of Furn. and Fixtures	2,400		Buildings	60,000	
Furniture and Fixtures	$ 6,000		Allow. for Depr. of Buildings	9,600		Land	15,000	
Less Allow. for Depreciation	2,400	3,600	Cash		33,800	Notes Payable		25,000
Buildings	$60,000		Notes Receivable		12,000	Accounts Payable		22,000
Less Allow. for Depreciation	9,600	50,400	Accounts Receivable		18,000	Accrued Interest on Notes Payable		300
Land		15,000	Accrued Interest on Notes Receivable		200	Accrued Interest on Mortgage		1,800
Total Assets		$168,550	Merchandise Inventory		36,000	Allow. for Bad Debts		450
Notes Payable		$ 25,000	Furniture and Fixtures		6,000	Allow. for Depr. of Furniture and Fixtures		2,400
Accounts Payable		22,000	Buildings		60,000	Allow. for Depr. of Bldgs.		9,600
Accrued Interest on Notes Payable		300	Land		15,000	I. B. Owens, Receiver		119,450
Accrued Interest on Mortgage		1,800						
Total Liabilities		$ 49,100						

Miles Corporation in Receivership
I. B. Owens, Receiver
Income Statement
March 31–December 31, 1967

Gross sales				$210,000
Less: Sales returns and allowances			$ 1,500	
Sales discounts			2,000	3,500
Net sales				$206,500
Cost of goods sold:				
Merchandise inventory, March 31, 1967			$ 50,000	
Purchases		$112,000		
Less: Purchases returns and allowances	$1,500			
Purchases discounts	2,500	4,000	108,000	
Merchandise available for sale			$158,000	
Deduct merchandise inventory, December 31, 1967			36,000	122,000
Gross profit on sales				$ 84,500
Operating expenses:				
Selling expenses:				
Sales salaries		$ 22,000		
Other selling expense		18,600	$ 40,600	
General expenses:				
Office expense		$ 8,000		
Depreciation of furniture and fixtures		450		
Depreciation of buildings		1,800		
Loss from bad debts		450		
Other general expense		12,000		
Receivership fees		6,500	29,200	69,800
Net operating income				$ 14,700
Other revenue and expense items:				
Interest income			$ 700	
Interest expense			600	100
Net income from receiver's operations				$ 14,800
Corporation profit and loss items:				
Corporation expenses:				
Interest expense on notes, old	$ 700			
Interest expense on mortgage, old	1,800	$ 2,500		
Corporation losses:				
Loss from bad debts, old	$2,000			
Loss on sale of X Co. stock	7,500	9,500		
Total corporation expenses and losses			$ 12,000	
Less corporation gains:				
Gain on sale of Y Co. stock			500	
Net corporation loss				11,500
Increase in retained earnings				$ 3,300

Miles Corpo
Working P

	Trial Balance	
	Dr.	C
Corporation's Books		
I. B. Owens, Receiver	116,150	.....
Accrued Interest on Mortgage	....	
6% First Mortgage Payable	....	40
Capital Stock	....	100
Retained Earnings	24,250	.....
Receiver's Books		
Cash	33,800	.....
Notes Receivable	12,000	.....
Accounts Receivable	18,000	.....
Merchandise Inventory	50,000	.....
Furniture and Fixtures	6,000	.....
Allowance for Depreciation of Furniture and Fixtures	....	1
Buildings	60,000	.....
Allowance for Depreciation of Buildings	....	7
Land	15,000	.....
Notes Payable	....	25
Accounts Payable	....	22
Miles Corporation in Receivership	....	181
Sales	....	21(
Sales Returns and Allowances	1,500	....
Sales Discounts	2,000	....
Purchases	112,000	....
Purchases Returns and Allowances	....	1
Purchases Discounts	....	2
Sales Salaries	22,000	....
Other Selling Expense	18,600	....
Office Expense	8,000	....
Other General Expense	12,000	....
Receivership Fees	6,500	....
Interest Income	....	
Interest Expense	300	....
Corporation — Interest Expense on Notes, Old	700	....
Corporation — Loss from Bad Debts, Old	2,000	....
Corporation — Loss on Sale of X Co. Stock	7,500	....
Corporation — Gain on Sale of Y Co. Stock	....	
Corporation Liability Paid — Accounts Payable, Old	30,000	....
Corporation Liability Paid — Notes Payable, Old	35,000	....
Corporation Liability Paid — Accrued Interest on Notes Payable, Old	250	....
	593,550	59
Profit and Loss	....	....
Loss from Bad Debts	....	....
Allowance for Bad Debts	....	....
Depreciation of Furniture and Fixtures	....	....
Depreciation of Buildings	....	....
Accrued Interest on Notes Receivable	....	....
Accrued Interest on Notes Payable	....	....
Corporation — Interest Expense on Mortgage, Old	....	....
Increase in Retained Earnings	....	....

vership
er 31, 1967

Adjustments		Eliminations		Income Statement		Balance Sheet	
	Cr.	Dr.	Cr.	Dr.	Cr.	Dr.	Cr.
			116,150				
	(21) 1,800						2,200
							40,000
							100,000
						24,250	
						33,800	
						12,000	
						18,000	
,000	(14) 50,000					36,000	
						6,000	
	(17) 450						2,400
						60,000	
	(18) 1,800						9,600
						15,000	
							25,000
							22,000
		181,400					
					210,000		
				1,500			
				2,000			
				112,000			
					1,500		
					2,500		
				22,000			
				18,600			
				8,000			
				12,000			
				6,500			
	(19) 200				700		
300				600			
				700			
				2,000			
				7,500			
					500		
			30,000				
			35,000				
			250				
,000	(15) 36,000			50,000	36,000		
450				450			
	(16) 450						450
450				450			
,800				1,800			
200						200	
	(20) 300						300
,800				1,800			
,000	91,000	181,400	181,400				
				247,900	251,200	205,250	201,950
				3,300			3,300
				251,200	251,200	205,250	205,250

Miles Corporation in Receivership
I. B. Owens, Receiver
Balance Sheet
December 31, 1967

Assets			
Current assets:			
Cash			$ 33,800
Notes receivable			12,000
Accounts receivable		$ 18,000	
Less allowance for bad debts		450	17,550
Accrued interest on notes receivable			200
Merchandise inventory			36,000
Total current assets			$ 99,550
Plant and equipment:			
Furniture and fixtures	$ 6,000		
Less allowance for depreciation	2,400	$ 3,600	
Buildings	$60,000		
Less allowance for depreciation	9,600	50,400	
Land		15,000	
Total plant and equipment			69,000
Total assets			$168,550
Liabilities and Stockholders' Equity			
Liabilities			
Current liabilities:			
Notes payable			$ 25,000
Accounts payable			22,000
Accrued interest on notes payable			300
Accrued interest on mortgage			2,200
Total current liabilities			$ 49,500
Long-term debt:			
6% First mortgage payable			40,000
Total liabilities			$ 89,500
Stockholders' Equity			
Capital stock		$100,000	
Less deficit		20,950	
Total stockholders' equity			79,050
Total liabilities and stockholders' equity			$168,550

1967. Creditors and stockholders agree that an attempt should be made to rehabilitate the business. If this proves unsuccessful, the receiver is to sell the business assets, pay off the creditors, and distribute remaining funds to the stockholders. The receiver is authorized to take over all of the business assets. A balance sheet prepared just prior to receivership appears on page 679.

The transactions and the entries on the books of the receiver and the corporation during the period of receivership are shown on pages 680 to 684.

Working papers are prepared at the end of the year in developing the financial statements. The working papers are shown on pages 686 and 687. The income statement prepared from these working papers is given on page 685. The balance sheet is given on page 688.

ACCOUNTING FOR COURT APPOINTEES

The qualifications, duties, and responsibilities of the assignee, trustee, or receiver are quite similar. Each will have to maintain records to show the course of operations, reorganization, or dissolution. The standards and the procedures that have been considered in the preceding pages are applicable in the case of any person who may be placed in charge of the assets of a debtor.

QUESTIONS

1. (a) Describe the nature of the receivership in equity. (b) What are the duties of the receiver?

2. Describe the accounting system that must be employed by an appointee of a court who is to take charge of a debtor's assets.

3. What reports and statements are required of the receiver by a court?

4. What circumstances should be considered in determining whether a receiver should continue with the use of original company books or should establish a new set of books to summarize receivership activities?

5. In accounting for a receivership, why are distinctions made between:

(a) Assets originally acquired by the company and assets subsequently acquired by the receiver?
(b) Liabilities originally incurred by the company and liabilities subsequently incurred by the receiver?
(c) Profit and loss items related to the company and profit and loss items related to the receiver?

6. When separate books are to be maintained by the receiver, what entries would be made on the books of the receiver and on the books of the corporation for each of the following transactions:

(a) The receiver takes over certain assets of the company.
(b) The receiver converts assets taken over into cash.

(c) The receiver pays off corporation debts.
(d) The receiver distributes remaining cash to stockholders in the form dividend in final liquidation.

7. Give two alternative procedures that may be followed on both company's books and the receiver's books for the payment of interest indebtedness originally incurred by the company.

8. What entry would be made on the books of the Success Corporat and on the separate books of receiver M. A. Turner for each transact of the receiver listed below:

(a) Took over control of the corporate assets.
(b) Sold merchandise on account.
(c) Received payment on accounts receivable, old.
(d) Received payment on accounts receivable, new.
(e) Wrote off worthless accounts, old, against allowance established p to receivership.
(f) Received payment on notes receivable, old, and interest earned pric receivership.
(g) Received interest on securities held by the corporation as an investm
(h) Sold part of the securities held at a loss.
(i) Purchased merchandise on account.
(j) Paid accounts payable, new.
(k) Paid mortgage note and accrued interest on the note, part of the in est having accrued prior to receivership.
(l) Paid expenses of receivership.
(m) Paid remaining operating expenses.
(n) Adjusted the accounts for the following items prior to return of the porate assets to the former management:
   (1) Ending inventory.
   (2) Accrued interest on securities held.
   (3) Depreciation on furniture and equipment.
   (4) Accrued operating expenses.
   (5) Provision for bad debts on accounts receivable, new.
   (6) Prepaid operating expenses.

9. (a) What entries are made in closing profit and loss items on receiver's books at the end of the period? (b) What entries are mad the company books in recognizing the results of receivership activities in closing profit and loss items that are reflected on the company bo

10. Assuming that financial solvency is restored and a receiver retur business to the control of its original owners, what entries would be n on the books of the receiver and on the books of the company upon a transfer?

11. Assuming that financial solvency cannot be restored and a rece makes payment to all of the creditors according to the terms of a c position, what entries would be made on the books of the receiver an the books of the company in recording the settlement and corporate solution?

12. What special procedures are followed in combining debtor receiver account balances in the preparation of financial statemen the end of the period?

EXERCISES

1. Give the entries that would appear on the separate books of Wesley Parks, receiver for the Madison Co., in recording the transactions that he completes as listed below. Assets were transferred to the receiver's books, but original liabilities were left on the company records.

(a) Merchandise is purchased for $15,000, receiver's certificates of indebtedness being issued for such goods.
(b) Sales on account are $80,000.
(c) Company accounts payable of $12,000 are paid.
(d) Receiver's certificates of $8,500 are paid.
(e) Collections on company accounts receivable of $14,000 are made; accounts totaling $1,500 prove worthless and are written off.
(f) Collections on receiver's accounts of $46,000 are made; accounts totaling $650 prove worthless and are written off.
(g) Company notes payable of $15,000 and accrued interest of $450 are paid; the company books report a liability for accrued interest of $150 as of the date of the last closing.
(h) Furniture and fixtures with a cost of $10,000 and a book value of $6,000 are sold for $5,600.

2. The receiver for the Monarch Co. keeps separate books. He completes the following transactions, among others, in July:

(1) He acquires company bonds of $10,000 at a market price of 86 plus accrued interest of $200; the bonds are retired. (The obligation was carried on the company's books.)
(2) He sells 500 shares of Wallace Corp. stock, cost to the company $15,750, at 22½, less brokerage commissions and costs of $140. (The asset was carried on the receiver's books.)

Give the entries that would appear on the books of the receiver and on the books of the company assuming that:

(a) Gains, losses, and expense items identified with the debtor are reflected on the receiver's books and are closed into his profit and loss account at the end of the period.
(b) Gains, losses, and expense items identified with the debtor are reflected on the company's books and are closed into a company profit and loss account at the end of the period.

3. The account balances reported below were taken from the books of A. L. Shaw, receiver for Bloom Motors, Inc., and from the books of the company:

Receiver's Books

Bloom Motors, Inc., in Receivership	$66,000
Liabilities Paid — Bloom Motors, Inc.	15,000
Sales	80,000
Cost of Goods Sold	56,000
Operating Expenses	14,000
Bloom Motors, Inc. — Loss on Sale of Investments	16,000

Company's Books

A. L. Shaw, Receiver	$51,000
Interest on Mortgage	2,500

Give the closing entries that are required on (a) the receiver's books and (b) the company's books.

4. The receiver for the Wescott Co. shows on his separate receivership books only the profit and loss items relating to normal trading transactions; company charges and gains and losses on the sale of assets or the liquidation of indebtedness are reported on the company books. The receiver's books carry both old and new assets and new liabilities; old liabilities are reported on the company books. What entries would be made on the two sets of books for the following:

(a) The receiver pays off company notes of $20,000 and interest of $500; the company books show accrued interest of $150 at the date of the last closing; $350 represents interest of the current period.
(b) Company investments, cost $22,500, are sold for $30,000.
(c) Company 6% bonds of $50,000 are acquired by the receiver at a price of 62 plus accrued interest for 3 months; bonds are canceled.
(d) Company plant and equipment items, cost $6,000, book value $4,400, are sold for $1,600.
(e) Normal operations are summarized in the receiver's profit and loss account and show a net income of $6,200. The profit and loss account is closed. The receiver's income is recognized on the company books, and this balance as well as company profit and loss accounts are closed.

5. The balance sheet of the Michigan Sales Company is summarized as follows:

Assets	$100,000	Liabilities	$50,000
Deficit	10,000	Capital stock	60,000

A receiver is appointed who conducts the business for 6 months. He pays all of the old liabilities and returns to the company assets of $120,000 and new liabilities of $40,000. Give the entries to be made on the receiver's books and on the company's books:

(a) At the time control is assumed by the receiver.
(b) At the time the receiver pays off the old liabilities.
(c) At the time the receiver determines the profit and closes the profit and loss account and the liabilities paid accounts.
(d) At the time the receiver turns the business back to the company.

6. The following account balances are found on the books of the Potter Co. and its assignee for the benefit of creditors, James Taylor. Taylor has converted all of the assets, with the exception of land and buildings, into cash.

	Assignee's Books Dr.	Assignee's Books Cr.	Company Books Dr.	Company Books Cr.
James Taylor, Assignee			$114,000	
Potter Co. in Receivership		$114,000		
Cash	$ 20,500			
Land and Buildings	65,000			
Trade Accounts Payable				$ 35,000
Mortgage Note				40,000
Capital Stock				50,000
Retained Earnings			12,500	
Profit and Loss	28,500			1,500
	$114,000	$114,000	$126,500	$126,500

Land and buildings are transferred to holders of the mortgage note in final settlement of this claim; available cash is distributed to trade creditors in final liquidation of their claims.

Give the entries that are required on each set of books in recording the settlements and the dissolution of the business.

PROBLEMS

19-1. The balance sheet for the McDonald Manufacturing Company on April 1, 1967, was as follows:

Assets			Liabilities and Stockholders' Equity	
Cash		$ 8,000	Notes payable	$ 41,000
Notes receivable		21,350	Accounts payable	61,300
Accounts receivable	$57,500		Accrued interest on notes payable	200
Less allow. for bad debts	1,200	56,300	Accrued interest on mortgage note	100
Accrued interest on notes receivable		150	6% Mortgage note payable	20,000
Raw materials inventory		19,000	Capital stock, $10 par	100,000
Goods in process inventory		18,500	Retained earnings	5,500
Finished goods inventory		24,800		
Machinery	$50,000			
Less allow. for depr.	17,000	33,000		
Buildings	$40,000			
Less allow. for depr.	8,000	32,000		
Land		15,000		
Total		$228,100	Total	$228,100

On this date W. A. Krell was appointed as receiver in equity to assume control of the business. The receiver conducted the business until December 31, 1967, returning the business to management on this date. Transactions completed by the receiver were:

Raw materials purchased on account, $36,000; $12,000 remains unpaid on December 31; discounts received were $650.
Freight paid on raw materials purchased, $3,200.
Direct labor paid, $41,000; $600 is accrued on December 31.
Manufacturing expenses paid, $27,600; $750 is accrued on December 31.
General expenses paid, $18,600; $960 is accrued on December 31.
Sales on account, $199,700; $21,500 remains uncollected on December 31; discounts allowed were $1,800.
Selling expenses paid, $26,500; $1,350 is accrued on December 31.
Collections on accounts of April 1, $51,050; remaining accounts were written off as bad.
Payments on accounts of April 1, $61,300.
Collections on notes of April 1, $20,000, and interest, $600; notes of $1,350 and accrued interest of $30 as of April 1 were written off as bad.
Payments on notes payable of April 1, $41,000, and interest on these notes, $1,360.
Payment of semiannual interest on mortgage notes, $600; $400 is accrued on December 31.

Additional adjustments required December 31, 1967, were:

Allowance for bad debts, 2% of accounts.
Depreciation of buildings, $1,500.
Depreciation of machinery, $3,750.
Raw materials inventory, $16,000.
Goods in process inventory, $17,600.
Finished goods inventory, $21,850.
Amount owed to receiver (payable in January), $9,000.

Instructions: (1) Prepare the necessary journal entries for the separate books of the receiver and for the books of the corporation: (a) to record transfer of corporation assets to the receiver; (b) to record the transactions for the period; (c) to adjust and close the books; (d) to record the return of the business to the corporation.

(2) Prepare (a) a balance sheet as of December 31, 1967, and (b) an income statement supported by a schedule to show the cost of goods manufactured for the period April 1–December 31, 1967.

19-2. A. T. Call was appointed receiver in equity on May 1, 1967, when the Robbins Corporation was unable to meet its current obligations as they matured. A balance sheet for the corporation prepared on this date is shown at the top of the following page.

The business was conducted by Call until December 31, 1967, when it was returned to the control of the corporation. Transactions completed by the receiver during the period of receivership were as follows:

Sales on account, $140,000.
Purchases on account, $80,000.

Assets			Liabilities and Stockholders' Equity	
Cash		$ 5,750	Notes payable	$ 35,000
Notes receivable		25,000	Accounts payable	65,000
Accounts receivable	$65,000		Accrued interest on notes payable	1,050
Less allow. for bad debts	1,300	63,700	Capital stock	50,000
			Retained earnings	10,050
Accrued interest on notes receivable		400		
Merchandise inventory		40,000		
Furniture and fixtures	$15,000			
Less allow. for depr.	3,750	11,250		
Vick Corporation stock (750 shares at $20)		15,000		
Total		$161,100	Total	$161,100

Reductions in accounts receivable (new):

Cash collections	$78,000	
Sales returns and allowances	3,000	
Sales discounts allowed	4,000	$85,000

Collections on notes receivable, old, $24,000, and interest, $650; notes receivable, old, of $1,000 and accrued interest of $100 as of May 1 were written off as bad.

Collections on accounts receivable, old, $55,000; remaining accounts were written off as worthless.

Sale of 500 shares of Vick Corporation stock, $12,000.

Reductions in accounts payable (new):

Cash payments	$12,500	
Notes issued in payment	18,000	
Purchases returns and allowances	2,000	
Purchases discounts received	500	$33,000

Payment of notes payable, old, $25,000, and interest, $1,400 (includes all of accrued interest as of May 1).

Payment of accounts payable, old, $65,000.

Payment of operating expenses:

Selling expenses	$18,500	
General expenses (including expenses of receivership)	23,300	$41,800

Additional data for adjustments on December 31 were as follows:

Merchandise inventory, $33,250.
Provision for bad debts, 2% of accounts receivable.
Depreciation of furniture and fixtures, 10% per year.

Accrued expenses:		
Selling expenses	$250	
General expenses	300	
Interest on notes payable (old)	150	
Interest on notes payable (new)	200	$900

Instructions: (1) Prepare the necessary journal entries for the separate books of the receiver and for the books of the corporation: (a) to record transfer of corporation assets to the receiver; (b) to record the transactions for the period; (c) to adjust and close the books; (d) to record the return of the business to the corporation.

(2) Prepare (a) a balance sheet as of December 31, 1967, and (b) an income statement for the period May 1–December 31, 1967.

19-3. X and Y, partners, were unable to meet their maturing obligations and were required to turn over their business to Z, a receiver in equity, on July 1, 1966. The condition of the business as shown by a balance sheet prepared on June 30, 1966, was as follows:

Assets			Liabilities and Capital	
Cash		$ 4,000	Notes payable	$ 7,500
Notes receivable		3,750	Accounts payable	34,700
Accounts receivable		28,450	Accrued interest on notes payable	300
Merchandise inventory		17,600	X, capital	10,000
Furniture and fixtures	$1,800		Y, capital	7,500
Less allow. for depr.	300	1,500		
Cash surrender value of life insurance		4,700		
Total		$60,000	Total	$60,000

Transactions completed by the receiver during the period of receivership, July 1, 1966, to June 30, 1967, were as follows:

Accounts receivable of $20,000 were pledged on an advance from the AAA Finance Co.; the receiver collected cash of $14,400 after a 4% deduction for finance charges.

Settlement was made on notes payable by payment of $7,850, which included accrued interest to date of payment, $350.

Of the unpledged accounts receivable, accounts of $7,500 were subsequently collected and remaining accounts were written off as uncollectible.

Notes receivable of $2,500 were collected; remaining notes were written off as worthless.

Settlement was made on accounts payable by the payment of cash of $15,500 and the balance in the form of 12 equal monthly installment notes. The notes are all dated July 1, 1966, and provide for interest at 5% payable upon their maturities; the first note is due on August 1, 1966.

All of the accounts that were pledged were subsequently collected. The loan from the AAA Finance Co. was paid off with interest at 6% for 2 months.

Purchases on account during the period of receivership were $40,000; sales on account were $75,000.

Operating expenses of $12,500 were paid in cash.
The installment notes were paid as they came due.
Receiver's expenses and fees totaled $6,500; $3,500 had been paid and the balance is payable on August 1, 1967.

On June 30, 1967, the receiver adjusted and closed his books preparatory to returning the business to its owners. On this date, customers' balances not yet collected amounted to $13,600; trade creditors' balances of $12,000 had not yet been paid; operating expenses of $760 were accrued. An inventory disclosed merchandise, cost $16,500, on hand. Depreciation was recognized on furniture and fixtures at 10%; on allowance on the balance of the customers' accounts was established at 5%.

Instructions: (1) Prepare journal entries for the separate books of the receiver and for the books of the partnership: (a) to record transfer of partnership assets to the receiver; (b) to record the receivership transactions for the period; (c) to adjust and close the books; (d) to record the return of the business to the partnership.

(2) Prepare (a) a balance sheet as of June 30, 1967, and (b) an income statement for the period of receivership ending June 30, 1967.

19-4. The Curtis Co. cannot meet its obligations and a general assignment of assets for the benefit of creditors is made at the beginning of 1967. Roger Wilson, assignee, attempts to restore solvency; but on April 30, 1967, it is decided that this is impossible and that interests of the creditor group will be best served by immediate liquidation. On this date balances on the books of the assignee and on the books of the company are:

	Assignee's Books		Company's Books	
	Dr.	Cr.	Dr.	Cr.
Cash	$ 25,500			
Accounts Receivable	30,000			
Merchandise Inventory	40,000			
Roger Wilson, Assignee			$135,000	
Land			15,000	
Buildings			60,000	
Allow. for Depr. of Buildings				$ 7,500
Machinery and Equipment	35,000			
Allow. for Depr. of Mach. and Eq.		$ 15,000		
Patents	25,000			
Accounts Payable		20,000		66,000
6% Mortgage Note Payable (interest payable 4/30 and 10/31)				50,000
Accrued Int. on Mortgage Note				500
Curtis Co. in Assignment		135,000		
Capital Stock				100,000
Retained Earnings			14,000	
Sales		30,000		
Cost of Goods Sold	28,000			
Selling Expenses	6,500			
General Expenses	10,000			
	$200,000	$200,000	$224,000	$224,000

Transactions for April 30–June 30 follow:

(a) On May 1, land and buildings are turned over to the holder of the mortgage note in full settlement of the note and unpaid interest to that date. No entries have been made for accrued interest and depreciation for 1967. The building is being depreciated over a 16-year life.

(b) Collections on accounts receivable total $15,000; remaining accounts are sold to the Crawford Finance Company for $4,500.

(c) Gordon Hall agrees to purchase the merchandise for $20,000 and the machinery and equipment for $9,800. Payment is made on June 30. No depreciation has been recognized on machinery and equipment for 1967; the depreciation rate on this asset is 8% per year. Hall also pays $2,000 for the patents.

(d) Payments of miscellaneous assignment expenses total $1,800. The assignee's fee is $3,000 and this is paid.

(e) Accounts payable incurred by the assignee are paid in full.

(f) The balance of cash is distributed as a final payment on June 30 to old trade creditors.

Instructions: (1) Give the entries on the books of the assignee and the company to record the course of liquidation and to close the two sets of books.

(2) Prepare an income statement summarizing activities of the assignee and the Curtis Co. for the period January 1–June 30.

19-5. James Cole took over the business of Wesson Stores, Inc., on July 1, 1967, as a receiver in equity. Trial balances of the company books and the receiver's books on December 31, 1967, follow. On this date the receiver has merchandise on hand amounting to $20,750.

	Wesson Stores, Inc.		James Cole, Receiver	
	Dr.	Cr.	Dr.	Cr.
Cash			$ 28,420	
Accounts Receivable — Old			37,800	
Accounts Receivable — New			39,680	
Merchandise Inventory, July 1, 1967			25,300	
Fixtures			91,500	
Allowance for Depreciation				$ 17,500
Trademark			12,500	
Accounts Payable — New				19,600
Wesson Stores, Inc., in Receivership				214,400
Sales				200,500
Purchases			126,400	
Depreciation			5,490	
Selling Expenses			22,800	
General Expenses			14,110	
Receiver's Expenses			1,500	
Wesson Stores, Inc., Liabilities Paid — Accounts Payable, Old			35,000	
Wesson Stores, Inc., Liabilities Paid — Interest on Mortgage			4,000	

	Wesson Stores, Inc.		James Cole, Receiver	
	Dr.	Cr.	Dr.	Cr.
Wesson Stores, Inc. — Loss from Accounts Receivable, Old.....			7,500	
James Cole, Receiver...........	$175,400			
Mortgage Payable (due December 31, 1972)................		$ 50,000		
Capital Stock..................		150,000		
Deficit........................	20,600			
Interest Expense...............	4,000			
	$200,000	$200,000	$452,000	$452,000

Instructions: Prepare as of December 31, 1967, an income statement and a balance sheet to be submitted to creditors as interim reports. Submit working papers in support of your statements.

19-6. Coast Sales Company, having insufficient cash to continue operations, turned over the business to L. E. King, a receiver in equity, on December 31, 1966. Account balances on the company's books as shown by a balance sheet prepared on this date were as follows:

Assets			Liabilities and Stockholders' Equity	
Cash....................		$ 10,860	Accounts payable.........	$125,000
Accounts receivable.......		54,700	Capital stock.............	150,000
Inventory (cost)..........		82,940	Retained earnings........	23,500
Advance to Cranston Co...		50,000		
Plant and equip..	$125,000			
Less allow. for depr.........	25,000	100,000		
Total..................		$298,500	Total..................	$298,500

The receiver took over the above assets at the balance sheet figures except for inventory, which was taken over on his books at the prevailing market price for the inventory, $70,000. The receiver operated the business for a year and then returned the business to the control of the stockholders on December 31, 1967.

The following transactions were completed by the receiver during the year of receivership:

Sales on account totaled $184,350, of which $145,400 had been collected.
Purchases on account amounted to $95,400, of which $75,400 had been paid.
All of the old accounts receivable were collected, except for balances of $9,500 that were written off as uncollectible.
At the time the receiver took over the assets, the Cranston Co. was undergoing liquidation; the receiver subsequently recovered 45¢ on the dollar on the advance made to this company.

Company accounts payable were all paid in cash, except for a $25,000 balance on which a 90-day non-interest-bearing note due January 15, 1968, was issued.

Payments representing general and selling expenses amounted to $27,440.

The receiver charged $6,000 for fees and expenses; $4,000 was paid in cash, and the balance is due February 15, 1968.

The merchandise inventory on December 31, 1967, amounted to $82,500.

Depreciation of $12,500 was recorded.

Instructions: (1) Prepare working papers to summarize the activities during the period of receivership.

(2) Prepare an income statement summarizing activities during the period of receivership.

(3) Prepare a balance sheet for the business on December 31, 1967, after its return to the stockholders.

19-7. The Triangle Corporation contemplates dissolution primarily because one of the three stockholders may be regarded as unfriendly. Arthur and Brooks, two of the stockholders, agree to form a partnership.

Applicable data are enumerated below:

(1) A balance sheet of the Triangle Corporation on December 16, 1967, is shown on the following page.

(2) The capital stock records of the corporation as at December 16, 1967, indicate that there are three stockholders who have retained their respective interests since corporate organization prior to 1947, as shown by the following tabulation:

	Total	Preferred		Common	
Stockholder	Paid in	Shares	Paid in	Shares	Paid in
Arthur....	$115,000	300	$30,000	35,000	$ 85,000
Brooks....	105,000	100	10,000	40,000	95,000
Crandall..	90,000	200	20,000	25,000	70,000
	$310,000	600	$60,000	100,000	$250,000

(3) In accordance with a reorganization agreement, the corporation will acquire the stock interest of Mr. Crandall, and thereafter the corporation will be dissolved by an appropriate disposition of its net assets.

(4) In order to finance the acquisition of the stock interest of Mr. Crandall, the property was appraised as a basis for an $80,000 mortgage satisfactorily arranged by the corporation with a bank. The appraisal made as at December 16, 1967, and reflected in the general books is summarized as follows:

	Appraisal	Books Before Appraisal	Revaluation Capital
Property............	$125,000	$70,000	$55,000
Allowance for depr....	27,500	22,500	5,000
	$ 97,500	$47,500	$50,000

The Triangle Corporation
Balance Sheet
December 16, 1967

Assets

Current assets:		
Cash		$ 95,000
Receivables — less allowance, $22,000		135,000
Inventories		225,000
Investments		20,000
Total current assets		$475,000
Property — stated at appraisal value determined as at December 16, 1967	$125,000	
Less allowance for depreciation	27,500	97,500
Treasury preferred stock (par value $40,000), at cost		47,250
Other assets		10,000
Prepaid expenses		4,500
Total assets		$634,250

Liabilities and Stockholders' Equity

Current liabilities:		
Note payable — Mr. Crandall, stockholder		$ 30,000
Accounts payable — trade		110,000
Accrued liabilities		8,000
Accrued federal income tax		24,000
Total current liabilities		$172,000
Reserve for contingencies		50,000
Stockholders' equity:		
Capital stock:		
Preferred stock — par value, $100 (entitled to $110 in liquidation); authorized, 1,000 shares; in treasury, 400 shares; outstanding, 600 shares	$100,000	
Common stock — no-par authorized, 200,000 shares; issued and outstanding, 100,000 shares stated at nominal value of $1 per share	100,000	
Additional paid-in capital	150,000	
	$350,000	
Revaluation capital arising from property appraisal as at December 16, 1967	50,000	
Retained earnings	12,250	412,250
Total liabilities and stockholders' equity		$634,250

(5) The stock interest of Mr. Crandall is to be acquired by the cash payment of $110 per share for the preferred stock and $3 per share for the common stock. Such reacquired stock is to be canceled.

(6) After acquisition of the stock interest of Mr. Crandall, disposition of the net assets of the corporation in complete liquidation and dissolution is to be made as follows:

(a) The note payable to Mr. Crandall is to be paid.

(b) The investments (having a quoted market value of $36,000 as at December 16, 1967) reflected in the balance sheet of the corporation are to be distributed at the market value (incident to the complete liquidation) to Mr. Brooks.

(c) The reserve for contingencies represents a contingent liability on account of guarantees under contract, which is to be settled by the corporation at 25 cents on the dollar.

(d) The remaining assets are to be acquired and the liabilities (including the $80,000 mortgage) are to be assumed by a partnership organized by Arthur and Brooks. Mr. Brooks invests cash in the partnership as necessary to equalize his partnership interest with that of Mr. Arthur.

Instructions: Prepare a balance sheet for the partnership of Arthur and Brooks as of December 16, 1967, after giving effect to the dissolution of the predecessor organization in accordance with the reorganization agreement.

(AICPA adapted)

19-8. The Bergstrom Manufacturing Company cannot meet its obligations and C. Phillips is appointed receiver on April 28, 1967. The books are closed on that date and the following trial balance drawn off:

Debits	
Cash	$ 800
Receivables	1,400
Finished goods	100,000
Materials and supplies	15,000
Goods on consignment (out)	220,000
Employees' bonds	4,700
Unexpired insurance	800
Machinery and equipment	507,300
	$850,000

Credits	
Accounts payable	$110,000
Bank overdraft	1,000
Bank loans	105,000
Baker, Inc.	250,000
Acceptances	23,000
Collateral notes payable	4,700
Lease — machinery	30,000
Accrued interest on lease	2,000
City taxes accrued	4,000
Mortgage on machinery	100,000
Accrued interest on mortgage	3,000
Allowance for depreciation	7,300
Capital stock — preferred	100,000
Capital stock — common	100,000
Retained earnings	10,000
	$850,000

On November 20, 1967, the receiver, having disposed of all assets except $400 of accounts receivable that he considers doubtful, calls upon you to prepare an interim statement for the information of shareholders and creditors. An examination of the company's and the receiver's books and records discloses the following:

(a) Cash receipts:

Collections of accounts receivable	$ 1,000
Rebate upon cancellation of all insurance	100
Proceeds from surrender of insurance policy on life of manager	1,000
Sales of finished goods during receivership	75,000
Rent of sublet portion of building	1,000
Unclaimed wages	500
Interest on bank account	200
Sale of all goods and supplies on hand after operations were discontinued	25,000
Sale of all machinery and equipment owned	200,000
	$303,800

(b) Cash disbursements:

City taxes	$ 4,000
Interest on city taxes	400
Mortgage	100,000
Interest on mortgage	5,000
Labor, materials, and other operating and general expenses during receivership	61,000
	$170,400

(c) Of the stocks on hand at April 28, finished goods costing $60,000 were sold during the receivership and $9,000 of materials and supplies were used.

(d) The accounts payable are understated by $10,000 and include an item of $5,000 in dispute.

(e) The merchandise on consignment was pledged as collateral to the advances by Baker, Inc. and was accepted by them in part payment of these advances at full book value.

(f) The collateral notes payable were for accommodation of employees and were secured by deposit of bonds. The notes were paid by the employees and the bonds returned to them.

(g) The lease covered machinery worth $30,000 used by the company under a lease agreement. It was returned by the receiver and was accepted in full satisfaction of this agreement and all interest accrued.

(h) Claims were filed for all liabilities except an item of $7,000 of accounts payable.

(i) Receiver's fees need not be considered.

Instructions: (1) Prepare a columnar work sheet summarizing the foregoing data in rational manner and form.

(2) Prepare a balance sheet and an income statement summarizing activities of the receiver. (AICPA adapted)

Chapter 20

STATEMENT OF REALIZATION AND LIQUIDATION

A summary of the course of operations of a business under the direction of a receiver or a trustee and involving the realization of assets and the liquidation of indebtedness may be presented in the form of a special report called the *statement of realization and liquidation.*

Operations by a receiver or a trustee are presented on the statement of realization and liquidation in a manner that permits a summary of the net business gain or loss for the period covered. The statement is usually accompanied by supplementary schedules summarizing changes in cash and in capital. It may also be accompanied by formal reports in the form of a balance sheet, an income statement, and a retained earnings statement.

The preparation of the statement of realization and liquidation in its conventional form is illustrated in the first part of the chapter. After the statement is presented in its conventional form, alternative forms that such reporting may take will be suggested.

STATEMENT OF REALIZATION AND LIQUIDATION IN CONVENTIONAL FORM

In its conventional form, the statement of realization and liquidation is composed of asset, liability, and profit and loss sections, with subdivisions in each of these sections as follows:

Assets	
Assets to be realized	Assets realized
Assets acquired	Assets not realized
Liabilities	
Liabilities liquidated	Liabilities to be liquidated
Liabilities not liquidated	Liabilities assumed
Profit and Loss	
Supplementary charges	Supplementary credits

The basic procedures that are employed in the preparation of the statement of realization and liquidation in its conventional form will be illustrated by means of a simple set of facts. Assume the information that follows for the Apex Company.

Harmon West is appointed receiver of the Apex Company on December 1, 1967. The financial position of the Apex Company as shown by a balance sheet prepared on this date is as follows:

Apex Company
Balance Sheet
December 1, 1967

Assets		Liabilities and Stockholders' Equity		
Cash	$ 5,000	Accounts payable		$ 65,000
Marketable securities	15,000	Capital stock	$50,000	
Accounts receivable	30,000	Less deficit	15,000	35,000
Merchandise (cost)	50,000			
Total	$100,000	Total		$100,000

Transactions in December that did not involve cash were as follows:

Sales of merchandise on account	$ 5,000
Purchases of merchandise on account	1,500

Cash receipts and disbursements for December are summarized as follows:

Cash receipts:	
Sale of merchandise	$25,000
Collection of accounts receivable	11,500
Sale of the marketable securities	18,500
Interest on marketable securities	150
	$55,150
Cash disbursements:	
Payment of accounts payable	$35,000
Payment of expenses of receivership	7,500
	$42,500

At the end of December, assets remaining to be realized and liabilities remaining to be liquidated are as follows:

Assets

Accounts receivable:		
Balance, December 1		$30,000
Add sales on account in December		5,000
		$35,000
Deduct: Collections on account in December	$11,500	
Balances determined to be uncollectible	1,500	13,000
Balance, December 31		$22,000

Merchandise:	
Balance, December 1	$50,000
Add merchandise acquired in December	1,500
	$51,500
Deduct cost of goods sold in December	31,500
Balance, December 31	$20,000

Liabilities

Accounts payable:	
Balance, December 1	$65,000
Add purchases on account in December	1,500
	$66,500
Deduct payments on account in December	35,000
Balance, December 31	$31,500
Accrued expenses balance, December 31	$ 350

A statement of realization and liquidation, together with cash and capital schedules, summarizing the foregoing appears on pages 707 and 708. The statement and the supporting schedules were developed by analyzing data in terms of debit and credit and by "posting" the data.

For purposes of posting, the left-hand side of the statement of realization and liquidation is viewed as composed of debit sections; the right-hand side of the statement is viewed as composed of credit sections. The following steps are employed in the process of summarizing receivership activities on the statement and the accompanying schedules:

(1) Opening balance sheet data are reported on the statement and the supplementary schedules as follows:

(a) The cash balance is reported as a debit in the cash schedule.
(b) Remaining assets are listed as debits in the asset section of the statement under the heading "Assets to be realized."
(c) Liabilities are listed as credits in the liability section of the statement under the heading "Liabilities to be liquidated."
(d) Capital balances are reported as credits in appropriately titled capital schedules.

(2) Current transactions other than those involving cash are analyzed and their effects are reported on the statement as follows:

(a) Sales on account are reported as a debit to Accounts Receivable in the asset section of the statement under the heading "Assets acquired" and a credit to Sales in the profit and loss section under the heading "Supplementary credits."
(b) Purchases on account are reported as a debit to Purchases in the profit and loss section of the statement under the heading "Supplementary

Apex Company in Receivership
Harmon West, Receiver
Statement of Realization and Liquidation
For Month Ended December 31, 1967

Assets

Assets to be realized:		Assets realized:	
(1) Marketable securities	$ 15,000	(3) Marketable securities	$ 18,500
(1) Accounts receivable	30,000	(3) Accounts receivable	11,500
(1) Merchandise	50,000	Assets not realized:	
Assets acquired:		(4) Accounts receivable	22,000
(2) Accounts receivable	5,000	(4) Merchandise	20,000

Liabilities

Liabilities liquidated:		Liabilities to be liquidated:	
(3) Accounts payable	35,000	(1) Accounts payable	65,000
Liabilities not liquidated:		Liabilities assumed:	
(4) Accounts payable	31,500	(2) Accounts payable	1,500
(4) Accrued expenses	350		

Profit and Loss

Supplementary charges:		Supplementary credits:	
(2) Purchases	1,500	(2) Sales on account	5,000
(3) Payment of expenses of receivership	7,500	(3) Interest on marketable securities	150
		(3) Sales for cash	25,000
			$168,650
		(5) Net loss	7,200
Total	$175,850	Total	$175,850

Apex Company in Receivership
Harmon West, Receiver
Supplementary Schedules to Accompany
Statement of Realization and Liquidation
For Month Ended December 31, 1967

Cash

1967			1967		
Dec. 1	(1) Balance	$ 5,000	Dec. 1–31	(2) Payment of accounts payable	$35,000
1–31	(3) Cash sales of merchandise	25,000		(2) Payment of expenses of receivership	7,500
	(3) Collections on accounts receivable	11,500	Dec. 31	Balance	17,650
	(3) Proceeds from sale of marketable securities	18,500			
	(3) Collection of interest on marketable securities	150			
		$60,150			$60,150
1968					
Jan. 1	Balance	$17,650			

Capital Stock

			1967		
			Dec. 1	(1) Balance	$50,000

Retained Earnings

1967			1967		
Dec. 1	(1) Balance	$15,000	Dec. 31	Balance	$22,200
31	(5) Net loss for December	7,200			
		$22,200			$22,200
1968					
Jan. 1	Balance	$22,200			

charges" and a credit to Accounts Payable in the liability section under the heading "Liabilities assumed."

(3) Cash receipts and disbursements are reported on the statement and the accompanying schedules as follows:

(a) Cash receipts are reported as debits in the cash schedule and as credits either in the asset section of the statement under the heading "Assets realized" or in the profit and loss section under the heading "Supplementary credits," whichever is appropriate.
(b) Cash disbursements are reported as debits either in the liability section of the statement under the heading "Liabilities liquidated" or in the profit and loss section under the heading "Supplementary charges," whichever is appropriate, and as credits in the cash schedule.

(4) Closing asset and liability balances are reported on the statement as follows:

(a) Assets still to be realized are listed under the asset section heading "Assets not realized."
(b) Liabilities still to be liquidated are listed under the liability section heading "Liabilities not liquidated."

(5) The loss or the gain on liquidation may now be summarized by adding up the amounts on the left-hand and the right-hand sides of the statement. A left-hand side excess indicates a loss emerging from liquidation, and the loss is reported on the right-hand side of the statement to bring the totals on each side of the statement into balance; a right-hand side excess would indicate a gain from liquidation, and such a gain would be reported on the left-hand side of the statement in bringing the totals on each side of the statement into balance. The loss or the gain may now be reported in the supplementary capital schedule; capital accounts then report the capital at the end of the period.

It should be observed that the final loss or gain on the statement of realization and liquidation represents a combination of three factors:

(1) The loss or the gain emerging from asset changes summarized in the asset section of the statement.

(2) The loss or the gain emerging from liability changes summarized in the liability section of the statement.

(3) Revenue and expense items summarized in the profit and loss section of the statement.

In the case of the Apex Company, the loss of $7,200 emerges from the foregoing categories as follows:

				Loss or (Gain)
Assets:				
Assets to be realized.....	$ 95,000	Proceeds from asset realization........	$30,000	
Assets acquired.........	5,000	Assets not realized.	42,000	
	$100,000		$72,000	$28,000
Liabilities:				
Applied to liability liquidation.................	$ 35,000	Liabilities to be liquidated........	$65,000	
Liabilities not liquidated.	31,850	Liabilities assumed.	1,500	
	$ 66,850		$66,500	350
Profit and loss:				
Supplementary charges...............	$ 9,000	Supplementary credits...........	$30,150	(21,150)
Net loss..				$ 7,200

Certain transactions can be treated in alternative manners on the statement of realization and liquidation. In the previous illustration, the following alternatives are available:

Transaction	Treatment	Alternative
Sale of merchandise on account.	Dr. Assets acquired Cr. Supplementary credits	Dr. Assets acquired Cr. Assets realized
Purchase of merchandise on account.	Dr. Supplementary charges Cr. Liabilities assumed	Dr. Assets acquired Cr. Liabilities assumed
Bad accounts written off.	No entry. (Loss emerges from recognition of accounts receivable at a reduced value under the heading "Assets not realized.")	Dr. Supplementary charges Cr. Assets realized
Accrued expenses at end of period.	No entry. (Charge emerges from recognition of amount payable under the heading "Liabilities not liquidated.")	Dr. Supplementary charges Cr. Liabilities assumed

The foregoing examples are simply suggestive of the different procedures that can be followed in developing the statement.

A check on the calculation of the loss or the gain on realization and liquidation may be provided by summarizing the balances reported on the statement and the accompanying schedules as follows: the balance of cash in the cash schedule plus other assets under the heading "Assets not realized" must be equal to the liabilities under the heading "Liabilities not liquidated" plus capital as reported in the capital schedules. Data for the Apex Company summarized in this manner follow:

Apex Company in Receivership
Balances per Statement of Realization and Liquidation
and Accompanying Schedules
December 31, 1967

Assets		Liabilities and Stockholders' Equity		
Cash	$17,650	Liabilities not liquidated		$31,850
Assets not realized	42,000	Capital stock	$50,000	
		Less deficit	22,200	27,800
Total	$59,650	Total		$59,650

Financial statements may be prepared to accompany the realization and liquidation summaries. Financial statements prepared for the Apex Company are shown below.

Apex Company in Receivership
Harmon West, Receiver
Income Statement
For Month Ended December 31, 1967

	Book Value	Proceeds	Loss or (Gain)
Losses and gains on asset realization:			
Marketable securities	$15,000	$18,500	$(3,500)
Merchandise	31,500	30,000	1,500
Accounts receivable	13,000	11,500	1,500
Excess of gains over losses			$ (500)
Expenses during course of realization and liquidation			7,850
			$ 7,350
Other revenue — interest on marketable securities			(150)
Net loss			$ 7,200

Apex Company in Receivership
Harmon West, Receiver
Balance Sheet
December 31, 1967

Assets		Liabilities and Stockholders' Equity			
Cash	$17,650	Accounts payable			$31,500
Accounts receivable	22,000	Accrued expenses			350
Merchandise	20,000				
		Total liabilities			$31,850
		Stockholders' equity:			
		Capital stock		$50,000	
		Deficit, Dec. 1	$15,000		
		Add loss for Dec.	7,200	22,200	27,800
Total	$59,650	Total			$59,650

Limitations of statement when prepared in conventional form. The statement of realization and liquidation prepared in the conventional form just illustrated is subject to certain limitations:

(1) The statement fails to point out those individual factors responsible for the gain or the loss for the period. The final net gain or loss results from a combination of elements — revenue and expense items summarized in a profit and loss section, gains and losses reflected in a summary of asset proceeds, gains and losses reflected in summaries of liability liquidation, and gains and losses reflected in changed values assigned to ending assets and liabilities.

(2) The statement fails to provide a full summary of the nature of asset and liability changes. Beginning and ending asset and liability account balances are presented, but there is no reconciliation of these balances in view of credits to assets for cash proceeds that may be more or less than asset book value and charges to liabilities for cash payments that similarly may involve amounts other than book value. Furthermore, the statement fails to offer support for asset and liability changes arising from adjusting data.

These limitations can be overcome by an alternative approach in the preparation of the statement described in the paragraphs that follow.

STATEMENT OF REALIZATION AND LIQUIDATION IN ALTERNATIVE FORM

Transactions can be reported on the statement of realization and liquidation in a manner that is fully consistent with the procedure that is employed in recording the transactions. All transactions are analyzed just as they would be for recording purposes and are then "posted" to the statement and its supporting schedules.

Sale of an asset is analyzed in terms of the reduction in the book value of the asset and the resulting loss or gain from realization; the reduction in asset book value is reported under the heading "Assets realized," and the loss or the gain on realization is reported as a supplementary charge or credit. Liquidation of a liability is analyzed in terms of the reduction in the book value of the liability and any loss or gain from settlement; the reduction in the liability book value is reported under the heading "Liabilities liquidated" and the loss or the gain on liquidation is reported as a supplementary charge or credit. Adjusting data require analysis in terms of their effects upon assets, liabilities, and profit and loss, and they are reported on the statement in accordance with such an analysis.

Recording transactions and adjustments on the statement and the schedules in accordance with the procedure that is followed in the accounts will make available a complete summary of profit and loss items in the profit and loss section of the statement. Furthermore, ending asset balances become the direct product of beginning asset balances, increases in assets arising from acquisitions, and decreases in assets resulting from asset sales; ending liability balances are the direct product of beginning liability balances, increases in liabilities arising from new obligations assumed, and decreases resulting from the liquidation of liabilities. An organized and clear reporting of profit and loss is made available through this procedure; a full reconciliation of changes in asset and liability items is afforded.

The examples that are listed below illustrate the nature of the analysis and the posting process that is employed on the statement of realization and liquidation in recording current transactions.

Realization of assets:	Cash received is reported as a debit in the cash schedule; the reduction in the book value of the asset is reported as a credit under the heading "Assets realized"; the loss or the gain on realization is reported as a debit or a credit under the heading "Supplementary charges" or "Supplementary credits."
Liquidation of liabilities:	The reduction in the book value of the liability is reported as a debit under the heading "Liabilities liquidated"; cash paid is reported as a credit in the cash schedule; a loss or a gain from settlement is reported as a debit or a credit under the heading "Supplementary charges" or "Supplementary credits."
Revenue:	Cash received is reported as a debit in the cash schedule; the revenue is reported as a credit under the heading "Supplementary credits." If the revenue is receivable, a debit to the receivable would be reported under the heading "Assets acquired."

Merchandise purchases or expense:	The cost or expense is reported as a debit under the heading "Supplementary charges." The payment of cash for purchases or expense is reported as a credit in the cash account. If the expense is payable, a credit to a payable would be reported under the heading "Liabilities assumed."

The following examples illustrate the procedures employed on the statement in recording the adjusting data at the end of the period:

Beginning inventory:	The beginning inventory, an element of cost of sales, is recorded as a debit under the heading "Supplementary charges"; the beginning inventory is canceled in the asset section by a credit under the heading "Assets realized."
Ending inventory:	The ending inventory as an asset item is recorded as a debit under the heading "Assets acquired"; the ending inventory as a subtraction from goods available for sale is recorded as a credit under the heading "Supplementary credits."
Depreciation:	The expense is recorded as a debit under the heading "Supplementary charges"; the reduction in the book value of the asset for cost amortization is recorded as a credit under the heading "Assets realized."
Accrued expense:	The expense is recorded as a debit under the heading "Supplementary charges"; the payable is recorded as a credit under the heading "Liabilities assumed."
Accrued revenue:	The receivable is recorded as a debit under the heading "Assets acquired"; the revenue is recorded as a credit under the heading "Supplementary credits."
Prepaid expense:	When an expense balance includes an amount that is to be deferred: the asset is recorded as a debit under the heading "Assets acquired"; the reduction in the expense balance is recorded as a credit under the heading "Supplementary credits."
Prepaid revenue:	When a revenue balance includes an amount that is to be deferred: the reduction in the revenue balance is recorded as a debit under the heading "Supplementary charges"; the liability is recorded as a credit under the heading "Liabilities assumed."

After recording the current transactions and the adjustments, the ending asset and liability balances are determined as follows:

To arrive at assets not realized —

Assets to be realized + Assets acquired − Assets realized = Assets not realized

To arrive at liabilities not liquidated —

Liabilities to be liquidated + Liabilities assumed − Liabilities liquidated = Liabilities not liquidated

As a final step in the preparation of the statement of realization and liquidation, the debits and the credits in the profit and loss section are summarized. The section is balanced and the net loss or gain is reported as a charge or a credit in the appropriate capital schedule.

Alternative form of statement of realization and liquidation illustrated. Preparation of the statement of realization and liquidation in the alternative form described is illustrated in the following example. Facts in this example are those for the Miles Corporation in receivership that were given in the preceding chapter. Asset, liability, and capital balances for the Miles Corporation at the beginning of receivership were given on page 679. Transactions and adjusting data for the Miles Corporation during the period of receivership are listed and analyzed in terms of their effects upon the statement in the section that follows. The statement of realization and liquidation and the supporting schedules prepared from the foregoing data are shown on pages 717–719. Transactions and adjustments are numbered the same as in the receivership illustration in the preceding chapter.

Opening balances, transactions, and adjustments and the analysis of these data for reporting on the statement of realization and liquidation follow:

Data	Analysis and Entry		
(1) Opening balances: Cash.... $ 1,000 — Liabilities.. $105,650 (List in detail.) Other Assets... 180,400 (List in detail.) — Capital Stock...... 100,000; Deficit..... (24,250) Total: $181,400 — $181,400	Dr. Cash — Cash Schedule.....	1,000	
	Dr. Other assets as named — "Assets to be realized"..........	180,400	
	Dr. Retained Earnings — Retained Earnings Schedule.......	24,250	
	Cr. Liabilities as named — "Liabilities to be liquidated"..		105,650
	Cr. Capital stock — Capital Stock Schedule.............		100,000
(2) Sales on account, $210,000.	Dr. Accounts Receivable — "Assets acquired".................	210,000	
	Cr. Sales — "Supplementary credits"...................		210,000
(3) Purchases on account, $112,000.	Dr. Purchases — "Supplementary charges".....................	112,000	
	Cr. Accounts Payable — "Liabilities assumed"............		112,000
(4) Accounts receivable (new) were reduced by the following: Cash collections............... $158,500 Notes received in payment...... 30,000 Sales returns and allowances..... 1,500 Sales discounts allowed......... 2,000 Total: $192,000	Dr. Cash — Cash Schedule......	158,500	
	Dr. Notes receivable — "Assets acquired"	30,000	
	Dr. Sales Returns and Allowances — "Supplementary charges"....	1,500	
	Dr. Sales Discounts — "Supplementary charges".............	2,000	
	Cr. Accounts Receivable — "Assets realized"...........		192,000

Data		Analysis and Entry		
(5) Collection on accounts receivable, old (carried at book value of $24,000), $22,000; remaining accounts were written off as worthless.		Dr. Cash — Cash Schedule......	22,000	
		Dr. Loss from Bad Accounts, Old — "Supplementary charges"....	2,000	
		Cr. Accounts Receivable, Old — "Assets realized"..........		24,000
(6) Collection on notes receivable, old:		Dr. Cash — Cash Schedule......	15,450	
Principal balances..............	$ 15,000	Cr. Notes Receivable, Old — "Assets realized"............		15,000
Accrued interest...............	150	Cr. Accrued Interest on Notes Receivable, Old — "Assets realized"......................		150
Interest.......................	300	Cr. Interest Income — "Supplementary credits"............		300
	$ 15,450			
(7) Collection on notes receivable (new):		Dr. Cash — Cash Schedule......	18,200	
Principal balances..............	$ 18,000	Cr. Notes Receivable — "Assets realized"................		18,000
Interest.......................	200	Cr. Interest Income — "Supplementary credits"............		200
	$ 18,200			
(8) Accounts payable (new) were reduced by the following:		Dr. Accounts Payable — "Liabilities liquidated".............	90,000	
Cash payments..................	$ 46,000	Cr. Cash — Cash Schedule....		46,000
Notes issued in payment........	40,000	Cr. Notes Payable — "Liabilities assumed".............		40,000
Purchases returns and allowances.	1,500	Cr. Purchases Returns and Allowances — "Supplementary credits"....................		1,500
Purchases discounts received.....	2,500	Cr. Purchases Discounts — "Supplementary credits"......		2,500
	$ 90,000			
(9) Payment of accounts payable, old, $30,000.		Dr. Accounts Payable, Old — "Liabilities liquidated".........	30,000	
		Cr. Cash — Cash Schedule....		30,000
(10) Payment of notes payable, old:				
Principal balances..............	$ 35,000	Dr. Notes Payable, Old — "Liabilities liquidated"...........	35,000	
Accrued interest...............	250	Dr. Accrued Interest on Notes Payable, Old — "Liabilities liquidated"...................	250	
Interest.......................	700	Dr. Interest Expense on Notes Payable, Old — "Supplementary charges".....................	700	
	$ 35,950	Cr. Cash — Cash Schedule....		35,950
(11) Payment of notes payable (new):				
Principal balances..............	$ 15,000	Dr. Notes Payable — "Liabilities liquidated"...................	15,000	
Interest.......................	300	Dr. Interest Expense — "Supplementary charges"..............	300	
	$ 15,300	Cr. Cash — Cash Schedule....		15,300
(12) Sale of securities:		Dr. Cash — Cash Schedule......	13,000	
Common stock of X Co. (book value, $16,000)................	$ 8,500	Dr. Loss on Sale of X Co. Stock — "Supplementary charges"......	7,500	
Preferred stock of Y Co. (book value, $4,000)................	4,500	Cr. Common Stock of X Co. — "Assets realized"............		16,000
	$ 13,000	Cr. Preferred Stock of Y Co. — "Assets realized"............		4,000
		Cr. Gain on Sale of Y Co. Stock — "Supplementary credits"...		500

Data	Analysis and Entry		
(13) Payment of operating expenses: Sales salaries .... $ 22,000 Other selling expense .... 18,600 Office expense .... 8,000 Other general expense .... 12,000 Receivership fees .... 6,500 $ 67,100	Dr. Sales Salaries — "Supplementary charges"	22,000	
	Dr. Other Selling Expense — "Supplementary charges"	18,600	
	Dr. Office Expense — "Supplementary charges"	8,000	
	Dr. Other General Expense — "Supplementary charges"	12,000	
	Dr. Receivership Fees — "Supplementary charges"	6,500	
	Cr. Cash — Cash Schedule		67,100
(14) To recognize beginning inventory as an element of cost of goods sold, $50,000.	Dr. Merchandise Inventory (March 31) — "Supplementary charges"	50,000	
	Cr. Merchandise Inventory (March 31) — "Assets realized"		50,000
(15) To recognize ending inventory as an asset and as a subtraction from goods available for sale in arriving at cost of goods sold, $36,000.	Dr. Merchandise Inventory (Dec. 31) — "Assets acquired"	36,000	
	Cr. Merchandise Inventory (Dec. 31) — "Supplementary credits"		36,000
(16) To provide for bad debts (new accounts), $450.	Dr. Loss from Bad Debts (Allowance provision) — "Supplementary charges"	450	
	Cr. Allowance for Bad Debts — "Assets realized"		450
(17) To record depreciation of furniture and fixtures, $450.	Dr. Depreciation of Furniture and Fixtures (Allowance provision) — "Supplementary charges"	450	
	Cr. Allowance for Depreciation of Furniture and Fixtures — "Assets realized"		450
(18) To record depreciation of buildings, $1,800.	Dr. Depreciation of Buildings (Allowance provision) — "Supplementary charges"	1,800	
	Cr. Allowance for Depreciation of Buildings — "Assets realized"		1,800
(19) To record accrued interest on notes receivable, $200.	Dr. Accrued Interest on Notes Receivable — "Assets acquired"	200	
	Cr. Interest Income (accrued) — "Supplementary credits"		200
(20) To record accrued interest on notes payable (new), $300.	Dr. Interest Expense (accrued) — "Supplementary charges"	300	
	Cr. Accrued Interest on Notes Payable — "Liabilities assumed"		300
(21) To record accrued interest on mortgage, $1,800.	Dr. Interest Expense on Mortgage, Old (accrued) — "Supplementary charges"	1,800	
	Cr. Accrued Interest on Mortgage — "Liabilities assumed"		1,800
(22) To transfer net gain to retained earnings, $3,300.	Dr. Increase in Retained Earnings — "Supplementary charges"	3,300	
	Cr. Increase in Retained Earnings — Retained Earnings Schedule		3,300

Miles Corporation in Receivership
I. B. Owens, Receiver
Statement of Realization and Liquidation
March 31–December 31, 1967

Assets

Assets to be realized:		
Notes receivable, old		$ 15,000
Accounts rec., old	$25,000	
Less allow. for bad debts	1,000	24,000
Accrued interest on notes receivable, old		150
Merchandise inventory (March 31)		50,000
Furniture and fixtures	$ 6,000	
Less allow. for depr.	1,950	4,050
Buildings	$60,000	
Less allow. for depr.	7,800	52,200
Land		15,000
Common stock of X Co.		16,000
Preferred stock of Y Co.		4,000
		$180,400
Assets acquired:		
(2) Accounts receivable		$210,000
(4) Notes receivable		30,000
(15) Merchandise inventory (Dec. 31)		36,000
(19) Accrued interest on notes receivable		200
		$276,200
		$456,600

Assets realized:		
(4) Accounts receivable		$192,000
(5) Accounts rec., old	$25,000	
Less allow. for bad debts	1,000	24,000
(6) Notes receivable, old		15,000
(6) Accrued interest on notes rec., old		150
(7) Notes receivable		18,000
(12) Common stock of X Co.		16,000
(12) Preferred stock of Y Co.		4,000
(14) Merchandise inventory (March 31)		50,000
(16) Allowance for bad debts		450
(17) Allow. for depr. of furniture and fixtures		450
(18) Allow. for depr. of bldgs.		1,800
		$321,850
Assets not realized:		
Notes receivable		$ 12,000
Accounts receivable	$18,000	
Less allow. for bad debts	450	17,550
Accrued interest on notes receivable		200
Merchandise inventory (Dec. 31)		36,000
Furniture and fixtures	$ 6,000	
Less allow. for depr.	2,400	3,600
Buildings	$60,000	
Less allow. for depr.	9,600	50,400
Land		15,000
		$134,750
		$456,600

Liabilities

Liabilities liquidated:	
(8) Accounts payable	$ 90,000
(9) Accounts payable, old	30,000
(10) Notes payable, old	35,000
(10) Accrued interest on notes payable, old	250
(11) Notes payable	15,000
	$170,250
Liabilities not liquidated:	
Notes payable	$ 25,000
Accounts payable	22,000
Accrued interest on notes payable	300
Accrued interest on mortgage	2,200
6% first mortgage payable	40,000
	$ 89,500
	$259,750

Liabilities to be liquidated:	
Notes payable, old	$ 35,000
Accounts payable, old	30,000
Accrued interest on notes payable, old	250
Accrued interest on mortgage	400
6% first mortgage payable	40,000
	$105,650
Liabilities assumed:	
(3) Accounts payable	$112,000
(8) Notes payable	40,000
(20) Accrued interest on notes payable	300
(21) Accrued interest on mortgage	1,800
	$154,100
	$259,750

Profit and Loss

Supplementary charges:		Supplementary credits:	
(3) Purchases	$112,000	(2) Sales	$210,000
(4) Sales returns and allowances	1,500	(6) Interest income	300
(4) Sales discounts	2,000	(7) Interest income	200
(5) Loss from bad accts., old	2,000	(8) Purchases returns and allowances	1,500
(10) Interest expense on notes, old	700	(8) Purchases discounts	2,500
(11) Interest expense	300	(12) Gain on sale of Y Co. stock	500
(12) Loss on sale of X Co. stock	7,500	(15) Merchandise inventory (Dec. 31)	36,000
(13) Sales salaries	22,000	(19) Interest income (accrued)	200
(13) Other selling expense	18,600		
(13) Office expense	8,000		
(13) Other general expense	12,000		
(13) Receivership expense	6,500		
(14) Merchandise inventory (March 31)	50,000		
(16) Loss from bad debts (allowance provision)	450		
(17) Depr. of furniture and fixtures (allowance provision)	450		
(18) Depr. of buildings (allowance provision)	1,800		
(20) Interest expense (accrued)	300		
(21) Interest expense on mortgage, old (accrued)	1,800		
	$247,900		
(22) Increase in retained earnings	3,300		
	$251,200		$251,200

Miles Corporation in Receivership
I. B. Owens, Receiver
Supplementary Schedules to Accompany Statement of Realization and Liquidation
March 31–December 31, 1967

Cash

Mar. 31 Balance	$ 1,000	(8) Payment of accts. payable	$ 46,000
(4) Collection of accounts receivable	158,500	(9) Payment of accts. pay., old	30,000
(5) Collection of accounts receivable, old	22,000	(10) Payment of notes payable, old, $35,000; accrued interest on notes payable, old, $250; and current interest, $700	35,950
(6) Collection of notes receivable, old, $15,000; accrued interest on notes receivable, old, $150; and current interest, $300	15,450	(11) Payment of notes payable, $15,000, and current interest, $300	15,300
(7) Collection of notes receivable, $18,000, and current interest, $200	18,200	(13) Payment of operating expenses	67,100
(12) Proceeds from sale of common stock of X Co., $8,500, and preferred stock of Y Co., $4,500	13,000	Dec. 31 Balance	33,800
	$228,150		$228,150
Jan. 1 Balance	$ 33,800		

Capital Stock

		Mar. 31 Balance	$100,000

Retained Earnings

Mar. 31 Balance	$ 24,250	Dec. 31 (22) Increase in retained earnings	$ 3,300
		31 Balance	20,950
	$ 24,250		$ 24,250
Jan. 1 Balance	$ 20,950		

A check on the accuracy of the statement of realization and liquidation and supporting schedules is afforded by the following summary:

Miles Corporation in Receivership
Balances per Statement of Realization and Liquidation and Accompanying Schedules
December 31, 1967

Assets		Liabilities and Stockholders' Equity		
Cash	$ 33,800	Liabilities not liquidated		$ 89,500
Assets not realized	134,750	Capital stock	$100,000	
		Less deficit	20,950	79,050
Total	$168,550	Total		$168,550

The financial statements that may be prepared to accompany the realization and liquidation statement for the Miles Corporation were illustrated in the previous chapter.

STATEMENT OF REALIZATION AND LIQUIDATION— WORK SHEET FORM

Previous illustrations utilized a statement and related schedules in summarizing the process of realization and liquidation. Realization and liquidation data can also be presented by means of a work sheet. Although such a presentation represents a departure from the conventional approach, nevertheless it offers a clearer and better organized presentation of data and is developed in a manner similar to that employed in preparing other financial statements. The work sheet approach may take a number of different forms. One form is illustrated on pages 720 and 721. The statement is based upon the facts in the previous example. The following steps are employed in the development of the statement:

(1) Opening balances are listed in the first pair of columns in trial balance form but are divided into four groups: (a) cash, (b) other assets, (c) liabilities, and (d) stockholders' equity. In listing the accounts, adequate space is left within each group to provide for transactions and new accounts to be added in summarizing activities for the period.

(2) Transactions are recorded in a second pair of columns. The four classes of items mentioned in (1) are headed in the second pair of columns as shown at the top of page 722.

Miles Corporation in Receivership
I. B. Owens, Receiver
Statement of Realization and Liquidation
March 31–December 31, 1967

Item	Balances March 31, 1967		Transactions: Cash Receipts	Transactions: Cash Disbursements	Balances December 31, 1967	
Cash Balance, March 31	1,000					
Collection of Accounts Receivable			(4) 158,500			
Collection of Accounts Receivable, Old			(5) 22,000			
Collection of Notes Receivable, Old; Accrued Interest on Notes Receivable, Old; and Current Interest			(6) 15,450			
Collection of Notes Receivable and Current Interest			(7) 18,200			
Payment of Accounts Payable				(8) 46,000		
Payment of Accounts Payable, Old				(9) 30,000		
Payment of Notes Payable, Old; Accrued Interest on Notes Payable, Old; and Current Interest				(10) 35,950		
Payment of Notes Payable and Current Interest				(11) 15,300		
Proceeds from Sale of Common Stock of X Co. and Preferred Stock of Y Co.			(12) 13,000			
Payment of Operating Expenses				(13) 67,100		
Cash Balance, December 31					33,800	
			Other Assets: Acquired	**Other Assets: Realized**		
Notes Receivable, Old	15,000			(6) 15,000		
Accounts Receivable, Old	25,000			(5) 25,000		
Allowance for Bad Debts, Old		1,000	(5) 1,000			
Accrued Interest on Notes Receivable	150		(19) 200	(6) 150	200	
Merchandise Inventory	50,000		(15) 36,000	(14) 50,000	36,000	
Common Stock of X Co.	16,000			(12) 16,000		
Preferred Stock of Y Co.	4,000			(12) 4,000		
Furniture and Fixtures	6,000				6,000	
Allowance for Depreciation of Furniture and Fixtures		1,950		(17) 450		2,400
Buildings	60,000				60,000	
Allowance for Depreciation of Buildings		7,800		(18) 1,800		9,600
Land	15,000				15,000	
Accounts Receivable			(2) 210,000	(4) 192,000	18,000	
Notes Receivable			(4) 30,000	(7) 18,000	12,000	
Allowance for Bad Debts				(16) 450		450

			Liabilities — Liquidated	Liabilities — Assumed		
Notes Payable, Old		35,000	(10) 35,000			
Accounts Payable, Old		30,000	(9) 30,000			
Accrued Interest on Notes Payable, Old		250	(10) 250			
Accrued Interest on Mortgage		400		(21) 1,800		2,200
6% First Mortgage Bonds		40,000				40,000
Accounts Payable			(8) 90,000	(3) 112,000		22,000
Notes Payable			(11) 15,000	(8) 40,000		25,000
Accrued Interest on Notes Payable				(20) 300		300
			Stockholders' Equity — Charges	**Stockholders' Equity — Credits**		
Capital Stock		100,000				100,000
Retained Earnings	24,250				24,250	
Sales				(2) 210,000		
Purchases			(3) 112,000			
Sales Returns and Allowances			(4) 1,500			
Sales Discounts			(4) 2,000			
Loss from Bad Debts, Old			(5) 2,000			
Interest Income				(6) 300 (7) 200 (19) 200		
Purchases Returns and Allowances				(8) 1,500		
Purchases Discounts				(8) 2,500		
Interest Expense on Notes, Old			(10) 700			
Interest Expense			(11) 300 (20) 300			
Loss on Sale of Common Stock of X Co.			(12) 7,500			
Gain on Sale of Preferred Stock of Y Co.				(12) 500		
Sales Salaries			(13) 22,000			
Other Selling Expense			(13) 18,600			
Office Expense			(13) 8,000			
Other General Expense			(13) 12,000			
Receivership Fees			(13) 6,500			
Profit and Loss (Beginning and Ending Inventories)			(14) 50,000			
Loss from Bad Debts			(16) 450	(15) 36,000		
Depreciation of Furniture and Fixtures			(17) 450			
Depreciation of Buildings			(18) 1,800			
Interest Expense on Mortgage			(21) 1,800			
	216,400	216,400	247,900	251,200	205,250	201,950
Increase in Retained Earnings			3,300			3,300
			251,200	251,200	205,250	205,250

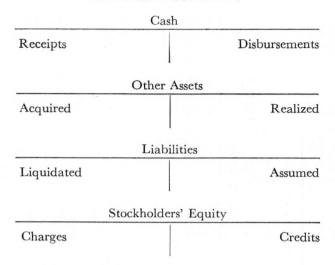

Cash	
Receipts	Disbursements

Other Assets	
Acquired	Realized

Liabilities	
Liquidated	Assumed

Stockholders' Equity	
Charges	Credits

Transactions are analyzed in terms of their effects on assets, liabilities, and stockholders' equity, and are then applied in debit and credit form to the accounts in the different sections within the Transactions columns. Transactions are thus analyzed and recorded on the work sheet in the same manner in which they would be analyzed and recorded on the books.

(3) Closing asset and liability balances are determined by combining opening balances and changes reported in the Transactions columns and are listed in the third pair of columns. The original balances for the stockholders' equity are carried to the third pair of columns. Profit and loss data in the last section of the Transactions columns are summarized and the net loss or gain is determined. The loss or the gain is entered as a balancing figure in the profit and loss section of the Transactions columns and as a balancing figure in the third pair of columns where it represents an addition to or a subtraction from the opening balances previously listed.

The work sheet form for realization and liquidation reporting offers in a single exhibit the following data:

(1) Beginning and ending asset, liability, and capital balances.
(2) A reconciliation of beginning and ending balances for each item.
(3) A full statement of cash receipts and disbursements.
(4) A full statement of profit and loss items and the net change in capital therefrom.

With a complete summary of financial and operating data available in this form, any data requested by the court, creditors, or other parties can be conveniently located on the work sheet and transferred to the appropriate reports and schedules.

QUESTIONS

1. Distinguish between the functions served by the statement of affairs and the statement of realization and liquidation.

2. Describe the nature of the statement of realization and liquidation.

3. How are original assets, liabilities, and capital reported for purposes of realization and liquidation reports?

4. (a) What sections of the statement of realization and liquidation or its supplementary schedules are affected by cash receipts? (b) What sections of the statement or the schedules are affected by cash payments?

5. How are the following data reported on the statement of realization and liquidation and the supplementary schedules?

(a) Assets taken over by a receiver.
(b) Sale of assets taken over at a loss.
(c) Payment to creditors of amounts owed.
(d) Distribution of cash to owners in the form of a final liquidating dividend.

6. How are the following data reported on the statement of realization and liquidation prepared in its conventional form?

(a) Additional assets discovered.
(b) Additional liabilities discovered.
(c) Assets determined in the course of receivership to be worthless.
(d) Composition of creditors, payments to be made to creditors in four equal quarterly installments.

7. Explain the sources that contribute to the net gain or loss when the statement of realization and liquidation is prepared in its conventional form, the gain or loss being determined by adding up the two sides of the statement.

8. What alternative analyses of the following transactions may be made in reflecting these transactions on the statement of realization and liquidation prepared in the conventional form?

(a) Sale of merchandise.
(b) Accrued revenue.
(c) Bad accounts written off.
(d) Settlement of an obligation at less than its book value.

9. (a) What are the limitations of the statement of realization and liquidation prepared in its conventional form? (b) What modifications can be introduced in the statement to overcome these limitations?

10. When transactions are analyzed in terms of debit and credit and are applied to the statement of realization and liquidation and the supplementary schedules, what are the offsetting debits and credits for each of the following transactions? (Give the statement section or schedule affected.)

(a) Sale of merchandise on account.
(b) Purchase of merchandise on account.
(c) Liquidation of liabilities at less than the book value of such obligations.
(d) Sale of securities at a profit.
(e) Payment of expenses.

11. When adjustments are analyzed in terms of debit and credit and are applied to the statement of realization and liquidation and the supplementary schedules, how would the following adjusting data be recorded in the statement sections and the schedules?

(a) Recognition of beginning inventory as an element in the calculation of cost of goods sold.
(b) Recognition of ending inventory as an asset and an element in the calculation of cost of goods sold.
(c) Accrued expenses.
(d) Amortization of deferred costs.
(e) Accrued revenue.
(f) Prepaid expense balances that have expired.
(g) Expense prepayments.
(h) Prepaid revenue balances that have been earned.
(i) Revenue prepayments.

12. The accountant for the Lea Co., which is in receivership, feels that the preparation of a statement of realization and liquidation makes unnecessary the development of the usual financial statements. Do you agree?

13. What advantages can you suggest for the preparation of the realization and liquidation report in work sheet form?

EXERCISES

1. The following balance sheet is prepared for the Warden Co. on December 1, when a receiver is appointed to take over control:

Assets		Liabilities and Stockholders' Equity	
Cash	$ 12,000	Accounts payable	$ 55,000
Receivables	36,000	Capital stock	50,000
Merchandise	40,000	Retained earnings	(2,000)
Furniture and fixtures (net)	15,000		
Total	$103,000	Total	$103,000

Transactions in December are summarized below.

Cash receipts:		
Sale of merchandise		$24,000
Collection of receivables:		
Company receivables	$18,500	
Receivership claims	450	18,950
		$42,950
Cash disbursements:		
Purchase of merchandise		$ 750
Expenses		1,400
		$ 2,150

Sales of merchandise on account in December totaled $1,800. Company receivables of $650 were written off as worthless.
At the end of December the merchandise on hand is valued at $22,500. Depreciation of furniture and fixtures is $250.

(a) Prepare a statement of realization and liquidation in conventional form together with supporting schedules as illustrated on pages 707 and 708.

(b) Prepare a condensed balance sheet as of December 31 to prove the gain or the loss for December.

2. Indicate how the following transactions for the Leo Sales Co. in receivership will be reported on the statement of realization and liquidation and the supplementary schedules prepared in the conventional form as illustrated on pages 707 and 708.

(a) Sale of merchandise on account, $25,000.
(b) Collections on accounts receivable, $13,500; bad accounts of $500 are written off.
(c) Sale of securities, cost $17,000, for $16,400.
(d) Purchase of merchandise on account, $17,500.
(e) Payment of selling expenses, $4,750, of which $800 had accrued prior to receivership.
(f) Depreciation of furniture and fixtures, $275.
(g) Trade of delivery truck with a book value of $1,200 for a new truck, cost $2,200; $1,000 is allowed on the trade in, and the balance is paid in cash.
(h) Payments on accounts payable, $9,800, after a $200 discount.

3. From the data and transactions given below, prepare a statement of realization and liquidation and supporting schedules for Jaspar and Kalman in the alternative form illustrated on pages 717–719.

(a) The opening balance sheet on October 1 is as follows:

Assets		Liabilities and Capital	
Cash	$ 5,000	Notes payable	$ 25,000
Marketable securities	20,000	Accounts payable	34,500
Accounts receivable	25,000	Accrued interest on notes payable	500
Merchandise	40,000	Jaspar, capital	30,000
Furniture and fixtures (net)	10,000	Kalman, capital	10,000
Total	$100,000	Total	$100,000

During October:

(b) Marketable securities are sold for $11,500.
(c) Merchandise sales are as follows: cash sales, $8,500; sales on account, $6,500.
(d) Collections of $12,000 are made from customers; accounts of $400 are written off as worthless.
(e) Payment of $10,000 is made on notes payable and $300 for accrued interest.

(f) Payment of $21,500 is made on account.
(g) Payment of $2,200 is made for expenses.
(h) At the end of October, the following adjusting data are recognized:
Merchandise on hand is valued at $22,500.
Accrued interest on notes payable on this date is $330.
Depreciation of furniture and fixtures for October is $250.

4. Assuming preparation of the statement of realization and liquidation and the supplementary schedules for the Wesley Co. in the alternative form illustrated on pages 717–719, give the effects of the following data on the statement and the schedules in terms of offsetting debits and credits:

(a) Balances relating to a company bond issue as of December 1 when receivership became effective were as follows: bonds payable, $100,000; discount on bonds, $2,500; accrued interest on bonds, $1,000. Outstanding bonds were acquired at a cost of $86,500, which included a payment of accrued interest of $1,500.
(b) Balances relating to a company investment as of December 1 were as follows: $20,000 bonds of Ward Co., book value (cost plus prior accumulation of discount), $17,750; accrued interest on bonds, $300. Bonds were sold at a price of $21,400, which includes receipt of accrued interest of $325.
(c) Balances relating to unsecured creditors were as follows: notes payable, $20,000; accrued interest on notes payable, $1,500; accounts payable, $38,500. Settlement was made with this group of creditors by means of a composition whereby they agreed to accept 60¢ on the dollar, 15¢ being paid in December, the balance to be paid in the first three months of the following year in equal monthly installments.

5. The partnership of L and M is unable to repay a maturing bank loan. Upon petition to the court by the bank, N is appointed as receiver and takes over the control of the firm on July 15. The following balance sheet is prepared from the books of the partnership on this date:

Assets		Liabilities and Capital	
Cash	$ 3,250	Accounts payable	$ 6,500
Accounts receivable	12,000	Bank loan	20,000
Inventory (at cost)	21,350	Accrued interest on bank loan	500
Supplies	800	L, capital	10,000
Furniture and fixtures (net)	7,600	M, capital	8,000
Total	$45,000	Total	$45,000

Transactions during the period of receivership from July 15–August 31 are as follows:

(a) The accounts receivable are sold for $8,000.
(b) A part of the inventory costing $5,000 is sold for $4,500; the balance of the inventory is accepted by the original supplier at a 30% discount.
(c) Supplies of $150 are used.
(d) The loan from the bank is paid, together with additional interest of $150.

(e) Accounts payable of $3,500 are paid.
(f) Receiver's expenses of $295 are paid.

Prepare a statement of realization and liquidation together with supporting schedules in the alternative form illustrated on pages 717–719.

6. Assuming preparation of the statement of realization and liquidation for the Process Co. in work sheet form as illustrated on pages 720 and 721, indicate in terms of offsetting debits and credits how the adjustments that are listed below would be reported on the working papers:

(a) Depreciation of equipment	$ 4,500
(b) Leasehold amortization	1,500
(c) Accrued interest on investments	350
(d) Accrued salaries and wages	600
(e) Interest expense that is prepaid	60
(f) Rental income that is prepaid	200
(g) Beginning inventory that is to be recognized in cost of sales	35,000
(h) Ending inventory	21,500

PROBLEMS

20-1. The Young Steamship Co. is unable to meet its current obligations, partly because of losses suffered and partly because of inability to transfer its foreign deposits back to the United States. Upon petition of creditors, the Moore Steamship Co. is appointed receiver. On February 12, 1967, the receiver takes over the control of the business. The following balance sheet is prepared from the books of the Young Steamship Co. on this date:

Assets		Liabilities and Stockholders' Equity		
Cash	$ 51,200	Accounts payable		$ 202,500
Freights receivable	81,800	Accrued expenses		39,500
Stores	42,000	6% mortgage payable		600,000
Prepaid expenses	35,000	Capital stock	$1,400,000	
Foreign deposits	123,500	Less deficit	83,500	1,316,500
Vessels (net)	1,800,000			
Furniture and fixtures (net)	25,000			
Total	$2,158,500	Total		$2,158,500

Transactions of the receiver up to December 31, 1967, are as follows:

(a) Cash receipts:

Collections on freights receivable (after a discount of $6,800 is allowed to a shipper in settlement of a dispute that may have cost more to arbitrate)	$ 75,000
Freights received on new shipping contracts (after 5% of the total freight being withheld by agents pending settlement)	427,500
Proceeds from sale of stores	91,800
	$594,300

(b) Cash disbursements:

Fuel oil	$165,000
Operating expenses (including accrual of $39,500)	133,000
Cash purchases of stores	50,000
Accounts payable (after discounts of $4,500)	198,000
Prepaid expenses	40,000
Receiver's expenses	17,500
Interest on mortgage	36,000
	$639,500

(c) Foreign deposits of $108,000 are utilized to pay for stores purchased abroad and shipped back by own vessels. The stores are subsequently sold to wholesalers at a 15% discount. (Proceeds are listed under cash receipts.)

(d) Adjustments are required at end of year for the following:

Accounts payable — fuel oil	$ 35,000
Stores on hand	25,000
Prepaid expenses	18,500
Accrued expenses	26,800
Depreciation of vessels	100,000
Depreciation of furniture and fixtures	5,000

Instructions: (1) Prepare a statement of realization and liquidation in conventional form together with supporting schedules as illustrated on pages 707 and 708.

(2) Prepare a balance sheet as of December 31, 1967.

20-2. The Bailey Storage Co. is unable to meet its obligations. On March 1, 1967, C. C. Hill is appointed receiver. A balance sheet prepared from the books of the Bailey Storage Co. on this date is as follows:

Assets			Liabilities and Stockholders' Equity	
Cash		$ 8,200	Accounts payable	$ 28,400
Notes receivable		14,500	6% mortgage on warehouse	50,000
Accounts receivable		31,050	Accrued interest on mortgage (up to March 1, 1967)	1,000
Supplies		2,050	Capital stock	40,000
Trucks	$25,000		Retained earnings	8,400
Less allow. for depr.	10,500	14,500		
Warehouse	$75,000			
Less allow. for depr.	17,500	57,500		
Total		$127,800	Total	$127,800

The receiver operates the business until the end of the year and returns control of the business to the stockholders at that time.

Transactions during the period of receivership are as follows:

(a) Cash receipts:

Notes receivable, old	$ 13,800
Accounts receivable, old	28,000
Accounts receivable, new	140,000
	$181,800

(b) Cash disbursements:

Accounts payable, old	$ 28,400
Accounts payable, new	27,600
Mortgage payable (installment payment on November 1, 1967)	15,000
Interest on mortgage (paid on May 1 and November 1)	3,000
Operating expenses	84,400
Receiver's expenses and fees	8,000
New trucks (after trade-in allowance of $12,500)	10,000
	$176,400

(c) Billings to customers for truckage and storage services, $153,450. Purchases on account for gas, oil, parts, and other supplies, $35,000.

(d) A 10-month, 6% note dated April 1, 1967, for $3,000 is received from a customer in settlement of an old account receivable. Balances of old accounts and notes receivable after collections are written off as worthless at the end of the year.

(e) Five trucks having a total book value of $10,000, but with an original cost to the company of $20,000, are traded in for 5 new trucks on July 1, 1967. The new trucks are estimated to have a total scrap value of $5,000 after a 5-year service life.

(f) Adjustments on December 31, 1967, are as follows:

Supplies on hand	$ 4,500
Accrued operating expenses	1,500
Depreciation of old trucks (including depreciation for the period March 1–July 1, 1967, for the 5 trucks traded)	3,000
Depreciation of warehouse	5% per year

Instructions: (1) Prepare a statement of realization and liquidation in conventional form together with supporting schedules as illustrated on pages 707 and 708.

(2) Prepare a balance sheet as of December 31, 1967.

20-3. A balance sheet prepared for Rusk Sales as of March 1, 1967, is given at the top of the next page. A summary of transactions of the receiver for this company for the period March 1–July 1 follows:

Transactions, March 1–July 1:

Sales on account, $36,000.
Purchases on account, $12,000.
Reductions in accounts receivable — new:
Cash collections, $30,000.
Sales returns, $1,000.

Assets			Liabilities and Capital	
Accounts receivable.	$20,000		Cash overdraft	$ 1,500
Less allow. for bad debts	1,000	$19,000	Notes payable	15,000
Merchandise inventory		30,000	Accrued interest on notes payable	500
Furniture and fix.	$ 5,000		Accounts payable	25,000
Less allow. for depr.	1,000	4,000	M. A. Rusk, capital	16,000
Securities		5,000		
Total		$58,000	Total	$58,000

Reductions in accounts receivable — old:
  Cash collections, $14,000.
  Accounts of $2,000 were written off as uncollectible; remaining accounts are believed to be collectible.
Sale of securities, $8,000.
Payment of accounts payable — new, $4,000.
Payment of notes payable — old, $15,000, and interest, $1,000.
Payment of accounts payable — old, $18,000.
Payment of operating expenses, $10,000.

Data for adjustments, July 1:
  Merchandise inventory, $18,500.
  Depreciation of furniture and fixtures, $100.
  Accrued operating expenses, $500.
  Prepaid operating expenses, $350.

Instructions: Prepare a statement of realization and liquidation in the alternative form together with supplementary schedules as illustrated on pages 717–719.

20-4. Using the data given in Problem 19-1 for the McDonald Manufacturing Company (page 693), prepare a statement of realization and liquidation in the alternative form together with supplementary schedules as illustrated on pages 717–719.

20-5. Using the data given in Problem 19-2 for the Robbins Corporation (page 694), prepare a statement of realization and liquidation in the alternative form together with supplementary schedules as illustrated on pages 717–719.

20-6. Using the data given in Problem 19-6 for the Coast Sales Company (page 699), prepare a statement of realization and liquidation in the work sheet form illustrated on pages 720 and 721.

20-7. Using the data given in Problem 19-3 for the X and Y partnership (page 696), prepare a statement of realization and liquidation in the work sheet form illustrated on pages 720 and 721.

20-8. The Sherbourne Company was unable to meet its obligations. As a result, William Bond was appointed receiver on February 5, 1967. The following trial balance was taken from the books as of that date:

Debits	
Cash	$ 764
Accounts Receivable	5,928
Merchandise	16,536
Prepayment of Expenses	704
Fixtures	12,342
Total debits	$36,274

Credits	
Accounts Payable	$15,987
Notes Payable	3,500
Accrued Wages, Taxes, etc.	1,275
Accrued Rent	600
Allowance for Depreciation	3,803
Capital Stock	10,000
Retained Earnings	1,109
Total credits	$36,274

In the period from February 5 to April 30, 1967, the receiver's actions resulted in the following:

(1) An audit of the accounts receivable disclosed that there were an additional $423 of accounts receivable that had not been brought on the books.
(2) Merchandise costing $8,310 was sold for cash.
(3) A portion of the fixtures, which cost $5,376 and had accumulated depreciation credits of $942, was sold.
(4) Accounts receivable totaling $1,882 were collected. Other accounts amounting to $741 have been determined to be worthless.
(5) Claims have been approved and paid for $903 of the wages and taxes that were accrued at February 5. Wage claims for $125 that were unrecorded on February 5 have also been approved and paid. Other claims have not yet been paid.
(6) Expenses for wages and supplies used in liquidating the business to April 30 amounted to $1,245. Fees for the receiver need not be considered.
(7) Rent under leases has continued to accrue in the amount of $900. Interest of $70 has accrued on notes payable.
(8) Cash receipts and cash disbursements show the following:

Cash Receipts	
Collection of accounts	$1,882
Sales of merchandise	9,108
Sale of fixtures	1,000

Cash Disbursements

Accrued wages and taxes	$1,028
Expenses of the receivership	1,245

Instructions: Prepare a statement of realization and liquidation in work sheet form for the period ended April 30, 1967.

(AICPA adapted)

20-9. Horace Sloan, a partner in the investment banking firm of Ross and Sloan, died on December 31, 1966.

The assets and the liabilities of the firm at that date were as follows:

Cash in bank	$ 11,526.90	
Life insurance funds receivable	44,700.02	
Marketable securities	978,663.77	
Notes and accounts receivable	23,268.63	
Bonds of Brown Lumber Co., bankrupt, at 25% of par	56,250.00	
75% interest in logs, lumber, machinery, and logging equipment	22,604.25	
Notes payable		$ 500,000.00
Accrued interest		1,500.00
Liability as guarantors of note of Brown Lumber Co., bankrupt		38,170.31
Accounts payable		14,357.33
Agreement to repurchase $10,000 of Brown Lumber Co. bonds at 97½		9,750.00
Capital — Phillip Ross, 40%		229,294.37
Capital — Horace Sloan, 60%		343,941.56
Totals	$1,137,013.57	$1,137,013.57

Phillip Ross, surviving partner, was appointed trustee to continue the business for a limited period of time.

The transactions to September 30, 1967, were as follows:

(1) The amount due for life insurance was collected.
(2) $712,554.07 was realized on securities that cost $619,483.
(3) $3,725 was expended in exercising rights, the original and newly acquired shares being among those unsold at September 30.
(4) Notes and accounts receivable realized $17,429.30, but of the balance outstanding at September 30 only $1,000 was considered good.
(5) Foreclosure proceedings were instituted on the bonds of the Brown Lumber Co. In the final settlement, $4,603.97 was realized in cash and the firm acquired a ¾ interest in 10,000 acres of timberland.
(6) The interest in logs, lumber, machinery, and logging equipment realized $2,725.09.
(7) A claim receivable for damages, which was pending on December 31, 1965, but not entered on the books, was settled for $3,000.
(8) The notes payable, with interest amounting to $27,500, were paid.
(9) The liability as guarantors of the note of the Brown Lumber Co. was discharged by payment of $36,149.73.

(10) One $1,000 bond of the Brown Lumber Co. had been lost or stolen and therefore could not be produced. The remaining bonds were repurchased. (It is assumed there will be no company liability on the bond that is not produced.)
(11) The accounts payable, together with an additional item of $1,275 owing at December 31 but not discovered until later, were duly paid.
(12) The sum of $200,000 was withdrawn in the proportion of the partners' investments.
(13) Expenses incurred, exclusive of interest, totaled $7,328.30, of which $432.15 was unpaid on September 30, 1967.
(14) Income amounted to $14,732.03, of which $2,500 had not been received on September 30, 1967.

Instructions: Prepare a realization and liquidation account in conventional form for the use of the trustee and of the executor of the estate of the deceased partner.

(AICPA adapted)

20-10. The Wain Sales Company was on the verge of insolvency. Accordingly, a receiver in equity, B. C. Bell, was appointed by the court to take legal possession of the company's assets as at February 1, 1966. A new set of books was opened by the receiver to reflect properly the transactions during the period of receivership. A proper segregation is to be made between transactions originating prior to and during the receivership. At January 31, 1967, the business was turned back to the company.

A post-closing trial balance of the company on February 1, 1966, is as follows:

Cash	$ 48,000	
Notes Receivable	90,000	
Notes Receivable Discounted		$ 10,000
Accrued Interest on Notes Receivable	3,000	
Accounts Receivable	138,000	
Allowance for Bad Debts		7,500
Inventory	174,200	
Subscribers to Capital Stock	20,500	
U.S. Government Bonds	25,000	
Buildings	121,400	
Allowance for Depreciation — Buildings		56,540
Prepaid Insurance	1,400	
Deficit	47,040	
Notes Payable		127,500
Accrued Interest on Notes Payable		9,800
Accounts Payable		296,000
Mortgage Payable on Buildings		60,000
Accrued Interest on Mortgage Payable		1,200
Common Stock		100,000
	$668,540	$668,540

The transactions during the year of receivership are summarized on the following page.

Cash collections:	
Notes receivable—old (gross $79,000, less notes written off $8,090)	$ 70,910
Interest on notes receivable, including accrued of $3,000	4,400
Accounts receivable — old (gross $110,000, less discount $2,000 and uncollectible accounts written off $3,500)	104,500
Subscribers to capital stock ($1,000 uncollectible)	19,500
Securities considered worthless February 1, 1966, and not included in post-closing trial balance	4,700
Receiver's certificates issued, interest at 4½%	120,000
Accounts receivable—new (gross $225,000, less discounts $10,600)	214,400
Interest on U. S. Government bonds	500
Total cash collections	$538,910

Cash payments:	
Notes receivable discounted, not paid by makers (remaining $7,500 as at February 1, 1966, paid by makers at maturity)	$ 2,500
Notes payable — old	65,200
Accounts payable — old (retired at a discount of 10%)	45,000
Accounts payable — old (retired at face amount)	210,000
Accounts payable — new (gross $124,000, less discount $2,000)	122,000
Interest on notes payable, including accrual of $9,800	11,000
Interest on mortgage payable, including accrual of $1,200	2,600
Receiver's certificates	40,000
Interest on receiver's certificates	5,810
Receiver's fees	8,000
Total cash payments	$512,110

Other transactions:	
Sales of merchandise (before discounts)	$260,000
Purchases of merchandise (before discounts)	110,000
Selling expenses	33,000
General expenses	13,000
Adjustments at January 31, 1967:	
Merchandise inventory	$120,000
Depreciation of buildings	3,600
Accrued taxes	3,700
Accrued interest on notes receivable	300
Provision for doubtful accounts — new accounts receivable	800
Insurance expired	300
Interest on old notes payable	2,800
Interest on old mortgage payable	1,200

Instructions: (1) Prepare a statement of realization and liquidation summarizing the receiver's transactions by setting forth his accountability at the beginning of receivership, the operations during receivership, and the condition at the consummation of receivership.

(2) Prepare summary statements of assets and liabilities conveyed to company management at the termination of the receivership period.

(AICPA adapted)

Chapter 21

ESTATES AND TRUSTS

GENERAL ESTATE PROCEDURES

Parties who are entrusted with the care, management, and disposition of properties on behalf of others and who are accountable for such activities act in a *fiduciary* capacity and are referred to as *fiduciaries*. Receivers, assignees, or trustees who are appointed to take over control of the assets of insolvents act in the capacity of fiduciaries; parties who are named by a court to assume control of an estate and parties who, by terms of a trust instrument, are appointed to manage properties for the benefit of others act in a similar capacity.

This chapter and the one that follows describe the accounting for those parties who are charged with the administration of properties of an estate and of a trust. For an understanding of the accounting, one must be familiar with the nature of the activities and responsibilities of such parties as well as with the legal framework within which they operate. It should be understood that the statutes and body of law governing the activities of those parties administering estates and trusts vary in the different states. Also the legal requirements as to accounting frequently differ. The rules and the procedures described are those that generally apply to estates and trusts. The accounting methods and reports illustrated are those that are normally adopted or required.

ADMINISTRATION OF AN ESTATE

Upon the death of a person, it becomes necessary for some party to assume control and administration of the property of the deceased and to make appropriate disposition of this property. If the decedent has left a will, the property will be disposed of in accordance with the terms of the will; in the absence of a will, state inheritance laws govern the disposition of the property.

When a person has left a will directing the disposal of his estate, he is said to have died *testate* and is referred to as the *testator*. In the absence of a will, the person is said to have died *intestate*. When there is a will, this document may name a person to carry out its provisions. If such a person is willing and able to administer the estate, the court will confirm the appointment, this party being referred to as an *executor*. When a will fails to name a person or when the party named is unqualified to act in settling the estate, the court will appoint a person to act in such a capacity, this party being referred to as an *administrator-with-the-will-annexed* or *administrator c.t.a.* (*cum testamento annexa*). In the absence of a will, the court appointee is simply referred to as an *administrator*. The executor or the administrator is referred to as the *personal representative* of the deceased.

The *law of decedent estates*, also known as the *probate law*, governs the administration and the distribution of the property of a decedent. Such law is administered by courts that are variously known as *probate*, *surrogate's*, or *orphans'* courts. A petition to the court of proper jurisdiction by any party having an interest in the estate begins estate proceedings. Such a petition is known as an *application for probate* or *application for grant of administration*. If there is a will, it must be ruled valid or *probated* by a court of probate jurisdiction before it becomes operative. If, after hearings, the court is satisfied that the will is genuine, that it was made by a party who was legally competent at the time, and that it represents the last expression of the decedent relative to the distribution of his property, the court will order that the terms of the will be carried out. The will is then said to be *admitted to probate*.

The court confirms the appointment of the executor named in a will by issuing *letters testamentary;* it confirms the appointment of an administrator by issuing *letters of administration*. These instruments evidence the authority of the individual to act as the personal representative of the deceased and authorize him to assume title to the properties of the estate. The executor or the administrator is considered a fiduciary operating under court control. In the case of any questions as to the appropriate distribution of properties of the estate, he may ask the court to interpret the terms of the will or to designate the legal rules that are applicable.

RESPONSIBILITIES OF THE EXECUTOR OR THE ADMINISTRATOR

Upon appointment by the court, the personal representative becomes responsible for the collection, conservation, and distribution of the property of the decedent. He prepares an inventory of the estate properties for court, tax, and accounting purposes. He pays funeral and administrative expenses, legal debts of the decedent, estate and inheritance taxes, and other expenses, converting properties into cash when necessary to meet such requirements. After providing for the payment of all estate expenses and debts, the personal representative distributes remaining properties to the legal beneficiaries. Finally, he is required to account to the court and to other parties of interest with respect to estate administration and distribution. These responsibilities are described in detail in the following pages.

Administration of estate properties. The personal representative takes title to the estate properties. Throughout the course of his administration, he continues to seek out and take possession of any properties that belong to the estate. Properties coming into his custody must be prudently managed, protected, and conserved until they are distributed. In the absence of special instructions in the will, the personal representative is normally not required to invest estate funds or to operate a business left by the decedent. When the estate includes a partnership interest, liquidation of the partnership will be required in the absence of special provisions in the will or in the articles of copartnership. The responsibility of the personal representative is ended only after all of the properties have been properly distributed and the court has formally approved the course of administration.

The personal representative is normally required to submit to the court an inventory of all the properties identified with the estate. A full description should be provided for each property item in the inventory, and values must be assigned to each item. The personal representative may be able to arrive at satisfactory valuations for many of the items in the inventory; for certain items he may find it necessary or may be required by law to consult outside authority.

State laws specify those assets that pass directly to beneficiaries in accordance with testamentary dispositions or rules of succession and those that pass to the estate. Ordinarily, laws provide that title to real property shall pass directly to the legal beneficiaries upon the death of the decedent and that only personal property shall pass into the possession and control of the personal representative. In many states a portion of the decedent's personal properties in the form of household and personal effects and a limited amount of cash pass directly to the surviving spouse or to the decedent's children. Ordinarily, real and personal properties that pass directly to beneficiaries are not included in the decedent's inventory, the inventory being limited to those properties for which the representative is held accountable by law; but schedules listing real and personal properties excluded from the inventory should be submitted to the court so that the court may be informed of all of the properties left by the decedent.

When a valid contract has been made by the decedent for the sale of real estate, the receivable for the contract sales price is recognized as personal property and comes into the possession of the personal representative for distribution. Although title to the real estate passes to the legal beneficiary, the latter is required to relinquish such title upon the fulfillment of the contract. A contract by the decedent to purchase real estate is recognized as realty and thus is identified with the legal beneficiary; any payment that is required on such a contract represents a claim against the personal property of the deceased. A mortgage receivable owned by the decedent represents personalty. A mortgage payable on real estate frequently follows the real estate and thus represents a claim to be met by the party acquiring title to the realty; in some states, however, the mortgage may have to be paid by the estate, the beneficiary taking the property free of the mortgage.

Among the property items that are included in the personal representative's inventory are the following:

Cash in checking and savings accounts, cash on hand, cash in decedent's safety deposit box, etc.
Shares in savings and loan associations.
Valuables in the decedent's possession, in safety deposit box, etc.
Advancements to legatees or heirs.
Notes and accounts receivable.
Accrued interest on notes (up to and including the date of the decedent's death).
Recoverable judgments and other claims.
Accrued rents receivable.
United States bonds.
Corporate bonds.
Accrued interest on bonds (up to and including the date of decedent's death.)
Corporate stock.
Dividends declared on corporate stock.
Ownership interest in a business or partnership.
Real estate that becomes a part of the estate by terms of the will.
Life insurance when the estate is named the beneficiary.

The values that are assigned to the individual property items are normally those that are applicable or acceptable for inheritance and estate tax purposes. For many items, satisfactory valuations may be found by consulting brokers, appraisers, or other experts or by referring to current market quotations. For certain items, valuation will present serious difficulties calling for various approaches under the different circumstances encountered. Particularly difficult problems are encountered in determining the value to be assigned to such properties as a going business, an interest in a partnership, stock in a closely held corporation, royalty rights, and copyrights.

When properties are discovered after the original inventory has been filed, supplements to the original inventory are prepared and submitted to the court.

Payment of debts of the estate. Debts of the estate must be fully met before any property may properly be distributed to the beneficiaries. State laws generally set a limited period, frequently six months, within which creditors of the decedent must file their claims or forfeit any legal rights that they may have. Ordinarily, laws require that the executor or the administrator must advertise for claims by legal notices in specified newspapers or journals for a certain period. He is required to reject invalid claims and to establish appropriate defenses where claims can be avoided. Approved claims are paid.

When assets of the estate are insufficient to meet all debts, the personal representative recognizes certain priorities as set by state statutes. The law frequently provides that claims against the estate shall have priority in the following order:

(1) Estate administration expenses.
(2) Funeral expenses.
(3) Expenses of last illness.
(4) Allowances for the support and the maintenance of the deceased's dependents for a limited period when provided by law.
(5) All debts entitled to preference under the laws of the United States and of the state.
(6) Certain wage claims of employees of the decedent.
(7) Judgment creditors.
(8) All other debts.

Taxes paid by the estate. The executor or the administrator is responsible for the settlement of all taxes relating to the decedent or to his estate, including income tax, inheritance tax, and estate tax.

Income tax. Income tax on the decedent's income for the period from the date of the last income tax return to his death will have to be paid from estate assets. Furthermore, the payment of income tax on the income of the estate during the period of its operation will be required. Federal tax laws require the preparation of fiduciary income tax returns for an estate with a gross income in its taxable year of $600 or more. Estate income is reduced by a $600 exemption in calculating the income subject to tax. The income tax rates applicable to estate income are the same as those applicable in the calculation of an individual's income tax liability.

State inheritance tax. The state inheritance tax is a levy on the individual's *right to receive* a portion of the decedent's estate. Thus, state inheritance taxes paid by the estate are recoverable by it either by collections from the various beneficiaries or by deductions from the amounts that would otherwise be payable to them. Inheritance taxes are normally based on the relationship of the various beneficiaries to the decedent, those persons more closely related to the decedent being allowed greater exemptions and lower tax rates than those beneficiaries more distantly related.

Federal estate tax. The federal estate tax is a levy on an individual's *right to give* his estate to others upon his death. This tax, the same as other expenses and debts of the decedent, is paid by the estate and reduces the amount ultimately available to the beneficiaries. The estate tax is based upon the decedent's total or *gross estate* less certain allowable deductions and exemptions. A decedent's gross estate includes all property, real or personal, tangible or intangible. Life insurance proceeds payable to the estate are includible in the gross estate; policies on which the decedent possessed no incident of ownership and payable to beneficiaries other than to the estate are not includible or subject to estate tax. In arriving at the value of the gross estate, the executor or the administrator is offered the option of stating property values as of (1) the date of the decedent's death or (2) the date one year after the decedent's death, or in the case of property disposed of at an earlier date, the value at such date of disposition. Deductions are allowed from the gross estate for funeral and administrative expenses, commissions and fees, claims against the estate, unpaid mortgages, bequests for public, charitable, and religious organizations, and a marital deduction for certain properties that pass to a surviving spouse. A $60,000 exemption is allowed for each estate. The gross estate, less allowable deductions and the $60,000 exemption, represents the *taxable estate*. Estate tax rates are applied to the taxable estate in arriving at a tentative estate tax balance.[1] A credit is allowed against this amount for state death taxes paid, such a credit being limited to a stated percentage of the taxable estate. The tentative tax less the credit is the net tax for which the estate is liable.

Distribution of estate properties after payment of debts and taxes. When a beneficiary other than the estate is named in a life insurance policy, insurance payment is made directly to the named beneficiary;

[1]Federal estate tax rates are graduated, current rates beginning at 3% for the first $5,000 subject to estate tax and rising to 77% for any amount in excess of $10,000,000.

when the estate is named as the beneficiary, payment is made to the personal representative. Title to all other personal property passes to the personal representative and from him to the beneficiaries. Title to real estate normally passes directly from the decedent to the beneficiary by will or by law unless (1) it becomes a part of the estate by the terms of the will or (2) it is made available to the personal representative by court order to provide cash for payment of debts of the estate.

After appropriate provisions have been made for the payment of all claims against the estate, the personal representative may take steps to distribute the remaining estate properties.

In the absence of a will naming the persons who are to receive the estate property available for distribution, property is distributed by the personal representative in accordance with the state laws relating to intestate succession. Such laws specify the distributions that are required in view of the various relationships by marriage and by blood that are found between the decedent and the surviving relatives. Certain states distinguish between the distribution of real and personal property of the intestate. In these states, the persons who are to inherit real property are determined by the *laws of descent* and the persons who are to share in the distribution of personal property are determined by the *laws of distribution.* The persons receiving properties under the laws of descent and distribution are referred to as the *heirs* or *next of kin.*

When there is a will, the disposition of personal property by the terms of the will is known as a *legacy* or *bequest*; the person named to receive such property is referred to as a *legatee*. The disposition of real property by the terms of a will is known as a *devise;* the person named to receive such property is called a *devisee.*

Testamentary dispositions of personal property are classified as follows:

Specific legacies: Dispositions of particular items. For example: "My gold watch to my son," "My 100 shares of X Co. common stock to my wife," or "Forgiveness of the $1,000 owed me by my brother, Jack."

Demonstrative legacies: Dispositions of cash or other personal property payable out of a particular fund or asset accumulation. For example: "$1,500 from the balance of my account at the State Bank to my chauffeur."[1]

General legacies: Dispositions that are not specifically designated and are payable out of the general assets of the estate. For example: "$10,000 to the Children's Hospital."

---

[1]When a fund is insufficient to satisfy the amount of the demonstrative legacy, the amount of the deficiency would be regarded as a general legacy.

Residuary legacies: Dispositions of the personal property remaining after distribution of the other legacies named. For example: "The rest, remainder, and residue of my personal property to be divided between my brothers, John and Henry."

Real property dispositions may be classified as *specific devises*, *general devises*, and *residuary devises*. A residuary disposition in the form of the "remainder of my property" would cover all remaining property, both real and personal.

It should be observed that if a will fails to dispose of all the property, such a failure is referred to as a condition of *partial intestacy*, and undisposed properties are distributed in accordance with the laws of descent and distribution. It should be further noted that state laws frequently provide that a surviving spouse, in lieu of testamentary dispositions, may elect to take a share of the estate as specified by law; such an elective share is frequently defined as that portion of the properties that the surviving spouse would have received if the decedent had died intestate.

It has already been suggested that the personal representative must make provision for the payment of all estate expenses and debts before distributing properties to the various beneficiaries. If the personal representative should make certain distributions and then find himself unable to satisfy estate claims in full, he may be held personally liable to creditors.

When payment of debts makes it impossible to pay the legacies in full as provided for in the will, the abatement or ademption of certain classes of legacies is necessary. *Abatement* refers to a proportionate reduction or scaling down of legacies of a certain class; *ademption* refers to the complete revocation of legacies of a certain class. In the absence of provisions to the contrary in a will, laws of the state normally call for the abatement or the complete revocation of legacies by classes in the following order: (1) residuary legacies, (2) general legacies, and (3) demonstrative and specific legacies. When all the personal property is insufficient to satisfy the claims against the estate, the court may approve the lease, mortgage, or sale of the real property descended or devised.

In certain cases a legacy may not require payment. This *failure of legacies* may be authorized by law or the court as a result of such circumstances as death of a legatee prior to the decedent's death, loss or destruction of specific property bequeathed, or a disposition that is regarded as contrary to public policy.

Amounts that are earned on specific legacies after the date of the decedent's death accrue to the respective beneficiaries; when collection of such earnings is made by the estate, the earnings are paid to the legatee together with the specific legacy. Certain legacies may be subject to deductions or offsets for such items as (1) payments made by the executor on behalf of respective beneficiaries, for example, inheritance and transfer taxes and fees, and (2) debts due to the decedent by respective beneficiaries. A parent during his lifetime may transfer properties to his children as *advancements* on the shares of the estate to which they will be entitled. When there is no will, a child who has received an advancement from the decedent for an amount that exceeds his distributable share of the estate is entitled to no further distribution but is not required to return such excess; if the advancement is less than his share, he is entitled to the difference between his distributable share of the estate and the advancement. A gratuitous transfer of property prior to death is construed as an absolute gift and not as an advancement except when the latter can be proved.

State laws normally provide that, at his discretion, the executor or the administrator can defer the distribution of legacies for a certain period, normally from six months to a year. Furthermore, laws frequently provide that interest shall accrue on legacies that are unpaid after a specified time after death or petition for probate. Payment by the estate of interest for such an overdue period is recognized as a charge against the earnings of the properties whose distribution was deferred. When a payment is made to a legatee in advance of a statutory waiting period, such a payment may be subject to a charge for interest for the period of advancement; in the latter instance, the distributable estate is increased by the amount of the interest earned. In making an advance payment, the personal representative should require bond to assure recovery of the advance if such action later becomes necessary.

Intermediate and final accountings. The executor or the administrator is required to report to the court and to other interested parties on the progress of estate administration and distribution. The nature of the report varies in character. In some cases certain reports may be required at regular intervals during the course of administration; when an estate is of short duration, reports may be required only when the personal representative has completed estate administration and requests a formal discharge. Reports summarizing activities and progress that are submitted during the course of estate administration are referred to as *intermediate accountings;* a report submitted upon fulfillment of the responsibilities of administration is called a *final accounting*. Vouchers evidencing completed transactions may be submitted to the court together with the reports. The report frequently found in accounting to the court takes the form of the *charge and discharge statement.* This report is illustrated later in the chapter.

The compensation or the commissions allowed to the executor or the administrator may be provided by terms of the will or may be fixed by the court or by statute. Commissions when computed in accordance with statute are based upon the value of the estate that is handled by the personal representative. A fund may be set aside for remuneration of the personal representative. The court must approve the payment of the commissions. In making the final accounting, the personal representative requests approval for the payment of commissions and for the distribution of remaining estate properties. If everything is in order, the court approves the accounting and issues a decree authorizing remaining distributions. Upon receiving further evidence from the personal representative that distributions have been completed, the court declares the estate to be closed and the settlements to be final and binding upon all parties.

ACCOUNTS MAINTAINED FOR THE ESTATE

The nature and the form of the books and the records to be maintained by the executor or the administrator are not prescribed by law. Books and accounts should be kept in sufficient detail to make possible the convenient preparation of the reports required by the court and other parties of interest. Ordinarily, the reports are prepared in a form that shows the properties coming into the possession of the personal representative and the disposition of such properties. Accounts, then, must provide a record of the estate properties and their changes. It is normally desirable to record transactions of the estate in double-entry form.

General principles of estate accounting. Data concerning properties and how the personal representative has met his responsibilities relative to such properties are provided by records maintained in the following manner:

(1) Asset accounts are charged and Estate Principal (or Estate Corpus) is credited for property items originally coming into the possession of the personal representative. Estate Principal summarizes the accountability of the personal representative for properties transferred to his custody.

(2) Increases in estate properties from asset discoveries, the sale or conversion of estate properties at a gain, proceeds from the lease, mortgage, or sale of real properties as authorized by the court, and estate in-

come are recorded by charges to appropriate asset accounts accompanied by credits to nominal accounts that indicate the sources of the increased accountability on the part of the personal representative; credit balances in the nominal accounts are ultimately closed into Estate Principal.

(3) Decreases in estate properties from the sale or the conversion of properties at a loss, the payment of expenses and debts of the decedent, the payment of estate expenses, and distributions to beneficiaries are recorded by credits to appropriate asset accounts accompanied by debits to nominal accounts that explain the reductions in the personal representative's accountability; debit balances in the nominal accounts are ultimately closed into Estate Principal. The full distribution of estate assets will cancel the balance in Estate Principal.

Recording transactions of an estate. Entries to record the transactions of the estate in accordance with the foregoing are made as follows:

Opening the estate books. The estate inventory is the basis for the opening entry on the books for the estate. Individual estate assets are debited and the account Estate Principal is credited. Debits are made to asset accounts at the appraised values as of the date of the decedent's death as reported on the asset inventory submitted to the court.

Discovery of assets after opening estate books. When assets of the decedent are discovered after the inventory has been filed with the court, appropriate asset accounts are debited and the account Assets Subsequently Discovered is credited. The assets are recorded at their value as of the date of the decedent's death.

Disposal of assets. As properties, including accrued income items as of the date of death, are converted into cash, Cash is debited and the appropriate asset accounts are credited. If assets realize less than their book values, Losses on Disposal of Assets is debited; if assets realize more than their book values, Gains on Disposal of Assets is credited.

Collection of income accruing to the estate. Collections of income earned after the date of the decedent's death on assets belonging to the estate are recorded by debits to Cash and credits to Collections of Income.

Collection of amounts accruing to a legatee. When the personal representative collects amounts that were earned after the date of the decedent's death on assets specifically bequeathed and thus accruing to a legatee, Cash is debited and an account with the legatee is credited. The subsequent payment of cash to the legatee is recorded by a debit to the account with the legatee and a credit to Cash.

Payment of funeral and administrative expenses. Payments of funeral expenses, expenses of the last illness, court fees, attorneys' fees, accountants' fees, appraisers' fees, fiduciaries' fees, bonding costs, estate tax, and other administrative expenses are recorded by debits to Funeral and Administrative Expenses and credits to Cash.

Payment of debts of decedent. Payments of debts of the decedent and income taxes on the income earned prior to death are recorded by debits to Debts of Decedent Paid and credits to Cash.

Payment or delivery of legacies. Payments or transfers of legacies are recorded by debits to the account Legacies Paid or Delivered and credits to the appropriate asset accounts. When it is required that legacies be recorded at their fair market values as of the date of distribution, Legacies Paid or Delivered is charged for such values, assets are credited at amounts reported on the books, and loss or gain balances are charged or credited for the differences.

Payment of amounts chargeable to a legatee. When the personal representative makes payment of a charge that is to be borne by the legatee (state inheritance taxes, for example), an account with the legatee is debited and Cash is credited. The subsequent receipt of cash from the legatee is recorded by a debit to Cash and a credit to the account with the legatee. If the legatee is not required to reimburse the estate but is paid his legacy less the amount previously paid on his behalf, the balance in the legatee's account is transferred to Legacies Paid or Delivered.

Payment of expenses chargeable to income. Payments of expenses incurred after the date of the decedent's death and applicable to the earnings of the estate are recorded by debits to Expenses Chargeable to Income and credits to Cash.

Distribution of net income. Distributions of cash representing estate net income — the difference between collections of income and payments of expenses chargeable against such income — are recorded by debits to Distributions of Income and credits to Cash.

Closing the executor's books. Accounts before closing appear with debit and credit balances as follows:

Debits	Credits
Losses on Disposal of Assets	Estate Principal
Funeral and Administrative Expenses	Assets Subsequently Discovered
Debts of Decedent Paid	Gains on Disposal of Assets
Legacies Paid or Delivered	Collections of Income
Expenses Chargeable to Income	
Distributions of Income	

In closing the books, the nominal accounts with debit and credit balances are transferred to Estate Principal. After closing the nominal accounts, Estate Principal will be equal to the assets still on hand. When all of the estate assets have been distributed, transfer of the nominal accounts to Estate Principal will cancel this balance.

ACCOUNTING FOR THE ESTATE ILLUSTRATED

Accounting for the estate is illustrated in the example that follows.[1] Assume that Walter Bragg dies testate on May 31, 1967. The will is admitted to probate on July 10, 1967. The will does not name an executor and the court appoints a son, Thomas Bragg, to act as administrator-with-the-will-annexed, and he is issued letters of administration.

The will provides for the following:

(1) Specific bequests of 500 shares of Gaylord Corp. preferred stock and all of the Gaylord Corp. bonds are made to the son, Thomas.
(2) A general bequest of $1,000 is made to the Children's Hospital.
(3) After payment of debts, expenses, and legacies, the home, the remaining estate properties, and any estate income are to be distributed to the widow, Anna Mae.

On July 25, Thomas Bragg files with the court of probate jurisdiction an inventory of estate assets as follows:[2]

Cash in bank	$ 2,400
Personal effects	350
Automobile	1,500
United States Savings Bonds, Series E, (redemption value on May 31)	6,250
Gaylord Corp. 6% Preferred Stock, 1,000 shares, par $10	10,550
Dividends declared on Gaylord Corp. 6% Preferred Stock	150
Gaylord Corp. 4% Bonds, par $6,000	5,675
Accrued interest on Gaylord Corp. 4% bonds from Feb. 1	80
Total inventory of assets	$26,955

[1]The example in this chapter is designed to illustrate the basic procedures that are required in accounting for the estate. The special problems that are encountered when estate assets are transferred to a trust and principal-income distinctions must be made are considered and illustrated in an example in the next chapter. The example in the next chapter also illustrates the schedules that are prepared to support the charge and discharge statement.

[2]In this example it is assumed that laws of the state do not require the executor to include in his inventory those assets for which he assumes no responsibility or control; hence the home that passes directly to the widow is not reported. In certain states it is required that real estate be inventoried even though it passes directly to heirs or devisees. Further, it may be desirable to report such property on the executor's books even though it passes directly to the named beneficiaries, since it must be included as a part of the estate subject to federal estate taxes. In the instances mentioned, real estate can be recorded on the books of the executor as a part of the opening inventory. Entries would follow to report that such assets had passed to respective beneficiaries.

Entries for transactions of the estate. The entries to record the inventory and the subsequent transactions completed by the administrator in accounting for the estate follow:

Transaction		Entry		
May 31 (1) Assets at appraised values per inventory filed with the court by Thomas Bragg:		Cash Personal Effects Automobile U.S. Savings Bonds	2,400 350 1,500 6,250	
Cash	$ 2,400	Gaylord Corp. 6% Preferred Stock	10,550	
Personal effects	350	Dividends Receivable on Gaylord Corp. 6% Preferred Stock	150	
Automobile	1,500	Gaylord Corp. 4% Bonds	5,675	
U.S. Savings Bonds	6,250	Accrued Interest on Gaylord Corp. 4% Bonds	80	
Gaylord Corp. 6% Preferred Stock, 1,000 shares, par $10	10,550	Estate Principal		26,955
Dividends declared on Gaylord Corp. 6% Preferred Stock	150			
Gaylord Corp. 4% Bonds, par $6,000	5,675			
Accrued interest on Gaylord Corp. 4% Bonds	80			
	$26,955			
June 10 (2) Collected dividends on Gaylord Corp. 6% Preferred Stock, $150.		Cash Dividends Receivable on Gaylord Corp. 6% Preferred Stock	150	 150
July 1 (3) Interest was credited on cash in bank, $20.		Cash Collections of Income	20	 20
July 15 (4) Paid funeral expenses, $850.		Funeral and Administrative Expenses Cash	850	 850
July 26 (5) Sold automobile for $1,325.		Cash Losses on Disposal of Assets Automobile	1,325 175	 1,500

Transaction		Entry		
July 31 (6) Sold 500 shares of Gaylord Corp. 6% Preferred Stock at 10¾.		Cash . . . . Gaylord Corp. 6% Preferred Stock . . . . Gains on Disposal of Assets	5,375	 5,275 100
Aug. 1 (7) Received semiannual payment on Gaylord Corp. 4% bonds, $120.		Cash . . . . Accrued Interest on Gaylord Corp. 4% Bonds . . . . Thomas Bragg	120	 80 40
Aug. 15 (8) Discovered deposit with Security Savings and Loan Association of $225.		Cash — Security Savings and Loan Association . . . . Assets Subsequently Discovered	225	 225
Sept. 11 (9) Received dividends on Gaylord Corp. 6% Preferred Stock, $75.		Cash . . . . Thomas Bragg	75	 75
Sept. 15 (10) Paid debts of decedent, $1,800.		Debts of Decedent Paid Cash	1,800	 1,800
Sept. 15 (11) Paid general legacy to Children's Hospital, $1,000.		Legacies Paid or Delivered . . . . Cash	1,000	 1,000
Dec. 1 (12) Paid inheritance tax: On legacies distributable to Thomas Bragg . . . . On legacies distributable to Anna Mae Bragg	 $ 180 150 $ 330	Thomas Bragg . . . . Anna Mae Bragg . . . . . Cash	180 150	 330
Dec. 6 (13) Paid court and administrative expenses, $240.		Funeral and Administrative Expenses . . . . . . Cash	240	 240

Transaction		Entry		
Dec. 8 (14) Received cash from Thomas Bragg in settlement of balance due:		Cash	65	
		Thomas Bragg		65
Inheritance tax paid by estate, due from Thomas	$ 180			
Less interest and dividends collected by estate on specific legacies, accruing to Thomas	115			
Balance due	$ 65			
Dec. 8 (15) Distributed specific legacies to Thomas Bragg: Gaylord Corp. 6% Preferred Stock, 500 shares; Gaylord Corp. 4% Bonds, par $6,000.		Legacies Paid or Delivered	10,950	
		Gaylord Corp. 6% Preferred Stock		5,275
		Gaylord Corp. 4% Bonds		5,675

Statement for the estate. A trial balance of the accounts maintained by Thomas Bragg as of December 10, 1967, appears below. A charge and discharge statement prepared from the data on the trial balance appears on the next page. This statement is submitted to the court with a request that the administrator be permitted to make final distribution of remaining estate properties.

Estate of Walter Bragg
Thomas Bragg — Administrator-with-the-Will-Annexed
Trial Balance
December 10, 1967

Cash	5,310	
Cash — Security Savings and Loan Association	225	
Personal Effects	350	
U.S. Savings Bonds	6,250	
Anna Mae Bragg	150	
Estate Principal		26,955
Assets Subsequently Discovered		225
Gains on Disposal of Assets		100
Collections of Income		20
Losses on Disposal of Assets	175	
Funeral and Administrative Expenses	1,090	
Debts of Decedent Paid	1,800	
Legacies Paid or Delivered	11,950	
	27,300	27,300

Estate of Walter Bragg
Thomas Bragg — Administrator-with-the-Will-Annexed
Charge and Discharge Statement
May 31, 1967 — December 10, 1967

I Charge Myself With:		
Original principal of estate	$26,955	
Assets subsequently discovered	225	
Gains on disposal of assets	100	
Collections of income	20	$27,300
I Credit Myself With:		
Losses on disposal of assets	$ 175	
Funeral and administrative expenses	1,090	
Debts of decedent paid	1,800	
Legacies paid or delivered	11,950	15,015
Balance		$12,285
Consisting of:		
Cash		$ 5,310
Cash — Security Savings and Loan Association		225
Personal effects		350
U.S. Savings Bonds		6,250
Claim against Anna Mae Bragg		150
Total		$12,285

Closing entries for the estate. The final accounting as submitted by Thomas Bragg is approved by the court, and the administrator is permitted to distribute remaining assets to the residuary beneficiary. Entries to record this distribution and to close the estate books follow.

Transaction		Entry		
Dec. 28 (16) Distributed residuary assets to Anna Mae Bragg:		Legacies Paid or Delivered	12,265	
		Distributions of Income	20	
Cash	$ 5,310	Cash		5,310
Cash — Security Savings and Loan Association	225	Cash—Security Savings and Loan Association		225
Personal Effects	350	Personal Effects		350
U.S. Savings Bonds	6,250	U.S. Savings Bonds		6,250
Claim against Anna Mae Bragg (inheritance tax paid)	150	Anna Mae Bragg		150
	$12,285			

Transaction	Entry		
(17) To close the nominal accounts into Estate Principal.	Estate Principal......	26,955	
	Assets Subsequently Discovered..........	225	
	Gains on Disposal of Assets..............	100	
	Collections of Income.	20	
	Losses on Disposal of Assets..........		175
	Funeral and Administrative Expenses..		1,090
	Debts of Decedent Paid..............		1,800
	Legacies Paid or Delivered............		24,215
	Distributions of Income.............		20

QUESTIONS

1. (a) Define the term *fiduciary*. (b) Give four different situations that require participation by a fiduciary.

2. Define each of the following terms: (a) testator, (b) intestate, (c) admission to probate, (d) letters of administration, (e) bequest.

3. Distinguish between:

(a) Administrator and executor.
(b) Legatee and devisee.
(c) Specific legacy and demonstrative legacy.
(d) General legacy and residuary legacy.
(e) Laws of descent and laws of distribution.
(f) Abatement and ademption.
(g) Intermediate accounting and final accounting.

4. Define each of the following terms: (a) partial intestacy, (b) advancement, (c) legacy failure.

5. List the duties of the executor or administrator.

6. (a) What properties normally appear on the inventory that is presented to the court by the personal representative of the decedent? (b) What values are reported for properties inventoried and how are such values ascertained? (c) Under what circumstances will real property be included in the inventory? (d) Under what circumstances will life insurance policies be included in the inventory?

7. State which of the following items are normally included in the inventory submitted to the court:

(a) Interest in a partnership.
(b) Down payment made by the decedent for purchase of land.
(c) Refundable advance to an heir.
(d) Mortgage note receivable on property sold by decedent.
(e) Deposit on real estate purchase contract entered into by decedent.
(f) Corporate first mortage bonds.

8. Distinguish between estate taxes and inheritance taxes and describe how these taxes are calculated.

9. (a) What priorities are set by law in the payment of claims against the estate? (b) What is the order of abatement or ademption of legacies when required in the settlement of estate claims? (c) Will real property generally or specifically devised ever be used for the payment of estate claims? Explain.

10. (a) State the sources for an increase in the personal representative's accountability. (b) State the sources for a decrease in his accountability.

11. In accounting for an estate, what entries are made when:

(a) Estate books are opened and properties are recorded at appraised values.
(b) Property is sold at more than its appraised value.
(c) Property belonging to the decedent is discovered during the course of administration.
(d) Income is collected, a part of which had accrued as of the date of the decedent's death and was included in the opening inventory.
(e) Expenses of last illness are paid.
(f) Property is sold at less than its appraised value.
(g) Income is collected on a legacy not yet distributed.
(h) The legacy referred to in (g) is paid, together with the income collected thereon.
(i) Debts of the decedent are paid.
(j) Remaining assets are distributed to the residuary legatee.
(k) Accounts of the estate are closed.

12. Give the entries that would be made on the books for the estate of Bernard Bailey as a result of the following:

(a) An inventory for the estate shows the decedent to have left cash, certain valuables, a first trust deed on property that the decedent had sold 3 months ago together with 3 months' accrued interest on the deed, and corporate bonds together with 2 months' accrued interest on the bonds. The trust deed is specifically bequeathed to a son, while the balance of the estate after payment of expenses, etc., is to be transferred to the surviving spouse.
(b) A dividend is received and investigation discloses that the decedent is an owner of certain shares of stock; the dividend had been declared prior to date of death.
(c) The bonds are sold at an amount in excess of their appraised value plus accrued interest for 5 months.
(d) Interest for 6 months is collected on the first trust deed.
(e) Funeral and administrative expenses are paid.
(f) Legacies are distributed and estate accounts are closed.

13. The estate of Henry Dakin pays the taxes that are listed below. State how each payment would be reflected in the accounts:

(a) Federal income tax on earnings of the decedent prior to date of death.
(b) Federal income tax on estate income for year after decedent's death.
(c) State death taxes requiring reimbursement from beneficiaries.
(d) Federal estate taxes.
(e) Local real estate taxes accrued prior to decedent's death.
(f) Local real estate taxes on property that is owned by the estate.

14. Describe the charge and discharge statement.

EXERCISES

1. A. C. Parker died on March 15. Give the entries that will appear on the estate books as a result of the following:

(a) An inventory was filed with the court as follows:

Cash	$4,560
R Co. common stock, 100 shares	6,000
S Co. 6% bonds, par $5,000	5,150
Accrued interest on bonds, Jan. 15–Mar. 15	50
Personal effects and household effects	2,600

(b) Funeral expenses and expenses of last illness were paid, $1,600.
(c) Interest was collected on S Co. bonds for 6 months.
(d) Dividends of $60 were received on R Co. common stock. The stock is bequeathed by will to Billy Parker, a son, and the stock together with the cash dividend is transferred to the son.
(e) S Co. 6% bonds are sold at 104 plus accrued interest on September 15.
(f) Debts of decedent are paid, $6,000.
(g) The court approves the payment of administrative expenses of $450 and the distribution of the balance of the estate to the surviving spouse.

2. What entries would be made on the books of the estate of Wilbur Massey for the following transactions:

(a) 500 shares of 6% preferred stock of the W Company, par value per share $50, are sold at 55. The shares are carried at a value of $53.50 as of date of decedent's death.
(b) 5% bonds of the X Company, face value $20,000, are sold at 103½ plus accrued interest for 3 months. The bonds are carried on the books at their appraised value, $20,250.
(c) 200 shares of stock of Y Company are discovered in a safety deposit box of the decedent; the stock had a value on the date of death of $4,000 and a dividend of 37½ cents per share had been declared on each share just prior to the date of the decedent's death.
(d) Interest for 6 months is collected on 6% bonds of the Z Company with a face value of $20,000; at the date of the decedent's death, interest for 2 months had accrued and had been recorded as a part of the estate inventory. The bonds are a specific legacy distributable to B.
(e) Certain personal effects of the decedent reported on the inventory as without value realized $350.

3. A trial balance for the estate of Joseph Kelly on March 31 follows:

Cash	$ 4,200	
Estate Principal		$46,250
Assets Subsequently Discovered		1,250
Gains on Disposal of Assets		3,700
Collections of Income		400
Losses on Disposal of Assets	6,500	
Funeral and Administrative Expenses	2,200	
Debts of Decedent Paid	12,000	
Legacies Paid or Delivered	11,550	
Devises Delivered	15,000	
Expenses Chargeable to Income	150	
	$51,600	$51,600

(a) Using the preceding data, prepare a charge and discharge statement.

(b) Assuming that the court authorizes the distribution of cash on hand to the residuary legatee, give the entry to record the distribution and to close the estate books.

4. Personal property left by Andrew Allen on the date of his death is valued at $40,000. Testamentary dispositions to his children include:

Specific legacy to Betty, property included in the inventory at		$ 3,500
Demonstrative legacy to Carl, cash in F & M Bank, included in the inventory at		1,650
General legacies:		
To Don	$25,000	
To Edward	10,000	
To Frank	5,000	40,000

Assets of the estate other than cash and the specific legacy are sold at $1,500 less than inventoried values. Funeral and administrative expenses and debts of the decedent totaling $12,500 are paid. The executor then distributes legacies to Don, Edward, and Frank. Assuming that the laws provide for the prorata abatement of general legacies in the event that all legacies cannot be met, state how the cash is to be distributed to the individual beneficiaries.

5. Residuary assets of the estate of Z are to be distributed among beneficiaries as follows: A, 25%; B, 25%; C, 12½%; D, 12½%; E, 8⅓%; F, 8⅓%; G, 8⅓%. Distribution of the residuary estate is authorized by the court on May 1, 1967. On this date there is cash on hand of $66,000 and the books show that there was an advance of $15,000 to A on July 1, 1965, on which interest at the rate of 6% per year has accrued. (a) How should the cash on hand be distributed? (b) Give the entries to close the estate books.

PROBLEMS

21-1. Warren Brent died on April 30, 1967. Brent left a will providing for the following disposition of his properties:

Personal residence — to widow, Ella Brent.
Household furniture — bequeathed to widow.
Jewelry — bequeathed to widow.
Cash of $10,000 — bequeathed to daughter, Edith B. Powers.
Balance of estate after payment of debts, expenses, taxes, and other distributions — to be divided equally between Edith B. Powers and son, James Brent.

James Brent was named executor of the estate. Assets of the decedent as of date of death were valued as follows:

Residence	$60,000
Life insurance payable to widow	50,000
Household furniture	4,200
Jewelry	6,000
Dividends on Kern Steel common, payable May 5 to stockholders of record April 10	1,250
Kern Steel common	52,375
Cash in checking account	4,400

A summary of cash receipts and disbursements related to estate activities up to December 1, 1967, follows:

Cash Receipts		Cash Disbursements	
Collection of dividends	$ 1,250	Expenses of last illness and funeral expenses	$ 3,600
Proceeds from sale of Kern Steel stock	50,650	Debts of the decedent	23,250
Collection of note receivable in name of decedent (note was found in July)	850	Federal and state death taxes.	1,250
		Attorneys' and accountants' fees	1,600

James Brent submitted a statement to the court on December 1, 1967, summarizing his activities as executor and requesting permission for the distribution of the remaining estate assets. Brent agreed to waive all commissions and fees.

Instructions: Prepare a charge and discharge statement for the period April 30–December 1, accompanied by a schedule showing the proposed distribution of estate assets on this date.

21-2. Clyde C. Cook died on January 20, 1967. An inventory filed by Harvey James, his executor, listed the following:

Cash in commercial account	515
Cash in savings account	4,400
Series E U.S. Savings Bonds (redemption value)	7,825
Stock, A Co., 500 shares	15,600
Stock, B Co., 100 shares	3,600
Dividends receivable on B Co. stock	100
Automobile	2,400

Cook's will provides for the following legacies:

To Children's Hospital, cash of $5,000
To son, Carl: automobile
250 shares of A Co. stock
50 shares of B Co. stock
To widow: properties not otherwise disposed of by will, and estate income.

The following transactions took place during the course of administration:

(a) Funeral expenses and expenses of last illness were paid, $1,350.
(b) Dividends were collected on B Co. stock, $100.
(c) Dividends were received on A Co. stock, $250.
(d) The U.S. Savings Bonds were redeemed at $7,875.

(e) Debts of the decedent were paid, \$4,410.
(f) The legacy to the Children's Hospital was paid.
(g) The legacy to the son was distributed.
(h) The executor received permission from the court to pay administration expenses and fees totaling \$1,450 and to distribute the estate income and remaining estate assets to the widow. This was done on July 31, 1967.

Instructions: (1) Give the entries to record the transactions of the executor.
(2) Prepare a charge and discharge statement summarizing the course of estate liquidation.
(3) Give the entries to close the books of the estate.

21-3. Alex Bender died on July 1, 1967. Richard Wells, who was named administrator-with-will-annexed, filed the following inventory with the probate court:

Cash	\$ 6,450
6% preferred stock, Y Co., 100 shares, par \$100	10,500
4% bonds, Z Co., par \$5,000	5,200
Accrued interest on Z Co. Bonds	50
Household furniture	1,600
Automobile	2,000

The following testamentary dispositions were made by Bender: (1) \$2,500 each to two nephews, James and Billy Bender; (2) the automobile, 50 shares of Y Co. preferred stock and \$2,500 in Z Co. bonds to a brother, Wallace Bender; (3) the remainder of the estate, including any estate income, to the Good Samaritan Foundation, a charitable organization.

During the course of administration, the following transactions were completed by Wells:

(a) Paid funeral and administrative expenses, \$2,200.
(b) Received interest on Z Co. bonds for 6 months, \$100.
(c) Received a semiannual dividend on Y Co. stock, \$300.
(d) Sold bonds of Z Co., par \$2,500, for \$2,525 plus accrued interest for 3 months.
(e) Sold 50 shares of Y Co. stock for \$5,000.
(f) Paid debts of the decedent, \$3,600.
(g) Distributed the specific and general legacies.
(h) Made application to the court and received its approval for the distribution of the estate income and remaining estate assets. The distribution was made on January 10, 1968.

Instructions: (1) Give the entries to record the estate transactions.
(2) Prepare a charge and discharge statement summarizing estate liquidation.
(3) Give the entries to close the books of the estate.

21-4. Robert Story died on May 1, 1967, and his son Russell was named executor for the estate. The will provided that, after payment of funeral and administrative expenses, debts of the decedent, and bequests to charitable organizations, the remaining estate was to be distributed to the widow, Rita, and to the son, Russell, in the ratio of 2 to 1 respectively.

The will also provided that the widow's share of the estate was to be invested in an annuity for her support during her lifetime.

Russell Story kept no records of the transactions of the estate, but he had a list of cash receipts and disbursements up to November 30, 1967, as follows:

Cash receipts:	
Cash on hand in banks, May 1, 1967	$27,500
Savings accounts discovered	6,500
Proceeds from sale of 1,000 shares of Fielding Corp. common stock (appraised at 21½ per share on May 1, 1967)	23,000
Cash payments:	
Funeral and administrative expenses	$ 1,150
Debts of decedent paid	3,500
Advance to Rita Story	3,500
Payment on exercise of 1,200 rights of Lane Co. common stock (received 600 shares of the Lane Co. common stock on exercise of rights)	33,000
General legacies to charity:	
Community Hospital	5,000
Community Home for Orphans	5,000
Inheritance tax paid on behalf of Rita Story	2,200

After the payment of funeral and administrative expenses, the debts of the decedent, and the general legacies, Russell Story distributed the shares of Fielding Corp. common stock in the ratio specified. Shares of Fielding Corp. common stock belonging to the widow were sold with the permission of the court. Russell Story withheld the proceeds from the sale and later used it for payment of part of the 600 shares of the Lane Co. common stock received through the exercise of rights. After exercising the rights of Lane Co. common stock, he made a similar distribution of the shares of Lane Co. common stock. Lane Co. common stock was valued at $50 on May 1, 1967.

On December 1, 1967, the court ordered Russell Story to submit a charge and discharge statement. He engaged an accountant to prepare the statement for him. In preparing the statement, the accountant found that Russell Story had made an overdistribution, both to himself and to the widow.

Instructions: (1) Prepare entries to record the inventory of the estate on May 1, 1967, and to record the transactions of the executor up to November 30, 1967, with proper charges to the accounts of the legatees for the excess distributions.

(2) Prepare a charge and discharge statement for the executor as of December 1, 1967.

21-5. On April 1, 1967, just before making final distribution of the estate of Henry Duncan, the executor's books show the following asset balances:

Cash	$42,800
Discount Sales Co. Stock	7,200
Claim against Norman Duncan	16,000

The estate is distributable as follows: ½ to the widow, Mary Jane Duncan; ⅓ to a son, Norman; and the balance equally to two daughters, Betty and Lorraine. An advance had been made by the estate to Norman on July 1, 1966, with the permission of the court; it was agreed that interest at 6% would be charged on the loan to the date when final distribution is made to estate beneficiaries.

On April 1 it is agreed that the widow shall take over the stock of the Discount Sales Co. at its present value of $7,500; the executor pays himself commissions of $1,200 and he distributes the remaining available cash to the appropriate parties.

Instructions: Give the entries in general journal form to record the final distribution of estate assets and to close the estate books on April 1. (Indicate how the cash is distributed among the various beneficiaries, showing calculations.)

21-6. Under the terms of the will of Jackson Holmes, who died in 1964, the beneficiaries were:

Mary Holmes, widow of testator, who was left a special bequest of $50,000 payable immediately, and in addition a life interest in ½ of the residuary estate, with the right of appointment.

Kathryn Holmes, his daughter, who was left ¼ of the residuary estate. One half of this was left outright and the other half was to remain in trust, with the right of appointment.

Jenny Holmes, his daughter, who was left a life interest in ⅛ of the residuary estate, with the right of appointment.

John Holmes, his son, who was also left a ⅛ interest in the residuary estate, to be paid to him outright.

The testator specified that, because of unsatisfactory market conditions, the trustees have the power and the right to defer liquidation of any of the assets until, in their opinion, conditions are favorable and may, in their discretion, make intermediate distributions of principal from the funds so realized to the beneficiaries who are entitled thereto. The income from the estate was to be distributed annually in the proportion of the beneficiaries' interests.

On December 31, 1966, the following advances were made on account of principal:

Kathryn Holmes	$150,000
John Holmes	100,000

The special bequest to Mary Holmes had not been paid on this date.

The trustees rendered their first accounting to the surrogate as at December 31, 1966, on which date all income, after paying therefrom all expenses applicable to income, was paid to the beneficiaries.

The surrogate's decree on the accounting of December 31, 1966, specified that (1) in considering the distribution of future income, all intermediary payments of principal should be treated as advances to the beneficiaries; (2) in order to make a fair and equitable division of income, interest at 6% per annum should be charged and credited.

The income for the year 1967 amounted to $450,000 after all expenses applicable to income had been paid. No further distribution of principal had taken place.

Instructions: Prepare a statement showing the amounts payable to each beneficiary on December 31, 1967.

(AICPA adapted)

21-7. John Thompson died on July 7, 1966. His will appointed two executors to administer his estate and provided for the payment of funeral and other necessary expenses and of general bequests as follows: $10,000 to the Cemetery on the Mount; $15,000 to Mary, a sister; and $5,000 to each executor in lieu of fees.

The testator at the date of death was possessed of the following: cash, $52,000; accounts receivable, $18,000; non-interest-bearing notes receivable, $10,000; first-mortgage bonds, 6%, interest payable on January 1 and July 1, principal amount $18,000, appraised value $15,000; Western Development Corp. bonds, 3%, interest payable on January 15 and July 15, par value $100,000, appraised value $101,500; 5,000 shares of Shell Mining Company stock, no-par value, cost $50,000, appraised as valueless; 1,000 shares of Atlas Amusement Corporation stock, par value $100, appraised at $102 per share; semiprecious stones, $5,280; clothing, $1,375; furniture, $7,500.

A summary of cash transactions from July 7, 1966, to September 30, 1967, is presented below:

Cash receipts:	
Accounts receivable collected (remainder uncollectible)...	$15,000
Proceeds from sale of $70,000 of Western Development Corp. bonds on January 15, 1967, at 102 without interest.	71,400
Dividends:	
$2.50 per share of Atlas Amusement Corporation stock, declared payable to stockholders of record on July 5, 1966, and paid on July 25, 1966	2,500
$2.50 per share of Atlas Amusement Corporation stock, declared payable to stockholders of record on January 5, 1967, and paid on January 25, 1967.............	2,500
Proceeds from sale of 5,000 shares of Shell Mining Company stock at $0.10 per share..........................	500
Refund of 1966 overpayment of United States income tax (declaration tax paid, $5,725; actual tax payable, $5,350)	375
Proceeds from sale of furniture.......................	5,150
Other transactions: short-term notes were collected at maturity; interest on all investments was collected.	
Cash disbursements:	
Funeral expenses, etc..............................	$ 1,750
Administrative expenses (corpus, $5,250; income, $1,250).	6,500
Legal and accounting services incident to probating will..	3,750
Debts of testator	14,450

United States Treasury Department — tax deficiency, 1963, and interest thereon, $72	$ 522
Playa Company, 4½% bonds — $20,000 acquired on September 16, 1966, at 101 (interest dates, March 15 and September 15; bonds mature on September 15, 1976)	20,580
Short-term notes, $5,000; 6% short-term notes purchased out of corpus on January 16, 1967, at 100½; interest payable on January 15 and July 15, maturing in 6 months from date of purchase.	
Other transactions: general bequests were paid in full, Mary taking semiprecious stones at appraised value to apply against bequest of $15,000; clothing was given to charity.	

Instructions: (1) Give the entries to be made on the books of the executors for the period July 7, 1966, to September 30, 1967, and on September 30, 1967.

(2) Prepare a charge and discharge statement covering activities for the period indicated.

(AICPA adapted)

21-8. The will of B. A. Brown, who died on December 31, 1961, provided cash bequests of $40,000 to Mrs. Brown and $15,000 each to two children, the residuary estate to be divided equally among the three beneficiaries. Mrs. Brown was appointed executrix and trustee without fees or other emoluments.

By court order Mrs. Brown was to receive a family allowance of $4,000 a month, commencing January 1, 1962, payable from income or from any cash principal available if the income should be inadequate. The estate never had enough cash available to pay up the full allowance nor could any part of the cash bequests be paid. Accordingly a considerable liability to Mrs. Brown had accumulated toward the end of 1967 for the unpaid portion of the family allowance, as shown by the following trial balance of the estate ledger at December 31 of that year:

	Dr.	Cr.
Cash	$ 200	
Securities	20,000	
Building A	200,000	
Reserve for Depreciation — Building A		$ 36,000
Building B	160,000	
Reserve for Depreciation — Building B		38,400
Mortgage — Building B		32,000
Revolving Fund — Building A	1,800	
Revolving Fund — Building B	2,400	
Mrs. B. A. Brown — Family Allowance		288,000
Mrs. B. A. Brown — Paid on Account	178,000	
Estate Corpus		168,000
	$562,400	$562,400

The balance in the estate corpus account was made up as follows:

Appraisal of assets	$365,000
Deduct — funeral expenses, etc.	15,000
	$350,000
Add — income:	
Dividends received	6,000
Rentals, after deducting expenses and mortgage interest to date	100,000
	$456,000
Deduct — family allowance	288,000
Balance	$168,000

For want of cash, the beneficiaries decided to settle all liabilities by transfer of property, and they requested their attorney to petition the court for approval of the following agreement to take effect as of December 31, 1967:

> Building B and its revolving fund are to be conveyed to Mrs. Brown subject to the mortgage. In turn she agrees to waive all of her claim against the estate for expenditures not refunded to her, including one of $5,000 for estate income taxes paid by her and not collected from the estate, and in addition to pay attorney's fees of $6,000 for the estate. Furthermore, all beneficiaries agree to have the family allowance discontinued after December 31, 1967, and also to waive their claims to the cash bequests.

The court gave its approval to the agreement and ordered an intermediary accounting by the trustee as of December 31, 1967.

Instructions: (1) Give the entries required to adjust the trial balance.

(2) Prepare a columnar work sheet showing the trial balance before and after adjustment.

(3) Prepare a statement of Mrs. Brown's account.

(4) Prepare a statement of estate corpus.

(5) Prepare the trustee's intermediary accounting in the form of a charge and discharge statement.

(AICPA adapted)

Chapter 22

ESTATES AND TRUSTS

PRINCIPAL AND INCOME

A *trust* relationship is formed when a person or persons are appointed to hold certain properties for the benefit of others. The person who creates the trust is variously known as the *donor*, *trustor*, *settlor*, *creator*, or *founder*. Those who are to receive the benefits of the trust are its *beneficiaries*. The person who assumes possession of the property and holds and manages it in the interests of the beneficiaries is known as the *trustee*. The trustee may be an individual or a corporate entity. The trustee acquires legal title to trust property; the beneficiaries possess equitable or beneficial title to such property.

Trusts commonly provide for two classes of beneficiaries: (1) those who are entitled to the income from the properties in trust for a certain time; (2) those who are entitled to the properties composing the principal of the trust at the end of the period indicated. The person who is to receive the income from a trust is known as the *income beneficiary* or *cestui que trust;* if he is entitled to the income during his life, he is referred to as a *life tenant* or *life beneficiary*. The person who is to receive the principal of the trust upon termination of the tenancy of the income beneficiary is called the *principal beneficiary* or *remainderman*. The income beneficiary may also be the principal beneficiary when the trust provides that trust income is to be distributed to a certain party until he reaches a certain age, whereupon this same party is to receive the principal properties of the trust. Trust income as well as trust principal may be distributable to more than one person.

LIVING AND TESTAMENTARY TRUSTS

A person may during his lifetime transfer title to properties to a trustee who is to hold them for the benefit of others. Such a trust is known as a *living trust* or *inter vivos trust*. Transfer of properties is generally effected by a written agreement known as a *declaration of trust*. The creator of the trust may make whatever provisions he wishes for the distribution of income and principal of the trust to the beneficiaries that he names. The trustor may reserve the right to revise the terms of the trust or actually to revoke the trust in the event that family circumstances or business conditions made such a change desirable. The trust is then known as a *revocable living trust.* A trust in which the trustor does not reserve the right to revoke or to alter constitutes an outright gift and is an *irrevocable living trust.* The declaration of trust should indicate the date on which the trust becomes effective.

A trust may be established by the terms of a will. A trust established by will is in effect a legacy or a devise of certain properties. A portion or all of the estate properties is made subject to the control and the management of a trustee for the benefit of the parties named as beneficiaries. Income and principal distributions are made in accordance with the terms of the trust. A trust established by terms of a will is known as a *testamentary trust.* The testamentary trust becomes effective upon the date of the decedent's death.

When real estate is left in trust by will, title passes directly from the deceased to the trustee. When personalty is left in trust, the trustee obtains title upon distribution of the property by the executor or the administrator. Amounts earned on such property and collected by the executor or the administrator from the date of the decedent's death but not distributed to the income beneficiary are also transferred to the trustee. When a trust is to be composed of the residuary assets of the estate, the trust properties are not finally determinable until the estate is declared terminated, and the trustee can assume no trust responsibilities until he is granted title to the properties.

RESPONSIBILITIES OF THE TRUSTEE

A trustee has those powers expressly granted to him by the trust as well as those powers that are required to carry out its purposes. The duties and the responsibilities of the trustee are normally similar to those of the executor or the administrator. A trustee acquires legal title to the trust property. It is his duty to manage, conserve, and protect properties that have been placed in his custody. He is required to keep principal funds invested and income-producing. Investments are made in accordance with the requirements of state laws except when contrary provisions are found in the trust declaration. Whenever necessary, properties are sold or exchanged. The trustee is responsible for the collection of income and its appropriate distribution. Upon termination of the trust, he is responsible for the distribution of principal. All income and principal distributions must be made in accordance with the instrument establishing the trust and also in accordance with statutory law. Finally, as in the case of the executor or the administrator, the trustee is required to render to the court of appropriate jurisdiction and to the other interested parties a full accounting for the properties subject to his control.

Periodic reports may be prepared; a final accounting may be required upon the final distribution of properties and request by the trustee for a formal discharge. The trustee is liable for any failure to meet his responsibilities under the trust in a reasonable and prudent manner.

A will may name the same individual as both executor of the estate and as trustee for a trust created by its terms. As executor, the individual acts to wind up the estate with powers and duties consistent with this responsibility. As trustee, the individual administers the trust in accordance with requirements of the trust declaration and with the statutory law pertaining to trusts. The fiduciary must maintain separate books for his activities as executor and separate books for his activities as trustee. When properties of the estate are formally turned over to the trust, the books of the estate will report the transfer of such properties out of the estate and the books of the trust will report their receipt. If several trusts are created by the will, a separate accountability for each trust is required.

PRINCIPAL AND INCOME OF THE TRUST DISTINGUISHED

In both living and testamentary trusts, careful distinction must be made between property composing the *principal* or *corpus* of the trust and property composing the *income* of the trust. The distinction between principal and income is made by law except when a contrary treatment is prescribed by the provisions of the trust instrument. This distinction is important because the principal of the trust belongs to the remainderman and is to be distributed to this party upon termination of the trust, while the income belongs to the income beneficiary and is distributable during the trust period. When the income beneficiary and the remainderman are different parties, failure to distinguish properly between principal and income will result in gain to one party and in loss to the other. Even when the income beneficiary is ultimately to receive the trust principal, improper distinctions between principal and income will result in trust distributions that do not meet the conditions set by the party who established the trust.

Properties acquired by the trust as a result of gift, legacy, or devise, and designated as ultimately to become available to the remainderman, form the trust principal. Proceeds from the sale of such properties, or any new properties acquired with the original assets or their proceeds, are likewise principal. Gains or losses on the disposal of principal assets, then, increase or decrease the amount of the trust principal. In the case of a testamentary trust, properties of the decedent on the date of death, whether determined and inventoried as of date of death or discovered at some later date, represent principal.

Debts relating to principal assets require payment from these assets. Thus a mortgage on real estate transferred to a trust requires settlement from principal assets. Proceeds from a mortgage placed after the asset transfer constitute principal, and settlement of such a mortgage is made from principal. When a trust is to be composed of the residuary assets of an estate, the debts of the decedent, as well as the debts relating to estate liquidation, including taxes, widow's sustenance when allowed, etc., are paid from principal assets and reduce the amount ultimately to be recognized as trust principal.

The earnings or yield from the use of principal assets, such as interest, dividends, rents, and royalties, represent trust income. Expenses that relate to the production of income, such as interest, taxes, costs of caring for income-producing properties, and legal expenses, are charges against trust income. The difference between the gross income and the expenses chargeable against such income becomes available for distribution to the income beneficiary. Distributions to the income beneficiary must leave trust principal unimpaired.

Accounting records of the trustee must maintain the distinction between principal and income items if the trustee is to be able to meet his responsibilities to principal and income beneficiaries. The trustee is required to submit periodically statements summarizing accountabilities to both principal and income beneficiaries. Such reports normally take the form of the charge and discharge statement prepared in two sections: the first section is devoted to principal assets and reports the principal assets held by the trustee at the beginning of the period, the changes in such principal assets during the period, and the balance of principal assets held at the end of the period; the second section is devoted to income assets and reports any income assets held by the trustee at the beginning of the period, income assets becoming available during the period, distributions and expenses paid out of income assets during the period, and any balance of income assets held at the end of the period. Statements submitted by the trustee must be accompanied by vouchers and other evidence offering full support for the summaries.

ANALYSIS OF TRUST RECEIPTS AND DISBURSEMENTS

Each receipt and disbursement by the trustee requires analysis to determine whether it is to be treated as principal or as income. In distinguishing between principal and income, the trustee is bound by any specific provisions in the trust instrument or by the intent of the creator when this can be determined from the trust instrument. In the absence of express or implied rules in the instrument creating the trust, the trustee follows statutory requirements of the state or the specific rulings of the court of trust jurisdiction. Some progress has been made towards uniformity on rules governing classification of items as principal and income. A number of states have adopted the Uniform Principal and Income Act. Many other states have adopted a part of the provisions embodied in this Act. The general rules governing the classification of cash receipts and payments are considered in the paragraphs that follow.

Interest income and expense. Statutory law generally provides that interest income is accruable for classification purposes. Accrued interest income at the beginning of an income beneficiary's tenancy (the date of death of the party creating a testamentary trust, for example) is considered principal. Accrued interest income at the date of termination of the income beneficiary's tenancy (the date of death of a life tenant, for example) is considered income. Only interest earned during the period of the income beneficiary's tenancy qualifies as income and is distributable to this party. Collections of interest, then, must be analyzed and identified as to that portion representing income and to be made available to an income beneficiary and that portion representing principal and to be retained for the principal beneficiary. Laws generally make an exception to the accrual rule for interest that is credited on savings accounts: interest credited by a bank during the period of tenancy is allowed in full to the income beneficiary; interest credited after termination of the tenancy is allowed to the principal beneficiary.

The "purchase" of accrued interest upon the acquisition of securities from principal funds calls for subsequent analysis of interest receipts and the replenishment of principal for such an outlay. A "sale" of accrued interest upon the disposal of securities calls for analysis of the sales proceeds with recognition of the accrued interest as income and the balance of the proceeds as a return of principal.

Ordinarily, interest expense is accruable. Thus an income beneficiary is chargeable only for interest accruing during his tenancy. Accrued interest expense at the beginning of an income beneficiary's tenancy is regarded as a principal debt. Accrued interest expense at the date of termination of an income beneficiary's tenancy is regarded as an income debt. Payments of interest expense, then, require analysis to determine that portion chargeable against principal and reducing the amount ultimately available to the principal beneficiary and that portion chargeable against income and thus reducing the amount distributable to the income beneficiary.

Rental income and rental expense. State laws generally require the accrual of rental income and rental expense. Thus rentals identified with the period of tenancy are income items, and rentals accruing prior to or after the period of tenancy are principal items. Similar rules of accrual commonly apply to royalty income. Ordinarily, compensation does not have to be made to an income beneficiary for rents and royalties applicable in part to the tenancy period but collected by the testator prior to his death.

Dividends. Dividends are not accruable. The general rule is that the declaration date determines the classification of dividends as principal or income: dividends that are declared within the period of the income beneficiary's tenancy are income; dividends declared prior to such tenancy or after such tenancy are principal. In some states, however, the classification is determined in terms of the record date, the date when the company refers to its books for a list of the stockholders who are entitled to dividends: when the record date falls within the tenancy period, the dividends are recognized as income; when the record date precedes the tenancy period, the dividends are recognized as principal. Dividend declaration dates or dividend payment dates have no significance when the latter rule is in effect.

To illustrate application of the rules mentioned above, assume that a trust becomes effective upon the death of the testator on November 10. Cash dividends on stock of the estate are declared on November 1 payable on December 1 to stockholders of record November 15. If the declaration date is controlling, dividends when collected are recognized as principal; if the record date is controlling, the dividends when collected are recognized as income.

State laws may provide that certain dividends or portions of certain dividends must be regarded as principal even though they are related to the period of the income beneficiary's tenancy. Laws of most states provide that all cash dividends within the tenancy period represent income accruing to the income beneficiary. Many states have adopted the view that whether ordinary and regular or extraordinary and irregular, all cash dividends shall be regarded as income and all stock dividends as principal. It is the form of the dividend that determines its classification. This is known as the "Massachusetts Rule" and has been adopted in the Uniform Principal and Income Act.

Some states, however, follow the "Pennsylvania Rule," which provides that a distinction must be made between ordinary dividends and extraordinary dividends. Although ordinary and regular dividends are regarded as income, extraordinary dividends must be apportioned between principal and income so that there is no impairment of principal. This rule applies to all dividends, whether cash, stock, property, or scrip.

Apportionment is based on the periods when the earnings used as a basis for dividends were accumulated: a dividend or that portion of a dividend declared from earnings accumulated prior to the commencement of the trust is regarded as principal; a dividend or that portion of a dividend declared from earnings accumulated during the period of the trust is regarded as income.

Liquidating dividends. The foregoing discussion was related to dividends representing distributions of corporate earnings. Liquidating dividends representing the proceeds from wasting assets or from corporate liquidation are generally regarded as distributions of capital and are classified as principal.

Stock rights. Stock rights and the proceeds from the sale of stock rights are generally regarded as principal. This rule has been adopted in the Uniform Principal and Income Act.

Profit realized on contract completed after death. When a contract remains to be completed after a person's death, the profit is not accrued but is calculated at the conclusion of the contract and the full amount is considered principal.

Income from crops and livestock. When farm lands are held in trust, any crops harvested during the income beneficiary's tenancy are regarded as income; costs of maintaining the farm lands and harvesting the land are chargeable to income. The income from a first crop of a testamentary trust, then, requires no apportionment but accrues to the income beneficiary. Livestock born during an income beneficiary's tenancy is likewise income. The income beneficiary is normally charged for any shrinkage in the original livestock supply; if principal is to be unimpaired, the supply of livestock at the termination of the income beneficiary's tenancy should be equal to the supply at the beginning of the tenancy period.

Depreciation, depletion, and amortization. No charge is generally required against income for depreciation or obsolescence of trust properties unless specifically provided for in the trust instrument. There is no reimbursement to principal for the normal impairment in properties through such natural causes. The prevailing view holds that, if the party creating the trust had intended that the principal beneficiary recover a sum equal to depreciation or obsolescence during the tenancy period, he would have included specific requirements to that effect in the trust instrument.

When trust properties include certain wasting assets such as mines, oil wells, or timberlands, or intangibles such as leaseholds, patents, and copyrights, it is generally held that income must be reduced by amounts equal to the depletion or the amortization charges. When a charge against income for asset depletion or amortization is appropriate, a portion of the proceeds from sales equal to this charge is withheld during the period of tenancy and is regarded as principal. Proceeds from activities relating to wasting assets, then, are divided into two parts: (1) the amount required to keep the principal unimpaired and (2) the balance representing income. It is possible to provide in the trust instrument, of course, that no charge shall be made against income for asset depletion or amortization.

Operating, maintenance, and repair charges. All ordinary expenses in the operation of income properties are chargeable to income. Thus such expenses as insurance, taxes, repairs, and rental fees are proper charges to income. Normal and recurring maintenance expenses and repairs on properties are chargeable against the income from properties; but extraordinary repairs, betterments, and additions are normally chargeable against principal on the theory that these result in principal benefits. When an expenditure benefits both principal and income, the court may authorize apportionment of the expenditure between principal and income. In the case of unimproved or non-income-producing properties, carrying charges are generally absorbed by principal.

Partnership profits. Profits of a partnership up to the date that the deceased partner's interest is calculated are generally regarded as principal. When the books are closed as of the date of death, the deceased's interest on this date represents principal, and any income related to this interest thereafter represents income. When the partnership agreement provides for closing the books at the end of the fiscal period in the regular manner, the interest of the decedent determined as of this date is generally regarded as principal.

Insurance premiums on real estate. Insurance premiums on properties are charged against income. Amounts collected on insurance policies as a result of a property loss are treated as a recovery of principal.

Property tax, estate tax, and income tax payments. In general, taxes on real estate are not considered to accrue. Taxes that were assessed and became a lien on the property prior to the period of tenancy are usually charges against principal; taxes becoming a lien during the tenancy period are usually charges against income. Special assessment taxes during the period of tenancy may be chargeable against either principal or income, or may be apportioned between both, depending upon the extent to which the levies are related to the permanent improvement of the properties. The federal estate tax is chargeable against principal. Income taxes on the gains resulting from the sale of principal assets are chargeable against principal; income taxes on accumulations of income are chargeable against income.

Trust fees and expenses. Fees and expenses of administering a trust are identified with principal or income depending upon the parties who benefit by the services performed. The expenses of creating the trust are generally charged against principal. When estate assets are to be transferred to a trust, all administrative expenses, including probate and legal expenses of preparing the estate for the trust, are chargeable to principal. After the trust has been set up, expenses pertaining to the production and the collection of income are charged to income; expenses relating to the preservation of principal are charged to principal. Charges identified with changes in investments are generally considered principal and reported as a cost of the principal assets acquired. Fees based upon sums of income and principal paid out would be charged against income and principal respectively. Certain fees and expenses may be related to both principal and income, suggesting allocation between the two. Under such circumstances, directions from the court may be sought as a basis for the allocation.

Receipt of bond interest — amortization of bond premium and accumulation of bond discount.[1] When a testamentary trust holds bonds originally acquired by the deceased, courts have held that bond interest collected during the period of tenancy accrues in full to the income beneficiary. No adjustment in income is required even though the bonds are inventoried at a premium or at a discount. Upon the sale of the bonds or upon their maturity, the difference between the value of the bonds at the date of death and the amount received on their sale is treated as a principal gain or loss. In the absence of specific provisions for bond premium amortization or bond discount accumulation, it is assumed that the intent of the testator was to make the interest actually collected on the bonds available to the income beneficiary.

When bonds are purchased by a trustee at a premium, courts generally have supported the amortization of premium and the payment to

[1]This discussion relates to bonds and also to other obligations for the payment of money whether inventoried or acquired at a premium or a discount.

the income beneficiary of the bond interest reduced by such amortization. Interest received, then, is considered to be composed of two parts: (1) an amount equal to the premium amortization that is principal; (2) the balance, representing income. However, when bonds are purchased by a trustee at a discount, courts generally have not supported the accumulation of discount on bonds and the payment to the income beneficiary of an amount in excess of the interest actually received. The ultimate recovery of an amount exceeding bond cost is treated as a principal gain.

The Uniform Principal and Income Act has adopted a consistent position for bonds taken over at the commencement of a trust as well as for bonds purchased at either a premium or a discount during a period of trust tenancy. The Act provides that no adjustment be made for premium amortization or discount accumulation, the income beneficiary being entitled to amounts actually received as interest; upon the sale or the maturity of the bonds, any loss or gain represented by the difference between their inventoried value or cost and their sales proceeds or maturity value applies to principal. When bonds are acquired at a discount, then, the income beneficiary still receives no more than the interest actually collected; however, he does not suffer a reduction in the amount of interest collected when bonds are acquired at a premium.

ACCOUNTING FOR THE TESTAMENTARY TRUST

Since the testamentary trust is normally operative from the date of the testator's death even though the assets are not to be turned over to the trustee until the estate is terminated, a careful distinction between principal and income items must be made on the books of the executor or the administrator until separate books for the trust are set up.

The following entries are made on the estate books in accounting for income items:

Collection of income. Receipts representing income accruing to the income beneficiary are recorded by debits to Income Cash and credits to Collections of Income. When an account is maintained for Income Cash, cash representing a part of the principal of the estate is designated as Principal Cash. With income from a number of different sources, a separate income account for each class of income may be maintained.

Payment of expenses identified with income. Expenses chargeable against income are paid out of income cash. The account Expenses Chargeable to Income is debited and Income Cash is credited. Here, too, separate accounts may be maintained to report the different expense items; the titles of such accounts should indicate the trust income relationship.

Distributions of income. Distributions of income cash to the income beneficiary are recorded by debits to the account Distributions of Income and by credits to Income Cash. When there are a number of income beneficiaries, separate distribution accounts with each beneficiary may be maintained.

Closing nominal income accounts. Nominal income account balances may be closed at regular intervals and also before trust assets on the estate books are transferred to the trustee. Income accounts before closing appear with debit and credit balances as follows:

Debits	Credits
Income Cash	Collections of Income
Distributions of Income	
Expenses Chargeable to Income	

To close the accounts, Collections of Income is debited, Distributions of Income and Expenses Chargeable to Income are credited, and Estate Income is credited. The balance in Estate Income is then equal to the balance of the income assets.

Transfer of trust assets to trustee. When the estate transfers principal assets to a trust, the asset accounts to form the principal of the trust are credited and an account Principal Assets Transferred to Trustee is debited. The balance of the latter account is ultimately closed into Estate Principal. When there are income assets that have not been distributed to the beneficiary, these too are transferred to the trust. The asset accounts are credited and an account Income Assets Transferred to Trustee is debited. The balance of the latter account is ultimately closed into Estate Income.

MAINTAINING BOOKS FOR THE TRUST

When trust books are opened, accounts with the principal assets are debited and Trust Principal is credited. Trust Principal measures the accountability of the trustee to the principal beneficiary. Any assets identified with the income beneficiary are recorded by debits to the income asset accounts and a credit to Trust Income. Trust Income measures the accountability to the income beneficiary. Thereafter transactions are recorded with appropriate distinction between principal and income items. At the end of the trust fiscal period, nominal accounts reporting changes in the trust principal, such as Gains on Disposal of Principal Assets, Losses on Disposal of Principal Assets, and Expenses Chargeable to Principal, are closed into Trust Principal; nominal accounts reporting changes in trust income, such as Collections of Income, Expenses Chargeable to Income, and Distributions of Income, are closed into Trust Income.

It should be observed that accounting for the trust is normally maintained on a cash basis. Distributions to an income beneficiary must be limited to the amount of the income cash available. Under these circumstances, the cash basis provides for income measurement that is consistent with the limitations that are found in income distribution. However, accruable income and expense must be recognized both at the beginning of the income beneficiary's tenancy and upon termination of his tenancy. For example, any accrued interest receivable on the date of the commencement of a trust must be recognized as increasing principal and any accrued interest payable on this date must be recognized as decreasing principal; receipts and disbursements relating to such accrued items during the trust period are recorded as changes in Principal Cash since income accrues to the income beneficiary only from the commencement of the tenancy. Furthermore, any accrued interest receivable on the date of the termination of an income beneficiary's tenancy must be recognized as a part of trust income and any accrued interest payable on this date must be recognized as a charge against trust income; while past distributions to the income beneficiary were limited to the income available in the form of cash, settlement upon termination of the tenancy period calls for the payment of income adjusted for accruable items.

ACCOUNTING FOR THE ESTATE-TO-TRUST DEVELOPMENT ILLUSTRATED

Accounting for an estate whose assets are ultimately transferred to a trust is illustrated in the example that follows. Paul Davis, who died on May 1, 1967, left a will naming William C. Ross as executor and trustee. The will was admitted to probate and letters testamentary were issued by the court to Ross on May 15. The will provided that:

Home, furniture, personal effects, and cash of $15,000 were to go to the widow.
The personal library was bequeathed to Southeastern University.
Co. X Bonds were bequeathed to the son, Henry.
After payment of debts, expenses, legacies, and estate and inheritance taxes, remaining property was to be held by William C. Ross in trust, the income from the trust to be paid to the widow and, upon her death, the trust principal to be paid to the son.

The inventory filed by the executor as of May 1 and subsequent transactions, together with entries to record the transactions, follow.

Transactions		Entries on Estate Books[1]		
May 1 (1) Assets at appraised values per inventory filed with the court by William C. Ross: Cash Automobile Furniture and personal effects Library Co. A Stock (100 shares) Dividends on Co. A Stock declared April 15, to stockholders of record April 25, payable May 25 Co. X 6% Bonds Accrued interest on Co. X Bonds, December 1–May 1 Co. Y 6% Bonds Accrued interest on Co. Y Bonds, December 1–May 1 Life insurance policy payable to estate	 $ 2,800 1,500 4,500 2,000 11,500 150 10,000 250 25,000 625 20,000	*Principal Cash Estate Principal Automobile Furniture and Personal Effects Library Co. A Stock Dividends Receivable on Co. A Stock Co. X 6% Bonds Accrued Interest on Co. X Bonds Co. Y 6% Bonds Accrued Interest on Co. Y Bonds Life Insurance Policy Estate Principal	2,800 1,500 4,500 2,000 11,500 150 10,000 250 25,000 625 20,000	 2,800 75,525
May 20 (2) Collected life insurance policy.		*Principal Cash Life Insurance Policy	20,000	 20,000
May 25 (3) Collected dividends on Co. A Stock.		*Principal Cash Dividends Receivable on Co. A Stock	150	 150
June 1 (4) Collected interest for 6 months on Co. X 6% Bonds.		*Principal Cash Accrued Interest on Co. X Bonds Henry Davis	300	 250 50
June 1 (5) Collected interest for 6 months on Co. Y 6% Bonds.		*Principal Cash Income Cash Accrued Interest on Co. Y Bonds Collections of Income	625 125	 625 125

[1]Entries with asterisks on this and following pages would appear in special cash journals as illustrated on pages 783 and 784.

Transactions	Entries on Estate Books		
June 10 (6) Sold automobile.	*Principal Cash	1,350	
	Losses on Disposal of Assets	150	
	Automobile		1,500
June 12 (7) Paid funeral expenses.	*Funeral and Administrative Expenses	600	
	Principal Cash		600
June 15 (8) Transferred cash, furniture, and personal effects to Mrs. Paul Davis.	*Legacies Paid or Delivered	15,000	
	Principal Cash		15,000
	Legacies Paid or Delivered	4,500	
	Furniture and Personal Effects		4,500
June 15 (9) Transferred library to Southeastern University.	Legacies Paid or Delivered	2,000	
	Library		2,000
June 18 (10) Transferred Co. X Bonds and interest collected on bonds from April 30 to Henry Davis.	Legacies Paid or Delivered	10,000	
	Co. X 6% Bonds		10,000
	*Henry Davis	50	
	Principal Cash		50
September 1 (11) Received payment of $1,000 note dated March 1 and interest at 6% for six months from R. G. Stapp. (The executor had no knowledge of this asset until September 1.)	*Principal Cash	1,010	
	Income Cash	20	
	Assets Subsequently Discovered		1,010
	Collections of Income		20
September 1 (12) Distributed available income cash to Mrs. Paul Davis.	*Distributions of Income	145	
	Income Cash		145
September 5 (13) Collected dividends on Co. A Stock.	*Income Cash	150	
	Collections of Income		150
September 15 (14) Paid debts filed against the decedent: A. C. Parker, $450; P. O. Thomas, $3,200; State Bank (on note), $2,000.	*Debts of Decedent Paid	5,650	
	Principal Cash		5,650

Transactions	Entries on Estate Books		
September 15 (15) Sold Co. A Stock.	*Principal Cash......	11,800	
	Company A Stock		11,500
	Gains on Disposal of Assets.........		300
October 1 (16) Paid estate taxes and miscellaneous administrative expenses.	*Funeral and Administrative Expenses...	6,385	
	Expenses Chargeable to Income..........	15	
	Principal Cash....		6,385
	Income Cash.....		15

STATEMENTS FOR THE ESTATE-TO-TRUST DEVELOPMENT ILLUSTRATED

A trial balance of principal and income accounts on October 1, 1967, taken from the estate books maintained by William C. Ross, executor, appears below. A charge and discharge statement prepared from the trial balance and the detail found in the ledger accounts is given on page 778. The schedules that are prepared in support of the balances reported on the charge and discharge statement appear on pages 778 and 779.

Estate of Paul Davis
William C. Ross, Executor
Trial Balance
October 1, 1967

	Principal Accounts		Income Accounts	
	Dr.	Cr.	Dr.	Cr.
Principal Cash.....................	10,350			
Co. Y 6% Bonds..................	25,000			
Estate Principal...................		78,325		
Assets Subsequently Discovered......		1,010		
Gains on Disposal of Assets..........		300		
Losses on Disposal of Assets.........	150			
Funeral and Administrative Expenses.	6,985			
Debts of Decedent Paid.............	5,650			
Legacies Paid or Delivered..........	31,500			
Income Cash.......................			135	
Collections of Income.............				295
Expenses Chargeable to Income......			15	
Distributions of Income............			145	
	79,635	79,635	295	295

Estate of Paul Davis
William C. Ross, Executor
Charge and Discharge Statement
May 1–October 1, 1967

First, as to Estate Principal

I Charge Myself With:		
Original principal of estate (Schedule A)	$78,325	
Assets subsequently discovered (Schedule B)	1,010	
Gains on disposal of assets (Schedule C)	300	$79,635
I Credit Myself With:		
Losses on disposal of assets (Schedule D)	$ 150	
Funeral and administrative expenses (Schedule E)	6,985	
Debts of decedent paid (Schedule F)	5,650	
Legacies paid or delivered (Schedule G)	31,500	44,285
Balance as to Estate Principal (Schedule H)		$35,350

Second, as to Estate Income

I Charge Myself With:		
Collections of income (Schedule I)		$ 295
I Credit Myself With:		
Expenses chargeable to income (Schedule J)	$ 15	
Distributions of income (Schedule K)	145	160
Balance as to Estate Income — Consisting of Income Cash		$ 135

(Balances of estate principal and estate income are subject to deductions for executor's commissions.)

Schedule A — Original Principal of Estate, May 1, 1967

Cash	$ 2,800
Automobile	1,500
Furniture and personal effects	4,500
Library	2,000
Co. A stock	11,500
Dividends receivable on Co. A stock	150
Co. X 6% bonds	10,000
Accrued interest on Co. X bonds	250
Co. Y 6% bonds	25,000
Accrued interest on Co. Y bonds	625
Life insurance policy	20,000
Total	$78,325

Schedule B — Assets Subsequently Discovered

Note dated March 1 accruing interest at 6%, signed by R. G. Stapp.	$ 1,000
Accrued interest on note on May 1	10
Total	$ 1,010

Schedule C — Gains on Disposal of Assets	
Proceeds on sale of Co. A stock on September 15	$11,800
Co. A stock, per inventory, May 1	11,500
Gain	$ 300
Schedule D — Losses on Disposal of Assets	
Automobile, per inventory, May 1	$ 1,500
Proceeds on sale of automobile on June 10	1,350
Loss	$ 150
Schedule E — Funeral and Administrative Expenses	
Funeral expenses	$ 600
Taxes	4,000
Administrative expenses	2,385
Total	$ 6,985
Schedule F — Debts of Decedent Paid	
A. C. Parker	$ 450
P. O. Thomas	3,200
State Bank	2,000
Total	$ 5,650
Schedule G — Legacies Paid or Delivered	
Mrs. Paul Davis	$19,500
Henry Davis	10,000
Southeastern University	2,000
Total	$31,500
Schedule H — Balance as to Estate Principal	
Principal cash	$10,350
Co. Y 6% bonds	25,000
Total	$35,350
Schedule I — Collections of Income	
Interest on Co. Y bonds for period May 1–June 1	$ 125
Interest on R. G. Stapp note, May 1–August 1	20
Dividends on Co. A stock, September 5	150
Total	$ 295
Schedule J — Expenses Chargeable to Income	
Administrative expenses	$ 15
Schedule K — Distributions of Income	
Payment to Mrs. Paul Davis, September 1	$ 145

CLOSING ENTRIES FOR THE ESTATE

The final accounting as submitted by William C. Ross is approved by the court, and the executor is allowed commissions of $2,025 allocable $2,000 to principal and $25 to income. The court authorizes William C.

Ross to act as trustee for the testamentary trust that names Mrs. Paul Davis, the life tenant, and Henry Davis, the remainderman. The entries that are required on October 1 in closing the temporary accounts on the estate books are as follows:

Transactions	Entries on Estate Books		
October 1 (17) Commissions paid for administration.	*Funeral and Administrative Expenses . . .	2,000	
	Expenses Chargeable to Income.	25	
	Principal Cash. . . .		2,000
	Income Cash		25
October 1 (18) To close principal accounts.	Estate Principal.	44,975	
	Assets Subsequently Discovered	1,010	
	Gains on Disposal of Assets	300	
	Losses on Disposal of Assets		150
	Funeral and Administrative Expenses		8,985
	Debts of Decedent Paid.		5,650
	Legacies Paid or Delivered		31,500
October 1 (19) To close income accounts.	Collections of Income	295	
	Distributions of Income.		145
	Expenses Chargeable to Income . . .		40
	Estate Income		110

Account balances on the executor's books after closing would be as follows:

	Principal Accounts		Income Accounts	
	Dr.	Cr.	Dr.	Cr.
Principal Cash.	8,350			
Co. Y 6% Bonds.	25,000			
Estate Principal		33,350		
Income Cash.			110	
Estate Income.				110
	33,350	33,350	110	110

The entries on the executor's books to record the transfer of principal and income assets to the trustee and to close the remaining accounts are as follows:

Transactions	Entries on Estate Books		
October 1 (20) Transferred principal assets to William C. Ross, trustee.	*Principal Assets Transferred to William C. Ross, Trustee	8,350	
	Principal Cash....		8,350
	Principal Assets Transferred to William C. Ross, Trustee	25,000	
	Co. Y 6% Bonds..		25,000
October 1 (21) To close principal accounts.	Estate Principal.....	33,350	
	Principal Assets Transferred to William C. Ross, Trustee..............		33,350
October 1 (22) Transferred income assets to William C. Ross, trustee.	*Income Assets Transferred to William C. Ross, Trustee.......	110	
	Income Cash.....		110
October 1 (23) To close income accounts.	Estate Income......	110	
	Income Assets Transferred to William C. Ross, Trustee..............		110

ACCOUNTING FOR THE TRUST ILLUSTRATED

The opening entries on the trustee's books and the entries that are made for the transactions that take place during the trust's fiscal period, which is to be the calendar year, are shown below. A charge and discharge statement would be prepared to summarize activities of the trust for the partial period ending December 31.

Transactions	Entries on Trust Books		
October 1 (24) Took over principal and income assets from William C. Ross, executor.	*Principal Cash......	8,350	
	Trust Principal...		8,350
	Co. Y 6% Bonds....	25,000	
	Trust Principal...		25,000
	*Income Cash.......	110	
	Trust Income.....		110
October 31 (25) Purchased $7,500 Co. Z 6% Bonds, interest payable annually on December 31, at 104 plus accrued interest. Bonds mature 50 months from this date.	*Co. Z 6% Bonds....	7,800	
	Accrued Interest on Co. Z Bonds........	375	
	Principal Cash....		8,175

Transactions		Entries on Trust Books		
December 1 (26) Collected interest for 6 months on Co. Y 6% Bonds.		*Income Cash . . . . Collections of Income	750	 750
December 15 (27) Distributed available income cash to Mrs. Paul Davis.		*Distributions of Income . . . . Income Cash	 860	 860
December 31 (28) Collected interest on Co. Z bonds, $450, interest being divided between principal and income as follows:		*Principal Cash . . . . . . Income Cash . . . . Accrued Interest on Co. Z Bonds . . . Co. Z 6% Bonds . . Collections of Income	387 63	 375 12 63
To principal —				
Accrued interest on date of purchase paid from principal cash	$375			
Premium amortization for two months, 2/50 x $300 (it is assumed that state laws provide for the principal recovery of original bond outlay)	12			
	$387			
To income —				
Interest collected, $75, less premium amortization, $12	63			
	$450			
December 31 (29) to close temporary accounts.		Collections of Income Trust Income . . . . Distributions of Income	813 47	 860

SPECIAL CASH JOURNALS FOR EXECUTOR AND TRUSTEE

Special columnar cash receipts and cash payments journals are generally desirable in recording cash transactions of the executor and the trustee. Cash transactions for William C. Ross, Executor, could be recorded in a cash receipts journal and a cash payments journal as illustrated on pages 783 and 784. Similar special columnar cash journals could be provided to record the cash transactions completed by William C. Ross acting as trustee.

CASH RECEIPTS

Date		Account Credited	Explanation	L. P.	Principal Cash Dr.	Income Cash Dr.	Disposal of Assets: Loss Dr.	Disposal of Assets: Asset Cr.	Disposal of Assets: Gain Cr.	Collections of Income Cr.	Sundry Credits
May	1	Estate Principal	Cash left by decedent		2,800						2,800
	20	Life Insurance Policy	Collected insurance		20,000			20,000			
	25	Dividends Receivable on Co. A Stock	Collected dividend		150			150			
June	1	Accrued Int. on Co. X Bonds	Collected accrued interest		300			250			
		Henry Davis	Collected legacy interest								50
	1	Accrued Int. on Co. Y Bonds	Collected accrued interest		625			625			
		Collections of Income	Collected interest income			125				125	
	10	Automobile	Sold automobile at loss		1,350		150	1,500			
Sept.	1	Assets Subsequently Discovered	Collected note and accrued int.		1,010						1,010
		Collections of Income	Collected interest income			20				20	
	5	Collections of Income	Collected dividend income			150				150	
	15	Co. A Stock — Gains on Disposal of Assets	Sold stock at gain		11,800			11,500	300		
					38,035	295	150	34,025	300	295	3,860

CASH PAYMENTS

Date		Account Debited	Explanation	L. P.	Principal Cash Cr.	Income Cash Cr.	Funeral and Administrative Expenses Dr.	Debts of Decedent Paid Dr.	Legacies Paid or Delivered Dr.	Expenses Chargeable to Income Dr.	Distributions of Income Dr.	Sundry Debits
June	12	Funeral and Adm. Exp.	Paid funeral expense		600		600					
	15	Legacies Paid or Delivered	Paid cash legacy to widow		15,000				15,000			
	18	Henry Davis	Paid interest collected on legacy		50				50			
Sept.	1	Distributions of Income	Paid income to widow			145					145	
	15	Debts of Decedent Paid	Paid creditors		5,650			5,650				
Oct.	1	Funeral and Administrative Expenses	Paid principal charges		6,385		6,385					
		Expenses Chargeable to Income	Paid income charges			15				15		
					27,685	160	6,985	5,650	15,050	15	145	
Oct.	1	Funeral and Administrative Expenses	Paid principal commissions		2,000		2,000					
		Expenses Chargeable to Income	Paid income commissions			25				25		
	1	Principal Assets Transferred to William C. Ross, Trustee	Transferred principal cash to trustee		8,350							8,350
	1	Income Assets Transferred to William C. Ross, Trustee	Transferred income cash to trustee			110						110
					10,350	135	2,000			25		8,460

QUESTIONS

1. (a) What is meant by a trust? (b) Name the parties to a trust.

2. Distinguish between:

(a) Trust principal and trust income.
(b) Testamentary trust and inter vivos trust.
(c) Income beneficiary and remainderman.
(d) Revocable trust and irrevocable trust.

3. What are the usual responsibilities of the trustee?

4. (a) When does the testamentary trust acquire title to (1) real properties and (2) personal properties? (b) When does the tenancy of the income beneficiary begin?

5. Which of the following credits are generally considered principal and which are considered income?

(a) Assets discovered after death of the testator.
(b) Gain on the sale of a principal asset.
(c) Cash dividend of which 30% is declared by the corporation to be liquidating.
(d) Extra cash dividend.
(e) Proceeds from sale of stock rights.
(f) Accrued interest on bonds as of death of the testator.
(g) Gain on sale of securities acquired and sold after death of the testator.
(h) Profit on executory contract completed after death of the testator.
(i) Income from sale of crops after death of the testator.
(j) Accrued interest on bonds as of termination of a trust.
(k) Recovery of insurance as a result of property loss by fire.

6. Which of the following charges are generally considered to decrease principal and which are considered to decrease income?

(a) Specific legacies distributed.
(b) Legal fees for defending estate against certain claims.
(c) Funeral and administrative expenses of the estate.
(d) Cost of supporting widow for short period after death of testator.
(e) Federal estate tax paid.
(f) Expenses of probating will.
(g) Commission to executor for distributing estate assets.
(h) Loss on failure to collect account receivable of testator.
(i) Legal fees for collection of rents on property.
(j) Depreciation of real estate.
(k) Depletion of wasting assets.
(l) Property taxes assessed after death of testator.
(m) Cost of harvesting crops after death of testator.
(n) Ordinary repairs on real estate.
(o) Commission to trustee on distribution of income cash.
(p) Special assessment tax on real estate for street improvements.
(q) Interest on mortgage on real estate.
(r) Federal income tax on gain from sale of real estate.
(s) Federal income tax on income accumulated for the benefit of the income beneficiary.
(t) Accounting and legal fees in winding up trust activities.
(u) Real estate taxes that were a lien on date of testator's death.
(v) Loss on sale of a principal asset.

(w) Principal asset written off as worthless.
(x) Inheritance taxes paid on a trust-estate.
(y) Federal income taxes on decedent's last tax return.
(z) Special amounts allowed by law to surviving spouse.

7. What two views are held with respect to the treatment as principal and income of "extraordinary" cash dividends? Which rule prevails?

8. What two views are held with respect to the treatment as principal and income of stock dividends? Which rule prevails?

9. Assuming conditions as indicated below for bonds held in trust, indicate in each case how the net income accruing to the income beneficiary is generally measured:

How Acquired	Value at which Carried
(1) Transfer from estate	Premium
(2) Purchase by trustee	Premium
(3) Transfer from estate	Discount
(4) Purchase by trustee	Discount

10. (a) What general rules are followed in the measurement of income accruing to the income beneficiary when property is subject to (1) depreciation and (2) depletion? (b) What entries are made in recording depreciation and depletion on the trustee's books?

11. The executor for P. M. Bours listed 1,000 shares of Uranium, Inc. at no value in the estate inventory. As a result of valuable discoveries on the properties of this company four months after date of death, the stock became actively traded in over-the-counter dealings. A dividend was declared and paid. Shortly after receiving the dividend, the executor sold the stock. Income of the estate is payable to the surviving widow; principal of the estate is ultimately to be distributed to a surviving daughter. How would the dividend and the sale of the stock be reported on the estate books?

12. What books should be maintained by a party who is named in a will as both executor of an estate and trustee of a trust created by the will?

13. In accounting for a trust, what entries would be made when:
(a) The trust is opened and principal assets are recorded at appraised values.
(b) Trust assets are sold at a gain.
(c) Bonds are purchased at a premium plus 2 months' accrued interest.
(d) Semiannual interest is collected on the bonds referred to in part (c). (The law requires that income be reduced by regular bond premium amortization.)
(e) The costs of setting up the trust are paid.
(f) Income is distributed, the trustee withdrawing 2% of the income distribution as his commission.
(g) All nominal accounts are closed at the end of the trust fiscal period.

14. Describe the special journals that may be employed for an estate whose assets will ultimately be transferred to a trust.

EXERCISES

1. Peter Green, executor for the estate of Lee Andrews, collects the following items. What entries would be made for each of the following receipts in distinguishing properly between principal and income?

(a) Dividends on X Company stock of $300, dividends having been declared prior to date of death.
(b) Interest on Y Company bonds of $450, $150 having accrued prior to date of death.
(c) Rentals from properties owned, $400, $250 having accrued prior to date of death.
(d) Interest on Z Company bonds of $600, $100 having accrued prior to date of death. One half of the Z Company bonds represents a specific legacy.

2. P. C. Thatcher died on June 30, 1967, leaving a will in which B. D. Schire was named executor. Among other assets, the executor took over bonds of $10,000 appraised at $10,275, interest at 6% payable annually on December 31. The bonds mature on December 31, 1972. What entries would be made on December 31, 1967, when interest is collected and the proper amount of cash is paid to the income beneficiary?

3. In Exercise 2, state how the entries would differ if Schire, as trustee, acquired the bonds at $10,275 on June 30 and made payment to the income beneficiary on December 31? (Assume that the law requires the amortization of bond premium in calculating income.)

4. Under the terms of the will of J. A. Bailey, $40,000 is to be transferred to a trust to be administered by Ben Barker. The transfer of cash is made on February 1, 1967, and on March 1 Barker acquires $35,000 of 6% bonds of the Wescott Co. at 104½ plus accrued interest for 3 months. Interest is collected on the bonds on June 1 and December 1. Bonds mature in 8 years and 9 months after date of purchase, and bond premium is amortized over this period in arriving at the income distributable to the income beneficiary, Paul Bailey. Income distributions are made on June 15 and December 15. The trustee recognizes no accruals at the end of the calendar year. (a) Give the entries that would be made on the books of the trustee in 1967. (b) Prepare a charge and discharge statement as to principal and income.

5. Jack Lemmon, named trustee under a testamentary trust for the benefit of Richard Hill, took control on April 1, 1967, of 250 acres of farm land, including unharvested crops, appraised at a value of $45,000; a house appraised at $8,500; and a savings account of $4,950. Income from the trust is to be distributed to Ruth Hill for the support of the income beneficiary until the time when Richard reaches 21, when the entire trust principal is to be turned over to him.

The trustee completed the following transactions for the period April 1, 1967–December 31, 1967:

(a) Paid $1,450 for harvesting crops planted by the deceased, and sold the entire crop for $8,800.
(b) Sold the house and the farm land for $52,000.
(c) Purchased $55,000 of California Power Co. bonds at 100½.
(d) Received bond interest of $1,100 and interest from savings deposit of $100.
(e) Distributed the trust income after deducting fees of $200.

Prepare entries to record the activities of the trustee.

6. The following trial balance is taken from the books of the estate of Richard Harmon on May 1, 1967:

	Principal Accounts		Income Accounts	
	Dr.	Cr.	Dr.	Cr.
Principal Cash	25,000			
Stock of Ramsey Co.	67,500			
York Co. 3% Bonds	48,000			
Estate Principal		179,500		
Assets Subsequently Discovered		3,500		
Gains on Disposal of Assets		2,000		
Losses on Disposal of Assets	4,800			
Funeral and Administrative Expenses	3,750			
Debts of Decedent Paid	7,950			
Legacies Paid or Delivered	28,000			
Income Cash			1,750	
Collections of Income				4,500
Expenses Chargeable to Income			250	
Distributions of Income			2,500	
	185,000	185,000	4,500	4,500

Prepare entries (a) to close the temporary accounts and to record the transfer of estate assets to the trust, and (b) to open the trust books.

PROBLEMS

22-1. Frank F. Culver died on November 12, 1966. His will named Gordon S. Scott executer of his estate and also trustee under a testamentary trust. The will provided that, upon settlement of the estate, remaining assets were to be placed in trust, the income being paid to the widow of the decedent for her lifetime, the principal of the trust passing to certain charities upon the widow's death. Scott winds up estate affairs and his estate books show the following account balances on September 15, 1967, just before he established separate books for the trust:

Principal Cash	$ 43,500
Securities — Stocks and Bonds	24,000
Culver Building on Wilshire Blvd.	135,000
Mortgage Payable on Culver Building	60,000
Income Cash	350
Losses on Disposal of Assets	2,800
Funeral and Administrative Expenses	8,500
Debts of Decedent Paid	14,000
Legacies Paid or Delivered	82,000
Expenses Chargeable to Income	4,200
Estate Principal	238,950
Distributions of Income	17,450
Assets Subsequently Discovered	1,850
Gains on Disposal of Assets	9,000
Collections of Income	22,000

Instructions: (1) Prepare a charge and discharge statement summarizing estate activities.

(2) Give the entries to close the accounts on the estate books and to report the transfer of assets to the trustee.

(3) Give the entries to open the books of the trust.

22-2. Curtis A. Stoneman died on June 1, 1967, leaving a will in which he named John Burke as executor and trustee, property to be disposed of as follows:

Home, furniture, and automobile to wife.
Library to Edgewood State College.
10 shares of X Co. preferred stock and $5,000 of Y Co. bonds to the executor as a legacy.
Proceeds of insurance policy of $10,000 as well as all of the rest, residue, and remainder of the real and personal property to be placed in the hands of Burke as trustee. Income from this property is to accrue to a son who will receive the trust principal upon reaching the age of 21.

An inventory was filed by the executor as follows:

Balance in checking account	$ 1,500
Household furniture	8,500
Automobile	3,500
Library	4,000
Apartment house	60,000
X Co. 6% preferred stock, $100 par, 50 shares	5,350
Regular quarterly dividend on preferred stock, declared May 10 and payable to stockholders of record May 25	75
Y Co. 6% bonds, interest payable semiannually on February 1 and August 1 (valued at par)	15,000
Accrued interest on Y Co. bonds	300
Insurance policy (payable to estate)	10,000

The following transactions are completed by the executor:

(a) Quarterly dividend on preferred stock is collected on June 10.

(b) Insurance policy is collected.

(c) Household furniture and automobile are turned over to wife.

(d) The library is transferred to Edgewood State College.

(e) Interest on bonds, $450, is collected on August 1.

(f) The executor withdraws his legacy on August 15.

(g) Remaining bonds are sold at 102 plus accrued interest on September 1.

(h) The preferred stock is sold for 102½.

(i) Funeral, administrative expenses, and taxes are paid, $7,200.

(j) A bank deposit of $1,250 in the name of Stoneman is discovered.

(k) Debts of the decedent are paid, $6,500.

(l) The apartment house is sold for $61,500 on August 20; $16,500 is received in cash, and a 6% mortgage note is received for the balance. Income collected on the real estate to date of the sale totaled $1,850; expenses paid were $1,200.

(m) Income cash was distributed to the son on September 1.

(n) On September 1 Burke closed executor accounts and opened new books to record his activities as trustee.

Instructions: (1) Prepare general journal entries for Burke as executor.

(2) Prepare a trial balance and a charge and discharge statement, together with supporting schedules.

(3) Prepare the journal entries to close the estate books.

(4) Give the entry to open the trust books.

22-3. The estate of Wilbur C. Ward, deceased, is appraised as of date of death, March 1, as follows:

Assets

Cash in bank	$ 3,600
Apartment house	40,000
6% trust deed note on 12th St. property, interest payable June 1 and December 1	30,000
Unimproved real estate	4,500
Personal and household effects	10,000
Billings Co. 6% bonds, interest payable January 1 and July 1 (valued at par)	15,000
Cross Co. common stock	3,000
Accrued interest on bonds	150
Accrued interest on trust deed note	450

Disposition of the property under the will is as follows:

Bert C. Parker is to act as executor and trustee and is to receive bonds of $5,000, plus expenses, as compensation for his services.

Personal and household effects are to be turned over to the widow. The son, John, is granted a legacy of $5,000, and two grandsons are allowed $2,500 each.

The executor shall dispose of such securities as may be necessary in liquidating the liabilities of the estate. After payment of legacies, expenses, and debts, residual property shall be held in trust by the trustee, income to be payable to the widow, trust assets to belong to son upon her death.

During the period of executorship, March 1 to November 1, the following took place:

Interest of $900 was collected on the trust deed note, and $450 was collected on the Billings Co. bonds.

Dividends of $60 were received on the Cross Co. common stock.

Cross Co. common stock was sold for $2,600, and Billings Co. bonds, face value $5,000, were disposed of for $5,100 plus accrued interest to date of sale, $25.

Apartment house rental receipts totaled $3,600; however, $150 represented collection of rentals accrued prior to March 1. Repairs, maintenance, and taxes paid on this property totaled $1,650.

The executor paid debts of $2,200, funeral expenses and expenses of last illness of $950, and legal, probate, and administrative expenses of $800. In addition, $1,500 was paid to the State Bank on a note dishonored by George Connally; this note had been endorsed by the decedent. It is believed that collection will be made from the maker of the note.

All of the legacies were distributed in accordance with the provisions of the will, except that the son, with the consent of all parties, accepted the unimproved real estate in full settlement of his legacy. In addition, cash of $2,000 was paid to the widow.

On November 1 the executor filed his report with the court. The court approved final distribution of the estate according to the terms of the will, and the executor thereupon closed the estate books and opened books as trustee.

Instructions: (1) Give the entries in general journal form to record the transactions of the executor on the estate books.

(2) Prepare a preclosing trial balance and a charge and discharge statement, together with accompanying schedules, to be submitted to the court.

(3) Give the entries to close the temporary principal accounts and income accounts.

(4) Give the entries to transfer principal and income assets to the trustee and to close the estate books.

(5) Give the opening entries on the books of the trustee.

22-4. Henry Briggs is appointed to act as trustee for a trust fund of $106,000, income to be paid to Andrew Scott and principal to be paid to Scott when he reaches the age of 25.

On June 30, 1967, Briggs receives the cash and on July 1 he purchases $100,000 of Coast Utilities Co. 4½% bonds, paying 103 plus accrued interest. Interest on the bonds is payable semiannually on April 1 and October 1. The bonds mature on October 1, 1973.

The trustee collects interest regularly in 1967 and 1968. In making income distributions out of the trust, the trustee is entitled to withdraw 5% of such amounts as his commission. Trust income is distributed at the end of 1967 and 1968. (State laws provide that bond premium shall be amortized in determining amounts available for income beneficiaries.)

Instructions: (1) Give in general journal form the entries to record the above transactions on the books of the trustee, including the closing entries that would be prepared at the end of 1967 and 1968.

(2) Prepare charge and discharge statements as to principal and income for 1967 and for 1968.

22-5. Clarence Ross acts as trustee under terms of a testamentary trust made by Robert Searles, deceased. Income of the trust is payable to Mrs. Searles. At her death, the trust principal is to be divided equally among four children, Andrew, Barbara, Charles, and Dolores. On December 31, 1966, trust account balances are as follows:

Valley County 5% Bonds, interest payable April 1 and October 1, bonds maturing on October 1, 1981; face value, $30,000	$34,500*
Principal Cash	5,500
Trust Principal	40,000

*Valley County bonds were purchased on October 1, 1966, after the trust was formed.

On March 1, 1967, the trustee purchased $5,000 of Riverside 4½% bonds, paying $5,150 plus accrued interest of $75. Interest is payable semiannually at the beginning of May and November, the bonds maturing on May 1, 1971.

Interest on bonds was collected regularly and all available income cash was distributed to the life tenant on July 1 and December 31, 1967 and 1968. The trustee in making remittances deducts 2% as commission. This rate is allowed Ross on all cash distributions made by him on behalf of the trust.

Mrs. Searles died on May 1, 1969. At the direction of the court, the trustee sold the bonds at the following amounts:

Valley County 5% Bonds	$32,000 plus accrued interest to June 1
Riverside 4½% Bonds	$ 5,100 plus accrued interest to June 1

Mrs. Searles's will provided that any equity that she might have in the trust income upon her death should be paid to her daughter Dolores. The trustee made final distribution of trust assets in accordance with the foregoing stipulations.

Instructions: (1) Give in general journal form the entries to record the above transactions on the books of the trustee, including the closing entries that would be prepared at the end of each calendar year and also upon termination of the trust on June 1, 1969. (Assume that state laws require premium amortization in determining amounts available to income beneficiary. Amortization entries are made only when interest is collected.)

(2) Prepare charge and discharge statements as to principal and income for 1967, for 1968, and for the period January 1–June 1, 1969.

22-6. Charles Murray, executor for the estate of Paul Warner, and trustee, takes charge of the following assets on January 4, 1967:

Cash	$ 45,000
Product Development Co. stock, 10,000 shares, market value.	82,500
Villa in Sky High Mountains, appraised value	56,500
Land in Sunset City, appraised value	250,000

The will provides that, after payments of funeral and administrative expenses, debts of the decedent, federal and state taxes, and bequests to charities, the residue and remainder of the real and personal property is to be placed in the hands of Murray as trustee. Mrs. Warner is to be sole life tenant of the trust income. Mrs. Warner is to receive a minimum of $15,000 per year; if net trust income, after allowance for expenses and trustee's fees, is unequal to this minimum, such deficiency is to be paid out of principal.

From January 4, 1967, to March 31, 1967, the executor made the following cash disbursements: funeral and administrative expenses, $4,200; debts of decedent, $8,500; advance to Mrs. Warner, $5,000; bequests to charity, $20,000; income tax of decedent for 1966, $1,720; and fees of executor, $2,000.

On March 31, 1967, the executor closed his accounts and opened new books to record his activities as trustee.

From April 1, 1967, to December 31, 1967, cash transactions of the trustee were as follows:

Cash receipts:

Dividends of Product Development Co. stock, declared after death of decedent		$ 5,000
Proceeds from sale of lots (the land was divided into 45 Class A lots, 80 Class B lots, and 40 Class C lots):		
Class A lots sold, 15 @ $3,600	$ 54,000	
Class B lots sold, 50 @ $2,600	130,000	
Class C lots sold, 20 @ $1,500	30,000	
Gross proceeds from sale	$214,000	
Less commissions to agents	10,700	
Net proceeds		203,300
Interest received on $150,000 Sunset City bonds		2,250
Net income from operations of the Sky High Villa as a resort hotel.		6,950

Cash disbursements:

Cost of grading, surveying, etc. in subdividing land into lots....	$ 8,000
Cost of remodeling the Sky High Villa..........................	21,500
Investment in Sunset City bonds at par........................	150,000
Other disbursements:	
Trustee's fees allowed and paid as follows:	
5% of net trust income before allowance for fees.	
2% of net gain on sale of principal assets.	
Allowance to Mrs. Warner less advance.	

Instructions: (1) Prepare general journal entries for the executor, including entries to close the estate books.

(2) Prepare entries for the trustee to record trust activities.

(3) Prepare a charge and discharge statement for the trustee covering the period April 1, 1967, to December 31, 1967.

22-7. The will of Arthur Benson, deceased, directed that his executor, Carl Dewing, liquidate the entire estate within two years of the date of Mr. Benson's death and pay the net proceeds and income, if any, to the Sunnydale Orphanage. Mr. Benson, who was a bachelor, died on February 1, 1967, after a brief illness.

An inventory of the decedent's property was prepared, and the fair market value of all items was determined. The preliminary inventory, before the computation of any appropriate income accruals on inventory items, follows:

	Fair Market Value
First National Bank checking account.................	$ 6,000
$60,000 City of Laguna School Bonds, interest rate 2% payable January 1 and July 1, maturity date 7/1/71..	59,000
2,000 shares Jones Corporation capital stock...........	220,000
Term life insurance. Beneficiary — Estate of Arthur Benson..	20,000
Personal residence ($45,000) and furnishings ($5,000)...	50,000

During 1967 the following transactions occurred:

(1) The interest on the City of Laguna School Bonds was collected. The Bonds were sold on July 1 for $59,000, and the proceeds and interest were paid to the Orphanage.

(2) The Jones Corporation paid cash dividends of $1 per share on March 1 and December 1, as well as a 10% stock dividend on July 1. All dividends were declared 45 days before each payment date and were payable to holders of record as of 40 days before each payment date. On September 2, 1,000 shares were sold at $105 per share, and the proceeds were paid to the Sunnydale Orphanage.

(3) Because of a depressed real estate market, the personal residence was rented furnished at $300 per month commencing April 1. The rent is paid monthly, in advance. Real estate taxes of $900 for the calendar year of 1967 were paid. The house and furnishings have estimated lives of 45 years and 10 years respectively. The part-time gardener-handyman was paid 4 months' wages totaling $500 on April 30 for services performed, and he was released.

(4) The First National Bank checking account was closed and the balance of $6,000 was transferred to an estate bank account.
(5) The term life insurance was paid on March 1 and deposited in the estate bank account.
(6) The following disbursements were made:
 (a) Funeral expenses, $2,000.
 (b) Final illness expenses, $1,500.
 (c) April 15 income tax remittance, $700.
 (d) Attorney's and accountant's fees, $12,000.
(7) On December 31, the balance of the undistributed income, except for $1,000, was paid to the beneficiary. The balance of the cash on hand derived from the corpus of the estate was also paid to the beneficiary on December 31. As of December 31, 1967, the executor resigned and waived all commissions.

Instructions: Prepare a charge and discharge statement separately stated as to principal and income, together with its supporting schedules, on behalf of the executor of the Estate of Arthur Benson for the period from February 1, 1967, through December 31, 1967.

(AICPA adapted)

22-8. Alfred Tucker died in an accident on May 31, 1967. His will, dated February 28, 1966, provided that all just debts and expenses be paid and that his property be disposed of as follows:

Personal residence — devised to Betty Tucker, widow.
United States Treasury bonds and Puritan Co. stock — to be placed in trust. All income to go to Betty Tucker during her lifetime, with right of appointment upon her death.
Seneca Co. mortgage notes — bequeathed to Carol Tucker Watson, daughter.
Cash — a bequest of $10,000 to Donald Tucker, son.
Remainder of estate — to be divided equally between the two children, Carol Tucker Watson and Donald Tucker.

The will further provided that during the administration period Betty Tucker was to be paid $300 a month out of estate income. Estate and inheritance taxes are to be borne by the residue. Donald Tucker was named as executor and trustee.

An inventory of the decedent's property was prepared. The fair market value of all items as of the date of death was determined. The preliminary inventory, before the computation of any appropriate income accruals on inventory items, follows:

Personal residence property	$ 45,000
Jewelry — diamond ring	9,600
York Life Insurance Co. — term life insurance policy on life of Alfred Tucker. Beneficiary — Betty Tucker, widow	120,000
Granite Trust Co. — 3% savings bank account, Alfred Tucker, in trust for Paul Watson (grandchild), interest credited January and July 1; balance May 31, 1967	400
Fidelity National Bank — checking account; balance May 31, 1967	143,000
$100,000 United States Treasury bonds, 3%, 1999, interest payable March 1 and September 1	100,000

$9,700 Seneca Co. first mortgage notes, 6%, 1971, interest payable May 31 and November 30	9,900
800 shares Puritan Co. common stock	64,000
700 shares Meta Mfg. Co. common stock	70,000

The executor opened an estate bank account to which he transferred the decedent's checking account balance. Other deposits, through July 1, 1968, were as follows:

Interest collected on bonds:	
$100,000 United States Treasury:	
September 1, 1967	$ 1,500
March 1, 1968	1,500
Dividends received on stock:	
800 shares Puritan Co.:	
June 15, 1967, declared May 7, 1967, payable to holders of record May 27, 1967	800
September 15, 1967	800
December 15, 1967	1,200
March 15, 1968	800
June 15, 1968	800
Net proceeds of June 19, 1967, sale of 700 shares Meta Mfg. Co.	68,810

Payments were made from the estate's checking account through July 1, 1968, for the following:

Funeral expenses	$ 2,000
Assessments for additional 1965 federal and state income taxes ($1,700) plus interest ($110) to May 31, 1967	1,810
1967 income taxes of Alfred Tucker for the period January 1, 1967, through May 31, 1967, in excess of amounts paid by the decedent on Declarations of Estimated Tax	9,100
Federal and state fiduciary income taxes, fiscal years ending June 30, 1967, ($75) and June 30, 1968 ($1,400)	1,475
Federal and state estate taxes	58,000
Monthly payments to Betty Tucker: 13 payments of $300	3,900
Attorney's and accountant's fees	25,000

The executor waived his commission. However, he desired to receive his father's diamond ring in lieu of the $10,000 specific legacy. All parties agreed to this in writing, and the courts approval was secured. All other specific legacies were delivered by July 15, 1967.

Instructions: Prepare a charge and discharge statement as to principal and income, together with its supporting schedules, to accompany the attorney's formal court accounting on behalf of the executor of the Estate of Alfred Tucker for the period from May 31, 1967, through July 1, 1968. (Alfred Tucker was not a resident of a community property state.) The following supporting schedules should be included: (1) Original Principal of Estate; (2) Gain on Disposal of Estate Assets; (3) Loss on Disposal of Estate Assets; (4) Funeral, Administration and Other Expenses; (5) Debts of Decedent Paid; (6) Legacies Paid or Delivered; (7) Balance as to Estate Principal, July 1, 1968; (8) Proposed Plan of Distribution of Estate Assets; (9) Collections of Income; (10) Distributions of Income.

(AICPA adapted)

22-9. Sam Williams, Jr. died on January 15, 1967. His records disclose the following estate:

Cash in bank	$ 3,750
6% note receivable, including $50 accrued interest	5,050
Stocks	50,000
Dividends declared on stocks	600
6% mortgage receivable, including $100 accrued interest	20,100
Real estate — apartment house	35,000
Household effects	8,250
Dividend receivable from Sam Williams, Sr. trust fund	250,000
Total	$372,750

On July 1, 1949, the late Sam Williams, Sr. created a trust, with his son Sam Williams, Jr. as life tenant and his grandson as remainderman. The assets in the fund consist solely of the outstanding capital stock of Williams, Inc., namely, 2,000 shares of $100 each. At the creation of the trust, the book value, as well as the market value, of the Williams, Inc., shares was $400,000, and at December 31, 1966, it was $500,000. On January 2, 1967, Williams, Inc. declared a 125% cash dividend payable February 2, 1967, to shareholders of record January 12, 1967.

The executor's transactions from January 15 to 31, 1967, were as follows:

Cash receipts:

Jan. 20	Dividends	$ 1,500.00
25	6% note receivable	5,000.00
	Interest accrued on note	58.33
	Stock sold, inventoried at $22,500	20,000.00
	6% mortgage sold	20,100.00
	Interest accrued on mortgage	133.33
28	Sale of assets not inventoried	250.00
29	Real estate sold	30,000.00
		$77,041.66

Cash disbursements:

Jan. 20	Funeral expenses	$ 1,750.00
23	Decedent's debts	8,000.00
25	Decedent's bequests	10,000.00
31	Advance to widow	1,500.00
		$21,250.00

Instructions: Prepare statements of principal and income for the executor, covering the period from January 15 to January 31, 1967.

(AICPA adapted)

22-10. Wallace Weber died January 1, 1963, and left his property in trust for his daughter, Amy. The income was to be paid to her as long as she lived, and at her death the trust was to go to his nephew, Werner Weber. He appointed Joseph Brooks trustee at a fixed fee of $5,000 per annum. All expenses of settling the estate were paid and accounted for by the executor before the trustee took it over.

Amy died on September 30, 1966, and left all her property in trust to her cousin, Phillip Marsh. Joseph Brooks was appointed executor and trustee of her estate, and he agreed not to make any additional charges for these services. All income was to be paid to Phillip Marsh. The estate, which consisted solely of Amy's unexpended income from the Wallace Weber trust, was immediately invested in 4% certificates of deposit.

The property received under the will of Wallace Weber on January 1, 1963, was:

10,000 shares of the K. O. Corporation, valued at $100 each.
$300,000 bonds of the K. O. Corporation, paying interest on June 30 and December 31 at 6% per annum.

In the 5 years ended December 31, 1967, the trustee received the following dividends on the stock:

February 1, 1963	$40,000
February 1, 1964	40,000
February 1, 1965	40,000
February 1, 1966	60,000
February 1, 1967	60,000

During this period the trustee made the following payments:

Expenses:		
$100 a month, totaling		$ 6,000
Trustees fees:		
$5,000 per annum, totaling		$ 25,000
To beneficiaries:		
Amy Weber:		
1963	$27,250	
1964	35,000	
1965	25,000	
1966	37,000	$124,250
Werner Weber:		
1966	$17,000	
1967	46,000	$ 63,000
Phillip Marsh:		
1967		$ 3,000

The undistributed income was left on deposit in the bank and drew no interest.

Instructions: Prepare trustee's statements covering the 5 years ended December 31, 1967, showing the beneficiaries' interests.

(AICPA adapted)

22-11. Sam Hill died September 30, 1966, leaving a will and appointing three executors to administer his estate. The will provided for the payment of funeral expenses, debts, and other necessary expenses, and for the following specific bequests:

Cemetery, for upkeep of burial plot	$ 2,500
Hospital	2,000
Church	5,000
Relative	10,000
Executors ($5,000 each in lieu of fees)	15,000
	$34,500

The balance of the estate was to be held in trust, and the income thereof was to be paid in equal shares to the three children of the testator during their natural lives. The first distribution from income was to be made December 31, 1967. On the death of each of the life beneficiaries, the proportionate part of the estate as at that date was to revert to that beneficiary's issue surviving, if any; otherwise to remain in trust.

At date of death the testator was possessed of the following: cash, $25,000; accounts receivable, $55,000; 5½% first-mortgage bonds, interest June 30 and December 31, par and appraised value, $100,000; U.S. 2¾% Treasury bonds, interest May 15 and November 15, par and appraised value, $50,000; 1,000 shares Astor Mining Company stock, par $5 per share, appraised as valueless; 1,000 shares of Boston Industries, Inc., stock, par $100, appraised at $110; clothing, $1,000; jewelry, $5,000; furniture, $10,000.

Receipts were as follows: $40,000 of U.S. Treasury bonds sold on November 15, 1966, at 102; accounts receivable collected, $50,000 (balance worthless); dividends on Boston Industries, Inc., declared prior, but paid subsequent, to death of testator, $4,000; dividend of same company declared and paid subsequent to death of testator, $2,000; furniture sold for $9,000; Astor Mining Company stock sold at 25 cents per share; bank interest earned after death, $1,250; refund of federal taxes, year 1965, $500; all interest collected on investments.

Disbursements were as follows: funeral expenses, $2,500; administration expenses (chargeable to corpus), $8,000; legal services, $3,000; debts of testator, $15,000; 1966 federal and state taxes to date of death, $3,100; all specific bequests paid, relative taking jewelry at appraised value against bequest of $10,000.

Other transactions: clothing given to charity.

Instructions: Prepare as of November 30, 1967, (a) a summary statement of executors as to principal, showing assets remaining in the estate; and (b) a summary statement of executors as to income. (For purposes of this problem, ignore the factors of inheritance, transfer, and other taxes not specified in the problem.)

(AICPA adapted)

Chapter 23

GOVERNMENTAL UNITS

THE GENERAL FUND

All phases of the financial activities of a governmental unit, whether federal, state, or local, are determined and controlled by law. Laws determine how revenues of the governmental unit are to be raised. Laws determine how the revenues are to be allocated among the different governmental activities and the specific purposes for which they may be spent. Standards and procedures for handling receipts and disbursements and for accounting and reporting for the governmental unit must likewise conform with the law.

The plan that is developed by a governmental unit for the expenditures of a given period and for the means of financing these is known as a *budget.* The budget when prepared in accordance with legal requirements and enacted into law becomes the basis for the management and control of the financial activities of the period. Changes in a budget may be made during the period by appropriate legislative action. Financial actions must adhere to the plans and requirements established by the budget and supplementary legislative provisions.

EFFECTS OF LEGAL CONTROLS UPON ACCOUNTING

There are many similarities in accounting for the private unit and for the governmental unit. In both cases transactions are analyzed and recorded in books of original entry and in ledger accounts, and are summarized periodically on statements reporting financial position and operating results.

In accounting for the private unit, emphasis is placed on the satisfactory measurement of net income arising from the sale of goods or services. Financial operations of the governmental unit, however, are not directed toward achieving a net income but toward raising sufficient revenue to meet the cost of the services that the unit is called upon to render. Although revenues and expenditures of the governmental unit are recorded and summarized in accounting for its activities, no adjustments are normally made for depreciation and certain accrued and prepaid items that would require recognition in measuring net income.

On the other hand, accounting for the governmental unit involves certain responsibilities that go beyond those found in accounting for the private unit. Accounts of the public unit must provide financial data that will enable officials of the government to administer affairs in accordance with the legislative intent as provided by the budget and other applicable laws and regulations. Further, the accounts must summarize governmental activities and show how these meet legal requirements.

Accounting for the governmental unit calls for the recognition of the different *funds* that have been established by such unit. A fund is defined by the National Committee on Governmental Accounting as "a sum of money or other resources segregated for the purpose of carrying on specific activities or attaining certain objectives in accordance with special regulations, restrictions, or limitations and constituting an independent fiscal and accounting entity."[1]

Funds are established by constitution, statute, charter, or ordinance, or by appropriate action by the legislative or administrative branch of the government. The number of separate funds established by a governmental unit may vary from one to more than a hundred. Each fund requires a separate accounting. The accounting for a fund will embrace assets, liabilities, surplus, and revenues and expenditures.

Governmental accounting is frequently referred to as *fund accounting* in view of the recognition of the fund as the accounting entity. Governmental accounting is also referred to as *budgetary accounting* because budgetary accounts are incorporated in the system of accounts. Fund or budgetary accounting is applicable to all levels of government including the federal government, state government, counties, cities, school districts, and other special taxing units. Such accounting is also employed with certain modifications by nonprofit service organizations whose activities are related to funds and whose operations are frequently controlled by budgets. Such organizations include schools, hospitals, charities, religious organizations, and fraternal groups.

Many governmental units carry on major business enterprises furnishing utilities or other special services to the public. The operations of such enterprises follow closely the operations that would be found in private enterprises. Such enterprises call for accounting and reporting procedures that parallel those found in a comparable private unit.

CLASSIFICATION OF ACCOUNTS OF A GOVERNMENTAL UNIT

As previously indicated, accounts of a governmental unit are classified by funds. Accounts within the funds are classified into balance sheet and operating statement accounts. Further classifications are applied to the revenue and expenditure accounts. Extended classifications may be called for in governmental accounting to facilitate effective planning,

[1] *Municipal Accounting and Auditing* (Chicago: National Committee on Governmental Accounting, September, 1951), p. 4. The Committee, formerly known as the National Committee on Municipal Accounting, is located at 1313 East 60th St., Chicago, Illinois 60637.

control, and reporting. Classification serves in budget preparation and execution, in reporting, in cost analysis, in comparative analyses, and in the development of statistical summaries.

Classes of funds. The National Committee on Governmental Accounting has classified governmental funds according to the types of activities that are financed, as follows:

(1) General fund (or general revenue fund).
(2) Special revenue funds.
(3) Bond funds.
(4) Special assessment funds.
(5) Sinking funds.
(6) Working capital funds.
(7) Trust and agency funds.
(8) Utility or other enterprise funds.

A general fund will be found for every governmental unit. This fund accounts for all revenues and finances all activities that are not directly identified with some special fund. The number of special funds that are found in any governmental unit will vary, depending upon the nature and variety of the special activities carried on by the unit and the legal provisions that have been adopted for separately financing such activities.

In addition to the eight classes of funds listed, the National Committee on Governmental Accounting recommends that two special groups of accounts be established to provide information concerning general fixed assets and general bonded debt and interest. Although the general fixed assets and the general bonded debt and interest groups of accounts do not qualify as funds as previously defined, nevertheless the terms "funds" and "fund accounting" are normally interpreted broadly to include these groups that are required for a full accounting.

Governmental revenues classified. A governmental unit normally has revenues from many sources. A primary classification of revenues for budgetary, recording, and statement purposes is normally made in terms of revenue *source*. Revenues of a municipality, for example, are normally classified under the following headings:

Taxes.
Licenses and permits.
Fines, forfeits, and penalties.
Revenue from other agencies.
Revenue from use of money and property.
Charges for current services.

Subclassifications would be provided for significant revenue sources within the above categories. For example, tax sources may be subdivided to show taxes on real property, taxes on personal property, sales taxes, and interest and penalties on delinquent taxes; licenses and permits may be subdivided in terms of motor vehicle licenses, building permit fees, and inspection charges.

Instead of classifying revenues by source as described above, revenues are frequently classified according to the *organization unit* making the collection. Revenues, then, would be classified in terms of the department, bureau, or division responsible for their collection.

Governmental expenditures classified. A primary classification of expenditures is usually made in terms of governmental *function*. Expenditures of a municipality, for example, may be classified by function under the following headings:

General government.
Public safety.
Highways.
Sanitation and waste removal.
Health and hospitals.
Public welfare.
Schools.
Libraries.
Recreation.
Public service enterprises.
Interest on debt.
Redemption of bonds.
Miscellaneous.

Expenditures according to function may be further subclassified in terms of *activities*, *character*, and *object*. To illustrate, general governmental expenditures may be subclassified in terms of *activities* as administrative, legislative, and judicial. Information concerning the *character* of expenditures is offered by subclassifying expenditures as (1) current expense, (2) capital outlay, and (3) debt retirement. Information concerning the *object* of expenditures is offered by further analysis of the current expense items just mentioned in terms of (1) personal services for salaries and wages, (2) contractual services, consisting of work done under special contract, (3) material and supply acquisitions, and (4) other charges.

A functional classification of expenditures may be accompanied by a further subclassification in terms of *organization units*. The basis for such classification is the department, bureau, or division responsible for certain activities. Here, too, further analyses would be provided in terms of activities, character, and object.

All of the classifications that have been suggested are shown in the headings of the following statement that summarizes expenditures for a department of health, one of the units involved in the health and hospitals function of a governmental unit:

Function: Health and Hospitals

	Current Expenses				Capital Outlays			Debt Retirement
	Personal Services	Contractual Services	Materials and Supplies	Other Charges	Land	Buildings	Equipment	
Department of Health								$10,000
Bureau of Regulation and Inspection							$6,500	
Inspection of Milk and Dairy Products	$4,000	$1,500	$1,200	$300				
Inspection of Other Foods and Drugs	5,000	2,000	1,500	200				
Sanitary Inspection	1,200		300	150				

Revenues and expenditures are classified only in certain funds. Classifications are appropriate in accounting for general fund revenues and expenditures when receipts are collected from many sources and are applied to many functions. Classification would not apply in the case of a sinking fund that is restricted to the accumulation of moneys for the retirement of bonds; in the latter case, revenues are normally acquired from a single source and applied to a single purpose.

ACCOUNTING FOR THE GOVERNMENTAL UNIT

Accounting for the governmental unit begins with the adoption of the budget. The budget lists the proposed expenditures and also the sources for financing such expenditures. It is adopted by passage of an appropriation act or ordinance by the responsible legislative body. Adoption of the budget provides legal authorization for expenditures in accordance with the plan. The budget that authorizes expenditures is at the same time a device that limits expenditures; expenditures should not exceed the amounts specified for each function or organization unit as well as for each object within the categories named and subject to such control. The statements that are prepared at the end of each period compare actual expenditures with the amounts appropriated in terms of the classifications established within the budget.

Upon adoption of the budget, certain revenue-producing measures may have to be put into effect. Although legislation may already be effective with respect to sales tax rates, licenses, and fees, special action may be required in setting tax rates for real and personal property and charges for certain services. Once the revenue-raising rates are set, no further action or control is involved. Accounting reports prepared in the future will provide comparisons of actual revenue with revenue requirements as established in the budget.

A general ledger is maintained for each fund with asset, liability, and surplus accounts, and also with revenue and expenditure accounts. Revenue and expenditure detail is provided in the accounts to make possible summaries of such information in accordance with the classifications to be used in reporting activities. Separate subsidiary ledgers are maintained where necessary.

A balance sheet is prepared for each fund at the end of the period. The balance sheet may be accompanied by a statement summarizing fund operations for the period. The nature of the latter statement varies with the different funds. In some instances operating data consist of a summary of revenues and expenditures; in other instances operating data are limited to a summary of cash receipts and disbursements; in certain instances both types of data are given. Balance sheets and operating statements are often supported by schedules offering supplementary detail. Governmental units may also prepare interim statements within the fiscal period. Frequently, separate statements for each fund are accompanied by combined statements showing the financial condition and the results of operations for a number of funds or all of the funds.

The National Committee on Governmental Accounting has recommended a body of principles and procedures that should be employed in accounting for municipalities and related units. The recommendations of this group are summarized below:[1]

Principles:

(1) The accounting system should make it possible (a) to show that legal provisions have been complied with and (b) to reflect the financial condition and the financial operations of the governmental unit.

(2) If legal and sound accounting provisions conflict, legal provisions should govern but the finance officer should seek to obtain changes in the law to bring it into harmony with sound principles.

(3) The general accounting system should be on a double-entry basis with all transactions summarized in a general ledger supported by subsidiary records where appropriate.

(4) Funds should be established consistent with legal provisions and requirements of sound financial administration, but the number of funds should be kept at a minimum to avoid undue inflexibility.

(5) The budget document and financial reports should recognize the following types of funds to the extent required: (1) General, (2) Special Revenue, (3) Bond, (4) Special Assessment, (5) Sinking, (6) Working Capital, (7) Trust and Agency, and (8) Utility or Other Enterprise.

(6) A complete balancing group of accounts should be established for each fund, including all of the accounts to set forth financial condition and financial operations and to reflect compliance with legal provisions.

(7) With the exception of Working Capital, Utility or Other Enterprise, or Trust Funds, fixed assets should not be carried in the same fund with current assets but should be set up in a self-balancing group of accounts known as the General Fixed Assets Group of Accounts; similarly, except in Special Assessment and Utility Funds, long-term liabilities should not be carried in the same fund with current liabilities but should be shown in a separate self-balancing group of accounts known as the General Bonded Debt and Interest Group of Accounts.

(8) Fixed assets should be maintained at original cost, or at estimated cost when original cost is not available; in the case of gifts, assets should be maintained at the appraised value at the time received.

(9) Depreciation on general fixed assets should not be reflected in the accounts unless cash for replacements can legally be set aside; however,

---

[1]For a full statement of recommended principles and procedures, refer to *Municipal Accounting and Auditing* (Chicago: National Committee on Governmental Accounting, September, 1951).

depreciation may be recognized for unit cost purposes and for memorandum purposes.

(10) The accounting system should provide for budgetary control for both revenues and expenditures, and financial statements should include such budgetary information.

(11) The accrual basis for revenues and expenditures is recommended to the extent applicable: revenues partially offset by provisions for estimated losses should be recognized when earned even though not received in cash; expenditures should be recognized as soon as liabilities are incurred.

(12) Revenues should be classified by fund and source; expenditures should be classified by fund, function, department, activity, character, and by main classes of objects in accordance with standard classifications.

(13) Cost accounting systems should be established wherever costs can be measured; depreciation should be recognized in determining unit costs.

(14) Common terminology and classification should be used consistently throughout the budget, the accounts, and the financial reports.

Procedures:

(1) Accounts should be centralized under the direction of one officer who should be responsible for keeping or supervising all accounts and preparing and issuing all financial reports.

(2) Budgets are essential for the proper management of the affairs of the governmental unit and should be prepared even if not required by law; fund distinctions should be made in such budgets.

(3) As soon as purchase orders or contracts are signed, obligations should be recorded as encumbrances of the funds and appropriations affected.

(4) Inventories of both consumable and permanent properties should be kept in subsidiary ledgers controlled by accounts in the general accounting system; physical inventories should be taken at least annually, and accounts and records brought into agreement with such inventories.

(5) Accounting for municipal business enterprises should follow the standard classifications employed by similar private enterprises; accounting for public institutions should follow the standard classifications for such institutions.

(6) Financial reports should be prepared monthly or oftener to show the current condition of budgetary accounts and the other information necessary to control operations, and a general financial report should be prepared and published at least once a year.

(7) Financial reports of all municipalities of similar size and type should be generally uniform.

(8) A periodic audit by independent accountants is desirable.

Remaining pages of this chapter and the chapter that follows describe the operations of governmental funds and illustrate the application of the principles and the procedures that have been described. Accounting for the general fund is described in this chapter; accounting for other funds and the special groups of accounts that have been mentioned is described in the following chapter.

GENERAL FUND

Every governmental unit has a general fund. This is the most important fund, for it finances all of the normal activities of the governmental unit. Revenues that are not specifically allocated by law to some special fund accrue to the general fund; activities or projects that are not to be financed by some special fund make their demands upon the resources of the general fund. The general fund, while financing the general activities of the governmental unit, may also be responsible for the payment for properties acquired by governmental departments and for the payment of principal and interest on governmental debt.

Accounting for the general fund illustrated. To illustrate the accounting for the general fund of a governmental unit, general fund transactions for the City of A and the entries to record these transactions are listed on pages 808–811. An explanation of these entries is given below and on pages 812–818.

Explanation of general fund entries — adoption of budget. (See transaction (1), page 808.) At the beginning of the fiscal period, the budgeted revenues and appropriations are recorded by a debit to Estimated Revenues and a credit to Appropriations. Estimated Revenues may be interpreted as the total estimated receivables for the period; Appropriations may be interpreted as the total estimated payables. When the budget shows an excess of estimated revenues over appropriations, Unappropriated Surplus is credited in the opening entry; this is the fund increase that is estimated to result from activities of the current period. When the budget shows an excess of appropriations over estimated revenues, Unappropriated Surplus is debited in the opening entry; in such an instance, assets carried over from prior periods are to be used in financing current activities.

Accounts that report budgetary estimates of revenues or budgetary limitations on expenditures are referred to as *budgetary accounts;* accounts that express the results of actual transactions of the governmental unit are termed *operating* or *proprietary accounts*. During the course of activities of the fiscal period, budgetary accounts serve as comparison and control devices; but at the end of the period the financial position and the results of activities have to be expressed in terms of what actually occurred — data reported in the operating or proprietary accounts.

Revenues. (See transactions (2), (3), (4), and (9), pages 808, 809, and 811.) When tax levies are made, when accrued revenue is recognized, or when collections of revenue are made, an appropriate asset account is debited and the account Revenues is credited. Certain revenues of the general fund may represent contributions from other funds.

General Fund Books

Transaction	Entry			
(1) Adoption of budget for fiscal year ending June 30, 1967, indicating estimated revenues of $1,000,000 and providing for appropriations of $960,000.	*General ledger:*			
	Estimated Revenues		1,000,000	
	Appropriations			960,000
	Unappropriated Surplus			40,000
	Subsidiary revenues ledger — debits:			
	General Property Taxes	$ 620,000		
	Business Taxes	45,000		
	Sales Taxes	105,000		
	Motor Vehicle Licenses	60,000		
	Municipal Court Fines	35,000		
	Interest on Bank Deposits	5,000		
	Rents	20,000		
	Return of Taxes Collected by State	100,000		
	Charges for Private Police Service	10,000		
		$1,000,000		
	Subsidiary appropriations ledger — credits:			
	General Government	$ 48,000		
	Police Department	242,000		
	Fire Department	122,500		
	Highways	85,000		
	Sanitation and Waste Removal	90,000		
	Health and Hospitals	137,500		
	Public Welfare	130,000		
	Bond Sinking Fund	10,000		
	Government's Share of Special Assessments	20,000		
	Establishment of Working Capital Fund	25,000		
	Establishment of Utility Fund	50,000		
		$ 960,000		
(2) Accrual of income resulting from property tax levy.	*General ledger:*			
	Taxes Receivable		600,000	
	Revenues			600,000
	Subsidiary taxpayers ledger — debits:			
	Individual taxpayers accounts	$600,000		
	Subsidiary revenues ledger — credit:			
	General Property Taxes	$600,000		

Transaction	Entry			
(3) Receipt of other revenues.	*General ledger:*			
	Cash		380,000	
	Revenues			380,000
	Subsidiary revenues ledger — credits:			
	Business Taxes	$ 43,500		
	Sales Taxes	96,000		
	Motor Vehicle Licenses	65,000		
	Municipal Court Fines	32,000		
	Interest on Bank Deposits	6,500		
	Rents	20,000		
	Return of Taxes Collected by State	106,250		
	Charges for Private Police Service	10,750		
		$380,000		
(4) Collection of taxes previously accrued.	*General ledger:*			
	Cash		560,000	
	Taxes Receivable			560,000
	Subsidiary taxpayers ledger — credits:			
	Individual taxpayers accounts	$560,000		
(5) Expenditures made in accordance with appropriations (expenditures include purchases of equipment, purchases of supplies from working capital fund, required contributions to bond sinking fund, and special assessment fund, and establishment of working capital and utility funds).	*General ledger:*			
	Appropriation Expenditures		700,000	
	Vouchers Payable			555,000
	Due to Working Capital Fund			65,000
	Due to Sinking Fund			10,000
	Due to Special Assessment Fund			20,000
	Due to Utility Fund			50,000
	Subsidiary appropriations ledger — debits:			
	General Government	$ 31,500		
	Police Department	197,200		
	Fire Department	35,000		
	Highways	40,000		
	Sanitation and Waste Removal	88,000		
	Health and Hospitals	86,500		
	Public Welfare	116,800		
	Bond Sinking Fund	10,000		
	Government's Share of Special Assessments	20,000		
	Establishment of Working Capital Fund	25,000		
	Establishment of Utility Fund	50,000		
		$700,000		

Transaction	Entry			
(6) Estimates of expenditures that will result from orders placed for supplies and equipment.	*General ledger:*			
	Encumbrances		250,000	
	Reserve for Encumbrances			250,000
	Subsidiary appropriations ledger — debits:			
	General Government	$ 15,200		
	Police Department	44,250		
	Fire Department	85,250		
	Highways	42,500		
	Sanitation and Waste Removal	1,800		
	Health and Hospitals	48,500		
	Public Welfare	12,500		
		$250,000		
(7) Liquidation of encumbrances ($200,000) upon receipt of invoices and determination of actual expenditures relating to encumbrances ($195,000).	*General ledger:*			
	Reserve for Encumbrances		200,000	
	Encumbrances			200,000
	Subsidiary appropriations ledger — credits:			
	General Government	$ 12,000		
	Police Department	38,400		
	Fire Department	60,800		
	Highways	36,000		
	Sanitation and Waste Removal	1,750		
	Health and Hospitals	39,500		
	Public Welfare	11,550		
		$200,000		
	General ledger:			
	Appropriation Expenditures		195,000	
	Vouchers Payable			195,000
	Subsidiary appropriations ledger — debits:			
	General Government	$ 11,200		
	Police Department	37,500		
	Fire Department	59,750		
	Highways	36,600		
	Sanitation and Waste Removal	1,750		
	Health and Hospitals	36,900		
	Public Welfare	11,300		
		$195,000		

Transaction	Entry			
(8) Payment of vouchers and billings.	*General ledger:*			
	Vouchers Payable		665,000	
	Due to Working Capital Fund		55,000	
	Due to Sinking Fund		10,000	
	Due to Special Assessment Fund		20,000	
	Due to Utility Fund		50,000	
	Cash			800,000
(9) To close revenues and estimated revenues accounts at the end of the fiscal year.	*General ledger:*			
	Revenues		980,000	
	Unappropriated Surplus		20,000	
	Estimated Revenues			1,000,000
	To close revenues ledger balances:	*Debits*	*Credits*	
	General Property Taxes		$20,000	
	Business Taxes		1,500	
	Sales Taxes		9,000	
	Motor Vehicle Licenses	$ 5,000		
	Municipal Court Fines		3,000	
	Interest on Bank Deposits	1,500		
	Return of Taxes Collected by State	6,250		
	Charges for Private Police Service	750		
		$13,500	$33,500	
	Unappropriated surplus decrease	20,000		
		$33,500	$33,500	
(10) To close appropriations, expenditures, and encumbrances accounts at the end of the fiscal year.	*General ledger:*			
	Appropriations		960,000	
	Appropriation Expenditures			895,000
	Encumbrances			50,000
	Unappropriated Surplus			15,000
	To close appropriations ledger balances:	*Debits*	*Credits*	
	General Government	$ 2,100		
	Police Department	1,450		
	Fire Department	3,300		
	Highways	1,900		
	Sanitation and Waste Removal	200		
	Health and Hospitals	5,100		
	Public Welfare	950		
		$15,000	—	
	Unappropriated surplus increase		$15,000	
		$15,000	$15,000	

For example, cash may be received regularly from public utilities or other public enterprises to finance general fund activities; cash balances in bond funds or other funds that have terminated may likewise be transferred to the general fund and thus become a source of revenue to the latter fund. The account Revenues may be viewed as an offset to the account Estimated Revenues. The collection of revenue that has already been recognized in the accounts by a receivable is recorded by a debit to Cash and a credit to the receivable.

At the end of the period the balances in the accounts Estimated Revenues and Revenues are closed. If actual revenues are greater than estimated revenues, the closing entry consists of a debit to Revenues, a credit to Estimated Revenues, and a credit to Unappropriated Surplus; if actual revenues are less than estimated revenues, Unappropriated Surplus is debited. Unappropriated Surplus is thus corrected to reflect the actual revenue of the period rather than the original estimated amount.

A subsidiary *revenues ledger* is maintained to show revenue detail. Individual revenue accounts are debited for original revenue estimates. The sum of the debits to these accounts must agree with the total reported in the account Estimated Revenues in the general ledger. As revenues are recognized, individual accounts are credited for revenue amounts. The sum of the credits must agree with the total reported in the account Revenues in the general ledger. The account Estimated Revenues thus controls the debits and the account Revenues controls the credits in the subsidiary revenues ledger.

A debit balance for a revenue item in the subsidiary revenues ledger account at the end of the period indicates that the revenue estimate exceeded the actual revenue; a credit balance indicates that the actual revenue exceeded the revenue estimate. A debit excess of Estimated Revenues over Revenues in the general ledger accounts should be matched by a similar net debit excess in the subsidiary ledger; a credit excess in the two controlling accounts should be matched by a similar net credit excess in the subsidiary accounts. The subsidiary account balances are closed when the controlling account balances are closed and the revenue excess or deficiency is carried to Unappropriated Surplus. In the example on pages 808–811, subsidiary accounts were indicated for only major revenue sources. Ordinarily, dozens, and in some cases hundreds, of subsidiary accounts would be maintained in reporting the individual sources of revenue.

The nature of the control of the balances of the accounts Estimated Revenues and Revenues over subsidiary revenue accounts is illustrated in the chart on the opposite page.

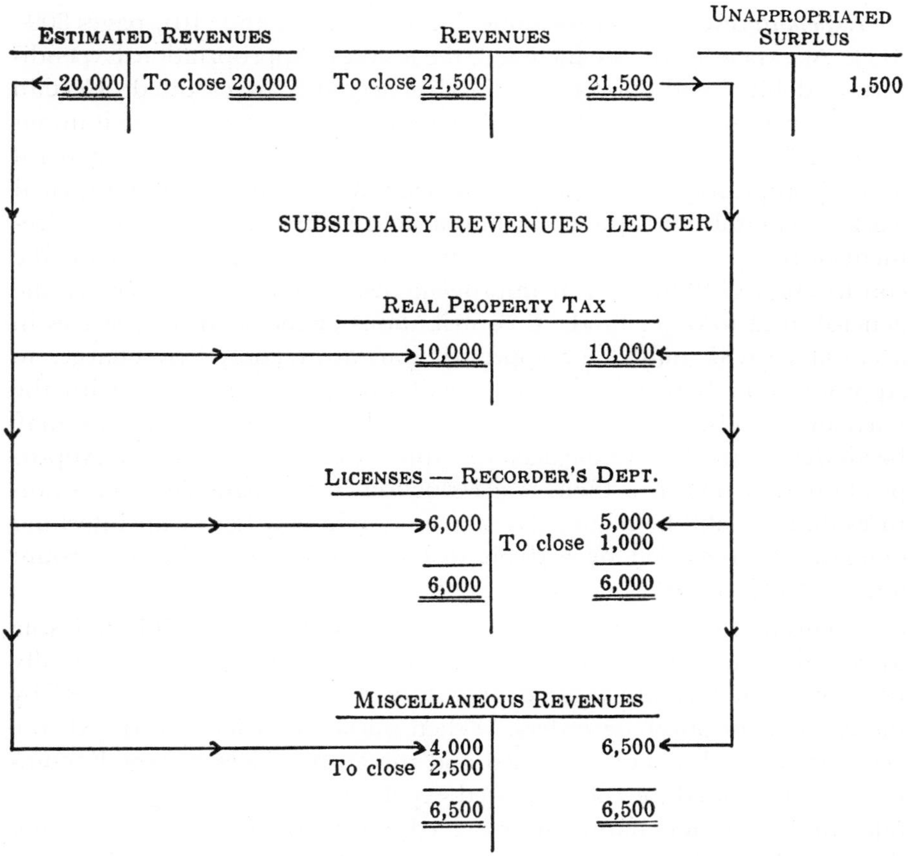

Explanation of Controlling Account — Subsidiary Relationships
Illustrated Above

Entries to record estimated revenues: In reporting estimated revenues and appropriations per budget at the beginning of the period, Estimated Revenues is charged, Appropriations is credited, and Unappropriated Surplus is credited; the charge to Estimated Revenues of $20,000 in the general ledger is accompanied by individual charges to the subsidiary revenue accounts for this total.

Entries to record actual revenues: In recording actual revenues for the period, Cash and Receivables are charged and Revenues is credited; the credit to Revenues of $21,500 in the general ledger is accompanied by individual credits to the subsidiary revenue accounts for this total.

Entries to close the revenues accounts: In closing an excess of actual revenues over estimated revenues at the end of the period, Revenues is charged, Estimated Revenues is credited, and Unappropriated Surplus is credited; the debit to Revenues of $21,500 and the credit to Estimated Revenues of $20,000 are accompanied by individual debits and credits to the subsidiary revenue accounts canceling a net credit excess in this group of accounts of $1,500.

Expenditures. (See transactions (5), (6), (7), (8), and (10), pages 809–811). As expenditures are incurred, the account Appropriation Expenditures is debited and appropriate liability accounts are credited. Certain expenditures that are made by the general fund represent contributions to other funds to finance their special activities. For example, general fund appropriations may include sums for the establishment of a special working capital fund, the contribution to a sinking fund for the retirement of bonds, or the contribution to a special assessment fund for the construction of certain local improvements. Amounts payable by the general fund to other funds as contributions or for goods or services in accordance with budgetary appropriations are recorded by charges to Appropriation Expenditures and credits to liability accounts with the particular funds. The appropriation expenditures account balance may be viewed as an offset to the account Appropriations; a charge to Appropriation Expenditures, then, is a reduction in the balance of expenditures that can still be made. The payment of a voucher or an interfund obligation is recorded by a debit to the appropriate liability account and a credit to Cash.

To insure that appropriations will not be overexpended, it is desirable to recognize in the accounts not only expenditures that have actually been incurred but also those expenditures that have been proposed by the issuance of purchase orders. When purchase orders are issued, the account Encumbrances is debited and the account Reserve for Encumbrances is credited for the estimated expenditures. When the orders are filled and the exact charges are received, the entries originally recording the commitments are reversed and the expenditures are recorded at their actual amounts. Although appropriations may be encumbered for such items as orders for supplies and contracts for services, encumbrances are not recognized for regularly recurring expenditures such as payrolls; charges for regularly recurring expenditures, then, are recognized only at the time expenditures are made. When encumbrances are recorded, the balances of the account Encumbrances and the account Appropriation Expenditures are both properly viewed as offsets to the account Appropriations.

Frequently there is authority for subdividing total appropriations into monthly or quarterly *allotments*. Allotments limit expenditures within the month or the quarter to fractional parts of the entire appropriation. Unexpended allotment balances are carried forward within the fiscal year to the next allotment period. Allotment schedules contribute to a continuing control over expenditures and help avoid the need for special appropriations to meet shortages in the later stages of the budget period.

Appropriations expire upon the close of the budget period. At the end of the period, the accounts Encumbrances, Appropriation Expenditures, and Appropriations are closed. When the sum of the actual and the proposed expenditures is less than the budgeted appropriations, the closing entry consists of a debit to Appropriations, credits to Encumbrances and to Appropriation Expenditures, and a credit to Unappropriated Surplus. Unappropriated Surplus then reports the effects of the actual charges and encumbrances of the fiscal period rather than the original appropriation amount. Closing the accounts as described leaves the Reserve for Encumbrances with a credit balance that is carried into the succeeding period. The reserve is viewed as a part of the fund balance rather than as a liability: the encumbrance procedure is no more than an earmarking of appropriations; a fund cannot be charged for goods and services before these are actually received.

A subsidiary *appropriations ledger* is maintained to offer information and control over expenditures. Accounts in this ledger normally provide full detail concerning original appropriations, allotments, expenditures, and encumbrances. Individual appropriation accounts are credited for original appropriations. The sum of the credits to these accounts must agree with the total reported in the account Appropriations in the general ledger.

Upon incurring expenditures, individual appropriation accounts are debited, thus reducing the credit balances that report amounts available for expenditure. Encumbrances are also recognized by debits reducing individual appropriation account balances. When the orders are received and the exact charges are known, the encumbrances are canceled and the actual expenditures are recorded, the credit balances in the appropriation accounts being corrected to show the actual unexpended and unencumbered balances at that point.

The sum of the debits to the individual appropriation accounts for expenditures must agree with the total reported in the appropriation expenditures account in the general ledger, and the sum of the debits for encumbrances must agree with the total reported in the encumbrances account in the general ledger. The account Appropriations thus controls the credits in the subsidiary ledger and the two accounts Appropriation Expenditures and Encumbrances summarize and control the debits made to the subsidiary accounts.

A debit balance will not appear in a subsidiary appropriation account at the end of the fiscal period when actual expenditures and encumbrances for an expenditure item have been limited to the amount of the appropriation. A credit balance in a subsidiary appropriation account at the end of the period indicates that the appropriation exceeded actual

Encumbrances	
36,000	34,000
	To close 2,000

Appropriation Expenditures	
62,600	To close 62,600

Appropriations	
To close 66,000	66,000

Unappropriated Surplus	
	1,400

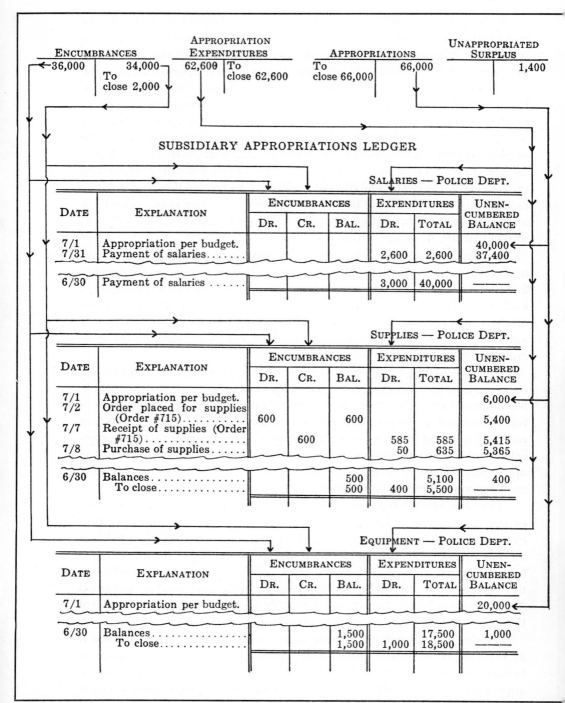

SUBSIDIARY APPROPRIATIONS LEDGER

Salaries — Police Dept.

Date	Explanation	Encumbrances Dr.	Encumbrances Cr.	Encumbrances Bal.	Expenditures Dr.	Expenditures Total	Unencumbered Balance
7/1	Appropriation per budget.						40,000
7/31	Payment of salaries.......				2,600	2,600	37,400
6/30	Payment of salaries				3,000	40,000	——

Supplies — Police Dept.

Date	Explanation	Encumbrances Dr.	Encumbrances Cr.	Encumbrances Bal.	Expenditures Dr.	Expenditures Total	Unencumbered Balance
7/1	Appropriation per budget.						6,000
7/2	Order placed for supplies (Order #715)...........	600		600			5,400
7/7	Receipt of supplies (Order #715)................		600		585	585	5,415
7/8	Purchase of supplies......				50	635	5,365
6/30	Balances................			500		5,100	400
	To close..............			500	400	5,500	——

Equipment — Police Dept.

Date	Explanation	Encumbrances Dr.	Encumbrances Cr.	Encumbrances Bal.	Expenditures Dr.	Expenditures Total	Unencumbered Balance
7/1	Appropriation per budget.						20,000
6/30	Balances................			1,500		17,500	1,000
	To close..............			1,500	1,000	18,500	——

Explanation of Controlling Account — Subsidiary Relationships Illustrated on Opposite Page

Entries to record budgeted appropriations: In reporting estimated revenues and appropriations per budget at the beginning of the period, Estimated Revenues is charged, Appropriations is credited, and Unappropriated Surplus is credited; the credit to Appropriations of $66,000 in the general ledger is accompanied by individual credits to the subsidiary appropriation accounts for this total.

Entries to record encumbrances: In recording encumbrances, Encumbrances is charged and Reserve for Encumbrances is credited; the charge to Encumbrances of $36,000 in the general ledger is accompanied by individual charges to the subsidiary appropriation accounts for this total.

Entries to record expenditures and the liquidation of encumbrances: In recording expenditures, Appropriation Expenditures is charged and Vouchers Payable is credited. When encumbrances are liquidated, an entry is made charging Reserve for Encumbrances and crediting Encumbrances. The charge to Appropriation Expenditures of $62,600 in the general ledger is accompanied by individual charges to the subsidiary accounts for this total. For encumbrances that are liquidated with the recognition of expenditures, a credit to Encumbrances of $34,000 in the general ledger is accompanied by individual credits to the subsidiary appropriation accounts for this total, unencumbered balances in the subsidiary accounts being adjusted for the differences between the credits for encumbrances that are canceled and the charges for expenditures that are now recognized.

Entries to close the expenditures accounts: In closing an excess of appropriations over encumbrances and expenditures at the end of the period, Appropriations is debited, Encumbrances and Appropriation Expenditures are credited, and Unappropriated Surplus is credited; the debit to Appropriations of $66,000 and credits to Encumbrances of $2,000 and Appropriation Expenditures of $62,600 are accompanied by debits of $1,400 to the subsidiary appropriation accounts canceling the unencumbered balances (credits) in this group of accounts.

expenditures and encumbrances for the expenditure item. A credit excess of Appropriations over Appropriation Expenditures and Encumbrances should be matched by a similar credit total in the subsidiary accounts. The subsidiary accounts are closed when the controlling account balances are closed and the net change in unappropriated surplus is recorded.

In the example on pages 808–811, subsidiary accounts were indicated only for expenditures summarized in terms of function. In practice, a separate account would be required for each appropriation as set by the budget; normally the budget would provide appropriations for the various governmental functions analyzed in terms of organization unit and object.

The nature of the control of the balances of the accounts Appropriations, Encumbrances, and Appropriation Expenditures over subsidiary appropriations accounts is illustrated in the chart on pages 816 and 817.

General fund statements. A general fund is established upon the organization of a governmental unit and continues for the life of that unit. Accounts are closed periodically, with assets, liabilities, and fund balances being carried into the subsequent period. Entries to record the budget and the transactions of the new period are then applied to the balances carried over. To simplify the illustration for the City of A, no opening balances were given. A general fund trial balance prepared on June 30, 1967, after the accounts are closed would appear as follows:

City of A
General Fund
Trial Balance
June 30, 1967

Cash	140,000	
Taxes Receivable	40,000	
Vouchers Payable		85,000
Due to Working Capital Fund		10,000
Reserve for Encumbrances		50,000
Unappropriated Surplus		35,000
	180,000	180,000

Statements are developed from this trial balance together with data supplied by the general ledger and the subsidiary account detail. At least four statements should be prepared: (1) a balance sheet, (2) a statement analyzing the changes in unappropriated surplus, (3) a statement comparing actual revenues with estimated revenues, and (4) a statement comparing expenditures and encumbrances with authorizations. Cash reports and various other analytical and comparative summaries may be developed to accompany the basic exhibits mentioned.

Balance sheet. The balance sheet that is prepared at the close of the fiscal period reports the assets, the liabilities, and the fund balances represented by the reserve for encumbrances and the unappropriated surplus balance. A general fund balance sheet for the City of A as of June 30, 1967, would reflect the closing entries for revenue and appropriation items previously given and would appear as shown below.

City of A
General Fund
Balance Sheet
June 30, 1967

Assets		Liabilities, Reserves, and Surplus	
Cash	$140,000	Vouchers payable	$ 85,000
Taxes receivable	40,000	Due to working capital fund	10,000
		Reserve for encumbrances	50,000
		Unappropriated surplus	35,000
Total assets	$180,000	Total liabilities, reserves, and surplus	$180,000

Other assets that might appear on the general fund balance sheet include petty cash funds, cash with fiscal agents for payment of bonded indebtedness, temporary investments, accrued interest on investments, delinquent taxes, interest and penalties receivable on taxes, tax liens receivable, amounts due from other funds, and supply inventories; other liabilities that might appear are items such as matured bonds and matured bond interest payable, contracts payable, amounts due to other funds, taxes collected in advance, notes payable, and accrued interest payable.

Although the balance sheet prepared at the end of a fiscal period reports the financial status of the city as it enters into a new fiscal period, balance sheets prepared at different intervals during the course of the period should reflect budgetary as well as operating or proprietary balances. A balance sheet for the City of A, prepared as of December 31, 1966, for example, should reflect those revenues estimated to be collectible for the remainder of the period as well as the appropriations that apply to the remainder of the period. Balance sheet data would be obtained from a trial balance prepared as of this date. To illustrate, assume that a trial balance for the City of A on December 31, 1966, shows the following information:

City of A
General Fund
Trial Balance
December 31, 1966

Cash	156,000	
Taxes Receivable	260,000	
Estimated Revenues	1,000,000	
Revenues		760,000
Vouchers Payable		110,000
Due to Working Capital Fund		12,000
Due to Special Assessment Fund		20,000
Reserve for Encumbrances		62,500
Appropriations		960,000
Appropriation Expenditures	486,000	
Encumbrances	62,500	
Unappropriated Surplus		40,000
	1,964,500	1,964,500

A balance sheet prepared on this date would be as follows:

City of A
General Fund
Balance Sheet
December 31, 1966 (Interim Report)

Assets and Estimated Revenues		
Cash		$156,000
Taxes receivable		260,000
Estimated revenues	$1,000,000	
Less revenues collected to date	760,000	240,000
Total assets and estimated revenues		$656,000

Liabilities, Reserves, Appropriations, and Surplus			
Vouchers payable			$110,000
Due to working capital fund			12,000
Due to special assessment fund			20,000
Reserve for encumbrances			62,500
Appropriations		$960,000	
Less: Expenditures to date	$486,000		
Encumbrances on Dec. 31, 1966	62,500	548,500	411,500
Unappropriated surplus			40,000
Total liabilities, reserves, appropriations, and surplus			$656,000

Analysis of changes in unappropriated surplus. The unappropriated surplus of the general fund indicates the resources that can be employed in financing future general fund appropriations. Changes in general fund unappropriated surplus arise during the fiscal period as a result of the difference between governmental revenues and the charges against such revenues. An unappropriated surplus statement is prepared to show changes in surplus for the past period. Ordinarily, the statement is prepared in a manner that discloses both budgetary estimates as to changes in surplus for the year and actual revenues, expenditures, encumbrances, and other charges and credits that affect surplus. The analysis of changes in unappropriated surplus for the City of A for the year ended June 30, 1967, may be prepared as follows:

City of A
General Fund
Analysis of Changes in Unappropriated Surplus
For Year Ended June 30, 1967

	Estimated	Actual	Excess or (Deficiency) of Actual Compared with Estimated
Unappropriated surplus, July 1, 1966[1]	—	—	
Add: Reserve for encumbrances, July 1, 1966[1]	—	—	
Revenues, 1966–1967	$1,000,000	$980,000	($20,000)
	$1,000,000	$980,000	($20,000)
Deduct: Expenditures chargeable to reserve for encumbrances, July 1, 1966[1]	—	—	
Expenditures, 1966–1967	$ 960,000	$895,000	($65,000)
Reserve for encumbrances, June 30, 1967		50,000	50,000
	$ 960,000	$945,000	($15,000)
Unappropriated surplus, June 30, 1967	$ 40,000	$ 35,000	($ 5,000)

[1]When there are beginning balances for unappropriated surplus and for the reserve for encumbrances, these balances would be shown in both estimated and actual columns.

It is possible to prepare the unappropriated surplus statement in a form that simply reports the net change in surplus arising from the difference between total revenues and total expenditures and encumbrances. Prepared in such condensed form, the statement would appear as shown at the top of the next page.

Statement of revenue — estimated and actual. Statements summarizing operations of the governmental unit are prepared at the end of the period to accompany statements reporting financial position. A revenue statement summarizes actual revenues for the period and compares these with original estimates in the budget. The statement thus shows the

City of A
General Fund
Analysis of Changes in Unappropriated Surplus
For Year Ended June 30, 1967

Unappropriated surplus, July 1, 1966		—
Add: Excess of revenues over expenditures and encumbrances for year ended June 30, 1967:		
Revenues	$980,000	
Expenditures and encumbrances	945,000	$35,000
Unappropriated surplus, June 30, 1967		$35,000

extent to which individual revenues met original expectations and offers a basis for developing revenue estimates for future budgets. The statement is prepared from the detail in the subsidiary revenue ledger. A revenue statement for the City of A is illustrated below. It will be observed that totals on this statement support the revenues summary as listed on the analysis of changes in unappropriated surplus on the preceding page.

City of A
General Fund
Statement of Revenue — Estimated and Actual
For Year Ended June 30, 1967

Revenue by Source	Estimated Revenue	Actual Revenue	Excess or (Deficiency) of Actual Compared with Estimated
General property taxes	$ 620,000	$600,000	($20,000)
Business taxes	45,000	43,500	(1,500)
Sales taxes	105,000	96,000	(9,000)
Motor vehicle licenses	60,000	65,000	5,000
Municipal court fines	35,000	32,000	(3,000)
Interest on bank deposits	5,000	6,500	1,500
Rents	20,000	20,000	—
Return of taxes collected by state	100,000	106,250	6,250
Charges for private police service	10,000	10,750	750
Totals	$1,000,000	$980,000	($20,000)

Statement of expenditures and encumbrances — compared with authorizations. An expenditures and encumbrances statement summarizes actual expenditures and encumbrances for the period and compares these with the expenditure authorizations for the period. The statement thus indi-

City of A
General Fund
Statement of Expenditures and Encumbrances
Compared with Authorizations
For Year Ended June 30, 1967

Expenditures by Functions, Activity, and Object	Authorizations			Expenditures	Unexpended Balance	Encumbrances Outstanding at End of Year	Unencumbered Balance
	Appropriations	Encumbrances Outstanding at Beginning of Year	Total				
General government:							
Legislative:							
Personal services	$ 15,000	—	$ 15,000	$ 15,000	—		
Other current expenses	5,000	—	5,000	4,000	$ 1,000	$ 750	$ 250
Equipment	3,000	—	3,000	—	3,000	2,800	200
	$ 23,000		$ 23,000	$ 19,000	$ 4,000	$ 3,550	$ 450
Executive:							
Personal services	$ 10,000	—	$ 10,000	$ 10,000	—	—	—
Other current services	2,000	—	2,000	1,000	$ 1,000	$ 600	$ 400
Totals	$960,000	—	$960,000	$895,000	$65,000	$50,000	$15,000

cates the extent to which departments have remained within the limits set by the budget and offers a basis for future appropriation planning. The statement is prepared from the detail reported in the subsidiary appropriations ledger. Part of an expenditures and encumbrances statement for the City of A is illustrated on the preceding page. It should be noted that totals on this statement support the expenditures summary as listed on the analysis of changes in unappropriated surplus on page 821.

SPECIAL CONSIDERATIONS RELATING TO REVENUES

Mention needs to be made of certain revenue matters that are not illustrated in the example for general fund accounting given in the preceding pages of this chapter.

Tax revenues. When losses are expected to emerge in the course of realization of a tax levy, it is appropriate to establish an allowance for bad debts upon recognizing the asset and the related revenue. For example, in the previous illustration for the City of A, the tax levy of $600,000 was recorded by a debit to Taxes Receivable and a credit to Revenues for this amount. Assuming that only $590,000 is estimated to be recoverable, the following entry would be made:

General ledger:			
Taxes Receivable		600,000	
Allowance for Uncollectible Taxes			10,000
Revenues			590,000
Subsidiary taxpayers ledger — debit:			
Individual taxpayers accounts	$600,000		
Subsidiary revenues ledger — credit:			
General Property Taxes	$590,000		

On the balance sheet prepared at the end of the period, the allowance account is subtracted from the asset balance.

When the due date for payment has passed and taxes are delinquent, both receivable and allowance balances should be transferred to accounts that indicate the delinquent nature of the taxes. Collection of delinquent taxes together with interest and penalties is recorded as a recovery of the delinquent taxes balance and as additional revenue. When interest and penalties have accrued on delinquent taxes at the end of a period, an asset would be established for the accrual and an allowance would be recognized for the estimated loss related to such accrual. The entries that follow record (1) tax delinquencies, (2) recoveries on delinquent balances, and (3) the accrual of interest and penalties on delinquent balances at the end of a period:

(1) *General ledger:*

Taxes Receivable — Delinquent		40,000	
Allowance for Uncollectible Taxes		10,000	
Taxes Receivable			40,000
Allowance for Taxes Receivable — Delinquent			10,000
Subsidiary taxpayers ledger:			
No entries.			

(2) *General ledger:*

Cash		11,000	
Taxes Receivable — Delinquent			10,000
Revenues			1,000
Subsidiary taxpayers ledger — credits:			
Individual taxpayers accounts	$10,000		
Subsidiary revenues ledger — credit:			
Interest and Penalties	$ 1,000		

(3) *General ledger:*

Interest and Penalties Receivable		1,200	
Allowance for Uncollectible Interest and Penalties Receivable			350
Revenues			850
Subsidiary taxpayers ledger — debits:			
Individual taxpayers accounts	$ 1,200		
Subsidiary revenues ledger — credit:			
Interest and Penalties	$ 850		

When delinquent taxes are converted into tax liens, receivable balances for taxes, interest, and penalties should be transferred to a tax lien receivable account and allowances balances related to the original asset accounts should be transferred to a tax lien allowance account. Any costs involved in establishing the tax liens are added to the tax lien balance. Collection of tax liens is recorded by debits to Cash and credits to Tax Liens Receivable; in the event of failure to collect a tax lien and upon appropriate authorization, the tax lien is offset against the allowance. Entries to record (1) the conversion of delinquent taxes into tax liens, (2) collections of tax liens, and (3) the write-off of uncollectible tax liens follow:

(1) *General ledger:*

Tax Liens Receivable		31,200	
Allowance for Uncollectible Taxes — Delinquent		10,000	
Allowance for Uncollectible Interest and Penalties Receivable		350	
Taxes Receivable — Delinquent			30,000
Interest and Penalties Receivable			1,200
Allowance for Uncollectible Tax Liens			10,350
Subsidiary tax liens ledger — debits:			
Individual taxpayers accounts	$31,200		
Subsidiary taxpayers ledger — credits:			
Individual taxpayers accounts	$31,200		

(2) *General ledger:*			
Cash		12,000	
Tax Liens Receivable			12,000
Subsidiary tax liens ledger — credits:			
Individual taxpayers accounts	$12,000		
(3) *General ledger:*			
Allowance for Uncollectible Tax Liens		5,000	
Tax Liens Receivable			5,000
Subsidiary tax liens ledger — credits:			
Individual taxpayers accounts	$ 5,000		

Revenues received in advance. In certain instances taxes may be collected in advance of the period in which they accrue or are due. In such cases a liability balance is recognized in the accounts. When the tax assessment is made, Taxes Receivable is charged and Revenues is credited for the amount of the assessment; at this time the advance may be applied against the receivable balance. The entries that are made upon (1) tax collection and (2) application of such collections to the receivables are as follows:

(1) *General ledger:*			
Cash		12,000	
Taxes Collected in Advance			12,000
Subsidiary taxpayers ledger (for succeeding period) — credits:			
Individual taxpayers accounts	$12,000		
(2) *General ledger:*			
Taxes Collected in Advance		12,000	
Taxes Receivable			12,000
Subsidiary taxpayers ledger:			
No entries — credits to receivable balances for amounts paid were recognized by previous entry.			

Revenues from issue of bonds. When cash from the issue of bonds is made available to the general fund, it is recognized in the accounts of the general fund as revenue. The bond liability balance is not reported in the general fund because bonds make no current claim on general fund resources; the liability balance, however, is reported in the general bonded debt and interest group of accounts to be described later. The receipt by the general fund of proceeds from a bond issue is recorded by the following entry:

General ledger:			
Cash		100,000	
Revenues			100,000
Subsidiary revenues ledger — credit:			
Proceeds from Issue of Bonds	$100,000		

Revenues from sale or salvage of fixed assets. When cash from the sale or salvage of fixed assets becomes available to the general fund, it is recognized in the general fund accounts as revenue. The decrease in the property item is not reported in the general fund but is reported in the separate general fixed assets group of accounts in which the asset was originally recorded. This procedure is described later. The receipt of cash from property sales or salvage is recorded as follows:

General ledger:		
Cash.	2,500	
Revenues.		2,500
Subsidiary revenues ledger — credit:		
Proceeds from Sale of Obsolete Equipment. $2,500		

SPECIAL CONSIDERATIONS RELATING TO EXPENDITURES

Mention needs to be made of certain expenditure matters that were not developed in the original illustration.

Expenditures in liquidation of encumbrances of prior period. In the illustration for the City of A, the credit to Reserve for Encumbrances was accompanied by a charge to Encumbrances. The encumbrance balance was treated as a charge against current revenues, the same as the expenditures balance. The reserve balance at the end of the period was regarded as a fund balance awaiting charges to emerge from the liquidation of encumbrances. In the new fiscal period, expenditures emerging from previous authority and commitments should be distinguished from those that are made under current appropriations: the liquidation of prior period encumbrances that are not related to current appropriations should be charged against the reserve; expenditures and encumbrances of the current period should be separately reported as charges related to current appropriations. To accomplish this, the reserve for encumbrances carried over from a prior period should be identified with the prior period and thus distinguished from the reserve relating to encumbrances of the current period.[1] As expenditures are made relating to prior year commitments, an expenditures account indicating a relationship to the prior period reserve should be debited. Ordinarily encumbrances can be fully liquidated within the succeeding period. At the end of this period, then, the expenditures balance is closed against the related reserve balance and any reserve excess or deficiency is carried to unappropriated surplus.

For example, assume in the previous illustration for the City of A that in the fiscal year ended June 30, 1968, expenditures of $48,500 are

[1]In practice, the reserve for encumbrances account would be dated to show the year to which it was related.

made in full liquidation of encumbrances of $50,000 existing at the end of the prior year. The entries to record the liquidation of the encumbrances during the period and the cancellation of related expenditures and reserve balances on June 30, 1968, follow:

General ledger:		
Expenditures Chargeable against Reserve for Encumbrances — Prior Year	48,500	
Vouchers Payable		48,500
General ledger:		
Reserve for Encumbrances — Prior Year	50,000	
Expenditures Chargeable against Reserve for Encumbrances — Prior Year		48,500
Unappropriated Surplus		1,500

The unappropriated surplus statement prepared for the year ended June 30, 1968, will show a surplus increase of $1,500 arising from the liquidation of prior year encumbrances.

Some governmental units offset the encumbrances and reserve for encumbrances balances at the end of the period and recognize outstanding encumbrances in making appropriations for the new period. Under such circumstances, the balance sheet prepared at the end of the period shows no reserve balance. Following the entry recognizing appropriations for the new period, an entry is made charging Encumbrances and crediting Reserve for Encumbrances for unliquidated balances of the preceding period. Liquidation of the encumbrances is then charged against appropriations of the new period instead of against a reserve balance carried over from a preceding period. Laws of the governmental unit should indicate the encumbrance procedure that is to be followed.

Purchases of fixed assets. Purchases of properties such as equipment, buildings, and land from resources of the general fund require authorization in the form of appropriations just as any current expense item. Acquisitions of assets are made in accordance with budgetary provisions and are recorded as expenditures in the usual manner. The property item does not appear as an asset of the general fund since it does not represent a resource that is to be employed in meeting claims against this fund; the property item, however, is reported in the general fixed assets group of accounts to be described later. The purchase of a property item by the general fund is recorded by the following entry:

General ledger:			
Appropriation Expenditures		40,000	
Vouchers Payable			40,000
Subsidiary appropriations ledger — debit:			
Acquisition of Land	$40,000		

Retirement of bonded debt. When payment of bonded debt is to be made by the general fund, such payment is viewed the same as any other expenditure that is to be made from the resources of this fund. Payment of debt by the general fund, then, can be made only if there is budgetary authorization for such payment; payment is recorded in the same manner as payments for current salaries and supplies or for materials and equipment. Recognition of the amount payable in accordance with the appropriation is made by an entry as follows:

General ledger:

Appropriation Expenditures	65,000	
Matured Bonds Payable (or Vouchers Payable)		65,000

Subsidiary appropriations ledger — debit:

Retirement of Bonds	$65,000

Payment of matured obligations is recorded as follows:

Matured Bonds Payable (or Vouchers Payable)	65,000	
Cash		65,000

Interest payments that are to be made currently on bonds outstanding as well as on maturing issues are similarly recorded in the accounts. Decreases in a governmental unit's total general bonded debt and interest are not shown in the general fund but are summarized in the separate general bonded debt and interest group of accounts to be described later.

Prepayments and inventories. In certain instances it may be the policy of the governmental unit to report on the balance sheet prepayments and supplies inventories. Since such assets are not in a form to become available in meeting subsequent appropriation demands, the fund should show a reserve balance equal to the sum of the asset balances. When materials and supplies inventories are to be reported on the balance sheet, the following entry may be made in the ledger at the end of the period:

Materials and Supplies Inventories	8,500	
Reserve for Materials and Supplies Inventories		8,500

No change needs to be made in these balances during the course of the fiscal period. Assuming that inventories at the end of the next period are valued at $8,200, an entry to recognize the change in the inventories balance is made as follows:

Reserve for Materials and Supplies Inventories	300	
Materials and Supplies Inventories		300

QUESTIONS

1. What are the essential differences between accounting for the private unit and accounting for the public unit?

2. What information should be provided by accounts and statements of a governmental unit?

3. (a) Define the term *fund* as employed in governmental accounting. (b) How is a fund established?

4. How may the major governmental revenues be classified?

5. Give five bases for classification of governmental expenditures. Show by example the expenditures that would be listed under each classification given.

6. Describe the nature and the purpose of the governmental budget.

7. Describe the purpose of the general fund.

8. Distinguish between *budgetary* accounts and *proprietary* accounts.

9. What entries would be made in the general and subsidiary ledgers in recording the general fund budget?

10. Explain how each of the following differ: (a) appropriation, (b) allotment, (c) encumbrance, and (d) appropriation expenditure.

11. What accounts in the general ledger control the detail reported in the revenues ledger and the appropriations ledger?

12. (a) What is the significance of the debit and credit entries in the subsidiary revenues ledger?

(b) What is the significance in the revenues ledger of an account with (1) a debit balance and (2) a credit balance?

(c) What is the significance of the debit and credit entries in the subsidiary appropriations ledger?

(d) What is the significance in the appropriations ledger of an account with a credit balance?

13. The City of Bell, after adoption of an appropriation ordinance, makes a number of supplementary appropriations during the course of the fiscal period. How should such supplementary appropriations be recorded in the general and subsidiary ledgers?

14. Give the entries that would be made in the general ledger and the subsidiary ledgers of the general fund for each of the following transactions:

(a) A budget is adopted providing for an excess of appropriations over estimated current revenues.

(b) General property taxes accrue; the accrual is recognized together with a provision for estimated losses on such taxes.

(c) Other revenues are collected.

(d) Orders are placed for materials, and encumbrances are recognized in the accounts for such orders.

(e) Certain items ordered in (d) are received and expenditures are recognized in the accounts.
(f) Payrolls are approved for payment.
(g) Checks are written in payment of vouchers.
(h) Collections are made on general property taxes.
(i) General property taxes not collected are recognized as delinquent in the accounts.
(j) Charges are made by a special fund for services rendered to the general fund and are recognized in the accounts.
(k) At the end of the period:
  (1) Accrued interest and penalties on delinquent taxes are recognized, together with a provision for possible losses on this item.
  (2) Stores on hand in the various departments are reported in the accounts.
(l) Estimated revenues exceed revenue balances for the period; revenue accounts are closed.
(m) Appropriations exceed expenditures and encumbrances for the period; accounts are closed.

15. Explain how you would treat the following matters in the accounts of a general fund:
(a) Taxes are assessed and it is estimated that 2% of the assessments will prove uncollectible.
(b) Uncollected taxes at the end of the year are delinquent; accrued interest and penalties are recognized on such delinquencies.
(c) Certain receivables are found uncollectible and the city council authorizes that they be written off against an allowance that was recognized on such uncollectibles.
(d) Sums are collected representing taxes not yet accrued or recorded on the books.

16. The town of Wescott wishes to show prepayments and materials and supplies on hand on the general fund balance sheet at the end of each period. What accounting procedures would you recommend be employed to achieve this purpose?

17. What statements are prepared to summarize general fund operations for the year? What information is offered by each of these?

18. How will the balance sheet for the general fund prepared during the fiscal year differ from that prepared at the end of the fiscal year?

19. Describe the form that may be employed for (a) the analysis of changes in unappropriated surplus, (b) the statement of revenues — estimated and actual, and (c) the statement of expenditures and encumbrances — compared with authorizations.

20. What arguments can you give for excluding fixed assets in the preparation of the general fund balance sheet?

21. What arguments can you give for excluding charges for depreciation in the preparation of the general fund operating reports?

EXERCISES

1. Give the entries that would be made to record the following general fund transactions for the City of Balfour:

(a) Revenues for 1966–67 are estimated at $150,000; appropriations, at $145,000.
(b) A general tax levy is set at $120,000; the tax accrual is recognized in the accounts, together with an allowance for uncollectible taxes estimated at $2,500.
(c) Orders estimated to cost $70,000 are placed for materials and supplies, and encumbrances are recorded.
(d) Certain materials and supplies ordered in (c) are received; invoices total $56,000 for items originally estimated to cost $57,500.
(e) Tax anticipation warrants of $25,000 are sold to obtain cash in advance of tax collections.
(f) Payrolls of $50,000 are approved for payment.
(g) Property taxes totaling $105,000 levied in (b) are collected; remaining taxes are recognized in the accounts as delinquent.
(h) Licenses, fines, fees, etc., totaling $40,000 are collected.
(i) Tax anticipation warrants are paid together with interest of $500.
(j) Payments totaling $90,000 are made on vouchers for materials, supplies, and payrolls relating to (d) and (f).
(k) An obligation of $6,000 to a city public service enterprise for services rendered during the year is recognized in the accounts.
(l) Vacant land is purchased for future construction at a cost of $15,000; cash payment is made on the purchase.
(m) Accounts are closed at the end of the year.

2. A trial balance for the general fund of the City of Grandview prepared on June 30, 1967, the end of a fiscal year, follows:

	Dr.	Cr.
Cash	$ 200,000	
Taxes Receivable, Delinquent	35,000	
Allowance for Estimated Loss on Taxes, Delinquent		$ 5,000
Estimated Revenues	1,200,000	
Vouchers Payable		45,000
Due to Other Funds		15,000
Taxes Collected in Advance		3,500
Reserve for Encumbrances, 1965–66		35,000
Reserve for Encumbrances, 1966–67		40,000
Appropriations		1,300,000
Unappropriated Surplus		138,000
Revenues		1,175,000
Encumbrances	40,000	
Appropriation Expenditures	1,250,000	
Expenditures Chargeable to Reserve for Encumbrances, 1965–66	31,500	
	$2,756,500	$2,756,500

All of the encumbrances relating to 1965–66 were liquidated during the year. Give the necessary adjusting and closing entries.

3. Give the entries required in the general fund to record the following transactions, assuming that required payments are made by the general fund and receipts become available to this fund:

(a) Desks were ordered for operating departments at an estimated cost of $15,000, the purchase to be financed out of the general fund.
(b) The desks were received. The actual cost was $15,400 and this was paid.
(c) Equipment costing $10,000 and carried in the general fixed asset group was sold for $650.
(d) A fire truck costing $5,000 was traded in for another truck. The price of the new truck was $6,200, but $1,000 was allowed on the old truck.
(e) A library building that had been financed through the issuance of bonds was torn down. The original cost of the building was $75,000 and the cost of dismantling the building was $2,500. Cash of $1,500 was realized from the salvage.

4. Give the entries affecting the general ledger as well as subsidiary accounts of the general fund for the following transactions:

(a) The appropriation for salaries in the public welfare department is increased by $400, a reserve for contingencies having been provided by the budget for salary changes of this nature.
(b) The appropriation for contractual services in the public welfare department is reduced by $500 and the appropriation for personal services is increased by this amount when it is decided that a project is to be completed by departmental employees.
(c) A supplementary appropriation for a permanent advance of $30,000 to a stores working capital fund is made after the budget has already been recorded in the accounts.
(d) A supplementary appropriation of $1,500 is made for salary of a collection clerk as a result of a new policy adopted whereby charges are to be made for certain services rendered by the public welfare department; it is estimated that revenues from this source will total $4,000.

5. A trial balance prepared for the City of Knox appears as follows:

Cash	$ 180,000	
Receivables (net)	215,000	
Payables		$ 160,000
Reserve for Encumbrances — Prior Year		45,000
Reserve for Encumbrances — Current Year		60,000
Unappropriated Surplus		187,500
Estimated Revenues	1,000,000	
Revenues		860,000
Appropriations		980,000
Appropriation Expenditures — Current Year	800,000	
Appropriation Expenditures — Prior Year	37,500	
Encumbrances — Current Year	60,000	
	$2,292,500	$2,292,500

(a) Prepare a balance sheet from the foregoing summary, assuming that the balances reflect transactions as of May 31, one month prior to the end of the city's fiscal period, and that budgetary accounts are to be reflected on the statement.

(b) Prepare a balance sheet from the foregoing summary, assuming that the balances reflect transactions as of June 30, the end of the city's fiscal period, and that budgetary accounts are not to be reflected on the statement.

6. From the account balances given below that were taken from the ledger of the general fund for the City of W at the end of the fiscal year ending June 30, 1967, prepare a statement summarizing fully the changes in unappropriated surplus for the year:

Balance of unappropriated surplus, June 30, 1966, $315,000.

Revenues, July 1, 1966–June 30, 1967: estimated, $750,000; actual, $734,000.

Expenditures, July 1, 1966–June 30, 1967: appropriations, $820,000; expenditures, $755,000; reserve for encumbrances, June 30, 1967, $35,000.

Reserve for encumbrances, July 1, 1966, $36,000; expenditures, July 1, 1966–June 30, 1967, in full liquidation of encumbrances as of July 1, 1966, $34,500.

Credit to unappropriated surplus, July 1, 1966–June 30, 1967: proceeds from sale of city properties no longer being used, $180,000.

PROBLEMS

23-1. A trial balance for Welcome City on July 1, 1966, was as follows:

Cash	$117,500	
Taxes receivable — delinquent	15,000	
Allowance for delinquent taxes		$ 10,000
Vouchers payable		70,000
Reserve for encumbrances		15,000
Unappropriated surplus		37,500
	$132,500	$132,500

During the fiscal year ended June 30, 1967, the following transactions took place:

(a) A budget was adopted reporting estimated revenues of $340,000 and authorizing expenditures of $350,000.

(b) Taxes were levied totaling $250,000, of which $15,000 was estimated uncollectible.

(c) Taxes were collected as follows:
Prior year $12,500 (remaining balances were written off).
Current year $225,000.

(d) Other revenues collected, $95,000.

(e) Orders were placed for equipment, materials, and supplies, $230,000.

(f) Vouchers were approved as follows:

In full liquidation of encumbrances outstanding on June 30, 1966	$ 12,500
In liquidation of current encumbrances reported at $200,000	205,000
For current salaries	115,000

(g) Vouchers were paid, $370,000.

(h) Unpaid taxes were transferred to the delinquent account.

Instructions: (1) Give general journal entries for the year to record the transactions and to close the accounts.

(2) Prepare (a) a balance sheet and (b) an analysis of changes in unappropriated surplus in condensed form.

23-2. A balance sheet for the general fund for Ocean View City shows balances as follows on June 30, 1966:

Cash	$22,500	Vouchers payable	$14,000
Taxes receivable-delinquent	16,000	Reserve for encumbrances	20,000
		Unappropriated surplus	4,500
	$38,500		$38,500

The following transactions took place during the fiscal year ended June 30, 1967:

(a) Budget estimate of revenue, $200,000.

(b) Budget appropriations, $195,000.

(c) Taxes levied for purposes of this fund, $100,000.

(d) Cash borrowed from a special revenue fund pending tax collections, $40,000.

(e) Delinquent taxes collected, $3,500, plus interest and penalties of $750.

(f) Current taxes collected, $90,000, plus interest and penalties, $1,500. Balance of current taxes was transferred to delinquent taxes account.

(g) Other revenues collected, $90,000.

(h) Repayments to the special revenue fund on balance borrowed, $30,000.

(i) Orders placed for equipment, materials, and supplies estimated to cost $60,000.

(j) Vouchers approved in full liquidation of encumbrances outstanding on June 30, 1966, $19,500.

(k) Vouchers approved for purchases of materials and supplies, $45,000.

(l) Vouchers approved for salaries, $90,000.

(m) Vouchers approved for purchases of equipment, $26,000.

(n) Vouchers approved for payment of matured bonds, $20,000, and interest, $1,000.

(o) Vouchers paid, $200,000.

(p) Unliquidated encumbrances on June 30, 1967, $12,000.

Instructions: (1) Give the entries in general journal form to record the transactions and to close the accounts at the end of the period.

(2) Prepare (a) a balance sheet and (b) an analysis of changes in unappropriated surplus in condensed form.

23-3. A balance sheet for the Lakeside City general fund on April 30, 1966, showed the following balances:

Cash	$172,500	Vouchers payable	$155,000
Taxes receivable (1965–66)	30,000	Reserve for encumbrances	35,000
Taxes receivable (1964–65)	10,000	Unappropriated surplus	22,500
	$212,500		$212,500

The following transactions took place during the fiscal year, May 1, 1966–April 30, 1967.

(a) A budget was approved:
Estimated revenues:
From taxes, licenses, fees, and other regular revenue sources $720,000
From issuance of general bonds 200,000
Appropriations:
For general governmental activities $600,000
For the retirement of general bonds maturing on January 1, 1967 300,000

(b) Taxes levied for general fund activities, $450,000.

(c) Collection of taxes:
1964–65, $7,500 plus interest and penalties, $3,150.
1965–66, $21,000 plus interest and penalties, $4,200.
1966–67, $425,000.

(d) Receipt of proceeds from general bond issue, $200,000.

(e) Collection of other revenues, $250,000.

(f) Orders placed at estimated costs as follows:
Equipment $ 65,000
Materials and supplies 200,000

(g) Vouchers approved in full liquidation of encumbrances outstanding on April 30, 1966, as follows:

	Encumbrances	Vouchers Payable
Equipment	$15,000	$15,000
Materials and supplies	20,000	19,200

(h) Vouchers approved in liquidation of encumbrances currently incurred as follows:

	Encumbrances	Vouchers Payable
Equipment	$ 50,000	$ 52,500
Materials and supplies	175,000	174,250

(i) Vouchers approved for payment of general bonds maturing on January 1, 1967, $300,000, plus interest, $7,500.

(j) Vouchers approved for payment of salaries, $260,000.

(k) Vouchers approved for payment of other current expenditures, $60,000.

(l) Vouchers paid, $900,000.

Instructions: (1) Give the entries in general journal form to record the transactions of the general fund and to close the accounts at the end of the period.

(2) Prepare (a) a balance sheet and (b) an analysis of changes in unappropriated surplus in the form illustrated on page 821.

23-4. The following is a general fund balance sheet for Fairfield City on June 30, 1966:

General Fund

Assets

Cash		$ 140,000
Taxes receivable:		
1964–65	$21,000	
1965–66	44,000	65,000
Total assets		$ 205,000

Liabilities, Reserves, and Surplus

Vouchers payable	$ 80,000
Tax anticipation notes	65,000
Reserve for encumbrances	25,000
Unappropriated surplus	35,000
Total liabilities, reserves, and surplus	$ 205,000

A budget for 1966–67 is adopted as follows:

Anticipated Revenues

Taxes	$ 765,000
Licenses and permits	125,000
Fines, forfeits, and penalties	30,000
Revenue from use of money and properties	20,000
Revenue from other agencies	200,000
Charges for current services	90,000
	$1,230,000

Appropriations

General government	$ 130,000
Public safety	300,000
Highways	90,000
Sanitation and waste removal	50,000
Health and hospitals	45,000
Public welfare	40,000
Schools	420,000
Libraries	35,000
Recreation	20,000
Contribution to pension fund	5,000
Interest on debt	30,000
Redemption of debt	40,000
Surplus receipts	25,000
	$1,230,000

Taxes levied for the year 1966–67 were $775,000.

A cash receipts and disbursements statement for the year ended June 30, 1967, follows:

Receipts

Taxes: 1964–65	$ 20,000	
1965–66	32,000	
1966–67	725,000	$ 777,000
Licenses and permits		130,000
Fines, forfeits, and penalties		32,000
Revenue from use of money and properties		16,500
Revenue from other agencies		190,000
Charges for current services		80,000
Tax anticipation notes		300,000
Total receipts		$1,525,500

Disbursements

General government		$ 110,000
Public safety		250,000
Highways		80,000
Sanitation and waste removal		50,000
Health and hospitals		44,000
Public welfare		32,000
Schools		350,000
Libraries		32,000
Recreation		20,000
Contribution to pension fund		5,000
Interest on debt		30,000
Redemption of debt		40,000
Prior year's indebtedness:		
Vouchers payable	$ 80,000	
Tax anticipation notes	303,000	
Reserve for encumbrances (in full liquidation of reserve)	23,500	406,500
Total disbursements		$1,449,500

Unpaid invoices and unliquidated encumbrances related to 1966–67 appropriations were outstanding on June 30, 1967, as follows:

	Unpaid Invoices	Encumbrances	Total
General government	$12,000	$ 4,500	$ 16,500
Public safety	35,000	10,000	45,000
Highways	6,000		6,000
Schools	15,000	40,000	55,000
	$68,000	$54,500	$122,500

Uncollected taxes for the year 1964–65, $1,000, were written off against the unappropriated surplus balance.

Instructions: (1) Give journal entries to record transactions for the year ended June 30, 1967, indicating postings to the general ledger accounts and also to the subsidiary ledger accounts.

(2) Prepare for the year ended June 30, 1967, (a) a balance sheet, (b) an analysis of changes in unappropriated surplus, (c) a statement of revenue — estimated and actual, and (d) a statement of expenditures and encumbrances compared with authorizations.

23-5. The following is a general fund balance sheet for Beach City on January 1, 1967:

General Fund

Assets		
Cash		$ 235,000
Taxes receivable:		
1965	$33,500	
1966	67,500	101,000
Total assets		$ 336,000

Liabilities, Reserves, and Surplus	
Vouchers payable	$ 140,000
Tax anticipation notes	90,000
Reserve for encumbrances	50,000
Unappropriated surplus	56,000
Total liabilities, reserves, and surplus	$ 336,000

A budget for 1967 is adopted as follows:

Anticipated Revenues	
Taxes	$1,250,000
Licenses and permits	150,000
Fines, forfeits, and penalties	55,000
Revenue from use of money and properties	40,000
Revenue from other agencies	275,000
Charge for current services	65,000
	$1,835,000

Appropriations

General government	$ 180,000
Public safety	350,000
Highways	250,000
Sanitation and waste removal	55,000
Health and hospitals	70,000
Public welfare	60,000
Schools	650,000
Libraries	50,000
Recreation	30,000
Contribution to pension fund	15,000
Interest on debt	35,000
Redemption of debt	60,000
Unappropriated surplus	30,000
	$1,835,000

Taxes levied for the year 1967 were $1,238,000.

A cash receipts and disbursements statement for the year ended December 31, 1967, follows:

Receipts

Taxes: 1965	$ 30,000	
1966	55,000	
1967	1,195,000	$1,280,000
Licenses and permits		152,000
Fines, forfeits, and penalties		58,000
Revenue from use of money and properties		45,000
Revenue from other agencies		280,000
Tax anticipation notes		500,000
Charge for current services		64,500
Total receipts		$2,379,500

Disbursements

General government		$ 145,000
Public safety		317,500
Highways		185,000
Sanitation and waste removal		48,000
Health and hospitals		65,000
Public welfare		59,500
Schools		612,000
Libraries		47,500
Recreation		28,000
Contribution to pension fund		15,000
Interest on debt		35,000
Redemption of debt		60,000
Prior year's indebtedness:		
Vouchers payable	$140,000	
Tax anticipation notes	550,000	
Reserve for encumbrances (in full liquidation of reserve)	52,000	742,000
Total disbursements		$2,359,500

Unpaid invoices and unliquidated encumbrances related to 1967 appropriations were outstanding on December 31, 1967, as follows:

	Unpaid Invoices	Encumbrances	Total
General government	$20,500	$ 12,000	$ 32,500
Public safety	18,000	14,000	32,000
Highways		57,500	57,500
Sanitation and waste removal	6,500		6,500
Schools	15,000	21,500	36,500
	$60,000	$105,000	$165,000

Uncollected taxes for the year 1965, $3,500, were written off against the unappropriated surplus balance.

Instructions: (1) Give journal entries to record transactions for the year ended December 31, 1967, indicating postings to the general ledger accounts and also to the subsidiary ledger accounts.

(2) Prepare for the year ended December 31, 1967, (a) a balance sheet, (b) an analysis of changes in unappropriated surplus, (c) a statement of revenue — estimated and actual, and (d) a statement of expenditures and encumbrances compared with authorizations.

23-6. The following information pertains to the operations of the general fund of Z County. Functions of this county government include operating the county jail and caring for the county courts.

Funds to finance the operations are provided from a levy of county tax against the various towns of the county, from the state distribution of unincorporated business taxes, from board of jail prisoners assessed against the towns and against the state, and from interest on savings accounts.

The balances in the accounts of the fund on January 1, 1967, were as follows:

Cash in savings accounts	$ 60,650
Cash in checking accounts	41,380
Cash on hand (undeposited prisoners' board receipts)	320
Inventory of jail supplies	3,070
Due from towns and state for board of prisoners	3,550
General fund surplus	108,970

The budget for the year 1967 as adopted by the county commissioners provided for the following items of revenue and expenditure:

(1) Town and county taxes	$ 20,000
(2) Jail operating costs	55,500
(3) Court operating costs	7,500
(4) Unincorporated business tax	18,000
(5) Board of prisoners (revenue)	5,000
(6) Commissioners' salaries and expenses	8,000
(7) Interest on savings	1,000
(8) Miscellaneous expenses	1,000

General fund surplus was appropriated in sufficient amount to balance the budget. At December 31, 1967, the jail supply inventory amounted to $5,120, cash of $380 was on hand, and $1,325 of prisoners' board bills were unpaid. The following items represent all of the transactions that occurred during the year, with all current bills vouchered and paid by December 31, 1967:

Item (1) was transacted exactly as budgeted.	
Item (2) cash expenditures amounted to	$ 55,230
Item (3) amounted to	7,110
Item (4) amounted to	18,070
Item (5) billings amounted to	4,550
Item (6) amounted to	6,670
Item (7) amounted to	1,050
Item (8) amounted to	2,310

During the year, $25,000 was transferred from the savings accounts to the checking accounts.

Instructions: From the above information, prepare a work sheet with columns to show:

(a) The transactions for the year. (Journal entries are not required.)
(b) Variances between budgeted and actual revenues and expenditures for the year.
(c) Balance sheet of the general fund, December 31, 1967.

(AICPA adapted)

23-7. The following data were taken from the accounts of the Town of Farmdale after the books had been closed for the fiscal year ended June 30, 1967:

	Balances 6-30-66	1967 Changes Debits	1967 Changes Credits	Balances 6-30-67
Cash	$180,000	$ 955,000	$ 880,000	$255,000
Taxes Receivable	20,000	809,000	781,000	48,000
	$200,000			$303,000
Allowances for Uncollectible Taxes	$ 4,000	6,000	9,000	$ 7,000
Vouchers Payable	44,000	880,000	889,000	53,000
Due to Working Capital Fund	2,000	7,000	10,000	5,000
Due to Sinking Fund	10,000	60,000	100,000	50,000
Reserve for Encumbrances	40,000	40,000	47,000	47,000
Unappropriated Surplus	100,000	20,000	61,000	141,000
	$200,000	$2,777,000	$2,777,000	$303,000

The following additional data are available:

(1) The budget for the year provided for estimated revenues of $1,000,000 and appropriations of $965,000.

(2) Expenditures totaling $895,000, in addition to those chargeable against Reserve for Encumbrances, were made.
(3) The actual expenditure chargeable against Reserve for Encumbrances was $37,000.

Instructions: Prepare a work sheet to compare estimated revenues with actual revenues and encumbrances and expenditures with appropriations and other authorizations. The work sheet should have the following column headings: Columns 1–4, "Name of Account"; Column 5, "Balance Sheet, June 30, 1966"; Columns 6 and 7, "1967 Transactions" (Debit and Credit); Column 8, "Estimated Revenues"; Column 9, "Actual Revenues"; Column 10, "Encumbrances and Expenditures"; Column 11, "Appropriations and Other Authorizations"; Column 12, "Balance Sheet, June 30, 1967." (Formal journal entries are not required.) (AICPA adapted)

23-8. The account balances of the general fund of McArthur Township at the beginning of 1967 include:

Cash	$ 1,300
Taxes receivable	3,500
Accounts payable	800
Reserve for unfilled orders and contracts	1,100

The cash receipts for the year were:

From taxes of prior years	$ 3,200
From taxes of the current year	76,000
Other current revenues	16,000
Sales of old equipment	600
Temporary loans	20,000

The disbursements for the year were as follows:

Accounts payable of preceding year	$ 800
Invoices for current expenses and interest:	
(a) Covering all orders and contracts outstanding at beginning of year	1,200
(b) Incurred during year	80,000
Payment of bonds falling due during year	10,000
Purchase of fixed assets	4,000
Permanent petty cash advance made to city finance office	500
Stores purchased for central storeroom established during year	4,000
Payment of temporary loans	15,000

During the year $1,600 of stores purchased were issued to departments whose expenses are met from this fund. The balance of stock on hand at the end of the year represents a minimum inventory that the municipality proposes to maintain in the storeroom.

The only taxes considered collectible at the end of 1967 are those of the current year amounting to $7,000. Unfilled orders and contracts outstanding at the end of 1967 amounted to $900.

Instructions: (1) Prepare a set of working papers to summarize activities of the general fund for 1967.

(2) Prepare a general fund balance sheet as of December 31, 1967.

(3) Prepare a statement summarizing in detail the changes in the general fund unappropriated surplus for 1967. (AICPA adapted)

23-9. Information relating to the general fund for the Town of Clayton for the year ended April 30, 1967, follows:

(a) Unappropriated surplus at May 1, 1966, consisting entirely of cash, $2,350.
(b) Budget estimate of revenue, $185,000.
(c) Budget appropriations, $178,600.
(d) Tax levy, $115,620, against which a reserve of $4,000 is set for estimated losses in collection.
(e) Tax receipts, $112,246, with penalties of $310 in addition.
(f) Receipts from temporary loans, $20,000, all of which were repaid during period with interest of $300.
(g) Balance of encumbrances unliquidated, April 30, 1967, $3,250.
(h) Vouchers approved for expenses, $146,421.
(i) Vouchers approved for capital expenditures, $21,000.
(j) Vouchers approved for payment of bonds falling due during the year, $5,000, and for interest on the bonds, $2,000.
(k) Miscellaneous revenue received, $74,319.
(l) Rebate of current year's taxes collected in error, $240.
(m) Warrants issued and payable on demand, $169,400.
(n) Refund on an expense voucher on which an excess payment was made, $116.

Instructions: (1) Give the entries to record the data listed.

(2) Prepare entries to close the books for the year ended April 30, 1967.

(3) Prepare a balance sheet as of April 30, 1967.

(4) Prepare a statement of revenue, expenditures, and surplus for the year ended April 30, 1967. (AICPA adapted)

23-10. Information concerning the general fund of the City of Homewood is given below.

Account balances on January 1, 1967, were as follows:

Cash	$1,000
Taxes Receivable — Delinquent	8,000
Accounts Payable	7,000
Reserve for Encumbrances	1,500
Unappropriated Surplus	500

Transactions for 1967 were as follows:

(a) The budget that was adopted for 1967 provided for taxes of $275,000, special assessments of $100,000, fees of $15,000, and license revenues of $10,000. Appropriations were $290,000 for general fund operations, and $100,000 for the purpose of establishing a working capital fund.
(b) All taxes and special assessments became receivable.
(c) Cash receipts for the general fund included:

Taxes from 1967	$260,000
Special assessments	100,000
Fees	16,000
Licenses	9,500
Taxes Receivable — Delinquent	5,000
Interest on Taxes Receivable — Delinquent	500

Tax liens were obtained on the remainder of the delinquent taxes.
(d) Contracts amounting to $75,000 were let by the general fund.
(e) Billings for services rendered by the working capital fund to the general fund totaled $40,000.

(f) General fund disbursements were as follows:

Working capital fund	$100,000
Accounts payable of the preceding year	7,000
Outstanding orders at beginning of the year were received and paid for	2,000
Expenses of fund incurred during year	145,000
Stores purchased for central storeroom established during year	5,000
Contracts let during year	30,000
Permanent advance to newly created petty cash fund	1,000
Services performed by working capital fund	35,000
Salaries paid during year	30,000

(g) All unpaid taxes became delinquent.

(h) Stores inventory in the general fund amounted to $2,000 on December 31, 1967.

Instructions: Prepare as of December 31, 1967, a work sheet reflecting the transactions, closing entries and balance sheet for the general fund.

(AICPA adapted)

23-11. The Good Haven Township's adjusted trial balance for the general fund at the close of its fiscal year ended June 30, 1967, is shown below.

Good Haven Township
General Fund Trial Balance
June 30, 1967

Cash	$ 1,100	
Taxes Receivable — Current (note 1)	8,200	
Allowance for Uncollectible Taxes — Current		$ 150
Taxes Receivable — Delinquent	2,500	
Allowance for Uncollectible Taxes — Delinquent		1,650
Miscellaneous Accounts Receivable	4,000	
Allowance for Uncollectible Accounts		400
Due from Working Capital Fund	5,000	
Appropiation Expenditures (note 2)	75,500	
Encumbrances	3,700	
Revenues (note 3)		6,000
Due to Utility Fund		1,000
Vouchers Payable		2,000
Reserve for Encumbrances — Prior Year		4,400
Reserve for Encumbrances		3,700
Surplus Receipts (note 4)		700
Appropriations		72,000
Unappropriated Surplus		8,000
	$100,000	$100,000

Note 1. The current tax roll and miscellaneous accounts receivable, recorded on the accrual basis as sources of revenue, amounted to $50,000 and $20,000 respectively. These items have been recorded on the books subject to a 2% provision for uncollectible accounts.

Note 2. Includes $4,250 paid during the fiscal year in settlement of all purchase orders outstanding at the beginning of the fiscal year.

Note 3. Represents the difference between the budgeted (estimated) revenue of $70,000 and the actual revenue realized during the fiscal year.
Note 4. Represents the proceeds from sale of equipment damaged by fire.

Instructions: (1) Prepare in columnar form an analysis of changes in unappropriated surplus for the year ending June 30, 1967, with column headings for "Estimated," "Actual," and "Excess or Deficiency of Actual Compared with Estimated."

(2) Prepare a balance sheet at June 30, 1967. (AICPA adapted)

23-12. Information concerning the accounting records of the City of Brookville at December 31, 1967, is presented below:

City of Brookville
General Fund
Partial General Ledger Trial Balance (Before Adjustments)
December 31, 1967

	Debit	Credit
Supplies Inventory (Physical Inventory 12/31/67)	$ 10,000	
Estimated Revenue — Miscellaneous	20,000	
Estimated Revenue — Taxes	95,000	
Appropriations		$112,000
Revenue — Miscellaneous		19,900
Revenue — Taxes		95,500
Encumbrances	20,000	
Expenditures	80,000	
Expenditures Chargeable Against Prior Years' Encumbrances	7,100	
Reserve for Encumbrances (Balance, 1/1/67, $7,000)		27,000
Reserve for Supplies Inventory (Balance at 1/1/67)		12,000
Unappropriated Surplus		3,300
Surplus Receipts		1,700

Supplementary information:

1. The unencumbered balance of the fire department's appropriation at December 31, 1967, was $10,025. As legally authorized, the city council voted to carry over to 1968 this balance in the rounded amount of $10,000. The action of the city council has not been recorded in the accounts.

2. Unfilled purchase orders for the general fund at December 31, 1967, totaled $20,000.

Instructions: (1) Prepare adjusting journal entry or entries for general fund accounts at December 31, 1967.

(2) Prepare closing journal entry or entries for general fund accounts at December 31, 1967.

(3) Prepare in columnar form an "Analysis of Changes in Unappropriated Surplus" for the year with the following column headings: "Estimated," "Actual," and "Excess or Deficiency of Actual Compared with Estimated."

(AICPA adapted)

Chapter 24

GOVERNMENTAL UNITS

SPECIAL FUNDS

Every governmental unit has a general fund that accounts for all revenues and that finances all activities not directly identified with some special fund. The number of special funds found in any governmental unit will vary with the nature of the special activities carried on by the unit and the legal provisions that have been adopted for separate financing of such activities. Accounting for the general fund was described in the preceding chapter; accounting for special funds and for special groups of accounts is discussed in this chapter.

SPECIAL REVENUE FUNDS

A *special revenue fund* is established when charter, statute, or ordinance requires that specific taxes or special revenue sources are to be used to finance a particular activity. Special revenue funds, then, are established when certain revenue is to be used exclusively for particular purposes such as schools, parks, libraries, or special improvements. A special revenue fund may be created to serve certain broad purposes or to serve some narrow and limited purpose; in either case resources can be applied only to the particular fund objective. A fund may be viewed as a special revenue fund by the general governmental unit but may actually occupy a general fund status. For example, the governmental unit views the "school fund" as a special revenue fund, whereas the school fund is the "general fund" in terms of operations of the school system as a whole.

The authority for administering a special revenue fund may rest with the general governing body, but frequently the authority is delegated to a special body. A special revenue fund to finance school activities may be administered by a school board; a special revenue fund to finance recreational activities may be administered by a recreational commission. In some instances, the body responsible for the administration of the fund has the power to levy taxes or to establish the revenue measures that are required to finance activities. When a special revenue fund is to finance a number of activities, planning and control of expenditures will be required. Expenditures may be controlled by a budget in the same manner as in the general fund.

A special revenue fund calls for the establishment of a general ledger and appropriate subsidiary ledgers. Upon adoption of a budget, entries are made in estimated revenues, appropriations, and unappropriated surplus accounts. During the course of activities, revenues and expenditures and encumbrances are summarized in the general ledger and are reported in detail in the subsidiary records. The statements that report the activities of a special revenue fund are similar to the statements of the general fund. Accounting for a special revenue fund, then, parallels accounting for the general fund.

BOND FUNDS

Every issue of governmental bonds gives rise to a *bond fund* with the exception of special assessment or utility or other enterprise bonds; the latter provide resources for their own respective funds. Bonds may be authorized and issued (1) to purchase or construct improvements, (2) to finance general or special revenue fund activities or to absorb fund deficits, (3) to refund certain bond issues, and (4) to establish working capital funds or to acquire utilities or other enterprises. A separate bond fund with a separate self-balancing set of accounts is established whether the bond proceeds are to be expended over a lengthy period, as in the case of their use for construction activities, or whether the bond proceeds are to be transferred in total to another fund, as in their application to the cancellation of a general fund deficit.

Bonds can be issued only after appropriate authorization by the legislative body or favorable vote by the electorate. Approval of a bond issue carries with it authorization for the application of the bond proceeds to certain objectives. Upon approval of an issue, a bond fund is established and the authorization as well as subsequent transactions are recorded in the bond fund books. A separate bond fund is established for each bond issue.

To continue the example for the City of A in the preceding chapter, assume that this city approves a general bond issue to finance the acquisition of land and the construction of governmental buildings. Bond fund transactions and the entries made to record these transactions follow:

Bond Fund Books

Transaction	Entry		
Authorization of bond issue.	Bonds Authorized — Unissued	100,000	
	Appropriations.		100,000
Sale of bonds.	Cash	100,000	
	Bonds Authorized — Unissued. . .		100,000
Expenditure for purchase of land made relative to purpose of bond issue.	Expenditures	20,000	
	Vouchers Payable		20,000

Transaction	Entry		
Placing of orders and estimate of expenditures that will arise from commitments.	Encumbrances	25,000	
	Reserve for Encumbrances......		25,000
Placing of contract with construction company for work on project.	Encumbrances	50,000	
	Reserve for Encumbrances......		50,000
Liquidation of certain encumbrances ($15,000) upon receipt of invoices, and determination of expenditures relating to encumbrances ($16,000).	Reserve for Encumbrances........	15,000	
	Encumbrances		15,000
	Expenditures	16,000	
	Vouchers Payable		16,000
Completion of contract by construction company and authorization for payment of same, less 10% retention pending final approval of project.	Reserve for Encumbrances........	50,000	
	Encumbrances		50,000
	Expenditures	50,000	
	Vouchers Payable		45,000
	Contracts Payable — Retained Percentage		5,000
Payment of vouchers.	Vouchers Payable	70,000	
	Cash		70,000
To close the expenditures account at the end of the period.	Appropriations..................	86,000	
	Expenditures		86,000

A trial balance for the bond fund after posting the foregoing entries is shown below:

City of A
Bond Fund
Trial Balance
June 30, 1967

Cash..................................	30,000	
Encumbrances	10,000	
Vouchers Payable		11,000
Contracts Payable — Retained Percentage		5,000
Reserve for Encumbrances..................		10,000
Appropriations..........................		14,000
	40,000	40,000

Explanation of bond fund entries — authorization of bond issue. The authorization of a bond issue is recorded by a debit to the account Bonds Authorized — Unissued and a credit to the account Appropriations for the amount of the bonds to be issued. Bonds Authorized — Unissued may be viewed as the total resources estimated to become available to the fund; Appropriations may be viewed as the total obligations to be met by the fund.

Proceeds from issuance of bonds. When bonds are sold at par, Cash is debited and Bonds Authorized — Unissued is credited. If the bonds are sold at a premium, a bond premium account is also credited. The disposition of the premium balance is made in accordance with applicable legal requirements. If the premium becomes available for bond fund purposes, the premium is transferred to the appropriations account. If the premium is to be made available to the general fund for general purposes or to a sinking fund for bond interest payments or for bond retirement, the premium may be transferred to a payable account with such a fund; the subsequent payment of cash cancels the payable. If the bonds are sold at a discount, a bond discount account is charged for the amount of the discount. As in the case of a premium, disposition of the discount depends upon legal requirements. If the discount reduces the amount available for bond fund purposes, the discount is closed into the appropriations account. If the discount is to be recovered from some other fund in meeting bond fund requirements, a receivable balance with such other fund is established and the discount balance is closed; the subsequent receipt of cash cancels the receivable. The liability arising from the issue of the bonds is not reported in the bond fund but is recognized in the general bonded debt and interest group of accounts.

Expenditures and encumbrances. When a bond fund is to finance construction activities, the orders or contracts that are placed in carrying out the purpose of the bond issue are recorded by debits to Encumbrances and credits to Reserve for Encumbrances. As orders are filled and contracts are completed, original encumbrance entries are reversed and the actual expenditures are recorded by debits to the account Expenditures and credits to the appropriate liability accounts.

The authorization for expenditures is not limited to a specified time but is effective until completion of the project; hence entries to close encumbrance and expenditure balances are not required until the project is completed. Ordinarily, however, it is desirable to close the expenditures account into the appropriations account at the end of each fiscal period so that the portion of the project that has been completed may be summarized. The encumbrances account is not closed at the end of the period; however, the balance in this account is subtracted from the appropriations balance in preparing a bond fund balance sheet.

Properties constructed for general governmental purposes from bond fund proceeds are not reported in the bond fund but are recognized in the separate general fixed assets group of accounts. When construction is only partly completed at the end of the period, expenditures to date are reported in the general fixed assets group of accounts as Construction in Progress.

When all of the encumbrances have been liquidated and the project is completed, the expenditures balance is closed into the appropriations account. Any unexpended balance in the appropriations account may now be transferred to unappropriated surplus. The unappropriated surplus balance is matched by cash of an equivalent amount.

Cash remaining in the bond fund is disposed of in accordance with legal requirements. Normally, the cash must be transferred to the fund that is responsible for ultimate retirement of the bonds. The transfer of cash to the general fund or to a bond sinking fund is recorded by a debit to Unappropriated Surplus and a credit to Cash. Bond fund accounts have now been closed and the bond fund is no longer operative. The fund receiving cash from the bond fund debits Cash and credits a revenue account. If Construction in Progress was previously recognized in the separate general fixed assets group of accounts, this balance is canceled and the property item is recorded at its full cost.

When bond fund proceeds are used for the purchase of certain properties, the purchase is recorded by a charge to Expenditures. When bond fund proceeds are simply transferred to another fund for such purposes as financing current activities, refunding a bond issue, or acquiring a public utility or other enterprise, the transfer is recorded by a charge to Expenditures. Accounts are closed as previously indicated. Recognition of the properties that are acquired or the debt that is terminated through bond fund expenditures is made in the fund or group of accounts responsible for carrying the properties or liability.

Statements. Statements for each bond fund are prepared periodically. These statements normally consist of a balance sheet, a statement comparing expenditures and encumbrances with appropriations, and a statement of cash receipts and disbursements. Statements may be accompanied by special schedules that offer detailed support of statement items. When there are a number of bond funds, combined statements may be prepared with separate columns reporting financial data relating to the individual bond funds and total columns summarizing the data for all of the bond funds. The statements for the bond fund for the City of A are illustrated on the following page. It should be observed that

City of A
Bond Fund
Balance Sheet
June 30, 1967

Assets		Liabilities, Reserves, Appropriations, and Surplus	
Cash	$30,000	Vouchers payable	$11,000
		Contracts payable—retained percentage	5,000
		Reserve for encumbrances	10,000
		Appropriations — unencumbered balance	4,000
Total assets	$30,000	Total liabilities, reserves, appropriations and surplus	$30,000

City of A
Bond Fund
Statement of Expenditures and Encumbrances — Compared with Appropriations
For Year Ended June 30, 1967

Amount appropriated, January 20, 1967	$100,000
Less Expenditures, January 20–June 30, 1967	86,000
Unexpended balance	$ 14,000
Less Encumbrances, June 30, 1967	10,000
Unencumbered balance, June 30, 1967	$ 4,000

City of A
Bond Fund
Statement of Cash Receipts and Disbursements
For Year Ended June 30, 1967

Receipts:		
Proceeds from sale of bonds, January 20, 1967		$100,000
Disbursements:		
Purchase of land	$20,000	
Payments on construction contract	45,000	
Payment of other miscellaneous costs and expenses	5,000	70,000
Cash balance, June 30, 1967		$ 30,000

the building project is still uncompleted with certain encumbrances remaining to be liquidated, certain invoices and contracts remaining to be paid, and a bond fund surplus yet to be determined.

A balance sheet for a bond fund may show asset and liability balances other than those listed in the example. Other assets that may be found include bonds authorized and unissued, accounts receivable, and amounts due from other funds; liabilities may include accounts payable, contracts payable, judgments payable, and amounts due to other funds.

The statement comparing expenditures and encumbrances with appropriations may show changes in the amount appropriated other than those in the illustration; for example, there may be additions to or deductions from the appropriations balance for bond premiums and discounts, for contributions from other funds, and for transfers to other funds. If an unencumbered fund balance has been transferred to Unappropriated Surplus, this would be reported on the statement.

SPECIAL ASSESSMENT FUNDS

A *special assessment fund* is established whenever public improvements are to be financed in part or in whole by special levies on properties benefiting therefrom. The special assessment fund accounts for the collection of special assessment levies and also reports the application of such monies to the particular purpose for which they were raised.

Special assessment improvements are made only after appropriate authorization by the legislative body or favorable vote by the property owners affected. When a project has been approved, a special assessment fund is established for the project, and the authorization as well as subsequent transactions are recorded in the special assessment fund books. A separate special assessment fund is established for each special assessment project authorized.

When cash is collected from property owners at the time improvements are made, accounting for a special assessment fund is similar to that for the bond fund previously illustrated. Ordinarily, however, special assessments are collected over a number of years and it becomes necessary to finance construction from the proceeds of special assessment bonds or other long-term loans. Such obligations are claims against the benefited properties and are retired as the special assessments are collected from property owners. Special assessment taxpayers are normally charged interest on any deferred payments and this interest is used to pay the interest on the special assessment indebtedness. When construction is financed by bonds or other loans, the special assessment fund must show the original receipt of funds and their use for the authorized project, and also the subsequent collection of special assessments and the application of such proceeds to the retirement of special assessment fund indebtedness.

To illustrate the accounting for a special assessment fund, assume that street improvements are authorized within the City of A, the cost of such improvements to be assumed by the city and by the property owners who benefit from the improvements. Special assessment fund transactions and the entries that are made to record such transactions follow:

Special Assessment Fund Books

Transaction	Entry		
Authorization of project.	Improvements Authorized	120,000	
	Appropriations		120,000
Charge to government for its share of cost, and assessments levied against property owners.	Due from General Fund — Government's Share of Cost	20,000	
	Special Assessments Receivable — Current	10,000	
	Special Assessments Receivable — Deferred	90,000	
	Improvements Authorized		120,000
Receipt of government's share of cost from general fund, and also first half of current assessments.	Cash for Construction	25,000	
	Due from General Fund — Government's Share of Cost		20,000
	Special Assessments Receivable — Current		5,000
Issuance of bonds to finance construction activities.	Cash for Construction	95,000	
	Bonds Payable		95,000
Payment of construction expenditures.	Expenditures	20,000	
	Vouchers Payable		20,000
Placing of orders and estimate of expenditures that will arise from commitments.	Encumbrances	10,000	
	Reserve for Encumbrances		10,000
Placing of contract with construction company for work on project.	Encumbrances	80,000	
	Reserve for Encumbrances		80,000
Completion of contract by construction company and authorization for payment of same, less 10% retention pending final approval of project.	Reserve for Encumbrances	80,000	
	Encumbrances		80,000
	Expenditures	85,000	
	Vouchers Payable		76,500
	Contracts Payable — Retained Percentage		8,500

Transaction	Entry		
Payment of vouchers.	Vouchers Payable	90,000	
	Cash for Construction		90,000
Receipt of second half of current assessments together with interest on unpaid assessments.	Cash for Bond Payments	5,000	
	Cash for Interest Payments	2,000	
	Special Assessments Receivable — Current		5,000
	Interest Income		2,000
Retirement of part of bond issue together with interest on bonds.	Bonds Payable	4,000	
	Interest Expense	1,900	
	Cash for Bond Payments		4,000
	Cash for Interest Payments		1,900
To record accrued interest on special assessments receivable — deferred at the end of the period.	Interest Receivable	450	
	Interest Income		450
To record accrued interest on bonds payable at the end of the period.	Interest Expense	400	
	Interest Payable		400
To close expenditures account at the end of the period.	Appropriations	105,000	
	Expenditures		105,000
To close interest accounts at the end of the period.	Interest Income	2,450	
	Interest Expense		2,300
	Unappropriated Surplus — Interest		150

A trial balance taken after recording the foregoing follows:

City of A
Special Assessment Fund
Trial Balance
June 30, 1967

Cash for Construction	30,000	
Vouchers Payable		6,500
Contracts Payable — Retained Percentage		8,500
Reserve for Encumbrances		10,000
Appropriations		15,000
Encumbrances	10,000	
Cash for Bond Payments	1,000	
Special Assessments Receivable — Deferred	90,000	
Bonds Payable		91,000
Cash for Interest Payments	100	
Interest Receivable	450	
Interest Payable		400
Unappropriated Surplus — Interest		150
	131,550	131,550

Explanation of special assessment fund entries — authorization of project. The authorization of a project to be financed by special assessments is recorded by a debit to the account Improvements Authorized and a credit to the account Appropriations. Improvements Authorized may be viewed as the total resources estimated to become available in fulfilling the objectives of the fund; Appropriations may be viewed as the total obligations to be met by the fund.

Proceeds from special assessments and from borrowing. The amount that the governmental unit is to contribute as its share of the project cost and the assessments against property owners are recorded by debits to appropriate receivable accounts and a credit to the account Improvements Authorized. Subsidiary ledgers are established and individual charges are made to accounts with special assessment taxpayers. As cash is received from the governmental unit and from taxpayers during the construction period, Cash for Construction is debited and the receivable balances are credited. Accounting for taxes follows procedures already described in the preceding chapter.

When borrowing is necessary to meet construction requirements, Cash for Construction is debited and Bonds Payable (or other appropriate liability account) is credited. Subsequent collections of assessments are applied to the liquidation of the bonded indebtedness; subsequent collections of interest on special assessments are applied to the payment of interest on the bonded indebtedness. Collections, then, are recorded by debits to Cash for Bond Payments and to Cash for Interest Payments; special assessment receivable accounts and Interest Income are credited. Accrued interest on special assessments receivable at the end of the period is recognized by a charge to Interest Receivable and a credit to Interest Income.

The issue of bonds at a premium or at a discount creates special problems. When bonds are issued at a premium, Cash for Construction is debited for the amount of the obligation, Cash for Interest is debited for the amount of the premium, and Bonds Payable and Premium on Bonds are credited. Cash for Interest is applied to interest payments. The premium balance is amortized over the life of the bond issue, periodic charges to the premium being accompanied by credits to Interest Expense. When bonds are issued at a discount, Cash for Construction is debited for the bond issue proceeds, Discount on Bonds is debited for the amount of the discount, and Bonds Payable is credited. The discount balance is amortized over the life of the bond issue, periodic credits to the discount being accompanied by charges to Interest Expense. Special assessment collections, in either case, require analysis in terms of the amount to be applied to the liquidation of bonded indebtedness and the amount to be applied to the payment of interest on such indebtedness.

Encumbrances and expenditures. Encumbrances and expenditures are recorded just as in the bond fund. Expenditures are closed at the end of each period, but encumbrances are carried into the new period. A credit excess in the appropriations account upon the completion of the project would indicate a surplus, this surplus to be used for the abatement of special assessments still owing, for rebates to be made to special assessment taxpayers, or for disposal in some other manner in accordance with the law. When special assessment expenditures are made for the acquisition or the development of properties properly recognized as fixed assets, the property items are recognized at their acquisition or during the course of their construction in the general fixed assets group of accounts just as projects financed by a bond fund.

Payments of bonds and interest on bonds from special assessment proceeds are recorded by debits to Bonds Payable and to Interest Expense, and by credits to Cash for Bond Payments and to Cash for Interest. Accrued interest on bonds at the end of the period is recognized by a charge to Interest Expense and a credit to Interest Payable.

Interest income and interest expense balances are closed periodically. An excess of interest income over interest expense results in a credit to Unappropriated Surplus — Interest; an excess of interest expense over interest income results in a debit to the interest surplus account. An interest surplus or deficit upon ultimate settlement of special assessment indebtedness calls for a cash transfer in accordance with legal requirements. The law frequently provides that upon an interest surplus, interest cash is to be transferred to the general fund; an interest deficit is generally made up by a transfer of cash from the general fund. An interest surplus normally calls for a transfer of interest cash to the general fund. The general fund charges Appropriation Expenditures upon transferring cash to a special assessment fund to finance construction activities, to absorb a construction deficit, or to cover an interest shortage; the general fund credits Revenues upon receiving excess construction cash or interest cash from a special assessment fund.

Statements. Statements are prepared periodically for each special assessment fund. These statements normally consist of a balance sheet, a statement comparing expenditures and encumbrances with appropriations, and a statement of cash receipts and disbursements. The statement of cash receipts and disbursements should offer an analysis of the changes in the three cash balances — cash for construction, cash for bond payments, and cash for interest payments. When there are a number of special assessment funds, combined statements may be prepared, with separate columns reporting financial data for the individual special assessment funds and total columns summarizing the data for all of the special assessment funds. The balance sheet for the special assessment fund of the City of A is illustrated below. The other statements are similar to those previously illustrated for the bond fund.

City of A
Special Assessment Fund
Balance Sheet
June 30, 1967

Assets		Liabilities, Reserves, Appropriations, and Surplus	
Cash for construction	$ 30,000	Vouchers payable	$ 6,500
Cash for bond payments	1,000	Contracts payable — retained percentage	8,500
Cash for interest payments	100	Bonds payable	91,000
Special assessments receivable — deferred	90,000	Interest payable	400
Interest receivable	450	Reserve for encumbrances	10,000
		Appropriations — unencumbered balance	5,000
		Unappropriated surplus — interest	150
Total assets	$121,550	Total liabilities, reserves, appropriations, and surplus	$121,550

A balance sheet for a special assessment fund may show assets and liabilities other than those reported in the example. Among the assets that may be found are assessments receivable — delinquent, current, and deferred; special assessment liens receivable; penalties receivable on special assessments; amounts due from the government for its share of cost; and amounts due from other funds. Liabilities may include contracts payable, judgments payable, and amounts due to other funds.

A special assessment fund is terminated only after its receivables have been fully realized and its obligations fully liquidated. Special assessments receivable to be collected in years to come and bonds to be paid from such proceeds are reported on successive balance sheets until receivables are fully realized and bonds are fully liquidated.

SINKING FUNDS

A *sinking fund* is established whenever resources are accumulated for the specific purpose of retiring term bonds of the governmental unit. Books of the sinking fund report the accumulation of the sinking fund and also the application of assets to the particular purpose for which they were accumulated.

Cash deposits are normally made to the sinking fund at regular intervals. The source of such deposits may be contributions from the general fund or a special revenue fund, or sinking fund levies included in the general tax assessments. Cash deposited in the sinking fund is invested, and the earnings on these investments further increase the amount available for bond retirement. When serial bonds are issued, the sinking fund accumulation is not required, for cash is applied periodically to the direct retirement of the serial maturities. Normally, serial bond maturities, as well as periodic interest on both serial bonds and term bonds, are met through direct payment by the general fund or special revenue funds.

Deposits to a sinking fund may be arbitrary sums or they may be equal periodic sums calculated actuarially so that such deposits at an assumed interest rate will accumulate to the desired amount at some future date.[1] When deposits are calculated actuarially and earnings differ from the assumed rate, deposits may be adjusted or cash transfers may be made to or from the general fund so that scheduled amounts are deposited.

Assume that the City of A is required to establish a sinking fund for the ultimate retirement of the bonds that were issued for the construction of certain public properties, referred to in an earlier example. Sinking fund transactions, the entries to record such transactions on the sinking fund books, and a trial balance after recording these transactions follow:

Sinking Fund Books

Transaction	Entry		
Determination of current required contributions and earnings.	Required Contributions..........	10,000	
	Required Earnings..............	400	
	Reserve for Retirement of Sinking Fund Bonds..................		10,400
Charge to source providing installment contribution.	Due from General Fund..........	10,000	
	Contribution Revenues.........		10,000
Receipt of revenues.	Cash..........................	10,000	
	Due from General Fund........		10,000
Investment of cash.	Investments....................	9,800	
	Cash........................		9,800
Receipt of income.	Cash..........................	300	
	Interest Income...............		300

[1]Calculation of the equal periodic deposits that when left at an assumed rate of interest will produce a given fund at some future date is described and illustrated in Chapter 26.

Transaction	Entry		
To record accrued income at the end of the period.	Interest Receivable	50	
	Interest Income		50
To close sinking fund requirement and revenue accounts at the end of the period.	Contribution Revenues	10,000	
	Required Contributions		10,000
	Interest Income	350	
	Unappropriated Surplus	50	
	Required Earnings		400

City of A
Sinking Fund
Trial Balance
June 30, 1967

Cash	500	
Interest Receivable	50	
Investments	9,800	
Reserve for Retirement of Sinking Fund Bonds		10,400
Unappropriated Surplus	50	
	10,400	10,400

Explanation of sinking fund entries — recording current requirements. Periodic sinking fund contributions and earnings requirements in accordance with the fund plan are recorded at the beginning of each period by debits to Required Contributions and Required Earnings and a credit to Reserve for Retirement of Sinking Fund Bonds. Required Contributions and Required Earnings may be viewed as the resources estimated to become available to the fund during the period; Reserve for Retirement of Sinking Fund Bonds may be viewed as the obligation that the fund has undertaken to meet.

Proceeds from contributions and from earnings. If a portion of the taxes is to be made directly available to the sinking fund in satisfying deposit requirements, Taxes Receivable is debited and Contribution Revenues is credited. Accounting for the collection of taxes will follow the procedures already described in the preceding chapter. If the contribution is to be made by the general fund or a special revenue fund, a receivable account with such a fund is debited to establish the claim and the revenues account is credited. When the contribution is received, Cash is debited and the receivable account is credited. The account Contribution Revenues may be regarded as an offset to the account Required Contributions. At the end of the period Required Contributions and Contribution Revenues are closed. An excess of actual contributions over required contributions results in a credit to Unappropriated Surplus; an excess of required contributions over actual contributions results in a charge to Unappropriated Surplus.

Accounting for sinking fund investments of a governmental unit is similar to accounting for sinking fund investments of a business unit. Amounts collected on investments are recorded by debits to Cash and credits to appropriate revenue accounts. The latter balances may be regarded as offsets to the account Required Earnings. At the end of the period, adjustments are made to recognize any revenue accruals. At this time, too, entries would be made for the amortization and accumulation of any premiums or discounts on sinking fund investments. After adjustments, Required Earnings and the individual revenue account balances are closed. An excess of actual earnings over required earnings results in a credit to Unappropriated Surplus; an excess of required earnings over actual earnings results in a charge to Unappropriated Surplus.

Payment of sinking fund bonds will require the sale of sinking fund securities. Gains and losses on such sales are carried to Unappropriated Surplus. A deficit in a bond sinking fund and insufficient funds to meet maturing indebtedness is made up in accordance with legal requirements. Generally, the shortage is met by a general fund contribution. The receipt of such a contribution is recorded by a debit to Cash and a credit to Unappropriated Surplus. A surplus balance and excessive cash in the sinking fund will result in a transfer of cash to some other fund in accordance with legal requirements. Such transfer is recorded by a debit to Unappropriated Surplus and a credit to Cash. The general fund records a transfer of cash to meet a sinking fund shortage by a charge to Appropriation Expenditures; the receipt of cash from a sinking fund is recorded by a credit to Revenues.

Expenditures. When bonds that are to be paid from the sinking fund mature, they should be recognized on the sinking fund books by a debit to Reserve for Retirement of Sinking Fund Bonds and a credit to Matured Bonds Payable. Upon payment of the bonds, the liability account is closed. Until the time the bonds mature, they are carried on the general bonded debt and interest group of accounts; when they mature and are recognized on the books of the sinking fund, the balances are closed on the general bonded debt and interest group of accounts.

Statements. Statements are prepared periodically for each sinking fund. Statements normally include a balance sheet, a statement comparing sinking fund revenues with requirements, a statement analyzing the changes in the reserve for retirement of sinking fund bonds, and a statement of cash receipts and disbursements. When there are a number of bond sinking funds, combined sinking fund statements may be prepared reporting individual fund data and combined data. Investment balance detail can be provided in the form of supporting schedules. Only the balance sheet for the sinking fund of the City of A is illustrated.

City of A
Sinking Fund
Balance Sheet
June 30, 1967

Assets		Liabilities, Reserves, and Surplus	
Cash	$ 500	Reserve for retirement of sinking fund bonds	$10,400
Interest receivable	50	Deficit	(50)
Investments	9,800		
Total assets	$10,350	Total liabilities, reserves, and surplus	$10,350

Assets other than those shown in the example may be found on a sinking fund balance sheet. Among these assets are cash with fiscal agents for payment of bonds; taxes receivable — current and delinquent — and related allowances for losses on such receivables; tax liens receivable; interest and penalties receivable; and amounts due from other funds. On an interim balance sheet actual contribution revenues and actual earnings would be listed as subtraction items from required contributions and required earnings balances, the debit excesses being reported as assets estimated to be realizable currently.

WORKING CAPITAL FUNDS

Working capital funds or *revolving funds* are created upon establishing service units that are to offer certain goods or services to the different governmental departments. Service units are established with the expectation that they will be able to provide goods and services at costs that are less than what the governmental departments would otherwise have to pay to outsiders. Representative of working capital funds are central stores, garages, printing establishments, cement and asphalt plants, and prison industries.

Operations of the service unit are normally similar to those of the private business organization, and accounting for the service unit normally parallels that of the private organization. Costs are incurred in connection with operations, but the service unit recovers its costs through charges that it makes to governmental departments that benefit from its services. Ordinarily expenditures of the unit are not restricted by appropriation measures; operations of the service unit are based upon the demands made upon it by the various departments, and such demands are limited to the amounts appropriated to respective departments for its goods or services.

Assume that the City of A establishes a central print shop offering printing services to the various city departments. Working capital fund transactions, the entries that are made to record such transactions, and a trial balance taken after recording the transactions follow:

Working Capital Fund Books

Transaction	Entry		
Establishment of working capital fund by contribution from general fund in accordance with budgetary appropriation.	Cash	25,000	
	Capital Contribution by General Fund		25,000
Purchase of equipment, materials, and supplies.	Equipment	10,000	
	Materials and Supplies	26,000	
	Vouchers Payable		36,000
Billings to general fund for services rendered.	Due from General Fund	40,000	
	Billings for Services		40,000
Expenses incurred.	Expenses	25,000	
	Vouchers Payable		25,000
Cash received from general fund on billings.	Cash	30,000	
	Due from General Fund		30,000
Payment of vouchers.	Vouchers Payable	50,000	
	Cash		50,000
Materials and supplies used during the period.	Expenses	14,000	
	Materials and Supplies		14,000
To record depreciation of equipment.	Expenses	500	
	Allowance for Depreciation of Equipment		500
To close revenue and expense accounts at the end of the period.	Billings for Services	40,000	
	Expenses		39,500
	Unappropriated Surplus		500

City of A
Working Capital Fund
Trial Balance
June 30, 1967

Cash	5,000	
Due from General Fund	10,000	
Materials and Supplies	12,000	
Equipment	10,000	
Allowance for Depreciation of Equipment		500
Vouchers Payable		11,000
Capital Contribution by General Fund		25,000
Unappropriated Surplus		500
	37,000	37,000

Explanation of working capital fund entries. The working capital fund is established by a contribution from the general fund or from some other fund, or possibly from funds provided by the issuance of bonds. Cash is debited and a capital account reporting the source of the contribution is credited. Revenue and expense items of the working capital fund are recorded just as they would be for a similar private enterprise. Materials and supplies purchased by the fund may be carried on a perpetual inventory basis, with charges to expense recognized as these items are consumed or transferred. Property and equipment items acquired by the fund are carried on its own books, and depreciation is recognized as a part of the cost of goods and services for billing purposes; billings thus recover the depreciation sustained and provide funds for the ultimate replacement of the depreciable properties. At the end of the period, adjustments are made for prepaid and accrued items, for depreciation and amortization, and for inventories, as in the case of the private unit. Revenue and expense balances are closed, and the net income or loss from operations is carried to Unappropriated Surplus.

Ordinarily a working capital fund bills the departments that it serves for no more than the cost of the services rendered. Cost accounting records may be maintained in arriving at charges that will cover material, labor, and overhead costs. When charges are made at approximate cost, the capital of the fund will remain steady. When charges are made that produce a net income, the transfer of cash to the general fund may be authorized at different intervals. Such transfers are recorded on the working capital fund books by debits to Unappropriated Surplus and credits to Cash. When a working capital fund operates regularly at a net loss, replenishment of its capital by the general fund at different intervals may be authorized. The transfer of cash in such an instance is recorded on the working capital fund books by a debit to Cash and a credit to

Unappropriated Surplus. The general fund in receiving cash from a working capital fund credits Revenues; the transfer of cash to a working capital fund in establishing the fund or in meeting a capital deficiency is recorded by a debit to Appropriation Expenditures.

Statements. Statements are prepared periodically for each working capital fund. Statements normally include a balance sheet, a statement of operations, and an analysis of changes in unappropriated surplus. When there are a number of working capital funds, combined working capital statements may be prepared reporting individual fund data and combined data. Only the working capital fund balance sheet for the City of A is shown below. The statement of operations and the analysis of changes in unappropriated surplus would be similar to those normally prepared for a private business unit.

City of A
Working Capital Fund
Balance Sheet
June 30, 1967

Assets			Liabilities, Capital, and Surplus	
Cash		$ 5,000	Vouchers payable	$11,000
Due from general fund		10,000	Capital contribution by general fund	25,000
Materials and supplies		12,000	Unappropriated surplus	500
Equipment	$10,000			
Less allow. for depr.	500	9,500		
Total assets		$36,500	Total liabilities, capital, and surplus	$36,500

TRUST AND AGENCY FUNDS

Governmental units frequently hold and operate assets in the capacity of trustee or agent. Separate *trust funds* and *agency funds* are established for properties so controlled. In its capacity as trustee or as agent, the governmental unit is faced with special responsibilities. It must carry out its duties in accordance with trust or agency requirements as well as the applicable general law. A full accounting for the discharge of its responsibilities in either capacity is required.

Trust and agency funds are so similar that they are generally treated as a single class for governmental accounting purposes. In certain cases the accounting for such funds is very simple and the fund books are maintained for only a short period. This is the case where the governmental unit receives a grant that is immediately spent, or where the governmental unit makes certain cash collections that are immediately distributed to other units. In other instances the accounting may be rather complex and the fund may continue for a considerable time or indefinitely. This would be the case where the governmental unit takes over tax-delinquent properties and makes cash distributions to other governmental units in satisfaction of their liens as cash is realized on such properties, or where the governmental unit receives a grant with the principal to remain intact and only the income to be used for public benefits. Whether simple or complex problems are involved, accounting for the governmental trust or agency is the same as that employed for such a relationship in the private field.

Assume that cash is received by the City of A for the establishment of a trust fund. Income of the fund is to become available for certain public benefits, but the principal of the fund is to remain unexpendable. Transactions for the trust fund and the entries to record the transactions appear below. A post-closing trial balance for the fund follows the entries.

Trust and Agency Fund Books

Transaction	Entry		
Receipt of cash whose income is to be used for a specific purpose.	Principal Cash................. Trust Fund Principal Balance...	50,000	 50,000
Investment of cash.	Investments.................... Principal Cash...............	45,000	 45,000
Receipt of income.	Income Cash.................... Income.......................	1,500	 1,500
Payments chargeable to income in accordance with trust requirements.	Payments Chargeable to Income... Income Cash..................	1,200	 1,200
To close the accounts at the end of the period.	Income......................... Payments Chargeable to Income. Trust Fund Income Balance....	1,500	 1,200 300

City of A
Trust Fund
Trial Balance
June 30, 1967

Principal Cash..................................	5,000	
Investments.....................................	45,000	
Trust Fund Principal Balance....................		50,000
Income Cash.....................................	300	
Trust Fund Income Balance.......................		300
	50,300	50,300

Explanation of trust fund entries. A clear distinction must be maintained between principal assets and income assets when only the latter are expendable. Income and income payment account balances are closed at the end of each period. An excess of income over income payments would indicate that income had not been wholly expended, and such a balance could be used to satisfy spending requirements in subsequent periods.

When a fund is nonexpendable both as to principal and as to income, as in the case of a fund established to make loans to public employees, no principal-income distinction for assets is necessary; fund capital can be summarized in a single account or can be divided into original capital and the surplus or the deficit emerging from the fund activities. The same procedures would apply for a fund that is fully expendable as to principal and income, as in the case of a fund for pensions to employees.

Statements. Statements are prepared periodically for each trust fund and each agency fund. Statements normally include a balance sheet, a statement accounting for changes in fund principal and income balances, and a statement of cash receipts and disbursements. When there are a number of agency and trust funds, combined statements may be prepared reporting individual and combined data. The balance sheet for the trust fund of the City of A is shown below. The remaining statements would be the same as those prepared for the private trust.

City of A
Trust Fund
Balance Sheet
June 30, 1967

Assets		Liabilities and Balances	
Principal cash	$ 5,000	Trust fund principal balance	$50,000
Investments	45,000	Trust fund income balance	300
Income cash	300		
Total assets	$50,300	Total liabilities and balances	$50,300

UTILITY OR OTHER ENTERPRISE FUNDS

Many governmental units own and operate certain utilities and other enterprises that offer services to the public. Examples of utilities include water plants, electric plants, gas plants, and transportation systems; examples of other enterprises include airports, docks, and public housing. Operations of such utilities and other enterprises are normally self-supporting, the rates charged to the public covering the costs of providing services. *Utility* or *other enterprise funds* are established to account for the properties and the operations of the public enterprises.

Accounting for utility or other enterprise funds. Operations of publicly owned utilities and enterprises are similar to those of privately owned utilities and enterprises, and accounting is normally the same as that for private units. Accounting for public units, as for private units, must provide at regular intervals full data concerning both the financial position and the results of operations.

Original acquisition of a utility or other enterprise may be financed from amounts contributed by the general fund or by a special revenue fund, from amounts raised by a general bond issue, or from amounts raised by the sale of utility or other enterprise bonds that are to be retired from earnings of this unit. When cash for the purchase of properties is received from a general or a special revenue fund, the utility or other enterprise fund debits Cash and credits a capital account that identifies the fund making the contribution. When cash is received from the issue of bonds of the general governmental authority, the utility or other enterprise fund debits Cash and credits Capital Contributed by General Bond Issue. When cash is raised by means of its own bonds secured by a lien on its revenues or a mortgage on its properties, the utility or other enterprise debits Cash and credits Revenue Bonds Payable or Mortgage Bonds Payable. Following the receipt of cash, entries are made on the books of the utility or other enterprise for the purchase of land and buildings and other properties.

Revenues and expenses are recorded on the books of the utility or other enterprise just as these would be recorded on the books for a similar private enterprise. At the end of each period appropriate adjustments are made in arriving at financial position and the results of operations. The net income or loss from operations is summarized and transferred to Unappropriated Earned Surplus. When cash representing a portion or all of the net income is transferred by the utility or other enterprise fund to the general fund or to some special revenue fund to finance governmental activities, the entry on the utility or other enterprise books is a debit to Unappropriated Earned Surplus and a credit to Cash. The general fund or special revenue fund in receiving cash from a utility or other enterprise credits Revenues; the general fund or special revenue fund in transferring cash to a utility or other enterprise fund to establish the fund, to pay for services, or to meet a capital deficiency debits Appropriation Expenditures.

Statements. Statements are prepared periodically for each utility or other enterprise fund. Statements normally include a balance sheet, a revenue and expense statement, and a statement analyzing changes in earned surplus. Supporting schedules normally accompany the statements. Statements and supporting schedules are similar to those for like private enterprises. A utility fund balance sheet for the City of A is presented below.

City of A
Utility Fund
Balance Sheet
June 30, 1967

Assets

Current assets:			
Cash		$ 35,500	
Accounts and notes receivable	$ 40,000		
Less allowance for bad debts	1,500	38,500	
Materials and supplies		12,000	
Prepaid expenses		6,500	$ 92,500
Bond sinking fund			30,000
Utility plant in service:			
Equipment	$ 60,000		
Less allowance for depreciation	15,000	$ 45,000	
Structures and improvements	$150,000		
Less allowance for depreciation	20,000	130,000	
Land		50,000	225,000
Deferred costs:			
Unamortized bond issue costs			2,500
Total assets			$350,000

Liabilities, Contributions, and Surplus

Liabilities:		
Current liabilities:		
Vouchers payable	$ 60,000	
Accrued expenses	5,000	$ 65,000
Bonds payable		200,000
		$265,000
Contributions and surplus:		
Capital contribution by general fund	$ 50,000	
Surplus appropriation for bond sinking fund	30,000	
Unappropriated earned surplus	5,000	85,000
Total liabilities, contributions, and surplus		$350,000

GENERAL FIXED ASSETS GROUP OF ACCOUNTS

The need for a full accountability for the fixed assets of a governmental unit is obvious. As indicated in previous sections, working capital, trust and agency, and utility and other enterprise funds reported fixed asset acquisitions on their respective books. However, the general fund, special revenue funds, bond funds, and special assessment funds in acquiring fixed assets did not report these on their respective books but simply charged an expenditures account. Fixed assets acquired by the latter funds are referred to as the *general fixed assets* and are summarized in a separate self-balancing *general fixed assets group* of accounts.

General fixed assets when acquired by purchase are recorded at cost. When properties are acquired by gift, they are recorded at their appraised value. Normally no recognition is made in the accounts for depreciation on this class of property items; cost allocation procedures for general fixed assets would serve little purpose when there is no concern with a determination of net income. Physical checks of property items are made at various intervals and differences between items on hand and items reported on the books are investigated and reconciled.

Transactions and entries affecting the general fixed assets records for the City of A and a trial balance after transactions have been recorded are as follows:

General Fixed Assets Books

Transaction	Entry		
Acquisition of equipment through appropriation expenditures of general fund.	Equipment	65,000	
	Investment in General Fixed Assets — From Current Revenues..		65,000
Equipment retired during period (original cost, $6,000, financed by general fund).	Investment in General Fixed Assets — From Current Revenues	6,000	
	Equipment		6,000
To record land acquired and buildings in process of construction at the end of the year through expenditures of bond fund.	Land	20,000	
	Structures and Improvements in Progress........................	66,000	
	Investment in General Fixed Assets — From Bonds		86,000
To record improvements in process at the end of the year through expenditures of special assessment fund.	Structures and Improvements in Progress........................	105,000	
	Investment in General Fixed Assets — From Property Owners' Share of Special Assessments		85,000
	Investment in General Fixed Assets — From Government's Share of Special Assessments..........		20,000

City of A
General Fixed Assets
Trial Balance
June 30, 1967

Equipment	59,000	
Structures and Improvements in Progress	171,000	
Land	20,000	
Investment in General Fixed Assets — From Current Revenues		59,000
Investment in General Fixed Assets — From Bonds		86,000
Investment in General Fixed Assets — From Property Owners' Share of Special Assessments		85,000
Investment in General Fixed Assets — From Government's Share of Special Assessments		20,000
	250,000	250,000

Explanation of general fixed assets group entries. The acquisition of a general fixed asset is recorded in the general fixed assets group of accounts by a debit to the appropriate asset account and a credit to Investment in General Fixed Assets. Frequently, instead of a single investment credit balance indicating total general asset holdings, separate investment balances are established to indicate the different sources of general fixed assets financing — financing from current revenues, bonds, special assessments, grants, etc. General fixed assets in the process of construction are reported as "in progress" until their completion, when the full cost is taken up. The entries for the expenditures for fixed assets are not made in the general fixed assets group of accounts but are made in the books of the funds financing the acquisitions as described in earlier sections.

Subsidiary accounts are provided to show general fixed assets detail. The subsidiary record describes each asset, reports its cost, and offers supplementary information including its location and other significant data.

When a general fixed asset is retired, the original entry recording the acquisition is reversed. The account Investment in General Fixed Assets, then, is debited and the appropriate asset balance is credited.

Statements. Statements are prepared periodically from the general fixed assets group books. Statements normally include a statement of general fixed assets and a statement summarizing changes in the different classes of general fixed assets during the course of the period. A statement of general fixed assets prepared for the City of A is shown at the top of the following page.

City of A
Statement of General Fixed Assets
June 30, 1967

Equipment	$ 59,000	Investment in general fixed assets financed from:	
Structures and improvements in progress	171,000	Current revenues	$ 59,000
Land	20,000	Bonds	86,000
		Property owners' share of special assessments	85,000
		Government's share of special assessments	20,000
Total	$250,000	Total	$250,000

GENERAL BONDED DEBT AND INTEREST GROUP OF ACCOUNTS

Bonded debt of the governmental unit, with the exception of that reported directly in special assessment funds or utility and other enterprise funds, is known as the *general bonded debt.* Total general bonded debt maturities, together with the total interest that will accrue during the lifetime of such indebtedness, is summarized in a separate self-balancing *general bonded debt and interest group* of accounts.

Transactions and entries affecting the general bonded debt records for the City of A and the resulting trial balance appear at the top of the following page.

Explanation of general bonded debt group entries. Total amounts owed as principal and interest on bonded debt are reported as liabilities, with offsets in the form of balances reporting the amounts available and the amounts to be provided in the future to meet such obligations. Upon the issuance of bonds, the accounts Amount to be Provided for Payment of Principal and Amount to be Provided for Payment of Interest are debited, and the accounts Bonds Payable and Interest Payable in Future Years are credited. Cash received upon issuing such bonds is not reported in the general bonded debt and interest books but is accounted for in the bond funds as described earlier.

When a sinking fund is established for the retirement of bonds, the addition of resources to the sinking fund is recorded in the general bonded debt and interest group of accounts by a debit to the account Amount in Sinking Fund and a credit to the account Amount to be Provided for Payment of Principal. When sinking fund bonds mature and the sinking fund establishes a liability for matured bonds payable, the issue is canceled on the general bonded debt and interest books by a debit to Bonds Payable and a credit to Amount in Sinking Fund.

General Bonded Debt Books

Transaction	Entry		
To record bonds issued to finance improvements, and total interest payable on bonds during their lifetime.	Amount to be Provided for Payment of Principal....................	100,000	
	Amount to be Provided for Payment of Interest......................	40,000	
	Sinking Fund Bonds Payable....		100,000
	Interest Payable in Future Years.		40,000
To record increase in sinking fund for retirement of bonds.	Amount in Sinking Fund.........	10,350	
	Amount to be Provided for Payment of Principal..............		10,350
To record matured interest recognized by general fund.	Interest Payable in Future Years..	2,000	
	Amount to be Provided for Payment of Interest...............		2,000

City of A
General Bonded Debt and Interest
Trial Balance
June 30, 1967

Amount in Sinking Fund..........................	10,350	
Amount to be Provided for Payment of Principal.....	89,650	
Amount to be Provided for Payment of Interest......	38,000	
Sinking Fund Bonds Payable........................		100,000
Interest Payable in Future Years..................		38,000
	138,000	138,000

When payment of bonds is to be made from current revenues, recognition of maturing serial bonds or term bonds on the books of the general fund or a special revenue fund calls for an entry in the general bonded debt and interest books debiting Bonds Payable and crediting Amount to be Provided for Payment of Principal. The recognition of maturing interest on the books of the general fund or a special revenue fund calls for similar accounting on the general bonded debt and interest books: Interest Payable in Future Years is debited and Amount to be Provided for Payment of Interest is credited.

Statements. Statements are prepared periodically from the general bonded debt and interest group books. Statements normally include a statement of general bonded debt and interest and statements summarizing changes in the individual bonded debt and interest balances during the course of the period. A statement of general bonded debt and interest for the City of A is shown at the top of the following page.

City of A
Statement of General Bonded Debt and Interest
June 30, 1967

Bond Principal:			General Bonds — Sinking fund bonds payable	$100,000
Amount in sinking fund	$10,350		Interest payable in future years	38,000
Amount to be provided for payment of principal	89,650	$100,000		
Amount to be provided for payment of interest		38,000		
Total		$138,000	Total	$138,000

It may be observed that many governmental units combine the general fixed assets and the general bonded debt items in a single set of books. In such instances the following procedures are frequently followed: (1) acquisition of fixed assets is recorded by a debit to the asset accounts and a credit to the account Excess of Fixed Assets over Bonded Debt; (2) the disposal of a fixed asset is recorded by an entry reversing the entry made at the time of the asset acquisition; (3) the issue of general bonds is recorded by a charge to the account Excess of Fixed Assets over Bonded Debt and a credit to Bonds Payable; (4) the retirement of general bonded debt is recorded by an entry reversing the entry made at the time of the bond issue. A statement for the general fixed assets and bonded debt group would show fixed assets balanced by bonds payable and an excess of fixed assets over bonded debt.

The foregoing practice can be criticized on the grounds that there is normally no relationship between a governmental unit's general fixed assets and general bonded debt that would suggest their presentation on a single statement with a surplus or a deficit balance. Many of the fixed assets are acquired from current revenues, special assessments, and grants rather than from bond issues; on the other hand, general bonded debt, although in some instances incurred to finance fixed asset acquisitions, is also incurred to meet general and special revenue fund deficits, to establish working capital funds, and to acquire public utilities and other enterprises. Normally bondholders can look only to the governmental unit's taxing powers and not to the fixed assets for settlement of its general bonded debt. Under these circumstances, general fixed assets and general bonded debt represent two separate aspects of a governmental unit's financial status. If a combined statement of general fixed assets and general bonded debt is to be presented, it would best be presented in the following form:

City of A
Statement of General Fixed Assets,
General Bonded Debt, and Interest
June 30, 1967

Amount available and to be provided for retirement of general bonded debt and interest:		
Bond Principal:		
Amount in sinking fund	$ 10,350	
Amount to be provided for payment of principal	89,650	
	$100,000	
Amount to be provided for payment of interest	38,000	$138,000
General fixed assets:		
Land	$ 20,000	
Structures and improvements in progress	171,000	
Equipment	59,000	250,000
Total		$388,000

General bonded debt and interest payable in future years:		
General Bonds—Sinking fund bonds payable	$100,000	
Interest payable in future years	38,000	$138,000
Investment in general fixed assets financed from:		
Current revenues	$ 59,000	
Bonds	86,000	
Property owners' share of special assessments	85,000	
Government's share of special assessments	20,000	250,000
Total		$388,000

COMBINED STATEMENTS

In addition to the separate statements for the different funds described in the preceding pages, it is normally desirable to prepare statements that show combined financial and operating data. A balance sheet may be prepared that shows assets, liabilities, and balances for all of the governmental funds. Certain summaries of revenues and expenditures for different funds can be presented in combined form to show the results of related activities. A statement of cash receipts and expenditures can be prepared to report the cash transactions for all of the governmental funds.

A combined balance sheet for the City of A may be prepared as illustrated on pages 876 and 877.

CITY OF A
Combined Balance Sheet — All Funds
June 30, 1967

	Total	General Fund	Bond Fund	Special Assess-ment Fund	Sink-ing Fund	Work-ing Capital Fund	Trust Fund	Utility Fund	General Fixed Asset Accounts	General Bonded Debt Accounts
Assets										
Cash	$ 247,400	$140,000	$ 30,000	$ 31,100	$ 500	$ 5,000	$ 5,300	$ 35,500		
Accounts and notes receivable (net)	38,500							38,500		
Taxes receivable	40,000	40,000								
Interest receivable	500			450	50					
Due from general fund	10,000					10,000				
Materials and supplies	24,000					12,000		12,000		
Prepaid expenses	6,500							6,500		
Investments	54,800				9,800		45,000			
Bond sinking fund	30,000							30,000		
Special assessments rec. — deferred	90,000			90,000						
Equipment (net)	113,500					9,500		45,000	$ 59,000	
Structures and improvements (net)	130,000							130,000		
Structures and improvements in progress	171,000								171,000	
Land	70,000							50,000	20,000	
Unamortized bond issuance costs	2,500							2,500		
Amount available and to be provided for retirement of bonds and interest	138,000									$138,000
Totals	$1,166,700	$180,000	$ 30,000	$121,550	$ 10,350	$ 36,500	$ 50,300	$350,000	$250,000	$138,000
Liabilities										
Vouchers payable	$ 173,500	$ 85,000	$ 11,000	$ 6,500		$ 11,000		$ 60,000		
Due to working capital fund	10,000	10,000								
Accrued expenses	5,000							5,000		
Interest payable	400			400						
Contracts pay. — retained percentage	13,500		5,000	8,500						
Bonds payable	391,000			91,000				200,000		$100,000
Interest payable in future years	38,000									38,000
Total liabilities	$ 631,400	$ 95,000	$ 16,000	$106,400		$ 11,000		$265,000		$138,000

Reserves, Appropriations, Contributions, Balances, and Surplus										
Reserve for encumbrances	$ 70,000	$ 50,000	$ 10,000	$ 10,000						
Reserve for retirement of sinking fund bonds	10,400				$ 10,400					
Appropriations — Unencumbered balance	9,000		4,000	5,000						
Unappropriated surplus (deficit)	35,450	35,000			(50)	$ 500				
Unappropriated surplus — interest	150			150						
Unappropriated earned surplus	5,000							$ 5,000		
Surplus appropriation for bond sinking fund	30,000							30,000		
Capital contribution by general fund	75,000					25,000		50,000		
Trust fund principal balance	50,000						$ 50,000			
Trust fund income balance	300						300			
Investment in general fixed assets	250,000								$250,000	
Total reserves, appropriations, contributions, balances, and surplus	$ 535,300	$ 85,000	$ 14,000	$ 15,150	$ 10,350	$ 25,500	$ 50,300	$ 85,000	$250,000	
Totals	$1,166,700	$180,000	$ 30,000	$121,550	$ 10,350	$ 36,500	$ 50,300	$350,000	$250,000	$138,000

QUESTIONS

1. (a) Name and describe eight classes of funds that might be found in a municipality. (b) Which of the funds named carry fixed assets among their resources? (c) Which of the funds named carry bonded indebtedness among their liabilities?

2. (a) What purposes are served by a special revenue fund? (b) How does such a fund originate? (c) How do special revenue fund operations compare with those of the general fund?

3. (a) Indicate the different purposes for which a general bonded debt may be incurred. (b) Assuming that bond proceeds are employed for public improvements, name the funds or account groups affected through such use and give the entries that would appear on the books of each. (c) What statements are prepared for a bond fund during the course of its operations?

4. Would you recommend that a system of encumbrances be employed in a bond fund? Give reasons for your answer.

5. What purposes are served by a special assessment fund? How does such a fund originate?

6. (a) Describe the nature of a bond sinking fund. (b) Assuming that the fund is ultimately applied to the retirement of bonds, name the funds affected by such action and give the entries that are made on the books of each.

7. (a) Describe the nature of a working capital fund. (b) What is the purpose of recognizing depreciation in summarizing activities in this fund? (c) Would you recommend that billings for goods and services be made at cost, at more than cost, or at less than cost? Give reasons for your answer.

8. Describe and give an example for each of the following:

(a) An agency fund.
(b) A trust fund that is expendable as to both principal and income.
(c) A trust fund that is expendable as to income but nonexpendable as to principal.
(d) A trust fund that is nonexpendable as to both principal and income.

9. (a) Give three examples of *utilities* that may be owned and operated by a governmental unit. (b) Give three examples of *other enterprises* that may be owned and operated by a governmental unit.

10. Give the entries that would be made on the general fixed assets books for each of the following transactions:

(a) Certain equipment is acquired by a general fund in accordance with special revenue fund appropriations.
(b) Certain equipment employed by a special revenue fund is scrapped.

(c) Bonds are issued for construction of public buildings and the buildings are partly completed in the current period.
(d) Certain special assessment improvements begun in a previous period are completed in the current period.
(e) Certain buildings originally financed from current revenues are destroyed by fire.

11. Give the entries that would be made on the general bonded debt and interest group of accounts for each of the following transactions:

(a) Sinking fund bonds are issued for the construction of a freeway.
(b) Cash is transferred from the general fund to a sinking fund to provide for the ultimate retirement of bonds issued in (a).
(c) Serial bonds are issued for the construction of public buildings.
(d) Payment is made by the general fund of current serial bond maturities as well as interest on serial bonds and sinking fund bond issues.

12. Indicate for each account that follows the different funds or other books of account in which it might appear:

(a) Required Contributions.
(b) Appropriations.
(c) Reserve for Encumbrances.
(d) Matured Bonds Payable.
(e) Bonds Authorized — Unissued.
(f) Equipment.
(g) Expenditures.
(h) Estimated Revenues.
(i) Taxes Receivable.
(j) Bonds Payable.
(k) Interest Receivable.
(l) Interest Payable in Future Years.

13. List the possible dispositions of an unappropriated surplus balance in (a) the general fund, (b) the bond fund, (c) the special assessment fund, (d) the sinking fund, and (e) the working capital fund.

14. Describe the nature of the combined balance sheet for a governmental unit.

EXERCISES

1. What entries would be made to record the following transactions of a special revenue fund for the City of X:

(a) The budget is adopted providing for estimated revenues of $100,000 and appropriations of $90,000.
(b) Revenues totaling $105,000 are collected.
(c) Orders are placed for materials and supplies estimated to cost $40,000.
(d) Materials and supplies billed at $34,000 are received. These were estimated to cost $35,000 and were included in (c) above.
(e) Payments of $30,000 on billings relating to (d) above are made.
(f) Salaries totaling $45,000 are paid.
(g) Accounts are closed at the end of the period.

2. What entries would be made to record the following transactions of a bond fund for the City of X:

(a) Bonds of $100,000 are authorized for the construction of a sewer system.
(b) Bonds are sold at par.
(c) Construction is completed at a cost of $95,000.
(d) Accounts are closed and the remaining cash is transferred to the general fund.

3. What entries would be made to record the following transactions of a special assessment fund for the City of X:

(a) Improvements are authorized at a cost of $100,000. Forty percent of the cost is to be borne by the city, the balance by taxpayers.
(b) Payment is received for the city's share of cost, and $60,000 is borrowed from a revolving fund to finance construction pending collection of assessments from taxpayers.
(c) Construction is completed at a cost of $100,000.
(d) Collection of special assessments of $60,000 is made.
(e) Payment is made to the revolving fund.
(f) Accounts are closed.

4. Give the entries to record the following transactions of a central materials storeroom on the books of this fund and on the books of any of the other funds that are affected:

(a) The general fund transfers $10,000 to a central materials storeroom in establishing the fund.
(b) Materials are purchased and paid for, $8,000.
(c) Salaries of $1,000 are paid.
(d) Materials that cost $5,000 are requisitioned by the general fund departments. Overhead at the rate of 6% is added to the cost of materials in the charge to these departments.
(e) The book inventory of materials at the end of the period exceeds the physical inventory by $150.
(f) The materials inventory remaining in the hands of the general fund departments at the end of the year is $3,000. The inventory at the end of the preceding year was $3,200 and the general fund books show materials, $3,200, and a reserve for materials of $3,200.

5. The following transactions, among others, were completed by the City of Monica during 1967. Prepare the journal entries to record the transactions on the books of all of the funds affected.

(a) Bonds of $100,000, for which a sinking fund had been established, matured and were paid by the sinking fund.
(b) Bonds of $100,000 were authorized and sold at par to finance a general fund deficit. Bonds pay 4% interest and are due in 10 years.
(c) Twenty-year 4½% sinking fund bonds of $200,000 were sold at par.
(d) The project financed from the bonds referred to in (c) was completed. The construction expenditures balance in the amount of $197,000 was closed; the balance in the bond fund was transferred to the bond sinking fund.
(e) Special assessment improvements in the amount of $500,000 were authorized. Special assessment notes of $350,000 were sold at par to finance current construction. Assessments of $350,000 were levied on

private property, the remainder of the cost to be paid by the municipality. The municipality authorized the issuance of 10-year 5% bonds in financing its share of the cost, $150,000. The bonds were sold at a premium of $1,000. Bond proceeds were transferred to the special assessment fund; $150,000 was recorded as Cash for Construction and $1,000 was recorded as Cash for Interest.

6. The following transactions are completed by the City of Fairview during the course of a fiscal period. Give the entries that would be made on the general fixed assets and general bonded debt and interest books.

(a) Equipment is ordered by the general fund at an estimated cost of $20,000 and is subsequently received at a cost of $19,400.
(b) Buildings originally acquired by expenditures from the general fund of $40,000 are dismantled, salvage of $1,500 being recovered; salvage proceeds were made available to the general fund.
(c) Equipment costing $2,500 is destroyed by fire.
(d) Equipment originally acquired by an expenditure of $5,000 from the general fund is found to be no longer useful and is traded in for similar new equipment costing $6,500, a $500 trade-in allowance being received on the old equipment.
(e) Bonds of $100,000 due in 10 years and with interest at 3½%, payable semiannually, are issued for the construction of a library. The library is completed at a cost of $95,000 and $5,000 is transferred from the bond fund to a bond sinking fund.

PROBLEMS

24-1. Trial balances for Bensonville City on July 1, 1966, were as follows:

General Fund

Cash	$ 35,000	
Delinquent Taxes	30,000	
Allowance for Losses on Delinquent Taxes		$ 10,000
Inventories	22,500	
Vouchers Payable		60,000
Reserve for Encumbrances		7,500
Reserve for Inventories		22,500
Unappropriated Surplus	12,500	
	$100,000	$100,000

General Fixed Assets

Land	$120,000	
Buildings and Improvements	400,000	
Equipment	66,500	
Investment in General Fixed Assets		$586,500
	$586,500	$586,500

General Bonded Debt and Interest

Amount to be Provided for Payment of Principal	$250,000	
Amount to be Provided for Payment of Interest	300,000	
Bonds Payable		$250,000
Interest Payable in Future Years		300,000
	$550,000	$550,000

The budget adopted for the fiscal year 1966–1967 was as follows:

Estimated Revenues	$220,000
Appropriations	207,500
Available Surplus	$ 12,500

The city council levied taxes for the year of $125,000; losses on delinquencies were estimated at 5%. Collections on the current tax levy totaled $115,000; collections on delinquent taxes were $12,500, which included penalties and interest of $1,000. Receipts from other sources during the year totaled $90,000.

Vouchers relating to current-year commitments were approved totaling $200,000 and included the following: salaries and services, $115,000; buildings and improvements, $50,000; equipment, $25,000; interest on bonds, $10,000. The cost of buildings and improvements was found to exceed the original estimate, and a supplementary appropriation of $15,000 was passed by the City Council to permit the completion of this project. Vouchers in liquidation of all of the prior-year commitments were approved totaling $7,000. On June 30, 1967, there were unliquidated commitments for equipment of $20,000; orders for the equipment had been placed pursuant to current appropriations, but equipment had not yet been received. Vouchers paid during the year totaled $215,000.

During the year, equipment of $11,500 that was no longer usable was retired. Inventories on hand at the end of the year were found to total $18,000. Unpaid taxes were transferred to the delinquent taxes account.

Instructions: (1) Give the entries in general journal form to record the transactions of the general fund and to close the accounts at the end of the year.

(2) Prepare a balance sheet and an analysis of changes in unappropriated surplus in condensed form for the general fund.

(3) Give the required entries in general journal form for (a) the general fixed assets group of accounts and (b) the general bonded debt and interest group of accounts.

(4) Prepare statements at the end of the year for (a) the general fixed assets and (b) the general bonded debt and interest.

24-2. Statements for Mills City at the end of 1966 show the following balances:

General Fund

Cash		$52,250	Vouchers payable	$36,000
Delinquent taxes	$25,000		Reserve for encumbrances	15,000
Less allowance for losses	10,000	15,000	Unappropriated surplus	16,250
		$67,250		$67,250

Statement of General Fixed Assets

Equipment	$ 850,000	Investment in fixed assets financed from:		
Land, buildings, and improvements	400,000	Current revenues	$ 800,000	
		Bonds	450,000	
	$1,250,000		$1,250,000	

Statement of General Bonded Debt and Interest

Amount to be provided for payment of principal	$600,000	Bonds payable	$600,000
Amount to be provided for payment of interest	280,000	Interest payable in future years	280,000
	$880,000		$880,000

Transactions of the city during 1967 were as follows:

(a) A budget for 1967 was adopted as follows:

Estimated revenues:		
Taxes — 1967	$400,000	
Licenses and permits	60,000	
Fines and penalties	40,000	
Revenues from other agencies	35,000	$535,000
Appropriations:		
General government	$100,000	
Public safety	180,000	
Highways	60,000	
Sanitation and health	45,000	
Charities	30,000	
Bond retirement and interest	120,000	$535,000

(b) Taxes of $420,000 were levied; an allowance of $20,000 was established for possible losses on tax collections, revenue of $400,000 being recognized on the levy.

(c) Cash receipts during 1967 were as follows:

Delinquent taxes	$ 6,000	
Current taxes	380,000	
Licenses and permits	64,000	
Fines and penalties	39,500	
Revenues accruing from state government	35,000	$524,500

(d) Vouchers were approved during 1967 for the following:

General government	$ 96,750	
Public safety	166,000	
Highways	49,600	
Sanitation and health	44,000	
Charities	29,800	
Bond retirement	100,000	
Interest on bonds	20,000	
In full liquidation of encumbrances outstanding on January 1, 1967	14,200	$520,350

Expenditures above included a total of $50,000 for equipment and $35,000 for buildings and improvements.

(e) Checks drawn in payment of vouchers totaled $525,250.

(f) Current encumbrances unliquidated at the end of 1967 were as follows:

General government	$ 1,800	
Public safety	11,600	
Highways	10,000	$ 23,400

Instructions: (1) Give the entries in general journal form to record the transactions of the general fund and to close the accounts at the end of the period.

(2) Prepare for the general fund: (a) a balance sheet, (b) a statement of revenue — estimated and actual, (c) a statement of expenditures and encumbrances — compared with authorizations, and (d) an analysis of changes in unappropriated surplus.

(3) Give the entries in general journal form required on (a) the general fixed assets books, and (b) the general bonded debt and interest books.

(4) Prepare statements at the end of the year for (a) the general fixed assets and (b) the general bonded debt and interest.

24-3. Bonds of $5,000,000 are authorized by the voters of Oak City for the construction of a health center. The following transactions take place in 1966:

(a) The bonds are sold at par, $5,000,000. Bonds pay interest at 4% and are due at the end of 10 years.
(b) Land is purchased for cash at a cost of $1,200,000.
(c) A contract is entered into for construction of the center at a cost of $3,200,000.
(d) Payments are authorized on the construction contract totaling $1,700,000.

The project is completed in 1967 when the following transactions take place:

(a) The contractors are paid the balance owed on the contract, $1,500,000, plus extras of $160,000.

(b) Payments are made for miscellaneous expenditures incurred during the course of construction totaling $406,200.
(c) A sinking fund is established through general fund appropriations of $300,000 per year. Transfer of $300,000 is made by the general fund and, in addition, bond interest amounting to $200,000 is paid from general fund appropriations.
(d) The balance of cash in the bond fund is transferred to the sinking fund.

Instructions: (1) Give all of the entries required on the bond fund books for 1966 and 1967. (Assume closing entries are made at the end of 1966 and also upon completion of the project.)

(2) Prepare a balance sheet for the bond fund as of December 31, 1966.

(3) Give any entries as a result of the above affecting (a) the general fund books, (b) the general fixed assets group of accounts, (c) the general bonded debt and interest group of accounts, and (d) the bond sinking fund books.

24-4. In 1962 Garden City authorizes the widening of First Street at a cost of $500,000. The project is to be financed as follows: ¼ by general fund contributions and the balance by property owners in the special assessment district.

The city pays its share of the cost in 1962, and $375,000 is borrowed from Garden City Bank to finance construction activities pending collection of special assessments.

Payments of $100,000 are made to property owners in 1962 for the land required in the street widening project. In December, 1962, a contract is awarded to the Peerless Construction Co. for the work to be done at an estimated cost of $400,000.

The project is completed in 1963 and settlement is made with the contractors at $415,000. The general fund contributes $15,000 to complete payment on the contract.

Collections are made from the property owners of the full amount of the special assessments, plus interest and penalties totaling $39,000, during the period 1963–1967. During this period collection proceeds are used to pay off the obligation to the bank, together with interest charges over the 5-year period totaling $33,200. At the end of 1967 the balance of special assessment fund cash is transferred to the general fund and the special assessment books are closed.

Instructions: (1) Give all of the entries that are required on the books of the special assessment fund for the period 1962–1967.

(2) Prepare a balance sheet for the special assessment fund showing its position as of December 31, 1962.

24-5. The following are the transactions of a central storehouse during 1967:

(a) The fund is established by a contribution of $100,000 by the general fund.
(b) Supplies of $125,000 are purchased on account.

(c) Salaries and miscellaneous expenses of $4,000 are paid.
(d) Supplies costing $56,000 are requisitioned by general fund departments. The general fund is billed for the cost of supplies plus 6% of such cost, which is estimated to cover departmental overhead.
(e) Cash of $45,000 is received on general fund billings.
(f) Payments of $112,500 are made on account.
(g) The following information is recorded at the end of the fiscal period.
Accrued salaries and expenses are $400.
A physical count of the supplies on hand shows an inventory that is $160 less than the book inventory.

Instructions: (1) Give the journal entries to record the transactions of the central storehouse fund, including adjusting and closing entries at the end of 1967.

(2) Prepare (a) a balance sheet and (b) a statement of operations for the year ended December 31, 1967.

24-6. Statements for the City of X on June 30, 1966, showed balances as follows:

General Fund

Cash	$50,000	Vouchers payable	$30,000
Taxes receivable — delinquent	25,000	Reserve for encumbrances	20,000
		Unappropriated surplus	25,000
	$75,000		$75,000

General Fixed Assets

Equipment	$250,000	Investment in general fixed assets financed from bonds	$950,000
Land and improvements	700,000		
	$950,000		$950,000

General Bonded Debt and Interest

Amount to be provided for payment of principal	$1,280,000	Bonds payable	$1,280,000
Amount to be provided for payment of interest	620,000	Interest payable in future years	620,000
	$1,900,000		$1,900,000

Transactions of the city for the year ended June 30, 1967, follow:

(a) The budget for the year showed revenues estimated at $750,000 and appropriations of $745,000.
(b) A bond issue was authorized for the construction of a recreation center at a cost of $100,000, and bonds were sold at par. The interest rate on the bonds is 4%; bonds mature at the end of 10 years.

(c) A sinking fund was established for retirement of the bonds: required contributions for the first year were $9,000, and required earnings were $400.

(d) Taxes of $500,000 were assessed to finance general fund activities.

(e) A street widening project of $125,000 was authorized.

(f) Property owners were assessed $75,000 for the street project, the city to contribute the balance. Contributions from each source were payable in 10 equal annual installments.

(g) Contracts were entered into with Fulton and Flagg, Inc. for construction of the recreation center at a cost of $80,000 and with Powers Construction Co. for the street widening at a cost of $85,000.

(h) Taxes were collected as follows:

General taxes — delinquent	$ 5,000
General taxes — current	480,000
Special assessment taxes	7,200

Unpaid current taxes were transferred to delinquent tax accounts.

(i) Additional revenues collected by the general fund totaled $235,000.

(j) General fund encumbrances outstanding on June 30, 1966, were fully liquidated by the approval of vouchers for $18,250. Various equipment items costing $2,400 were included in this total.

(k) Vouchers were approved for current expenditures of the general fund totaling $690,000. This included $50,000 for the current maturities of general bonds, $20,000 for interest on bonds, and $65,000 representing the cost of various equipment items.

(l) General fund encumbrances outstanding on June 30, 1967, total $35,000.

(m) Vouchers totaling $716,500 were paid by the general fund.

(n) The general fund transferred cash of $9,000 to the sinking fund and $5,000 to the special assessment fund. (These items are not included in the expenditures or payments above.)

(o) Bonds of $112,500 were sold by the special assessment fund at par to finance completion of the project.

(p) The sinking fund acquired U.S. Government bonds at par as an investment, paying $8,500 plus accrued interest, $150.

(q) Interest of $450 was collected on investments by the sinking fund. Accrued interest on the bonds on June 30, 1967, is $60.

(r) Payment of $20,500 was made to property owners for land required in the street widening project.

(s) Billing was received for work done to date and payment was made as follows: to Fulton and Flagg, Inc., $50,000; to Powers Construction Co., $25,000.

Instructions: (1) Give the entries in general journal form that would be required on the books of each of the funds and account groups for the City of X, including any entries required on June 30, 1967, the close of the fiscal year.

(2) Prepare a combined balance sheet for the City of X as of June 30, 1967.

24-7. The board of education of the Valerie School District is developing a budget for the school year ending June 30, 1968. The budgeted expenditures follow:

Valerie School District
Budgeted Expenditures
For the Year Ending June 30, 1968

Current operating expenditures:			
Instruction:			
General	$1,401,600		
Vocational training	112,000	$1,513,600	
Pupil service:			
Bus transportation	$ 36,300		
School lunches	51,700	88,000	
Attendance and health service		14,000	
Administration		46,000	
Operation and maintenance of plant		208,000	
Pensions, insurance, etc.		154,000	
Total current operating expenditures			$2,023,600
Other expenditures:			
Capital outlays from revenues		$ 75,000	
Debt service (annual installment and interest on long-term debt)		150,000	
Total other expenditures			225,000
Total budgeted expenditures			$2,248,600

The following data are available:

(a) The estimated average daily school enrollment of the school district is 5,000 pupils, including 200 pupils enrolled in a vocational training program.

(b) Estimated revenues include equalizing grants-in-aid from the state of $150 per pupil. The grants were established by state law under a plan intended to encourage raising the level of education.

(c) The federal government matches 60% of state grants-in-aid for pupils enrolled in a vocational training program. In addition the federal government contributes towards the cost of bus transportation and school lunches a maximum of $12 per pupil based on total enrollment within the school district but not to exceed 6⅔% of the state per-pupil equalization grants-in-aid.

(d) Interest on temporary investment of school tax receipts and rents of school facilities are expected to be $75,000 and are earmarked for special equipment acquisitions listed as "Capital outlays from revenues" in the budgeted expenditures. Cost of the special equipment acquisitions will be limited to the amount derived from these miscellaneous receipts.

(e) The remaining funds needed to finance the budgeted expenditures of the school district are to be raised from local taxation. An allowance of 9% of the local tax levy is necessary for possible tax abatements and losses. The assessed valuation of the property located within the school district is $80,000,000.

Instructions: (1) Prepare a schedule computing the estimated total funds to be obtained from local taxation for the ensuing school year ending June 30, 1968, for the Valerie School District.

(2) Prepare a schedule computing the estimated current operating cost per regular pupil and per vocational pupil to be met by local tax funds. Assume that costs other than instructional costs are assignable on a per capita basis to regular and vocational students.

(3) Without prejudice to your solution to part (1), assume that the estimated total tax levy for the ensuing school year ending June 30, 1968, is $1,092,000. Prepare a schedule computing the estimated tax rate per $100 of assessed valuation of the property within the Valerie School District.

(AICPA adapted)

24-8. The city hall bond fund was established on July 1, 1966, to account for the construction of a new city hall financed by the sale of bonds. The building was to be constructed on a site owned by the city.

The building construction was to be financed by the issuance of 10-year $2,000,000 general obligation bonds bearing interest at 4%. Through prior arrangements, $1,000,000 of these bonds were sold on July 1, 1966. The remaining bonds are to be sold on July 1, 1967.

The only funds in which transactions pertaining to the new city hall were recorded were the city hall bond fund and the general fund. The bond fund's trial balance follows:

City of LaVerne
City Hall Bond Fund
June 30, 1967

	Debit	Credit
Cash	$ 893,000	
Appropriation Expenditures	140,500	
Encumbrances	715,500	
Accounts Payable		$ 11,000
Reserve for Encumbrances		723,000
Appropriations		1,015,000
	$1,749,000	$1,749,000

An analysis of the appropriation expenditures account follows:

	Debit
(a) A progress billing invoice from General Construction Company (with which the city contracted for the construction of the new city hall for $750,000 — other contracts will be let for heating, air conditioning, etc.) showing 10% of the work completed	$ 75,000
(b) A charge from the General Fund for work done in clearing the building site	11,000
(c) Payments to suppliers for building materials and supplies purchased	14,500
(d) Payment of interest on bonds outstanding	40,000
	$140,500

An analysis of the reserve for encumbrances account follows:

	Debit (Credit)
(a) To record contract with General Construction Company	($750,000)
(b) Purchase orders placed for materials and supplies	(55,000)
(c) Receipt of materials and supplies and payment therefor	14,500
(d) Payment of General Construction Company invoice less 10% retention	67,500
	($723,000)

An analysis of the appropriations account follows:

	Debit (Credit)
(a) Face value of bonds sold	($1,000,000)
(b) Premium realized on sale of bonds	(15,000)
	($1,015,000)

Instructions: (1) Prepare a work sheet for the city hall bond fund at June 30, 1967, showing:

(a) Preliminary trial balance.
(b) Adjustments.
(c) Adjusted trial balance.

(2) Prepare the adjusting journal entries for the following funds and groups of accounts (closing entries are not required):

(a) General fixed assets fund.
(b) General fund.
(c) General bonded debt and interest fund.

(AICPA adapted)

24-9. The following budget was proposed for 1967 for the Blue Valley School District general fund:

Unappropriated surplus, January 1, 1967	$128,000
Revenues:	
Taxes	112,000
Investment income	4,000
Total	$244,000
Expenditures:	
Operating	$120,000
County treasurer's fees	1,120
Bond interest	50,000
Unappropriated surplus, December 31, 1967	72,880
Total	$244,000

A general obligation bond issue of the school district was proposed in 1966. The proceeds are to be used for a new school. There are no other outstanding bond issues. Information about the bond issue follows:

Face: $1,000,000
Interest rate: 5%
Bonds dated: January 1, 1967
Coupons mature: January 1 and July 1 beginning July 1, 1967
Bonds mature serially at $100,000 per year starting January 1, 1969.

The school district uses a separate bank account for each fund. The general fund trial balance at December 31, 1966, follows:

	Debit	Credit
Cash	$ 28,000	
Temporary Investments — U.S. 4% Bonds, interest payable May 1 and November 1	100,000	
Unappropriated Surplus		$128,000
	$128,000	$128,000

The county treasurer will collect the taxes and charge a standard fee of 1% on all collections. The transactions for 1967 were as follows:

January 1 — The proposed budget was adopted, the general obligation bond issue was authorized, and the taxes were levied.

February 28 — Tax receipts from the county treasurer, $49,500, were deposited.

April 1 — The bond issue was sold at 101 plus accrued interest. It was directed that the premium be used for payment of interest.

April 2 — The school district disbursed $47,000 for the new school site.

April 3 — A contract for $950,000 for the new school was approved.

May 1 — Interest was received on temporary investments.

July 1 — Interest was paid on bonds.

August 31 — Tax receipts from the county treasurer, $59,400, were deposited.

November 1 — Payment was made on new school construction contract, $200,000.

December 31 — Operating expenses of $115,000 were paid during the year.

Instructions: Prepare journal entries to record the foregoing 1967 transactions in the following funds or groups of accounts (each entry should be dated the same as its related transaction as given above):

(1) General fund.
(2) Bond fund.
(3) General fixed assets.
(4) General bonded debt and interest.

(AICPA adapted)

24-10. Sunshine City entered into the following transactions during the year 1967:

(a) A bond issue was authorized by vote to provide funds for the construction of a new municipal building, which it was estimated would cost

$500,000. The bonds were to be paid in 10 equal installments from a sinking fund, payments being due March 1 of each year. Any balance of the bond fund is to be transferred directly to the sinking fund.

(b) An advance of $40,000 was received from the general fund to underwrite a deposit on the land contract of $60,000. The deposit was made.

(c) Bonds of $450,000 were sold for cash at 102. It was decided not to sell all of the bonds because the cost of the land was less than was expected.

(d) Contracts amounting to $390,000 were let to Michela and Company, the lowest bidder, for the construction of the municipal building.

(e) The temporary advance from the general fund was repaid and the balance on the land contract was paid.

(f) Based on the architect's certificate, warrants were issued for $320,000 for the work completed to date.

(g) Warrants paid in cash by the treasurer amounted to $310,000.

(h) Due to changes in the plans, the contract with Michela and Company was revised to $440,000; the remainder of the bonds were sold at 101.

(i) Before the end of the year the building had been completed and additional warrants amounting to $115,000 were issued to the contractor in final payment for the work. All warrants were paid by the treasurer.

Instructions: (1) Record the above transactions and the closing entries in bond fund T-accounts. Designate the entries in the T-accounts by the letters that identify the data.

(2) Prepare applicable fund balance sheets as of December 31, 1967, considering only the proceeds and the expenditures from bond fund transactions.

(AICPA adapted)

24-11. The Village of Hope, by referendum on November 30, 1966, was authorized to sell bonds, the proceeds of which were to be used for constructing a municipal building to provide adequate facilities for the offices and departments of the village. The cost of the building was estimated to be $90,000, and the ordinance provided for the issuance of general obligation bonds in that amount, at an interest rate of 3% per annum. Bonds were to be dated January 1, 1967, and were to become due and payable in equal annual installments on January 1 of each of the years 1969 to 1977, inclusive. Interest was to be due semiannually on January 1 and July 1, except that the first coupon was to be due on July 1, 1968. Bonds were to be payable out of the proceeds of a direct annual tax sufficient to pay the principal and interest when due.

The village advertised for bids on the bonds, and on January 15, 1967, the bids were opened and the bonds were awarded to Municipal Bond Co.

The following transactions occurred:

(a) November 30, 1966 — Bonds were authorized in accordance with the referendum.

(b) February 1, 1967 — Bonds were sold to Municipal Bond Co. and a certified check was received in the amount of $93,636, including premium and accrued interest of 3% to date of sale.

(c) February 10, 1967 — Initial architectural fees of $2,000 were paid to the firm that prepared the plans and specifications and was to have construction supervision. The fee for their services was to be 6% of the building cost.

(d) April 15, 1967 — The general contractor had bid $81,400 to construct the building. The first contractor's estimate in the amount of $30,000 was received from the architect, properly approved. The estimate was paid, less 10% retained until the building was accepted by the village.

(e) July 30, 1967 (entry as of September 1, 1967) — The appropriation ordinance of the village for the fiscal year ending August 31, 1968 was adopted. The ordinance contained provision for the retirement of the bonds due on January 1, 1969, and interest due through that date. It has been the experience of the village that the tax levy should provide an additional 3% to provide for losses and costs on collection.

(f) September 20, 1967 — The final contractor's invoice was received in the amount of $54,500, including approved extras totaling $3,100. The invoice was paid less a 10% retention. At the same time, an invoice in the amount of $2,000 was paid to the architects.

(g) December 21, 1967 — Final approval of the building was given by the architect and the board of trustees and final payments were made to the general contractor and the architect.

Instructions: Journalize the preceding transactions. Prepare entries for each of the applicable funds, and key the entries to the transaction number indicated. No entries need be considered to close out the various revenue and expenditure accounts at August 31, 1967.

(AICPA adapted)

24-12. The ledger balances of the Water Department of Valley City on December 31, 1967, were as follows:

Cash — operating fund	$ 588,800	Accounts payable — trade	$ 47,000
Cash — consumers' deposits	17,000	Accounts payable — township	56,000
Postage on meter	1,000	Water consumers' deposits	67,000
Accounts receivable:		Revenue bonds payable	300,000
Consumer billing	65,000	Accumulated depreciation	1,200,000
Service	17,000	Surplus	4,500,000
Sundry	700	Revenue	1,500,000
Due from other funds	—	Expense:	
Supplies inventory	140,000	Production	340,000
Merchandise on order and in transit	145,000	Distribution	151,000
Investments — consumers' deposits	50,000	Office	90,000
Property	6,000,000	Administrative and general	105,000
Unfilled orders and contracts	145,000	Cost of installations, repairs and parts	140,000
Warrants payable	50,100	Interest on consumers' deposits	600
Due to other funds	—	Interest on bonds	9,000
Advance service payments	—	Allowances and adjustments	5,000

NOTE: Revenue bonds mature serially $30,000 each year.

Examination of the records disclosed the following additional data:

(a) Included in error in accounts payable — trade:		
(1) For reimbursement of metered postage		$ 500
(2) Due to other city funds		18,500
(b) Items included in book inventory that were not received until 1968		2,000
(c) Computation of inventory items chargeable to distribution expense understated		1,000
(d) Classified as accounts payable trade, should be accounts payable township		10,000
(e) Unfilled orders not of record		1,000
(f) 1968 expense purchases recorded as 1967 liabilities and charged to expense as follows:		
(1) Production expense	$500	
(2) Distribution expense	500	
(3) Office expense	500	
(4) Administrative and general expense	500	
(g) Included in accounts receivable — service, but actually due from other funds		500
(h) Credit balances included in accounts receivable — service, advance service payments		1,000
(i) Included in accounts receivable sundry but due from other city funds		50
(j) Required adjustment to reduce unfilled orders and contracts to proper estimates		2,600
(k) Purchase order included in unfilled orders and contracts. This order is a duplication of a previously recorded expenditure		40,000
(l) Unrecorded receivable from township for water		5,000

Instructions: (1) Prepare working papers showing the original trial balance, the adjustments, and the extended profit and loss and balance sheet accounts for the Water Department of Valley City for the year ended December 31, 1967.

(2) Prepare a balance sheet as of December 31, 1967.

(3) Prepare an operating statement for the year ended December 31, 1967.

(AICPA adapted)

24-13. The following information pertains to the operation of the water fund of the City of S. Included in the operations of this fund are those of a special replacement fund for the Water Department, the accounts of which are a part of the accounts of the water fund.

The balances in the accounts of this fund on January 1, 1967, were:

Cash	$ 6,126
Accounts receivable	7,645
Stores	13,826
Investments of replacement fund	21,700
Permanent property	212,604
Accounts payable	4,324
Customers' deposits	1,500
Replacement fund reserve	21,700
Operating surplus	21,773
Bonds payable	60,000
Capital surplus	152,604

The following items represent the total transactions of the fund for the year ended December 31, 1967.

(a) Services billed	$146,867
(b) Accounts collected	147,842
(c) Uncollectible accounts of prior years written off	1,097
(d) Invoices and payrolls approved for current expense	69,826
(e) Invoices approved for purchase of water department stores	31,424
(f) Stores issued for use in operation	32,615
(g) Supplies secured from general fund stores and used in operation (cash transferred to general fund)	7,197
(h) Vouchers approved for payment of bonds and interest of $3,000	23,000
(i) Depreciation entered as charge against current income and credited to replacement reserve	10,600
(j) Deposits received	400
Deposits refunded	240
(k) Invoices approved for replacements of equipment that cost $6,200	7,800
(l) Invoices approved for additions to plant	12,460
(m) Vouchers approved for purchase of securities necessary to fully invest the replacement fund	compute
(n) Income received on investments	1,102
(o) Warrants drawn for invoices, payrolls and vouchers approved	147,316

Instructions: Prepare from the above information (1) a balance sheet of the fund as of December 31, 1967, (2) an operating statement of the water department for 1967, and (3) an analysis of the operating surplus of the department for 1967.

(AICPA adapted)

24-14. The City of Fairview, organized on January 1, 1953, has never kept accounts on a double-entry system. During 1967 the city council employed you to install a system of accounts. You made a study and determined the values of assets and liabilities in order to inaugurate the proper system as of January 1, 1968, the beginning of the city's fiscal year, as follows:

(a) City taxes receivable — 1967 and prior years (including 10% considered uncollectible)	$ 21,900
(b) Investment in securities:	
(1) Earmarked to bond retirement	136,680
(2) Donated by J. C. Belmont on July 1, 1967, the net income from which is to supplement library operations. The cost of all the stock to Belmont was $50,000. Appraised value on July 1	65,400
(c) Cash:	
(1) For general operations, including $3,000 in petty cash	18,000

(2) Earmarked to investments for bond retirement (represents interest earned over the actuarial estimate)	840
(3) Balance of cash donated by J. C. Belmont, the net income from which is to supplement library operations	12,000
(4) Undistributed balance of cash received from J. C. Belmont investments and apartment rents	3,000
(d) Buildings:	
(1) For general operations	235,000
(2) Apartment building donated by J. C. Belmont on July 1, 1967. Net income to be used in the operation of the library. Cost of completion to Belmont, July 1, 1957, $96,000 (exclusive of cost of land) with estimated life of 50 years, no salvage. Appraised value on July 1, 1967	90,000
(e) Equipment:	
(1) For general use	280,000
(2) Apartment furniture purchased with donated cash, October 1, 1967, estimated life 10 years, no salvage. Cost	36,000
(f) Streets and curbs built by special assessment funds in prior years. (All collected.) The city contributed ⅓ of the cost	300,000
(g) Land:	
(1) For general use	60,000
(2) For apartment building site	10,000
(h) Supplies:	
(1) For general operation	1,800
(2) For apartment house operation, purchased by income cash	300
(3) Originally purchased for general operation were transferred to and used in library operations; no settlement has been made	2,400
(i) Vouchers payable — for general operations	16,000
(j) 3%, 30-year bonds payable, due on December 31, 1985. (Issued for purchase of land, buildings and equipment.)	400,000

Instructions: List the funds or group titles that would be required for the city on the basis of the above information, leaving at least 15 lines between each title. Under each title make one summary journal entry that will record all of the required accounts and amounts in the appropriate fund.

(AICPA adapted)

24-15. The balance sheet for the Town of Z was prepared on June 30, 1967, in the form shown at the top of the following page.

During the first month of its fiscal year starting July 1, 1967, the following events took place relative to the general fund:

(a) A budget was adopted that provided for property taxes of $210,000 for general municipal purposes and for estimated revenue from fees, etc., of

Town of Z
Balance Sheet
June 30, 1967

Assets		
Current:		
Cash	$ 50,000	
Taxes receivable (including special assessments $80,000)	100,000	
Supply inventories	10,000	
Investments of trust funds	30,000	$ 190,000
Fixed:		
Land	$100,000	
Buildings	800,000	
Equipment	50,000	950,000
		$1,140,000
Liabilities		
Current:		
Accounts payable		$ 10,000
Fixed:		
General obligations bonds payable	$350,000	
Special assessment bonds payable	75,000	425,000
Fund equities:		
General fund	$ 35,000	
Trust funds	40,000	
Bond fund	25,000	
Special assessment fund	5,000	
Capital fund	600,000	705,000
		$1,140,000

$23,000. Appropriations were $180,000 for current operations, $20,000 for debt service, and $35,000 for street and other capital improvements.

(b) During July purchase orders of $9,400 were placed, $3,150 of which were received and vouchered at an actual net cost of $3,078. Payroll amounting to $5,185 was vouchered, and $14,000 of accounts payable were paid.

(c) The tax roll was not completed; but $21,000 of 1966–67 taxes were collected, $18,350 of which were special assessments. Also, $466 of delinquent taxes and penalties were collected. These taxes had been written off and no amount was in the current budget for such collections. Miscellaneous fees, etc., collected amounted to $2,060.

(d) Inventory of supplies at the end of the month was $10,400.

Instructions: (1) Rearrange the balance sheet as of June 30, 1967, in acceptable form.

(2) Prepare a balance sheet for the general fund at the end of the first month of the new fiscal year, July 31, 1967.

(AICPA adapted)

Chapter 25

NONPROFIT SERVICE ORGANIZATIONS

Our society is made up of a large number of privately organized nonprofit service organizations that possess many of the characteristics of the governmental unit. These organizations include schools and colleges, hospitals, churches, charities, and social service groups. Services of these units may be offered only to closed membership groups or they may be offered to the general public.

Privately organized service organizations differ widely as to size, nature, and diversity of operations. They may also differ in the means that they employ to finance their activities. Contributions are generally an important part of the financing program, but the nature of the contributions and the use of such resources also differ.

Service organizations require books and records to summarize receipts and expenditures as well as assets, liabilities, and equities. Systems for achieving accounting and administrative control are required. Budgets that provide for direction and control of proposed activities and financial statements that summarize past activities are indispensable parts of an accounting program.

Although privately organized service organizations are not subject to the rigid legal controls that are found in the governmental unit, nevertheless they are subject to special conditions that suggest an accounting similar to that employed by the governmental unit. Service organizations ordinarily engage in a core of general activities that are accompanied by a number of auxiliary activities. Gifts and grants from both private and public channels in the form of cash and other properties are frequently accompanied by detailed requirements on exactly how such resources are to be spent or utilized. Instead of emphasis upon operating at a profit, emphasis centers upon the resources that are available and the proper and efficient use of such resources in meeting the service objectives for which the units were organized. These factors call for the use of fund accounting.

The discussion in this chapter will focus upon accounting for two types of service organizations in which fund accounting finds extensive use: (1) the privately organized educational institution — school, college, or university; and (2) the privately organized hospital. Educational institutions and hospitals have received particularly extensive study, and systems of accounting for such units, recommended by certain authoritative groups, have been widely adopted. These systems should not be regarded as limited to educational and hospital units but should be viewed as frameworks within which the needs of the wide variety of privately organized nonprofit service organizations can be met.

THE EDUCATIONAL INSTITUTION

The activities of an educational institution may be classified as (1) instructional, (2) administrative, and (3) auxiliary. Instructional activities include both resident and extension instruction, public services, organized research, and the operation of libraries. Administrative activities include staffing and promotion, registration and enrollment, operation of the business office, and operation and maintainance of the educational plant. Auxiliary activities include the operation of residence halls, dining rooms, college unions and bookstores, health centers, and athletic and cultural programs. Revenues in support of these different activities are provided by such varied sources as contributions, governmental appropriations, student fees, endowment income, and revenues from the sale of goods and services.

Funds for the educational institution. Recommendations of the American Council on Education on the application of fund accounting to educational institutions have won wide acceptance, and the discussion that follows is based largely on such recommendations.[1] The Council, in viewing the special accounting problems of the educational institution, recognizes a need for six major fund groupings:

(1) Current funds, divided into (a) a general fund and (b) restricted funds.
(2) Loan funds.
(3) Endowment and other nonexpendable funds.
(4) Annuity funds.
(5) Plant funds, divided into (a) unexpended plant funds, (b) retirement of indebtedness funds, and (c) an invested in plant section.
(6) Agency funds.

Each fund group or subdivision thereof calls for a separate set of self-balancing accounts and the recognition of related asset, liability, and fund balances. When a number of different revenues and expenditures affect a fund balance, nominal accounts are established to summarize them, and the nominal accounts are closed at the end of each period; when relatively few transactions affect a fund balance, they may be recorded directly in the fund balance. At the end of each period, finan-

[1]*College and University Business Administration* (Washington, D.C.: American Council on Education, National Committee on the Preparation of a Manual on College and University Business Administration); Vol. I, 1952; Vol. II, 1955.

cial statements are prepared to summarize the operations and to report on the financial position of each of the funds or fund groups maintained.

Before considering the activities of the educational institution and how these activities are recorded, it is necessary to discuss certain special practices that are found in accounting for the educational unit.

The accrual basis. A "modified accrual basis" is generally employed in summarizing the operations of the educational unit. Such a basis is described by the American Council on Education as follows:

> In general, the accounts of colleges and universities should be kept on the accrual basis. This means that bills for materials received or for services rendered, whether or not paid, should be reported to the fullest extent practicable. Income should be reported when it becomes due or when a bill has been rendered for it, and appropriate allowances should be made for probable losses. Since the primary purpose of accounting in educational institutions is to report on the stewardship of the funds and property entrusted to the institution rather than to determine net profits and net worth, some items of income need not be accrued and certain expenditures need not be prorated. For example, few institutions find it either necessary or desirable to report accrued interest receivable, or to allocate insurance premiums to subsequent periods. Consequently, it may be said that the accounts of educational institutions generally are maintained on a modified accrual basis.

Depreciation. Charges for depreciation are rarely recognized on properties that are used for the educational function. The educational institution normally relies on gifts and grants for original plant financing as well as for plant renewals and replacements. In the absence of a net income objective and in the absence of a need to accumulate funds for property replacement, the omission of charges for depreciation can be defended. Charges for depreciation are appropriate, however, under the following circumstances:

(1) When certain properties of the educational plant render a service function and the institution plans to replace such properties from operating revenue.
(2) When properties are identified with auxiliary enterprises that are expected to be self-supporting — bookstores, cafeterias, and dormitories, for example.
(3) When properties are transferred to the educational unit under terms of an endowment that limit expenditures from endowment resources for general or specific purposes to periodic net income after recognition of appropriate charges for depreciation.

Descriptions and examples of the accounting for the different funds of an educational institution are given in the sections that follow.

Current funds. Current funds are composed of current resources that are to be employed in meeting obligations arising from the general operations of the educational institution. The educational unit establishes the following funds within this grouping: (1) a *general current fund* that consists of the resources that can be applied to current purposes without restriction, and (2) *restricted current funds* consisting of resources that, while available for current purposes, are subject to certain limitations in their application. Student fees and resources from gifts or from income of endowment funds that carry no specific limitations as to use, then, are reported in the general current fund. On the other hand, resources from gifts or grants and from the income of endowment funds that can be spent only for specified purposes, such as for a library, for scholarships, for an athletic program, or for research, would be reported in restricted current funds.

Operations of the educational institution normally include the establishment of a number of auxiliary enterprises that offer services to students and staff on a self-supporting basis. Activities of such auxiliary enterprises are generally reported in the general current fund. It would be possible, however, to establish a third subgrouping within the current funds category for *revolving funds* or *working capital funds* and thus provide a separate accounting for auxiliary units.

To illustrate the accounting for current funds, transactions affecting the current funds of Cal University and the entries to record these transactions are listed on pages 902–905. An explanation of the entries follows.

Explanation of general current fund entries. The general current fund books report the resources that can be used for general current needs, the liabilities that apply against such resources, and the fund balance. During the period, changes in these assets and liabilities and related revenues and expenditures arising from operations are recorded. At the end of the period, revenue and expenditure balances are closed and the change in net assets is carried to the general current fund balance. The general current fund recognizes neither long-term assets nor long-term liabilities; receipts and expenditures relating to these items are recorded directly in the fund balance. The accounting for the general current fund is closely comparable to the accounting for the general fund of the governmental unit.

The American Council on Education, in considering financial reports for educational institutions, recommends three principal classifications for revenues and expenditures: (1) educational and general, (2) auxiliary enterprises, and (3) student aid. The Council recommends the following subclassifications for educational and general revenues: (a) student fees, (b) governmental appropriations, (c) endowment income, (d) gifts and grants, (e) sales and services — educational departments, (f) income from organized activities relating to educational departments, and (g) income from other sources. Subclassifications for expenditures are recommended in terms of educational function as follows: (a) general administration, (b) general expense, (c) instruction and departmental research, (d) organized activities relating to educational departments, (e) organized research, (f) extension and public services, (g) libraries, and (h) operation and maintenance of the physical plant. Accounts for Cal University have been established in accordance with these classifications.

Current Funds — General Current Fund Books

Transaction	Entry		
(1) Educational and general revenue for the year ended June 30, 1967, $3,000,000, of which $150,000 has not yet been collected.	Cash	2,850,000	
	Accounts Receivable	150,000	
	Student Fees		1,620,000
	Governmental Appropriations		920,000
	Endowment Income		60,000
	Gifts and Grants		300,000
	Sales and Services — Educational Departments		25,000
	Income from Organized Activities Relating to Educational Departments.		40,000
	Income from Other Sources		35,000
(2) Revenue related to auxiliary enterprise — bookstore, $262,500, of which $25,000 has not yet been collected.	Cash	237,500	
	Accounts Receivable	25,000	
	Revenue — Auxiliary Enterprise		262,500
(3) Revenue for student aid, $400,000, all of which was collected.	Cash	400,000	
	Revenue for Student Aid		400,000
(4) Educational and general expenditures (salaries and supplies), $2,750,000, of which $180,000 has not yet been paid.	General Administration	190,000	
	General Expense	60,000	
	Instruction and Departmental Research.	1,230,000	
	Organized Activities Relating to Educational Departments	35,000	
	Organized Research	415,000	
	Extension and Public Services	160,000	
	Libraries	360,000	
	Operation and Maintenance of Physical Plant	300,000	
	Cash		2,570,000
	Vouchers Payable		180,000
(5) Expenditures related to auxiliary enterprise — bookstore (materials and supplies, salaries, and other expenses), $300,000, of which $55,000 has not yet been paid.	Expenses — Auxiliary Enterprise	300,000	
	Cash		245,000
	Vouchers Payable		55,000

Transaction	Entry		
(6) Payments representing student aid, $415,000.	Student Aid Cash	415,000	 415,000
(7) Payments of interest on current and long-term indebtedness, $100,000, and payment of installment due on mortgage carried as a liability in invested in plant section, $25,000.	General Expense Unappropriated Surplus Cash	100,000 25,000	 125,000
(8) Acquisition of equipment to be carried as an asset in invested in plant section, $15,000.	Unappropriated Surplus Cash TRANSFERS TO OTHER ACCTS.	15,000	 15,000
(9) Transfer to unexpended plant funds of cash to be used for plant renewals and replacements, $30,000.	Unappropriated Surplus Cash	30,000	 30,000
(10) Transfer to endowment fund of cash to be employed as an endowment until alternative use is authorized by the board of directors, $50,000.	Unappropriated Surplus Cash	50,000	 50,000
(11) Adjustments required on June 30, 1967:			
(a) Earnings of $2,500 reported by annuity fund that are to become available in the next period for educational and general purposes.	Due from Annuity Fund Deferred Income from Annuity Fund	2,500	 2,500

(b) Adjustments related to auxiliary enterprise — bookstore:
Inventory of materials and supplies $50,000
Prepaid expenses 2,500
Accrued expenses 5,000
	Inventory of Materials and Supplies
	Prepaid Expenses
	  Accrued Expenses
	  Expenses — Auxiliary Enterprise
		50,000
		2,500
			
			5,000
			47,500

(c) Adjustments related to educational and general activities: Allowance for uncollectible accounts $ 5,000	General Expense Allowance for Uncollectible Accounts	5,000	 5,000

Transaction	Entry		
(12) To close educational and general revenue and expenditure accounts at the end of the fiscal period.	Student Fees	1,620,000	
	Governmental Appropriations	920,000	
	Endowment Income	60,000	
	Gifts and Grants	300,000	
	Sales and Services — Educational Departments	25,000	
	Income from Organized Activities Relating to Educational Departments	40,000	
	Income from Other Sources	35,000	
	General Administration		190,000
	General Expense		165,000
	Instruction and Departmental Research		1,230,000
	Organized Activities Relating to Educational Departments		35,000
	Organized Research		415,000
	Extension and Public Services		160,000
	Libraries		360,000
	Operation and Maintenance of Physical Plant		300,000
	Unappropriated Surplus		145,000
(13) To close auxiliary enterprise revenue and expense accounts at the end of the fiscal period.	Revenue — Auxiliary Enterprise	262,500	
	Expenses — Auxiliary Enterprise		252,500
	Unappropriated Surplus		10,000
(14) To close student aid revenue and expenditure accounts at the end of the fiscal period.	Revenue for Student Aid	400,000	
	Unappropriated Surplus	15,000	
	Student Aid		415,000

Current Funds — Restricted Current Funds Books

Transaction	Entry		
(1) Revenues for the year ended June 30, 1967, $182,500, of which $15,000 applies to expenditures of the next fiscal period.	Cash	182,500	
	Deferred Income		15,000
	Endowment Income		50,000
	Gifts and Grants		37,500
	Revenues — Auxiliary Enterprise		80,000
(2) Expenditures, $140,000, of which $7,500 has not yet been paid.	General Administration	10,000	
	Instruction and Departmental Research	35,000	
	Extension and Public Services	5,000	
	Libraries	32,500	
	Expenses — Auxiliary Enterprise	57,500	
	Cash		132,500
	Vouchers Payable		7,500

Transaction	Entry		
(3) Investment of cash in securities, $30,000.	Temporary Investments	30,000	
	Cash		30,000
(4) Required transfer to endowment fund of $10,000 representing charge for depreciation on endowment properties (dormitory) employed in producing auxiliary income.	Expenses — Auxiliary Enterprise	10,000	
	Due to Endowment Fund D		10,000
(5) To close educational and general revenue and expenditure accounts at the end of the fiscal period.	Endowment Income	50,000	
	Gifts and Grants	37,500	
	General Administration		10,000
	Instruction and Departmental Research		35,000
	Extension and Public Services		5,000
	Libraries		32,500
	Restricted Current Funds Balance		5,000
(6) To close auxiliary enterprise revenue and expense accounts at the end of the fiscal period.	Revenues — Auxiliary Enterprise	80,000	
	Expenses — Auxiliary Enterprise		67,500
	Restricted Current Funds Balance		12,500

Cal University
Current Funds
Balance Sheet
June 30, 1967

Assets				Liabilities, Reserves, and Balances		
General fund:				General fund:		
Cash		$ 37,500		Vouchers payable	$235,000	
Due from annuity fund		2,500		Accrued expenses	5,000	
Accounts receivable . .	$175,000			Deferred income from annuity fund	2,500	
Less allowance for uncollectible accounts . . .	5,000	170,000		Total liabilities	$242,500	
Inventories of materials and supplies . . .		50,000		Unappropriated surplus	20,000	
Prepaid expenses		2,500		Total		$262,500
Total			$262,500			
Restricted funds:				Restricted funds:		
Cash		$ 20,000		Vouchers payable	$ 7,500	
Temporary investments		30,000		Due to Endowment Fund D	10,000	
				Deferred income	15,000	
				Total liabilities	$ 32,500	
				Restricted current funds balance	17,500	
Total			50,000	Total		50,000
Total assets			$312,500	Total liabilities, reserves, and balances		$312,500

Cal University
Current Funds
Summary of Current Income and Expenditures
For Year Ended June 30, 1967

	Total	General Current Fund	Restricted Current Funds
Current income:			
Educational and general			
Student fees	$1,620,000	$1,620,000	
Governmental appropriations	920,000	920,000	
Endowment income	110,000	60,000	$ 50,000
Gifts and grants	337,500	300,000	37,500
Sales and services—educational departments	25,000	25,000	
Income from organized activities relating to educational departments	40,000	40,000	
Income from other sources	35,000	35,000	
Total educational and general income	$3,087,500	$3,000,000	$ 87,500
Auxiliary enterprises			
Bookstore	$ 262,500	$ 262,500	
Dormitory	80,000		$ 80,000
Total auxiliary enterprise income	$ 342,500	$ 262,500	$ 80,000
Student aid	$ 400,000	$ 400,000	
Total current income	$3,830,000	$3,662,500	$167,500
Current expenditures:			
Educational and general			
General administration	$ 200,000	$ 190,000	$ 10,000
General expense	165,000	165,000	
Instruction and departmental research	1,265,000	1,230,000	35,000
Organized activities relating to educational departments	35,000	35,000	
Organized research	415,000	415,000	
Extension and public services	165,000	160,000	5,000
Libraries	392,500	360,000	32,500
Operation and maintenance of physical plant	300,000	300,000	
Total educational and general expenditures	$2,937,500	$2,855,000	$ 82,500
Auxiliary enterprises			
Bookstore	$ 252,500	$ 252,500	
Dormitory	67,500		$ 67,500
Total auxiliary expenditures	$ 320,000	$ 252,500	$ 67,500
Student Aid	$ 415,000	$ 415,000	
Total current expenditures	$3,672,500	$3,522,500	$150,000
Excess of current income over current expenditures	$ 157,500	$ 140,000	$ 17,500

Cal University
Current Funds
Summary of Changes in Fund Balances
For Year Ended June 30, 1967

	Total	Current Fund Balance (Unappropriated Surplus)	Restricted Current Funds Balance
Fund balances, July 1, 1966	—	—	—
Add:			
Increase for year ended June 30, 1967, per summary of current income and expenditures	$157,500	$140,000	$17,500
Total	$157,500	$140,000	$17,500
Deduct:			
Payment on mortgage note reported in invested in plant section	$ 25,000	$ 25,000	
Acquisition of equipment reported in invested in plant section	15,000	15,000	
Transfer to unexpended plant funds	30,000	30,000	
Transfer to endowment fund	50,000	50,000	
Total deductions	$120,000	$120,000	
Fund balances, June 30, 1967	$ 37,500	$ 20,000	$17,500

Special attention is directed to entries (7), (8), (9), and (10) on page 903. Payment of an obligation that is carried by the plant funds is reported by a charge to Unappropriated Surplus and a credit to Cash (entry 7). Similar entries are made for the purchase of equipment that is to be carried in the plant funds (entry 8), the transfer of cash to the plant funds to finance subsequent plant renewals and replacements (entry 9), and the transfer of cash to establish an endowment fund (entry 10). These expenditures should not be considered in summarizing and evaluating the results of educational and general operations.[1]

Explanation of restricted current funds entries. The restricted current funds books report resources that are to be used for certain designated purposes, the liabilities that are to be paid from these resources, and a funds balance. During the period, changes in assets and liabilities and related revenues and expenditures arising from operations are recorded. The restricted current funds, like the general current fund, recognize neither long-term assets nor long-term liabilities; receipts and expenditures relating to these items are recorded directly in the funds balance.

[1]It may be noted that some authorities would distinguish between acquisitions of equipment for new buildings and acquisitions of equipment other than for new buildings. They would charge acquisitions of equipment for new buildings against fund surplus, but would recognize all other acquisitions of equipment as current fund expenditures and would report these in the summary of operations within appropriate functional classifications.

The relationship of the restricted current funds and the general current fund may be compared to that of the special funds and the general fund of the governmental unit.

Special attention should be directed to entry (4) on page 905. In the example, the net earnings of a dormitory become available for certain designated current purposes and hence revenues and expenditures of this enterprise are reported in the restricted current funds. It is assumed, however, that terms of the dormitory grant call for a periodic charge against revenue for depreciation and a transfer of cash to the endowment fund equal to the depreciation charge. The depreciation is recognized by a charge to expense and a credit to a liability account; subsequent payment to the endowment fund will call for a charge to the liability account and a credit to Cash.

Statements. Statements for the current funds to report financial position, revenues and expenditures, and changes in the funds balances are prepared periodically. Statements for Cal University offering separate data for the general current fund and restricted current funds as well as combined data are given on pages 905–907.

Loan funds. Loan funds consist of resources that are available for loans to students. Loan funds may originate from gifts, or they may be built up over a period of years from student fees collected for such purpose or from cash transfers from an endowment fund whose income is available for such purpose. Loans may be made with or without interest depending upon the conditions established by those providing the loan fund. Loan funds are regarded as nonexpendable funds. However, loan fund balances will change as a result of charges arising from uncollectible loans, fund administrative expenses, and losses on the sale of fund investments, and as a result of credits arising from interest on loans, income from fund investments, and gains on the sale of fund investments.

Transactions related to the loan fund of Cal University and the entries to record these transactions are listed on page 909. An explanation of the entries follows.

Explanation of loan fund entries. Loan fund resources are balanced by the account Loan Fund Balance. During the period, entries are made to record the operations of the fund. Nominal accounts may be established to summarize the separate sources of fund increases and decreases for the period; when fund changes are few in number, changes are recorded directly in the loan fund balance. This was done in the example.

Statements. Statements to report the financial position of the loan fund and the changes in the loan fund balances are prepared periodically. Statements for Cal University are given on page 909.

Loan Fund Books

Transaction	Entry		
(1) Receipt of cash gift to be used for loans to students, $50,000.	Cash. Loan Fund Balance.	50,000	 50,000
(2) Purchase of securities for $25,600, which includes accrued interest of $600.	Investments. Accrued Interest. Cash.	25,000 600	 25,600
(3) Loans to students, $20,000.	Notes Receivable. Cash.	20,000	 20,000
(4) Collections of interest on investments, $1,500.	Cash. Accrued Interest. Loan Fund Balance.	1,500	 600 900
(5) Collections on loans, $7,650, which includes interest of $150.	Cash. Notes Receivable. Loan Fund Balance.	7,650	 7,500 150
(6) Uncollectible loans written off, $300.	Loan Fund Balance. Notes Receivable.	300	 300

Cal University
Loan Fund
Balance Sheet
June 30, 1967

Assets		Liabilities, Reserves, and Balances	
Cash.	$13,550	Loan fund balance.	$50,750
Investments.	25,000		
Notes receivable.	12,200		
Total assets.	$50,750	Total liabilities, reserves, and balances.	$50,750

Cal University
Loan Fund
Summary of Changes in Loan Fund Balance
For Year Ended June 30, 1967

Loan fund balance, July 1, 1966.		—
Add: Increase from gift.	$50,000	
Interest on investments.	900	
Interest on loans.	150	$51,050
Deduct uncollectible loans written off.		300
Loan fund balance, June 30, 1967.		$50,750

Endowment and other nonexpendable funds. An endowment fund is formed when cash or other properties are transferred to the institution under conditions that provide that only the income produced by such resources can be used for the benefit of the institution. Fund principal, then, is unexpendable; although fund principal may change as a result of the sale of fund assets at a gain or a loss, it cannot be impaired by income distributions. When no restrictions are placed on the use of the fund income by the institution, the endowment is referred to as an *unrestricted endowment*. When the use of the fund income is limited to certain objectives, the endowment is called a *restricted endowment*. Income from an unrestricted endowment becomes available to the general current fund; income from a restricted endowment is transferred to the appropriate restricted current fund or to the plant fund.

Endowments are generally created by transfers of assets directly to the institution. The governing body of the institution then takes steps to carry out the terms of the endowment. In some instances, assets are transferred to a trustee who assumes the responsibility for administering the endowment. Here, the trustee transfers endowment income to the institution for use in accordance with the terms of the endowment. In other instances, resources not currently required by a general current fund may be transferred out of this fund to be administered as an endowment until the resources are required for alternative use. These resources are referred to as *funds temporarily functioning as an endowment*. Authority for the establishment of the latter funds, the use of income from such funds, and the ultimate disposition of such funds rests with the governing body of the institution.

The proper management of an endowment fund calls for measuring income accurately so that income distributions do not impair fund principal. Terms of the endowment may define certain practices for calculating distributable income. When specific provisions for distinguishing between principal and income are not included in the endowment instrument, reference is made to the law. Principal and income distinctions are the same as those that were recognized in the discussion of trusts in Chapter 22.

In maintaining a single set of books for the endowment fund group, investments and other property items should be identified with specific endowments, and separate endowment fund balances should be reported for each endowment. Earnings of the different endowments do not need to be reflected on the books for the endowment funds but may be entered directly on the books of the funds receiving the earnings.

An institution may arrange for pooling the resources of some or all of its endowments when such action is not prohibited by terms of the individual endowments. Pooling frequently makes possible more attractive investment opportunities. It also reduces the amount of detailed record keeping. Furthermore, arrangements may be made for assuring regularity in periodic income distributions by adopting conservative distribution rates that permit an accumulation of income for distribution in periods of below-normal investment return. Under the latter circumstances, both investment income and distributions of income would be reported in the endowment fund books and any undistributed earnings balance would be carried forward.

Transactions related to the endowment funds of Cal University and the entries to record these transactions appear on pages 912 and 913. An explanation of the entries follows.

Explanation of endowment and other nonexpendable fund entries. The receipt of endowment fund resources is recorded by charges to appropriate asset accounts and credits to properly identified endowment fund balances. In the example, resources from Endowment Funds A, B, and C are pooled. Securities and endowment fund balances are restated in terms of the values of the respective contributions on the date of the pooling (see entry 3).

Revenues of $107,500 are related to pooled investments (see entry 5), but these revenues are reduced by bond premium amortization of $2,500 to assure that endowment principal balances remain unimpaired (see entry 6). It is assumed in the example that the total revenue from pooled investments is distributed, and consequently distribution is made in proportion to the respective fund contributions (see entry 7). With endowment fund principal balances of $2,000,000 and income available for distribution of $105,000, the return on principal balances is 5¼%. An agreement to distribute earnings at a lesser rate, say 4½%, would have resulted in a distribution limited to $90,000 and would have left a balance of $15,000 to be carried forward as undistributed pooled income.

A sale of pooled securities is made during the year at a gain of $10,000 (see entry 8). The gain is reported separately in an account titled Reserve for Realized Gains and Losses on Pooled Investments. Gains and losses in subsequent periods can also be carried to this account. Ultimately, any balance in this account will be transferred to the individual endowment fund balances in proportion to the respective fund interests in the pooling.

Endowment Funds D, E, and F are examples of funds carried separately. Fund D arises from a gift of land and buildings whose net income is to be used for certain restricted purposes. Properties forming the endowment are recorded in the endowment fund (see entry 9). Revenues

Endowment Funds Books

Transaction	Entry		
(1) Receipt of cash from donor in establishment of Endowment Fund A, $1,000,000. No restrictions are made as to use of endowment income.	Cash Endowment Fund A Balance	1,000,000	 1,000,000
(2) Receipt of securities from two donors in establishment of Endowment Funds B and C: Endowment Fund B — 10,000 shares of X Co. common stock, value on date of transfer $715,000. Endowment Fund C — 2,500 shares of Y Co. preferred stock, value on date of transfer $245,000. No restrictions are made as to use of endowment income.	Investments — Common Stock Investments — Preferred Stock Endowment Fund B Balance Endowment Fund C Balance	715,000 245,000	 715,000 245,000
(3) Pooling of Endowment Funds A, B, and C. Endowment fund balances were restated in terms of market values of securities as of date of pooling as follows: Common shares market value, $750,000. Preferred shares market value, $250,000.	Pooled Cash Pooled Investments — Common Stock Pooled Investments — Preferred Stock Cash Investments — Common Stock Investments — Preferred Stock Endowment Fund B Balance Endowment Fund C Balance	1,000,000 750,000 250,000	 1,000,000 715,000 245,000 35,000 5,000
(4) Purchase of $900,000 of Z Co. bonds at a price of 105.	Pooled Investments — Bonds Pooled Investments — Unamortized Bond Premium Pooled Cash	900,000 45,000	 945,000
(5) Collection of interest and dividends on pooled investments, $107,500.	Pooled Cash Undistributed Pooled Income	107,500	 107,500
(6) Premium amortization on pooled investments, $2,500.	Undistributed Pooled Income Pooled Investments — Unamortized Bond Premium	2,500	 2,500

Transaction	Entry		
(7) Distribution of income on pooled endowments to general current and restricted current funds: Endowment Fund A: 1,000,000/2,000,000 x $105,000, or $52,500. Endowment Fund B: 750,000/2,000,000 x $105,000, or $39,375. Endowment Fund C: 250,000/2,000,000 x $105,000, or $13,125.	Undistributed Pooled Income .... Pooled Cash	105,000	 105,000
(8) Sale of Y Co. preferred shares for $260,000.	Pooled Cash .... Pooled Investments — Preferred Stock Reserve for Realized Gains and Losses on Pooled Investments	260,000	 250,000 10,000
(9) Receipt of gift of properties to be used as a dormitory. Net income after recognizing an annual charge for depreciation of $10,000 is to be used for certain restricted purposes. Appraised values of properties on date of gift: Land $125,000 Buildings 175,000	Land .... Buildings.......................... Endowment Fund D Balance........	125,000 175,000	 300,000
(10) Receipt of cash from general current fund to be used as an endowment fund until alternative use is authorized, $50,000.	Cash.............................. Principal Temporarily Functioning as Endowment Fund E Balance........	50,000	 50,000
(11) To recognize resources of $400,000 held by trustee as an endowment. No restrictions are made as to use of endowment income.	Fund Held by Trustee .... Endowment Fund F Balance........	400,000	 400,000
(12) Amount receivable from restricted current fund representing recovery of depreciation on endowment properties (dormitory), $10,000.	Due from Restricted Current Fund..... Allowance for Depreciation of Buildings	10,000	 10,000

Cal University
Endowment and Other Nonexpendable Funds
Balance Sheet
June 30, 1967

Assets		
Cash		$ 50,000
Due from restricted current fund		10,000
Pooled cash		317,500
Pooled investments:		
Common stock	$750,000	
Bonds	900,000	
Unamortized bond premium	42,500	1,692,500
Land		125,000
Buildings	$175,000	
Less allowance for depreciation	10,000	165,000
Fund held by trustee		400,000
Total assets		$2,760,000

Liabilities, Reserves, and Balances		
Reserve for realized gains and losses on pooled investments		$ 10,000
Fund balances:		
Unrestricted —		
Endowment Fund A	$1,000,000	
Endowment Fund B	750,000	
Endowment Fund C	250,000	
Endowment Fund F	400,000	
	$2,400,000	
Restricted —		
Endowment Fund D	300,000	
Principal temporarily functioning as Endowment Fund E	50,000	2,750,000
Total liabilities, reserves, and balances		$2,760,000

Cal University
Endowment and Other Nonexpendable Funds
Summary of Changes in Fund Balances
For Year Ended June 30, 1967

	Total	Fund A	Fund B	Fund C	Fund D	Fund E	Fund F
Fund balances, July 1, 1966	—	—	—	—	—	—	—
Increases for year:							
Gifts or transfers establishing funds	$2,710,000	$1,000,000	$715,000	$245,000	$300,000	$50,000	$400,000
Restatement of investments of Endowment Funds A, B, and C upon pooling of resources	40,000		35,000	5,000			
Fund balances, June 30, 1967	$2,750,000	$1,000,000	$750,000	$250,000	$300,000	$50,000	$400,000

and expenses relating to operations of the properties are reported in the restricted current funds. The recognition of a claim against a restricted current fund for the recovery of cash equal to the depreciation on endowment properties, as required by terms of the endowment, is recorded by a charge to a receivable account and a credit to an allowance for depreciation (see entry 12). Fund E arises from a transfer of general current fund cash for use as an endowment until some alternative employment of funds is authorized (see entry 10). Fund F is established to recognize resources that are held for the benefit of the institution by a trustee (see entry 11). Upon notification from the trustee of a change in fund principal, an appropriate adjustment would be made in the endowment fund balance. Income distributions by the trustee are recognized by the fund receiving such income.

Statements. Statements to report assets, liabilities, reserves, and balances identified with the endowment funds and to summarize the changes in fund balances are prepared periodically. Statements for Cal University are given on page 914.

Annuity funds. An annuity fund is formed when cash or other properties are transferred to the institution subject to the requirement that specified payments be made to a designated beneficiary during his lifetime. The payments to an annuitant may be variable amounts or they may be fixed; they may be equal to the income produced by the fund assets or they may be more or less than such amounts. Upon the death of an annuitant, undistributed fund resources become available for use in accordance with the terms of the annuity agreement.

Annuity funds are sometimes included with the endowment funds for accounting and reporting purposes. In the absence of limitations in the annuity agreements, assets may be pooled just as in the case of endowment funds. Annuity fund balances are increased by gifts subject to annuity agreements, gains on the sale of annuity fund assets, and annuity fund income; annuity fund balances are decreased by losses on the sale of assets, payments to annuitants, and asset transfers.

Transactions related to an annuity fund of Cal University and the entries to record these transactions appear on page 916. An explanation of the entries follows.

Explanation of annuity fund entries. The receipt of annuity fund resources is recorded by charges to appropriate asset accounts and credits to properly identified annuity fund balances. Investments in securities are recorded in the usual manner. Earnings from investments as well as losses and gains on the sale of investments are usually entered directly in the fund balance. Payment to an annuitant is recorded by a charge to the annuity fund balance and a credit to Cash. In the example, recognition of the amount payable to the annuitant is recorded by a credit to a liability account; the liability account would be closed when payment is made.

Statements. Statements to report the financial position of annuity funds and to summarize the changes in fund balances are prepared periodically. Statements for Cal University are given following the entries.

Annuity Fund Books

Transaction	Entry		
(1) Receipt of cash of $125,000 subject to condition that $5,000 per year be paid to the donor during his lifetime, any balance becoming available for educational and general purposes.	Cash	125,000	
	Annuity Fund Balance		125,000
(2) Purchase of securities for $120,000 that includes accrued interest of $2,000.	Investments	118,000	
	Accrued Interest	2,000	
	Cash		120,000
(3) Collections of income for the year ended June 30, 1967, $9,500.	Cash	9,500	
	Accrued Interest		2,000
	Annuity Fund Balance		7,500
(4) Recognition of amount payable to annuitant, $5,000.	Annuity Fund Balance	5,000	
	Due to Annuitant		5,000
(5) Amount becoming available for educational and general purposes according to the annuity agreement, $2,500.	Annuity Fund Balance	2,500	
	Due to General Current Fund		2,500

Cal University
Annuity Fund
Balance Sheet
June 30, 1967

Assets		Liabilities, Reserves, and Balances	
Cash	$ 14,500	Due to annuitant	$ 5,000
Investments	118,000	Due to general current fund	2,500
		Annuity fund balance	125,000
Total assets	$132,500	Total liabilities, reserves, and balances	$132,500

Cal University
Annuity Fund
Summary of Changes in Annuity Fund Balance
For Year Ended June 30, 1967

Annuity fund balance, July 1, 1966		—
Add: Increase from gift subject to annuity	$125,000	
Increase from income for year	7,500	$132,500
		$132,500
Deduct: Amount payable to annuitant for year.	$ 5,000	
Amount payable to general current fund	2,500	7,500
Annuity fund balance, June 30, 1967		$125,000

Plant funds. Resources related to the educational plant may be divided into three groups: (1) resources that are held for plant expansion and replacement, (2) resources that are held for the retirement of long-term debt incurred in the acquisition of the plant, and (3) the specific physical resources comprising the plant. This division has suggested the use of three self-balancing groups of accounts for plant resources that are designated by the American Council on Education as (1) unexpended plant funds, (2) retirement of indebtedness funds, and (3) invested in plant.

Resources of the unexpended plant funds grouping consist of cash, securities, receivables, and other assets that are to be used for the acquisition of new plant or the replacement of existing plant. Present obligations against these resources for construction in progress or for current plant acquisitions are recognized on the unexpended plant funds books as liabilities. The difference between the assets and the liabilities is reported as the unexpended plant funds balance. This balance is commonly divided into (1) the portion to be applied to plant additions and (2) the portion to be applied to renewals and replacements.

Resources of the retirement of indebtedness funds grouping consist of cash, securities, and other assets that are to be used for the retirement of plant indebtedness. Fund accounts are balanced by a single funds balance reporting total resources available for retirement of indebtedness.

Resources of the invested in plant grouping consist of the individual property items that compose the educational plant. This grouping also carries any long-term indebtedness relating to plant acquisitions. The difference between plant assets and related liabilities is reported as an investment in plant balance. This balance is commonly divided to show the different sources of plant financing — gifts, current funds, and endowment funds.

Plant Funds — Unexpended Plant Funds Books

Transaction	Entry		
(1) Receipt of cash gift to be used for plant acquisitions, $100,000.	Cash	100,000	
	Unexpended Plant Funds Balance — Plant Additions		100,000
(2) Payment for additions to buildings, $85,000.	Unexpended Plant Funds Balance — Plant Additions	85,000	
	Cash		85,000
(3) Issue of bonds to raise funds for construction of buildings, $1,500,000.	Cash	1,500,000	
	Unexpended Plant Funds Balance — Plant Additions		1,500,000
(4) Completion of buildings at contract price of $1,500,000.	Unexpended Plant Funds Balance — Plant Additions	1,500,000	
	Contracts Payable		1,500,000
(5) Payment of contract, $1,500,000.	Contracts Payable	1,500,000	
	Cash		1,500,000
(6) Receipt of cash from general current fund for plant renewals and replacements in subsequent periods, $30,000.	Cash	30,000	
	Unexpended Plant Funds Balance — Renewals and Replacements		30,000
(7) Purchase of securities, $30,000.	Investments	30,000	
	Cash		30,000
(8) Collection of interest on investments, $750.	Cash	750	
	Unexpended Plant Funds Balance — Renewals and Replacements		750

Plant Funds — Retirement of Indebtedness Funds

Transaction	Entry		
(1) Receipt of cash from general current fund for payment of mortgage installment due, $25,000.	Cash	25,000	
	Retirement of Indebtedness Funds Balance		25,000
(2) Payment of mortgage installment due, $25,000.	Retirement of Indebtedness Funds Balance	25,000	
	Cash		25,000
(3) Receipt of cash gift to be used for payment of installments due on mortgage in 1968–1970, $75,000.	Cash	75,000	
	Retirement of Indebtedness Funds Balance		75,000

Plant Funds — Invested in Plant Books

Transaction	Entry		
1) Receipt of gift of land, ›uildings, and equipment or educational and gen- ral purposes valued at 4,000,000; properties are ubject to mortgage for 1,000,000.	Land	850,000	
	Improvements Other Than Buildings	150,000	
	Buildings	2,500,000	
	Equipment	500,000	
	Mortgage Payable		1,000,000
	Investment in Plant — From Gifts		3,000,000
2) Addition to buildings nanced by gifts reported n unexpended plant unds, $85,000.	Buildings	85,000	
	Investment in Plant — From Gifts		85,000
3) Issue of bonds to be sed for construction of uildings, $1,500,000.	Buildings to be Acquired	1,500,000	
	Bonds Payable		1,500,000
4) Completion of build- ngs financed by bond ssue.	Buildings	1,500,000	
	Buildings to be Acquired		1,500,000
5) Payment by retire- nent of indebtedness unds of current install- nent due on mortgage, 25,000.	Mortgage Payable	25,000	
	Investment in Plant — From Current Funds		25,000
6) Acquisition by gen- ral current fund of quipment, $15,000.	Equipment	15,000	
	Investment in Plant — From Current Funds		15,000
7) Acquisition by en- owment fund of a dor- nitory valued at 300,000.	Land	125,000	
	Buildings	175,000	
	Investment in Plant — From Endowments		300,000
8) To record deprecia- on on buildings repre- ented by endowment, 10,000.	Investment in Plant — From Endowments	10,000	
	Allowance for Depreciation of Buildings		10,000
9) Retirement of equip- nent carried at $5,000.	Investment in Plant — From Gifts	5,000	
	Equipment		5,000

Cal
Plant
Balance
June 30,

Assets			
Unexpended plant funds:			
Cash		$ 15,750	
Investments		30,000	$ 45,750
Retirement of indebtedness funds:			
Cash			75,000
Invested in plant:			
Land		$ 975,000	
Improvements other than buildings		150,000	
Buildings	$4,260,000		
Less allowance for depreciation	10,000	4,250,000	
Equipment		510,000	
		$5,885,000	
Deduct items carried in endowment funds		290,000	5,595,000
Total assets			$5,715,750

Transactions related to the plant funds of Cal University and the entries to record these transactions are given on pages 918 and 919. An explanation of the entries follows.

Explanation of unexpended plant funds entries. Cash or other assets for plant additions or for renewals and replacements received from gifts or grants, from transfers from current funds, or from the issue of long-term indebtedness are recorded by debits to appropriate asset account balances and credits to unexpended plant funds balances that designate the purpose to be served by the resources (see entries 1, 3, and 6). Expenditures for plant expansion or for renewals and replacement are recorded by debits to unexpended plant funds balances and credits to Cash or to payable balances (see entries 2 and 4). Investments in securities are recorded in the usual manner. Earnings are recorded by debits to asset accounts and credits to appropriate unexpended funds balances (see entry 8).

Explanation of retirement of indebtedness funds entries. Resources that are specifically provided for the retirement of long-term debt are recorded by debits to appropriate asset accounts and credits to Retirement of

University
Funds
Sheet
1967

Liabilities, Reserves, and Balances				
Unexpended plant funds:				
Balance — plant additions			$ 15,000	
Balance — renewals and replacements			30,750	$ 45,750
Retirement of indebtedness funds:				
Balance				75,000
Invested in plant:				
Mortgage payable	$ 975,000			
Bonds payable	1,500,000	$2,475,000		
Investment in plant —				
From gifts	$3,080,000			
From current funds	40,000	3,120,000		5,595,000
Total liabilities, reserves, and balances				$5,715,750

Indebtedness Funds Balance. Payments of long-term debit are recorded by debits to the funds balance and credits to Cash.

Explanation of invested in plant section entries. Acquisitions of educational plant items are recorded by debits to appropriate asset accounts and credits to investment in plant balances that designate the plant financing sources. The issue of bonds to finance construction is recorded by a debit to Buildings to be Acquired and a credit to the liability; the proceeds from the bond issue are recorded in the unexpended plant funds books. Completion of the construction is recorded by a debit to Buildings and a credit to Buildings to be Acquired; payment for construction is recorded in the unexpended plant funds books (see entries 3 and 4). Retirement of a plant item is recorded by a debit to the appropriate investment in plant balance and a credit to the asset account (see entry 9).

Special attention is directed to entries (7) and (8). In order that the invested in plant group may report all of the properties owned by the institution, land and buildings reported in an endowment fund are also reported here; asset accounts are debited and Investment in Plant — From Endowments is credited. Depreciation on endowment fund properties that was recognized in the endowment fund is also reported in the invested in plant group; the investment in plant balance is debited and an allowance for depreciation account is credited.

Statements. A balance sheet is prepared periodically to report assets, liabilities, reserves, and balances for each of the plant fund groupings. The plant funds balance sheet for Cal University is given on pages 920 and 921. Observe that the credit balance summarizing the investment in plant from endowments is subtracted from total assets rather than being reported as a balance item. This is done to cancel the effects of reporting endowment fund properties both in endowment funds books and in plant funds books.

Agency funds. The educational institution frequently acts as an agent or trustee, holding certain assets on behalf of others. When agency operations are simple and of limited duration, both asset accounts and accounts expressing the institution's accountability to others may be carried in the general current fund. On the other hand, when operations are involved and continuing, an agency fund may be recognized and special agency books established for the properties subject to agency control. Agency funds may be established for pension and retirement resources, special organization resources, student deposits, and tax withholding amounts. Accounting for the agency is the same as it would be for a private business; hence it is not illustrated here.

Combined balance sheet for the educational unit. Preceding pages offered examples of the statements that are prepared for the funds of the educational institution. The statements included (1) balance sheets, (2) statements of income and expenditures, and (3) statements of changes in fund balances. Instead of balance sheets for individual funds or groups of funds, the educational institution frequently prepares a combined statement offering balance sheet data for all of its funds. Balance sheet data on the combined statement may be listed in either sectional form or in columnar form. The sectional form simply reports the separate balance sheets in a series of sections; the balance sheet for current funds would be followed by that for loan funds, endowment funds, etc. The columnar form employs a separate column for each fund balance sheet and is similar in form to the combined statement for the governmental unit that was illustrated on pages 876 and 877.

THE HOSPITAL

Hospitals provide for reception, care, and medical and surgical treatment of the sick or injured. Rooms are provided and meals are supplied. Although major activities center about inpatients, hospitals frequently render outpatient care and emergency services. Hospitals may also carry on special activities such as research and nurses training. They also operate a number of auxiliary enterprises such as pharmacies for outpatients and cafeterias for staff members and visitors. Hospital operations call for important administrative activities. The latter include: hospital staffing; registration of patients; operation of the physical plant; food, laundry, and housekeeping management; and budgeting, accounting, billing, and collecting.

The major source of hospital support is normally the charges that are made to patients for services. However, such charges frequently fail to cover the full cost of hospital operations, and significant sums must be sought from contributions and grants from private, public, and charitable sources.

Funds for the hospital. Accounting for hospitals is quite similar to that for educational institutions. The hospital, like the educational institution, acquires revenues that must be applied to specific objectives; hence, a funds approach is used in the recognition of resources. There are certain accounting differences, however, that should be pointed out.

The hospital generally does not require the variety of funds required by the educational institution. A further difference is found with respect to the operating summaries of the two units. For the educational institution, *revenues* were compared with *expenditures*, a "modified accrual basis" was employed, and depreciation of the educational plant was generally ignored. In the case of hospitals, an analysis and a summary of operations that comes closer to that of private business is normally warranted. Hospitals sell specific services. There is the expectation by patients, group purchasers of insurance protection, and insurance companies selling hospital protection that charges for services will bear a close relationship to the costs of these services. Furthermore, although contributions may be available for original hospital properties, the lack of assurance that replacement moneys will be available suggests that hospital revenues should be set at levels that will provide for the ultimate replacement of properties. In summarizing activities for the hospital unit, then, these factors suggest that *revenues* be compared with *expenses*, that a "full accrual basis" be employed, and that depreciation of hospital properties be recognized in arriving at total operating costs.

Recommendations of the American Hospital Association on the application of fund procedures to hospitals have won wide acceptance, and the discussion that follows is based largely on these recommendations.[1] The Association recognizes four major fund groupings:

[1] *Handbook on Accounting, Statistics and Business Office Procedures for Hospitals* (Chicago: American Hospital Association, Committee on Accounting and Statistics, 1950), Section I, "University Hospital Statistics and Classification of Accounts."

(1) General fund.
(2) Temporary funds.
(3) Endowment funds.
(4) Plant funds.

A description of the funds and illustrations of their operation follow. Descriptions are brief since funds of the hospital compare closely with those of the educational institution.

General fund. The general fund of the hospital summarizes the current resources that are to be used in meeting the obligations arising from general operations. Resources that can be applied without restriction are reported here; expenditures for which specific funds have not been provided are financed from these resources. The general fund of the hospital is the same in nature and function as the general current fund of the educational institution.

To illustrate the accounting for the general fund, transactions affecting the general fund of Cal Hospital and the entries to record these transactions are listed on pages 924–926. An explanation of the entries follows.

Explanation of general fund entries. The American Hospital Association, in considering the presentation of hospital revenues for statement purposes, suggests the following classifications: (1) gross revenues from patients, (2) deductions from revenue, and (3) other revenue sources. In considering operating expenses, it recognizes the following classifications: (1) administration and general, (2) dietary, (3) household and property, (4) professional care of patients, (5) outpatient and emergency, and (6) other expenses. Accounts in the general fund for Cal Hospital have been established in accordance with the above.

General Fund Books

Transaction	Entry		
(1) Charges for services to patients for year ended December 31, 1967, $580,000, of which $45,000 is still due; adjustments and allowances of $60,000 apply to charges.	Cash	475,000	
	Accounts Receivable	45,000	
	Free Service and Adjustments — Contractual Patients	40,000	
	Free Service and Adjustments — General Patients	16,500	
	Courtesy and Miscellaneous Allowances	3,500	
	Earnings from Routine Services — Inpatients		320,000
	Earnings from Routine Services — Outpatients		50,000
	Earnings from Special Services		210,000

Transaction	Entry		
(2) Other hospital revenues, $420,000, of which $10,000 is still due from temporary fund in reimbursement of research expenditures.	Cash	410,000	
	Due from Temporary Fund	10,000	
	General Contributions, Donations, Legacies, and Bequests		180,000
	Grants from Community Chests, Foundations, and Governmental Agencies		122,500
	Donated Services and Commodities		10,000
	Income Transfers from Temporary Funds		57,500
	Miscellaneous Revenues		50,000
(3) Collections of interest and dividends on endowment funds securities, $85,000, of which $5,000 is due to Endowment Fund #1 representing bond premium amortization.	Cash	85,000	
	Due to Endowment Fund #1		5,000
	Income from Investments		80,000
(4) Expenditures for hospital supplies, $200,000, of which $25,000 has not yet been paid.	Inventory of Supplies	200,000	
	Cash		175,000
	Vouchers Payable		25,000
(5) Hospital supplies charged out, $170,000.	Administrative and General	5,000	
	Dietary	120,000	
	Household and Property	10,000	
	Professional Care of Patients	15,000	
	Outpatient and Emergency	5,000	
	Other Expenses	15,000	
	Inventory of Supplies		170,000
(6) Payments of hospital salaries and wages, $490,000.	Administrative and General	85,000	
	Dietary	60,000	
	Household and Property	45,000	
	Professional Care of Patients	220,000	
	Outpatient and Emergency	30,000	
	Other Expenses	50,000	
	Cash		490,000
(7) Payments of hospital expenses other than salaries and wages, $75,000.	Administrative and General	20,000	
	Dietary	7,500	
	Household and Property	10,000	
	Professional Care of Patients	25,000	
	Outpatient and Emergency	2,500	
	Other Expenses	10,000	
	Cash		75,000
(8) Payments of interest on mortgage, $60,000, and payment of installment due on mortgage carried as a liability in the plant funds, $50,000.	Interest Expense	60,000	
	General Fund Balance	50,000	
	Cash		110,000

Transaction	Entry		
(9) Adjustments required on December 31, 1967:			
(a) Allowance for uncollectible accounts, $2,500.	Provision for Uncollectible Accounts	2,500	
	Allowance for Uncollectible Accounts		2,500
(b) Accrued salaries and wages, $5,000.	Administrative and General	1,000	
	Dietary	750	
	Household and Property	250	
	Professional Care of Patients	1,250	
	Outpatient and Emergency	250	
	Other Expenses	1,500	
	Accrued Salaries and Wages		5,000
(c) Charges for depreciation on properties carried as assets by plant funds, $85,000.	Provision for Depreciation	85,000	
	General Fund Balance		85,000
(d) To recognize amount to be paid to plant funds equal to depreciation on properties.	General Fund Balance	85,000	
	Due to Plant Funds		85,000
(10) To close general operating revenue and expense accounts at the end of the fiscal period.	Earnings from Routine Services — Inpatients	320,000	
	Earnings from Routine Services — Outpatients	50,000	
	Earnings from Special Services	210,000	
	General Fund Balance	222,500	
	Free Service and Adjustments — Contractual Patients		40,000
	Free Service and Adjustments — General Patients		16,500
	Courtesy and Miscellaneous Allowances		3,500
	Provision for Uncollectible Accounts		2,500
	Administrative and General		111,000
	Dietary		188,250
	Household and Property		65,250
	Professional Care of Patients		261,250
	Outpatient and Emergency		37,750
	Other Expenses		76,500
(11) To close other revenue and expense accounts at the end of the fiscal period.	General Contributions, Donations, Legacies, and Bequests	180,000	
	Grants from Community Chests, Foundations, and Governmental Agencies	122,500	
	Donated Services and Commodities	10,000	
	Income Transfers from Temporary Funds	57,500	
	Income from Investments	80,000	
	Miscellaneous Revenues	50,000	
	Interest Expense		60,000
	Provision for Depreciation		85,000
	General Fund Balance		355,000

Cal Hospital
General Fund
Statement of Revenue and Expense
For Year Ended December 31, 1967

Gross revenues from service to patients:				
Routine services — inpatients		$320,000		
Routine services — outpatients		50,000		
Special services (see schedule)		210,000		$580,000
Deductions from gross revenues:				
Free service and adjustments — contractual patients		$ 40,000		
Free service and adjustments — general patients		16,500		
Courtesy and miscellaneous allowances		3,500		
Provision for uncollectible accounts		2,500		62,500
Net revenues from services to patients				$517,500
Operating expenses:				
	Salaries and wages	Other		
Administrative and general	$ 86,000	$ 25,000		$111,000
Dietary	60,750	127,500		188,250
Household and property	45,250	20,000		65,250
Professional care of patients (see schedule)	221,250	40,000		261,250
Outpatient and emergency	30,250	7,500		37,750
Other expenses	51,500	25,000		76,500
	$495,000	$245,000		$740,000
Deficit from operations				$222,500
Other revenue:				
General contributions, donations, legacies, and bequests		$180,000		
Grant from community chests, foundations, and governmental agencies		122,500		
Donated services and commodities		10,000		
Income transfers from temporary funds		57,500		
Income from investments		80,000		
Miscellaneous revenues		50,000		500,000
				$277,500
Other expense:				
Interest expense		$ 60,000		
Provision for depreciation		85,000		145,000
Net income				$132,500

Cal Hospital
General Fund
Schedule of Gross Revenues from Special Services
For Year Ended December 31, 1967

Operating rooms	$ 30,000
Delivery rooms	12,500
Anesthesiology	3,000
Radiology	8,000
Laboratory	40,000
Pharmacy	106,000
Medical and surgical supplies	2,500
Emergency	8,000
Total	$210,000

Cal Hospital
General Fund
Schedule of Salaries and Wages for Professional Care of Patients
For Year Ended December 31, 1967

Nursing services	$ 25,000
Medical and surgical services	90,000
Pharmacy	17,500
Medical library	15,000
Operating rooms	27,500
Delivery rooms	10,000
Department of anesthesiology	5,000
Department of radiology	12,500
Laboratory	18,750
Total	$221,250

Cal Hospital
General Fund
Balance Sheet
December 31, 1967

Assets			Liabilities, Reserves, and Balances	
Cash		$120,000	Vouchers payable	$ 25,000
Accounts receivable	$45,000		Due to Endowment Fund #1	5,000
Less allowance for uncollectible accounts	2,500	42,500	Due to plant funds	85,000
			Accrued salaries and wages	5,000
Due from temporary funds		10,000	Total liabilities	$120,000
Inventory of supplies		30,000	General fund balance	82,500
Total assets		$202,500	Total liabilities, reserves, and balances	$202,500

Cal Hospital
General Fund
Summary of Changes in General Fund Balance
For Year Ended December 31, 1967

General fund balance, January 1, 1967		—
Add: Increase for year ended December 31, 1967, per statement of revenue and expense	$132,500	
Recognition of depreciation charge on properties reported in plant funds	85,000	$217,500
Deduct: Payment of mortgage reported in plant funds	$ 50,000	
Transfer to plant funds	85,000	135,000
General fund balance, December 31, 1967		$ 82,500

Special attention is directed to entries (8) and (9). Payment of an installment due on an obligation that is carried by the plant funds is reported by a debit to General Fund Balance and a credit to Cash (entry 8). Depreciation on hospital properties that are reported in plant funds is recognized by a debit to an expense account and a credit to General Fund Balance (entry 9c). The transfer of cash to plant funds to finance the ultimate replacement of properties is recorded by a debit to General Fund Balance and a credit to Cash. In the example, recognition of reimbursement due to plant funds is reported by a credit to a payable (entry 9d); the payable would be closed when the cash is transferred.

Statements. Statements for the general fund include a balance sheet, a statement of revenue and expense, and a summary of changes in the general fund balance. Revenue and expense schedules, as well as summaries offering additional detail and cost analyses, frequently accompany the operating statements. Statements for Cal Hospital are given on pages 927–929.

Temporary funds. Temporary funds are composed of current resources that, while available for current purposes, are subject to certain limitations in their use. For example, resources from gifts or grants and income from endowment funds that can be spent only for specified purposes, such as research, a medical library, or nurses training, would be reported as temporary funds. Temporary funds of the hospital, then, are identical in nature and function to the restricted current funds of the educational institution.

Temporary funds transactions of Cal Hospital and the entries to summarize these transactions are listed on page 930. An explanation of the entries follows.

Temporary Funds Books

Transaction	Entry		
(1) Receipt of cash gift to be used for medical research, $100,000.	Cash Temporary Fund A Balance	100,000	 100,000
(2) Purchase of securities, $85,000.	Temporary Investments — Fund A Cash	85,000	 85,000
(3) Receipt of cash gift to be used for books and journals for hospital patients, $10,000.	Cash Temporary Fund B Balance	10,000	 10,000
(4) Sale of securities, book value $25,000, for $23,500.	Cash Temporary Fund A Balance Temporary Investments — Fund A	23,500 1,500	 25,000
(5) Collection of interest and dividends on temporary investments, $5,000.	Cash Temporary Fund A Balance	5,000	 5,000
(6) Expenditures during year by general fund for research chargeable to Temporary Fund A, $50,000; cash transferred to general fund, $40,000.	Temporary Fund A Balance Cash Due to General Fund	50,000	 40,000 10,000
(7) Payment to general fund for books and journals chargeable to Temporary Fund B, $7,500.	Temporary Fund B Balance Cash	7,500	 7,500
(8) Adjustments required on December 31, 1967: Accrued interest on securities, $250.	Accrued Interest on Temporary Investments Temporary Fund A Balance	250	 250

Cal Hospital
Temporary Funds
Balance Sheet
December 31, 1967

Assets		Liabilities, Reserves, and Balances		
Cash	$ 6,000	Due to general fund		$10,000
Temporary investments	60,000	Fund balances:		
Accrued interest on temporary investments	250	Fund A	$53,750	
		Fund B	2,500	56,250
Total assets	$66,250	Total liabilities, reserves, and balances		$66,250

Cal Hospital
Temporary Funds
Summary of Changes in Balances
For Year Ended December 31, 1967

	Total	Fund A	Fund B
Balances, January 1, 1967	—	—	—
Increases for year:			
Gifts establishing funds	$110,000	$100,000	$10,000
Income from dividends and interest	5,250	5,250	
	$115,250	$105,250	$10,000
Decreases for year:			
Loss on sale of securities at less than book value	$ 1,500	$ 1,500	
Charges in fulfillment of fund objectives	57,500	50,000	$ 7,500
	$ 59,000	$ 51,500	$ 7,500
Balances, December 31, 1967	$ 56,250	$ 53,750	$ 2,500

Explanation of temporary funds entries. In the example, the temporary funds books summarize two temporary funds, and separate fund balances are maintained to report the respective fund equities. It should be observed that changes in temporary fund balances arising from revenues, expenses, and distributions are recorded directly in the fund balances; when there are many changes and these are to be reported in special operating statements, nominal accounts would be established to accumulate profit and loss detail.

Statements. Statements for the temporary funds of Cal Hospital consist of a balance sheet and a summary of changes in fund balances. These are illustrated on pages 930 and 931.

Endowment funds. Endowment funds for a hospital, like those for an educational unit, represent resources that have been transferred under conditions that limit expenditures to the income that is produced by such resources. Assets may be transferred directly to the hospital, or they may be transferred to a trustee who administers them for the benefit of the institution. An endowment may also be created by the action of the governing board of the hospital. Terms of an endowment may place no restrictions on the use of endowment income or they may specify a particular purpose for which the income is to be used. In the absence of restrictions, endowment income becomes available to the general fund; when there are restrictions, income is reported in a temporary fund.

Endowment funds transactions for Cal Hospital and the entries to summarize these transactions are listed below. An explanation of the entries follows.

Explanation of endowment funds entries. In the example, endowment funds books summarize two endowments, and separate endowment fund balances summarize the respective fund equities. It should be observed in the example that endowment income is reported directly in the fund that is entitled to such income. When revenue and expenses are involved

Endowment Funds Books

Transaction	Entry		
(1) Receipt of bonds in establishment of Endowment Fund #1 as follows: Co. R bonds, face value $500,000, market value on date of transfer $550,000. Co. S bonds, face value $500,000, market value on date of transfer $470,000. No restrictions are made on the use of endowment income.	Investments — Bonds at Face Value (Endowment Fund #1)	1,000,000	
	Investments — Unamortized Bond Premium (Endowment Fund #1)	50,000	
	Investments — Unamortized Bond Discount (Endowment Fund #1)		30,000
	Endowment Fund #1 Balance		1,020,000
(2) Receipt of cash in establishment of Endowment Fund #2, $250,000. Endowment income is to be used for a specified research project.	Cash	250,000	
	Endowment Fund #2 Balance		250,000
(3) Purchase of 1,000 shares of Co. T preferred stock, $240,000.	Investments — Preferred Stock (Endowment Fund #2)	240,000	
	Cash		240,000
(4) Collection of interest by general fund that includes $5,000 reimbursable to Endowment Fund #1 for bond premium amortization.	Due from General Fund	5,000	
	Investments — Unamortized Bond Premium (Endowment Fund #1)		5,000
(5) Sale of Co. S bonds at face value, $250,000.	Cash	250,000	
	Investments — Unamortized Bond Discount (Endowment Fund #1)	15,000	
	Investments — Bonds at Face Value (Endowment Fund #1)		250,000
	Endowment Fund #1 Balance		15,000

in a determination of net income, revenue and expenses can be summarized in the endowment fund books; the fund net income, when determined, is then transferred to the appropriate fund.

Statements. Statements for the endowment funds of Cal Hospital consist of a balance sheet and a summary of changes in endowment fund balances. The statements are illustrated on pages 934 and 935.

Plant funds. Hospital plant resources may be divided into two groups: (1) physical resources comprising the hospital properties, and (2) cash and other assets that are available for the improvement and the replacement of the hospital properties. Although the American Hospital Association recognizes the two asset groups, they would nevertheless combine these within a single plant funds category. When there are claims against plant fund resources in connection with original financing of properties, construction in progress, or current property acquisitions, such obligations would be recognized in the plant funds. Funds are balanced by two plant fund balances: (1) investment in plant and (2) reserve for plant improvement and expansion.

Transactions affecting the plant funds of Cal Hospital and the entries to record these transactions are given on pages 935 and 936. An explanation of the entries follows.

Explanation of plant funds entries. Alternative approaches have been suggested for analyzing and recording plant funds transactions of the hospital. Probably the best approach would recognize two self-balancing sets of accounts, one summarizing the existing physical plant and the other summarizing resources that are held for plant improvement and replacement. With such an approach, the analysis of transactions affecting hospital plant assets, liabilities, and fund balances is the same as that employed for the educational unit. However, the entries relating to existing plant and to improvement and replacement resources are made in self-balancing form within a single set of books instead of in separate sets of books as in the case of the educational unit.

In applying the above, the acquisition of hospital properties is recorded by debits to asset accounts and credits to an investment in plant balance; the recognition of a liability in connection with the acquisition of properties would reduce the credit to the investment in plant balance (see entry 1). The acquisition of assets that are to be used for plant improvement and replacement is recorded by debits to asset accounts and credits to Reserve for Plant Improvements and Replacements. Two entries are required when an addition or an improvement is made through plant fund expenditures: (1) Reserve for Plant Improvements and Replacements is debited and Cash is credited; (2) an asset account

Cal
Endowment
Balance
December 31,

Assets			
Cash			$ 260,000
Due from general fund			5,000
Investments:			
Preferred stock (Endowment Fund #2)		$ 240,000	
Bonds at face value (Endowment Fund #1)	$ 750,000		
Unamortized bond premium	45,000		
	$ 795,000		
Less unamortized bond discount	15,000	780,000	1,020,000
Total assets			$1,285,000

Cal Hospital
Endowment Funds
Summary of Changes in Balances
For Year Ended December 31, 1967

	Total	Fund #1	Fund #2
Balances, January 1, 1967	—	—	—
Increases for year:			
Gifts establishing funds	$1,270,000	$1,020,000	$ 250,000
Gain on sale of securities at more than book value	15,000	15,000	
Balances, December 31, 1967	$1,285,000	$1,035,000	$ 250,000

is debited and Investment in Plant is credited (see entry 3). When the expenditure represents an asset replacement, an additional entry is required to cancel the asset that is retired and the related investment in plant balance.

The recognition of depreciation on plant fund assets when reimbursement is to be made for such depreciation by another fund is recorded by two entries: (1) Investment in Plant is debited and an asset valuation account is credited, and (2) a receivable balance is debited and Reserve for Improvements and Replacements is credited (see entries 5b and 5c). The subsequent collection of cash is recorded by a debit to Cash and a credit to the receivable account.

Hospital
Funds
Sheet
1967

Liabilities, Reserves, and Balances	
Fund balances:	
Endowment Fund #1 — for general purposes	$1,035,000
Endowment Fund #2 — for restricted purposes	250,000
Total liabilities, reserves, and balances	$1,285,000

Statements. The plant funds balance sheet summarizes hospital properties and resources held for plant improvement and replacement. The plant funds balance sheet for Cal Hospital is given on page 936.

Plant Funds Books

Transaction	Entry		
(1) Acquisition of land and construction of hospital financed by gifts of cash, $1,500,000, and cash raised through a mortgage, $1,000,000.	Land	250,000	
	Buildings	1,750,000	
	Equipment	500,000	
	Mortgage Payable		1,000,000
	Investment in Plant		1,500,000
(2) Receipt of gifts of cash of $50,000 and securities valued at $100,000 for plant improvements and replacements.	Cash	50,000	
	Investments	100,000	
	Reserve for Plant Improvements and Replacements		150,000
(3) Acquisition of equipment, $30,000.	Reserve for Plant Improvements and Replacements	30,000	
	Cash		30,000
	Equipment	30,000	
	Investment in Plant		30,000
(4) Payment by general fund of mortgage installment due, $50,000.	Mortgage Payable	50,000	
	Investment in Plant		50,000

Transaction	Entry		
(5) Adjustments required on December 31, 1967:			
(a) Accrued interest on investments, $1,500.	Accrued Interest on Investments	1,500	
	Reserve for Plant Improvements and Replacements		1,500
(b) Depreciation on plant assets for year, $85,000.	Investment in Plant	85,000	
	Allowance for Depreciation of Buildings		35,000
	Allowance for Depreciation of Equipment		50,000
(c) Amount recoverable from general fund equal to depreciation on plant assets, $85,000.	Due from General Fund	85,000	
	Reserve for Plant Improvements and Replacements		85,000

Cal Hospital
Plant Funds
Balance Sheet
December 31, 1967

Assets			Liabilities, Reserves, and Balances	
Invested in plant:			Invested in plant:	
Land		$ 250,000	Mortgage payable	$ 950,000
Buildings	$1,750,000		Investment in plant	1,495,000
Less allowance for depreciation	35,000	1,715,000		$2,445,000
Equipment	$ 530,000		Reserve for plant improvements and replacements	206,500
Less allowance for depreciation	50,000	480,000		
		$2,445,000		
For plant improvements and replacements:				
Cash	$ 20,000			
Due from general fund	85,000			
Investments	100,000			
Accrued interest on investments	1,500	206,500		
Total assets		$2,651,500	Total liabilities, reserves, and balances	$2,651,500

Combined balance sheet for the hospital. Instead of providing balance sheets for individual funds or groups of funds, the hospital, like the educational institution, normally prepares a combined balance sheet that offers the financial data for all of the funds. The combined statement is prepared in either sectional or columnar form as described for the educational institution.

BUDGETARY CONTROLS

Discussions and illustrations in this chapter made no reference to budgetary controls and accompanying budgetary accounts. This was done to simplify presentations. Ordinarily, the educational institution or hospital prepares and adopts a budget and then controls operations within such a budgetary framework.

In developing the budget, revenues are classified by source and expenditures are classified by function with further subclassifications related to activity, character, and object. Upon adoption of the budget, entries are made establishing controls for estimated revenues and for appropriations with detailed support in subsidiary revenues and appropriations ledgers. Thereafter, accounting for revenues, expenditures, appropriations, and encumbrances is the same as that which was described for the governmental unit. At the end of the period, both budgetary and operating accounts are closed, and accounts then reflect the ending asset, liability, reserve, and fund balances. Special summaries are generally prepared, in addition to the statements that were illustrated, to report how closely actual revenues compare with estimated revenues and also the degree to which limitations on expenditures were observed.

It should be noted that budgetary accounting procedures are normally employed only in funds related to the general activities of the institution — the general current fund of the educational unit and the general fund of the hospital.

QUESTIONS

1. Name the funds groups maintained by the educational institution and describe the purpose of each group.

2. Name the funds groups maintained by the hospital and describe the purpose of each group.

3. What funds of the educational unit carry fixed assets among their resources? What funds carry fixed liabilities among their obligations?

4. Compare the accounting for nonprofit service institutions with that for governmental units.

5. (a) Describe the "modified accrual basis" employed by the educational institution. (b) Would you prefer the use of a full accrual basis? Give reasons for your answer.

6. Do you see any serious objections to the use of the "modified accrual basis" by a hospital? Explain.

7. What circumstances would suggest the recognition of depreciation on properties of a nonprofit service organization?

8. The Seamans Hospital recognizes a charge for depreciation but accumulates no funds for the replacement of hospital properties. Under what circumstances would you consider such procedure acceptable?

9. Describe the differences in accounting for the general fixed assets of the governmental unit and those of the educational institution.

10. Describe the differences in accounting for the general fixed assets of the educational institution and those of the hospital.

11. Distinguish between the "general purpose" endowment and the "restricted purpose" endowment.

12. What entries would be made on the plant fund books of an educational institution for each of the following transactions:

(a) The purchase of certain equipment is paid for by the general current fund.
(b) Certain equipment financed from gifts is scrapped.
(c) Bonds are issued for the construction of additional classroom space and the building is partly completed in the current period.
(d) A building financed from current funds on which fire insurance is carried is destroyed by fire.

13. In what fund of an educational institution should each of the following properties be listed:

(a) Physical education building acquired by funds from the issue of long-term bonds.
(b) Dormitory acquired from a donor, with income to become available for general purposes of the institution.
(c) Student union building acquired from gifts by alumni.
(d) Apartment building acquired from a donor with the provision that net income from the building shall become available to donor for life; upon his death, the building may be sold and proceeds employed for any educational purpose.

14. Indicate for each account of an educational institution that follows the different fund groups in which it might appear:

(a) Unappropriated Surplus.
(b) Due from Annuity Fund.
(c) Inventory of Materials and Supplies.
(d) Cash.
(e) Accrued Expenses.
(f) Investments (or Temporary Investments).
(g) Pooled Investments.
(h) Land and Buildings.
(i) Funds Held by Trustee.
(j) Mortgage Payable.
(k) Cash — Student Deposits.
(l) Vouchers Payable.
(m) Construction Contracts Payable.
(n) Due to General Current Fund.

15. Describe two forms that may be used in preparing the combined balance sheet of an institution.

EXERCISES

1. Assuming that a gift of $100,000 is received by a school, for each case below name the fund that is affected and give the required entry:

(a) The gift is received for general educational purposes.
(b) The gift is received under conditions that permit only income to be used for general educational purposes.
(c) The gift is received for the acquisition of plant and equipment.
(d) The gift is received under conditions that permit only income to be used for the acquisition of faculty club buildings.
(e) The gift is received under conditions that permit only income to be used for loans to students.
(f) The gift is received for the payment of current interest on long-term debt.
(g) The gift is received for the payment of subsequent installments of long-term debt.
(h) The gift is received under conditions that permit income to be used for certain specified purposes only after a fixed periodic payment is made to the donor.

2. A number of transactions of the Wilson School are listed below. For each transaction, state the funds that are affected and give the entries that would be made on the fund books.

(a) Dividends and interest of $5,000 from investments in a restricted endowment fund were collected and became available for plant and equipment purchases.
(b) A restricted current fund received the income of $25,000 from an endowment fund and spent this for organized research activities.
(c) The general current fund spent $30,000 for equipment.
(d) The school received a bequest in the form of marketable securities valued at $10,000 to be used for general educational purposes.
(e) The general current fund paid bondholders $155,000, which represented interest, $50,000, and payment on the redemption of bonds of $100,000 at 105.
(f) A charge of $12,500 was made for depreciation on buildings used for auxiliary enterprises, and cash of this amount was transferred by the general current fund to the plant funds.

3. Plant funds transactions for the Western School of Law are listed below. For each transaction, state the different funds that are affected and give the entries that would be made on the fund books.

(a) A gift is received of land and buildings; land is valued at $50,000, buildings at $125,000.
(b) The general current fund makes $50,000 available for additions to buildings, and $47,500 is expended for this purpose.
(c) Serial bonds of $250,000 are issued to finance new plant; $150,000 is paid for the construction of a new building and $95,000 is paid for new equipment.
(d) Cash of $15,000 representing endowment income that is available for plant renewals and replacements is received.

(e) $10,000 is received from the general current fund, and this is applied to the retirement of current bond maturities.
(f) Land valued at $200,000 and buildings valued at $350,000 are transferred to the school in an annuity arrangement providing for the payment of net income on the property to the donor for the rest of his life.

4. A university loan fund on July 1, 1966, reports the following assets: cash, $18,500; notes receivable, $48,600; investments, $40,000; accrued interest on investments, $750. Give the entries that would be made for the year ended June 30, 1967, for loan fund transactions that are summarized below.

(a) Loans to students, $45,600; loan repayments, $54,200, which includes interest of $1,600; loans written off as uncollectible, $350.
(b) A bequest in the form of securities valued at $24,000 was received, the bequest providing that both principal and interest be available for loan purposes.
(c) Interest and dividend collections on investments totaled $3,000.
(d) Bonds carried at a book value of $19,600 were sold for $20,750, which included accrued interest of $350.
(e) Accrued interest on investments on June 30, 1967, was $800.

5. An annuity funds balance sheet for the Merced School shows the following balances on December 31, 1966:

Cash	$ 7,500	Annuity Fund A	$25,000
Investments	72,500	Annuity Fund B	25,000
		Annuity Fund C	30,000
	$80,000		$80,000

Terms of the annuity funds were as follows:

Fund A — Fund net income is to be paid to the annuitant for life.
Fund B — $2,500 per year is to be paid to the annuitant for life.
Fund C — $5,000 per year is to be paid to the annuitant for life.

Assets were pooled under terms providing that periodic net income as well as losses and gains on sales of securities are to be related to the individual endowments in proportion to the annuity fund balances at the beginning of each calendar year.

During 1967, interest and dividends were collected totaling $6,000. Securities, cost $22,500, were sold for $26,500. Distributions of income were made in accordance with annuity agreements. The income beneficiary named in Annuity Fund C died at the end of the year, and cash equal to the annuity fund balance was transferred to the unexpended plant fund to be used for plant additions in accordance with terms of the annuity agreement.

Give the entries required for the above transactions on the annuity funds books.

PROBLEMS

25-1. A trial balance of the general current ledger for the Sawyer School on July 1, 1966, was as follows:

Cash	$155,000	
Accounts Receivable	140,000	
Allowance for Uncollectible Accounts		$ 5,000
Inventories and Supplies	35,000	
Prepaid Expenses	7,500	
Vouchers Payable		185,000
Accrued Expenses		10,000
Deferred Income		15,000
Unappropriated Surplus		122,500
	$337,500	$337,500

Transactions of the general current fund for the period July 1, 1966–June 30, 1967, are summarized below.

(a) Educational and general revenues, $3,200,000, of which $155,000 has not been collected on June 30, 1967.
(b) Revenues related to auxiliary enterprises, $385,000, of which $12,500 has not been collected on June 30, 1967.
(c) Revenues related to student aid, $300,000, all of which has been collected.
(d) Collections during the year on the accounts receivable balance as of July 1, 1966, $130,000; accounts of $1,500 were written off as uncollectible.
(e) Educational and general expenditures, $3,050,000, of which $212,500 has not been paid on June 30, 1967.
(f) Expenses related to auxiliary enterprises, $305,000, of which $25,000 has not been paid on June 30, 1967.
(g) Expenses related to student aid, $315,000, all of which was paid.
(h) Payments during the year on vouchers payable as of June 30, 1966, $185,000.
(i) Acquisition of equipment for $300,000, $60,000 being paid currently and the balance to be paid in subsequent years; the property item and related liability are to be carried in the plant funds.
(j) Payment of $177,500 on mortgage payable, representing $125,000 on principal and $52,500 interest; the mortgage is carried in the plant funds.
(k) Transfer from general current fund of $40,000, money to be employed as an endowment fund.
(l) Collection of $17,500 on the sale of equipment no longer required; the equipment was carried in the plant funds.
(m) Adjustments required on June 30, 1967:

Related to auxiliary enterprises:	
Inventory of materials and supplies	$42,500
Prepaid expenses	6,000
Accrued expenses	10,000
Related to educational and general activities:	
Allowance for uncollectible accounts — required balance	6,500
Deferred income	22,500

Instructions: (1) Give the entries to record the transactions of the general current fund and to close the accounts at the end of the period.

(2) Prepare (a) a balance sheet, (b) a summary of current income and expenditures, and (c) a summary of changes in the general current fund balance for the year.

25-2. A trial balance for the general fund of Meridith Hospital on January 1, 1967, was as follows:

Cash	$ 27,500	
Accounts Receivable	85,000	
Allowance for Uncollectible Accounts		$ 3,500
Due from Temporary Funds	15,000	
Inventory of Supplies	45,000	
Accounts Payable		47,500
Due to Plant Fund		65,000
Accrued Salaries and Wages		4,000
General Fund Balance		52,500
	$172,500	$172,500

The following transactions affected the general fund during 1967:

(a) Gross charges to patients and adjustments and allowances against such charges were:

	Gross Charges	Free Service and Adjustments	Courtesy and Misc. Allowances
Routine services — inpatients	$410,000	$35,000	$4,500
Routine services — outpatients	40,000	15,000	1,000
Special services	192,500	12,500	500
	$642,500	$62,500	$6,000

It is estimated that $5,000 of the net billings will prove uncollectible.

(b) Collections on receivables were $605,000; uncollectible accounts of $4,000 were written off.

(c) Other hospital revenues were:

General contributions, donations, legacies, and bequests	$195,000
Grants from governmental agencies	180,000
Donated services and commodities	5,000
Income transfers from temporary funds	65,000
Miscellaneous revenues	15,000

All of these were collected in 1967, with the exception of $17,500 that is still due from temporary funds; the balance due from temporary funds on January 1 of $15,000 had been collected.

(d) Expenditures for hospital supplies that were placed into the inventory totaled $210,000. All supplies were paid for, except for purchases in December totaling $54,000; the accounts payable on January 1, 1967, of $47,500 had all been paid.

(e) Supplies were charged out of the inventory as follows:

Administrative and general	$ 12,500
Dietary	145,000
Household and property	15,000
Professional care patients	20,000
Outpatient and emergency	5,000
Other expenses	10,000
	$207,500

(f) Payroll information for 1967 is summarized as follows:

	Amount Accrued on Jan. 1	Total Paid during 1967	Amount Accrued on Dec. 31
Administrative and general	$ —	$100,000	$ —
Dietary	1,250	75,000	1,050
Household and property	—	35,000	—
Professional care of patients	2,400	275,000	4,750
Outpatient and emergency	250	30,000	450
Other expenses	100	45,000	—
	$4,000	$560,000	$6,250

(g) Payments of hospital expenses other than salaries and wages were as follows:

Administrative and general	$ 23,500
Dietary	10,000
Household and property	12,000
Professional care of patients	42,500
Outpatient and emergency	1,500
Other expenses	12,500
	$102,000

(h) Payments of $105,000 were made to bondholders, including interest on bonds of $30,000 and payment of serial maturities due of $75,000. (Bonds are reported in the plant fund.)

(i) Payment of $65,000 was made to the plant fund, representing depreciation on the hospital properties recognized for 1966. A charge for depreciation on hospital properties for 1967 of $82,500 is recognized, and a liability to the plant fund is set up for this amount as of December 31.

Instructions: (1) Give the entries to record the transactions of the general fund and to close the accounts at the end of 1967.

(2) Prepare (a) a balance sheet, (b) a statement of revenue and expense, and (c) a summary of changes in the general fund balance for the year.

25-3. A trial balance of the endowment funds for Oceanside College as of June 30, 1966, follows:

Cash	$ 566,000	
Endowment Fund #1, for general purposes		$ 566,000
A County Bonds (face value, $300,000)	317,500	
B County Bonds (face value, $200,000)	205,000	
Endowment Fund #2, for restricted purposes		522,500
	$1,088,500	$1,088,500

During the year July 1, 1966–June 30, 1967, the following transactions affecting endowment funds took place:

(a) Resources of the two endowments were pooled, with the following conditions applying to the pooling:
(1) Cash is to be invested in top-rated bonds.
(2) Income distributions at the rate of 4% on the endowment balances are to be made at the end of each year.
Bonds were restated to market on the date of the pooling as follows: A County Bonds, $312,500; B County Bonds, $197,500.

(b) Cash of $250,000 was received from a donor in establishing Endowment Fund #3, the income to be used for certain designated college purposes. This cash was pooled with resources of Endowment Funds #1 and #2 under the same conditions applying to the original pooling.

(c) C Company Bonds, face value $750,000, were acquired for $812,500, which includes accrued interest of $15,000.

(d) Properties were received from a donor to be used as a dormitory. Dormitory income is to be used for certain restricted purposes and is to be accounted for in the restricted current funds. Depreciation is to be recognized in calculating net income, and cash equal to this charge is to be transferred to the endowment fund periodically to maintain fund principal intact. The endowment is designated as Endowment Fund #4. Properties are recorded at appraised values as follows:

Land	$52,500
Buildings	85,000
Equipment	35,000

(e) The following assets were received from a donor, the income to be used for general educational purposes:

Cash	$50,000
D Company Stock, 1,000 shares	12,500

The fund is designated as Endowment Fund #5.

(f) D Company stock was sold for $12,350.

(g) Cash of $100,000 was received from the general current fund, the board of trustees authorizing that the cash transferred shall function as an endowment. The fund is designated as Endowment Fund #6.

(h) Notification was received of the transfer of assets under terms of a will to a trustee who is to administer certain assets for the benefit of the college. Assets in the trust are valued at $136,250 on the date of its creation; income of the trust is to be made available for general college purposes. This fund is designated as Endowment Fund #7.

(i) Interest collections on pooled resources for the year were $77,750. Premium amortization of $3,750 and discount amortization of $500 was recognized on investments. An income distribution at the agreed 4% rate was made to current and plant funds in accordance with terms of the endowment funds.

(j) Cash of $11,250 was received from the restricted current funds, representing depreciation on endowment properties as follows: buildings, $4,250; equipment, $7,000.

(k) Notification was received from the trustee of Endowment Fund #7 of the sale of certain principal assets at a gain of $30,000.

Instructions: (1) Give the entries to record the transactions of the endowment funds for the year.

(2) Prepare a balance sheet for the endowment funds as of June 30, 1967.

25-4. The Parker Prep School was organized at the beginning of 1967 as a private nonprofit educational institution. At the time of its organization, it received four gifts of cash that were to be administered as endowments as follows:

Endowment A — $100,000, income to be used for educational purposes.
Endowment B — $80,000, income to be used for student scholarships.
Endowment C — $50,000, income to be used for student loans
Endowment D — $20,000, income to be used to pay off general long-term debt.

Terms of the endowments permitted the pooling of resources and the distribution of income in amounts to be determined by the school's governing board.

During 1967, the following transactions took place:

(a) Endowment resources were merged and investments were made as follows:
$125,000 X Co. bonds, purchased at 102½ plus accrued interest, $500.
1,000 shares Y Co. preferred stock, purchased at 88.
1,000 shares Z Co. common stock, purchased at 30½.

(b) Interest collected on bonds during the year totaled $6,875; premium amortization of $625 was recognized.

(c) Cash dividends on preferred and common stocks totaled $8,250.

(d) The Z Co. common stock was sold at 36; the gain was carried directly to endowment fund balances in proportion to their beginning balances.

(e) The board of trustees of the school authorized the distribution of income of $12,500 in proportion to the beginning fund balances. The balance of the income is to be reserved to assure stability of income distributions in future periods.

Instructions: (1) Give the entries to record the foregoing transactions on the books of the endowment fund, and prepare a balance sheet for the endowment funds as of December 31, 1967.

(2) Name the other funds affected by the foregoing transactions and give the entries that would be required on the books of each of these funds.

25-5. Trial balances of the plant funds for Carlson College on June 30, 1966, follow:

Cash	$ 22,500	
Investments	180,000	
Unexpended Plant Fund — Plant Additions (from Gifts)		$ 65,000
Unexpended Plant Fund — Plant Renewals and Replacements (from General Current Fund)		137,500
	$202,500	$202,500
Land	$ 650,000	
Buildings	800,000	
Equipment	1,400,000	
Bonds Payable		$1,200,000
Investment in Plant — from Gifts		1,650,000
	$2,850,000	$2,850,000

The following transactions affected the plant funds during the year July 1, 1966–June 30, 1967:

(a) A gift of $500,000 cash was received, $200,000 to be used for financing plant additions and the balance to be invested and ultimately applied to the retirement of plant debt.

(b) The cash received in (a) is invested in the purchase of 5,000 shares of 5% preferred stock of United Steel at par.

(c) $50,000 was received from the general current fund to finance plant and equipment replacements.

(d) Equipment carried on the books at $40,000 was retired; $3,500 was recovered on the sale of such equipment and the cash was retained by the plant funds.

(e) Equipment that was retired was replaced by new equipment costing $65,000.

(f) The general current fund sent checks to bondholders of $104,000, $54,000 representing interest on bonds and the balance representing payment on current serial maturities.

(g) A fire destroyed a part of the plant reported on the books at $65,000; cash of $30,000 was recovered on an insurance policy and the cash was retained by the plant funds.

(h) Revenues for the year ended June 30, 1967, were:

On investments included in unexpended plant fund resources	$21,150
On investments included in retirement of indebtedness fund resources	15,000

Instructions: (1) Give the entries to record the transactions of the plant funds for the year.

(2) Prepare a combined balance sheet for the plant funds as of June 30, 1967.

25-6. Transactions of Orange County College for 1967 are as follows:

January 1

Orange County College, which previously held no endowment funds, received five gifts as a result of an appeal for funds. The campaign closed December 31 and all gifts are to be recorded as of January 1. Gifts were as follows:

(1) From A. B. Smith, $10,000, the principal to be held intact and the income to be used for any purpose that the Board of Control of Orange County College should indicate.

(2) From C. D. Jones, $20,000, the principal to be held intact and the income to be used to endow scholarships for worthy students.

(3) From E. F. Green, $30,000, the principal to be held intact and the interest only to be loaned to students. All income is to be again loaned, and all losses from student loans are to be charged against income.

(4) From G. H. White, $200,000. During the lifetime of the donor, semiannual payments of $2,500 are to be made to him. Upon his death the fund is to be used to construct or purchase a residence hall for housing men students.

(5) From I. J. Brown, 1,000 shares of XYZ stock, which had a market value on this date of $150 per share. Such shares are to be held for not more than 5 years and all income received thereon held intact. At any date during this period, designated by the Board of Control, all assets are to be liquidated and the proceeds used to build a student hospital.

(6) The Board of Control consolidated the Smith and Jones funds as to assets into Merged Investments Account (in the proportion of their principal accounts) and purchased $25,000 of Electric Power Company bonds at par. Interest rate, 4%; interest dates, January 1 and July 1.

(7) The cash of the Green fund was used to purchase $30,000 of Steam Power Company 5% bonds at par and accrued interest. Interest dates, April 1 and October 1.

(8) The $200,000 cash of the White fund was used to purchase $200,000 of 2% U.S. Treasury notes at par. Interest dates, January 1 and July 1.

July 1

(9) All interest has been received as stipulated on bonds owned, and $4,000 dividends were received on XYZ stock.

(10) Payment was made to G. H. White in accordance with the terms of his gift. A loan of cash was authorized from endowment funds to cover the overdraft created.

(11) $20,000 par of Electric Power Company bonds were sold at 102. No commission was involved.

(12) A loan was made to M. N. Black, $300, from the Green student loan fund.

October 1

(13) Notice was received of the death of G. H. White. There is no liability to his estate.

(14) A scholarship award of $200 was made to G. P. Gray from the Jones Scholarship fund.

(15) $200,000 par of U.S. Treasury notes held by the White fund were sold at 101 and accrued interest. The endowment funds loan was repaid.

(16) Interest due on bonds was received.

December 31

(17) M. N. Black paid $100 principal and $5 interest on his student loan.

(18) The Board of Control purchased a building suitable for a residence hall for $250,000, using the available funds from the G. H. White gift as part payment therefor and giving a 20-year mortgage payable for the balance.

Instructions: (1) Prepare skeleton ledger accounts and record the transactions of the college for 1967. In setting up ledger accounts, classify them into suitable groups by funds. In entering transactions, key these to the transaction numbers given. Accounts need not be ruled or formally balanced.

(2) Prepare a trial balance, listing all of the accounts used even if they do not have a balance.

(AICPA adapted)

25-7. The Jones Medical Foundation was established in 1959 to finance research in the field of medical science. It leased building facilities from others from the date of its foundation to December, 1966, at which time land and buildings adaptable to its operation were purchased.

Since it was desired to operate its plant property as a self-supporting entity, the board decided to account for its plant as a separate fund, by establishment of a general fund and of a plant fund. All cash is to be handled by the general fund, with the plant fund being charged or credited with amounts applicable to it until after the close of each year. At this time settlement will be made if possible. The plant property is to be depreciated effective as of January 1, 1967 at the rate of 5% per annum. A depreciation fund is to be established.

The assets, debts, and capital accounts as of December 31 show the following:

Jones Medical Foundation

	December 31	
Assets	1967	1966
Cash	$ 42,000	$ 36,000
Investments	217,000	67,000
Plant Account	96,000	75,000
Unexpired Insurance Premiums	1,000	
Plant Operations		1,000
Total	$356,000	$179,000
Liabilities		
Accounts Payable	$ 6,000	$ 4,000
Rents	3,000	
Balance	347,000	175,000
Total	$356,000	$179,000

Upon analysis of the plant account, you find the following:

Date	Item	Dr.	Cr.
9/30/66	Cash donation for purchase of plant..		$100,000
12/15/66	Purchase of property...............	$175,000	
1/31/67	Building improvements............	24,000	
3/31/67	Building improvements............	15,000	
12/31/67	Plant operation..................		18,000

Debit entries in the plant operation account consisted of:

12/31/66	Coal, cleaning supplies, etc..........	$ 1,000
2/28/67	Coal, cleaning supplies, etc..........	4,000
6/30/67	Grading and seeding of grounds.....	6,000
7/31/67	Cleaning supplies, etc...............	1,200
12/31/67	Coal, cleaning supplies, etc..........	4,000
12/31/67	Expired insurance premiums........	1,800
12/31/67	Plant account......................	18,000

Rents consisted of $3,000 per month received in 1967 and rent for January, 1968, which was received on December 31, 1967.

You obtain an appraisal of the land owned by the Foundation, which gives a value of $75,000 at date of purchase.

Instructions: (1) Prepare journal entries setting up the plant fund and recording the transactions in the fund to December 31, 1967.

(2) Prepare a sectional balance sheet presenting the funds as of December 31, 1967.

(AICPA adapted)

25-8. The X Society, a fraternal order, which operated the A County Hospital for indigent members of the community, donated it on September 1, 1966, to the Village of H, in which it is located. The gift included all of the securities in the endowment fund (the hospital's principal source of income), as well as the real estate, equipment, and other assets. Since the village had made no appropriation for the operation and maintenance of a hospital, gifts from public-spirited citizens supplemented the endowment fund income to provide for operating costs during the first year of its operation by the village, which coincided with the village fiscal year. No part of the principal of endowments may be used for operations. Before the end of the year, preparations were under way for a drive to raise funds to enlarge and improve the plant. Since no money was collected in connection with this drive during the year under consideration, all expenditures for plant improvements were paid out of the general fund, but they will be reimbursed from the proceeds of the drive.

The transactions given on the following page occurred during the first year:

Contributions and Receipts

(1)	Hospital site — value	$ 25,000
(2)	Hospital buildings — value	200,000
(3)	U.S. Treasury bonds contributed as endowment, principal amount	100,000
(4)	Accrued interest on U.S. bonds at August 31, 1966	1,250
(5)	Stocks and bonds contributed as endowments (no accrued dividends or interest) — market value	1,300,000
(6)	Equipment — value	60,000
(7)	Life insurance policies assigned to hospital as endowments— Cash value $5,000 Face amount $150,000 (Hospital to pay future premiums)	
(8)	Contribution from A County for hospital operations	10,000
(9)	Contributions from numerous individuals for hospital operations	20,000
(10)	Proceeds from sponsored charity bazaar	500
(11)	Interest received from U.S. Treasury bonds	2,500
(12)	Dividends from stocks	44,000
(13)	Interest from bonds, other than U.S. Treasury	12,000
(14)	Sale of stocks included in endowments at $27,000	52,000

Disbursements

(15)	Building improvements	20,000
(16)	Equipment	15,000
(17)	Salaries	15,000
(18)	Food and dietary supplies	10,000
(19)	Medicinal supplies	20,000
(20)	Life insurance premium paid	2,000
(21)	Property insurance	5,000
(22)	Light, heat, and water	1,000
(23)	Expenses of charity bazaar, announcements, etc.	15
(24)	Other operating expenses	4,000

Other Information

(25)	Cash value of life insurance held for benefit of hospital at August 31, 1967	6,500
(26)	Contributions subscribed but not collected	5,000
(27)	Prepaid insurance at end of year	500
	Balance in bank per bank statement at end of period	51,085
	Outstanding checks amount to $3,300, and the last day's deposit of $1,200 is not included on the bank statement.	
(28)	Upon completion of the $20,000 improvements, the hospital building was appraised at $250,000.	

Instructions: (1) Prepare a work sheet to record the transactions relative to the A County Hospital for the year ended August 31, 1967.

(2) Prepare a balance sheet for the A County Hospital as of August 31, 1967, that reflects a general fund, an endowment fund, and a plant fund.

(AICPA adapted)

25-9. The Town of Hot Springs built a town hospital on land previously owned by the town. The building was completed on March 1, 1967. Since that date the hospital has been under the control of a superintendent. He has rendered monthly reports to the town mayor, but these reports have been on a cash basis and have not shown separation of amounts by funds. You have been employed by the town government to prepare financial statements for the 10 months ended December 31, 1967, and to do certain other work in connection with setting up an accounting system for the hospital operations. The town wants the financial statements to be on an accrual basis, to the extent such basis is appropriate, and to follow usual fund accounting practices. The data listed below are assembled.

(1) The total contract price of the buildings was $240,000. The contractor was paid in the following manner:
   (a) Cash of $120,000, which was a contribution by the federal government toward the hospital cost.
   (b) Cash of $25,000, contributed by the county government toward the cost.
   (c) Hospital bonds issued by the town to the contractor in the amount of $100,000. These bonds are 5% bonds dated 1/1/67, due in 10 years, interest payable semiannually. They are general obligation bonds of the town, but the town wishes to carry them in the hospital fund.

(2) Equipment was initially obtained as follows:
   (a) Purchased by the town for cash — $35,300.
   (b) Purchased out of cash donations made by citizens for that purpose — $9,800.
   (c) Donated equipment that had an estimated value of — $11,000.

(3) The statement of cash receipts and disbursements, exclusive of items described above, for the 10 months was as follows:

Received from patients:	
Room and meals	$105,314
Fees	6,170
Out-patients	4,201
Miscellaneous income from meals, etc.	515
Received from estate of James Johnson, M.D.	25,000
Miscellaneous donations	10,410
Received from Beulah Jenkins	32,500
Donations from churches	1,850
Received from county for county charity patients — room and meals	940
Income from rents	2,000
Income from bonds	2,125
Total cash received	$191,025
Payroll and taxes thereon paid	$ 96,200
Stores and supplies purchased	34,180
Equipment purchased	27,250
Expense of operating rented property	700
Miscellaneous expenses (including bond interest of $2,500)	4,170
Total cash disbursed	$162,500
Balance of cash 12/31/67	$ 28,525

(4) Investigation revealed the following additional information:

(a) Patients' accounts on the books as of December 31, 1967, amounted to \$9,403, distributed as follows: for room and meals — \$7,310; for laboratory and other fees — \$1,095; for outpatients — \$998. It is estimated that \$500 of these accounts will never be collected.

(b) As of December 31, 1967, accrued unpaid wages, etc. amounted to \$5,234, unpaid supply invoices amounted to \$6,810, and accrued utilities amounted to \$174. The analysis of miscellaneous expenses showed that there was \$330 of prepaid insurance. Kitchen and other supplies on hand amounted to \$1,760 at cost.

(c) It has been decided to charge current income with depreciation on general hospital property at the following annual rates based on the year-end balance of the asset accounts:
Buildings — 2%.
Equipment — 10% and 20%.
All equipment will take the 10% rate except for \$18,500 of minor items of equipment, which will be depreciated at the 20% rate. Depreciation is to be computed for a full year. The allowance is not to be funded.

(d) The following facts were determined in respect to the donations:

(1) The donation from the estate of James Johnson, M.D. was received July 1, 1967. It consisted of two houses and \$25,000 in cash. The terms of the bequest provided that the cash is to be invested and that the income therefrom and from the houses is to be used for the purchase of surgical equipment. The houses had a market value of approximately \$30,000, of which amount \$5,000 was for the land. The estimated life of the properties from date of the gift was 25 years. The houses were rented, and in addition to the \$2,000 of rent received there was \$150 receivable as of December 31, 1967. All expenses on the houses for the year were paid and were included in the disbursements. No purchase of surgical equipment has been approved.

(2) The miscellaneous donations were made for general purposes of the operation of the hospital.

(3) The Beulah Jenkins donation received on June 1, 1967, consisted of cash and of \$50,000 face value of X Corporation 4¼% bonds. Interest dates are June 1 and December 1. The provisions of the gift were: "The amounts are to be invested by said trustees in accordance with applicable law governing trust investments and the income derived therefrom is to be used to defray or help to defray the necessary hospitalization of such indigent women as the trustees shall designate upon application by their physician." The trustees were designated in the document. These trustees have accepted but have never met or transacted any business.

(4) The donations from churches are to apply toward purchase of an "iron lung." No order has yet been placed for such equipment.

Instructions: From the information that is given, prepare a statement of revenue and expense for the general fund, a summary of changes in the general fund balance, and a combined fund balance sheet.

(AICPA adapted)

25-10. The balances of the general ledger accounts for the Prep School as at July 1, 1967, are as follows:

Cash — For General Use	$ 1,000	
Cash — From Alumni Subscriptions for New Dormitory	2,000	
Cash — Endowment	45,000	
Cash — For Student Loans	1,000	
Tuition Receivable	12,500	
Investments — Temporary Investments of General Cash	4,000	
Investments — Endowment	250,000	
Stores	15,000	
Alumni Subscriptions for New Dormitory (due Sept. 30, 1966)	8,000	
Student Loans Receivable	3,500	
Educational Plant:		
Financed from Original and Subsequent Endowments	600,000	
Financed from Tuition Funds	50,000	
Financed from Alumni Subscriptions	200,000	
Financed by Grant from State and Local Government	50,000	
Accounts Payable for Supplies		$ 3,500
Unpaid Expenses of Alumni Subscription Campaign		1,000
Balance		1,237,500
	$1,242,000	$1,242,000

Transactions completed by the Prep School in the period July 1, 1967–June 30, 1968, follow:

(1) Endowment investments and $40,000 of the endowment cash represent the principal of endowment funds held under terms providing that the income therefrom shall be used only for operating expenses of the school. The balance of endowment fund cash represents accumulated income not transferred from the endowment to the general fund.

(2) Student population was 150 students. The tuition rate was $1,000 per school year per student, except for 6 full scholarships and 3 partial (½) scholarships.

(3) 90% of current tuition was collected, and $100 of the balance is considered uncollectible.

(4) Tuition receivable of prior years was collected in the amount of $12,000 and the balance is considered uncollectible.

(5) Charges for operating expenses incurred and supplies purchased during the year totaled $135,000.

(6) Inventory of operating supplies at June 30, 1968, amounted to $13,500.

(7) Accounts payable for operating supplies and expenses amounted to $2,000 at June 30, 1968.

(8) All temporary investments of general cash were sold on July 1, 1967, for $4,300 and accrued interest of $100.

(9) Endowment investments having a book value of $25,000 were sold for $27,500, including accrued interest of $500.

(10) Investments were purchased by the endowment fund trustees at a cost of $50,000.

(11) Interest on endowment fund investments not sold during the year amounted to $20,500 for the year and was all collected in cash.

(12) The endowment fund trustees transferred $22,500 to the general fund bank account.

(13) As a result of the continued alumni subscription campaign, additional subscriptions in the amount of $65,000 were received for the purpose of providing a new dormitory. These subscriptions were payable ⅕ at the date of the pledge and ⅕ quarterly beginning January 15, 1968.

(14) 5% bonds in the amount of $50,000 were issued for cash on January 1, 1968, to provide funds for immediate construction of the new dormitory. Interest was payable annually.

(15) Contracts in the amount of $70,000 were let for construction of the new dormitory out of subscriptions.

(16) The contract for construction of the new dormitory was 50% completed on June 1, 1968, and payment for half of the total amount, less a retained percentage of 10%, was made on that date.

(17) All alumni subscriptions of the current year were paid on the due dates; those due previously were also paid in full.

(18) Tuition receipts amounting to $5,000 were used to build additional bleachers at the athletic stadium.

(19) A riding stable costing $4,000 and financed during a previous year from tuition receipts was destroyed by fire. Insurance recovery was $4,500; the building will not be replaced.

(20) Student loans amounting to $3,500 were made.

(21) Student loan collections amounted to $4,000, including $200 interest.

(22) Expenses of the alumni subscription campaign were paid in full in the amount of $1,500.

Instructions: Prepare work sheets showing opening balances, transactions, and adjustments for the year ended June 30, 1968, and closed trial balances as of June 30, 1968, for each of the four funds into which the general ledger is divided: general fund, plant fund, endowment fund, and student loan fund.

(AICPA adapted)

25-11. The following balances appear on the books of Memorial Hospital as of January 1, 1967:

	Debits	Credits
Cash on Hand and in Banks	$ 143,866	
Accounts Receivable — Patients	48,740	
Sundry Accounts Receivable	508	
Inventory of Supplies	17,583	
Prepaid Insurance	3,294	
Stocks and Bonds	3,702,010	
Other Investments	225,950	
Land	25,000	
Buildings	402,305	
Equipment	106,500	
Allowance for Loss on Accounts		$ 10,385
Accounts Payable		29,227
Other Current Liabilities		38,014
Bonds Payable — 1st mortgage 5%		300,000
Advance Payments by Patients		6,364
Balance		4,291,766
	$4,675,756	$4,675,756

A summary of transactions of the hospital for 1967 follows:

(1) The stocks and bonds, together with $112,808 of the cash, belong to endowment funds, the income of which may be used for general purposes of the hospital. An additional $12,150 of cash belongs to specific expendable funds. Buildings and equipment are stated net of depreciation, which has been charged to the current expenses of each year. There is no intention to provide a fund for replacement of assets, and as assets are replaced, payments are made out of general cash. The other investments belong to endowment funds for specific purposes. The income from these funds may be used only for the designated purposes.

(2) Cash income from endowment fund stocks and bonds amounted to $138,710. Income from other investments amounted to $11,765.

(3) Cash donations received amounted to $41,305, all except $10,500 of which was for current use. The $10,500 was expendable only for a designated purpose.

(4) Services rendered pay patients amounted to $930,480, which was all recorded through Accounts Receivable — Patients.

(5) Cash collected from patients and prospective patients amounted to $925,428, of which $12,890 represented advance payments.

(6) Cash of $1,375 was collected on sundry accounts receivable.

(7) The allowance for loss on accounts was increased by $10,000. Patients' accounts totaling $6,302 were considered to be uncollectible and were written off.

(8) Depreciation on the buildings was $11,307. Depreciation on equipment was $18,541.

(9) The following vouchers were approved:
Storeroom supplies, $78,240; insurance, $11,624; general operating expenses, $979,731; maintenance, $7,448; replacement of equipment, $11,432; interest on bonds, $15,000; retirement of bonds, $10,000. Other Current Liabilities was created with $505,212 of these $1,113,475 of vouchers.

(10) The carrying value of equipment replaced was $2,710.

(11) Free services rendered during the year amounted to $108,000.

(12) Services rendered patients (see No. 4) were covered by advance payments amounting to $14,105.

(13) Cash disbursements of $502,701 in payment of other current liabilities and $610,043 in payment of accounts payable were made. Discounts on accounts payable amounted to $2,305.

(14) Storeroom supplies of $72,578 were issued for general use, and $1,073 of supplies were sold to employees and charged to Sundry Accounts Receivable. Insurance expired amounted to $10,445.

(15) Cash expenditures from specific expendable funds were $5,875.

(16) Cash receipts for the year included unexpendable cash contributions of $50,000, proceeds from sale of stocks and bonds of $502,164, and proceeds from sale of other investments of $52,125.

(17) Cash disbursements not vouchered consisted of $507,892 for purchase of stocks and bonds and $48,100 of the proceeds from sale of other investments that was invested in bonds.

(18) There was a loss of $7,354 sustained on the sale of stocks and bonds and a $9,978 loss sustained on the sale of other investments.

Instructions: From the foregoing information and summary of the transactions for the year ended December 31, 1967, prepare work sheets showing by appropriate funds all information needed for (a) a statement of revenue and expense for the year and (b) a balance sheet for each fund as of December 31, 1967. Changes in surplus accounts or in fund balances should be shown in additional columns unless all such changes are clearly identified in the balance sheet columns.

(AICPA adapted)

Chapter 26

COMPOUND INTEREST

AMOUNTS

Actuarial science is the study of compound interest and insurance probabilities. It is the actuary who is called upon to solve complex problems requiring the application of the principles of actuarial science. Nevertheless, the accountant should be familiar with the fundamentals of actuarial science, for he may have to interpret or solve certain problems that require the application of these principles. Such problems include those relating to investments, long-term obligations, sinking funds, depreciation, and leaseholds. The principles of compound interest are described in this and the following chapter. The application of these principles to certain problems that the accountant may encounter is discussed and illustrated in Chapter 28.

COMPOUND INTEREST

By *compound interest* is meant interest that accrues upon the unpaid interest of past periods as well as upon the principal. Interest that accrues during the period is considered to increase the principal. Compound interest must be distinguished from *simple interest*, which is interest upon the original principal regardless of interest amounts that may have accrued upon the principal in past periods.

Amount and present value. Problems involving the application of the principles of compound interest require interpretation in terms of "amount" and "present value."

Amount. The value at a later date of a given sum that is left at compound interest is known as the *amount* or the *compound amount* of the given sum. An amount may be sought for a single sum left to accumulate interest or for a series of equal sums left at regular intervals to accumulate interest. In the latter case the amount consists of the increased values of all of the original sums. The calculation of amounts is considered in this chapter.

Present value. The value at an earlier date of a given sum discounted at compound interest is known as the *present value* of the given sum. A present value may be sought for a single sum or for a series of equal sums that are due at regular intervals. In the latter case the present value consists of the discounted values of all of the original sums. The calculation of present values is discussed in the next chapter.

AMOUNT OF SINGLE GIVEN SUM

In determining the amount to which a single sum will accumulate at compound interest, the principal, the interest rate per period, and the number of periods during which the principal is left to accumulate interest must be known.

Although interest is commonly expressed as a certain rate per year, the interest period for purposes of compounding may be less than a year. When interest is expressed as an annual rate but the interest period is less than a year, the interest rate for the shorter period must be determined. This is done by dividing the annual rate by the number of interest periods in the year. For example, "interest at 6% compounded semiannually" indicates 2 interest periods a year and an interest rate of 3% for each 6-month period. If interest at 6% is compounded quarterly, the frequency of compounding is 4 times a year and the interest rate for each period is 1½%; if 6% is compounded monthly, the frequency of compounding is 12 times a year and the interest rate for each period is ½%.

Computation of amount of single given sum. In computing the amount of a single given sum left at compound interest, the amount to which $1 will accumulate for the given number of periods at the given interest rate is determined. The number of dollars left at interest is then multiplied by this amount.

Example: What is the amount of $1,500 left from January 1, 1966, to January 1, 1972, at interest of 4% compounded annually?

The amount of 1, which may be interpreted as $1, £1, or any other monetary unit, for 6 periods at 4% can be determined arithmetically as follows:

1.000000 × 1.04 = 1.040000, amount of 1 for 1 period at 4%
1.040000 × 1.04 = 1.081600, amount of 1 for 2 periods at 4%
1.081600 × 1.04 = 1.124864, amount of 1 for 3 periods at 4%
1.124864 × 1.04 = 1.169859, amount of 1 for 4 periods at 4%
1.169859 × 1.04 = 1.216653, amount of 1 for 5 periods at 4%
1.216653 × 1.04 = 1.265319, amount of 1 for 6 periods at 4%

The amount of $1,500 left for 6 years at 4% compounded annually is:

Sum deposited	$1,500.00
Multiply by amount of 1 for 6 periods at 4%	1.265319
Amount of $1,500 for 6 periods at 4%	$1,897.98

It may be observed that the amount of \$1,500 left for 3 years at interest of 8% compounded semiannually is identical with the above, for the number of interest periods is 6 and the interest rate for each period is 4%.

Formula for "amount of 1." Using "1" to represent a single unit of value, "i" the interest rate per single period, and "n" the number of periods, the amount of 1, represented by "a", may be expressed as a formula as follows:

$$a = (1 + i)^n$$

The foregoing example, then, may be expressed as follows:

$$\$1{,}500\ (1.04)^6 = \$1{,}500 \times 1.265319 = \$1{,}897.98$$

In finding 1.04 to the sixth power, it is not necessary to multiply six successive times as was done above. Powers of numbers may be used in the following manner:

$$(1.04 \times (1.04) = (1.04)^2 \text{ or } 1.04 \times 1.04 = 1.0816$$
$$(1.04)^2 \times (1.04)^2 = (1.04)^4 \text{ or } 1.0816 \times 1.0816 = 1.169859$$
$$(1.04)^4 \times (1.04)^2 = (1.04)^6 \text{ or } 1.169859 \times 1.0816 = 1.265319$$

It should be noted that the sum of the exponents of the interest factors gives the power of the product of the interest factors. Thus $(1 + i)^4 \times (1 + i)^2 = (1 + i)^6$.

"Amount of 1" table. Compound interest tables that show the amounts of 1 for given numbers of periods at given interest rates are available and may be used, thereby eliminating the need for multiplication in raising the interest factor to the required power. Part of a table showing amounts follows. More complete tables are given on pages 1030 and 1031.

AMOUNT OF 1 $(1 + i)^n$

Periods	2½%	3%	3½%	4%	4½%	5%
1	1.025	1.03	1.035	1.04	1.045	1.05
2	1.050625	1.0609	1.071225	1.0816	1.092025	1.1025
3	1.076891	1.092727	1.108718	1.124864	1.141166	1.157625
4	1.103813	1.125509	1.147523	1.169859	1.192519	1.215506
5	1.131408	1.159274	1.187686	1.216653	1.246182	1.276282
6	1.159693	1.194052	1.229255	1.265319	1.302260	1.340096
7	1.188686	1.229874	1.272279	1.315932	1.360862	1.407100
8	1.218403	1.266770	1.316809	1.368569	1.422101	1.477455
9	1.248863	1.304773	1.362897	1.423312	1.486095	1.551328
10	1.280085	1.343916	1.410599	1.480244	1.552969	1.628895

With the table, the amount of 1 for 6 periods at 4% is immediately found to be 1.265319. The amount table may be used in computing the amount of 1 for periods greater in number than those shown. For example, the amount of 1 for 15 periods at 4% can be computed in the following ways:

$$(1.04)^{10} \times (1.04)^{5} \text{ or } 1.480244 \times 1.216653 = 1.800944$$
$$(1.04)^{8} \times (1.04)^{7} \text{ or } 1.368569 \times 1.315932 = 1.800944$$

Computation of compound interest. *Compound interest* is the difference between a given sum and its amount. Compound interest on 1 may be determined by subtracting 1 from the amount of 1 for the given number of periods at the given rate. To find the compound interest accumulating on a given sum, the number of dollars in the given sum is multiplied by the compound interest on 1.

Example: What is the compound interest on $1,500 left from January 1, 1966, to January 1, 1972, at interest of 4% compounded annually?

The compound interest on 1 may be determined as follows:

Amount of 1 for 6 periods at 4%, $(1.04)^6$	1.265319
Less principal	1.000000
Compound interest on 1 for 6 periods at 4%	.265319

The compound interest on $1,500 for 6 years at 4% compounded annually is:

Sum deposited	$1,500.00
Multiply by compound interest on 1 for 6 periods at 4%	.265319
Compound interest on $1,500 for 6 periods at 4%	$ 397.98

Formula for "compound interest on 1." Using "I" to represent the compound interest on 1, the formula for compound interest may be stated as follows:

$$I = (1 + i)^n - 1, \text{ or}$$
$$I = a - 1$$

Using the first formula, the foregoing example may be expressed as follows:

$$\$1,500\left[(1.04)^6 - 1\right] = \$1,500(1.265319 - 1) = \$1,500 \times .265319 = \$397.98$$

With tables showing the amounts of 1, the compound interest on 1 is readily determined by subtracting 1 from the amount of 1 for the given number of periods at the given interest rate.

ANNUITIES

A series of equal payments at regular intervals with interest compounded at a certain rate is known as an *annuity*. The equal periodic payments are called *rents*. The regular interval between payments may be any period such as a month, a quarter-year, a half-year, or a year.

AMOUNT OF AN ANNUITY

The *amount of an annuity* is the amount of a series of rents left at compound interest. Stated differently, it is the accumulated total that results from a series of equal deposits at regular intervals left at compound interest. Both deposits and interest serve to increase the accumulation.

The total becoming available immediately after the last rent of a series is known as the *amount of an ordinary annuity*. If interest continues for one period after the last rent, the total is known as the *amount of an annuity due*. The distinction is presented graphically below.

Amount of an Ordinary Annuity

Amount on Dec. 31, 1970, to be determined; interest at 4% is compounded annually.

1st Deposit of $1.00	2nd Deposit of $1.00	3rd Deposit of $1.00	4th Deposit of $1.00	5th Deposit of $1.00
*	*	*	*	*
Dec. 31 1966	Dec. 31 1967	Dec. 31 1968	Dec. 31 1969	Dec. 31 1970

Amount of an Annuity Due

Amount on Dec. 31, 1971, to be determined; interest at 4% is compounded annually.

1st Deposit of $1.00	2nd Deposit of $1.00	3rd Deposit of $1.00	4th Deposit of $1.00	5th Deposit of $1.00	
*	*	*	*	*	|
Dec. 31 1966	Dec. 31 1967	Dec. 31 1968	Dec. 31 1969	Dec. 31 1970	Dec. 31 1971

In the first example, the amount of an ordinary annuity is to be determined since interest does not accumulate after the last deposit. Here, the amount of an ordinary annuity of 5 rents of $1 at 4% is to be computed. In the second example, the amount of an annuity due is to be determined since interest continues to accumulate for 1 period following the last deposit. In this case, the amount of an annuity due of 5 rents of $1 at 4% is to be computed.

It is apparent from the illustrations that the amount of an annuity due is greater than the amount of an ordinary annuity of the same number of rents by the interest for one period following the last rent. The amount of an ordinary annuity of 5 rents of $1 when multiplied by the rate of increase for one period, then, gives the amount of an annuity due of 5 rents of $1. Or, if the amount of an ordinary annuity of 6 rents of $1 is known, this amount less $1 gives the amount of an annuity due of 5 rents. This is the case because the accumulation of the annuity due of 5 rents is identical with that of an ordinary annuity of 6 rents except for the absence of the sixth rent of $1.

Computation of the amount of an annuity. To find the amount of an annuity, the total accumulation for a series of rents of 1 is determined. The number of dollars in each rent for which the amount is required is then multiplied by the amount for the annuity of 1.

Example 1: Amount of an ordinary annuity. What is the accumulated amount on December 31, 1970, of a series of 5 annual deposits of $2,500, the first deposit being made on December 31, 1966? Interest of 4% is compounded annually.

Example 2: Amount of an annuity due. What is the accumulated amount of the above annuity on December 31, 1971, 1 period after the last deposit?

Amount of the ordinary annuity computed. The amount of an ordinary annuity of 5 rents of 1 at 4% may be determined arithmetically as follows:

Amount of 1 (deposit, Dec. 31, 1966), interest for 4 periods at 4% = $(1.04)^4$	= 1.169859
Amount of 1 (deposit, Dec. 31, 1967), interest for 3 periods at 4% = $(1.04)^3$	= 1.124864
Amount of 1 (deposit, Dec. 31, 1968), interest for 2 periods at 4% = $(1.04)^2$	= 1.081600
Amount of 1 (deposit, Dec. 31, 1969), interest for 1 period at 4%.	= 1.040000
Final rent of 1 (deposit, Dec. 31, 1970), that accumulates no interest	= 1.000000
Amount of an ordinary annuity of 5 rents of 1 at 4%	5.416323

The amount of the ordinary annuity of 5 rents of $2,500 at 4% is:

Periodic rents.	$ 2,500.00
Multiply by amount of an ordinary annuity of 5 rents of 1 at 4%.	5.416323
Amount of ordinary annuity of 5 rents of $2,500 at 4% . .	$13,540.81

The process of accumulation of the annuity through deposits and interest takes place as shown in the table below:

Date	Interest Accruing on Balance in Fund During Period	Amount Deposited in Fund	Total Increase in Fund for Period	Accumulated Total on Deposit
Dec. 31, 1966		$2,500.00	$2,500.00	$ 2,500.00
Dec. 31, 1967	$100.00	2,500.00	2,600.00	5,100.00
Dec. 31, 1968	204.00	2,500.00	2,704.00	7,804.00
Dec. 31, 1969	312.16	2,500.00	2,812.16	10,616.16
Dec. 31, 1970	424.65	2,500.00	2,924.65	13,540.81

Amount of the annuity due computed. If the accumulated amount on December 31, 1971, is to be determined, each rent will bear interest for one more period. The amount of an annuity due of 5 rents of 1 at 4% may be determined arithmetically as follows:

Amount of 1 (deposit, Dec. 31, 1966), interest for 5 periods at 4% = $(1.04)^5$	= 1.216653
Amount of 1 (deposit, Dec. 31, 1967), interest for 4 periods at 4% = $(1.04)^4$	= 1.169859
Amount of 1 (deposit, Dec. 31, 1968), interest for 3 periods at 4% = $(1.04)^3$	= 1.124864
Amount of 1 (deposit, Dec. 31, 1969), interest for 2 periods at 4% = $(1.04)^2$	= 1.081600
Amount of 1 (deposit, Dec. 31, 1970), interest for 1 period at 4%.	= 1.040000
Amount of an annuity due of 5 rents of 1 at 4%.	5.632976

The amount of the annuity due of 5 rents of $2,500 at 4% is:

Periodic rents.	$ 2,500.00
Multiply by amount of an annuity due of 5 rents of 1 at 4%	5.632976
Amount of annuity due of 5 rents of $2,500 at 4%.	$14,082.44

A table to show the process of accumulation follows:

Date	Interest Accruing on Balance in Fund During Period	Amount Deposited in Fund	Total Increase in Fund for Period	Accumulated Total on Deposit
Dec. 31, 1966		$2,500.00	$2,500.00	$ 2,500.00
Dec. 31, 1967	$100.00	2,500.00	2,600.00	5,100.00
Dec. 31, 1968	204.00	2,500.00	2,704.00	7,804.00
Dec. 31, 1969	312.16	2,500.00	2,812.16	10,616.16
Dec. 31, 1970	424.65	2,500.00	2,924.65	13,540.81
Dec. 31, 1971	541.63		541.63	14,082.44

Formula for "amount of an annuity of 1." Compound interest accumulates in exactly the same manner as an annuity. The compound interest on $1 for 5 periods at 4%, for example, is the equivalent of an ordinary annuity of 5 rents of 4 cents at 4% compounded periodically. This equality is illustrated in the two tables below.

ACCUMULATION OF COMPOUND INTEREST ON $1 FOR 5 PERIODS AT 4%

End of Period	Interest on Interest Already Accumulated	Interest on Principal $1	Total Increase for Period	Total Compound Interest Accumulation
1		.04	.04	.04
2	.0016	.04	.0416	.0816
3	.003264	.04	.043264	.124864
4	.0049946	.04	.0449946	.1698586
5	.0067943	.04	.0467943	.2166529

ACCUMULATION OF ORDINARY ANNUITY OF 5 RENTS OF 4 CENTS AT INTEREST OF 4%

End of Period	Interest Accruing on Balance in Fund During Period	Amount Deposited in Fund	Total Increase in Fund for Period	Accumulated Total on Deposit
1		.04	.04	.04
2	.0016	.04	.0416	.0816
3	.003264	.04	.043264	.124864
4	.0049946	.04	.0449946	.1698586
5	.0067943	.04	.0467943	.2166529

The compound interest on $1 for a given number of periods, then, is equal to the amount of an ordinary annuity of the interest amount for the same number of rents at the stated interest rate. To determine the amount of an annuity of $1 instead of an annuity of the interest amount, the following procedure may be used:

Since: the amount of an ordinary annuity of 5 rents of 4¢ at 4%. . . . . = .2166529

Then: the amount of an ordinary annuity of 5 rents of 1¢ at 4%. . . . . = .2166529 ÷ 4, or $.054163225

And: the amount of an ordinary annuity of 5 rents of $1 at 4% . . . . = .054163225 × 100, or $5.416323

The foregoing may be summarized as follows:

The amount of an ordinary annuity of 5 rents of $1 at interest of 4% is the compound interest for 5 periods at 4%, .2166529, divided by the interest rate, .04, or $5.416323. Division by .04 is equivalent to dividing by 4 to get an annuity for 1 cent and multiplying by 100 to raise this to an annuity of $1.

From the procedures just developed, the following rule may be formulated: To calculate the amount of an ordinary annuity of 1, divide the compound interest on 1 at the interest rate effective between rents and for a number of periods equal to the number of rents by the interest rate. Using "A" to represent the amount of an annuity of 1, the amount of an ordinary annuity may be expressed as a formula as follows:

$$A = \frac{(1+i)^n - 1}{i}, \text{ or in shorter form, } A = \frac{a-1}{i}, \text{ or simply, } A = \frac{I}{i}$$

Example 1, then, may be expressed as follows:

$$\$2{,}500\left[\frac{(1.04)^5 - 1}{.04}\right] = \$2{,}500\left(\frac{1.2166529 - 1}{.04}\right) = \$2{,}500\left(\frac{.2166529}{.04}\right) =$$

$$\$2{,}500 \times 5.416323 = \$13{,}540.81$$

It was pointed out on page 962 that, in determining the amount of an annuity due, the amount of an ordinary annuity of the same number of rents may be increased by the interest for one more period. The amount of an annuity due determined in this manner may be expressed as a formula as follows:

$$A \text{ due} = \left[\frac{(1+i)^n - 1}{i}\right](1+i)$$

Example 2, then, may be expressed as follows:

$$\$2{,}500\left[\frac{(1.04)^5 - 1}{.04}\right](1.04) = \$2{,}500\left(\frac{1.2166529 - 1}{.04}\right)(1.04) = \$2{,}500\left(\frac{.2166529}{.04}\right)(1.04) =$$

$$\$2{,}500 \times 5.416323 \times 1.04 = \$14{,}082.44$$

As indicated on page 962, the amount of an annuity due of 1 may be regarded as the equivalent of an ordinary annuity of one more rent minus 1. Computation in this way is more convenient when compound interest tables are available. The formula for the amount of an annuity due as thus defined is:

$$A \text{ due} = \left[\frac{(1+i)^{n+1} - 1}{i} - 1\right]$$

Example 2 would be expressed:

$$\$2{,}500\left[\frac{(1.04)^{5+1} - 1}{.04} - 1\right] = \$2{,}500\left[\frac{(1.04)^6 - 1)}{.04} - 1\right] = \$2{,}500\left[\frac{1.265319 - 1}{.04} - 1\right]$$

$$= \$2{,}500\left[\frac{.265319}{.04} - 1\right] = \$2{,}500\ (6.632975 - 1) = \$2{,}500 \times 5.632975 = \$14{,}082.44$$

"Amount of annuity of 1" table. Compound interest tables that show the amount of ordinary annuities of 1 for the given number of rents at given interest rates are available. Part of such a table is reproduced below. More complete tables are given on pages 1032 and 1033.

AMOUNT OF AN ORDINARY ANNUITY OF 1 $\frac{(1 + i)^n - 1}{i}$

Rents	2½%	3%	3½%	4%	4½%	5%
1	1.	1.	1.	1.	1.	1.
2	2.025	2.03	2.035	2.04	2.045	2.05
3	3.075625	3.0909	3.106225	3.1216	3.137025	3.1525
4	4.152516	4.183627	4.214943	4.246464	4.278191	4.310125
5	5.256329	5.309136	5.362466	5.416323	5.470710	5.525631
6	6.387737	6.468410	6.550152	6.632975	6.716892	6.801913
7	7.547430	7.662462	7.779408	7.898294	8.019152	8.142008
8	8.736116	8.892336	9.051687	9.214226	9.380014	9.549109
9	9.954519	10.159106	10.368496	10.582795	10.802114	11.026564
10	11.203382	11.463879	11.731393	12.006107	12.288209	12.577893

With the table, the amount of an ordinary annuity of 5 rents of 1 at 4% is immediately found to be 5.416323. Tables that show the amounts of ordinary annuities may also be used in determining the amount of an annuity due by applying the procedure just explained. For example, in determining the amount of an annuity due of 5 rents of 1 at 4%, the amount of an ordinary annuity of 6 rents at 4% is found; this amount, 6.632975, less 1, or 5.632975, is the amount of the annuity due.

Further application of amount of annuity. In the preceding examples, the periodic rents were given; the amount to which the series of rents would accumulate was to be computed. In certain instances the amount to be accumulated may be given; the periodic rents that are to provide the given amount are to be computed. When the rents are to be computed, the amount to which rents of 1 will accumulate is first determined. The amount to be accumulated when divided by the amount of an annuity of 1 then gives the required rents.

Example: What equal annual deposits are required to provide a total of $10,000 immediately after the fifth deposit, interest at 4% to be compounded annually on the accumulated balance?

As already indicated, the amount of an ordinary annuity of 5 rents of 1 at 4% is 5.416323; 5 deposits of $1 left at 4% interest, then, will provide a total of $5.416323. Since the desired accumulation is $10,000, this amount is divided by 5.416323 to determine the equal periodic deposits, which would then be $1,846.27. The procedure may be expressed as follows:

$$\frac{\text{Amount to be accumulated (\$10,000)}}{\text{Amount of an annuity of 1 (ordinary annuity of 5 rents of 1 at 4\%, 5.416323)}} = \text{Rents (\$1,846.27)}$$

Assuming annual deposits of $1,846.27 left at interest of 4%, the process of accumulation would be as follows:

Date	Interest Accruing on Balance in Fund During Period	Amount Deposited in Fund	Total Increase in Fund for Period	Accumulated Total on Deposit
End of 1st year		$1,846.27	$1,846.27	$ 1,846.27
End of 2nd year	$ 73.85	1,846.27	1,920.12	3,766.39
End of 3rd year	150.66	1,846.27	1,996.93	5,763.32
End of 4th year	230.53	1,846.27	2,076.80	7,840.12
End of 5th year	313.60	1,846.28[1]	2,159.88	10,000.00

If, in the foregoing example, the fund of $10,000 was required one year following the date of the fifth deposit, the series of deposits would represent an annuity due; consequently, $10,000 would be divided by the amount of the annuity due of 5 rents at 4%, or 5.632975. The deposits would then be $1,775.26. A table to show the accumulation follows:

Date	Interest Accruing on Balance in Fund During Period	Amount Deposited in Fund	Total Increase in Fund for Period	Accumulated Total on Deposit
End of 1st year		$1,775.26	$1,775.26	$ 1,775.26
End of 2nd year	$ 71.01	1,775.26	1,846.27	3,621.53
End of 3rd year	144.86	1,775.26	1,920.12	5,541.65
End of 4th year	221.67	1,775.26	1,996.93	7,538.58
End of 5th year	301.54	1,775.26	2,076.80	9,615.38
End of 6th year	384.62		384.62	10,000.00

AMOUNT OF AN ANNUITY LEFT TO ACCRUE INTEREST

A series of rents may be left to accrue interest for more than one period after the date of the last deposit.

[1]By showing computations to the nearest cent in the process of accumulation, an element of error is introduced. Compensation for the error may be made with the last payment. In this example the final payment is increased by one cent to produce the required fund.

Computation of amount of an annuity left to accrue interest. To find the amount of an annuity that is left to accrue interest, the amount for a series of rents of 1 may first be determined. The number of dollars in each rent for which the amount is required is then multiplied by the amount for the series of rents of 1.

Example: What is the accumulated amount on December 31, 1970, of a series of 6 semiannual deposits of $1,000, the first deposit being made on December 31, 1966? Interest is 5% compounded semiannually.

The problem may be presented graphically as follows:

AMOUNT OF AN ANNUITY LEFT TO ACCRUE INTEREST

Amount accumulated on Dec. 31, 1970, to be determined; interest at 5% is compounded semiannually.

1st Deposit of $1,000	2nd Deposit of $1,000	3rd Deposit of $1,000	4th Deposit of $1,000	5th Deposit of $1,000	6th Deposit of $1,000			
*	*	*	*	*	*	|	|	|
Dec. 31 1966	June 30 1967	Dec. 31 1967	June 30 1968	Dec. 31 1968	June 30 1969	Dec. 31 1969	June 30 1970	Dec. 31 1970

Ordinary annuity of 6 rents — Period of accrual — 3 periods

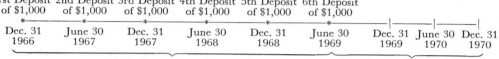

The foregoing indicates the amount of an ordinary annuity of 6 rents that accrues interest for 3 more periods. If the amount were to be determined as of June 30, 1969, the series of rents would represent an ordinary annuity of 6 rents. The amount of an ordinary annuity of 6 rents of 1 at 2½% is 6.387737. Since, however, the amount is to be determined as of December 31, 1970, the question is: what amount will be reached if 6.387737 is left for 3 periods at 2½%? The amount of the ordinary annuity of 6 rents of 1 at 2½%, 6.387737, when multiplied by the amount of 1 for 3 periods at 2½%, 1.076891, gives 6.878896, the amount at 2½% of an ordinary annuity of 6 rents left to accrue interest for 3 periods. Since the periodic rents are $1,000, the accumulated amount provided by these rents is $1,000 × 6.878896, or $6,878.90. The process of accumulation is as follows:

Date	Interest Accruing on Balance in Fund During Period	Amount Deposited in Fund	Total Increase in Fund for Period	Accumulated Total on Deposit
Dec. 31, 1966		$1,000.00	$1,000.00	$1,000.00
June 30, 1967	$ 25.00	1,000.00	1,025.00	2,025.00
Dec. 31, 1967	50.63	1,000.00	1,050.63	3,075.63
June 30, 1968	76.89	1,000.00	1,076.89	4,152.52
Dec. 31, 1968	103.81	1,000.00	1,103.81	5,256.33
June 30, 1969	131.41	1,000.00	1,131.41	6,387.74
Dec. 31, 1969	159.69		159.69	6,547.43
June 30, 1970	163.69		163.69	6,711.12
Dec. 31, 1970	167.78		167.78	6,878.90

Formula for amount of annuity of 1 left to accrue interest. Using "n" to indicate the number of rents and "m" to indicate the number of periods of interest accrual after the last rent, the amount of an annuity of 1 left to accrue interest may be expressed as a formula as follows:

$$\text{A accrued} = \left[\frac{(1+i)^n - 1}{i}\right](1+i)^m$$

The foregoing example, then, may be expressed as follows:

$$\$1{,}000\left[\frac{(1.025)^6 - 1}{.025}\right](1.025)^3 = \$1{,}000\left(\frac{1.15969342 - 1}{.025}\right)(1.025)^3 =$$

$$\$1{,}000\left(\frac{.15969342}{.025}\right)(1.025)^3 = \$1{,}000 \times 6.387737 \times 1.076891 = \$6{,}878.90$$

With tables giving the amounts of ordinary annuities, the amount of an annuity left to accrue interest may be determined by a shorter process. The amount of an annuity is first determined for the sum of the rents in the given annuity and the rents that would be applicable to the periods of accrual; the amount of an annuity for the rents applicable to the periods of accrual is then subtracted from the first value. In the foregoing example, using the table, the amount of an annuity of 9 rents of 1 at 2½%, 9.954519, minus the amount of an annuity of 3 rents of 1 at 2½%, 3.075625, gives 6.878894, the amount at 2½% of an annuity of 6 rents left to accrue interest for 3 periods.

The effect of this procedure is illustrated as follows:

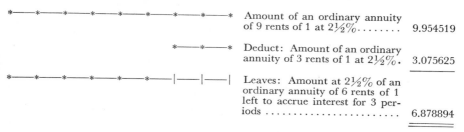

————*——*——*——*——*——*——*	Amount of an ordinary annuity of 9 rents of 1 at 2½%........	9.954519
————*	Deduct: Amount of an ordinary annuity of 3 rents of 1 at 2½%.	3.075625
————*——*——*——*——|——|——|	Leaves: Amount at 2½% of an ordinary annuity of 6 rents of 1 left to accrue interest for 3 periods	6.878894

The amount of the annuity as thus determined may be expressed as a formula as follows:

$$\text{A accrued} = \frac{(1+i)^{n+m} - 1}{i} - \frac{(1+i)^m - 1}{i}$$

SPECIAL PROBLEMS

The preceding pages have described the basic amount patterns, and examples were provided in each section to illustrate the particular pattern described. Frequently a problem is encountered that consists of a series or combination of amounts. Under such circumstances special analysis of the problem is necessary; when the various elements of the problem are clearly identified, it is possible to determine the procedures to be followed and the tables to be used in arriving at a solution. Graphic analysis of a problem is frequently helpful. Several examples of problems that call for special analysis follow.

Example 1: Amount combination; interest rate change. Ashby deposits \$10,000 on January 1, 1961, and \$5,000 on January 1, 1966. What will be the sum on deposit on January 1, 1972, if interest is compounded annually and is 3% from January 1, 1961 through 1964, and 3½% from January 1, 1965 to 1972?

The problem is analyzed in graphic form as follows:

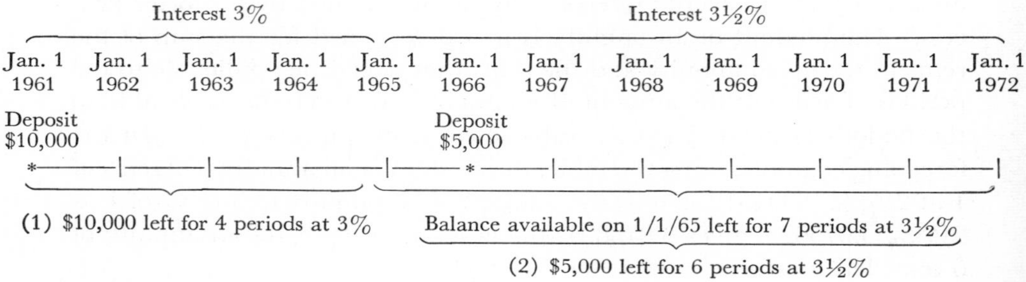

Solution:

(1) Amount deposited 1/1/61, \$10,000, times amount of 1, 4 periods at 3%, 1.125509, equals amount on deposit on 1/1/65, \$11,255.09. Amount on deposit 1/1/65, \$11,255.09, times amount of 1, 7 periods at 3½%, 1.272279, equals amount available on 1/1/72..........	\$14,319.61
(2) Amount deposited 1/1/66, \$5,000, times amount of 1, 6 periods at 3½%, 1.229255, equals amount available on 1/1/72..........	6,146.28
Total accumulation on 1/1/72..........	\$20,465.89

Example 2: Amount and amount of an annuity combination. Benson makes 4 annual deposits of \$1,000, the first deposit being made on January 1, 1962. This is to be followed by 4 more annual deposits of \$2,500 each, the first deposit in this series being made on January 1, 1968. What will be the amount on deposit on December 31, 1971, if interest is compounded annually at the rate of 4%?

The problem is analyzed as follows:

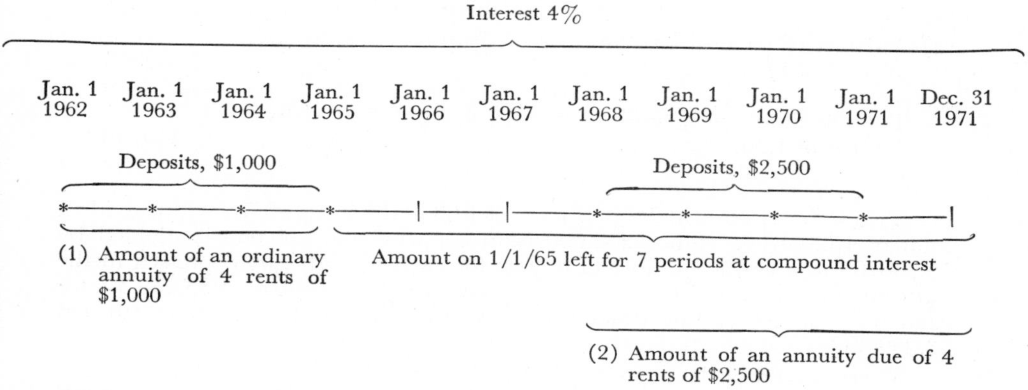

Solution:

(1) Rents beginning 1/1/62, $1,000, times amount at 4% of an ordinary annuity of 4 rents of 1 left for 7 periods (equivalent to the amount of an ordinary annuity of 11 rents of 1 at 4%, 13.486351, minus the amount of an ordinary annuity of 7 rents of 1 at 4%, 7.898294), 5.588057, equals amount available on 12/31/71	$ 5,588.06
(2) Rents beginning 1/1/68, $2,500, times amount of an annuity due of 4 rents of 1 at 4% (equivalent to amount of an ordinary annuity of 5 rents of 1 at 4%, 5.416323, minus 1), 4.416323, equals amount available on 12/31/71	11,040.81
Total accumulation on 12/31/71	$16,628.87

Example 3: Amount of annuity combination. Caldwell wishes to accumulate a fund of $50,000 on December 31, 1975. The fund is to be accumulated by 10 annual deposits, the first to be made beginning on December 31, 1966. The first 5 deposits are to be equal in amount; the last 5 deposits are to be equal in amount but are to be 50% larger than the first 5. The sum on deposit will earn interest at 5% compounded annually. What are the deposits?

The problem is analyzed as follows:

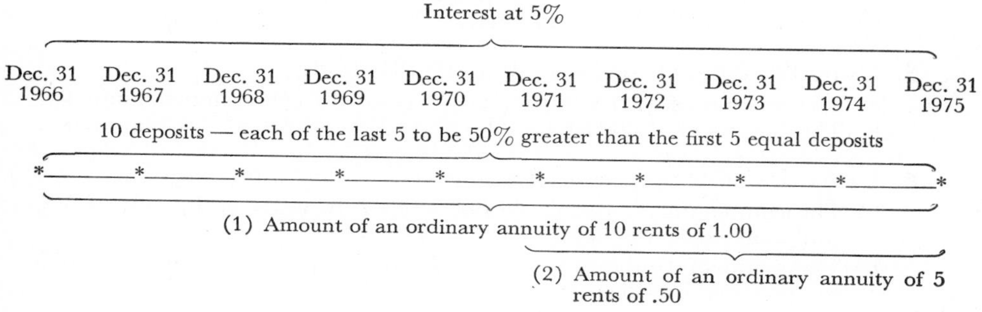

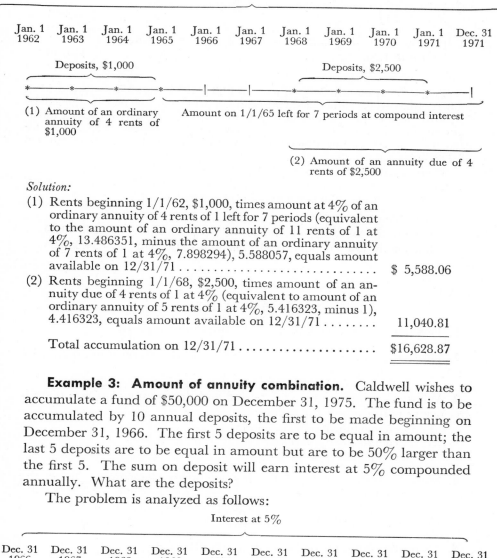

Solution:

(1) Amount of an ordinary annuity of 10 rents of 1.00 at 5%.	12.577893
(2) Amount of an ordinary annuity of 5 rents of .50 at 5%, .5(5.525631)	2.762816
Total available as a result of 5 rents of 1.00 followed by 5 rents of 1.50	15.340709

Two series of rents at 5%, 10 rents of 1.00 and 5 rents of .50, will provide a total of 15.340709. Since $50,000 is to be provided, $50,000 is divided by 15.340709 to give the number of dollars for each unit of 1.00 expressed in the pattern. The required sum, $50,000, divided by 15.340709 gives $3,259.30; for each unit of 1.00 in the deposit pattern, then, there should be substituted $3,259.30.

There should be 10 deposits of 1.00 × $3,259.30, or $3,259.30.

There should be 5 additional deposits of .50 × $3,259.30, or $1,629.65, concurrent with the last 5 deposits of the first series.

Stated differently:

Each of the first 5 deposits is	$3,259.30
Each of the last 5 deposits is $3,259.30 plus $1,629.65, or.	$4,888.95

QUESTIONS

1. Distinguish between simple and compound interest.

2. Distinguish between the amount of 1 and the amount of an annuity of 1.

3. What is the interest rate per period and the frequency of compounding per year in each of the following:
- (a) 6% compounded semiannually?
- (b) 5% compounded quarterly?
- (c) 9% compounded monthly?

4. State how each of the following would be determined, using the table on page 959:
- (a) The amount of 1 left for 15 years at 5% compounded annually.
- (b) The amount of 1 left for 11 years at 7% compounded semiannually.

5. Using the table on pages 1030 and 1031, find:
- (a) The amount of $1,000 left for 20 years at 5% compounded annually.
- (b) The amount of $1,000 left for 20 years at 5% compounded semiannually.

6. Using the table on pages 1030 and 1031, determine:
- (a) The compound interest on $1,000 left for 10 years at interest of 5% compounded semiannually.
- (b) The compound interest on $1,000 left for 10 years at interest of 6% compounded quarterly.

7. (a) Give a formula for each of the following values:

(1) The amount of 1.
(2) The compound interest on 1.
(3) The amount of an ordinary annuity of 1.
(4) The amount of an annuity due of 1.
(5) The amount of an annuity left at compound interest.

(b) Give an example of a situation in which each of the foregoing values is applicable.

8. The compound interest on 1 divided by the interest rate gives the amount of an annuity of 1 at such an interest rate. Explain why this is so.

9. What two methods may be used in determining the amount of an annuity due? What method is more convenient when annuity tables are available?

10. Explain how each of the following would be solved in the absence of tables:

(a) The amount of $2,500 left for 8 years at 7% compounded annually.
(b) The amount of $5,000 left for 5 years at 5% compounded quarterly.
(c) The compound interest on $1,000 left for 4 years at 6% compounded monthly.
(d) The sum that will reach a total of $10,000 after 5 years if left at 6% compounded semiannually.

11. Explain how, in the absence of tables, each of the following problems would be solved:

(a) What is the accumulated amount on January 1, 1971, of a series of 5 annual deposits, the first deposit being made on January 1, 1966? Interest of 7% is compounded annually on the sum on deposit.
(b) What is the accumulated amount on January 1, 1968, of a series of 5 semiannual deposits, the first deposit being made on January 1, 1966? Interest of 7% is compounded semiannually on the sum on deposit.
(c) What is the accumulated amount on January 1, 1976, of a series of 5 annual deposits, the first deposit being made on January 1, 1966? Interest of 6% is compounded annually on the sum on deposit.

12. Analyze the following problems, stating the procedures to be followed and the tables to be used in developing solutions:

(a) Abbott makes 6 deposits at annual intervals; the first 3 deposits are $1,000 each, and the next 3 are $2,000 each. Deposits are left at 6% compounded annually. How much is available 4 years after the last deposit?
(b) Bauer makes 5 annual deposits of $1,000. For a 5-year period no further deposits are made, then Bauer once more makes 5 annual deposits of $1,000. Deposits are left at 5% compounded annually. How much is available immediately after the last deposit?
(c) Clark makes 10 equal annual deposits of $5,000 to a sinking fund. The interest rate is 5%, but it drops to 4% immediately after the fifth deposit. How much is available immediately after the tenth deposit?

EXERCISES

1. Using the amount tables on pages 1030 and 1031, solve the following:

(a) What is the amount on January 1, 1971, of a deposit of $10,000 left on January 1, 1967, to accumulate interest at 5% compounded annually?
(b) What is the amount on January 1, 1971, of a deposit of $1,500 left on July 1, 1967, to accumulate interest at 6% compounded quarterly?
(c) What is the compound interest on an investment of $2,500 left for 5 years at 6% compounded semiannually?

2. Stan Kabrins deposited $5,000 in a special savings account that provides for interest at the rate of 6% compounded monthly if the deposit is maintained for 4 years. Using the amount tables on pages 1030 and 1031, calculate the balance of the savings account at the end of the 4-year period.

3. Using the amount tables on pages 1032 and 1033, solve the following:

(a) What is the accumulated amount on December 31, 1970, of a series of 5 annual deposits of $1,000, the first deposit being made on December 31, 1966? Interest of 4% is compounded annually on the sum on deposit.
(b) What is the accumulated amount on January 1, 1971, of a series of 5 annual deposits of $1,000, the first deposit being made on January 1, 1966? Interest of 5% is compounded annually on the sum on deposit.
(c) What is the accumulated amount on January 1, 1976, of a series of 10 semiannual deposits of $1,000, the first deposit being made on July 1, 1966? Interest of 5% is compounded semiannually on the sum on deposit.

4. Five equal annual contributions are to be made to a fund, the first deposit to be made on December 31, 1966. Using the amount tables on pages 1030–1033, determine the equal contributions that, if invested at 5% compounded annually, will produce a fund of $10,000, assuming that this sum is desired on:

(a) Dec. 31, 1970. (b) Dec. 31, 1971. (c) Dec. 31, 1985.

5. Using the amount tables on pages 1030–1033, solve the following:

(a) Moore deposits $10,000 on January 1, 1966, at interest of 4% compounded annually. On January 1, 1969, the annual interest rate is increased to 4½%. Moore makes a second deposit of $5,000 on January 1, 1971. Interest continues at 4½% until the end of 1976. What is the sum on deposit at the end of 1976?
(b) Nolte makes 10 annual deposits of $2,500 in a fund, the first being made on December 31, 1966. Interest is 4% compounded annually for the years 1967, 1968, and 1969, and is 3% thereafter. What is the accumulated amount immediately after the tenth deposit?
(c) Olson makes 10 annual deposits in a fund, the first 5 being $5,000 and the last 5 being $7,500. Interest is 5% compounded annually. How much is available 5 years after the tenth deposit?
(d) Pater wishes to make 10 annual deposits into a fund, the first 5 to be double the size of the last 5. A total of $20,000 is to become available 1 year after the last deposit. It is assumed that interest will be 5% compounded annually. What are the required deposits?

PROBLEMS

(*Use the amount tables given on pages 1030–1033.*)

26-1. Parks borrows $25,000 on December 31, 1966, promising to repay this amount together with accrued interest at 4½% compounded annually on December 31, 1976. Parks plans to make 5 equal deposits at annual intervals in a special savings fund in order to retire the obligation at its maturity, the first deposit to be made on January 1, 1968. He believes that the fund will earn 5% compounded annually. What amounts are to be deposited?

26-2. Scoville deposits $5,000 semiannually on January 1 and July 1. His first deposit was made on January 1, 1966. Interest was compounded semiannually at the following rates:

January 1, 1966	4% per year
Beginning July 1, 1967	5% per year

What was his account balance after his deposit on January 1, 1970?

26-3. The Burnside Co. deposits the following amounts in a fund for the replacement of buildings:

On December 31, 1961, 1962, 1963, 1964	$10,000
On December 31, 1965	15,000
On December 31, 1966, 1967	20,000

Interest was compounded annually as follows:

1962–1963 inclusive	3½%
1964–1965 inclusive	4 %
1966–1967 inclusive	4½%

What was the amount in the fund on December 31, 1967?

26-4. Masters needs $20,000 to pay off a mortgage due on December 31, 1975. He plans to make 10 annual deposits beginning on January 1, 1966, in accumulating a fund to pay off the mortgage. Three annual deposits of $2,000 have been made. What equal amounts should be deposited in the next 7 years to reach the fund objective, assuming interest at 4% compounded annually?

26-5. (a) B. J. Brooks owns an annuity that pays $3,000 on May 1 of each year. If, beginning in 1966, Brooks deposits the proceeds of the annuity as each payment is received at 4% interest, compounded annually, what amount will he have accumulated after his deposit on May 1, 1980?

(b) What additional equal amounts must Brooks deposit annually at the time the annuity receipts are deposited if his balance is to be $100,000 after the deposit on May 1, 1980?

26-6. The Carter Supply Co. has been setting aside \$50,000 on December 31 of each year to provide for the retirement of 20-year bonds of \$1,000,000, due January 1, 1980. In reviewing the corporation books on January 2, 1966, the auditor finds that the company has failed to invest the amounts set aside. He suggests that the amounts already accumulated be immediately invested and that future amounts also be invested. Assuming interest of 5% compounded annually on the sum on deposit, what equal amounts should be set aside annually until the retirement date of the bonds to complete the retirement fund?

26-7. Weber deposits his Christmas bonus in a special savings account. For the years 1957–1962 inclusive, his bonus was \$1,000. He did not receive a bonus in 1963 and 1964. Since 1965 his annual bonus was \$2,000. Deposits were made on December 31. Interest was compounded annually at 4% until January 1, 1962; thereafter it was compounded annually at 5%. What was the balance of Weber's savings account after the deposit on December 31, 1967?

26-8. White Fabricators, Inc., has been setting aside \$50,000 annually since December 31, 1962, in providing a fund for plant expansion. In January, 1966, an audit discloses an accumulated total in the fund of \$212,800. It is assumed that in 1966 and thereafter the fund will earn 4% annually. What equal annual deposits are required, beginning with the one in 1966, to produce a fund of \$1,000,000 immediately after the deposit at the end of 1971?

26-9. Keith-Jenson, Inc., establishes a fund to provide for the retirement of a mortgage of \$1,000,000 on December 31, 1975. Ten annual deposits to the fund are to be made, the first deposit to be made on December 31, 1966. It is expected that the fund will earn 4½% a year.

(a) What equal annual deposits should be made?
(b) Assuming that the last 5 deposits are to be 50% greater than the first 5, what are the respective annual deposits?

26-10. Cunningham receives \$5,000 at the beginning of each year on an insurance policy. The final payment is due January 1, 1971. Cunningham decides to deposit each payment in a bank beginning with the one due January 1, 1966. In addition to these amounts, he plans to make 10 additional equal deposits annually on January 1, beginning in 1966, so that he will have a total of \$100,000 available at the end of 1975. Assuming interest on fund deposits at 4% compounded annually, calculate the equal deposits required to produce the desired fund.

26-11. Quality Products, Inc., has been setting aside \$75,000 annually since December 31, 1965, in providing a fund for the retirement of bonds of $1,000,000 that are payable on December 31, 1974. The fund earns 4% annually.

(a) Assuming that annual deposits remain unchanged through 1973, what deposit will be required on December 31, 1974, to bring the fund up to $1,000,000?

(b) Assuming that annual deposits are increased beginning with the one December 31, 1971, so that enough is available to retire the bonds at maturity, give the amount of the equal increased deposits.

26-12. Parker wishes to accumulate a fund of $100,000 for the purchase of an annuity. He plans to deposit $2,000 quarterly.

(a) Assuming interest at 4% a year compounded quarterly, how many deposits will be required and what is the amount of the last deposit?

(b) Assuming that the thirty-fifth deposit is increased to bring the fund to $100,000 on that date, give the amount of this deposit.

26-13. Williams plans to deposit $1,500 at annual intervals, interest accruing at the rate of 4%.

(a) What amount will Williams have available immediately after his tenth deposit?

(b) Assuming that he requires a total of $30,000, give the number of annual deposits required and the amount of the last deposit that will bring the fund to this amount.

26-14. The Pacific Construction Company offers to build a bridge across the Narrows at a cost of $20,000,000 and to accept in payment the city's 4% bonds, redeemable in 25 years, interest payable semiannually. The annual maintenance charges are estimated at $50,000 a year. It is proposed to charge tolls of 5 cents for foot passengers and 50 cents for vehicles. Based on these charges and assuming a ratio of foot passengers to vehicles of 1 to 20, how many tolls of each class would be necessary each year in order to provide for maintenance, interest, and semiannual deposits to a sinking fund sufficient to retire the bonds at maturity? Assume that the sinking fund will earn 4% compounded semiannually.

(AICPA adapted)

26-15. The Winthrop Corporation is issuing $100,000 of 4%, 20-year bonds that it wishes to pay at maturity by means of a sinking fund in which equal annual deposits are to be made. The board of directors wishes to assume that this fund will earn 3½% interest for the first 5 years, 3% for the next 5 years, and 2% for the last 10 years. What is the annual deposit required?

(AICPA adapted)

Chapter 27

COMPOUND INTEREST

PRESENT VALUES

PRESENT VALUE OF SINGLE GIVEN SUM

In determining the amount, a certain sum was given and an equivalent later value was sought; in determining the present value, a certain sum is given and an equivalent earlier value is sought.

Computation of present value of single given sum. To compute the present value of a single given sum, the present value of 1 for the given number of periods at the given interest rate is determined. The number of dollars in the given sum is then multiplied by the present value of 1.

Example: What is the present value of $2,500 discounted for 3 years at 6% compounded semiannually?

The purpose of calculating the foregoing may be to determine (1) the sum to be paid in settlement of a claim of $2,500 due at the end of 3 years if discounted at 6% compounded semiannually, or (2) the sum that will accumulate to $2,500 at the end of 3 years if left at 6% compounded semiannually.

Using the same number of periods and interest rate, the ratio of increase from 1 to the amount of 1 is the same as the ratio of increase from the present value of 1 to 1. Applying this principle, the present value of 1 for 1 period at 3% may be found by dividing 1 by the amount of 1 for 1 period at 3%, or 1.03. It should be observed that the quotient .970874, when multiplied by the rate of increase for 1 period, 1.03, equals 1. To find the present value of 1 for more than 1 period arithmetically, successive divisions may be completed as follows:

1.000000 ÷ 1.03 = .970874, present value of 1 discounted for 1 period at 3%
.970874 ÷ 1.03 = .942596, present value of 1 discounted for 2 periods at 3%
.942596 ÷ 1.03 = .915142, present value of 1 discounted for 3 periods at 3%
.915142 ÷ 1.03 = .888487, present value of 1 discounted for 4 periods at 3%
.888487 ÷ 1.03 = .862609, present value of 1 discounted for 5 periods at 3%
.862609 ÷ 1.03 = .837484, present value of 1 discounted for 6 periods at 3%

One dollar discounted for 6 periods at 3% is $.837484, or $.837484 left for 3 years to accumulate interest at 6% compounded semiannually will amount to $1. The present value of $2,500 discounted for 3 years at 6% compounded semiannually is:

Sum discounted	$2,500.00
Multiply by present value of 1 for 6 periods at 3%.......	.837484
Present value of $2,500 discounted for 6 periods at 3%....	$2,093.71

It may be observed that the present value of $2,500 discounted for 6 years at interest of 3% compounded annually is identical with the above, for the number of interest periods is 6 and the interest rate for each period is 3%.

In finding the present value of 1 for 6 periods at 3%, it is not necessary to divide 1 by 1.03 six successive times as was done earlier; 1 may simply be divided by the amount of 1 for 6 periods at 3%.

Formula for "present value of 1." The present value of 1 represented by "p" may be expressed as a formula as follows:

$$p = \frac{1}{(1+i)^n}, \text{ or } p = \frac{1}{a}$$

The foregoing example, then, may be expressed as follows:

$$\$2{,}500\left[\frac{1}{(1.03)^6}\right] = \$2{,}500\left(\frac{1}{1.194052}\right) = \$2{,}500 \times .837484 = \$2{,}093.71$$

"Present value of 1" table. Compound interest tables that show the present value of 1 for given numbers of periods at given interest rates are available. Part of a table showing present values is reproduced below. More complete tables are given on pages 1034 and 1035.

PRESENT VALUE OF 1 $\frac{1}{(1+i)^n}$

Periods	2½%	3%	3½%	4%	4½%	5%
1	.975610	.970874	.966184	.961538	.956938	.952381
2	.951814	.942596	.933511	.924556	.915730	.907029
3	.928599	.915142	.901943	.888996	.876297	.863838
4	.905951	.888487	.871442	.854804	.838561	.822702
5	.883854	.862609	.841973	.821927	.802451	.783526
6	.862297	.837484	.813501	.790315	.767896	.746215
7	.841265	.813092	.785991	.759918	.734828	.710681
8	.820747	.789409	.759412	.730690	.703185	.676839
9	.800728	.766417	.733731	.702587	.672904	.644609
10	.781198	.744094	.708919	.675564	.643928	.613913

With the table, the present value of 1 for 6 periods at 3% is immediately found to be .837484. The present value table may be used in determining the present value of 1 for periods greater in number than those shown. For example, the present value of 1 for 15 periods at 3% can be computed in the following manners:

$$\frac{1}{(1.03)^{10}} \times \frac{1}{(1.03)^5} = \frac{1}{(1.03)^{15}}, \text{ or } .744094 \times .862609 = .641862$$

$$\frac{1}{(1.03)^8} \times \frac{1}{(1.03)^7} = \frac{1}{(1.03)^{15}}, \text{ or } .789409 \times .813092 = .641862$$

Computation of compound discount. *Compound discount* is the difference between a given sum and its present value. The compound discount on 1 may be determined by subtracting the present value of 1 for the given number of periods at the given interest rate from 1. To find the compound discount on a given sum, the number of dollars in the sum is multiplied by the compound discount on 1.

Example: What is the compound discount on $2,500 for 3 years at 6% compounded semiannually?

The compound discount on 1 may be determined as follows:

Principal	1.000000
Less present value of 1 for 6 periods at 3%, 1 ÷ $(1.03)^6$	.837484
Compound discount on 1 for 6 periods at 3%	.162516

The compound discount on $2,500 for 3 years at 6% compounded semiannually is:

Sum discounted	$2,500.00
Multiply by compound discount on 1 for 6 periods at 3%	.162516
Compound discount on $2,500 for 6 periods at 3%	$ 406.29

Formula for "compound discount on 1." Using "D" to represent compound discount on 1, the formula for compound discount is:

$$D = 1 - \frac{1}{(1+i)^n}, \text{ or } D = 1 - p$$

The foregoing example, then, may be expressed as follows:

$$\$2,500\left[1 - \frac{1}{(1.03)^6}\right] = \$2,500\left(1 - \frac{1}{1.194052}\right) = \$2,500\ (1 - .837484) =$$

$$\$2,500 \times .162516 = \$406.29$$

With tables showing the present values of 1, the compound discount on 1 is readily determined by subtracting the present value of 1 for the given number of periods at the given interest rate from 1.

PRESENT VALUE OF AN ANNUITY

The *present value of an annuity* is the present value of a series of rents discounted at compound interest. Stated differently, it is the sum which if left at compound interest will permit a series of equal withdrawals at regular intervals. The present value balance is *increased* periodically for interest and *decreased* periodically for the withdrawal. The last rent in the series exhausts the balance on deposit.

If the first rent is payable 1 period after the date of determination of the present value of an annuity, the series of rents is known as an *ordinary annuity*. If the first rent is payable on the date of determination of the present value, the series is known as an *annuity due*. The distinction is presented graphically below:

Present Value of an Ordinary Annuity

Deposit on June 30, 1966, to be determined; interest at 6% is compounded semiannually.

	1st With-drawal of $1.00	2nd With-drawal of $1.00	3rd With-drawal of $1.00	4th With-drawal of $1.00	5th With-drawal of $1.00	6th With-drawal of $1.00
|	*	*	*	*	*	*
June 30 1966	Dec. 31 1966	June 30 1967	Dec. 31 1967	June 30 1968	Dec. 31 1968	June 30 1969

Present Value of an Annuity Due

Deposit on Dec. 31, 1966, to be determined; interest at 6% is compounded semiannually.

1st With-drawal of $1.00	2nd With-drawal of $1.00	3rd With-drawal of $1.00	4th With-drawal of $1.00	5th With-drawal of $1.00	6th With-drawal of $1.00
*	*	*	*	*	*
Dec. 31 1966	June 30 1967	Dec. 31 1967	June 30 1968	Dec. 31 1968	June 30 1969

In the first example, the present value of an ordinary annuity is to be determined since the first rent is payable 1 period after the date of the deposit. Here, the present value of an ordinary annuity of 6 rents of $1 at 3% is to be computed. In the second example, the present value of an annuity due is to be determined since the first rent is payable on the date of the deposit. Here, the present value of an annuity due of 6 rents of $1 at 3% is to be computed.

It should be observed from the preceding illustrations that the present value of an annuity due is greater than the present value of an ordinary annuity for the same number of rents by the interest on the present value of the ordinary annuity for 1 period. The present value of an ordinary annuity of 6 rents of $1 when multiplied by the rate of increase for 1 period, then, gives the present value of an annuity due of 6 rents of \$1. Or, if the present value of an ordinary annuity of 5 rents of \$1 is known, this sum plus \$1 gives the present value of the annuity due of 6 rents. This is true because the present value of the annuity due of 6 rents is identical with that of an ordinary annuity of 5 rents except for an additional dollar that is immediately payable.

Computation of present value of an annuity. To find the present value of an annuity, the present value of a series of rents of 1 is determined. The number of dollars in each rent for which the present value is required is then multiplied by the present value of the series of rents of 1.

Example 1: Present value of an ordinary annuity. What is the present value on June 30, 1966, of a series of 6 semiannual rents of \$1,500, the first rent being payable on December 31, 1966? Interest is 6% compounded semiannually.

Example 2: Present value of an annuity due. What is the present value of the above annuity on December 31, 1966, the date when the first rent is payable?

The purpose of calculating the foregoing may be to determine (1) the sum left at interest of 6% compounded semiannually that will provide for 6 semiannual withdrawals of \$1,500, or (2) the sum that is payable in settlement of a series of 6 obligations of \$1,500 that are due at semiannual intervals, the obligations being discounted at 6% compounded semiannually.

Present value of the ordinary annuity computed. The following procedure may be used in computing the present value of an ordinary annuity of 6 rents of 1 at 3%:

Present value of 1 (withdrawal, Dec. 31, 1966), 1 period at 3%	$= \dfrac{1}{(1.03)} =$	.970874
Present value of 1 (withdrawal, June 30, 1967), 2 periods at 3%	$= \dfrac{1}{(1.03)^2} =$	.942596
Present value of 1 (withdrawal, Dec. 31, 1967), 3 periods at 3%	$= \dfrac{1}{(1.03)^3} =$	.915142
Present value of 1 (withdrawal, June 30, 1968), 4 periods at 3%	$= \dfrac{1}{(1.03)^4} =$	.888487
Present value of 1 (withdrawal, Dec. 31, 1968), 5 periods at 3%	$= \dfrac{1}{(1.03)^5} =$	.862609
Present value of 1 (withdrawal, June 30, 1969), 6 periods at 3%	$= \dfrac{1}{(1.03)^6} =$	.837484
Present value of an ordinary annuity of 6 rents of 1 at 3%		5.417192

The present value of the ordinary annuity of 6 rents of $1,500 at 3% is:

Periodic rents.	$1,500.00
Multiply by present value of an ordinary annuity of 6 rents of 1 at 3%.	5.417192
Present value of an ordinary annuity of 6 rents of $1,500 at 3%.	$8,125.79

Assuming that $8,125.79 is invested at 6% compounded semiannually to make possible 6 semiannual withdrawals of $1,500, the increases in the fund through interest and the decreases in the fund through withdrawals take place as follows:

Date	Interest Accruing on Balance in Fund During Period	Withdrawal from Fund	Net Decrease in Fund	Balance on Deposit
June 30, 1966				$8,125.79
Dec. 31, 1966	$243.77	$1,500.00	$1,256.23	6,869.56
June 30, 1967	206.09	1,500.00	1,293.91	5,575.65
Dec. 31, 1967	167.27	1,500.00	1,332.73	4,242.92
June 30, 1968	127.29	1,500.00	1,372.71	2,870.21
Dec. 31, 1968	86.11	1,500.00	1,413.89	1,456.32
June 30, 1969	43.69	1,500.01	1,456.32	

Present value of the annuity due computed. If the present value of the series of rents is to be determined as of December 31, 1966, and the first rent is due on this date, each rent is discounted for 1 less period as compared with the ordinary annuity computed above. The present value of an annuity due of 6 rents of 1 at 3% may be computed as follows:

1 (withdrawal, Dec. 31, 1966) that is not discounted since it is immediately payable		= 1.000000
Present value of 1 (withdrawal, June 30, 1967), 1 period at 3%	$= \frac{1}{(1.03)}$	= .970874
Present value of 1 (withdrawal, Dec. 31, 1967), 2 periods at 3%	$= \frac{1}{(1.03)^2}$	= .942596
Present value of 1 (withdrawal, June 30, 1968), 3 periods at 3%	$= \frac{1}{(1.03)^3}$	= .915142
Present value of 1 (withdrawal, Dec. 31, 1968), 4 periods at 3%	$= \frac{1}{(1.03)^4}$	= .888487
Present value of 1 (withdrawal, June 30, 1969), 5 periods at 3%	$= \frac{1}{(1.03)^5}$	= .862609
Present value of an annuity due of 6 rents of 1 at 3%. .		5.579708

The present value of the annuity due of 6 rents of $1,500 at 3% is:

Periodic rents	$1,500.00
Multiply by present value of an annuity due of 6 rents of 1 at 3%	5.579708
Present value of an annuity due of 6 rents of $1,500 at 3%	$8,369.56

The increases in the fund through interest and the decreases in the fund through withdrawals take place as indicated below.

Date	Interest Accruing on Balance in Fund During Period	Withdrawal from Fund	Net Decrease in Fund	Balance on Deposit
Dec. 31, 1966				$8,369.56
Dec. 31, 1966		$1,500.00	$1,500.00	6,869.56
June 30, 1967	$206.09	1,500.00	1,293.91	5,575.65
Dec. 31, 1967	167.27	1,500.00	1,332.73	4,242.92
June 30, 1968	127.29	1,500.00	1,372.71	2,870.21
Dec. 31, 1968	86.11	1,500.00	1,413.89	1,456.32
June 30, 1969	43.69	1,500.01	1,456.32	

Formula for "present value of annuity of 1." As previously shown on page 964, the compound interest on 1 is equal to the amount of an ordinary annuity of the interest amount at the stated interest rate. Conversely, the compound discount on 1 is equal to the present value of an ordinary annuity whose rents are the interest amounts discounted at the stated interest rate. Since the compound discount on 1 is equal to the present value of an ordinary annuity of the interest amount, the following rule may be formulated: to determine the present value of an ordinary annuity of 1, divide the compound discount on 1 at the interest rate effective between rents and for a number of periods equal to the number of rents by the interest rate. To illustrate: the compound discount on 1 for 6 periods at 3% is 1 − .8374843, or .1625157. The compound discount, .1625157, divided by the interest rate, .03, gives the present value of an ordinary annuity of 6 rents at 3%, 5.41719.

The present value of an ordinary annuity of 1 determined in this manner, using "P" to represent the annuity, may be expressed as a formula as follows:

$$P = \frac{1 - \frac{1}{(1+i)^n}}{i}, \text{ or in shorter form, } P = \frac{1-p}{i}, \text{ or simply, } P = \frac{D}{i}$$

Example 1, then, may be expressed as follows:

$$\$1{,}500 \left[\frac{1 - \frac{1}{(1.03)^6}}{.03}\right] = \$1{,}500 \left(\frac{1 - .8374843}{.03}\right) = \$1{,}500 \left(\frac{.1625157}{.03}\right)$$

$$= \$1{,}500 \times 5.41719 = \$8{,}125.79$$

It was pointed out on page 981 that the present value of an annuity due may be determined by increasing the present value of an ordinary annuity of the same number of rents and at the same interest rate by the interest for 1 period. The present value of an annuity due determined in this manner may be expressed as a formula as follows:

$$\text{P due} = \left[\frac{1-\dfrac{1}{(1+i)^n}}{i}\right](1+i)$$

Example 2, then, may be expressed as follows:

$$\$1{,}500\left[\frac{1-\dfrac{1}{(1.03)^6}}{.03}\right](1.03) = \$1{,}500\left(\frac{1-.8374843}{.03}\right)(1.03) =$$

$$\$1{,}500\left(\frac{.1625157}{.03}\right)(1.03) = \$1{,}500 \times 5.41719 \times 1.03 = \$8{,}369.56$$

As indicated on page 982, the present value of an annuity due of 1 may be regarded as the present value of an ordinary annuity of 1 less rent plus 1. Computation in this way is more convenient when compound interest tables are available. The formula for the present value of an annuity due as thus defined is:

$$\text{P due} = \frac{1-\dfrac{1}{(1+i)^{n-1}}}{i}+1$$

Example 2 would be expressed:

$$\$1{,}500\left[\frac{1-\dfrac{1}{(1.03)^{6-1}}}{.03}+1\right] = \$1{,}500\left[\frac{1-\dfrac{1}{(1.03)^5}}{.03}+1\right] = \$1{,}500\left(\frac{1-.8626088}{.03}+1\right)$$

$$= \$1{,}500\left(\frac{.1373912}{.03}+1\right) = \$1{,}500\ (4.579707+1) = \$1{,}500 \times 5.579707 = \$8{,}369.56$$

"Present value of annuity of 1" table. Compound interest tables that show the present value of ordinary annuities of 1 for given numbers of rents at given interest rates are available. Part of such a table is reproduced at the top of the following page. More complete tables are given on pages 1036 and 1037.

With the table, the present value of an ordinary annuity of 6 rents of 1 at 3% is immediately found to be 5.417191. Tables that show the present values of ordinary annuities may also be used in determining the present value of an annuity due by applying the procedure just explained. For example, in determining the present value of an annuity due of 6 rents of 1 at 3%, the present value of an ordinary annuity of 5 rents at 3%

PRESENT VALUE OF ORDINARY ANNUITY OF 1 $\dfrac{1 - \dfrac{1}{(1+i)^n}}{i}$

Rents	2½%	3%	3½%	4%	4½%	5%
1	.975610	.970874	.966184	.961538	.956938	.952381
2	1.927424	1.913470	1.899694	1.886095	1.872668	1.859410
3	2.856024	2.828611	2.801637	2.775091	2.748964	2.723248
4	3.761974	3.717098	3.673079	3.629895	3.587526	3.545951
5	4.645829	4.579707	4.515052	4.451822	4.389977	4.329477
6	5.508125	5.417191	5.328553	5.242137	5.157872	5.075692
7	6.349391	6.230283	6.114544	6.002055	5.892701	5.786373
8	7.170137	7.019692	6.873956	6.732745	6.595886	6.463213
9	7.970866	7.786109	7.607687	7.435332	7.268791	7.107822
10	8.752064	8.530203	8.316605	8.110896	7.912718	7.721735

is found; this sum, 4.579707, plus 1, or 5.579707, is the present value of the annuity due.

Further application of present value of annuity. In the preceding examples, the periodic rents were given; the present value of the series of rents was to be computed. In certain instances the present value of an annuity may be given; the periodic rents that will result from this value are to be computed.

Example: What 6 semiannual rents will be provided by $5,000 left on June 30, 1966, at 6% compounded semiannually, if the date of the first rent is December 31, 1966?

The purpose of calculating the foregoing may be to determine (1) the equal semiannual withdrawals that may be made as the result of a deposit of $5,000, interest on the balance on deposit accruing at 6% compounded semiannually, or (2) the equal semiannual payments that are required in settlement of a liability of $5,000, interest on the unpaid balance accruing at 6% compounded semiannually.

The present value of an annuity of 1 is first determined. The given sum when divided by the present value of the annuity of 1 gives the series of rents that will be provided. As already indicated, the present value of an ordinary annuity of 6 rents of 1 at 3% is 5.417191; $5.417191, then, will provide a series of 6 rents of $1, the first rent payable after 1 period. Since the sum given is $5,000, this sum is divided by 5.417191 to determine the periodic rents, which would then be $922.99. The procedure that is followed may be expressed as follows:

$$\frac{\text{Given sum (\$5,000)}}{\text{Present value of an annuity of 1 (ordinary annuity of 6 rents of 1 at 3\%, 5.417191)}} = \text{Rents (\$922.99)}$$

A table summarizing the increases and the decreases in the balance invested or the balance owed may be prepared as follows:

Date	Interest Accruing on Balance in Fund (or Interest Accruing on Unpaid Balance of Liability)	Withdrawal from Fund (or Payment on Liability)	Net Decrease in Fund (or Net Decrease in Liability)	Balance on Deposit (or Balance of Liability)
June 30, 1966				$5,000.00
Dec. 31, 1966	$150.00	$922.99	$772.99	4,227.01
June 30, 1967	126.81	922.99	796.18	3,430.83
Dec. 31, 1967	102.92	922.99	820.07	2,610.76
June 30, 1968	78.32	922.99	844.67	1,766.09
Dec. 31, 1968	52.98	922.99	870.01	896.08
June 30, 1969	26.88	922.96	896.08	

If, in the example above, the date of the first rent was June 30, 1966, the series of rents would represent an annuity due; consequently, $5,000 would be divided by the present value of an annuity due of 6 rents at 3%, or 5.579707. The rents would then be $896.10. A table showing the changes in the balance invested or the balance owed would be as follows:

Date	Interest Accruing on Balance in Fund (or Interest Accruing on Unpaid Balance of Liability)	Withdrawal from Fund (or Payment on Liability)	Net Decrease in Fund (or Net Decrease in Liability)	Balance on Deposit (or Balance) of Liability)
June 30, 1966				$5,000.00
June 30, 1966		$896.10	$896.10	4,103.90
Dec. 31, 1966	$123.12	896.10	772.98	3,330.92
June 30, 1967	99.93	896.10	796.17	2,534.75
Dec. 31, 1967	76.04	896.10	820.06	1,714.69
June 30, 1968	51.44	896.10	844.66	870.03
Dec. 31, 1968	26.10	896.13	870.03	

PRESENT VALUE OF DEFERRED ANNUITY

When the first rent of an annuity is due after the expiration of more than 1 period from the date of the original deposit, the series of rents is known as a *deferred annuity*.

Computation of present value of a deferred annuity. To find the present value of a deferred annuity, the present value of a series of rents of 1 is first determined. The number of dollars in each rent for which the present value is required is then multiplied by the present value of the series of rents of 1.

Example: What is the present value on December 31, 1966, of a series of 4 annual rents of $1,000, the first rent being payable on December 31,

1969? Interest of 4% is compounded annually. The problem may be presented graphically as follows:

Present Value of a Deferred Annuity

Present value on Dec. 31, 1966, to be determined; interest at 4% is compounded annually.

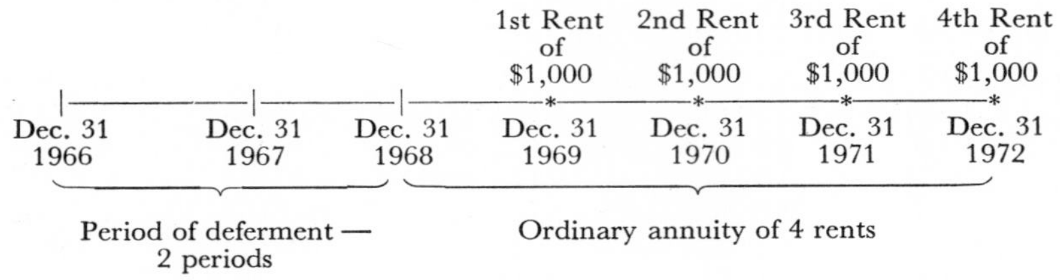

The foregoing indicates an ordinary annuity of 4 rents deferred 2 periods. If the present value were to be found as of December 31, 1968, the series of rents would represent an ordinary annuity of 4 rents. The present value of an ordinary annuity of 4 rents of 1 at 4% is 3.629895. Since the present value is to be determined as of December 31, 1966, however, the question is: What sum on December 31, 1966, will increase to 3.629895 on December 31, 1968, thus allowing for 4 annual rents of 1, the first rent becoming due December 31, 1969? The present value of the ordinary annuity of 4 rents of 1 at 4%, 3.629895, when multiplied by the present value of 1 for 2 periods at 4%, .9245562, gives 3.356042, the present value at 4% of an ordinary annuity of 4 rents deferred 2 periods. Since the periodic rents are $1,000, the present value to provide these rents is $1,000 × 3.356042, or $3,356.04. Assuming that $3,356.04 is deposited, a table to show the increases and the decreases in the fund would be:

Date	Interest Accruing on Balance in Fund	Withdrawal from Fund	Net Increase* or Decrease in Fund	Balance on Deposit
Dec. 31, 1966				$3,356.04
Dec. 31, 1967	$134.24		$134.24*	3,490.28
Dec. 31, 1968	139.61		139.61*	3,629.89
Dec. 31, 1969	145.20	$1,000.00	854.80	2,775.09
Dec. 31, 1970	111.00	1,000.00	889.00	1,886.09
Dec. 31, 1971	75.44	1,000.00	924.56	961.53
Dec. 31, 1972	38.46	999.99	961.53	

Formula for "present value of deferred annuity of 1." Using "n" to indicate the number of rents and "m" to indicate the number of periods of deferment, the present value of a deferred annuity of 1 may be expressed as a formula as follows:

$$\text{P deferred} = \left[\left(\frac{1 - \frac{1}{(1+i)^n}}{i} \right) \left(\frac{1}{(1+i)^m} \right) \right]$$

The foregoing example, then, may be expressed as follows:

$$\$1{,}000 \left[\left(\frac{1 - \frac{1}{(1.04)^4}}{.04} \right) \left(\frac{1}{(1.04)^2} \right) \right] = \$1{,}000 \left[\left(\frac{1 - .854804}{.04} \right) \left(\frac{1}{1.0816} \right) \right]$$

$$= \$1{,}000 \left[\left(\frac{.145196}{.04} \right) \left(\frac{1}{1.0816} \right) \right] = \$1{,}000 \times (3.629895 \times .924556)$$

$$= \$1{,}000 \times 3.356042 = \$3{,}356.04$$

With tables giving the present value of ordinary annuities, the present value of a deferred annuity can be determined by a shorter process. The present value of an annuity is first determined for the sum of the rents in the given annuity and the rents that would be applicable to the period of deferment; the present value of an annuity for the rents applicable to the periods of deferment is then subtracted from the first value. In the foregoing example, using the table, the present value of an annuity of 6 rents of 1 at 4%, 5.242137, minus the present value of an annuity of 2 rents of 1 at 4%, 1.886095, gives 3.356042, the present value of an annuity of 4 rents of 1 deferred 2 periods.

The effect of this procedure is illustrated as follows:

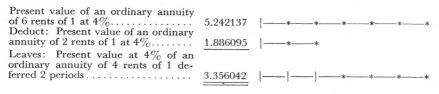

Present value of an ordinary annuity of 6 rents of 1 at 4%.	5.242137	|——*——*——*——*——*——*
Deduct: Present value of an ordinary annuity of 2 rents of 1 at 4%.	1.886095	|——*——*
Leaves: Present value at 4% of an ordinary annuity of 4 rents of 1 deferred 2 periods	3.356042	|——|——|——*——*——*——*

The present value of a deferred annuity as thus determined may be expressed as a formula as follows:

$$\text{P deferred} = \frac{1 - \frac{1}{(1+i)^{m+n}}}{i} - \frac{1 - \frac{1}{(1+i)^m}}{}$$

AMOUNT AND PRESENT VALUE COMPARED

It should be observed from the previous discussions that the terms *amount* and *present value* suggest no more than differences in the point of reference that is taken for purposes of valuation. The valuation of a sum as of an earlier date involves a determination of *present value*; the valuation of a sum as of a later date involves a determination of *amount*. For example, in the following:

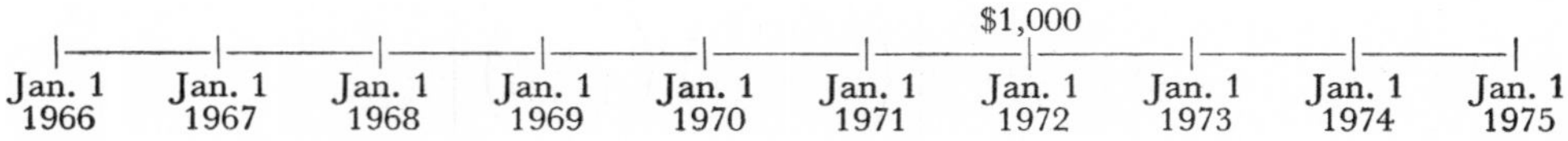

(a) Viewing the $1,000 sum on January 1, 1972, in terms of its value on January 1, 1966, calls for the determination of a present value.

(b) Viewing the $1,000 sum on January 1, 1972, in terms of its value on January 1, 1975, calls for the determination of an amount.

The point of reference is also the determining factor in defining annuities as "amounts" or "present values" and in further designating these by special terms. This may be illustrated by the following example:

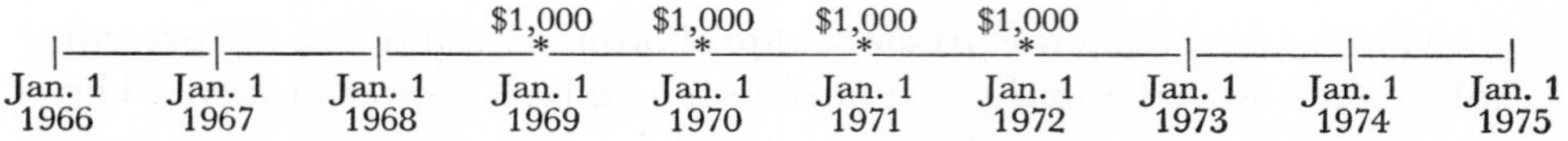

(a) Viewing the rents of $1,000 in terms of their value on January 1, 1966, calls for a determination of *the present value of a deferred annuity.*

(b) Viewing the rents in terms of their value on January 1, 1968, calls for a determination of the *present value of an ordinary annuity.*

(c) Viewing the rents in terms of their value on January 1, 1969, calls for a determination of *the present value of an annuity due.*

(d) Viewing the rents in terms of their value on January 1, 1972, calls for a determination of *the amount of an ordinary annuity.*

(e) Viewing the rents in terms of their value on January 1, 1973, calls for a determination of *the amount of an annuity due.*

(f) Viewing the rents in terms of their value on January 1, 1975, calls for a determination of *the amount of an annuity left at compound interest.*

SPECIAL PROBLEMS

Preceding pages have presented the basic present value patterns; an example was offered to illustrate each of the patterns described. Problems may be encountered that represent a series or a combination of present values; in certain instances both present values and amounts may be involved. Such circumstances call for an identification of the various elements of the problem before procedures may be developed and compound interest tables applied in its solution. Examples of problems that call for special analysis follow.

Example 1: Present value combination. Kent wishes to deposit on January 1, 1967, a sum that will enable him to make 3 withdrawals of $5,000 each at 2-year intervals, the first withdrawal to be made on December 31, 1969. It is assumed that the deposit will earn interest at 3% compounded semiannually. What is the required deposit?

The problem is analyzed as follows:

Interest at 3% compounded semiannually

Jan. 1 1967 | Dec. 31 1967 | Dec. 31 1968 | Dec. 31 1969 | Dec. 31 1970 | Dec. 31 1971 | Dec. 31 1972 | Dec. 31 1973

Withdrawal $5,000 (Dec. 31, 1969) | Withdrawal $5,000 (Dec. 31, 1971) | Withdrawal $5,000 (Dec. 31, 1973)

(1) $5,000 discounted 6 periods at 1½%

(2) $5,000 discounted 10 periods at 1½%

(3) $5,000 discounted 14 periods at 1½%

Solution:

(1) Sum required on 12/31/69, $5,000, times present value of 1, 6 periods at 1½%, .914542, equals present value on 1/1/67 of first withdrawal	$ 4,572.71
(2) Sum required on 12/31/71, $5,000, times present value of 1, 10 periods at 1½%, .861667, equals present value on 1/1/67 of second withdrawal.	4,308.34
(3) Sum required on 12/31/73, $5,000, times present value of 1, 14 periods at 1½%, .811849, equals present value on 1/1/67 of third withdrawal	4,059.25
Deposit required on 1/1/67.	$12,940.30

Example 2: Present value and present value of annuity combination. On December 31, 1965, Brown owes King a balance of $12,500 on a non-interest-bearing note; this balance is payable in $1,000 installments on January 1 of each of the years 1966–70, with a lump sum payment of the balance of $7,500 on January 1, 1971. King agrees to accept full settlement of the note on January 1, 1966, and agrees to a discount compounded at 5%. What payment is required in settlement?

The problem is analyzed as follows:

Interest 5%

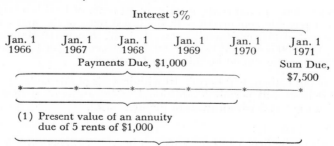

Jan. 1 1966 | Jan. 1 1967 | Jan. 1 1968 | Jan. 1 1969 | Jan. 1 1970 | Jan. 1 1971

Payments Due, $1,000 (Jan. 1, 1966–1970) | Sum Due, $7,500 (Jan. 1, 1971)

(1) Present value of an annuity due of 5 rents of $1,000

(2) Present value of $7,500 discounted for 5 periods

Solution:

(1) Payments due beginning 1/1/66, \$1,000, times present value of an annuity due of 5 rents of 1 at 5%, (3.545951 + 1), equals present value on 1/1/66 of series of payments due	\$ 4,545.95
(2) Sum due 1/1/71, \$7,500, times present value of 1, 5 periods at 5%, .783526, equals present value on 1/1/66 of sum due	5,876.45
Payment required on 1/1/66.	\$10,422.40

Example 3: Present value of annuity combination. Carter deposits \$10,000 on January 1, 1967, at 4% compounded annually. He plans to make 10 annual withdrawals from the fund, beginning on January 1, 1968, the first 5 withdrawals to be equal and the last 5 withdrawals to be equal but double the amount of the first 5. What are the withdrawals?

The problem is analyzed as follows:

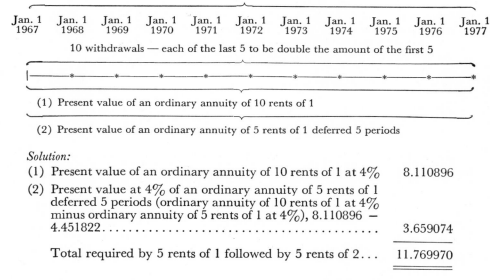

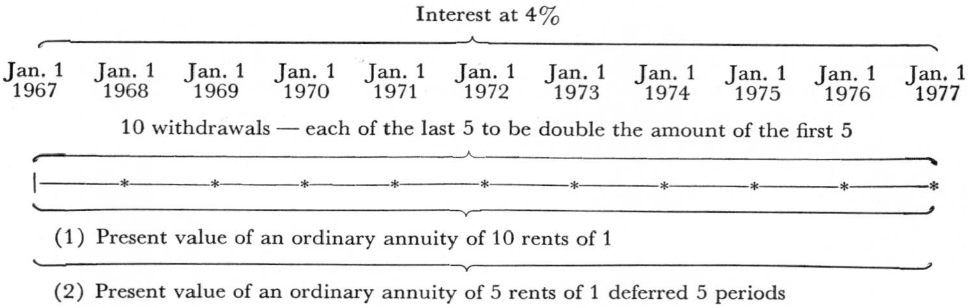

Solution:

(1) Present value of an ordinary annuity of 10 rents of 1 at 4%	8.110896
(2) Present value at 4% of an ordinary annuity of 5 rents of 1 deferred 5 periods (ordinary annuity of 10 rents of 1 at 4% minus ordinary annuity of 5 rents of 1 at 4%), 8.110896 − 4.451822.	3.659074
Total required by 5 rents of 1 followed by 5 rents of 2. . .	11.769970

Two series of annual rents, a series of 10 rents of 1 with a second series of 5 rents of 1 payable concurrent with the last 5 rents of the first series, requires an investment of 11.769970 on January 1, 1967. Since \$10,000 is deposited on this date, \$10,000 is divided by 11.769970; for each unit of 1 in the withdrawal pattern, then, there should be substituted \$849.62.

The deposit, then, will permit 10 withdrawals of \$849.62.
The deposit will permit 5 additional withdrawals of \$849.62 concurrent with the last 5 withdrawals of the first series.

Stated differently:

Each of the first 5 withdrawals will be.	\$ 849.62
Each of the last 5 withdrawals will be.	\$ 1,699.24

Example 4: Amount and present value combination. Dwight borrows \$10,000 on January 1, 1966. This is to be repaid together with interest at 4% compounded annually in the form of (1) a series of 5 annual payments of \$1,000 on January 1 of each year, 1967–1971, and (2) the balance on January 1, 1972. What amount will be payable on January 1, 1972? The problem is analyzed as follows:

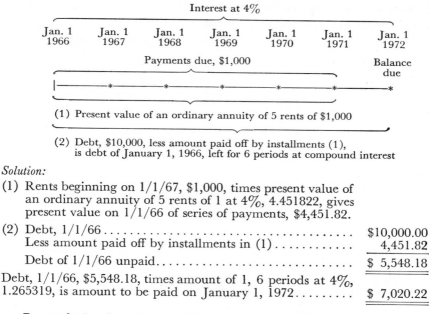

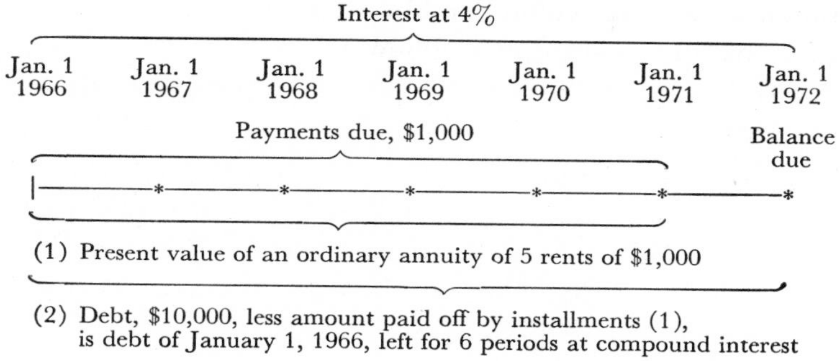

Solution:

(1) Rents beginning on 1/1/67, \$1,000, times present value of an ordinary annuity of 5 rents of 1 at 4%, 4.451822, gives present value on 1/1/66 of series of payments, \$4,451.82.

(2) Debt, 1/1/66	\$10,000.00
Less amount paid off by installments in (1)	4,451.82
Debt of 1/1/66 unpaid	\$ 5,548.18
Debt, 1/1/66, \$5,548.18, times amount of 1, 6 periods at 4%, 1.265319, is amount to be paid on January 1, 1972	\$ 7,020.22

Example 5: Amount and present value combination. Egan wishes to establish a fund that will make it possible for him to withdraw \$8,000 at 8 annual intervals beginning on January 1, 1971. The fund is to be established by 5 equal deposits, the first to be made on January 1, 1966. Interest at 5% compounded annually will be earned on the balance on deposit. What are the annual deposits? The problem is analyzed as follows:

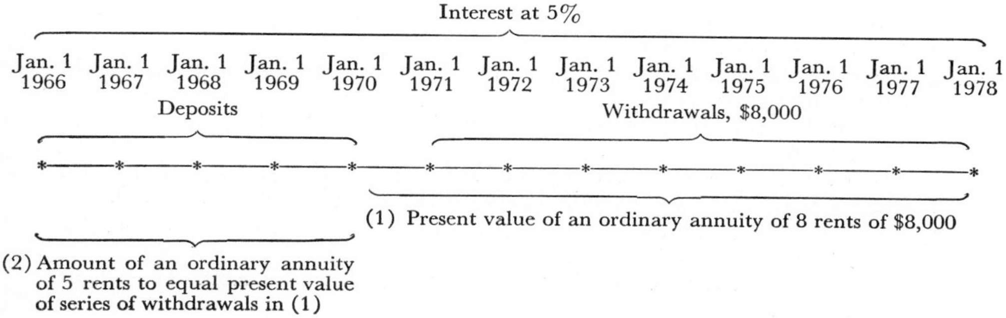

Solution:

(1) Rents beginning on 1/1/71, \$8,000, times present value of an ordinary annuity of 8 rents of 1 at 5%, 6.463213, equals present value on 1/1/70 of series of payments, \$51,705.70.

(2) Amount required on 1/1/70, \$51,705.70 in (1), divided by amount of an ordinary annuity of 5 rents of 1 at 5%, 5.525631, gives annual deposits to be made beginning 1/1/66, \$9,357.43.

Example 6: Present value combination. The Fisher Company has bonded indebtedness maturing as follows:

Due January 1, 1976	\$100,000
Due January 1, 1981	\$100,000

The company wishes to establish a redemption fund to provide for the retirement of the bonds. Fifteen equal annual deposits are to be made, the first being made on January 1, 1967. Assuming interest at 5% compounded annually, what are the equal deposits? The problem is analyzed as follows:

Interest at 5%

Jan. 1 1967 | Jan. 1 1968 | Jan. 1 1969 | Jan. 1 1970 | Jan. 1 1971 | Jan. 1 1972 | Jan. 1 1973 | Jan. 1 1974 | Jan. 1 1975 | Jan. 1 1976 | Jan. 1 1977 | Jan. 1 1978 | Jan. 1 1979 | Jan. 1 1980 | Jan. 1 1981

Deposits

Withdrawal \$100,000 (Jan. 1, 1976) — Withdrawal \$100,000 (Jan. 1, 1981)

————*——*——*——*——*——*——*——*——*——*——*——*——*

(1) (Present value of first withdrawal)
Present value of \$100,000 discounted 9 periods

(2) (Present value of second withdrawal)
Present value of \$100,000 discounted 14 periods

(3) (Present value of series of deposits to meet debts to be retired)
Present value of an annuity due of 15 rents of 1
[Equal periodic rents have present value equal to theoretical present value of debt (sum of (1) and (2)]

Solution:

(1) Using 1/1/67 as a focal date and computing the present value of the first debt retirement:

Sum due 1/1/76, \$100,000 times present value of 1, 9 periods at 5%, .644609, is \$64,460.90.

(2) Using 1/1/67 as a focal date and computing the present value of the second debt retirement:

Sum due 1/1/81, \$100,000 times present value of 1, 14 periods at 5%, .505068, is \$50,506.80.

Theoretical value of obligations as of 1/1/67, date that fund accumulation begins, \$64,460.90 + \$50,506.80 [sum of (1) and (2)], or \$114,967.70.

(3) Using 1/1/67 as a focal date and computing the present value of the deposits to meet the obligations:

Present value of an annuity due of 15 rents of 1 at 5%, 9.898641 + 1, or 10.898641.

Then, theoretical present value of obligations on 1/1/67, $114,967.70, divided by present value of an annuity due of 15 rents of 1 as of 1/1/67, 10.898641 in (3), gives the equal annual installments to meet the debt retirement needs, $10,548.81.

COMPOUND INTEREST VALUE RELATIONSHIPS

Frequently the specific value that is to be applied in solving a problem is not given. When certain values are known, however, remaining values can be determined by the following processes:

(a) Given: Amount of 1.
To find: Present value of 1.
Divide 1 by the amount of 1.

Example: Given, 1.628895, amount of 1, 10 periods at 5%. 1 ÷ 1.628895 = .613913, present value of 1, 10 periods at 5%.

(b) Given: Present value of 1.
To find: Present value of an annuity of 1.
Subtract the present value of 1 from 1 to obtain the compound discount on 1 and divide this by the interest rate.

Example: Given, .613913, present value of 1, 10 periods at 5%. 1 − .613913 = .386087, compound discount on 1, 10 periods at 5%. .386087 ÷ .05 = 7.72174.

(c) Given: Present value of an annuity of 1.
To find: Amount of an annuity of 1.
Additional value required: Amount of 1.
Multiply the present value of an annuity of 1 by the amount of 1 for a number of periods equal to the number of rents.

Example: Given, 7.721735, present value of an annuity of 10 rents of 1 at 5%. 7.721735 × 1.628895, amount of 1, 10 periods at 5%, = 12.5779, amount of an annuity of 10 rents of 1 at 5%.

(d) Given: Amount of an annuity of 1.
To find: Amount of 1.
Multiply the amount of an annuity of 1 by the interest rate to obtain compound interest on 1, and add 1.

Example: Given, 12.577893, amount of an annuity of 10 rents of 1 at 5%. 12.577893 × .05 = .628895, compound interest on 1, 10 periods at 5%. .628895 + 1 = 1.628895, amount of 1, 10 periods at 5%.

(e) Given: Amount of 1.
To find: Amount of an annuity of 1.
Subtract 1 from the amount of 1 to obtain compound interest on 1, and divide this by the interest rate.

Example: Given, 1.628895, amount of 1, 10 periods at 5%. 1.628895 − 1 = .628895, compound interest on 1, 10 periods at 5%. .628895 ÷ .05 = 12.5779, amount of an annuity of 10 rents of 1 at 5%.

(f) Given: Amount of an annuity of 1.
To find: Present value of an annuity of 1.
Additional value required: Present value of 1.
Multiply the amount of an annuity of 1 by the present value of 1 for a number of periods equal to the number of rents.

Example: Given, 12.577893, amount of an annuity of 10 rents of 1 at 5%. 12.577893 × .613913 = 7.7217, present value of an annuity of 10 rents of 1 at 5%.

(g) Given: Present value of an annuity of 1.
To find: Present value of 1.
Multiply the present value of an annuity of 1 by the interest rate to obtain the compound discount and subtract this from 1.

Example: Given, 7.721735, present value of an annuity of 10 rents of 1 at 5%. 7.721735 × .05 = .386087, compound discount on 1, 10 periods at 5%. 1 − .386087 = .613913, present value of 1, 10 periods at 5%.

(h) Given: Present value of 1.
To find: Amount of 1.
Divide 1 by the present value of 1.

Example: Given, .613913, present value of 1, 10 periods at 5%. 1 ÷ .613913 = 1.628895, amount of 1, 10 periods at 5%.

The relationships described in the preceding examples are illustrated by the following diagram:

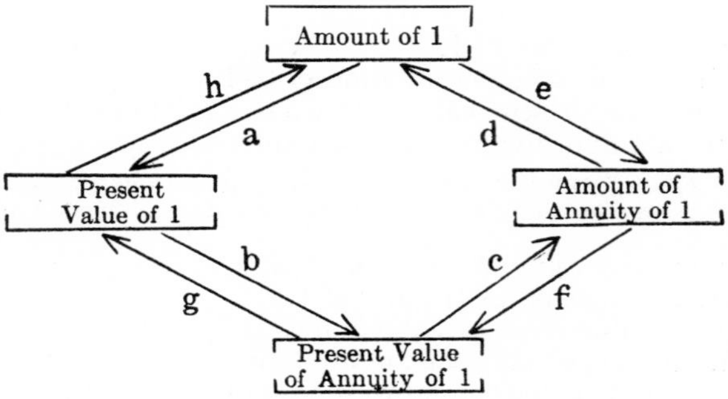

In computing a value from information that is given, it may be necessary to develop an intermediate value. For example, given the amount of 1 and working to obtain the present value of an annuity of 1, it is first necessary to compute the present value of 1. Or, given the present value of 1 and working to obtain the amount of an annuity of 1, it is first necessary to compute the amount of 1.

QUESTIONS

1. Distinguish between the amount of 1 and the present value of 1.

2. Distinguish between the present value of 1 and the present value of an annuity of 1.

3. State how each of the following would be determined with the use of the table on page 979:
(a) The present value of 1 for 12 years at 4% compounded annually.
(b) The present value of 1 for 13 years at 7% compounded semiannually.

4. Using the table on pages 1034 and 1035, find:
(a) The present value of $1,000 for 6 years at 4½% compounded annually.
(b) The present value of $1,000 for 10 years at 5% compounded semiannually.

5. Using the table on pages 1034 and 1035, determine:

(a) The compound discount on \$1,000 for 12 years at 3½% compounded annually.

(b) The compound discount on \$1,000 for 12 years at 6% compounded semiannually.

6. What two methods may be used in determining the present value of an annuity due? Which method is more convenient when annuity tables are available?

7. Explain how each of the following would be solved without tables:

(a) The present value of \$1,000 for 5 years at 6% compounded annually.

(b) The present value of \$2,000 for 4 years at 5% compounded semiannually.

(c) The compound discount on \$1,000 for 12 years at 4% compounded quarterly.

8. Explain how each of the following problems would be solved in the absence of annuity tables:

(a) The sum to be deposited on December 31, 1966, to provide for 15 annual withdrawals of \$1,000, the first withdrawal to be made on December 31, 1967. Interest of 3% is compounded annually on the sum on deposit.

(b) The sum to be deposited on December 31, 1966, to provide for 15 annual withdrawals of \$1,000, the first withdrawal to be made on December 31, 1972. Interest of 3% is compounded annually on the sum on deposit.

9. Analyze the following problems, stating the procedures to be followed and the tables to be used in developing solutions:

(a) Smith wishes to deposit a sum that at interest of 5% compounded semiannually will permit 2 withdrawals: \$10,000 at the end of 5 years and \$10,000 at the end of 10 years. What is the required deposit?

(b) Torgen borrows \$10,000, promising to repay this amount in 4 equal annual installments of \$2,000 beginning 1 year hence, and the balance at the end of 5 years. Assuming interest at 4% compounded annually, what balance will be payable at the end of 5 years?

(c) Unger wishes to make 5 annual deposits of \$5,000 to a fund. This fund is to provide for a series of 20 equal annual withdrawals, the first to be made 1 year after the last deposit. Assuming that the fund will earn 4% compounded annually, what are the equal annual withdrawals?

EXERCISES

1. Using the present value tables on pages 1034 and 1035, solve each of the following problems:

(a) What is the present value on January 1, 1967, of \$10,000 due January 1, 1971, and discounted at 5% compounded annually?

(b) What is the present value on July 1, 1967, of \$2,500 due January 1, 1971, and discounted at 6% compounded quarterly?

(c) What is the compound discount on \$1,000 for 5 years at 6% compounded quarterly?

2. Using the tables given on pages 1036 and 1037, solve each of the following problems:

(a) What sum shall be deposited on June 30, 1966, to provide for 5 semiannual withdrawals of $1,000, the first withdrawal to be made on June 30, 1966? Interest of 5% is compounded semiannually on the sum on deposit.
(b) What sum shall be deposited on June 30, 1966, to provide for 5 annual withdrawals of $1,000, the first withdrawal to be made June 30, 1967? Interest of 5% is compounded annually on the sum on deposit.
(c) What sum shall be deposited on June 30, 1966, to provide for 5 annual withdrawals of $1,000, the first withdrawal to be made June 30, 1969? Interest of 4% is compounded annually on the sum on deposit.

3. Five equal annual withdrawals are to be made beginning December 31, 1971. Using the proper table, determine the equal annual withdrawals if $10,000 is invested at interest of 5% compounded annually on:

(a) December 31, 1971.
(b) January 1, 1971.
(c) January 1, 1966.

4. Using the tables given on pages 1036 and 1037, solve each of the following problems:

(a) Ten payments of $1,000 are due at annual intervals beginning June 30, 1966. What amount will be accepted in cancellation of this series of payments on June 30, 1966, assuming a discount rate of 5% compounded annually?
(b) Ten payments of $1,000 are due at annual intervals beginning December 31, 1966. What amount will be accepted in cancellation of this series of payments on January 1, 1966, assuming a discount rate of 4% compounded annually?
(c) $5,000 is owed on January 1, 1966. This amount is to be paid in 5 equal annual installments to include both principal and interest at 4% compounded annually, the first payment to be made January 1, 1967. What are the equal payments?
(d) $5,000 is owed on January 1, 1966. This amount is to be paid in 10 equal semiannual installments to include both principal and interest at 5% compounded semiannually, the first payment to be made January 1, 1966. What are the equal payments?
(e) $5,000 is owed on January 1, 1966. This is to be paid in 4 equal semiannual installments to include principal and interest at 6% compounded semiannually, the first payment to be made January 1, 1968. What are the equal payments?

5. Assuming compound interest at 5%, solve each of the following problems, using the proper tables:

(a) The sum to be deposited on June 30, 1966, to provide for 5 equal annual withdrawals of $1,000, the first withdrawal to be made on June 30, 1967.
(b) The accumulated amount on January 1, 1971, of a series of 5 equal annual deposits of $1,000, the first deposit being made on January 1, 1966.

(c) The 5 equal annual withdrawals to be made beginning January 1, 1966, if $1,000 is deposited on January 1, 1966.
(d) The 5 equal annual contributions to be made to produce a fund of $1,000 on December 31, 1970, the first contribution to be made on December 31, 1966.

6. Using the present value tables on pages 1034–1037, solve each of the following problems:

(a) Ritter wishes to make 2 withdrawals of $5,000 each, the first on January 1, 1972, and the second on July 1, 1972. What sum should he deposit on January 1, 1966, to make possible such withdrawals if it is assumed that interest will be earned on the deposit at 5% compounded semiannually?
(b) Jansen wishes to make 5 annual withdrawals of $5,000 followed by 5 annual withdrawals of $10,000; the first withdrawal from the fund is to be made on January 1, 1969. What sum should be deposited on January 1, 1967, to make possible such withdrawals, assuming that interest will be earned on the deposit at 6% compounded annually?
(c) Green deposits $10,000 on January 1, 1967, at 4% compounded annually. He wishes to make 8 annual withdrawals beginning January 1, 1969, the first 4 withdrawals to be double the amount of the last 4. What are the withdrawals?
(d) Lamb owes Stine $10,000 due December 31, 1971, and $15,000 due December 31, 1976. Lamb wishes to establish a fund to make possible the payment of amounts coming due. Ten equal deposits are to be made to the fund, the first to be made on December 31, 1967. What are the equal deposits, assuming the fund will earn 5% per year compounded annually?

7. Fritch borrows $1,000 that is to be repaid in 24 equal monthly installments with interest at the rate of 1% per month. Using the tables on pages 1036 and 1037, calculate the equal installments.

8. Duffy holds a secured note for $10,000 that is due at the end of 5 years together with interest at 5% compounded annually. He is willing to sell this note to offer a yield of 6%. Using the tables on pages 1030–1037, calculate the sum he will accept.

9. Given 1.216653, the amount of 1, 5 periods at 4%, calculate:

(a) The present value of 1, 5 periods at 4%.
(b) The present value of an ordinary annuity of 5 rents of 1 at 4%.
(c) The amount of an ordinary annuity of 5 rents of 1 at 4%.

10. Given 7.360087, the present value of an ordinary annuity of 10 rents at 6%, calculate:

(a) The present value of 1, 10 periods at 6%.
(b) The amount of 1, 10 periods at 6%.
(c) The amount of an ordinary annuity of 10 rents of 1 at 6%.

11. Given 5.637093, the amount of an ordinary annuity of 5 rents at 6%, calculate the present value of 1, 5 periods at 6%.

12. Given .873154, the present value of 1, 5 periods at 2¾%, calculate the present value of an annuity due of 6 rents of 1 at 2¾%.

PROBLEMS

(*Use the tables given on pages 1030–1037.*)

27-1. Anderson deposits $50,000 on January 1, 1966. How much can he withdraw in 5 equal annual installments beginning January 1, 1972, if the interest rate is 5% compounded annually during this period?

27-2. On January 1, 1966, Kane invests $25,000 in an annuity to provide 6 equal annual payments. Interest is compounded annually at 5%. Compute the equal amounts that Kane will receive, assuming that the first payment is due:

(a) January 1, 1966.
(b) December 31, 1966.
(c) January 1, 1969.
(d) December 31, 1973.

27-3. On July 1, 1966, Wallace purchases real estate for $75,000 to be paid in 10 equal annual installments including interest of 6% on any unpaid balance. The first installment is due on the date of purchase. What are the equal payments?

27-4. On July 31, Cooper purchases a lot for $27,500, payable 20% down and the balance in 30 equal monthly installments that are to include interest on any unpaid balance at 6% compounded monthly. What are the equal installments?

27-5. Young holds a non-interest-bearing note, signed by T. C. Bailey, for $40,000, payable in 8 annual installments of $5,000 beginning December 31, 1970. Assuming that the parties agree to cancel the note using a rate of 5% compounded annually, give the amount that would be paid by Bailey if the date of settlement is:

(a) January 1, 1966
(b) January 1, 1968.
(c) December 31, 1969.
(d) December 31, 1970.

27-6. Carter purchases an annuity that is to provide 10 annual rents, the first 5 rents to be $5,000 each, the remaining rents to be $7,500 each. The first rent is payable on December 31, 1969.

(a) What is the cost of the annuity on a 3% basis compounded annually, assuming that the purchase is made on: (1) December 31, 1966; (2) January 1, 1969; (3) December 31, 1969.
(b) Assume that Carter invests $100,000 on a 3% basis compounded annually in order to obtain 10 annual rents, each of the last 5 rents to be double the amount of each of the first 5 and the first rent to be payable on December 31, 1969. What amounts will he receive, assuming that the purchase is made on: (1) January 1, 1967; (2) December 31, 1968; (3) December 31, 1969.

27-7. The Washington Co. acquires land on January 1, 1967, making payment as follows:

Cash, $100,000.
Non-interest-bearing notes as follows:
$25,000 due 5 years hence.
$75,000 due in 5 equal annual installments, the first due 10 years hence.

What purchase price should be assigned to the land? Assume an interest rate of 6%.

27-8. The Peerless Supply Co. is offered the following plans in the acquisition of a delivery truck:

(1) Purchase of the truck for a cash price of $12,000.
(2) Lease of the truck at the rate of $250 per month, payable at the beginning of each month.

The service life of the truck is estimated at 4 years with a residual value at the end of that time of $2,500. Assuming an interest rate of 6% and disregarding all factors other than those stated above, indicate which alternative you would select and state the amount of the savings thereby.

27-9. The Donner Film Co. leases a piece of property, agreeing to pay $10,000 a year for the first 5-year period, $15,000 annually for the second 5-year period, and $20,000 annually for the third 5-year period, rentals being payable at the beginning of each year. The lessor agrees to accept the full amount of the rentals in advance on a 6% basis. What amount should be paid?

27-10. Evans wishes to provide for the college education of his son and estimates that the cost will be approximately $3,000 a year for a 4-year period beginning January 1, 1973. To provide for the annual college costs, Evans will set aside equal amounts annually, beginning January 1, 1966, and including a final deposit on January 1, 1973. What are the equal payments if it is assumed that amounts set aside will earn interest at 4%?

27-11. On January 1, 1966, Jim Hill borrows $50,000 from his father to open a business. The son is the beneficiary of a trust from which he is to receive $20,000 on January 1, 1975. He agrees to make this amount payable to his father and further to pay his father equal annual amounts from January 1, 1967, to January 1, 1974, inclusive, in retirement of the debt. Interest is to be charged at 5%. What are the annual payments?

27-12. Taylor purchases a home for $50,000, paying $10,000 down. The balance is to be paid in equal monthly payments over a 4-year period, payments to apply first as interest at ½% a month on the balance owed, the balance as a reduction of principal.

(a) What are the equal monthly payments?
(b) Assuming that Taylor is permitted to pay off the balance owed on the date of the fortieth payment, what amount would he pay in settlement of the contract?

27-13. McMillan has deposited $7,500 at the end of each year from 1957–1966 inclusive. He plans to make annual withdrawals of $5,000 per year from this fund, the first withdrawal to be made at the end of 1967. Assuming interest at 4% compounded annually throughout the duration of this plan, how many withdrawals can McMillan make and what is the amount of the final withdrawal?

27-14. On January 1, 1966, Crawford borrows $80,000 from Miller and agrees to repay this amount in payments of $4,000 a year until the debt is paid off. Payments are to include interest at 4% on the unpaid balance of the debt. Assuming that the annual payments are made beginning on January 1, 1967, state the number of payments to be made and give the amount of the final payment.

27-15. Gilbert buys a store for $22,500, paying $7,500 down, the balance to be paid in monthly installments of $450. The rate of interest on the obligation is 6% compounded monthly and payments are to apply first to interest due to date, the balance reducing the principal.

(a) How many payments will be required in paying off the obligation? What is the amount of the final payment?

(b) Assuming that the contract is settled on the date of the twentieth payment, give the settlement amount.

27-16. The premiums on a fire insurance policy covering a certain building for the amount of $500,000 on a 1-year, 3-year, and 5-year basis are as follows:

1 year	$1,120
3 years	2,800
5 years	4,480

In each case the entire premium for the full term of the policy is payable in advance. Compute the annual cost of this insurance to the insured on each of the three bases, assuming that money is worth 6% per annum. (AICPA adapted)

27-17. The Westwood Corporation wants to retire a debt of $105,000 bearing 5% interest payable annually. The tenth payment, including the interest, is to be $15,000. The other 9 periodical payments are all to include interest and to be of the same amount. Calculate the amount of each of such 9 payments. (AICPA adapted)

27-18. A series of 5% bonds totaling $100,000 is issued, dated January 1, 1966, redeemable at par by 10 annual payments of $10,000 each, beginning December 31, 1976.

(a) What equal annual sinking fund payments are required on a 4% basis to pay off the bonds as they mature if the first payment to the sinking fund trustee is to be made on December 31, 1966, and annually thereafter?

(b) What is the status of the sinking fund on December 31, 1975, 1976, and 1977? (AICPA adapted)

Chapter 28

COMPOUND INTEREST

SPECIAL PROBLEMS

The principles of compound interest were discussed in the previous chapters. The application of these principles to a number of problems that the accountant encounters are considered in this chapter. The problems to be considered include those relating to leaseholds, installment payments, bonds, sinking funds, and depreciation.

LEASEHOLDS

In acquiring a leasehold, rentals may be paid for a number of years in advance. The amount paid in advance is frequently the present value of the amounts that would otherwise be due periodically. To illustrate the calculation of the amount that would be paid for a leasehold acquired on such a basis, assume that on January 1, 1967, a leasehold is acquired for a 5-year period at an annual rental of $5,000. The rents are to be paid at the beginning of the lease, compound discount at 4% per year being allowed on the prepayments. Since rents would be due at the beginning of each year, the amount payable represents the present value of an annuity due of 5 rents of $5,000 at 4%. The present value of an annuity due of 5 rents of 1 at 4% is 4.629895. The amount payable, then, is $5,000 × 4.629895, or $23,149.48. A table showing the changes that take place in the leasehold balance follows:

TABLE OF REDUCTION IN LEASEHOLD BALANCE

Date	Rent	Interest (4% of leasehold balance)	Leasehold Balance
January 1, 1967........			$23,149.48
January 1, 1967........	$5,000.00		18,149.48
December 31, 1967.....		$725.98	18,875.46
January 1, 1968........	5,000.00		13,875.46
December 31, 1968.....		555.02	14,430.48
January 1, 1969........	5,000.00		9,430.48
December 31, 1969.....		377.22	9,807.70
January 1, 1970........	5,000.00		4,807.70
December 31, 1970.....		192.30	5,000.00
January 1, 1971........	5,000.00		

Entries that would be made in recording the leasehold and rents for 1967 and 1968 appear below. Entries for rents in subsequent periods would be similar to those given.

Transaction	Books of the Lessee			Books of the Lessor		
January 1, 1967 Made payment for leasehold.	Leasehold........	23,149.48		Cash............	23,149.48	
	Cash..........		23,149.48	Deferred Leasehold Income...		23,149.48
To record rent for 1967.	Rent............	5,000.00		Deferred Leasehold Income.....	5,000.00	
	Leasehold......		5,000.00	Rental Income..		5,000.00
December 31, 1967 To record interest at 4% on leasehold balance.	Leasehold........	725.98		Interest Expense..	725.98	
	Interest Income.		725.98	Deferred Leasehold Income...		725.98
January 1, 1968 To record rent for 1968.	Rent............	5,000.00		Deferred Leasehold Income.....	5,000.00	
	Leasehold......		5,000.00	Rental Income..		5,000.00
December 31, 1968 To record interest at 4% on leasehold balance.	Leasehold........	555.02		Interest Expense..	555.02	
	Interest Income.		555.02	Deferred Leasehold Income...		555.02

INSTALLMENT PAYMENTS

An obligation may provide that it is to be liquidated by a series of equal payments that are to include both principal and accrued interest. The obligation represents the present value of an annuity, the equal payments being calculated by dividing the sum owed by the present value of an annuity of 1. To illustrate, a debt of $10,000 incurred at the end of 1966 is to be paid off by 10 equal semiannual installments including both principal and interest. Interest at the rate of 5% compounded semiannually accrues on the unpaid balance, and the first payment is to be made on June 30, 1967. Semiannual payments are determined by dividing $10,000 by 8.752064, the present value of an ordinary annuity of 10 rents of 1 at 2½%. The equal payments, then, are $1,142.59. A table summarizing the changes in the balance owed is given at the top of the following page.

Entries that would be made on June 30 and December 31, 1967, appear below. Similar entries would be made in subsequent periods.

Transaction	Books of the Party Making Payment			Books of the Party Receiving Payment		
June 30, 1967 Made first semiannual payment.	Interest Expense......	250.00		Cash................	1,142.59	
	Contracts Payable....	892.59		Interest Income....		250.00
	Cash..............		1,142.59	Contracts Receivable.........		892.59
December 31, 1967 Made second semiannual payment.	Interest Expense......	227.69		Cash................	1,142.59	
	Contracts Payable....	914.90		Interest Income....		227.69
	Cash..............		1,142.59	Contracts Receivable........		914.90

TABLE OF REDUCTION IN INSTALLMENT DEBT

Date	A Payment	B Interest Accruing on Principal (2½% of principal balance)	C Net Decrease in Principal (A–B)	D Balance of Principal (D–C)
January 1, 1967...				$10,000.00
June 30, 1967.....	$1,142.59	$250.00	$ 892.59	9,107.41
December 31, 1967.	1,142.59	227.69	914.90	8,192.51
June 30, 1968.....	1,142.59	204.81	937.78	7,254.73
December 31, 1968.	1,142.59	181.37	961.22	6,293.51
June 30, 1969.....	1,142.59	157.34	985.25	5,308.26
December 31, 1969.	1,142.59	132.71	1,009.88	4,298.38
June 30, 1970.....	1,142.59	107.46	1,035.13	3,263.25
December 31, 1970.	1,142.59	81.58	1,061.01	2,202.24
June 30, 1971.....	1,142.59	55.06	1,087.53	1,114.71
December 31, 1971.	1,142.58*	27.87	1,114.71	

*Corrected for 1 cent discrepancy.

PREMIUM AND DISCOUNT ON BONDS

The interest rate that is paid periodically on bonds is known as the *nominal* or *coupon rate*. The nominal interest rate as adjusted for premium or discount amortization is the *effective* or *yield rate*. When bonds are issued at a premium, the effective rate is less than the nominal rate; when bonds are issued at a discount, the effective rate is greater than the nominal rate.

Sale at a premium. When, at the time of issue, bonds provide for an interest rate that is greater than the going market rate for securities of this class, the bonds will command a premium that will bring the interest to the market rate. The premium may be computed by discounting at the market rate the benefits to be received by bondholders in the form of (1) the principal payment and (2) interest payments at the nominal rate. To illustrate, assume the issuance on January 1, 1967, of 5-year bonds of $100,000 that pay interest annually at 5%. On the date of issue the prevailing rate for bonds of this class is 4½%.

The bonds will produce benefits as follows: (1) $100,000 at maturity, 5 years hence; (2) 5 annual interest payments of $5,000, the first payment due at the end of the first year. Since the 5% bonds are sold to yield 4½%, the benefits are discounted at 4½%, the series of interest payments being considered an ordinary annuity of 5 rents. The amount received on the issue, then, is $102,194.99, computed as follows:

$100,000 × .802451 (present value of 1 for 5 periods at 4½%)	$ 80,245.10
$5,000 × 4.389977 (present value of an ordinary annuity of 5 rents of 1 at 4½%)	21,949.89
Present value of principal and interest payments at 4½%. . .	$102,194.99

The sales price for the bonds may be computed by an alternative method. Since bonds offering a 4½% return would sell at face value, 5% bonds will sell for face value plus the present value at 4½% of the interest payments in excess of the normal return. For example, bonds of $100,000 offer the same benefits at maturity regardless of the stated interest rate. Bonds on a 4½% basis would provide interest of $4,500 annually; however, 5% bonds provide interest of $5,000 annually. Five percent bonds of $100,000 acquired to yield 4½% would be valued at face value plus the present value of 4½% of 5 rents of $500, the difference between the payment rate, $5,000, and the market rate, $4,500. Computation of the sales price of the bonds in this manner follows:

Present value at 4½% of 5-year bonds of $100,000 paying interest of $4,500 annually	$100,000.00
Add present value at 4½% of an ordinary annuity of 5 rents of $500, difference between return on 5% bonds and 4½% bonds, $500 × 4.389977	2,194.99
Present value of principal and interest payments at 4½%. . .	$102,194.99

In recording the annual interest payments, interest is reported at the effective rate applied to the carrying value of the bonds. The premium on the bonds is reduced annually by the difference between the cash payment and the effective interest. Bond premium amortization over the life of the bond issue is shown below.

TABLE OF PREMIUM AMORTIZATION

$100,000 of 5-Year Bonds, Interest at 5% Payable Annually, Sold at $102,194.99 to Yield 4½%

Date	A Interest Payment (5% of face value)	B Effective Interest (4½% of carrying value)	C Premium Amortization (A–B)	D Bond Carrying Value (D–C)
January 1, 1967. . . .				$102,194.99
December 31, 1967. .	$5,000	$4,598.77	$401.23	101,793.76
December 31, 1968. .	5,000	4,580.72	419.28	101,374.48
December 31, 1969. .	5,000	4,561.85	438.15	100,936.33
December 31, 1970. .	5,000	4,542.13	457.87	100,478.46
December 31, 1971. .	5,000	4,521.54*	478.46	100,000.00

*Corrected for 1 cent discrepancy.

Entries to record the issuance of the bonds and the interest payments for the first two years are shown below.

Transaction	Books of the Issuing Company			Books of the Buyer		
January 1, 1967 Issued $100,000 of 5-year 5% bonds to yield 4½%.	Cash.......... Bonds Payable Bond Premium	102,194.99	 100,000.00 2,194.99	Investment in Bonds......... Cash........	102,194.99	 102,194.99
December 31, 1967 Made first annual interest payment on bonds: paid 5%; effective rate, 4½%.	Interest Expense Bond Premium. Cash........	4,598.77 401.23	 5,000.00	Cash.......... Interest Income........ Investment in Bonds.......	5,000.00	 4,598.77 401.23
December 31, 1968 Made second annual interest payment on bonds: paid 5%; effective rate, 4½%.	Interest Expense Bond Premium. Cash........	4,580.72 419.28	 5,000.00	Cash.......... Interest Income........ Investment in Bonds.......	5,000.00	 4,580.72 419.28

Sale at a discount. At the time of issue, bonds may provide for an interest rate that is less than the prevailing market rate. When this is the case, the bonds will have to be sold at a discount that adjusts the interest to the market rate. The proceeds of the issue may be computed by discounting at the market rate the bond principal and the interest benefits. To illustrate, assume that on January 1, 1967, 5-year bonds of $100,000 are issued with interest at 4% payable semiannually. On the date of issue the prevailing interest rate is 5% compounded semiannually. The bonds will produce benefits as follows: (1) $100,000 at maturity, 5 years hence; (2) 10 semiannual interest payments of $2,000, the first payment due at the end of the first 6-month period. The benefits are discounted at 2½%, the series of interest payments being considered an ordinary annuity of 10 rents. The amount received on the issue is $95,623.93, computed as follows:

$100,000 × .781198 (present value of 1 for 10 periods at 2½%)	$78,119.80
$2,000 × 8.752064 (present value of an ordinary annuity of 10 rents of 1 at 2½%)	17,504.13
Present value of principal and interest payments at 2½%....	$95,623.93

As in the case of bonds sold at a premium, the sales price may be computed by an alternative method. Since bonds offering a 5% return would sell at face value, 4% bonds will sell for face value less the present value at 5% of the normal return deficiency. Bonds on a 5% basis would provide a return of $2,500 semiannually; however, a 4% rate provides only $2,000 semiannually. Four percent bonds of $100,000 acquired to yield 5%, with interest paid semiannually, would be valued at face amount less the present value at 2½% of 10 rents of $500, the difference between the market rate, $2,500, and the payment rate, $2,000. Computation of the sales price of the bonds in this manner follows:

Present value at 5% compounded semiannually of 5-year bonds of $100,000 paying interest of $2,500 semiannually .	$100,000.00
Deduct present value at 2½% of an ordinary annuity of 10 rents of $500, difference between semiannual return on 5% bonds and 4% bonds, $500 × 8.752064.	4,376.03
Present value of principal and interest payments at 2½%. . .	$ 95,623.97

In recording the semiannual interest payments, interest is reported at the effective rate based upon the carrying value of the bonds. The discount on the bonds is reduced semiannually by the difference between the cash payment and the effective interest. Bond discount amortization that would be recognized over the life of the bond issue is shown in the table below.

TABLE OF DISCOUNT AMORTIZATION

$100,000 of 5-Year Bonds, Interest at 4% Payable Semiannually, Sold at $95,623.93 to Yield 5%

Date	A Interest Payment (2% of face value)	B Effective Interest (2½% of carrying value)	C Discount Amortization (B − A)	D Bond Carrying Value (D + C)
January 1, 1967. . . .				$ 95,623.93
June 30, 1967.	$2,000	$2,390.60	$390.60	96,014.53
December 31, 1967. .	2,000	2,400.36	400.36	96,414.89
June 30, 1968.	2,000	2,410.37	410.37	96,825.26
December 31, 1968. .	2,000	2,420.63	420.63	97,245.89
June 30, 1969.	2,000	2,431.15	431.15	97,677.04
December 31, 1969. .	2.000	2,441.93	441.93	98,118.97
June 30, 1970.	2,000	2,452.97	452.97	98,571.94
December 31, 1970. .	2,000	2,464.30	464.30	99,036.24
June 30, 1971.	2,000	2,475.91	475.91	99,512.15
December 31, 1971. .	2,000	2,487.85*	487.85	100,000.00

*Corrected for 5 cent discrepancy.

Entries to record the issuance of the bonds and the periodic interest payments for the first year are given at the top of the following page.

Transaction	Books of the Issuing Company			Books of the Buyer		
January 1, 1967 Issued $100,000 of 5-year 4% bonds to yield 5%.	Cash..........	95,623.93		Investment in Bonds..........	95,623.93	
	Bond Discount...	4,376.07		Cash.........		95,623.93
	Bonds Payable.		100,000.00			
June 30, 1967 Made first semiannual interest payment on bonds: paid 2%; effective rate, 2½%.	Interest Expense.	2,390.60		Cash...........	2,000.00	
	Bond Discount		390.60	Investment in Bonds..........	390.60	
	Cash........		2,000.00	Interest Income.		2,390.60
December 31, 1967 Made second semiannual interest payment on bonds: paid 2%; effective rate, 2½%.	Interest Expense.	2,400.36		Cash...........	2,000.00	
	Bond Discount		400.36	Investment in Bonds..........	400.36	
	Cash........		2,000.00	Interest Income.		2,400.36

Bond tables. Bond tables may be used in obtaining bond values. Part of such a table for 4% bonds, interest payable semiannually, is illustrated below. From this table the value of a 4%, $1,000 bond with a remaining life of 5 years that is to yield 5% is immediately found to be $956.24. Bonds of $100,000, then, would sell on this basis for $95,624.

BOND VALUES TO THE NEAREST CENT PER $1,000 BOND
INTEREST AT 4% PAYABLE SEMIANNUALLY

Effective Rate	Remaining Life of Bonds			
	4 Years	4½ Years	5 Years	5½ Years
3.50	$1,018.51	$1,020.65	$1,022.75	$1,024.82
3.60	1,014.78	1,016.48	1,018.15	1,019.80
3.70	1,011.06	1,012.33	1,013.58	1,014.81
3.75	1,009.21	1,010.26	1,011.30	1,012.32
3.80	1,007.36	1,008.20	1,009.03	1,009.84
3.90	1,003.67	1,004.09	1,004.50	1,004.91
4.00	1,000.00	1,000.00	1,000.00	1,000.00
4.10	996.35	995.93	995.52	995.12
4.20	992.71	991.88	991.06	990.27
4.25	990.89	989.86	988.84	987.85
4.30	989.08	987.84	986.63	985.44
4.40	985.47	983.83	982.22	980.65
4.50	981.88	979.84	977.83	975.88
4.60	978.30	975.86	973.47	971.13
4.70	974.74	971.90	969.13	966.42
4.75	972.97	969.93	966.97	964.07
4.80	971.20	967.97	964.81	961.73
4.90	967.67	964.05	960.51	957.07
5.00	964.15	960.15	956.24	952.43

CALLABLE BONDS

When bonds are redeemable before the maturity date at the option of the company issuing the bonds, this factor must be considered by the buyer in determining the price to be paid for the bonds. The value of the bonds should be computed on the assumption that (1) the bond is called on the earliest optional redemption date and (2) the bond is paid at maturity. The buyer should pay the lower of the two values so that he is protected against loss on possible bond redemption.

If callable bonds are selling at a discount, computation on the basis of the full life always gives the lower value; if the bonds are selling at a premium, computation on the basis of the shorter optional period will give the lower value. However, in cases in which the issuing corporation agrees to pay a premium if it should choose to redeem bonds prior to their maturity, such a premium must be considered in arriving at the lower value. If the bonds are selling at a discount, computation on the basis of the full life will still offer the lower value. If the bonds are selling at a premium, however, both values in terms of both a full life and an accelerated life must be computed in determining the lower value. To illustrate, assume that a $1,000, 10-year bond that pays interest at 6% semiannually is bought to yield 4%. Bonds are redeemable by the issuer at any time after the end of the fifth year upon payment of a premium of 10%. Bond values are computed as follows:

Assuming redemption at the option date:

$1,100 (principal payment) × .820348 (present value of 1 for 10 periods at 2%)..	$ 902.38
$30 (interest payments) × 8.982585 (present value of an ordinary annuity of 10 rents of 1 at 2%)............................	269.48
Present value of principal and interest payments at 2%..........	$1,171.86

Assuming redemption at the maturity date:

$1,000 (principal payment) × .672971 (present value of 1 for 20 periods at 2%)..	$ 672.97
$30 (interest payments) × 16.351433 (present value of an ordinary annuity of 20 rents of 1 at 2%)............................	490.54
Present value of principal and interest payments at 2%..........	$1,163.51

In this case, the assumption of redemption at maturity gives the lower bond value, $1,163.51. This is the amount, then, that the buyer should pay. If the bond had been redeemable at a premium of only 5%, the lower value would have been found on the assumption that the bonds would be called, the bond then having a value of only $1,130.85 computed as follows:

Assuming redemption at the option date:

$1,050 (principal payment) × .820348 (present value of 1 for 10 periods at 2%)	$ 861.37
$30 (interest payments) × 8.982585 (present value of an ordinary annuity of 10 rents of 1 at 2%)	269.48
Present value of principal and interest payments at 2%	$1,130.85

Under these circumstances the buyer should pay no more than $1,130.85.

BOND VALUATION BETWEEN INTEREST DATES

In finding the value of bonds at a date other than an interest date, it is necessary to compute (1) the present value of the benefits provided by the bond issue at the date of purchase, and (2) the accrued interest at the nominal rate for the fractional interest period elapsed. The first figure may be obtained by finding the difference in values, assuming the purchase was made at the beginning of the interest period and at the beginning of the next interest period; by interpolation, the beginning value may then be adjusted for the fractional period elapsed. To illustrate, assume that 5-year bonds of $100,000, dated January 1, 1967, interest at 5% payable annually, are sold on March 1, 1967, at a price to yield 4½%. Their value is computed as follows:

Value on January 1, 1967:

Present value at 4½% of 5-year bonds of $100,000	$100,000.00
Add present value at 4½% of an ordinary annuity of 5 rents of $500, difference between return on 5% bonds and 4½% bonds, $500 × 4.389977	2,194.99
Present value of bonds, January 1, 1967	$102,194.99

Value on January 1, 1968:

Present value at 4½% of 4-year bonds of $100,000	$100,000.00
Add present value at 4½% of an ordinary annuity of 4 rents of $500, difference between return on 5% bonds and 4½% bonds, $500 × 3.587526	1,793.76
Present value of bonds, January 1, 1968	$101,793.76

Value on March 1, 1967, including accrued interest:

Present value of bonds on January 1, 1967	$102,194.99
Subtract premium for period January 1, 1967–March 1, 1967, $\frac{2}{12}$ × $401.23 ($2,194.99 − $1,793.76, premium for year)	66.87
Bond value on March 1, 1967	$102,128.12
Add accrued interest January 1–March 1, 1967, at the nominal rate, 5%, $\frac{2}{12}$ (.05 × $100,000)	833.33
Value of bonds and accrued interest on March 1, 1967	$102,961.45

Bonds would be recorded at $102,128.12 and accrued interest at $833.33. Upon payment of interest on December 31, 1967, the carrying value of the bonds is reduced by $\frac{10}{12}$ of $401.23 ($2,194.99 minus $1,793.76), or $334.36, the premium identified with the 10-month period. Thereafter regular amortization is required, the premium balance being reduced by the difference between interest at the nominal rate and interest on the bond carrying value at the effective rate.

The value of bonds at a date other than an interest date may be computed in an alternative manner: the value of the bonds may be computed as of the beginning of the interest period; to this value is added interest based on the computed value for the fractional period elapsed at the effective rate. In arriving at the charge to the investment account, accrued interest at the nominal rate is subtracted from the total value of the bonds and accrued interest as computed on the date of purchase. Computation of the bond value for the previous example in this manner is made as follows:

Value on March 1, 1967, including accrued interest:

Present value of bonds on January 1, 1967	$102,194.99
Add accrued interest at the yield rate, 4½%, January 1–March 1, 1967, $\frac{2}{12}$ (.045 × $102,194.99)	766.46
Value of bonds and accrued interest on March 1, 1967	$102,961.45
Deduct accrued interest January 1–March 1, 1967, at the nominal rate, 5%, $\frac{2}{12}$ (.05 × $100,000)	833.33
Bond value on March 1, 1967	$102,128.12

Upon the payment of interest on December 31, 1967, bond premium amortization may be calculated as follows:

Interest at nominal rate for 1967, 5% of $100,000	$5,000.00
Interest at effective rate for 1967, 4½% of $102,194.99	4,598.77
Bond premium amortization for 1967	$ 401.23
Bond premium amortization for holding period, March 1–December 31, 1967, $\frac{10}{12}$ × $401.23	$ 334.36

Entries to record the issuance of the bonds on March 1, 1967, and the periodic interest payments for 1967 and 1968 are shown at the top of the following page.

It should be observed that on December 31, 1967, the premium is reduced by $334.36, representing $\frac{10}{12}$ of $401.23, the premium applicable to the entire year. Interest for the 10-month period is then reported at $3,832.31, representing $4,665.64, interest charge after amortization of the premium, less $833.33, the accrued interest on the date of pur-

Transaction	Books of the Issuing Company			Books of the Investor		
March 1, 1967 Issued $100,000 of 5-year 5% bonds dated January 1, 1967, to yield 4½%.	Cash..........	102,961.45		Investment in Bonds.........	102,128.12	
	Bonds Payable		100,000.00	Interest Income.	833.33	
	Bond Premium		2,128.12	Cash........		102,961.45
	Interest Expense........		833.33			
December 31, 1967 Made first annual interest payment on bonds: paid 5%; effective rate, 4½%.	Interest Expense	4,665.64		Cash..........	5,000.00	
	Bond Premium.	334.36		Interest Income........		4,665.64
	Cash........		5,000.00	Investment in Bonds.......		334.36
December 31, 1968 Made second annual interest payment on bonds: paid 5%; effective rate, 4½%.	Interest Expense	4,580.72		Cash..........	5,000.00	
	Bond Premium.	419.28		Interest Income........		4,580.72
	Cash........		5,000.00	Investment in Bonds.......		419.28

chase. This is equivalent to interest at 4½% for 10 months on bonds valued at the beginning of the period at $102,194.99.

When bonds are sold between interest dates at a discount, values at the beginning of the interest period and at the beginning of the following interest period are determined, and the beginning value is increased for the fractional period elapsed. Or, as in the case of bonds acquired at a premium, it would be possible to compute the bond value as of the beginning of the interest period and to add to this value interest for the fractional period elapsed at the effective rate.

SERIAL BONDS

When serial bonds are sold on a basis other than the stated interest rate, the benefits provided by the bond issue must be analyzed in determining the sales price of the issue. Benefits are represented by payments consisting of (1) retirement of the principal obligation and (2) interest on the amount owed. Present values at the interest rate that the issue must yield are applied to the benefits that are to be provided. To illustrate, assume that bonds of $1,000,000, interest of 4% payable annually, are issued on January 1, 1967, bonds of $200,000 to be retired at the end of each year beginning on December 31, 1967. Principal and interest payments are analyzed below.

	Dec. 31 1967	Dec. 31 1968	Dec. 31 1969	Dec. 31 1970	Dec. 31 1971
Principal payments	$200,000	$200,000	$200,000	$200,000	$200,000
Interest payments on bonds outstanding	40,000	32,000	24,000	16,000	8,000
Total payments	$240,000	$232,000	$224,000	$216,000	$208,000

If the issue is sold to yield 3½% compounded annually, the present value of the issue may be calculated as follows:

$240,000 × .96618357 (present value of 1, 1 period at 3½%)	=	$ 231,884.06
232,000 × .93351070 (present value of 1, 2 periods at 3½%)	=	216,574.48
224,000 × .90194271 (present value of 1, 3 periods at 3½%)	=	202,035.17
216,000 × .87144223 (present value of 1, 4 periods at 3½%)	=	188,231.52
208,000 × .84197317 (present value of 1, 5 periods at 3½%)	=	175,130.42
Present value of principal and interest payments at 3½%		$1,013,855.65

When bond tables are available, it is more convenient to regard each serial maturity as a separate bond issue and to obtain the price at which each issue would sell in yielding the required rate. The sum of the prices of the individual series is the price of the entire issue. The use of bond tables for the serial bonds mentioned above provides the following analysis and summary:

Par Value of Bonds	Maturity	Value of $1,000 4% Bond to Yield 3½%	Value of Bond Series
$200,000	1 year	$1,004.830913	$ 200,966.18
200,000	2 years	1,009.498471	201,899.69
200,000	3 years	1,014.008189	202,801.64
200,000	4 years	1,018.365398	203,673.08
200,000	5 years	1,022.575265	204,515.05
Value of bond issue			$1,013,855.64

Assuming that the serial bonds are sold at the price calculated above, amortization of the bond premium over the life of the issue would be recorded as shown in the table below.

TABLE OF PREMIUM AMORTIZATION

$1,000,000 Serial Bonds Maturing $200,000 per Year, Interest at 4% Payable Annually, Sold at $1,013,855.64 to Yield 3½%

Date	A Interest Payment (4% of face value)	B Effective Interest (3½% of carrying value)	C Premium Amortization (A − B)	D Retirement of Principal	E Decrease in Bond Carrying Value (C + D)	F Bond Carrying Value (F − E)
Jan. 1, 1967						$1,013,855.64
Dec. 31, 1967	$40,000.00	$35,484.95	$4,515.05	$200,000.00	$204,515.05	809,340.59
Dec. 31, 1968	32,000.00	28,326.92	3,673.08	200,000.00	203,673.08	605,667.51
Dec. 31, 1969	24,000.00	21,198.36	2,801.64	200,000.00	202,801.64	402,865.87
Dec. 31, 1970	16,000.00	14,100.31	1,899.69	200,000.00	201,899.69	200,966.18
Dec. 31, 1971	8,000.00	7,033.82	966.18	200,000.00	200,966.18	

Entries to record the issuance of the bonds and the payment of interest and serial maturities at the end of 1967 and 1968 follow:

Transaction	Books of the Issuing Company			Books of the Investor		
January 1, 1967 Issued $1,000,000 of 5-year 4% serial bonds to yield 3½%.	Cash.......	1,013,855.64		Investment in Bonds....	1,013,855.64	
	Bonds Payable......		1,000,000.00	Cash.....		1,013,855.64
	Bond Premium....		13,855.64			
December 31, 1967 Made first annual interest payment on bonds: paid interest on $1,000,000 at 4%; effective rate 3½%.	Interest Expense	35,484.95		Cash..........	40,000.00	
	Bond Premium.	4,515.05		Interest Income........		35,484.95
	Cash........		40,000.00	Investment in Bonds.......		4,515.05
December 31, 1967 Paid off serial maturities of $200,000.	Bonds Payable..	200,000.00		Cash..........	200,000.00	
	Cash........		200,000.00	Investment in Bonds.......		200,000.00
December 31, 1968 Made second annual interest payment on bonds: paid interest on $800,000 at 4%; effective rate, 3½%.	Interest Expense	28,326.92		Cash..........	32,000.00	
	Bond Premium.	3,673.08		Interest Income........		28,326.92
	Cash........		32,000.00	Investment in Bonds.......		3,673.08
December 31, 1968 Paid off serial maturities of $200,000.	Bonds Payable..	200,000.00		Cash..........	200,000.00	
	Cash........		200,000.00	Investment in Bonds.......		200,000.00

SINKING FUND ACCUMULATION

When equal periodic deposits are to be made to a sinking fund, the series of rents represents an annuity. The total to be accumulated is the amount of an annuity, the equal periodic deposits being determined by dividing the required total by the amount of an annuity of 1.

To illustrate, assume that a fund of $100,000 is desired on December 31, 1971. Ten equal semiannual contributions to the fund are to be made, the first contribution to be made on June 30, 1967. It is estimated that the fund will earn 5% compounded semiannually. Since the last contribution is made on the date that the total fund is desired, the series of deposits represents an ordinary annuity. The equal deposits, then, are $8,925.88, determined by dividing the amount required, $100,000, by the amount of an ordinary annuity of 10 rents of 1 at 2½%, 11.203382. A table summarizing the fund accumulation follows:

TABLE OF FUND ACCUMULATION

Date	A Interest Accruing on Balance in Fund	B Amount Deposited in Fund	C Total Increase in Fund for Period (A + B)	D Accumulated Total on Deposit (D + C)
June 30, 1967......		$8,925.88	$ 8,925.88	$ 8,925.88
December 31, 1967..	$ 223.15	8,925.88	9,149.03	18,074.91
June 30, 1968......	451.87	8,925.88	9,377.75	27,452.66
December 31, 1968..	686.32	8,925.88	9,612.20	37,064.86
June 30, 1969......	926.62	8,925.88	9,852.50	46,917.36
December 31, 1969..	1,172.93	8,925.88	10,098.81	57,016.17
June 30, 1970......	1,425.40	8,925.88	10,351.28	67,367.45
December 31, 1970..	1,684.19	8,925.88	10,610.07	77,977.52
June 30, 1971......	1,949.44	8,925.88	10,875.32	88,852.84
December 31, 1971..	2,221.32	8,925.84*	11,147.16	100,000.00

*Corrected for 4 cent discrepancy.

The entries to record the fund deposits and interest accumulations for the period June 30, 1967, through June 30, 1968, are shown below.

Transaction	Entry		
June 30, 1967 First fund deposit.	Sinking Fund Cash..... Cash................	8,925.88	 8,925.88
December 31, 1967 Increase in fund for (a) interest on fund, and (b) second fund deposit.	Sinking Fund Cash..... Cash................ Interest Income on Sinking Fund........	9,149.03	 8,925.88 223.15
June 30, 1968 Increase in fund, for (a) interest on fund, and (b) third fund deposit.	Sinking Fund Cash..... Cash................ Interest Income on Sinking Fund........	9,377.75	 8,925.88 451.87

It was assumed in the foregoing example that the rate of interest did not change throughout the 5-year period. In practice it may be impossible to assure a fixed return on the fund balance. When this is the case, deposits may be calculated on the basis of estimated returns, and deposits may be corrected periodically for actual earnings that differ from estimated amounts. To illustrate, assume in the foregoing example that, although a semiannual return of 2½% was anticipated, the actual semiannual return was 2¾% during the first year and 2½% thereafter until the last year, when the rate dropped to 2%. The fund accumulation is shown in the table at the top of the next page.

TABLE OF FUND ACCUMULATION

Date	A Interest Schedule (at 2½%)	B Interest Accruing on Balance in Fund	C Interest Shortage or Overage* (A − B)	D Deposit Schedule	E Amount Deposited (C + D)	F Total Increase in Fund for Period (B + E)	G Accumulated Total on Deposit (G + F)
June 30, 1967				$8,925.88	$8,925.88	$ 8,925.88	$ 8,925.88
Dec. 31, 1967	$ 223.15	$ 245.46	$ 22.31*	8,925.88	8,903.57	9,149.03	18,074.91
June 30, 1968	451.87	497.06	45.19*	8,925.88	8,880.69	9,377.75	27,452.66
Dec. 31, 1968	686.32	686.32		8,925.88	8,925.88	9,612.20	37,064.86
June 30, 1969	926.62	926.62		8,925.88	8,925.88	9,852.50	46,917.36
Dec. 31, 1969	1,172.93	1,172.93		8,925.88	8,925.88	10,098.81	57,016.17
June 30, 1970	1,425.40	1,425.40		8,925.88	8,925.88	10,351.28	67,367.45
Dec. 31, 1970	1,684.19	1,684.19		8,925.88	8,925.88	10,610.07	77,977.52
June 30, 1971	1,949.44	1,559.55	389.89	8,925.88	9,315.77	10,875.32	88,852.84
Dec. 31, 1971	2,221.32	1,777.06	444.26	8,925.84*	9,370.10	11,147.16	100,000.00

*Corrected for 4 cent discrepancy.

DEPRECIATION

Depreciation is sometimes calculated by compound interest methods. The methods to be discussed here are (1) the *annuity method* and (2) the *sinking fund method.*

Annuity method of depreciation. The annuity method is employed when it is desired to charge operations not only with the cost of the property but with the interest that the amount applied to the property might have earned if it had been employed for other purposes. The cost of the asset, then, is regarded as the discounted value of a series of benefits to be received. In recording depreciation periodically, a charge is made for the sum of depreciation on cost and interest on the book value of the asset, and credits are made to the allowance account and to interest income.

To illustrate the use of the annuity method, assume that equipment is acquired at a cost of $10,000. The asset has an estimated life of 5 years and a scrap value at the end of that time of $500. The annual depreciation is found as follows:

$$\frac{\text{Asset Cost minus Present Value of Estimated Scrap Value}}{\text{Present Value of Annuity}}$$

Assuming an interest rate of 5%, depreciation is calculated as follows:

$$\frac{\$10{,}000 - (\$500 \times .783526^{*})}{4.329477^{**}} = \$2{,}219.26$$

*Present value of 1 for 5 periods at 5%.
**Present value of an ordinary annuity of 5 rents of 1 at 5%.

A table summarizing depreciation and changes in the asset book value follows:

TABLE OF ASSET DEPRECIATION — ANNUITY METHOD

Year	A Depreciation Charge	B Interest Credit (5% of Book Value)	C Allowance Credit (A − B)	D Allowance Balance (D + C)	E Asset Book Value
					$10,000.00
1	$ 2,219.26	$ 500.00	$1,719.26	$1,719.26	8,280.74
2	2,219.26	414.04	1,805.22	3,524.48	6,475.52
3	2,219.26	323.78	1,895.48	5,419.96	4,580.04
4	2,219.26	229.00	1,990.26	7,410.22	2,589.78
5	2,219.27*	129.49	2,089.78	9,500.00	500.00
	$11,096.31	$1,596.31	$9,500.00		

*Corrected for 1 cent discrepancy.

Entries to record depreciation for the first two years follow:

Transaction	Entry		
End of first year To record depreciation for year.	Depr. of Equipment.....	2,219.26	
	Interest Income......		500.00
	Allow. for Depr. of Equipment.........		1,719.26
End of second year To record depreciation for year.	Depr. of Equipment.....	2,219.26	
	Interest Income......		414.04
	Allow. for Depr. of Equipment.........		1,805.22

It should be noted that the periodic depreciation charge is uniform. Although the depreciation over the 5-year period exceeds the cost of the asset, this overstatement is canceled by the recognition of interest income. The net charge to operations, then, is the actual cost, $9,500, or $11,096.31 (depreciation) less $1,596.31 (interest income).

Sinking fund method of depreciation. The sinking fund method of depreciation is based upon the assumption that a fund is being accumulated to replace the property item when it is fully depreciated. Periodic depreciation is charged at amounts equal to the increase in the fund arising from deposits and from interest accruals. Decreases in the carrying value of the asset are accompanied by corresponding increases in the fund balance.

To illustrate the use of the sinking fund method, assume that equipment is acquired at a cost of $10,000. The asset has an estimated life of 5 years and a scrap value at the end of that time of $500. Equal fund contributions would first be found as follows:

$$\frac{\text{Asset Cost minus Estimated Scrap Value}}{\text{Amount of an Annuity}}$$

Assuming an interest rate of 5%, fund contributions are calculated as follows:

$$\frac{\$10{,}000 - \$500}{5.525631^*} = \$1{,}719.26$$

*Amount of an ordinary annuity of 5 rents of 1 at 5%.

A table to show the fund accumulation and depreciation charges follows:

TABLE OF FUND ACCUMULATION AND ASSET DEPRECIATION—SINKING FUND METHOD

	Fund Accumulation				Asset Item		
Year	A Interest Credit (5% of fund balance)	B Fund Deposit	C Total Fund Increase (A + B)	D Fund Balance (D + C)	E Depreciation Charge (C)	F Allowance Balance (F + E)	G Asset Book Value
							$10,000.00
1		$1,719.26	$1,719.26	$1,719.26	$1,719.26	$1,719.26	8,280.74
2	$ 85.96	1,719.26	1,805.22	3,524.48	1,805.22	3,524.48	6,475.52
3	176.22	1,719.26	1,895.48	5,419.96	1,895.48	5,419.96	4,580.04
4	271.00	1,719.26	1,990.26	7,410.22	1,990.26	7,410.22	2,589.78
5	370.51	1,719.27*	2,089.78	9,500.00	2,089.78	9,500.00	500.00

*Corrected for 1 cent discrepancy.

Entries to record the fund accumulation and the charges for depreciation for the first two years follow:

Transaction	Entry		
End of first year Increase in fund for year as a result of cash deposit.	Cash Fund for Replacement of Equipment.....	1,719.26	
	Cash................		1,719.26
To record depreciation for year.	Depr. of Equipment.....	1,719.26	
	Allow. for Depr. of Equipment.........		1,719.26
End of second year Increase in fund for year as a result of cash deposit and interest on accumulated amount.	Cash Fund for Replacement of Equipment.....	1,805.22	
	Cash................		1,719.26
	Interest Income......		85.96
To record depreciation for year.	Depr. of Equipment.....	1,805.22	
	Allow. for Depr. of Equipment.........		1,805.22

It should be observed that the sinking fund method of depreciation is sometimes used without the actual accumulation of a replacement fund. When a fund is not maintained, depreciation charges would still be made on the basis of theoretical fund increases.

QUESTIONS

1. (a) What entries are made on the books of a lessee when (1) payment is made for a leasehold, the sum paid representing the present value of the rental payments due under the lease, and (2) the rental charge for the current period is recognized?

(b) What entries will appear on the books of the lessor relative to (1) and (2) above?

2. The purchase of a home is to be paid for by a down payment followed by a series of equal monthly payments to include principal and interest for a 10-year period.

(a) How are the equal monthly payments calculated?

(b) What entries will appear on the books of both the buyer and the seller for (1) the sale of the property and (2) the periodic payments on the contract?

3. Distinguish between *nominal interest* and *effective interest.*

4. \$100,000 of 6% bonds are issued at a price to yield 5½%. Describe two methods for calculating the sales price of the issue.

5. State how the prices would be determined for the following bond issues, using the bond table on page 1009.

(a) Bonds of \$100,000, due in 5 years, with interest at 4% payable semiannually, are sold at a price to yield 4.25%.
(b) Bonds of \$100,000, due in 4 years, with interest at 4% payable semiannually, are sold at a price to yield 3.60%.
(c) Serial bonds of \$200,000 with interest at 4% payable semiannually are sold at a price to yield 3.75%; bonds of \$50,000 mature at the end of 4 years, with bond maturities of \$50,000 at 6-month intervals thereafter until the issue is retired.

6. A company issues \$100,000 of 20-year, 5% bonds with the provision that the bonds may be called in and retired at the end of 10 years. State what life and what maturity value should be considered by the investor in calculating the price to be paid for the bonds under each set of conditions given below.

(a) The bonds are sold on a 5½% basis; there is no call premium on accelerated redemption.
(b) The bonds are sold on a 5½% basis; there is a 5% call premium on accelerated redemption.
(c) The bonds are sold on a 4½% basis; there is no call premium on accelerated redemption.
(d) The bonds are sold on a 4½% basis; there is a 5% call premium on accelerated redemption.

7. How would you calculate the price to be paid for bonds when the yield is to differ from nominal interest and the bonds are sold at a time other than an interest date?

8. Describe two methods for arriving at the price to be paid for serial bonds when the yield rate is to differ from the nominal rate on the issue.

9. The West Co. has developed a redemption fund deposit schedule providing for an accumulation of $100,000 at the end of 10 years, assuming that fund deposits earn 5% per year. What procedure would you recommend that the company follow to attain its objective in the event periodic earnings prove to be more or less than assumed earnings?

10. Distinguish between depreciation by the annuity method and depreciation by the sinking fund method.

EXERCISES

(*Use the tables given on pages 1030–1037.*)

1. Osborne leases land and buildings from Chase Enterprise, Inc. for 10 years. The rental is $5,000 annually, amounts being payable at the beginning of each year. Osborne is permitted to pay the rent for the entire period, rents to be discounted at 4% compounded annually. (a) What amount would be paid by Osborne? (b) What entries would appear on the books of Osborne and of Chase Enterprise, Inc. at the beginning and the end of the first and second years?

2. Parks owes $10,000 on a non-interest-bearing note that matures on June 30, 1967. On this date he agrees with the holder of the note to pay it off in 10 equal semiannual installments to include interest at 6% compounded semiannually, the first payment to be made on June 30, 1967. (a) What are the equal payments? (b) Prepare a table similar to the one illustrated on page 1005 to show the reduction of the debt principal. (c) What entries would be made on the books of Parks and the payee on June 30, 1967, and December 31, 1967?

3. Webster purchases an automobile for $5,500, paying $1,500 down, the balance to be paid in 48 equal monthly installments to include interest at the rate of 6% on the unpaid balance. What entries are required to record (a) the purchase of the automobile, (b) the first monthly payment, and (c) the second monthly payment?

4. Reed buys a $1,000, 20-year, 6% bond, interest payable semiannually, at a price to yield 5%. What entries are required to record (a) the purchase of the bond and (b) the receipt of the first and the second interest payments?

5. The Lynch Corporation sells $100,000 of 6% bonds, payable in 10 years, interest payable semiannually, at a price to yield 7%. What entries are required to record (a) the sale of the bonds and (b) the first and the second interest payments?

6. What amounts would be paid for the bonds in each case below:

(a) \$1,000, 10-year, 5% bonds, interest payable semiannually, sold to yield 6%.

(b) \$1,000, 10-year, 6% bonds, interest payable semiannually, sold to yield 5%.

(c) \$1,000, 10-year, 6% bonds, interest payable semiannually, sold to yield 5%, the bonds being acquired 3 months after their issuance.

7. In Exercise 6, what amount would be paid in each case assuming that the bonds were redeemable at the option of the corporation at the end of 5 years at a premium of 5%?

8. Lux and Landy, Inc., issue serial bonds of \$500,000 on January 1, 1967. The bonds pay interest at 4% annually. Bonds of \$100,000 mature annually on December 31, beginning on December 31, 1967. What are the proceeds on the issue if the bonds are sold on a 5% basis?

9. In Exercise 8, what would the proceeds be assuming that the bonds provide for interest at 4% paid semiannually and that they are sold on a 5% basis?

10. Richards and Tanner, Inc., decide to establish a bond redemption fund to accumulate \$1,000,000 on December 31, 1977. The fund is expected to earn 3%. What are the equal annual deposits if:

(a) Ten deposits are to be made, the first being made on December 31, 1967?

(b) Ten deposits are to be made, the first being made on December 31, 1968?

(c) Five deposits are to be made, the first being made on December 31, 1968?

11. The Wayne Corporation acquires equipment at a cost of \$250,000. The estimated life of the asset is 25 years with an estimated salvage value of 10%. Assuming a 5% interest rate, what entry would be made to record depreciation for the first and the second years if (a) the annuity method is used and (b) the sinking fund method is used?

PROBLEMS

(Use the tables given on pages 1030–1037.)

28-1. Bradshaw acquires a 10-year leasehold on January 1, 1967, from Crest Properties, Inc., on the following basis: rentals are payable annually in advance, the rate to be \$15,000 for each of the first 5 years and \$17,500 thereafter. Crest Properties, Inc., agrees to accept payment for the entire leasehold in advance, a discount rate of 6% annually to be used.

Instructions: (1) Prepare a table similar to the one illustrated on page 1003 to show the changes in the leasehold balance during the 10-year period.

(2) Give the journal entries that would be made on the books of each party for the years 1967 and 1968.

28-2. Hillman owes Turner the following amounts on 3 non-interest-bearing notes:

Note 1, \$ 5,000 due June 30, 1967
Note 2, \$12,000 due June 30, 1968
Note 3, \$15,000 due June 30, 1970

Hillman and Turner agree that the notes are to be paid off by a single series of 8 equal semiannual payments to include interest at 5% compounded semiannually, the first payment to be made on June 30, 1967. What are the equal periodic payments?

28-3. Chatfield owes \$25,000 on a non-interest-bearing note that matures on June 30, 1967. On this date he agrees with the holder of the note to pay it off in a series of 10 semiannual installments that are to include interest at 5% compounded semiannually.

(a) What are the amounts payable if the installments are to be equal, the first to be payable on June 30, 1967?
(b) What are the amounts payable if the installments are to be equal, the first to be payable on December 31, 1967?
(c) What are the amounts payable if the installments are to be equal, the first to be payable on December 31, 1969?
(d) What are the amounts payable if the last 5 installments are to be ½ as large as the first 5, the first installment being payable on June 30, 1967?
(e) What are the last 5 equal installments if the first 5 are \$2,500 each, the first installment being payable on December 31, 1967?

28-4. The Burbank Co. is negotiating for the purchase of the Freiden Co. It agrees to pay book value for the net tangible assets acquired. Calculate the amount that it should pay for goodwill on each of the following assumptions, using a 6% interest rate:

(a) Above-normal annual earnings of \$15,000 are expected to continue indefinitely.
(b) Above-normal annual earnings of \$30,000 are expected to be limited to the next 10 years.
(c) Above-normal annual earnings are expected to be limited to the next 10 years as follows: for the first 5 years, \$50,000; for the remaining 5 years, \$25,000.

28-5. On July 1, 1967, Polk and Owen, Inc., issues \$1,000,000 of 20-year, 5% bonds, interest payable semiannually, at a price to yield 6%. On this date Stillman acquires bonds of \$100,000 on this basis.

Instructions: Give the journal entries for the corporation and for the investor upon (a) the issuance of the bonds, (b) the first interest payment, and (c) the second interest payment.

28-6. On January 1, 1967, the Harriman Co. sells \$1,000,000 of 10-year, 5% bonds, interest payable semiannually, at a price to yield 4%. On this date Klein acquires bonds of \$25,000 on this basis.

Instructions: (1) Prepare an amortization table similar to that illustrated on page 1006 to show the decrease in the carrying value of the bonds.

(2) Give the journal entries for the corporation and for the investor upon (a) the issuance of the bonds, (b) the first interest payment, and (c) the second interest payment.

28-7. West buys $25,000 of 10-year, 5% bonds, interest payable annually, at a price to yield 4½%. The bonds are redeemable at the end of 5 years at a premium of 5%.

Instructions: (1) Calculate the amount to be paid for the bonds.
(2) Assuming that West purchased the bonds 3 months after they had been issued, how much should he have paid?

28-8. Gamble buys $10,000 of 10-year, 6% bonds, interest payable annually, at a price to yield 5%. The bonds are redeemable at the end of 5 years at a premium of 5%.

Instructions: (1) Calculate the amount to be paid for the bonds.
(2) Assuming that Gamble purchased the bonds 2 months after they had been issued, how much should he have paid?

28-9. On July 1, 1967, Wells pays $10,206.51 for $10,000 of Orange County bonds that mature on January 1, 1972. The bonds pay 4% but are acquired at a price to yield 3.5%. Wells receives interest on January 1 and July 1. On October 1, 1968, he sells the bonds at 99¾.

Instructions: Give the journal entries to record the foregoing transactions, assuming that Wells recognizes the effective yield in his accounts.

28-10. The Monterey Co. issues $1,000,000 in serial bonds on July 1, 1967. Interest at 6% is payable annually on July 1. Bonds of $200,000 mature annually, the first payment being due on July 1, 1968. The bonds are sold on a 5% basis.

Instructions: (1) Calculate the proceeds of the issue.
(2) Prepare a table similar to that illustrated on page 1014 to show the decrease in the bond carrying value.
(3) Give the journal entries that would be made on the books of the corporation: (a) to record the sale of the bonds on July 1, 1967; (b) to adjust the books for accrued interest on December 31, 1967, the end of the fiscal year; and (c) to record the payment of interest and bond principal on July 1, 1968.

28-11. The Keith Manufacturing Co. sets up a preferred stock retirement fund that is to accumulate to $800,000 on December 31, 1967. Equal deposits are made annually on December 31, beginning in 1963 and including 1967. Deposits are based on an estimated return of 4%, deposits being corrected periodically for earnings of the past period that may have been greater or less than the expected return. Earnings on the fund balance for 1964–1967 are as follows:

1964	$ 5,756.10
1965	$13,022.50
1966	$19,500.62
1967	$26,605.00

Instructions: Prepare a table similar to that illustrated on page 1017 to summarize the fund accumulation.

28-12. The Moore Trading Co. maintained a stock redemption fund to accumulate to $100,000 on December 31, 1971. Equal deposits were made annually on December 31 beginning in 1967 and including 1971. Deposits were based on an estimated return of 4%, deposits being corrected periodically for earnings of the past period that may have been greater or less than the expected return. The fund earned 4% in 1968 but only 3½% thereafter.

Instructions: Give the journal entries for the redemption fund for the period December 31, 1967, to December 31, 1971.

28-13. The board of directors of Ward Sales Co. decides to set up a fund to provide for the replacement of buildings at the end of 1976. Deposits to the fund are to be made annually, beginning on December 31, 1967, the first 5 deposits to be $100,000, and the remaining deposits to be equal amounts to produce a total fund of $1,000,000. It is expected that the fund will earn 3% compounded annually.

Instructions: (1) Prepare a table similar to that illustrated on page 1016 to summarize the fund accumulation.

(2) Give the journal entries that will appear on the books of the corporation at the end of 1967, 1968, and 1969.

28-14. A $200,000 mortgage of Bragan and Brooks, Inc., is payable in 2 equal installments on January 1, 1976, and January 1, 1981. A fund is to be established whereby 10 equal annual deposits are to be made to provide for the payment of mortgage installments, the first deposit to the fund to be made on January 1, 1967. It is expected that the fund will earn 3%.

Instructions: (1) Give the amount of the equal annual deposits to the mortgage retirement fund.

(2) Construct a table that will summarize all of the changes in the fund resulting from deposits and mortgage retirements.

28-15. Rayburn, Inc., acquires equipment at a cost of $200,000. The estimated life of the equipment is 5 years and the estimated scrap value at the end of that time is 15% of cost.

Instructions: (1) Assuming that depreciation is recorded by the annuity method using an interest rate of 4%, (a) prepare a table similar to that illustrated on page 1018 to show the periodic charges and credits and the decreases in the asset book value, and (b) prepare entries to record depreciation for the first 2 years.

(2) Assuming that depreciation is recorded by the sinking fund method using an interest rate of 4%, (a) prepare a table similar to that illustrated on page 1019 to show the periodic decreases in the asset book value and the accumulation of an asset replacement fund, and (b) prepare entries to record depreciation and the replacement fund deposits for the first 2 years.

28-16. The Southern Sales Co. issues serial bonds of $1,000,000 on January 1, 1967, bonds of $200,000 to be retired annually beginning on January 1, 1972. Interest of 4½% is payable annually, but the bonds are sold at a price to yield 5%.

Instructions: (1) Calculate the proceeds of the issue.

(2) Prepare a table similar to that illustrated on page 1014 to show the decrease in the bond carrying value, assuming amortization that recognizes the effective rate.

(3) Prepare a table similar to that in part (2) assuming that the bonds outstanding method is employed for amortization purposes.

28-17. The West Coast Electric Co. issues serial bonds of $10,000,000 on January 1, 1967. Interest at 5% is payable annually on December 31. Bonds of $1,000,000 are to be retired at the end of 1970, 1971, 1972, and 1973. Remaining bonds are to be retired at the rate of $2,000,000 per year, beginning on December 31, 1974. Bonds are sold at a price to yield 4%.

Instructions: (1) Calculate the proceeds of the issue.

(2) Prepare a table similar to that illustrated on page 1014 to show the decrease in the bond carrying value.

(3) Give the journal entries that would appear on the books of the company to record (a) the issuance of the bonds on January 1, 1967, (b) the payment of interest on December 31, 1967, and (c) the payments of interest and principal amounts on December 31, 1970.

28-18. The Caldwell Company is planning a pension system for certain of its employees and wishes to provide funds for meeting the payments under the pension plan. The company does not contemplate making any pension payments under the plan until January, 1977. Payments in 1977 and thereafter to the present group of covered employees are expected to be as follows:

January 1, 1977	$ 5,000
January 1, 1978	7,000
January 1, 1979	10,000
January 1, 1980	14,000
January 1, 1981	16,000
January 1, 1982	20,000
January 1, 1983	25,000
January 1, 1984	22,000
January 1, 1985	17,000
January 1, 1986	12,000
January 1, 1987	8,000
January 1, 1988	5,000
January 1, 1989	2,000
January 1, 1990	2,000

Starting on January 1, 1967, and continuing for 10 years, the company will deposit $10,000 a year in a special fund. On January 1, 1966, the company wishes to make a lump sum deposit of an amount sufficient to provide the remaining funds needed for meeting the pensions. It is expected that all the above funds will earn 3½% interest compounded annually during the entire life of the fund.

Instructions: Using the tables of value at 3½% as needed, compute the amount of the payment that should be made on January 1, 1966. Show all supporting computations in good form.

(AICPA adapted)

28-19. Reproduced below are the first three lines from the 2% columns of each of several tables of mathematical values:

Periods	Table A	Table B	Table C	Table D	Table E	Table F
0	1.0000		1.0000			
1	0.9804	1.0200	1.02	1.0000	0.9804	1.0200
2	0.9612	2.0604	1.0404	0.4950	1.9416	0.5150
3		3.1216		0.3268	2.8839	0.3468

Instructions: (1) For each of the following items, select from among the fragmentary tables given above the one from which the amount required can be obtained *most directly* (assuming that the complete table was available in each instance). Indicate your selections by naming the *capital letter* that identifies the table which you would use.

(a) The amount to which a single sum would accumulate at compound interest by the end of a specified period (interest compounded annually).

(b) The amount that must be appropriated at the end of each of a specific number of years to provide for the accumulation, at annually compounded interest, of a certain sum.

(c) The amount that must be deposited in a fund which will earn interest at a specified rate, compounded annually, in order to make possible the withdrawal of certain equal sums annually over a specified period starting one year from date of deposit.

(d) The amount of interest that will accumulate on a single deposit by the end of a specified period (interest compounded semiannually).

(e) The amount, net of compound discount, that if paid now would settle a debt of larger amount due at a specified future date.

(2) Use the tables of values at 4% interest given on pages 1030–1037 as needed in answering the following questions:

(a) Your client has made annual payments of $2,500 into a fund at the close of each year for the past 9 years. The fund balance immediately after the ninth payment totaled $26,457. He has asked you how many more $2,500 annual payments will be required to bring the fund to $50,000, assuming that the fund continues to earn interest at 4% compounded annually. Compute the number of full payments required and the amount of the final payment if it does not require the entire $2,500. Carefully label all computations supporting your answer.

(b) Your client wishes to provide for the payment of an obligation of $200,000 due on July 1, 1975. He plans to deposit $20,000 in a special fund each July 1 for 8 years, starting July 1, 1968. He wishes to make an initial deposit on July 1, 1967, of an amount that, with its accumulated interest, will bring the fund up to $200,000 at the maturity of the obligation. He expects that the fund will earn interest at the rate of 4% compounded annually. Compute the amount to be deposited July 1, 1967. Carefully label all computations supporting your answer.

(AICPA adapted)

28-20. (a) Your client has agreed to sell a property for \$60,000. He is to receive \$20,000 cash at date of sale and 20 notes of equal amount that will not bear interest. The notes are due serially, one each 6 months starting 6 months from date of sale. It is agreed that the notes will include in their face an amount that will equal 5% interest to be compounded semiannually.

Compute to the nearest dollar the amount of each note. Show your computations in good form, with each part explained or labeled.

(b) Jones, an employee of the Union Company, asks your advice on the following matter:

He is eligible to participate in a company insurance and retirement plan. His payment into the company plan would amount to \$500 each 6 months for the next 10 years, and starting with the eleventh year he would receive an annual payment of \$1,080 for life. He does not need insurance protection and states that he can save and invest each 6 months the amounts to be paid into the company plan so that he will earn 6% compounded semiannually. Also he can continue to earn the same rate on his capital after retirement. He would like to have an equal amount per year of funds for 15 years after retirement.

Assuming that he can carry out his personal saving and investing plan, how much can he expect to have available *each 6 months* for the 15 years following his retirement? Compute to the nearest dollar and show your computations in good form.

(c) (1) The X Company has outstanding \$2,000,000 of 20-year, 5% bonds that were issued 10 years ago. Unamortized discount and expense of \$100,000 remains on the books. The bonds are callable at 105. The company has the opportunity to refinance by issuing, at par, \$2,150,000 of 4%, 10-year bonds. Expenses that would be incurred in connection with the issue are estimated to be \$50,000. Interest on both issues is payable semiannually.

Determine whether the refinancing would be desirable. Show your computations in good form and explain the basis used in reaching your conclusion. Ignore any tax difference that might arise out of the refinancing.

(2) If X Company carries out the refunding of the long-term debt, a decision must be made concerning the accounting treatment to be accorded the unamortized portion of discount and expense pertaining to the old bonds. Three different treatments of this item have received support from various accountants.

Describe these treatments and give a brief statement of the central argument offered in support of each of them.

(AICPA adapted)

COMPOUND INTEREST TABLES

Amount of 1

(1 + i)^n

n	½%	1%	1½%	2%	2½%	3%	n
1	1.005 000	1.010 000	1.015 000	1.020 000	1.025 000	1 030 000	1
2	1.010 025	1.020 100	1.030 225	1.040 400	1.050 625	1.060 900	2
3	1.015 075	1.030 301	1.045 678	1.061 208	1.076 891	1.092 727	3
4	1.020 151	1.040 604	1.061 364	1.082 432	1.103 813	1.125 509	4
5	1.025 251	1.051 010	1.077 284	1.104 081	1.131 408	1.159 274	5
6	1.030 378	1.061 520	1.093 443	1.126 162	1.159 693	1.194 052	6
7	1.035 529	1.072 135	1.109 845	1.148 686	1.188 686	1.229 874	7
8	1.040 707	1.082 857	1.126 493	1.171 659	1.218 403	1.266 770	8
9	1.045 911	1.093 685	1.143 390	1.195 093	1.248 863	1.304 773	9
10	1.051 140	1.104 622	1.160 541	1.218 994	1.280 085	1.343 916	10
11	1.056 396	1.115 668	1.177 949	1.243 374	1.312 087	1.384 234	11
12	1.061 678	1.126 825	1.195 618	1.268 242	1.344 889	1.425 761	12
13	1.066 986	1.138 093	1.213 552	1.293 607	1.378 511	1.468 534	13
14	1.072 321	1.149 474	1.231 756	1.319 479	1.412 974	1.512 590	14
15	1.077 683	1.160 969	1.250 232	1.345 868	1.448 298	1.557 967	15
16	1.083 071	1.172 579	1.268 986	1.372 786	1.484 506	1.604 706	16
17	1.088 487	1.184 304	1.288 020	1.400 241	1.521 618	1.652 848	17
18	1.093 929	1.196 147	1.307 341	1.428 246	1.559 659	1.702 433	18
19	1.099 399	1.208 109	1.326 951	1.456 811	1.598 650	1.753 506	19
20	1.104 896	1.220 190	1.346 855	1.485 947	1.638 616	1.806 111	20
21	1.110 420	1.232 392	1.367 058	1.515 666	1.679 582	1.860 295	21
22	1.115 972	1.244 716	1.387 564	1.545 980	1.721 571	1.916 103	22
23	1.121 552	1.257 163	1.408 377	1.576 899	1.764 611	1.973 587	23
24	1.127 160	1.269 735	1.429 503	1.608 437	1.808 726	2.032 794	24
25	1.132 796	1.282 432	1.450 945	1.640 606	1.853 944	2.093 778	25
26	1.138 460	1.295 256	1.472 710	1.673 418	1.900 293	2.156 591	26
27	1.144 152	1.308 209	1.494 800	1.706 886	1.947 800	2.221 289	27
28	1.149 873	1.321 291	1.517 222	1.741 024	1.996 495	2.287 928	28
29	1.155 622	1.334 504	1.539 981	1.775 845	2.046 407	2.356 566	29
30	1.161 400	1.347 849	1.563 080	1.811 362	2.097 568	2.427 262	30
31	1.167 207	1.361 327	1.586 526	1.847 589	2.150 007	2.500 080	31
32	1.173 043	1.374 941	1.610 324	1.884 541	2.203 757	2.575 083	32
33	1.178 908	1.388 690	1.634 479	1.922 231	2.258 851	2.652 335	33
34	1.184 803	1.402 577	1.658 996	1.960 676	2.315 322	2.731 905	34
35	1.190 727	1.416 603	1.683 881	1.999 890	2.373 205	2.813 862	35
36	1.196 681	1.430 769	1.709 140	2.039 887	2.432 535	2.898 278	36
37	1.202 664	1.445 076	1.734 777	2.080 685	2.493 349	2.985 227	37
38	1.208 677	1.459 527	1.760 798	2.122 299	2.555 682	3.074 783	38
39	1.214 721	1.474 123	1.787 210	2.164 745	2.619 574	3.167 027	39
40	1.220 794	1.488 864	1.814 018	2.208 040	2.685 064	3.262 038	40
41	1.226 898	1.503 752	1.841 229	2.252 200	2.752 190	3.359 899	41
42	1.233 033	1.518 790	1.868 847	2.297 244	2.820 995	3.460 696	42
43	1.239 198	1.533 978	1.896 880	2.343 189	2.891 520	3.564 517	43
44	1.245 394	1.549 318	1.925 333	2.390 053	2.963 808	3.671 452	44
45	1.251 621	1.564 811	1.954 213	2.437 854	3.037 903	3.781 596	45
46	1.257 879	1.580 459	1.983 526	2.486 611	3.113 851	3.895 044	46
47	1.264 168	1.596 263	2.013 279	2.536 344	3.191 697	4.011 895	47
48	1.270 489	1.612 226	2.043 478	2.587 070	3.271 490	4.132 252	48
49	1.276 842	1.628 348	2.074 130	2.638 812	3.353 277	4.256 219	49
50	1.283 226	1.644 632	2.105 242	2.691 588	3.437 109	4.383 906	50

Amount of 1

(1 + i)ⁿ

n	3½%	4%	4½%	5%	5½%	6%	n
1	1.035 000	1.040 000	1.045 000	1.050 000	1.055 000	1.060 000	1
2	1.071 225	1.081 600	1.092 025	1.102 500	1.113 025	1.123 600	2
3	1.108 718	1.124 864	1.141 166	1.157 625	1.174 241	1.191 016	3
4	1.147 523	1.169 859	1.192 519	1.215 506	1.238 825	1.262 477	4
5	1.187 686	1.216 653	1.246 182	1.276 282	1.306 960	1.338 226	5
6	1.229 255	1.265 319	1.302 260	1.340 096	1.378 843	1.418 519	6
7	1.272 279	1.315 932	1.360 862	1.407 100	1.454 679	1.503 630	7
8	1.316 809	1.368 569	1.422 101	1.477 455	1.534 687	1.593 848	8
9	1.362 897	1.423 312	1.486 095	1.551 328	1.619 094	1.689 479	9
10	1.410 599	1.480 244	1.552 969	1.628 895	1.708 144	1.790 848	10
11	1.459 970	1.539 454	1.622 853	1.710 339	1.802 092	1.898 299	11
12	1.511 069	1.601 032	1.695 881	1.795 856	1.901 207	2.012 196	12
13	1.563 956	1.665 074	1.772 196	1.885 649	2.005 774	2.132 928	13
14	1.618 695	1.731 676	1.851 945	1.979 932	2.116 091	2.260 904	14
15	1.675 349	1.800 944	1.935 282	2.078 928	2.232 476	2.396 558	15
16	1.733 986	1.872 981	2.022 370	2.182 875	2.355 263	2.540 352	16
17	1.794 676	1.947 901	2.113 377	2.292 018	2.484 802	2.692 773	17
18	1.857 489	2.025 817	2.208 479	2.406 619	2.621 466	2.854 339	18
19	1.922 501	2.106 849	2.307 860	2.526 950	2.765 647	3.025 600	19
20	1.989 789	2.191 123	2.411 714	2.653 298	2.917 757	3.207 135	20
21	2.059 431	2.278 768	2.520 241	2.785 963	3.078 234	3.399 564	21
22	2.131 512	2.369 919	2.633 652	2.925 261	3.247 537	3.603 537	22
23	2.206 114	2.464 716	2.752 166	3.071 524	3.426 152	3.819 750	23
24	2.283 328	2.563 304	2.876 014	3.225 100	3.614 590	4.048 935	24
25	2.363 245	2.665 836	3.005 434	3.386 355	3.813 392	4.291 871	25
26	2.445 959	2.772 470	3.140 679	3.555 673	4.023 129	4.549 383	26
27	2.531 567	2.883 369	3.282 010	3.733 456	4.244 401	4.822 346	27
28	2.620 172	2.998 703	3.429 700	3.920 129	4.477 843	5.111 687	28
29	2.711 878	3.118 651	3.584 036	4.116 136	4.724 124	5.418 388	29
30	2.806 794	3.243 398	3.745 318	4.321 942	4.983 951	5.743 491	30
31	2.905 031	3.373 133	3.913 857	4.538 039	5.258 069	6.088 101	31
32	3.006 708	3.508 059	4.089 981	4.764 941	5.547 262	6.453 387	32
33	3.111 942	3.648 381	4.274 030	5.003 189	5.852 362	6.840 590	33
34	3.220 860	3.794 316	4.466 362	5.253 348	6.174 242	7.251 025	34
35	3.333 590	3.946 089	4.667 348	5.516 015	6.513 825	7.686 087	35
36	3.450 266	4.103 933	4.877 378	5.791 816	6.872 085	8.147 252	36
37	3.571 025	4.268 090	5.096 860	6.081 407	7.250 050	8.636 087	37
38	3.696 011	4.438 813	5.326 219	6.385 477	7.648 803	9.154 252	38
39	3.825 372	4.616 366	5.565 899	6.704 751	8.069 487	9.703 507	39
40	3.959 260	4.801 021	5.816 365	7.039 989	8.513 309	10.285 718	40
41	4.097 834	4.993 061	6.078 101	7.391 988	8.981 541	10.902 861	41
42	4.241 258	5.192 784	6.351 615	7.761 588	9.475 526	11.557 033	42
43	4.389 702	5.400 495	6.637 438	8.149 667	9.996 679	12.250 455	43
44	4.543 342	5.616 515	6.936 123	8.557 150	10.546 497	12.985 482	44
45	4.702 359	5.841 176	7.248 248	8.985 008	11.126 554	13.764 611	45
46	4.866 941	6.074 823	7.574 420	9.434 258	11.738 515	14.590 487	46
47	5.037 284	6.317 816	7.915 268	9.905 971	12.384 133	15.465 917	47
48	5.213 589	6.570 528	8.271 456	10.401 270	13.065 260	16.393 872	48
49	5.396 065	6.833 349	8.643 671	10.921 333	13.783 849	17.377 504	49
50	5.584 927	7.106 683	9.032 636	11.467 400	14.541 961	18.420 154	50

Amount of an Annuity of 1

$$\frac{(1+i)^n - 1}{i}$$

n	½%	1%	1½%	2%	2½%	3%	n
1	1.000 000	1.000 000	1.000 000	1.000 000	1.000 000	1.000 000	1
2	2.005 000	2.010 000	2.015 000	2.020 000	2.025 000	2.030 000	2
3	3.015 025	3.030 100	3.045 225	3.060 400	3.075 625	3.090 900	3
4	4.030 100	4.060 401	4.090 903	4.121 608	4.152 516	4.183 627	4
5	5.050 251	5.101 005	5.152 267	5.204 040	5.256 329	5.309 136	5
6	6.075 502	6.152 015	6.229 551	6.308 121	6.387 737	6.468 410	6
7	7.105 879	7.213 535	7.322 994	7.434 283	7.547 430	7.662 462	7
8	8.141 409	8.285 671	8.432 839	8.582 969	8.736 116	8.892 336	8
9	9.182 116	9.368 527	9.559 332	9.754 628	9.954 519	10.159 106	9
10	10.228 026	10.462 213	10.702 722	10.949 721	11.203 382	11.463 879	10
11	11.279 167	11.566 835	11.863 262	12.168 715	12.483 466	12.807 796	11
12	12.335 562	12.682 503	13.041 211	13.412 090	13.795 553	14.192 030	12
13	13.397 240	13.809 328	14.236 830	14.680 332	15.140 442	15.617 790	13
14	14.464 226	14.947 421	15.450 382	15.973 938	16.518 953	17.086 324	14
15	15.536 548	16.096 896	16.682 138	17.293 417	17.931 927	18.598 914	15
16	16.614 230	17.257 864	17.932 370	18.639 285	19.380 225	20.156 881	16
17	17.697 301	18.430 443	19.201 355	20.012 071	20.864 730	21.761 588	17
18	18.785 788	19.614 748	20.489 376	21.412 312	22.386 349	23.414 435	18
19	19.879 717	20.810 895	21.796 716	22.840 559	23.946 007	25.116 868	19
20	20.979 115	22.019 004	23.123 667	24.297 370	25.544 658	26.870 374	20
21	22.084 011	23.239 194	24.470 522	25.783 317	27.183 274	28.676 486	21
22	23.194 431	24.471 586	25.837 580	27.298 984	28.862 856	30.536 780	22
23	24.310 403	25.716 302	27.225 144	28.844 963	30.584 427	32.452 884	23
24	25.431 955	26.973 465	28.633 521	30.421 862	32.349 038	34.426 470	24
25	26.559 115	28.243 200	30.063 024	32.030 300	34.157 764	36.459 264	25
26	27.691 911	29.525 632	31.513 969	33.670 906	36.011 708	38.553 042	26
27	28.830 370	30.820 888	32.986 679	35.344 324	37.912 001	40.709 634	27
28	29.974 522	32.129 097	34.481 479	37.051 210	39.859 801	42.930 923	28
29	31.124 395	33.450 388	35.998 701	38.792 235	41.856 296	45.218 850	29
30	32.280 017	34.784 892	37.538 681	40.568 079	43.902 703	47.575 416	30
31	33.441 417	36.132 740	39.101 762	42.379 441	46.000 271	50.002 678	31
32	34.608 624	37.494 068	40.688 288	44.227 030	48.150 278	52.502 759	32
33	35.781 667	38.869 009	42.298 612	46.111 570	50.354 034	55.077 841	33
34	36.960 575	40.257 699	43.933 092	48.033 802	52.612 885	57.730 177	34
35	38.145 378	41.660 276	45.592 088	49.994 478	54.928 207	60.462 082	35
36	39.336 105	43.076 878	47.275 969	51.994 367	57.301 413	63.275 944	36
37	40.532 785	44.507 647	48.985 109	54.034 255	59.733 948	66.174 223	37
38	41.735 449	45.952 724	50.719 885	56.114 940	62.227 297	69.159 449	38
39	42.944 127	47.412 251	52.480 684	58.237 238	64.782 979	72.234 233	39
40	44.158 847	48.886 373	54.267 894	60.401 983	67.402 554	75.401 260	40
41	45.379 642	50.375 237	56.081 912	62.610 023	70.087 617	78.663 298	41
42	46.606 540	51.878 989	57.923 141	64.862 223	72.839 808	82.023 196	42
43	47.839 572	53.397 779	59.791 988	67.159 468	75.660 803	85.483 892	43
44	49.078 770	54.931 757	61.688 868	69.502 657	78.552 323	89.048 409	44
45	50.324 164	56.481 075	63.614 201	71.892 710	81.516 131	92.719 861	45
46	51.575 785	58.045 885	65.568 414	74.330 564	84.554 034	96.501 457	46
47	52.833 664	59.626 344	67.551 940	76.817 176	87.667 885	100.396 501	47
48	54.097 832	61.222 608	69.565 219	79.353 519	90.859 582	104.408 396	48
49	55.368 321	62.834 834	71.608 698	81.940 590	94.131 072	108.540 648	49
50	56.645 163	64.463 182	73.682 828	84.579 401	97.484 349	112.796 867	50

Amount of an Annuity of 1

$$\frac{(1+i)^n - 1}{i}$$

n	3½%	4%	4½%	5%	5½%	6%	n
1	1.000 000	1.000 000	1.000 000	1.000 000	1.000 000	1.000 000	1
2	2.035 000	2.040 000	2.045 000	2.050 000	2.055 000	2.060 000	2
3	3.106 225	3.121 600	3.137 025	3.152 500	3.168 025	3.183 600	3
4	4.214 943	4.246 464	4.278 191	4.310 125	4.342 266	4.374 616	4
5	5.362 466	5.416 323	5.470 710	5.525 631	5.581 091	5.637 093	5
6	6.550 152	6.632 975	6.716 892	6.801 913	6.888 051	6.975 319	6
7	7.779 408	7.898 294	8.019 152	8.142 008	8.266 894	8.393 838	7
8	9.051 687	9.214 226	9.380 014	9.549 109	9.721 573	9.897 468	8
9	10.368 496	10.582 795	10.802 114	11.026 564	11.256 260	11.491 316	9
10	11.731 393	12.006 107	12.288 209	12.577 893	12.875 354	13.180 795	10
11	13.141 992	13.486 351	13.841 179	14.206 787	14.583 498	14.971 643	11
12	14.601 962	15.025 805	15.464 032	15.917 127	16.385 591	16.869 941	12
13	16.113 030	16.626 838	17.159 913	17.712 983	18.286 798	18.882 138	13
14	17.676 986	18.291 911	18.932 109	19.598 632	20.292 572	21.015 066	14
15	19.295 681	20.023 588	20.784 054	21.578 564	22.408 664	23.275 970	15
16	20.971 030	21.824 531	22.719 337	23.657 492	24.641 140	25.672 528	16
17	22.705 016	23.697 512	24.741 707	25.840 366	26.996 403	28.212 880	17
18	24.499 691	25.645 413	26.855 084	28.132 385	29.481 205	30.905 653	18
19	26.357 181	27.671 229	29.063 562	30.539 004	32.102 671	33.759 992	19
20	28.279 682	29.778 079	31.371 423	33.065 954	34.868 318	36.785 591	20
21	30.269 471	31.969 202	33.783 137	35.719 252	37.786 076	39.992 727	21
22	32.328 902	34.247 970	36.303 378	38.505 214	40.864 310	43.392 290	22
23	34.460 414	36.617 889	38.937 030	41.430 475	44.111 847	46.995 828	23
24	36.666 528	39.082 604	41.689 196	44.501 999	47.537 998	50.815 577	24
25	38.949 857	41.645 908	44.565 210	47.727 099	51.152 588	54.864 512	25
26	41.313 102	44.311 745	47.570 645	51.113 454	54.965 981	59.156 383	26
27	43.759 060	47.084 214	50.711 324	54.669 126	58.989 109	63.705 766	27
28	46.290 627	49.967 583	53.993 333	58.402 583	63.233 510	68.528 112	28
29	48.910 799	52.966 286	57.423 033	62.322 712	67.711 354	73.629 798	29
30	51.622 677	56.084 938	61.007 070	66.438 848	72.435 478	79.058 186	30
31	54.429 471	59.328 335	64.752 388	70.760 790	77.419 429	84.801 677	31
32	57.334 502	62.701 469	68.666 245	75.298 829	82.677 498	90.889 778	32
33	60.341 210	66.209 527	72.756 226	80.063 771	88.224 760	97.343 165	33
34	63.453 152	69.857 909	77.030 256	85.066 959	94.077 122	104.183 755	34
35	66.674 013	73.652 225	81.496 618	90.320 307	100.251 364	111.434 780	35
36	70.007 603	77.598 314	86.163 966	95.836 323	106.765 189	119.120 867	36
37	73.457 869	81.702 246	91.041 344	101.628 139	113.637 274	127.268 119	37
38	77.028 895	85.970 336	96.138 205	107.709 546	120.887 324	135.904 206	38
39	80.724 906	90.409 150	101.464 424	114.095 023	128.536 127	145.058 458	39
40	84.550 278	95.025 516	107.030 323	120.799 774	136.605 614	154.761 966	40
41	88.509 537	99.826 536	112.846 688	127.839 763	145.118 923	165.047 684	41
42	92.607 371	104.819 598	118.924 789	135.231 751	154.100 464	175.950 545	42
43	96.848 629	110.012 382	125.276 404	142.993 339	163.575 989	187.507 577	43
44	101.238 331	115.412 877	131.913 842	151.143 006	173.572 669	199.758 032	44
45	105.781 673	121.029 392	138.849 965	159.700 156	184.119 165	212.743 514	45
46	110.484 031	126.870 568	146.098 214	168.685 164	195.245 719	226.508 125	46
47	115.350 973	132.945 390	153.672 633	178.119 422	206.984 234	241.098 612	47
48	120.388 257	139.263 206	161.587 902	188.025 393	219.368 367	256.564 529	48
49	125.601 846	145.833 734	169.859 357	198.426 663	232.433 627	272.958 401	49
50	130.997 910	152.667 084	178.503 028	209.347 996	246.217 476	290.335 905	50

Present Value of 1

$$\frac{1}{(1+i)^n}$$

n	½%	1%	1½%	2%	2½%	3%	n
1	0.995 025	0.990 099	0.985 222	0.980 392	0.975 610	0.970 874	1
2	0.990 075	0.980 296	0.970 662	0.961 169	0.951 814	0.942 596	2
3	0.985 149	0.970 590	0.956 317	0.942 322	0.928 599	0.915 142	3
4	0.980 248	0.960 980	0.942 184	0.923 845	0.905 951	0.888 487	4
5	0.975 371	0.951 466	0.928 260	0.905 731	0.883 854	0.862 609	5
6	0.970 518	0.942 045	0.914 542	0.887 971	0.862 297	0.837 484	6
7	0.965 690	0.932 718	0.901 027	0.870 560	0.841 265	0.813 092	7
8	0.960 885	0.923 483	0.887 711	0.853 490	0.820 747	0.789 409	8
9	0.956 105	0.914 340	0.874 592	0.836 755	0.800 728	0.766 417	9
10	0.951 348	0.905 287	0.861 667	0.820 348	0.781 198	0.744 094	10
11	0.946 615	0.896 324	0.848 933	0.804 263	0.762 145	0.722 421	11
12	0.941 905	0.887 449	0.836 387	0.788 493	0.743 556	0.701 380	12
13	0.937 219	0.878 663	0.824 027	0.773 033	0.725 420	0.680 951	13
14	0.932 556	0.869 963	0.811 849	0.757 875	0.707 727	0.661 118	14
15	0.927 917	0.861 349	0.799 852	0.743 015	0.690 466	0.641 862	15
16	0.923 300	0.852 821	0.788 031	0.728 446	0.673 625	0.623 167	16
17	0.918 707	0.844 377	0.776 385	0.714 163	0.657 195	0.605 016	17
18	0.914 136	0.836 017	0.764 912	0.700 159	0.641 166	0.587 395	18
19	0.909 588	0.827 740	0.753 607	0.686 431	0.625 528	0.570 286	19
20	0.905 063	0.819 544	0.742 470	0.672 971	0.610 271	0.553 676	20
21	0.900 560	0.811 430	0.731 498	0.659 776	0.595 386	0.537 549	21
22	0.896 080	0.803 396	0.720 688	0.646 839	0.580 865	0.521 893	22
23	0.891 622	0.795 442	0.710 037	0.634 156	0.566 697	0.506 692	23
24	0.887 186	0.787 566	0.699 544	0.621 721	0.552 875	0.491 934	24
25	0.882 772	0.779 768	0.689 206	0.609 531	0.539 391	0.477 606	25
26	0.878 380	0.772 048	0.679 021	0.597 579	0.526 235	0.463 695	26
27	0.874 010	0.764 404	0.668 986	0.585 862	0.513 400	0.450 189	27
28	0.869 662	0.756 836	0.659 099	0.574 375	0.500 878	0.437 077	28
29	0.865 335	0.749 342	0.649 359	0.563 112	0.488 661	0.424 346	29
30	0.861 030	0.741 923	0.639 762	0.552 071	0.476 743	0.411 987	30
31	0.856 746	0.734 577	0.630 308	0.541 246	0.465 115	0.399 987	31
32	0.852 484	0.727 304	0.620 993	0.530 633	0.453 771	0.388 337	32
33	0.848 242	0.720 103	0.611 816	0.520 229	0.442 703	0.377 026	33
34	0.844 022	0.712 973	0.602 774	0.510 028	0.431 905	0.366 045	34
35	0.839 823	0.705 914	0.593 866	0.500 028	0.421 371	0.355 383	35
36	0.835 645	0.698 925	0.585 090	0.490 223	0.411 094	0.345 032	36
37	0.831 487	0.692 005	0.576 443	0.480 611	0.401 067	0.334 983	37
38	0.827 351	0.685 153	0.567 924	0.471 187	0.391 285	0.325 226	38
39	0.823 235	0.678 370	0.559 531	0.461 948	0.381 741	0.315 754	39
40	0.819 139	0.671 653	0.551 262	0.452 890	0.372 431	0.306 557	40
41	0.815 064	0.665 003	0.543 116	0.444 010	0.363 347	0.297 628	41
42	0.811 009	0.658 419	0.535 089	0.435 304	0.354 485	0.288 959	42
43	0.806 974	0.651 900	0.527 182	0.426 769	0.345 839	0.280 543	43
44	0.802 959	0.645 445	0.519 391	0.418 401	0.337 404	0.272 372	44
45	0.798 964	0.639 055	0.511 715	0.410 197	0.329 174	0.264 439	45
46	0.794 989	0.632 728	0.504 153	0.402 154	0.321 146	0.256 737	46
47	0.791 034	0.626 463	0.496 702	0.394 268	0.313 313	0.249 259	47
48	0.787 098	0.620 260	0.489 362	0.386 538	0.305 671	0.241 999	48
49	0.783 183	0.614 119	0.482 130	0.378 958	0.298 216	0.234 950	49
50	0.779 286	0.608 039	0.475 005	0.371 528	0.290 942	0.228 107	50

Present Value of 1

$$\frac{1}{(1+i)^n}$$

n	3½%	4%	4½%	5%	5½%	6%	n
1	0.966 184	0.961 538	0.956 938	0.952 381	0.947 867	0.943 396	1
2	0.933 511	0.924 556	0.915 730	0.907 029	0.898 452	0.889 996	2
3	0.901 943	0.888 996	0.876 297	0.863 838	0.851 614	0.839 619	3
4	0.871 442	0.854 804	0.838 561	0.822 702	0.807 217	0.792 094	4
5	0.841 973	0.821 927	0.802 451	0.783 526	0.765 134	0.747 258	5
6	0.813 501	0.790 315	0.767 896	0.746 215	0.725 246	0.704 961	6
7	0.785 991	0.759 918	0.734 828	0.710 681	0.687 437	0.665 057	7
8	0.759 412	0.730 690	0.703 185	0.676 839	0.651 599	0.627 412	8
9	0.733 731	0.702 587	0.672 904	0.644 609	0.617 629	0.591 898	9
10	0.708 919	0.675 564	0.643 928	0.613 913	0.585 431	0.558 395	10
11	0.684 946	0.649 581	0.616 199	0.584 679	0.554 911	0.526 788	11
12	0.661 783	0.624 597	0.589 664	0.556 837	0.525 982	0.496 969	12
13	0.639 404	0.600 574	0.564 272	0.530 321	0.498 561	0.468 839	13
14	0.617 782	0.577 475	0.539 973	0.505 068	0.472 569	0.442 301	14
15	0.596 891	0.555 265	0.516 720	0.481 017	0.447 933	0.417 265	15
16	0.576 706	0.533 908	0.494 469	0.458 112	0.424 581	0.393 646	16
17	0.557 204	0.513 373	0.473 176	0.436 297	0.402 447	0.371 364	17
18	0.538 361	0.493 628	0.452 800	0.415 521	0.381 466	0.350 344	18
19	0.520 156	0.474 642	0.433 302	0.395 734	0.361 579	0.330 513	19
20	0.502 566	0.456 387	0.414 643	0.376 889	0.342 729	0.311 805	20
21	0.485 571	0.438 834	0.396 787	0.358 942	0.324 862	0.294 155	21
22	0.469 151	0.421 955	0.379 701	0.341 850	0.307 926	0.277 505	22
23	0.453 286	0.405 726	0.363 350	0.325 571	0.291 873	0.261 797	23
24	0.437 957	0.390 121	0.347 703	0.310 068	0.276 657	0.246 979	24
25	0.423 147	0.375 117	0.332 731	0.295 303	0.262 234	0.232 999	25
26	0.408 838	0.360 689	0.318 402	0.281 241	0.248 563	0.219 810	26
27	0.395 012	0.346 817	0.304 691	0.267 848	0.235 605	0.207 368	27
28	0.381 654	0.333 477	0.291 571	0.255 094	0.223 322	0.195 630	28
29	0.368 748	0.320 651	0.279 015	0.242 946	0.211 679	0.184 557	29
30	0.356 278	0.308 319	0.267 000	0.231 377	0.200 644	0.174 110	30
31	0.344 230	0.296 460	0.255 502	0.220 359	0.190 184	0.164 255	31
32	0.332 590	0.285 058	0.244 500	0.209 866	0.180 269	0.154 957	32
33	0.321 343	0.274 094	0.233 971	0.199 873	0.170 871	0.146 186	33
34	0.310 476	0.263 552	0.223 896	0.190 355	0.161 963	0.137 912	34
35	0.299 977	0.253 415	0.214 254	0.181 290	0.153 520	0.130 105	35
36	0.289 833	0.243 669	0.205 028	0.172 657	0.145 516	0.122 741	36
37	0.280 032	0.234 297	0.196 199	0.164 436	0.137 930	0.115 793	37
38	0.270 562	0.225 285	0.187 750	0.156 605	0.130 739	0.109 239	38
39	0.261 413	0.216 621	0.179 665	0.149 148	0.123 924	0.103 056	39
40	0.252 572	0.208 289	0.171 929	0.142 046	0.117 463	0.097 222	40
41	0.244 031	0.200 278	0.164 525	0.135 282	0.111 339	0.091 719	41
42	0.235 779	0.192 575	0.157 440	0.128 840	0.105 535	0.086 527	42
43	0.227 806	0.185 168	0.150 661	0.122 704	0.100 033	0.081 630	43
44	0.220 102	0.178 046	0.144 173	0.116 861	0.094 818	0.077 009	44
45	0.212 659	0.171 198	0.137 964	0.111 297	0.089 875	0.072 650	45
46	0.205 468	0.164 614	0.132 023	0.105 997	0.085 190	0.068 538	46
47	0.198 520	0.158 283	0.126 338	0.100 949	0.080 748	0.064 658	47
48	0.191 806	0.152 195	0.120 898	0.096 142	0.076 539	0.060 998	48
49	0.185 320	0.146 341	0.115 692	0.091 564	0.072 549	0.057 546	49
50	0.179 053	0.140 713	0.110 710	0.087 204	0.068 767	0.054 288	50

Present Value of an Annuity of 1

$$\frac{1 - \frac{1}{(1+i)^n}}{i}$$

n	½%	1%	1½%	2%	2½%	3%	n
1	0.995 025	0.990 099	0.985 222	0.980 392	0.975 610	0.970 874	1
2	1.985 099	1.970 395	1.955 883	1.941 561	1.927 424	1.913 470	2
3	2.970 248	2.940 985	2.912 200	2.883 883	2.856 024	2.828 611	3
4	3.950 496	3.901 966	3.854 385	3.807 729	3.761 974	3.717 098	4
5	4.925 866	4.853 431	4.782 645	4.713 460	4.645 829	4.579 707	5
6	5.896 384	5.795 476	5.697 187	5.601 431	5.508 125	5.417 191	6
7	6.862 074	6.728 195	6.598 214	6.471 991	6.349 391	6.230 283	7
8	7.822 959	7.651 678	7.485 925	7.325 481	7.170 137	7.019 692	8
9	8.779 064	8.566 018	8.360 517	8.162 237	7.970 866	7.786 109	9
10	9.730 412	9.471 305	9.222 185	8.982 585	8.752 064	8.530 203	10
11	10.677 027	10.367 628	10.071 118	9.786 848	9.514 209	9.252 624	11
12	11.618 932	11.255 077	10.907 505	10.575 341	10.257 765	9.954 004	12
13	12.556 151	12.133 740	11.731 532	11.348 374	10.983 185	10.634 955	13
14	13.488 708	13.003 703	12.543 382	12.106 249	11.690 912	11.296 073	14
15	14.416 625	13.865 053	13.343 233	12.849 264	12.381 378	11.937 935	15
16	15.339 925	14.717 874	14.131 264	13.577 709	13.055 003	12.561 102	16
17	16.258 632	15.562 251	14.907 649	14.291 872	13.712 198	13.166 118	17
18	17.172 768	16.398 269	15.672 561	14.992 031	14.353 364	13.753 513	18
19	18.082 356	17.226 009	16.426 168	15.678 462	14.978 891	14.323 799	19
20	18.987 419	18.045 553	17.168 639	16.351 433	15.589 162	14.877 475	20
21	19.887 979	18.856 983	17.900 137	17.011 209	16.184 549	15.415 024	21
22	20.784 059	19.660 379	18.620 824	17.658 048	16.765 413	15.936 917	22
23	21.675 681	20.455 821	19.330 861	18.292 204	17.332 110	16.443 608	23
24	22.562 866	21.243 387	20.030 405	18.913 926	17.884 986	16.935 542	24
25	23.445 638	22.023 156	20.719 611	19.523 456	18.424 376	17.413 148	25
26	24.324 018	22.795 204	21.398 632	20.121 036	18.950 611	17.876 842	26
27	25.198 028	23.559 608	22.067 617	20.706 898	19.464 011	18.327 031	27
28	26.067 689	24.316 443	22.726 717	21.281 272	19.964 889	18.764 108	28
29	26.933 024	25.065 785	23.376 076	21.844 385	20.453 550	19.188 455	29
30	27.794 054	25.807 708	24.015 838	22.396 456	20.930 293	19.600 441	30
31	28.650 800	26.542 285	24.646 146	22.937 702	21.395 407	20.000 428	31
32	29.503 284	27.269 589	25.267 139	23.468 335	21.849 178	20.388 766	32
33	30.351 526	27.989 693	25.878 954	23.988 564	22.291 881	20.765 792	33
34	31.195 548	28.702 666	26.481 728	24.498 592	22.723 786	21.131 837	34
35	32.035 371	29.408 580	27.075 595	24.998 619	23.145 157	21.487 220	35
36	32.871 016	30.107 505	27.660 684	25.488 842	23.556 251	21.832 253	36
37	33.702 504	30.799 510	28.237 127	25.969 453	23.957 318	22.167 235	37
38	34.529 854	31.484 663	28.805 052	26.440 641	24.348 603	22.492 462	38
39	35.353 089	32.163 033	29.364 583	26.902 589	24.730 344	22.808 215	39
40	36.172 228	32.834 686	29.915 845	27.355 479	25.102 775	23.114 772	40
41	36.987 291	33.499 689	30.458 961	27.799 489	25.466 122	23.412 400	41
42	37.798 300	34.158 108	30.994 050	28.234 794	25.820 607	23.701 359	42
43	38.605 274	34.810 008	31.521 232	28.661 562	26.166 446	23.981 902	43
44	39.408 232	35.455 454	32.040 622	29.079 963	26.503 849	24.254 274	44
45	40.207 196	36.094 508	32.552 337	29.490 160	26.833 024	24.518 713	45
46	41.002 185	36.727 236	33.056 490	29.892 314	27.154 170	24.775 449	46
47	41.793 219	37.353 699	33.553 192	30.286 582	27.467 483	25.024 708	47
48	42.580 318	37.973 959	34.042 554	30.673 120	27.773 154	25.266 707	48
49	43.363 500	38.588 079	34.524 683	31.052 078	28.071 369	25.501 657	49
50	44.142 786	39.196 118	34.999 688	31.423 606	28.362 312	25.729 764	50

Present Value of an Annuity of 1

$$\frac{1 - \frac{1}{(1+i)^n}}{i}$$

n	3½%	4%	4½%	5%	5½%	6%	n
1	0.966 184	0.961 538	0.956 938	0.952 381	0.947 867	0.943 396	1
2	1.899 694	1.886 095	1.872 668	1.859 410	1.846 320	1.833 393	2
3	2.801 637	2.775 091	2.748 964	2.723 248	2.697 933	2.673 012	3
4	3.673 079	3.629 895	3.587 526	3.545 951	3.505 150	3.465 106	4
5	4.515 052	4.451 822	4.389 977	4.329 477	4.270 284	4.212 364	5
6	5.328 553	5.242 137	5.157 872	5.075 692	4.995 530	4.917 324	6
7	6.114 544	6.002 055	5.892 701	5.786 373	5.682 967	5.582 381	7
8	6.873 956	6.732 745	6.595 886	6.463 213	6.334 566	6.209 794	8
9	7.607 687	7.435 332	7.268 791	7.107 822	6.952 195	6.801 692	9
10	8.316 605	8.110 896	7.912 718	7.721 735	7.537 626	7.360 087	10
11	9.001 551	8.760 477	8.528 917	8.306 414	8.092 536	7.886 875	11
12	9.663 334	9.385 074	9.118 581	8.863 252	8.618 518	8.383 844	12
13	10.302 738	9.985 648	9.682 852	9.393 573	9.117 079	8.852 683	13
14	10.920 520	10.563 123	10.222 825	9.898 641	9.589 648	9.294 984	14
15	11.517 411	11.118 387	10.739 546	10.379 658	10.037 581	9.712 249	15
16	12.094 117	11.652 296	11.234 015	10.837 770	10.462 162	10.105 895	16
17	12.651 321	12.165 669	11.707 191	11.274 066	10.864 609	10.477 260	17
18	13.189 682	12.659 297	12.159 992	11.689 587	11.246 074	10.827 603	18
19	13.709 837	13.133 939	12.593 294	12.085 321	11.607 654	11.158 116	19
20	14.212 403	13.590 326	13.007 936	12.462 210	11.950 382	11.469 921	20
21	14.697 974	14.029 160	13.404 724	12.821 153	12.275 244	11.764 077	21
22	15.167 125	14.451 115	13.784 425	13.163 003	12.583 170	12.041 582	22
23	15.620 410	14.856 842	14.147 775	13.488 574	12.875 042	12.303 379	23
24	16.058 368	15.246 963	14.495 478	13.798 642	13.151 699	12.550 358	24
25	16.481 515	15.622 080	14.828 209	14.093 945	13.413 933	12.783 356	25
26	16.890 352	15.982 769	15.146 611	14.375 185	13.662 495	13.003 166	26
27	17.285 365	16.329 586	15.451 303	14.643 034	13.898 100	13.210 534	27
28	17.667 019	16.663 063	15.742 874	14.898 127	14.121 422	13.406 164	28
29	18.035 767	16.983 715	16.021 889	15.141 074	14.333 101	13.590 721	29
30	18.392 045	17.292 033	16.288 889	15.372 451	14.533 745	13.764 831	30
31	18.736 276	17.588 494	16.544 391	15.592 811	14.723 929	13.929 086	31
32	19.068 865	17.873 552	16.788 891	15.802 677	14.904 198	14.084 043	32
33	19.390 208	18.147 646	17.022 862	16.002 549	15.075 069	14.230 230	33
34	19.700 684	18.411 198	17.246 758	16.192 904	15.237 033	14.368 141	34
35	20.000 661	18.664 613	17.461 012	16.374 194	15.390 552	14.498 246	35
36	20.290 494	18.908 282	17.666 041	16.546 852	15.536 068	14.620 987	36
37	20.570 525	19.142 579	17.862 240	16.711 287	15.673 999	14.736 780	37
38	20.841 087	19.367 864	18.049 990	16.867 893	15.804 738	14.846 019	38
39	21.102 500	19.584 485	18.229 656	17.017 041	15.928 662	14.949 075	39
40	21.355 072	19.792 774	18.401 584	17.159 086	16.046 125	15.046 297	40
41	21.599 104	19.993 052	18.566 109	17.294 368	16.157 464	15.138 016	41
42	21.834 883	20.185 627	18.723 550	17.423 208	16.262 999	15.224 543	42
43	22.062 689	20.370 795	18.874 210	17.545 912	16.363 032	15.306 173	43
44	22.282 791	20.548 841	19.018 383	17.662 773	16.457 851	15.383 182	44
45	22.495 450	20.720 040	19.156 347	17.774 070	16.547 726	15.455 832	45
46	22.700 918	20.884 654	19.288 371	17.880 067	16.632 915	15.524 370	46
47	22.899 438	21.042 936	19.414 709	17.981 016	16.713 664	15.589 028	47
48	23.091 244	21.195 131	19.535 607	18.077 158	16.790 203	15.650 027	48
49	23.276 565	21.341 472	19.651 298	18.168 722	16.862 751	15.707 572	49
50	23.455 618	21.482 185	19.762 008	18.255 925	16.931 518	15.761 861	50

INDEX

D

E

F

DATE DUE

APR 12 '74			
APR 4 1974			
MAY 3 '74			
MAY 3 1974			
NOV 7 1974			
APR 23 1975			
FEB 02 1976			
JAN 20 1977			
FEB 14 1977			
NOV 12 '79			
AP 27 '82			
MAY 10 '82			
MY 14 [illegible]			
OCT 22 '85			
GAYLORD			PRINTED IN U.S.A.